THE  TIMES
GUIDE TO
THE HOUSE
OF COMMONS
April 1992

Edited by Alan H Wood
and Roger Wood
Parliamentary Editor of The Times

TIMES BOOKS
A Division of HarperCollinsPublishers

Published by **Times Books**
A division of HarperCollins*Publishers*
77-85 Fulham Palace Road
London W6 8JB

© **Times Newspapers Ltd, 1992**

Compiled by Julian Desborough,
Steve Gibbs, Arthur Leathley,
Robert Morgan, Bernard West,
and John Winder

Typeset by
London Post (Printing) Ltd

Printed and bound in Great Britain by
Mackays of Chatham Ltd, Kent

British Library Cataloguing in Publication Data

"Times" Guide to the House of Commons 1992
 I. Wood, Alan H.
 328.41

ISBN 0-7230-0497-8

Contents

Her Majesty's Government

The Cabinet

Prime Minister, First Lord of the Treasury and Minister for the Civil Service
John Major

Lord Chancellor
Lord Mackay of Clashfern

Secretary of State for Foreign and Commonwealth Affairs
Douglas Hurd

Chancellor of the Exchequer
Norman Lamont

Home Secretary
Kenneth Clarke

Secretary of State for Trade and Industry
Michael Heseltine

Secretary of State for Transport
John MacGregor

Secretary of State for Defence
Malcolm Rifkind

Lord Privy Seal and Leader of the House of Lords
John Wakeham

Lord President of the Council and Leader of the House of Commons
Tony Newton

Minister of Agriculture, Fisheries and Food
John Gummer

Secretary of State for Environment
Michael Howard

Secretary of State for Wales
David Hunt

Secretary of State for Social Security
Peter Lilley

Chancellor of the Duchy of Lancaster and Minister for Citizen's Charter
William Waldegrave

Secretary of State for Scotland
Ian Lang

Secretary of State for National Heritage
David Mellor

Secretary of State for Northern Ireland
Sir Patrick Mayhew

Secretary of State for Education
John Patten

Secretary of State for Health
Virginia Bottomley

Secretary of State for Employment
Gillian Shephard

Chief Secretary to the Treasury
Michael Portillo

Departments of State and Ministers

AGRICULTURE, FISHERIES AND FOOD

Minister
John Gummer

Minister of State
David Curry

Parliamentary Secretaries
Earl Howe
Nicholas Soames

DEFENCE
Secretary of State
Malcolm Rifkind
Ministers of State
Archie Hamilton
Jonathan Aitken
Under Secretary of State
Viscount Cranborne

DUCHY OF LANCASTER
Chancellor
William Waldegrave

EDUCATION

Secretary of State
John Patten

Minister of State
Baroness Blatch

Under Secretaries of State
Eric Forth
Nigel Forman

EMPLOYMENT

Secretary of State
Gillian Shephard

Minister of State
Michael Forsyth

Under Secretaries of State
Patrick McLoughlin
Viscount Ullswater

ENVIRONMENT

Secretary of State
Michael Howard

Ministers of State
John Redwood
David Maclean

**Minister for Housing
and Planning**
Sir George Young

Under Secretaries of State
Tony Baldry
Robin Squire
Lord Strathclyde

FOREIGN AND COMMONWEALTH AFFAIRS

Secretary of State
Mr Douglas Hurd

**Minister for Overseas
Development**
Lynda Chalker

Ministers of State
Alastair Goodlad
Douglas Hogg
Tristan Garel-Jones

Under Secretary of State
Mark Lennox-Boyd

HEALTH

Secretary of State
Virginia Bottomley

Minister of State
Brian Mawhinney

Under Secretaries of State
Tim Yeo
Tom Sackville
Baroness Cumberlege

HOME OFFICE

Secretary of State
Kenneth Clarke

Ministers of State
Peter Lloyd
Michael Jack
Earl Ferrers (Deputy Leader of House of Lords)

Under Secretary of State
Charles Wardle

LAW OFFICERS

Attorney General
Sir Nicholas Lyell

Solicitor General
Sir Derek Spencer

Lord Advocate
Alan Rodger

Solicitor General for Scotland
Thomas Dawson

LORD CHANCELLOR'S DEPARTMENT

Lord Chancellor
Lord Mackay of Clashfern

Parliamentary Secretary
John M Taylor

NATIONAL HERITAGE

Secretary of State
David Mellor

Under Secretary of State
Robert Key

NORTHERN IRELAND OFFICE

Secretary of State
Sir Patrick Mayhew

Ministers of State
Michael Mates
Robert Atkins

Under Secretaries of State
Jeremy Hanley
The Earl of Arran

PAYMASTER GENERAL'S DEPARTMENT

Paymaster General
Sir John Cope

PRIVY COUNCIL OFFICE

Lord President of the Council and Leader of the Commons
Tony Newton

Lord Privy Seal and Leader of the House of Lords
John Wakeham

Minister for the Civil Service
Robert Jackson

SCOTTISH OFFICE

Secretary of State
Ian Lang

Minister of State
Lord Fraser of Carmyllie

Under Secretaries of State
Lord James Douglas-Hamilton
Allan Stewart
Sir Hector Monro

SOCIAL SECURITY

Secretary of State
Peter Lilley

Minister for Social Security and Disabled People
Nicholas Scott

Under Secretaries of State
Alistair Burt
Ann Widdecombe
Lord Henley

TRADE AND INDUSTRY

Secretary of State
Michael Heseltine

Ministers of State
Tim Eggar
Richard Needham

Minister for Trade
Tim Sainsbury

Under Secretary of State for Industry and Consumer Affairs
Edward Leigh

Under Secretaries of State
Neil Hamilton
Baroness Denton of Wakefield

TRANSPORT

Secretary of State
John MacGregor

Minister of State
The Earl of Caithness

Minister for Public Transport
Roger Freeman

Under Secretaries of State
Kenneth Carlisle
Steven Norris

TREASURY

Prime Minister, First Lord of the Treasury and Minister for the Civil Service
John Major

Chancellor of the Exchequer
Norman Lamont

Chief Secretary
Michael Portillo

Financial Secretary
Stephen Dorrell

Paymaster General
Sir John Cope

Economic Secretary
Anthony Nelson

WELSH OFFICE

Secretary of State
John Hunt

Minister of State
Sir Wyn Roberts

Under Secretary of State
Gwilym Jones

GOVERNMENT WHIPS

House of Commons
Parliamentary Secretary to the Treasury (Government Chief Whip)
Richard Ryder

Treasurer of HM Household (Deputy Chief Whip)
David Heathcoat-Amory

Comptroller of HM Household
David Lightbown

Vice Chamberlain of HM Household
Sydney Chapman

Lords Commissioners of the Treasury
Nicholas Baker
Gregory Knight
Irvine Patnick
Timothy Wood
Timothy Boswell

Assistant Whips
Timothy Kirkhope
David Davis
Robert G Hughes
James Arbuthnot
Andrew MacKay

House of Lords
Captain, Gentlemen-at-Arms (Government Chief Whip)
Lord Hesketh

Captain, Yeomen of the Guard (Deputy Chief Whip)
Earl of Strathmore and Kinghorne

Lords in Waiting (Government whips)
Viscount Long
Lord Cavendish of Furness
Viscount Astor
Viscount St Davids
Viscount Goschen

Baroness-in-Waiting (Government whip)
Baroness Trumpington

Second Church Estates Commissioner, representing Church Commissioners
Mr Michael Alison

The General Election 1992

The general election on April 9 1992 gave the Conservatives under John Major, an historic fourth successive victory. They were returned with an overall majority of 21 and a majority of 64 over Labour, enough to ensure another full parliament.

Mr Major's new cabinet, swiftly in place, included two women, Virginia Bottomley as health secretary, and Gillian Shephard as employment secretary. John Wakeham, who did not seek re-election to the Commons, became leader of the House of Lords and Michael Heseltine, whose challenge to Mrs Thatcher's leadership paved the way for Mr Major's succession, became trade and industry secretary, an office from which he resigned over the Westlands affair.

Kenneth Baker, Home Secretary, was replaced by Kenneth Clarke and Malcolm Rifkind was appointed defence secretary to succeed Tom King. Tony Newton became leader of the Commons in place of John MacGregor, who became transport secretary. David Mellor took charge of the new department of national heritage and William Waldegrave became the new minister for the citizen's charter. Sir Patrick Mayhew succeeded Peter Brooke as Northern Ireland secretary.

Neil Kinnock, the Labour leader, and his deputy, Roy Hattersley, announced their resignations.

The state of the parties in the Commons compared with dissolution and the outcome of the 1987 election is:

	April 1992	Gains	Losses	Dissolution	June 1987
Conservative	336	5	44	367	375
Labour	271	44	1	229	229
Liberal Democrat	20	4	3	22	—
Liberal/Alliance	—	—	—	—	17
Social Democrat/ SDP/All	—	—	2	3	5
Scottish National	3	—	1	5	3
Plaid Cymru	4	1	—	3	3
Ulster Unionist	9	—	—	9	9
Democratic Unionist	3	—	—	3	3
Ulster Popular Unionist	1	—	—	1	1
Social Democratic and Labour	4	1	0	3	3
Ind C	—	—	1	1	—
Sinn Fein	—	—	1	1	1
The Speaker	—	—	1	1	1
Ind Lab	—	—	1	1	—
Socialist Lab	—	—	1	1	—
Totals	651			650	650

Details of seats that changed hands in 1992 from the 1987 general election (thus excluding by-election changes):

From Conservative to Labour: Barrow and Furness, Birmingham Northfield, Birmingham Selly Oak, Birmingham Yardley, Bristol East, Cambridge, Cannock and Burntwood, Cardiff Central, Croydon North West, Darlington, Delyn, Dulwich, Ellesmere Port and Neston, Feltham and Heston, Hampstead and Highgate, Hornsey and Wood Green, Hyndburn, Ilford South, Ipswich, Kingswood, Lancashire West, Lewisham East, Lewisham West, Nottingham East, Nottingham South, Nuneaton, Pembroke, Pendle, Rossendale and Darwen, Sherwood, Southampton Itchen, Stockport, Streatham, Thurrock, Wallasey, Walthamstow, Warrington South, Warwickshire North, Wolverhampton North East, York.

From Social Democrat to Labour: Greenwich, Plymouth Devonport, Woolwich.

From Conservative to Liberal Democrat: Bath, Cheltenham, Cornwall North, Devon North.

From Labour to Conservative: Aberdeen South.

From Liberal Democrat to Conservative: Brecon and Radnor, Southport.

From Liberal Democrat to Plaid Cymru: Ceredigion and Pembroke North.

From Sinn Fein to Social Democratic and Labour Party: Belfast West.

Croydon North East, the seat of the retiring Speaker, Bernard Weatherill, was held by the Conservaties. After Boundary Commission recommendations Milton Keynes, held by the Conservatives, was split into two and the Conservatives took both, thus gaining them one seat.

In by-elections during the 1987-92 Parliament, the Conservatives lost seven seats: Vale of Glamorgan (to Labour); Mid-Staffordshire (to Labour); Eastbourne (to Liberal Democrats); Ribble Valley (to Liberal Democrats); Monmouth (to Labour), Kincardine and Deeside (to Liberal Democrats), and Langbaurgh (to Labour). All were regained on April 9. Labour lost Glasgow Govan to the Scottish National Party in a by-election but regained it in the general election.

The House of Commons

The following have been elected members of the House of Commons in the 1992 general election: * denotes new members. The abbreviations used to designate political parties are:
C - Conservative; Lab - Labour; LD - Liberal Democrat; UU - Ulster Unionist; SDLP - Social Democratic and Labour Party; UPUP - Ulster Popular Unionist Party; DUP - Democratic Unionist Party; SNP - Scottish National Party; PC - Plaid Cymru.

A

Abbott, Diane: *Hackney North and Stoke Newington*	Lab
Adams, Irene: *Paisley North*	Lab
Adley, Robert: *Christchurch*	C
*Ainger, Nick: *Pembroke*	Lab
*Ainsworth, Peter: *Surrey East*	C
*Ainsworth, Robert: *Coventry North East*	Lab
Aitken, Jonathan: *Thanet South*	C
Alexander, Richard: *Newark*	C
Alison, Michael: *Selby*	C
Allason, Rupert: *Torbay*	C
Allen, Graham: *Nottingham North*	Lab
Alton, David: *Liverpool, Mossley Hill*	LD
Amess, David: *Basildon*	C
*Ancram, Michael: *Devizes*	C
Anderson, Donald: *Swansea East*	Lab
*Anderson, Janet: *Rossendale and Darwen*	Lab
Arbuthnot, James: *Wanstead and Woodford*	C
Armstrong, Hilary: *Durham North West*	Lab
Arnold, Jacques: *Gravesham*	C
Arnold, Sir Thomas: *Hazel Grove*	C
Ashby, David: *Leicestershire North West*	C
Ashdown, Paddy: *Yeovil*	LD
Ashton, Joe: *Bassetlaw*	Lab
Aspinwall, Jack: *Wansdyke*	C
Atkins, Robert: *South Ribble*	C
Atkinson, David: *Bournemouth East*	C
*Atkinson, Peter: *Hexham*	C
*Austin-Walker, John: *Woolwich*	Lab

B

Baker, Kenneth: *Mole Valley*	C
Baker, Nicholas: *Dorset North*	C
Baldry, Tony: *Banbury*	C
Banks, Robert: *Harrogate*	C
*Banks, Matthew: *Southport*	C
Banks, Tony: *Newham North West*	Lab
Barnes, Harry: *Derbyshire North East*	Lab
Barron, Kevin: *Rother Valley*	Lab
*Bates, Michael: *Langbaurgh*	C
Batiste, Spencer: *Elmet*	C
Battle, John: *Leeds West*	Lab
*Bayley, Hugh: *York*	Lab
Beckett, Margaret: *Derby South*	Lab

Beggs, Roy: *Antrim East*	UU
Beith, Alan: *Berwick-upon-Tweed*	LD
Bell, Stuart: *Middlesbrough*	Lab
Bellingham, Henry: *Norfolk North West*	C
Bendall, Vivian: *Ilford North*	C
Benn, Tony: *Chesterfield*	Lab
Bennett, Andrew: *Denton and Reddish*	Lab
Benton, Joe: *Bootle*	Lab
*Beresford, Sir Paul: *Croydon Central*	C
Bermingham, Gerald: *St Helens South*	Lab
*Berry, Roger: *Kingswood*	Lab
*Betts, Clive: *Sheffield, Attercliffe*	Lab
Biffen, John: *Shropshire North*	C
Blackburn, John: *Dudley West*	C
Blair, Tony: *Sedgefield*	Lab
Blunkett, David: *Sheffield, Brightside*	Lab
Boateng, Paul: *Brent South*	Lab
Body, Sir Richard: *Holland with Boston*	C
Bonsor, Sir Nicholas: *Upminster*	C
*Booth, Hartley: *Finchley*	C
Boothroyd, Betty: *West Bromwich West*	Lab
Boswell, Timothy: *Daventry*	C
Bottomley, Peter: *Eltham*	C
Bottomley, Virginia: *Surrey South West*	C
Bowden, Andrew: *Brighton, Kemptown*	C
Bowis, John: *Battersea*	C
*Boyce, James: *Rotherham*	Lab
Boyes, Roland: *Houghton and Washington*	Lab
Boyson, Sir Rhodes: *Brent North*	C
Bradley, Keith: *Manchester, Withington*	Lab
*Brandreth, Gyles: *Chester, City of*	C
Bray, Dr Jeremy: *Motherwell South*	Lab
Brazier, Julian: *Canterbury*	C
Bright, Graham: *Luton South*	C
Brooke, Peter: *City of London and Westminster South*	C
Brown, Gordon: *Dunfermline East*	Lab
Brown, Michael: *Brigg and Cleethorpes*	C
Brown, Nicholas: *Newcastle upon Tyne East*	Lab
*Browning, Angela: *Tiverton*	C
Bruce, Ian: *Dorset South*	C
Bruce, Malcolm: *Gordon*	LD
Budgen, Nicholas: *Wolverhampton South West*	C
*Burden, Richard: *Birmingham, Northfield*	Lab
Burns, Simon: *Chelmsford*	C
Burt, Alistair: *Bury North*	C
Butcher, John: *Coventry South West*	C
*Butler, Peter: *Milton Keynes North East*	C
Butterfill, John: *Bournemouth West*	C
*Byers, Stephen: *Wallsend*	Lab

C

Caborn, Richard: *Sheffield Central*	Lab
Callaghan, James: *Heywood and Middleton*	Lab
*Campbell, Anne: *Cambridge*	Lab
Campbell, Menzies: *Fife North East*	LD
Campbell, Ronald: *Blyth Valley*	Lab
Campbell-Savours, Dale: *Workington*	Lab
Canavan, Dennis: *Falkirk West*	Lab
*Cann, Jamie: *Ipswich*	Lab
Carlile, Alexander: *Montgomery*	LD
Carlisle, John: *Luton North*	C
Carlisle, Kenneth: *Lincoln*	C
Carrington, Matthew: *Fulham*	C
Carttiss, Michael: *Great Yarmouth*	C
Cash, William: *Stafford*	C

Channon, Paul: *Southend West* — C
*Chaplin, Judith: *Newbury* — C
Chapman, Sydney: *Chipping Barnet* — C
*Chisholm, Malcolm: *Edinburgh, Leith* — Lab
Churchill, Winston: *Davyhulme* — C
*Clapham, Michael: *Barnsley West and Penistone* — Lab
*Clappison, James: *Hertsmere* — C
Clark, Dr David: *South Shields* — Lab
Clark, Dr Michael: *Rochford* — C
*Clarke, Eric: *Midlothian* — Lab
Clarke, Kenneth: *Rushcliffe* — C
Clarke, Tom: *Monklands West* — Lab
Clelland, David: *Tyne Bridge* — Lab
*Clifton-Brown, Geoffrey: *Cirencester and Tewkesbury* — C
Clwyd, Ann: *Cynon Valley* — Lab
*Coe, Sebastian: *Falmouth and Camborne* — C
*Coffey, Anne: *Stockport* — Lab
Cohen, Harry: *Leyton* — Lab
Colvin, Michael: *Romsey and Waterside* — C
*Congdon, David: *Croydon North East* — C
*Connarty, Michael: *Falkirk East* — Lab
Conway, Derek: *Shrewsbury and Atcham* — C
Cook, Frank: *Stockton North* — Lab
Cook, Robin: *Livingston* — Lab
Coombs, Anthony: *Wyre Forest* — C
Coombs, Simon: *Swindon* — C
Cope, Sir John: *Northavon* — C
Corbett, Robin: *Birmingham, Erdington* — Lab
Corbyn, Jeremy: *Islington North* — Lab
Cormack, Patrick: *Staffordshire South* — C
*Corston, Jean: *Bristol East* — Lab
Couchman, James: *Gillingham* — C
Cousins, Jim: *Newcastle upon Tyne Central* — Lab
Cox, Thomas: *Tooting* — Lab
Cran, James: *Beverley* — C
Critchley, Julian: *Aldershot* — C
Cryer, Robert: *Bradford South* — Lab
Cummings, John: *Easington* — Lab
Cunliffe, Lawrence: *Leigh* — Lab
*Cunningham, Jim: *Coventry South East* — Lab
Cunningham, Dr John: *Copeland* — Lab
Currie, Edwina: *Derbyshire South* — C
Curry, David: *Skipton and Ripon* — C

D

*Dafis, Cynog: *Ceredigion and Pembroke North* — PC
Dalyell, Tam: *Linlithgow* — Lab
Darling, Alistair: *Edinburgh Central* — Lab
*Davidson, Ian: *Glasgow, Govan* — Lab
*Davies, Bryan: *Oldham Central and Royton* — Lab
Davies, Denzil: *Llanelli* — Lab
Davies, Quentin: *Stamford and Spalding* — C
Davies, Ronald: *Caerphilly* — Lab
Davis, David: *Boothferry* — C
Davis, Terry: *Birmingham, Hodge Hill* — Lab
Day, Stephen: *Cheadle* — C
*Denham, John: *Southampton, Itchen* — Lab
*Deva, Nirj: *Brentford and Isleworth* — C
Devlin, Timothy: *Stockton South* — C
Dewar, Donald: *Glasgow, Garscadden* — Lab
Dickens, Geoffrey: *Littleborough and Saddleworth* — C
Dicks, Terence: *Hayes and Harlington* — C
Dixon, Donald: *Jarrow* — Lab
Dobson, Frank: *Holborn and St Pancras* — Lab
*Donohue, Brian: *Cunninghame South* — Lab

Dorrell, Stephen: *Loughborough* — C
Douglas-Hamilton, Lord James: *Edinburgh West* — C
Dover, Den: *Chorley* — C
*Dowd, Jim: *Lewisham West* — Lab
*Duncan, Alan: *Rutland and Melton* — C
*Duncan-Smith, Iain: *Chingford* — C
Dunn, Robert: *Dartford* — C
Dunnachie, Jimmy: *Glasgow, Pollok* — Lab
Dunwoody, Gwyneth: *Crewe and Nantwich* — Lab
Durant, Sir Anthony: *Reading West* — C
Dykes, Hugh: *Harrow East* — C

E

*Eagle, Angela: *Wallasey* — Lab
Eastham, Kenneth: *Manchester, Blackley* — Lab
Eggar, Timothy: *Enfield North* — C
*Elletson, Harold: *Blackpool North* — C
Emery, Sir Peter: *Honiton* — C
Enright, Derek: *Hemsworth* — Lab
*Etherington, William: *Sunderland North* — Lab
Evans, David: *Welwyn Hatfield* — C
Evans, John: *St Helens North* — Lab
*Evans, Jonathan: *Brecon and Radnor* — C
*Evans, Nigel: *Ribble Valley* — C
*Evans, Roger: *Monmouth* — C
Evennett, David: *Erith and Crayford* — C
Ewing, Margaret: *Moray* — SNP

F

*Faber, David: *Westbury* — C
*Fabricant, Michael: *Staffordshire Mid* — C
Fairbairn, Sir Nicholas: *Perth and Kinross* — C
Fatchett, Derek: *Leeds Central* — Lab
Faulds, Andrew: *Warley East* — Lab
Fenner, Dame Peggy: *Medway* — C
Field, Barry: *Isle of Wight* — C
Field, Frank: *Birkenhead* — Lab
Fishburn, Dudley: *Kensington* — C
Fisher, Mark: *Stoke-on-Trent Central* — Lab
Flynn, Paul: *Newport West* — Lab
Fookes, Dame Janet: *Plymouth, Drake* — C
Forman, Nigel: *Carshalton and Wallington* — C
Forsyth, Michael: *Stirling* — C
Forsythe, Clifford: *Antrim South* — UU
Forth, Eric: *Worcestershire Mid* — C
Foster, Derek: *Bishop Auckland* — Lab
*Foster, Don: *Bath* — LD
Foulkes, George: *Carrick, Cumnock and Doon Valley* — Lab
Fowler, Sir Norman: *Sutton Coldfield* — C
*Fox, Dr Liam: *Woodspring* — C
Fox, Sir Marcus: *Shipley* — C
Fraser, John: *Norwood* — Lab
Freeman, Roger: *Kettering* — C
French, Douglas: *Gloucester* — C
Fry, Peter: *Wellingborough* — C
Fyfe, Maria: *Glasgow, Maryhill* — Lab

G

Galbraith, Samuel: *Strathkelvin and Bearsden* — Lab
Gale, Roger: *Thanet North* — C
*Gallie, Phil: *Ayr* — C
Galloway, George: *Glasgow, Hillhead* — Lab

*Gapes, Mike: *Ilford South*	Lab
Gardiner, Sir George: *Reigate*	C
Garel-Jones, Tristan: *Watford*	C
*Garnier, Edward: *Harborough*	C
Garrett, John: *Norwich South*	Lab
George, Bruce: *Walsall South*	Lab
*Gerrard, Neil: *Walthamstow*	Lab
Gilbert, Dr John: *Dudley East*	Lab
Gill, Christopher: *Ludlow*	C
*Gillan, Cheryl: *Chesham and Amersham*	C
Godman, Dr Norman: *Greenock and Port Glasgow*	Lab
*Godsiff, Roger: *Birmingham, Small Heath*	Lab
Golding, Llin: *Newcastle-under-Lyme*	Lab
Goodlad, Alastair: *Eddisbury*	C
Goodson-Wickes, Dr Charles: *Wimbledon*	C
Gordon, Mildred: *Bow and Poplar*	Lab
Gorman, Teresa: *Billericay*	C
Gorst, John: *Hendon North*	C
Gould, Bryan: *Dagenham*	Lab
Graham, Thomas: *Renfrew West and Inverclyde*	Lab
Grant, Sir Anthony: *Cambridgeshire South West*	C
Grant, Bernie: *Tottenham*	Lab
Greenway, Harry: *Ealing North*	C
Greenway, John: *Ryedale*	C
Griffiths, Nigel: *Edinburgh South*	Lab
Griffiths, Peter: *Portsmouth North*	C
Griffiths, Win: *Bridgend*	Lab
Grocott, Bruce: *Wrekin, The*	Lab
Grylls, Sir Michael: *Surrey North West*	C
Gummer, John: *Suffolk Coastal*	C
*Gunnell, John: *Leeds South and Morley*	Lab

H

Hague, William: *Richmond, Yorks*	C
Hain, Peter: *Neath*	Lab
*Hall, Mike: *Warrington South*	Lab
Hamilton, Archie: *Epsom and Ewell*	C
Hamilton, Neil: *Tatton*	C
Hampson, Dr Keith: *Leeds North West*	C
Hanley, Jeremy: *Richmond and Barnes*	C
Hannam, Sir John: *Exeter*	C
*Hanson, David: *Delyn*	Lab
Hardy, Peter: *Wentworth*	Lab
Hargreaves, Andrew: *Birmingham, Hall Green*	C
Harman, Harriet: *Peckham*	Lab
Harris, David: *St Ives*	C
*Harvey, Nick: *Devon North*	LD
Haselhurst, Alan: *Saffron Walden*	C
Hattersley, Roy: *Birmingham, Sparkbrook*	Lab
*Hawkins, Nick: *Blackpool South*	C
*Hawksley, Warren: *Halesowen and Stourbridge*	C
Hayes, Jerry: *Harlow*	C
*Heald, Oliver: *Hertfordshire North*	C
Heath, Sir Edward: *Old Bexley and Sidcup*	C
Heathcoat-Amory, David: *Wells*	C
Henderson, Douglas: *Newcastle upon Tyne North*	Lab
*Hendron, Dr Joseph: *Belfast West*	SDLP
*Hendry, Charles: *High Peak*	C
*Heppell, John: *Nottingham East*	Lab
Heseltine, Michael: *Henley*	C
Hicks, Robert: *Cornwall South East*	C
Higgins, Terence: *Worthing*	C
Hill, James: *Southampton, Test*	C
*Hill, Keith: *Streatham*	Lab
Hinchliffe, David: *Wakefield*	Lab

Hoey, Kate: *Vauxhall*	Lab
Hogg, Douglas: *Grantham*	C
Hogg, Norman: *Cumbernauld and Kilsyth*	Lab
Home Robertson, John: *East Lothian*	Lab
Hood, Jimmy: *Clydesdale*	Lab
*Hoon, Geoffrey: *Ashfield*	Lab
*Horam, John: *Orpington*	C
Hordern, Sir Peter: *Horsham*	C
Howard, Michael: *Folkestone and Hythe*	C
Howarth, Alan: *Stratford-on-Avon*	C
Howarth, George: *Knowsley North*	Lab
Howell, David: *Guildford*	C
Howell, Ralph: *Norfolk North*	C
Howells, Dr Kim: *Pontypridd*	Lab
Hoyle, Douglas: *Warrington North*	Lab
*Hughes, Kevin: *Doncaster North*	Lab
Hughes, Robert: *Aberdeen North*	Lab
Hughes, Robert G.: *Harrow West*	C
Hughes, Roy: *Newport East*	Lab
Hughes, Simon: *Southwark and Bermondsey*	LD
Hume, John: *Foyle*	SDLP
Hunt, David: *Wirral West*	C
Hunt, Sir John: *Ravensbourne*	C
Hunter, Andrew: *Basingstoke*	C
Hurd, Douglas: *Witney*	C
*Hutton, John: *Barrow and Furness*	Lab

I

Illsley, Eric: *Barnsley Central*	Lab
Ingram, Adam: *East Kilbride*	Lab

J

Jack, Michael: *Fylde*	C
*Jackson, Glenda: *Hampstead and Highgate*	Lab
*Jackson, Helen: *Sheffield, Hillsborough*	Lab
Jackson, Robert: *Wantage*	C
*Jamieson, David: *Plymouth, Devonport*	Lab
Janner, Greville: *Leicester West*	Lab
*Jenkin, Bernard: *Colchester North*	C
Jessel, Toby: *Twickenham*	C
Johnson Smith, Sir Geoffrey: *Wealden*	C
Johnston, Sir Russell: *Inverness, Nairn and Lochaber*	LD
Jones, Barry: *Alyn and Deeside*	Lab
Jones, Gwilym: *Cardiff North*	C
Jones, Ieuan Wyn: *Ynys Mon*	PC
*Jones, Dr Lynne: *Birmingham, Selly Oak*	Lab
Jones, Martyn: *Clwyd South West*	Lab
*Jones, Nigel: *Cheltenham*	LD
Jones, Robert: *Hertfordshire West*	C
Jopling, Michael: *Westmorland and Lonsdale*	C
*Jowell, Tessa: *Dulwich*	Lab

K

Kaufman, Gerald: *Manchester, Gorton*	Lab
*Keen, Alan: *Feltham and Heston*	Lab
Kellett-Bowman, Dame Elaine: *Lancaster*	C
Kennedy, Charles: *Ross, Cromarty and Skye*	LD
*Kennedy, Jane: *Liverpool, Broadgreen*	Lab
Key, Robert: *Salisbury*	C
*Khabra, Piara: *Ealing, Southall*	Lab
Kilfedder, James: *Down North*	UPUP

Kilfoyle, Peter: *Liverpool, Walton* — Lab
King, Tom: *Bridgwater* — C
Kinnock, Neil: *Islwyn* — Lab
Kirkhope, Timothy: *Leeds North East* — C
Kirkwood, Archy: *Roxburgh and Berwickshire* — LD
Knapman, Roger: *Stroud* — C
*Knight, Angela: *Erewash* — C
Knight, Gregory: *Derby North* — C
Knight, Dame Jill: *Birmingham, Edgbaston* — C
Knox, David: *Staffordshire, Moorlands* — C
*Kynoch, George: *Kincardine and Deeside* — C

L

*Lait, Jacqui: *Hastings and Rye* — C
Lamont, Norman: *Kingston upon Thames* — C
Lang, Ian: *Galloway and Upper Nithsdale* — C
Lawrence, Ivan: *Burton* — C
*Legg, Barry: *Milton Keynes South West* — C
Leigh, Edward: *Gainsborough and Horncastle* — C
Leighton, Ronald: *Newham North East* — Lab
Lennox-Boyd, Mark: *Morecambe and Lunesdale* — C
Lester, James: *Broxtowe* — C
Lestor, Joan: *Eccles* — Lab
Lewis, Terry: *Worsley* — Lab
*Lidington, David: *Aylesbury* — C
Lightbown, David: *Staffordshire South East* — C
Lilley, Peter: *St Albans* — C
Litherland, Robert: *Manchester Central* — Lab
Livingstone, Ken: *Brent East* — Lab
Lloyd, Tony: *Stretford* — Lab
Lloyd, Peter: *Fareham* — C
*Llwyd, Elfyn: *Meirionnydd Nant Conwy* — PC
Lofthouse, Geoffrey: *Pontefract and Castleford* — Lab
Lord, Michael: *Suffolk Central* — C
Loyden, Edward: *Liverpool, Garston* — Lab
*Luff, Peter: *Worcester* — C
Lyell, Sir Nicholas: *Bedfordshire Mid* — C
*Lynne, Elizabeth: *Rochdale* — LD

M

Macdonald, Calum: *Western Isles* — Lab
MacGregor, John: *Norfolk South* — C
MacKay, Andrew: *Berkshire East* — C
*MacKinlay, Andrew: *Thurrock* — Lab
Maclean, David: *Penrith and the Border* — C
Maclennan, Robert: *Caithness and Sutherland* — LD
McAllion, John: *Dundee East* — Lab
McAvoy, Thomas: *Glasgow, Rutherglen* — Lab
McCartney, Ian: *Makerfield* — Lab
McCrea, Rev William: *Ulster Mid* — DUP
McFall, John: *Dumbarton* — Lab
McGrady, Eddie: *Down South* — SDLP
McKelvey, William: *Kilmarnock and Loudoun* — Lab
McLeish, Henry: *Fife Central* — Lab
McLoughlin, Patrick: *Derbyshire West* — C
McMaster, Gordon: *Paisley South* — Lab
McNair-Wilson, Sir Patrick: *New Forest* — C
McNamara, Kevin: *Hull North* — Lab
McWilliam, John: *Blaydon* — Lab
Madden, Max: *Bradford West* — Lab
Madel, David: *Bedfordshire South West* — C
Maginnis, Kenneth: *Fermanagh and South Tyrone* — UU
Mahon, Alice: *Halifax* — Lab

*Maitland, Lady Olga: *Sutton and Cheam*	C
Major, John: *Huntingdon*	C
Mallon, Seamus: *Newry and Armagh*	SDLP
*Malone, Gerald: *Winchester*	C
*Mandelson, Peter: *Hartlepool*	Lab
Mans, Keith: *Wyre*	C
Marek, Dr John: *Wrexham*	Lab
Marland, Paul: *Gloucestershire West*	C
Marlow, Antony: *Northampton North*	C
Marshall, David: *Glasgow, Shettleston*	Lab
Marshall, James: *Leicester South*	Lab
Marshall, John: *Hendon South*	C
Marshall, Sir Michael: *Arundel*	C
Martin, David: *Portsmouth South*	C
Martin, Michael: *Glasgow, Springburn*	Lab
Martlew, Eric: *Carlisle*	Lab
Mates, Michael: *Hampshire East*	C
Mawhinney, Dr Brian: *Peterborough*	C
Maxton, John: *Glasgow, Cathcart*	Lab
Mayhew, Sir Patrick: *Tunbridge Wells*	C
Meacher, Michael: *Oldham West*	Lab
Meale, Alan: *Mansfield*	Lab
Mellor, David: *Putney*	C
*Merchant, Piers: *Beckenham*	C
Michael, Alun: *Cardiff South and Penarth*	Lab
Michie, Ray: *Argyll and Bute*	LD
Michie, William: *Sheffield, Heeley*	Lab
*Milburn, Alan: *Darlington*	Lab
*Miller, Andrew: *Ellesmere Port and Neston*	Lab
*Milligan, Stephen: *Eastleigh*	C
Mills, Iain: *Meriden*	C
Mitchell, Andrew: *Gedling*	C
Mitchell, Austin: *Great Grimsby*	Lab
Mitchell, Sir David: *Hampshire North West*	C
Moate, Roger: *Faversham*	C
Molyneaux, James: *Lagan Valley*	UU
Monro, Sir Hector: *Dumfries*	C
Montgomery, Sir Fergus: *Altrincham and Sale*	C
Moonie, Dr Lewis: *Kirkcaldy*	Lab
Morgan, Rhodri: *Cardiff West*	Lab
Morley, Elliot: *Glanford and Scunthorpe*	Lab
Morris, Alfred: *Manchester, Wythenshawe*	Lab
*Morris, Estelle: *Birmingham, Yardley*	Lab
Morris, John: *Aberavon*	Lab
Morris, Michael: *Northampton South*	C
Moss, Malcolm: *Cambridgeshire North East*	C
Mowlam, Marjorie: *Redcar*	Lab
*Mudie, George: *Leeds East*	Lab
Mullin, Christopher: *Sunderland South*	Lab
Murphy, Paul: *Torfaen*	Lab

N

Needham, Richard: *Wiltshire North*	C
Nelson, Anthony: *Chichester*	C
Neubert, Sir Michael: *Romford*	C
Newton, Tony: *Braintree*	C
Nicholls, Patrick: *Teignbridge*	C
Nicholson, David: *Taunton*	C
Nicholson, Emma: *Devon West and Torridge*	C
Norris, Steven: *Epping Forest*	C

O

*O'Brien, Michael: *Warwickshire North*	Lab
O'Brien, William: *Normanton*	Lab

15

O'Hara, Edward: *Knowsley South*	Lab
O'Neill, Martin: *Clackmannan*	Lab
Oakes, Gordon: *Halton*	Lab
*Olner, William: *Nuneaton*	Lab
Onslow, Cranley: *Woking*	C
Oppenheim, Phillip: *Amber Valley*	C
Orme, Stanley: *Salford East*	Lab
*Ottaway, Richard: *Croydon South*	C
*Owen Jones, Jonathan: *Cardiff Central*	Lab

P

Page, Richard: *Hertfordshire South West*	C
Paice, James: *Cambridgeshire South East*	C
Paisley, Rev Ian: *Antrim North*	DUP
Parry, Robert: *Liverpool, Riverside*	Lab
Patchett, Terry: *Barnsley East*	Lab
Patnick, Irvine: *Sheffield, Hallam*	C
Patten, John: *Oxford West and Abingdon*	C
Pattie, Sir Geoffrey: *Chertsey and Walton*	C
Pawsey, James: *Rugby and Kenilworth*	C
Peacock, Elizabeth: *Batley and Spen*	C
Pendry, Tom: *Stalybridge and Hyde*	Lab
*Pickles, Eric: *Brentwood and Ongar*	C
*Pickthall, Colin: *Lancashire West*	Lab
Pike, Peter: *Burnley*	Lab
*Pope, Greg: *Hyndburn*	Lab
Porter, Barry: *Wirral South*	C
Porter, David: *Waveney*	C
Portillo, Michael: *Enfield, Southgate*	C
Powell, Ray: *Ogmore*	Lab
Powell, William: *Corby*	C
*Prentice, Bridget: *Lewisham East*	Lab
*Prentice, Gordon: *Pendle*	Lab
Prescott, John: *Hull East*	Lab
Primarolo, Dawn: *Bristol South*	Lab
*Purchase, Kenneth: *Wolverhampton North East*	Lab

Q

Quin, Joyce: *Gateshead East*	Lab

R

Radice, Giles: *Durham North*	Lab
Randall, Stuart: *Hull West*	Lab
Rathbone, Tim: *Lewes*	C
*Raynsford, Nick: *Greenwich*	Lab
Redmond, Martin: *Don Valley*	Lab
Redwood, John: *Wokingham*	C
Reid, Dr John: *Motherwell North*	Lab
Renton, Timothy: *Sussex Mid*	C
*Richards, Rod: *Clwyd North West*	C
Richardson, Jo: *Barking*	Lab
Riddick, Graham: *Colne Valley*	C
Rifkind, Malcolm: *Edinburgh, Pentlands*	C
*Robathan, Andrew: *Blaby*	C
Roberts, Sir Wyn: *Conwy*	C
Robertson, George: *Hamilton*	Lab
*Robertson, Raymond: *Aberdeen South*	C
Robinson, Geoffrey: *Coventry North West*	Lab
*Robinson, Mark: *Somerton and Frome*	C
Robinson, Peter: *Belfast East*	DUP
*Roche, Barbara: *Hornsey and Wood Green*	Lab

Roe, Marion: *Broxbourne*	C
Rogers, Allan: *Rhondda*	Lab
Rooker, Jeffrey: *Birmingham, Perry Barr*	Lab
Rooney, Terry: *Bradford North*	Lab
Ross, Ernest: *Dundee West*	Lab
Ross, William: *Londonderry East*	UU
Rowe, Andrew: *Kent Mid*	C
Rowlands, Edward: *Merthyr Tydfil and Rhymney*	Lab
Ruddock, Joan: *Lewisham Deptford*	Lab
Rumbold, Dame Angela: *Mitcham and Morden*	C
Ryder, Richard: *Norfolk Mid*	C

S

Sackville, Tom: *Bolton West*	C
Sainsbury, Tim: *Hove*	C
Salmond, Alex: *Banff and Buchan*	SNP
Scott, Nicholas: *Chelsea*	C
Sedgemore, Brian: *Hackney South and Shoreditch*	Lab
Shaw, David: *Dover*	C
Shaw, Sir Giles: *Pudsey*	C
Sheerman, Barry: *Huddersfield*	Lab
Sheldon, Robert: *Ashton-under-Lyne*	Lab
Shephard, Gillian: *Norfolk South West*	C
Shepherd, Colin: *Hereford*	C
Shepherd, Richard: *Aldridge-Brownhills*	C
Shersby, Michael: *Uxbridge*	C
Shore, Peter: *Bethnal Green and Stepney*	Lab
Short, Clare: *Birmingham, Ladywood*	Lab
*Simpson, Alan: *Nottingham South*	Lab
Sims, Roger: *Chislehurst*	C
Skeet, Sir Trevor: *Bedfordshire North*	C
Skinner, Dennis: *Bolsover*	Lab
Smith, Andrew: *Oxford East*	Lab
Smith, Christopher: *Islington South and Finsbury*	Lab
Smith, Sir Dudley: *Warwick and Leamington*	C
Smith, John: *Monklands East*	Lab
*Smith, Llewellyn: *Blaenau Gwent*	Lab
Smith, Timothy: *Beaconsfield*	C
Smyth, Rev Martin: *Belfast South*	UU
Snape, Peter: *West Bromwich East*	Lab
Soames, Nicholas: *Crawley*	C
Soley, Clive: *Hammersmith*	Lab
Spearing, Nigel: *Newham South*	Lab
Speed, Keith: *Ashford*	C
*Spellar, John: *Warley West*	Lab
*Spencer, Sir Derek: *Brighton, Pavilion*	C
Spicer, Sir James: *Dorset West*	C
Spicer, Michael: *Worcestershire South*	C
*Spink, Robert: *Castle Point*	C
*Spring, Richard: *Bury St Edmunds*	C
*Sproat, Iain: *Harwich*	C
*Squire, Rachel: *Dunfermline West*	Lab
Squire, Robin: *Hornchurch*	C
Stanley, Sir John: *Tonbridge and Malling*	C
Steel, Sir David: *Tweeddale, Ettrick and Lauderdale*	LD
Steen, Anthony: *South Hams*	C
Steinberg, Gerald: *Durham, City of*	Lab
*Stephen, Michael: *Shoreham*	C
Stern, Michael: *Bristol North West*	C
*Stevenson, George: *Stoke-on-Trent South*	Lab
Stewart, Allan: *Eastwood*	C
Stott, Roger: *Wigan*	Lab
Strang, Gavin: *Edinburgh East*	Lab
Straw, Jack: *Blackburn*	Lab

*Streeter, Gary: *Plymouth, Sutton*	C
Sumberg, David: *Bury South*	C
*Sweeney, Walter: *Vale of Glamorgan*	C
*Sykes, John: *Scarborough*	C

T

Tapsell, Sir Peter: *Lindsey East*	C
Taylor, Ann: *Dewsbury*	Lab
Taylor, Sir Teddy: *Southend East*	C
Taylor, Ian: *Esher*	C
Taylor, John David: *Strangford*	UU
Taylor, John Mark: *Solihull*	C
Taylor, Matthew: *Truro*	LD
Temple-Morris, Peter: *Leominster*	C
*Thomason, Roy: *Bromsgrove*	C
Thompson, Sir Donald: *Calder Valley*	C
Thompson, Jack: *Wansbeck*	Lab
Thompson, Patrick: *Norwich North*	C
Thornton, Malcolm: *Crosby*	C
Thurnham, Peter: *Bolton North East*	C
*Tipping, Paddy: *Sherwood*	Lab
Townend, John: *Bridlington*	C
Townsend, Cyril: *Bexleyheath*	C
Tracey, Richard: *Surbiton*	C
Tredinnick, David: *Bosworth*	C
*Trend, Michael: *Windsor and Maidenhead*	C
Trimble, David: *Upper Bann*	UU
Trotter, Neville: *Tynemouth*	C
Turner, Dennis: *Wolverhampton South East*	Lab
Twinn, Dr Ian: *Edmonton*	C
*Tyler, Paul: *Cornwall North*	LD

V

Vaughan, Sir Gerard: *Reading East*	C
Vaz, Keith: *Leicester East*	Lab
Viggers, Peter: *Gosport*	C

W

Waldegrave, William: *Bristol West*	C
Walden, George: *Buckingham*	C
Walker, Cecil: *Belfast North*	UU
Walker, Harold: *Doncaster Central*	Lab
Walker, William: *Tayside North*	C
Wallace, James: *Orkney and Shetland*	LD
Waller, Gary: *Keighley*	C
Walley, Joan: *Stoke-on-Trent North*	Lab
Ward, John: *Poole*	C
Wardell, Gareth: *Gower*	Lab
Wardle, Charles: *Bexhill and Battle*	C
Wareing, Robert: *Liverpool, West Derby*	Lab
*Waterson, Nigel: *Eastbourne*	C
Watson, Michael: *Glasgow Central*	Lab
Watts, John: *Slough*	C
Wells, Bowen: *Hertford and Stortford*	C
Welsh, Andrew: *Angus East*	SNP
Wheeler, Sir John: *Westminster North*	C
Whitney, Raymond: *Wycombe*	C
*Whittingdale, John: *Colchester South and Maldon*	C
*Wicks, Malcolm: *Croydon North West*	Lab
Widdecombe, Ann: *Maidstone*	C

Wiggin, Jerry: *Weston-Super-Mare* — C
Wigley, Dafydd: *Caernarfon* — PC
Wilkinson, John: *Ruislip, Northwood* — C
*Willetts, David: *Havant* — C
Williams, Alan J: *Swansea West* — Lab
Williams, Alan W: *Carmarthen* — Lab
Wilshire, David: *Spelthorne* — C
Wilson, Brian: *Cunninghame North* — Lab
Winnick, David: *Walsall North* — Lab
Winterton, Ann: *Congleton* — C
Winterton, Nicholas: *Macclesfield* — C
Wise, Audrey: *Preston* — Lab
Wolfson, Mark: *Sevenoaks* — C
Wood, Timothy: *Stevenage* — C
Worthington, Tony: *Clydebank and Milngavie* — Lab
Wray, James: *Glasgow, Provan* — Lab
*Wright, Tony: *Cannock and Burntwood* — Lab

Y

Yeo, Timothy: *Suffolk South* — C
Young, David: *Bolton South East* — Lab
Young, Sir George: *Ealing, Acton* — C

Call me madam

By Robert Morgan, *The Times* Parliamentary Staff

Few events in the House of Commons are unprecedented, but the occasion of the election of Betty Boothroyd as Speaker on April 27 1992 certainly was. After seven centuries and 154 previous Speakers of the House of Commons, she became the first woman to occupy the chair.

The scenes that followed the annoucement of the result of the vote were also unprecedented. As Miss Boothroyd was conducted from the Labour benches to her new place, the packed House burst into spontaneous and sustained applause. All members, including the government, stood and joined in. Clapping is out of order in the House, but no one seemed to notice or indeed care.

For some months Miss Boothroyd had been the front-runner to succeed Bernard Weatherill to become the highest commoner in the land. She had been a deputy Speaker for five years and shown the toughness of a Yorkshire-born lass who had spent the greater part of her adult life in or around the higher echelons of the Labour party. And in the chair she had shown wit and understanding. When appointed deputy Speaker she advised one MP: "Call me madam".

In the 18 days between polling and the election of the Speaker, a number of Tory back-benchers had let it be known that they were interested in the job. Peter Brooke was popular and the best known outside Westminster, but many argued that he should not be chosen because he had just relinquished cabinet office as Northern Ireland secretary. Other possible contenders were Terence Higgins and Sir Giles Shaw, both highly experienced and respected House of Commons figures.

But when Sir Edward Heath, Father of the House, set in motion the election process , only two candidates were mentioned. Mr Brooke's name was put forward with Miss Boothroyd as an alternative. After about an hour's debate, the House voted by 372 votes to 238 in favour of the Labour MP for West Bromwich West. Peter Brooke was among the first to congratulate her.

PARLIAMENTARY SEATS HELD SINCE THE WAR

	1945	1950	1951	1955	1959	1964	1966	1970	Feb 1974	Oct 1974	1979	1983	1987	1992
Consevative	213	298	321	345	365	303	253	330	296	276	339	397	375	336
Labour	393	315	295	277	258	317	363	287	301	319	268	209	229	271
Lib/Dem	12	9	6	6	6	9	12	6	14	13	11	23	22	20
Others*	22	3	3	2	—	2	2	7	24	27	17	21	24	24
Total	640	625	625	630	630	630	630	630	635	635	635	650	650	651

* Including the Speaker

Major defies the odds in all-or-nothing campaign

by Robin Oakley, Political Editor of *The Times*

The general election campaign of 1992 was a story of prime ministerial gambles which came off and Labour and Liberal Democrat gambles which did not, leaving opinion pollsters and pundits with bloodied noses and the Tories with a majority of 21.

Once again, as in 1987, Labour was commonly held to have won the campaign and once again it lost the election, John Major leading his party to their fourth successive victory and securing a marginally higher share of the vote for the Conservatives in a recession than Margaret Thatcher had done in a comparative boom.

All through an election in which Labour had led in the vast majority of the opinion polls and in which the Tory campaign had been criticised as negative and lacklustre, the prime minister retained his composure and insisted that he was "stone cold certain" of victory. Many about him had their doubts and the hung parliament industry was working overtime before election day proved him right.

After a long "phoney war" the election was called on March 11, the day after Norman Lamont's "Budget for recovery" had concentrated limited tax cuts on the lower paid with a new 20p tax band for the first £2,000 of taxable income and shaken the City with a forecast doubling of the public sector borrowing requirement to £28 billion in the next financial year. Labour said it was morally wrong to borrow to finance tax cuts and voted against them as a truncated finance bill was rushed through in the dying days of the parliament.

The election was called three months before it had to be. In interviews during the campaign Mr Major said that he had regarded it as immoral to go to the country the previous spring, cashing in on the end of the Gulf war, and that he had ruled out a November 1991 contest because he had not wanted to go to the polls until he had completed the Maastricht negotiations on European union in December and put through parliament a replacement for the poll tax, the scuttled "flagship" of Mrs Thatcher's legislative programme.

John Major and Chris Patten, his party chairman, knew that they were taking on a daunting task. They were trying in a sophisticated democracy to arrest the natural swing of the pendulum and have their party elected for the fourth time in a row. What is more, they were doing so against the background of a recession which had hit hardest with high interest rates many of the people the Tories liked to call their own — the C2s who had purchased their council houses, those encouraged by the enterprise ethos to start their own businesses.

Their attempt to re-run the almost traditional "Don't let Labour ruin it" argument was, they knew, complicated by having to paraphrase it on this occasion to "Don't let Labour make things even worse". But Mr Patten and the Tory admen were proved right in believing that the strongest line of all for them was the oft-repeated slogan "You can't trust Labour". Mr Major and Norman Lamont, the Chancellor of the Exchequer, remained convinced that they would prosper by harping on the cost of the spending programmes implied by Labour's manifesto and the tax increases which they asserted would follow the election of a Labour government.

The Tories faced the problem of all long-term governments: the appeal to a fair-minded electorate of the "time for a change" argument which Labour made its theme song. Neil Kinnock and his team underlined the theme by insisting that the Tories were supine in the face of the recession and its accompanying rise in unemployment.

Tory problems were compounded by the Scottish picture. There devolution and separatism appeared to have developed new appeal, with more than half the population backing separatism in one early 1992 poll.

The Tory leadership decided to run several risks. First was the risk of a largely negative campaign based on highlighting the fears about Labour's likely tax burden and on contrasting the experience and approach of John Major and Neil Kinnock, an already proven election fighter.

Secondly, against the background of a stack of opinion polls suggesting that a hung parliament was a likely outcome, Mr Major decided on an all-or-nothing strategy. He insisted on every opportunity that he would do no deals with Liberal Democrats or others and would not contemplate proportional representation, which he derided in his opening campaign speech in Torquay as "Paddy's Roundabout", a gibe at the expense of the Liberal Democrat leader.

Thirdly, despite the urgings of many within his own party that it was time for a concession to the rising tide for Scottish devolution, he took the view that there was nothing for the Tories in being the fourth best devolution party. Instead he played the union card vigorously, losing no opportunity to insist that any concession to devolution would lead inevitably to separatism, threatening the strength of the whole United Kingdom. Against widespread predictions of a wipeout that would leave the Tories without enough MPs in Scotland to man the Scottish Office that seemed to verge on the foolhardy. But with Labour and the Liberal Democrats backing the half-way house of a devolved Scottish parliament there was tactical advantage for the Tories in polarising the debate between unionism and separatism and they finished the election with two seats extra in Scotland.

Labour's national strategy, by contrast, was a safety first one of leaving the government to lose the election. Labour's press conferences were polished, drilled and regimented, with supplementary questions ruthlessly ruled out. The aim was to drive to the top of the agenda the "caring" issues of health, education and pensions on which the party knew it struck a chord with the voters. Despite all Mr Major's denials, culminating in his assertion that he was as likely to do so as he was to join the Labour party, they continued to insist that a Conservative government would privatise the NHS.

Secondly, Mr Kinnock and his team relentlessly pushed home the idea that the Tories had no answer to the recession and that only a Labour government would take "action" to counter it with jobs, training and investment packages. And thirdly came their one big risk. They decided to tackle head on the fears about their taxation policies with the much-publicised introduction of a "shadow budget" by the canny and comforting John Smith, a man on whom no interviewer ever laid a glove.

Mr Major told friends that John Smith's shadow budget, including the removal of the £21,000 ceiling on national insurance contributions, had presented the Tories with the election by hitting the middle classes with an unexpected savagery. But voters, the vast majority of them earning less than £22,000 a year and ending as net gainers (if only marginally) under Mr Smith's carefully drawn plans, appeared initially to respond favourably to the Labour initiative.

After several days the Tories had to recalibrate their tax attack, focusing instead on the claimed impact on lower earning taxpayers of implementing Labour's manifesto promises. Totting up Labour's spending promises at £38 billion, Mr Lamont insisted that this would mean an all-round average increase in tax of £1,250 per head. Even then, ministers did not succeed throughout the campaign in elevating taxation or management of the economy to the levels of health and education in the "issue" tables of public concerns. Such questions, it seems, were not confronted by many until they were in the polling booths.

Labour was able to give the impression of a fresh party with new ideas by recycling in daily segments sections of its already published policy documents and announcing new programmes for the first week, the first month and the first year of a Labour government. There was the feminist point too: Harriet Harman and Margaret Beckett, with or without anything to say, were constantly paraded on the Labour platform in deliberate contrast with the Tories' array of masculine grey suits.

In the first opinion poll of the campaign, taken on March 11-12, Mori measured party support at Labour 41 per cent, Conservatives 38 per cent and Liberal Democrats 16 per cent, indicating that the Budget had failed to provide the stimulus to Conservative support which the government had been seeking.

Neil Kinnock was first off the mark on the Friday with a speech to the previously arranged Scottish Labour conference. Calling the budget a "£2 billion flop", Mr Kinnock promised that Labour would "invest, invest, invest" to build a strong economy in partnership with industry and condemned what he called the sourness and the selfishness, the staleness and the stagnation of the Tory years. He pledged: "We want people to be free of the fear of falling ill, free of fear of walking the dark streets at night, free of fear of being old and lonely."

John Major opened his campaign at the Conservative Central Council meeting in Torquay the next day, insisting that the economy was "poised for recovery" and promising to bury the old divisions in British society between north and south, white collar and blue collar, university and polytechnic. He made a point of declaring that the Liberal Democrat campaign for proportional representation was "a sham" offering the "government of smoke-filled rooms".

While Labour would treat the people as pawns, he said, the Conservatives, as the party of low tax and personal choice, would give them power. Underlining the Tory strategy, Michael Heseltine, a key figure in the Tory campaign, said that the election would be about tax, tax and tax. And both he and Douglas Hurd suggested that Neil Kinnock lacked the experience and authority for Number Ten. On the Sunday came the first of the John Major talkabouts, with the prime minister perched on a bar stool taking questions from an invited audience. Modelled on his talks to Gulf war troops, the "meet John Major" sessions were designed to play to his strengths in handling detail across a wide range of subjects. But they never made news and failed to help the Tories win control of the election agenda.

The next day the Liberal Democrats were first into the field with their manifesto, a glossy magazine-style document which insisted that PR was the minimum price for Liberal Democrat participation in any coalition government. It committed the party to the integration of tax and national insurance systems, a 10p a year increase in petrol prices to tackle pollution, an increase in borrowing to fund a £6 billion "kick-start" programme for jobs and investment, a break-up of privatised monopolies and Scottish and Welsh parliaments.

One of the more controversial elements was the promise to increase income tax by 1p to provide an extra £2 billion for education. That was one of several risks taken by Paddy Ashdown and his team in the election. Another was the way they deliberately raised the "wasted vote" argument and tackled it head on. So too was the decision to stay out of the row about "Jennifer's ear", Labour's election broadcast about NHS waiting lists and queue jumping. But as the Liberal Democrats picked up 5 points in the polls during the campaign the "penny on tax" for education and the other gambles appeared to be succeeding, at least until polling day. Issues polls showed the Liberal Democrat policy on education earning them their best rating ever on a particular issue and advancing on the Conservatives.

Labour launched their big gamble the same day with the shadow budget from shadow chancellor John Smith. He and his team posed in front of the Treasury and issued a "red book" resembling the traditional Treasury document. Aimed to kill off speculation about any "hidden agenda" of planned tax increases, the shadow budget was presented as "a fair deal for the average taxpayer" and the most explicit revelation of taxation plans ever given by an Opposition. Measures included scrapping of the new 20p band and increasing personal allowances by £330, taking 740,000 people out of taxation altogether. A 50p tax band was to be introduced at a taxable income of £36,375 and the £21,060 upper earnings limit on NICs would be removed. But Mr Smith dropped Labour's previous plan for a tax on savings income of more than £3,000 a year.

On the spending side the absolute commitments were a pensions increase of £5 for single pensioners and £8 for couples, an uprating of child benefit to £9.95 and a £2.7 billion recovery programme of investment in training, health and education. There would be no increase beyond Tory plans in borrowing and Mr Smith and Mr Kinnock then and through the campaign promised that a Labour government would not raise the standard rate or the new top rate of tax, nor the 9 per cent contribution level on NICs nor the VAT rate of 17.5 per cent.

Mr Lamont said Labour's plans would push up interest rates, clobber those on whom the country was depending to come out of recession and "devastate" house prices.

The Conservatives released the education section of their manifesto a day early to show the priority attached to the subject and promised money for over-subscribed schools to be able to expand, new types of grant-maintained schools and a breakdown in barriers between academic and vocational education.

The two major party manifestos, issued on Wednesday, March 18, contained no new "big ideas" and few surprises, but the Conservative document *The Best Future for Britain* did announce plans for a new cabinet minister to oversee the Citizen's Charter, a new ministry, soon nicknamed the Ministry of Fun, to cover arts, heritage, broadcasting and sport, and the demise of the Department of Energy. The Conservative document, detailed enough to include a "hedgerow incentive scheme" included promises to franchise British Rail services to outside companies, special help for the inner cities and an attempt to open up Whitehall. In future the membership of cabinet committees will be revealed.

On Europe, the Tory document struck a distinctly pragmatic note, with much talk of the Conservatives' readiness to "resist" Brussels initiatives and "stoutly defend" British interests.

Labour's manifesto *It's time to get Britain working again* was shorter, pithier and proved to be the most distant of cousins to the Labour documents at the previous two elections. It contained strong commitments to the European community and promised to retain a nuclear deterrent for Britain until the world's stock of nuclear weapons had been eliminated. The nearest thing to any renationalisation was the pledge to take the national grid and the privatised water companies into "public control".

It took up Neil Kinnock's promise of fixed-term parliaments, pledged a £1 billion recovery package (derided by the Tories as pointless in its effect on a £630 billion economy) and promised tax incentives to encourage firms to invest. With an eye to Liberal Democrat floaters, the document promised an upgrading under a Labour government of the party committee under Professor Raymond Plant studying electoral systems.

As the campaign then settled into the routine of leader's tours and daily press conferences (the Liberal Democrats starting the day promptly each day at an unfriendly 7.15 am), Labour had the greater success in framing the agenda while Conservatives grew edgy at their party's apparent inability to peg back Labour's small but visible lead in the opinion polls. A media pack long bored with the preliminary skirmishing of the phoney war, during which the Conservatives had been forced to expend much of their ammunition on Labour's tax plans to prevent Mr Kinnock developing momentum, criticised the Tories in particular for concentrating all their efforts on attacking Labour. The youthful team at Conservative Central Office under director of communications Shaun Woodward, aged 33, was nicknamed the "brat pack" and past luminaries of Thatcher campaigns, resentful in some cases at not being part of the latest effort, were not slow to air their criticisms.

There was, however, curiously little excitement. The long practice period ensured that most acts were well rehearsed and there were few gaffes. Roy Hattersley, Labour's deputy leader, erred one day on his party's plans for tackling the privatised public utilities and another day on taxation policy being smartly corrected by John Smith. There was a minor difference between Mr Kinnock and Mr Smith on privatisation proceeds. John Major had a tricky time at one press conference when harried for a promise that the next Tory government would reduce the overall burden of taxation. Labour was embarrassed by revelations that millionaires living off their interest would fare better under the party's tax plans than middle-rank managers. But there was a curious lack of buzz or movement about the campaign. Few stories were hastily rewritten late at night.

The government continued to be dogged by poor economic statistics, notably the unemployment figures on March 19 which showed 2.6 million without a job in February, more than at any time since September 1987. Trade figures a week later disappointed with a larger than expected deficit and there were reports that the government's spending plans would not be adequately covered by its tax receipts. Later still came a Dun and Bradstreet report showing that businesses were failing at the rate of 1,200 a week.

Mr Major, more exposed than Mr Kinnock, was jostled by demonstrators and forced to end a walkabout in Bolton. But, the odd egg apart, the campaign proved generally violence-free and far cleaner than commentators had predicted.

As the polls continued to suggest a hung parliament with Labour the largest party, the Liberal Democrats steadily upped the ante for their participation in any coalition government. On March 22 Margaret Thatcher boosted Tory morale in a joint appearance with John Major to bless her successor. Labour derided her appearance at a long-arranged rally of Tory candidates as a sign of government desperation. In fact, Mrs Thatcher's intervention, before leaving the country for an American lecture tour in the last week, probably served as a reminder of the change at the top even without a change of government, so undermining a central plank of Labour's campaign. Significantly, opinion polls continued all through to indicate a much larger number of floating voters than at a similar stage in the past two campaigns.

Then in mid campaign came the bizarre affair of "Jennifer's ear". A glossy Labour party political broadcast, designed to lift health to the top of the political agenda, highlighted the cases of two little girls needing the same ear operation, one of them rich enough to have it privately. The film was loosely based on a real life case and the identity of the family concerned was leaked. It was never quite established by whom. The Tories complained of the exploitation of children and the besmirching of the NHS, accusing Neil Kinnock of being unfit to govern. Labour, unrepentant, accused the Tories of smear tactics and creating diversions. Even the parents of the girl concerned were at odds about the film. William Waldegrave, the health secretary, was given a torrid time at a Tory press conference, in the course of which he revealed that the party had put the consultant in the case in touch with the *Daily Express*. Labour was forced to withdraw case histories it had offered in support of its claims and in an extraordinary episode Neil Kinnock's press secretary Julie Hall took to a press conference rostrum to deny emotionally that she had leaked the name of the girl concerned.

Labour succeeded in raising the profile of health, but not quite in the way it had intended. A vote of no confidence in the government's health reforms by the British Medical Association conference passed almost unnoticed amid the furore.

The wrangle continued for days before both parties retired hurt and dropped the subject. The public appeared to have retired bemused long before that point.

By the end of March, the worries about the Tory campaign were being openly discussed in the party, with Mrs Thatcher said to feel that it lacked "oomph and fizz". On March 28 John Major, jostled and persecuted by demonstrators in Luton, stood up on a soapbox with a loudhailer and shouted back. The stratagem proved such a success that he announced he would take his soapbox with him for the rest of the campaign, and so he did. Some criticised the move as one which diminished his advantage as an incumbent prime minister. But the soapbox become the symbol of a Tory fightback and may well have been the turning point of the campaign.

On March 30 Paddy Ashdown, displaying prodigious energy as he dashed from end to end of the country to enthusiastic Liberal Democrat rallies, even took his party's "My Vote" campaign to the continent with a day trip to Boulogne. The sharper bite of Liberal Democrat policies and the party's refusal to participate in the war of Jennifer's ear had increased its support and the campaign moved into the final week with the Liberal Democrat subjects of fair votes and constitutional reform apparently topping the agenda.

As the campaign moved into April John Major promised to "take the gloves off" and the Liberal Democrats began a surge in the polls, at Tory expense rather than by dividing the anti-Conservative opposition.

Then a Mori opinion poll published in *The Times* on April 1 gave Labour its biggest lead so far of 7 points, opening the prospect of an overall Labour majority. City markets took fright and that night Labour staged an exultant rally of 10,000 supporters in Sheffield, full of showbusiness glamour and American-style razzmatazz. Labour leaders, understandably buoyed up by polls which seemed to show them breaking clear, allowed the tone to become too triumphalist and what came to be known as "Red Wednesday" was seen by many in retrospect as the day which tipped the election away from them as voters were forced to consider if they really wanted to swap a John Major government for one led by Neil Kinnock.

The near level pegging in the polls for most of the campaign despite the recession had argued that there was no "sea change" mood running in the electorate of the kind likely to deliver the record 8 per cent swing Labour needed for victory. In the final week of the campaign, as both leaders sharpened their rhetoric, it seems that the Tories' relentless campaign on the potential tax cost of Labour's plans began to sink home. The five-point improvement in Liberal Democrat support began to slip away again as pocket book concerns reasserted themselves.

The Tories, in one of their more effective election broadcasts, revealed how the past CND affiliations of Labour candidates had been expunged from their official biographies. And John Major tackled the Liberal Democrats directly. At a West Country rally and on his soapbox he condemnded them as the "Trojan horse to a Labour Britain". Support for Paddy Ashdown, he declared, would let Neil Kinnock into Downing Street. And the prime minister took the risk of devoting a Tory press conference in the final week to the perils of a hung parliament. A defeatist move, said virtually every commentator, revealing the state of Tory alarm. But, as with his stark presentation of Scottish devolution as the precursor to the break-up of Britain, it clearly served to concentrate minds.

Mr Kinnock meanwhile attacked the Tories as a "spent force". He declared: "They have no vitality and they are rapidly losing their integrity". Conservative government had increased the numbers of unemployed and homeless and created two-tier systems of health and education. They had shrunk the economy, lowered investment and taken Britain to the bottom of the international league tables. While Mr Major mounted his soapbox thousands more slept in cardboard boxes. Labour, said Mr Kinnock, would govern positively, looking to the future.

As the polls continued to indicate at least a hung parliament if not a Labour majority, the Tory effort to target Mr Kinnock personally and to emphasise the likely tax increases under a Labour government was redoubled in the final days. Labour, possibly fearing that the Liberal Democrat surge could harm its own prospects and eager to detach Mr Ashdown's looser supporters, flirted ever more openly with PR, suggesting that the membership of the Plant committee could be widened to include those in other parties and hinting it would back PR for elections to the European Parliament. That may have served to underline the prime minister's message three days before polling that Labour and the Liberal Democrats would happily climb into bed together and eased his task in warning of the dangers of a hung parliament.

Mr Kinnock's talk turned more and more to "consensus" government. Mr Ashdown, aware of the danger that Liberal Democrat supporters might slip away if they feared he was helping to bring in a high-taxing Labour government, made plain in an interview with *The Times* that in a hung parliament he would veto Labour's tax package and ensure that tax increases were introduced more gradually up the scale.

In response to reports that Mr Ashdown would want four cabinet posts for his party in a coalition government Mr Kinnock said that none would be available. Mr Ashdown appeared to soften slightly on how much progress he would be demanding towards PR as his price for cooperation with a minority government.

At their final rallies Mr Major urged the country not to don the "tatty red vest of socialism" just when the rest of the world was choosing to run in blue. Mr Kinnock insisted that the people's choice was building up the National Health Service with Labour or breaking it up with the Tories. The opinion polls indicated that we were in for a desperately close contest with a hung parliament the most likely outcome.

Labour had begun the election campaign with an average lead in the opinion polls of 1.6 per cent and ended it with an average lead of 2.3 per cent. That in itself was enough to raise the query: do campaigns matter?

Certainly the 1992 campaign justified the prime minister's quiet optimism all through. It testified to his coolness under fire and it vindicated his judgment, just as it underlined once more Neil Kinnock's fine qualities as a platform orator and demonstrated a new discipline in the Labour effort. But history has since been rewritten about the campaign simply because of the result. Mr Kinnock did cut John Major's lead as the most popular prime minister through the campaign, although not by enough. The Tory effort was at times diffuse and unfocused. The Conservatives seemed ambivalent themselves about whether they wanted Mr Major to remain Mr Nice Guy or to mix it with Mr Kinnock, whether they wanted him to be a simple guy on a soapbox or a star amid the special £500,000 set they took around the country for his rallies. But either way, there was no doubt whose election it was. In the end the only positive part of the Tory message was "Trust John Major", and the people did.

Europe and poll tax spell end of the Thatcher decade

by Philip Webster, Chief Political Correspondent of *The Times*

In the early hours of April 10, 1992, a tired but smiling Margaret Thatcher, suffering from a heavy cold, announced her pleasure at the way the general election results were going. The Conservatives were heading for their fourth outright election victory in succession and, Mrs Thatcher remarked, everything she had worked for would be preserved.

But it was not Mrs Thatcher who returned to Downing Street later that morning to pick up the reins of government. It was a 49-year-old man who had entered parliament on the day she became prime minister in 1979, and who had been a junior social security minister when she secured her third victory back in 1987.

The intervening tumultuous years had seen Mrs Thatcher suddenly, perhaps cruelly, removed from office. She had spearheaded three election wins but Conservative MPs decided she should not be given another chance. Their collective wisdom was that another leader would win the election for them.

On that April morning John Major, the man who had emerged from obscurity to take the nation's top job, duly rewarded their judgment. Against the predictions of virtually every pundit and pollster in the land Mr Major, who never wavered in his confidence, led his party to majority government yet again.

In South Wales that same April morning another leader arrived for his election count in his Islwyn constituency. He had been expecting to make a speech of triumph. But during the night things had gone wrong, horribly wrong. All the polls, private and public, had told Neil Kinnock that later that day his eight-and-a-half-year struggle to make the Labour party an electable force would culminate in him, not Mr Major, becoming the occupant of 10 Downing Street. Now, voice cracked with emotion, the Labour leader declared: "I take this opportunity to dedicate myself to the service of my constituents, and in any capacity whatsoever to the people of my country."

They were the words of a man who knew he had been beaten. No one had ever done more for his party; his personal campaign could hardly have been faulted. But power had eluded him, this time forever. Within days he had announced his resignation. If politics, in the end, had been cruel to Margaret Thatcher, how much more so for Neil Kinnock.

Mr Kinnock's swift departure from the leadership of his party was the poignant postcript to a Parliament that had more than its share of super-charged personal and political drama. The pundits who thought Mrs Thatcher's 1987 general election landslide would mean a period of relative calm were hopelessly wrong.

Mrs Thatcher, seemingly invincible, was brought down by a combination of a hated new local government tax that she had promised in the 1987 manifesto, her hardline opposition to closer integration in the European Community, mistakes in the running of the economy that tipped it over into recession, and a personal style that her Cabinet, MPs and the voters found increasingly difficult to take.

Hers was the last, and most sensational, of a series of departures from a Cabinet that now contains no faces from 1979.

Nigel Lawson, the chancellor whom she described as brilliant, went at the end of a simmering dispute over the European exchange-rate mechanism. Nicholas Ridley, her closest ally, had to go for rudely castigating the Germans. Finally, the quiet and apparently emollient Sir Geoffrey Howe, once her most important lieutenant, resigned over Europe, leaving her fatally wounded with one of the most devastating Commons speeches of modern times. In Mr Major the Conservatives chose a leader who had never even served in opposition.

The excitement was not confined to the Conservative party. The parliament saw the birth under Paddy Ashdown of the old Liberal and Social Democrat parties as a merged new party and the death of an independent SDP which staggered on for a time under David Owen. Dr Owen bowed out as well.

Neil Kinnock saw off a leftwing challenge to his leadership and cast aside the ideological baggage that helped Labour lose three elections. He converted Labour to the market economy and multilateralism and left his opponents claiming he had forsaken all his principles in the pursuit of power.

It was a parliament in which public opinion veered wildly between lengthy periods of support for Labour and the Conservatives. There was even a truce on the political front as Britain went to war with Iraq. President Gorbachev was ousted and quickly returned, but the Soviet Union passed into history and Mr Gorbachev went for good.

The Maastricht summit in December 1991 saw Europe take important steps towards economic and political union. John Major secured a deal that satisfied most of his party and kept Mrs Thatcher's objections in check.

Margaret Thatcher was returned to Downing Street for the third time on June 11, 1987. She had a 101-seat majority but was not satisfied. Her immediate pledge to tackle the problems of the inner cities was personal recognition that the Conservatives should do more to improve their image in the Labour heartlands.

For the opposition parties it was a period of speedy reappraisal. On June 15 David Steel, disappointed by the Alliance's performance, soon tabled proposals for the merger of his own Liberal party and David Owen's Social Democratic Party. Labour quickly decided to "review" the policies that had cost it three elections.

It was too much for Dr Owen. Two months later he resigned as leader of the SDP after it voted by 57 per cent to 42 per cent for a merger with the Liberals. He was to go it alone with two other MPs, Rosie Barnes and John Cartwright.

For the government the seeds of later trouble were sown as the Queen's speech contained as its centrepiece a bill to introduce the community charge to replace the rates. Within a month it had decided that the poll tax should be phased in over four years. In October a self-congratulatory Tory conference held a debate on the poll tax in which calls were made for it to be introduced in one go rather than phased. It gave Nicholas Ridley, then environment secretary, the ammunition he needed. The next month the Cabinet decided to introduce it in one go. The consequences would be heavy. By December Michael Heseltine, still in the political wilderness after the Westland affair, was leading a Tory backbench rebellion against the community charge. He called it a Tory tax and the government's majority fell to 72.

On October 19 that year came another event that was to have lasting repercussions. Black Monday saw the collapse of world stock markets, with £50 billion wiped off London share values. Next day there was a drop of £40 billion, and in response Nigel Lawson, the Chancellor, cut interest rates.

At the beginning of 1988 Lord Whitelaw, sheet anchor of the government, resigned as deputy prime minister on doctor's advice. His departure from the centre-stage was to be sharply felt by Mrs Thatcher as the troubles piled up for her later on.

In the Labour party all was reasonably quiet. John Prescott was dissuaded from challenging for Labour's deputy leadership; the Liberals backed the merger with the SDP, and a few days later the SDP conference backed merger with the Liberals.

March 15, 1988, was a fateful day in the history of the Parliament. Mr Lawson cut the basic rate of tax to 25p and the top rate to 40p, adding fuel to an already overheated economy. Mrs Thatcher called the Budget a "humdinger" but privately she was in deep disagreement with the Chancellor over his policy of shadowing the D-mark, referred to privately by Mr Lawson as "living in sin" with the European exchange-rate mechanism. She was furious at his policy of holding down the pound by selling it heavily on the foreign exchanges. "You cannot buck the markets," she said. Mr Lawson again cut interest rates and the economy moved towards an inflationary boom. It was later to be admitted that serious policy errors had been made.

Later that month Labour came alive as the left objected to the direction in which Mr Kinnock was taking it. Tony Benn challenged Neil Kinnock for the leadership and Eric Heffer challenged Roy Hattersley for the deputy's job. Prominent leftwingers resigned from the far left Campaign Group in protest. Mr Prescott entered the contest for the deputy leadership and Mr Kinnock staked his authority on the reelection of Mr Hattersley. The policy review was proceeding apace. Nationalisation without compensation was one of the first sacred cows sent to the slaughter.

Some time afterwards Mr Kinnock explicitly abandoned unilateralism for the first time. "There is now no need for something-for-nothing unilateralism," he said in a television interview. In the kerfuffle that followed, Denzil Davies resigned as his defence spokesman over an alleged lack of consultation before the Kinnock statement. The confusion over Labour's defence stance and the leadership election created internal turmoil and helped the Tories to a 12 per cent opinion poll lead.

It was some relief for ministers because until then the real trouble seemed to be occurring on the government benches. Mr Heseltine was accused bitterly by ministers of being the inspiration behind an imminent revolt on the poll tax and on April 18 the government majority slumped to 25 as the rebels attempted to wreck the poll tax bill with an amendment trying to relate it to the ability to pay.

There was worse on the economic front. In May Mr Lawson cut interest rates from 8 to 7.5 per cent, the lowest since 1978. But next month he suddenly had to start applying the brakes. Between June and November interest rates soared from 7.5 per cent to 13 per cent, with eight increases between June and August 23. Edward Heath, still a rumbling presence, said Mr Lawson was a one-club man, and that club was interest rates. A consumer boom resulted in a July £2.15 billion trade deficit.

In July, Labour's position had improved with a good result in the Kensington by-election. In the same month Paddy Ashdown became leader of the SLD, heavily defeating Alan Beith.

On September 21, 1988, Mrs Thatcher made a speech that was to reverberate around Europe and lay down the battle lines on an issue that ultimately contributed to her demise. She went to Bruges, in Belgium, and set her face against European political and economic union in a speech that became a rallying-point for the anti-federalists, and a source of discontent for the Euro-enthusiasts.

The next month, at the Labour conference, Mr Kinnock and Mr Hattersley routed their opponents in the leadership election. They were defeated on nuclear defence but pledged to change it all the same.

As Mrs Thatcher made a visit to Washington in November to say farewell to Ronald Reagan — both hailed their periods in office as a turning point in world history — there was more pressure on the government at home over interest rates. Sir Alan Walters, Mrs Thatcher's former economic adviser, wrote of the wasted years in the battle against inflation and called the ERM "half-baked." It was suspected, rightly or wrongly, that he was speaking for his former boss.

December of that year was dominated by eggs. Edwina Currie, then health minister, dropped the biggest bombshell of her illustrious career when she suggested that most of the country's egg production was infected with salmonella. In the row that followed there was a huge drop in egg demand. After an outcry from the farming lobby Mrs Currie resigned.

The new year, 1989, started badly for Mr Lawson. In January he told MPs that inflation was worsening. Things got much worse in May when Mrs Thatcher recalled Sir Alan Walters to Downing Street. The writing was on the wall.

For Labour the portents were good. In February its defence policy review team was boosted by Kremlin backing for its multilateralist approach. As the policy review proceeded, with the policy of renationalisation watered down so far that now only water and BT would be returned to the public sector, it moved in February into a poll lead for the first time since the 1987 election. In May, Mr Kinnock won national executive backing for the end of unilateralism, a switch that would have been unthinkable a few years before. Mr Kinnock even said he might press the nuclear button.

On May 4, 1989, a Cabinet dinner saluted Mrs Thatcher's decade as prime minister. But times were not happy. Labour captured Vale of Glamorgan in a by-election and the ubiquitous Sir Alan Walters was reported to have criticised Mr Lawson at City lunches. The Lawson-Walters-Thatcher row spilled over into a loss of confidence in the pound. Inflation hit 8 per cent, Mrs Thatcher blamed Lawson for letting the economy get out of hand but then she was forced publicly to back him as the pound slid.

Meanwhile Conservative unhappiness over Mrs Thatcher's hardline stance on Europe was increasing. Edward Heath said she would leave Britain a "second rate power in a second tier community". Discontent with the government increased on June 15 when Labour triumphed in the European Parliament elections after a disastrous Tory campaign dogged by rows over Mrs Thatcher's policy.

On June 27 Mrs Thatcher agreed at the historic Madrid summit that, subject to conditions, Britain would one day join the ERM. It was revealed much later that she did so only after a threat to resign from Sir Geoffrey Howe, her Foreign Secretary, and Mr Lawson.

The world did not know it at the time but the behind-the-scenes drama was the reason for Mrs Thatcher's decision the following month dramatically to reconstruct her cabinet. Sir Geoffrey was moved, against his will, from the Foreign Office because Mrs Thatcher disliked his preference for speedy European integration. John Major was promoted to Foreign Secretary to become the Crown Prince of the Conservative party, and Kenneth Baker to party chairman.

Sir Geoffrey took the consolation of the deputy prime ministership but it soon emerged that he had almost resigned during the reshuffle negotiations and had turned down the post of Home Secretary.

If that was not enough trouble for Mrs Thatcher, there was also a Conservative backbench outcry over the effects of the safety net to cushion poll tax, with MPs warning that marginal seats were at risk because high-spenders would be bailed out by the prudent.

By now the Thatcher-Lawson dispute was moving rapidly to a conclusion. On October 5 1989 interest rates were raised from 14 per cent to 15 per cent, guaranteeing a miserable Tory conference week for the Chancellor.

On October 24 Tory MPs and Mr Lawson asked for Sir Alan Walters to be silenced after his remark that the "ERM is half-baked" seemed to be trying to undermine him.

On an unforgettable day, October 26, Mr Lawson resigned from office complaining that he could no longer accept the presence of Sir Alan at Number 10. Mrs Thatcher had not wanted to lose the man she once called "brilliant" but she refused his demand for Sir Alan's scalp. Within hours the adviser had gone too. Mrs Thatcher was forced to reshuffle her three main departments of state. Mr Major, moving onward and upwards, became Chancellor and Douglas Hurd became Foreign Secretary.

It was the beginning of the end. On November 22, 1989, a little-known backbencher, Sir Anthony Meyer, announced he would be a "stalking-horse" challenger to Mrs Thatcher in the first leadership contest since she was elected in 1975. The future of the EC was the battleground.

On December 5 she secured a convincing victory, but 60 MPs voted against her or abstained and many warned that they would not back her again. How seriously that warning was taken no one will ever know.

Poll tax worries dominated the start of 1990. On February 27 Chris Patten, then the environment secretary, warned of huge poll tax bills being drawn up by councils and the backbench 1922 Committee was told that it was a "political cyanide pill" for the Tories. In March there were violent town hall protests over poll tax.

Tory nerves were stretched further when on March 22 Labour secured its best by-election success for 50 years, overturning a 14,000 Tory majority to take Mid Staffordshire. A review of the poll tax was promised with doubts resurfacing over Mrs Thatcher's leadership. Norman Tebbit said he would be ready to stand if she stood down, a move designed to spike Michael Heseltine who admitted that he, too, would be a candidate.

On April 1 1990 the poll tax was finally introduced in England and Wales and two days later Mr Heseltine unveiled plans to reform it. In July Mr Patten secured an extra £2.5 billion from the Treasury to try to hold bills down. The previous month David Owen had wound up the SDP because it was no longer big enough to carry on as a national force.

In *The Spectator* of July 12 Nicholas Ridley, the industry secretary, told Dominic Lawson, its editor, that the Germans were trying to take over Europe. A furore followed which ended with Mr Ridley's resignation two days later. Mrs Thatcher had lost her closest friend and ideological soulmate in the Cabinet.

On August 1 that year Saddam Hussein of Iraq sent his troops into Kuwait. Britain quickly began sending air and naval forces to the Gulf.

But while talk of war in the Middle East was in the air the Mother of all Battles was about to engulf the Tory party. On October 4 the government chose the last day of the Labour conference to announce entry into the ERM. Mr Major and Mr Hurd had quietly persuaded Mrs Thatcher over the previous months that there was no alternative. Conservative divisions over the speed towards economic union and a single currency resurfaced at a subdued party conference and on October 18, against all the odds, the Tories lost Eastbourne, the seat formerly held by Ian Gow, who was murdered by the IRA.

On October 28, against Mrs Thatcher's furious opposition, the Rome European Council summit set a 1994 deadline for the start of the second stage of EMU. She told the Commons it was "the back door to a federal Europe" and appeared to undermine Mr Major's plan for a "hard ecu" common currency. Sir Geoffrey Howe reached the end of his tether, and on November 1 he resigned as Commons leader. Mrs Thatcher's last days were upon her.

On November 13 Sir Geoffrey made a devastating resignation speech to the Commons which was widely seen as virtually inciting a challenge to her leadership. She was risking Britain's future by her attitude to Europe. "The time has come for others to consider their own response to the tragic conflict of loyalties with which I have myself wrestled for perhaps too long," he said, stunning his colleagues.

Mr Heseltine had been wavering about making a challenge, but Sir Geoffrey had made up his mind for him. On November 14 he flung down the gauntlet.

Mrs Thatcher's campaign team were far too confident. On November 20 she polled 204 votes to Mr Heseltine's 152, insufficient under the party's complex rules for an overall first ballot victory. It seemed to be the end for her but in Paris that night she declared she would fight the second ballot.

The next day Mrs Thatcher declared: "I fight on, I fight to win." But support was slipping away. One by one members of the Cabinet visited her in her room at the Commons to tell her that she would lose and hand the leadership to Mr Heseltine. By midnight she had decided to go.

It was the nearest Mr Heseltine would come to the leadership. On November 22 a tearful prime minister told the cabinet at 9 am that she was resigning. Nominations for the second ballot were to close at midday. Nothing is certain in politics but it is likely that Mr Heseltine was only three hours away from the job he coveted most. Instead, freed of their loyalty to Mrs Thatcher, Mr Hurd and Mr Major had time to throw their hats into the ring.

By the afternoon the ever-resilient Mrs Thatcher had recovered to make a bravura speech in the Commons no confidence debate. "We will not see her like again" was the tribute that echoed round the political world as an era ended.

On November 27, after a friendly contest from which all the bitterness of the first ballot had been removed, John Major, aged 47, became the new Tory leader. The man who promised to create a truly classless society in the 1990s scored 185 votes, to Mr Heseltine's 131 and Mr Hurd's 56. He was two short of the figure required for outright victory but his rivals quickly conceded.

The following day Mr Heseltine was recalled by Mr Major to the Cabinet as environment secretary to oversee the reform of the poll tax. Chistopher Patten became party chairman. Mr Major gave Mr Heseltine a free hand to scrap the poll tax. In a sense the 1992 election campaign began here. There was talk that Mr Major would make a quick rush to the country to secure his own mandate, but he apparently did not give it a thought.

1991 began with the economy plunging into recession. On January 17 the Gulf war started, the first of a series of international events that propelled Mr Major into the international limelight.

For a time, as the nation was gripped by the first televised war, it seemed that it would cause political trouble at home for Mr Kinnock. A mysterious gathering of Labour's soft left, calling itself the Supper Club, met in secret to try to limit the Labour leader's backing for the government line. Five Labour front-benchers resigned over Mr Kinnock's stance on the Gulf.

The Gulf war ended on February 28 with the rout of the Iraqi forces. The first serious option for a general election emerged but it was dished on March 7 when the Liberal Democrats captured the tenth safest Tory seat with a by-election triumph at Ribble Valley. The outcome strengthened Mr Heseltine's hand to get rid of poll tax with a new property tax, to be called the "council tax".

The next election option was June. This was favoured by Mr Major himself but Labour and the Liberal Democrats made widespread gains in the May local elections and a Labour victory at the Monmouth by-election on May 16 turned the speculators' gaze towards the autumn.

The government hit another rough patch. On June 6 Mrs Thatcher said she had no regrets over introducing the community charge and there was sharp Conservative irritation over the comments allegedly made by the former PM criticising her successor. The Bruges group, set up after Mrs Thatcher's famous speech in that city to defend the anti-federalist cause, attacked Mr Major over what they saw as his over-friendly approach to Europe. Labour's opinion poll lead widened to 10 per cent, and two old bruisers, Mrs Thatcher and Mr Heath, clashed angrily over Europe, the latter accusing the former of telling lies.On June 28 1991, Mrs Thatcher announced she would be bowing out as an MP at the general election. She said that she wanted to speak more loudly against a single currency, and her decision would show she was not a threat to Mr Major.

Mr Kinnock's incessant battle to oust the Militant left from Labour had continued throughout the parliament and on July 4 it reached a watershed. Forced out into the open to fight Labour for the first time a Militant-backed candidate was crushed in the Liverpool Walton by-election, caused by the death of the veteran leftwinger Eric Heffer.

In July Mr Major, battling to put his own stamp on the government, unveiled his Citizens' Charter, including guaranteed maximum waiting times for operations, fixed appointments for the gas man, and refunds for rail travellers if the trains were late.

Labour entered that summer recess well ahead in polls but it was dominated by foreign events which saw Mr Major's stature rising. On August 18 President Gorbachev was toppled by reactionaries and imprisoned in his holiday home. With Boris Yeltsin leading the resistance in Moscow Mr Gorbachev was to be reinstated after three days, but for him retirement beckoned.

Mr Major flew to Washington to see President Bush about the Soviet upheavals. His performance there, and immediately afterwards in Moscow and Peking boosted his personal standing. Suddenly the Tories had leapt ahead of Labour in the opinion polls and speculation about a November election rose sharply, particularly after interest rate cuts.

It did not last. On September 30 the Labour conference was electrified by the news that ministers had formally ruled out a November general election. Labour, believing it had succeeded yet again in closing down Mr Major's options, went back into the lead.

The rest of the year was dominated by Europe and Mr Major's efforts to hold his party together as the EC discussed progress towards economic and political union.

The omens looked unfavourable when, on November 17, a Commons debate before the crucial Maastricht summit was hijacked by Mrs Thatcher who called for a referendum and warned against "the conveyor belt to federalism". Mr Major decided that Mrs Thatcher could not be placated and rejected the referendum idea.

On December 11 Mr Major brought off a negotiating triumph at Maastricht as his European colleagues agreed to a treaty allowing Britain an opt-out on the single currency and decided to go ahead without Britain on the "social chapter". These were the two big sticking points and Mr Major managed to keep both wings of his party happy. Such was his success that Europe never again became an issue up to and during the election campaign.

After the summer coup events had moved fast in the Soviet Union. Mr Gorbachev tried in vain to hold it together and on Christmas Day he resigned. The Soviet republics became a Commonwealth of Independent States with Mr Yeltsin taking over the leadership of Russia.

By January the election campaign was truly under way, and this time there could be no pulling back. July was Mr Major's last possible option but no one expected him to wait until then.

On January 22 Norman Lamont set the Budget day for March 10. With the parties neck-and-neck in the polls the general assumption was that April 9 would be the day. In a bizarre diversion, Paddy Ashdown admitted a brief affair five years earlier with his former secretary. Early polls suggested his party had not been damaged.

It was not working out as Tory strategists had hoped. Mr Major had been persuaded by his party chiefs and his Chancellor to delay until 1992 when, he had been assured, the economic prospects would have been brighter. Now, he was on the threshold of an election, the recession was still biting and Labour was at least level-pegging in the national opinion polls.

The decision, however, had been made. On March 10 Mr Lamont unveiled his Budget. Its most novel feature was a new 20p in the pound income tax band for the first £2,000 of taxable income; its biggest surprise was a massive borrowing requirement of £28 billion. The next day, March 11, Mr Major, who had occupied 10 Downing Street for 16 months, went to the Palace. It was to be April 9.

The media and the message

By Brian MacArthur

At general elections, our political leaders go out to meet the people. Or do they? The most enduring images of the 1992 campaign will be of John Major, Neil Kinnock and Paddy Ashdown on stage-managed photo-opportunities surrounded by jostling throngs of reporters and cameramen who prevented them meeting the voters. It often seemed as if what mattered most was a few seconds on the evening news bulletins.

That was demonstrated in a telling report on the BBC's *Newsnight* exposing the management of the media that was ruthlessly practised by all three parties. Although it exposed the tactics used by Mr Kinnock's team of minders, it could have applied equally to the Major or Ashdown campaigns. The venue was Redditch an hour before Mr Kinnock was due to arrive for a brief walkabout. His advance team were shown preparing the scene so that it looked good for the cameras. Up went the red and yellow posters, but only in the area that would be filmed. Stickers and balloons were handed out, but only to those who would be in sight of the cameras. Enter Neil Kinnock.

Whatever the shots on television that night, and a smiling Neil Kinnock works a crowd well, *Newsnight* exposed the truth which was that he was shielded from the voters by his minders and journalists and had to reach over them to grasp a few hands. Within half an hour of his departure, the shopping centre was almost empty, peopled only by voters who had failed to shake his hand or speak to him. As they stood amid the litter left behind, their sense of frustration was eloquent. If elections are won or lost on television, which is the conventional wisdom, that quick photo-opportunity in a Midlands shopping centre was a typical example of a media lie, a short item of theatre in which Mr Kinnock met nobody, answered no questions, looked good on television but disappointed the voters.

Perhaps the most perplexing period of the media election, however, occurred during the controversy over Jennifer's Ear after the Labour party election broadcast on the National Health Service. The policy issues raised by the broadcast were ignored as reporters from newspapers and television started to hunt the mole who had leaked the name of Jennifer Bennett, the girl featured in the broadcast — and also trapped the hapless William Waldegrave, then health secretary, into revealing that he had suggested that the surgeon involved call the *Daily Express*. On several bulletins, reporters were shown interviewing Peter Hitchens, the *Daily Express* reporter who had discovered her name. Where were the politicians and where were the issues are the questions posed by this incestuous reporting.

So central was television to the three campaigns, and so directed were they to television, that many of the most experienced political commentators complained that democratic debate was being stifled. According to Hugo Young in *The Guardian*, the people did speak, but only as persons aggregated into faceless, nameless statistics in polls or as extras to walkabouts. They were a "multitude in a wasteland" made to deceive the cameras, passive receivers, no longer active participants in a dialogue nobody controlled. "These are the politics of condescension," he declared, echoed by Peter Jenkins in *The Independent* who said that a medium that had the potential to extend the democratic process stood in danger of subverting it.

The central role of television in what was undoubtedly a campaign waged in the American presidential style was convincingly demonstrated in research by the Communications Research Centre at Loughborough University and published by *The Guardian*. John Major made 175 appearances in news bulletins to 162 by Mr Kinnock and 152 by Paddy Ashdown, compared with 62 by Norman Lamont, 55 by John Smith and 48 by Des Wilson.

That research also showed that both the BBC and ITN maintained balanced coverage — belying a persistent view among senior Conservative ministers, allegedly including Mr Major, that the BBC was biased against the Tories. Conservative and Labour got an equal share of time on the BBC *Nine O'Clock News*, with ITN allocating a slightly higher proportion to the Tories than Labour. On all broadcast coverage during the campaign, the Conservatives got 15,000 seconds, Labour nearly 14,000 and the Liberal Democrats about 9,000. That the extent of media coverage is now assessed in such detail is a measure of the crucial importance given to the role of the media in British election campaigns. There are instant complaints to news editors if parties detect any hint of bias or unequal coverage.

There is no statutory obligation of balanced reporting on Fleet Street, where the mass-market tabloids, albeit occasionally distracted by the separation of the Duke and Duchess of York, the death of Earl Spencer, father of the Princess of Wales, and a libel action involving Jason Donovan, a former star of the soap opera *Neighbours*, campaigned with characteristic partisan relish, with the *Daily Mirror* rooting as strongly if solitarily for Labour as *The Sun*, the *Daily Mail* and the *Daily Express* supported the Tories.

Aware that the three main Tory tabloids would exploit any gaffe, Mr Kinnock's minders guarded him closely, allowing few opportunities for reporters to try to trip him up. He refused interviews with both *The Sun* and the *Daily Mail* (which responded by printing a page with its questions and blanks where Mr Kinnock's answers should have been). Yet if the Tory papers were frustrated by Mr Kinnock's minders, they were equally irritated by the lacklustre Tory campaign. On the second Saturday, the *Daily Mail* vented that irritation by lamenting the absence of Margaret Thatcher and told the Tories that they deserved to lose the election unless they "raised their game". John Major duly obliged with his soapbox.

Although editors of the tabloids always worry about how much election news their readers will tolerate, and millions complain there is too much coverage in newspapers and on television, the evidence of research by Market & Opinion Research International was that millions, many more than watch *Match of the Day*, follow election news closely and find it useful, although the number saying there is too much coverage has risen sharply over the past three elections. One in three electors told Mori they had spent more than an hour a day watching election news on television and more than 30 minutes reading election coverage in newspapers. Eight in ten readers of *The Times*, *The Guardian* and *The Independent* said they were interested in the campaign, compared with just over half the readers of the tabloids. On an average election day, at least one elector in four also listened to election news on the radio and watched a party election broadcast, while 43 per cent said they were interested in politicians' speeches and 40 per cent in opinion polls.

Fleet Street "voted" overwhelmingly for the Tories. Newspapers accounting for 67 per cent of sales backed John Major, corresponding exactly with the 1987 election. Although more papers backed Labour than in 1987 — the most surprising of which was the *Financial Times* — seven of the 11 dailies were Tory, three Labour and one, *The Independent*, remained neutral, stating the positive case for all three parties. Of the nine Sunday papers, five were Tory and four either Labour or anti-Tory. Most papers were voting with their readers' voting intentions, but a majority of readers of *The Sun*, *Today* , the *News of the World* and the *Financial Times* voted against their paper's political endorsement.

The biggest media controversy of the election occurred after it was over when Mr Kinnock, quoting the view of Lord McAlpine, a former treasurer of the Conservative party, blamed the editors of *The Sun*, the *Daily Mail* and the *Daily Express* for his defeat. Those three papers undoubtedly launched a blitz against him and his party in the last four days of the campaign. "If Kinnock wins today will the last person to leave Britain please turn out the lights", said the front page of *The Sun*, which sells more than 3.6 million copies, on polling day. Alongside a picture of Mr Kinnock inside a lightbulb, it added: "You know our views on the subject but we don't want to influence you in your final judgment on who will be prime minister! But if it's a bald bloke with wispy red hair and two Ks in his surname, we'll see you at the airport. Good night and thank you for everything".

It was *The Sun* "wot won it", the paper declared after the election was over, saying that its front page had been used in car windows to rally voters in the crucial marginal seat of Basildon — only to deny its influence after Mr Kinnock made his accusation. Lord McAlpine's view was reportedly shared by Mrs Thatcher but was vehemently denied by all three named editors. Opinion remains divided on whether voters are influenced by their papers but there can be no doubt about the extent of the anti-Labour bias in those three papers, based on a study on polling day by European Information Technology demonstrates. Yet whether that bias sways votes will be debated hotly for several years.

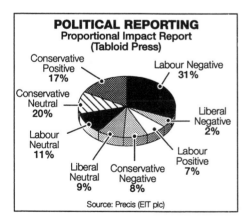

POLITICAL REPORTING
Proportional Impact Report
(Tabloid Press)

Conservative Positive 17%
Labour Negative 31%
Conservative Neutral 20%
Liberal Negative 2%
Labour Neutral 11%
Labour Positive 7%
Liberal Neutral 9%
Conservative Negative 8%

Source: Precis (EIT plc)

How readers voted

	Circ*	C	Lab	Lib
	'000			
Sun	3,629	45	36	14
Mirror/Record	3,607	20	64	14
Star	816	31	54	12
Mail	1,682	65	15	18
Express	1,538	67	15	14
Today	521	43	32	23
Telegraph	1,042	72	11	16
Guardian	428	15	55	24
Times	391	64	16	19
Independent	374	25	37	34
Financial Times	288	65	17	16

* ABC, March 1992

House of Commons, April 1992

The voting statistics for the 651 parliamentary constituencies of the United Kingdom contested at the general election are set out in alphabetical order. Constituencies in cities or towns are listed under that city or town.

Abbreviations used to designate the principal political parties are: C — Conservative; Lab — Labour; LD — Liberal Democrat (in 1987: L/All — Liberal/Alliance; SDP/All — Social Democrat/Alliance); SNP — Scottish National Party; PC — Plaid Cymru; UU —Ulster Unionist Party; DUP — Democratic Unionist Party; SDLP — Social Democratic and Labour Party; UPUP — Ulster Popular Unionist Party; SF — Sinn Fein; All — Alliance Party (Northern Ireland); Grn — Green Party; NLP — Natural Law Party; SD — Social Democrat; Lib — Liberal Party; Anti Fed — Anti Federalist League.

Abbreviations used in the biographies of MPs and candidates are tabulated on page 250.

The percentage of the constituency turnout, the votes cast for candidates and the majority of the winner have been calculated to the nearest decimal place.

The electoral register on which this general election was fought came into effect on February 16, 1992. The electorate figures consist of those eligible to vote when the register came into force including the relevant proportion of those reaching 18 years of age between February 16 and polling day. On appointment to office, ministers resign directorships.

*Denotes member of the last Parliament.

Guide to election result tables

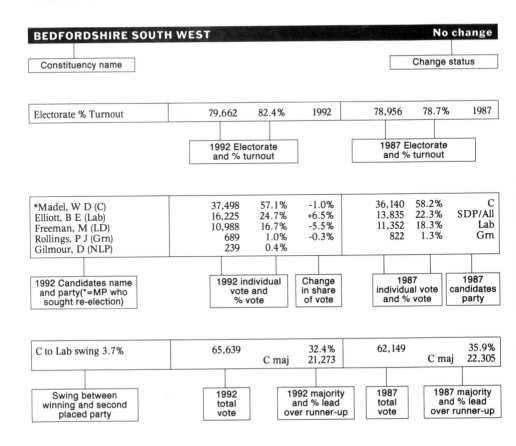

ABERAVON						No change
Electorate % Turnout	51,650	77.6%	1992	52,280	77.7%	1987
*Morris, J (Lab)	26,877	67.1%	+0.3%	27,126	66.8%	Lab
Williams, H (C)	5,567	13.9%	-0.5%	6,517	16.0%	L/All
Harris, Mrs M (LD)	4,999	12.5%	-3.6%	5,861	14.4%	C
Saunders, D (PC)	1,919	4.8%	+2.0%	1,124	2.8%	PC
Beany, Capt (Real Bean)	707	1.8%				
C to Lab swing 0.4%	40,069		53.2%	40,628		50.7%
		Lab maj	21,310		Lab maj	20,609

John Morris, QC, has been chief Opposn spokesman on legal affairs since 1983; Sec of State for Wales, 1974-9. On back-benches 1981-3 after a spell as spokesman on Wales and then on legal affairs. Opposn spokesman on defence, 1970-4; Minr of Defence for Equipment, 1968-70; PC 1970; Parly Sec, Ministry of Transport, 1966-8, and Min of Power, 1964-6. Mbr, Cmte of Privileges, 1984-7 and 1989- ; vice-chmn, barristers gp. Elected in 1959. Barrister; recorder of crown court, 1982- . B Nov 1931; ed Univ Coll of Wales, Aberystwyth; Gonville and Caius Coll,
Cambridge; Acad of International Law, The Hague.
Hywel Williams, sixth form master at Rugby Sch and Tudor of School House. Ed Llandeilo GS; Bishop Gore Sch, Swansea; St John's Coll, Cambridge.
Marilyn Harris, an analyst/programmer, BP Chemicals, Baglan Bay, contested this seat 1987. Mbr, Port Talbot BC, 1991- . B May 14 1945; ed Univ of Wales, Swansea.
David Saunders, transport manager; chmn, Clydach and Mawr district pty; Clydach community cllr. B Nov 2 1942; ed Cirencester GS; Swansea Tech Coll. TGWU.

ABERDEEN NORTH						No change
Electorate % Turnout	60,217	66.5%	1992	63,214	69.9%	1987
*Hughes, R (Lab)	18,845	47.0%	-7.6%	24,145	54.7%	Lab
McGugan, J A (SNP)	9,608	24.0%	+10.8%	7,867	17.8%	SDP/All
Cook, P (C)	6,836	17.1%	+2.7%	6,330	14.3%	C
Ford, Dr M A (LD)	4,772	11.9%	-5.9%	5,827	13.2%	SNP
Lab to SNP swing 9.2%	40,061		23.1%	44,169		36.9%
		Lab maj	9,237		Lab maj	16,278

Robert Hughes was chief Opposn spokesman on transport, 1985-8, being in shadow cabinet, 1985-6 and 1987-8; chief spokesman on agriculture, 1983-4; a transport spokesman, 1981-3. Convenor and campaign officer, 1990-1, and vice-convenor, 1989-90, Scottish Lab MPs; jt vice-chmn, Southern Africa parly gp; chmn, Select Cmte on Scottish Affairs, 1981-2. Under Sec of State for Scotland, 1974-5. Engineering draughtsman. Elected in 1970; contested North Angus and Mearns, 1959. Unpaid director, Freedom Productions Ltd. B Jan 3 1932; ed Benoni HS, Transvaal; Pietermaritzburg Technical Coll, Natal. Chmn, Anti-Apartheid Movement, 1976- . Mbr, Movement for Colonial Freedom, 1955- . Sponsored by AEU.
Jim McGugan, exporter of Scottish farm produce; importer of flowers, plants and florist goods. Contested this seat 1983, twice in 1974, and N Angus and Mearns 1970. Mbr, Arbroath TC, 1968-71. B Jul 27 1937; ed Forfar Acad.
Paul Cook, director of personnel company in N Sea oil and gas industry. Proprietor, Coach and Horses Inn, Balmedie, 1979-83. Contested Dundee E 1987. Mbr, Grampian health bd, 1985-89. B May 27 1949; ed Aberdeen GS; Robert Gordon's Inst of Tech.
Martin Ford, research scientist; mbr, Scottish exec of LDs; exec, Scottish assocn of LD cllrs; vice-chmn, Gordon LDs. B Oct 25 1959; ed Hele's Sch, Exeter; Newcastle Univ; Univ Coll, Swansea. IPMS.

ABERDEEN SOUTH						C gain
Electorate % Turnout	58,881	69.8%	1992	62,943	67.1%	1987
Robertson, R S (C)	15,808	38.5%	+3.6%	15,917	37.7%	Lab
*Doran, F (Lab)	14,291	34.8%	-2.9%	14,719	34.8%	C
Davidson, J C (SNP)	6,223	15.1%	+8.6%	8,844	20.9%	SDP/All
Keith, Mrs I (LD)	4,767	11.6%	-9.3%	2,776	6.6%	SNP
Lab to C swing 3.3%	41,089		3.7%	42,256		2.8%
		C maj	1,517		Lab maj	1,198

Raymond Robertson, NE political director, Scottish Cons pty, since 1989, regained this seat for Cons in 1992; contested Clydesdale 1987. Ex-teacher of history and modern studies at Dumbarton Acad. Chmn, Scottish Cons candidates assocn, 1987-8; mbr, Scottish Cons pty exec cmte, 1986- and 1982-4. Chmn, Scottish society of Cons teachers, 1985-7; Scottish YCs, 1982-4. B Dec 11 1959; ed Garrion Acad; Glasgow Univ; Jordanhill Coll of Ed.
Frank Doran, solicitor, was an Opposn spokesman on energy, 1988-92. MP for this seat 1987-92; contested
Scotland North East in 1984 Euro election. B Apr 13 1949; ed Ainslie Park Sec Sch; Leith Acad; Dundee Univ. Asst editor, Scottish legal action gp bulletin, 1975-8. GMB.
Jim Davidson, writer; former teacher, missionary, coll lecturer. Mbr, Grampian reg cl, 1990- ; Banff/Buchan DC, 1988- . Church of Scotland elder and lay preacher. B Jul 19 1932; ed Peterhead; Hong Kong and Aberdeen Univs.
Irene Keith, legal asst with firm of solicitors in Aberdeen. Mbr, Aberdeen city cl. B Mar 12 1954; ed Camphill HS, Paisley; Paisley Coll of Commerce.

ALDERSHOT						No change
Electorate % Turnout	81,754	78.7%	1992	80,797	74.0%	1987
*Critchley, J M G (C)	36,974	57.5%	-1.5%	35,272	59.0%	C
Collett, A P (LD)	17,786	27.6%	-1.6%	17,488	29.2%	L/All
Anthony Smith, J (Lab)	8,552	13.3%	+1.5%	7,061	11.8%	Lab
Robinson, D (Lib)	1,038	1.6%				
LD to C swing 0.0%	64,350		29.8%	59,821		29.7%
		C maj	19,188		C maj	17,784

Julian Critchley, author, freelance journalist and columnist, was elected in 1970; MP for Rochester and Chatham, 1959-64; contested seat, 1966. Vice-chmn, all-pty Gulf families parly gp 1991. Steward, British Boxing Board of Control, 1987- . B Dec 8 1930; ed Shrewsbury, Sorbonne, and Pembroke Coll, Oxford. Chmn, Bow Group, 1966-7; jt vice-chmn, Cons back-bench defence cmte, 1976-87; chmn, media cmte, 1976-80. Delegate to WEU (chmn, WEU defence cmte, 1974-7) and Cl of Europe; N Atlantic Assembly. Pres, Atlantic Assocn of Young Political Leaders,

1968-70.
Adrian Collett, house husband, former retail manager; ex-associate, Inst of Grocery Distribution. Mbr, Hants CC, 1983- ; Hart DC, 1980- ; Yateley TC, 1983-7. Former mbr Lib pty cl. B Mar 30 1958; ed Salesian Coll, Farnborough.
John A Smith, financial consultant, has own mortgage broking company; previously engineer, teacher. B Jan 5 1947; ed Edgbarrow Sec Mod Sch, Berkshire; Sussex Univ. MSF.

ALDRIDGE-BROWNHILLS						No change
Electorate % Turnout	63,404	82.6%	1992	62,129	79.8%	1987
*Shepherd, R C S (C)	28,431	54.3%	+1.0%	26,434	53.3%	C
Fawcett, N (Lab)	17,407	33.3%	+4.9%	14,038	28.3%	Lab
Reynolds, S (LD)	6,503	12.4%	-5.9%	9,084	18.3%	SDP/All
C to Lab swing 2.0%	52,341		21.1%	49,556		25.0%
		C maj	11,024		C maj	12,396

Richard Shepherd, founder-director of London retail food business, won the seat 1979; fought Nottingham E, Feb 1974. Vice-pres, Inst of Environmental Health Officers, 1987- ; co-chmn, Campaign for Freedom of Information. B Dec 6 1942; ed LSE and The Johns Hopkins Univ Sch of Advanced International Studies. Underwriting mbr of Lloyd's, 1974- . Mbr, Select Cmtes on Severn Bridges Bill, 1991; Treasury and Civil Service, 1979-83. Sec, all-pty civil liberties parly gp. Director, Shepherd Foods (London) Ltd, 1970- , and Partridges of Sloane Street Ltd, 1972- .

Neil Fawcett, solicitor and partner in Walsall firm; mbr, Walsall MBC, 1974-8 and 1987-91. B Apr 3 1945; ed Kings Langley cty primary sch; Apsley GS, Herts; Cotham GS, Bristol; Bristol Coll of Commerce.
Stewart Reynolds, teacher; mbr, Cannock Chase DC, 1982-90; Heath Hayes PC, 1991- . Contested Amber Valley 1987 and B'ham W in 1989 Euro elections. B Jul 22 1947; ed Chesterfield Sch; Westminster Coll, Oxford; Open Univ. NAS/UWT.

ALTRINCHAM AND SALE						No change
Electorate % Turnout	65,897	80.7%	1992	67,611	76.7%	1987
*Montgomery, Sir Fergus (C)	29,066	54.7%	+1.2%	27,746	53.5%	C
Atherton, Mrs M E (Lab)	12,275	23.1%	+2.6%	13,518	26.1%	L/All
Mulholland, J H (LD)	11,601	21.8%	-4.2%	10,617	20.5%	Lab
Renwick, J (NLP)	212	0.4%				
C to Lab swing 0.7%	53,154		31.6%	51,881		27.4%
		C maj	16,791		C maj	14,228

Sir Fergus Montgomery became chmn, Commons information cmte, in 1991; mbr Commons services cmte, 1979-91 (chmn, library sub-cmte, 1991); mbr, Commons selection cmte, 1987- ; select cmtes on home affairs, 1983-7; environment, 1979-83. Chmn, 1989- , and jt vice-chmn, 1987-9, NW gp of Cons MPs. Elected Oct 1974; MP for Brierley Hill, 1967 to Feb 1974, when he contested Dudley W; MP for Newcastle E, 1959-64; contested Consett, 1955. Non-exec director, Messenger Television Productions Ltd, 1989- ; consultant to Welbeck Public Relations Ltd; teacher, 1950-9. Mbr, exec cmte, UK branch of CPA, 1983- . B Nov 25 1927; ed Hebburn Methodist Sch;

Jarrow GS; Bede Coll, Durham.
Mary Atherton, primary head teacher; mbr, Trafford MBC, 1990- ; pty offices held include exec cmte mbr, CLP and Gtr Manchester Metropolitan Lab pty. B Jul 27 1944; ed Sale GS; Doncaster Coll of Ed. NAS/UWT; TGWU. Pres NAS/UWT Stockport 1988 and Warrington 1991.
John Mulholland, industrial relations consultant and Acas arbitrator and mediator, contested this seat 1987, Stockton-on-Tees 1964 and 1962 by-election; Gtr Manchester Central in 1989 Euro elections. Mbr, LD NW region exec, 1988-91; Runcorn RDC, 1959-62. B May 23 1933; ed St Mary's Coll, Middlesbrough; UMIST.

ALYN AND DEESIDE						No change
Electorate % Turnout	60,477	80.1%	1992	58,674	80.4%	1987
*Jones, S B (Lab)	25,206	52.0%	+3.5%	22,916	48.6%	Lab
Riley, J J (C)	17,355	35.8%	+0.8%	16,533	35.0%	C
Britton, R (LD)	4,687	9.7%	-5.7%	7,273	15.4%	SDP/All
Rogers, J (PC)	551	1.1%	+0.1%	478	1.0%	PC
Button, V (Grn)	433	0.9%				
Cooksey, J (Ind)	200	0.4%				
C to Lab swing 1.3%	48,432		16.2%	47,200		13.5%
		Lab maj	7,851		Lab maj	6,383

Barry Jones was reappointed chief Opposn spokesman on Wales in 1988 when re-elected to shadow cabinet; chief spokesman, 1983-7, when mbr shadow cabinet; employment spokesman, 1980-3. Under Sec of State for Wales, 1974-9. Elected for this seat 1983; MP for E Flint, 1970-83; contested Northwich 1966. Mbr, PAC, 1979-82. Teacher and former regional organiser, NUT. B Jun 1938; ed Hawarden GS; Bangor coll of ed. PPS to Denis Healey, 1972-4. Sponsored by TGWU.

Jeff Riley, sales manager. Former Cons pty agent in Cardiff S and Penarth and Oxford East. Chmn, Alyn and Deeside Cons assocn, 1990. B Feb 4 1962; ed Hawarden HS.
Robert Britton, barrister. B Jul 4 1945; ed Monkton House sch, Cardiff; Inns of Court Sch of Law.
John Rogers, teacher, contested this seat 1987, Flint East 1979 and Ebbw Vale Feb 1974. Founder, Cambrian Coast Line Action Gp. B Feb 1943; ed Glyndwr sec mod sch, Rhyl; Rhyl GS; St Mary's coll, Crosby; Leeds univ.

AMBER VALLEY						No change
Electorate % Turnout	70,155	84.7%	1992	68,478	81.2%	1987
*Oppenheim, P A C L (C)	27,418	46.1%	-5.3%	28,603	51.4%	C
Cooper, J G (Lab)	26,706	44.9%	+10.6%	19,103	34.4%	Lab
Brocklebank, G (LD)	5,294	8.9%	-5.3%	7,904	14.2%	L/All
C to Lab swing 7.9%	59,418		1.2%	55,610		17.1%
		C maj	712		C maj	9,500

Phillip Oppenheim became PPS to Kenneth Clarke, Home Secretary and former health and ed and science sec in 1988. Author; founder and former director of What to Buy plc sold to Reed International 1989. Mbr of Lloyd's. Elected in 1983. Jt vice-chmn (1987-8) and sec (1986-7), Cons back-bench Euro Affairs cmte; jt sec, Cons trade and industry cmte, 1987-8; Cons party organization cmte, 1985-87. B Mar 20 1956; ed Harrow; Oriel coll, Oxford. Mbr, cl, parly IT cmte, 1984- . Vice-pres, Videotex industry assocn, 1985-90. Jt founder and co-editor, 1980-85, of

business consumer magazine covering high tech what to buy for business products.
John Cooper, barrister and writer, contested Surrey NW 1987. Watford cllr. B Sep 15 1958; ed Newcastle univ; Cl of Legal Ed. TGWU.
Graham Brocklebank, training consultant; chmn at Chesterfield, 1986-88; sec, Sherwood, 1982; cty rep to regional exec, 1989- . B Jun 26 1950; ed Hull Univ; Leicester Coll of Ed; Open Univ.

ANGUS EAST						No change
Electorate % Turnout	63,170	75.0%	1992	61,060	75.5%	1987
*Welsh, A (SNP)	19,006	40.1%	-2.3%	19,536	42.4%	SNP
Harris, R O (C)	18,052	38.1%	-0.9%	17,992	39.0%	C
Taylor, D G (Lab)	5,994	12.6%	+1.9%	4,971	10.8%	Lab
McLeod, C A (LD)	3,897	8.2%	+0.4%	3,592	7.8%	SDP/All
McCabe, D M (Grn)	449	0.9%				
SNP to C swing 0.7%	47,398		2.0%	46,091		3.3%
		SNP maj	954		SNP maj	1,544

Andrew Welsh, vice-pres of SNP since 1987 and Provost of Angus DC, 1984-7, and mbr, Angus DC, 1984-7, won this seat in 1987; contested it 1983; SNP MP for Angus S, Oct 1974-9; contested Dunbartonshire Central, Feb 1974. Mbr, select cmte on members' interests, 1990- . SNP spokesman on housing, 1987- and 1974-8, on self-employed affairs and small businesses, 1987- and 1975-9, and on agriculture, 1987- and 1976-9; SNP chief whip, 1987- and 1978-9. Exec vice-chmn of SNP responsible for local govt, 1984-7, and for administration, 1979-87. Snr lecturer in business studies and public administration, Angus Tech Coll, Arbroath, 1983-7; lecturer in public administration and economics, Dundee Coll of Commerce, 1979-83. B Apr 19 1944; ed Govan HS; Glasgow Univ. Mbr, Stirling DC, 1974. SFHEA and EIS.
Ronald Harris, self-employed in family retail and domestic

property business since 1976; mbr, Angus DC, 1986-8. B May 4 1937; ed Montrose acad; St Andrews and Toronto univs. Professor of chemistry, Toronto univ, 1967-76. Vice-chmn, Montrose branch, 1986- .
Geoffrey Taylor, depute rector, Arbroath HS; chmn Carnoustie Lab pty; vice-chmn, Tayside reg Lab pty. B Feb 22 1935; ed Univ of Wales; Dundee univ. EIS.
Mr Callum McLeod, teacher; chmn, St Andrews LD branch; mbr, Royal Burgh of St Andrews community cl, 1986- . B Nov 11 1960; ed Dollar acad; St Andrews univ. EIS.
Duncan McCabe, biochemist, now an organic horticulturist. Pty co-ordinator on Scottish Grn pty nat exec; convenor, coastal pollution working gp. B Jan 27 1960; ed Morgan Acad, Dundee; Dundee Univ.

ANTRIM EAST						No change
Electorate % Turnout	62,839	62.5%	1992	60,587	55.2%	1987
*Beggs, J R (UU)	16,966	43.2%	-28.3%	23,942	71.6%	UU
Dodds, N (DUP)	9,544	24.3%		8,582	25.6%	All
Neeson, S (All)	9,132	23.3%	-2.4%	936	2.8%	WP
Boal, Miss M (C)	3,359	8.6%				
Palmer, Ms A (NLP)	250	0.6%				
No swing calculation.	39,251		18.9%	33,460		45.9%
		UU maj	7,422		UU maj	15,360

Roy Beggs, a director of Larne Enterprise Development Co, was elected in 1983. Resigned seat in 1985 in protest at Anglo-Irish Agreement and retained it in 1986 by-election. Mbr, Public Accounts Commission; has also served on PAC. Mbr for N Antrim, N Ireland Assembly, 1982-6; chmn, Economic Development Cmte, 1982-4. Mbr, Larne BC, 1973- ; Mayor of Larne, 1978-83. B Feb 20 1936; ed Ballyclare HS; Stranmillis Training Coll.
Nigel Dodds, Lord Mayor of Belfast.

Sean Neeson, public affairs consultant; alderman on Carrick cl, 1977- ; Alliance chief whip and spokesman on transport and energy. Mbr, NI Assembly, 1982-6. B Feb 6 1946; ed St Malachys Coll, Belfast; Queens Univ, Belfast; Ulster Univ, Jordanstown.
Myrtle Boal, regional sales manager for international pharmaceutical manufacturers; vice-chmn, South Belfast Cons assocn. B 1939; ed Ashleigh House Sch, Belfast; Queen's Univ, Belfast; Trinity Coll, Dublin.

ANTRIM NORTH						No change
Electorate % Turnout	69,124	65.8%	1992	65,733	62.8%	1987
*Paisley, Rev I R K (DUP)	23,152	50.9%	-17.8%	28,383	68.7%	DUP
Gaston, J (UU)	8,216	18.1%		5,149	12.5%	SDLP
Farren, S (SDLP)	6,512	14.3%	+1.8%	5,140	12.4%	All
Williams, G (All)	3,442	7.6%	-4.9%	2,633	6.4%	SF
Sowler, R (C)	2,263	5.0%				
McGarry, J (SF)	1,916	4.2%	-2.2%			
No swing calculation.	45,501		32.8%	41,305		56.2%
		DUP maj	14,936		DUP maj	23,234

The Rev Ian Paisley, ldr of Democratic Unionist Pty; MP for Antrim N since 1970. Resigned seat in 1985 in protest at Anglo-Irish Agreement and retained it in 1986 by-election. Mbr, European Parliament, 1979- ; N Ireland Assembly, 1982-6. Minister of Martyrs Memorial Free Presbyterian Church, Belfast, 1946- . Hon director, Voice Newspapers Ltd and Protestant Telegraph Ltd. Founded Protestant Unionist Pty and sat as Prot U MP, 1970-4. B Apr 6 1926; ed Model Sch, Ballymena; Ballymena Tech Coll; S Wales Bible Coll; Reformed Presbyterian Theological Hall, Belfast. Pres, Whitefield Coll of the Bible, 1979- . Mbr Stormont, 1970-2. Dem U mbr NI Assembly, 1973-5, and UUUC mbr, NI Constitutional Convention, 1975-6.

Joe Gaston, farmer; Ballymena cllr since 1983 (mayor for five years). B Dec 20 1927; ed Bellaghy Primary Sch; Ballymena Model. Mbr education board, 1977- ; former mbr, NI police authority.
Sean Farren, univ lecturer; mbr, Coleraine BC, 1977-81. Chmn, SDLP, 1980-4; Assemblyman, 1982-6. B Sep 6 1939; ed Univ Coll, Dublin; Essex and Ulster Univs.
Gareth Williams, pharmacist, Alliance spokesman on overseas development; Ballymena cllr, 1989- .
Richard Sowler, solicitor, contested Carlisle 1983 and Newcastle Central by-election 1976. Mbr, Tynedale DC, 1983- . B 1943; ed Harrow; Univ Coll, Oxford.
James McGarry, mbr, Moyle DC.

ANTRIM SOUTH						No change
Electorate % Turnout	68,013	62.1%	1992	61,649	59.1%	1987
*Forsythe, C (UU)	29,956	70.9%	+1.2%	25,395	69.8%	UU
McClelland, D (SDLP)	5,397	12.8%	+2.9%	5,808	16.0%	All
Blair, J (All)	5,224	12.4%	-3.6%	3,611	9.9%	SDLP
Cushinan, H (SF)	1,220	2.9%	-1.5%	1,592	4.4%	SF
Martin, D (Loony G)	442	1.0%				
UU to SDLP swing 0.8%	42,239		58.1%	36,406		53.8%
		UU maj	24,559		UU maj	19,587

Clifford Forsythe became mbr select cmte on social security, 1991. Plumbing and heating contractor; former professional footballer with Linfield and Derry City. Elected in 1983. Resigned seat in 1985 in protest at Anglo-Irish Agreement and retained it at 1986 by-election. UU spokesman on transport, local govt and communications. Sec, all-pty paper industry parly gp; vice-chmn, plumbing gp. B Aug 24 1929; ed Glengormley public elementary sch. Mbr, Newtownabbey BC, 1981-85, mayor, 1983; NI Assembly, 1982-6; dep chmn, DHSS cmte of assembly, 1982-6.
Donovan McClelland, univ lecturer, contested this seat 1987; local cllr; mbr, pty exec. B Jan 14 1949..
John Blair, electrical salesman; Newtownabbey cllr, 1988- ; Alliance spokesman on youth.
Henry Cushinan, SF mbr of Antrim BC, 1985- . Released from Maze prison in 1983 after serving six years for terrorist offences.

ARGYLL AND BUTE						No change
Electorate % Turnout	47,894	76.2%	1992	48,700	75.5%	1987
*Michie, Mrs J R (LD)	12,739	34.9%	-2.4%	13,726	37.3%	L/All
Corrie, J (C)	10,117	27.7%	-5.8%	12,332	33.5%	C
MacCormick, Prof D N (SNP)	8,689	23.8%	+6.7%	6,297	17.1%	SNP
Browne, D (Lab)	4,946	13.6%	+1.5%	4,437	12.1%	Lab
C to LD swing 1.7%	36,491		7.2%	36,792		3.8%
		LD maj	2,622		L/All maj	1,394

Ray Michie became LD spokeswoman on Scotland and women's issues in 1988; Lib spokeswoman on transport and rural environment, 1987-8. Won this seat 1987; contested it 1983 and Argyll 1979. Jt chmn all-pty parly gp on UN convention on rights of child; jt vice-chmn parly cmte on whisky industry. Area speech therapist with Argyll and Clyde health board, 1977-87; vice-pres, Coll of Speech and Language Therapists. Vice-chmn, Scottish Lib pty, 1977-9; chmn, Argyll Lib assocn, 1973-6. Served on L/SDP commission on constitutional reform. B Feb 4 1934; ed Aberdeen HS for Girls; Lansdowne House sch, Edinburgh; Edinburgh Sch of Speech Therapy.
John Corrie, partner in firm of financial consulants, farmer, was MP for Cunninghame N, 1983-7; MP for Ayrshire N and Bute, Feb 1974-83; contested Ayrshire Central, 1966, and Lanark N, 1964. Chmn, Transport Users Consultative Cmte for Scotland, 1989- ; mbr, Central Transport Consultative Cmte, 1989- . PPS to Sec of State for Scotland, 1979-81; mbr, Select Cmte on Scottish Affairs, 1981-7; Cl of Europe and WEU, 1982-7; EP, 1975-6 and 1977-9. B Jul 29 1935; ed Kirkcudbright Acad; George Watson's Coll, Edinburgh; Lincoln Agricultural Coll, New Zealand. Opposn Scottish whip, 1975-6, resigning over devolution.
Neil MacCormick professor of public law, Edinburgh Univ, since 1972, contested Edinburgh, Pentlands, 1987 and 1983; Edinburgh N, 1979. Mbr SNP nat cl, 1978-83, 84-5 and 1988- ; SNP nat exec, 1978-81. B May 27 1941; ed Glasgow HS; Glasgow Univ; Balliol Coll, Oxford (Pres of Union, 1965); LLD Edinburgh 1982. Director, New Iona Press, 1991- . AUT, 1965-88.
Des Browne, solicitor; cl mbr, Law Society of Scotland. B Mar 22 1952; ed Glasgow Univ. Usdaw.

ARUNDEL						No change
Electorate % Turnout	79,241	77.1%	1992	78,683	71.2%	1987
*Marshall, Sir Michael (C)	35,405	58.0%	-3.4%	34,356	61.3%	C
Walsh, Dr J M M (LD)	15,542	25.5%	-2.2%	15,476	27.6%	L/All
Nash, R A (Lab)	8,321	13.6%	+2.6%	6,177	11.0%	Lab
Renson, Mrs D (Lib)	1,103	1.8%				
Corbin, R (Grn)	693	1.1%				
C to LD swing 0.6%	61,064		32.5%	56,009		33.7%
		C maj	19,863		C maj	18,880

Sir Michael Marshall was Under Sec of State for Industry, 1979-81. Mbr, Select Cmte on Defence, 1982-7. Chmn (1987-) and vice-chmn (1982-7), Parly Information Tech Cmte. Chmn (1987-90), jt vice-chmn (1982-7) and still mbr, exec cmte, British Gp, IPU; Jt vice-chmn, Interparly Cl against Anti-Semitism, 1991- . Elected in Feb 1974; contested Hartlepool, 1970. Chmn, Direct Business Satellite Systems Ltd, 1984-90; managing partner, Marshall Consultants; non-exec director, Integrated Information Tech Ltd, 1984-8. Chmn, all-pty space cmte. Parly adviser to British Aerospace plc, 1989- ; BAe, Space and Communications Div, 1982-9; Cable and Wireless, 1982- ; Comsat; Soc of West End Theatre, 1984- ; Wm Holdings plc, 1988- . B Jun 21 1930; ed Bradfield Coll; Harvard and Stanford Univs. Mbr, Lloyd's.
Dr James Walsh, general practitioner, contested this seat 1987 and 1983; Hove 1979 and Oct 1974, and Sussex W in 1989, 1984 and 1979 Euro elections. Mbr W Sussex CC, 1985- ; Arun DC, 1976- ; Littlehampton TC, 1976- (mayor, 1989-90). B Jan 11 1943; ed Wimbledon Coll; London Hospital Medical Sch.
Roger Nash, teacher; mbr, Bognor TC (ldr Lab gp); Arun DC, 1986-7. Director of holiday business in France. B Apr 14 1948; ed Kent, Leicester and Sussex Univs. NUT.

ASHFIELD						No change
Electorate % Turnout	75,075	77.7%	1992	70,937	77.2%	1987
Hoon, G W (Lab)	32,018	54.9%	+13.2%	22,812	41.7%	Lab
Robertson, L A (C)	19,031	32.6%	-1.0%	18,412	33.6%	C
Turton, J S (LD)	7,291	12.5%	-12.2%	13,542	24.7%	L/All
C to Lab swing 7.1%	58,340		22.3%	54,766		8.0%
		Lab maj	12,987		Lab maj	4,400

Geoffrey Hoon, elected in 1992, has been MEP for Derbyshire since 1984. Mbr, EP Legal Affairs and Citizens' Rights Cmte, being Lab gp spokesman, 1984- ; EP delegation on relations with Gulf states. Barrister. B Dec 6 1953; ed Nottingham HS; Jesus Coll, Cambridge. Lab pty agent in Leeds for both Westminster and Euro elections in 1979. Worked in local furniture factory before reading law at Cambridge. Lecturer in law, Leeds univ, 1972-82; Visiting Professor of Law, Sch of Law, Louisville univ, Kentucky, 1979-80. TGWU.
Laurence Robertson, proprietor of public relations consultancy, contested Makerfield 1987. Mbr, Cons nat advisory cmte on ed; Soc of Cons Lawyers. B Mar 29 1958; ed Farnworth GS. Former treas Bolton SE Cons assocn.
James Turton, employed in transport office of Charcon Tunnels Ltd, Kirkby-in-Ashfield; was local pty sec and branch chmn. Served in Army, 1959-76 in RASC and Royal Corps of Transport. B Feb 5 1941; ed Claremont Sec Mod Sch, Nottingham.

ASHFORD						No change
Electorate % Turnout	71,767	79.2%	1992	70,052	75.7%	1987
*Speed, H K (C)	31,031	54.6%	-1.9%	29,978	56.5%	C
Headley, C L B (LD)	13,672	24.1%			14,490	27.3% SDP/All
Cameron, Ms D (Lab)	11,365	20.0%	+5.3%	7,775	14.7%	Lab
Porter, Dr C A (Grn)	773	1.4%	-0.1%	778	1.5%	Grn
LD to C swing 0.7%	56,841		30.5%	53,021		29.2%
		C maj	17,359		C maj	15,488

Keith Speed, company director and marketing consultant; jt chmn, all-pty Channel tunnel parly gp; chmn, Friends of Northern Cyprus gp; treas, British-Vietnam parly gp. Mbr, Select Cmte on Defence, 1983-7; UK delegation, Cl of Europe and WEU, 1987- . Under Sec of State for Defence for Royal Navy, 1979-81; an Opposition spokesman on environment and local govt, 1975-9; Under Sec of State for Environment, 1972-4; govt whip, 1971-2; asst govt whip, 1970-1. Elected for this seat Oct 1974; MP for Meriden, Mar 1968 to Feb 1974. B Mar 11 1934; ed Greenhill Sch, Evesham; Bedford Modern Sch; Dartmouth and Greenwich RNCs. Parly adviser, PAT, 1982- ; parly consultant,

Assocn for Instrumentation Control and Automation Industry in UK; Machine Tool Assocn.
Christine Headley, indexer; mbr, Lambeth BC, 1984-90; first woman elected to Kent County Cricket Club gen cmte. B Aug 7 1954; ed Friends Sch, Saffron Walden; B'ham Poly; S Bank Poly.
Doreen Cameron, lecturer; mbr management cmte family services unit, Thamesmead. B Feb 29 1952 in Portland, Jamaica; ed Avery Hill and Goldsmiths Colls, London.
Dr Andrew Porter, consultant paediatrician, contested Ashford 1987 and 1983. B Apr 9 1936; ed Bryarston Sch, Dorset; Middlesex Hospital Medical Sch.

ASHTON-UNDER-LYNE						No change
Electorate % Turnout	58,701	73.9%	1992	58,440	74.0%	1987
*Sheldon, R E (Lab)	24,550	56.6%	+4.8%	22,389	51.8%	Lab
Pinniger, J (C)	13,615	31.4%	+1.1%	13,103	30.3%	C
Turner, C W (LD)	4,005	9.2%	-8.7%	7,760	17.9%	L/All
Hall, C (Lib)	907	2.1%				
Brannigan, J (NLP)	289	0.7%				
C to Lab swing 1.9%	43,366		25.2%	43,252		21.5%
		Lab maj	10,935		Lab maj	9,286

Robert Sheldon has been chairman, Commons PAC since 1983; mbr, 1965-70 and 1975-9; mbr, Public Accounts Commission. An Opposition spokesman on Treasury and economic affairs, 1979-83; Financial Sec to the Treasury, 1975-9; Minr of State, Treasury, 1974-5; Minr of State, Civil Service Dept, 1974. PC 1977. Mbr, Treasury and Civil Service Select Cmte, 1979-81; Public Expenditure Cmte, 1972-4; Fulton Cmte on Civil Service, 1966-8. Elected in 1964; contested Manchester, Withington, 1959. Director, Manchester Chamber of Commerce, 1964-74 and since 1979. B Sep 13 1923; ed elementary, GS, and tech colls; external graduate, London Univ. Chmn, NW gp,

Lab MPs, 1970-4. TGWU.
John Pinniger, communications manager with Financial Intermediaries, Managers and Brokers Regulatory Assocn (Fimbra), 1988- ; press and PR officer, British Insurance Brokers Assocn, 1986-7. Mbr, Lambeth Cl, 1986- . B Jul 11 1955; ed Cambridge GS; Dundee Univ.
Charles Turner, teacher; pty offices held include constituency sec, branch membership sec and campaigns asst. B Mar 22 1964; ed Magna Carta Comprehensive Sch, Staines, Middlesex; Strode's Sixth Form Coll, Egham, Surrey; Manchester Univ; Manchester Poly.

AYLESBURY						No change
Electorate % Turnout	79,208	80.3%	1992	76,919	74.5%	1987
Lidington, D R (C)	36,500	57.4%	-0.1%	32,970	57.5%	C
Bowles, S M (LD)	17,640	27.7%			16,412	28.6% SDP/All
Priest, R (Lab)	8,517	13.4%	-0.5%	7,936	13.8%	Lab
Foster, N (Grn)	702	1.1%				
D'Arcy, B (NLP)	239	0.4%				
LD to C swing 0.4%	63,598		29.7%	57,318		28.9%
		C maj	18,860		C maj	16,558

David Lidington was elected in 1992. Special adviser to Douglas Hurd as home secretary and foreign secretary, 1987-90. He was then on secondment from Rio Tinto-Zinc where he was in charge of media relations, 1986-7. Contested Vauxhall 1987. With British Petroleum, 1983-6, working in external affairs division and corporate press office. B Jun 30 1956; ed Haberdashers' Aske's Sch, Elstree; Sidney Sussex Coll, Cambridge (chmn, univ Cons assocn, 1978). Treas, Enfield North Cons assocn, 1984-6, and a branch chmn, 1982-5; hon sec, Cons Nat Advisory Cmte on education, 1983-5. Choral singer.

Sharon Bowles, Euro patent attorney, is sec, Chilterns region Lib Dems. Partner, Bowles Horton; director, Dacorum Enterprise Agency. On LD science, tech and innovation green paper working pty; a founder, LD Engineers and Scientists. B Jun 12 1953; ed Our Lady's Convent, Abingdon; Reading Univ; Lady Margaret Hall, Oxford.
Roger Priest, industrial consultant in printing industry and director of printing company. Mbr, Bucks CC, 1984-8. B Jan 26 1930; ed primary sch, Barking; SE Essex Tech Coll. GMPU (FoC).

AYR						No change
Electorate % Turnout	65,481	83.1%	1992	66,450	79.9%	1987
Gallie, P R (C)	22,172	40.8%	+1.3%	20,942	39.4%	C
Osborne, A (Lab)	22,087	40.6%	+1.5%	20,760	39.1%	Lab
Mullin, Mrs B (SNP)	5,949	10.9%	+4.3%	7,859	14.8%	L/All
Boss, J A (LD)	4,067	7.5%	-7.3%	3,548	6.7%	SNP
Scott, R (NLP)	132	0.2%				
C to Lab swing 0.1%	54,407		0.2%	53,109		0.3%
		C maj	85		C maj	182

Phil Gallie an engineer and power stations manager in electricity supply industry, retained the seat for the Cons in 1992; contested Dunfermline W, 1987 and Cunninghame S 1983. Chmn W of Scotland Area Cons cl, 1989-90; Strathclyde W Euro cl, 1987-9; Bute and N Ayrshire Cons assocn, 1978-80; Cunninghame N assocn, 1985-87. Mbr, Cunninghame DC, 1980-4. B Jun 3 1939; ed Dunfermline HS; Kirkcaldy Tech Coll. EPEA.

Alastair Osborne, community worker and former Church of Scotland minister; CLP sec, press officer and vice-chmn.

B Mar 10 1948; ed Royal HS, Edinburgh; Edinburgh Univ; Jordanhill Coll of Ed, Glasgow. TGWU (ACTS).

Barbara Mullin is an education and training consultant. Mbr SNP nat cl and spokeswoman on employment and training. B Jun 8 1949; ed Ayr GS; Queen's Coll, Glasgow; Open Univ.

John Boss, personnel officer, contested Cunninghame S 1987 and 1983. Chmn, Cunninghame LDs. B Dec 31 1940; ed Reading sch; Trinity coll, Dublin; LSE. JP; Rotary mbr.

BANBURY						No change
Electorate % Turnout	71,840	81.5%	1992	69,455	76.2%	1987
*Baldry, A B (C)	32,215	55.0%	-1.2%	29,716	56.2%	C
Billingham, Ms A (Lab)	15,495	26.5%	+6.1%	12,386	23.4%	SDP/All
Fisher, G J (LD)	10,602	18.1%	10,789		20.4%	Lab
Ticciati, Dr R (NLP)	250	0.4%				
C to Lab swing 3.6%	58,562		28.6%	52,891		32.8%
		C maj	16,720		C maj	17,330

Tony Baldry was appointed Under Sec of State for Environment in 1990; Under Sec of State for Energy, Jan-Dec 1990. Barrister, former publisher and company director. Elected in 1983; contested Thurrock, 1979. PPS to John Wakeham, Ld President of Cl and Ldr of Commons and then Sec of State for Energy, 1987-90, and to Lynda Chalker, Minr of State for Transport and then FCO, 1985-7. B Jul 10 1950; ed Leighton Park; Sussex Univ. Director, Newpoint Publishing Gp Ltd, 1983-90. Mbr, Select Cmte on Employment, 1983-86. Dep chmn, Carlton Club political cmte. Awarded Robert Schumann Silver Medal, 1978, for contributions to European politics. Chmn, nat

appeals cmte, National Childrens Home.

Angela Billingham, teacher; former mbr, Cherwell DC (gp ldr, 1974-84); mbr Banbury BC, 1970-4. B Jul 31 1939; ed Dartford coll; Oxford Univ. Mbr, southern reg sports cl; Oxfordshire cty ladies tennis capt. With her two daughters, has for past four years reached finals of national mothers and daughters tennis championships.

Geoff Fisher, chmn and director, St Ebbes coll, Oxford, contested seat Feb 1974 and 1970. Chmn, Banbury LDs; mbr, Banbury BC, 1965-6. B May 23 1936; ed Banbury GS; Oxford coll of tech.

BANFF AND BUCHAN						No change
Electorate % Turnout	64,873	71.2%	1992	62,149	70.8%	1987
*Salmond, A E A (SNP)	21,954	47.5%	+3.3%	19,462	44.3%	SNP
Manson, S (C)	17,846	38.6%	-0.1%	17,021	38.7%	C
Balcombe, B (Lab)	3,803	8.2%	+0.8%	4,211	9.6%	SDP/All
Kemp, Mrs R (LD)	2,588	5.6%	-4.0%	3,281	7.5%	Lab
C to SNP swing 1.7%	46,191		8.9%	43,975		5.6%
		SNP maj	4,108		SNP maj	2,441

Alex Salmond was elected ldr of SNP in 1990. Won this seat in 1987 and appointed mbr select cmte on energy. SNP/PlC spokesman on Treasury and economic affairs, energy and fishing, 1987-8; on economy, energy and oil, fisheries, 1988- . Non-exec director, Eala Bhan, a Gaelic TV independent production company, 1992- . Energy economist with Royal Bank of Scotland, 1980-7; asst economist, with Dept of Agriculture and Fisheries, Scotland, 1978-80. Snr vice-convenor (dep ldr and former senior vice-chmn) SNP, 1987-90; SNP vice-chmn (publicity) 1985-7; mbr, SNP nat exec, 1981- . B Dec 31 1954; ed Linlithgow Acad; St Andrews Univ. BIFU.

Sandy Manson, chartered accountant, with W D

Johnstone and Carmichael; previously with Arthur Andersen and Co, Edinburgh from 1982 and worked in Zurich, Switzerland, office, 1985-7. Scottish Cons spokesman on agriculture, fisheries and countryside. B Dec 16 1961; ed Robert Gordon's coll, Aberdeen; Edinburgh Univ.

Brian Balcombe, self-employed computer operator; mbr, Grampian reg cl, 1985- . B Sep 28 1958; ed St Geo Monoux Sch, London; Aberdeen univ.

Rhona Kemp, manager; mbr, Grampian reg cl, 1986- (LD gp ldr, 1990- ; chmn, finance cmte, 1989-); Grampian health bd, 1986-91. B Mar 15 1939; ed Morgan Acad. Vice-chmn, Royal Workshops for Blind, 1990- .

BARKING						No change
Electorate % Turnout	50,454	70.0%	1992	51,639	66.9%	1987
*Richardson, Ms J (Lab)	18,224	51.6%	+7.3%	15,307	44.3%	Lab
Kennedy, J G (C)	11,956	33.9%	-0.6%	11,898	34.4%	C
Churchman, S W (LD)	5,133	14.5%	-6.7%	7,336	21.2%	L/All
C to Lab swing 3.9%	35,313		17.7%	34,541		9.9%
		Lab maj	6,268		Lab maj	3,409

Jo Richardson, chief Opposn front bencher on women's rights since 1983, was elected to shadow cabinet 1987; mbr Lab pty NEC, 1979-91; former chmn women's cmte and black and Asian advisory gp; mbr, Lab working pty on electoral systems, 1990- . Elected in Feb 1974; contested Harrow E, 1964; Hornchurch, 1959; Monmouth, 1955 and 1951. B Aug 28 1923; ed Southend HS for Girls. Former mbr, select cmtes on home affairs, nationalized industries, procedure and expenditure. Chmn Tribune gp of Lab MPs, 1978-9 (sec, 1948-78, when it was known as Keep Left Gp and later Bevan Gp). Sponsored by MSF.

John Kennedy, public relations and political consultant. Personal asst to John Moore when cabinet minister, 1986-9. Former mbr exec Carshalton Cons assocn; vice-chmn, Carshalton CPC, 1988-9; sec, Gtr London area YCs, 1986-87; sec, Cons cl on eastern Europe. B Jun 18 1965; ed Royal Russell sch, Addington, Surrey.

Steve Churchman, draftsman, was mbr and dep LD gr ldr, Barking and Dagenham BC, 1986-90. Pty press officer, Barking, 1984-6. B Aug 4 1962; ed Mayesbrook comprehensive, Dagenham. TSSA.

BARNSLEY CENTRAL						No change
Electorate % Turnout	55,373	70.5%	1992	55,902	70.0%	1987
*Illsley, E E (Lab)	27,048	69.3%	+2.5%	26,139	66.8%	Lab
Senior, D (C)	7,687	19.7%	+1.6%	7,088	18.1%	C
Cowton, S (LD)	4,321	11.1%	-4.1%	5,928	15.1%	L/All
C to Lab swing 0.5%	39,056		49.6%	39,155		48.7%
		Lab maj	19,361		Lab maj	19,051

Eric Illsley, elected in 1987, became mbr, select cmte on procedure, 1991- ; on energy, 1987-91; on broadcasting, 1988-91. Treas, 1987- . Campaign officer 1990- , Yorkshire gp of Lab MPs. Sec and election agent Yorkshire S Euro constituency Lab pty, 1983-7. Jt chmn all-pty glass parly gp, 1990- . B Apr 9 1955; ed Barnsley Holgate GS; Leeds univ. Sponsored by NUM. Worked for Yorkshire area NUM from 1978 being compensation officer, 1978-81; asst head of general dept, 1981-4, and hd of general

dept and chief administrative officer, 1984-7. Sponsored by NUM.

David Senior, an international marketing manager for ICI; mbr of ICI's education task force. Contested Dundee W 1983; elected to Macclesfield BC 1982. B Feb 22 1959; ed Kings sch, Macclesfield; Jesus coll, Cambridge (Pres of Union).

Steve Cowton, in road transport; does work in care of elderly. B Aug 11 1949; ed in Filey.

BARNSLEY EAST						No change
Electorate % Turnout	54,051	72.7%	1992	53,505	72.6%	1987
*Patchett, T (Lab)	30,346	77.2%	+2.7%	28,948	74.5%	Lab
Procter, J (C)	5,569	14.2%	+0.2%	5,437	14.0%	C
Anginotti, Ms S (LD)	3,399	8.6%	-2.9%	4,482	11.5%	L/All
C to Lab swing 1.3%	39,314		63.0%	38,867		60.5%
		Lab maj	24,777		Lab maj	23,511

Terry Patchett, miner, was on Select Cmte on Social Services, 1985-8. Elected in 1983. B Jul 11 1940; ed state schs; Sheffield univ. Jt vice-chmn, PLP energy cmte, 1985-9 and 1990- . NUM Houghton Main branch delegate, 1966-83; mbr, Yorkshire miners' executive, 1976-83; Wombwell UDC, 1969-73. Former mbr, appeals tribunals, community health cl. NUM sponsored.

John Procter, businessman, owns industrial contract maintenance company supplying caretaking, commissionaire, security and cleaning services. With Post Office, becoming higher grade postal officer, 1983-7. Mbr, Cons

nat union exec and gen purposes cmtes, 1990- ; vice-chmn, Yorkshire area cl; mbr, Yorkshire area finance and gp cmtes; Leeds NW and Elmet exec; chmn, Yorkshire area YCs, 1990- ; vice-chmn, Leeds NW assocn, 1985- . B Nov 7 1966; ed Ralph Thoresby, Leeds.

Sylvia Anginotti is a lecturer. Local pty chmn 1988-90; city-wide strategy chmn 1987- ; co-ordinator in Sheffield Heeley and Attercliffe in 1987; and Euro coordinator for Chesterfield, Sheffield and Derbyshire NE 1989. B Apl 22 1949; ed Sheffield Univ. NATFHE (branch chmn Norton Coll, 1990-).

BARNSLEY WEST AND PENISTONE						No change
Electorate % Turnout	63,374	75.8%	1992	61,091	75.6%	1987
Clapham, M (Lab)	27,965	58.3%	+0.9%	26,498	57.3%	Lab
Sawyer, G (C)	13,461	28.0%	+1.4%	12,307	26.6%	C
Nicolson, I H (LD)	5,610	11.7%	-4.3%	7,409	16.0%	SDP/All
Jones, D (Grn)	970	2.0%				
Lab to C swing 0.2%	48,006		30.2%	46,214		30.7%
		Lab maj	14,504		Lab maj	14,191

Michael Clapham was elected in 1992; national industrial relations officer of NUM; sponsored by union; mbr branch cmte of NUM, 1965-70. Joined Lab pty 1979. B May 15 1943; ed Barnsley Tech Coll; Leeds Univ; Leeds Poly; Bradford Univ. Mbr NUM and GMB/Apex, Greenpeace, British-Soviet Friendship Society, Co-op Pty.

Graham Sawyer, communications consultant. Mbr, staff of Dragon Sch, Oxford, 1986-90, and York Minster Choir Sch, 1983-5. Treas, Oxford W and Abingdon Cons assocn. B Mar 29 1961; ed St Paul's sch, London; Durham univ; Inst of Linguists. AMMA.

Hugh Nicolson, nurse manager; health spokesman, Yorks and Humberside LD region. B Jul 9 1944; ed Park St Jnr Sch; Wombwell Sec Mod Sch; Open Univ. RCN.

BARROW AND FURNESS						Lab gain
Electorate % Turnout	67,764	82.1%	1992	69,288	79.0%	1987
Hutton, J M P (Lab)	26,568	47.7%	+8.5%	25,432	46.5%	C
*Franks, C S (C)	22,990	41.3%	-5.1%	21,504	39.3%	Lab
Crane, C J (LD)	6,089	10.9%	-3.3%	7,799	14.2%	SDP/All
C to Lab swing 6.8%	55,647		6.4%	54,735		7.2%
		Lab maj	3,578		C maj	3,928

John Hutton, lecturer at Newcastle Poly and lawyer, won this seat in 1992; contested Penrith and the Border 1987 and Cumbria and Lancs N in 1989 Euro elections. B May 6 1955; ed Westcliff HS, Essex; Magdalen coll, Oxford. TGWU; NATFHE.

Cecil Franks, solicitor and company director, was MP for this seat 1983-92. Mbr select cmte on energy, 1991-2. Sec, all-pty British-Moroccan parly gp. Mbr Manchester City cl, 1975-84, being ldr of Cons gp; Salford City cl, 1960-74 (ldr of Cons gp, 1968-74, and ldr of cl, 1968-72). B Jul 1 1935; ed Manchester GS; Manchester Univ. Director Pryde Investments Ltd. Mbr, North West RHA, 1973-5.

Clive Crane, computer analyst/programmer; mbr Kendal DC, 1990- . B Dec 24 1964; ed W Suffolk CFE, Bury St Edmunds.

BASILDON						No change
Electorate % Turnout	67,585	79.6%	1992	68,500	73.3%	1987
*Amess, D A (C)	24,159	44.9%	+1.4%	21,858	43.5%	C
Potter, J (Lab)	22,679	42.2%	+3.9%	19,209	38.3%	Lab
Williams, G (LD)	6,967	12.9%	-5.3%	9,139	18.2%	L/All
C to Lab swing 1.3%	53,805		2.8%	50,206		5.3%
		C maj	1,480		C maj	2,649

David Amess was elected in 1983; contested Newham NW, 1979. PPS to Michael Portillo, Minr of State, Transport, then for Environment, and Chief Sec to Treasury, 1989- ; to Under Secs of State for Health (including Mr Portillo), 1987-9. Chmn, Accountancy Aims; snr partner, 1981-7, Employment Agency (Accountancy Aids), a specialist agency. Consultant to Horner Collis and Kirwan. B Mar 26 1952; ed St Bonaventure GS; Bournemouth Coll of Tech. Mbr, Redbridge BC, 1982-6.

John Potter, computer manager; mbr, Basildon DC, 1970- (cl ldr, 1973-9; ldr Lab gp, 1975-9). B Jul 5 1937; ed Loughborough Coll of Tech. MSF.

John Potter, computer manager; mbr, Basildon DC, 1970- ldr, Lab gp, Assocn of DCs, 1975-79. B Jul 5 1937; ed Melton Mowbray GS; Loughborough Coll of Advanced Tech. MSF.

Geoff Williams, snr lecturer in modern languages; Basildon LD cllr and gp ldr, 1981-4 and 1986-91; chmn, Basildon Lib assocn and LDs, 1985-90. B Jan 26 1947; ed Fryerns sch, Basildon; London univ. NATFHE.

BASINGSTOKE						No change
Electorate % Turnout	82,952	82.8%	1992	78,003	77.0%	1987
*Hunter, A R F (C)	37,521	54.6%	-1.4%	33,657	56.0%	C
Bull, D J C (Lab)	16,323	23.8%	+6.1%	15,764	26.3%	SDP/All
Curtis, C (LD)	14,119	20.6%		10,632	17.7%	Lab
Oldaker, Ms V (Grn)	714	1.0%				
C to Lab swing 3.7%	68,677		30.9%	60,053		29.8%
		C maj	21,198		C maj	17,893

Andrew Hunter became mbr select cmte on environment in 1986; mbr select cmte on agriculture 1985. Vice-chmn Monday Club 1990-; British-S Africa gp 1990- ; vice-chmn Cons backbench agriculture cmte 1987-91; all-pty Friends of Croatia parly gp 1991- ; jt sec Cons N Ireland cmte 1990- ; all-pty lighting parly gp 1990- . Company director (unpaid). Political adviser, European Land Ltd; consultant to Plessey-Telnet, Kaye Enterprises Ltd and Scott, Wilson, Kirkpatrick, consulting engineers. Elected in 1983; contested Southampton, Itchen 1979. Asst master Harrow, 1971-83. B Jan 8 1943; ed St George's sch, Harpenden; Durham Univ; Jesus Coll, Cambridge. Hon mbr Society of Sealed Knot, 1990- . Chmn falconry cmte, British Field Sports Society, 1988- . Vice-pres Nat Prayer Book Society, 1987- .

David Bull, transportation planner, Hammersmith and Fulham BC. Mbr Southampton City Cl, 1979-90; chmn Southampton City Bus Co, 1986-90. B Nov 27 1952; ed sec mod sch; Southampton univ. Nalgo.

Chris Curtis, print production consultant; mbr Hants CC, 1981- (gp ldr, 1983-9); Tadley TC 1983- (chmn 1985-6 and 1987-); Basingstoke and Dene DC 1990- (gp ldr, 1991-). B Feb 24 1948; ed GS. Mbr British Fed of Master Printers.

BASSETLAW						No change
Electorate % Turnout	69,375	78.5%	1992	68,043	77.6%	1987
*Ashton, J W (Lab)	29,061	53.4%	+5.3%	25,385	48.1%	Lab
Spelman, Mrs C A (C)	19,064	35.0%	-2.5%	19,772	37.5%	C
Reynolds, M (LD)	6,340	11.6%	-2.8%	7,616	14.4%	SDP/All
C to Lab swing 3.9%	54,465		18.4%	52,773		10.6%
		Lab maj	9,997		Lab maj	5,613

Joe Ashton became a director (unpaid) of Sheffield Wednesday Football Club in 1990. Journalist and broadcaster; formerly a design engineer. Elected in 1968 by-election. Mbr select cmtes on home affairs 1989- ; trade and industry 1987-; members' interests 1979-83; members' salaries 1981-2, and nationalized industries, 1974-6. Opposn spokesman on energy 1979-81. Asst govt whip, 1976-7; PPS to Tony Benn 1974-6. Mbr Sheffield City Cl 1962-9. B Oct 9 1933; ed High Storrs GS, Sheffield; Rotherham tech coll. Sponsored by MSF.

Caroline Spelman, freelance political consultant on agricultural affairs, was dep director, International Confed of European Beetgrowers, 1984-9, and administrative sec to sugar beet cmte of NFU of England and Wales, 1980-4. Lay asst and choir mbr, St Michael's Church, Paris, 1987-9. B May 4 1958; ed Herts and Essex girls' GS; Queen Mary coll, London univ.

Michael Reynolds, univ lecturer; recruitment officer, E Midlands LD region and reg spokesman on ed. B Aug 11 1942; ed Durham, Lancaster and Manchester univs.

BATH						LD gain
Electorate % Turnout	63,689	82.5%	1992	65,246	79.4%	1987
Foster, D M E (LD)	25,718	48.9%	+6.3%	23,515	45.4%	C
*Patten, C F (C)	21,950	41.8%	-3.6%	22,103	42.7%	SDP/All
Richards, Mrs P M (Lab)	4,102	7.8%	-2.8%	5,507	10.6%	Lab
McCanlis, D (Grn)	433	0.8%	-0.5%	687	1.3%	Grn
Barker, Ms M (Lib)	172	0.3%				
Sked, Dr A (Anti-Fed)	117	0.2%				
Rumming, J (Ind)	79	0.2%				
C to LD swing 4.9%	52,571		7.2%	51,812		2.7%
		LD maj	3,768		C maj	1,412

Don Foster, managing consultant public sector consultant, won this seat in 1992. Former teacher and univ education lecturer; contested Bristol East in 1987. Mbr Avon CC 1981-89, being Alliance gp ldr 1981-86 and chmn ed cmte 1986- . B Mar 31 1947; ed Lancaster Royal GS; Keele and Bath Univs. Former mbr, NUT.

Christopher Patten, after being defeated in April 1992, was appointed governor of Hong Kong. Cons Pty chmn and Chancellor of Duchy of Lancaster, 1990-92; enviroment sec 1986-9; Minr for Overseas Development with rank of Minr of State 1986-7; Minr of State for Ed and Science, 1985-6; Under Sec of State for N Ireland, 1983-5. PC 1989. Director, Cons Research Dept 1974-9 and served in it 1966-70; in Cabinet Office, 1970-2; voluntary services unit, Home Office, 1972; personal asst and political sec to Lord Carrington, chmn of Cons pty, 1972-4. MP for this seat 1979-92; contested Lambeth Central, Feb 1974. B May 12 1944; ed St Benedict's Sch, Ealing; Balliol Coll, Oxford.

Pam Richards, social worker; mbr Bath City cl, 1980- (gp ldr 1984-9). B Oct 9 1947; ed Simon Langton GS for Girls, Canterbury; Essex and Bristol Univs. Nalgo.

Duncan McCanlis, director of stationery company that sells green office products; mbr pty exec. B May 10 1949; ed in Ghana and Nigeria; Dartington Hall Sch.

BATLEY AND SPEN				No change		
Electorate % Turnout	76,417	79.6%	1992	74,347	79.0%	1987
*Peacock, Mrs E J (C)	27,629	45.4%	+2.0%	25,512	43.4%	C
Durkin, Mrs E (Lab)	26,221	43.1%	+2.0%	24,150	41.1%	Lab
Beever, G J (LD)	6,380	10.5%	-3.8%	8,372	14.3%	SDP/All
Lord, C (Grn)	628	1.0%	689	1.2%		ML
C to Lab swing 0.0%	60,858		2.3%	58,723		2.3%
		C maj	1,408		C maj	1,362

Elizabeth Peacock was elected in 1983. PPS to Angela Rumbold when home office minr 1991-2. Mbr exec 1922 Cmte 1987- ; Commons Services Cmte 1987-91; Unopposed Bills Panel 1987- ; Select Cmte on Employment 1983-7. Jt vice-chmn 1991- and mbr 1987-91 exec cmte UK branch CPA. Chmn all-pty Trans-Pennine parly gp; wool textile gp; jt vice-chmn prevention of solvent abuse gp; sec Commons motor club. Director Transpennine Gp Ltd 1988- ; Shilton Investments Ltd 1989- ; consultant to Nat Bed Federation and Mettings Industry Assocn. B Sep 4 1937; ed St Monica's Convent, Skipton. Magistrate. Mbr BBC general advisory cl 1987- . Pres 1991- and vice-pres 1987-91 Yorks area CTU.

Eunice Durkin, a development education worker. Mbr Kirklees MDC. Former vice-chmn women's reg TUC of Yorkshire and Humberside. B Sep 30 1937; ed St Joseph's Girls ch; Bradford and Ilkley Community Coll. TGWU.

Gordon Beever, chartered accountant. Mbr Kirklees MBC 1982- . Chmn Colne Valley Lib assocn 1981-4. B Jul 18 1946; ed Holme Valley GS; Pembroke Coll, Oxford.

BATTERSEA				No change		
Electorate % Turnout	68,218	76.6%	1992	66,979	70.7%	1987
*Bowis, J C (C)	26,390	50.5%	+6.2%	20,945	44.2%	C
Dubs, A (Lab)	21,550	41.2%	-1.2%	20,088	42.4%	Lab
O'Brien, R (LD)	3,659	7.0%	-4.9%	5,634	11.9%	SDP/All
Wingrove, I (Grn)	584	1.1%	-0.1%	559	1.2%	Grn
Stevens, W (NLP)	98	0.2%	116	0.2%		WRP
Lab to C swing 3.7%	52,281		9.3%	47,342		1.8%
		C maj	4,840		C maj	857

John Bowis gained this seat in 1987. Mbr Select Cmte on Members' Interests 1987-90. PPS to David Hunt, Sec of State for Wales and fomerly Minr for Local Govt 1989- . Chmn all-pty parly youth affairs lobby; jt sec social science and policy gp 1988- . Adviser to Assocn of Colls of Further and Higher Ed 1987- ; parly adviser to Assocn of Coll Management. Director (unpaid) London Actors Theatre Co 1989- and Battersea Arts Centre. Public affairs director British Insurance Brokers' Assocn 1983-7 and campaign director 1981-2. B Aug 2 1945; ed Tonbridge Sch; Brasenose Coll, Oxford. Vice-pre, International Society for Human Rights 1988- ; Hon jt pres British Youth Cl 1987- . Mbr Kingston BC 1982-6.

Alfred Dubs was MP for this seat 1983-7 when he was defeated and for Battersea S 1979-83; contested Cities of London and Westminster, 1970; S Herts twice in 1974. Appointed director British Refugee Cl 1988. Mbr Broadcasting Standards Cl, 1988- . Mbr Opposn front bench team on home affairs 1983-7. B Dec 1932; ed LSE. Exec mbr Liberty; Fabian Society and Catholic Inst for International Relations; Nicaragua Health Fund; trustee Action Aid. Jt vice-chmn Gtr London gp of Lab MPs 1985-87. TGWU.

Roger O'Brien, solicitor. Sec Battersea & Tooting LDs; mbr London reg LDs. B Aug 1 1964; ed Hull GS; Manchester Univ; Colls of Law, Chester and Chancery Lane.

Ian Wingrove has been library asst, van driver, lay trade unionist. Mbr Grn pty policy cmte, 1990-1; nat speaker on employment 1990-1. B Sep 10 1961; ed Hynburn Comprehensive; Ruskin Coll.

BEACONSFIELD				No change		
Electorate % Turnout	64,268	82.3%	1992	67,713	74.6%	1987
*Smith, T J (C)	33,817	64.0%	-2.0%	33,324	66.0%	C
Purse, Ms P A (LD)	10,220	19.3%	-4.4%	11,985	23.7%	L/All
Smith, D G (Lab)	7,163	13.5%	+3.2%	5,203	10.3%	Lab
Foulds, W (Ind C)	1,317	2.5%				
Foss, A (NLP)	196	0.4%				
Martin, Ms J (ERIP)	166	0.3%				
LD to C swing 1.2%	52,879		44.6%	50,512		42.2%
		C maj	23,597		C maj	21,339

Timothy Smith, chartered accountant, was elected for this seat at 1982 by-election; MP for Ashfield, 1977-9. Appointed to PAC in 1987. PPS to Leon Brittan when Home Sec 1983-5. Director,Gartmore Value Investments plc 1991- . Adviser to Price Waterhouse, Financial Intermediaries, Managers and Brokers Regulatory Assocn, British Venture Capital Assocn, Commodity Traders' Gp, Lloyd's Gp Union and Omitec Ltd. B Oct 5 1947; ed Harrow; St Peter's Coll, Oxford. Jt vice-chmn (1986-8) and jt sec (1988-90 and 1985-6) Cons backbench trade and industry cmte; jt vice-chmn (1987-) and sec (1985-7) Cons finance cmte. Sec all-pty British-Oman parly gp.

Anne Purse, speech therapist. Mbr Henley LD exec; policy officer Henley LD. B Sep 17 1943; ed Radcliffe Sch, Wolverton; Elizabeth Gaskell Coll, Manchester (now Manchester Poly). MSF.

Graham Smith, teacher. Mbr Ealing BC 1986- . B Feb 27 1959; ed Stamford Sch; St Catherine's, Oxford Univ. NUT.

BECKENHAM				No change		
Electorate % Turnout	59,440	77.9%	1992	60,110	73.6%	1987
Merchant, P R G (C)	26,323	56.9%	+0.6%	24,903	56.3%	C
Ritchie, K G H (Lab)	11,038	23.8%	+6.0%	11,439	25.9%	L/All
Williams, Ms M C (LD)	8,038	17.4%	-8.5%	7,888	17.8%	Lab
Williams, G (Lib)	643	1.4%				
Shaw, P (NLP)	243	0.5%				
C to Lab swing 2.7%	46,285		33.0%	44,230		30.4%
		C maj	15,285		C maj	13,464

Piers Merchant was returned for this seat in 1992; MP for Newcastle Central, 1983-7; contested seat in 1979. Public affairs director of Advertising Assocn 1990- . Journalist and editor of *Newsline*, the Cons pty newspaper, 1982-4, and has edited *Newsline North*, regional pty newspaper; on staff of *The Journal*, Newcastle, 1973-82, being chief reporter, 1978-80 and news editor, 1980-2. Director (corporate publicity) NEI plc, now part of Rolls-Royce plc, 1987-90. B Jan 2 1951; ed Nottingham HS; Durham Univ (treas, then chmn, univ Cons assocn, 1970-3); elected Fellow Univ Coll, Durham, 1975. Director Tyne and Wear Wastesaver Ltd, and of tall ships appeal, 1986-90; jt pres free flow of information cmte, international parly gp on human rights; mbr exec Northern Area Cons pty. NUJ, former FoC of Newcastle chapel.

Ken Ritchie, dep director, Refugee Cl, contested this seat 1987. Chmn Beckenham CLP. Exec mbr cl for advancement of Arab-British understanding. B Dec 8 1946; ed Edinburgh and Aston Univs. ACTSS.

Mary Williams, Citizens Advice Bureau adviser and teacher of English to foreign adults, contested London SE in 1989 Euro elections. B Nov 25 1936; ed St Ursula's, Greenwich; London Univ. Voluntary worker for Oxfam.

BEDFORDSHIRE MID				No change		
Electorate % Turnout	81,864	84.5%	1992	80,673	78.6%	1987
*Lyell, Sir Nicholas (C)	40,230	58.2%	-0.8%	37,411	59.0%	C
Clayton, R (Lab)	15,092	21.8%	+3.8%	14,560	23.0%	SDP/All
Hills, N C (LD)	11,957	17.3%	-5.7%	11,463	18.1%	Lab
Cottier, P (Lib)	1,582	2.3%				
Lorys, M (NLP)	279	0.4%				
C to Lab swing 2.3%	69,140		36.4%	63,434		36.0%
		C maj	25,138		C maj	22,851

Sir Nicholas Lyell, QC, was appointed Attorney-general in April 1992; solicitor-general, 1987-92; Under Sec of State for Health and Social Security, 1986-7. PC 1990. PPS to Sir Michael Havers, Attorney-general, 1979-86; a recorder, 1985-7. Chmn 1985-6 and vice-chmn 1982-5 executive Soc of Cons Lawyers; chmn Bow Gp home affairs standing cmte 1979-85. Elected for this seat 1983; MP for Hemel Hemstead, 1979-83; contested Lambeth Central, Oct 1974. B Dec 6 1938; ed Stowe (governor, 1990-); Christ Church, Oxford. Mbr of Lloyd's; Select Cmte on Procedure (Finance), 1982-3. Vice-chmn, British Field Sports Soc, 1983-6.

Richard Clayton, barrister. B May 25 1954; ed Westminster Sch; Oxford Univ. TGWU.

Nick Hills, marketing consultant, contested this seat 1987. Mbr Bedfordshire CC, 1988- . Vice-chmn Beds region of Nat Deaf Childrens Society. B Apr 26 1950; ed Royal Liberty GS, Gidea Park, Essex; NE London Poly.

BEDFORDSHIRE NORTH				No change		
Electorate % Turnout	73,789	80.0%	1992	73,536	77.2%	1987
*Skeet, Sir Trevor (C)	29,920	50.7%	-1.9%	29,845	52.6%	C
Hall, P (Lab)	18,302	31.0%	+7.8%	13,340	23.5%	L/All
Smithson, M (LD)	10,014	17.0%	-6.5%	13,140	23.2%	Lab
Smith, Ms L (Grn)	643	1.1%		435	0.8%	OOBPC
Bench, B (NLP)	178	0.3%				
C to Lab swing 4.9%	59,057		19.7%	56,760		29.1%
		C maj	11,618		C maj	16,505

Sir Trevor Skeet, barrister and industrial consultant, won this seat 1983; MP for Bedford, 1970-83; for Willesden E, 1959-64; contested Llanelli, 1955, and Stoke Newington and Hackney N, 1951. B Jan 28 1918; ed King's Coll, Auckland; Univ of NZ. Chmn, Cons trade cmte, 1971-4; mbr, select cmte on wealth tax, 1975-6; sec, all-pty parly gp on airships, 1971-8; chmn, Cons Middle East cmte, 1973-8; co-chmn, all-pty parly gp on minerals, 1971- . Chmn (1985-8) vice-pres (1988-91) and mbr (1982-) steering cmte parly and scientific cmte.

Patrick Hall, town planner; mbr Bedfordshire CC, 1989- . B Oct 20 1951; ed Bedford Modern Sch. Nalgo.

Mike Smithson, marketing consultant; owner Pemberley Associates; director Bravo Communications Systems; Finite Investment Co. Mbr Bedfordshire CC, 1989- . Worked for BBC for 14 years; nat exec mbr for broadcasting NUJ 1977-82. B May 11 1946; ed Burnage GS, Mancghester, LSE.

Louise Smith, mature student. B Jul 17 1963; ed VCC, Oatham.

BEDFORDSHIRE SOUTH WEST						No change
Electorate % Turnout	79,662	82.4%	1992	78,956	78.7%	1987
*Madel, W D (C)	37,498	57.1%	-1.0%	36,140	58.2%	C
Elliott, B E (Lab)	16,225	24.7%	+6.5%	13,835	22.3%	SDP/All
Freeman, M (LD)	10,988	16.7%	-5.5%	11,352	18.3%	Lab
Rollings, P J (Grn)	689	1.0%	-0.3%	822	1.3%	Grn
Gilmour, D (NLP)	239	0.4%				
C to Lab swing 3.7%	65,639		32.4%	62,149		35.9%
		C maj	21,273		C maj	22,305

David Madel has served on select cmtes on Euro legislation since 1986, members' interests 1979-87 and ed, science and the arts 1979-83. Parly consultant to BET plc and BIFU; advertising exec Thomson Organization 1964-70. Elected for this seat 1983; MP for Bedford S 1970-83; contested Erith and Crayford 1965 by-election and 1966. B Aug 6 1938; ed Uppingham; Keble Coll, Oxford. Chmn Cons backbench ed cmte 1983-5. Jt vice-chmn Cons backbench employment cmte 1974-81.
Barry Elliott, accountant; accounting systems manager, European Passengers Services Ltd; mbr, S Beds DC, 1979-

83, 1984-8 and 1990- . Sec, Leighton-Linslade LP. B Mar 2 1938; ed Univ Coll, London. TSSA.
Mark Freeman, computer software support consultant; mbr South Beds DC 1986-90 (gp ldr, 1987-90); Leighton Linslade TC 1979-83. Agent SW Beds Libs 1980-8 but not in 1983 when seat was SDP led. B Aug 20 1953; ed Cedars Sch, Leighton Buzzard.
Peter Rollings, draughtsman, contested this seat 1987. Mbr, Eaton Bray PC. B Oct 27 1955; ed Dunstable GS; Luton Coll of Tech.

BELFAST EAST						No change
Electorate % Turnout	52,833	67.7%	1992	54,627	60.2%	1987
*Robinson, P D (DUP)	18,437	51.5%	-10.4%	20,372	61.9%	DUP
Alderdice, Dr J (All)	10,650	29.8%	-2.4%	10,574	32.1%	All
Greene, D (C)	3,314	9.3%		1,314	4.0%	WP
Dunlop, D (Ind U)	2,256	6.3%		649	2.0%	SF
O'Donnell, J (SF)	679	1.9%	-0.1%			
Bell, J (WP)	327	0.9%	-3.1%			
Redden, G (NLP)	128	0.4%				
DUP to All swing 4.0%	35,791		21.8%	32,909		29.8%
		DUP maj	7,787		DUP maj	9,798

Peter Robinson, who won the seat in 1979, became dep ldr, Democratic Unionist pty, in 1980; gen secretary, 1975-80. Resigned seat in 1985 in protest at Anglo-Irish agreement and retained it in 1986 by-election. Mbr, N Ireland Assembly, 1982-6; chmn of its environment cmte. Mbr, Castlereagh BC, 1977- ; dep mayor 1978; mayor 1986. B Dec 29 1948; ed Annadale GS; Castlereagh CFE. Director Crown Publications, Belfast, and hon director Voice Newspapers.

Dr John Alderdice is ldr of the Alliance Pty of N Ireland. Contested this seat 1987. Psychiatrist. B May 28 1955; ed Ballymena Acad; Queen's Univ, Belfast. Belfast City cllr, 1989- . BMA.
David Greene owns a firm of solicitors; elected first Cons mbr, Lisburn BC, in 1989; dep chmn, N Ireland Area Cl; sec to Cons cllrs assocn. B 1956; ed Queen's Univ, Belfast; Inst of Professional Legal Studies, Belfast.
Joe O'Donnell, SF speaker on discrimination.

BELFAST NORTH						No change
Electorate % Turnout	55,062	65.2%	1992	59,124	62.3%	1987
*Walker, A C (UU)	17,240	48.0%	+9.0%	14,355	39.0%	UU
Maginness, A (SDLP)	7,615	21.2%	+5.5%	5,795	15.7%	SDLP
McManus, P (SF)	4,693	13.1%	-0.7%	5,671	15.4%	Prot U
Campbell, T (All)	2,246	6.3%	-1.5%	5,062	13.7%	SF
Redpath, Mrs M (C)	2,107	5.9%		3,062	8.3%	WP
Lynch, S (NA)	1,386	3.9%		2,871	7.8%	All
Smith, Ms M (WP)	419	1.2%	-7.2%			
O'Leary, D (NLP)	208	0.6%				
SDLP to UU swing 1.8%	35,914		26.8%	36,816		23.3%
		UU maj	9,625		UU maj	8,560

Cecil Walker, a former sales manager, was elected in 1983; contested the seat, 1979. Resigned seat in 1985 in protest at Anglo-Irish Agreement and re-elected at 1986 by-election. Unsuccessfully contested N Ireland Assembly, 1973. B Dec 17 1924; ed Methodist Coll, Belfast. In timber business with James P Corry & Co Ltd, Belfast, from 1941; joinery sales manager, 1951-83.
Alban Maginness, barrister; mbr Belfast City Cl. B Jul 9 1950; ed St Malachy's Coll, Belfast; Ulster Univ; Queen's Univ, Belfast.

Paddy McManus, former welder, contested this seat 1987. Mbr Belfast City Cl; SF speaker on legal affairs. Interned in the early Seventies.
Tom Campbell, solicitor, contested this seat 1987; mbr, Belfast City Cl, 1985- (pty chief whip); chmn, Alliance clls assocn. B Aug 31 1958; ed St McNissis GS, Garron Tower, Co Antrim; Queen's Univ, Belfast.
Margaret Redpath, teacher; founder mbr, Belfast N Cons assocn. B 1943; ed Belfast Royal Acad; Stranmillis Coll; Queen's Univ, Belfast.

BELFAST SOUTH				No change		
Electorate % Turnout	52,032	64.5%	1992	54,208	60.3%	1987
*Smyth, Rev W M (UU)	16,336	48.6%	-9.2%	18,917	57.8%	UU
McDonnell, Dr A (SDLP)	6,266	18.7%	+5.6%	6,963	21.3%	All
Montgomery, J (All)	5,054	15.0%	-6.2%	4,268	13.0%	SDLP
Fee, L (C)	3,356	10.0%	1,528		4.7%	WP
Hayes, S (SF)	1,123	3.3%	+0.2%	1,030	3.1%	SF
Hadden, P (LTU)	875	2.6%				
Lynn, P (WP)	362	1.1%	-3.6%			
Mullan, Ms T (NLP)	212	0.6%				
UU to SDLP swing 7.4%	33,584		30.0%	32,706		36.5%
		UU maj	10,070		UU maj	11,954

The Rev Martin Smyth held seat for UU at 1982 by-election caused by murder of the Rev Robert Bradford. Resigned seat 1985 in protest at Anglo-Irish Agreement and held it in 1986 by-election. Pty spokesman on health and social services; mbr select cmte on health 1991- ; select cmte on social services 1984-6 and 1987-90; sec all-pty personal social services parly panel; pro-life gp. Vice-pres UU Cl since 1974. Vice-chmn all-pty cmte on Soviet Jewry, 1983- ; mbr exec cmte British gp IPU 1984- ; exec cmte UK branch CPA 1989- ; jt vice-chmn all-pty British-Malawi parly gp and Brazilian gp.
Dr Alasdair McDonnell, GP, contested this seat 1987; 1986 by-election; 1983; 1982 by-election; and 1979. Stood as Nat Democratic pty candidate in Antrim N in 1970 when medical student. Mbr, Belfast City Cl, 1977-81 and 1985-92. Asst treas, SDLP, 1985-90. B Sep 1949; ed St MacNissi's Coll, Cty Antrim; Univ Coll, Dublin. First elected to SDLP exec in 1976.
John Montgomery, teacher, hon press officer of Alliance pty and spokesman on environment. Belfast cllr, 1985-9.
Andrew Fee, manufacturer's representative for motor supplies; founder and chmn, Gilnahirk branch, North Down Cons assocn; mbr, gen purposes and CPC cmtes, N Down assocn. B 1948; ed Belfast Royal acad; Belfast tech coll.
Sean Hayes is an Irish language teacher.

BELFAST WEST				SDLP gain		
Electorate % Turnout	54,609	73.2%	1992	59,324	69.1%	1987
Hendron, Dr J G (SDLP)	17,415	43.6%	+7.8%	16,862	41.2%	SF
*Adams, G (SF)	16,826	42.1%	+0.9%	14,641	35.7%	SDLP
Cobain, F (UU)	4,766	11.9%	-6.7%	7,646	18.7%	UU
Lowry, J (WP)	750	1.9%	-2.6%	1,819	4.4%	WP
Kennedy, M (NLP)	213	0.5%				
SF to SDLP swing 3.4%	39,970		1.5%	40,968		5.4%
		SDLP maj	589		SF maj	2,221

Dr Joe Hendron, a general practitioner, won the seat in 1992; contested it in 1987 and 1983. SDLP mbr NI Convention 1975 and of Assembly 1982-6. Ldr SDLP gp Belfast City Cl 1985- (mbr since 1981). B Nov 12 1933; ed St Nalachy's coll, Belfast; Queen's univ, Belfast.
Gerry Adams was elected in 1983 and re-elected 1987 but did not take his seat at Westminster. B Oct 6 1948; ed St Mary's GS, Belfast. President of SF 1984- ; former vice-pres. Elected NI Assembly 1982 for West Belfast. In Feb 1978 charged with membership of IRA and spent seven months imprisoned on remand but freed when charge was dropped. Served with exclusion order in Dec 1982 banning him from entering London for talks with Ken Livingstone then GLC leader. Exclusion order lifted when elected MP for Belfast West.

BERKSHIRE EAST				No change		
Electorate % Turnout	90,365	81.4%	1992	87,820	73.8%	1987
*Mackay, A J (C)	43,898	59.7%	-0.6%	39,094	60.3%	C
Murray, Ms L (LD)	15,218	20.7%	-4.7%	16,468	25.4%	SDP/All
Dibble, K (Lab)	14,458	19.7%	+5.3%	9,287	14.3%	Lab
LD to C swing 2.0%	73,574		39.0%	64,849		34.9%
		C maj	28,680		C maj	22,626

Andrew MacKay was appointed an asst govt whip in 1992; PPS to Tom King, when Sec of State for N Ireland and for Defence, 1986-92. Former adviser to Morgan Grenfell plc, D Y Davies plc, and Henry Burcher and Co, chartered surveyors; director Cabra Estates plc 1989-92, was non-exec director Barnett Consulting Gp Ltd. Former estate agent. Elected in 1983; MP for B'ham, Stechford, 1977-9. Mbr select cmte on environment 1985-6; nat exec Cons pty 1979-82. Sec Cons backbench foreign affairs cmte, 1985-6; sec Cons Friends of Israel parly gp, 1986-92. B Aug 27 1949; ed Solihull Sch.
Linda Murray, univ lecturer in psychology, contested seat 1987; mbr, Berks CC, 1985- (LD gp ldr). B Nov 25 1949; ed Stoke Dameral HS for Girls, Plymouth; City Univ, London; Univ Coll, London. AUT.
Keith Dibble, an administration manager, was chmn Aldershot branch Lab Pty 1990-1; mbr Rushmoor BC, 1984- . B Jul 4 1955; ed Woolmer Hill Comprehensive Sch, Haslemere, Surrey. EETPU.

BERWICK-UPON-TWEED				No change		
Electorate % Turnout	54,919	79.1%	1992	54,378	77.3%	1987
*Beith, A J (LD)	19,283	44.4%	-7.7%	21,903	52.1%	L/All
Henfrey, Dr A W (C)	14,240	32.8%	+3.3%	12,400	29.5%	C
Adam, Dr G J (Lab)	9,933	22.9%	+5.4%	7,360	17.5%	Lab
				379	0.9%	Grn
LD to C swing 5.5%	43,456		11.6%	42,042		22.6%
		LD maj	5,043		L/All maj	9,503

Alan Beith won the seat as Lib in 1973 by-election; contested it, 1970. Contested leadership of LDs in 1988. Convenor of LD team on economic affairs and chief Treasury spokesman, 1988- ; spokesman on Treasury matters from 1987 when he joined Select Cmte on Treasury and Civil Service. Also spokesman on trade and industry, 1990- . Dep Ldr of Lib Pty, 1985-8; spokesman on foreign affairs, 1985-7; Alliance spokesman on foreign affairs in 1987 election. Lib Chief Whip, 1976-85. Mbr, HoC Commission, 1979- ; select cmte on sittings of Commons, 1991-2. B Apr 20 1943; ed King's Sch, Macclesfield; Balliol and Nuffield Coll, Oxford. Jt vice-chmn, all-pty arts and heritage parly gp; Methodist gp, 1990- . Parly adviser to AUT. Methodist local preacher.

Tony Henfrey, chartered chemist, is chmn, Oceonics Gp plc, an offshore marine surveying company, 1991- ; non-exec director, Hornbeck Offshore Services, Galveston, Texas, US, 1990- . Managing director and partner, Simmons and Co International Houston, Texas, 1979-90. Vice-chmn, Cons abroad, 1991- ; chmn, Cons abroad Texas branch, 1987-90. B Dec 24 1944; ed Stationers' Company's Sch, London; St Catherine's Coll, Oxford.

Gordon Adam, a mining engineer with NCB 1959-79, has been MEP for Northumbria since 1979; a vice-chmn of European Parliament's cmte on energy, research and technology, 1979- . Contested Tynemouth, 1966 general election, and Berwick-upon-Tweed in 1973 by-election and Feb 1974. Mbr Whitley Bay BC 1971-4; North Tyneside MBC 1973-80 (chmn 1973-4; mayor 1974-5; dep ldr 1975-80); Northern Economic Planning Cl 1974-9; Northern Arts General Cl 1975- . B Mar 28 1934; ed Carlisle GS; Leeds Univ.

BETHNAL GREEN AND STEPNEY				No change		
Electorate % Turnout	55,675	65.5%	1992	55,769	57.6%	1987
*Shore, P D (Lab)	20,350	55.8%	+7.6%	15,490	48.2%	Lab
Shaw, J A (LD)	8,120	22.3%	-9.5%	10,206	31.8%	L/All
Emmerson, Miss J E (C)	6,507	17.9%	-1.4%	6,176	19.2%	C
Edmonds, R (BNP)	1,310	3.6%		232	0.7%	Comm
Kelsey, S (Comm GB)	156	0.4%				
LD to Lab swing 8.6%	36,443		33.6%	32,104		16.5%
		Lab maj	12,230		Lab maj	5,284

Peter Shore was elected for this seat in 1983; MP for Stepney and Poplar, 1974-83, and Stepney, 1964-74; contested St Ives, 1950; Halifax, 1959. Appointed to select cmte on foreign affairs in 1987; mbr, privileges cmte, 1984-7 and 1989- ; on sittings of Commons, 1991-92; exec cmte, UK branch, CPA, being jt vice-chmn, 1989-90. Jt pres, race and community parly gp; chmn, all-pty maritime parly gp, 1987- ; jt vice-chmn, interparly cl against Anti-Semitism. Mbr shadow cabinet, 1979-87, being chief spokesman on Commons affairs, 1984-7. Sec of State for Environment, 1976-9; Sec of State for Trade, 1974-6. Minr without Portfolio and Dep Ldr of House, 1969-70; Sec of State for Economic Affairs, 1967-9; Parly Sec, Min of Techn, 1966-7. B May 20 1924; ed Quarry Bank HS, Liverpool; King's Coll, Cambridge. Sponsored by TGWU.

Jeremy Shaw, training mgr, contested this seat 1987; mbr, Tower Hamlets BC, 1982- (mayor, 1989-90). B Apr 18 1959; ed Latymer Sch, Edmonton; Queen's Coll, Oxford.

Jane Emmerson, accounts exec, has chaired Bethnal Green and Stepney Cons assocn since 1990; mbr, Nat Advisory Cl for Ed, 1989- . Former mbr, exec cl, Toynbee Hall; self-employed, Flamborough Pottery, E Yorks 1983-85. Hon mbr, Nat Fed of Fishermen's Org, 1989- . B Aug 10 1957; ed Headlands Sch, Bridlington; Scarborough CFE.

BEVERLEY				No change		
Electorate % Turnout	81,198	79.7%	1992	78,923	76.3%	1987
*Cran, J D (C)	34,503	53.3%	+1.1%	31,459	52.2%	C
Collinge, A (LD)	17,986	27.8%	-3.5%	18,864	31.3%	L/All
Challen, C R (Lab)	12,026	18.6%	+2.1%	9,901	16.4%	Lab
Hetherington, D (NLP)	199	0.3%				
LD to C swing 2.3%	64,714		25.5%	60,224		20.9%
		C maj	16,517		C maj	12,595

James Cran was elected in 1987 and became mbr, Select Cmte on Trade and Industry; contested Gordon, 1983; Glasgow, Shettleston, Oct 1974. Sec, Cons backbench Euro affairs cmte, 1990-1; Cons constitutional affairs cmte, 1989-90; all-pty Order of St John parly gp. W Midlands director of CBI, 1984-7, and Northern director, 1979-84. Sec and then chief exec, Nat Assocn of Pension Funds, 1971-9. Mbr, Ct, Hull Univ, 1987- ; Sutton BC, 1974-9. B Jan 28 1944; ed Ruthrieston Sch, Aberdeen; Aberdeen Coll of Commerce; Kings Coll, Univ of Aberdeen.

Arthur Collinge, freelance lecturer and management consultant/trainer, contested Darlington 1987; Bishop Auckland 1983; York in 1989 Euro election. Mbr, N Yorks CC, 1985- ; Harrogate BC, 1991- . Chmn, Harrogate LD. B Jul 6 1939; ed Queen Elizabeth's GS, Blackburn; univs of Wales and Durham.

Colin Challen, publisher; mbr, Hull City Cl, 1986- . B Jun 12 1953; ed Norton Sec Sch; Hull Univ. GPMU.

BEXHILL AND BATTLE						No change
Electorate % Turnout	65,850	79.0%	1992	65,288	77.4%	1987
*Wardle, C F (C)	31,330	60.2%	-6.2%	33,570	66.4%	C
Prochak, Ms S M (LD)	15,023	28.9%	+3.0%	13,051	25.8%	SDP/All
Taylor, F W (Lab)	4,883	9.4%	+1.7%	3,903	7.7%	Lab
Prus, J (Grn)	594	1.1%				
Smith, Mrs M (CSP)	190	0.4%				
C to LD swing 4.6%	52,020		31.3%	50,524		40.6%
		C maj	16,307		C maj	20,519

Charles Wardle was appointed under sec, Home Office, in 1992. Elected in 1983. PPS to Ian Lang, Sec of State for Scotland, in 1990; PPS to Sir Norman Fowler, Sec of State for Social Services, 1984-7. Mbr, select cmte on trade and industry 1983-4. Chmn One Nation Forum. Director Wardle and Co Ltdd chmn, Ray Powell Ltd, 1990; Benjamin Priest Gp 1977-84; Warne, Wright and Rowland, 1978-84; director, Ray Powell Holdings Ltd, 1990-2; Asset Special Situations Trust plc, 1982-4. Former Consultant to Peat Marwick McLintock and to UniChem. B Aug 23 1939; ed Tonbridge sch; Lincoln Coll, Oxford; Harvard Business sch. Mbr, CBI central cl and CBI West Midlands reg cl, 1980-84.

Susan Prochak, teacher; mbr, Rother DC, 1989- (LD gp ldr). B Nov 9 1946; ed state sch. Cot deaths counsellor.

Frank Taylor, actor. B Oct 17 1935; ed St Albans; Northampton Eng Coll. Equity; TGWU.

BEXLEYHEATH						No change
Electorate % Turnout	57,684	82.2%	1992	59,448	77.8%	1987
*Townsend, C D (C)	25,606	54.0%	+0.3%	24,866	53.7%	C
Browning, J (Lab)	11,520	24.3%	+6.5%	13,179	28.5%	L/All
Chaplin, Ms A W (LD)	10,107	21.3%	-7.2%	8,218	17.8%	Lab
Cundy, R (Ind)	170	0.4%				
C to Lab swing 3.1%	47,403		29.7%	46,263		25.3%
		C maj	14,086		C maj	11,687

Cyril Townsend was jt vice-chmn Cons backbench defence cmte 1985-91 and jt sec 1982-5; jt vice-chmn Cons backbench foreign and Commonwealth affairs cmte 1991- . Chmn, cl for advancement of Arab-British understanding 1982- ; S Atlantic Cl 1983- ; British-Cyprus parly gp, 1980- . Vice-chmn Cons Middle East cl, 1988- (previously sec); Hansard Society, 1988- ; Friends of Cyprus, 1980- ; political cmte UNA 1980- ; treas all-pty Euro Arab co-operation parly gp . Elected in Feb 1974. B Dec 21 1937; ed Bradfield coll, Berkshire; RMA Sandhurst.

John Browning, finance officer; mbr Bexley BC 1986- . B Jan 17 1948; ed Erith GS; Portsmouth Poly; E Ham Coll of Tech.

Wendy Chaplin, town planner; mbr LD housing working pty; Bromley CHC; Bromley visitors panel; Chislehurst and Bexley HA. B Sep 13 1938; ed Brockenhurst Cty HS, Hants; LSE; Univ coll, London.

BILLERICAY						No change
Electorate % Turnout	80,388	82.3%	1992	79,535	77.2%	1987
*Gorman, Mrs T E (C)	37,406	56.5%	+1.6%	33,741	54.9%	C
Bellard, F (LD)	14,912	22.5%	-3.1%	15,725	25.6%	SDP/All
Miller, Ms A (Lab)	13,880	21.0%	+1.5%	11,942	19.4%	Lab
LD to C swing 2.3%	66,198		34.0%	61,408		29.3%
		C maj	22,494		C maj	18,016

Teresa Gorman was jt sec Cons backbench social security cmte, 1988-9. Founder and former co-proprietor of Banta, a company making biological and nursing teaching aids. Elected in 1987. Mbr Cons women's nat cmte 1983- ; Westminster City Cl 1982-6. Chmn, ASP (Alliance of Small Firms and Self Employed People), a pressure gp for small businesses; also chmn of Amarant Trust, a registered charity for medical research. Stood in Streatham in Oct 1974 as Ind (Small Business) candidate. B Sep 1931; ed Fulham Cty sch; London univ.

Frank Bellard, civil servant; mbr Essex CC, 1987- ; Basildon DC, 1986-90. B Aug 3 1946; ed St Margaret's HS for Boys, Liverpool. CPSA.

Alison Miller, systems engineer. B Feb 2 1954; ed NE London poly; Garnett coll. Mbr, Society of Telecom Execs.

BIRKENHEAD						No change
Electorate % Turnout	62,682	73.0%	1992	65,662	72.3%	1987
*Field, F (Lab)	29,098	63.6%	+4.9%	27,883	58.7%	Lab
Hughes, R G M (C)	11,485	25.1%	-1.2%	12,511	26.3%	C
Williams, Mrs P M (LD)	4,417	9.7%	-5.3%	7,095	14.9%	L/All
Fox, Ms T R (Grn)	543	1.2%				
Griffiths, Ms B (NLP)	190	0.4%				
C to Lab swing 3.1%	45,733		38.5%	47,489		32.4%
		Lab maj	17,613		Lab maj	15,372

Frank Field became chmn of select cmte on social security in 1991: chmn, select cmte on social services, 1987-91; an Opposn spokesman on health and social security, 1983-4; a spokesman on ed, 1979-81. Elected 1979; contested Buckinghamshire S, 1966. Director, Child Poverty Action Gp, 1969-79, and of Low Pay Unit, 1974-80. Teacher at Southwark and Hammersmith CFEs, 1964-9. B Jul 16 1942; ed St Clement Danes GS; Hull Univ. Parly consultant to CPSA. TGWU.

Glyn Mon Hughes, public relations executive. With BBC North, Manchester, 1989-90, being publicity officer, BBC Philharmonic. B Jul 4 1956; ed Birkenhead Sch; Univ of Wales, Bangor; Trinity Hall, Cambridge. Former exec cl mbr and media officer Birkenhead Cons assocn.

Pat Williams, self-employed market research interviewer. Mbr Wirral MBC, 1987- ; Birkenhead choral society. Former chmn Oxton Ward LDs, Birkenhead. B Feb 12 1937; ed local primary and sec schs.

BIRMINGHAM, EDGBASTON						No change
Electorate % Turnout	53,041	71.3%	1992	54,416	68.6%	1987
*Knight, Dame Jill (C)	18,529	49.0%	-0.8%	18,595	49.8%	C
Wilton, J (Lab)	14,222	37.6%	+10.8%	10,014	26.8%	Lab
Robertson-Steel, I (LD)	4,419	11.7%	-9.3%	7,843	21.0%	SDP/All
Simpson, P M (Grn)	643	1.7%	+0.2%	559	1.5%	Grn
				307	0.8%	Ind C
C to Lab swing 5.8%	37,813		11.4%	37,318		23.0%
		C maj	4,307		C maj	8,581

Dame Jill Knight was re-elected to exec cmte of 1922 Cmte of Cons backbenchers in 1989; first woman vice-chmn of cmte, 1987-8; sec 1983-7; mbr of exec cmte 1979-83. Chmn Cons backbench health cmte 1988- , and of the former health and social services cmte 1982-8. Mbr exec cmte British gp IPU 1991- . Elected in 1966; contested Northampton, 1959 and 1964. Director, Computeach International and its subsidiary Teachware Ltd 1990- . Journalist and broadcaster. B Jul 9 1927; ed Fairfield Sch, Bristol; King Edward VI GS, Birmingham. Vice-pres Nat Union of Townswomen's Guilds 1986- . Mbr Cl of Europe and WEU 1977-88 Chmn Lords and Commons all-pty

family and child protection gp, 1978- .

John Wilton, lecturer, contested this seat 1987. Mbr W Midlands Lab pty reg exec cmte, 1989-91; CLP sec, 1983-4. B Jan 14 1947; ed Raines Foundation GS, Stepney; Bristol Poly; Birmingham and Keele Univs. MSF.

Dr Iain Robertson-Steel is a general practitioner and RAF doctor until 1992. B Nov 26 1954; ed Ramsey Abbey GS, Cambs; B'ham Univ. BMA.

Phil Simpson, civil engineer (municipal and highway), contested this seat 1987 and Birmingham East in 1989 Euro elections. B May 22 1947; ed Coalville GS; Birmingham Univ.

BIRMINGHAM, ERDINGTON						No change
Electorate % Turnout	52,398	70.2%	1992	54,179	68.5%	1987
*Corbett, R (Lab)	18,549	50.5%	+4.6%	17,037	45.9%	Lab
Hope, S N (C)	13,814	37.6%	-1.7%	14,570	39.2%	C
Campbell, Dr J (LD)	4,398	12.0%	-2.9%	5,530	14.9%	SDP/All
C to Lab swing 3.1%	36,761		12.9%	37,137		6.6%
		Lab maj	4,735		Lab maj	2,467

Robin Corbett was elected in for this seat in 1983; MP for Hemel Hempstead, Oct 1974-9; contested the seat, 1966 and Feb 1974; W Derbyshire by-election, 1967. Opposn spokesman on home affairs, 1985- . Communication and public affairs consultant. Journalist with IPC Magazines, 1969-74. Jt vice-chmn, all-pty motor industry parly gp, 1987- ; mbr, cl, Save the Children Fund, 1986-90; cl, Royal Coll of Vet Surgeons, 1989- ; sponsor, Terrence Higgins Trust, 1987- . B Dec 22 1933; ed Holly Lodge GS, Smethwick. Chmn, farm animal welfare co-ordinating cmte, 1977- . Jt vice-chmn, all-pty Friends of Cyprus parly

gp, 1987- ; jt sec, Anzac gp, 1985- . NUJ. Sponsored by Usdaw.

Stanley Hope is a power station operations engineer. Mbr, Sefton MBC, 1974-88, being re-elected four months later in by-election in different ward, retiring from cl in 1991; Crosby BC, 1971-74. B Jul 26 1947.

John Campbell, chartered chemist and schoolmaster; press officer, Sutton Coldfield and Erdington LDs. B Aug 29 1930; ed Lenzie Acad, nr Glasgow; Glasgow Univ; Queen's Univ, Belfast.

BIRMINGHAM, HALL GREEN						No change
Electorate % Turnout	60,091	78.2%	1992	61,148	74.7%	1987
*Hargreaves, A (C)	21,649	46.1%	+1.2%	20,478	44.9%	C
Slowey, Ms J E (Lab)	17,984	38.3%	+10.1%	12,857	28.2%	Lab
McGrath, D A (LD)	7,342	15.6%	-11.4%	12,323	27.0%	SDP/All
C to Lab swing 4.4%	46,975		7.8%	45,658		16.7%
		C maj	3,665		C maj	7,621

Andrew Hargreaves was elected in 1987; contested Blyth Valley, 1983. Jt sec, Cons backbench urban and inner cities cmte, 1987- ; Cons backbench defence cmte, 1991- ; sec, all-pty Anglo-Belgian parly gp. Consultant to J Henry Schroder Wagg and Co Ltd (assistant director of bank, 1981-7) and to Midlands Electricity plc. Fine art auctioneer and valuer with Christie's, 1977-81. B May 15 1955; ed Eton; St Edmund Hall, Oxford. Joint proprietor of fitness centre.

Jane Slowey, researcher for MEP; mbr, Birmingham City Cl, 1988- (chairman, jt leisure and learning and employment support sub-cmte). Mbr, Nat Lab women's cmte, 1985-9; W Midlands reg women's cmte, 1983-9; chairman of branch women's section. B Apr 3 1952; ed Birmingham Univ; Chiswick Poly. MSF.
David McGrath, business development manager; chmn Birmingham LDs, 1989-90. Mbr, B'ham City Cl, 1986- . B Feb 10 1960.

BIRMINGHAM, HODGE HILL						No change
Electorate % Turnout	57,651	70.8%	1992	59,296	68.8%	1987
*Davis, T A G (Lab)	21,895	53.6%	+4.9%	19,872	48.7%	Lab
Gibson, Miss E (C)	14,827	36.3%	-0.6%	15,083	36.9%	C
Hagan, S (LD)	3,740	9.2%	-5.2%	5,868	14.4%	L/All
Whicker, E (NF)	370	0.9%				
C to Lab swing 2.8%	40,832		17.3%	40,823		11.7%
		Lab maj	7,068		Lab maj	4,789

Terry Davis was elected for this seat 1983; MP for Birmingham, Stechford, 1979-83, and for Bromsgrove, 1971-4; contested that seat, 1970; Bromsgrove and Redditch, Feb and Oct 1974, and Birmingham, Stechford, 1977 by-election. Appointed mbr PAC in 1987; an Opposn spokesman on industry, 1986-7; on Treasury and economic affairs, 1983-6; on health and social services, 1980-3. Parly adviser to Inland Revenue Staff Fed. Mbr, Advisory Cl on Public Records, 1989- . Manager in motor industry, 1974-9. B Jan 5 1938; ed King Edward VI GS, Stourbridge; London Univ and Michigan Univ. Sponsored

by MSF.
Elizabeth Gibson, teacher and part-time; partner in small business. Mbr, W Midlands Cons area cl; dep chmn, Chelsea Cons assocn, 1987-90; mbr, Cons Greater London area cl, 1988-90; chmn, Cons parly candidates assocn, 1990- . B Oct 7 1951; ed St Bernard's Convent, Westcliff-on-Sea; Convent of Notr Dame, Teignmouth; Maria Assumpta Coll, London. PAT.
Sean Hagan, solicitor; chmn, B'ham Selly Oak LDs; mbr, Law Society. B Apr 2 1963; ed Hayling comprehensive sch; Rhyl HS; UCW, Aberystwyth; Chester Coll of Law.

BIRMINGHAM, LADYWOOD						No change
Electorate % Turnout	56,970	65.9%	1992	58,761	64.8%	1987
*Short, Ms C (Lab)	24,887	66.3%	+8.6%	21,971	57.7%	Lab
Ashford, Mrs B (C)	9,604	25.6%	-5.8%	11,943	31.3%	C
Worth, B L (LD)	3,068	8.2%	-1.1%	3,532	9.3%	SDP/All
				650	1.7%	Grn
C to Lab swing 7.2%	37,559		40.7%	38,096		26.3%
		Lab maj	15,283		Lab maj	10,028

Clare Short was elected in 1983. Mbr, Opposn front bench social security team, 1989-91; employment team, 1985-8. Mbr, select cmte on home affairs, 1983-5; chmn, all-pty parly gp on race relations, 1985-6. Mbr, Labour Party NEC, 1988- . B Feb 5 1946; ed Keele and Leeds Univs. Served at Home Office, 1970-5; director, All Faiths in One Race, Birmingham, 1976-8; director, Youthaid, 1979-83, and the Unemployment Unit, 1981-3. Sponsored by Nupe.
Barbara Ashford, barrister, was dep chief clerk to

Marylebone justices, 1977-82. Mbr, Waverley BC, 1987- . Has held office in Surrey SW Cons Assocn. B Apr 8 1953; ed King Edward VI GS, Birmingham; King's Coll, London; Inns of Court Sch of Law.
Mr Brian Worth, chartered accountant; cl mbr, Inst of Chartered Accountants in England and Wales. Hon treas, British Cl of Churches, 1973-80. B Jan 25 1938; ed Haberdashers' Aske's Hatcham sch.

BIRMINGHAM, NORTHFIELD						Lab gain
Electorate % Turnout	70,533	76.1%	1992	73,319	72.6%	1987
Burden, R (Lab)	24,433	45.5%	+6.3%	24,024	45.1%	C
*King, R D (C)	23,803	44.4%	-0.8%	20,889	39.2%	Lab
Cropp, D (LD)	5,431	10.1%	-5.5%	8,319	15.6%	SDP/All
C to Lab swing 3.5%	53,667		1.2%	53,232		5.9%
		Lab maj	630		C maj	3,135

Richard Burden, full-time Nalgo official since 1979, won this seat in 1992; contested Meriden 1987. B Sep 1 1954; ed Wallasey Tech GS; Bramhall comprehensive sch; St John's CFE, Manchester; York and Warwick univs. Mbr, Lab Middle East Cl; TU Friends of Palestine. Held numerous Lab Pty offices including CLP chairman, political ed officer and ward sec. TGWU.
Roger King was PPS to Michael Howard, Sec of State for Employment, previously Minr for Local Govt and then for Water and Planning, 1987-92. Mbr, Select Cmte on Transport, 1984-7; jt chmn, 1991-2, and jt vice-chmn,

1985-91, all-pty motor industry parly gp. Was parly adviser to Retread Manufacturers Assocn. Elected in 1983; contested Cannock, Feb 1974. B Oct 26 1943; ed Solihull sch. Auto engineering apprentice, British Motor Corporation, 1960-6; sales rep, 1966-74; had own motor products design, production and marketing business, 1974-81; self-employed distributor of motor products, 1982-3.
David Cropp, head of special ed unit, contested Bromsgrove 1987. Mbr, West Midlands LD exec, 1990-92; chairman, Leominster LDs, 1989-92. B Aug 16 1946; ed Reading Sch; Birmingham and Warwick Univs.

BIRMINGHAM, PERRY BARR						No change
Electorate % Turnout	72,161	71.6%	1992	73,767	69.6%	1987
*Rooker, J W (Lab)	27,507	53.2%	+2.8%	25,894	50.4%	Lab
Green, G G (C)	18,917	36.6%	-0.3%	18,961	36.9%	C
Philpott, T (LD)	5,261	10.2%	-2.5%	6,514	12.7%	L/All
C to Lab swing 1.6%	51,685		16.6%	51,369		13.5%
		Lab maj	8,590		Lab maj	6,933

Jeffrey Rooker, a chartered engineer, joined Opposn front bench health team in 1990 as spokesman on community care and personal social services. Unsuccessfully contested election for Labour chief whip in 1988; Opposn spokesman on housing and construction, 1984-7; spokesman on local govt, 1987-8; mbr, PAC, 1988-90. Chmn, Lab campaign for electoral reform, 1989- ; mbr, Lab working pty on electoral systems, 1990- . Elected in Feb 1974. B Jun 5 1941; ed Handsworth Tech School and Coll; Aston and

Warwick univs. Jt vice-chmn, Interparly Cl against Anti-Semitism, 1991- . Mbr, cl, Inst of Production Engineers, 1975-81.
Graham Green, engineer, elected to Brimingham City Cl in 1988. Precision grinder, W J Wild Ltd, from 1986; casting controller/superviser, Delta Tubes Ltd, 1980-6. B Apr 12 1955; ed Slade Rd secondary sch.
Toby Philpott, economist. B Aug 2 1969; ed B'ham Poly. Mbr, Royal Statistical Society.

BIRMINGHAM, SELLY OAK						Lab gain
Electorate % Turnout	72,150	76.6%	1992	72,213	73.1%	1987
Jones, Ms L M (Lab)	25,430	46.0%	+6.7%	23,305	44.2%	C
*Beaumont-Dark, A M (C)	23,370	42.3%	-1.9%	20,721	39.3%	Lab
Osborne, D (LD)	5,679	10.3%	-5.1%	8,128	15.4%	L/All
Slatter, P G (Grn)	535	1.0%	-0.2%	611	1.2%	Grn
Barwood, C (NLP)	178	0.3%				
Malik, K (Rev Comm)	84	0.2%				
C to Lab swing 4.3%	55,276		3.7%	52,765		4.9%
		Lab maj	2,060		C maj	2,584

Lynne Jones, housing manager, won this seat 1992. Mbr, Birmingham City cl, 1980- (chairman, housing cmte, 1984-7). Former exec mbr, Lab housing gp. B Apr 26 1951; ed Ley Hill primary sch, Northfield; Bartley Green Girls' GS, Birmingham; B'ham univ; B'ham poly. Branch treas. MSF since 1972.
Anthony Beaumont-Dark was MP for this seat 1979-92; contested B'ham, Aston, 1964 and 1959. Investment analyst; partner of Smith Keen Cutler, stockbrokers, 1959-85, then consultant to them; former consultant to Sedgwick UK Ltd, insurance brokers. Mbr, Select Cmte on Treasury and Civil Service, 1979-92. Mbr, B'ham Stock Exchange, 1958- . Trustee, B'ham Copec Housing Trust, 1975- . B

Oct 11 1932; ed Cedarhurst sch, Solihull; B'ham Coll of Arts; Birmingham univ. Non-exec director, J Saville Gordon plc, 1989- ; T R Higher Income Trust plc, 1989- . Mbr, Birmingham City Cl, 1957-67 (alderman from 1967); W Midland Met CC, 1973-80. Governor, Aston univ, 1980- ; Birmingham univ, 1984- .
David Osborne, lecturer; nat hon tres, NATFHE, 1988-9; chmn, NATFHE finance and gen purposes cmte, 1991- . B Feb 25 1942; ed Queen Elizabeth's Boys' GS, Mansfield; City of Worcester teachers' traing coll; B'ham univ.
Paul Slatter, local govt advice and information worker. Mbr, Birmingham Grn Pty cmte. B Nov 10 1966; ed Charters Comprehensive Sch, Ascot; B'ham Univ.

BIRMINGHAM, SMALL HEATH						No change
Electorate % Turnout	55,213	63.0%	1992	56,722	60.6%	1987
Godsiff, R D (Lab)	22,675	65.2%	-1.1%	22,787	66.3%	Lab
Qayyum Chaudhary, A (C)	8,686	25.0%	+3.8%	7,266	21.1%	C
Thomas, H (LD)	2,575	7.4%	-3.1%	3,600	10.5%	L/All
Clawley, Mrs H M (Grn)	824	2.4%	+0.7%	559	1.6%	Grn
				154	0.4%	Comm
Lab to C swing 2.5%	34,760		40.2%	34,366		45.2%
		Lab maj	13,989		Lab maj	15,521

Roger Godsiff won this seat in 1992; contested Birmingham Yardley, 1983. Former political officer, Apex, and snr research officer, GMB. Mbr, Lewisham BC, 1971-90; held various offices in CLPs. B Jun 28 1946; ed Catford Comprehensive Sch. GMB/Apex.

Abdul Quayym Chaudhary has been in legal practice in Britain since 1984; came to England 1965. Snr counsellor with UK Immigrants Advisory Service, 1979-83; joined advisory service 1974; an exec mbr, 1985-90, and its vice-chmn, 1990- . From 1976-8, being seconded at request of Pakistan Govt, he was director, immigrants advisory service of Pakistan in liaison with British embassy, Islamabad. B May 1 1941; ed Punjab Univ; Cl of Legal Ed. From 1984, chmn, Cl of British Pakistanis; mbr, Anglo-Asian Cons assocn and One Nation Forum. Chmn, Pakistan Forum, Birmingham, 1989; dep chmn, Small Heath Cons assocn, 1989.

Haydn Thomas, retired director of nurse education; vice-chairman, Kenilworth community care cl, 1987- ; mbr, Warwick DC, 1973-83 and 1991- . B Jul 12 1927.

Hazel Clawley, part-time local govt officer, proof reader, teacher; business interests in local community credit union and housing co-operative. B Nov 22 1939; ed Kings Coll, London Univ; LSE; Salvation Army Intnl Training Coll.

BIRMINGHAM, SPARKBROOK						No change
Electorate % Turnout	51,677	66.8%	1992	53,093	63.5%	1987
*Hattersley, R S G (Lab)	22,116	64.1%	+3.2%	20,513	60.8%	Lab
Khamisa, M J (C)	8,544	24.8%	-0.9%	8,654	25.7%	C
Parry, D (LD)	3,028	8.8%	-2.5%	3,803	11.3%	SDP/All
Alldrick, C (Grn)	833	2.4%	+0.9%	526	1.6%	Grn
				229	0.7%	RF
C to Lab swing 2.1%	34,521		39.3%	33,725		35.2%
		Lab maj	13,572		Lab maj	11,859

Roy Hattersley resigned as deputy leader of the Labour party immediately after the 1992 election. Elected dep ldr in 1983; became chief Opposn spokesman on home affairs in 1987; chief spokesman on Treasury and economic affairs, 1983-7; mbr, shadow Cabinet, 1979- ; chief spokesman on home affairs, 1980-83; on environment, 1979-80. Sec of State for Prices and Consumer Protection 1976-9; Minr of State, FCO, 1974-6. PC 1975; Minr of Defence for Administration, 1969-70; Under Sec of State for Employment and Productivity, 1968-9; Parly Sec, Min of Labour, 1967-8. Elected in 1964; contested Sutton Coldfield, 1959. Journalist and author. B Dec 28 1932; ed Sheffield City GS; Hull univ. Visiting Fellow, Nuffield Coll, Oxford, 1984- . Sponsored by Usdaw.

Mohammed Khamisa, barrister, arrived in UK as a Ugandan refugee in 1972. Ward chmn in constituency from 1986. Appointed in 1988 to serve on One Nation Forum whose main aim is to encourage greater integration of ethnic minorities in Cons Pty; is vice-chmn of London cmte of forum. B Feb 16 1962; ed Whitings Hill Jnr, Barnet; Queen Elizabeth Boys' Sch, Barnet; Barnet CFE; City of London Poly; Cl of Legal Ed.

David Parry, architectural consultant; mbr, St Albans DC, 1984-88. B Jun 30 1957; ed St Albans Boys GS; Reading Univ.

BIRMINGHAM, YARDLEY						Lab gain
Electorate % Turnout	54,749	78.0%	1992	56,957	73.9%	1987
Morris, Ms E (Lab)	14,884	34.9%	-1.8%	17,931	42.6%	C
*Gilroy Bevan, A D (C)	14,722	34.5%	-8.1%	15,409	36.6%	Lab
Hemming, J A M (LD)	12,899	30.2%	+9.5%	8,734	20.8%	L/All
Read, Miss P (NF)	192	0.4%				
C to Lab swing 3.2%	42,697		0.4%	42,074		6.0%
		Lab maj	162		C maj	2,522

Estelle Morris, a teacher, won seat from the Conservatives in 1992. Mbr, Warwick DC, 1979-91 (Lab gp ldr, 1982-9). B Jun 17 1952; ed Whalley Range HS, Manchester; Coventry Coll of Ed. Mbr, Shelter; NUT.

David Gilroy Bevan had held the seat since 1979. Mbr, Select Cmte on Transport, 1983-92. Sole principal, A Gilroy Bevan, incorporated estate agents, auctioneer, valuer and surveyor; parly adviser and leisure and recreation consultant. B Apr 10 1928; ed Woodrough's Sch, Moseley; King Edward's Sch, Birmingham. Chmn, Cons backbench tourism cmte, 1984-92; jt chmn, all-pty leisure and recreation industries parly gp, 1979-92, and all-pty road passenger transport gp, 1987-92; vice-chmn (1987-92) and jt sec (1980-7), Cons urban and inner cities cmte. Commodore (1989) and sec (1987-9), Hse of Commons Yacht Club. Mbr, Birmingham City Cl, 1959-74; West Midlands CC, 1974-81.

John Hemming, businessman, contested B'ham Small Heath 1987; B'ham Hall Green 1983, and was agent for B'ham E in 1989 Euro elections. Mbr, B'ham City Cl, 1990- . B Mar 16 1960; ed King Edward's Sch, Edgbaston; Magdalen Coll, Oxford.

BISHOP AUCKLAND						No change
Electorate % Turnout	72,572	76.5%	1992	72,147	74.1%	1987
*Foster, D (Lab)	27,763	50.0%	+2.0%	25,648	48.0%	Lab
Williamson, D (C)	17,676	31.8%	-3.0%	18,613	34.8%	C
Wade, W P (LD)	10,099	18.2%	+1.0%	9,195	17.2%	L/All
C to Lab swing 2.5%	55,538		18.2%	53,456		13.2%
		Lab maj	10,087		Lab maj	7,035

Derek Foster was elected Lab Chief Whip in 1985; PPS to Neil Kinnock, 1983-5. Chmn (1988-9) and vice-chmn (1987-8), Northern gp of Lab MPs. An Opposition spokesman on social security, 1982-3; mbr, Select Cmte on Trade and Industry, 1980-2; asst director of education in Sunderland, 1974-9. Elected in 1979. B Jun 25 1937; ed Bede GS, Sunderland; Oxford Univ. Chmn, North of England Development Cl, 1974-6. Vice-chmn, Youthaid, 1979-86. Mbr, Sunderland CBC, 1972-4; Tyne and Wear Met CC, 1973-7. Mbr of Salvation Army. Sponsored by Usdaw.

David Williamson, mbr of Stock Exchange since 1977, is partner in independent Stock Exchange firm; company director, former investment analyst and dealer in securities. Contested Hemsworth 1983. Chmn, Bridlington Cons assocn since 1988; mbr, Yorkshire area finance and GP cmte, 1984- ; cmte mbr, Foreign Affairs Forum. B 1950; ed King Edward VI Sch, Lichfield; Southampton Univ; Birmingham Coll of Commerce. Mbr, Lichfield DC, 1976-9.

William Wade, snr residential social worker; mbr, Wear Valley DC, Co Durham, 1989-. B Nov 7 1940; ed Douglas HS for Boys, Isle of Man; Selly Oak Colls, Birmingham; Teesside Poly.

BLABY						No change
Electorate % Turnout	81,790	83.4%	1992	77,094	80.9%	1987
Robathan, A (C)	39,498	57.9%	-2.6%	37,732	60.5%	C
Ranson, Ms E (Lab)	14,151	20.7%	+6.2%	15,556	25.0%	L/All
Lewin, Ms M (LD)	13,780	20.2%	-4.8%	9,046	14.5%	Lab
Peacock, J (BNP)	521	0.8%				
Lincoln, Ms S (NLP)	260	0.4%				
C to Lab swing 4.4%	68,210		37.2%	62,334		35.6%
		C maj	25,347		C maj	22,176

Andrew Robathan was returned for this seat in 1992. Personnel adviser for BP. Mbr, Hammersmith and Fulham BC, 1990-2, winning the ward in May 1990 for Cons for first time since 1968, defeating Lab mayor. Officer, Coldstream Guards, 1974-89, resigning to pursue political career. Served all over world, including Hong Kong, Belize, New Zealand, South Georgia and Northern Ireland. Rejoined Army in Jan 91 to serve in Gulf war as Chief of Staff of Prisoner of War Force in Saudi Arabia, Iraq and Kuwait. Fellow, Royal Geographical Society; mbr, Woodland Trust, World Wildlife Fund and Civic Trust. B July 17 1951; ed Merchant Taylors' Sch, Northwood; Oriel Coll, Oxford; RMA, Sandhurst; Army Staff Coll, Camberley. Freeman, City of London.

Ethel Ranson, community teacher. B Jun 23 1953; ed Haywards Heath GS; Maria Assumpta Coll of Ed, London. NUT.

Marjorie Lewin, exec PA with Bostik Ltd; mbr, Blaby DC, 1983-5; Braunstone TC, 1985- (Town mayor, 1989-). B Apr 9 1933; ed GS.

BLACKBURN						No change
Electorate % Turnout	73,251	75.1%	1992	74,801	74.9%	1987
*Straw, J W (Lab)	26,633	48.4%	-1.5%	27,965	49.9%	Lab
Coates, R M (C)	20,606	37.5%	-2.6%	22,468	40.1%	C
Mann, D (LD)	6,332	11.5%	+1.5%	5,602	10.0%	SDP/All
Field, R (Grn)	878	1.6%				
Carmichael-Grimshaw, Mrs M (LP)	334	0.6%				
Ayliffe, W (NLP)	195	0.4%				
C to Lab swing 0.6%	54,978		11.0%	56,035		9.8%
		Lab maj	6,027		Lab maj	5,497

Jack Straw has been chief Opposn spokesman on education since 1987 when elected to shadow cabinet; a housing and local govt spokesman, 1983-7; a spokesman on Treasury and economic affairs, 1980-3. Parly adviser to AUT. Vice-pres, Assocn of DCs, 1984- ; mbr, ccl, Inst for Fiscal Studies, 1983- . Elected in 1979; contested Tonbridge and Malling, Feb 1974. Visiting Fellow, Nuffield Coll, Oxford, 1990- ; governor, Blackburn Coll, 1990- . Barrister. B Aug 3 1946; ed Brentwood Sch, Essex; Leeds Univ; Inns of Court Sch of Law. Special adviser to Barbara Castle when Sec of State for Social Services, 1974-6, and to Peter Shore, Sec of State for Environment, 1976-7.

Ross Coates, solicitor, is vice-chmn, nat CPC cmte; chmn, Ipswich Cons Assocn, 1984-8, and dep chmn, 1983-4; chmn, Ipswich CPC, 1977-83; Eastern area CPC, 1986-9; Vice-chmn, Suffolk Euro constituency, 1989-91. Author; mbr, bd of examiners, Inst of Legal Execs. B Mar 28 1954; ed Woodbridge Sch, Suffolk; Chelmer Inst, Chelmsford.

Derek Mann, educational book representative; retired teacher; contested Oldham East 1966. Co-opted mbr, Bacup Cl, 1969-74. Sch governor; snr athletics coach. B Nov 13 1935; ed George Dixons, B'ham; Chorley Coll of Ed; Open univ.

Robin Field, teacher. B Apr 15 1947; ed St John's Coll, Southsea; Christ's Coll, Cambridge. NUT.

BLACKPOOL NORTH				No change	
Electorate % Turnout	58,087	77.6%	1992	58,893	73.1%	1987
Elletson, H D H (C)	21,501	47.7%	-0.3%	20,680	48.0%	C
Kirton, E (Lab)	18,461	41.0%	+10.0%	13,359	31.0%	Lab
Lahiff, A (LD)	4,786	10.6%	-10.3%	9,032	21.0%	L/All
Francis, Sir Guy (Loony)	178	0.4%				
Walker, H (NLP)	125	0.3%				
C to Lab swing 5.1%	45,051		6.7%	43,071		17.0%
		C maj	3,040		C maj	7,321

Harold Elletson won the seat in 1992; contested Burnley in 1987. Self-employed consultant to companies seeking to develop business in former Soviet Union and Eastern Europe. Retained as consultant by ECO Ltd and has assisted with various trading and development projects in the Commonwealth of Independent States. In 1988-90, worked for Alan Lewis, chmn of Illingworth Morris plc and chmn of CBI Initiative 1992, as PR director of CBI Initiative 1992 and as business development manager (USSR) for Illingworth Morris. Organised negotiations in Moscow between board of Illingworth Morris and Russian textile industry; accompanied company chmn to negotiations in Kremlin and to fourth Anglo-Soviet economic conference. Former exec of public affairs company, freelance journalist and researcher. Mbr, Lancashire CC, 1984-8. B Dec 8 1960; ed Eton; Exeter Univ; Voronezh Univ, USSR; Central London Poly; Bradford univ. Fluent in Russian, French and German.

Eric Kirton, unemployed turner, contested this seat 1987. Mbr, Lancashire CC, 1981- ; Blackpool BC, 1971-6; Blackpool Advice Centre for Unemployed; Blackpool Play Cl. AEU branch pres, 1971- . Pres, Blackpool district Lab Pty. B Nov 29 1929; ed Normanton Mod Sch and Whitworth Tech Coll, W Yorks.

Andre Lahiff, industrial sales rep. B Nov 21 1961.

BLACKPOOL SOUTH				No change	
Electorate % Turnout	56,801	77.4%	1992	57,567	73.5%	1987
Hawkins, N J (C)	19,880	45.2%	-2.8%	20,312	48.0%	C
Marsden, G (Lab)	18,213	41.4%	+9.4%	13,568	32.1%	Lab
Wynne, R (LD)	5,675	12.9%	-7.0%	8,405	19.9%	SDP/All
Henning, D (NLP)	173	0.4%				
C to Lab swing 6.1%	43,941		3.8%	42,285		15.9%
		C maj	1,667		C maj	6,744

Nick Hawkins, who was elected for the seat in 1992, is a barrister and company lawyer; gp legal adviser, Lloyds Abbey Life plc, 1989- . Research sec, Bow Gp, 1990-91; Bow Gp campaign director, 1991-92; elected to gp cl 1989 being managing director, Bow Publications Ltd, 1989-90. Elected to Bar Cl, 1988, serving on law reform cmte and, from 1989, on international cmte, and, from 1991, on public affairs cmte. Company legal adviser to Access (Jt Credit Card Co Ltd), 1987-9. Practised at Bar, Midland and Oxford Circuit, 1979-86. Contested Huddersfield 1987. B Mar 27 1957; ed Bedford Modern Sch; Lincoln Coll, Oxford; Middle Temple (Harmsworth Scholar); Inns of Court Sch of Law. Vice-chmn, Rochford Cons assocn, Essex, 1989-91. Natsopa, 1976-7.

Gordon Marsden, editor of *History Today*, since 1985; former consultant editor, *New Socialist;* Open Univ tutor. Nat exec mbr, Fabian Society; has held pty offices in Brighton, Hendon S and Hazel Grove, and chaired Young Fabians. B Nov 28 1953; ed Stockport GS; New Coll, Oxford; London and Harvard Univs. GMB/Assocn of British Editors.

Robert Wynne is a restaurateur. Mbr, Blackpool BC, 1991. B Aug 16 1956; ed Thames and Arnold Schs, Blackpool; Keele Univ.

BLAENAU GWENT				No change	
Electorate % Turnout	55,638	78.1%	1992	56,011	77.2%	1987
Smith, L T (Lab)	34,333	79.0%	+3.1%	32,820	75.9%	Lab
Melding, D (C)	4,266	9.8%	-1.7%	4,959	11.5%	C
Burns, A (LD)	2,774	6.4%	-2.5%	3,847	8.9%	L/All
Davies, T A R (PC)	2,099	4.8%	+1.1%	1,621	3.7%	PC
C to Lab swing 2.4%	43,472		69.2%	43,247		64.4%
		Lab maj	30,067		Lab maj	27,861

Llewellyn Smith elected for this seat in 1992, was elected MEP for SE Wales in 1984 and has served on its Cmte on Energy, Research and Technology; former mbr, Cmte on Economic and Monetary Affairs and Industrial Policy. Former labourer with Pilkington Glass and George Wimpey, builders; computer operator with British Steel Corporation; tutor-organizer, WEA. B Apr 16 1944; ed Cardiff Univ. Former chmn, Abertillery CLP and exec mbr, Welsh Lab Pty. Vice-pres, Anti-Apartheid Wales. TGWU.

David Melding, exec officer, Welsh Centre for International Affairs, Cardiff; at Welsh affairs desk, Cons research dept, 1986-9. B Aug 28 1962; ed Dwy-y-Felin comprehensive sch, Neath; Univ Coll, Cardiffa; Coll of William and Mary, Virginia, US.

Alastair Burns, laboratory technician. B Jan 5 1962; ed Dollar Acad; Open Univ. Mbr, Inst of Professionals, Managers and Specialists.

Alun Davies, conservationist with a wildlife charity; mbr, PlC nat cl; former pres, Welsh Nat Union of Students. B Feb 12 1964; ed Tredegar Comprehensive Sch; UCW, Aberystwyth (mbr, ct of governors).

BLAYDON					No change	
Electorate % Turnout	66,044	77.7%	1992	66,301	75.7%	1987
*McWilliam, J D (Lab)	27,028	52.7%	+2.3%	25,277	50.3%	Lab
Pescod, P R (C)	13,685	26.7%	+2.5%	12,789	25.5%	SDP/All
Nunn, P (LD)	10,602	20.7%		12,147	24.2%	C
Lab to C swing 0.1%	51,315	26.0%		50,213	24.9%	
		Lab maj	13,343		Lab maj	12,488

John McWilliam appointed to Select Cmte on Defence in 1987; mbr, Commons Chairmen's Panel, 1987- . Opposn whip, 1984-7. Mbr, Commons Services Cmte, 1983-7, and Select Cmte on Procedure, 1984-7; Select Cmte on Ed, Science and the Arts, 1980-3. Jt vice-chmn, all-pty Info Tech parly cmte; jt vice-chmn, all-pty space cmte. Elected in 1979; contested Edinburgh, Pentlands, Feb 1974. Chmn, Northern gp, Lab MPs, 1985-6. Former Post Office engineer. B May 16 1941; ed Leith Acad; Herriott Watt Coll; Napier Coll of Science and Tech. Mbr, Edinburgh Corpn, 1970-5; treas, City of Edinburgh, 1974-5. Mbr, Gen Advisory Cl, BBC, 1984-9. Sponsored by NCU (Engineering Section).

Peter Pescod, solicitor and partner in Newcastle upon Tyne practice, contested this seat in 1987. Mbr, Northumberland CC; exec cmte, Blaydon Cons assocn. Chmn, Northumberland medical services cmte; past pres, Newcastle upon Tyne trainee solicitors' gp. B Jun 29 1951; ed Queen Elizabeth GS, Darlington; Newcastle Univ.

Paul Nunn, journalist, contested this seat in 1987; Gateshead East 1983. Mbr, Gateshead MBC, 1986- (ldr of opposition, 1987-). B Aug 28 1948; ed Woodhouse Grove Sch, Bradford; Bristol Univ. Former Gateshead area SDP sec. NUJ.

BLYTH VALLEY					No change	
Electorate % Turnout	60,913	80.8%	1992	59,104	78.1%	1987
*Campbell, R (Lab)	24,542	49.9%	+7.4%	19,604	42.5%	Lab
Tracey, P M (LD)	16,498	33.5%	-7.1%	18,751	40.6%	SDP/All
Revell, M J (C)	7,691	15.6%	-1.3%	7,823	16.9%	C
Tyley, S (Grn)	470	1.0%				
LD to Lab swing 7.3%	49,201	16.3%		46,178	1.8%	
		Lab maj	8,044		Lab maj	853

Ronnie Campbell was an unemployed miner when elected for this seat in 1987. Mbr, Select Cmte on Parliamentary Commissioner for Administration, 1987- ; vice-chmn, all-pty Euro information marketplace parly gp; sec, Romanian children gp. Mbr Blyth BC, 1969-74; Blyth Valley Cl, 1974-88 (chmn, environmental health, and vice-chmn, housing). B Aug 14 1943; ed Ridley HS, Blyth. Mbr of and sponsored by NUM.

Peter Tracey, teacher; mbr, Blyth Valley Cl, 1984- (ldr, LD gp). B May 2 1945; ed King James GS, Huddersfield; Manchester and Newcastle Univs.

Michael Revell has professional, manufacturing and property interests; visiting lecturer at City Univ; optometrist. Founder chmn, Basildon Cons businessmen's gp, 1985. B Dec 21 1943; ed Borden GS; City univ.

BOLSOVER					No change	
Electorate % Turnout	66,693	78.9%	1992	65,452	77.3%	1987
*Skinner, D E (Lab)	33,973	64.5%	+8.3%	28,453	56.2%	Lab
James, T D R (C)	13,313	25.3%	-3.0%	14,333	28.3%	C
Barber, Ms S P (LD)	5,363	10.2%	-5.3%	7,836	15.5%	SDP/All
C to Lab swing 5.7%	52,649	39.2%		50,622	27.9%	
		Lab maj	20,660		Lab maj	14,120

Dennis Skinner was chmn, Labour Party, 1988-89, and vice-chmn, 1987-8; mbr, Lab Pty NEC, since 1978. Unsuccessfully contested chmnship of PLP, 1990. Miner, 1949-70. Chmn, East Midlands gp of Lab MPs; Miners gp of Lab MPs, 1977-8. Elected in 1970. B Feb 11 1932; ed Tupton Hall GS; Ruskin Coll, Oxford. Pres, Derbyshire Miners (NUM), 1966-70; NE Derbyshire CLP, 1968-71. Mbr, Clay Cross UDC, 1960-70; Derbyshire CC, 1964-70. Mbr, Campaign Gp of Lab MPs, 1981- . Sponsored by NUM.

Timothy James, career consultant; dep director, Manage-ment Consultancies Assocn. Mbr, Royal United Services Inst for Defence Studies; International Inst for Strategic Subjects; Inst for European Defence and Strategic Studies. B Jan 22 1952; ed Marlborough Coll; RMA Sandhurst; B'ham Univ.

Sue Barber is a medical laboratory scientific officer; Fellow, Inst of Medical Laboratory Sciences. Vice-chairman and press officer, High Peak LDs. Founder and sec, High Peak diabetic self-help gp; pres, Soroptimist International. B Dec 14 1943; ed Eccles GS; Cavendish GS, Burton; Manchester Poly. NHS local MSF rep.

BOLTON NORTH EAST						**No change**
Electorate % Turnout	58,659	82.3%	1992	59,382	78.7%	1987
*Thurnham, P G (C)	21,644	44.9%	+0.5%	20,742	44.4%	C
Crausby, D A (Lab)	21,459	44.5%	+1.8%	19,929	42.6%	Lab
Dunning, B F (LD)	4,971	10.3%	-2.7%	6,060	13.0%	SDP/All
Tong, P (NLP)	181	0.4%				
C to Lab swing 0.7%	48,255		0.4%	46,731		1.7%
		C maj	185		C maj	813

Peter Thurnham, chartered engineer and company director, was elected in 1983. PPS to Eric Forth and Robert Jackson at employment dept, 1991- ; and to Norman Fowler when employment sec, 1987-90. Mbr, Select Cmte on Employment, 1983-7. B Aug 21 1938; ed Oundle; Peterhouse Coll, Cambridge; Cranfield Inst of Tech; Harvard Business Sch. Mbr, S Lakeland DC, 1982-4. Director, Wathes Holdings Ltd (chmn, 1972-) and subsidiaries; consultant to Electrical Contractors' Assocn and Inst of Civil Engineers. Jt vice-chmn, all-pty gp for children, 1986- . Founder mbr, 1985, and cmte mbr, 1985- , Progress, Campaign for Research into Reproduction; vice-pres, Campaign for Inter-Country Adoption, 1991- .

David Crausby, engineer, contested Bury North in 1987. Mbr, Bury MDC 1979- (chairman, housing, 1986). Chaired Bury N CLP 1987. B Jun 17 1946; ed Derby GS, Bury. AEU, being convenor at Bolton engineering works.

Brian Dunning, teacher, is on Bolton LD exec; ward/constituency treas. B Dec 6 1938; ed Bolton Cty GS; Bolton Tech Coll; Bolton Training Coll of Tech Teachers. C of E church warden.

BOLTON SOUTH EAST						**No change**
Electorate % Turnout	65,600	75.5%	1992	65,932	74.9%	1987
*Young, D W (Lab)	26,906	54.3%	+0.0%	26,791	54.3%	Lab
Wood-Dow, N J S (C)	14,215	28.7%	-2.5%	15,410	31.2%	C
Lee, D (LD)	5,243	10.6%	-3.9%	7,161	14.5%	L/All
Hardman, W (Ind Lab)	2,894	5.8%				
Walch, L (NLP)	290	0.6%				
C to Lab swing 1.3%	49,548		25.6%	49,362		23.1%
		Lab maj	12,691		Lab maj	11,381

David Young, former teacher and insurance executive, was elected for this seat 1983; MP for Bolton E, Feb 1974-83; contested Bath 1970, Banbury 1966, and S Worcs 1959. Mbr, Select Cmte on Employment, 1987- ; Public Accounts Commission, 1983- . B Oct 12 1930; ed Greenock Acad; Glasgow univ; St Paul's coll, Cheltenham. Vice-chmn, all-pty cable and satellite TV parly gp, 1990- ; HoC Motor Club. Vice-chmn or jt vice-chmn, British-Burmese, Gibraltar, Danish, Singapore and other gps. PPS to Fred Mulley, defence secretary, 1977-9. Sponsored by TGWU.

Nicholas Wood-Dow, director of public affairs, Chelgate Public Relations Ltd, is founder and chmn of Tory Green Initiative. Mbr, Spelthorne BC (vice-chmn, policy and resources cmte); Spelthorne crime prevention panel; Hounslow and Spelthorne CHC. B Dec 27 1952; ed Gordonstoun and Haileybury Jnr Sch; St Catharine's Coll, Cambridge. Chmn, Egham Royal Agricultural Show.

Dennis Lee, computer engineer, contested Stretford for SDP/All in 1987; treas, constituency pty, 1983-87. British Amateur Athletics Bd coach; represented Lancashire in athletics. B Aug 28 1936; ed Horwich Tech Coll; Bolton Inst of Tech; Salford Univ. MFS, 1968- ; dept rep for technical support gp, 1983-88; ETU, 1960-68.

BOLTON WEST						**No change**
Electorate % Turnout	71,344	83.5%	1992	69,843	80.0%	1987
*Sackville, T G (C)	26,452	44.4%	+0.1%	24,779	44.3%	C
Morris, C (Lab)	25,373	42.6%	+6.5%	20,186	36.1%	Lab
Ronson, Ms B (LD)	7,529	12.6%	-6.9%	10,936	19.6%	SDP/All
Phillips, Ms J (NLP)	240	0.4%				
C to Lab swing 3.2%	59,594		1.8%	55,901		8.2%
		C maj	1,079		C maj	4,593

Thomas Sackville was appointed under secretary for health, 1992; a Lord Commissioner of the Treasury (govt whip), 1989-92; an asst Govt whip, 1988-9. Won this seat, 1983; contested Pontypool, 1979. Mbr, Select Cmte on Broadcasting, 1990-1; Commons administration cmte, 1991-2. With Deltec Banking Corporation, New York, 1971-4; Grindlays Bank, 1974-8; and International Bullion and Metal Brokers (London) Ltd, 1978-83, being a divisional director, 1981-3. Sec, all-pty cmte on drug misuse, 1984-8. B Oct 26 1950; ed St Aubyn's, Rottingdean, Sussex; Eton; Lincoln Coll, Oxford. Sec, all-pty British-Columbian parly gp; treas, British-Spanish gp.

Clifford Morris, managing director of local catering complex. Mbr, Bolton BC, 1986- . B Jan 6 1942; ed Castle Hill Sch, Bolton. TGWU; Co-op Pty.

Barbara Ronson, coll lecturer; mbr Horwich TC, 1987- (LD gp ldr, 1987-); Bolton BC, 1986-90. B Dec 16 1942; ed Manchester Coll of Commerce; Bolton Inst of HE. Associate, Library Assocn.

BOOTHFERRY						No change
Electorate % Turnout	80,747	79.7%	1992	75,176	75.8%	1987
*Davis, D M (C)	35,266	54.8%	-0.9%	31,716	55.7%	C
Coubrough, Ms L (Lab)	17,731	27.5%	+5.6%	12,746	22.4%	L/All
Goss, J M (LD)	11,388	17.7%	-4.7%	12,498	21.9%	Lab
C to Lab swing 3.3%	64,385		27.2%	56,960		33.3%
		C maj	17,535		C maj	18,970

David Davis was appointed an asst govt whip in 1990. PPS to Francis Maude, Under Sec of State, DTI, 1989-90. Elected in 1987. Former director, Tate and Lyle, which he joined in 1974; strategic planning director, Tate and Lyle plc, 1984-7; pres, Zymaize, a Canadian sweetener manufacturer, 1982-4; managing director, Tate and Lyle Transport, 1980-2; and financial director, Manbre and Garton, 1976-80. Non-exec director, Globe Investment, 1989-90. B Dec 23 1948; ed Warwick univ (chmn, Univ Cons Assocn, 1971); London Business Sch (chmn of its assocn, 1972); Harvard (AMP).
Louise Coubrough, solicitor. B Nov 27 1961; ed Exeter univ. TGWU.
John Goss, industrial consultant, contested Plymouth Sutton as C in 1970; Torbay for L Oct 1974; Wessex in 1979 Euro elections; Dorset E and Hants W in 1989 Euro elections. B Dec 26 1933; ed King's Sch, Rochester; LSE; Amsterdam univ. Mbr Lib pty cl, 1974-89.

BOOTLE						No change
Electorate % Turnout	69,308	72.5%	1992	71,765	72.9%	1987
*Benton, J (Lab)	37,464	74.6%	+7.7%	34,975	66.9%	Lab
Varley, C (C)	8,022	16.0%	-4.1%	10,498	20.1%	C
Cunningham, J (LD)	3,301	6.6%	-6.5%	6,820	13.0%	SDP/All
Hall, Ms M (Lib)	1,174	2.3%				
Haynes, T (NLP)	264	0.5%				
C to Lab swing 5.9%	50,225		58.6%	52,293		46.8%
		Lab maj	29,442		Lab maj	24,477

Joe Benton won the second by-election for this seat in 1990. Appointed to Select Cmte on Energy in 1991; mbr, Select Cmte on Severn Bridges Bill, 1991. Employed by Girobank, 1982-90; former personnel manager, Pacific Steam Navigation Co. Mbr, Sefton BC, 1970-90 (Lab gp ldr, 1985-1990). Chmn, governors, Hugh Baird Coll of Tech. B Sep 28 1933; ed St Monica's Primary and Secondary Sch; Bootle Tech Coll.
Christopher Varley, manager with Bull HN Information Systems Ltd; formerly with managerial consultancy and engineer with British Aerospace plc. Held party offices in Richmond upon Thames. Ed City Univ; Kingston Management Centre; City of London Freemans.
John Cunningham, cllr, contested both 1990 by-elections for this seat. B Aug 22 1965.
Details of 1990 by-elections on page 287

BOSWORTH						No change
Electorate % Turnout	80,234	84.1%	1992	77,186	81.3%	1987
*Tredinnick, D A S (C)	36,618	54.2%	-0.2%	34,145	54.4%	C
Everitt, D (Lab)	17,524	26.0%	+8.8%	17,129	27.3%	L/All
Drozdz, G M (LD)	12,643	18.7%	-8.6%	10,787	17.2%	Lab
Fewster, B (Grn)	716	1.1%	+0.0%	660	1.1%	Grn
C to Lab swing 4.5%	67,501		28.3%	62,721		27.1%
		C maj	19,094		C maj	17,016

David Tredinnick became PPS to Sir Wyn Roberts, Minr of State, Welsh Office, in 1991; jt sec, Cons backbench defence cmte and Cons foreign and Commonwealth affairs cmte, 1990-1; chmn, British-Atlantic gp of Young Politicians, 1990-91; chmn, Future of Europe Trust, 1991; treas, all-pty world govt parly gp. Chmn, Anglo East European Co, 1990- ; adviser, Malden Mitcham Properties. Elected in 1987; contested Cardiff S and Penarth 1983. Mbr of Lloyd's. Research assistant to Kenneth Warren MP and Angela Rumbold MP, 1981-7. B Jan 19 1950; ed Ludgrove Sch, Wokingham; Eton; Mons Officer Cadet Sch; Graduate Business Sch, Capetown Univ; St John's Coll, Oxford.
David Everitt, telephone engineer; mbr, Hinkley and Bosworth DC, 1983-91; chairman, Bosworth CLP, 1983-8; Nuneaton Post Office Advisory Cmte. B Jan 24 1943; ed Swinnerton Sec HS, Nuneaton.
Gregory Drozdz, asst director (fieldwork), Age Concern, Lambeth. Press officer, Bosworth LD, 1987-8. B Sep 28 1958; ed John Cleveland Coll, Hinckley; Edinburgh and Pennsylvania Univs; SW London Coll. Nalgo.
Brian Fewster, teacher, contested Leicester S 1987 and Harborough 1983; co-chair, Leicester Grn Pty. B Jul 10 1942; ed Nottingham HS; Jesus Coll, Cambridge. NUT.

BOURNEMOUTH EAST				No change		
Electorate % Turnout	75,089	72.8%	1992	75,232	70.5%	1987
*Atkinson, D A (C)	30,820	56.4%	-1.9%	30,925	58.3%	C
Russell, N R (LD)	15,997	29.3%	-1.4%	16,242	30.6%	L/All
Brushett, P (Lab)	7,541	13.8%	+2.7%	5,885	11.1%	Lab
Holmes, Ms S (NLP)	329	0.6%				
C to LD swing 0.3%	54,687		27.1%	53,052		27.7%
		C maj	14,823		C maj	14,683

David Atkinson was parliamentary private secretary to Paul Channon in his ministerial posts, 1979-87; jt vice-chmn, Cons backbench health cmte, 1988- , and of previous health and social services cmte, 1987-8; vice-chmn, Cons backbench space sub-cmte, 1987- . Elected at 1977 by-election; contested Newham NW, Feb 1974, and Basildon, Oct 1974. B Mar 24 1940; ed St George's Coll, Weybridge; Southend Coll of Tech; the Coll of Automobile and Aeronautical Engineering, Chelsea. Treas, all-pty British-USSR parly gp; chmn, Albanian and Cameroon gps. Nat YC chmn, 1970-1. Mbr, Essex CC, 1973-8;

Southend CBC, 1969-72; Cl of Europe and WEU, 1979-86, 1987- . Pres, Christian Solidarity International (UK), 1983- (chmn, 1979-83); International Society for Human Rights (UK), 1985- .
Neil Russell, community worker; chmn, constituency LDs; mbr, Dorset CC, 1985-9. B Nov 23 1951; ed Dartford Tech Sch for Boys. Manager, under-nines football team.
Peter Brushett. self-employed poultry distributor; mbr, Dorset CC, 1981- ; Bournemouth BC, 1983- ; vice-chairman, Bournemouth West LP; CHC mbr. Ed Seale Hayne Coll of Ag.

BOURNEMOUTH WEST				No change		
Electorate % Turnout	74,738	75.8%	1992	74,444	73.3%	1987
*Butterfill, J V (C)	29,820	52.6%	-2.5%	30,117	55.2%	C
Dover, Ms J (LD)	17,178	30.3%	-1.7%	17,466	32.0%	SDP/All
Grower, B B (Lab)	9,423	16.6%	+3.8%	7,018	12.9%	Lab
Springham, A (NLP)	232	0.4%				
C to LD swing 0.4%	56,653		22.3%	54,601		23.2%
		C maj	12,642		C maj	12,651

John Butterfill, PPS to Brian Mawhinney, Minr of State Health; PPS to Cecil Parkinson when energy secretary and transport secretary. Chmn, Cons Gp for Europe, 1989- . Snr partner in firm of chartered surveyors; pres, European Property Associates, 1979- . Director, Conservation Investments Ltd and subsidiary companies. Elected in 1983; contested Croydon NW, 1981 by-election; London S Inner in 1979 Euro elections. B Feb 14 1941; ed Caterham Sch; Coll of Estate Management, London. Jt sec, Cons trade and industry cmte, 1987-88 and 1991. Mbr, nat cl,

European Movement, 1982-90; vice-chmn, Foreign Affairs Forum.
Janet Dover, partner in childcare consultancy; chairman, E Dorset Play Assocn, and Dorset Childminding Assocn. Mbr, E Dorset Cl, 1988-; Colehill PC, 1987- . Jul 24 1953; ed Open univ.
Ben Grower, chartered accountant; chmn, Bournemouth East LP, 1982-91. Mbr Bournemouth DC, 1976- ; Dorset CC, 1974-7 and 1981-5. B Nov 13 1945; ed Ringwood GS. GMB/Apex.

BOW AND POPLAR				No change		
Electorate % Turnout	56,685	65.8%	1992	59,178	57.4%	1987
*Gordon, Mrs M (Lab)	18,487	49.5%	+3.1%	15,746	46.4%	Lab
Hughes, P (LD)	10,083	27.0%	-5.7%	11,115	32.7%	L/All
Pearce, S (C)	6,876	18.4%	-1.6%	6,810	20.1%	C
Tyndall, J (BNP)	1,107	3.0%		276	0.8%	WRP
Petter, S (Grn)	612	1.6%				
Hite, W (NLP)	158	0.4%				
LD to Lab swing 4.4%	37,323		22.5%	33,947		13.6%
		Lab maj	8,404		Lab maj	4,631

Mildred Gordon, teacher from 1945-85, was elected in 1987; contested London NW in 1979 Euro elections. Mbr, Select Cmte on Ed, Science and Arts, 1991- ; jt vice-chairman, PLP ed, science and arts cmte, 1989- ; PLP social security cmte, 1991- . Mbr, London Lab Pty exec, 1983-6 (women's cmte and anti-racism sub-cmte); jt chairman, Gtr London Lab Cmte's policy cmte, 1985-6; sch governor; has taught English, history, and English as a second language in Brent, and typing to prisoners in Holloway. B Oct 24 1923; ed Raines Foundation Sch; Forest Teacher Training Coll. NUT.
Peter Hughes, health service manager; mbr, Tower

Hamlets BC, 1982-6 and 1990- (ldr, 1991- ; dep ldr, 1990-1). B Dec 2 1959; ed Trinity Sch, Warwickshire; City univ, London.
Simon Pearce, public affairs consultant; was press officer for Cons London borough and public relations adviser to some local authorities. Chmn, Newham NW Cons Assocn, 1985-87. B Dec 28 1958; ed Stratford GS; York Univ (vice-chmn, univ Cons students, 1979-80).
Stephen Petter, freelance computer programmer; chairman, Tower Hamlets Grn pty. B May 10 1937; ed Leyton GS; Open univ.

BRADFORD NORTH				No change from 1987		
Electorate % Turnout	66,719	73.4%	1992	67,430	72.7%	1987
*Rooney, T (Lab)	23,420	47.8%	+5.0%	21,009	42.8%	Lab
Riaz, M (C)	15,756	32.2%	-7.3%	19,376	39.5%	C
Ward, D (LD)	9,133	18.7%	+1.0%	8,656	17.7%	SDP/All
Beckett, W (Loony)	350	0.7%				
Nasr, Dr H (Islamic)	304	0.6%				
C to Lab swing 6.2%	48,963		15.7%	49,041		3.3%
		Lab maj	7,664		Lab maj	1,633

Terry Rooney won the 1990 by-election and in 1991 became chmn, PLP social security cmte. Was welfare rights advice worker, Bierley Community Centre; former commercial insurance broker. Mbr, Bradford Cl, 1983-90 (chaired Lab gp, 1988-90; dep ldr of cl, 1990). B Nov 11 1950; ed Buttershaw Comprehensive Sch; Bradford Coll.

Mohammed Riaz, director of property development company since 1980; owner of number of shops. Mbr, Bradford City Cl, 1985-90; Yorkshire Cons area training team, 1990- ; W Yorkshire police authority, 1986-90

(chmn, complaints cmte, 1986-90); mbr, AMA police cmte, 1986-90; Bradford Community Relations Cl, 1986-90. Research officer in economics, Bradford univ, 1975-80. B Sep 19 1951; ed London and Bradford univs.

David Ward, lecturer, contested 1990 by-election. Mbr, Bradford MDC, 1984- (ldr, LD gp, 1989-). B Jun 24 1953; ed Boston GS; Bradford Univ Management Centre. NATFHE.

Details of 1990 by-election on page 288

BRADFORD SOUTH				No change		
Electorate % Turnout	69,914	75.6%	1992	69,588	73.7%	1987
*Cryer, G R (Lab)	25,185	47.6%	+6.2%	21,230	41.4%	Lab
Popat, A S (C)	20,283	38.4%	-2.4%	20,921	40.8%	C
Boulton, B J (LD)	7,243	13.7%	-4.1%	9,109	17.8%	SDP/All
Naseem, M (Islamic)	156	0.3%				
C to Lab swing 4.3%	52,867		9.3%	51,260		0.6%
		Lab maj	4,902		Lab maj	309

Robert Cryer, elected for this seat 1987, was MP for Keighley, 1974-83; contested Darwen, 1964; MEP for Sheffield, 1984-9 (mbr, EP Transport Cmte). Chmn, Select Cmte and Jt Select Cmte on Statutory Instruments, 1987- , and also chmn, 1979-83; mbr, Select Cmte on Members' Interests, 1989- . Chmn, PLP employment cmte, 1987-90; PLP films gp, 1987- ; vice-chmn, PLP defence cmte, 1988- . Resigned in 1978 as Under Sec of State for Industry, to which he was appointed in 1976, in protest at decision to cut off public funds to a Merseyside workers' co-operative. B Dec 3 1934; ed Salt HS, Shipley; Hull univ. Vice-pres (and founder), Keighley and Worth Valley Railway. TGWU since 1971.

Andrew Popat, barrister practising in criminal and EC law; prosecuting counsel for attorney-general, DPP and Crown Prosecution Service; associate attorney with Wall St law firm, New York, 1970-5. Personal legal adviser on law and order to John Patten when Minister of State, Home Office, 1987-92. B Dec 31 1943; ed London and California univs. Freeman, City of London, 1987.

Brian Boulton, teacher, contested Yorkshire South in 1989 Euro elections. B Jan 28 1943; ed Carlton GS, Bradford; James Graham Coll of Ed, Leeds. Chmn of local pty. AMMA.

BRADFORD WEST				No change		
Electorate % Turnout	70,016	69.9%	1992	70,763	70.2%	1987
*Madden, M F (Lab)	26,046	53.2%	+1.3%	25,775	51.9%	Lab
Ashworth, Dr A J (C)	16,544	33.8%	-2.9%	18,224	36.7%	C
Griffiths, Dr A O (LD)	5,150	10.5%	-0.9%	5,657	11.4%	SDP/All
Braham, P (Grn)	735	1.5%				
Pidcock, D (Islamic)	471	1.0%				
C to Lab swing 2.1%	48,946		19.4%	49,656		15.2%
		Lab maj	9,502		Lab maj	7,551

Max Madden was an Opposn spokesman on health and social security, 1983-4. Vice-chmn, all-pty wool textile parly gp. Lab Pty director of publicity, 1979-82; previously press and information officer, British Gas Corpn, and journalist on the *East Essex Gazette, Tribune, The Sun* and *The Scotsman*. Elected for this seat 1983; MP for Sowerby, 1974-9; contested Sudbury and Woodbridge, 1966. B Oct 29 1941; ed Lascelles Sec Mod Sch, South Harrow; Pinner GS. TGWU sponsored.

Dr Andrew Ashworth, general practitioner, served in the RN, including the Falklands task force, 1977-90, reaching

rank of Surgeon Lt Cmdr; latterly a medical officer to MoD (staff trainee). Has business links with health support and medical communications. Dep chmn, Yorkshire area Cons candidates' assocn. B Jan 22 1956; ed Greenhill Sch, Rochdale; Leeds Univ; RN Staff Coll. BMA; MRCGP. Plays the euphonium.

Dr Alun Griffiths, general practitioner; membership sec, Bradford South West LDs. B Jul 19 1957; ed Millhouse Primary Sch; Penistone GS; Woodhouse Grove Sch; Univ of Wales — Welsh Sch of Medicine.

BRAINTREE				No change		
Electorate % Turnout	78,880	83.4%	1992	76,994	79.0%	1987
*Newton, A H (C)	34,415	52.3%	-1.9%	32,978	54.2%	C
Willmore, I (Lab)	16,921	25.7%	+6.4%	16,121	26.5% SDP/All
Wallis, Ms D (LD)	13,603	20.7%	-5.8%	11,764	19.3%	Lab
Abbott, J E (Grn)	855	1.3%				
C to Lab swing 4.1%	65,794		26.6%	60,863		27.7%
		C maj	17,494		C maj	16,857

Tony Newton was appointed Lord President of the Council and Leader of the Commons, 1992; social security secy, 1989-92; appointed to cabinet in 1988 as Chancellor of Duchy of Lancaster and chief Commons spokesman for DTI as Minr for Trade and Industry; Minr of Health, 1986-8; Minr for Social Security and Disabled, 1984-6; Under Sec, DHSS, 1982-4; Ld Commissioner of Treasury (govt whip), 1981-82; asst govt whip, 1979-81. PC 1988. Elected in Feb 1974; contested Sheffield, Brightside, 1970. Economist. B Aug 29 1937; ed Friends' Sch, Saffron Walden; Trinity Coll, Oxford (Pres of Union, 1958).

Ian Willmore, researcher for TGWU, contested Herts SW 1987. Mbr, Haringey BC, 1988- . B Nov 8 1958; ed Oriel Coll, Oxford. TGWU/ACTSS.

Diana Wallis, solicitor. B Jun 28 1954; ed London and Kent Univs.

James Abbott, landscape gardener, tree grower and forester. Treas, Essex Grn pty; speaker for E Anglian pty. B Oct 15 1960; ed Gilberd Sch, Colchester; Univ Coll, London.

BRECON AND RADNOR						C gain
Electorate % Turnout	51,509	85.9%	1992	49,394	84.4%	1987
Evans, J P (C)	15,977	36.1%	+1.4%	14,509	34.8%	L/All
*Livsey, R A L (LD)	15,847	35.8%	+1.0%	14,453	34.7%	C
Mann, C J (Lab)	11,634	26.3%	-2.9%	12,180	29.2%	Lab
Mereudd, Ms S (PC)	418	0.9%	-0.3%	535	1.3%	PC
Richards, H W (Grn)	393	0.9%				
LD to C swing 0.2%	44,269		0.3%	41,677		0.1%
		C maj	130		L/All maj	56

Jonathan Evans won the seat in 1992 having contested it in 1987; Wolverhampton NE 1979; Ebbw Vale twice in 1974. Solicitor and managing partner in Leo Abse and Cohen. Mbr, exec cmte, Nat Union, 1991- ; chmn, Welsh Cons parly candidates, 1985-91, and of Welsh Cons policy gp, 1987-91. Dep-chmn, Housing for Wales (the Welsh housing corporation), 1988- ; vice-chmn, NSPCC in Wales; trustee, Welsh nat sports centre for disabled. B Jun 2 1950; ed Lewis Sch, Pengam; Howardian HS, Cardiff; Coll of Law, Guildford; Lancaster Gate, London.

Richard Livsey won the seat for the Liberals in the 1985 by-election having contested it in 1983; Pembroke, 1979; Perth and E Perthshire, 1970. Elected Ldr, Welsh LDs in 1988; LD spokesman on Wales from 1987-92 and on water, 1988-9; Alliance spokesman on countryside in 1987 election. Lib spokesman on Wales, 1987; spokesman on agriculture, 1985-7. Mbr, Select Cmte on Welsh Affairs, 1987-92. Farmer and lecturer in farm management. B May 2 1935; ed Talgarth Cty Primary Sch; Bedales Sch; Seale-Hayne Ag Coll; Reading Univ.

Chris Mann, probation officer; sec, Brecon and Radnor CLP, 1983-85; constituency agent, 1985-6. Mbr, Powys CC, 1985- (ldr, Lab gp, 1989-). B Oct 1 1950; ed Kingsbury HS; Dundee Univ.

Sian Mereudd, retired teacher; mbr, Llandrindod TC; PC policy director on environment. Ed Bristol Univ.

Hugh Richards, chartered town planner; self-employed planning, design and environment consultant. B Jul 5 1945; ed Whitchurch GS; Welsh Sch of Architecture; Sheffield Univ.

BRENT EAST				No change		
Electorate % Turnout	53,319	68.8%	1992	61,020	64.5%	1987
*Livingstone, K R (Lab)	19,387	52.8%	+10.2%	16,772	42.6%	Lab
Green, D (C)	13,416	36.6%	-1.9%	15,119	38.4%	C
Cummins, M (LD)	3,249	8.9%	-5.7%	5,710	14.5% SDP/All
Dean, Ms T (Grn)	548	1.5%	-0.3%	1,035	2.6% Ind Lab
Murphy, Ms A (Comm GB)	96	0.3%		716	1.8%	Grn
C to Lab swing 6.0%	36,696		16.3%	39,352		4.2%
		Lab maj	5,971		Lab maj	1,653

Ken Livingstone was elected for this seat 1987; mbr, Lab Pty nat exec cmte, 1987-89. Ldr, GLC, 1981-86, when it was abolished; GLC mbr for Paddington, 1981-86, and for Hackney N, 1973-81. Joint editor, *Labour Herald*, 1981-85. Author and director. Contested Hampstead, 1979. B Jun 17 1945; ed Tulse Hill Comprehensive Sch; Philippa Fawcett Coll of Ed. Former laboratory technician. Mbr, regional exec, Gtr London Lab Pty, 1974-86; Lambeth BC, 1971-78; Camden BC, 1978-82.

Damian Green, presenter and City editor of Channel 4 *Business Daily* programme, since 1987; business editor, ITN Channel 4 news, 1985-7; news editor, *The Times Business News*, 1984-5; business producer, ITN Channel 4 News, 1982-4; producer/presenter, BBC radio news financial programme, 1978-82. Speech writer/researcher for John Major, 1988- . B Jan 17 1956; ed Reading Sch; Balliol Coll, Oxford (Pres of Union, 1977).

Mark Cummins, photographer, graphic designer and higher ed lecturer. Mbr, Brent BC, 1988- . B Nov 12 1937.

Theresa Dean, carer for homeless people; press officer, Brent pty. B Oct 6 1954; ed Sacred Heart Convent, Woldingham, Surrey; London Univ.

BRENT NORTH						No change
Electorate % Turnout	58,917	70.6%	1992	63,081	71.0%	1987
*Boyson, Sir Rhodes (C)	23,445	56.4%	-3.5%	26,823	59.9%	C
Moher, J G (Lab)	13,314	32.0%	+7.2%	11,103	24.8%	Lab
Lorber, P (LD)	4,149	10.0%	-5.4%	6,868	15.3%	SDP/All
Vipul, T (Ind)	356	0.9%				
Davids, A (NLP)	318	0.8%				
C to Lab swing 5.4%	41,582		24.4%	44,794		35.1%
		C maj	10,131		C maj	15,720

Sir Rhodes Boyson was Minr for Local Govt, with rank of Minr of State, DoE, 1986-7; Minr of State, N Ireland, 1984-6; Minr for Social Security, with rank of Minr of State, DHSS, 1983-4; Under Sec of State for Ed and Science, 1979-83; an Opposn spokesman on ed, 1976-9. PC 1987. Mbr, exec, 1922 Cmte, 1987- ; chmn, all-pty Methodist parly gp, 1990- . Elected in Feb 1974; contested Eccles, 1970. Headmaster, 1955-74, including Highbury Grove Sch, 1967-74. Non-exec director, Blacks Leisure plc; consultant, ARC International. B May 11 1925; ed Haslingden GS; Univ Coll, Cardiff; Manchester Univ; LSE; Corpus Christi Coll, Cambridge.

Jim Moher, nat legal officer of Nat Communications Union; chairman, Brent Lab Pty; mbr, exec, Gtr London Lab Pty, 1989- ; Brent BC (local govt cmte chairman, 1988-91). B Apr 14 1946; ed Univ Coll, Cork; London univ. NCU; GMB/Apex.

Paul Lorber, chartered accountant; tax adviser to Texaco Ltd; mbr, Brent BC, 1982- ; organiser, Brent S LDs. B Sep 3 1955; ed Kilburn HS; Manchester Univ.

BRENT SOUTH						No change
Electorate % Turnout	56,034	64.1%	1992	62,772	64.9%	1987
*Boateng, P (Lab)	20,662	57.5%	+5.6%	21,140	51.9%	Lab
Blackman, R J (C)	10,957	30.5%	-1.9%	13,209	32.4%	C
Harskin, M T (LD)	3,658	10.2%	-5.5%	6,375	15.7%	L/All
Johnson, D P (Grn)	479	1.3%				
Jani, C (NLP)	166	0.5%				
C to Lab swing 3.8%	35,922		27.0%	40,724		19.5%
		Lab maj	9,705		Lab maj	7,931

Paul Boateng became a member of Opposn Treasury and economic affairs team in 1989. Barrister; unpaid director, English National Opera Co Ltd, 1984- , and Cities in Schools Ltd, registered charity. Elected in 1987; contested Hertfordshire W 1983. Vice-chmn, all-pty British-Bermuda parly gp, 1989- ; jt vice-chmn, race and community parly panel; sec, British-Caribbean gp; sec/treas, British-Ghana gp, 1989- . Mbr, Select Cmte on Environment, 1987-9; GLC, 1981-6; World Cl of Churches Commission on programme to combat racism, 1984- ; bd, Christian Aid, 1991- . B Jun 14 1951; ed Ghana International Sch; Accra Acad; Apsley GS; Bristol Univ; Coll of Law. Sponsored by GMB.

Robert Blackman, snr nat account executive manager with BT, chaired Brent S Cons assocn, 1987-90. Mbr, Brent cl, 1986- (chmn, Cons gp, 1989-90, gp ldr, 1990-). B Apr 26 1956; ed Wembley HS; Preston Manor HS, Wembley; Liverpool Univ (pres, Guild of Undergraduates, 1978-79).

Mike Harskin, journalist, became editor of *Liberal Democrat News* in 1990. Contested this seat 1987. Former director of labour unit at Liberal whips office, House of Commons. Chaired YLDs of England, 1988-9 Mbr, Brent BC, 1990- . B Dec 19 1963; ed Wallington HS for Boys, Surrey; Harlow Tech Coll. NUJ.

Darren Johnson, accounts clerk; former press officer, Hull N Grn pty; Humberside area election agent; co-chairman, Brent pty. B May 20 1966; ed Penwortham Priory HS; colls at Preston, Blackpool and Willesden.

BRENTFORD AND ISLEWORTH						No change
Electorate % Turnout	70,880	76.2%	1992	71,715	76.7%	1987
Deva, N J A (C)	24,752	45.8%	-1.9%	26,230	47.7%	C
Keen, Mrs A L (Lab)	22,666	42.0%	+8.7%	18,277	33.2%	Lab
Salmon, Ms J C N (LD)	5,683	10.5%	-7.0%	9,626	17.5%	SDP/All
Bradley, J W (Grn)	927	1.7%	+0.2%	849	1.5%	Grn
C to Lab swing 5.3%	54,028		3.9%	54,982		14.5%
		C maj	2,086		C maj	7,953

Nirj Deva returned for this seat in 1992; contested Hammersmith 1987. Environmental scientist, aeronautical engineer, company director and co-founder of small businesses in London,. Chmn, One Nation Forum, 1987- ; vice-chmn, Anglo-Asian Cons Assocn, 1978-89; joined Nat Consumer Cl in 1984; chaired Govt cmte on cheaper air travel; served on cmte seeking reform of Euro agriculture. Editor, Bow Gp political magazine *Crossbow*, 1983-5. B 1948 in Sri Lanka; ed Loughborough Univ. Dep Lieut for Gtr London, since 1985.

Ann Keen, head of faculty for advanced nursing at Hammersmith Hospital, contested this seat 1987. Mbr, Lab Pty health advisory forum. B Nov 26 1948; ed Elfed Sec Mod Sch, Clwyd. GMB/Apex.

Janet Salmon, self-employed management consultant. Organises annual remuneration survey of leisure industry in UK and since 1992 in Europe. Adviser, Prince's Trust. B Oct 28 1948; ed Bournemouth Sch for Girls; Leicester Univ; Wm Balmain Coll of Advanced Tech, Sydney; Cape Town Univ Business Sch.

John Bradley, quantity surveyor; treas and election agent, Hounslow Grn Pty. B Jan 10 1956; ed Aston Univ.

BRENTWOOD AND ONGAR — No change

Electorate % Turnout	65,830	84.7%	1992	67,521	79.0%	1987
Pickles, E J (C)	32,145	57.6%	-2.8%	32,258	60.5%	C
Bottomley, Mrs E T (LD)	17,000	30.5%	+5.5%	13,337	25.0%	L/All
Keohane, Ms F (Lab)	6,080	10.9%	-2.3%	7,042	13.2%	Lab
Bartley, Ms C (Grn)	535	1.0%	-0.3%	686	1.3%	Grn
C to LD swing 4.2%	55,760		27.2%	53,323		35.5%
		C maj	15,145		C maj	18,921

Eric Pickles was ldr of Bradford Cl, 1988-90; mbr since 1979 and ldr of Cons gp, 1987-91; dep ldr, Cons gp, AMA, 1989-91 ; mbr, Yorkshire RHA, 1982-90. Consultant in employment practice. Local govt editor, Cons Newsline, 1990- . Mbr, Nat Union exec cmte, 1975-86 and 1987-91; Yorkshire area finance and gen purposes cmte, 1974- ; One Nation Forum, 1987- ; Cons nat advisory cmte on local govt, 1985- ; lecturer at Cons agents examination courses, 1988- . Vice-chmn, Keighley Cons Assocn, 1986-90; chmn, YCs, 1980-1. Cons co-chmn, Jt Cmte Against Racialism, representing Nat Union, 1982-7. B Apr 20 1952; ed Greenhead GS, Keighley; Leeds Poly.

Liz Bottomley, teacher, was area agent for SE, 1986-9; agent Epping Forest by-election, 1988. Mbr, Brentwood DC, 1983- (chmn environment and community services cmte); Ingatestone and Fryering PC, 1979-91. B Feb 28 1943; ed Slough HS for Girls; Queen Mary Coll, London Univ.

Francis Keohane, employed in voluntary housing assocn. B Apr 22 1939; ed Fircroft Coll; London Univ. AEU.

Carolyn Bartley, mother, Open Univ student, photographer. East Anglia Grn pty spokeswoman and press officer. B Mar 24 1955; ed Penarth GS; Barry CFE; Open Univ.

BRIDGEND — No change

Electorate % Turnout	58,531	80.4%	1992	57,389	80.3%	1987
*Griffiths, W J (Lab)	24,143	51.3%	+3.7%	21,893	47.5%	Lab
Unwin, D A (C)	16,817	35.7%	-2.3%	17,513	38.0%	C
Mills, D (LD)	4,827	10.3%	-1.9%	5,590	12.1%	SDP/All
Lloyd Jones, A (PC)	1,301	2.8%	+0.5%	1,065	2.3%	PC
C to Lab swing 3.0%	47,088		15.6%	46,061		9.5%
		Lab maj	7,326		Lab maj	4,380

Win Griffiths became an Opposn spokesman on environmental protection in 1990. Won this seat 1987 and was mbr, Select Cmte on Ed, Science and Arts until 1990; chmn, PLP ed, science and arts cmte, 1988-90. Sec, all-pty British-East African parly gp. MEP for S Wales, 1979-89; a vice-pres, EP, 1984-7. B Feb 11 1943; ed Brecon Boys' GS; Univ Coll, Cardiff. Mbr, Vale of Glamorgan BC, 1973-6; Dinas Powys community cl, 1974-9. Methodist Church lay preacher since 1966. TGWU (ACTS); in NUT 22 years; head of history, Cowbridge comprehensive sch, 1976-9.

David Unwin was full-time constituency agent for Bridgend, 1983-9; voluntary agent for Ogmore and Bridgend, 1973-83; sports mail order manager; chmn, Brackla Nodor Gp jt works cmte. UK distribution and export shipping manager with Royal Mint, Tower Hill, London, 1964-70, and at Llantrisant, 1970-83. Mbr, Bridgend TC, 1984- (Mayor, 1990-1); Ogwr BC, 1976- ; St Brides Major community Cl, 1979- ; Mid-Glamorgan CC, 1977-85. B Jan 21 1947; ed Southgate County GS, Cockfosters, Herts.

David Mills, RSPCA official. B Jul 20 1961; ed Brynteg comprehensive sch; Bridgend; Seale-Hayne Ag Coll, Devon.

Alun Lloyd Jones, exec medical rep with Pfizer International Pharmaceuticals. Mbr, nat cl, Pl Cymru; vice-chmn, Ceredigion/Pembroke N pty; mbr, Ceredigion DC, 1991- . B Jun 4 1946; ed Ardwyn GS, Aberystwyth.

BRIDGWATER — No change

Electorate % Turnout	71,567	79.5%	1992	67,480	78.2%	1987
*King, T J (C)	26,610	46.8%	-4.8%	27,177	51.5%	C
Revans, W J (LD)	16,894	29.7%	-0.6%	15,982	30.3%	SDP/All
James, P E (Lab)	12,365	21.7%	+3.5%	9,594	18.2%	Lab
Dummett, G (Grn)	746	1.3%				
Body, A (Ind)	183	0.3%				
Sanson, Ms G (NLP)	112	0.2%				
C to LD swing 2.1%	56,910		17.1%	52,753		21.2%
		C maj	9,716		C maj	11,195

Tom King resigned from government after 1992 general election. Defence sec., 1989-1992; N Ireland sec., 1985-9; Employment sec., 1983-5; Transport sec., Jun-Oct 1983; Environment sec., Jan-Jun 1983; Minr for Local Govt and Environmental Services at DoE, 1979-83. PC 1979. Opposn spokesman on energy, 1976-9, industry, 1975-6. Elected 1970 by-election. B Jun 13 1933; ed Rugby; Emmanuel Coll, Cambridge. Chmn, Sale, Tilney and Co Ltd, 1971-9 (director, 1965-79); general manager, E.S.and A. Robinson, Bristol, 1964-9, joining company in 1956.

William Revans, computer journalist. Nat sec, 1986-7, and vice-chmn, 1987-8, Young SDP. B Jun 24 1968; ed Taunton Sch; Lancaster Univ (chmn Student Dems, 1988-9). Worked for US Congressman Gerry Sikorski 1988.

Peter James, an operating dept assistant, NHS, contested Wells in 1987 and Devon N 1983. B Sep 9 1953; ed West Bridgeford GS. Sch governor. Mbr, nat exec cmte, Nupe, 1986- ; shop steward, 1978- ; sponsored by union.

Graham Dummett, retired engineer involved in oil and zinc extraction. B Feb 2 1932; ed Colston's, Bristol.

BRIDLINGTON					No change	
Electorate % Turnout	84,829	77.9%	1992	80,126	73.7%	1987
*Townend, J E (C)	33,604	50.8%	-4.0%	32,351	54.8%	C
Leeman, J A (LD)	17,246	26.1%	+0.6%	15,030	25.5%	SDP/All
Hatfield, S (Lab)	15,263	23.1%	+5.0%	10,653	18.1%	Lab
				983	1.7%	Grn
C to LD swing 2.3%	66,113		24.7%	59,017		29.3%
		C maj	16,358		C maj	17,321

John Townend, wine merchant and chartered accountant, was elected in 1979; contested Hull N, 1970. Mbr, Select Cmte on Treasury and Civil Service, 1983- . Chmn (1988-) and jt vice-chmn (1985-8), Cons backbench small businesses cmte; jt vice-chmn, Cons finance cmte, 1983- . Mbr, Commons catering cmte, 1991- ; exec cmte, British gp, IPU; jt sec, all-pty British-Argentina parly gp; sec, United Arab Emirates gp. B Jun 12 1934; ed Hymers Coll, Hull. Mbr, Hull City Cl, 1966-74; Humberside CC, 1973-9; chmn, Humber Bridge bd, 1969-71. Chmn (1977-), managing director (1966-77) and co sec/director (1959-67), J Townend and Sons (Hull) Ltd and associated companies; Surrey Building Society, and AAH Holdings Ltd, 1989- ; mbr of Lloyd's.

John Leeman, teacher, contested Sheffield, Brightside, 1987. Chmn, Humberside LDs. Mbr, Holderness BC, 1987- (Oppsn ldr, 1991- ; LD gp ldr, 1987-). B Apr 3 1952; ed Riley Tech HS, Hull; Endsleigh coll of ed, Hull. NUT.

Steve Hatfield, snr scientific officer. Mbr, Bilton PC, Holderness; vice-chmn and treas, Holderness Lab pty. B May 25 1957; ed Hull GS. MSF hospital rep.

BRIGG AND CLEETHORPES					No change	
Electorate % Turnout	82,377	78.0%	1992	80,096	76.3%	1987
*Brown, M R (C)	31,673	49.3%	+0.6%	29,725	48.7%	C
Cawsey, I A (Lab)	22,404	34.9%	+12.2%	17,475	28.6%	L/All
Cockbill, Ms M R (LD)	9,374	14.6%	-14.0%	13,876	22.7%	Lab
Jacques, D N (Grn)	790	1.2%				
C to Lab swing 5.8%	64,241		14.4%	61,076		20.1%
		C maj	9,269		C maj	12,250

Michael Brown was elected for this seat 1983; MP for Brigg and Scunthorpe, 1979-83. Mbr Select Cmte on Energy, 1986-9. PPS to Douglas Hogg, Minr of State for Industry and then at FCO, 1989- . Parly adviser to Nat Assocn of Licensed Opencast Operators, 1990- ; Associated British Ports plc; Alexander Stenhouse UK Ltd. Lecturer and tutor, Swinton Cons Coll, 1974-5; parly assistant to MP, 1976-9. B Jul 3 1951; ed Andrew Cairns County Sec Mod Sch, Littlehampton; York Univ. Mbr, British-Irish Inter-Parly Body.

Ian Cawsey, research asst to Elliot Morley, Lab MP for Glanford and Scunthorpe. Mbr, Humberside CC, 1989-; director, Humberside International Airport. B Apr 14 1960; ed Wintringham Sch, Grimsby. GMB.

Margaret Cockbill, state registered nurse; snr lecturer, Humberside Coll of Health. B Jan 11 1938; ed Erdington GS, B'ham. Treas, Mid-Holderness LD branch. Sec, Humberside Assocn of Counselling. RCN.

Neil Jacques, local govt leisure services country park manager, contested Sunderland S 1987 and Newcastle Central 1983. Nat sec, Grn pty, 1986-8. Mbr, Glanford DC, 1991- . B Feb 28 1955; ed Wycliffe Coll, Glos. Nalgo; mbr Newcastle branch exec.

BRIGHTON, KEMPTOWN					No change	
Electorate % Turnout	57,646	76.1%	1992	60,271	74.5%	1987
*Bowden, A (C)	21,129	48.1%	-5.4%	24,031	53.5%	C
Haynes, Ms G O (Lab)	18,073	41.2%	+8.3%	14,771	32.9%	Lab
Scott, P (LD)	4,461	10.2%	-3.4%	6,080	13.5%	L/All
Overall, Ms E (NLP)	230	0.5%				
C to Lab swing 6.8%	43,893		7.0%	44,882		20.6%
		C maj	3,056		C maj	9,260

Andrew Bowden, a personnel consultant, has been chmn, all-party parly gp for pensioners, since 1972; the all-party British Limbless Ex-servicemen's Assocn gp, 1975- ; and People to People International, 1981- ; jt vice-chmn, all-pty pre-1973 war widows gp. Mbr, Cl of Europe, 1987- . Won the seat 1970; contested it 1966; Kensington N, 1964; Hammersmith N 1955. Parly and public affairs consultant to Ewbank Preece Gp, consulting engineers, 1989- . Mbr, Select Cmte on Employment, 1979-83. B Apr 8 1930; ed Ardingly Coll, Sussex (mbr of school cl since 1982). Pres, Captive Animals Protection Soc, since 1978.

Gill Haynes, personnel officer; former chmn, Kemptown CLP. Mbr, Brighton BC, 1984- (dep ldr cl, 1986-9; chmn housing, 1988-91; chmn, police and public safety, 1991-). B Feb 14 1948; ed Barking Abbey GS; Nottinghan and E Anglia univs. Nalgo.

BRIGHTON, PAVILION						No change
Electorate % Turnout	57,616	76.8%	1992	58,910	73.7%	1987
Spencer, Sir Derek (C)	20,630	46.6%	-4.2%	22,056	50.8%	C
Lepper, D (Lab)	16,955	38.3%	+8.6%	12,914	29.7%	Lab
Pearce, T H (LD)	5,606	12.7%	-6.8%	8,459	19.5%	SDP/All
Brodie, I (Grn)	963	2.2%				
Turner, Ms E (NLP)	103	0.2%				
C to Lab swing 6.4%	44,257		8.3%	43,429		21.1%
		C maj	3,675		C maj	9,142

Sir Derek Spencer, QC, was appointed solicitor-general and knighted on his election for this seat in 1992. MP for Leicester South, 1983-7. Crown court recorder, 1979-92; Bencher, Gray's Inn, 1991- ; PPS to Sir Michael Havers, attorney-general, 1986-7, and to David Mellor, Minister of State, Home Office, 1986. Treas, City of London and Westminster Cons Assocn, 1990-1. B Mar 31 1936; ed Clitheroe Royal GS; Keble Coll, Oxford. Mbr, Camden BC, 1978-83; dep Cons leader, 1980-2. Vice-chmn, St Pancras North Cons Assocn, 1977-8.

David Lepper, teacher, was first Lab ldr of Brighton Cl, 1986-7; elected to cl 1980; chmn, police and public safety cmte; former ldr and dep ldr of Lab gp. A director of the Gardner arts centre and exec cmte mbr, South East Arts. B Sep 15 1945; ed Wimbledon Cty Sec; Kent and Sussex Univs; Central London Poly. NUT.

Tom Pearce, lecturer; cartoonist and caricaturist; sculptor (Associate, Royal Soc of British Sculptors). Contested Old Bexley and Sidcup for L/All 1987. Sec, SE LD region; regional spokesman on further and higher ed; mbr, exec cl, regions of England. B Nov 21 1934; ed Porth Cty GS for Boys; Cardiff Coll of Art. Mbr, Nat Soc for Ed in Art and Design.

BRISTOL EAST						Lab gain
Electorate % Turnout	62,577	80.4%	1992	63,840	78.7%	1987
Corston, Ms J (Lab)	22,418	44.6%	+9.1%	21,906	43.6%	C
*Sayeed, J (C)	19,726	39.2%	-4.4%	17,783	35.4%	Lab
Kiely, J F (LD)	7,903	15.7%	-4.7%	10,247	20.4%	L/All
Anderson, I (NF)	270	0.5%		286	0.6%	NFFG
C to Lab swing 6.8%	50,317		5.4%	50,222		8.2%
		Lab maj	2,692		C maj	4,123

Jean Corston, barrister, gained this seat for Lab in 1992. Worked at Lab regional office, Bristol, 1976-85, being first SW regional women's organiser then SW regional organiser; at Lab Pty HQ, 1985-6. B May 5 1942; ed Yeovil Girls' HS, Somerset; Coll of Art and Tech; Open Univ; LSE. Apex, 1976-85; Nat Union Lab Organisers, 1974-86; TGWU-ACTTS, 1985- .

Jonathan Sayeed was MP for this seat, 1983-92. PPS to Lord Belstead, Paymaster General and Minr of State for N Ireland, 1991-2. Mbr select cmte on defence, 1987-91; select cmte on environment, 1987. Vice-chmn (1985-91) and former sec, Cons backbench shipping and shipbuild-ing sub-cmte; jt dep chmn (1987-92) and former sec, all-pty maritime parly gp. B Mar 20 1948; ed primary sch in Hampstead, London; Wolverstone Hall, Suffolk; RNC Dartmouth; Royal Naval Engineering Coll, Manadon. Served in Royal Navy, 1965-72; RNR, 1972-6. Director, then chmn, insurance and shipping consultancy, 1973-82. Mbr of Lloyd's.

John Kiely, distribution manager; mbr, Bristol City Cl. 1983-90; chmn, constituency LD. B Apr 22 1957; ed Cardinal Manning Sch, Ladbroke Grove, W London. TGWU.

BRISTOL NORTH WEST						No change
Electorate % Turnout	72,726	82.4%	1992	72,876	79.4%	1987
*Stern, M C (C)	25,354	42.3%	-4.3%	26,953	46.6%	C
Naysmith, J D (Lab)	25,309	42.3%	+7.7%	20,001	34.6%	Lab
Taylor, J D (LD)	8,498	14.2%	-4.6%	10,885	18.8%	SDP/All
Long, Mrs H (Soc Dem)	729	1.2%				
C to Lab swing 6.0%	59,890		0.1%	57,839		12.0%
		C maj	45		C maj	6,952

Michael Stern, partner in firm of chartered accountants, was elected in 1983; fought Derby S, 1979. Vice-chmn, Conservative Pty, 1991- ; PPS to John Redwood, Minr of State for Corporate Affairs at DTI, 1990-1; to Peter Brooke, Minr of State, Treasury and then Paymaster Gen and chmn Cons Pty, 1986-9. Mbr select cmtes on sittings of House, 1991-2; Energy, 1989-91; Environment, 1986. Chief finance officer, Cons Pty, 1990-1. Chmn (1987-91) and jt vice-chmn (1983-7), West Country Cons MPs; chmn, all-pty chess parly gp. B Aug 3 1942; ed Christ's Coll GS, Finchley.

Dr Doug Naysmith, medical scientist and lecturer, contested Cirencester and Tewkesbury 1987; Bristol in 1979 Euro elections. Nat pres, Socialist Health Assocn. Mbr, Bristol City Cl, 1981- (chmn, docks cmte; chief whip, Lab gp, 1988- ; chmn, Port of Bristol, 1976-). B Apr 1 1941; ed Musselburgh Burgh Sch; George Heriot Sch, Edinburgh; Edinburgh and Yale Univs. Past chmn, Bristol district Lab Pty; chmn, Bristol Co-op Pty reg cl. IPCS 1958-61; NUS 1961-71; AUT 1973- (past pres, sec, treas, Bristol AUT). Sponsored by Co-op Pty.

John Taylor, pensions administrator. B Mar 11 1964; ed Univ Coll, Swansea.

BRISTOL SOUTH						No change
Electorate % Turnout	64,309	78.0%	1992	68,733	74.0%	1987
*Primarolo, Ms D (Lab)	25,164	50.1%	+9.3%	20,798	40.9%	Lab
Bercow, J S (C)	16,245	32.4%	-5.7%	19,394	38.1%	C
Crossley, P N (LD)	7,892	15.7%	-3.8%	9,952	19.6%	SDP/All
Boxall, J H (Grn)	756	1.5%	+0.3%	600	1.2%	Grn
Phillips, N (NLP)	136	0.3%		149	0.3%	RF
C to Lab swing 7.5%	50,193		17.8%	50,893		2.8%
		Lab maj	8,919		Lab maj	1,404

Dawn Primarolo, a researcher, was elected in 1987. Mbr, Select Cmte on Members' Interests, 1990- . Mbr, Avon CC, 1985-7. Sec, Bristol SE CLP; chmn Bristol District Lab pty; SW rep, Nat Lab Women's Cmte. B May 2 1954; ed Thomas Bennett Comprehensive Sch, Crawley; Bristol Poly; Bristol Univ. MSF.

John Bercow, vice-chmn, Cons Collegiate Forum since 1987. Contested Motherwell S 1987. Account director with public affairs company. Nat chmn, FCS, 1986-7; mbr, nat union exec cmte, 1985- ; nat union gen purposes cmte,

1986- ; Lambeth BC, 1986-90 (dep Cons gp ldr, 1987-9). B Jan 19 1963; ed Finchley Manorhill Sch; Essex Univ. Qualified lawn tennis instructor.

Paul Crossley is a self-employed computer analyst/programmer. Contested Wiltshire in 1989 Euro elections. Mbr, Bath City Cl, 1988- ; membership sec, LDs against Apartheid. B Jan 19 1952; ed Gosport GS; Brighton Poly.

John Boxall, local govt officer. B Oct 9 1962; ed Bristol GS. Nalgo.

BRISTOL WEST						No change
Electorate % Turnout	70,579	74.4%	1992	72,357	75.0%	1987
*Waldegrave, W A (C)	22,169	42.2%	-3.3%	24,695	45.5%	C
Boney, C R (LD)	16,098	30.7%	-0.7%	16,992	31.3%	L/All
Bashforth, H (Lab)	12,992	24.8%	+3.9%	11,337	20.9%	Lab
Sawday, G A R (Grn)	906	1.7%	-0.3%	1,096	2.0%	Grn
Cross, D (NLP)	104	0.2%		134	0.2%	Comm
Brent, B (Rev Comm)	92	0.2%				
Hammond, P (SOADDA)	87	0.2%				
Hedges, T (Anti-Fed)	42	0.1%				
C to LD swing 1.3%	52,490		11.6%	54,254		14.2%
		C maj	6,071		C maj	7,703

William Waldegrave was appointed Chancellor of the Duchy of Lancaster and Minister for the Citizen's Charter in April 1992. Appointed to cabinet in 1990 as health secretary; Minr of State, FCO, 1988-90; Minr of State, Environment, 1985-8; Under Sec Environment, 1981-3. PC 1990. Elected in 1979. Mbr, Central Policy Review Staff, Cabinet Office, 1971-3; mbr political staff, No 10 Downing Street, 1973-4; head of Edward Heath's political office, 1974-5. With GEC Ltd, 1975-81. B Aug 15 1949; ed Eton; Corpus Christi, Oxford (Pres of Union and of Cons Assocn); Harvard (Kennedy Fellow in Politics).

Charles Boney, teacher, contested Bristol for LDs in 1989 Euro elections, and Salisbury for Lab in 1979 gen election. Mbr Bristol City Cl, 1979-81 for Lab, 1981-2 for Libs, and 1986- as Lib and LD (ldr, LD gp, 1989-). B Mar 21 1950; ed Felstead Sch, Essex; Bristol Univ.

Hedley Bashforth, teacher; mbr, Bristol City Cl, 1986- ; sec, Bristol district LP, 1985-6. B Nov 25 1951; ed Barnsley GS, S Yorks; Bath Univ. NATFHE.

Alastair Sawday, director of own tour design company and consultancy, and of own company promoting green products and services. B Aug 5 1945; ed Charterhouse; Trinity Coll, Oxford.

BROMSGROVE						No change
Electorate % Turnout	71,111	82.5%	1992	69,494	76.4%	1987
Thomason, R (C)	31,709	54.1%	-0.7%	29,051	54.7%	C
Mole, Ms C (Lab)	18,007	30.7%	+7.4%	12,366	23.3%	Lab
Cassin, Ms A J (LD)	8,090	13.8%	-8.2%	11,663	22.0%	SDP/All
Churchman, J C (Grn)	856	1.5%				
C to Lab swing 4.0%	58,662		23.4%	53,080		31.4%
		C maj	13,702		C maj	16,685

Roy Thomason was returned for the seat in 1992; contested Newport East 1983. Solicitor and adviser to a number of companies. Vice-chmn Cons nat local govt advisory cmte, 1988-91; mbr nat union exec cmte. 1988-91. Mbr Bournemouth BC, 1970-92 (cl ldr, 1974-82). Chmn Assocn of DCs, 1987-91; mbr of cl, 1979-91; ldr, 1981-7; and chmn, housing, 1983-7. B Dec 14 1944; ed Cheney Sch, Oxford. Chmn Bournemouth West Cons assocn, 1981-2; chmn Wessex area local govt advisory cmte, 1983-86.

Catherine Mole, commercial manager; mbr, Bromsgrove DC, 1973-9 and 1981- . B Aug 7 1947; ed Bishop Challenor Sch, Birmingham. GMB/Apex.

Alexis Cassin, solicitor; mbr, Cheltenham BC, 1979- (gp ldr, 1988-). B Apr 29 1952; ed Pate's GS for Girls, Cheltenham; Kingston upon Thames and Birmingham Polys.

John Churchman, radiographer, contested this seat 1983. Ex-mbr, Grn pty cl as W Midlands rep. B Jul 24 1948; ed City of London Sch; Manchester Univ.

BROXBOURNE				No change		
Electorate % Turnout	72,116	80.0%	1992	70,631	75.2%	1987
*Roe, Ms M A (C)	36,094	62.6%	-0.6%	33,567	63.2%	C
Hudson, M (Lab)	12,124	21.0%	+4.1%	10,572	19.9%	L/All
Davies, Mrs J M (LD)	9,244	16.0%	-3.9%	8,984	16.9%	Lab
Woolhouse, G (NLP)	198	0.3%				
C to Lab swing 2.4%	57,660		41.6%	53,123		43.3%
		C maj	23,970		C maj	22,995

Marion Roe was elected in 1983; contested Barking, 1979. Appointed to Select Cmtes on Procedure and on sittings of Commons in 1991; mbr, Commons administration cmte, 1991- ; Select Cmte on Social Services, 1988-89. Chmn, Cons backbench social security cmte, 1990- , and Cons horticulture and markets sub-cmte, 1989- ; jt vice-chmn, Cons environment cmte, 1990- . Parly consultant to Horticultural Trades Assocn, 1990-. Under Sec of State for Environment, 1987-8. Mbr, women's panel, Nat and Provincial Building Society, 1988- ; advisory cmte on women's employment, Dept of Employment, 1989- ; UK delegation to Cl of Europe and WEU, 1989- . Managing trustee, Parly Contributory Pension Fund, 1990-. Jt chmn, all-pty fairs and showgrounds parly gp, 1989- ; sec, hospice gp, 1990- ; British Canadian gp, 1991- . B Jul 15 1936; ed Bromley HS; Croydon HS; English Sch of Languages, Vevey. Freeman, City of London and Worshipful Company of Gardeners.

Martin Hudson, public housing professional. Chmn Lab campaign for travellers' rights; Herts cty LP and Herts Euro pty, 1986-9; former chmn CLP; CLP sec, E Herts, 1979-83. Mbr, Broxbourne DC, 1984- ; Hammersmith BC, 1971-4. B Aug 20 1946; ed St Albans Cty GS for Boys. Nalgo; Nupe.

Julia Davies, teacher; GCSE assessor and team ldr. Vice-chmn Broxbourne LD, 1990- ; press officer, 1986- . Mbr Herts Conservation Trust. B Jul 7 1952; ed Merchant Taylors' Girls' Sch, Crosby; Bedford Coll, London Univ. NAS.

BROXTOWE				No change		
Electorate % Turnout	73,123	83.4%	1992	71,780	79.2%	1987
*Lester, J T (C)	31,096	51.0%	-2.6%	30,462	53.6%	C
Walker, J R W (Lab)	21,205	34.8%	+10.5%	13,811	24.3%	Lab
Ross, J (LD)	8,395	13.8%	-8.3%	12,562	22.1%	L/All
Lukehurst, D (NLP)	293	0.5%				
C to Lab swing 6.5%	60,989		16.2%	56,835		29.3%
		C maj	9,891		C maj	16,651

James Lester was Under Secretary of State for Employment, 1979-81; mbr, select cmte on foreign affairs, since 1982. Chmn, Cons backbench employment cmte, 1987-9 and 1983; vice-chmn, all-pty gp on overseas development, 1983- ; sec, association football gp. Founder mbr and current chmn, CARE (Conservative Action to Revive Employment). Parly consultant to Direct Selling Assocn, Assocn of First Div Civil Servants, BAT Industries, Communication Managers Assocn, Phonographic Performance Ltd, and Regency Park Ltd. Elected for this seat 1983; MP for Beeston, 1974-83; contested Bassetlaw, 1968 by-election and 1970. B May 23 1932; ed Nottingham HS.

James Walker, teacher; agent in Broxtowe 1987; chmn Broxtowe CLP, 1986-88; mbr, bd of governors, Broxtowe Coll, 1986-88. B Jul 2 1956; ed Nottingham Bluecoat Sch; King Alfred's Coll of HE, Winchester; Birmingham Univ. NUT.

John Ross, computer consultant; chmn, Braintree, Essex, constituency, 1988-91. Lib mbr, Braintree DC, 1973-80 and 1983-7. B Jul 15 1946; ed Giggleswick Sch; Reading and Essex Univs.

BUCKINGHAM				No change		
Electorate % Turnout	56,063	84.2%	1992	70,036	78.3%	1987
*Walden, G G H (C)	29,496	62.5%	+3.8%	32,162	58.6%	C
Jones, H T (LD)	9,705	20.6%	-4.3%	13,636	24.9%	L/All
White, K M (Lab)	7,662	16.2%	-0.3%	9,053	16.5%	Lab
Sheaff, L (NLP)	353	0.7%				
LD to C swing 4.1%	47,216		41.9%	54,851		33.8%
		C maj	19,791		C maj	18,526

George Walden, who was elected in 1983, was Under Sec of State for Ed and Science 1985-7 as minr for higher ed. Consultant to Samuel Montagu and Co Ltd; feature writer for *The Daily Telegraph*, 1989- ; consultant on international affairs to Chase Manhattan Bank. Director, Ashchurch Enterprises, family business. Former diplomat; head of policy planning, FCO, 1982-3; principal private sec to Lord Carrington and Dr David Owen, 1978-81; British Embassy, Paris, 1974-8; FCO, 1970-3; British Mission, Peking, 1967-70;. Fellow of Harvard Univ, 1981-2. B Sep 15 1939; ed Latymer Upper Sch; Jesus Coll, Cambridge; postgraduate at Moscow Univ.

Tudor Jones, polytechnic lecturer, contested Coventry NW 1987. Mbr, Oxford branch cmte of Oxford West and Abingdon LDs. B Jan 25 1946; ed Univ Coll Sch, London; Oxford Univ; LSE; Southampton Univ. NATFHE.

Keith White is a snr analyst/programmer. Mbr, St Albans DC, 1989- . B Sep 16 1963; ed Appleton Hall GS, Warrington; Hatfield Poly. MSF; previously Apex as shop steward, Stevenage photographic branch, and CPSA.

BURNLEY				No change		
Electorate % Turnout	68,952	74.4%	1992	65,956	78.8%	1987
*Pike, P L (Lab)	27,184	53.0%	+4.6%	25,140	48.4%	Lab
Binge, Mrs B (C)	15,693	30.6%	-3.2%	17,583	33.8%	C
Birtwistle, G (LD)	8,414	16.4%	-1.4%	9,241	17.8%	SDP/All
C to Lab swing 3.9%	51,291		22.4%	51,964		14.5%
		Lab maj	11,491		Lab maj	7,557

Peter Pike joined Opposn front bench team on agriculture in 1990 with responsibility for rural affairs. Elected in 1983. Mbr Select Cmte on Environment 1985-90. Chmn (1987-90) and jt vice-chmn (1985-7) PLP environment cmte; vice-chmn PLP anti-apartheid gp; treas civil liberties gp. Production worker (inspection) 1973-83. B Jun 26 1937; ed Hinchley Wood cty sec sch; Kingston Tech Coll. Mbr Merton and Morden UDC, 1962-3; Burnley BC, 1976-84 (Lab gp ldr 1980-3). With Mullard (Simonstone) Ltd 1973-83; Lab pty organiser and agent, 1963-73; Twinings Tea, 1962-3; Midland Bank, 1954-62. Sponsored by GMB.

Brenda Binge, writer and freelance journalist, Surrey and Sth London Newspaper Gp; former owner of rest home for elderly. Mbr Reigate DC 1981-6. Vice-chmn SE Area CPC; former vice-chmn Families for Defence. Mbr European Union of Women. B Dec 24 1945; ed St Margarets, Johnstone, Scotland; NE Surrey Coll of Tech, Ewell; Hillcroft Coll, Surbiton; LSE. IOJ.

Gordon Birtwistle, director of engineering company; LD gp ldr on BC. B Sep 6 1943.

BURTON				No change		
Electorate % Turnout	75,292	82.4%	1992	73,252	78.5%	1987
*Lawrence, I J (C)	30,845	49.7%	-1.0%	29,160	50.7%	C
Muddyman, Ms P K (Lab)	24,849	40.0%	+6.4%	19,330	33.6%	Lab
Renold, R (LD)	6,375	10.3%	-5.5%	9,046	15.7%	L/All
C to Lab swing 3.7%	62,069		9.7%	57,536		17.1%
		C maj	5,996		C maj	9,830

Ivan Lawrence, QC, was elected in Feb 1974; contested Peckham, 1966 and 1970. Mbr Select Cmte on Foreign Affairs 1983- . Chmn (1988-) and jt vice-chmn (1982-8) Cons backbench home affairs cmte; chmn (1987-) and vice-chmn (1979-87) Cons legal cmte. Elected Governing Master, Bench of Inner Temple, 1991. Crown court recorder 1987- ; asst recorder, 1983-7. Mbr exec Society of Cons Lawyers, 1989- . Chmn all-pty barristers parly gp 1987- ; all-pty anti-flouridation cmte 1978- ; jt vice-chmn (1990-1) and mbr (1991-) exec cmte UK branch CPA; sec all-pty cmte for release of Soviet Jewry 1977- ; vice-chmn Euro Interparly Conference for Soviet Jewry 1980- ; treas

Cons Friends of Israel parly gp. B Dec 24 1936; ed Brighton, Hove and Sussex GS; Christ Church, Oxford.

Patricia Muddyman, local govt officer. Mbr W Midlands CC 1981-6. Former pty officer in Birmingham, Perry Barr; W Midlands cty pty delegate. B Feb 17 1956; ed Perry Common Comprehensive Sch, Erdington and Birmingham Poly. Nupe/Nalgo.

Rob Renold, management consultant, contested Rutland and Melton for L/All 1987 and Leicester S 1983. Mbr Leicestershire CC 1985-9. B Apl 20 1952; ed Gordonstoun; Birmingham Univ; Cranfield Inst.

BURY NORTH				No change		
Electorate % Turnout	69,529	84.8%	1992	67,961	82.5%	1987
*Burt, A J H (C)	29,266	49.7%	-0.5%	28,097	50.1%	C
Dobbin, J (Lab)	24,502	41.6%	+3.8%	21,168	37.8%	Lab
McGrath, C F L (LD)	5,010	8.5%	-3.6%	6,804	12.1%	L/All
Sullivan, M (NLP)	163	0.3%				
C to Lab swing 2.1%	58,941		8.1%	56,069		12.4%
		C maj	4,764		C maj	6,929

Alistair Burt was appointed under sec for social services in 1992. Elected in 1983. Former PPS to Kenneth Baker. Mbr Select Cmte on sittings of Commons 1991-2. Jt vice-chmn Cons backbench European affairs cmte 1991-2; jt sec Cons backbench energy cmte, 1983-5; sec NW Cons MPs 1984-8; Parly Christian Fellowship, 1984- ; all-pty home safety parly gp; jt vice-chmn tertiary colleges association parly gp 1990- . Solicitor and consultant. Former parly adviser to British Fibreboard Packaging

Assocn and to AMMA. B May 25 1955; ed Bury GS; St John's Coll, Oxford.

Jim Dobbin, medical microbiologist is dep ldr Rochdale Cl and chmn of neighbourhood services; former chmn district Lab pty. Mbr Rochdale HA; chmn Rochdale credit union. B May 26 1941; ed St Columbus HS, Cowdenbeath. MSF.

Colin McGrath, personnel director; adviser to business on human resources. B Nov 25 1942.

BURY SOUTH						No change
Electorate % Turnout	65,793	82.1%	1992	65,039	79.7%	1987
*Sumberg, D A G (C)	24,873	46.0%	-0.0%	23,878	46.1%	C
Blears, Ms H A (Lab)	24,085	44.6%	+3.7%	21,199	40.9%	Lab
Cruden, A H (LD)	4,832	8.9%	-4.1%	6,772	13.1%	SDP/All
Sullivan, Mrs N (NLP)	228	0.4%				
C to Lab swing 1.9%	54,018		1.5%	51,849		5.2%
		C maj	788		C maj	2,679

David Sumberg, solicitor and consultant partner, was elected in 1983; contested Manchester, Wythenshawe, 1979. Appointed to Select Cmte on Home Affairs, 1991; PPS to Sir Patrick Mayhew, as solicitor-general and then attorney-general, 1986-90. Consultant to Jaques & Lewis, solicitors, and Burgher Properties (North West) Ltd. B Jun 2 1941; ed Tettenhall Coll, Wolverhampton; Coll of Law, London. Mbr, Manchester City Cl, 1982-4. Jt vice-chmn, all-pty war crimes parly gp; treas, British-Singapore gp; jt hon sec, Cons Friends of Israel parly gp, 1986. Fellow, Industry and Parliament Trust.

Hazel Blears, solicitor in local govt, contested Tatton 1987. Mbr, Salford City Cl, 1984- . Mbr, Gtr Manchester low pay unit; Salford "Relate"; trustee, Working Class Museum and Library. Former chmn Bury and Radcliffe CLP; vice-chmn and asst sec, Eccles CLP; campaigns co-ordinator, Salford Dist LP. B May 14 1956; ed Wardley GS; Eccles VIth Form; Trent Poly; Chester Coll of Law. TGWU (ACTSS); sponsored by TGWU.

Adrian Cruden, personnel officer, contested Gtr Manchester West in 1989 Euro elections. Vice-chmn, Bradford S and W LDs, 1990-1; chmn, One World Democrats, 1988-90. B May 30 1963; ed Hutchesons GS, Glasgow; Glasgow Univ, Bell Coll, Hamilton. Chmn, Scottish YSDs, 1983-6.

BURY ST EDMUNDS						No change
Electorate % Turnout	79,967	78.4%	1992	76,619	74.1%	1987
Spring, R J G (C)	33,554	53.5%	-5.8%	33,672	59.3%	C
Sheppard, T (Lab)	14,767	23.6%	+6.2%	12,214	21.5%	SDP/All
Williams, J B (LD)	13,814	22.0%	+0.5%	9,841	17.3%	Lab
Lillis, Ms J (NLP)	550	0.9%		1,057	1.9%	Grn
C to Lab swing 6.0%	62,685		30.0%	56,784		37.8%
		C maj	18,787		C maj	21,458

Richard Spring was returned for this seat in 1992. Managing director of Xerox Furman Selz, financial services company and advisers to pension funds, banks and unit trusts. Contested Ashton-under-Lyne in 1983. B Sep 24 1946; ed Rondebosch, Cape; Cape Town Univ; Magdalene Coll, Cambridge. Ward chmn; mbr of exec, Westminster S Cons assocn; chmn, Westminster CPC; campaign co-ordinator, 1989 Euro elections. Trustee, Thornham Field Study Centre, Suffolk.

Tom Sheppard, local govt officer; mbr, Hackney BC, 1986- (cl dep ldr). B Mar 6 1959; ed Coleraine Academical Institution; Aberdeen Univ. Nupe.

John Williams, computer manager; mbr, St Edmundsbury BC, 1979- . B Oct 12 1951; ed Altrincham GS; York Univ.

CAERNARFON						No change
Electorate % Turnout	46,468	78.2%	1992	45,661	78.0%	1987
*Wigley, D W (PC)	21,439	59.0%	+1.9%	20,338	57.1%	PC
Fowler, P E H (C)	6,963	19.2%	-2.0%	7,526	21.1%	C
Mainwaring, S (Lab)	5,641	15.5%	-0.3%	5,652	15.9%	Lab
Arwel Williams, R (LD)	2,101	5.8%	-0.1%	2,103	5.9%	L/All
Evans, G (NLP)	173	0.5%				
C to PC swing 1.9%	36,317		39.9%	35,619		36.0%
		PC maj	14,476		PC maj	12,812

Dafydd Wigley, president of Plaid Cymru, 1991- and 1981-84, became PC parly whip in 1987. Won the seat, Feb 1974; contested Merioneth, 1970. Mbr, Select Cmte on Welsh Affairs, 1983-7; mbr, all-pty disablement gp; sponsored Disabled Persons Act 1981; pres, Spastic Soc of Wales, 1985-90; vice-pres, Wales Cl for the Disabled. Awarded Grimshaw Memorial Award (1982) by Nat Fed of the Blind. Industrial economist. Pres, S Caernarfon Creamery, 1989- ; director, Alpha Cysylltiadau Cyf, 1991- . Vice-pres, Nat Fed of Industrial Development Authorities, 1981- . Mbr, Merthyr BC, 1972-4. B Apr 1 1943; ed Caernarfon GS; Rydal Sch, Colwyn Bay; Manchester Univ. Mbr, Nat Cmte for Electoral Reform.

Peter Fowler, chartered accountant, was vice-chmn, Conwy Cons assocn, 1989-91. Mbr of Lib Pty, 1974-81, and Anglesey vice-chmn, 1980-1 and press officer. Mbr Press Cl, 1983-8. B May 10 1949; ed Loughborough Coll Sch; Hertford GS.

Sharon Mainwaring, dep director of Shelter (Cymru); mbr, Lliw Valley BC, 1983- ; sec, district Lab pty. B Dec 31 1953; ed Ystalyfera GS. TGWU/ACTTS.

Robert Arwel Williams, legal officer; treas, constituency pty; community cllr; elder of Methodist Church. B Apr 28 1956; ed Brynhyfryd Sch, Ruthin; NE Wales Inst; W Cheshire Coll.

CAERPHILLY				No change		
Electorate % Turnout	64,529	77.2%	1992	64,154	76.5%	1987
*Davies, R (Lab)	31,713	63.7%	+5.2%	28,698	58.4%	Lab
Philpott, H (C)	9,041	18.1%	-1.3%	9,531	19.4%	C
Whittle, L G (PC)	4,821	9.7%	+1.6%	6,923	14.1%	L/All
Wilson, S (LD)	4,247	8.5%	-5.6%	3,955	8.1%	PC
C to Lab swing 3.2%	49,822		45.5%	49,107		39.0%
		Lab maj	22,672		Lab maj	19,167

Ron Davies, an Opposition spokesman on food, agriculture and rural affairs 1987- ; Opposition whip, 1985-7. Chmn, 1990-1, and vice-chmn, 1989-90, Welsh gp of Lab MPs. Contested election for Opposn chief whip, 1988. Further ed adviser, Mid-Glamorgan CC, 1974-83; tutor-organiser, WEA, 1970-4; teacher, 1968-70. Elected in 1983. B Aug 6 1946; ed Bassaleg GS; Portsmouth Poly; Univ Coll of Wales. Mbr, Bedwas and Machen UDC and Rhymney Valley DC, 1969-84. Nupe sponsored.
Howard Philpott is the owner of furniture company and printing business. In 1988, appointed research officer to the Cons South Glamorgan CC co-ordinating cmte. B Jan 29 1966; ed Willows HS; Univ Coll, Cardiff.
Lindsay Whittle, housing officer, contested this seat 1987 and 1983. Mbr, Rhymni Valley DC, 1976; Mid-Glamorgan CC, 1977-81; Penyrheol Community Cl, 1985. B Mar 24 1953; ed Caerffili Grammar Tech Sch. Nalgo
Stanley Wilson, retired teacher; Mbr, Langbaurgh DC, 1987- ; Redcar BC, 1963-66; Lib Pty Cl, 1986-89; exec, LDTU. B Nov 12 1931; ed King Alfred's Coll, Winchester. NUT.

CAITHNESS AND SUTHERLAND				No change		
Electorate % Turnout	30,905	71.9%	1992	31,279	73.6%	1987
*Maclennan, R A R (LD)	10,032	45.1%	12,338	53.6%	SDP/All	
Bruce, G (C)	4,667	21.0%	+4.3%	3,844	16.7%	C
MacGregor, K (SNP)	4,049	18.2%	+7.9%	3,437	14.9%	Lab
Coyne, M F (Lab)	3,483	15.7%	+0.7%	2,371	10.3%	SNP
				686	3.0%	Ind L
				333	1.4%	Grn
LD to C swing 6.4%	22,231		24.1%	23,009		36.9%
		LD maj	5,365		SDP/All maj	8,494

Robert Maclennan became convenor of LD home affairs team and home affairs and arts spokesman in 1988. Leader of SDP, 1987-8 until merger with Liberals to form SLD pty; jt interim ldr in 1988. Alliance spokesman on agriculture and fisheries in 1987 election; SDP spokesman on home and legal affairs and N Ireland, 1983-7, on Scotland, 1982-3, and on agriculture and fisheries, 1982-3. Mbr, nat and policy cmtes, SDP, 1981-8; fed exec and fed policy cmtes, LD, 1988-. Won seat for Lab in 1966; joined SDP in 1981 retained seat 1983 and 1987. Mbr, PAC, 1979- . Under Sec for Prices and Consumer Protection, 1974-9. B Jun 26 1936; ed Glasgow Acad; Balliol Coll, Oxford; Trinity Coll, Cambridge; Columbia Univ, New York.
George Bruce, company director. Past chmn, Caithness and Sutherland Cons assocn; chmn, Caithness chamber of commerce. Chmn, Caithness local health cl, 1985-7; mbr Highland Health Bd, 1987-91; Wick TC, 1962-8, and Caithness CC, 1963-8. B Mar 29 1936; ed Wick HS; Aberdeen Univ.
Kerr MacGregor, inventor/lecturer; snr lecturer in energy engineering Napier Polytechnic . Contested this seat 1987. SNP spokesman on energy. B Jul 14 1940; ed Edinburgh and Strathclyde univs. Chmn, Moorfoot Community Cl.
Michael Coyne is GMB branch sec, Scottish regional cl mbr and on regional appeals tribunal. Director/treas, Rights Office, Fife; mbr, Fife children's panel. B Jul 20 1949; ed St Andrew's HS, Fife; Elmwood Tech Coll; Fife Coll of Tech. Fellow, Royal Horticultural Society.

CALDER VALLEY				No change		
Electorate % Turnout	74,417	82.1%	1992	73,398	81.1%	1987
*Thompson, Sir Donald (C)	27,753	45.4%	+1.9%	25,892	43.5%	C
Chaytor, D M (Lab)	22,875	37.4%	+4.1%	19,847	33.4%	Lab
Pearson, S (LD)	9,842	16.1%	-7.0%	13,761	23.1%	L/All
Smith, Ms V (Grn)	622	1.0%				
C to Lab swing 1.1%	61,092		8.0%	59,500		10.2%
		C maj	4,878		C maj	6,045

Sir Donald Thompson was Parly Sec, Min of Ag, Fish and Food, 1986-9; a Ld Commissioner of Treasury (govt whip), 1983-6; asst govt whip, 1981-3. Elected for this seat 1983; MP for Sowerby, 1979-83; contested it in both 1974 elections and Batley and Morley, 1970. Mbr, exec, 1922 Cmte, 1989- . Mbr, cross pty team of advisers to British Nuclear Forum; adviser to Nat Fed of Meat Traders; British Agrochemicals Assocn; British West Indian Airways. Farmer and owner of contract butchering firm, 1952-74; director, 1979-86, and managing director, 1974-9, Armadillo Plastics, glass fibre manufacturers. B Nov 13 1931; ed Hipperholme GS.
David Chaytor, snr lecturer, contested seat 1987; mbr, Calderdale BC, 1982- (chmn ed cmte). B Aug 3 1949; ed Huddersfield Poly; London and Bradford Univs. NATFHE; TGWU.
Stephen Pearson, chartered sec; company director; mbr, Calderdale MBC, 1990- . B Jul 4 1955; ed Bradford Univ.
Viv Smith, family centre worker. B Aug 16 1943; ed Fulwell Grange private school, Sunderland. Nalgo.

CAMBRIDGE						Lab gain
Electorate % Turnout	69,022	73.2%	1992	69,336	78.0%	1987
Campbell, Ms A (Lab)	20,039	39.7%	+11.4%	21,624	40.0%	C
Bishop, M (C)	19,459	38.5%	-1.4%	16,564	30.6%	SDP/All
Howarth, D R (LD)	10,037	19.9%	15,319	28.3%	Lab	
Cooper, T (Grn)	720	1.4%	+0.3%	597	1.1%	Grn
Brettell-Winnington, R (Loony)	175	0.3%				
Chalmers, R (NLP)	83	0.2%				
C to Lab swing 6.4%	50,513		1.1%	54,104		9.4%
		Lab maj	580		C maj	5,060

Anne Campbell, employed as head of statistics and data processing dept, Nat Inst of Agricultural Botany, won this seat in 1992. Mbr, Cambridgeshire CC, 1985-9; Cambridge Progressive Cooperators; Socialist Ed Assocn. B Apr 6 1940; ed Cambridge Univ. Fellow, Inst of Staticians and Royal Statistical Society. MSF; former mbr, NATFHE.
Mark Bishop, barrister, contested Cynon Valley 1987. Former standing counsel to DTI; public inquiry work including Clapham Junction rail disaster; prosecution work for Customs and Excise on drug smuggling; health and safety executive work. B Jul 12 1958; ed The Leys Sch, Cambridge; Downing Coll, Cambridge (Pres of Union

1980). Treas, Battersea Cons Assocn, 1983-5. Chmn, Coningsby Club, 1987-8. C of E lay reader.
David Howarth, univ lecturer; mbr, Cambridge City Cl, 1987- (gp ldr, 1990-); LD fed policy cmte; chmn, LD nat working gp on economic policy. B Nov 10 1958; ed Queen Mary's GS, Walsall; Clare Coll, Cambridge (now Fellow); Yale Law Sch.
Tim Cooper, economist, contested Brentford and Isleworth 1987 and Westminster N 1983. Co-chmn, Grn Pty Cl, 1987-8; nat coordinator, Christian Ecology Link. B Jan 20 1957; ed Queen Elizabeth's Boys GS, Barnet; Bath Univ.

CAMBRIDGESHIRE NORTH EAST						No change
Electorate % Turnout	79,935	79.4%	1992	74,231	77.4%	1987
*Moss, M D (C)	34,288	54.0%	+7.1%	26,983	47.0%	C
Leeke, M L (LD)	19,195	30.3%	-14.2%	25,555	44.5%	L/All
Harris, R J (Lab)	8,746	13.8%	+5.3%	4,891	8.5%	Lab
Ash, C (Lib)	998	1.6%				
Chalmers, Mrs M (NLP)	227	0.4%				
LD to C swing 10.6%	63,454		23.8%	57,429		2.5%
		C maj	15,093		C maj	1,428

Malcolm Moss became PPS to Tristan Garel-Jones, Minr of State, FCO, in 1991; mbr, select cmte on energy, 1988-91; jt vice-chmn (1989-91) and sec (1987-9), Cons backbench energy cmte; sec, all-pty British-Bermuda parly gp; treas, Anglo-Swiss gp. Financial services company director and consultant. Won this seat 1987. Mbr, Wisbech TC, 1979-87; Fenland DC, 1983-7; Cambridgeshire CC, 1985-7. Non-exec chmn (1986-) and former managing director, Mandrake Associates Ltd, previously known as Mandrake (Insurance and Finance Brokers) Ltd (director, 1974-). B Mar 6 1943; ed Audenshaw GS; St John's Coll,

Cambridge. Director, Fens Business Enterprise Trust, 1983- .
Maurice Leeke, financial accountant; mbr, Cambridgeshire CC, 1985- . Director, Peterborough Development Agency Ltd, 1988- . B Dec 16 1952; ed Cambridgeshire HS for Boys.
Ron Harris, manager of psychiatric day centre, qualified social worker, teacher of blind. Contested this seat 1987 and 1983. Pres of CLP. Director, Anglia regional Co-op. Mbr, Fenland DC, 1980-87. B Jul 12 1934; ed John Clare Sec Mod, Northampton. Nalgo.

CAMBRIDGESHIRE SOUTH EAST						No change
Electorate % Turnout	78,600	80.6%	1992	73,216	76.5%	1987
*Paice, J E T (C)	36,693	57.9%	-0.8%	32,901	58.8%	C
Wotherspoon, R E (LD)	12,883	20.3%	-7.2%	15,399	27.5%	SDP/All
Jones, A M (Lab)	12,688	20.0%	+6.3%	7,694	13.7%	Lab
Marsh, J (Grn)	836	1.3%				
Langridge, B (NLP)	231	0.4%				
LD to C swing 3.2%	63,331		37.6%	55,994		31.3%
		C maj	23,810		C maj	17,502

James Paice became PPS to John Gummer, Minr of Agriculture, Fisheries and Food, in 1991; PPS to Minr of State for Agriculture, 1989-91. Mbr select cmte on employment, 1987-90; jt sec, Cons back-bench employment cmte, 1988-9. Non-exec director, United Framlingham Farmers Ltd, being training manager, 1982-5, and training officer, 1979-82. Public affairs adviser to Dixons plc; parly adviser to Nat Training Fed. Farmer, 1973-9; farm manager, 1970-3. Elected in 1987; fought Caernarfon 1979. B Apr 24 1949; ed Framlingham Coll, Suffolk; Writtle Agricultural Coll, Essex (now a

governor). Mbr, Suffolk Coastal DC, 1976-87 (cl chmn, 1982-3).
Ron Wotherspoon, company director, contested Hertford and Stortford 1987 and 1983. B Nov 18 1948; ed St Bonaventure RC Sch, London; Univ Coll, Swansea. In Cons Pty 18 years to 1981; from 1981, SDP area chmn; now mbr, Eastern LD region exec. JP.
Murray Jones, retired primary sch head teacher; mbr, Cambridgeshire CC, 1990- ; held CLP and branch offices B Nov 25 1928; ed Grove Park GS, Wrexham. NUT.

CAMBRIDGESHIRE SOUTH WEST						No change
Electorate % Turnout	84,418	81.1%	1992	81,658	77.7%	1987
*Grant, Sir Anthony (C)	38,902	56.8%	-0.9%	36,622	57.7%	C
Sutton, S M (LD)	19,265	28.1%	-0.8%	18,371	29.0%	L/All
Price, K (Lab)	9,378	13.7%	+0.4%	8,434	13.3%	Lab
Whitebread, Ms L J (Grn)	699	1.0%				
Chalmers, F (NLP)	225	0.3%				
C to LD swing 0.0%	68,469		28.7%	63,427		28.8%
		C maj	19,637		C maj	18,251

Sir Anthony Grant joined select cmte on trade and industry in 1987; select cmte on broadcasting, 1988- . Mbr, exec, 1922 Cmte. Under Sec of State for Industrial Development, DTI, 1972-4; Under Sec of State for Trade, DTI, 1970-2; Parly Sec, Bd of Trade, 1970. Pres, Guild of Experienced Motorists. Elected for this seat 1983; MP for Harrow Central, 1964-83; contested Hayes and Harlington, 1959. Vice-chmn, Cons Pty, 1974-6. Business consultant; former solicitor. B May 29 1925; ed St Paul's Sch; Brasenose Coll, Oxford. Liveryman, Worshipful Co of Solicitors; Freeman, City of London; Master of Guild of Freemen. Mbr, UK delegation to Cl of Europe (chmn, economic cmte, 1980-4).

Sue Sutton, freelance editor/writer; mbr, Cambridgeshire CC, 1985- (speaker on social services, 1991- ; environment, 1989-91). Chaired Cambs SDP; mbr, SW Cambs LD exec; Eastern region exec. B Jun 17 1946; ed George Watson's Ladies' Coll, Edinburgh; Edinburgh and Leeds Univs.

Kevin Price, Lithographic machine manager. B Jan 16 1957; ed Impington Village Coll. NGA (now GPMU), 1974- ; Father of Chapel, 1981-8. and on nat cl, 1987-90.

Linda Whitebread, NHS administrator; parish cllr. B Apl 25 1950; ed Keele Univ. On Nalgo local exec in 1970s.

CANNOCK AND BURNTWOOD						Lab gain
Electorate % Turnout	72,600	84.2%	1992	68,137	79.8%	1987
Wright, A W (Lab)	28,139	46.0%	+6.5%	24,186	44.5%	C
*Howarth, J G D (C)	26,633	43.6%	-0.9%	21,497	39.5%	Lab
Treasaden, P (LD)	5,899	9.6%	-6.3%	8,698	16.0%	L/All
Hartshorne, M (Loony)	469	0.8%				
C to Lab swing 3.7%	61,140		2.5%	54,381		4.9%
		Lab maj	1,506		C maj	2,689

Tony Wright, univ lecturer/reader, won this seat 1992; contested Kidderminster 1979; former exec mbr, Fabian Society; former chair, S Birmingham CHC. B Mar 11 1948; ed Desborough Cty Primary Sch; Kettering GS; LSE; Harvard Univ; Balliol Coll, Oxford. AUT.

Gerald Howarth was MP for seat, 1983-92. PPS to Margaret Thatcher, 1991-2; to Sir George Young, Minr for Housing and Planning, 1990-1, and to Michael Spicer, Under Sec of State for Energy, 1987-90. International banker with Standard Chartered Bank, 1981-7, later consultant to bank; director, Richard Unwin International Ltd, 1983-7. Former parly consultant to British Cable Makers Confed; Astra Holdings plc; Trade Indemnity plc, George House Holdings, and parly adviser to British Constructional Steelwork Assocn; Consumer Credit Assocn. B Sep 12 1947; ed Haileybury and ISC junior sch; Bloxham sch, Banbury; Southampton Univ.

Peter Treasaden, water industry supervisor; mbr, Cannock Chase DC, 1988- (gp ldr, 1991-); Rugeley TC, 1988-91 (chair, 1988-90). B Mar 27 1945.

CANTERBURY						No change
Electorate % Turnout	75,181	78.1%	1992	76,062	74.0%	1987
*Brazier, J W H (C)	29,827	50.8%	-3.0%	30,273	53.8%	C
Vye, M (LD)	19,022	32.4%	+5.0%	15,382	27.3%	L/All
Whitemore, M F (Lab)	8,936	15.2%	-1.7%	9,494	16.9%	Lab
Arnall, W J (Grn)	747	1.3%	-0.4%	947	1.7%	Grn
Curphey, S (NLP)	203	0.3%		157	0.3%	ICN
C to LD swing 4.0%	58,735		18.4%	56,253		26.5%
		C maj	10,805		C maj	14,891

Julian Brazier became PPS in 1990 to Gillian Shephard, Minr of State, Treasury, and now Employment Sec. Elected in 1987. Jt sec, all-pty parly maritime gp, 1987-90; jt sec, then vice-chmn, Cons back-bench defence cmte, 1988-90. Former project manager with HB Maynard, international management consultants; was sec, exec cmte of bd of Charter Consolidated plc. Fought Berwick-upon-Tweed 1983. B Jul 24 1953; ed Wellington Coll, Berkshire; Brasenose Coll, Oxford. Chmn (1974) and former treas, univ Cons assocn. Serving officer in 5 (HSF) Company, 10th Battalion, Parachute Regt.

Martin Vye, schoolmaster; mbr, Kent CC, 1989- ; chmn, Canterbury L and then LD assocn. B Dec 8 1936; ed Kingston GS; Christ's Coll, Cambridge.

Fred Whitemore, univ lecturer; mbr, Canterbury Cl, 1972-4 and 1983-91. B Feb 20 1941; ed Worcester and Nuffield Colls, Oxford. AUT (former local assocn pres).

Wendy Arnall, sessional lecturer. B Dec 3 1937; ed Nat Art Sch, Sydney, Australia; Sittingbourne Coll of Ed.

CARDIFF CENTRAL						**Lab gain**
Electorate % Turnout	57,716	74.4%	1992	52,980	77.6%	1987
Owen Jones, J (Lab)	18,014	42.0%	+9.7%	15,241	37.1%	C
*Grist, I (C)	14,549	33.9%	-3.2%	13,255	32.3%	Lab
Randerson, Mrs J E (LD)	9,170	21.4%	-8.0%	12,062	29.4%	L/All
Marshall, H (PC)	748	1.7%	+0.4%	535	1.3%	PC
von Ruhland, C (Grn)	330	0.8%				
Francis, B (NLP)	105	0.2%				
C to Lab swing 6.5%	42,916		8.1%	41,093		4.8%
		Lab maj	3,465		C maj	1,986

Jonathan Owen Jones, teacher, won this seat in 1992; contested it 1987. Mbr, Cardiff city cl, 1987- (vice-chmn, finance cmte). Pres, Campaign for Welsh Assembly. B Apr 19 1954; ed Ysgol Gyfun Rhydfelin; Norwich Univ; Univ Coll, Cardiff. Pres, Mid-Glamorgan NUT, 1986.
Ian Grist, who lost the seat, was Under Sec of State for Wales, 1987-90. Chmn, Welsh Cons MPs, 1990- ; mbr, select cmte on MPs interests, 1984-7; select cmte for Welsh Affairs, 1981-3 and 1986-7. Elected for this seat 1983; MP for Cardiff N, Feb 1974-83; contested Aberavon, 1970. B Dec 5 1938; ed Repton; Jesus Coll, Oxford. Mbr, Ct of Governors, Univ of Wales, since 1983; Univ of Wales Inst of Science and Tech, since 1983; Cons anti-hunt cl. Chmn,

Cons west African affairs cmte, 1978-87 and 1991- .
Jenny Randerson, further ed lecturer, contested Cardiff S and Penarth 1987. Vice-chmn (previously chmn), Welsh LDs, 1989- ; environment spokesperson, Welsh LDs. Mbr, Cardiff city cl 1983- . B May 26 1948; ed Wimbledon HS; Bedford Coll; Inst of Ed, London Univ. NATFHE.
Huw Marshall is a TV producer and director of TV production company. B Feb 28 1969; ed Ysgol Morgan Llwyd, Wrexham.
Christopher von Ruhland, research technician. B Aug 2 1962; Haydn Comp, Northwood; NE Surrey Coll of Tech; Plymouth Poly; S Glamorgan Inst of HE.

CARDIFF NORTH						**No change**
Electorate % Turnout	56,721	84.2%	1992	54,704	81.0%	1987
*Jones, G H (C)	21,547	45.1%	-0.1%	20,061	45.3%	C
Morgan, Ms J (Lab)	18,578	38.9%	+12.2%	11,827	26.7%	Lab
Warlow, Ms E (LD)	6,487	13.6%	-12.9%	11,725	26.5%	SDP/All
Bush, Ms E M (PC)	916	1.9%	+0.4%	692	1.6%	PC
Morse, J (BNP)	121	0.3%				
Palmer, D (NLP)	86	0.2%				
C to Lab swing 6.2%	47,735		6.2%	44,305		18.6%
		C maj	2,969		C maj	8,234

Gwilym Jones was appointed under secretary, Welsh Office, 1992. Former insurance broker and director, Bowring Wales Ltd. Elected in 1983. Mbr select cmte on Welsh affairs, 1983- ; Cardiff city cl, 1969-72 and 1973-83. B 1947; ed London and S Wales. Vice-pres, Kidney Research Unit for Wales Foundation, 1986- ; founder chmn, Friendship Force in Wales, 1978-81. Sec, Welsh Cons MPs, 1984-92; jt sec, all-pty gp for Replacement of Animals in Medical Experiments, 1987-92.

Julie Morgan, social worker; mbr, S Glamorgan CC (chmn, women's cmte). B Nov 2 1944; ed London, Manchester and Cardiff Univs. TGWU.
Eve Warlow, teacher; chmn, Cardiff N LD; mbr, Welsh LD exec and policy cmtes. B Jun 15 1947; ed Jordanhill Teachers Training Coll, Glasgow.
Eluned Bush, careers adviser, contested this seat 1987. B Mar 10 1944; ed Ferndale GS; Exeter and Reading Univs; Univ of Wales. Nalgo.

CARDIFF SOUTH AND PENARTH						**No change**
Electorate % Turnout	61,484	77.3%	1992	58,714	76.4%	1987
*Michael, A E (Lab)	26,383	55.5%	+8.8%	20,956	46.7%	Lab
Hunter Jarvie, T (C)	15,958	33.6%	-2.9%	16,382	36.5%	C
Verma, P (LD)	3,707	7.8%	-7.6%	6,900	15.4%	L/All
Anglezarke, Ms B (PC)	776	1.6%	+0.3%	599	1.3%	PC
Davey, L (Grn)	676	1.4%				
C to Lab swing 5.9%	47,500		21.9%	44,837		10.2%
		Lab maj	10,425		Lab maj	4,574

Alun Michael became an Opposn spokesman on Wales in 1988; political coordinator for Vale of Glamorgan (1989), Neath and Monmouth (1991) by-elections. Elected in 1987; Opposn whip, 1987-8. Chmn, Co-op gp of MPs, 1990- . Area community ed officer, Grangetown and Butetown, 1984-7; youth and community worker, Cardiff, 1972-84. Mbr, Cardiff city cl, 1973-89. B Aug 22 1943; ed Colwyn Bay GS; Keele Univ. Sponsored by Co-op pty.
Thomas Hunter Jarvie, self-employed solicitor. Mbr, bd, Cardiff Bay Development Cmte, 1991- . Former dep chmn, Vale of Glamorgan Cons Assocn. Mbr, Vale of Glamorgan

BC, 1982- (mayor, 1988); pres, Bridgend district law society, 1986. B 1944; ed Ilfield GS, Crawley; Birmingham Univ.
Prabhat Verma, mining engineer, contested Merthyr Tydfil and Rhymney 1987 and S Wales in 1989 Euro elections. B Nov 15 1941; ed Univ of Wales. Co-opted mbr, Wales Cl for Voluntary Action.
Barbara Anglezarke, housing development officer working with special needs housing assocn based in Cardiff. B Jun 4 1959; ed Univ Coll, Cardiff.

CARDIFF WEST						No change
Electorate % Turnout	58,898	77.6%	1992	57,363	77.8%	1987
*Morgan, H R (Lab)	24,306	53.2%	+7.7%	20,329	45.5%	Lab
Prior, M (C)	15,015	32.9%	-3.6%	16,284	36.5%	C
Gasson, Ms J (LD)	5,002	10.9%	-5.4%	7,300	16.3%	SDP/All
Bestic, Ms P (PC)	1,177	2.6%	+0.9%	736	1.6%	PC
Harding, A (NLP)	184	0.4%				
C to Lab swing 5.6%	45,684		20.3%	44,649		9.1%
		Lab maj	9,291		Lab maj	4,045

Rhodri Morgan, industrial analyst, became an Opposn spokesman on energy in 1988; mbr select cmte on energy, 1987-9; select cmte on members' interests, 1987-9. Elected in 1987. Jt chmn, all-pty dolphins parly gp, 1989- . Head of bureau for press and information, EC commission office for Wales, 1980-7; adviser to Lab pty economic planning cmtes in Wales; economic development officer for S Glamorgan CC, 1974-80; economic adviser, DTI, 1972-4; research officer, Cardiff City Cl, Welsh Office and DoE, 1965-71; tutor organiser, S Wales area WEA, 1963-5. B Sep 29 1939; ed state schs in Cardiff; St John's Coll, Oxford; Harvard Univ. TGWU.
Michael Prior, solicitor; partner with Morgan Bruce,

Cardiff, 1985- . Mbr (Vale of Glamorgan NE Ward), S Glamorgan CC, 1989- ; Community cllr for Wenvoe, 1977-91. Chmn, Welsh Cons candidates gp, 1991- . B May 6 1955; ed St George's Coll, Weybridge; Durham Univ.
Jacqui Gasson, voluntary community advice worker; mbr, Cardiff City Cl, 1988- ; S Glamorgan CC, 1989- ; Cardiff CHC. Vice-chmn, Cardiff W LDs. B Mar 15 1938; Univ of Wales Inst of Science and Tech; Univ Coll, Cardiff.
Penni Bestic, graphic designer based in Cardiff; mbr, design and photographjy co-operative, Argraff; PC policy director on employment. B May 4 1953; ed in Johannesburg; W Sussex Coll of Art and Design.

CARLISLE						No change
Electorate % Turnout	55,140	79.4%	1992	55,053	78.8%	1987
*Martlew, E A (Lab)	20,479	46.8%	+4.5%	18,311	42.2%	Lab
Condie, C W (C)	17,371	39.7%	-0.4%	17,395	40.1%	C
Aldersey, R E (LD)	5,740	13.1%	-4.5%	7,655	17.7%	SDP/All
Robinson, Ms N (NLP)	190	0.4%				
C to Lab swing 2.5%	43,780		7.1%	43,361		2.1%
		Lab maj	3,108		Lab maj	916

Eric Martlew was elected in 1987 when he became mbr select cmte on agriculture; vice-chmn, PLP agriculture cmte, 1987- . With Nestle Co Ltd, 1966-87, joining as laboratory technician, later becoming personnel manager, Dalston factory, Carlisle. Former unpaid director, Inward, promotion organisation for NW England. Chmn, Carlisle CLP, 1980-5; mbr, Cumbria CC, 1973-87 (chmn, 1983-85); East Cumbria HA, 1981-7; Cumbria AHA, 1975-81 (chmn, 1977-9); Carlisle City Cl, 1972-4. B Jan 3 1949; ed Harraby Sec Sch, Carlisle; Carlisle Tech Coll. Sponsored by TGWU.
Clive Condie, senior manager (development) with responsi-

bility for expansion of Manchester airport, contested Rochdale 1987; previously project manager at airport; planning asst and asst projects officer for former Manchester international airport authority. B Jul 19 1960; ed Hulme Hall Sch; Cheadle Hulme Sch; Stirling Univ. Treas, Hazel Grove Cons Assocn, 1988-91; chmn, Hazel Grove YCs, 1986-7; vice-chmn and treas, High Lane Cons Assocn, 1985-7.
Ralph Aldersey, British Rail carriage and wagon electrician; mbr, Cumbria CC, 1981- ; Carlisle DC, 1983- . B Sep 25 1940; ed Carlisle Tech Coll. EEPTU, former shop steward.

CARMARTHEN						No change
Electorate % Turnout	68,887	82.7%	1992	65,252	82.9%	1987
*Williams, A W (Lab)	20,879	36.6%	+1.3%	19,128	35.4%	Lab
Glyn Thomas, R (PC)	17,957	31.5%	+8.5%	14,811	27.4%	C
Cavenagh, S J (C)	12,782	22.4%	-5.0%	12,457	23.0%	PC
Hughes, Mrs J M (LD)	5,353	9.4%	-3.9%	7,203	13.3%	SDP/All
				481	0.9%	Grn
Lab to PC swing 3.6%	56,971		5.1%	54,080		8.0%
		Lab maj	2,922		Lab maj	4,317

Alan W Williams was elected in 1987 and became mbr, select cmte on Welsh affairs and jt select cmte on consolidation bills. Jt vice-chmn, PLP environment cmte, 1990- . Senior lecturer in environmental science, Trinity Coll, Carmarthen, 1971-87. B Dec 21 1945; ed Carmarthen GS; Jesus Coll, Oxford. Sec, Carmarthen Lab Pty, 1981-4; election agent, 1983. NATFHE.
Rhodri Glyn Thomas, director of TV production company; PC spokesperson on ed. B Apr 11 1953; ed Univs of Wales,

Aberstwyth, Bangor and Lampeter.
Stephen Cavenagh, farmer. Mbr, NFU, sitting on Carmarthen county milk, parliamentary, legal and executive cmtes; chmn, local NFU branch; former chmn, local Young Farmers' club. B 1964; ed Malvern Coll.
Juliana Hughes, house manager; previously teacher. Been chmn and sec, Carmarthen pty. JP Carmarthen S bench. Hon mbr, Nat Eisteddfod Bardic Gorsedd. B Nov 30 1944; ed Llanelli Girls' GS; UCW, Aberystwyth.

CARRICK, CUMNOCK AND DOON VALLEY				No change		
Electorate % Turnout	55,330	76.9%	1992	56,360	75.8%	1987
*Foulkes, G (Lab)	25,142	59.1%	-1.0%	25,669	60.1%	Lab
Boswell, J A D (C)	8,516	20.0%	-0.7%	8,867	20.7%	C
Douglas, C E (SNP)	6,910	16.2%	+6.7%	4,106	9.6%	SDP/All
Paris, Ms M (LD)	2,005	4.7%	-4.9%	4,094	9.6%	SNP
Lab to C swing 0.1%	42,573		39.1%	42,736		39.3%
		Lab maj	16,626		Lab maj	16,802

George Foulkes, an Opposition spokesman on foreign and Commonwealth affairs, 1985- ; on European and community affairs, 1983-5. Jt vice-chmn (1990-1) and mbr (1987-90 and 1991-), exec cmte, UK branch, CPA; mbr, exec cmte, British gp, IPU, 1989- ; cl, parliamentarians for global action, 1987- ; exec, British-China centre, 1987- . Director, Co-operative Press Ltd. Chmn, all-pty low flying parly gp; jt chmn, release of hostages gp; pensioners' gp, 1983- , and sec-treas, 1979-83; vice-chmn, British-Canadian gp; jt vice-chmn, Action on Smoking and Health (ASH) Gp. Chmn, John Wheatley Centre. Won this seat 1983; MP for S Ayrshire, 1979-83; contested Edinburgh, Pentlands, Oct 1974, and Edinburgh W, 1970. B Jan 21 1942; ed Keith GS, Banffshire; Haberdashers' Aske's Sch; Edinburgh Univ. Apex. Sponsored by Co-op Pty.

James Boswell, director of leisure development company and of Auchinleck Estate; farmer. B Oct 1 1945; ed Ardvreck, Perthshire; Blanerne, Borders; Fettes Coll, Edinburgh.

Charles Douglas, lecturer in finance and accounting; mbr, management cmte, of nature reserve. B Aug 10 1935.

Mary Paris, snr counsellor, Open Univ. Chmn, Glasgow Hillhead, 1986-91. B Nov 17 1942; ed Oxford, London, Glasgow and Strathclyde Univs.

CARSHALTON AND WALLINGTON				No change		
Electorate % Turnout	65,179	80.9%	1992	69,120	75.0%	1987
*Forman, F N (C)	26,243	49.7%	-4.2%	27,984	54.0%	C
Brake, T A (LD)	16,300	30.9%	+4.7%	13,575	26.2%	SDP/All
Moran, Ms M (Lab)	9,333	17.7%	-0.5%	9,440	18.2%	Lab
Steel, R W (Grn)	614	1.2%	-0.5%	843	1.6%	Grn
Bamford, D (Loony G)	266	0.5%				
C to LD swing 4.5%	52,756		18.8%	51,842		27.8%
		C maj	9,943		C maj	14,409

Nigel Forman became an Under Sec of State for Education in 1992. Mbr select cmte on foreign affairs, 1990-2. PPS to Nigel Lawson, Chancellor of the Exchequer, 1987-9; to Lord Privy Seal, 1979-81, and to Minr of State, FCO, 1979-83. Elected in 1983; MP for Sutton, Carshalton, 1976-83; contested Coventry NE, Feb 1974. Was consultant to Kleinwort Benson Securities; Merck, Sharp and Dohme; Alexander Consulting Gp; Newton Investment Management Ltd. Mbr economic and social research cl; hon treas, Federal Trust. Vice-chmn, all-pty social science and policy cmte, 1984-92. B Mar 25 1943; ed Dragon Sch, Oxford; Shrewsbury Sch; New Coll, Oxford; Coll of Europe, Bruges; Harvard and Sussex Univs. Hon chmn, governing body, Gt Britain-E Europe Centre.

Tom Brake, computer consultant; mbr, Hackney BC, 1988-91; transport speaker for London region LDs; on LD environment policy working gp. B May 6 1962; ed Lycee International, France; Imperial Coll, London.

Margaret Moran, housing assocn director; mbr, Lewisham BC, 1984- (chmn, housing cmte, 1985-91; direct labour cmte, 1991-). Chmn, London housing unit; vice-chmn, AMA housing cmte. B Apl 24 1955; ed Birmingham Univ. TGWU.

Bob Steel, teacher; chmn, Sutton Grn Pty; contested seat 1987 and 1983. B Jan 31 1955; ed John Fisher Sch, Purley; Southampton and Nottingham Univs. NAS/UWT.

CASTLE POINT				No change		
Electorate % Turnout	66,229	80.5%	1992	65,992	75.1%	1987
Spink, Dr R M (C)	29,629	55.6%	-4.3%	29,681	59.9%	C
Flack, D (Lab)	12,799	24.0%	+5.0%	10,433	21.1%	SDP/All
Petchey, A R K (LD)	10,208	19.1%	-1.9%	9,422	19.0%	Lab
Willis, Ms I L (Grn)	683	1.3%				
C to Lab swing 4.7%	53,319		31.6%	49,536		38.9%
		C maj	16,830		C maj	19,248

Robert Spink, engineer; management consultant since 1984, was elected in 1992. Director, Bournemouth international airport plc, 1989- ; director and co-owner, Seafarer Navigation International Ltd, 1980-4; engineer with EMI Electronics Ltd, 1966-77; started as textile mill labourer, 1962-4. Mbr, Dorset CC, 1985- (chmn, ed policy sub-cmte, 1989-); Dorset police authority, 1985- . Dep chmn, Poole Cons Assocn, 1984- ; pres, Canford Heath branch. B Aug 1 1948; ed Holycroft sec mod sch, Keighley; Manchester Univ; Cranfield. Mbr, NEC, Bliss (charity).

David Flack, teacher; chmn, Rochford CLP; mbr, Rochford DC, 1986- (gp ldr); Essex CC, 1989- . Chmn, Southend Community Health Cl. B May 29 1948; ed NE London Poly. NUT.

Allan Petchey, health service internal auditor. Mbr, Essex CC, 1985-9. B Jun 20 1961; ed Fairfax HS, Westcliff-on-Sea, Essex. CPSA, 1978-86.

Irene Willis, teacher. Convenor, decentralist working gp, Grn Pty; Castle Pt Grn Pty; Essex and Anglia coordinator. B Feb 24 1945; ed Southend HS for Girls; Avery Hill Coll. NUT.

CEREDIGION AND PEMBROKE NORTH						PC gain
Electorate % Turnout	66,180	77.4%	1992	63,141	76.5%	1987
Dafis, C G (PC)	16,020	31.3%	+15.0%	17,683	36.6%	L/All
*Howells, G W (LD)	12,827	25.1%	-11.6%	12,983	26.9%	C
Williams, O J (C)	12,718	24.8%	-2.0%	8,965	18.6%	Lab
Davies, J R (Lab)	9,637	18.8%	+0.3%	7,848	16.2%	PC
				821	1.7%	Grn
LD to PC swing 13.3%	51,202		6.2%	48,300		9.7%
		PC maj	3,193		L/All maj	4,700

Cynog Dafis won this seat in 1992; contested this seat 1987 and 1983. A researcher, ed dept, Univ Coll, Swansea; former comprehensive sch teacher; PC speaker on agriculture and environment. Editor of *Ddraig Goch*, monthly newspaper. B Apr 1 1938; ed Aberavon Cty Sec Sch; Neath Boys' GS; UCW Aberystwyth.

Geraint Howells, farmer, was ldr, Welsh Lib pty, 1979-88 (Pres, 1974-8). Chmn, Lib by-election unit, 1987-8. Alliance spokesman on Wales in 1987 election; Lib spokesman on agriculture, 1976-85, and Wales, 1976-87; Lib and then LD spokesman on agriculture, 1987-92. Elected as L/All MP for this seat 1983; Lib MP for Cardigan, 1974-83; contested Brecon and Radnor, 1970. Mbr, Commons Chairmen's Panel, 1987-92; Commons

accommodation and works cmte, 1991-2; Commons Services Cmte, 1987-91; Select Cmte on Welsh Affairs, 1979-87. B Apr 15 1925; ed Ardwyn GS. Mbr, Cardiganshire CC, 1952-73. Chmn, Wool Producers of Wales Ltd, 1977- ; sec, Ponterwyd Eisteddfod, 1944- .

John Williams, barrister, chmn of family business and company director, contested Mid and West Wales in 1989 Euro elections and this seat in 1987. A non-exec director, East Dyfed HA. B May 17 1950; ed Ysgol Abermad, Aberystwyth; Harrow; Univ Coll, Oxford.

John Davies, teacher, contested seat 1987. Mbr, Walsall TC, 1970-4. B Jun 23 1937; ed Gwendraeth GS, Llanelli; St Luke's Coll, Exeter. NUT; mbr, Wales Advisory Cl (Secondary).

CHEADLE						No change
Electorate % Turnout	66,131	84.4%	1992	68,332	81.0%	1987
*Day, S R (C)	32,504	58.2%	+3.2%	30,484	55.1%	C
Calton, Mrs P (LD)	16,726	30.0%	-5.9%	19,853	35.9%	L/All
Broadhurst, Ms S (Lab)	6,442	11.5%	+2.4%	5,037	9.1%	Lab
Whittle, Ms P (NLP)	168	0.3%				
LD to C swing 4.5%	55,840		28.3%	55,374		19.2%
		C maj	15,778		C maj	10,631

Stephen Day was elected in 1987; contested Bradford W 1983. Appointed mbr, Select Cmte on Social Security, in 1991; jt sec, Cons backbench health cmte, 1991- . Parly consultant to Nalgo. Jt-chmn, parly advisory cl for transport safety, 1989- . Sales executive with Photographic Laboratories Ltd, Leeds, 1986-7; with PPL Chromacopy, photographic labs, Leeds and Manchester, 1984-6. Mbr, Otley TC, 1975-6 and 1979-83; Leeds City Cl, 1975-80. B Oct 30 1948; ed Otley sec mod sch; Park Lane Coll, Leeds; Leeds Poly. Vice-pres, Stockport Chamber of Commerce,

1987- .

Patsy Calton, teacher (head of chemistry); chairman, Bramhall LDs; LEA governor. B Sep 19 1948; ed Wymondham Coll, Norfolk; Umist.

Sandra Broadhurst, teacher; mbr, Stockport MBC, 1987- (speaker on leisure services). Past chairman, Heaton Mersey branch; delegate to Stockport CLP; past political ed officer for constituency. B May 28 1946; ed Surrey Univ. NUT since 1969. Sch rep and past chairman of Manchester Teachers Association's special schools section.

CHELMSFORD						No change
Electorate % Turnout	83,441	84.6%	1992	82,564	82.2%	1987
*Burns, S H M (C)	39,043	55.3%	+3.4%	35,231	51.9%	C
Nicholson, H P (LD)	20,783	29.4%	-11.1%	27,470	40.5%	L/All
Chad, Dr R K (Lab)	10,010	14.2%	+7.3%	4,642	6.8%	Lab
Burgess, E (Grn)	769	1.1%	+0.4%	486	0.7%	Grn
LD to C swing 7.2%	70,605		25.9%	67,829		11.4%
		C maj	18,260		C maj	7,761

Simon Burns was elected in 1987; contested Alyn and Deeside 1983. PPS to Tim Eggar, Minr of State for Employment, for Ed and Science and then for Trade and Industry, 1989- ; director, What to Buy Ltd, 1981-3; political adviser to Sally Oppenheim, MP, 1975-81. B Sep 6 1952; ed Christ the King Sch, Accra, Ghana; Stamford Sch; Worcester Coll, Oxford (sec, univ Cons assocn, 1972-5).

Hugh Nicholson, chartered accountant and pension fund manager with ICI plc. Contested Ipswichin 1987. Treas,

NW Essex SDP, 1982-5; mbr, working pty on tax and benefits, 1985-6. Mbr, Northampton BC, 1968-71; Redbridge BC, 1974-5. B Jun 2 1941; ed Northampton Town and Cty GS.

Dr Roy Chad, consultant psychiatrist. Pty offices held: vice-chairman, Chelmsford CLP; district Lab pty chairman, Chelmsford; also in Tottenham CLP. B Nov 4 1950; ed Holland Park comprehensive sch; Birmingham Univ medical sch. MPU/MFS.

CHELSEA						No change
Electorate % Turnout	42,371	63.3%	1992	49,534	57.7%	1987
*Scott, N P (C)	17,471	65.1%	+0.5%	18,443	64.6%	C
Horton, Ms R E (Lab)	4,682	17.5%	+2.0%	5,124	17.9%	L/All
Broidy, Mrs S N (LD)	4,101	15.3%	-2.7%	4,406	15.4%	Lab
Kortvelyessy, Ms N (Grn)	485	1.8%	-0.2%	587	2.1%	Grn
Armstrong, D (Anti-Fed)	88	0.3%				
C to Lab swing 0.7%	26,827		47.7%	28,560		46.6%
		C maj	12,789		C maj	13,319

Nicholas Scott became Minr of State for Social Security and Minr for Disabled People at Dept of Social Security, in 1988 when DHSS was split into two; Minr for Social Security (with rank of Minr of State) and Minr for Disabled, at DHSS, 1987-8; Minr of State for N Ireland, 1986-7; Under Sec of State for N Ireland, 1981-6; Under Sec of State for Employment, Jan-Feb 1974. PC 1989. Mbr, shadow Cabinet and chief Opposn spokesman on housing, 1974. Elected for this seat, Oct 1974; MP for Paddington S, 1966-74; contested Paddington, Feb 1974; Islington SW, 1964 and 1959. B Aug 5 1933; ed Clapham Coll. Pres, Tory Reform Gp. Mbr, Holborn BC, 1956-9 and 1962-5. Freeman, City of London, 1979; Liveryman, Guild of Air Pilots and Navigators, 1988- .

Rima Horton, snr lecturer in economics; mbr, Kensington and Chelsea BC, 1984- (chief whip, Lab gp and spokesperson on ed). B Jan 31 1947; ed City of London Sch for Girls; Southampton Univ; LSE. NATFHE.
Susan Broidy, writer/activist; mbr, exec cmte, Chelsea LDs. B Dec 25 1940; ed Suva Girls GS, Fiji; London Univ, Westfield and Univ coll. Sec, S Kensington Assocn of Traders.
Niki Kortvelyessy, self-employed designer, contested this seat 1987 and London Central in 1989 Euro elections. Grn Pty speaker on international affairs; convenor of Grn international cmte. B May 10 1947 in Budapest; ed Victoria Univ, Wellington, New Zealand.

CHELTENHAM						LD gain
Electorate % Turnout	79,808	80.3%	1992	79,234	78.9%	1987
Jones, N D (LD)	30,351	47.3%	+5.0%	31,371	50.2%	C
Taylor, J D B (C)	28,683	44.7%	-5.4%	26,475	42.3%	L/All
Tatlow, Ms P R (Lab)	4,077	6.4%	-1.2%	4,701	7.5%	Lab
Rendall, M (AFE)	665	1.0%				
Brighouse, H (NLP)	169	0.3%				
Bruce-Smith, M (Ind)	162	0.3%				
C to LD swing 5.2%	64,107		2.6%	62,547		7.8%
		LD maj	1,668		C maj	4,896

Nigel Jones, computer consultant with International Computers, won this seat in 1992. Mbr for Cheltenham Park, Gloucestershire CC, 1989- (vice-chairman, public protection cmte, 1990-91). Contested seat 1979. B Mar 30 1948; ed Prince Henry's GS, Evesham. Mbr, Swindon Town FC; Friends of the Earth.
John Taylor, adviser on immigration at Home Office until 1990; barrister, being selected for DPP's list in 1985; former lecturer and professional cricketer. Contested Birmingham Perry Barr in 1987. Elected secretary of the

Nat Cons Parly Candidates' Assocn in 1986; mbr, Solihull DC, 1985- . B Sep 21 1952; ed Moseley GS, Birmingham; Keele Univ; Inns of Court Sch of Law. Mbr, One Nation Forum.
Pam Tatlow, lecturer, contested Bristol W 1983. Mbr, Lab Pty NEC women's cmte, 1990- ; chairman, regional women's cmte, 1990- ; mbr, SW regional exec cmte, 1990- . On Bristol City Cl, 1983-91. B Jul 13 1950; ed Tynemouth HS. TGWU

CHERTSEY AND WALTON						No change
Electorate % Turnout	70,465	80.5%	1992	71,448	75.5%	1987
*Pattie, G E (C)	34,164	60.2%	+0.7%	32,119	59.5%	C
Kremer, A (LD)	11,344	20.0%	-7.2%	14,650	27.2%	SDP/All
Hamilton, Ms I (Lab)	10,793	19.0%	+5.7%	7,185	13.3%	Lab
Bennell, S (NLP)	444	0.8%				
LD to C swing 3.9%	56,745		40.2%	53,954		32.4%
		C maj	22,820		C maj	17,469

Sir Geoffrey Pattie was appointed a vice-chmn, Cons Pty, in 1990 with responsibility for liaising with other centre-right parties in Europe and emerging democracies in Eastern Europe. Mbr, Select Cmte on Social Services, 1989-90. Minr for Information Technology, with rank of Minr of State, DTI, 1984-87; Minr of State for Defence Procurement, 1983-4; Under Sec of State for Defence Procurement, 1981-3; Under Sec of State for Defence for RAF, 1979-81. PC 1987. Jt-chmn, GEC-Marconi, 1991- (chmn 1990-1); chmn, CDP Nexus; non-exec director, Fairy Gp Ltd; Leica plc (formerly Cambridge Instruments

Co plc), 1988- ; Carroll Gp; partner, Terrington Management. Elected in 1974; contested Barking, 1966 and 1970. Jt dep chmn, 1991- , and treas (1988-91), Parly and Scientific Cmte, 1988- . B Jan 17 1936; ed Durham sch; St Catharine's Coll, Cambridge. Barrister.
Tony Kremer, specialist in European business; former mbr, Woking Cl. Ed London Univ.
Irene Hamilton, researcher and advice worker for city centre project (voluntary sector). Mbr, Elmbridge BC, 1984- (dep ldr, Lab gp). B May 15 1941; ed Bloomfield Collegiate Sch, Belfast. TGWU/ACTSS.

CHESHAM AND AMERSHAM						No change
Electorate % Turnout	69,895	81.9%	1992	71,751	77.3%	1987
Gillan, Mrs C E K (C)	36,273	63.3%	+1.2%	34,504	62.2%	C
Ketteringham, A T (LD)	14,053	24.5%	-2.6%	15,064	27.1%	L/All
Atherton, Ms C (Lab)	5,931	10.4%	+1.0%	5,170	9.3%	Lab
Strickland, Ms C (Grn)	753	1.3%	-0.1%	760	1.4%	Grn
Griffith-Jones, T (NLP)	255	0.4%				
LD to C swing 1.9%	57,265		38.8%	55,498		35.0%
		C maj	22,220		C maj	19,440

Cheryl Gillan, marketing director, Kidsons Impey, chartered accountants, 1991- , contested Gtr Manchester Central in 1989 Euro elections. Former snr marketing consultant, Ernst and Young, chartered accountants and management consultants. Former special events director, British Film Year; previously with International Management Gp. Chmn, Bow Gp, 1987-8 (sec, 1986-7); sec, political standing cmte, Bow Gp, 1989-91; managing director, Bow Functions Ltd, 1984-6. Founder mbr, Families for Defence. B Apr 21 1952; ed Cheltenham Ladies Coll; Coll of Law. Mbr, Inst of Public Relations and Chartered Inst of Marketing. Ex-mbr, LSO chorus.

Andrew Ketteringham, public affairs director for banking and insurance gp, contested this seat 1987; Brent N, 1979; London NW 1984 Euro election. Mbr, Chesham TC, 1982- . B Jul 15 1950; ed Lascelles Sec Mod Sch; Harrow Cty Boys' Sch; Hull univ.

Candy Atherton, journalist; partner in press agency. Mbr, Islington BC, 1986-91; Islington HA, 1986-90. B Sep 21 1955; ed Sutton HS; Midhurst GS; N London Poly. NUJ.

CHESTER, CITY OF						No change
Electorate % Turnout	63,370	83.8%	1992	65,845	79.8%	1987
Brandreth, G D (C)	23,411	44.1%	-0.8%	23,582	44.9%	C
Robinson, D (Lab)	22,310	42.0%	+6.4%	18,727	35.6%	Lab
Smith, J G (LD)	6,867	12.9%	-6.6%	10,262	19.5%	L/All
Barker, T (Grn)	448	0.8%				
Cross, S (NLP)	98	0.2%				
C to Lab swing 3.6%	53,134		2.1%	52,571		9.2%
		C maj	1,101		C maj	4,855

Gyles Brandreth, author and broadcaster, became chmn, Victorama Ltd in 1974 and of Complete Editions Ltd, in 1988; director, Newarke Wools Ltd, 1988- , and J W Spear and Sons plc 1990- . Chmn, Nat Playing Fields Assocn, 1989- , and of its appeals cmte, 1983-9. Freelance journalist since 1968; broadcaster from 1969, TV-am presenter from 1983. Author of over 100 books. Record holder for longest after-dinner speech, lasting 12hrs 30mins in 1982. B Mar 8 1948; ed Lycee Francais de Londres; Betteshanger Sch, Kent; Bedales Sch; New Coll, Oxford (Pres of union).

David Robinson, teacher, contested this seat 1987. Mbr, Chester City Cl, 1979- (Lab ldr, 1989-90; chmn, highways cmte, 1990-1). B Sep 19 1946; ed Bede Coll, Durham; Sheffield Poly. NUT.

Gordon Smith, civil engineer, contested Shropshire N 1987. Sheriff of Chester, 1986-7; mbr, Chester City Cl, 1978- . B Dec 14 1941; ed Bury GS; Leeds Univ. Nalgo.

Tom Barker, coordinator of alternative tech assocn. B Nov 5 1955. Chester Grn pty officer.

CHESTERFIELD		·				No change
Electorate % Turnout	71,783	78.0%	1992	70,357	76.7%	1987
*Benn, A N W (Lab)	26,461	47.3%	+1.8%	24,532	45.5%	Lab
Rogers, A H (LD)	20,047	35.8%	+6.2%	15,955	29.6%	L/All
Lewis, P G (C)	9,473	16.9%	-8.0%	13,472	25.0%	C
Lab to LD swing 2.2%	55,981		11.5%	53,959		15.9%
		Lab maj	6,414		Lab maj	8,577

Tony Benn, writer and broadcaster, unsuccessfully contested Labour leadership against Neil Kinnock, 1988. Elected for this seat by-election in 1984. Contested dep leadership of Lab pty, 1981; candidate for party ldr, 1976, and for dep ldr, 1971. Mbr, Privileges Cmte, 1984-7 and 1989- . President, Campaign Gp of Lab MPs, 1987- . Energy sec., 1975-9; Industry sec. and Minr for Posts and Telecommunications, 1974-5; Minr of Technology, 1966-70; Postmaster-General, 1964-6. PC 1964. MP for Bristol SE, 1950-60 and 1963-83, when he contested Bristol E. Debarred from Commons on death of his father, Viscount Stansgate, in Nov 1960, he won by-election in May 1961, but Election Court declared his Cons opponent elected. Renounced title under the Peerage Act; re-elected in Aug 1963. Mbr, Lab Party NEC, 1959-60 and since 1962; chmn, 1971-2. B Apr 3 1925; ed Westminster; New Coll, Oxford. Four hon doctorates from British and US univs. Author of 14 books on politics, including Benn Diaries, 1963-80. NUJ and TGWEU; hon mbr, NUM, GMB and Sogat.

Tony Rogers, food shops businessman; landlord; contested seat 1987, S Hams 1983, Totnes 1979 and twice in 1974. B Apr 9 1938; ed Kingsbridge Sec Mod Sch. Mbr, Kingsbridge UDC, 1963-74; then on Kingsbridge TC and South Hams DC (former mayor).

Peter Lewis, lecturer in English, Loughborough Univ, since 1977; Visiting Professor, State Univ of New York, 1980-1. B Mar 2 1942; ed Taunton's Sch, Southampton; Nottingham Univ. Mbr, nat union exec, 1988-90; hon sec, nat advisory cmte on ed, 1988-90; vice-chmn, Loughborough Cons Assocn, 1990- ; Leicester Cons Euro Cl, 1990- . AUT.

CHICHESTER					No change	
Electorate % Turnout	82,124	77.8%	1992	81,019	74.4%	1987
*Nelson, R A (C)	37,906	59.3%	-2.5%	37,274	61.8%	C
Gardiner, Dr P (LD)	17,019	26.6%	-1.7%	17,097	28.3%	L/All
Andrewes, Mrs D M (Lab)	7,192	11.3%	+3.4%	4,751	7.9%	Lab
Paine, E (Grn)	876	1.4%	-0.6%	1,196	2.0%	Grn
Weights, Ms J (Lib)	643	1.0%				
Jackson, Ms J (NLP)	238	0.4%				
C to LD swing 0.4%	63,874		32.7%	60,318		33.5%
		C maj	20,887		C maj	20,177

Anthony Nelson was appointed economic secretary to the Treasury in 1992. Elected, Oct 1974; contested Leeds E, Feb 1974. Merchant banker; Former consultant to European Investments and Development and to GEC plc; trustee, Business Against Drugs; director, Chichester Festival Theatre Productions and Festival Theatre Trust; Sussex Training (West); Job Training (Sussex); Downs Enterprise Agency. Mbr, Select Cmte on Broadcasting, 1988-91. B Jun 11 1948; ed Harrow; Christ's Coll, Cambridge. FRSA.

Dr Peter Gardiner, professor of civil engineering; mbr, exec cmte, Chichester LD. B Feb 1940; ed Nottingham, Liverpool and Surrey univs.
Diane Andrewes, lecturer and former officer, NATFHE; West Midlands TUC organiser of services for unemployed people. Mbr, SW Hampshire CHC. B Mar 1 1934; ed Rugby HS; Swansea HS; Bristol univ.
Eric Paine, unwaged; hon sec, Thomas Paine Society. B Jun 9 1927; ed in Oxford until 14.

CHINGFORD					No change	
Electorate % Turnout	55,401	78.4%	1992	56,797	76.7%	1987
Duncan-Smith, G I (C)	25,730	59.2%	-3.0%	27,110	62.3%	C
Dawe, P J (Lab)	10,792	24.8%	+9.6%	9,155	21.0%	L/All
Banks, S (LD)	5,705	13.1%	-7.9%	6,650	15.3%	Lab
Green, D (Lib)	602	1.4%		634	1.5%	Grn
Baguley, J (Grn)	575	1.3%	-0.1%			
John, Rev C (Ind)	41	0.1%				
C to Lab swing 6.3%	43,445		34.4%	43,549		41.2%
		C maj	14,938		C maj	17,955

Iain Duncan-Smith elected for this seat in 1992. Contested Bradford W in 1987. Publisher; director, Janes Information Gp; director, Bellwinch plc, a property co, 1988-9; GEC/Marconi, 1981-8; Scots Guards officer 1975-81. Vice-chmn, Fulham Cons assocn, 1991; mbr, Cons Central Office task force; Foreign Affairs Forum. B Apr 9 1954; ed Dunchurch Coll of Management; RMA Sandhurst; Universita di Peruguia, Italy; HMS Conway (cadet sch), Anglesey. Trustee, Lygon Almshouses, sheltered housing, 1985-91.
Peter Dawe, teacher, chmn Christian Socialist Movement since 1983; Methodist local preacher since 1968; mbr, Methodist divisional bd of social responsibility, 1982-88.

Contested Chipping Barnet 1979, Dorset W Oct 1974. B Nov 18 1947; ed Hardye's Sch, Dorchester; Univ Coll and Inst of ERd, London. Mbr GLC 1981-6, Lee Valley park authority, 1981-6; Waltham Forest CHC, 1975-80. NUT.
Simon Banks, health service manager, contested Leyton 1987; Plymouth, Sutton twice, 1974; London NE, 1989 Euro elections. Mbr, Waltham Forest BC, 1982- (ldr, All gp, 1982-87); London LD exec. B Nov 20 1946; ed Welwyn Garden City GS; King's Coll, Cambridge; Bristol Univ. Nalgo.
John Baguley, head of fundraising, Amnesty International; Grn pty cl mbr, 1990-91. B Nov 22 1947; ed Churston Ferrers GS, Devon; NE London Poly; Open Univ. ACTSS.

CHIPPING BARNET					No change	
Electorate % Turnout	57,153	78.6%	1992	60,876	70.0%	1987
*Chapman, S B (C)	25,589	57.0%	-0.9%	24,686	57.9%	C
Williams, A (Lab)	11,638	25.9%	+6.9%	9,815	23.0%	L/All
Smith, D (LD)	7,247	16.1%	-6.9%	8,115	19.0%	Lab
Derksen, Ms D (NLP)	222	0.5%				
Johnson, C (Fun)	213	0.5%				
C to Lab swing 3.9%	44,909		31.1%	42,616		34.9%
		C maj	13,951		C maj	14,871

Sydney Chapman was appointed Vice-Chamberlain of the Household (govt whip) April 1992; a Lord Commissioner of the Treasury 1990-2; asst govt whip, 1988-90. Chartered architect and town and country planning consultant. Mbr, Select Cmtes on Environment, 1983-7, and Commons Services, 1983-7. Elected for this seat 1979; MP for B'ham, Handsworth, 1970-Feb 1974; fought Stalybridge and Hyde, 1964. B Oct 17 1935; ed Rugby; Manchester Univ. Vice-Pres, RIBA, 1974-5; mbr of cl, 1972-7. Hon mbr, Landscape Inst; hon Fellow, Incorporated Assocn of

Architects and Surveyors; Faculty of Building; FRSA.
Alan Williams, building surveyor; mbr, Southwark BC, 1989. B Jun 5 1959; ed Kingsway HS, Chester; Cambs Coll of Arts and Tech; LSE; Imperial Coll. GMB.
David Smith, operational research manager, British Gas; chmn, Chipping Barnet LDs, 1988-90. Mbr, cl, Electoral Reform Society, 1985-86; trustee, Electoral Reform (Ballot Services). B Aug 14 1941; ed King's Sch, Worcester; Trinity Coll, Cambridge; LSE. Coastal skipper, British Gas Seafarers, 1983- ; Thames barge sailor.

CHISLEHURST				No change		
Electorate % Turnout	53,782	78.9%	1992	55,535	75.5%	1987
*Sims, R E (C)	24,761	58.4%	+0.7%	24,165	57.6%	C
Wingfield, Dr R I (Lab)	9,485	22.4%	+3.0%	9,658	23.0%	L/All
Hawthorne, T W M (LD)	6,683	15.8%	-7.3%	8,115	19.3%	Lab
Richmond, I (Lib)	849	2.0%				
Speed, Ms F (Grn)	652	1.5%				
C to Lab swing 1.1%	42,430		36.0%	41,938		34.6%
		C maj	15,276		C maj	14,507

Roger Sims was elected in Feb 1974; contested Shoreditch and Finsbury, 1966 and 1970. Appointed to select cmtes on health and on sittings of Commons, in 1991; select cmtes on social services, 1987-90; ed, science and the arts, 1984-7; procedure, 1980-91. Mbr, Gen Medical Cl, 1989-. Director, Inchcape International, 1981-90; former consultant to Dodwell and Co Ltd for whom he worked as export manager; parly adviser to Scotch Whisky Assocn. B Jan 27 1930; ed City Boys' GS, Leicester; St Olave's GS, London. Jt vice-chmn, Cons backbench health cmte, 1988-, and of health and social services cmte, 1983-8; chmn, ASH parly gp, 1983-90; sec, Gulf families gp, 1991. Mbr, central exec cmte, NSPCC, 1980.

Dr Ian Wingfield, trade union researcher. Mbr, Southwark BC, 1989- (chief whip, Lab gp, since 1990). B Jun 5 1959; ed schs in Chester; Cambridgeshire Coll of Arts and Technology; LSE; Imperial Coll, London. GMB/Apex.

Bill Hawthorne, area training manager; political organiser. B Sep 6 1956; ed Woolwich Poly. Communication Managers' Assocn.

Frances Speed, freelance writer, TV producer and director; mbr, Grn pty cl, 1991-2. B Feb 14 1927; ed St Peters Collegiate Sch; Wolverhampton Girls HS; Wolverhampton Acad of Arts.

CHORLEY				No change		
Electorate % Turnout	78,531	82.8%	1992	78,541	76.9%	1987
*Dover, D R (C)	30,715	47.2%	-0.8%	29,015	48.0%	C
McManus, R C (Lab)	26,469	40.7%	+6.0%	20,958	34.7%	Lab
Ross-Mills, Ms J (LD)	7,452	11.5%	-4.6%	9,706	16.1%	L/All
Leadbetter, P (NLP)	402	0.6%		714	1.2%	Grn
C to Lab swing 3.4%	65,038		6.5%	60,393		13.3%
		C maj	4,246		C maj	8,057

Den Dover, civil engineer and mbr, Institution of Civil Engineers, was elected in 1979; fought Caerphilly, Oct 1974. Mbr Select Cmte on Transport, 1979-87; chmn, Select Cmte on Severn Bridges Bill, 1991. Director, Cosalt plc, 1988- ; M P Holdings Ltd, 1991- , and Arcaster Investments Ltd, 1991-. B Apr 4 1938; ed Manchester GS; Manchester Univ. Mbr, Barnet Cl, 1968-71. Pres, CTU nat engineering gp; chmn, all-pty UK-Manx parly gp. Director of housing construction, GLC, 1977-9; contracts manager, Wimpey Laing, Iran, 1975-7; projects director, Capital and Counties Property Co Ltd, 1972-5; chief exec, 1971-72, dep chief exec, 1969-70, Nat Building Agency; with John Laing and Son Ltd, 1959-68.

Ray McManus, district offical of TGWU; mbr, W Lancs DC, 1976-81. Former local election agent, vice-chairman CLP and branch chairman. B Jan 30 1943; ed Walton Tech Coll, Liverpool.

Janet Ross-Mills, teacher of children with special ed needs, contested Lancs Central in 1989 Euro elections. Mbr, NW reg exec, LD; nat membership sec, Women in Ed, 1990-1. B Jul 4 1955; ed Chorley Coll of HE; Lancaster Univ. NUT.

CHRISTCHURCH				No change		
Electorate % Turnout	71,438	80.7%	1992	70,964	76.3%	1987
*Adley, R J (C)	36,627	63.5%	-2.4%	35,656	65.9%	C
Bussey, Rev D (LD)	13,612	23.6%		13,282	24.5%	SDP/All
Lloyd, A (Lab)	6,997	12.1%	+2.6%	5,174	9.6%	Lab
Barratt, J (NLP)	243	0.4%				
Wareham, A (CRA)	175	0.3%				
C to LD swing 0.7%	57,654		39.9%	54,112		41.3%
		C maj	23,015		C maj	22,374

Robert Adley, director and marketing consultant, Scotts Hotels Ltd (Marriott Corporation). Elected for this seat 1983; MP for Christchurch and Lymington, Feb 1974-83; MP for Bristol NE, 1970-4; contested Birkenhead, 1966. Mbr, Select Cmte on Members' Interests, 1979- . Chmn (1991-) and vice-chmn (1975-91), Cons backbench transport cmte. Director, General and Wholesale Representation Ltd; William Jacks plc, 1984- ; Home Rouxl, 1990- . Underwriting mbr of Lloyd's, 1988- ; author. B Mar 2 1935; ed Falconbury and Uppingham. First chmn and founder mbr, Brunel Soc; mbr, cmte, Nat Railway Museum. Patron, SS Gt Britain project. Trustee, Brunel Engineering Centre Trust. Chmn, all-pty railways parly gp; book publishing gp.

The Rev Dennis Bussey, Methodist minister and probation officer; chairman Verwood branch LDs; mbr, exec cl, Dorset East constituency. B May 20 1932; ed Rostrick GS, W Yorks; London and B'ham Univs. Preaches in America; graphologist.

Alan Lloyd, vehicle assembler (Fords), contested Gosport 1987. Mbr, Southampton City Cl, 1986- ; Hampshire CC, 1985- ; exec cmte, Southampton Lab pty. Chairman, Southampton Road Safety Cl, 1988- . B Jul 13 1952; ed Taunton's Sch, Southampton. TGWU.

CIRENCESTER AND TEWKESBURY						No change
Electorate % Turnout	88,299	82.1%	1992	84,071	77.9%	1987
Clifton-Brown, G R (C)	40,258	55.6%	+0.2%	36,272	55.4%	C
Weston, E J (LD)	24,200	33.4%	-2.6%	23,610	36.0%	L/All
Page, T (Lab)	7,262	10.0%	+1.9%	5,342	8.2%	Lab
Clayton, R (NLP)	449	0.6%		283	0.4%	M OAP
Trice-Rolph, P (Ind)	287	0.4%				
LD to C swing 1.4%	72,456		22.2%	65,507		19.3%
		C maj	16,058		C maj	12,662

Geoffrey Clifton-Brown, managing director of farming company. Chmn, North Norfolk Cons Assocn, 1986-90; Grandfather, Lt Colonel G B Clifton-Brown, was MP for Bury St Edmunds, 1945-50, and great uncle, Colonel D Clifton-Brown, MP for Hexham, was Commons Speaker, 1943-51. B Mar 23 1953; ed Tormore Sch, Upper Deal, Kent; Eton; Royal Agricultural Coll, Cirencester. Investment surveyor with Jones, Lang, Wootton in London,

1975-9. Freeman, City of London; Liveryman, Worshipful Company of Farmers. ARICS.
Edward Weston, management consultant and electrical engineer. B Jul 6 1946; ed Lancastrian Sch, Chichester. Chmn, Assocn of Small Historic Towns and Villages of UK; sec, Society for Architecture.
Trevor Page, union researcher. B Aug 29 1965; ed Harvey GS; Poly SW, Devon.

CITY OF LONDON AND WESTMINSTER SOUTH						No change
Electorate % Turnout	55,021	63.1%	1992	57,428	58.3%	1987
*Brooke, P L (C)	20,938	60.3%	+2.5%	19,333	57.8%	C
Smith, A C (Lab)	7,569	21.8%	+1.4%	7,299	21.8%	SDP/All
Smithard, Ms J C G (LD)	5,392	15.5%	-6.3%	6,821	20.4%	Lab
Herbert, G (Grn)	458	1.3%				
Stockton, P (Loony)	147	0.4%				
Farrell, A (IFM)	107	0.3%				
Johnson, R (NLP)	101	0.3%				
Lab to C swing 0.6%	34,712		38.5%	33,453		36.0%
		C maj	13,369		C maj	12,034

Peter Brooke resigned from the government after the general election. N Ireland secretary. 1989-92; chmn, Cons pty, 1987-9; Paymaster General, 1987-9, continuing duties he had as Treasury Minr, 1985-7; Under Sec for Ed and Science, 1983-5; Ld Commissioner of Treasury (Govt whip), 1981-3; asst Govt whip, 1979-81. PC 1988. Elected at 1977 by-election; contested Bedwellty, Oct 1974. B Mar 3 1934; ed Marlborough; Balliol Coll, Oxford (pres of Union, 1957); Harvard Business Sch (Commonwealth Fund Fellow). Presentation Fellow, King's Coll London, 1989; Snr Fellow, Royal Coll of Art, 1987. Mbr of Lloyd's. Lay adviser, St Paul's Cathedral, 1980.

Charlie Smith, housing assocn surveyor. B Apr 18 1948; ed Buckingham Gate Sec Sch, London; Westminster Coll. Ucatt.
Jane Smithard, barrister; legal consultant; contested this seat 1987. Chairman, LD Parly Candidates' Assocn; B May 2 1954; ed St Paul's Girls Sch; St Mary's Hall, Brighton; Kingston Poly; Inns of Court Sch of Law.
Guy Herbert, administration manager for literary agency; treas, London Fed of Grn parties; on Grn pty policy cmte. B Dec 22 1961; ed King Edward VI Sch, Stratford-upon-Avon; Bristol univ.

CLACKMANNAN						No change
Electorate % Turnout	48,963	78.3%	1992	49,083	77.0%	1987
*O'Neill, M J (Lab)	18,829	49.1%	-4.6%	20,317	53.7%	Lab
Brophy, A (SNP)	10,326	26.9%	+6.0%	7,916	20.9%	SNP
Mackie, J A (C)	6,638	17.3%	+2.4%	5,620	14.9%	C
Watters, Mrs A M (LD)	2,567	6.7%	-3.8%	3,961	10.5%	SDP/All
Lab to SNP swing 5.3%	38,360		22.2%	37,814		32.8%
		Lab maj	8,503		Lab maj	12,401

Martin O'Neill became chief Opposition spokesman on defence, disarmament and arms control in 1988 after resignation of Denzil Davies; spokesman on defence, 1984-8, and on Scotland, 1980-4. Mbr, Select Cmte on Scottish Affairs, 1979-80. Elected for this seat 1983; MP for Stirlingshire East and Clackmannan, 1979-83. Teacher of modern studies, Boroughmuir HS, Edinburgh, 1974-7; social science tutor, 1976-9. B Jan 6 1945; ed Wardie Primary Sch; Trinity Acad; Heriot Watt univ; Moray House Coll of Ed, Edinburgh. Sponsored by GPMU.
Andrew Brophy, solicitor, contested Glasgow Garscadden 1987. Past chairman, Garscadden SNP, and a former local

sec and organiser. B 1960; ed Glasgow univ.
Jim Mackie, self-employed, supplier of nutritional products for agriculture; founder mbr and trustee, Forth Fisheries Conservation Trust; hon inspector of fisheries, Forth Dist Salmon Fishery Bd. B May 21 1950; ed Garmouth public sch and Milnes HS, both in Morayshire. Police office, Central Scotland, 1969-77.
Ann Watters, science/environmental studies adviser, contested this seat 1987. Mbr, Scottish LD exec; Kirkcaldy DC, 1984- . B Sep 23 1926; ed London univ; Moray House Coll of Ed. PAT.

CLWYD NORTH WEST						No change
Electorate % Turnout	67,351	78.6%	1992	66,118	75.2%	1987
Richards, R (C)	24,488	46.2%	-2.3%	24,116	48.5%	C
Ruane, C (Lab)	18,438	34.8%	+10.0%	12,335	24.8%	Lab
Ingham, R V (LD)	7,999	15.1%	-7.6%	11,279	22.7%	L/All
Taylor, N (PC)	1,888	3.6%	-0.4%	1,966	4.0%	PC
Swift, Ms M (NLP)	158	0.3%				
C to Lab swing 6.1%	52,971		11.4%	49,696		23.7%
		C maj	6,050		C maj	11,781

Rod Richards, former special adviser to Secretary of State for Wales, David Hunt, was elected in 1992; contested Vale of Glamorgan by-election 1989 and Carmarthen 1987. Presenter, BBC TV news and current affairs, 1983-9; with defence intelligence staff, Ministry of Defence, 1976-83; economic forecaster, 1975-6; short service commission, Royal Marines, 1969-71. B Mar 12 1947; ed Llandovery Coll; UCW, Swansea. Former mbr, Development Bd for Rural Wales and Welsh Consumer Cl. Has served as exec mbr, Brecon and Radnor Cons Assocn; mbr, Special Forces Club; patron, Llanelli Rugby Club.
Christopher Ruane, dep head of primary sch. Mbr, Rhyl TC, 1988- . Chairman, founder mbr and press officer, Rhyl Anti-Apartheid and Rhyl Environment Assocn. B Jul 18 1958; ed Blessed Edward Jones HS, Rhyl; UCW, Aberystwyth; Liverpool univ. Pres, W Clwyd NUT, 1990.
Robert Ingham, physicist on control and safety at nuclear power stations. Contested Knutsford by-election and gen election 1979. Mbr, Macclesfield BC, 1986- . B Nov 8 1931; ed Llangollen GS; univ coll of N Wales, Bangor; UKAEA Harwell.
Neil Taylor, solicitor, contested Flint E Feb 1974 and Flint W Oct 1974. B Mar 11 1941; ed John Bright GS, Llandudno; Liverpool Poly; Coll of Law, Chester. Mbr, Rhyl TC, 1974-87; Rhuddlan BC, 1976-87 (Mayor 1984); Clwyd CC, 1981-4.

CLWYD SOUTH WEST						No change
Electorate % Turnout	60,607	81.5%	1992	58,158	81.1%	1987
*Jones, M D (Lab)	21,490	43.5%	+8.1%	16,701	35.4%	Lab
Owen, G (C)	16,549	33.5%	+0.2%	15,673	33.2%	C
Williams, W G (LD)	6,027	12.2%	-10.7%	10,778	22.9%	SDP/All
Lloyd Jones, E (PC)	4,835	9.8%	+1.3%	3,987	8.5%	PC
Worth, N (Grn)	351	0.7%				
Leadbetter, Mrs J (NLP)	155	0.3%				
C to Lab swing 3.9%	49,407		10.0%	47,139		2.2%
		Lab maj	4,941		Lab maj	1,028

Martyn Jones won this seat 1987; mbr, Select Cmte on Agriculture and chmn, PLP agriculture cmte, 1987- . An Opposn whip, 1988- . Microbiologist in brewing industry, 1968-87, and mbr of Inst of Biology. B Mar 1 1947; ed Grove Park GS, Wrexham; Liverpool and Trent Polys. Mbr, Clwyd, CC, 1981-9. Chmn, Clwyd Lab pty. Area rep, TGWU, and sponsored by that union.
Gwilym Owen, retail banking Cardiff area manager, Midland Bank plc and formerly area manager, Carnarfon and Oswestry. Mbr, Welsh Language Bd; past financial sec, Nat Eisteddfod of Wales, Cardiff; past pres, Cardiff Centre of Chartered Inst of Bankers and Fellow of Inst. B Dec 13 1938; ed Tywyn GS.
Gwyn Williams, farmer; mbr, Clwyd CC, 1986- ; Clwyd HA, 1989-90; mbr, exec cmte, Welsh LD. B Oct 30 1960; ed Ruthin Sch; Reading univ.
Eifon Lloyd Jones, TV producer and lecturer, contested seat 1987. B Oct 13 1938; ed UCNW Bangor.

CLYDEBANK AND MILNGAVIE						No change
Electorate % Turnout	47,337	77.8%	1992	50,152	78.9%	1987
*Worthington, A (Lab)	19,637	53.3%	-3.6%	22,528	56.9%	Lab
Hughes, G (SNP)	7,207	19.6%	+7.1%	6,224	15.7%	C
Harvey, W A (C)	6,654	18.1%	+2.3%	5,891	14.9%	SDP/All
Tough, A G (LD)	3,216	8.7%	-6.2%	4,935	12.5%	SNP
Barrie, Ms J (NLP)	112	0.3%				
Lab to SNP swing 5.3%	36,826		33.8%	39,578		41.2%
		Lab maj	12,430		Lab maj	16,304

Tony Worthington became an Opposn spokesman on Scotland in 1989. Elected for this seat 1987. Mbr, Select Cmte on Home Affairs, 1987-9; jt vice-chmn, PLP home affairs cmte, 1987-8; jt sec, all-pty population and development parly gp. Director (unpaid) Scottish Chamber Orchestra, 1987- . Chmn, Lab Campaign for Criminal Justice, 1987-9. Social policy and sociology lecturer, Jordanhill Coll, Glasgow, 1971-87; Monkwearmouth CFE, Sunderland, 1967-71; HM Borstal, Dover, 1962-6. Mbr, Strathclyde Reg Cl, 1974-87. B Oct 11 1941; ed City Sch, Lincoln; LSE; York and Glasgow univs. GMB.
Gordon Hughes, community ed worker, contested Dun-fermline W 1987. B May 7 1954; ed Graeme HS, Falkirk; Callender Park and Moray House Colls of Ed; Open univ. Founder mbr, Cumbernauld and Kilsyth branch, Heritage Society of Scotland. Nalgo.
William Harvey, partner in financial services company, contested Glasgow, Cathcart in 1987 and Glasgow Central 1983. Elder, Church of Scotland. B Oct 27 1955; ed Woodside Sch, Glasgow; Central Coll of Commerce, Glasgow; Glasgow Coll of Tech.
Alistair Tough, achivist, Glasgow univ; chmn, Coventry LDs, 1989-90. B Apr 27 1953; ed Robert Gordon's Coll; Aberdeen univ; Univ Coll, London. AUT.

CLYDESDALE						No change
Electorate % Turnout	61,878	77.6%	1992	61,620	78.2%	1987
*Hood, J (Lab)	21,418	44.6%	-0.7%	21,826	45.3%	Lab
Goodwin, Ms C E (C)	11,231	23.4%	-0.1%	11,324	23.5%	C
Gray, I G M (SNP)	11,084	23.1%	+8.3%	7,909	16.4%	SDP/All
Buchanan, Ms E (LD)	3,957	8.2%	-8.2%	7,125	14.8%	SNP
Cartwright, S (BNP)	342	0.7%				
Lab to C swing 0.3%	48,032		21.2%	48,184		21.8%
		Lab maj	10,187		Lab maj	10,502

Jimmy Hood was elected in 1987 and joined the select cmte on European legislation. Miner/coal face engineer in Nottingham coalfield; previously at Douglas and Auchlochan collieries. Chmn miners parly gp, 1992. NUM official, 1973-85. Mbr Newark and Sherwood DC, 1979-87; exec mbr East Midlands regional Lab pty; NUM branch president and secretary, 1973-84, and mbr of area political cmte. B May 16 1949; ed Lesmahagow higher grade sch, Coatbridge; Motherwell Tech Coll; Nottingham Univ. WEA. Sponsored by NUM.
Carol Goodwin, chartered accountant with Glasgow consultancy. District cllr since 1988; chaired Strathkelvin and Bearsden YCs, 1987-8; vice-chmn, Bearsden Cons branch; assocn vice-chmn. B Nov 15 1860; ed Westbourne Sch for Girls, Glasgow; Stirling Univ.
Iain Gray, teacher; convenor, Carluke branch, SNP; mbr Clydesdale DC, 1988- . B Aug 23 1947; ed Hutchesons' GS; Glasgow Univ; Jordanhill Coll of Ed.
Elspeth Buchanan further ed lecturer, 1976-87; previously history teacher. Contested Paisley S 1983; S of Scotland 1984 Euro elections. Exec mbr Hillhead LDs. B Jun 18 1927; ed Glasgow HS for Girls; Glasgow Univ; Moray Hse Coll of Ed.

COLCHESTER NORTH						No change
Electorate % Turnout	86,479	79.1%	1992	82,420	76.0%	1987
Jenkin, B C (C)	35,213	51.5%	-0.8%	32,747	52.3%	C
Raven, Dr J R (LD)	18,721	27.4%	-3.2%	19,124	30.5%	SDP/All
Lee, D J (Lab)	13,870	20.3%	+3.1%	10,768	17.2%	Lab
Tariq Shabbeer, M (Grn)	372	0.5%				
Mears, M (NLP)	238	0.3%				
LD to C swing 1.2%	68,414		24.1%	62,639		21.7%
		C maj	16,492		C maj	13,623

Bernard Jenkin worked as fund manager with Legal and General Ventures Ltd; was with Investors in Industry plc from 1986. Contested Glasgow Central 1987. Research asst to Sir Leon Brittan MP, 1986-9; election asst to Sir Hugh Rossi MP, 1979 and 1983. Sales and marketing executive, Ford Motor Co Ltd, 1983-6. B Apr 9 1959; ed Highgate Sch; William Ellis Sch; Corpus Christi Coll, Cambridge (Pres of Union, 1982). Past chmn, Matching PC.
Dr James Raven, univ lecturer; chmn, Cambridge English Speaking Union; director, Project for the Book Trust. B Apr 13 1959; ed Gilberd Sch, Colchester; Clare Coll, Cambridge.
David Lee, dep sec to CHC; mbr Waltham Forest BC, 1990- ; sec, Colchester N CLP, 1987-8. B Mar 29 1966; ed ILEA comprehensive; Essex Univ (Vice-pres, NUS, 1987-8). Nalgo.
Tariq Shabbeer, unemployed. B Apl 18 1962; ed Swansea, Southampton and Essex univs.

COLCHESTER SOUTH AND MALDON						No change
Electorate % Turnout	86,410	79.2%	1992	84,392	75.3%	1987
Whittingdale, J F L (C)	37,548	54.8%	-0.1%	34,894	54.9%	C
Thorn, I L (LD)	15,727	23.0%	-7.6%	19,411	30.6%	SDP/All
Pearson, C A (Lab)	14,158	20.7%	+6.2%	9,229	14.5%	Lab
Patterson, M (Grn)	1,028	1.5%				
LD to C swing 3.8%	68,461		31.9%	63,534		24.4%
		C maj	21,821		C maj	15,483

John Whittingdale was political secretary to Margaret Thatcher when she was Prime Minister, 1988-90; manager of her private office since 1990; manager, N M Rothschild and Sons, 1987; special adviser to Secretary of State for Trade and Industry, 1984-7; head of political section, Cons research dept, 1982-4. B Oct 16 1959; ed Sandroyd Sch, Wiltshire; Winchester Coll; Univ Coll, London. Mbr Bow Gp, Selsdon Gp and British Mensa.
Ian Thorn, in public relations; mbr Maldon DC, 1991- . B Apr 13 1965; ed Plume Sch, Maldon; Colchester Inst.
Chris Pearson, regional manager with national charity. Mbr Essex CC, 1990- ; and parish cllr. Been CLP chmn, vice-chmn and youth officer. B Apr 4 1957; ed City Univ of New York. MSF.
Matthew Patterson, postgraduate student; mbr of NUS and Grn pty students; mbr Grn pty standing orders cmte, 1990- . B Jun 10 1967; ed Newcastle and Essex Univs.

COLNE VALLEY						No change
Electorate % Turnout	72,043	82.0%	1992	70,199	80.1%	1987
*Riddick, G E G (C)	24,804	42.0%	+5.6%	20,457	36.4%	C
Harman, J A (Lab)	17,579	29.8%	+0.7%	18,780	33.4%	L/All
Priestley, N J (LD)	15,953	27.0%	-6.4%	16,353	29.1%	Lab
Stewart, R J A (Grn)	443	0.8%	-0.3%	614	1.1%	Grn
Staniforth, Mrs M (Loony)	160	0.3%				
Hasty, J (Ind)	73	0.1%				
Tattersall, J (NLP)	44	0.1%				
Lab to C swing 2.5%	59,056		12.2%	56,204		3.0%
		C maj	7,225		C maj	1,677

Graham Riddick was PPS to Francis Maude, Financial Sec to Treasury, 1990-2. Won this seat in 1987. Vice-chmn Cons backbench employment cmte, 1988-90; sec Cons trade and industry cmte, 1990; all-pty wool textile parly gp, 1987- ; treas all-pty British-Mexican parly gp, 1987- . Mbr nat cl, Freedom Assocn, 1988- . In sales management with Procter and Gamble, 1977-82, and Coca-Cola, 1982-7. Mbr of Lloyd's. B Aug 26 1955; ed Stowe; Warwick univ (chmn, univ Cons assocn).

John Harman, lecturer, contested this seat 1987. Mbr Kirklees MDC, 1986- (ldr of cl); West Yorkshire CC, 1981-

6; vice chmn Huddersfield CLP, 1982-3; mbr W Yorks pty exec, 1981-6. Dep chmn AMA, 1988- . B Jul 30 1950; ed St George's Coll, Weybridge; Manchester Univ; Huddersfield Coll of Ed (Tech). NATFHE.

Nigel Priestley, solicitor, contested this seat 1987. Mbr, Meltham Town Cl, 1983-7. Chmn Colne Valley Lib Assocn, 1984-5. Lay reader. B Sep 22 1952; ed King James GS, Almondbury, Huddersfield; Warwick Univ. Mbr, Huddersfield Choral Society.

Robin Stewart, self-employed. Policy coordinator, Huddersfield Grn Pty. B Aug 25 1965; ed Aberystwyth Univ.

CONGLETON						No change
Electorate % Turnout	70,477	84.5%	1992	68,172	80.5%	1987
*Winterton, Mrs J A (C)	29,163	49.0%	+0.7%	26,513	48.3%	C
Brodie-Browne, I M (LD)	18,043	30.3%	-3.5%	18,544	33.8%	L/All
Finnegan, M (Lab)	11,927	20.0%	+2.2%	9,810	17.9%	Lab
Brown, P (NLP)	399	0.7%				
LD to C swing 2.1%	59,532		18.7%	54,867		14.5%
		C maj	11,120		C maj	7,969

Ann Winterton became a mbr of the select cmte on agriculture in 1987. Elected in 1983. Chmn all-pty parly Pro-Life gp; sec all-pty chemical industry gp; jt sec Parly and Scientic Cmte, 1991- ; sec parly office of science and technology (POST), 1991- . Wife of Nicholas Winterton, MP for Macclesfield. B Mar 6 1941; ed Erdington GS for Girls. Mbr West Midlands Cons Women's Advisory Committee, 1969-71. Joint Master, South Staffordshire Hunt, 1959-64.

Iain Brodie-Browne, a charity director, contested this seat 1987, Southport 1983 and Warrington 1979. Mbr, Cheshire CC, 1989- ; Congleton BC, 1988- ; Southport Cl, 1983-7. B Jan 16 1953; ed Blackdown HS; City of London Poly.

Matthew Finnegan, journalist; chmn, Bury S CLP and Holyrood ward Lab Pty, Prestwich. B Nov 24 1956; ed St Kevins comprehensive sch, Kirkby; Univ Coll, Cardiff. NUJ/GMB.

CONWY						No change
Electorate % Turnout	53,576	78.9%	1992	52,862	76.9%	1987
*Roberts, Sir Wyn (C)	14,250	33.7%	-5.0%	15,730	38.7%	C
Roberts, Rev J R (LD)	13,255	31.4%	+0.1%	12,706	31.2%	L/All
Williams, Mrs B H (Lab)	10,883	25.8%	+3.5%	9,049	22.3%	Lab
Davies, R (PC)	3,108	7.4%	-0.5%	3,177	7.8%	PC
Wainwright, O (Ind C)	637	1.5%				
Hughes, Ms D (NLP)	114	0.3%				
C to LD swing 2.5%	42,247		2.4%	40,662		7.4%
		C maj	995		C maj	3,024

Sir Wyn Roberts became Minr of State for Wales in Jun 1987; Under Sec of State for Wales, 1979-87; Opposn spokesman on Welsh affairs, 1974-9; PPS to Sec of State for Wales, 1970-4. PC 1991. Elected for this seat 1983; MP for Conway, 1970-83. B Jul 10 1930; ed Beaumaris County Sch; Harrow; University Coll, Oxford. Journalist; formerly Welsh controller, TWW (with company, 1957-68), and a former programme exec, Harlech Television. Mbr Ct of Governors, Nat Library of Wales, Nat Museum of Wales, and Univ Coll of Wales, Aberystwyth, and of Gorsedd, Royal Nat Eisteddfod of Wales.

The Rev Roger Roberts, Methodist superintendent minister of Llandudno, was elected president Welsh LDs in 1990;

pres Welsh Lib Pty, 1981-4. Contested this seat 1987, 1983 and 1979. Mbr Aberconwy BC, 1976- . B Oct 23 1935; ed John Bright GS, Llandudno; Univ Coll, Bangor; Handsworth Coll, Birmingham.

Betty Williams, housewife, contested this seat 1987 and Caernarfon 1983. Mbr, Gwynedd CC, 1976- ; Arfon BC, 1970-91 (Mayor, 1990-91). B Jul 31 1944; ed Ysgol Dyffryn Nantlle.

Rhodri Davies contested this seat 1987. Solicitor; was local govt solicitor, Anglesey; lecturer at Bristol Poly, 1971-79. PlC spokesman on housing. B Nov 25 1947; ed Friars GS, Bangor; Univ of Wales, Aberystwyth; Coll of Law, Guildford.

COPELAND						No change
Electorate % Turnout	54,911	83.5%	1992	54,695	81.3%	1987
*Cunningham, Dr J A (Lab)	22,328	48.7%	+1.5%	20,999	47.2%	Lab
Davies, P (C)	19,889	43.4%	+0.4%	19,105	43.0%	C
Putnam, R (LD)	3,508	7.6%	-1.5%	4,052	9.1%	SDP/All
Sinton, J (NLP)	148	0.3%		319	0.7%	Grn
C to Lab swing 0.5%	45,873		5.3%	44,475		4.3%
		Lab maj	2,439		Lab maj	1,894

Dr John Cunningham was elected to shadow cabinet in 1983; shadow Ldr of the House and campaigns coordinator, 1989- ; mbr privileges cmte, 1989- ; broadcasting cmte, 1989-91, and services cmte, 1989-91; chief Opposn spokesman on environment, 1983-9; an Opposn spokesman on industry, 1979-83. Under Sec of State for Energy, 1976-9. Elected for this seat 1983; MP for Whitehaven, 1970-83. PPS to James Callaghan, 1974-6. B Aug 4 1939; ed Jarrow GS; Bede Coll, Durham Univ. Full-time officer, GMWU, 1969-70; sponsored by union. Policy adviser to Albright and Wilson (UK) Ltd, to Leather Chemicals and to Dow Ltd.

Philip Davies, hotelier, and former proprietor, *North West*

Evening Mail; chmn British Magazine Publishing Corporation, 1986-7, and Ladbroke Publishing, 1984-6. Founder chmn Home and Law Magazines, 1978-84; special reports manager, *The Guardian*, 1974-8. Contested Farnham for Libs in both 1974 elections. Mbr, Farnham UDC, 1970-4; Surrey CC, 1973-6, and Waverley DC, 1973-6. B Sep 26 1945; ed Woking Cty GS.

Roger Putnam, education and training consultant; business interests in guest house, outdoor holidays and as training consultant. Planning officer, Middlesex CC, 1960-2. B Jul 27 1936; ed Wellingborough Sch; St John's Coll, Oxford.

CORBY						No change
Electorate % Turnout	68,333	82.9%	1992	66,119	79.6%	1987
*Powell, W R (C)	25,203	44.5%	+0.2%	23,323	44.3%	C
Feather, H A (Lab)	24,861	43.9%	+3.0%	21,518	40.9%	Lab
Roffe, M W (LD)	5,792	10.2%	-4.6%	7,805	14.8%	L/All
Wood, Ms J (Lib)	784	1.4%				
C to Lab swing 1.4%	56,640		0.6%	52,646		3.4%
		C maj	342		C maj	1,805

William Powell was appointed PPS to Michael Heseltine, Sec of State for Environment, in 1990. Mbr select cmte on foreign affairs, 1990-1; select cmte on procedure, 1987-90; jt parly ecclesiastical cmte, 1987- ; jt sec Cons backbench foreign affairs cmte, 1985 and 1987-90, and Cons defence cmte, 1988-90. PPS to Minr for Overseas Development, 1985-6. Non-practising barrister. Elected in 1983. Mbr bd federation against software theft; director, Anchorwise Ltd, 1989-91; adviser to Unquoted Companies Gp and Betting Offices Licensees Assocn. B Aug 3 1948; ed Lancing Coll;

Emmanuel Coll, Cambridge. Mbr, cl, British Atlantic Cmte, 1985-90.

Harry Feather, nat negotiating officer with Iron and Steel Trades Confederation, former steel worker, contested seat 1987. Mbr, Northants CC, 1968-71. B Aug 3 1938; ed Chiswick Cty Sch; Univ of NSW; Leicester Coll. Sponsored, ISTC.

Melvyn Roffe, teacher; sec of constituency pty; mbr, Oundle TC, 1987- . B Jun 15 1964; ed Noel-Baker comprehensive sch, Derby; York and Durham univs. AMMA.

CORNWALL NORTH						LD gain
Electorate % Turnout	76,844	81.5%	1992	72,375	79.8%	1987
Tyler, P A (LD)	29,696	47.4%	+5.5%	29,862	51.7%	C
*Neale, Sir Gerry (C)	27,775	44.3%	-7.4%	24,180	41.9%	L/All
Jordan, F (Lab)	4,103	6.6%	+0.1%	3,719	6.4%	Lab
Andrews, P (Lib)	678	1.1%				
Rowe, G (Ind)	276	0.4%				
Treadwell, Mrs H (NLP)	112	0.2%				
C to LD swing 6.5%	62,640		3.1%	57,761		9.8%
		LD maj	1,921		C maj	5,682

Paul Tyler, public relations and environmental campaign consultant, won this seat for the LDs in 1992. Lib MP for Bodmin, Feb to Oct 1974, contesting that seat 1979 and 1970, Beaconsfield by-election 1982, Totnes 1966. Contested Cornwall and Plymouth in 1989 Euro elections. Spokesman on housing and transport, 1974. Managing director, Western Approaches Public Relations Ltd; managing director, Cornwall Courier Newspapers, 1976-81; director, Good Relations Gp plc, 1984-6. Chmn Lib pty, 1983-6; campaign adviser to David Steel, 1983 and 1987. B Oct 29 1941; ed Mount House Sch, Tavistock; Sherborne Sch; Exeter Coll, Oxford. With RIBA 1966-72, director of public affairs in 1972. Mbr, Devon CC, 1964-

70.

Sir Gerrard Neale had held seat since 1979; contested it, Oct 1974. Chmn campaign for defence and multilateral disarmament, 1986; vice-chmn, Cons legal cmte, 1991-2. PPS to George Younger, defence sec, 1987-9; to Nicholas Ridley, environment sec 1986-7, and transport sec, 1985-6. Mbr statutory instruments cmte, 1991-2; procedure ctee, 1991-2. Partner in solicitors, 1988- ; director, Telephone Rentals Ltd, 1979-88. B Jun 25 1941; ed Bedford Sch. Mbr, Milton Keynes Cl, 1973-9; mayor, 1976-7

Frank Jordan is a psychiatric nurse; mbr Bodmin TC, 1985- ; N Cornwall DC, 1989-91. B Jul 20 1957. Cohse.

CORNWALL SOUTH EAST						No change
Electorate % Turnout	73,027	82.1%	1992	70,248	79.5%	1987
*Hicks, R A (C)	30,565	51.0%	-0.6%	28,818	51.6%	C
Teverson, R (LD)	22,861	38.1%	-1.6%	22,211	39.8%	L/All
Gilroy, Mrs L (Lab)	5,536	9.2%	+0.6%	4,847	8.7%	Lab
Cook, Miss M (Lib)	644	1.1%				
Quick, A (Anti-Fed)	227	0.4%				
Allen, Miss R (NLP)	155	0.3%				
LD to C swing 0.5%	59,988		12.8%	55,876		11.8%
		C maj	7,704		C maj	6,607

Robert Hicks has been mbr select cmte on Euro legislation since 1976; also mbr, 1973. Chmn (1988-9) and vice-chmn (1974-82 and 1972-3), Cons backbench ag, fish and food cmte. Parly adviser, British Hotels, Restaurants and Caterers Assocn, 1974- ; Milk Marketing Bd, 1985- . Elected for this seat 1983; MP for Bodmin, 1970-Feb 1974 and Oct 1974-83; contested Aberavon 1966. Asst Govt whip, 1973-4. B Jan 18 1938; ed Queen Elizabeth GS, Crediton; Univ Coll, London; Exeter Univ. Treas, Cons Middle East Cl, 1980- . Chmn UK gp Parly Assocn for Euro-Arab Cooperation, 1983- .

Robin Teverson, distribution managing director; vice-chmn, Stroud LD. B Mar 31 1952; ed Chigwell Sch; Waltham Forest Tech Coll; Exeter Univ.

Linda Gilroy, SW reg manager, Gas Consumers' Cl; sec Plymouth Drake CLP, 1987-8; chmn Cornwall Cty Lab Pty, 1991. Parish cllr, Maker with Rame, 1991- . B Jul 19 1949; ed Edinburgh and Strathclyde Univs. Chaired Nalgo gas consumers' Cl staffs branch, 1989-90.

COVENTRY NORTH EAST						No change
Electorate % Turnout	64,787	73.2%	1992	67,479	70.6%	1987
Ainsworth, R W (Lab)	24,896	52.5%	-1.8%	25,832	54.3%	Lab
Perrin, K R (C)	13,220	27.9%	-1.5%	13,965	29.3%	C
McKee, V J (LD)	5,306	11.2%	-4.6%	7,502	15.8%	L/All
*Hughes, J (Ind Lab)	4,008	8.5%		310	0.7%	Comm
Lab to C swing 0.2%	47,430		24.6%	47,609		24.9%
		Lab maj	11,676		Lab maj	11,867

Robert Ainsworth, sheet metal worker, elected in 1992, was dep ldr, 1988-90, and chmn of finance cmte, 1989-90, Coventry city cl, to which he was elected in 1984. Shop steward, 1974-9, for TGWU and then joined MSF; senior steward and stewards' sec throughout 1980s at Jaguar Cars Ltd; branch pres for a period in early 1980s. Chmn, Coventry NE CLP 1987-92; also been LP branch chmn. B Jun 19 1952; ed Foxford Comprehensive Sch, Coventry.

Keith Perrin, snr exec, Exclusive Gp; was gp gen manager, Weston Records Management plc, London, from 1989. Sandy, Beds, cllr since 1989. Chmn/organiser of Peace through Nato, Kent, 1983-7, and for Beds, 1987- . Mbr, Maidstone division exec, 1978-87. Sec, Sandy Cons Assocn, and mbr, Mid-Beds exec, 1988- . B 1953; ed Dame Alice Owens, Angel, Islington; SW and W London colls.

Vincent McKee, political studies lecturer and contributor to political science journals. Chmn, Coventry area LD policy cmte; Coventry NE LDs. B Feb 19 1958; ed Downpatrick Tech Coll, NI; Belfast Coll of Business Studies; Coventry Poly; B'ham and City of London polys. Nat cl mbr, Electoral Reform Society.

John Hughes was Lab MP for this seat 1987-92. Deselected by CLP in Dec 1989 and his appeal to pty NEC was rejected. Unemployed when elected MP; former warehouse man and TGWU convenor at Unipart, Canley; chmn, Coventry NE CLP, 1978-81. Mbr, Coventry City Cl, 1974-82. B May 29 1925; ed in Durham.

COVENTRY NORTH WEST						No change
Electorate % Turnout	50,670	77.6%	1992	53,090	74.8%	1987
*Robinson, G (Lab)	20,349	51.7%	+2.7%	19,450	49.0%	Lab
Hill, Mrs A A B (C)	13,917	35.4%	+0.6%	13,787	34.7%	C
Simpson, Ms E A (LD)	5,070	12.9%	-3.4%	6,455	16.3%	SDP/All
C to Lab swing 1.0%	39,336		16.4%	39,692		14.3%
		Lab maj	6,432		Lab maj	5,663

Geoffrey Robinson was in Opposn front bench team on trade and industry, 1983-7, speaking on industry and regional affairs; spokesman on science, 1982-3. On select cmte on trade and industry, 1983-4. Won by-election 1976. Financial controller, British Leyland, 1971-2; managing director, Leyland Innocenti, Italy, 1972-3; chief exec, Triumph Motorcycles (Meriden) Ltd (a workers' co-op), 1977-80, director 1980-2. Director, Agie UK Ltd; Transfer Technology Gp plc, 1991- ; director (unpaid), W Midlands Enterprise Bd, 1980-4. B May 25 1938; ed Emanuel Sch; Cambridge Univ; Yale.

Agnes Hill, a home economist (Cordon Bleu) and local govt consultant, has been St Albans district and Herts cty cllr since 1978 being first woman ldr of St Albans DC; mbr, Herts family practitioner cmte, 1981- ; NW Herts DHA, 1982-6. B 1940; ed private and state schs.

Ann Simpson, teacher of English; mbr, Stratford-on-Avon DC, 1990- ; chmn, Stratford-on-Avon and S Warwickshire LDs, 1988-91. B Sep 12 1938; ed Barrs' Hill GS, Coventry. NUT.

COVENTRY SOUTH EAST						No change
Electorate % Turnout	48,796	74.9%	1992	51,880	73.0%	1987
Cunningham, J (Lab)	11,902	32.6%	-14.9%	17,969	47.5%	Lab
Hyams, Mrs M (C)	10,591	29.0%	-0.9%	11,316	29.9%	C
*Nellist, D J (Ind Lab)	10,551	28.9%			8,095	21.4% SDP/All
Armstrong, A (LD)	3,318	9.1%	-12.3%	479	1.3%	Grn
Tompkinson, N (NF)	173	0.5%				
Lab to C swing 7.0%	36,535		3.6%	37,859		17.6%
		Lab maj	1,311		Lab maj	6,653

Jim Cunningham, engineer, won this seat in 1992. Mbr, Coventry City Cl, 1972- (Lab gp ldr); chmn West Midlands jt cmte. MSF, being shop steward and snr steward, for union since 1972. B Feb 4 1941.
Martine Hyams was director of small electronics company, 1988-91. Has served as officer of Spelthorne Cons assocn; mbr Thames Valley Euro constituency cl. B Nov 18 1939; ed Kingston Poly. Mbr, Cons womens parly sub-cmte.

David Nellist, formerly a storeman, engineering and building supplies, was Lab MP for this seat, 1983-91, when he was expelled from pty and deprived of PLP whip for links with Militant Tendency. Mbr West Midlands County Council, 1982-6. B Jul 1952. MSF.
Anthony Armstrong, computer help desk specialist; City pty treas and exec mbr. B Dec 12 1956; ed Salisbury Jnr HS, London. ACTS.

COVENTRY SOUTH WEST						No change
Electorate % Turnout	63,474	80.1%	1992	65,567	78.7%	1987
*Butcher, J P (C)	23,225	45.7%	+2.4%	22,318	43.3%	C
Slater, R E G (Lab)	21,789	42.8%	+5.8%	19,108	37.0%	Lab
Sewards, G B (LD)	4,666	9.2%	-10.5%	10,166	19.7%	L/All
Wheway, R (Lib)	989	1.9%				
Morris, D (NLP)	204	0.4%				
C to Lab swing 1.7%	50,873		2.8%	51,592		6.2%
		C maj	1,436		C maj	3,210

John Butcher was an Under Sec of State for Ed and Science, 1988-9; became Minr for Consumers Affairs after 1987 election, continuing as an Under Sec of State for Trade and Industry at DTI to which he was appointed in 1982. Non-exec chmn, bd of Texas Instruments Ltd; non-exec director, Landis and Gyr (UK) Ltd, 1990- . Elected in 1979; contested B'ham, Northfield, Feb 1974. Marketing executive and product manager, computer industry, 1968-79. B Feb 13 1946; ed Huntingdon GS; Birmingham Univ. Did research into guerrilla warfare and Nato at Inst of Strategic Studies. FRSA. Mbr Birmingham City Cl, 1972-8.

Robert Slater, further ed coll lecturer, contested this seat 1987 and Burton 1983. Mbr Leicester City Cl, 1979-87. Offices held include CLP and cty pty exec cmtes; vice-chmn CLP and ward sec; chmn, Leicester low pay campaign. B Dec 13 1948; ed George Gascoigne sec mod sch, Walthamstow; Sir George Monoux GS; Leicester and Warwick univs. NATFHE since 1972 and GMB/Apex.
Geoff Sewards, poly maths lecturer; chmn, Coventry Lib pty, 1978-88; sec, Coventry LDs, 1988- . B Feb 4 1936; ed Emanuel Sch, London; Clare Coll, Cambridge; Nottingham univ.

CRAWLEY						No change
Electorate % Turnout	78,277	79.2%	1992	72,076	81.9%	1987
*Soames, A N W (C)	30,204	48.7%	-0.8%	29,259	49.5%	C
Moffatt, Mrs L (Lab)	22,439	36.2%	+7.2%	17,121	29.0%	Lab
Seekings, G K (LD)	8,558	13.8%	-7.7%	12,674	21.5% SDP/All
Wilson, M (Grn)	766	1.2%				
C to Lab swing 4.0%	61,967		12.5%	59,054		20.6%
		C maj	7,765		C maj	12,138

Nicholas Soames was appointed Parly Sec, Min of Agriculture, Fisheries and Food in 1992. Elected in 1983; contested Central Dumbartonshire, 1979. Son of Lord Soames and grandson of Sir Winston Churchill. Was non-exec director, Robert Fraser & Partners, bankers; Tolgate Holdings plc, 1990-2; Abela Holdings (UK), 1989-90; Roche Products Ltd, 1989-92; Sedgwick James (London), and Sedgwick Gp Development Ltd. PPS to Nicholas Ridley, Sec of State for Environment and for Trade and Industry, 1987-90; and to John Gummer, when Minr of State for Employment and chmn of Cons Pty, 1984-85. Jt

sec, Cons backbench foreign and Commonwealth affairs cmte, 1985-7. B Feb 12 1948; ed St Aubyns, Sussex; Eton.
Laura Moffatt, state registered nurse. Mbr, Crawley BC, 1984- ; Mayor of Crawley, 1989-90. B Apr 9 1954; ed Hazelwick Comprehensive Sch, Crawley; Crawley Coll. Cohse.
Gordon Seekings, telecommunications quality manager; mbr, Crawley BC, 1987- ; Mensa. B Dec 28 1953; ed Honeywell primary and Spencer Park comprehensive, both in Battersea.

CREWE AND NANTWICH				No change		
Electorate % Turnout	74,993	81.9%	1992	72,961	79.3%	1987
*Dunwoody, Mrs G P (Lab)	28,065	45.7%	+1.7%	25,457	44.0%	Lab
Silvester, B G (C)	25,370	41.3%	-0.8%	24,365	42.1%	C
Griffiths, G (LD)	7,315	11.9%	-2.0%	8,022	13.9%	SDP/All
Wilkinson, Ms N (Grn)	651	1.1%				
C to Lab swing 1.3%	61,401		4.4%	57,844		1.9%
		Lab maj	2,695		Lab maj	1,092

Gwyneth Dunwoody became mbr, Select Cmte on Transport, in 1987; chief Opposn spokesman on transport, 1983-5, and spokesman on health, 1981-3. Mbr, shadow Cabinet, 1983-85; Lab Pty NEC, 1981-89. Pty campaign coordinator, 1983-5. Chmn, Lab Friends of Israel; jt vice-pres, all-pty British-Israeli parly gp. Elected 1983; MP for Crewe, Feb 1974-83; Exeter, 1966-70; contested that seat, 1964. MEP, 1975-9; mbr, Totnes BC, 1963-6. Parly Sec, Bd of Trade, 1967-70. B Dec 12 1930; ed Fulham Cty Sec Sch; Convent of Notre Dame. Parly consultant, British Fur Trade Assocn. Sponsored by RMT.

Brian Sylvester, director, Crewe Development Agency, contested Stalybridge and Hyde 1983. Mbr, Crewe and Nanwich BC, 1976- ;(cl ldr, 1984-90; Cons gp ldr, 1984-); Shavington-cum-Gresty PC, 1976- (chmn, 1987-8). B Jan 18 1952; ed Manor Rd Primary Sch, Nantwich; Nantwich and Acton GS; Smithfield Coll of Distributive Trade, London; N Staffs Poly. Former self-employed butcher.

Gwyn Griffiths, clerical officer, British Rail; mbr, Crewe and Nantwich BC, 1983- (LD gp ldr, 1988-). B Jul 6 1957; ed Ysgol Maelgwn, Llandudno; Crewe Cty GS for Boys; Univ Coll, Cardiff. TSSA.

Natalie Wilkinson, chemist and systems engineer. B Oct 29 1960; ed Croham Hurst Sch, Croydon; King's Sch, Ely; Guildford Univ.

CROSBY				No change		
Electorate % Turnout	82,537	82.5%	1992	83,914	79.6%	1987
*Thornton, G M (C)	32,267	47.4%	+1.3%	30,842	46.2%	C
Eagle, Ms M (Lab)	17,461	25.7%	+7.7%	23,989	35.9%	SDP/All
Clucas, Ms H F (LD)	16,562	24.3%	-11.6%	11,992	17.9%	Lab
Marks, J (Lib)	1,052	1.5%				
Brady, S (Grn)	559	0.8%				
Paterson, N (NLP)	152	0.2%				
C to Lab swing 3.2%	68,053		21.8%	66,823		10.3%
		C maj	14,806		C maj	6,853

Malcolm Thornton became chmn of Select Cmte on Ed and Science in 1989, mbr since 1985; mbr, Select Cmte on Environment, 1979-81. River Mersey pilot, 1955-79. Jt vice-chmn, all-pty Mersey barrage parly gp, 1990- . Won this seat 1983; MP for Liverpool, Garston, 1979-83. Jt vice-chmn, Cons back-bench constitutional affairs cmte, 1988-9. Parly consultant to Building Employers Confed. and Keene Public Affairs Ltd. B Apr 3 1939; ed Wallasey GS; Liverpool Nautical Coll. Mbr, Wallasey CBC, 1965-74; Wirral MBC, 1973-9. Former mbr, marine pilotage branch, TGWU.

Maria Eagle, trainee solicitor; chairman, Formby LP; sec, Formby women's section. B Feb 17 1961; ed Formby HS; Pembroke Coll, Oxford; Lancaster Gate Coll of Law. TGWU/ACTS; former NUJ.

Flo Clucas contested Merseyside W for LD in 1989 Euro elections; Halton in 1987. Mbr, Liverpool City Cl, 1986- (LD speaker on ed, 1990-). Teacher. B May 9 1947; ed Bellerive GS; St Mary's Coll, Bangor; Liverpool Inst of Higher Ed; Liverpool Univ. NAS/UWT.

CROYDON CENTRAL				No change		
Electorate % Turnout	55,798	71.7%	1992	55,410	70.5%	1987
Beresford, Sir Paul (C)	22,168	55.4%	-1.2%	22,133	56.6%	C
Davies, G R (Lab)	12,518	31.3%	+6.9%	9,516	24.3%	Lab
Richardson, Ms D (LD)	5,342	13.3%	-5.7%	7,435	19.0%	SDP/All
C to Lab swing 4.1%	40,028		24.1%	39,084		32.3%
		C maj	9,650		C maj	12,617

Sir Paul Beresford was elected in 1992. Became ldr in 1983 of Wandsworth BC, the council that levied the lowest poll tax; mbr of cl since 1978 and has chaired public accountability sub-cmte, housing policy, policy and finance and ed. Wandsworth rep on London Borough Assocn since 1980-1; AMA; Wandsworth, Sutton and Merton AHA; Wandsworth HA; Richmond, Twickenham and Roehampton HA. Dental surgeon. B Apr 6 1946; ed Richmond Primary Sch and Waimea Coll, Nelson, New Zealand; Otago Univ, Dunedin, New Zealand; Eastman Dental Hospital, London Univ. Has served on Cons Gtr London area exec and advisory cmtes; mbr, Dept of Environment Cons manifesto gp; Western Riverside Waste Authority. Governor, Riverside Sch, Westminster Coll.

Geraint Davies, managing director, Purecrete (Green tour operator) and business consultant, contested Croydon S 1987. Mbr, Croydon BC, 1986- . B May 3 1960; ed Llanishen Comprehensive Sch, Cardiff; Jesus Coll, Oxford. MSF.

Deborah Richardson, policy administrator. Mbr, NHS Support Fed. B Apr 13 1954; ed Sussex Univ.

CROYDON NORTH EAST						C gain
Electorate % Turnout	64,405	72.0%	1992	63,129	69.7%	1987
Congdon, D L (C)	23,835	51.4%		24,188	55.0%	Speaker
Walker, Ms M M (Lab)	16,362	35.3%	+8.7%	11,669	26.5%	Lab
Fraser, J (LD)	6,186	13.3%	-5.1%	8,128	18.5%	SDP/All
No swing calculation.	46,383		16.1%	43,985		28.5%
		C maj	7,473		Speaker maj	12,519

David Congdon was returned for this seat in 1992. Computer consultant with Philips Electronics. Vice-chmn, Croydon NE Cons assocn, 1979-82. Mbr, Croydon Cl, 1976- (dep ldr of cl and former chmn, social services cmte); Croydon Society; Nat Trust. Governor, Croydon Coll, 1979- . B Oct 16 1949; ed Alleyn's Sch; Thames Poly.
Mary Walker, employed in political and voluntary organisations; former teacher. Mbr, Croydon BC, 1973- (ldr, Lab gp, 1986-). Trustee, Nat Energy Foundation. Mbr, Croydon CHC. B Jul 1 1947; ed Elizabeth Coll, Guernsey; NW London Poly; LSE. TGWU.
John Fraser, credit controller; vice-pres, YLDs. B Nov 5 1963; ed Furzedown Sec Sch; Keele Univ.

CROYDON NORTH WEST						Lab gain
Electorate % Turnout	57,241	70.8%	1992	57,369	69.2%	1987
Wicks, M H (Lab)	19,152	47.3%	+10.3%	18,665	47.0%	C
*Malins, H J (C)	17,626	43.5%	-3.5%	14,677	37.0%	Lab
Hawkins, Mrs L F (LD)	3,728	9.2%	-6.8%	6,363	16.0%	L/All
C to Lab swing 6.9%	40,506		3.8%	39,705		10.0%
		Lab maj	1,526		C maj	3,988

Malcolm Wicks, director, Family Policy Studies Centre, won this seat in 1992; contested it 1987; chmn and sec, Croydon S CLP and Croydon local govt cmte. Worked in Home Office urban deprivation unit, 1974-7; research director and sec, study commission on the family, 1978-83. Trustee, Nat Energy Foundation. Mbr, Croydon CHC. B Jul 1 1947; ed Elizabeth Coll, Guernsey; NW London Poly; LSE. TGWU.
Humfrey Malins held the seat, 1983-92; contested Liverpool, Toxteth in both 1974 elections, and Lewisham E, 1979. PPS to Virginia Bottomley, Minr of State for Health, 1989-92, and to Minr of State and Under Sec of State, Home Office, 1987-9. Mbr, select cmtes on broadcasting, 1991-2; statutory instruments, 1991-2; consolidation bills, 1983-87. A solicitor and asst recorder. Consultant to Tuck and Mann, solicitors, Wena Hotels. Jt vice-chmn, Cons backbench legal cmte, 1986-7; jt sec, 1983-6. B Jul 31 1945; ed St John's Sch, Leatherhead; Brasenose Coll, Oxford; Coll of Law, Guildford. Mbr, Mole Valley DC, 1973-82.
Linda Hawkins, state registered chiropodist in NHS; exec mbr, Lewisham LDs. B Jun 21 1959; ed in Beeston, Notts; CFE; Notts Univ; London Foot Hospital. Mbr, Soc of Chiropodists; British Diabetic Assocn (professional section).

CROYDON SOUTH						No change
Electorate % Turnout	64,768	77.6%	1992	65,085	73.7%	1987
Ottaway, R G J (C)	31,993	63.7%	-0.4%	30,732	64.1%	C
Billenness, P H (LD)	11,568	23.0%	-1.3%	11,669	24.3%	L/All
Salmon, Ms H (Lab)	6,444	12.8%	+3.1%	4,679	9.8%	Lab
Samuel, M (Choice)	239	0.5%		900	1.9%	Grn
LD to C swing 0.5%	50,244		40.7%	47,980		39.7%
		C maj	20,425		C maj	19,063

Richard Ottaway was returned for this seat in 1992; MP for Nottingham N, 1983-7, Specialist in international, maritime and commercial law and former partner in Wm A Crump, solicitors. Director and legal adviser to Coastal States Petroleum (UK) Ltd. Served in RN, 1961-9; RNR, 1970-80. Cmte mbr of Population Concern. PPS to Minrs of State, FCO, 1985-7. B May 24 1945; ed Backwell Sec Mod Sch, Somerset; RNC Dartmouth; Bristol Univ.
Peter Billenness, international marketing consultant, was contesting his tenth election (eight UK and two Euro). Stood at London S and Surrey E in 1989 Euro elections and Kent West 1984. Contested Streatham 1983 and stood at Croydon S 1979, E Grinstead Feb 1974, Epsom 1970, Bromley 1966, Hendon S 1964 and 1959. B May 12 1927; ed Eastbourne GS; Eastbourne Coll; Cheltenham Tech Coll; Univ Coll, London. Treas, LD Europe gp; mbr, exec, Lib International (British gp); on cmte of Cl of Regions of England; chmn, LD land value taxation campaign.
Helen Salmon, press officer; mbr, Croydon BC, 1988- ; regional women's cmte, Lab pty, London; women's officer in local CLP. B Oct 11 1963; ed in Huddersfield and Lincoln. Apex, 1987-90 (staff rep); NUJ, 1991- .

CUMBERNAULD AND KILSYTH						No change
Electorate % Turnout	46,489	79.1%	1992	45,427	78.5%	1987
*Hogg, N (Lab)	19,855	54.0%	-6.0%	21,385	60.0%	Lab
Johnston, T (SNP)	10,640	28.9%	+9.4%	6,982	19.6%	SNP
Mitchell, I G (C)	4,143	11.3%	+2.2%	4,059	11.4%	SDP/All
Haddow, Ms J (LD)	2,118	5.8%	-5.6%	3,227	9.1%	C
Lab to SNP swing 7.7%	36,756		25.1%	35,653		40.4%
		Lab maj	9,215		Lab maj	14,403

Norman Hogg appointed to chairmen's panel, in 1988; Public Accounts Cmte, 1990- ; an Opposn spokesman on Scotland, 1987-8; Opposn dep chief whip, 1983-7; Scottish Lab whip, 1982-3. Non-exec director, Kelvin Buses, 1991- ; parly adviser, Bus and Coach cl; jt chmn, all-pty road passenger transport parly gp. Mbr, Select Cmte on Commons Services, 1983-7. Elected for this seat 1983; MP for E Dunbartonshire, 1979-83. Local govt official, Aberdeen TC, 1953-67. B Mar 12 1938; ed Causewayend Sch, Aberdeen; Ruthrieston sec sch, Aberdeen. TGWU.

Tom Johnston, teacher, fought seat 1987 and Monklands E 1983. Mbr, Cumbernauld and Kilsyth DC. B 1947; ed Glasgow univ; Jordanhill Coll of Ed; London univ. Pty spokesman on housing, 1985-7.
Iain Mitchell, advocate, fought Kirkcaldy 1987 and Falkirk W 1983. Part-time mercantile law, Edinburgh univ, 1974-83. B Nov 15 1951; ed Perth Acad; Edinburgh univ. FRSA; Fellow, Society of Antiquaries of Scotland.
Jean Haddow, training consultant; mbr, Kirkcaldy DC, 1989- ; Fife Health Cl. B Aug 5 1930; ed Edinburgh univ.

CUNNINGHAME NORTH						No change
Electorate % Turnout	54,803	78.2%	1992	54,817	78.2%	1987
*Wilson, B D H (Lab)	17,564	41.0%	-3.4%	19,016	44.4%	Lab
Clarkson, Ms E (C)	14,625	34.1%	+0.1%	14,594	34.0%	C
Crossan, D M (SNP)	7,813	18.2%	+8.7%	5,185	12.1%	SDP/All
Herbison, D (LD)	2,864	6.7%	-5.4%	4,076	9.5%	SNP
Lab to C swing 1.7%	42,866		6.9%	42,871		10.3%
		Lab maj	2,939		Lab maj	4,422

Brian Wilson became an Opposn spokesman on Scotland in 1988. Won this seat 1987; contested Western Isles 1983, Inverness 1979 and Ross and Cromarty, Oct 1974. Journalist, investigative reporter, having written for Glasgow Herald and The Observer, and Scottish football corr of The Guardian. Founding editor and director, West Highland Free Press, 1972- ; first winner in 1975 of Nicholas Tomalin Memorial Award for outstanding journalism. Mbr, Select Cmte on Broadcasting, 1988-90. B Dec 13 1948; ed Dunoon GS; Dundee univ; Univ Coll, Cardiff. NUJ and TGWU.
Edith Clarkson, housewife, former teacher, district cllr, 1984- (Cons gp ldr, 1988-). Chmn, Cunninghame local

govt advisory cmte, 1986- ; area crime prevention panel, 1987- . B Mar 26 1939. Mbr, Glasgow DC, 1977-80; Strathclyde Reg Cl, 1982-6. Vice-chmn, Scottish S African Society, 1986- .
David Crossan, consultant town planner; constituency convenor, Glasgow Hillhead, 1990-1; Gaelic spokesman, 1991. B Nov 28 1960; ed Hyndland Sch, Glasgow; Glasgow and Manchester univs.
Douglas Herbison, EC affairs, 1985- , fought this seat 1987; Cumbernauld and Kilsyth 1983; Strathclyde W in 1984 and 1989 Euro elections. Sec-Gen, European Confed of Retailers, 1978-85. B Jun 25 1951; ed London univ.

CUNNINGHAME SOUTH						No change
Electorate % Turnout	49,010	75.9%	1992	49,842	75.0%	1987
Donohue, B H (Lab)	19,687	52.9%	-7.9%	22,728	60.8%	Lab
Bell, R (SNP)	9,007	24.2%	+13.2%	6,095	16.3%	C
Leslie, S A (C)	6,070	16.3%	+0.0%	4,426	11.8%	L/All
Ashley, B (LD)	2,299	6.2%	-5.7%	4,115	11.0%	SNP
Jackson, W (NLP)	128	0.3%				
Lab to SNP swing 10.5%	37,191		28.7%	37,364		44.5%
		Lab maj	10,680		Lab maj	16,633

Brian Donohue, Nalgo official, was elected in 1992.Convenor to Scottish political and ed cmte, AUEW (Tass); sec, Irvine and District Trades Cl, 1973-81, and chmn of ICI contract draughtsmen's cmte. Became treas, Cunninghame South CLP in 1985. Chmn, Cunninghame industrial development cmte, 1976-80; N Ayrshire and Arran local health cl, 1977-9. In TASS, from 1970, and TGWU-ACTSS from 1981. Apprentice fitter/turner, Ailsa shipyard, finishing apprenticeship in drawing office; also worked at Hunterston power station and ICI organic division as draughtsman, and with Nalgo as a district officer. B Sep 10 1948; ed Patna Primary Sch; Waterside Primary Sch; Loudoun Montgomery Primary Sch; Irvine Royal Acad; Kilmarnock Tech Coll.

Ricky Bell, accounts clerk. Convenor, constituency pty; Young Scot Nats, 1988-90; elected mbr, SNP nat cl, and a spokesman on housing. B Dec 9 1965. Sogat '82 mbr, Scottish exec.
Sebastian Leslie, telecoms management consultant; financial controller, Rowco International Ltd, 1980-1; with Coopers and Lybrand, accountants, 1975-90. B Mar 5 1954; ed Ampleforth Coll, York; Grenoble univ.
Brian Ashley, community services consultant in Sweden since 1982; fought Motherwell S 1983; lecturer in community studies, Moray House, 1960-82. Chmn, Scottish Cl for Racial Equality. B May 30 1927; ed Univ Coll, Hull.

CYNON VALLEY						No change
Electorate % Turnout	49,695	76.5%	1992	49,621	76.7%	1987
*Clwyd, Ms A (Lab)	26,254	69.1%	+0.2%	26,222	68.9%	Lab
Smith, A M (C)	4,890	12.9%	+0.7%	4,651	12.2%	SDP/All
Benney, T (PC)	4,186	11.0%	+4.3%	4,638	12.2%	C
Verma, M (LD)	2,667	7.0%			2,549	6.7%	PC
Lab to C swing 0.2%	37,997		56.2%	38,060		56.7%
		Lab maj	21,364		Lab maj	21,571

Ann Clwyd contested the deputy leadership of Lab pty in 1992. Elected to shadow cabinet 1989 and appointed shadow aid minister; mbr Opposn team on ed, 1987-8; also spoke on women's rights, 1987-8. Broadcaster and journalist. Mbr, Select Cmte on Euro Legislation, 1987-8; treas, Europe gp, 1988- ; chairman PLP health and social security cmte, 1985-7; chmn, 1991- , and vice-chmn, 1990-1, Welsh Lab MPs; jt vice-chmn, PLP defence cmte, 1985-7. Elected at 1984 by-election; contested Gloucester, Oct 1974; Denbigh, 1970. MEP for Mid and West Wales, 1979-84. Mbr Lab NEC, 1983-4. B Mar 21 1937; ed Holywell GS; Queen's Sch, Chester; Univ Coll, Bangor. Mbr, Royal Commission on NHS, 1976-9. Parly adviser to Soc of Telecom Executives. NUJ. Sponsored by TGWU.

Andrew Smith, public affairs consultant; dep managing director, Ian Greer Associates Ltd; vice-pres, Cynon Valley Cons Assocn. Mbr, 1990 Task Force, Gtr London Cons area. B Jul 5 1962; ed St Columba RC Sch, Bexleyheath.

Terry Benney, legal exec; mbr, Cynon Valley BC, 1987- . B Apr 13 1947. Founder mbr, Cynon Valley Hospital broadcasting service and Merthyr Cynon action for single homeless.

Marcello Verma, estate agent. Party official in Cardiff S and Penarth. B Oct 4 1968; ed Chafyan Grove Sch, Salisbury; Poly of Wales.

DAGENHAM						No change
Electorate % Turnout	59,645	70.7%	1992	61,714	67.3%	1987
*Gould, B C (Lab)	22,027	52.3%	+7.8%	18,454	44.4%	Lab
Rossiter, D (C)	15,294	36.3%	-2.2%	15,985	38.5%	C
Marquand, C N H (LD)	4,824	11.4%	-5.6%	7,088	17.1%	SDP/All
C to Lab swing 5.0%	42,145		16.0%	41,527		5.9%
		Lab maj	6,733		Lab maj	2,469

Bryan Gould contested the party leadership and deputy leadership in 1992. Chief Opposition spokesman on environment 1989- ; chief spokesman on trade and industry 1987-9, mbr DTI front bench team, 1983-6. Elected to shadow cabinet in 1986 becoming pty campaigns co-ordinator and shadow Chief Sec to the Treas, 1986-7; chmn, Lab economic policy gp, 1985-7. Mbr Lab NEC, 1987-; mbr, Lab working pty on electoral systems, 1990-. Jt vice-chmn (1988-9) and mbr (1986-8 and 1989-), exec cmte, UK branch, CPA. Presenter and reporter, *TV Eye*, Thames Television, 1979-83. Elected for this seat 1983; MP for Southampton, Test, Oct 1974-9; contested that seat, Feb 1974. B Feb 11 1939; ed Dannevirke HS, New Zealand; Victoria and Auckland Univs; Balliol Coll, Oxford. Fellow and tutor in law, Worcester Coll, Oxford, 1968-74; diplomatic service in Brussels, 1966-8, and Foreign Office, 1964-6. Former mbr, Select Cmte on Euro Legislation and chmn, Safeguard Britain Campaign.

Don Rossiter, a professional footballer with Arsenal, 1950-56, and non-league player, 1956-63. Director of property development company. Mbr, Rochester upon Medway City Cl, 1976-91. B Jun 8 1935; ed sec sch.

Charles Marquand, barrister. B Oct 22 1962; ed City of London Sch; Magdalen Coll, Oxford; City Univ.

DARLINGTON						Lab gain
Electorate % Turnout	66,094	83.6%	1992	65,940	80.8%	1987
Milburn, A (Lab)	26,556	48.1%	+6.5%	24,831	46.6%	C
*Fallon, M (C)	23,758	43.0%	-3.6%	22,170	41.6%	Lab
Bergg, P (LD)	4,586	8.3%	-3.5%	6,289	11.8%	L/All
Clarke, Dr D (BNP)	355	0.6%				
C to Lab swing 5.0%	55,255		5.1%	53,290		5.0%
		Lab maj	2,798		C maj	2,661

Alan Milburn won the seat in 1992. Senior business devopment officer in local govt; exec mbr, Northern region Lab pty; chairman, Newcastle Central CLP; MSF NE regional pres, 1989- . B Jan 27 1958; ed comprehensive sch; Lancaster and Newcastle univs.

Michael Fallon was Under Sec of State for Ed and Science, 1990-2; a Lord Commissioner of Treasury (govt whip), 1990; asst govt whip, 1988-90; PPS to Cecil Parkinson, Sec of State for Energy, 1987-8. MP for the seat, 1983-92; contested Darlington by-election, 1983. Political research-er, writer and lecturer. B May 14 1952; ed Epsom Coll; St Andrews Univ. Political asst and adviser to Lord Carrington, 1974-7; EEC adviser, Cons research dept, 1977-9. Sec, Lord Home's cmte on future of House of Lords, 1977-8. Jt managing director, European Consul-tants Ltd, 1979-81.

DARTFORD						No change
Electorate % Turnout	72,366	83.1%	1992	72,632	79.0%	1987
*Dunn, R J (C)	31,194	51.8%	-1.6%	30,685	53.5%	C
Stoate, Dr H J A (Lab)	20,880	34.7%	+7.2%	15,756	27.5%	Lab
Bryden, Dr P J (LD)	7,584	12.6%	-5.6%	10,439	18.2%	SDP/All
Munro, A (FDP)	262	0.4%	-0.4%	491	0.9%	FDP
Holland, Ms A (NLP)	247	0.4%				
C to Lab swing 4.4%	60,167		17.1%	57,371		26.0%
		C maj	10,314		C maj	14,929

Robert Dunn was chmn of Cons back-bench transport cmte, 1990-1; jt vice-chmn, Cons environment cmte, 1989-90; chmn, Cons social security cmte, 1988-9; jt vice-chmn, Cons party organisation cmte, 1988-91; chmn, Cons unpaired MPs, 1989- . Under Sec of State for Ed and Science, 1983-8. Elected in 1979; contested Eccles, Feb and Oct 1974. Mbr, exec, 1922 Cmte, 1988- ; Commons selection cmte, 1991- ; select cmte on environment, 1981-2; jt sec, Cons back-bench ed cmte, 1980-3. B Jul 1946; ed Manchester Poly; Brighton Poly; Salford Univ. Senior buyer, J Sainsbury, 1973-9, . PPS to Under Secs of State at DES, 1981-2, and to Cecil Parkinson, 1982-3. Pres, SE Area YCs, 1989- ; Mbr, Southwark BC, 1974-8.

Dr Howard Stoate, general practitioner, contested Old Bexley and Sidcup in 1987. Vice-chmn, Dartford CLP, 1984- ; mbr, Dartford BC; nat exec cmte, Fabian society; chmn, Dartford Fabian Soc, 1984-90. B Apr 14 1954; ed Kingston GS; Kings Coll, London Univ. MSF; BMA.

Dr Peter Bryden, medical practitioner, medical management adviser and company director. Mbr, district management team, Hastings HA, 1984-9; E Sussex local medical cmte, 1979- ; chmn, Hastings GP cmte, 1984-9. B Sep 5 1950; ed Eastbourne GS; Queen Elizabeth Coll, London Univ; Royal Free Hosp sch of medicine.

DAVENTRY						No change
Electorate % Turnout	71,824	82.8%	1992	69,241	78.2%	1987
*Boswell, T E (C)	34,734	58.4%	+0.5%	31,353	57.9%	C
Koumi, Ms L M A W (Lab)	14,460	24.3%	+3.8%	11,663	21.6%	L/All
Rounthwaite, A S (LD)	9,820	16.5%	-5.0%	11,097	20.5%	Lab
France, R (NLP)	422	0.7%				
C to Lab swing 1.7%	59,436		34.1%	54,113		36.4%
		C maj	20,274		C maj	19,690

Timothy Boswell was appointed a Lord Commissioner to the Treasury after the general election. Asst Govt whip from 1990-2. Farmer. Elected in 1987. PPS to Peter Lilley, Financial Sec to Treasury, 1989-90. Mbr, Select Cmte on Agriculture, 1987-9; Contested Rugby, Feb 1974. Managed family farm business, 1974-87; agricultural specialist, Cons research dept, 1970-3. B Dec 2 1942; ed Marlborough Coll; New Coll, Oxford. Pres (1984-90) and cl mbr (1966-90), Perry Foundation (agriculture research). Chmn, Northants, Leics and Rutland NFU, 1983;

Lesley Koumi, teacher, contested this seat 1987. Former Lab pty sec at branch, district, constituency, county and Euro levels. Mbr, Daventry DC, 1988- ; Weedon PC, 1988- . B Oct 6 1948; ed St Joseph's Convent GS, London; Essex Univ. NUT.

Tony Rounthwaite, general manager, contested Northampton N in 1987, 1983 and 1979. Mbr Northampton BC, 1983-7. Pres, Northampton LDs. B Feb 6 1951; ed King's Sch, Tynemouth; Newcastle upon Tyne Poly.

DAVYHULME						No change
Electorate % Turnout	61,679	81.8%	1992	65,558	77.3%	1987
*Churchill, W S (C)	24,216	48.0%	+1.4%	23,633	46.6%	C
Brotherton, B (Lab)	19,790	39.2%	+8.8%	15,434	30.4%	Lab
Pearcey, Dr J (LD)	5,797	11.5%	-11.5%	11,637	23.0%	L/All
Brotheridge, T (NLP)	665	1.3%				
C to Lab swing 3.7%	50,468		8.8%	50,704		16.2%
		C maj	4,426		C maj	8,199

Winston Churchill, author, journalist and broadcaster, was Cons party coordinator for defence and multilateral disarmament, 1982-4; mbr, select cmte on defence, 1983- ; Commons services cmte, 1985-6; vice-chmn, Cons defence cmte, 1979-83; an Opposition spokesman on defence, 1976-8. Treas, 1922 Cmte, 1987-8, and mbr of exec, 1979-85. Mbr of Lloyd's. Jt vice-chmn, NW gp of Cons MPs, 1989-91; Interparly cl against anti-Semitism, 1991- . Elected for this seat 1983; MP for Stretford, 1970-83; contested Manchester, Gorton, by-election, 1967. B Oct 10 1940; ed Eton; Christ Church, Oxford. Trustee, Winston Churchill Memorial Trust, 1968- ; Nat Benevolent Fund for Aged, 1974- . IoJ.

Barry Brotherton, electrical engineer; bd mbr, Trafford Park Urban Development Corpn; mbr, Trafford MBC, 1973-5 and 1980- (cl ldr, 1986-8; Lab gp ldr); Sale BC, 1970-4; Bredbury and Romiley UDC, 1966-70. Ex-treas, Davyhulme CLP. B Dec 28 1942; edx Stockport GS; UMIST; London Univ (external). EPEA.

Jacqueline Pearcey, systems analyst (radiological safety); mbr, Manchester City Cl, 1991- ; vice-chmn, City of Manchester LDs; Manchester Gorton LDs. B Sep 23 1963; ed Leeds Girls' HS; Bristol and Manchester Univs. IPMS.

DELYN						Lab gain
Electorate % Turnout	66,591	83.4%	1992	63,541	82.6%	1987
Hanson, D G (Lab)	24,979	45.0%	+5.9%	21,728	41.4%	C
Whitby, M J (C)	22,940	41.3%	-0.1%	20,504	39.1%	Lab
Dodd, R C (LD)	6,208	11.2%	-5.8%	8,913	17.0%	L/All
Drake, A (PC)	1,414	2.5%	-0.0%	1,339	2.6%	PC
C to Lab swing 3.0%	55,541		3.7%	52,484		2.3%
		Lab maj	2,039		C maj	1,224

David Hanson was returned for this seat in 1992; contested it 1987, Eddisbury 1983 and Cheshire W in 1984 Euro election. Director of national charity and former regional manager with Spastics Society. Mbr Vale Royal BC, 1983-91 (ldr, Lab gp, 1988-90); Northwich TC, 1987-91. B Jul 5 1957; ed Verdin Comprehensive Sch, Winsford, Cheshire; Hull Univ. MSF.

Michael Whitby contested Midlands W in 1989 Euro elections and 1987 Euro by-election; Warley E in 1983 general election. Director, clothing and textile distribution company; lecturer in business studies. Former vice-chmn W Midlands CPC; hon sec, W Midlands Cons clubs advisory cmte, 1986; mbr W Midlands area exec cl, 1987- ; nat

union exec cmte, 1987-8; Nat Fed of Self-Employed and Small Businesses. Mbr Sandwell MBC, 1984-8. B Feb 1948; ed James Watt Tech GS; Coll of Michaelshoven, Germany; Birmingham Univ.

Raymond Dodd, community centre manager; organising sec British Novelty Salt and Pepper Collectors Club. Mbr Delyn BC, 1976- (LD gp ldr, 1979-91); Mold TC, 1987- ; chmn Mold L and LD branch, 1984-6 and 1989-91. B Sep 26 1945; ed Birkenhead Inst GS; Nat Coll for Youth Ldrs; Liverpool Univ (part-time).

Ashley Drake, sales rep, marketing agency for publishers. PlC youth and student organiser, 1989-91; NUS area organiser and mbr, NUS Wales exec, 1987-9.

DENTON AND REDDISH						No change
Electorate % Turnout	68,463	76.8%	1992	69,533	75.5%	1987
*Bennett, A F (Lab)	29,021	55.2%	+5.6%	26,023	49.6%	Lab
Horswell, J (C)	16,937	32.2%	-1.6%	17,773	33.9%	C
Ridley, Dr H F (LD)	4,953	9.4%	-7.1%	8,697	16.6%	SDP/All
Powell, M (Lib)	1,296	2.5%				
Fuller, J (NLP)	354	0.7%				
C to Lab swing 3.6%	52,561		23.0%	52,493		15.7%
		Lab maj	12,084		Lab maj	8,250

Andrew Bennett was elected for this seat 1983; MP for Stockport N, Feb 1974-83; contested Knutsford, 1970. Appointed to select cmtes on social security and on sittings of Commons in 1991; mbr select cmte on social services, 1989-91 and 1979-83; Commons information cmte, 1991- ; select cmte on members' interests, 1979-83; mbr and former chmn, select cmte on statutory instruments and jt select cmte, 1983-7. An Opposition spokesman on education, 1983-8. Former teacher. B Mar 9 1939; ed Birmingham Univ. NUT. Sec, PLP civil liberties gp.

Jeff Horswell, building society manager. Mbr exec cmte, Makerfield Cons assocn, 1989- ; CPC nat advisory cmte, 1987-9; treas Plymouth Devonport Cons assocn, 1988-9; chmn Western area CPC, 1988-9, and Western area YCs, 1983-5. B Jan 31 1962; ed Sutton HS, Plymouth.

Fred Ridley, self-employed political organiser and PR consultant; chmn Hazel Grove LD; former mbr working gp on transport; mbr Stockport MBC, 1987- . B Dec 26 1937; ed St Albans Cty GS for Boys; London Univ (part-time). Collector of Lloyd-George memorabilia.

DERBY NORTH						No change
Electorate % Turnout	73,176	80.7%	1992	71,738	75.7%	1987
*Knight, G (C)	28,574	48.4%	-0.4%	26,516	48.8%	C
Laxton, R (Lab)	24,121	40.9%	+3.6%	20,236	37.3%	Lab
Charlesworth, R (LD)	5,638	9.6%	-3.8%	7,268	13.4%	L/All
Wall, E (Grn)	383	0.6%	+0.1%	291	0.5%	Grn
Hart, P (NF)	245	0.4%				
Onley, N (NLP)	58	0.1%				
C to Lab swing 2.0%	59,019		7.5%	54,311		11.6%
		C maj	4,453		C maj	6,280

Gregory Knight was appointed a Lords Commissioner of the Treasury (govt whip) in 1990; an asst govt whip, 1989-90. Mbr select cmte on broadcasting, 1990-1. Solicitor. Compiler of Honourable Insults: a century of political invective. Elected in 1983. PPS to David Mellor and Lord Glenarthur, when Minrs of State, FCO, 1987-9, and to Mr Mellor when at Home Office, 1987. B Apr 4 1949; ed Alderman Newton's GS, Leicester; Coll of Law, Guildford. Mbr, Leicester city Cl, 1976-9; Leics CC, 1977-83.

Robert Laxton, telecommunications engineer; mbr Derby

city Cl, 1979- (cl ldr, 1986-8). B Sep 7 1944; ed Allestree Woodlands Sec Sch; Derby coll of tech.

Robert Charlesworth, maintenance electrician and EEPTU shop steward and part-time snr steward at Rolls-Royce. B Jun 23 1953; ed Aldercar comprehensive; Trent poly.

Eric Wall, stress counsellor and therapist, contested Derby N in 1987, Derby S in 1983 and Derbyshire in 1989 Euro elections. B Oct 22 1938; ed Durham and Hull Univs.

DERBY SOUTH						No change
Electorate % Turnout	66,328	75.5%	1992	68,825	69.9%	1987
*Beckett, Mrs M M (Lab)	25,917	51.7%	+8.1%	21,003	43.7%	Lab
Brown, N P (C)	18,981	37.9%	-2.6%	19,487	40.5%	C
Hartropp, S J (LD)	5,198	10.4%	-5.4%	7,608	15.8%	SDP/All
C to Lab swing 5.3%	50,096		13.8%	48,098		3.2%
		Lab maj	6,936		Lab maj	1,516

Margaret Beckett contested the Labour deputy leadership after general election. Elected to shadow cabinet in 1989, became shadow Treasury Chief Secretary; a spokesman on health and social security, 1984-9. Mbr, Lab pty NEC, 1980-1, 1985-6 and 1988- ; Lab working pty on electoral systems, 1990- . Elected for this seat 1983; MP for Lincoln, Oct 1974-9; contested the seat, Feb 1974. Ed and Science Sec., 1976-9; asst Govt whip, 1975-6. Principal researcher, Granada TV, 1979-83. B Jan 15 1943; ed Notre Dame HS, Manchester and Norwich; Manchester Coll of Science and Tech, John Dalton Poly. TGWU sponsored.

Nicholas Brown was elected ldr of Derby city cl in 1989; mbr since 1984. Partner in financial control systems business in Derby; chief rating officer, Derby city cl, 1979-84; rating gp officer, Leicester city cl, 1976-9; rating clerk, Bradford MDC, 1974-6. Chmn Derby S Cons Assocn, 1987-90. B Dec 25 1952; ed High Pavement GS, Nottingham; Bradford Univ; Leicester Poly.
Simon Hartropp, chartered engineer employed by Rolls Royce plc; parly spokesman for Derby city LDs. B Apr 7 1956; ed Univ Coll, Swansea; Bemrose Sch, Derby. Dept rep for MSF.

DERBYSHIRE NORTH EAST						No change
Electorate % Turnout	70,707	83.6%	1992	70,314	79.3%	1987
*Barnes, H (Lab)	28,860	48.8%	+4.4%	24,747	44.4%	Lab
Hayes, J H (C)	22,590	38.2%	+0.5%	21,027	37.7%	C
Stone, D (LD)	7,675	13.0%	-4.9%	9,985	17.9%	SDP/All
C to Lab swing 2.0%	59,125		10.6%	55,759		6.7%
		Lab maj	6,270		Lab maj	3,720

Harry Barnes joined select cmte on Euro legislation in 1989 and select cmte on members' interests in 1990. Elected in 1987. Jt vice-chmn PLP N Ireland cmte, 1989- ; vice-chmn, 1990- , E Midlands gp of Lab MPs. Lecturer in politics and industrial relations at Sheffield Univ, 1966-87; previously lectured at North Notts Further Ed Coll; former railway clerk. B Jul 22 1936; ed Easington Colliery primary and sec mod schs; Ryhope GS; Ruskin Coll, Oxford; Hull Univ. MSF.

John Hayes, sales director. Mbr Nottinghamshire CC, 1985- . B Jun 23 1958; ed Colfe's GS, SE London; Nottingham Univ. Mbr nat cmte of FCS, 1982-4; chmn Aspley Ward, Nottingham, Cons, 1980-3.
David Stone, residential social worker; mbr Chesterfield BC, 1984- (Gp ldr and opposn ldr). B Jun 24 1947; ed St Hugh's Seminary, Buckden, Huntingdon.

DERBYSHIRE SOUTH						No change
Electorate % Turnout	82,342	85.5%	1992	80,045	81.3%	1987
*Currie, Mrs E (C)	34,266	48.7%	-0.4%	31,927	49.1%	C
Todd, M W (Lab)	29,608	42.1%	+8.8%	21,616	33.2%	Lab
Brass, Ms D (LD)	6,236	8.9%	-8.8%	11,509	17.7%	SDP/All
Mercer, T (NLP)	291	0.4%				
C to Lab swing 4.6%	70,401		6.6%	65,052		15.9%
		C maj	4,658		C maj	10,311

Edwina Currie, lecturer, writer and broadcaster, was Under Sec of State for Health from 1986, with special responsibility for women's health issues. Resigned in Dec 1988 following controversy among egg producers over her comments on salmonella. PPS to Sir Keith Joseph, Sec of State for Ed and Science, 1985-6. Teacher and lecturer in economics, economic history and business studies, 1972-81. Elected in 1983. Mbr, select cmte on social services, 1983-6. B Oct 13 1946; ed Liverpool Inst; St Anne's Coll,

Oxford; LSE. Mbr, Birmingham City Cl, 1975-84; Birmingham AHA, 1975-82. Chmn, Central Birmingham HA, 1981-3.
Mark Todd, publisher in electronic media; mbr Cambridge city cl, 1980- (ldr, 1987-90); Lab Coordinating Cmte. B Dec 29 1954; ed Cambridge Univ. MSF.
Diana Brass, teacher. B Jan 10 1939; ed Sir William Perkis' Sch for Girls, Chertsey; Lady Margaret Hall, Oxford. AMMA.

DERBYSHIRE WEST				No change	
Electorate % Turnout	71,201	85.0%	1992	70,782	83.1%	1987
*McLoughlin, P A (C)	32,879	54.3%	+1.2%	31,224	53.1%	C
Fearn, R (LD)	14,110	23.3%	-11.9%	20,697	35.2%	L/All
Clamp, S J (Lab)	13,528	22.4%	+10.7%	6,875	11.7%	Lab
LD to C swing 6.6%	60,517		31.0%	58,796		17.9%
		C maj	18,769		C maj	10,527

Patrick McLoughlin was appointed Under Secretary for Employment in 1992; Under Sec for Transport, 1989-92. Elected at 1986 by-election; contested Wolverhampton SE, 1983. Minr of State for Ed and Science, 1987-8. Sec, E Midlands gp of Cons MPs, 1987-9; jt sec, Cons environment cmte, 1986-7. Mineworker at Littleton Colliery, 1979-85; marketing official, NCB, 1985-6. B Nov 30 1957; ed Cardinal Griffin RC Sch, Cannock; Staffordshire Coll of Agriculture. Mbr Staffordshire CC, 1981-7; Cannock Chase DC, 1980-7.

David Fearn, teacher; mbr, Derbyshire Dales DC, 1973- ; chmn, constituency LDs. Ed Ernest Bailey GS, Matlock; St Peter's Coll, Birmingham; Sch of Ed, Manchester Univ. NAS/UWT.

Steve Clamp, teacher and head of special needs at sec sch. Mbr, Wirksworth TC, 1982- (mayor, 1984-85); Derbyshire Dales DC, 1987- . B Jun 6 1956; ed Royal HS, Edinburgh; Southampton and Nottingham Univs. NUT.

DEVIZES				No change	
Electorate % Turnout	89,745	81.7%	1992	86,047	77.2%	1987
Ancram, M A F J K (C)	39,090	53.3%	-1.4%	36,372	54.8%	C
Mactaggart, Ms J (LD)	19,378	26.4%	-1.5%	18,542	27.9%	L/All
Berry, Ms R J (Lab)	13,060	17.8%	+0.5%	11,487	17.3%	Lab
Coles, S (Lib)	962	1.3%				
Ripley, J D (Grn)	808	1.1%				
LD to C swing 0.0%	73,298		26.9%	66,401		26.9%
		C maj	19,712		C maj	17,830

Michael Ancram was returned for this seat in 1992; MP for Edinburgh S, 1979-87; MP for Berwick and E Lothian, Feb to Oct 1974; fought W Lothian, 1970. Under Sec of State for Scotland, 1983-7. Mbr select cmte on energy, 1979-83. Former advocate, company director and columnist, *The Daily Telegraph*, Chmn Northern Corporate Communicatons; director, CSM Parly Consultants. B Jul 7 1945; ed Ampleforth; Christ Church, Oxford; Edinburgh Univ. Chmn Scottish Cons pty, 1980-3, and vice-chmn, 1975-80. Mbr, bd, Scottish Homes, 1988-90.

Jane Mactaggart, former organisation and method analyst; mbr Wanborough cl, 1989- ; Wilts CC, 1985-9; Wanborough PC, 1984- . Trustee, Wilts Community Fund, 1991- ; exec mbr Wilts charities information bureau, 1990- . B Feb 6 1949; ed City Poly; Bristol Poly; Cranfield Inst of Tech.

Rosemary Berry, teacher. B Dec 15 1946; ed Marlborough GS; Leeds, Bristol and Bordeaux Univs. NUT.

David Ripley, computer consultant. Sec Devizes and Marlborough Grn pty. B Apl 19 1958; ed Colne Valley HS; Kings Coll and Imperial Coll, London.

DEVON NORTH				LD gain	
Electorate % Turnout	68,998	84.4%	1992	67,474	81.7%	1987
Harvey, N B (LD)	27,414	47.1%	+4.3%	28,071	50.9%	C
*Speller, A (C)	26,620	45.7%	-5.2%	23,602	42.8%	L/All
Donner, P B (Lab)	3,410	5.9%	-0.4%	3,467	6.3%	Lab
Simmons, Ms C H (Grn)	658	1.1%				
Treadwell, G (NLP)	107	0.2%				
C to LD swing 4.7%	58,209		1.4%	55,140		8.1%
		LD maj	794		C maj	4,469

Nick Harvey won this seat in 1992; contested Enfield, Southgate for L/All 1987. Parliamentary lobbyist. Mbr Lib pty cl, 1981-2 and 1984-8;, London Lib pty exec, 1984-6; nat vice-chmn, ULS, 1981-2. B Aug 3 1961; ed Queen's Coll, Taunton; Middlesex Poly (pres, students' union, 1981-2).

Tony Speller represented the seat 1979-92; contested it in Oct 1974. Mbr select cmte on energy, 1982-8; jt sec Cons backbench energy cmte, 1987-8; chmn Westcountry Cons MPs, 1983-7. Non-exec director, Exeter Photo-Copying Ltd, 1963- . Chmn all-pty alternative energy gp, 1983- ; Cons West Africa Cmte, 1988- ; pres, catering industry liaison cmte, 1982- ; sec franchise development parly gp, 1990- ; treas all-pty fairs and showgrounds parly gp, 1989- . B Jun 12 1929; ed Exeter Sch; London and Exeter Univs. Mbr Exeter City Cl, 1963-74. Major, TA.

Paul Donner, opthalmic optician; sec Devon N CLP. B Feb 27 1949; ed St John's Sch, Leatherhead; Aston Univ. MSF.

Cathrine Simmons is undertaking further ed studies and assists husband with building design business. Mbr Gt Torrington TC, 1991- ; Torridge DC, 1987-1991. Chmn, N Devon Grn pty, 1989- . B Jul 13 1948; ed Sudbury HS for Girls, Suffolk.

DEVON WEST AND TORRIDGE						No change
Electorate % Turnout	76,933	81.5%	1992	74,550	78.7%	1987
*Nicholson, Miss E H (C)	29,627	47.3%	-3.0%	29,484	50.3%	C
McBride, D (LD)	26,013	41.5%	+2.3%	23,016	39.2%	L/All
Brenton, D G (Lab)	5,997	9.6%	+1.1%	4,990	8.5%	Lab
Williamson, Dr F (Grn)	898	1.4%	-0.6%	1,168	2.0%	Grn
Collins, D (NLP)	141	0.2%				
C to LD swing 2.6%	62,676		5.8%	58,658		11.0%
		C maj	3,614		C maj	6,468

Emma Nicholson, elected in 1987, was a Cons pty vice-chmn, 1983-7. Chmn 1990-1, jt sec 1989-90, Cons backbench environment cmte; mbr select cmte on employment, 1990- ; exec cmte, British gp IPU, 1989-91; chmn all-pty Euro Information Marketplace parly gp; jt chmn Romanian children gp. Fund raising director, Save the Children Fund 1977-85. Contested Blyth 1979. Computer and management consultant. B Oct 16 1941; ed Portsdown Lodge Sch, Bexhill-on-Sea; St Mary's Sch, Wantage; Royal Acad of Music, London. Mbr Howard League cl.
David McBride, chartered accountant, contested Blaenau Gwent 1987. Mbr LD nat campaigns gp; Welsh LD exec, 1988-90; Lib Pty Cl, 1978-82 and 1983-7. B June 23 1960; ed Stockport Sch; Univ Coll, Swansea.
David Brenton, basket maker, contested seat 1987. B Aug 15 1945; ed Barnstaple GS; St Luke's Coll, Exeter. Former chmn Bideford branch, and chmn Devon W and Torridge CLP. Mbr, Bideford TC (Mayor, 1991-2). NAS/UWT.
Frank Williamson, coll lecturer, contested seat 1987. On Grn Pty Cl, 1987-9. Mbr W Devon BC, 1987- ; Northlew PC, 1987-91. B Apr 16 1946; ed Cockermouth GS, Cumbria; Univs of London and Sydney (Aus). NATFHE.

DEWSBURY						No change
Electorate % Turnout	72,839	80.2%	1992	70,836	78.8%	1987
*Taylor, W A (Lab)	25,596	43.8%	+1.4%	23,668	42.4%	Lab
Whitfield, J (C)	24,962	42.7%	+1.1%	23,223	41.6%	C
Meadowcroft, R S (LD)	6,570	11.2%	-4.7%	8,907	16.0%	SDP/All
Birdwood, J (BNP)	660	1.1%				
Denby, N M (Grn)	471	0.8%				
Marsden, J (NLP)	146	0.2%				
C to Lab swing 0.1%	58,405		1.1%	55,798		0.8%
		Lab maj	634		Lab maj	445

Ann Taylor, elected to shadow cabinet in 1990, became Opposn spokesman on environmental protection; Mbr nat exec, Fabian Society, 1990- . Advisor to AMMA. Elected in 1987; an Opposn spokesman on home Affairs, 1987-8. MP for Bolton W Oct 1974-83 before contesting Bolton NE; contested Bolton W Feb 1974. An Opposn spokesman on education 1979-81. PPS to Ed and Science Sec., 1975-6, and Defence Sec., 1976-7; an asst Govt whip, 1977-9. Former teacher. B Jul 2 1947; ed Bolton Sch; Bradford and Sheffield Univs. Sponsored by GMB.
John Whitfield was MP for this seat, 1983-7; contested Hemsworth, 1979. B Oct 31 1941; ed Sedbergh Sch; Leeds Univ. Solicitor and partner in family firm; Director, Ashwood Chemicals Ltd; Thomas Carr Ltd; company sec and director, Caldaire Independent Hospital plc, 1982-9. Governor, Bretton Hall Coll of Higher Ed, 1990- . Sec, Tanfield Angling Club, 1972- .
Robert Meadowcroft, asst director, Royal Nat Inst for Blind; mbr, Kirklees Cl, 1983-1991 (LD gp ldr, 1986-91). B Apl 28 1950; ed King George V GS, Southport; Huddersfield Poly; Leeds Univ. MSF.
Neil Denby, teacher; editor "The Fellrunner". B Nov 1 1953; ed High Pavement GS, Nottingham; UCW Aberystwyth. Tass; NUT.

DON VALLEY						No change
Electorate % Turnout	76,327	76.3%	1992	74,500	73.8%	1987
*Redmond, M (Lab)	32,008	55.0%	+1.9%	29,200	53.1%	Lab
Paget-Brown, N (C)	18,474	31.7%	-0.5%	17,733	32.3%	C
Jevons, M (LD)	6,920	11.9%	-2.7%	8,027	14.6%	L/All
Platt, S (Grn)	803	1.4%				
C to Lab swing 1.2%	58,205		23.3%	54,960		20.9%
		Lab maj	13,534		Lab maj	11,467

Martin Redmond, a former heavy goods vehicle driver, was elected in 1983. Vice-chmn all-pty British-Thai parly gp; British-Bahrain gp; treas all-pty British-Malta parly gp; sec British-Asean gp. Director (unpaid), Doncaster Leisure (Management) Ltd, 1989- . B Aug 15 1937; ed Woodlands RC Sch; Sheffield Univ. Mbr, Doncaster BC, 1975- ; leader, 1982- ; chmn, Lab gp, 1982- . Vice-chmn, Doncaster AHA. Sponsored by NUM.
Nicholas Paget-Brown, international marketing manager with Reuters plc since 1988; with Finsbury Data Services, London, 1979-88. Mbr Kensington and Chelsea BC, 1986- . On cl, Bow Gp, 1984-86. B Mar 28 1957; ed Cranleigh Sch, Surrey; York Univ (chmn, univ Cons assocn, 1978).
Malcolm Jevons, computer systems engineer; chmn and press officer, Doncaster LD; S Yorks area vice-chmn, Yorks and Humberside LD. B Feb 17 1944; ed Mexborough schs; Leeds Univ.

DONCASTER CENTRAL					No change	
Electorate % Turnout	68,890	74.2%	1992	69,699	73.7%	1987
*Walker, H (Lab)	27,795	54.3%	+3.2%	26,266	51.2%	Lab
Glossop, G W (C)	17,113	33.5%	-1.7%	18,070	35.2%	C
Hampson, C (LD)	6,057	11.8%	-1.8%	7,004	13.6%	SDP/All
Driver, M (WRP)	184	0.4%				
C to Lab swing 2.5%	51,149		20.9%	51,340		16.0%
		Lab maj	10,682		Lab maj	8,196

Harold Walker was Chairman of Ways and Means and Deputy Speaker 1983-1992. Elected for this seat 1983; MP for Doncaster, 1964-83. An Opposn spokesman on employment, 1979-83; Minr of State for Employment, 1976-9; Under Sec of State for Employment, 1974-6; a spokesman on employment, 1970-4; Under Sec of State for Employment and Productivity, 1968-70; asst govt whip, 1967-8. Engineer. B Jul 12 1927; ed cl sch; Manchester Coll of Tech. Sponsored by AUEW.

George Glossop, barrister and small hill farmer in Peak district. Mbr, High Peak livestock society. Vice-chmn, Holborn and St Pancras Cons assocn. Mbr Cons Gp for Europe, society of Cons lawyers and Bow Gp advisory cmtes for agriculture, foreign representation and defence. Lt Cmdr RN, naval reserve. Ed Rowlinson sch, Sheffield; Keele Univ (chmn, univ Cons assocn); Lincoln's Inn.
Clifford Hampson, aircraft fitter. B Apr 17 1951; ed Sale Moor Sec Sch. Vintage car enthusiast.

DONCASTER NORTH					No change	
Electorate % Turnout	74,732	73.9%	1992	72,986	73.1%	1987
Hughes, K (Lab)	34,135	61.8%	+0.0%	32,953	61.8%	Lab
Light, R C (C)	14,322	25.9%	+1.5%	13,015	24.4%	C
Whiting, S (LD)	6,787	12.3%	-1.6%	7,394	13.9%	SDP/All
Lab to C swing 0.7%	55,244		35.9%	53,362		37.4%
		Lab maj	19,813		Lab maj	19,938

Kevin Hughes, coal miner, is mbr of and sponsored by NUM; mbr exec cmte, Yorkshire NUM, 1983-6; Doncaster BC, 1986- (chmn, social services cmte, 1987-); sec/agent, Doncaster N CLP. B Dec 15 1952; ed local state schs; Sheffield Univ on day release.
Robert Light, self-employed in farming and contracting business; mbr, Kirklees MBC, 1987- . Mbr, Cons nat advisory cmte on education, 1987- ; nat union exec cmte,

1988-90; Yorkshire Area and Batley and Spen Cons assocn cmtes; Yorks and Humberside sports cl. B Oct 12 1964; ed Whitcliffe Mount Sch, Cleckheaton, W Yorkshire.
Steven Whiting, legal exec (associate level); probate, trust and tax specialist; employed by firm of solicitors; chmn, Thorne and dist LDs, a sub-branch of Doncaster LDs. B Jul 26 1965; ed Thorne GS; Doncaster Inst of HE.

DORSET NORTH					No change	
Electorate % Turnout	76,718	81.8%	1992	72,844	79.1%	1987
*Baker, N B (C)	34,234	54.6%	-2.5%	32,854	57.0%	C
Siegle, Mrs L E (LD)	24,154	38.5%	+2.1%	20,947	36.4%	L/All
Fitzmaurice, J F (Lab)	4,360	6.9%	+0.3%	3,819	6.6%	Lab
C to LD swing 2.3%	62,748		16.1%	57,620		20.7%
		C maj	10,080		C maj	11,907

Nicholas Baker was appointed a Lord Commissioner of Treasury (govt whip) in 1990; an asst govt whip, 1989-90. Solicitor specialising in company and commercial law and mbr of Lloyd's. Elected in 1979; contested Southwark, Peckham, Feb and Oct 1974. PPS to Ld Young of Graffham, Sec of State for Trade and Industry, 1987-8; and from 1981-7 PPS to minrs at MoD including Michael Heseltine, sec of state, 1984-6. Jt vice-chmn, Cons backbench N Ireland cmte, 1988-9. B Nov 23 1938; ed St Neot's Sch, Hampshire; Clifton Coll; Exeter Coll, Oxford. Mbr select cmte on broadcasting, 1991- ; on Agriculture,

1986-7.
Linda Siegle, marketing director, PS Mailing Ltd, Wincanton, Somerset, contested Devizes for L/All in 1987. Mbr Somerset CC, 1989- ; Dorset CC, 1985-9. Former mbr, Lib pty cl. B Jul 30 1945; ed Purley Cty GS for Girls; Guys Hosp Sch of Dental Hygiene.
John Fitzmaurice, European civil servant, contested Yeovil 1987. Sec, Brussels Lab gp; vice-chair, Brussels Co-op pty. B Nov 18 1947; ed Shaftesbury GS; Bristol and Oxford Univs. Mbr European public service union, 1974- .

DORSET SOUTH						No change
Electorate % Turnout	75,788	76.9%	1992	72,855	75.5%	1987
*Bruce, I C (C)	29,319	50.3%	-4.5%	30,184	54.8%	C
Ellis, B E J (LD)	15,811	27.1%	-0.3%	15,117	27.5%	L/All
Chedzoy, Dr A (Lab)	12,298	21.1%	+3.8%	9,494	17.2%	Lab
Nager, Mrs J (Ind)	673	1.2%	+0.7%	244	0.4%	Ind
Griffiths, M (NLP)	191	0.3%				
C to LD swing 2.1%	58,292		23.2%	55,039		27.4%
		C maj	13,508		C maj	15,067

Ian Bruce joined select cmte on employment in 1990; sec Cons back-bench social security cmte, 1990- . Elected in 1987; contested Burnley 1983; Yorkshire W in 1984 Euro elections. Chmn and founder Ian Bruce Associates Ltd, a gp of employment agencies and management consultants, 1975- . Parly consultant to telecommunications managers assocn, 1989- ; parly adviser to Saudi-American Bank. Factory manager, Sinclair Electronics, 1974-5; factory and work study manager, BEPI (Pye), 1971-4. B Mar 14 1947; ed Chelmsford Tech HS; Mid-Essex Tech Coll; Bradford Univ.

Brian Ellis, legal executive, contested this seat 1987. Mbr Weymouth and Portland BC, 1984- (gp ldr, 1984- ; cmte chmn, 1988-91). B Sep 15 1950; ed Bridgwater Boys' Sch, Somerset.
Alan Chedzoy, freelance lecturer/writer, contested seat 1979 and twice in 1974. Dorset dialect expert. Mbr Weymouth and Portland BC, 1972-9 and 1986-; Dorset CC, 1986- . B Mar 23 1935; ed Beckenham GS for Boys; Bognor Regis Training Coll; Reading and Southampton Univs. NATFHE.

DORSET WEST						No change
Electorate % Turnout	67,256	81.2%	1992	64,360	78.3%	1987
*Spicer, Sir James (C)	27,766	50.8%	-5.3%	28,305	56.2%	C
Legg, R (LD)	19,756	36.2%	+4.5%	15,941	31.6%	L/All
Mann, J (Lab)	7,082	13.0%	+0.8%	6,123	12.2%	Lab
C to LD swing 4.9%	54,604		14.7%	50,369		24.5%
		C maj	8,010		C maj	12,364

Sir James Spicer has been a Cons Pty vice-chmn since 1984 and chmn International Office; company director. Mbr European Parliament, 1975-84, being elected MEP for Wessex, 1979-84; chief whip European Democratic Gp, 1975-9. Chmn, Cons Abroad, 1986- ; Director of Cons Gp for Europe, 1972-4. B Oct 4 1925; ed Latymer. Elected in Feb 1974; contested Southampton Itchen by-election, 1971. Chmn, Fitness for Industry Ltd; director, Thames and Kennet Marina Ltd.

Robin Legg, solicitor in local govt; mbr, Dorset CC, 1981- (dep ldr, LD gp, 1991-); Sherborne TC, 1987- ; Bradford Abbas PC, 1979-87. Chmn, W Dorset Lib Assocn, 1983-5. B Oct 26 1953; ed St Aldhelm's Sch and Foster's Sch, Sherborne; Bath Univ; Coll of Law, Guildford.
Joe Mann TGWU member for 20 years; on regional exec, 1986-90. B Oct 18 1951; ed Sexeys GS, Bruton, Somerset. Mbr Co-op Pty.

DOVER						No change
Electorate % Turnout	68,962	83.5%	1992	68,997	79.8%	1987
*Shaw, D L (C)	25,395	44.1%	-1.9%	25,343	46.0%	C
Prosser, G M (Lab)	24,562	42.6%	+8.5%	18,802	34.1%	Lab
Sole, M J (LD)	6,212	10.8%	-9.1%	10,942	19.9%	SDP/All
Sullivan, A (Grn)	637	1.1%				
Sherred, P (Ind)	407	0.7%				
Philp, B (Ind C)	250	0.4%				
Percy, C (NLP)	127	0.2%				
C to Lab swing 5.2%	57,590		1.4%	55,087		11.9%
		C maj	833		C maj	6,541

David Shaw, chartered accountant, was elected in 1987. Mbr select cmte on social security, 1991- . Jt vice-chmn, 1990- , and sec, 1987-90, Cons back-bench smaller businesses cmte; jt sec, Cons finance cmte, 1990- . Founder and managing director, Sabrelance Ltd; director, Adscene Gp plc, Palladian Estates plc, Hoskins Brewery plc. Contested Leigh in 1979. B Nov 14 1950; ed King's Coll Sch, Wimbledon; City of London Poly.
Gwyn Prosser, chief engineer on Sealink cross Channel ferries; exec cmte mbr, Dover CLP; vice-chmn, Dover Central branch. Mbr Dover DC, 1987- ; Kent CC, 1989- . B Apr 27 1943; ed Swansea Tech Sch. On exec cmte of Nat

Union of Marine and Shipping Transport Officers, 1985- ; Coordinator, local opposn gps against Channel tunnel, 1985-7; parly agent for petitioners against Channel Tunnel Bill, 1986-7.
Mike Sole, accounting technician with Dover chartered accountants; self-employed partner, market gardeners. Mbr Worth PC, 1990- ; exec cmte, SE region, YLDs. B Sep 1 1967; ed Sir Roger Manwoods GS, Sandwich.
Adrian Sullivan, photographer, teacher, univ tutor. Coordinator, Dover-Deal Grn Pty; Kent Pty, 1990-1. B Oct 20 1950; ed King's Hosp, Dublin; Goldsmiths Coll, London Univ.

DOWN NORTH						No change
Electorate % Turnout	68,662	65.5%	1992	65,018	62.8%	1987
*Kilfedder, J A (UPUP)	19,305	42.9%	-2.2%	18,420	45.1%	UPUP
Kennedy, Dr L (C)	14,371	32.0%		14,467	35.4%	Real U
Morrow, Ms A (All)	6,611	14.7%	-4.7%	7,932	19.4%	All
Vitty, D (DUP)	4,414	9.8%				
Wilmot, A (NLP)	255	0.6%				
No swing calculation.	44,956		11.0%	40,819		9.7%
		UPUP maj	4,934		UPUP maj	3,953

James Kilfedder, ldr of Ulster Popular Unionist Pty since 1980, was UPUP MP for N Down and Speaker of N Ireland Assembly, 1982-6. MP at Westminster for N Down since 1970. Resigned seat 1985 in protest at Anglo-Irish agreement and re-elected in 1986 by-election. UU MP for Belfast W, 1964-6. Official Unionist mbr, NI Assembly, 1973-5; UUUC mbr, NI Constitutional Convention, 1975-6. Barrister. B Jul 16 1928; ed Portora Royal Sch, Enniskillen; Trinity Coll, Dublin.

Dr Laurence Kennedy, consultant physician; ldr, Cons gp, North Down BC; founder mbr, North Down Cons assocn, 1988. B 1948; ed Queen's Univ, Belfast; Florida Univ.
Addie Morrow, chmn Alliance pty, 1992- ; vice-chmn 1990-2 and dep ldr, 1984-7; farmer; pty spokesman on agriculture. Castlereagh cllr, 1973-89; mbr NI Assembly, 1982-6. B Jul 17 1928; ed Campbell Coll.
Denny Vitty, stockbroker. Mbr, North Down DC.

DOWN SOUTH						No change
Electorate % Turnout	76,093	80.9%	1992	71,235	79.4%	1987
*McGrady, E K (SDLP)	31,523	51.2%	+4.2%	26,579	47.0%	SDLP
Nelson, D (UU)	25,181	40.9%	-4.8%	25,848	45.7%	UU
Fitzpatrick, S (SF)	1,843	3.0%	-1.2%	2,363	4.2%	SF
Healey, M (All)	1,542	2.5%	+0.6%	1,069	1.9%	All
McKenzie-Hill, Mrs S (C)	1,488	2.4%		675	1.2%	WP
UU to SDLP swing 4.5%	61,577		10.3%	56,534		1.3%
		SDLP maj	6,342		SDLP maj	731

Eddie McGrady, chartered accountant, won seat in 1987 defeating Enoch Powell; contested seat 1986 by-election, 1983 and 1979. Vice-chmn, all-pty UK-Manx parly gp. B Jun 3 1935; ed St Patrick's HS, Downpatrick; Belfast Coll of Tech. SDLP mbr for S Down of NI Assembly, 1973-5 and minr in NI power-sharing exec, 1973-4; NI Constitutional Convention, 1975-6 and NI Assembly, 1982-6. First chmn of SDLP, 1971-3, and first chmn of SDLP Assembly pty. Mbr Downpatrick UDC, 1961-89 being cl chmn, 1964-73; chmn or vice-chmn, Down DC, most years from 1973 to 1982. FCA.
Drew Nelson, solicitor; chmn UU legal cmte; hon sec SW

Down Unionist Assocn. Mbr, Banbridge DC, 1988- . BAug 3 1956; ed Queen's Univ, Belfast.
Sean Fitzpatrick is SF speaker on housing.
Michael Healey, univ research officer (chemical engineering); Alliance spokesman on ed. Mbr, Down DC, 1989- . B Nov 16 1950; ed Queen's Univ, Belfast. AUT.
Stephanie Mckenzie-Hill is mbr Cons nat women's cmte; vice-chmn Lewes Cons assocn and Lewes women's cmte. Owns and runs nursery sch. Mbr Wandsworth Cl, 1978-82; mbr Ilea, 1980-4; European Union of Women 1978- . B 1944; ed Richmond Lodge, Belfast; Salem, Germany; Diplome, Sorbonne, Paris; LSE, London Univ.

DUDLEY EAST						No change
Electorate % Turnout	75,355	75.0%	1992	75,206	72.3%	1987
*Gilbert, Dr J W (Lab)	29,806	52.8%	+6.9%	24,942	45.9%	Lab
Holland, C J (C)	20,606	36.5%	-3.0%	21,469	39.5%	C
Jenkins, I C (LD)	5,400	9.6%	-5.1%	7,965	14.6%	SDP/All
Cartwright, G (NF)	675	1.2%				
C to Lab swing 4.9%	56,487		16.3%	54,376		6.4%
		Lab maj	9,200		Lab maj	3,473

Dr John Gilbert was elected for this seat, Feb 1974; MP for Dudley, 1970-4; contested Dudley by-election, 1968, and Ludlow, 1966. Mbr select cmte on trade and industry, 1987- ; select cmte on defence, 1979-87. Minr of State for Defence, 1976-9; Financial Sec to Treasury, 1974-5; Minr for Transport, DoE, 1975-6. PC 1978. Chmn John Gilbert and Associates; non-exec director, Edmund Nuttall Ltd; Kyle Stewart Ltd, 1989- ; adviser to James F Byrnes International Center, Univ of South Carolina; mbr international advisory bd, Royal Jordanian Airlines. Chartered accountant and economist. B Apr 5 1927; ed Merchant Taylors' Sch, Northwood; St John's Coll, Oxford; New York Univ. Mbr, Cl for Arms Control; cl, Royal Utd

Services Inst; RIIA. GMB.
Jim Holland, director of plant hire company and proprietor of firm contracting trucks and crane hire. Chmn of EPOCH, an environmental pressure gp, Kates Hill, Dudley. Vice-chmn Dudley East Cons assocn. B Dec 10 1954; ed Roseland/Blue Coat Sch, Dudley; Dudley Coll of Tech. Owner of classic Mercedes sports car and judge at Dudley classic cars show.
Ian Jenkins, sales manager; chmn Wolverhampton NE LD; former regional vice-chmn. B Jan 10 1951; ed King Henry VII GS, Abergavenny; Wolverhampton Poly. Gp sec, MSF.

DUDLEY WEST						No change
Electorate % Turnout	86,632	82.1%	1992	81,789	79.1%	1987
*Blackburn, J G (C)	34,729	48.8%	-1.0%	32,224	49.8%	C
Lomax, K J (Lab)	28,940	40.7%	+6.7%	21,980	34.0%	Lab
Lewis, G P T (LD)	7,446	10.5%	-5.7%	10,477	16.2%	L/All
C to Lab swing 3.8%	71,115		8.1%	64,681		15.8%
		C maj	5,789		C maj	10,244

John **Blackburn** became gp exec chmn, Kudos gp of companies in 1990; chmn, Kudos Inns Ltd, 1991- ; regional sales manager with international engineering company, 1966-80; unpaid director, Shoalway Engineering Ltd. Parly adviser to Nat Assocn of Retired Police Officers. Elected 1979. Nat vice-pres, 1988- , and chmn, 1985-8, Cons Friends of Israel. Jt vice-chmn (1986-) and jt sec (1980-6), Cons back-bench cmte on arts and heritage; sec, all-pty child and family protection parly gp. Served in Royal Military Police, 1949-53; detective constable and then sergeant, Liverpool Police, 1953-65. B Sep 2 1933; ed Liverpool Collegiate sch; Liverpool and Berlin Univs. Mbr Wolverhampton Cl, 1970-80; Ecclesiastical Cl, 1979- . Freeman, City of London, 1980; City of Tel Aviv, 1981. Rear Commodore, Hse of Commons Yacht Club. MSF since 1966.

Kevin **Lomax**, economics and business studies teacher; mbr, Dudley MBC, 1988- (vice-chmn economic development cmte); exec, Dudley W CLP. B Oct 8 1945; ed N Staffs Poly; Worcester Coll of HE. NAS/UWT.

Gerry **Lewis**, retired counsellor at Dudley Coll, contested this seat 1987 and 1983 and Dudley E 1979. Treas, Dudley community relations cl. B Mar 17 1926; ed Aberdeen, Belfast, and Aston univs.

DULWICH						Lab gain
Electorate % Turnout	55,141	67.9%	1992	56,355	69.3%	1987
Jowell, Ms T (Lab)	17,714	47.3%	+5.3%	16,563	42.4%	C
*Bowden, G F (C)	15,658	41.8%	-0.6%	16,383	42.0%	Lab
Goldie, Dr A (LD)	4,078	10.9%	-3.6%	5,664	14.5%	SDP/All
				432	1.1%	Grn
C to Lab swing 3.0%	37,450		5.5%	39,042		0.5%
		Lab maj	2,056		C maj	180

Tessa **Jowell**, charity programme director, contested Redbridge, Ilford North, by-election 1978 and 1979. Mbr Camden BC, 1971-86; chaired AMA social services cmte, 1984-86. B Sep 17 1947; ed St Margaret's sch, Aberdeen; Aberdeen and Edinburgh Univs. In TGWU since 1975 (sponsored candidate) and MSF since 1987.

Gerald **Bowden**, elected, 1983, mbr select cmte on education, science and arts, 1989-91. PPS to Tim Renton, arts minr 1990-. Parly adviser to Periodical Publishers Assocn, 1990- . Principal lecturer, Dept of Estate Management, South Bank Polytechnic, 1972-83. Jt vice-chmn (1987-90) and sec (1985-7), Cons back-bench arts and heritage cmte; jt vice-chmn (1987-9) and jt sec (1985-7), Cons education cmte. Barrister and chartered surveyor; mbr of Lloyd's. B Aug 26 1935; ed Battersea GS; Magdalen Coll, Oxford; Gray's Inn; Coll of Estate Management, London. GLC mbr for Dulwich, 1977-81.

Dr Alex **Goldie**, polytechnic lecturer and researcher, contested seat for Green Pty 1987. Mbr Southwark BC, 1990- . B Jun 21 1929; ed London Univ; Thames Poly; Cranfield Inst of Tech. Mbr Divorce Law Reform Assocn. Past mbr, NATFHE.

DUMBARTON						No change
Electorate % Turnout	57,222	77.1%	1992	58,968	77.9%	1987
*McFall, J (Lab)	19,255	43.6%	+0.6%	19,778	43.0%	Lab
Begg, T N A (C)	13,126	29.7%	-1.9%	14,556	31.7%	C
McKechnie, W (SNP)	8,127	18.4%	+6.3%	6,060	13.2%	SDP/All
Morrison, J (LD)	3,425	7.8%	-5.4%	5,564	12.1%	SNP
Krass, D (NLP)	192	0.4%				
C to Lab swing 1.3%	44,125		13.9%	45,958		11.4%
		Lab maj	6,129		Lab maj	5,222

John **McFall** was elected in 1987 and joined select cmte on defence in 1988; mbr select cmte on sittings of Commons, 1991-2; Commons information cmte, 1991-. Jt vice-chmn all-pty Scotch whisky industry parly gp; jt chmn Romanian children gp; mbr exec cmte, parly gp for energy studies. Teacher and assistant head teacher, a Glasgow comprehensive school, 1974-87. B Oct 4 1944; ed St Patrick's primary and sec schs, Dumbarton; Paisley Coll; Strathclyde Univ; Open Univ. Visiting professor, Strathclyde Univ graduate business sch. Unpaid director, Dumbarton Equitable Co-op Society. EIS; GMB; sponsored by Co-op Pty.

Tom **Begg**, manufacturer and distributor, contested Glasgow, Garscadden 1987; materials systems coordinator with Britoil, 1980-7. Maker of "John Major jigsaw", launched at 1991 Scottish Cons pty conference. Cmte mbr Cons computer forum. B Jun 7 1944; ed Uddingston GS; Strathclyde Univ. Fellow, Inst of Petroleum.

Bill **McKechnie**, principal teacher of modern languages at Glasgow sch. Convenor, Dumbarton SNP; mbr Dumbarton DC, 1988- . An SNP rep on Cosla. B Jan 1 1949; ed Perth Acad; St Andrews univ; Moray House Coll of Ed.

John **Morrison**, solicitor, contested Glasgow Provan 1987 and Glasgow in 1989 Euro elections. Mbr Scottish exec LDs, 1988-90; Scottish Cl of SDP, 1986-8; chmn (1986-87) and sec (1986), Glasgow North SDP; convenor, Scottish SDP Students, 1983-4; pres (founder), Glasgow univ SDP, 1981-82, 1983. B Jun 14 1962; ed North Kelvinside sec sch; Glasgow Univ.

DUMFRIES						No change
Electorate % Turnout	61,145	80.0%	1992	59,347	75.6%	1987
*Monro, Sir Hector (C)	21,089	43.1%	+1.3%	18,785	41.9%	C
Rennie, P R (Lab)	14,674	30.0%	+4.8%	11,292	25.2%	Lab
Morgan, A (SNP)	6,971	14.3%	+0.0%	8,064	18.0%	SDP/All
Wallace, N C (LD)	5,749	11.8%	-6.2%	6,391	14.2%	SNP
McLeod, G (Ind Green)	312	0.6%		349	0.8%	Grn
Barlow, T (NLP)	107	0.2%				
C to Lab swing 1.8%	48,902		13.1%	44,881		16.7%
		C maj	6,415		C maj	7,493

Sir Hector Monro, farmer and company director, was appointed Under Sec of State for Scotland in 1992, an office he held in 1971-4; chmn, Scottish gp of Cons MPs, 1983-92; all-pty Scotch whisky industry parly gp; vice-chmn, RAF gp; jt vice-chmn, Scottish sports gp; low flying gp; racing and bloodstock industries cmte. Minister for Sport, 1979-81; Govt whip, 1970-1. Elected in 1964. B Oct 4 1922; ed Canford Sch; King's Coll, Cambridge. Was on Scottish Adv Bd, Abbey National. Pres, Scottish Rugby Union, 1976-7; Auto-cycle Union, 1983-90; Nat Small-bore Rifle Assocn, 1987- . RAF pilot, 1941-6; Inspector General, RAuxAF, 1990- ; Hon Air Commodore, No 2622

RAuxAF Regt Sqdn, 1982- .
Peter Rennie, fire brigade station officer; mbr Nithsdale DC, 1984- . B Nov 24 1952; ed New Abbey Primary Sch; Cargenbridge Jnr Sec; Dumfries Acad Snr Sec. FBU.
Alasdair Morgan, computer project manager; snr vice-convenor and election campaign director, SNP. Contested Dundee W 1987 and Tayside N 1983. B Apr 21 1945; ed Breadalbane Acad, Aberfeldy; Glasgow Univ.
Neil Wallace, sec sch teacher; chmn, Dumfries LDs, 1988-90; agent at Dumfries, 1985-90. B Mar 10 1957; ed Annan Acad; Edinburgh Univ; Moray House Coll of Ed. SSTA.

DUNDEE EAST						No change
Electorate % Turnout	58,959	72.1%	1992	60,805	75.9%	1987
*McAllion, J (Lab)	18,761	44.1%	+1.8%	19,539	42.3%	Lab
Coutts, D (SNP)	14,197	33.4%	-6.8%	18,524	40.1%	SNP
Blackwood, S F (C)	7,549	17.8%	+4.9%	5,938	12.9%	C
Yuill, I (LD)	1,725	4.1%	-0.6%	2,143	4.6%	L/All
Baird, Ms S (Grn)	205	0.5%				
Baxter, R (NLP)	77	0.2%				
SNP to Lab swing 4.3%	42,514		10.7%	46,144		2.2%
		Lab maj	4,564		Lab maj	1,015

John McAllion joined select cmte on energy in 1989. Won this seat 1987; chmn and campaign officer (1989-90) and vice-chmn (1988-9), Scottish Lab MPs; sec, all-pty Scotch whisky industry parly gp, 1987- ; Scottish sports gp, 1990- . Parly consultant to Union of Civil and Public Servants. Mbr, Tayside Reg Cl, 1984-7, being convener, 1986-7. Research asst, 1982-6, to late Robert MacTaggart, Lab MP for Glasgow Central; history and social studies teacher in Dundee, 1973-82. B Feb 13 1948; ed St Augustine's

comprehensive sch, Glasgow; St Andrews Univ; Dundee Coll of Ed. GMB.
David Coutts has own travel business. Mbr Dundee DC, 1984- ; elected mbr, SNP nat cl and spokesman on sport. B Dec 2 1957; ed in Edinburgh; Dundee Coll of Ed.
Steve Blackwood, procurement analyst; mbr, Dundee DC, 1977- . B Oct 15 1939; ed Rockwell, Dundee. Apex.
Ian Yuill, parly researcher; exec mbr, Scottish LDs. B Feb 12 1964; ed Robert Gordon's Coll, Aberdeen.

DUNDEE WEST						No change
Electorate % Turnout	59,953	69.8%	1992	61,926	75.4%	1987
*Ross, E (Lab)	20,498	49.0%	-4.4%	24,916	53.4%	Lab
Brown, K J (SNP)	9,894	23.6%	+8.3%	8,390	18.0%	C
Spearman, A (C)	7,746	18.5%	+0.5%	7,164	15.3%	SNP
Dick, Dr E G (LD)	3,132	7.5%	-5.2%	5,922	12.7%	SDP/All
Hood, Ms E (Grn)	432	1.0%		308	0.7%	Comm
Arnold, D (NLP)	159	0.4%				
Lab to SNP swing 6.3%	41,861		25.3%	46,700		35.4%
		Lab maj	10,604		Lab maj	16,526

Ernest Ross, mbr select cmte on employment, 1987- ; select cmte on standing orders and the unopposed bills panel, 1981- ; Court of Referees, 1987- . Chmn, PLP foreign affairs cmte, 1987- ; PLP CND gp, 1987- ; jt vice-chmn, PLP trade and industry cmte, 1987-8; chmn (1988-9) and vice-chmn (1987-8), Scottish gp of Lab MPs. Mbr exec cmte, British gp, IPU, 1991- ; chmn all-pty British-Palestine parly gp; jt vice-chmn Italian gp; sec Bangladesh and Cuban gps; jt sec space cmte. Elected in 1979. B Jul 1942; ed St Joseph's and St Mary's primary sch; St John's junior sec sch. Sponsored by MSF.

Keith Brown, local govt officer. B Dec 20 1961; ed Tynecastle HS, Edinburgh; Dundee Univ (convenor, Young Scot Nats). Nalgo.
Andrew Spearman manages family farm in Perthshire; political researcher. B Jun 4 1960; ed St Andrews Univ. Was personal asst to John Major, 1989-90.
Dr Elizabeth Dick, medical researcher, contested Falkirk E 1987 and this seat 1983. Mbr, Dundee LD exec. B Mar 17 1935; ed Oxford, London and Dundee Univs.
Elly Hood, secretary. B Jan 18 1939; ed Apeldoorn, Netherlands.

DUNFERMLINE EAST						No change
Electorate % Turnout	50,179	75.6%	1992	51,175	76.6%	1987
*Brown, J G (Lab)	23,692	62.4%	-2.3%	25,381	64.8%	Lab
Tennant, M E (C)	6,248	16.5%	+1.7%	5,792	14.8%	C
Lloyd, J V (SNP)	5,746	15.1%	+5.2%	4,122	10.5%	L/All
Little, Mrs T M (LD)	2,262	6.0%	-4.6%	3,901	10.0%	SNP
Lab to C swing 2.0%	37,948		46.0%	39,196		50.0%
		Lab maj	17,444		Lab maj	19,589

Gordon Brown became chief Opposn spokesman on trade and industry in 1989; elected to shadow cabinet 1987; shadow Chief Sec to Treasury, 1987-9; a spokesman on regional affairs in Opposn DTI front-bench team, 1985-7. Elected in 1983; contested Edinburgh S 1979. Mbr select cmte on employment, 1983-5. B Feb 20 1951; ed Kirkcaldy HS; Edinburgh Univ. Journalist with, then editor, current affairs dept, Scottish Television, 1980-3; lecturer in politics, Glasgow Coll of Tech, 1976-80; rector, Edinburgh Univ, 1972-5. NUJ. Sponsored by TGWU; has research into new tech funded by Inland Revenue Staff Fed.
Mark Tennant, director for Scotland of Chase Manhattan Bank, became treas, Scottish Cons Pty, in 1990. Chmn Hill Samuel Unit Trust Managers Ltd and Bell Lawrie White and Co Ltd. B May 9 1947; ed Eton. Dist cllr, Surrey Heath, 1977-9. Plays the bagpipes.
John Lloyd, principal teacher of modern studies; freelance journalist and author; convenor, Inverkeithing branch, SNP. B Jun 10 1951; ed St Andrew's HS, Kirkcaldy; Stirling and Aberdeen Univs. EIS.
Teresa Little, teacher, contested Fife Central 1987 and 1983. Mbr, Fife Regional Cl, 1982-6. B Feb 15 1949; ed St Joseph's Convent, Girvan; Edinburgh Univ; Craiglockart Coll of Ed. EIS.

DUNFERMLINE WEST						No change
Electorate % Turnout	50,948	76.4%	1992	51,063	77.0%	1987
Squire, Ms R (Lab)	16,374	42.0%	-5.0%	18,493	47.0%	Lab
Scott-Hayward, M D A (C)	8,890	22.8%	-0.3%	9,091	23.1%	C
Smith, J (SNP)	7,563	19.4%	+10.7%	8,288	21.1%	SDP/All
Harris, Ms E B A (LD)	6,122	15.7%	-5.4%	3,435	8.7%	SNP
Lab to C swing 2.4%	38,949		19.2%	39,307		23.9%
		Lab maj	7,484		Lab maj	9,402

Ms Rachel Squire was elected for this seat in 1992. Fulltime official with Nupe since 1981 having joined union in 1975; education officer with responsibility for Scotland since 1985; previously Nupe area officer in Ayrshire, Dumfries and Galloway (1982) and Renfrewshire (1982-5) and Liverpool (1981); snr social worker with B'ham social services dept, 1975-81. Mbr, Scottish exec of Lab Pty; former chair, Linlithgow CLP, and also political ed officer and press officer; former sec, Lothians European CLP. Has served on Scottish Cl political ed cmte. B Jul 13 1954; ed Godolphin and Latymer Girls' sch; Durham and Birmingham Univs.
Michael Scott-Hayward is chmn Tory Green Initiative, Scotland; Scottish Cons candidates assocn; mbr NE Fife DC, 1987- . Private businessman; owner of franchise outlet: Poppies (Dundee and NE Fife). Vice-chmn NE Fife Cons Assocn, 1988-9. In Royal Artillery, 1969-86 (Major). B Sep 7 1947; ed Mansfield HS, Durban, S Africa.
Jay Smith, hd of dept in CFE, contested Lothian in 1989 Euro elections. Mbr Dunfermline DC, 1986-91. Freelance presenter/broadcaster. B May 24 1951; ed Ayr Acad; Royal Scottish Acad of Music and Drama. EIS and Equity.
Elizabeth Harris, teacher, contested Dunfermline E 1987. Mbr, Dunfermline DC, 1984- ; Scottish exec, Lib Pty and LD, 1986-90; Scottish LD policy cmte, 1988- , and ed panel, 1988- . B Apr 29 1957; ed Beath Senior HS; Dundee Coll of Ed; Open Univ. EIS.

DURHAM NORTH						No change
Electorate % Turnout	73,694	76.1%	1992	72,115	76.0%	1987
*Radice, G H (Lab)	33,567	59.9%	+3.7%	30,798	56.2%	Lab
Sibley, Mrs E A (C)	13,930	24.8%	+3.6%	12,365	22.6%	SDP/All
Appleby, P J (LD)	8,572	15.3%	-7.3%	11,627	21.2%	C
C to Lab swing 0.0%	56,069		35.0%	54,790		33.6%
		Lab maj	19,637		Lab maj	18,433

Giles Radice became a mbr of select cmte on Treasury and civil service in 1987. Chief Opposn spokesman on ed, 1983-7, when in shadow cabinet. Elected for this seat 1983; MP for Chester-le-Street, 1973-83; contested Chippenham, 1964 and 1966. An Opposn spokesman on employment, 1981-3; on foreign affairs, 1981. Chmn (1987-8) and vice-chmn (1986-7), Northern gp of Lab MPs; chmn PLP employment gp, 1979-81. B Oct 4 1936; ed Winchester; Magdalen Coll, Oxford. Mbr, cl, Policy Studies Inst, 1978-83. PPS to Shirley Williams, Sec of State for Ed and Science, 1978-9. Sponsored by GMB.
Elizabeth Sibley, medical sec in NHS, was part-time personal asst in 1988 to Sir Ian Lloyd, then MP for Havant and chmn select cmte on energy; personal asst to Peter Lilley MP, 1985-7. B Nov 16 1957; ed Notre Dame HS, Southwark; LSE. Mbr Cons women's working pty on family income, 1989.
Philip Appleby, retired police officer, now student. B Feb 24 1958; ed Mangla International Sch, Pakistan; Bedford Sch; Newcastle Univ.

DURHAM NORTH WEST						No change
Electorate % Turnout	61,139	75.6%	1992	61,302	73.5%	1987
*Armstrong, Miss H J (Lab)	26,734	57.9%	+7.0%	22,947	50.9%	Lab
May, Mrs T M (C)	12,747	27.6%	-0.8%	12,785	28.4%	C
Farron, T (LD)	6,728	14.6%	-6.2%	9,349	20.7%	L/All
C to Lab swing 3.9%	46,209		30.3%	45,081		22.5%
		Lab maj	13,987		Lab maj	10,162

Hilary Armstrong joined Opposn front bench ed team in 1988 to speak on pre-school and primary ed; mbr, Select Cmte on sittings of Commons, 1991-2; on Ed, Science and Arts until Jan 1989; consultant to NUT; mbr, parly panel, Royal Coll of Nursing. Director (unpaid), Project Genesis Ltd, which is examining feasibility of redeveloping Consett steelworks site. Elected in 1987; chaired PLP ed, science and arts cmte, 1987-8. Vice-pres, Nat Children's Homes; treas, Methodist Church division of ed and youth. Lecturer in community and youth work, Sunderland Poly, 1975-86. Mbr, Durham CC, 1985-7 B Nov 30 1945; ed Monkwearmouth Comprehensive Sch; West Ham Coll of Tech; Birmingham Univ. Sponsored by MSF.

Theresa May, head of European affairs unit, Assocn for Payment Clearing Services. Mbr, Merton BC, 1986- ; Merton and Sutton CHC, 1986-8. B Oct 1 1956; ed Wheatley Park Comprehensive Sch, Oxfordshire; St Hugh's Coll, Oxford. Mbr, Surrey CCC. Fellow, Royal Geographical Society.

Tim Farron is pres, students' union, Newcastle univ; mbr, NUS exec. B May 27 1970; ed Runshaw Tertiary Coll, Leyland; Newcastle Univ.

DURHAM, CITY OF						No change
Electorate % Turnout	68,165	74.6%	1992	66,567	78.2%	1987
*Steinberg, G N (Lab)	27,095	53.3%	+8.3%	23,382	44.9%	Lab
Woodroofe, M I (C)	12,037	23.7%	+1.7%	17,257	33.2%	SDP/All
Martin, Dr N (LD)	10,915	21.5%		11,408	21.9%	C
Jane Banks, Ms S (Grn)	812	1.6%				
C to Lab swing 3.3%	50,859		29.6%	52,047		11.8%
		Lab maj	15,058		Lab maj	6,125

Gerry Steinberg was elected in 1987 when he became mbr, Select Cmte on Ed, Science and Arts; chmn, PLP ed, science and arts cmte, 1990- (jt vice-chmn, 1988-90); arts sub-cmte, 1991- . Adviser to Educational Psychologists Assocn, 1989- . Headmaster, Whitworth House Special School, 1979-87; teacher (1969-75) and dep head (1975-9), Elemore Hall. Mbr, Durham City Cl, 1975-87. B Apr 20 1945; ed St Margaret's Primary Sch; Whinney Hill Sec Mod Sch; Johnstone GS; Sheffield Coll of Ed; Newcastle Poly. Sponsored by TGWU.

Martin Woodroofe, personnel manager. Chmn, Durham Euro Constituency Cons cl, 1990- ; nat chmn, YCs, 1988-9; nat vice-chmn, 1986-8. B Sep 14 1959; ed Scorton GS; Univ of Wales; Bradford Univ.

Nigel Martin, univ lecturer and vice-principal, Collingwood Coll, Durham Univ, contested Newcastle Central 1987. Research fellow, Downing Coll, Cambridge, 1971-5. Mbr, Durham CC, 1985- . Local pty chrm, 1988-90. B Apr 26 1945; ed Clee Humberstone Foundation Sch, Cleethorpes; Christ's Coll, Cambridge. AUT.

EALING NORTH						No change
Electorate % Turnout	63,528	78.8%	1992	71,634	75.1%	1987
*Greenway, H (C)	24,898	49.7%	-6.3%	30,147	56.0%	C
Stears, M J (Lab)	18,932	37.8%	+10.0%	14,947	27.8%	Lab
Hankinson, P C D (LD)	5,247	10.5%	-4.7%	8,149	15.1%	L/All
Earl, D (Grn)	554	1.1%	+0.0%	577	1.1%	Grn
Hill, C (NF)	277	0.6%				
Davis, R (CD)	180	0.4%				
C to Lab swing 8.2%	50,088		11.9%	53,820		28.2%
		C maj	5,966		C maj	15,200

Harry Greenway won the seat 1979; contested Stepney and Poplar twice in 1974; Stepney, 1970. Dep head, Sedgehill Comprehensive Sch, London, 1972-9. Mbr, Select Cmte on Ed, Science and Arts, 1979-92. Part-time lecturer; part-time consultant, Taylor Woodrow. B Oct 4 1934; ed Warwick Sch; Coll of St Mark and St John, London; Caen Univ. Mbr, Cl of British Horse Soc, 1973- ; founder and chmn, London Schs Horse Soc, 1968- ; promoted Animal Protection Act, 1987, and Horses (Protection of Young Riders) Act, 1990. Vice-chmn, Gtr London Cons MPs, 1981- ; Cons backbench ed cmte, 1985-6; vice-chmn (1987-) and sec (1986-7), Cons sports cmte; sec, Cons Nat Advisory Cmte on Ed, 1981- . AMMA.

Martin Stears, lecturer in computing and information technology, contested Broxbourne 1983. N Herts cllr, 1979-88; mbr, Eastern regional Lab pty cl, 1980- (chairman, policy and local govt cmte, 1987-). Hon director, Centre for Alternative Industrial and Technological Systems. B May 11 1950; ed Carisbrooke GS, Isle of Wight; London Univ. MSF and NATFHE.

Peter Hankinson, industrial relations officer; former pres, Ealing-Southall Lib assocn. B May 31 1943; ed St Benedict's Sch, Ealing; Worcester Coll, Oxford.

EALING, ACTON						No change
Electorate % Turnout	58,687	76.0%	1992	67,176	71.1%	1987
*Young, Sir George (C)	22,579	50.6%	-2.8%	25,499	53.4%	C
Johnson, Ms Y (Lab)	15,572	34.9%	+7.1%	13,266	27.8%	Lab
Rowe, L (LD)	5,487	12.3%	-6.5%	8,973	18.8%	SDP/All
Seibe, Ms A (Grn)	554	1.2%				
Pitt-Aikens, Dr T (Ind C)	432	1.0%				
C to Lab swing 5.0%	44,624		15.7%	47,738		25.6%
		C maj	7,007		C maj	12,233

Sir George Young was appointed Minr for Housing and Planning in Nov 1990: Comptroller of HM Household (govt whip) 1990; an Under Sec of State for Environment, 1981-6; Under Sec of State for Health and Social Security, 1979-81. Chmn, Cons backbench social security cmte, 1989-90. Economist; non-exec director, Lovell Partnerships Ltd, 1987-90. Trustee, Guinness Trust, 1986-90. Elected in Feb 1974. Pres, all-pty Friends of Cycling parly gp. B Jul 16 1941; ed Eton; Christ Church, Oxford. Chmn, Acton Housing Assocn, 1972-9. Mbr, Select Cmte on Violence in Marriage, 1975; GLC, 1970-3; Lambeth BC, 1968-71.
Yvonne Johnson, teacher. Mbr Ealing BC, 1986- . B Feb 1 1954; ed St Edmunds Sch; Digby Stuart Roehampton Inst; Open Univ. NUT.

EALING, SOUTHALL						No change
Electorate % Turnout	65,574	75.5%	1992	74,843	69.7%	1987
Khabra, P (Lab)	23,476	47.4%	-3.3%	26,480	50.7%	Lab
Treleaven, Prof P C (C)	16,610	33.6%	-1.9%	18,503	35.5%	C
*Bidwell, S J (True Lab)	4,665	9.4%		6,947	13.3%	L/All
Nandhra, Mrs P K N (LD)	3,790	7.7%	-5.7%	256	0.5%	WRP
Goodwin, N (Grn)	964	1.9%				
Lab to C swing 0.7%	49,505		13.9%	52,186		15.3%
		Lab maj	6,866		Lab maj	7,977

Piara Khabra, social and welfare voluntary worker; school teacher. Won selection contest in Apl 1991 and endorsed by Lab Pty NEC in Dec 1991. Active in Indian workers' assocn in Ealing. Mbr Ealing BC 1978-82. B Nov 20 1924; ed Punjab Univ. MSF.
Prof Philip Treleaven, professor of computing, London univ; adviser to international high-tech companies; to EC Commission and foreign govts. Chmn Wokingham Cons assocn; Thames Valley Euro-constituency. B Mar 15 1950; ed Cornwall Tech Coll; Brunel and Manchester Univs.
Sydney Bidwell was Labour MP for this seat, 1974-92; de-selected by CLP but decided, after appeal to Lab NEC was rejected, to stand at election. Contested SW Herts, 1964; E Herts, 1959 Lab MP for Southall, 1966-74; select cmte on transport 1979-92; select cmte on race relations and immigration, 1968-79; former officer PLP transport cmte and Tribune gp. Treas all-pty British-Gibraltar parly gp. B Jan 14 1917; ed elementary sch and evening classes and trade union movement. Lecturer; previously railway worker. Mbr, Southall BC, 1951-55.
Pash Nandhra travel business owner; teacher. Mbr Harrow BC, 1986- (Chmn equal opportunities cmte tertiary and further ed; tertiary speaker on coll matters). Mbr Lib Pty ed panel, commission for racial activity working gp on reviving cities. B Nov 13 1939; ed Kenya Univ, Nairobi; Inst of Ed, London univ.
Nicholas Goodwin, computer instructor and youth training manager employed by Southall Information Tech Centre. B Aug 6 1961; ed Whitgift Sch, Croydon; Girton Coll, Cambridge. Assocn of Christian Teachers; NATFHE.

EASINGTON						No change
Electorate % Turnout	65,061	72.5%	1992	64,863	73.4%	1987
*Cummings, J S (Lab)	34,269	72.7%	+4.6%	32,396	68.1%	Lab
Perry, W J (C)	7,879	16.7%	+0.4%	7,757	16.3%	C
Freitag, P (LD)	5,001	10.6%	-5.0%	7,447	15.6%	L/All
C to Lab swing 2.1%	47,149		56.0%	47,600		51.8%
		Lab maj	26,390		Lab maj	24,639

John Cummings was elected in 1987 when he became mbr, select cmte on environment; treas, all-pty British-Czechoslovak parly gp. Electrician (1963-87) at Murton Colliery, where he started work in 1958. Vice-chmn, coalfields community campaign, 1985-7. Mbr Easington DC 1973-87 (ldr 1979-87; chmn, 1975-6); Easington RDC, 1970-3; Aycliffe and Peterlee Development Corporation, 1980-7; Northumbrian Water Authority, 1977-83. Vice-chmn, coalfield community campaign, 1985-7. B Jul 6 1943; ed Murton local schs; Easington Tech Coll. Sponsored by NUM.
William Perry, snr partner of oldest firm of solicitors in England contested this seat 1987. Chmn nat BCCI solicitors' co-ordinating cmte. Chmn London Handel abroad ltd; director, London Handel Society Ltd. Mbr Merton BC, London, 1980-6; Windsor and Maidenhead BC, 1974-9. Vice-chmn, Easington Cons assocn, 1987- . B Nov 19 1952; ed Malvern Coll; Univ Coll, Oxford; Coll of Law.
Peter Freitag, business consultant, contested Jarrow 1987, Middlesbrough 1979; Darlington twice in 1974; Durham in 1987 Euro elections and Tyne and Wear in 1979 Euro elections. Pres 1992- , and chmn 1989-92, Darlington LDs. Bd mbr Euro Movement. B Apr 23 1929; ed Haberdashers' Aske's. Mbr Darlington DC, 1970-6; Durham CC, 1970-7.

EAST KILBRIDE						No change
Electorate % Turnout	64,080	80.0%	1992	63,097	79.2%	1987
*Ingram, A P (Lab)	24,055	46.9%	-2.1%	24,491	49.0%	Lab
McAlorum, Mrs K (SNP)	12,063	23.5%	+11.0%	11,867	23.7%	SDP/All
Lind, G M (C)	9,781	19.1%	+4.4%	7,344	14.7%	C
Grieve, Mrs S (LD)	5,377	10.5%		6,275	12.6%	SNP
Lab to SNP swing 6.5%	51,276		23.4%	49,977		25.3%
		Lab maj	11,992		Lab maj	12,624

Adam Ingram became PPS to Kinnock, then Ldr of Opposition, in 1988. Elected in 1987; Opposn whip, 1987-8; contested Strathkelvin and Bearsden 1983. Mbr Scottish exec Lab MPs, 1987-8. Nalgo official, 1977-87; programmer and systems analyst, S of Scotland Electricity Bd, 1970-7; programmer/analyst, Associated British Foods, 1969-70; computer programmer, 1966-9. Mbr E Kilbride DC, 1980-7 (ldr of cl, 1984-7); mbr policy cmte Cosla 1984-7. Former treas, E Kilbride arts cl. B Feb 1 1947; ed Cranhill Sec Sch. Chmn E Kilbride CLP, 1981-5; sec, jt trades union side gas staffs and snr officers Scottish

Gas, 1978-82. Sponsored by TGWU.
Kathleen McAlorum, housewife, mbr, Motherwell DC; elected mbr SNP nat cl; sec SNP steel action cmte; pty rep on Strathclyde Reg Cl's steel cmte. B Sep 16 1939; ed Elmwood Snr Sec Sch, Bothwell. Nalgo.
Gordon Lind, principal teacher at Hamilton GS, Lanarkshire, contested Monklands W 1987. Mbr Coatbridge BC, 1969-72. B Apr 9 1945.
Sandra Grieve, training consultant, contested Monklands E 1987. Mbr fed policy cmte; Scottish LD policy convenor. B May 17 1954; ed Uddingston GS; Bell Coll, Hamilton.

EAST LOTHIAN						No change
Electorate % Turnout	66,699	82.4%	1992	65,046	78.7%	1987
*Home Robertson, J D (Lab)	25,537	46.5%	-1.6%	24,583	48.0%	Lab
Hepburne Scott, J P (C)	15,501	28.2%	-0.1%	14,478	28.3%	C
Thomson, G (SNP)	7,776	14.2%	+6.9%	7,929	15.5%	L/All
McKay, T (LD)	6,126	11.2%	-4.3%	3,727	7.3%	SNP
				451	0.9%	Grn
Lab to C swing 0.7%	54,940		18.3%	51,168		19.7%
		Lab maj	10,036		Lab maj	10,105

John Home Robertson appointed select Cmte on defence in 1990. An Opposn spokesman on food, agriculture and rural affairs in 1988, and spokesman on agriculture, particularly for Scotland, 1984-7; a spokesman on Scotland, 1987-8; Opposn Scottish whip, 1983-4. Elected for this seat 1983; MP for Berwick and E Lothian, 1978-83. Farmer. B Dec 5 1948; ed Ampleforth; W of Scotland Agricultural Coll.
James Hepburne Scott, grain merchant; sales consultant to

tree nursery. With RHM Agriculture, Stroud, Gloucs, 1978-82. B Jul 21 1947; ed Eton; RMA Sandhurst; RM Coll of Science, Shrivenham; Royal Agric Coll, Cirencester.
George Thomson, postal officer. Mbr E Lothian DC, 1988; area officer for UCW. B Feb 2 1961; ed Ross HS, Tranent, East Lothian.
Tim McKay, chartered accountant and investment analyst, contested Hamilton 1987. Convenor Scottish Enterprise Cmte 1990- . B Sep 17 1957; ed St Andrews Univ.

EASTBOURNE						No change from 1987
Electorate % Turnout	76,103	81.0%	1992	74,144	75.6%	1987
Waterson, N C (C)	31,792	51.6%	-8.3%	33,587	59.9%	C
*Bellotti, D F (LD)	26,311	42.7%	+13.0%	16,664	29.7%	L/All
Gibbons, I (Lab)	2,834	4.6%	-4.2%	4,928	8.8%	Lab
Aherne, D (Grn)	391	0.6%	-0.9%	867	1.5%	Grn
Williamson, Ms T (Lib)	296	0.5%				
C to LD swing 10.7%	61,624		8.9%	56,046		30.2%
		C maj	5,481		C maj	16,923

Nigel Waterson, solicitor and barrister, regained the seat for Cons in 1992 after the 1990 by-election reverse. Founder and snr partner of law firm providing services to shipping and energy industries. Contested Islington S and Finsbury 1979. Chmn Bow Gp 1986-7; Hammersmith Cons Assocn 1987-90. Mbr Cons Gtr London area exec cmte 1990-1; CPC advisory cmte, 1986-90; CPC gen purposes cmte 1990-1; London West Euro constituency cl 1987-91. B Oct 12 1950; ed Leeds GS; Queen's Coll, Oxford (pres, univ Cons assocn). Mbr management cmte, Sonham housing assocn hostel for ex-offenders, 1988-90. Patron, Eastbourne branch, multiple sclerosis society. Mbr foreign affairs forum; centre for policy studies, CPRE; small business bureau; society of Cons lawyers; Hammersmith BC 1974-78.
David Bellotti gained seat for LDs in 1990 by-election,

former director of Hove YMCA until end of 1990, youth and community worker, . LD spokesman on local govt and community care, 1991-2. Contested Lewes for L/All in 1987 and 1983 and Eastbourne for L in 1979. Mbr E Sussex CC, 1981- (chmn, ed cmte, 1986-7); nat local govt forum for drug misuse. B Aug 13 1943; ed Exeter Sch; YMCA Nat Coll; Brighton Poly.
Ivan Gibbons, adult ed lecturer; mbr Hammersmith and Fulham BC, 1982- (chmn leisure and recreation cmte 1987-). B Aug 9 1950; ed London Oratory Sch, Chelsea; Queen's univ, Belfast. NATFHE, 1980- .
David Aherne, journalist, contested 1990 by-election and W Sussex for Ecology Pty in 1984 Euro elections. Cons mbr, Brighton Cl, 1972-79, when he joined Ecol Pty. B Jul 24 1943; ed St Christopher's, Letchworth, Herts. NUJ.
For details of by-election see page 287.

EASTLEIGH						No change
Electorate % Turnout	91,736	82.9%	1992	87,552	79.3%	1987
Milligan, S D W (C)	38,998	51.3%	+0.0%	35,584	51.3%	C
Chidgey, D W G (LD)	21,296	28.0%	-4.0%	22,229	32.0%	L/All
Sugrue, Ms J E (Lab)	15,768	20.7%	+4.0%	11,599	16.7%	Lab
LD to C swing 2.0%	76,062		23.3%	69,412		19.2%
		C maj	17,702		C maj	13,355

Stephen Milligan was elected in 1992. BBC TV Europe correspondent, 1988-90; Washington correspondent and foreign editor, *The Sunday Times*, 1984-8. Journalist with *The Economist*; home editor, 1983; European editor, 1981-2; foreign reports editor, 1980-1; chief EC correspondent, 1975-80; industrial editor, 1972-5. Presenter, Radio 4's *The World Tonight*, 1980-3. Mbr, European advisory bd, Royal Inst of International Affairs, 1989- ; sec Cons foreign and Commonwealth cl, 1991- . B May 12 1948; ed Bradfield Coll; Magdalen Coll, Oxford (pres of union 1970; univ Cons assocn 1970).

David Chidgey contested Hampshire Central in 1989 Euro elections and 1988 Euro by-election. Civil engineer.Mbr, Winchester CC 1987-90; B Jul 9 1942; ed Brune Park Cty HS, Gosport; RNC Portsmouth; Portsmouth Poly.

Jo Sugrue, fund-raising and information officer. Mbr Portsmouth City Cl 1979-89. B Dec 15 1954; ed Usk Agricultural Coll. Exec mbr Shelter.

EASTWOOD						No change
Electorate % Turnout	63,685	81.0%	1992	61,872	79.4%	1987
*Stewart, J A (C)	24,124	46.8%	+7.3%	19,388	39.5%	C
Grant-Hutchison, P A (Lab)	12,436	24.1%	-0.9%	13,374	27.2%	SDP/All
Craig, Miss M (LD)	8,493	16.5%	-10.8%	12,305	25.1%	Lab
Scott, P (SNP)	6,372	12.4%	+4.1%	4,033	8.2%	SNP
Fergusson, Dr L (NLP)	146	0.3%				
Lab to C swing 4.1%	51,571		22.7%	49,100		12.2%
		C maj	11,688		C maj	6,014

Allan Stewart was reappointed Under Secretary of State for Scotland in 1992; under sec 1981-6. Elected for this seat 1983; MP for E Renfrewshire 1979-83; contested Dundee E, 1970. Jt chmn all-pty licensed trade parly gp 1989-90; sec Scottish Cons MPs 1987-90; jt vice-chmn Cons backbench pty organization cmte 1987-90; all-pty Scottish sports gp 1987-90. Former director Scotlander plc; Peter A Hawkins Ltd. Former consultant to the Brewers' Society, Decision Makers Ltd, and Inst of Chartered Accountants of Scotland. PPS to Minr of State for Energy 1981. Mbr Select Cmte on Scottish Affairs 1979-81. Economist. B Jun 1 1942; ed Bell Baxter HS, Cupar; St Andrews Univ and Harvard. Mbr Bromley BC, 1974-6. Head of Regional Development Dept CBI, 1971-3. Lecturer in political economy, St Andrews Univ, 1965-70.

Peter Grant-Hutchison, advocate, contested this seat 1987; political ed officer Glasgow Central CLP. B Jul 7 1956; ed Dundee Univ; Largs HS; Ardrossan Acad. GMB.

Moira Craig, psychologist, contested Glasgow Cathcart 1987 and Clydesdale 1983. Vice-convenor Campaign for Scottish Assembly; LD rep on STUC. B 1929; ed Queen's Park Sch; Glasgow Univ; Jordanhill Coll.

Paul Scott, retired diplomat, writer; contested Edinburgh E 1983. Mbr SNP nat exec cmte. B Nov 7 1920; ed Royal HS, Edinburgh; Edinburgh Univ.

ECCLES						No change
Electorate % Turnout	64,910	74.1%	1992	66,961	74.5%	1987
*Lestor, Miss J (Lab)	27,357	56.9%	+6.1%	25,346	50.8%	Lab
Ling, G (C)	14,131	29.4%	-2.0%	15,647	31.3%	C
Reid, Rev G C (LD)	5,835	12.1%	-5.8%	8,924	17.9%	SDP/All
Duriez, R (Grn)	521	1.1%				
Garner, Miss J (NLP)	270	0.6%				
C to Lab swing 4.0%	48,114		27.5%	49,917		19.4%
		Lab maj	13,226		Lab maj	9,699

Joan Lestor was elected for this seat 1987; MP for Eton and Slough and then for Slough, 1966-83; contested Lewisham W, 1964. Mbr of shadow cabinet 1989-90; spokesman on children 1989- ; on overseas development and co-operation 1987-9; on women's rights and welfare 1981-3. Under sec for ed and science 1969-70 and 1975-6, resigning in protest at public spending cuts; Under Sec FCO 1974-5; Sec all-pty British-Zimbabwe parly gp 1987- ; jt sec all-pty fund for replacement of animals in medical experiments 1987- . Chmn defence for children international (UK), a children's rights gp; mbr CND nat cl 1983- . Chmn Lab Pty 1977-8; vice-chmn 1976-7; mbr Labour NEC 1987- and 1967-82. B Nov 13 1931; ed Blaenavon Sec Sch, Monmouth; William Morris HS, Walthamstow; London Univ. Mbr Wandsworth Cl 1957-8; LCC 1963-5. Sponsored by GMB.

Gary Ling, management consultant. Royal Army Ordnance Corps officer 1985-9. Mbr Watford BC 1990- . B Apr 28 1959; ed Greenwich HS, US; Cassio Coll, Watford; Aberdeen Univ; RMA, Sandhurst; City Univ Business Sch.

The Rev Geoff Reid, Methodist minister with Salford Urban Mission, contested Barnsley Central 1983 and Rother Valley, Oct 1974. B Sep 5 1946; ed Heaton GS, Newcastle; Newcastle and Cambridge Univs. Mbr Camra; Nupe.

Richard Duriez, self-employed wall and floor tiler. B Mar 18 1956.

EDDISBURY						No change
Electorate % Turnout	75,089	82.6%	1992	73,894	78.0%	1987
*Goodlad, A R (C)	31,625	51.0%	-0.1%	29,474	51.1%	C
Edwards, Ms N (Lab)	18,928	30.5%	+7.0%	13,639	23.7%	L/All
Lyon, D W (LD)	10,543	17.0%	-6.6%	13,574	23.5%	Lab
Basden, A (Grn)	783	1.3%	-0.4%	976	1.7%	Grn
Pollard, N (NLP)	107	0.2%				
C to Lab swing 3.5%	61,986		20.5%	57,663		27.5%
		C maj	12,697		C maj	15,835

Alastair Goodlad was appointed a minister of state, Foreign and Commonwealth Office in 1992. Treas of HM Household and govt deputy chief whip 1990-2; PC 1992; Comptroller of HM Household (govt whip), 1989-90; mbr, broadcasting select cmte, 1987-9; services cmte, 1989-91. Under Sec of State for Energy, 1984-7; a govt whip, 1982-4; asst govt whip, 1981-2. Director, Fuel Tech Europe Ltd, 1988-9; Mersey Barrage Co Ltd, 1988-9. Elected for this seat 1983; MP for Northwich, Feb 1974-83; contested Crewe, 1970. B Jul 4 1943; ed St Faith's Sch, Cambridge; Marlborough Coll; King's Coll, Cambridge. Chmn NW gp of Cons MPs 1987-9.

Norma Edwards was elected to Cheshire CC in 1988. B Apr 19 1947; ed St Edmunds C of E Sch, Liverpool. GMB.

Derrick Lyon, director of small companies; constituency chmn 1988-90. B Sep 21 1942; ed Slough Tech HS; City univ, London; St John's Coll, Cambridge (rugby capt 1969).

Andrew Basden, lecturer, contested seat 1987. B Jul 31 1948; ed George Heriot's Sch, Edinburgh; Southampton univ.

EDINBURGH CENTRAL						No change
Electorate % Turnout	56,527	69.3%	1992	59,529	69.0%	1987
*Darling, A M (Lab)	15,189	38.8%	-1.4%	16,502	40.2%	Lab
Martin, P (C)	13,063	33.4%	-1.3%	14,240	34.7%	C
Devine, Ms L J (SNP)	5,539	14.1%	+7.9%	7,333	17.9%	L/All
Myles, A B (LD)	4,500	11.5%	-6.4%	2,559	6.2%	SNP
Harper, R C M (Grn)	630	1.6%	+0.5%	438	1.1%	Grn
Wilson, R (Lib)	235	0.6%				
Lab to C swing 0.0%	39,156		5.4%	41,072		5.5%
		Lab maj	2,126		Lab maj	2,262

Alistair Darling became an Opposn spokesman on home affairs in 1988; mbr, Lab working pty on electoral systems, 1990- . Won this seat 1987; jt vice-chmn, PLP transport cmte, 1987-8. Advocate. Mbr, Lothian Reg Cl 1982-7 (chmn transport cmte 1986-7). Lothian and Borders Police Bd, 1982-6. B Nov 28 1953; ed Aberdeen Univ. Governor, Napier Coll, Edinburgh, 1982-7. Apex.

Paul Martin is enterprise adviser, Moray House Coll, Edinburgh; an asst director CBI Scotland, 1987-8. Contested Edinburgh E 1983. Mbr, Edinburgh City Cl 1980- (chmn Cons gp 1988- ; ldr 1984-7). B May 1958; ed Royal HS, Edinburgh; Edinburgh Univ. Mbr Edinburgh Festival Cl 1980-5.

Lynne Devine, teacher spokesman, speaks for SNP on third world issues. B Nov 30 1948; ed Ayr Acad; Strathclyde univ. EIS.

Andrew Myles, NHS manager, contested seat 1987. Mbr Scottish LD exec. B Oct 25 1957; ed Dundee univ. Nalgo.

Robin Harper, teacher, contested Lothians in 1989 Euro elections. Edinburgh Grn pty co-ordinator since 1985. B Aug 4 1940; ed St Marylebone GS, London; Aberdeen univ.

EDINBURGH EAST						No change
Electorate % Turnout	45,687	73.9%	1992	48,895	74.1%	1987
*Strang, Dr G S (Lab)	15,446	45.7%	-4.6%	18,257	50.4%	Lab
Ward, K F (C)	8,235	24.4%	-0.3%	8,962	24.7%	C
McKinney, D (SNP)	6,225	18.4%	+9.0%	5,592	15.4%	L/All
Scobie, D S (LD)	3,432	10.2%	-5.3%	3,434	9.5%	SNP
Farmer, G (Grn)	424	1.3%				
Lab to C swing 2.1%	33,762		21.4%	36,245		25.6%
		Lab maj	7,211		Lab maj	9,295

Gavin Strang Elected in 1970. Mbr Select Cmte on Agriculture 1991, also a mmbr 1984-7; an Opposn spokesman on employment, 1987-9; chmn PLP defence cmte 1985-7; chmn Scottish Lab MPs 1986-7; chmn Labour Action for Peace, 1985-9; chmn or sec, PLP CND gp, 1982-6. An Opposn spokesman on ag, fish and food, 1979-82. Parly Sec Min of Ag, Fish and Food, 1974-9; Under Sec of State, Energy, 1974. Mbr, select cmte on science and tech, 1970-4. An Opposn spokesman on trade and industry, 1973-4. Agricultural scientist. B Jul 10 1943; ed Morrison's Acad; Edinburgh univ; Churchill Coll, Cambridge. Sponsored by TGWU.

Ken Ward, accountant with Scottish Power; director of Lothian Enterprise Bd. Pres, Edinburgh E Cons assocn. Mbr Lothian Reg Cl, 1982-90. B June 7 1942; ed Tynecastle Snr Sec Sch; Torhicen St and Regent Rd FE Insts.

Donald McKinney, self-employed director of E Lothian tutoring business. Convenor, Dunbar SNP. B Aug 23 1960; ed Paisley GS; Stirling and Strathclyde univs.

Devin Scobie, marketing manager, design/PR consultancy; collector of political autograph material; editor, Scottish LD magazine 1988- . B Oct 31 1965; ed Douglas Ewart HS, Newton Stewart; Edinburgh Univ.

EDINBURGH SOUTH						No change
Electorate % Turnout	61,355	72.7%	1992	63,842	75.7%	1987
*Griffiths, N (Lab)	18,485	41.5%	+3.8%	18,211	37.7%	Lab
Stevenson, S J S (C)	14,309	32.1%	-1.7%	16,352	33.8%	C
McCreadie, Dr R A (LD)	5,961	13.4%	-9.2%	10,900	22.5%	SDP/All
Knox, R T (SNP)	5,727	12.8%	+7.8%	2,455	5.1%	SNP
Manclark, G (NLP)	108	0.2%		440	0.9%	Grn
C to Lab swing 2.8%	44,590		9.4%	48,358		3.8%
		Lab maj	4,176		Lab maj	1,859

Nigel Griffiths joined the Opposn trade and industry team in 1989 as spokesman on consumers. Won this seat 1987; Lab whip 1987-9. Treasurer parly cl against anti-semitism; jt treas race and community parly gp. Exec mbr and convenor finance cmte Scottish Constitutional Convention. Mbr Edinburgh DC 1980-7 (chmn 1986-7). B May 20 1955; ed Hawick Comprehensive Sch; Edinburgh univ; Moray Coll of Ed. Mbr Edinburgh cl of soc service, 1984-7. TGWU shop steward, 1980-6. Sponsored by Usdaw.
Struan Stevenson, farmer and director of tourist business, contested Carrick, Cumnock and Doon Valley 1987. Ldr, Tory gp on Cosla 1986-8. Mbr Girvan DC 1972-5; Kyle

and Carrick DC 1974- . B Apr 4 1948; ed Strathallan Sch; W of Scotland Agric Coll. Chmn Carrick, Cumnock and Doon Valley Cons assocn 1982-9. NFU.
Bob McCreadie, univ lecturer, contested Glasgow Central by-election 1989; Livingston 1987; Edinburgh S for Lab 1983. Vice-chmn Scottish LDs 1988- . B Aug 17 1948; ed Madras Coll, St Andrews; Edinburgh univ; Christ's Coll, Cambridge. AUT.
Roger Knox, snr lecturer and information systems consultant, contested E Lothian 1983; Kirkcaldy twice 1974. B Oct 29 1942; ed Harris Acad, Dundee; St Andrews and Heriot-Watt univs.

EDINBURGH WEST						No change
Electorate % Turnout	58,998	82.7%	1992	62,214	79.4%	1987
*Douglas Hamilton, Lord (C)	18,071	37.0%	-0.3%	18,450	37.4%	C
Gorrie, D C E (LD)	17,192	35.2%	+0.4%	17,216	34.9%	L/All
Kitson, Ms I (Lab)	8,759	18.0%	-4.2%	10,957	22.2%	Lab
Sutherland, G D (SNP)	4,117	8.4%	+2.8%	2,774	5.6%	SNP
Fleming, A (Lib)	272	0.6%				
Hendry, Ms L M (Grn)	234	0.5%				
Bruce, D (BNP)	133	0.3%				
C to LD swing 0.3%	48,778		1.8%	49,397		2.5%
		C maj	879		C maj	1,234

Lord James Douglas-Hamilton, advocate and author, second son of the 14th Duke of Hamilton, became Under Sec of State for Scotland in 1987; Ld Commissioner of Treasury (govt whip) 1979-81; Scottish whip 1976-9. Former PPS to Malcolm Rifkind. Elected in Oct 1974; contested Hamilton, Feb 1974. B Jul 31 1942; ed Eton; Balliol Coll, Oxford (pres of union, 1964); Edinburgh univ. Boxing Blue; hon pres, Scottish ABA, 1975- .
Donald Gorrie, small business director, contested Edinburgh W 1970 and twice in 1974. Mbr, Edinburgh DC, 1980- ; Lothian Regional cl 1974-B Apr 2 1933; ed Hurst Grange Sch, Stirling; Oundle; Corpus Christi Coll, Oxford.
Irene Kitson, trade union official; mbr Edinburgh DC

since 1989. B Mar 10 1945; ed Boroughmuir Sec Sch, Edinburgh; Open univ for which she is now tutor in women's studies. Director, Edinburgh Women's Training Centre. EIS and MSF.
Graham Sutherland is a teacher. B Nov 28 1956; ed Inverness HS; Heriot-Watt univ, Edinburgh; Jordanhill Coll of Ed. Collector of historical vocal recordings. EIS.
Linda Hendry is self-employed. Contested Edinburgh Central 1987 and Edinburgh S 1983; Lothians in 1984 Euro elections. UK chmn Grn pty 1988. B Mar 7 1950; ed Dumfries Acad; Edinburgh univ; Moray House TC. Legalise cannabis campaigner.

EDINBURGH, LEITH						No change
Electorate % Turnout	56,520	71.3%	1992	60,359	70.9%	1987
Chisholm, M (Lab)	13,790	34.2%	-15.1%	21,104	49.3%	Lab
Hyslop, Ms F (SNP)	8,805	21.8%	+12.4%	9,777	22.9%	C
Bin Ashiq Rizvi, M (C)	8,496	21.1%	-1.8%	7,843	18.3%	SDP/All
Campbell, Mrs H (LD)	4,975	12.3%	-6.0%	4,045	9.5%	SNP
*Brown, R D M (Ind Lab)	4,142	10.3%				
Swan, A (NLP)	96	0.2%				
Lab to SNP swing 13.8%	40,304		12.4%	42,769		26.5%
		Lab maj	4,985		Lab maj	11,327

Malcolm Chisholm, teacher, was elected in 1992. Chmn Leith CLP; vice-chairman, Edinburgh District LP. Mbr EIS sch rep Castlebrae HS, 1976-87, and Broughton HS, 1989-90. B Mar 7 1949; ed Edinburgh univ.
Fiona Hyslop, marketing controller for insurance co. Mbr SNP and SNP Treasury team. B Aug 1 1964; ed Ayr Acad; Glasgow univ; Scottish Coll of Textiles. MSF.

Mo Rizvi, insurance consultant. Mbr Lothian Reg Cl 1986- . B Dec 15 1936; ed in India, Pakistan and London.
Hilary Campbell, economist, Scottish sports cl. B Jul 13 1952; ed Univ of W Ontario; Middlesex Poly.
Ron Brown was Lab MP for this seat, 1979-92. De-selected after court conviction. B Jun 1940; ed Ainslie Park HS; Bristol TI, Edinburgh. Mbr Lothian Reg Cl 1974-9.

EDINBURGH, PENTLANDS						No change
Electorate % Turnout	55,567	80.2%	1992	58,125	77.7%	1987
*Rifkind, M L (C)	18,128	40.7%	+2.4%	17,278	38.3%	C
Lazarowicz, M (Lab)	13,838	31.1%	+1.1%	13,533	30.0%	Lab
Caskie, Ms K M (SNP)	6,882	15.4%	+8.2%	11,072	24.5%	SDP/All
Smith, Dr K A (LD)	5,597	12.6%	-12.0%	3,264	7.2%	SNP
Rae, D (NLP)	111	0.2%				
Lab to C swing 0.7%	44,556		9.6%	45,147		8.3%
		C maj	4,290		C maj	3,745

Malcolm Rifkind, QC (Scot), was appointed defence sec, 1992; transport sec 1990-2; Scottish sec 1986-90; Minr of State, FCO 1983-6; Under Sec 1982-3; Under Sec of State for Scotland 1979-82. PC 1986. Opposn spokesman on Scotland from 1975 until he resigned in 1977 over devolution. Elected in 1974; contested Edinburgh, Central, 1970. B Jun 21 1946; ed George Watson's Coll, Edinburgh; Edinburgh Univ. Mbr select cmte on overseas development 1978-9 and on European secondary legislation, 1975-6; Edinburgh Cl 1970-4. Lecturer in politics, Univ Coll of Rhodesia, 1967-9.

Mark Lazarowicz contested this seat 1987. Mbr Edin-

burgh DC 1980- (ldr of cl 1986-); chmn Lab pty Scottish cl, 1989-90. B Aug 8 1953; ed St Andrews Univ. TGWU; mbr of and sponsored by Co-op pty.

Kathleen Caskie, campaign worker with Shelter; mbr SNP standing cmte on housing, and of nat cl. B Nov 2 1965; ed Williamwood Sch, Glasgow; Glasgow Coll of Tech. Shop steward, ACTSS.

Dr Keith Smith, agricultural and environmental scientist, contested this seat 1987 and 1983. Treas Scottish LDs 1988- ; mbr Fed policy cmte; SDP nat cl 1981-7. B Feb 9 1940; ed King Alfred's Sch, Wantage; Durham and Reading Univs.

EDMONTON						No change
Electorate % Turnout	63,052	75.7%	1992	66,080	72.5%	1987
*Twinn, Dr I D (C)	22,076	46.3%	-4.9%	24,556	51.2%	C
Love, A (Lab)	21,483	45.0%	+9.0%	17,270	36.0%	Lab
Jones, E V (LD)	3,940	8.3%	-4.5%	6,115	12.8%	SDP/All
Solley, Ms E (NLP)	207	0.4%				
C to Lab swing 7.0%	47,706		1.2%	47,941		15.2%
		C maj	593		C maj	7,286

Dr Ian Twinn, who won this seat in 1983, was a snr lecturer in planning, South Bank Polytechnic, 1975-83. PPS to David Trippier, Minr of State for Environment, 1990-2, and to Sir Peter Morrison, in his ministerial offices, 1985-90 and dep chmn Cons pty 1986-9. B Apr 26 1950; ed Netherhall Sec Mod Sch, Cambridge; Cambridge Boys GS; Univ Coll of Wales, Aberystwyth; Reading Univ. Jt chmn lighting industries gp; parly consultant to British Surgical Trades Assocn; consultant TNT; parly adviser to Chartered Soc of Physiotherapy. Vice-chmn, British

Caribbean assocn, 1986- . FRSA 1989. NATFHE.

Andy Love, political sec to Co-op RS London political cmte; mbr Haringey BC 1980-6; bd gtr London enterprise; former mbr NE Thames RHA. B Mar 21 1949; ed state schs; Strathclyde Univ. TGWU/ACTSS; sponsored by Co-op pty.

Elwyn Jones is a teacher. B Sep 25 1938; ed in Pengam, Glamorgan; Hull Univ; Kings Coll, London. Chmn, Enfield SDP, 1984-7 and first chmn, Southgate LD, 1987-8. NUT.

ELLESMERE PORT AND NESTON						Lab gain
Electorate % Turnout	71,572	84.1%	1992	71,344	81.0%	1987
Miller, A (Lab)	27,782	46.1%	+4.9%	25,664	44.4%	C
Pearce, A (C)	25,793	42.8%	-1.6%	23,811	41.2%	Lab
Jewkes, Ms E (LD)	5,944	9.9%	-4.2%	8,143	14.1%	SDP/All
Money, Dr M C (Grn)	589	1.0%		185	0.3%	Prot Ref
Rae, Dr A (NLP)	105	0.2%				
C to Lab swing 3.3%	60,213		3.3%	57,803		3.2%
		Lab maj	1,989		C maj	1,853

Andrew Miller won this seat in 1992. Trade union official being mbr ASTMS (now MSF) from 1967 and officer since 1976. Mbr Lab economic strategies gp; Lab regional exec mbr; former chmn Eddisbury CLP. B Mar 23 1949; ed Hayling sec sch; LSE. Co-author of Lab plan for regional govt in NW and Lab economic plan for NW.

Andrew Pearce became European Community affairs adviser, Littlewoods retail gp, Liverpool, in 1989; MEP for Cheshire West, 1979-89 when he was defeated. Served on EP cmtes on development and co-operation, on women's rights, environment, public health and consumer protection. Official in customs dept, EC commission, Brussels, 1974-9; previously in construction industry. Vice-pres,

Consultative Assembly of Lomé Convention, 1980-9. Founder, past chmn, and vice-pres British Cons assocn in Belgium. Contested Islington N in 1970 gen election and 1969 by-election. B Dec 1 1937; ed Rydal Sch, Colwyn Bay; Durham Univ. Chmn ED gp working pty on agriculture, 1980.

Elizabeth Jewkes, administrator of charity-run care home. B May 28 1957; ed GS, poly, Open Univ. Musketeer in English Civil War Society.

Dr Mike Money, lecturer. Dep co-ordinator, Wirral Grn Pty; former Grn pty cl. B Aug 24 1944; ed Calday Grange GS, W Kirby. NATFHE.

ELMET						No change
Electorate % Turnout	70,558	82.5%	1992	69,024	79.3%	1987
*Batiste, S L (C)	27,677	47.5%	+0.6%	25,658	46.9%	C
Burgon, C (Lab)	24,416	41.9%	+4.8%	20,302	37.1%	Lab
Beck, Mrs A (LD)	6,144	10.5%	-5.5%	8,755	16.0%	SDP/All
C to Lab swing 2.1%	58,237		5.6%	54,715		9.8%
		C maj	3,261		C maj	5,356

Spencer Batiste, solicitor, is a former legal adviser to Cutlery and Silverware assocn of UK; Law Clerk to Sheffield Assay Office, 1973- . PPS to Sir Leon Brittan, vice-pres European commission 1989- ; Lord Trefgarne, Minr of State for Defence Procurement 1987-9; and Sir Geoffrey Pattie, Minr of State for Info Tech 1985-7. Consultant to Music Industries Assocn; mbr British Hallmarking cl. Elected in 1983; contested Euro seat of Sheffield 1979. Jt vice-chmn Cons backbench trade and industry cmte, 1989- . Mbr jt select cmte on consolidation bills 1991- ; Commons information cmte 1991- . Nat pres 1990- , and vice-pres 1987-90, cons trade Unionists; pres, Yorkshire CTU. B Jun 5 1945; ed Carmel Coll, Sorbonne; Cambridge Univ. Vice-chmn Small Business Bureau, 1983- . EETPU.

Colin Burgon, policy and research officer, contested this seat 1987. Chmn and sec Elmet Lab pty; mbr Yorks reg exec LP; former chmn Leeds Euro pty; election agent at Elmet 1983 and Euro election at Leeds, 1989. B Apr 22 1948; ed St Michael's Coll, Leeds; Carnegie Coll, Leeds; Huddersfield Poly. Nupe and MSF; NUT mbr for 16 years. **Paddy Beck**, chartered company sec; former teacher. Agent at Elmet 1987. Chmn Elmet LDs, 1988; founder mbr Barkston Ash Lib assocn, 1973. Mbr Collingham PC, W Yorks, 1991- . B Nov 8 1938; ed Poles Convent, Ware, Herts; Channing Sch, Highgate, London; Parktown Convent, Johannesburg. Previously NUT then AMMA.

ELTHAM						No change
Electorate % Turnout	51,989	78.7%	1992	54,063	76.9%	1987
*Bottomley, P J (C)	18,813	46.0%	-1.5%	19,752	47.5%	C
Efford, C (Lab)	17,147	41.9%	+9.9%	13,292	32.0%	Lab
McGinty, C P (LD)	4,804	11.7%	-8.8%	8,542	20.5%	L/All
Graham, A (Ind C)	165	0.4%				
C to Lab swing 5.7%	40,929		4.1%	41,586		15.5%
		C maj	1,666		C maj	6,460

Peter Bottomley was elected for this seat 1983; MP for Woolwich W, 1975-83; fought that seat, Feb and Oct 1974. Jt vice-chmn of Cons backbench N Ireland cmte 1990- and vice-chmn of Cons media cmte. Minr for agriculture and environment in N Ireland, with rank of under sec of state, 1989-90; Minr for roads and traffic, with rank of under sec of state for transport, 1986-9; under sec of state for employment, 1984-6. B Jul 30 1944; ed mixed comprehensive, Washington, DC; Westminster Sch; Trinity Coll, Cambridge. Parly swimming champion, 1980-1 and 1984-6; capt, parly football team; parly dinghy sailing champion 1990. TGWU. His wife, Virginia, is health secretary and Cons MP for Surrey South West.

Clive Efford, London taxi driver; mbr Greenwich BC, 1986- (chief whip, 1990-1; gp sec, 1986-7). B July 10 1958; ed Walworth Comprehensive Sch. TGWU.

Christopher McGinty, investment manager, has been chmn of Greenwich borough LD since 1989; vice-chmn, City LD, 1991- . B May 8 1961; ed Bedford Sch; Goldsmiths Coll, London.

ENFIELD NORTH						No change
Electorate % Turnout	67,421	77.9%	1992	69,488	74.5%	1987
*Eggar, T J C (C)	27,789	52.9%	-2.6%	28,758	55.5%	C
Upham, M (Lab)	18,359	34.9%	+6.5%	14,743	28.5%	Lab
Tustin, Ms S (LD)	5,817	11.1%	-3.7%	7,633	14.7%	SDP/All
Markham, J (NLP)	565	1.1%		644	1.2%	Grn
C to Lab swing 4.6%	52,530		18.0%	51,778		27.1%
		C maj	9,430		C maj	14,015

Tim Eggar was appointed Minr of State, Trade and Ind, 1992; Minr of State for Education and Science 1990-2; Minr of State for Employment, 1989-90; an Under Sec of State, FCO, 1985-9; PPS to Minr for overseas development, 1982-5; mbr select cmte on Treasury and civil service, 1979-82. Elected in 1979. Merchant banker (with European Banking Co, 1975-83); director, Charterhouse Petroleum Ltd, 1984-5, and former parliamentary adviser. B Dec 19 1951; ed Winchester Coll; Magdalene Coll, Cambridge; Coll of Law, London. Called to Bar, 1976.

Martin Upham, freelance writer and lecturer; former research officer for ISTC. Contested this seat 1987 and Harborough 1983. B Mar 11 1947; ed Manchester, Bristol, Hull univs. Former sec Lab parly assocn. AUT.

Sara Tustin, bank manager. Nat chmn of YLDs 1991- ; exec mbr Student LDs; nat exec mbr football supporters assocn 1989. B Jun 1 1965; ed Latymer Sch, Edmonton.

ENFIELD, SOUTHGATE						No change
Electorate % Turnout	64,311	76.3%	1992	66,600	72.6%	1987
*Portillo, M D X (C)	28,422	57.9%	-0.9%	28,445	58.8%	C
Livney, Ms K R (Lab)	12,859	26.2%	+7.4%	10,100	20.9%	L/All
Keane, K (LD)	7,080	14.4%	-6.5%	9,114	18.8%	Lab
Hollands, Ms M (Grn)	696	1.4%	-0.0%	696	1.4%	Grn
C to Lab swing 4.1%	49,057		31.7%	48,355		37.9%
		C maj	15,563		C maj	18,345

Michael Portillo was appointed Chief Secretary to the Treasury, 1992; Minr for Local Govt, 1990-2; Minr for public transport, 1988-90; Under Sec of State for Health and Social Security, 1987-8; an asst govt whip, 1986-8; PPS to Minr of Transport, 1986. Elected in 1984 by-election; contested Birmingham, Perry Barr, 1983. Former oil industry consultant and TV political researcher. Mbr select cmte on energy, 1985-6 B May 26 1953; ed Harrow Cty Sch; Peterhouse, Cambridge. Special adviser to Sec of State for Trade and Industry, 1983, and to Chancellor of Exchequer, 1983-4.

Karen Livney, British Airways sales agent. Constituency agent, Hayes and Harlington 1989-91; mbr Hillingdon BC 1986-90. B Mar 11 1954; ed Walker primary sch; St Angelas convent; Southgate sch. GMB/Apex.

Kevin Keane, strategy consultant. B Apr 15 1958; ed Finchley Catholic GS; Loughborough Univ; Manchester Business Sch.

EPPING FOREST						No change
Electorate % Turnout	67,585	80.6%	1992	67,804	76.3%	1987
*Norris, S J (C)	32,407	59.5%	-1.4%	31,536	60.9%	C
Murray, S W (Lab)	12,219	22.4%	+4.1%	10,023	19.4%	SDP/All
Austen, Mrs B (LD)	9,265	17.0%	-2.3%	9,499	18.4%	Lab
O'Brien, A (Epping)	552	1.0%		695	1.3%	Grn
C to Lab swing 2.8%	54,443		37.1%	51,753		41.6%
		C maj	20,188		C maj	21,513

Stephen Norris was appointed under sec for transport in 1992 with responsibility for London's transport. Returned at 1988 by-election; MP for Oxford E 1983-7. Company director. PPS to trade and industry sec 1990; to home sec 1990-2; to William Waldegrave at DoE 1985-7. Mbr Select Cmte on Social Services 1984-5. B May 24 1945; ed Liverpool Inst; Worcester Coll, Oxford. Mbr Berkshire CC, 1977-85; Berkshire AHA 1979-82; vice-chmn W Berkshire Dist HA, 1982-5. Liveryman Coachmakers and Coach Harness Makers Company; Freeman City of London.

Stephen Murray, teacher, contested this seat 1987 and 1988 by-election. B May 8 1959; ed Bristol and London Univs. Mbr Epping Forest DC 1982- .

Mrs Beryl Austen, retired self-employed hotelier. B Nov 12 1930; ed sec; tech; Open Univ. Sec Rowcroft hospice 1990-2. Founder and first chmn, grant maintained schs trust and crime concern trust.

Details of 1988 by-election on page 287

EPSOM AND EWELL						No change
Electorate % Turnout	68,138	80.1%	1992	70,683	75.4%	1987
*Hamilton, A G (C)	32,861	60.2%	-2.0%	33,145	62.2%	C
Emerson, M P (LD)	12,840	23.5%	+0.3%	12,384	23.2%	L/All
Warren, R (Lab)	8,577	15.7%	+1.2%	7,751	14.5%	Lab
Hatchard, G (NLP)	334	0.6%				
C to LD swing 1.2%	54,612		36.7%	53,280		39.0%
		C maj	20,021		C maj	20,761

Archie Hamilton was appointed Minr of State for Armed Forces in 1988; PPS to Margaret Thatcher 1987-8; Under Sec of State for Defence Procurement 1986-7; Lord Commissioner of Treasury (govt whip) 1984-6; asst govt whip 1982-4. PPS to Sec of State for Energy, 1979-81, and Sec of State for Transport, 1981-2. PC 1991. Elected at 1978 by-election; contested Dagenham, Feb and Oct 1974. Farmer; mbr of Lloyd's. B Dec 30 1941; ed Eton. Mbr Kensington and Chelsea BC 1968-71.

Martin Emerson is in local ed authority advisory service. Vice-chmn Richmond and Barnes LDs; mbr Richmond-upon-Thames BC 1982-9 (mayor, 1987-8). B Jan 30 1944; ed Cathays HS, Cardiff; Loughborough Coll; Sheffield City Poly. NUT

Richard Warren, consultant surgeon at London hospital. B Apr 24 1953; ed Liverpool Univ Medical Sch. MSF.

EREWASH						No change
Electorate % Turnout	75,627	83.8%	1992	76,545	77.4%	1987
Knight, Mrs A A (C)	29,907	47.2%	-1.4%	28,775	48.6%	C
Stafford, S (Lab)	24,204	38.2%	+6.1%	19,021	32.1%	Lab
Tuck, P R (LD)	8,606	13.6%	-5.7%	11,442	19.3%	SDP/All
Johnson, L (BNP)	645	1.0%				
C to Lab swing 3.7%	63,362		9.0%	59,238		16.5%
		C maj	5,703		C maj	9,754

Angela Knight was returned for this seat in 1992. Chemist and engineer; adviser to engineering company. Mbr Sheffield city cl 1987- , being Cons chief whip. Held company directorships including that of managing director of engineering components heat treatment company which she started in 1977. B Oct 31 1950; ed Penrhos Coll, N Wales; Sheffield Girls HS; Bristol Univ.

Sean Stafford, mbr Derbyshire CC 1981- ; Clowne PC 1983- (chmn, 1984-5 and 1988-9). B Oct 29 1944. Nupe; former mbr NUM.

Philip Tuck, teacher. Local branch chmn. B Jul 2 1938; ed Caterham Sch, Surrey; Imperial Coll, London.

ERITH AND CRAYFORD						No change
Electorate % Turnout	59,213	79.7%	1992	59,292	75.4%	1987
*Evennett, D A (C)	21,926	46.5%	+1.3%	20,203	45.2%	C
Beard, C N (Lab)	19,587	41.5%	+12.0%	13,209	29.5%	Lab
Jamieson, Mrs M J (LD)	5,657	12.0%	-13.3%	11,300	25.3%	SDP/All
C to Lab swing 5.3%	47,170		5.0%	44,712		15.6%
		C maj	2,339		C maj	6,994

David Evennett, mbr of Lloyd's since 1976 and director of Lloyd's underwriting agency since 1982, won the seat in 1983; contested Hackney S and Shoreditch, 1979. Marine insurance broker, Lloyd's, 1974-81. Mbr select cmte on ed, science and the arts 1986- . Consultant to Octavian Gp Ltd. Sec House of Commons motor club 1984-6. B Jun 3 1949; ed Buckhurst Hill County HS for Boys; LSE. Mbr Redbridge BC, 1974-8; Bow Gp, 1971- .

Nigel Beard has been a snr manager/scientist with ICI plc gp HQ since 1979 dealing with technology and new business development. Contested Portsmouth N 1983; Woking 1979. Chmn Woking CLP and Surrey W Euro constituency. Mbr southern region Lab pty exec; CWS SE political cmte; SW Thames RHA, 1978-86; bd Royal Marsden Hospital 1982- , and Inst of Cancer Research 1981- . B Oct 10 1936; ed Castleford GS, Yorkshire; Univ Coll, London univ. Chief planner for strategy, GLC, 1973-4; director, London Docklands development team, 1974-9. FRSA. GMB.

Maisie Jamieson, teacher, contested this seat in 1979. B Dec 17 1928; ed Bexley Tech HS for Girls and Stockwell Coll of Ed.

ESHER						No change
Electorate % Turnout	58,840	80.8%	1992	62,117	76.9%	1987
*Taylor, I C (C)	31,115	65.4%	-0.1%	31,334	65.6%	C
Richling, J H (LD)	10,744	22.6%	-3.1%	12,266	25.7%	L/All
Reay, Ms J (Lab)	5,685	12.0%	+3.2%	4,197	8.8%	Lab
LD to C swing 1.5%	47,544		42.8%	47,797		39.9%
		C maj	20,371		C maj	19,068

Ian Taylor became PPS to William Waldegrave in 1990. Mbr select cmte on foreign affairs 1987-90. Elected in 1987; contested Coventry SE in Feb 1974. Chmn Cons foreign and Commonwealth cl 1990- ; chmn (1988-9) and sec (1987-8) Cons backbench Euro affairs cmte; chmn Cons Gp for Europe 1985-8. Vice-chmn assocn of Cons clubs 1988- . Director Mathercourt Securities Ltd 1980-91; Mathercourt Gp plc, a corporate finance and management services advisory gp, 1990- ; Fentiman Consultants Ltd; non-exec director Glenesk School Ltd 1988- ; American Community Schools Ltd 1991- . B Apr 18 1945; ed Whitley Abbey Sch, Coventry; Keele Univ; LSE (Ford Foundation Research Scholar).

John Richling, coll lecturer in industrial studies; vice-chmn Putney LDs. B Jul 28 1937; ed Loughborough Coll sch; Bede Coll, Durham; King's Coll and Imperial Coll, London; Middlesex Poly. NATFHE. Personal interests include graphology and pianolas.

Julie Reay an administration clerk; chmn of Kingston CLP for two years; elected cllr in 1990. B Jul 25 1953; ed Plymouth HS. Cohse.

EXETER						No change
Electorate % Turnout	76,723	80.9%	1992	75,208	80.6%	1987
*Hannam, J G (C)	25,543	41.1%	-3.3%	26,922	44.4%	C
Lloyd, J (Lab)	22,498	36.2%	+13.7%	19,266	31.8%	SDP/All
Oakes, G J (LD)	12,059	19.4%	-12.3%	13,643	22.5%	Lab
Micklem, A (Lib)	1,119	1.8%		597	1.0%	Grn
Brenan, T J R (Grn)	764	1.2%	+0.2%	209	0.3%	LAPP
Turnbull, M (NLP)	98	0.2%				
C to Lab swing 8.5%	62,081		4.9%	60,637		12.6%
		C maj	3,045		C maj	7,656

Sir John Hannam, mbr govt advisory cmte on transport for the disabled, 1983- , and sec all-pty disablement gp, 1974- ; jt sec, 1922 Cmte, 1987- . Won seat 1970. Parly adviser to Pharmaceutical Soc. Non-exec director, Brompton Holdings plc, 1988- ; Greyfriars Investment Co plc, 1989- . B Aug 2 1929; ed Yeovil GS. Hon master's degree, Open Univ, 1986. Chmn Cons backbench energy cmte, 1979- ; vice-chmn British cmte of rehabilitation international, 1979- . Vice-pres, disablement income gp; royal assocn for disability and rehabilitation; cl action research for crippled child; Altzheimer's disease soc; disabled motorists gp; bd,

Nat Theatre. Mbr cl British Youth Opera, 1989- .
John Lloyd, barrister. Mbr Exeter city cl, 1983- (chmn development cmte, 1984-); Devon CC, 1981-5. Former sec and chmn, Exeter Lab Pty. B Jul 29 1941; ed Durban HS; Natal and Exeter Univs. TGWU.
Graham Oakes is a nurse. Mbr Somerset CC, 1981-91; Yeovil TC 1982-7. B Oct 29 1959; ed Yeovil sch; Westfield comprehensive; Yeovil Coll. RCN.
Tim Brenan, computer network support analyst in NHS; co-editor, Devon *Green News*. B Sep 12 1961; ed St Paul's sch, Barnes; Exeter Univ; Bristol Poly. Nalgo.

FALKIRK EAST						No change
Electorate % Turnout	51,918	76.9%	1992	52,564	75.0%	1987
Connarty, M (Lab)	18,423	46.1%	-8.1%	21,379	54.2%	Lab
Halliday, R N F (SNP)	10,454	26.2%	+10.8%	7,356	18.7%	C
Harding, K (C)	8,279	20.7%	+2.1%	6,056	15.4%	SNP
Storr, Miss D (LD)	2,775	6.9%	-4.8%	4,624	11.7%	SDP/All
Lab to SNP swing 9.5%	39,931		20.0%	39,415		35.6%
		Lab maj	7,969		Lab maj	14,023

Michael Connarty, teacher of disabled children, was elected in 1992; contested Stirling 1987 and 1983. Bd mbr voluntary action resource centre Falkirk. Mbr Stirling DC 1977-90 (ldr 1980-90); exec cmte Scottish Lab pty 1981-92 (chmn local govt cmte 1988-90; represented Scotland on UK local govt cmte 1988-91); vice-chmn Lab gp Cosla 1988-90; former chmn Scottish working parties on ed, local govt, finance, sport and housing. B Sep 3 1947; ed Stirling and Glasgow univs; Jordanhill coll of ed. Exec mbr, central region EIS 1976-84. Vice-chmn Scottish Medical

Aid for Palestinians 1988- . Chmn Stirlingshire Co-op pty.
Ronald Halliday, administrator at Stirling univ, contested this seat 1987 and Edinburgh Central 1983. B Aug 16 1949; ed Boroughmuir Snr Sec Sch, Edinburgh; Edinburgh univ; Aberdeen coll of ed. AUT.
Keith Harding, self-employed newsagent; vice-chmn Stirling Cons assocn; mbr Stirling DC 1986- (ldr Cons gp); Forth Valley Health Bd. B Nov 21 1938; ed GS.
Debra Storr, business systems analyst; treas, Edinburgh Central LDs. B Feb 8 1960; ed Loughborough Univ.

FALKIRK WEST						No change
Electorate % Turnout	50,126	76.8%	1992	50,222	75.9%	1987
*Canavan, D A (Lab)	19,162	49.8%	-3.4%	20,256	53.2%	Lab
Houston, W (SNP)	9,350	24.3%	+7.8%	6,704	17.6%	C
Macdonald, M (C)	7,558	19.6%	+2.0%	6,296	16.5%	SNP
Reilly, M (LD)	2,414	6.3%	-6.4%	4,841	12.7%	L/All
Lab to SNP swing 5.6%	38,484		25.5%	38,097		35.6%
		Lab maj	9,812		Lab maj	13,552

Dennis Canavan was elected for this seat 1983; MP for W Stirlingshire, Oct 1974-83. Mbr select cmte on foreign affairs 1982- . Chmn PLP N Ireland cmte 1990- ; jt vice-chmn PLP foreign affairs cmte 1985-91 ; PLP defence cmte 1990- . Chmn all-pty Scottish sports parly gp 1987- ; jt vice-chmn Scottish hospice gp 1990- . Chmn Scottish PLP gp 1980-1. Parly spokesman for Scottish cmte on mobility for disabled 1977- . Ldr of Lab gp Stirling DC 1974 and mbr 1973-4. B Aug 8 1942; ed St Columba's HS, Cowdenbeath; Edinburgh Univ. Asst headmaster Holyrood HS, Edinburgh, 1974. Chmn parly branch, EIS, 1983- . Sponsored

by Cohse.
Bill Houston, community ed officer, contested Stirling 1983; B 1952; ed Crookston Castle Sch; Jordanhill coll.
Michael Macdonald, deputy nurse education director Forth Valley health bd; organising sec, Scottish CTU. B Apr 10 1948; ed St Joseph's sec sch, Inverness; Strathclyde Univ Business Sch. RCN.
Martin Reilly, student at Edinburgh Univ, is pres of univ LDs; mbr exec, Scottish student and YLDs. Mbr British Computing Society. B Feb 10 1970.

FALMOUTH AND CAMBORNE						No change
Electorate % Turnout	70,702	81.1%	1992	68,612	78.8%	1987
Coe, S N (C)	21,150	36.9%	-7.0%	23,725	43.9%	C
Jones, Mrs T L (LD)	17,883	31.2%		18,686	34.6%	SDP/All
Cosgrove, J D (Lab)	16,732	29.2%	+8.3%	11,271	20.9%	Lab
Holmes, P (Lib)	730	1.3%		373	0.7%	Loony
Saunders, K J (Grn)	466	0.8%				
Wall, J (Loony)	327	0.6%	-0.1%			
Pringle, A (NLP)	56	0.1%				
C to LD swing 1.8%	57,344		5.7%	54,055		9.3%
		C maj	3,267		C maj	5,039

Sebastian Coe, international athlete, was elected in 1992. Vice-chmn of Sports Cl, 1986-9 and cl mbr, 1983-9. Mbr health education authority, 1987- ; medical commission Olympic cmte, 1987- ; athletes commission, international Olympic cmte, Lausanne. Won gold medal for 1500 metres and silver for 800m at Moscow Olympics, 1980; gold for 1500m and silver for 800m at Los Angeles Olympics, 1984; Euro 800m champion, Stuttgart, 1986; set world records at 800m, 1000m and mile in 1981. B Sep 29 1956; ed Loughborough Univ where he was a research asst, 1981-4. Chmn Olympic review gp, sports cl, 1984-5. Associate mbr academie des sports, France.

Terrye Jones, company director and partner, Kerrier Computer Services. Mbr Kerrier DC 1986- (chmn, 1991-2); Breage PC, 1987- . Treas Camborne LDs; chmn, Keep Kerrier Tidy Gp. B Nov 5 1952; ed Helston GS; Camborne Coll.

John Cosgrove contested this seat in 1987 and Cornwall and Plymouth in 1984 Euro elections. B May 22 1955; ed Holy Cross sch, Plymouth; St Boniface's Coll, Plymouth; Trinity and All Saints' coll, Leeds. Mbr Camborne TC 1985-7.

Kevin Saunders, health food retailer. Press officer, local and cty Grn pty. B Oct 23 1960; ed Downer GS, Harrow.

FAREHAM						No change
Electorate % Turnout	81,124	81.9%	1992	76,974	78.2%	1987
*Lloyd, P R C (C)	40,482	61.0%	-0.1%	36,781	61.1%	C
Thompson, J (LD)	16,341	24.6%	-5.3%	17,986	29.9%	L/All
Weston, Ms E M (Lab)	8,766	13.2%	+4.1%	5,451	9.1%	Lab
Brimecome, M (Grn)	818	1.2%				
LD to C swing 2.6%	66,407		36.4%	60,218		31.2%
		C maj	24,141		C maj	18,795

Peter Lloyd was appointed Minr of State, Home Office in 1992; Under Sec Home Office 1989-92; Under Sec for Social Security 1988-9; Ld Commissioner of Treasury (govt whip) 1986-8; an asst govt whip 1984-6. Former marketing manager of United Biscuits plc. Mbr of Lloyd's. Elected in 1979; contested Nottingham W, Feb and Oct 1974. B Nov 12 1937; ed Tonbridge sch; Pembroke coll, Cambridge. Vice-chmn Cons European affairs cmte 1980-1; sec Cons employment cmte 1979-81; mbr select cmte on employment 1983-4. PPS to Minr of State for N Ireland,

1982-3; to sec of state for ed and science 1983-4.
John Thompson, broadcaster and audio visual producer; proprietor of John Thompson Productions, media training consultancy. Press and media relations officer, Fareham LDs. B Mar 14 1948; ed Portsmouth Southern GS; Highbury Tech Coll.
Liz Weston, arts consultant; partner in alternative arts company. Chmn Fareham CLP and its central branch. B Jun 28 1943; ed Heanor GS; Manchester Univ; Univ Coll, Cardiff; City Univ. Equity; MSF.

FAVERSHAM						No change
Electorate % Turnout	81,977	79.7%	1992	79,039	76.9%	1987
*Moate, R D (C)	32,755	50.1%	-1.0%	31,074	51.1%	C
Brinton, Mrs H R (Lab)	16,404	25.1%	+4.3%	17,096	28.1%	SDP/All
Truelove, R (LD)	15,896	24.3%	-3.8%	12,616	20.8%	Lab
Bradshaw, R (NLP)	294	0.4%				
C to Lab swing 2.7%	65,349		25.0%	60,786		23.0%
		C maj	16,351		C maj	13,978

Roger Moate, insurance broker, consultant, unpaid company director and former mbr of Lloyd's, won this seat 1970; contested it, 1966. Mbr Court of Referees; former mbr statutory instruments cmte; former jt vice-chmn Cons backbench transport cmte. Consultant for Wollams, Moira, Gaskin, O'Malley; Robinco AG, and to Fujitec UK Ltd. B May 12 1938; ed Latymer Upper Sch, Hammersmith. Vice-chmn Greater London YCs 1964-5; mbr YC nat advisory cmte 1963-6. Chmn British-Norwegian parly gp; sec British-American gp 1974-81.
Helen Brinton, freelance examiner in A and GCSE

literature and oral communication and employed by Cambridge, London and Northern bds. Held many pty offices including sec, Kent cty pty; asst sec and women's officer, Sevenoaks CLP. Chmn Tonbridge and Tunbridge Wells Fabian Society. B Dec 23 1954; ed Spondon Park GS, Derby; Bristol Univ. TGWU and Co-op Pty.
Roger Truelove, teacher. Mbr Swale DC, 1987- (chmn environment strategy, 1989- ; health and environment, 1990-). Treas, English schs cricket assocn. B Dec 8 1944; ed Abbey and Stanhope GS; St Edmund Hall, Oxford.

FELTHAM AND HESTON						Lab gain
Electorate % Turnout	81,221	73.9%	1992	81,062	73.7%	1987
Keen, A (Lab)	27,660	46.1%	+8.7%	27,755	46.5%	C
*Ground, R P (C)	25,665	42.8%	-3.7%	22,325	37.4%	Lab
Hoban, M F (LD)	6,700	11.2%	-5.0%	9,623	16.1%	SDP/All
C to Lab swing 6.2%	60,025		3.3%	59,703		9.1%
		Lab maj	1,995		C maj	5,430

Alan Keen won the seat for Labour in 1992. Fire protection consultant; mbr Hounslow BC, 1986-90; Public Enterprise Gp. B Nov 25 1937; ed Sir Wm Turners, Redcar. Mbr of and sponsored by Co-op pty; GMB

Patrick Ground, won the seat in 1983; contested Hounslow, Feltham and Heston in both 1974 elections and in 1979. PPS to Sir Nicholas Lyell, then solicitor-general, 1987-2; mbr select cmte on MPs' interests, 1983-7. B Aug 9 1932; ed Beckenham and Penge County GS; Lycee Guy Lussac, Limoges; Selwyn Coll, Cambridge; Magdalen Coll, Oxford. Pres Oxford Univ Cons Assocn, 1958. Mbr Hammersmith BC, 1968-71.

Mike Hoban, marketing manager for bakery company. B Jul 6 1965; ed Furness Comprehensive ch; York Univ. Pensioners Alone volunteer.

FERMANAGH AND SOUTH TYRONE						No change
Electorate % Turnout	70,192	78.5%	1992	68,979	80.3%	1987
*Maginnis, K (UU)	26,923	48.8%	-0.7%	27,446	49.6%	UU
Gallagher, T (SDLP)	12,810	23.2%	+4.1%	14,623	26.4%	SF
Molloy, F (SF)	12,604	22.9%	-3.5%	10,581	19.1%	SDLP
Kettyles, D (Prog Soc)	1,094	2.0%		1,784	3.2%	WP
Bullick, E (All)	950	1.7%	+0.0%	941	1.7%	All
Cullen, G (NA)	747	1.4%				
UU to SDLP swing 2.4%	55,128		25.6%	55,375		23.2%
		UU maj	14,113		UU maj	12,823

Kenneth Maginnis is party spokesman on internal security and defence, and on employment. Adviser to Royal Ulster Constabulary Fed. A director of N Ireland Centre in Europe. Former teacher. Won seat 1983; resigned in 1985 in protest at Anglo-Irish Agreement and retained it at 1986 by-election; also contested 1981 by-election. Mbr select cmte on defence, 1983-5. B Jan 21 1938; ed Royal Sch, Dungannon, Co Tyrone; Stranmillis teacher training coll, Belfast. Mbr N Ireland Assembly, 1982-6; Dungannon DC, since 1981. Mbr UDR, 1970-81 (Commissioned 1972; gained rank of major).

Tommy Gallagher, teacher; pty spokesman on ed; constituency chmn; mbr Fermanagh DC. B Aug 17 1942; ed St Joseph's coll of ed; Queens univ. NAS/UWT.

Francie Molloy, mbr Dungannon DC; SF speaker on prison issues.

Eric Bullick, school principal; mbr Alliance pty exec.

FIFE CENTRAL						No change
Electorate % Turnout	56,152	74.3%	1992	56,090	76.2%	1987
*McLeish, H B (Lab)	21,036	50.4%	-3.0%	22,827	53.4%	Lab
Marwick, Mrs T (SNP)	10,458	25.1%	+10.3%	7,118	16.7%	C
Cender, Mrs C E (C)	7,353	17.6%	+1.0%	6,487	15.2%	L/All
Harrow, C T A (LD)	2,892	6.9%	-8.3%	6,296	14.7%	SNP
Lab to SNP swing 6.7%	41,739		25.3%	42,728		36.8%
		Lab maj	10,578		Lab maj	15,709

Henry McLeish became an Opposn spokesman on employment in 1989; a spokesman on Scotland, 1988-9. Elected in 1987; contested NE Fife 1979. Planning officer, Dunfermline DC, 1975-87, and part-time lecturer/tutor, Heriot-Watt Univ, 1973-87. Part-time employment consultant, 1984-7. B Jun 15 1948; ed Buckhaven HS; Heriot Watt Univ, Edinburgh. Mbr Fife regional cl, 1978- (ldr of cl, 1982-7); Kirkcaldy DC. Planning officer, Fife CC, 1974-5; research officer, social work dept, Edinburgh, 1973-4. Sponsored by Nupe.

Tricia Marwick, training consultant; constituency convenor and press officer. B Nov 5 1953.

Carol Cender, writer; mbr Barnet BC, 1986-90. B Jan 2 1956 in Glasgow; ed Univ of Wales law graduate. Was competitive Highland dancer being successful at Edinburgh Festival.

Craig Harrow, LD information officer; chmn Kirkcaldy and Central Fife LDs, 1991- . Mbr Scottish history society; Scottish Lib Club; Malt whisky society. B Feb 20 1969; ed Kirkcaldy HS; Glasgow and Edinburgh univs.

FIFE NORTH EAST						No change
Electorate % Turnout	53,747	77.8%	1992	52,266	76.2%	1987
*Campbell, W M (LD)	19,430	46.4%	+1.6%	17,868	44.8%	L/All
Scanlon, Mrs M E (C)	16,122	38.5%	-2.7%	16,421	41.2%	C
Roche, F D (SNP)	3,589	8.6%	+2.0%	2,947	7.4%	Lab
Clark, Dr L M (Lab)	2,319	5.5%	-1.9%	2,616	6.6%	SNP
Flynn, T (Grn)	294	0.7%				
Senior, D (Lib)	85	0.2%				
C to LD swing 2.1%	41,839		7.9%	39,852		3.6%
		LD maj	3,308		L/All maj	1,447

Menzies Campbell, QC (Scot), became LD spokesman on defence and disarmament in 1988, and on sport in 1988. Mbr select cmte on trade and industry, 1990- . Won this seat 1987; contested it 1983; Lib and then LD spokesman on arts, broadcasting and sport, 1987-8. Mbr select cmte on members' interests, 1987-90; advisory cmte on Commons works of art, 1988- ; UK delegation, N Atlantic Assembly, 1989- ; jt vice-chmn, all-pty Scottish sports parly gp, 1987- ; treas, defence heritage gp. Contested E Fife 1979, and Greenock and Port Glasgow, twice in 1974. Was Lib spokesman in Scotland on legal and home affairs; chmn Scottish Lib pty, 1975-7. Advocate Depute, 1977-80; mbr legal aid central cmte, 1983-7; Scottish legal aid bd, 1987; broadcasting cl for Scotland, 1984-7. B May 22 1941; ed Hillhead HS, Glasgow; Glasgow Univ; Stanford Univ, California. Chmn Royal Lyceum Theatre Co, Edinburgh, 1984-7. International athlete; governor, Scottish sports aid foundation, 1981-91; trustee, Scottish international ed trust, 1984- .

Mary Scanlon, lecturer in economics, Dundee inst of tech; previously with Tayside reg cl, manpower services dept. Sec, 1986-8, Dundee E Cons assocn. B May 25 1947; ed Craigo sch, Montrose; Dundee Univ. Mbr inst of personnel management.

David Roche, freelance designer and architect; former chief architect, NE Fife DC. Contested this seat 1987. Former convenor NE Fife SNP and Cupar branch. B Mar 5 1941; ed St Michael's coll, Irvine; Aberdeen Sch of Arch. Nalgo.

Lynda Clark, QC. B Feb 26 1949; ed St Andrews Univ; Edinburgh Univ. Nupe.

FINCHLEY						No change
Electorate % Turnout	52,907	77.6%	1992	57,727	69.4%	1987
Booth, E H (C)	21,039	51.2%	-2.7%	21,603	53.9%	C
Marjoram, Ms A C (Lab)	14,651	35.7%	+4.0%	12,690	31.7%	Lab
Leighter, Ms H F (LD)	4,568	11.1%	-2.8%	5,580	13.9%	L/All
Gunstock, A (Grn)	564	1.4%		131	0.3%	Grmld
Johnson, Ms S (Loony)	130	0.3%		59	0.1%	GP
Macrae, J (NLP)	129	0.3%				
C to Lab swing 3.3%	41,081		15.5%	40,063		22.2%
		C maj	6,388		C maj	8,913

Hartley Booth, a barrister, was returned for this seat in 1992; contested Hackney North and Stoke Newington in 1983. Margaret Thatcher's adviser on law and order in Downing St policy unit, 1984-8. Chmn British urban regeneration assocn; director, British urban development corp, 1988-90. Former leader writer, The Daily Telegraph. B 1946; ed Bristol and Cambridge Univs.

Anni Marjoram, teacher, contested Devon N 1987. Has held various pty offices B Dec 10 1949; ed St Thomas More Girls Sec Mod, Wigan; Notre Dame Convent VI form, Wigan; Bretton Hall. NUT.

Hilary Leighter, management consultant, contested Enfield N in 1987 and London N in 1989 Euro elections. Mbr LD women's organisation campaigns cmte. B Sep 21 1956; ed Claremont High Sch, Brent; New Hall, Cambridge. Chmn, MSF London computer staffs branch.

Ashley Gunstock, actor and artistic director. B Feb 3 1957; ed Belmont, Harrow; Finchley, Manorhill; Arts Education, London EC1.

FOLKESTONE AND HYTHE						No change
Electorate % Turnout	65,856	79.6%	1992	64,406	78.3%	1987
*Howard, M (C)	27,437	52.3%	-3.0%	27,915	55.4%	C
Cufley, Mrs L F (LD)	18,527	35.3%	-1.9%	18,789	37.3%	L/All
Doherty, P (Lab)	6,347	12.1%	+4.7%	3,720	7.4%	Lab
Hobbs, A (NLP)	123	0.2%				
C to LD swing 0.6%	52,434		17.0%	50,424		18.1%
		C maj	8,910		C maj	9,126

Michael Howard, QC, was appointed environment sec in 1992; employment sec, 1990-2; Minr of State for Environment 1987 with responsibilities for local govt, and 1988-90, with same rank, was Minr for housing and planning. Piloted through Commons bills on community charge and water privatization. Minr for corporate and consumer affairs, with the rank of Under Sec of State for Trade and Industry, 1985-7. PC 1990. Elected in 1983; contested Liverpool, Edge Hill, 1966 and 1970. B Jul 7 1941; ed Llanelli GS; Peterhouse, Cambridge (Pres of Union, 1962). PPS to Sir Patrick Mayhew, solicitor-general, 1984-5.

Linda Cufley, personnel officer; mbr Kent CC, 1990- ; Shepway DC, 1983- (ldr, LD gp, 1987- ; cl ldr, 1989-90). B Feb 18 1946; ed Haberdashers Askes' Sch, London.

Peter Doherty, electrical commercial asst; mbr, Shepway DC, 1990- . B Nov 23 1958; ed Brockhill Sch, Saltwood; Dover Tech Coll. Mbr of and sponsored by EETPU.

FOYLE						No change
Electorate % Turnout	74,585	69.6%	1992	70,519	69.0%	1987
*Hume, J (SDLP)	26,710	51.5%	+2.7%	23,743	48.8%	SDLP
Campbell, G (DUP)	13,705	26.4%	-2.1%	13,883	28.5%	DUP
McGuinness, M (SF)	9,149	17.6%	-0.3%	8,707	17.9%	SF
McIlroy, Ms L (All)	1,390	2.7%	+0.1%	1,276	2.6%	All
McKenzie, G (WP)	514	1.0%	-1.1%	1,022	2.1%	WP
Burns, J (NLP)	422	0.8%				
DUP to SDLP swing 2.4%	51,890		25.1%	48,631		20.3%
		SDLP maj	13,005		SDLP maj	9,860

John Hume, a founder mbr of the SDLP, has been ldr since 1979; dep ldr, 1970-9. Teacher. Won this seat 1983; contested Londonderry, Oct 1974. B Jan 18 1937; ed St Columb's Coll, Londonderry; St Patrick's Coll, Maynooth. Mbr, European Parliament, since 1979, serving on bureau of Socialist Gp. MP for Foyle, N Ireland Parliament, 1969-73. Elected for Londonderry to NI Assembly, 1973-5; NI Constitutional Convention, 1975-6; NI Assembly, 1982-6. Mbr, NI Forum, 1983-4. Minister for Commerce in NI

power sharing executive, 1974.
Gregory Campbell is DUP spokesman on employment.
Martin McGuinness, mbr of PSF nat exec, contested this seat 1987 and 1983. B May 23 1950; educated Christian Brothers Tech Coll. PSF assembly member, 1982-6.
Lara McIlroy, trainee solicitor; mbr, Alliance Pty exec, 1990- ; chairman, Young Alliance, 1991; local branch, 1991- . B Aug 14 1967; ed univ coll, Cardiff.

FULHAM						No change
Electorate % Turnout	52,740	76.2%	1992	54,498	77.1%	1987
*Carrington, M H M (C)	21,438	53.4%	+1.6%	21,752	51.8%	C
Moore, N (Lab)	14,859	37.0%	+0.3%	15,430	36.7%	Lab
Crystal, P M (LD)	3,339	8.3%	-2.1%	4,365	10.4%	SDP/All
Streeter, Ms E (Grn)	443	1.1%	-0.0%	465	1.1%	Grn
Darby, J (NLP)	91	0.2%				
Lab to C swing 0.7%	40,170		16.4%	42,012		15.0%
		C maj	6,579		C maj	6,322

Matthew Carrington regained seat for Cons in 1987; contested by-election, 1986; Haringey, Tottenham, 1979. Appointed PPS to John Patten and Earl Ferrers, Minrs of State, Home Office, in 1990; PPS to Lord Trefgarne, Minr for Trade at DTI, 1989-90. Banker. Jt sec, Gtr London gp of Cons MPs, 1987- ; sec, Cons unpaired MPs, 1988-9. B Oct 19 1947; ed French Lycee, London; Imperial Coll of Science and Tech, London univ; London Graduate Sch of Business Studies. With First Nat Bank of Chicago, 1974-8, and Saudi International Bank, 1978-87, now adviser to

bank. Production foreman, GKN Ltd, 1969-72.
Nick Moore, manager of children's home; mbr exec cmte; local tenants and residents assocn; mbr, local CHC and Fulham Society. B Jan 5 1955; ed Eastbourne GS; Liverpool and Middlesex polys. Nalgo.
Peter Crystal, solicitor, contested Leeds NE in 1987 and 1983. B Jan 7 1948; ed Leeds GS, Oxford univ, McGill univ, Montreal.
Elizabeth Streeter, restaurateur. B Aug 10 1935; ed Roedean Sch, Brighton.

FYLDE						No change
Electorate % Turnout	63,573	78.5%	1992	63,246	77.0%	1987
*Jack, J M (C)	30,639	61.4%	+0.7%	29,559	60.7%	C
Cryer, N (LD)	9,648	19.3%	-4.9%	11,787	24.2%	L/All
Hughes, Ms C (Lab)	9,382	18.8%	+4.5%	6,955	14.3%	Lab
Leadbetter, P (NLP)	239	0.5%		405	0.8%	RCP
LD to C swing 2.8%	49,908		42.1%	48,706		36.5%
		C maj	20,991		C maj	17,772

Michael Jack was appointed Minr of State, Home Office in 1992; Under Sec for Social Security, 1990-2. Elected in 1987. PPS to John Gummer, local govt minr and agriculture minr, 1988-90. Former sales director of horticultural produce. Chmn, Cons horticulture and markets sub-cmte, 1987-8; jt sec, Cons transport cmte, 1987-8; sec, North West Cons MPs, 1988-90. Vice-pres, Think Green, 1989-90. Mbr, Mersey RHA, 1984-7. Contested Newcastle Central, Feb 1974. B Sep 17 1946; ed Bradford GS; Bradford Tech Coll; Leicester univ. With

Procter & Gamble, 1970-5; personal asst to Sir Derek Rayner, Marks & Spencer, 1975-80; sales director, L O Jeffs Ltd, 1980-87.
Nigel Cryer, scientific auditor employed by ICI Pharmaceuticals. Mbr, Macclesfield BC, 1988- ; treas, Christian Forum. B Jan 9 1957; ed Manchester Poly. MSF.
Carol Hughes, housewife; former civil servant. Held pty offices as press officer, treas, ward organiser, GMC delegate and exec cmte. B Jul 10 1953; ed Essex and Open univs. TGWU.

GAINSBOROUGH AND HORNCASTLE						No change
Electorate % Turnout	72,038	80.9%	1992	69,760	76.9%	1987
*Leigh, E J E (C)	31,444	54.0%	+0.6%	28,621	53.3%	C
Taylor, N (LD)	15,199	26.1%	-9.1%	18,898	35.2%	L/All
Jones, Mrs F E A (Lab)	11,619	19.9%	+8.5%	6,156	11.5%	Lab
LD to C swing 4.9%	58,262		27.9%	53,675		18.1%
		C maj	16,245		C maj	9,723

Edward Leigh was appointed Under Sec of State for Trade and Industry in 1990. Mbr, select cmte on defence, 1983-7. Consultant to Vickers plc, 1989-90. PPS to John Patten, Minr of State, Home Office, 1990. Jt sec, Cons backbench N Ireland cmte, 1988-90; jt vice-chmn, Cons employment cmte, 1987-8; sec, Cons defence cmte, 1983-84; Cons agriculture cmte, 1983-5, and former chmn, cereals sub-cmte. Barrister. Elected in 1983; contested Teeside Middlesbrough, Oct 1974. B Jul 20 1950; ed St Philip's Sch, Kensington; Oratory Sch; French Lycee, London;

Durham univ (pres of union and chmn, univ Cons assocn). Mbr, Richmond BC, 1974-8; GLC, 1977-81.
Neil Taylor is a teacher. Chairman, constituency pty; mbr, Market Rasen TC, 1979-90 (mayor, 1983-4); W Lindsey DC, 1982- . B Jan 31 1954; ed Ashmole Sec Mod Sch, N17; Radcliffe Comprehensive, Wolverton, Bucks; Coll of All Saints, N14. NAS/UWT.
Fiona Jones, journalist. Mbr, West Lindsey DC, 1990- . B Feb 27 1957; ed Mary Help of Christians GS, Liverpool; Preston/Wirral Coll. NUJ; chmn Lincs branch, 1989- .

GALLOWAY AND UPPER NITHSDALE						No change
Electorate % Turnout	54,474	81.7%	1992	53,429	76.8%	1987
*Lang, I B (C)	18,681	42.0%	+1.6%	16,592	40.4%	C
Brown, M (SNP)	16,213	36.4%	+5.0%	12,919	31.5%	SNP
Dowson, J (Lab)	5,766	13.0%	+0.1%	6,001	14.6%	L/All
McKerchar, J E (LD)	3,826	8.6%	-6.0%	5,298	12.9%	Lab
				230	0.6%	Retired
C to SNP swing 1.7%	44,486		5.5%	41,040		8.9%
		C maj	2,468		C maj	3,673

Ian Lang was appointed Sec of State for Scotland in 1990; Minr of State, Scottish Office, 1987-90; Minr for industry and home affairs at Scottish Office, with rank of Under Sec of State for Scotland, 1986-7; Under Sec of State for Employment, 1983-6; a Ld Commissioner of Treasury (govt whip), 1983-6; asst govt whip, 1981-3. Elected for this seat 1983; MP for Galloway, 1979-83; contested Ayrshire Central, 1970; Glasgow, Pollok, Feb 1974. B Jun 27 1940; ed Rugby; Sidney Sussex Coll, Cambridge. Former company director; director, Glasgow Chamber of Commerce, 1978-81. Vice-chmn, Scottish Cons pty, 1983-7. Mbr of Lloyd's; Queen's Bodyguard for Scotland (Royal Company of Archers), since 1974.
Matthew Brown, solicitor and engineer, contested Scot-

land S in 1989 Euro elections; Cunninghame N 1987 and Bute and N Ayrshire 1979. Provost of Cunninghame DC, 1977-80. An SNP speaker on home affairs. B Jan 1940; ed Larkhall Acad; Stow Coll.
John Dowson is an antique and fine art dealer; director of local charity. Mbr, Nithsdale DC, 1988- ; Dumfries and Galloway Reg Cl, 1990- . B Feb 16 1948; ed Paisley GS; Dundee Coll of Art; Royal Coll of Art, London. TGWU.
John McKerchar, managing director of own company producing health care products, contested this seat 1987 and Scotland S in 1989 Euro elections. Borders reg cllr, 1978-83. B May 11 1947; ed Burnage GS, Manchester; Salford univ.

GATESHEAD EAST						No change
Electorate % Turnout	64,355	73.6%	1992	67,953	71.8%	1987
*Quin, Miss J G (Lab)	30,100	63.5%	+4.3%	28,895	59.2%	Lab
Callanan, J M (C)	11,570	24.4%	+0.5%	11,667	23.9%	C
Beadle, R W A L (LD)	5,720	12.1%	-4.8%	8,231	16.9%	SDP/All
C to Lab swing 1.9%	47,390		39.1%	48,793		35.3%
		Lab maj	18,530		Lab maj	17,228

Joyce Quin joined Opposn front bench trade and industry team in 1989. Elected in 1987; mbr select cmte on Treasury and Civil Service, 1987-9. Jt vice-chmn, all-pty social science and policy cmte. MEP for Tyne and Wear, 1979-89, serving on the EP economic and monetary affairs and industrial policy cmte, and previously on agriculture and women's rights cmtes. Researcher, international dept, Lab pty HQ, 1969-72; lecturer in French, Bath univ, 1972-6, and in French and politics, Durham univ, 1977-9. B Nov 26 1944; ed Whitley Bay GS (HS); Newcastle and London univs; LSE. FRSA 1991. Hon Fellow, Sunderland Poly, 1986. Sponsored by TGWU.

Martin Callanan, project manager with Scottish and Newcastle Breweries, contested Houghton and Washington 1987. Mbr, Gateshead MBC, 1987- (ldr, Cons gp); Tyne and Wear CC, 1983-6. Political adviser to MP, 1983-7. Nat chmn, YC Initiative, 1989- ; mbr, nat union exec cmte, 1984-8; vice-chmn, Northern area exec cmte, 1987-9. B Aug 8 1961; ed Heathfield HS, Gateshead; Newcastle Poly.
Ronald Beadle, employed by British Gas in personnel management; sec, Gateshead LDs. B Jan 28 1966; ed Westminster City Sch; LSE.

GEDLING						No change
Electorate % Turnout	68,953	82.3%	1992	68,398	79.1%	1987
*Mitchell, A J B (C)	30,191	53.2%	-1.3%	29,492	54.5%	C
Coaker, V R (Lab)	19,554	34.4%	+10.5%	12,953	23.9%	Lab
George, D G (LD)	6,863	12.1%	-9.5%	11,684	21.6%	SDP/All
Miszeweka, Ms A (NLP)	168	0.3%				
C to Lab swing 5.9%	56,776		18.7%	54,129		30.6%
		C maj	10,637		C maj	16,539

Andrew Mitchell was appointed chmn, Cons Collegiate Forum, in 1991. Banker. Elected in 1987; contested Sunderland S in 1983. PPS to John Wakeham, Sec of State for Energy, 1990-2; and to William Waldegrave, Minr of State, FCO, 1988-90. With Lazard Brothers and Co, 1979-87; adviser to Lazards, 1987- , LEP, El Vino Co, 1981- , Scope Communications Management, and Cray Electronics. B Mar 23 1956; ed Rugby; Jesus Coll, Cambridge (Pres of Union, 1978; chmn, univ Cons assocn, 1977). Mbr, Islington HA, 1985-7.

Vernon Coaker, teacher, contested seat 1987; Rushcliffe 1983. Mbr, Rushcliffe BC, 1983- (cl ldr, 1987-); regional exec, Lab pty. B Jun 17 1953; ed Drayton Manor GS; Warwick univ. NUT.
David George, town planner employed by Lincolnshire CC; previously with Dorset, Surrey, Notts and Leics CCs. Membership sec, Nottingham N and S LDs; chairman, 1988-90; jt convenor Mitcham and Morden Alliance cmte, 1984-85. B Dec 16 1951; ed Lawrence Sheriff Sch, Rugby; Sheffield univ. Nalgo.

GILLINGHAM						No change
Electorate % Turnout	71,851	80.3%	1992	71,847	75.3%	1987
*Couchman, J R (C)	30,201	52.3%	-0.7%	28,711	53.1%	C
Clark, P G (Lab)	13,563	23.5%	+6.4%	16,162	29.9%	L/All
Wallbank, M (LD)	13,509	23.4%	-6.5%	9,230	17.1%	Lab
MacKinlay, C (Ind)	248	0.4%				
Jolicoeur, D (NLP)	190	0.3%				
C to Lab swing 3.6%	57,711		28.8%	54,103		23.2%
		C maj	16,638		C maj	12,549

James Couchman was elected in 1983; fought Chester-le-Street, 1979. PPS to Sec of State for Social Security, 1989-90; to Chancellor of Duchy of Lancaster, 1988-9; to Minr for Health, 1986-8; and to Minr of State for Social Security, 1984-6. Appointed to select cmte on health in 1991; mbr, select cmte on social services, 1983-5. Mbr, British-Irish inter-parly body. Director (since 1980) family licensed trade company. Director Chiswick Caterers; adviser to Gin Rectifiers and Distillers Assocn, Pfizer and

Denplan. B Feb 11 1942; ed Cranleigh Sch, Surrey; King's Coll, Newcastle upon Tyne; Durham univ. Mbr, Bexley BC, 1974-82. Freeman, City of London, and Vintner. NLVA.
Paul Clark, administrative asst sec, TUC; mbr, Gillingham BC, 1982-90 (Lab gp ldr, 1989-90; dep ldr, 1983-9). B Apr 29 1957; ed Gillingham GS; Keele univ. AEU.
Mark Wallbank, section head of Lloyd's broker; mbr, Gillingham BC, 1986- ; Kent CC, 1989- . B Apr 22 1963; ed Mid Kent Coll; Medway Coll of Design.

GLANFORD AND SCUNTHORPE						No change
Electorate % Turnout	73,479	78.9%	1992	72,816	78.0%	1987
*Morley, E A (Lab)	30,623	52.8%	+9.3%	24,733	43.5%	Lab
Saywood, Dr A M (C)	22,211	38.3%	-4.3%	24,221	42.6%	C
Paxton, W (LD)	4,172	7.2%	-6.5%	7,762	13.7%	SDP/All
Nottingham, C (Soc Dem)	982	1.7%		104	0.2%	Ind
C to Lab swing 6.8%	57,988		14.5%	56,820		0.9%
		Lab maj	8,412		Lab maj	512

Elliot Morley became an Opposn spokesman on food, agriculture and rural affairs in 1989. Won this seat 1987; contested Beverley, 1983. Mbr, Select Cmte on Agriculture, 1987-9; vice-chmn, PLP ed, science and arts cmte, 1987-9. Sec, all-pty British-Cyprus parly gp. Remedial teacher at Hull comprehensive school, then head of the individual learning centre until 1987. Mbr, Hull City Cl, 1979-86. Ornithologist. B Jul 6 1952; ed St Margaret's CE HS, Liverpool. Sponsored by GMB.
Dr Andrew Saywood, independent consultant in medico-legal affairs and forensic physician; consultant to NHS

research centre, Cons Central Office; chmn, CPC, Duffield; on area CPC and CTU. Mbr, BMA; Derby local medical cmte, 1984-9. Chmn, Ripley Round Table, 1988-9. B Feb 3 1951; ed Queen Elizabeth's GS, Mansfield; London univ Barts Hospital. Ex-Lt-Cmdr, RN.
Wesley Paxton, a lecturer, has been teaching with Humberside CC since 1974; mbr, nat exec, PAT, since 1986; cmte mbr since 1979. B Jun 23 1946; ed Brunts GS, Mansfield; Bilboro' GS, Nottingham; Warwick and Hull univs. Mbr Salvation Army.

GLASGOW CENTRAL						No change
Electorate % Turnout	48,107	63.1%	1992	51,137	65.6%	1987
*Watson, M (Lab)	17,341	57.2%	-7.3%	21,619	64.5%	Lab
O'Hara, B (SNP)	6,322	20.8%	+10.9%	4,366	13.0%	C
Stewart, E N (C)	4,208	13.9%	+0.9%	3,528	10.5%	L/All
Rennie, Dr A (LD)	1,921	6.3%	-4.2%	3,339	10.0%	SNP
Brandt, Ms I F (Grn)	435	1.4%	+0.6%	290	0.9%	Grn
Burn, T (Comm GB)	106	0.3%		265	0.8%	Comm
				126	0.4%	RF
Lab to SNP swing 9.1%	30,333		36.3%	33,533		51.5%
		Lab maj	11,019		Lab maj	17,253

Mike Watson won the seat at 1989 by-election. Former union official. Chmn PLP overseas aid development cmte, 1991- ; jt vice-chmn PLP employment cmte 1990- ; B May 1 1949; ed Dundee HS; Heriot-Watt Univ, Edinburgh. Sponsored by MSF.

Brendan O'Hara, student, former housing official, contested Glasgow, Springburn, 1987. B Apr 27 1963; ed St Andrews RC Comprehensive Sch, Glasgow; Strathclyde Univ.

Ewen Stewart, investment analyst . B Apr 15 1965; ed Daniel Stewart's and Melville Coll, Edinburgh; Aberdeen Univ.

Dr Alan Rennie, GP, contested Monklands East 1983 and Glasgow Hillhead Oct 1974. B Mar 4 1940; ed Glasgow Acad; Glasgow Univ. BMA.

Irene Brandt, teacher, contested 1989 by-election. B Jan 12 1947; ed Glasgow Univ; Jordanhill Coll.

Details of 1989 by-election results on page 287

GLASGOW, CATHCART						No change
Electorate % Turnout	44,689	75.4%	1992	49,307	76.4%	1987
*Maxton, J A (Lab)	16,265	48.3%	-3.8%	19,623	52.1%	Lab
Young, J H (C)	8,264	24.5%	+2.2%	8,420	22.4%	C
Steven, W A (SNP)	6,107	18.1%	+7.8%	5,722	15.2%	SDP/All
Dick, G C (LD)	2,614	7.8%	-7.4%	3,883	10.3%	SNP
Allan, Mrs K M (Grn)	441	1.3%				
Lab to C swing 3.0%	33,691		23.7%	37,648		29.8%
		Lab maj	8,001		Lab maj	11,203

John Maxton became an Opposn spokesman on Scotland in 1985; Scottish and Treasury whip, 1984-5. Mbr, PAC, 1983-5. Gained seat for Lab 1979. Lecturer in social studies at Hamilton coll of education; B May 5 1936; ed Lord Williams' GS, Thame; Oxford univ. Former parly representative, Civil Service Union and Scottish branch, Inst of Housing. EIS, MSFU.

John Young, public relations and export consultant, contested Rutherglen 1966. Mbr Glasgow Cl 1974- (ldr 1977-9); mbr Glasgow Corporation 1964-73. B Dec 21 1930; ed Hillhead HS, Glasgow; Scottish Coll of Commerce; Glasgow univ management course. .

William Steven, snr science laboratory technician, contested this seat 1987 and 1983. B Jul 2 1955; ed Glenwood Sec Sch, Glasgow. Nalgo.

Callan Dick, computer manager; . B Dec 21 1957; ed Allan Glen's Sch; Glasgow Univ.

Kay Allan, part-time social researcher; mbr local community cl; mbr victim support gp. B Jul 23 1937; ed Possil Snr Sec Sch, Glasgow; Glasgow Coll of Tech.

GLASGOW, GARSCADDEN						No change
Electorate % Turnout	41,289	71.1%	1992	47,958	71.4%	1987
*Dewar, D C (Lab)	18,920	64.4%	-3.3%	23,178	67.7%	Lab
Douglas, R G (SNP)	5,580	19.0%	+6.7%	4,201	12.3%	SNP
Scott, J (C)	3,385	11.5%	+0.8%	3,660	10.7%	C
Brodie, C (LD)	1,425	4.9%	-4.5%	3,211	9.4%	SDP/All
Orr, W (NLP)	61	0.2%				
Lab to SNP swing 5.0%	29,371		45.4%	34,250		55.4%
		Lab maj	13,340		Lab maj	18,977

Donald Dewar, chief Opposn spokesman on Scotland 1983- and a spokesman on Scotland, 1981-3, elected to shadow cabinet in 1984. Chmn select cmte on Scottish affairs, 1979-81. Elected for this seat at 1978 by-election; MP for Aberdeen S, 1966-70; contested the seat, 1964 and 1970. Solicitor. B Aug 21 1937; ed Glasgow Acad and Glasgow univ (pres of union 1961-2). Fellow, Industry and Parliament Trust. Sponsored by RMT.

Dick Douglas, economic consultant, marine engineer; elected Lab MP for Dunfermline W 1983; resigned Lab pty 1990 and joined SNP. Lab MP for Dunfermline, 1979-83; MP for E Stirlingshire and Clackmannan, 1970-Feb 1974; contested that seat, Oct 1974; Glasgow, Pollock, 1967 by-

election; Edinburgh W, 1966; S Angus, 1964. Mbr select cmte on defence 1983-90; PAC 1979-83. Former chmn and vice-chmn Scottish gp of Lab MPs; B Jan 4 1932; ed Govan Sec Sch; Co-op Coll, Stanford Hall, Loughborough; Strathclyde Univ; LSE. Hon lecturer, Strathclyde, 1980- .

Jim Scott, building and management consultant, contested Bothwell, 1979. B Nov 19 1930; ed Whitehill Sch, Glasgow; Glasgow Sch of Architecture; Royal Coll of Science and Tech.

Chic Brodie, finance manager and admin director, contested Surrey NW in 1987; Ayr 1983; Dundee E 1979 and Oct 1974. B May 8 1944; ed Morgan Acad, Dundee; St Andrew's Univ.

GLASGOW, GOVAN				No change from 1987		
Electorate % Turnout	45,822	76.0%	1992	50,616	73.4%	1987
Davidson, I (Lab)	17,051	48.9%	-15.9%	24,071	64.8%	Lab
*Sillars, J (SNP)	12,926	37.1%	+26.7%	4,562	12.3%	SDP/All
Donnelly, J A (C)	3,458	9.9%	-2.0%	4,411	11.9%	C
Stewart, R (LD)	1,227	3.5%	-8.8%	3,851	10.4%	SNP
Spaven, D L (Grn)	181	0.5%		237	0.6%	Comm
Lab to SNP swing 21.3%	34,843		11.8%	37,132		52.5%
		Lab maj	4,125		Lab maj	19,509

Ian Davidson, voluntary services consultant, regained this seat for Labour in 1992; mbr, Strathclyde Regional Cl, 1978- convenor, Cosla ed cmte. B Sep 8 1950; ed Galashiels Acad; Edinburgh univ; Jordanhill Coll. MSF; mbr and sponsored by Scottish Co-op Pty.
James Sillars, dep ldr and snr vice-convenor of SNP, was MP for seat from 1988-92; contested Linlithgow 1987. Vice-pres of SNP from 1987. Elected Lab MP for S Ayrshire in 1970 by-election; held seat until 1979; resigned Lab Pty in 1976; Joined SNP in 1980. B Oct 1937; ed Newton Park Sch, Ayr; Ayr Acad.

Alan Donnelly, North Sea oil/gas operations technician, contested Dundee W 1987. Merchant Navy engineering officer, 1974-80, mbr, Numast, B Jul 15 1954; ed St Bedes sec mod sch, Jarrow.
Bob Stewart, law consultant, 1991- ; local authority solicitor, 1985-91. B Feb 6 1938; ed Hutcheson's GS, Glasgow; Glasgow univ.
David Spaven, British Rail manager, contested Glasgow in 1989 Euro elections and Glasgow, Maryhill, 1987. B Apr 18 1952; ed Edinburgh univ; Central London Poly. TSSA.
Details of 1988 by-election on page 287

GLASGOW, HILLHEAD				No change		
Electorate % Turnout	57,223	68.8%	1992	57,836	72.4%	1987
*Galloway, G (Lab)	15,148	38.5%	-4.4%	17,958	42.9%	Lab
Mason, Dr C M (LD)	10,322	26.2%	-8.9%	14,707	35.1%	SDP/All
Bates, Mrs A K (C)	6,728	17.1%	+2.6%	6,048	14.4%	C
White, Ms S (SNP)	6,484	16.5%	+10.0%	2,713	6.5%	SNP
Collie, Ms L R (Grn)	558	1.4%	+0.4%	443	1.1%	Grn
Gold, Ms H (Rev Comm)	73	0.2%				
Patterson, D (NLP)	60	0.2%				
LD to Lab swing 2.2%	39,373		12.3%	41,869		7.8%
		Lab maj	4,826		Lab maj	3,251

George Galloway was elected in 1987 and was jt vice-chmn, PLP foreign affairs cmte until 1991. Jt vice-chmn, all-pty British-Lebanese parly gp; sec, British-Iranian gp; Former chmn and vice-chmn, Scottish Lab Pty. Gen sec of War on Want, 1983-7; former organiser, Lab Pty, and engineering worker. B Aug 16 1954; ed Charleston primary sch; Harris Acad, Dundee. Sponsored by TGWU.
Christopher Mason, univ lecturer; mbr, Strathclyde Regional Cl, 1982- (ldr, LD gp, 1986-); contested Glasgow for L/All in 1984 Euro elections. Chmn, Clyde Maritime Trust Ltd; Scottish Lib Pty, 1987-8. B Mar 8 1941; ed

Marlborough Coll; Magdalene Coll, Cambridge. AUT.
Aileen Bates, lecturer at Glasgow Coll of Nursing and Midwifery, contested Kilmarnock and Loudoun 1987 and Glasgow in 1989 Euro elections. Mbr, Ayrshire and Arran Health Bd, 1989- ; Scottish pty exec, 1988- . B Apr 24 1947; ed Thurso HS; Glasgow univ; Jordanhill Coll.
Sandra White, student; mbr, Renfrew DC, 1989- . B Aug 8 1951; ed Garthamlock Snr Sec Sch; Cardonald Coll.
Lizbeth Collie, lecturer, contested Paisley S by-election, Nov 1990. Mbr, Scottish Grn Pty nat cl. B Dec 19 1963; ed Perth Acad; Glasgow univ.

GLASGOW, MARYHILL				No change		
Electorate % Turnout	48,426	65.2%	1992	52,371	67.5%	1987
*Fyfe, Mrs M (Lab)	19,452	61.6%	-4.8%	23,482	66.4%	Lab
Williamson, C (SNP)	6,033	19.1%	+8.1%	4,118	11.7%	L/All
Godfrey, J P (C)	3,248	10.3%	+0.9%	3,895	11.0%	SNP
Alexander, J (LD)	2,215	7.0%	-4.6%	3,307	9.4%	C
O'Brien, P (Grn)	530	1.7%	+0.2%	539	1.5%	Grn
Henderson, M (NLP)	78	0.2%				
Lab to SNP swing 6.4%	31,556		42.5%	35,341		54.8%
		Lab maj	13,419		Lab maj	19,364

Maria Fyfe was an Opposn spokesman on women, 1988-91. Co-chairman, Scottish Labour against War in Gulf, 1991. Elected in 1987. Convener and campaign officer, Scottish gp of Lab MPs 1991-; jt vice-chairman, PLP employment cmte, 1987-8. Former lecturer, Central Coll of Commerce, Glasgow 1976-87. Mbr, Glasgow DC, 1980-7; Scottish Lab Pty exec, 1982-8. B Nov 25 1938; ed state primary and sec schools in Scotland; Strathclyde univ. Sponsored by TGWU.
Cliff Williamson, arts student; former health service

worker; agent at Glasgow, Springburn, 1987. SNP nat exec, 1987- ; B Dec 23 1965; ed Alexandra Parade primary sch; Whitehill sec sch; Glasgow Sch of Art. Nalgo.
John Godfrey, investment banker, special adviser to Home Office, 1988-90. B Mar 21 1963; ed Lochaber HS; Oriel Coll, Oxford (Pres, univ Cons Assocn, 1983).
Jim Alexander, engineer; sales and marketing manager; constituency sec, 1989- . Mbr, LD Friends of Israel. B May 28 1959; ed Glasgow Poly.

GLASGOW, POLLOK						No change
Electorate % Turnout	46,139	70.7%	1992	51,396	71.7%	1987
*Dunnachie, J F (Lab)	14,170	43.4%	-19.7%	23,239	63.1%	Lab
Sheridan, T (SML)	6,287	19.3%			5,256	14.3%	C
Gray, R (C)	5,147	15.8%	+1.5%	4,445	12.1%	L/All
Leslie, G (SNP)	5,107	15.6%	+6.1%	3,528	9.6%	SNP
Jago, D M (LD)	1,932	5.9%	-6.2%	362	1.0%	Grn
No swing calculation.	32,643		24.1%	36,830		48.8%
		Lab maj	7,883		Lab maj	17,983

Jimmy Dunnachie was elected in 1987. An Opposn whip, 1988- ; Scottish whip, 1989- . Former Rolls Royce engineer, mainly at Hillington factory. Mbr, Glasgow Corporation, 1972-4; City of Glasgow DC, 1974-7; Strathclyde Regional Cl, 1978-87 (vice-chmn, social work cmte, 1982-7) serving on Greater Glasgow Health Bd. B Nov 17 1930. Sponsored by AEU.

Tommy Sheridan, anti-poll tax campaigner, fought the election for Scottish Militant Labour from HM prison, Edinburgh, where he was serving six months for breach of court order banning him from attending warrant sales.

Russell Gray, financial consultancy manager; chmn, W of Scotland YCs, 1988-90; vice-chmn, Glasgow Rutherglen Cons Assocn, 1989- . B Dec 8 1960; ed Madras coll, St Andrews; Napier Coll, Edinburgh.

George Leslie, veterinary surgeon, contested Strathclyde E in 1989 and 1984 Euro elections and Glasgow in 1979 Euro elections; Kilmarnock and Loudoun in 1987 gen election; Glasgow Hillhead, 1983 and 1982 by-election; Glasgow Pollok, 1970 and 1967 by-election; Glasgow Craigton, 1966. B Nov 21 1936; ed Hillhead HS; Glasgow univ vet sch. Mbr, Strathclyde Reg Cl, 1976-79; Glasgow City Cl, 1968-71.

David Jago, Strathclyde univ lecturer; chmn, Pollok and S Glasgow LDs. B Jul 16 1938; ed RGS, High Wycombe; Cambridge and Leicester univs. Sec, Strathclyde AUT.

GLASGOW, PROVAN						No change
Electorate % Turnout	36,560	65.3%	1992	43,744	69.1%	1987
*Wray, J (Lab)	15,885	66.5%	-6.4%	22,032	72.9%	Lab
MacRae, Ms A (SNP)	5,182	21.7%	+9.6%	3,660	12.1%	SNP
Rosindell, A R (C)	1,865	7.8%	+0.1%	2,336	7.7%	C
Bell, C (LD)	948	4.0%	-3.3%	2,189	7.2%	SDP/All
Lab to SNP swing 8.0%	23,880		44.8%	30,217		60.8%
		Lab maj	10,703		Lab maj	18,372

James Wray, heavy goods vehicle driver, elected in 1987 and joined select cmte on Euro legislation. Vice-convener, Scottish gp of Lab MPs, 1991- ; chmn, Glasgow MPs gp; vice-chmn, all-pty anti-fluoridation cmte, 1990- ; sec, all-pty boxing parly gp. Mbr, Strathclyde Reg Cl, 1976- led Gorbals rent strike and anti-dampness campaign. Pres, Scottish Pure Water Assocn; Scottish Fed of the Blind, 1987 (vice-pres, 1986); Gorbals Utd FC; St Enoch's Drug Centre; Scottish Ex-Boxers' Assocn. B Apr 28 1938. Sponsored by TGWU.

Sandra MacRae, solicitor, coordinator of the SNP anti-dumping campaign and mbr, SNP local govt cmte.

Director/solicitor, ethnic minorities law centre, Glasgow. Contested Edinburgh Central twice 1974; Edinburgh Pentlands 1970; Midlothian 1966. Local govt solicitor for 14 years. Nalgo. B Jun 20 1941; ed Dundee HS; George Watsons Coll; Lycée Henri IV, Paris.

Andrew Rosindell, freelance journalist and political researcher. International sec of YCs; mbr, nat union exec, 1986-88. B Mar 17 1966; ed Marshalls Park Sec Sch, Romford. IOJ.

Charles Bell, area sales manager; mbr, Scottish LD exec; chmn, Clackmannan local pty. B Jan 17 1937; ed Burton-on-Trent GS; Lincoln Coll, Oxford.

GLASGOW, RUTHERGLEN						No change
Electorate % Turnout	52,709	75.2%	1992	57,313	77.2%	1987
*McAvoy, T M (Lab)	21,962	55.4%	-0.6%	24,790	56.0%	Lab
Cooklin, B D (C)	6,692	16.9%	+5.4%	10,795	24.4%	L/All
Higgins, J (SNP)	6,470	16.3%	+8.2%	5,088	11.5%	C
Baillie, D S (LD)	4,470	11.3%	-13.1%	3,584	8.1%	SNP
Slaughter, Ms B (Int Comm)	62	0.2%				
Lab to C swing 3.0%	39,656		38.5%	44,257		31.6%
		Lab maj	15,270		Lab maj	13,995

Tommy McAvoy was elected in 1987 and became an Opposn whip in Dec 1990. Jt vice-chmn, all-pty home safety parly gp. Engineering storeman, worked for Hoover at Cambuslang. Mbr, Strathclyde Regional Cl, 1982-7. Former chmn, Rutherglen Community Cl and Fed of Tenants' Assocns. B Dec 14 1943; ed St Columbkilles primary and junior sec schs. AEU. Sponsored by Co-op Pty.

Brian Cooklin, asst head teacher, contested Glasgow, Hillhead 1987; Edinburgh, Leith, 1983. Chmn, Scottish YCs, 1977-9. B Mar 26 1954; ed Hyndland Snr Sec Sch; Glasgow univ; Jordanhill Coll of Ed. SSTA.

John Higgins, private hire driver, fought seat 1987. Convener, Rutherglen SNP. B Aug 17 1944; ed Our Lady's HS, Motherwell. Boys' Brigade first aid instructor.

David Baillie, asst principal, Cardonald Coll. Mbr, Scottish LD ed gp. B Aug 22 1942; ed Uddingston GS; Glasgow and Strathclyde univs.

GLASGOW, SHETTLESTON — No change

Electorate % Turnout	51,910	68.9%	1992	53,604	70.4%	1987
*Marshall, D (Lab)	21,665	60.6%	-3.0%	23,991	63.6%	Lab
Sturgeon, Ms N (SNP)	6,831	19.1%	+6.4%	5,010	13.3%	C
Mortimer, N R (C)	5,396	15.1%	+1.8%	4,807	12.7%	SNP
Orskov, Ms J (LD)	1,881	5.3%	-5.2%	3,942	10.4%	L/All
Lab to SNP swing 4.7%	35,773		41.5%	37,750		50.3%
		Lab maj	14,834		Lab maj	18,981

David Marshall became chmn of select cmte on transport in 1987, mbr since 1985; mbr, select cmte on Scottish affairs, 1881-3. Elected in 1979. Sec and treas, Scottish gp of Lab MPs, 1981- ; chmn (1987-) and jt vice-chmn (1983-7), PLP transport cmte; jt chmn, parly advisory cl on transport safety; parly road passenger transport gp, 1986-90. B May 1941; ed Larbert HS, Denny HS, Falkirk HS and Woodside senior secondary sch. Mbr, Glasgow Corp, 1972-75; Strathclyde Reg Cl, 1974-79 (Chmn, Manpower Cmte and Cosla Manpower Cmte). Sponsored by TGWU.
Nicola Sturgeon, law student; elected mbr, SNP nat cl; nat convenor, Young Scottish Nats. B Jul 19 1970; ed Greenwood acad, Irvine; Glasgow univ.
Norman Mortimer, teacher of physical ed. Former exec cmte mbr, Nat Cl for School Sport; mbr, Scottish sabre squad, 1979-90, and former capt, Scottish sabre team. Former officer of Scottish and British Handball Assocns. B Nov 17 1956; ed Hillhead HS, Glasgow; Scottish Sch of Physical Ed.
Joan Orskov, art teacher; mbr, Grampian Reg Cl, 1986- (gp sec); sec, Gordon local pty exec. B Mar 20 1938; ed Bristol univ.

GLASGOW, SPRINGBURN — No change

Electorate % Turnout	45,842	65.7%	1992	51,563	67.5%	1987
*Martin, M J (Lab)	20,369	67.7%	-6.0%	25,617	73.6%	Lab
Miller, S (SNP)	5,863	19.5%	+9.3%	3,554	10.2%	SNP
Barnett, A C R (C)	2,625	8.7%	+0.5%	2,870	8.3%	C
Ackland, R (LD)	1,242	4.1%	-3.8%	2,746	7.9%	L/All
Lab to SNP swing 7.6%	30,099		48.2%	34,787		63.4%
		Lab maj	14,506		Lab maj	22,063

Michael Martin, former trade union official and sheet metal worker, served on select cmte on trade and industry, 1983-7. Mbr, Commons chairmen's panel, 1987- ; Commons services cmte, 1987-91; Commons catering cmte, 1991- ; jt vice-chmn, PLP N Ireland cmte, 1987-8; sec, British-Italian gp. Elected for Glasgow, Springburn, in 1979. Mbr, Glasgow Corporation, 1973-4, and Glasgow DC, 1974-9. B Jul 3 1945; ed St Patrick's Sch, Glasgow. PPS to Mr Denis Healey, when Dep Ldr, Lab Pty, 1981-83. Fellow, Industry and Parliament Trust. Sponsored by MSF.
Stuart Miller, electrician employed by Strathclyde Reg Cl. B Dec 10 1965; ed Bishopbriggs HS; Thomas Muir HS. EEPTU.
Andrew Barnett, public affairs exec and journalist; vice-chmn, Scottish Tory Reform Gp, 1990- ; mbr, exec cmtes, Edinburgh Central and NE Fife Cons assocns, 1988- . B Mar 1 1968; ed King's Sch, Bruton, Somerset; St Andrew's univ (pres, univ Cons, 1989-90).
Rod Ackland, computer analyst, contested Clydebank and Milngavie 1987; Monklands W 1983. Mbr, Scottish LD exec. B Mar 8 1945; ed Sussex and Oxford univs.

GLOUCESTER — No change

Electorate % Turnout	80,578	80.2%	1992	76,910	78.1%	1987
*French, D (C)	29,870	46.2%	-3.5%	29,826	49.7%	C
Stephens, K E (Lab)	23,812	36.8%	+7.2%	17,791	29.6%	Lab
Sewell, L M (LD)	10,978	17.0%	-3.7%	12,417	20.7%	L/All
C to Lab swing 5.3%	64,660		9.4%	60,034		20.0%
		C maj	6,058		C maj	12,035

Douglas French was PPS to Lynda Chalker, Minr of State for Foreign and Commonwealth Affairs and then Minr for Overseas Development, 1988-90. Elected in 1987; contested Sheffield, Attercliffe 1979. Barrister; executive, then director, P W Merkle; director, Westminster and City Programmes. Special adviser to Sir Geoffrey Howe, Chancellor of the Exchequer, 1981-83, and personal assistant to him when shadow Chancellor, 1976-79; nat chmn, Bow Gp, 1978-79. B Mar 20 1944; ed Glyn GS, Epsom; St Catharine's Coll, Cambridge; Inns of Court Sch of Law.
Kevin Stephens, an asst manager, became ldr, Lab gp, Gloucester City Cl, in 1988 (mbr since 1983; past cl ldr and chmn, policy and resources and housing cmtes); mbr, SW reg exec, Lab Pty, 1984- . B Sep 11 1955; ed Sir Thomas Rich's GS, Gloucester. Nupe; past vice-pres, Gloucester Trades Cl; vice-pres, Gloucestershire assocn trades cncls.
John Sewell, technician for the disabled; mbr, Gloucestershire CC, 1985- (cl ldr, 1986- ; chairman policy and resources cmte, 1989-); mbr, LD coordinating cmte for England. B Jan 23 1944; ed Chipping Campden GS.

GLOUCESTERSHIRE WEST						No change
Electorate % Turnout	80,007	83.9%	1992	77,994	81.1%	1987
*Marland, P (C)	29,232	43.6%	-2.7%	29,257	46.2%	C
Organ, Mrs D M (Lab)	24,274	36.2%	+8.4%	17,578	27.8%	Lab
Boait, Mrs J E (LD)	13,366	19.9%		16,440	26.0%	SDP/All
Reeve, A (Brit Ind)	172	0.3%				
Palmer, C (Century)	75	0.1%				
C to Lab swing 5.5%	67,119		7.4%	63,275		18.5%
		C maj	4,958		C maj	11,679

Paul Marland is a farmer. Mbr Select Cmte on Agriculture 1986- . Chmn 1989- and jt vice-chmn, 1987-9 Cons backbench agriculture fish and food cmte; treas all-pty Anglo-Irish parly gp. Elected in 1979; contested the seat, Feb and Oct, 1974; Bedwellty, 1970. Parly consultant to British Scrapmetal Fed. PPS to Minr of Ag, Fish and Food 1983-6; to Financial Sec to Treasury and to Economic Sec 1981-3. B Mar 19 1940; ed Gordonstoun sch; Trinity Coll, Dublin. Former mbr North Cotswold RDC. Mbr of Lloyd's. NFU.

Diana Organ, a special needs teacher, contested Somerset and Dorset W in 1989 Euro elections. Dist cllr. Former asst sec Somerset and Frome CLP; Somerset delegate women's cmte; mbr regional exec; political advisory bd Television South West. B Feb 21 1952; ed Edgbaston C of E Coll for Girls; St Hugh's Coll, Oxford; Univ Sch of Ed, Bath; Bristol Poly. Nupe.

Liz Boait, lecturer. Mbr Gloucs CC 1989- ; Forest of Dean DC 1983- . Chmn Gloucester CHC. Constituency sec 1987-9; agent/organiser 1986-90. B Jul 24 1950; ed Cty Sch for Girls, Guildford; Southampton and Sussex univs. NATFHE, 1977-83; NUT, 1972- .

GORDON						No change
Electorate % Turnout	80,103	73.9%	1992	73,479	73.7%	1987
*Bruce, M G (LD)	22,158	37.4%	-12.0%	26,770	49.5%	L/All
Porter, J A (C)	21,884	37.0%	+5.1%	17,251	31.9%	C
Adam, B J (SNP)	8,445	14.3%	+7.1%	6,228	11.5%	Lab
Morrell, P (Lab)	6,682	11.3%	-0.2%	3,876	7.2%	SNP
LD to C swing 8.6%	59,169		0.5%	54,125		17.6%
		LD maj	274		L/All maj	9,519

Malcolm Bruce was elected ldr of Scottish LDs in 1988 and in 1990 became chief LD spokesman on Scotland; spokesman on environment and natural resources, covering energy and conservation, 1988-90; Lib and then LD spokesman on trade and industry 1987-8; Alliance spokesman on employment in 1987 election; Lib spokesman on energy 1985-7; on Scotland 1983-5. Mbr Select Cmte on Trade and Industry 1987-90; on Scottish Affairs 1983-87. Marketing director, Noroil Publishing House (UK) Ltd, 1975-81. Elected for L/All 1983, becoming LD MP 1988; contested W Aberdeenshire, 1979; N Angus and Mearns, Oct 1974. B Nov 17 1944; ed Wrekin Coll, Shropshire; St Andrew's and Strathclyde univs.

John Porter, corporate finance consultant; corporate and industrial executive with Bowmaker, later Lloyds Bowmaker, 1959-86. Grampian regional cllr, 1978- (gp ldr, 1986-). Director, Aberdeen Exhibition Centre; NE Scotland tourism strategy cmte. B Dec 15 1931; ed Lumsden Primary sch; Gordon's sch, Huntly; Aberdeen Central snr sec sch.

Brian Adam, biochemist. Mbr Aberdeen DC 1988- (SNP gp ldr). B Jun 10 1948; ed Keith GS; Aberdeen Univ. MSF.

Peter Morrell, British Telecom engineer. B Apr 12 1963; ed Bankhead Acad; Aberdeen CFE.

GOSPORT						No change
Electorate % Turnout	69,638	76.8%	1992	68,113	74.8%	1987
*Viggers, P J (C)	31,094	58.1%	-0.4%	29,804	58.5%	C
Russell, M (LD)	14,776	27.6%	-3.9%	16,081	31.6%	L/All
Angus, Ms M F (Lab)	7,275	13.6%	+3.7%	5,053	9.9%	Lab
Ettie, P (Pensioners)	332	0.6%				
LD to C swing 1.8%	53,477		30.5%	50,938		26.9%
		C maj	16,318		C maj	13,723

Peter Viggers was an Under Sec of State for N Ireland 1986-9; PPS to solicitor-general 1979-83 and to Chief Sec to Treasury 1983-6. Mbr,Select Cmte on Members' Interests 1991- . Jt sec Cons backbench defence cmte 1991-. Director, Nynex CableComms Solent Ltd 1989- and other CableComms companies; Premier Consolidated Oilfields Ltd 1973-86. Mbr management cmte RNLI 1979-89 and vice-pres 1989- . Elected in Feb 1974. B Mar 13 1938; ed Portsmouth GS and Trinity Hall, Cambridge. Solicitor; underwriting mbr of Lloyd's; elected mbr (unpaid) Cl of Lloyds 1992- . Delegate N Atlantic Assembly 1980-6.

Michael Russell, Royal Mail manager. Mbr Hants CC 1985- ; Gosport Cl, 1986- . B Nov 14 1949; state ed.

Lynne Angus, shop steward/pre-production operater for TV manufacturer. B Aug 11 1947; ed Milton Sec Sch, Portsmouth. Mbr of and sponsored by EETPU.

GOWER					No change	
Electorate % Turnout	57,231	81.8%	1992	58,871	80.7%	1987
*Wardell, G L (Lab)	23,455	50.1%	+3.5%	22,138	46.6%	Lab
Donnelly, A L (C)	16,437	35.1%	+0.6%	16,374	34.5%	C
Davies, C G (LD)	4,655	9.9%	-6.2%	7,645	16.1%	SDP/All
Price, A (PC)	1,658	3.5%	+0.7%	1,341	2.8%	PC
Kingzett, B (Grn)	448	1.0%				
Egan, G (Loony G)	114	0.2%				
Beresford, M (NLP)	74	0.2%				
C to Lab swing 1.4%	46,841		15.0%	47,498		12.1%
		Lab maj	7,018		Lab maj	5,764

Gareth Wardell has been chmn select cmte on Welsh affairs since 1984. Former economics schoolmaster and college lecturer. Elected for this seat at 1982 by-election. Jt vice-chmn all-pty British-Sri Lanka parly gp; jt sec Burmese gp. B Nov 29 1944; ed Gwendraeth GS and LSE. Tutor/counsellor in social science with Open univ 1971-82; snr lecturer in geography, Trinity Coll, Carmarthen, 1973-82. Fellow and trustee Industry and Parliament Trust. Sponsored by GMB.
Tony Donnelly, company director, small businesses.

Voluntary election agent Walthamstow 1987. Mbr Brentwood DC, 1976-80; Essex CC 1981-89. B Sep 1 1950; ed St Martins Sec Sch; Chelmsford Coll.
Chris Davies, sales manager with Allied Dunbar, Swansea. Mbr Portsmouth City Cl 1986-90. B Sep 28 1961; ed Gowerton Comprehensive Sch; W Glamorgan Inst; Portsmouth Poly.
Adam Price, research asst, univ coll, Cardiff. Student rep on PC NEC. B Sep 1968.

GRANTHAM					No change	
Electorate % Turnout	83,463	79.3%	1992	79,434	75.0%	1987
*Hogg, D M (C)	37,194	56.2%	-0.9%	33,988	57.1%	C
Taggart, S (Lab)	17,606	26.6%	+6.1%	12,685	21.3%	L/All
Heppell, J P (LD)	9,882	14.9%	-6.4%	12,197	20.5%	Lab
Hiley, J (Lib)	1,500	2.3%		700	1.2%	Grn
C to Lab swing 3.5%	66,182		29.6%	59,570		35.8%
		C maj	19,588		C maj	21,303

Douglas Hogg was appointed Minr of State for Foreign and Commonwealth Affairs in 1990; Minr for Industry, with rank of Minr of State for Trade and Industry, 1989-90; Under Sec of State, Home Office, 1986-9; an asst govt whip, 1983-4. Elected in 1979. Barrister (non-practising). Chmn exec cmte Soc of Cons Lawyers. B Feb 5 1945; ed Eton; Christ Church, Oxford (pres of union); Lincoln's Inn. Elder son of Lord Hailsham of St Marylebone, the former Lord Chancellor. Mbr Select Cmte on Agriculture 1979-82. PPS to Chief Sec of the Treasury 1982-3.
Steven Taggart, community psychiatric nurse. Contested Lincolnshire in 1989 Euro election. Mbr Lincoln City cl

1986-7. Nat vice-chmn Lab rural revival. Mbr E Midlands regional Lab pty and rural affairs working pty. Mbr Nupe; District chmn, N Lincs health service. B Oct 26 1949; ed Middlesex Poly. Mbr and sponsored by Co-op pty.
James Heppell, environmental planning consultant, principal of 3SPA environmental consultancy. Contested this seat 1987, Stroud 1979, Gloucester 1970, Shipley 1966 and 1964 and three Euro elections — Lincolnshire 1989; London NE 1984; Bristol 1979. Vice-chmn Yorkshire regional LDs. Former cty and dist cllr in Gloucs and Kent. Methodist local preacher. B Jul 19 1938; ed Carre's GS, Sleaford.

GRAVESHAM					No change	
Electorate % Turnout	70,740	83.5%	1992	72,759	79.3%	1987
*Arnold, J A (C)	29,322	49.7%	-0.4%	28,891	50.1%	C
Green, G A (Lab)	23,829	40.4%	+5.5%	20,099	34.8%	Lab
Deedman, D R (LD)	5,269	8.9%	-6.2%	8,724	15.1%	L/All
Bunstone, A (Ind)	273	0.5%				
Khilkoff-Boulding, R (ILP)	187	0.3%				
Buxton, B (Socialist)	174	0.3%				
C to Lab swing 3.0%	59,054		9.3%	57,714		15.2%
		C maj	5,493		C maj	8,792

Jacques Arnold, an international banker, held the seat for the Cons in 1987. Contested Coventry SE 1983. Mbr Select Cmte on Ed Science and Arts, 1989- ; Commons administration cmte, 1991- ; sec Cons backbench foreign and Commonwealth affairs cmte 1990- . Director American Express Europe Ltd 1985-7; asst trade finance director Midland Bank plc, 1984-5; regional director Thomas Cook Gp 1978-84; asst gp representative, Midland Bank, Sao Paulo, 1976-8. Trustee Environment Foundation, 1989- . Mbr exec cmte British gp IPU 1991- .

B Aug 27 1947; ed schools in Brazil and LSE. Mbr, Northamptonshire CC, 1981-85.
Graham Green, solicitor, contested Sevenoaks 1987; mbr, Gravesham BC, 1989- ; Kent CC, 1981-9. Pty offices have included sec Kent Cty LP and CLP sec. B Feb 16 1954; ed Springhead sch, Northfleet; Bristol univ. EETPU.
Derek Deedman, local govt officer with E Sussex CC. Mbr Adur DC 1976-84 and 1986-90 (chmn 1981-3; dep ldr 1987-90). B Mar 25 1947; ed Stourfield/Beaufort sec sch, Bournemouth.

GREAT GRIMSBY						No change
Electorate % Turnout	67,427	75.3%	1992	68,501	75.3%	1987
*Mitchell, A V (Lab)	25,895	51.0%	+5.5%	23,463	45.5%	Lab
Jackson, P (C)	18,391	36.2%	+7.8%	14,679	28.4%	C
Frankish, Ms P (LD)	6,475	12.8%	-13.3%	13,457	26.1%	SDP/All
Lab to C swing 1.1%	50,761		14.8%	51,599		17.0%
		Lab maj	7,504		Lab maj	8,784

Austin Mitchell was an Opposn spokesman on trade and industry 1987-9 when he was dismissed by Neil Kinnock after becoming co-presenter of current affairs programme on Sky Television. Associate editor *House Magazine*. Mbr Select Cmte on Treasury and Civil Service 1979-87; chmn PLP Treasury and Civil Service Cmte 1989-90 and 1985-7; vice-chmn from 1990. Elected for this seat 1983; MP for Grimsby 1977-83. Journalist, Yorkshire Television, 1969-71 and 1973-7. Sec all-pty gp on TV in Commons 1987-9; jt vice-chmn all-pty Trans-Pennine parly gp. B Sept 19 1934: ed Woodbottom Cl Sch; Bingley GS; Manchester and Oxford univs. Vice-chmn E Midlands gp of Lab MPs 1986-90. Fellow Ind and Parly Trust. NUJ; sponsored by GMB.

Philip Jackson, senior process safety chemist; mbr, Gt Grimsby BC 1984- (gp ldr 1991-); treas Gt Grimsby CPC. B 1958; ed Wistringham GS, Grimsby; Grimsby Coll of Tech. Mbr Royal Soc of Chemistry.

Pat Frankish, chartered clinical psychologist. Mbr Brigg TC 1983-9. B Nov 12 1947; ed Caistor GS; Hull and Liverpool univs; Leeds Poly; Open Univ. MSF.

GREAT YARMOUTH						No change
Electorate % Turnout	68,263	77.9%	1992	65,770	74.5%	1987
*Carttiss, M R H (C)	25,505	47.9%	-3.8%	25,336	51.7%	C
Baughan, Ms B (Lab)	20,196	38.0%	+6.8%	15,253	31.1%	Lab
Scott, M J (LD)	7,225	13.6%	-3.5%	8,387	17.1%	SDP/All
Larkin, Ms P (NLP)	284	0.5%				
C to Lab swing 5.3%	53,210		10.0%	48,976		20.6%
		C maj	5,309		C maj	10,083

Michael Carttiss was elected for this seat in 1983. Constituency agent for Yarmouth, 1969-82. Mbr Norfolk CC 1966-85 (education cmte vice-chmn 1972; chmn 1980-5); Great Yarmouth BC 1973-82 (ldr 1980-2); East Anglian RHA 1981-5. Chmn Norfolk Museums Service 1981-5. Commissioner Great Yarmouth Port and Haven Commission 1982-6. B Mar 11 1938; ed Filby CP Sch; Great Yarmouth Tech HS; Goldsmiths' Coll, London Univ; LSE. Teacher, 1961-9.

Barbara Baughan, mbr Gt Yarmouth BC 1986- ; Warwick DC 1973-9. B Jul 2 1947. Chmn maritime pollution information forum. TGWU.

Malcolm Scott, sales and marketing agent, fought Norfolk SW 1987 and Norfolk S twice in 1974. Former chmn/agent Gt Yarmouth LDs; Gt Yarmouth BC 1991- . B Nov 26 1946; ed Duncan Hall Sch, Gt Yarmouth; St Joseph's Coll, Birkfield; Norwich City Coll. TSSA.

GREENOCK AND PORT GLASGOW						No change
Electorate % Turnout	52,053	73.7%	1992	57,756	75.4%	1987
*Godman, Dr N A (Lab)	22,258	58.0%	-5.9%	27,848	63.9%	Lab
Black, I (SNP)	7,279	19.0%	+10.4%	7,793	17.9%	L/All
McCullough, Dr J (C)	4,479	11.7%	+2.0%	4,199	9.6%	C
Lambert, C (LD)	4,359	11.4%	-6.5%	3,721	8.5%	SNP
Lab to SNP swing 8.2%	38,375		39.0%	43,561		46.0%
		Lab maj	14,979		Lab maj	20,055

Norman Godman was an Opposn spokesman on agriculture and rural affairs, 1987-90. Appointed select cmte on Euro legislation 1990; mbr select cmte on Scottish affairs 1983-7. Jt vice-chmn PLP foreign affairs cmte 1991- ; chmn all-pty Tibet parly gp. Former teacher in Scottish further and higher education and former shipwright. Elected for this seat in 1983; contested Aberdeen S, 1979. B Apr 19 1938; ed Westbourne Street Boys' School, Hull; Hull Univ; Heriot-Watt Univ.

Ian Black, local govt officer. Convenor Lanark SNP. B May 8 1947; ed Lanark GS; Newbattle Abbey Coll; Hull and Glasgow univs. GMB/Apex.

John McCullough, chartered engineer, consulting engineer, company director. Chmn Scottish region Inst of Energy 1984-5; mbr Glasgow enterprise zone task force 1980-2. B Mar 23 1949; ed Model sch, Belfast; Paisley Coll of Tech; Portsmouth Poly. Chmn, Kilmacolm Cons, Renfrewshire.

Chris Lambert, depute project ldr, Key housing assocn. Mbr Argyll and Bute DC 1988- (LD gp ldr); chmn Cowall branch and exec cmte mbr Argyll and Bute LDs. Mbr Scottish homes liaison cmte; Strathclyde region area liaison gp. B Sep 29 1956; ed Dunoon GS. ACTS.

GREENWICH						Lab gain
Electorate % Turnout	47,789	74.6%	1992	50,830	73.4%	1987
Raynsford, W R N (Lab)	14,630	41.0%	+6.2%	15,149	40.6%	SDP/All
*Barnes, Mrs R S (Soc Dem)	13,273	37.2%	-3.4%	13,008	34.9%	Lab
McNair, Mrs A (C)	6,960	19.5%	-3.8%	8,695	23.3%	C
McCracken, R (Grn)	483	1.4%	+0.4%	346	0.9%	Grn
Mallone, R (Fellowship)	147	0.4%	+0.3%	59	0.2%	Flwshp
Hardee, M (UTCHAP)	103	0.3%		58	0.2%	Comm
Small, J (NLP)	70	0.2%				
Soc Dem to Lab swing 4.8%	35,666		3.8%	37,315		5.7%
		Lab maj	1,357	SDP/All maj		2,141

Nick Raynsford was elected for this seat in 1992. Won Fulham for Labour in 1986 by-election but was defeated in 1987. Former PPS to Roy Hattersley. Director Raynsford and Morris, housing consultants, since 1987. Director of SHAC, London housing aid centre 1976-86. Mbr Lab housing gp; Notting Hill housing trust; family housing assocn; nat energy foundation. Gen sec soc for co-op dwellings 1972-3; market research for A C Nielsen Co Ltd, 1966-8. B Jan 28 1945; ed Repton Sch; Sidney Sussex Coll, Cambridge; Chelsea Sch of Art. Mbr, Hammersmith and Fulham BC, 1971-5. TGWU.

Rosie Barnes, freelance market researcher, won the seat from Labour in the Feb 1987 by-election and retained it in 1987 general election. SDP spokesman on health and education; former mbr Cl for Social Democracy. B May 16 1946; ed Bilborough GS; Birmingham univ. Product manager, Yardley of London Ltd, 1969-72.

Alison McNair, a chartered accountant, is financial director of family business. Former mbr Lewisham BC; N Wiltshire DC. Chmn Blackheath Cons. B Dec 19 1941; ed Pate's GS, Cheltenham; Manchester univ.

Robert McCracken, barrister. B Mar 15 1950; ed Rugby; Worcester Coll, Oxford.

GUILDFORD						No change
Electorate % Turnout	77,265	78.5%	1992	77,872	75.3%	1987
*Howell, D A R (C)	33,516	55.3%	-0.2%	32,504	55.5%	C
Sharp, Mrs M L (LD)	20,112	33.2%	-0.8%	19,897	33.9%	SDP/All
Mann, H L (Lab)	6,781	11.2%	+0.6%	6,216	10.6%	Lab
Law, A (NLP)	234	0.4%				
LD to C swing 0.3%	60,643		22.1%	58,617		21.5%
		C maj	13,404	C maj		12,607

David Howell, economic consultant, journalist, author and company director, became chmn foreign affairs select cmte, 1987; previously mbr. Chmn Cons One Nation Gp 1987- ; UK-Japan 2000 Gp. Mbr International Advisory Cl Swiss Bank Corporation 1988- ; economic adviser Coopers, Lybrand Deloittes; Swiss Bank Corporation (UK); non-exec director Trafalgar House plc 1990- ; Queens Moat Houses plc 1989- ; Jardine Insurance Brokers plc 1991- . Transport sec 1981-3; Energy sec, 1979-81. Energy minister 1974; NI minister 1972-4, under sec 1972; employment 1971-2; parly sec Civil Service dept 1970-2; govt whip 1970-1. Elected 1966; contested Dudley, 1964.

B Jan 18 1936; ed Eton; King's Coll, Cambridge.

Margaret Sharp, senior research fellow, science policy research unit, Sussex univ, fought the seat in 1987 and 1983. British Rail Southern Rgn advisory bd. Chmn Guildford LD 1988-91 and working gp on science, technology and innovation. Former mbr CSD; cmte Tawney Society. B Nov 21 1938; ed Tonbridge Girls' GS; Newnham Coll, Cambridge. AUT.

Howard Mann, Inland Revenue staff fed official; former tax inspector. Mbr Islington BC 1986- . B Jan 21 1958; ed Ald Newton's GS, Leicester; Durham univ. GMB/Apex.

HACKNEY NORTH AND STOKE NEWINGTON						No change
Electorate % Turnout	54,655	63.5%	1992	66,771	58.1%	1987
*Abbott, Ms D J (Lab)	20,083	57.8%	+9.1%	18,912	48.7%	Lab
Manson, C (C)	9,356	26.9%	-2.0%	11,234	28.9%	C
Fitchett, K (LD)	3,996	11.5%	-7.7%	7,446	19.2%	SDP/All
Hunt, Ms H M (Grn)	1,111	3.2%	+0.6%	997	2.6%	Grn
Windsor, J (NLP)	178	0.5%		228	0.6%	RF
C to Lab swing 5.6%	34,724		30.9%	38,817		19.8%
		Lab maj	10,727	Lab maj		7,678

Diane Abbott was elected in 1987. Appointed to Treasury and Civil Service select cmte in 1989. Press officer with Lambeth BC. Former civil servant, former employee, NCCL, Thames TV, Breakfast TV and ACTT. Mbr Westminster Cl 1982-6; Anti-Apartheid; CND; Campaign for Lab Pty Democracy. B Sep 27 1953; ed Harrow County Girls' GS; Newnham Coll, Cambridge. ACTT; NUJ.

Cole Manson, founder and owner, Hayloft Woodwork,

furniture design and manufacturing business. Grenadier Guards 1976-9. Dep chmn Hammersmith Cons assocn, 1987-9. B Oct 12 1956; ed Creighton Comprehensive; Mountview Theatre Coll.

Heather Hunt, consultant community psychologist; mbr Hackney cl 1983-8. B Apl 18 1946; ed Liverpool, London and Nottingham univs. MSF.

HACKNEY SOUTH AND SHOREDITCH						No change
Electorate % Turnout	57,935	63.8%	1992	70,873	55.4%	1987
*Sedgemore, B C J (Lab)	19,730	53.4%	+5.5%	18,799	47.8%	Lab
Turner, A J (C)	10,714	29.0%	+0.3%	11,277	28.7%	C
Wintle, G (LD)	5,533	15.0%	-7.5%	8,812	22.4%	L/All
Lucas, L (Grn)	772	2.1%		403	1.0%	Comm
Norman, Ms G (NLP)	226	0.6%				
C to Lab swing 2.6%	36,975		24.4%	39,291		19.1%
		Lab maj	9,016		Lab maj	7,522

Brian Sedgemore, was elected for this seat 1983; MP for Luton West, Feb 1974-9. Barrister and researcher with Granada Television 1979-83, and freelance journalist. Mbr Treasury and civil service select cmte 1983- . B Mar 17 1937; ed Newtown Primary Sch; Heles School, Exeter; Oxford Univ. PPS to Tony Benn, 1977-8. Mbr Wandsworth BC 1971-4.

Andrew Turner, director of Choice in Education, grant-maintained school trust, 1988- ; special adviser to Sec of State for Social Services 1987-8; Cons Research Dept 1984-7; geography and economics teacher 1977-84. B Oct 24 1953; ed Rugby; Keble Coll, Oxford; Birmingham Univ. Mbr Oxford City Cl 1979- ; vice-chmn Oxford E Cons Assocn 1984-7 and 1988-90.

George Wintle, pharmacist; mbr Hackney BC 1982- (gp ldr 1985-6 and 1988-90). B Jan 24 1933; Bristol Coll of Tech.

HALESOWEN AND STOURBRIDGE						No change
Electorate % Turnout	77,644	82.3%	1992	78,017	79.4%	1987
Hawksley, P W (C)	32,312	50.6%	+0.5%	31,037	50.1%	C
Hankon, A (Lab)	22,730	35.6%	+7.8%	17,229	27.8%	Lab
Sharma, V (LD)	7,941	12.4%	-9.6%	13,658	22.1%	SDP/All
Weller, T (Grn)	908	1.4%				
C to Lab swing 3.7%	63,891		15.0%	61,924		22.3%
		C maj	9,582		C maj	13,808

Warren Hawksley, hotelier, was elected for this seat in 1992; MP for The Wrekin, 1979-87; contested Wolverhampton NE, Feb and Oct 1974. Mbr select cmte on employment in 1987; jt sec Cons backbench urban and new towns cmte 1985-7. Employed by Lloyds Bank 1960-79. B Mar 10 1943; ed Mill Mead, Stourbridge; Denstone Coll, Staffs. Mbr Shropshire CC 1970-81; West Mercia police authority 1977-81. Governor Wolverhampton Poly 1973-7. Has held various offices in YCs and in South Worcestershire, Ludlow and Oswestry constituencies.

Alan Hankon, car worker. Mbr Dudley MBC 1982-7 and 1989- . TGWU shop steward at Rover Cars, Longbridge, B'ham, 1978- . B Feb 25 1947; ed St Paul's C of E Primary Sch; Hill and Cakemore Boys Sch.

Vinod Sharma, British Gas technical manager. Mbr Sutton BC 1990- (vice-chmn ed cmte). Former chmn Sutton local LDs and SDP. B Aug 14 1947; ed Sir Gilbert Claughton GS, Dudley; Univ Coll, London. Mbr Gas Higher Managers' Assocn.

Tim Weller, local govt social worker. Sec Halesowen Wildlife Gp. B Jan 23 1948; ed Mayfield Cty Sec Sch, Ilford, Essex.

HALIFAX						No change
Electorate % Turnout	73,401	78.7%	1992	73,392	77.7%	1987
*Mahon, Ms A (Lab)	25,115	43.5%	+0.1%	24,741	43.4%	Lab
Martin, T R (C)	24,637	42.7%	+1.4%	23,529	41.3%	C
Howell, I R (LD)	7,364	12.7%	-2.6%	8,758	15.4%	SDP/All
Pearson, R (Nat)	649	1.1%				
Lab to C swing 0.6%	57,765		0.8%	57,028		2.1%
		Lab maj	478		Lab maj	1,212

Alice Mahon was elected for this seat in 1987. Apppinted mbr select cmte on health 1991. Jt vice-chmn PLP health and personal social services cmte 1989- . Lecturer at Bradford and Ilkley Community Coll. Mbr Calderdale MDC; Calderdale DHA. School governor. B Sep 28 1937.

Terry Martin, director of van hire company. Treas Halifax Cons assocn. Mbr Calderdale MBC. B Feb 24 1946; ed Heath GS, Halifax; Keele Univ.

Ian Howell, motor claims administration manager. Mbr Hebden Royd TC 1991- ; exec cmte Yorks and Humberside regional LDs. B Oct 20 1964; ed King James Sch, Knaresborough.

HALTON						No change
Electorate % Turnout	74,906	78.3%	1992	73,848	78.3%	1987
*Oakes, G J (Lab)	35,025	59.7%	+4.2%	32,065	55.5%	Lab
Mercer, G (C)	16,821	28.7%	-1.6%	17,487	30.2%	C
Reaper, D (LD)	6,104	10.4%	-3.9%	8,272	14.3%	SDP/All
Herley, S (Loony)	398	0.7%				
Collins, Ms N (NLP)	338	0.6%				
C to Lab swing 2.9%	58,686		31.0%	57,824		25.2%
		Lab maj	18,204		Lab maj	14,578

Gordon Oakes was elected for this seat in 1983; MP for Widnes 1971-83; Bolton W 1964-70; contested Bebington 1959; Manchester, Moss Side 1961. An Opposn spokesman on environment 1979-83. Minr of State Education and Science, 1976-9; Under Sec of State for Environment, 1974-6; and for Energy, 1976. PC 1979. B Jun 22 1931; ed Wade Deacon Sch, Widnes; Liverpool univ. Public affairs consultant to 3M UK Ltd. Solicitor not in practice. Chmn all-pty chemical industry gp 1990; jt chmn licensed trade gp 1986; jt hon treas UK branch of CPA 1987-90 and mbr exec cmte 1979. Vice-pres ACC 1982; Environ-mental Officers' Assocn 1973; Building Soc Assocn, 1984-9. Sponsored by TGWU.

Grant Mercer, account manager, WRCS advertising agency, 1990- . Vice-chmn 1990-1 and treas 1989-90 Nat Assocn of Cons Graduates; vice-chmn Pudsey Cons Assocn and Pudsey CPC 1988. B Jan 22 1965; ed Stand GS, Manchester; Leeds univ.

David Reaper, teacher, contested Northwich twice in 1974. Mbr Vale Royal DC 1974-83. Chmn Eddisbury LDs. B Apr 14 1947; ed Robert Richardson GS, Ryhope, Co Durham; Sunderland Coll of Ed. NUT.

HAMILTON						No change
Electorate % Turnout	61,531	76.2%	1992	62,205	76.9%	1987
*Robertson, G I M (Lab)	25,849	55.2%	-4.5%	28,563	59.7%	Lab
Morrison, W (SNP)	9,246	19.7%	+7.0%	6,901	14.4%	C
Mitchell, Mrs J M (C)	8,250	17.6%	+3.2%	6,302	13.2%	L/All
Oswald, J (LD)	3,515	7.5%	-5.7%	6,093	12.7%	SNP
Lab to SNP swing 5.8%	46,860		35.4%	47,859		45.3%
		Lab maj	16,603		Lab maj	21,662

George Robertson, Opposn spokesman on European affairs 1984- ; dep spokesman on foreign and Common-wealth affairs 1981- ; spokesman on defence 1980-1; and on Scotland 1979-80. Vice-chmn bd British Cl 1985- ; all-pty British-Germany parly gp; governing body GB/E Europe Centre 1990-1. Jt chmn lighting gp; sec photographic gp. Won by-election in 1978. Adviser to Halton-Gill Associates. Mbr cl RIIA 1984- . Mbr British Atlantic Cmte 1981- ; cl Operation Raleigh 1982- ; steering cmte Atlantic conference 1987- ; steering cmte Königswinter conference 1983- ; advisory bd Know How Fund for Eastern Europe 1990- ; cl GB/USSR Assocn 1986- ; editorial bd European Business Journal 1988- ; cl, British Executive Service overseas 1991- B Apr 12 1946; ed Dunoon GS; Dundee univ. Chm, Seatbelt Survivors Club 1981- . Sponsored by GMB.

Bill Morrison, chemical engineer. Convenor Kincardine and Deeside SNP. B May 30 1956; ed Govan HS; Glasgow univ.

Margaret Mitchell, law student; former primary sch teacher. Mbr Hamilton DC 1988- ; Scottish Cons ed policy cmte; vice-chmn Hamilton Cons assocn exec cmte 1989- . B Nov 15 1952; ed Coatbridge HS; Hamilton Coll of Ed; Open univ; Strathclyde univ. EIS.

John Oswald, self-employed landscape gardener; previous-ly worked for Hamilton DC. B Aug 22 1954.

HAMMERSMITH						No change
Electorate % Turnout	47,229	71.9%	1992	48,285	72.7%	1987
*Soley, C S (Lab)	17,329	51.0%	+6.0%	15,811	45.0%	Lab
Hennessy, J A (C)	12,575	37.0%	-1.1%	13,396	38.1%	C
Bates, J H (LD)	3,380	10.0%	-5.0%	5,241	14.9%	L/All
Crosskey, R (Grn)	546	1.6%	+0.3%	453	1.3%	Grn
Turner, K (NLP)	89	0.3%		125	0.4%	RF
Szamuely, Ms H (Anti-Fed)	41	0.1%		98	0.3%	Human
C to Lab swing 3.6%	33,960		14.0%	35,124		6.9%
		Lab maj	4,754		Lab maj	2,415

Clive Soley was elected for this seat in 1983; MP for Hammersmith N 1979-83. Appointed to Opposn DoE team as spokesman on housing in 1987; a spokesman on home affairs, 1984-7; and on N Ireland, 1981-4. Probation officer and snr probation officer, 1970-9. Chmn, Alcohol Ed Centre, 1977-83. B May 7 1939; ed Downshall sec mod sch, Ilford; Newbattle Abbey Adult Ed Coll; Strathclyde and Southampton univs. Hammersmith cllr 1974-8. Former parly consultant to Soc of Civil and Public Servants. Chmn Lab Campaign for Criminal Justice, 1983-7. Fellow Industry and Parliament Trust. GMB.

John Hennessy works in laundry industry and since 1989 been district linen services manager, St George's Hospital, Tooting. Mbr Hammersmith and Fulham BC 1978- . Mbr Gtr London Cons local authority advisory cmte; exec Irish welfare bureau. Nat sec Assocn of NHS Linen and Laundry Managers. B Nov 20 1935; ed tech coll; Cork Sch of Commerce. Nalgo.

John Bates, barrister, contested Romford for L/All in 1987, 1983 and for L in 1979. B May 29 1951; ed Harrow; Inns of Court Sch of Law. Vice-chmn UK Environmental Law Assocn 1990- .

HAMPSHIRE EAST						No change
Electorate % Turnout	92,139	80.4%	1992	86,363	77.4%	1987
*Mates, M J (C)	47,541	64.2%	-0.3%	43,093	64.5%	C
Baring, Ms S (LD)	18,376	24.8%	-4.1%	19,307	28.9%	L/All
Phillips, J A (Lab)	6,840	9.2%	+2.6%	4,443	6.6%	Lab
Foster, I C (Grn)	1,113	1.5%				
Hale, S (RCC)	165	0.2%				
LD to C swing 1.9%	74,035		39.4%	66,843		35.6%
		C maj	29,165		C maj	23,786

Michael Mates appointed minr of state for Northern Ireland after the general election. Chmn, Select Cmte on Defence, 1987-92; mbr since 1979. Mbr, British-Irish Inter-Parly Body. Chmn (1987-8) and vice-chmn (1979-87), Cons back-bench home affairs cmte; jt sec, 1922 Cmte, 1987-8. Partner in Chelsham Consultants. Elected 1983; MP for Petersfield, 1974-83. Army officer from 1954-74. B Jun 9 1934; ed Blundell's; King's Coll, Cambridge. Master, Farriers' Co, 1986-7; liveryman from 1975. Sec (1974-9) and vice-chmn (1979-81), Cons back-bench N Ireland cmte; chmn, all-pty Anglo-Irish gp, 1979- .

Susan Baring has served on Parole Bd and Inner London probation cmte. Contested Reading E 1987. B Jun 5 1930; ed Heathfield Sch, Ascot.

Jim Phillips, lecturer and company director, contested Havant 1987 and Wight and Hampshire E in 1984 Euro elections. Mbr, Havant BC, 1980- (Lab gp ldr). B Nov 13 1940; ed Portsmouth Coll of Tech; Open univ. Sec, Portsmouth branch, NATFHE, 1985- .

Ian Foster, potter, local govt litter picker, houseperson and gardener. Sec, Grn pty elections cmte; press officer. B Nov 11 1952; ed Woolmer Hill Cty Sec Mod Sch.

HAMPSHIRE NORTH WEST						No change
Electorate % Turnout	73,101	80.8%	1992	69,965	77.9%	1987
*Mitchell, Sir David (C)	34,310	58.1%	+0.4%	31,470	57.8%	C
Simpson, M (LD)	16,462	27.9%	-5.2%	18,033	33.1%	L/All
Stockwell, M A D (Lab)	7,433	12.6%	+3.5%	4,980	9.1%	Lab
Ashley, Ms D A (Grn)	825	1.4%				
LD to C swing 2.8%	59,030		30.2%	54,483		24.7%
		C maj	17,848		C maj	13,437

Sir David Mitchell was jt sec, Cons back-bench finance cmte, 1990-1. Transport minr, 1986-8; transport under sec, 1983-6; N Ireland under sec, 1981-3; industry under sec, 1979-81. Mbr, British-Irish inter-parly body. Elected for this seat 1983; MP for Basingstoke, 1964-83; contested St Pancras N, 1959. Farming, 1945-50; businessman and wine merchant, 1951-79. Director, El Vino Co Ltd, 1988- . B Jun 20 1928; ed Aldenham. Mbr, St Pancras BC, 1956-9. Chmn, back-bench smaller business cmte, 1974-9; founder chmn, 1976, and trustee mbr, 1989- , Small

Business Bureau.

Michael Simpson, consultant; mbr, Berkshire CC, 1989-Newbury DC, 1987-91. B Apr 14 1959. Chmn, Care in Crisis, a pregnancy counselling service; Newbury YMCA.

Michael Stockwell, area manager for educational publisher; mbr, Basingstoke and Deane BC, 1990- . B May 30 1957; ed Peter Symonds GS, Winchester; Nottingham univ. NUT.

Doreen Ashley, youth worker; mbr, Andover Grn Pty. B Jul 12 1954; ed Marlborough Sec Mod Sch.

HAMPSTEAD AND HIGHGATE						Lab gain
Electorate % Turnout	58,203	73.0%	1992	63,301	71.5%	1987
Jackson, Ms G (Lab)	19,193	45.1%	+7.6%	19,236	42.5%	C
Letwin, O (C)	17,753	41.8%	-0.7%	17,015	37.6%	Lab
Wrede, Dr C D H (LD)	4,765	11.2%	-8.1%	8,744	19.3%	SDP/All
Games, S N (Grn)	594	1.4%		137	0.3%	Rnbow
Prosser, Dr R (NLP)	86	0.2%		134	0.3%	Human
Hall, Ms A (Raver)	44	0.1%				
Wilson, C S (Scally)	44	0.1%				
Rizz, C (Rizz)	33	0.1%				
C to Lab swing 4.1%	42,512		3.4%	45,266		4.9%
		Lab maj	1,440		C maj	2,221

Glenda Jackson, actress; director, United British Artists 1983- ; pres, Play Matters 1976- . B May 9 1936; ed West Kirby Cty GS for Girls; RADA. Repertory company actress, 1957-63; joined RSC, 1963. Awarded Oscars in 1971 and 1974 and best film actress awards. Equity; sponsored by Aslef.

Oliver Letwin, director and head of utilities and privatisation team at Rothschilds; former manager and corporate finance asst director. Contested Hackney N in 1987. Special adviser to PM's policy unit, 1983-6. Cambridge don, financial adviser and journalist; B May 19 1956; ed

Hall Sch, Hampstead; Eton; Trinity Coll, Cambridge; London Business Sch. Mbr, manifesto preparation policy gps, 1987. Sailing instructor.

Dr David Wrede, Research Fellow at St Mary's; trainee gynaecologist; chmn, Hospital Doctors' Assocn; mbr, nat hospital jnr staff cmte. B Aug 27 1958; ed Ibstock Place; Bedales; St Paul's Sch; Cambridge univ; St Thomas' Hosp.

Stephen Games, broadcaster and journalist. Director, Green Fund Ltd and Metronome Ltd. Chmn, Grn Pty nat fundraising cmte. B Jul 11 1952; ed Harrow Cty GS; Central sch of art; Magdalene coll, Cambridge. Equity.

HARBOROUGH						No change
Electorate % Turnout	76,514	82.1%	1992	74,700	79.3%	1987
Garnier, E H (C)	34,280	54.6%	-4.9%	35,216	59.4%	C
Cox, M (LD)	20,737	33.0%	+5.3%	16,406	27.7%	L/All
Mackay, Ms C (Lab)	7,483	11.9%	-1.0%	7,646	12.9%	Lab
Irwin, A (NLP)	328	0.5%				
C to LD swing 5.1%	62,828		21.6%	59,268		31.7%
		C maj	13,543		C maj	18,810

Edward Garnier, barrister in private practice specialising in defamation and media law, contested Hemsworth 1987. Hon sec foreign affairs forum; general cl Cons gp for Europe. B Oct 26 1952; ed Wellington Coll; Jesus Coll, Oxford; Coll of Law, London. Parliamentary assistant to Sir Paul Hawkins, MP, 1984-7. Former mbr Greater London area education cmte; Wandsworth ed sub-cmte. Mbr Soc of Cons Lawyers.

Mark Cox, credit controller. Mbr Leics CC 1985- (gp ldr 1990-); Harborough DC, 1987-91; Oadby and Wigston BC, 1991- . B May 6 1963.

Cynthia MacKay, teacher. B Sep 24 1945; ed Hastings, Richmond and Leicester Colls of Ed. NUT.

HARLOW						No change
Electorate % Turnout	68,615	82.6%	1992	70,286	78.4%	1987
*Hayes, J J J (C)	26,608	47.0%	-0.3%	26,017	47.2%	C
Rammell, W E (Lab)	23,668	41.8%	+5.2%	20,140	36.6%	Lab
Spenceley, Mrs L H (LD)	6,375	11.3%	-4.9%	8,915	16.2%	SDP/All
C to Lab swing 2.7%	56,651		5.2%	55,072		10.7%
		C maj	2,940		C maj	5,877

Jerry Hayes, barrister, won the seat in 1983. Mbr select cmte on health 1991; mbr select cmte on social services 1987-90. Jt vice-chmn Cons backbench constitutional cmte 1986-8 (jt sec 1983-6); jt sec Cons backbench health cmte 1988- ; Cons N Ireland cmte 1987-8; jt chmn all-pty glass parly gp 1990- ; jt treas race and community parly gp. B Apr 20 1953; ed Oratory Sch; Chelmer Inst. Hon director State Legislative Leaders Foundation of US. Freeman, City of London; Liveryman, Worshipful Co of Fletchers; Freeman, Co of Watermen and Lightermen. Sponsor of Video Recordings Act.

Bill Rammell, general manager, student services, Kings Coll, London. Mbr Harlow cl 1985- (chairman local govt cmte); management bd mbr nat local govt information unit. B Oct 10 1959; ed Burnt Mill Comprehensive Sch; Univ coll, Cardiff. MSF.

Lorna Spenceley, mother and chmn of local playgroup. Mbr Charter 88; sch governor. Mbr Harlow DC 1991- (gp ldr). B Dec 13 1958; ed Hautlieu Sch, Jersey; Selwyn Coll, Cambridge.

HARROGATE						No change
Electorate % Turnout	76,250	78.0%	1992	75,761	74.1%	1987
*Banks, R G (C)	32,023	53.9%	-1.7%	31,167	55.6%	C
Hurren, T J (LD)	19,434	32.7%	-1.7%	19,265	34.3%	SDP/All
Wright, A J (Lab)	7,230	12.2%	+2.0%	5,671	10.1%	Lab
Warneken, A (Grn)	780	1.3%				
C to LD swing 0.0%	59,467		21.2%	56,103		21.2%
		C maj	12,589		C maj	11,902

Robert Banks, a mbr of Lloyd's and company director, was elected in Feb 1974. B Jan 18 1937; ed Haileybury. Jt vice-chmn Yorkshire Cons MP, 1983- . Chmn (1981-7) and vice-chmn (1987- and 1979-81) all-pty tourism group; chmn (1982-) and sec (1978-82) British-Sudanese all-pty gp. Mbr Cl of Europe and WEU 1977-81 and of N Atlantic Assembly, 1981- . PPS to Minr of State FCO 1979-82. Mbr Alcohol Ed and Research Cl 1982- . Managing director Princes Design Works Ltd. Sponsored Licensing (Alcohol Education and Research) Act 1981 and Licensing (Restaurant Meals) Act 1987. Mbr Paddington BC 1959-65.

Tim Hurren, manager. Chmn and vice-chmn of policy cmte Harrogate LDs. Mbr Harrogate BC 1987-9 and 1991- (chmn finance cmte). B Sep 15 1946; ed Dartford GS; York univ. Chmn Harrogate district Relate; tutor Christian Listeners 1989- .

Andrew Wright contested this seat 1987. Mbr, Knaresborough DC, 1986- . B May 4 1953; ed King James's GS, Knaresborough; Northern Coll, Barnsley. Nalgo.

Arnold Warneken, organic horticulturist. Dist cllr 1990- . B Nov 18 1957; ed in Harrogate and Leeds.

HARROW EAST				No change		
Electorate % Turnout	74,733	77.8%	1992	81,124	73.4%	1987
*Dykes, H J M (C)	30,752	52.9%	-1.3%	32,302	54.2%	C
McNulty, A K (Lab)	19,654	33.8%	+10.2%	14,029	23.5%	Lab
Chamberlain, Ms V M (LD)	6,360	10.9%	-11.3%	13,251	22.2%	L/All
Burrows, P (Lib)	1,142	2.0%				
Hamza, Mrs S (NLP)	212	0.4%				
Lester, Ms J (Anti-Fed)	49	0.1%				
C to Lab swing 5.8%	58,169		19.1%	59,582		30.7%
		C maj	11,098		C maj	18,273

Hugh Dykes, stockbroker, director and consultant, became chmn, European Movement in Britain, in 1990 (jt hon sec, 1982-7). Mbr, Select Cmte on Euro Legislation, 1979- ; British-Irish Inter-Parly Body. Elected in 1970; contested Tottenham, 1966. Mbr, International Stock Exchange, London; chmn, ADA Video Systems Ltd; B May 17 1939; ed Weston-super-Mare GS; Pembroke Coll, Cambridge. Jt vice-chmn, Cons Friends of Israel parly gp, 1986- . MEP, 1974-6. Chmn, Cons Euro affairs cmte, 1979-81 (vice-chmn, 1974-9); chmn, all-pty Europe parly gp, 1988- ; jt vice-chmn, all-pty Franco-British Parly Relations Cmte.

Governor, N London Collegiate Sch, 1982- .
Tony McNulty, snr poly lecturer; mbr, Harrow BC, 1986- (dep ldr, Lab gp, and planning spokesman). Sec, Gtr London Lab exec, 1987-90. B Nov 3 1958; ed Salvatorian Coll, Harrow; Stanmore Sixth Form Coll; Liverpool univ; Virginia Poly Inst and state univ. NATFHE.
Veronica Chamberlain, charity manager, was chmn, Westminster N Lib Assocn; sec, London LDs. Governor, Marlborough First and Middle Sch, Harrow. B Apr 21 1956; ed Friends Sch, Saffron Walden; Utd World Coll of the Atlantic; Queen Mary Coll, London univ.

HARROW WEST				No change		
Electorate % Turnout	69,616	78.7%	1992	74,041	74.5%	1987
*Hughes, R G (C)	30,240	55.2%	-0.0%	30,456	55.2%	C
Moraes, C A (Lab)	12,343	22.5%	+5.0%	15,012	27.2%	SDP/All
Noyce, C (LD)	11,050	20.2%		9,665	17.5%	Lab
Aitman, G (Lib)	845	1.5%				
Argyle, Mrs J (NLP)	306	0.6%				
C to Lab swing 2.5%	54,784		32.7%	55,133		28.0%
		C maj	17,897		C maj	15,444

Robert G Hughes was appointed an assistant govt whip in 1992. PPS to Nicholas Scott, when minr for social security, 1990-2; mbr, select cmte on broadcasting, 1988-92; jt vice-chmn, 1989-90, and jt sec, 1987-9, Cons back-bench environment cmte; jt vice-chmn, Cons European affairs cmte, 1988-9; jt sec, race and community parly panel; all-pty film industry parly gp, 1987-92. Mbr, governing body, British Film Inst, 1990- ; freelance consultant for TV presentation; Elected in 1987; contested Southwark and Bermondsey twice in 1983; Stepney and Poplar, 1979. With BBC TV news, 1973-87. GLC mbr for Croydon Central, 1980-6; mbr, Hounslow BC, 1974-8. B Jul 14 1951; ed Spring Grove GS; Harrow Coll of Tech and Art.

BETA and NUJ.
Claude Moraes, lawyer; TUC official; mbr, TGWU. Exec mbr, Jt Cl for Welfare of Immigrants; founder mbr, Standing Conference on Race Equality in Europe; former research asst to MPs. B Oct 22 1966 in Aden; ed St Modans Comprehensive, Stirling; London and Dundee Univs.
Christopher Noyce, solicitor, contested London NW in 1989 Euro elections. Vice-chmn, Harrow West LD, 1988-90; chmn, Harrow West Lib Assocn, 1982-7; sec Harrow Lib Fed, 1982-8. Mbr, Harrow BC, 1986- . B Oct 14 1957; ed Harrow Cty GS for Boys; Pembroke Coll, Oxford; Coll of Law, Guildford. MSF.

HARTLEPOOL				No change		
Electorate % Turnout	67,968	76.1%	1992	68,686	73.0%	1987
Mandelson, P J (Lab)	26,816	51.9%	+3.4%	24,296	48.5%	Lab
Robb, G M (C)	18,034	34.9%	+1.0%	17,007	33.9%	C
Cameron, I J H (LD)	6,860	13.3%	-0.8%	7,047	14.1%	L/All
				1,786	3.6%	Ind
C to Lab swing 1.2%	51,710		17.0%	50,136		14.5%
		Lab maj	8,782		Lab maj	7,289

Peter Mandelson, industrial consultant with SRU Gp since 1990, was elected in 1992; Labour Pty director of campaigns and communications, 1985-90; producer, London Weekend Television, 1982-5. B Oct 21 1953; ed Hendon Snr HS; St Catherine's Coll, Oxford. In Economics Dept, TUC, 1977-8; chmn, British Youth Cl, 1978-80; mbr, Lambeth BC, 1979-82. GMB; NUJ.
Graham Robb, public relations consultant; former

presenter with BBC Radio Cleveland. Chmn, Northern area candidates' assocn; PR officer, Cleveland CC Cons gp. B Apr 7 1964; ed Hustler and Nunthorpe comprehensive schs, Middlesbrough; Longlands CFE. Mbr, Cleveland Wildlife Trust; CHC.
Ian Cameron, taxi and garage proprietor, contested this seat as Ind in 1987. B Sep 27 1948; ed Hartlepool Tech Day Sch.

HARWICH						No change
Electorate % Turnout	80,260	77.7%	1992	77,149	73.5%	1987
Sproat, I M (C)	32,369	51.9%	+0.1%	29,344	51.8%	C
Bevan, Mrs P A (LD)	15,210	24.4%	-6.1%	17,262	30.5%	L/All
Knight, R (Lab)	14,511	23.3%	+5.8%	9,920	17.5%	Lab
McGrath, Mrs E (NLP)	279	0.4%		161	0.3%	OFP
LD to C swing 3.1%	62,369		27.5%	56,687		21.3%
		C maj	17,159		C maj	12,082

Iain Sproat was Under Sec of State for Trade, 1981-3; MP for Aberdeen South, 1970-83; PPS to Sec of State for Scotland, 1973-4; contested Roxburgh and Berwickshire 1983, Rutherglen by-election and gen election 1964. Chmn, Milner and Co Ltd; Cricketers' Who's Who Ltd (editor since 1980); director, D'Arcy Masius Benton and Bowles Ltd. B Nov 8 1938; ed St Mary's Sch, Melrose; Winchester Coll; univ of Aix-en-Provence; Magdalen Coll, Oxford. Chmn, Scottish Cons MPs, 1979-81; ldr, Cons gp, Scottish Select Cmte, 1979-81.
Ann Bevan, company sec and director of family joinery

manufacturing business; Mbr, Essex CC, 1989- ; Tendring DC, 1976- . Pres, Clacton branch, Save the Children. B Mar 8 1941; ed Fleetwood GS; Collegiate Sch for Girls, Blackpool. Political adviser, ALC, 1982-3.
Ralph Knight, electrical supervisor, contested this seat 1987 and 1983. Mbr, Essex CC, 1981-91; Harwich Town, Dist and Borough Cls from 1970 being Mayor 1975-6, 1990-1. Chmn, local TUC; Harwich Conservation Panel; Harwich Development Gp. B Sep 22 1934; ed in Manchester and Harwich. TGWU/ACTSS.

HASTINGS AND RYE						No change
Electorate % Turnout	71,838	74.9%	1992	72,758	71.8%	1987
Lait, Mrs J (C)	25,573	47.6%	-2.5%	26,163	50.1%	C
Palmer, M E (LD)	18,939	35.2%	-0.8%	18,816	36.0%	L/All
Stevens, R (Lab)	8,458	15.7%	+2.7%	6,825	13.1%	Lab
Phillips, Ms S (Grn)	640	1.2%		242	0.5%	Loony
Howell, T (Loony)	168	0.3%	-0.2%	194	0.4%	NPR
C to LD swing 0.9%	53,778		12.3%	52,240		14.1%
		C maj	6,634		C maj	7,347

Jacqui Lait has run a Westminster and European parliamentary consultancy since 1984; contested Tyne Bridge in 1985 by-election and Strathclyde West in 1984 Euro elections. Chmn, City of London Cons, 1986-9; City and E London family health services authority, 1989-91. Parly adviser to Chemical Industries Association, 1980-4. In govt information service for seven years. Chmn, European Union of Women (British section). Mbr, Lloyd's; exec mbr, Cons Medical Society. B Dec 10 1947; ed Paisley

GS; Strathclyde univ.
Monroe Palmer, chartered accountant, contested Hendon S 1987, 1983 and 1979. Mbr, Barnet BC, 1986- (gp ldr, 1986-). Chairman, LD Friends of Israel; director, LD Publications. Former treas, Lib Pty. B Nov 30 1938; ed Orange Hill GS, Edgware.
Richard Stevens, painter; mbr, Hastings BC, 1983- (Lab gp ldr; chairman, personnel cmte). B Feb 5 1947; ed Isleworth Poly; Borough Road Coll. Nupe.

HAVANT						No change
Electorate % Turnout	74,217	79.0%	1992	76,344	74.6%	1987
Willetts, D L (C)	32,233	55.0%	-2.2%	32,527	57.1%	C
van Hagen, S F (LD)	14,649	25.0%	-3.1%	16,017	28.1%	SDP/All
Morris, G (Lab)	10,968	18.7%	+4.6%	8,030	14.1%	Lab
Mitchell, T (Grn)	793	1.4%		373	0.7%	Bread
LD to C swing 0.5%	58,643		30.0%	56,947		29.0%
		C maj	17,584		C maj	16,510

David Willetts was elected for this seat in 1992. Appointed director of studies, centre for policy studies, 1987; consultant director, Cons research dept, 1987. Research asst to Nigel Lawson, 1978; official in HM Treasury, 1978-84; Private sec to Financial Sec to Treasury, 1981-2; principal monetary policy division, 1982-4; mbr prime minister's policy unit, 1984-6. Director, Retirement Security Ltd, 1988- ; Electra Corporate Ventures Ltd, 1988- . Mbr social security advisory cmte, 1989-92; Parkside HA, 1988-90; Lambeth, Lewisham and South-

wark family practitioner cmte, 1987-90. B Mar 9 1956; ed King Edward's sch, Birmingham; Christ Church, Oxford.
Steve van Hagen, international information system manager, IBM; chmn Havant SDP, 1986-7; Havant LDs, 1988-90; mbr Havant BC, 1990- . B May 30 1940; ed Nottingham univ; LSE.
Graham Morris, head teacher. Former pres N Somerset NUT. B Feb 13 1942; ed Harrow cty sch for boys; Oxford and Bristol univs.

HAYES AND HARLINGTON						No change
Electorate % Turnout	54,449	79.7%	1992	58,240	74.5%	1987
*Dicks, T P (C)	19,489	44.9%	-4.3%	21,355	49.2%	C
McDonnell, J (Lab)	19,436	44.8%	+9.3%	15,390	35.5%	Lab
Little, A (LD)	4,472	10.3%	-5.0%	6,641	15.3%	SDP/All
C to Lab swing 6.8%	43,397		0.1%	43,386		13.7%
		C maj	53		C maj	5,965

Terence Dicks was elected in 1983; contested Bristol South, 1979. Mbr select cmte on transport 1986- . Consultant to FCDM Airport Services Ltd; C & L Country Club. Administrative officer with GLC, 1971-86. B Mar 17 1937; ed Oxford univ; LSE. Mbr Hillingdon BC 1974- (deputy leader and housing chmn 1982-4). Former head of Opposition secretariat and personal assistant to former ldr of opposition on GLC 1981-3. Employed by Ministry of Labour, 1959-66; Imperial Tobacco Co Ltd, 1952-9.

John McDonnell, sec of Assocn of London Authorities. Former mbr GLC; dep ldr Lab gp and chmn finance cmte. B Sep 8 1951; ed Gt Yarmouth GS; Burnley Tech Coll; Brunel and Birkbeck Univs. Mbr Nupe; Lab cmte on Ireland; Lab Irish society.
Tony Little, investment manager. Mbr Hillingdon-Harlington BC 1982-90 (gp ldr, 1982-90). B Jan 6 1947; ed Reading Univ. Assoc mbr society of investment analysts. Chmn, local hospice assocn.

HAZEL GROVE						No change
Electorate % Turnout	64,302	84.9%	1992	65,717	81.6%	1987
*Arnold, Sir Tom (C)	24,479	44.8%	-0.7%	24,396	45.5%	C
Stunell, R A (LD)	23,550	43.1%	+1.1%	22,556	42.0%	L/All
McAllister, C D (Lab)	6,390	11.7%	-0.1%	6,354	11.8%	Lab
Penn, M (NLP)	204	0.4%		346	0.6%	Grn
C to LD swing 0.9%	54,623		1.7%	53,652		3.4%
		C maj	929		C maj	1,840

Sir Thomas Arnold, theatre producer and publisher, has been a vice-chmn, Cons Pty, since 1983 with responsibility for the research and candidates departments. Won this seat Oct 1974; contested it Feb 1974; Manchester, Cheetham, 1970. B Jan 25 1947; ed Bedales; Le Rosey (Geneva); Pembroke Coll, Oxford. PPS to Sec of State for N Ireland, 1979-81, and to Lord Privy Seal, Foreign Office, 1981-2. Mbr Society of West End Theatre. Director Tom Arnold Ltd and Piccadilly Radio plc. Owner of musical and dramatic copyrights under Ivor Novello's will.
Andrew Stunell, political sec ASLDC, the Liberal Democrat cllrs organisation. Contested City of Chester for L/All

in 1987 and 1983 and for L in 1979. Chmn LD working pty on local govt; mbr English policy cmte. Mbr Chester City Cl 1979-90; Cheshire CC, 1981-91; vice-chmn ACC 1985-90. B Nov 24 1942; ed Surbiton GS; Manchester Univ; Liverpool poly. Nalgo, 1967-81; staff side mbr Whitley cl for new towns 1977-80. Former Baptist lay preacher.
Colin MacAlister, taxi owner; chmn, Denton and Reddish CLP, and agent to Andrew Bennett MP; mbr, Stockport MBC, 1979- (Dep ldr, Lab gp); Gtr Manchester NW regional exec. B Nov 9 1954; ed St Augustine's GS; Stockport Coll. MSF.

HEMSWORTH						No change
Electorate % Turnout	55,679	75.9%	1992	54,951	75.7%	1987
*Enright, D A (Lab)	29,942	70.8%	+3.8%	27,859	67.0%	Lab
Harrison, G (C)	7,867	18.6%	+1.4%	7,159	17.2%	C
Megson, Ms V (LD)	4,459	10.5%	-5.2%	6,568	15.8%	L/All
C to Lab swing 1.2%	42,268		52.2%	41,586		49.8%
		Lab maj	22,075		Lab maj	20,700

Derek Enright, special adviser to EC on the Third World, 1988-91, was elected at 1991 by-election. Director, Dega '92, 1987- . Lab MEP for Leeds, 1979-84; contested Kent East for Lab in 1984 Euro elections. British Lab gp spokesman on third world affairs and women's rights, 1979-84. Hd of classics, John Fisher Sch, Purley, Surrey, 1959-67; dep hd, St Wilfrid's Sch, N Featherstone, W Yorkshire, 1967-79; EC delegate in Guinea Bissau, 1985-7 and awarded Order of Merit (Guinea Bissau), 1987. B Aug 2 1935; ed St Joseph's Pontefract; St Michael's Coll, Leeds; Wadham Coll, Oxford.

Garnet Harrison, director of investment management gp and of UK listed investment trusts. Fought 1991 by-election and Huyton 1979 against Harold Wilson. Past constituency and NW area officer. B Sep 1 1951; ed Stand GS for Boys, Manchester. Founder and managing director of Australian investment management and life insurance gp, 1982-86.
Valerie Megson, owner of fast food businesses, contested 1991 by-election. Mbr, South Elmsall PC. B Jan 12 1951. *For 1991 by-election details see page 287.*

HENDON NORTH						No change
Electorate % Turnout	51,513	75.1%	1992	55,095	65.8%	1987
*Gorst, J M (C)	20,569	53.2%	-2.4%	20,155	55.6%	C
Hill, D J (Lab)	13,447	34.8%	+9.3%	9,223	25.5%	Lab
Kemp, P (LD)	4,136	10.7%	-8.2%	6,859	18.9%	SDP/All
Duncan, Mrs P A (Grn)	430	1.1%				
Orr, Ms P (NLP)	95	0.2%				
C to Lab swing 5.9%	38,677		18.4%	36,237		30.2%
		C maj	7,122		C maj	10,932

John Gorst was elected in 1970; contested Bodmin, 1966, and Chester-le-Street, 1964. Mbr select cmte on employment, 1980-7; chmn (1987-90) and vice-chmn (1986-7), Cons backbench media cmte; vice-chmn, all-pty war crimes cmte, 1987- . Director, John Gorst & Associates Ltd, public affairs consultancy, since 1964, with clients including British Amusements Caterers' Trade Assocn, Radnor (Management Advisory Services) Ltd, Alfred Marks Gp and Eastman Kodak Ltd. B Jun 28 1928; ed Ardingly Coll; Corpus Christi Coll, Cambridge. Founder (1964-80) and sec (1964-70), Telephone Users' Assocn; and the Local Radio Assocn (sec, 1964-71).

David Hill, clinical psychologist; director, Mind in Camden, 1987- . Mbr Ealing, Southall CLP exec cmte 1989-91; sec West London socialist health assocn, 1989-91. Founder mbr (1987) London alliance for mental health action and chmn 1989-91; mbr Ealing CHC, 1986-90. B Mar 4 1952; ed Hereford Tech Coll; Univ Coll, Cardiff; Cincinnati Univ, US. TGWU, previously Nalgo.
Peter Kemp, owner and director of travel retail company. B Dec 3 1953; ed Ambrose Fleming Tech GS, Enfield.
Patricia Duncan, product designer. Grn campaigns coordinator. Mbr ed appeals cmte. B Dec 6 19456; ed Middlesex Poly. Mbr chartered society of designers.

HENDON SOUTH						No change
Electorate % Turnout	48,401	72.4%	1992	54,560	63.8%	1987
*Marshall, J L (C)	20,593	58.8%	+3.2%	19,341	55.5%	C
Lloyd, Ms L (Lab)	8,546	24.4%	+3.5%	8,217	23.6%	L/All
Cohen, J (LD)	5,609	16.0%	-7.6%	7,261	20.9%	Lab
Leslie, J (NLP)	289	0.8%				
C to Lab swing 0.2%	35,037		34.4%	34,819		31.9%
		C maj	12,047		C maj	11,124

John Marshall was elected in 1987; contested Lewisham E, Feb 1974; Dundee E, 1964 and 1966. MEP for London N, 1979-89; whip ED gp, EP, 1986-9. Appointed PPS to Tony Newton, then Sec of State for Social Security, in 1990; PPS to Nicholas Scott, Minr of State and Minr for Disabled People, 1989-90. Stockbroker with Kitcat & Aitken (director, Kitcat & Aitken & Co, 1986-90; partner, 1983-6); director, Beta Global Emerging Markets Investment Trust plc, 1990- . Mbr, Stock Exchange, 1979- . Parly consultant to bus and coach cl. Chmn, all-pty, British-Israeli parly gp, 1990- ; vice-chmn, Cons Friends of Israel

parly gp; all-pty gp for Soviet Jewry. B Aug 19 1940; ed Harris Acad, Dundee; Glasgow Acad; St Andrews univ.
Leonora Lloyd, co-ordinator, Nat Abortion Campaign; vice-chmn CLP; former sec Hammersmith LPYS; branch chmn. B Nov 11 1040; ed Tiffin Girls' Sch, Kingston; Ruskin Coll of Ed, Acton. MSF (branch chmn and regional delegate).
Jack Cohen, snr probation officer. Mbr Barnet BC, 1986- . B Oct 30 1946; ed GS. Sec, Middlesex branch, Nat Assocn of Probation Officers, 1983-6.

HENLEY						No change
Electorate % Turnout	64,702	79.8%	1992	65,443	74.9%	1987
*Heseltine, M R D (C)	30,835	59.7%	-1.4%	29,978	61.1%	C
Turner, D G (LD)	12,443	24.1%	-2.2%	12,896	26.3%	L/All
Russell-Swinnerton, I J (Lab)	7,676	14.9%	+2.3%	6,173	12.6%	Lab
Plane, A (Anti H)	431	0.8%				
Banerji, Ms S (NLP)	274	0.5%				
LD to C swing 0.4%	51,659		35.6%	49,047		34.8%
		C maj	18,392		C maj	17,082

Michael Heseltine was appointed trade and industry secretary in 1992; environment sec 1990-2. Contested leadership of Cons pty in 1990. Defence sec 1983-Jan 1986, when he resigned over future of Westland helicopter company; environment sec 1979-83. PC 1979. Chmn, Haymarket Press, 1966-70 and director, 1974-9. Minr for aerospace and shipping, DTI, 1972-4; Under sec for environment, 1970-2; Parly sec, transport ministry 1970. Elected for this seat in Feb 1974; MP for Tavistock, 1966-74; contested Coventry N, 1964, and Gower, 1959. B Mar 21 1933; ed Shrewsbury Sch; Pembroke Coll, Oxford (hon

fellow 1986; pres of union, 1954). Mbr cl Zoological Society of London, 1987- .
David Turner, electronics sales manager. Mbr Oxfordshire CC; parish cllr. B Jul 4 1944; ed Worcester CFE.
Ivan Russell-Swinnerton is a schoolmaster. Wantage town cllr for six years; coll and poly governor; pres, Vale of White Horse Assocn (NUT); chmn teachers consultative cmte, Oxon; mbr Oxon ed cmte. Former chmn and sec of local pty branches. B Jul 24 1945; ed Taunton GS, Southampton; Southampton Univ; Univ Coll, London.

HEREFORD						No change
Electorate % Turnout	69,676	81.3%	1992	67,075	78.0%	1987
*Shepherd, C R (C)	26,727	47.2%	-0.3%	24,865	47.5%	C
Jones, G G (LD)	23,314	41.2%	-3.6%	23,452	44.8%	L/All
Kelly, Ms J (Lab)	6,005	10.6%	+2.9%	4,031	7.7%	Lab
Mattingly, C (Grn)	596	1.1%				
LD to C swing 1.7%	56,642		6.0%	52,348		2.7%
		C maj	3,413		C maj	1,413

Colin Shepherd, marketing director of The Haigh Engineering Co Ltd, Ross-on-Wye, 1963-85; parly adviser to Balfour Beatty Ltd. PPS to Peter Walker, Sec of State for Wales, 1987-90. Governor, Commonwealth Inst, 1989- . Chmn, 1991- ; jt vice-chmn, 1989-90, and mbr, 1987-9 and 1990-1, exec cmte, UK branch, CPA; British Islands and Mediterranean regional rep, international exec, CPA, 1989-91. Elected in Oct 1974. B Jan 13 1938; ed Oundle; Caius Coll, Cambridge; McGill Univ, Montreal. Jt vice-chmn, Cons back-bench ag, fish and food cmte, 1991- and 1979-87; vice-chmn, Cons horticulture sub-cmte, 1979-87. Chmn, Commons catering cmte, 1991- ; mbr, Commons Services cmte, 1979-91 (chmn, library sub-cmte, 1982-91, and catering sub-cmte, 1991). Chmn, all-pty Fund for Replacement of Animals in Medical Experiments. Mbr, cl,

Royal Coll of Vet Surgeons, 1983- .
Gwynoro Jones unsuccessfully contested leadership of LDs in 1988; mbr, LD nat exec, 1988-90; vice-chmn, LD policy cmte, 1988-9. Snr education officer. Lab MP for Carmarthen, 1970-4; joined SDP 1981; contested Gower 1982 by-election and 1983; Carmarthen in 1987. Lab Pty PRO in Wales, 1969-70; PPS to Roy Jenkins, Home Sec, 1970-4; chmn, SDP Cl for Wales, 1982-4 and 1987-8; mbr, SDP nat cmte 1981-4; jt chmn, Alliance cmte for Wales, 1982-8; chmn, SDP Cl for Wales policy cmte, 1985-7. B Nov 21 1942; ed Gwenddraeth GS; Cardiff Univ.
Josephine Kelly, lecturer; mbr, Hereford DC, 1983- . B Nov 9 1945; ed Strathclyde univ. NATFHE; chmn, cty branch, 1984-8; sec, Hereford TUC, 1983-8.
Chris Mattingly, engineer; former mbr, Grn Pty Cl.

HERTFORD AND STORTFORD						No change
Electorate % Turnout	76,654	81.0%	1992	75,508	77.7%	1987
*Wells, P B (C)	35,716	57.5%	-0.0%	33,763	57.5%	C
White, C J (LD)	15,506	25.0%	-3.4%	16,623	28.3%	SDP/All
Bovaird, A J (Lab)	10,125	16.3%	+3.5%	7,494	12.8%	Lab
Goth, J (Grn)	780	1.3%	-0.1%	814	1.4%	Grn
LD to C swing 1.7%	62,127		32.5%	58,694		29.2%
		C maj	20,210		C maj	17,140

Bowen Wells has served on select cmtes on Euro legislation since 1983 and on foreign affairs since 1981; mbr, exec cmte, UK branch, CPA, since 1984 and was jt vice-chmn. Sec, Cons environment cmte, 1991- ; jt sec, Cons trade and industry cmte, 1988-90, 1984-7 and 1979-81, and vice-chmn, 1983-4. Elected for this seat 1983; MP for Hertford and Stevenage, 1979-83. Chmn, UN parly gp, 1983- ; jt sec, all-pty Overseas Development gp, 1984- . Associate director, London Radio Jazz FM; parly consultant to International Distillers and Vintners Ltd; Geest Industries; ADT. Trustee, Industry and Parliament Trust, 1985- . B Aug 4 1935; ed St. Paul's Sch, London; Exeter Univ;

Regent St Poly Sch of Management. Governor, Inst of Development Studies, 1980- .
Chris White, chartered accountant; managing director, accountancy tuition company. Chmn, St Albans LD, 1989-90; treas, Chilterns region LD, 1988-91. B Jun 8 1959; ed Merchant Taylors' Sch, Northwood; Corpus Christi Coll, Oxford.
Alasdair Bovaird, research officer with Herts CC; sec, Hertford and Stortford CLP; treas, Scottish Lab Students, 1984-5. B Aug 12 1963; ed Richard Hale Sch, Hertford; Aberdeen Univ. Mbr, Hertford RFC. Nalgo.

HERTFORDSHIRE NORTH						No change
Electorate % Turnout	80,066	84.4%	1992	78,694	81.1%	1987
Heald, O (C)	33,679	49.8%	+0.1%	31,750	49.7%	C
Liddle, R (LD)	17,148	25.4%	-6.4%	20,308	31.8%	L/All
Bissett Johnson, Miss S (Lab)	16,449	24.3%	+5.9%	11,782	18.5%	Lab
Irving, B (NLP)	339	0.5%				
LD to C swing 3.3%	67,615		24.4%	63,840		17.9%
		C maj	16,531		C maj	11,442

Oliver Heald, barrister, contested Southwark and Bermondsey in 1987, vice-pres of constituency assocn. Vice-pres, Herts N Cons Assocn and chmn 1984-6; has served on Cons eastern area exec cmte. B Dec 15 1954; ed Reading sch; Pembroke coll, Cambridge (Ziegler law scholar). Mbr, British Atlantic Cmte, Bow Gp. Speaks French and German.
Roger Liddle contested Fulham by-election for SDP/All 1986 and Vauxhall 1983. Managing director, public affairs consultancy. Chmn, LD policy gp on transport; vice-chmn, Euro policy gp; mbr, Fed policy cmte; was on SDP

nat cmte and policy cmte. B Jun 14 1947; ed Carlisle GS; Queen's Coll, Oxford. Ldr, All gp, Lambeth BC, 1982-6; mbr, Oxford City Cl, 1971-6 (dep ldr, 1973-6). Apex.
Sarah Bissett Johnson, head of economic research unit, SE Economic Development Strategy, 1986- ; with GLC majority pty secretariat, 1984-6. Has served on Lab planning and policy review gps. B Aug 12 1948; ed in Australia; Architectural Assocn; Central London Poly. Nalgo and Nupe; founder mbr, TGWU branch, Amnesty International.

135

HERTFORDSHIRE SOUTH WEST				No change		
Electorate % Turnout	70,836	83.8%	1992	75,643	77.7%	1987
*Page, R L (C)	33,825	57.0%	+1.2%	32,791	55.8%	C
Shaw, Mrs A (LD)	13,718	23.1%	-5.8%	17,007	28.9%	L/All
Gale, A P (Lab)	11,512	19.4%	+4.1%	8,966	15.3%	Lab
Adamson, C (NLP)	281	0.5%				
LD to C swing 3.5%	59,336		33.9%	58,764		26.9%
		C maj	20,107		C maj	15,784

Richard Page was returned at 1979 by-election; MP for Workington, 1976-9; contested Workington, Feb and Oct 1974. Appointed mbr PAC 1987; jt vice-chmn all-pty cable and satellite TV gp 1990- ; Cons backbench trade and industry cmte, 1990- and 1988-9; jt sec parly space cmte. PPS to John Biffen, when Ldr of Commons, 1982-7; to Sec of State for Trade, 1981-2. Director of family company, Page Holdings Ltd and associated companies. Adviser to Electrical Installations Equipment Manufacturers Assocn Ltd and to Assocn of British Travel Agents. B Feb 22 1941; ed Hurstpierpoint coll; Luton tech coll.

Ann Shaw is a nursery teacher. Mbr Three Rivers DC 1971-6 and 1980 - (cl ldr 1986-90 and 1991-2; chmn 1990-1; chmn planning cmte 1986-90 and 1991-2; cl gp ldr 1981-90 and 1991-). Constituency sec. Ed St Helen's Sch, Northwood; Oxford Univ.
Andy Gale, principal officer (housing/homelessness), Ealing BC. Mbr Kings Langley PC, 1989- ; holder of various CLP branch officer posts 1983- . B Aug 17 1959; ed Cantonian HS (comprehensive); Worcester CHE. Competed in London marathon 1991. Nalgo.

HERTFORDSHIRE WEST				No change		
Electorate % Turnout	78,573	82.4%	1992	78,966	80.9%	1987
*Jones, R B (C)	33,340	51.5%	+1.8%	31,760	49.7%	C
McNally, Mrs E (Lab)	19,400	30.0%	+6.0%	16,836	26.3%	SDP/All
Trevett, M J (LD)	10,464	16.2%	-10.2%	15,317	24.0%	Lab
Hannaway, J (Grn)	674	1.0%				
McAuley, J (NF)	665	1.0%				
Harvey, G (NLP)	175	0.3%				
C to Lab swing 2.1%	64,718		21.5%	63,913		23.4%
		C maj	13,940		C maj	14,924

Robert Jones, elected in 1983, contested Teesside, Stockton, 1979; Kirkcaldy, Oct 1974. Director, Yarsley Quality Assured Firms Ltd, 1989- . PPS to Michael Spicer, aviation minr, and Peter Bottomley, roads and traffic minr 1986-7. Mbr select cmte on environment, 1987- and 1983-6. B Sep 26 1950; ed Merchant Taylors' Sch; St Andrews univ. Mbr St Andrews BC 1972-5; Fife CC 1973-5; Chiltern DC, 1979-83. Vice-pres assocn of DCs 1983- . Jt vice-chmn Cons backbench ed cmte 1989- ; mbr Inland Waterways Amenity Advisory Cl 1985- ; chmn all-pty inland waterways parly gp; vice-pres Wildlife Hospital Trust 1985- . Freeman, City of London; Liveryman,

Merchant Taylors' Co.
Eryl McNally, cty co-ordinator, modern languages, for teacher support and in-service training. Mbr Herts CC 1986- (Lab ed ldr); Abbots Langley PC 1970-4; Watford RDC 1972-4; Three Rivers DC 1974-6. Former CLP sec; cty chmn and sec. B Apl 11 1942; ed Newbridge GS, Gwent; Bristol univ; Univ Coll, Swansea. NUT, 1964- .
Martin Trevett, electrical contractor; mbr, Three Rivers DC 1986- (chmn highways and transport cmtes during LD control of cl 1986-90; chmn environment cmte, 1991-). B Jun 1 1949; ed Wm Grimshaw sch, London; Southgate tech coll.

HERTSMERE				No change		
Electorate % Turnout	69,951	80.9%	1992	73,367	75.4%	1987
Clappison, W J (C)	32,133	56.8%	+0.2%	31,278	56.6%	C
Souter, Dr D (Lab)	13,398	23.7%	+4.1%	13,172	23.8%	L/All
Gifford, Mrs Z (LD)	10,681	18.9%	-4.9%	10,835	19.6%	Lab
Harding, Ms D (NLP)	373	0.7%				
C to Lab swing 1.9%	56,585		33.1%	55,285		32.8%
		C maj	18,735		C maj	18,106

James Clappison, a barrister, retained the seat for Cons in 1992. Contested both Bootle by-elections in 1990; Barnsley E in 1987, and Yorkshire S in 1989 Euro elections. B Sep 14 1956; ed St Peter's Sch, York; Queen's Coll, Oxford; Central London Poly; Gray's Inn.
David Souter, head of research, Nat Communications Union; former full-time official, Lab pty policy directorate; former sec, Dulwich CLP. Chmn Fabian Society trade union forum. B Jul 17 1955; ed Royal GS, Newcastle; St

John's Coll, Cambridge; Wolfson Coll, Oxford.
Zerbanoo Gifford, author and adviser to Paddy Ashdown on community affairs. Contested Harrow E for L/All 1987 and this seat 1983. Mbr LD fed exec; chmn Lib pty community relations panel, 1985-8; commission on ethnic involvement, 1985-6; mbr Lib status of women commission, 1984-6. Mbr Harrow BC, 1982-6. B May 11 1950; ed Roedean; Watford coll of tech; London sch of journalism; Open univ.

HEXHAM				No change		
Electorate % Turnout	57,812	82.4%	1992	56,360	80.0%	1987
Atkinson, P (C)	24,967	52.4%	+2.8%	22,370	49.6%	C
Swithenbank, I C F (Lab)	11,529	24.2%	+6.2%	14,304	31.7%	L/All
Wallace, J C (LD)	10,344	21.7%	-10.0%	8,103	18.0%	Lab
Hartshorne, J (Grn)	781	1.6%	+0.9%	336	0.7%	Grn
C to Lab swing 1.7%	47,621		28.2%	45,113		17.9%
		C maj	13,438		C maj	8,066

Peter Atkinson, public affairs consultant since 1983; clients include British field sports society and a newspaper gp. Mbr Wandsworth BC, 1978-82; Wandsworth HA, 1982-89. Elected to Suffolk CC in 1989. *Evening Standard*, London, reporter, 1961-73, becoming broadcasting writer, dep news editor and then news editor, 1973-81. Joined *S London Guardian* Gp and was chmn, *Southern Free Press* Gp and on bd of *Deben Journal*, Suffolk, 1981-7. B 1943; ed Cheltenham coll.

Ian Swithenbank, electrician; mbr Northumberland CC, 1977- (cl ldr). B Sep 21 1944; ed Shiremoor sec mod sch, N Tyneside. NUM, 1960-87; GMB since 1987.
Jonathan Wallace, post-graduate student; mbr Gateshead MBC, 1987- ; dep chmn Northern region LDs, 1988-91; sec Gateshead LDs, 1988-90; Gateshead SDP, 1985-8; mbr CSD, 1985-8; LD fed conference, 1988- . B Nov 24 1963; ed Lobley Hill Primary and Whickham comprehensive, Gateshead; Newcastle univ.

HEYWOOD AND MIDDLETON				No change		
Electorate % Turnout	57,176	74.9%	1992	59,487	73.8%	1987
*Callaghan, J (Lab)	22,380	52.2%	+2.4%	21,900	49.9%	Lab
Ollerenshaw, E (C)	14,306	33.4%	-0.9%	15,052	34.3%	C
Taylor, Dr M (LD)	5,262	12.3%	-3.6%	6,953	15.8%	SDP/All
Burke, P (Lib)	757	1.8%				
Scott, Ms A (NLP)	134	0.3%				
C to Lab swing 1.6%	42,839		18.8%	43,905		15.6%
		Lab maj	8,074		Lab maj	6,848

Jim Callaghan was elected in 1983; MP for Middleton and Prestwich, 1974-83. Chmn NW gp of Lab MPs, 1987- . Art lecturer at St John's coll, Manchester, 1959-74. B Jan 28 1927; ed Manchester and London univs. Mbr select cmte on transport, 1987- ; on Cardiff Bay barrage bill, 1991- ; on education, science and arts, 1983-7; advisory cmte on Commons works of art, 1988- ; standing orders cmte, 1981-3; Middleton MBC, 1971-4. Football coach and referee.

Eric Ollerenshaw, teacher; chmn Hackney N and Stoke Newington Cons Assocn, 1988- ; mbr Gtr London ed advisory cmte; cllr and Cons gp dep ldr, Hackney BC, 1990- . Elected mbr ILEA, 1986-90 (Ldr of opposition, 1988-90). B Mar 26 1951; ed Hyde Cty GS, Cheshire; LSE. AMMA
Dr Michael Taylor, general practitioner; sec small practices assocn, 1991- ; GP tutor, Manchester univ, 1989- . B Sep 25 1944; ed Bolton sch; Edinburgh univ. BMA.

HIGH PEAK				No change		
Electorate % Turnout	70,793	84.6%	1992	69,926	80.5%	1987
Hendry, C (C)	27,538	46.0%	+0.3%	25,715	45.7%	C
Levitt, T (Lab)	22,719	37.9%	+9.1%	16,199	28.8%	Lab
Molloy, S P (LD)	8,861	14.8%	-10.8%	14,389	25.6%	SDP/All
Floyd, R (Grn)	794	1.3%				
C to Lab swing 4.4%	59,912		8.0%	56,303		16.9%
		C maj	4,819		C maj	9,516

Charles Hendry was political adviser to Tony Newton, when Sec of State for Social Security and Minr for Trade and Industry, 1988-90; political adviser to John Moore, Sec of State for Social Services, May-Aug 1988. Public relations consultant to PR agency, Burson-Marsteller, and to Ogilvy & Mather, 1982-8. Contested Mansfield 1987 and Clackmannan 1983. Trustee, Drive for Youth, a training charity. B May 6 1959; ed Rugby; Edinburgh univ (Pres, univ Cons assocn, 1979-80). Vice-chmn Scottish FCS, 1980-1. Vice-chmn Battersea Cons assocn, 1981-3. FRSA.

Tom Levitt, teacher, contested Cotswold in 1989 Euro elections and Stroud 1987. Mbr Stroud DC, 1989- ; Cirencester TC, 1983-7; Lab Coordinating Cmte. B Apr 10 1954; ed Westwood HS, Leek, Staffs; Lancaster and Oxford univs. NUT since 1975 (cty chmn 1985); Nupe, 1989- .
Simon Molloy, actor; coordinator of volunteer bureau. Contested Derbyshire in 1989 Euro elections. Former chmn High Peak Libs and LDs. B Oct 24 1947; ed Challoner sch, Finchley; Rose Bruford Coll, Sidcup; Open univ. Equity; Nupe.

HOLBORN AND ST PANCRAS — No change

Electorate % Turnout	64,480	63.0%	1992	70,589	64.3%	1987
*Dobson, F G (Lab)	22,243	54.8%	+4.1%	22,966	50.6%	Lab
McHallam, A (C)	11,419	28.1%	-3.0%	14,113	31.1%	C
Horne-Roberts, Mrs J (LD)	5,476	13.5%	-4.1%	7,994	17.6%	L/All
Wolf-Light, P (Grn)	959	2.4%		300	0.7%	RF
Hersey, M (NLP)	212	0.5%				
Headicar, R (Socialist)	175	0.4%				
Lewis, N (WAR)	133	0.3%				
C to Lab swing 3.6%	40,617		26.6%	45,373		19.5%
		Lab maj	10,824		Lab maj	8,853

Frank Dobson, elected to shadow cabinet in 1987, became chief Opposn spokesman on energy in 1989; shadow ldr of Commons and Lab campaigns co-ordinator 1987-9; mbr Commons services cmte 1987-9; select cmte on televising Commons, 1988-9; chief Opposn spokesman on health in front bench DHSS team, 1985-7; a spokesman on ed, 1981-3. Elected for this seat 1983; MP for Holborn and St Pancras South, 1979-83. Mbr Camden BC 1971-6. B Mar 15 1940; ed Archbishop Holgate GS, York; LSE (a governor since 1986). Chmn NHS Unlimited, 1981-9. Mbr select cmte on environment, 1979-81. Chmn PLP Greater London gp 1983-7. Sponsored by RMT.

Andrew McHallam, asst staff manager, John Lewis Partnership, since 1980. Chmn Islington CPC. 1986- ; dep chmn Islington S and Finsbury Cons Assocn, 1986-8. B Apr 3 1957; ed Haberdashers' Aske's Sch, Elstree; Queens Coll, Cambridge.
Jennifer Horne-Roberts is a barrister specialising in human rights law and company director. Contested Medway 1987; Fareham for Lab Feb 1974. B Feb 15 1949; ed state schs, NW London; Univ of Perugia, Italy; London univ; Cl of Legal Ed; Coll of Law, Chancery Lane. Chmn Holborn and St Pancras LDs; UK Assocn of Women Barristers.

HOLLAND WITH BOSTON — No change

Electorate % Turnout	67,900	77.9%	1992	65,539	72.3%	1987
*Body, Sir Richard (C)	29,159	55.1%	-2.8%	27,412	57.9%	C
Hough, J D (Lab)	15,328	29.0%	+8.4%	9,817	20.7%	L/All
Ley, N (LD)	8,434	15.9%	-4.8%	9,734	20.5%	Lab
				405	0.9%	L Voice
C to Lab swing 5.6%	52,921		26.1%	47,368		37.1%
		C maj	13,831		C maj	17,595

Sir Richard Body was elected for this seat in 1966. MP for Billericay, 1955-9; contested Leek, 1951, Rotherham, 1950, and Abertillery by-election, 1950. Chmn select cmte on agriculture, 1983-7 and mbr, 1979-87. Mbr jt cmte on consolidation bills, 1975-91. Barrister, farmer and Royal Show judge, underwriting mbr of Lloyd's. Chmn centre for European studies. B May 18 1927; ed Reading Sch. Vice-pres small farmers' assocn, 1985- . Jt Master, Windsor forest bloodhounds, 1988- . Chmn open seas forum, 1971- ;

society for individual freedom, 1987- ; consumer watch, 1988- . Jt chmn Get Britain Out (of EEC) Campaign, 1975. Pres Cobden club, 1981- ; vice-pres Selsdon Gp.
John Hough contested this seat in 1987 and Brigg and Cleethorpes 1983. Mbr of workers' co-operative. B Aug 22 1946; ed LSE. Chmn Lab pty rural revival, 1988- ; E Midland regional exec cmte Lab pty, 1986-7. TGWU.
Nigel Ley, barrister. B Jan 2 1947; ed Manchester Univ.

HONITON — No change

Electorate % Turnout	79,223	80.7%	1992	77,259	76.4%	1987
*Emery, Sir Peter (C)	33,533	52.4%	-6.7%	34,931	59.2%	C
Sharratt, Mrs J M (LD)	17,022	26.6%	-4.5%	18,369	31.1%	SDP/All
Davison, R (Lab)	8,142	12.7%	+4.3%	4,988	8.4%	Lab
Owen, D (Ind C)	2,175	3.4%		747	1.3%	Loony
Hughes, S (Loony G)	1,442	2.3%				
Halliwell, G (Lib)	1,005	1.6%				
Tootill, A (Grn)	650	1.0%				
C to LD swing 1.1%	63,969		25.8%	59,035		28.1%
		C maj	16,511		C maj	16,562

Sir Peter Emery has been chmn select cmte on procedure since 1983 and a mbr since 1973; mbr select cmte on sittings of Commons, 1991-2. Jt vice-pres parly and scientific cmte. Mbr advisory bd Centre for Strategic and International Studies, Washington DC; exec British-American parly gp, 1964- . Director Shenley Trust Services Ltd, Winglaw Gp Ltd; unpaid director, Purchasing Management Services Ltd, National Asthma Campaign (a charity company) and other companies. Mbr N Atlantic Assembly, 1983- . Capt Hse of Commons bridge team, 1984- . Under sec for energy 1974; under sec for trade and

industry, 1972-4. Elected for this seat at 1967 by-election; MP for Reading, 1959-66; contested Poplar, 1951, and Lincoln, 1955. B Feb 27 1926; ed Scotch Plains HS, New Jersey, US; Oriel Coll, Oxford.
Jennifer Sharratt, retired lecturer. Mbr E Devon DC 1989-91. B Sep 25 1930; ed Ladies' Coll, Cheltenham; London and Bristol Univs. NATFHE.
Ray Davison, lecturer in French studies, Exeter Univ. Held various constituency and branch offices. B Aug 4 1945; ed Stratford GS; Leeds Univ. AUT, 1969- ; TGWU, 1988- .

HORNCHURCH						No change
Electorate % Turnout	60,522	79.8%	1992	62,397	75.3%	1987
*Squire, R C (C)	25,817	53.5%	+2.3%	24,039	51.2%	C
Cooper, Ms L (Lab)	16,652	34.5%	+6.1%	13,345	28.4%	Lab
Oddy, B J (LD)	5,366	11.1%	-9.3%	9,609	20.4%	L/All
Matthews, T (Soc Dem)	453	0.9%				
C to Lab swing 1.9%	48,288		19.0%	46,993		22.8%
		C maj	9,165		C maj	10,694

Robin Squire, chartered accountant, became PPS to Christopher Patten, Chancellor of Duchy of Lancaster and Cons Pty chmn, in 1991. Mbr select cmte on environment, 1987-91 and 1979-83, and on Eu.) legislation, 1985-8. Chmn, 1989-91, and jt vice-chmi 1985-9, Cons back-bench environment cmte. Gained this seat 1979; contested it Oct 1974. Mbr bd of Shelter, 1982- ; chmn all-pty plumbing gp. Director, Link Assured Homes series of companies, 1988- ; Link Assured Homes Guaranteed Growth gp of companies, 1990- . Financial consultant to Lombard North Central plc, 1979- (dep chief accountant with company, 1972-9). Presenter, Left, Right and Centre, for British Satellite Broadcasting, 1990; programme presenter, Capital Radio, 1982-7. B Jul 12 1944; ed Tiffin Sch, Kingston upon Thames.

Leonie Cooper, director of housing assocn; nat organiser, Labour women's action cmte; chmn Nat Fed of Housing Assocn's women in housing gp; mbr Wandsworth CHC; vice-chmn CLP, 1988-9. B Dec 27 1959; ed Broxbourne Sch, Herts; Univ Coll, London. MSF.

Barry Oddy, mobile communication engineer; mbr Havering BC, 1989- (LD gp ldr, 1990-); vice-chmn Havering LDs. B Jun 11 1952; ed N Romford comprehensive sch.

HORNSEY AND WOOD GREEN						Lab gain
Electorate % Turnout	73,491	75.9%	1992	80,594	73.3%	1987
Roche, Mrs B M R (Lab)	27,020	48.5%	+8.5%	25,397	43.0%	C
Boff, A (C)	21,843	39.2%	-3.8%	23,618	40.0%	Lab
Dunphy, P G (LD)	5,547	10.0%	-5.2%	8,928	15.1%	SDP/All
Crosbie, Ms E M (Grn)	1,051	1.9%	-0.1%	1,154	2.0%	Grn
Davies, P (NLP)	197	0.4%				
Massey, W (Rev Comm)	89	0.2%				
C to Lab swing 6.1%	55,747		9.3%	59,097		3.0%
		Lab maj	5,177		C maj	1,779

Barbara Roche, barrister; works for local authority on crime prevention; previously with SE London law centre. Contested this seat 1987 and Surrey SW by-election 1984. Chmn Battersea Lab Pty, 1981-5. Former exec cmte mbr NCCL. B April 13 1954; ed comprehensive sch; Lady Margaret Hall, Oxford Univ. Mbr Lab coordinating cmte; society of Lab lawyers; Nalgo.

Andrew Boff, technical consultant on personal computers; mbr Hillingdon BC, 1982- (cl ldr, 1990-2). B 1958; ed Abbotsfield comprehensive sch; Middlesex poly.

Peter Dunphy, recruitment account executive. Nat chmn 1986-7, and nat sec 1985-6, YSD. B Jun 24 1966; ed St Bedes comprehensive, Lanchester, Co Durham; Liverpool univ. Personal interests include Cossack dancing.

HORSHAM						No change
Electorate % Turnout	84,158	81.3%	1992	86,135	72.5%	1987
*Hordern, Sir Peter (C)	42,210	61.7%	-2.0%	39,775	63.7%	C
Stainton, Ms J (LD)	17,138	25.1%	-0.3%	15,868	25.4%	SDP/All
Uwins, S P P (Lab)	6,745	9.9%	+1.2%	5,435	8.7%	Lab
Elliott, Ms J (Lib)	1,281	1.9%		1,383	2.2%	Grn
King, T (Grn)	692	1.0%	-1.2%			
Duggan, J (PPP)	332	0.5%				
C to LD swing 0.8%	68,398		36.7%	62,461		38.3%
		C maj	25,072		C maj	23,907

Sir Peter Hordern became chmn public accounts commission, in 1987, mbr since 1984; on PAC, 1970-87. Mbr cmte on privileges, 1989- . Jt sec, 1988- , and mbr exec, 1968-88, 1922 Cmte of Cons backbenchers. MP for Horsham, 1964-74, and 1983- ; MP for Horsham and Crawley, 1974-83. Director, Fina plc, formerly Petrofina (UK) plc, 1973- ,chmn, 1987- ; F. and C. Smaller Companies Investment plc, 1976- , chmn, 1986- ; and T.R. Technology plc, 1975- . B Apr 18 1929; ed Geelong GS, Australia; Christ Church, Oxford. Chmn, 1990-1 and mbr, 1986-90 and 1991- , exec cmte, UK branch, CPA. Consultant to Fisons plc, and Pannell, Kerr, Forster. Mbr of Lloyd's.

Julie Stainton, social worker; former publicity officer for nat charity; mbr Horsham DC, 1985-, cl rep, 1987-90, on W Sussex family practitioner cmte. B Jan 27 1953; ed Hull and London univs.

Steve Uwins, registered nurse for mentally handicapped; mbr West Sussex cty party; constituency chmn 1990-1. B Oct 3 1960; ed Weald comprehensive sch, Billingshurst; Forest Hospital sch of nursing. Cohse shop steward and health and safety rep.

HOUGHTON AND WASHINGTON						No change
Electorate % Turnout	79,325	70.6%	1992	77,906	71.2%	1987
*Boyes, R (Lab)	34,733	62.0%	+2.9%	32,805	59.1%	Lab
Tyrie, A G (C)	13,925	24.9%	+2.1%	12,612	22.7%	C
Dumpleton, O (LD)	7,346	13.1%	-5.1%	10,090	18.2%	SDP/All
C to Lab swing 0.4%	56,004		37.2%	55,507		36.4%
		Lab maj	20,808		Lab maj	20,193

Roland Boyes became an Opposn spokesman on defence, disarmament and arms control in 1988; mbr front bench environment team 1985-8 and from 1987 was spokesman on inner cities. Chmn 1990-1 and vice-chmn 1989-90, Northern gp of Lab MPs; jt vice-chmn PLP defence cmte, 1985-6; mbr select cmte on European legislation, 1983-7; founder chmn all-pty photography gp, 1987- ; dep chmn all-pty Europe gp 1988- . Elected for this seat 1983; MEP for Durham, 1979-84. B Feb 12 1937. Chmn Tribune gp 1985-6. Mbr Peterlee TC 1976-9; Easington DC, 1973-6. GMB.

Andrew Tyrie, special adviser to John Major, Chancellor of the Exchequer, 1986-90 and to Nigel Lawson, when Chancellor, 1986-9, and to Patrick Jenkin, when evironment sec, and to Richard Luce, arts minr 1985-6. Fellow Nuffield Coll, Oxford. Head of economic section Cons research dept, 1984-5. B Jan 15 1957; ed Trinity coll, Oxford; Coll of Europe, Bruges.

Owen Dumpleton, chartered engineer and company director, contested Cleveland and Yorkshire N for Grn pty in 1989 Euro elections. Worked for Babcock and Wilcox; Esso as design engineer for large tankers; and British Shipbuilders, retiring in 1988. Former engineer on Rainbow Warrior the Greenpeace vessel. B Nov 11 1924; ed Romford Royal Liberty; Regent St poly.

HOVE						No change
Electorate % Turnout	67,450	74.3%	1992	72,626	67.8%	1987
*Sainsbury, T A D (C)	24,525	49.0%	-9.9%	28,952	58.8%	C
Turner, D K (Lab)	12,257	24.5%	+6.2%	10,734	21.8%	SDP/All
Jones, Ms A (LD)	9,709	19.4%	-2.4%	9,010	18.3%	Lab
Furness, N (Hove C)	2,658	5.3%		522	1.1%	SE
Sinclair, G (Grn)	814	1.6%				
Morilly, J (NLP)	126	0.3%				
C to Lab swing 8.0%	50,089		24.5%	49,218		37.0%
		C maj	12,268		C maj	18,218

Tim Sainsbury was appointed Minr for Trade in 1990; Under Sec of State, FCO, 1989-90; Under Sec of State for Defence Procurement, 1987-9; Lord Commissioner of Treasury (govt whip) 1985-7; asst govt whip 1983-5. PC 1992. Director, J Sainsbury plc, 1962-83. Elected in 1973. B Jun 11 1932; ed Eton; Worcester Coll, Oxford. PPS to Sec of State for Environment 1979-83 and to Sec of State for Defence 1983. Chmn, all-pty gp for retail trade 1979-83; all-pty cmte for release of Soviet Jewry 1976-9 and vice-chmn 1979-83; former jt hon treas Cons Friends of Israel. Sponsored Indecent Displays (Control) Act 1981.

Don Turner, area representative, contested this seat 1987. Mbr East Sussex CC 1985- ; Brighton HA. B Jan 19 1935; ed Hove County GS; Open univ. MSF.

Anne Jones, voluntary worker. Mbr Mid-Sussex DC 1981-91. B Apr 24 1941; ed Fairlight Sch. B Apr 24 1941.

Gordon Sinclair, postman. B Apr 8 1956; ed Wellington CSS, Bury; Bolton coll of art and design. UCW.

HUDDERSFIELD						No change
Electorate % Turnout	67,604	72.3%	1992	66,413	75.5%	1987
*Sheerman, B J (Lab)	23,832	48.7%	+2.9%	23,019	45.9%	Lab
Kenyon, Miss J M (C)	16,574	33.9%	+2.5%	15,741	31.4%	C
Denham, Mrs A E (LD)	7,777	15.9%	-5.6%	10,773	21.5%	L/All
Harvey, N A L (Grn)	576	1.2%	-0.1%	638	1.3%	Grn
Cran, M (NLP)	135	0.3%				
C to Lab swing 0.2%	48,894		14.8%	50,171		14.5%
		Lab maj	7,258		Lab maj	7,278

Barry Sheerman became an Opposn spokesman on home affairs and deputy to Roy Hattersley in 1988; spokesman on employment and ed 1983-8 with responsibility for training, small businesses, tourism and youth affairs. Chmn Lab campaign for criminal justice. Elected for this seat 1983; MP for Huddersfield E 1979-83; contested Taunton, Oct 1974. B Aug 17 1940; ed Hampton GS; Kingston Tech Coll; LSE; London univ. Chmn nat ed research and development trust. Jt vice-chmn all-pty British-Latin American parly gp. Mbr Loughor UDC 1972-4; Lliw Valley BC 1973-9. Fellow Industry and Parliament Trust. Partner in Coptech (Co-operative technology and development). Academic adviser to Cornell Univ and Beaver Coll, Pennsylvania. Mbr of and sponsored by Co-op pty.

Jane Kenyon, sales negotiator. Mbr Whitby TC (mayor, 1987-9); Scarborough BC; N Yorks CC; Scarborough and District CHC. B Mar 24 1947; ed Queen Margaret's Sch, York; Wakefield Girls' HS; N of England Secretarial Coll, Leeds.

Ann Denham, former teacher and voluntary advice worker for CAB. B Jan 17 1941; ed Longley Hall Sec Tech; Huddersfield coll of tech; Leicester TTC; London univ.

Nicholas Harvey, caretaker, contested seat 1987. Area membership sec, Yorkshire Grn pty. B Aug 5 1964; ed Friary Grange comprehensive sch, Lichfield. Nupe.

HULL EAST					No change	
Electorate % Turnout	69,036	69.3%	1992	68,657	70.6%	1987
*Prescott, J L (Lab)	30,092	62.9%	+6.6%	27,287	56.3%	Lab
Fareham, J L (C)	11,373	23.8%	-2.2%	12,598	26.0%	C
Wastling, J (LD)	6,050	12.6%	-5.0%	8,572	17.7%	L/All
Kinzell, C (NLP)	323	0.7%				
C to Lab swing 4.4%	47,838		39.1%	48,457		30.3%
		Lab maj	18,719		Lab maj	14,689

John Prescott unsuccessfully contested dep ldrship of Lab pty in 1988; mbr, Lab pty NEC, 1989- . Elected to shadow cabinet in 1983 being chief Opposn spokesman on transport, 1988- ; energy, 1987-8; employment, 1985-7; and transport, 1983-5. Opposn spokesman on regional affairs, 1981-3; a spokesman on transport, 1979-81. Mbr, Euro Parliament 1975-79 (ldr of Lab delegation, 1976-9). Former official of and sponsored by Nat Union of Seamen; steward on passenger lines, Merchant Navy, 1955-63. Elected in 1970; contested Southport, 1966. B May 31 1938; ed Grange sec mod sch, Ellesmere Port; Ruskin Coll, Oxford; Hull univ.

John Fareham, self-employed publisher, book seller; previously property and investment manager; non-exec director of private companies. Mbr, Hull City Cl, 1983- ; Humberside local radio advisory cmte, 1984-90. Chmn, Hull and District rail users' gp, 1988- . B Jun 30 1958; ed Hull univ.

Jim Wastling was elected to Humberside CC in 1989 (LD speaker on social services). B May 14 1944; ed E Riding Inst of Agriculture.

HULL NORTH					No change	
Electorate % Turnout	71,363	66.7%	1992	73,288	69.6%	1987
*McNamara, J K (Lab)	26,619	55.9%	+4.7%	26,123	51.2%	Lab
Coleman, B G (C)	11,235	23.6%	-3.7%	13,954	27.3%	C
Meadowcroft, A (LD)	9,504	20.0%	-1.5%	10,962	21.5%	SDP/All
Richardson, G (NLP)	253	0.5%				
C to Lab swing 4.2%	47,611		32.3%	51,039		23.8%
		Lab maj	15,384		Lab maj	12,169

Kevin McNamara became chief Opposn spokesman on N Ireland in 1987; spokesman on defence and disarmament, 1982-87. Sec, all-pty Anglo-Irish parly gp. Lecturer in law. Elected this seat 1983; MP for Hull Central, Feb 1974-83, and Hull N, 1966-74; contested Bridlington, 1964. Mbr (unpaid), Irish Information Partnership. B Sep 5 1934; ed St Mary's Coll, Crosby; Hull univ. Mbr, UK delegation, N Atlantic Assembly, 1984-88. Vice-pres, League Against Cruel Sports. Former chmn, PLP N Ireland group. Sec, TGWU parly gp. Sponsored by TGWU.

Barry Coleman, teacher, contested Ashfield 1987. Mbr, Gt Yarmouth BC, 1976-92 (Mayor, 1983-4; ldr, Cons gp, 1989-92). Chmn, Gt Yarmouth Cons Assocn. B Jun 5 1943; ed Paston Sch, N Walsham; Kesteven Coll of Ed. AMMA

Andrew Meadowcroft, lecturer in performing arts, Hull CFE; mbr, Hull City Cl; dep chmn, Humberside LDs. B May 31 1963; ed W Leeds Boys HS; Hull Univ.

HULL WEST					No change	
Electorate % Turnout	56,111	65.7%	1992	55,636	67.6%	1987
*Randall, S J (Lab)	21,139	57.3%	+5.4%	19,527	51.9%	Lab
Stewart, D M (C)	10,554	28.6%	-1.7%	11,397	30.3%	C
Tress, R D (LD)	4,867	13.2%	-4.5%	6,669	17.7%	SDP/All
Franklin, B (NLP)	308	0.8%				
C to Lab swing 3.5%	36,868		28.7%	37,593		21.6%
		Lab maj	10,585		Lab maj	8,130

Stuart Randall, who was elected in 1983, became an Opposn spokesman on home affairs in 1987; a spokesman on ag, fish and food, 1985-7. Jt vice-chmn, all-pty Methodist parly gp, 1990- ; British-Taiwan gp; treas/sec, jazz gp; treas, British-Bahrain, Kuwait and United Arab Emirates gps. Consultant with Inter-Bank Research Organization, 1968-71; manager with BSC (1971-6) and British Leyland (1976-80); then with Nexos Office Systems, 1980-1; Plessey Communications Systems, 1981-3. Contested S Worcestershire, Oct 1974, and Euro seat of Midlands W, 1979. B Jun 22 1938; ed Univ Coll, Cardiff.

Donald Stewart, farmer; mbr, Boothferry BC, 1973- (mayor, 1987-88; dep ldr, 1982-); Humberside CC, 1973- (ldr, Cons gp). B Apr 30 1941; ed Gilmourton Sch; Kerswell Agricultural Coll. Former chmn and treas, Boothferry Cons Assocn.

Bob Tress, retired lecturer; sec, Hull W LDs; mbr, Beverley BC, 1979- (ldr, LD gp); Hessle TC (chair, 1990-1). B Jul 22 1941; ed Manchester GS; Oxford Univ. Ex-NATFHE.

HUNTINGDON				No change	
Electorate % Turnout	92,913	79.2%	1992	86,186	74.0%	1987
*Major, J (C)	48,662	66.2%	+2.6%	40,530	63.6%	C
Seckleman, H A (Lab)	12,432	16.9%	+3.0%	13,486	21.1%	SDP/All
Duff, A N (LD)	9,386	12.8%	-8.4%	8,883	13.9%	Lab
Wiggin, P (Lib)	1,045	1.4%	874		1.4%	Grn
Birkhead, Miss D (Grn)	846	1.2%	-0.2%			
Sutch, D (Loony)	728	1.0%				
Flanagan, M (C Thatch)	231	0.3%				
Buckethead, Lord (Gremloids)	107	0.1%				
Cockell, C (FTM)	91	0.1%				
Shepheard, D (NLP)	26	0.0%				
C to Lab swing 0.2%	73,554		49.3%	63,773		42.4%
		C maj	36,230		C maj	27,044

John Major became Prime Minister and First Lord of the Treasury in Nov 1990 following his election as ldr of the Conservative pty; Chancellor of the Exchequer, 1989-90; Sec of State for Foreign and Commonwealth Affairs, Jul to Oct 1989; Chief Sec to Treasury with seat in Cabinet, 1987-9; Minr for Social Security and Disabled, with rank of Minr of State at DHSS, 1986-7; Under Sec of State for Social Security, 1985-6; a Ld Commissioner of Treasury (govt whip), 1984-5; asst govt whip, 1983-4. PC 1987. Elected for this seat 1983; MP for Huntingdonshire, 1979-83; contested Camden, St Pancras N, Feb and Oct 1974. Executive, Standard Chartered Bank, 1965-79; Associate of Inst of Bankers. B Mar 29 1943; ed Rutlish GS. Mbr, Lambeth BC 1968-71; bd of Warden housing assocn, 1975-83. Jt sec, Cons backbench environment cmte 1979-81. PPS to minrs of state Home Office, 1981-3. Parly consultant Guild of Glass Engravers, 1979-83. Pres, eastern area YCs, 1983-5.

Hugh Seckleman, sales manager. District cllr and Lab branch sec. B Nov 20 1963; ed London Univ. MSF.

Andrew Duff, EC consultant, contested Cambridge and Beds N in 1989 and 1984 Euro elections. Chmn Eastern region LDs and LD EC working gp. Mbr Cambridge City Cl, 1982-90. B Dec 25 1950; ed St John's Coll, Cambridge; Free Univ of Brussels.

Deborah Birkhead, adult ed lecturer and partner in shop. B Jun 6 1944; ed Perse Sch for Girls, Cambridge; Goldsmiths Coll, London; City of London Poly; Salford Univ.

HYNDBURN				Lab gain	
Electorate % Turnout	58,539	84.0%	1992	60,529	80.5%	1987
Pope, G J (Lab)	23,042	46.9%	+7.1%	21,606	44.4%	C
*Hargreaves, J K (C)	21,082	42.9%	-1.5%	19,386	39.8%	Lab
Stars, Mrs Y (LD)	4,886	9.9%	-5.3%	7,423	15.2%	SDP/All
Whittle, S (NLP)	150	0.3%	297		0.6%	Grn
C to Lab swing 4.3%	49,160		4.0%	48,712		4.6%
		Lab maj	1,960		C maj	2,220

Greg Pope, local govt officer with Lancashire CC, won this seat in 1992; contested Ribble Valley 1987. Mbr Hyndburn BC 1984-8; Blackburn BC, 1989-91. Held numerous pty offices including CLP sec. Mbr Lab co-ordinating cmte; anti-apartheid movement. B Aug 29 1960; ed local state schs; St Mary's Coll, Blackburn; Hull univ. Nalgo/Nupe.

Kenneth Hargreaves represented the seat 1983-92. Office manager with Shopfitters (Lancashire) Ltd, Oswaldtwistle, 1963-83. Sec Cons backbench housing improvement sub-cmte, 1985-92; Cons constitutional affairs cmte, 1990-2; jt vice-chmn NW gp of Cons MPs, 1989-2; jt sec all-pty tertiary colleges association parly gp, 1990-2; treas Friends of Croatia gp 1991-2. B Mar 1 1939; ed St Mary's Coll, Blackburn; Burnley coll; Manchester Coll of Commerce.

Yvonne Stars is a superintendent radiographer. Mbr Hyndburn Cl 1984- (gp ldr, 1988-). B Sep 25 1938; ed Notre Dame Convent GS, Blackburn; Manchester Coll of Tech; Lancaster Sch of Radiography. MSF; Soc of Radiographers.

ILFORD NORTH				No change	
Electorate % Turnout	58,670	78.0%	1992	60,433	72.6%	1987
*Bendall, V W H (C)	24,698	54.0%	-1.0%	24,110	54.9%	C
Hilton, Ms L (Lab)	15,627	34.2%	+6.8%	12,020	27.4%	Lab
Scott, R J (LD)	5,430	11.9%	-5.8%	7,757	17.7%	SDP/All
C to Lab swing 3.9%	45,755		19.8%	43,887		27.5%
		C maj	9,071		C maj	12,090

Vivian Bendall was elected for this seat at 1978 by-election; contested Hertford and Stevenage, Feb and Oct 1974. Jt vice-chmn Cons backbench employment cmte, 1984-7 (jt sec 1981-4). Sole principal of Bendall's; consultant to London Taxi Drivers' Assocn. B Dec 14 1938; ed Coombe Hill House, Croydon; Broadgreen Coll, Croydon. Mbr Croydon BC 1964-78; GLC 1970-4. Chmn, Greater London YCs 1967-8. Vice-chmn Cons backbench transport cmte, 1982-3; sec foreign and Commonwealth affairs cmte 1981-4.

Lesley Hilton, market stall holder, contested Wanstead and Woodford 1987 and 1983. Mbr, Redbridge BC, 1986-90. B Jul 30 1949; ed Beckenham Girls GS; Maidstone Girls GS. GMB.

Ralph Scott, procurement manager, contested Ilford S 1987, 1983 and 1979, and Waltham Forest, Leyton, in Oct 1974. B Jan 10 1939; ed SE Essex Cty Tech Sch; NE London Poly. Nalgo.

ILFORD SOUTH						Lab gain
Electorate % Turnout	55,741	76.8%	1992	58,572	71.8%	1987
Gapes, M J (Lab)	19,418	45.3%	+7.8%	20,351	48.4%	C
*Thorne, N G (C)	19,016	44.4%	-4.0%	15,779	37.5%	Lab
Hogarth, G G (LD)	4,126	9.6%	-4.5%	5,928	14.1%	L/All
Bramachari, N (NLP)	269	0.6%				
C to Lab swing 5.9%	42,829		0.9%	42,058		10.9%
		Lab maj	402		C maj	4,572

Mike Gapes, senior international officer, Lab pty, since 1988; research officer, 1980-88; nat student organiser, 1977-80; chmn, nat organisation of Lab students, 1976-77. Elected in 1992; contested Ilford N 1983. B Sep 4 1952; ed schs in Loughton and Chigwell; Buckhurst Hill Cty HS, Essex; Fitzwilliam Coll, Cambridge; Middlesex Poly. Mbr of, and sponsored by, Co-op Pty; TGWU.
Neil Thorne on Select Cmte on Defence, 1983-92. Mbr Court of Referees, 1987-92. Chmn Nat Cl for Civil Defence, 1982-6; Commons motor club, 1985-91; jt sec, all-pty parly gp on war crimes, 1987-92. Founder and chmn, Armed Forces Parly Scheme, 1988- . Jt vice-chmn (1987-90) and still mbr, exec cmte, UK branch, IPU. Chartered surveyor, consultant and Lloyd's underwriter. MP for this seat 1979-

92; contested it, Oct 1974. B Aug 8 1932; ed City of London sch; London univ. Dep Lieut for Gtr London, 1991; Freeman and liveryman, City of London. Consultant to Hull and Co, chartered surveyors (senior partner of firm, 1962-76). Mbr, Chapter General, Order of St John, 1990, and chmn, all-pty Order of St John parly gp; mbr, TA, 1952-82; Redbridge BC, 1965-8 (alderman, 1975-8); GLC, 1967-73.
George Hogarth, accountant/accounts manager, was LD local govt agent 1990; agent for this seat 1992. B Nov 13 1938; ed Ilford primary and sec schs; Redbridge and Havering Tech Coll; London Business Sch. Churchwarden, St Clements, Ilford. Treas, Friends of Valentines Park, 1990- ; adviser, Valentines Residents Assocn, 1986-.

INVERNESS, NAIRN AND LOCHABER						No change
Electorate % Turnout	69,468	73.3%	1992	66,743	70.9%	1987
*Johnston, Sir Russell (LD)	13,258	26.0%	-10.8%	17,422	36.8%	L/All
Stewart, D (Lab)	12,800	25.1%	-0.2%	11,991	25.3%	Lab
Ewing, F S (SNP)	12,562	24.7%	+9.9%	10,901	23.0%	C
Scott, J (C)	11,517	22.6%	-0.4%	7,001	14.8%	SNP
Martin, J (Grn)	766	1.5%				
LD to Lab swing 5.3%	50,903		0.9%	47,315		11.5%
		LD maj	458		L/All maj	5,431

Sir Russell Johnston became LD Dep Ldr and President, Scottish LDs, in 1988; LD spokesman on Euro affairs including East-West relations, 1989- ; Lib and then LD spokesman on foreign and Commonwealth affairs, 1979-89. Vice-pres, Euro Lib, Democratic and Reform parties (ELDR), 1990- . Ldr, Scottish Lib pty, 1974-88, and spokesman on Scotland, 1981-7; Alliance spokesman on Scotland and Europe in 1987 election. Mbr, Cmte of Privileges, 1989- . Elected for this seat 1983, becoming LD MP 1988; MP for Inverness 1964-83. First UK Lib MEP (1973-5, 1976-9); contested Highlands and Islands 1979 and 1984 Euro elections. Delegate, Cl of Europe and WEU, 1985-6 and 1987- . B Jul 28 1932; ed Portree HS, Isle of Skye; Edinburgh univ; Moray House Coll of Ed.

David Stewart, social work manager, Highland reg cl, contested this seat 1987. Mbr, Lab pty Scottish exec, 1985-; Nithsdale DC, 1984-6; Inverness DC, 1988-. B May 5 1956; ed Paisley Coll; Stirling univ. Nalgo and Nupe.
Fergus Ewing, solicitor; mbr, SNP nat exec; spokesman for small business. Husband of Mrs Margaret Ewing, MP for Moray, and son of Mrs Winnie Ewing, MEP for Highlands and Islands. B Sep 23 1957; ed Glasgow univ.
John Scott retired early at end of 1991 from Rank Xerox (UK) Ltd where he was govt account exec; joined company in 1972. Depute chmn, Ross Cromarty and Skye Cons ssocn, 1987-. B Mar 9 1940; ed Queen Mary's GS, Walsall.
John Martin, self-employed computer consultant.

IPSWICH						Lab gain
Electorate % Turnout	67,261	80.3%	1992	68,165	77.1%	1987
Cann, J (Lab)	23,680	43.8%	+1.1%	23,328	44.4%	C
*Irvine, M F (C)	23,415	43.3%	-1.1%	22,454	42.7%	Lab
White, J (LD)	6,159	11.4%	-1.2%	6,596	12.6%	SDP/All
Scott, Ms J (Grn)	591	1.1%		174	0.3%	WRP
Kaplan, E (NLP)	181	0.3%				
C to Lab swing 1.1%	54,026		0.5%	52,552		1.7%
		Lab maj	265		C maj	874

Jamie Cann, deputy head of primary sch, won this seat in 1992. Mbr Ipswich BC, 1973- (ldr Lab gp, 1976-91; cl ldr 1979-91); non-exec director, Ipswich port authority. B June 28 1946; ed Barton on Humber GS; Kesteven Coll of Ed. NUT, 1967- .
Michael Irvine was PPS to Sir Patrick Mayhew, then Attorney General, 1990-2. MP for seat 1987-92; mbr, select cmte on parliamentary commissioner for administra-

tion. Sec, Cons back-bench European affairs cmte, 1989-90; Cons unpaired MPs, 1989-90. Contested Bishop Auckland in 1979. Barrister and son of the late Sir Arthur Irvine, QC MP, Labour Solicitor General. B Oct 21 1939; ed Rugby; Oriel Coll, Oxford.
Joseph White, financial director of printing company; mbr Basildon DC, 1987- (dep gp ldr); CHC mbr 1988-92. B Mar 10 1938; ed GS.

ISLE OF WIGHT				No change		
Electorate % Turnout	99,838	79.8%	1992	98,694	79.6%	1987
*Field, B J A (C)	38,163	47.9%	-3.2%	40,175	51.2%	C
Brand, Dr P (LD)	36,336	45.6%	+2.7%	33,733	43.0%	L/All
Pearson, K (Lab)	4,784	6.0%	+0.1%	4,626	5.9%	Lab
Daly, C (NLP)	350	0.4%				
C to LD swing 3.0%	79,633		2.3%	78,534		8.2%
		C maj	1,827		C maj	6,442

Barry Field, a company director, won the seat from L/All in 1987. Appointed to environment select cmte in 1991. Vice-chmn 1991- and sec 1987-91 Cons backbench shipping and shipbuilding sub-cmte; sec, Cons backbench party organisation cmte, 1988- ; Cons sports cmte, 1990- ; jt sec, Cons tourism cmte, 1988- ; all-pty maritime parly gp, 1990- . Mbr, Isle of Wight CC, 1986-9; Horsham DC, 1983-6. Parly consultant to Nat Assocn of Holiday Centres. Director, J D Field & Sons Ltd, 1981- . Major in TA with 17 Port Regiment TCT Marchwood, Southampton. B Jul 4 1946; ed Collingwood Boys' Sch; Mitcham GS; Bembridge Sch; Victoria St Coll. Liveryman Turners' Co; mbr Watermen and Lightermen's Co; Island Sailing Club 1964- .

Dr Peter Brand, family doctor, was elected to Isle of Wight CC in 1984 (dep ldr of cl). B May 16 1947; ed Thornbury GS; Birmingham Univ. Mbr, BMA; Royal Coll of General Practitioners.

Kenn Pearson, self-employed driver, contested this seat 1987. Former mbr, Lab southern region exec cmte. B Apr 5 1940; ed St Marylebone GS; City of Westminster Coll, London; Corpus Christi Coll, Oxford. TGWU.

ISLINGTON NORTH				No change		
Electorate % Turnout	56,270	67.3%	1992	58,917	66.5%	1987
*Corbyn, J B (Lab)	21,742	57.4%	+7.5%	19,577	50.0%	Lab
Champagnie, Mrs L (C)	8,958	23.7%	-1.6%	9,920	25.3%	C
Ludford, Miss S A (LD)	5,732	15.1%	-6.7%	8,560	21.8% SDP/All
Ashby, C M (Grn)	1,420	3.8%	+0.9%	1,131	2.9%	Grn
C to Lab swing 4.6%	37,852		33.8%	39,188		24.6%
		Lab maj	12,784		Lab maj	9,657

Jeremy Corbyn was elected in 1983. Vice-chmn of London Lab pty; jt vice-chmn, London gp of Lab MPs 1985- ; vice-chmn, PLP health cmte, 1989-90, and PLP health and social security cmte 1985-9; jt vice-chmn PLP N Ireland cmte 1988-9 and 1990- . Nupe official, 1975-83 and sponsored by the union. Appointed to select cmte on social security in 1991. B May 26 1949; ed Adams GS, Newport, Shropshire. Mbr Haringey BC 1974-83. Sec PLP Central and Latin America and Caribbean gp 1984- . Mbr Campaign Gp of Labour MPs 1987-. Trustee N Islington Red Rose Labour and Socialist Club.

Lurline Champagnie, self-employed specialist nursing consultant in mastectomy care. Cons Pty's first woman Afro-Caribbean candidate. Mbr assocn of plastic surgery nurses; the burn assocn; Cons medical society; RCN. Mbr Harrow BC 1986- ; exec cl Harrow W Cons assocn; Harrow community relations cl. B 1942; ed C of E schs; HS and business studies coll; CFHE.

Sarah Ludford, a barrister and European affairs consultant. Contested Wight and Hampshire E in 1984 Euro election and London Central 1989 Euro election. Mbr LD fed policy cmte 1990- ; exec ELDR 1989- ; vice-chmn London LDs 1990- . B Mar 14 1951; ed Portsmouth HS for Girls; LSE; Inns of Court Sch of Law.

Chris Ashby, teacher, contested seat 1987. B Aug 15 1945; ed City of London Poly.

ISLINGTON SOUTH AND FINSBURY				No change		
Electorate % Turnout	55,541	72.5%	1992	57,910	71.2%	1987
*Smith, C R (Lab)	20,586	51.1%	+11.0%	16,511	40.1%	Lab
Jones, M V (C)	9,934	24.7%	+4.1%	15,706	38.1% SDP/All
Pryce, C J (LD)	9,387	23.3%	-14.8%	8,482	20.6%	C
Hersey, Ms R (JBR)	149	0.4%		382	0.9%	Grn
Avino, Ms M (Loony)	142	0.4%		81	0.2%	SPGB
Spinks, M (NLP)	83	0.2%		56	0.1%	HP
C to Lab swing 3.5%	40,281		26.4%	41,218		2.0%
		Lab maj	10,652		Lab maj	805

Chris Smith became an Opposn spokesman on Treasury and economic affairs in 1987. Mbr exec cmte and chmn research and publications cmte Fabian Society 1989- . Chmn PLP home affairs cmte 1985-7; Tribune Gp of Lab MPs, 1988-9 (sec 1985-8); jt vice-chmn all-pty parly gp on Aids; parly cmte on drug misuse. Elected 1983; contested Epsom and Ewell, 1979. Unpaid director Sadlers's Wells Theatre (governor, 1987-); *Tribune* Newspaper; British Defence and Aid Fund for Southern Africa; John Muir Trust. Mbr bd of Shelter 1986- . B Jul 24 1951; ed George Watson's Coll, Edinburgh; Pembroke Coll, Cambridge (pres of union, 1972); Harvard Univ. Completed ascent of all Scottish "Munro" mountains. Sponsored by MSF, ACTT and UCW.

Mark Jones, regional director Taylor Walker Ltd and regional bd director Allied Breweries. Mbr Brent BC, 1984- . B Oct 16 1960; ed Salesian Coll, Battersea; Westfield and Luton Colls, London Univ.

Chris Pryce, economist and management consultant with Touche Ross. Mbr nat bd Shelter 1978- , chmn finance cmte 1990- . Islington cllr 1978-82 and 1983- (LD ldr, 1990-). B Feb 22 1948; ed Canton HS, Cardiff; LSE.

ISLWYN				No change		
Electorate % Turnout	51,079	81.5%	1992	50,414	80.4%	1987
*Kinnock, N G (Lab)	30,908	74.3%	+3.0%	28,901	71.3%	Lab
Bone, P W (C)	6,180	14.8%	+0.2%	5,954	14.7%	C
Symonds, M (LD)	2,352	5.7%	-3.6%	3,746	9.2%	SDP/All
Jones, Ms H (PC)	1,636	3.9%	-0.8%	1,932	4.8%	PC
Sutch, D (Loony)	547	1.3%				
C to Lab swing 1.4%	41,623		59.4%	40,533		56.6%
		Lab maj	24,728		Lab maj	22,947

Neil Kinnock was Leader of Labour Party and Ldr of the Opposn from 1983 until 1992, when he announced after April general election his decision to stand down. PC 1983. Elected to shadow cabinet in 1979; chief Opposn spokesman on education, 1979-83. Trade union tutor with WEA, 1966-70. Elected for this seat 1983; MP for Bedwelty, 1970-83. Chmn, Lab Pty, 1987-8; mbr, Lab Pty NEC, since 1978. B Mar 28 1942; ed Lewis Sch, Pengam, Glamorgan; Univ Coll, Cardiff (Pres of union, 1965-6). PPS to Mr Michael Foot, Sec of State for Employment, 1974-5; chmn, PLP Welsh gp, 1977-8. Mbr, Public Expenditure Cmte, 1971-3; Select Cmte on Nationalized Industries, 1973-7; also served on Select Cmte on Euro Legislation. Director (unpaid) Tribune Publications, 1974-82; Mbr, Welsh Hospital Bd, 1969-71; BBC Gen Advisory Cl, 1975-9. Sponsored by TGWU; mbr of union since 1966; chmn, TGWU parly gp, 1974-76.

Peter Bone, chartered accountant owning his firm; managing director of Welsh-based tour operator and travel agency and of property sales company. Mbr, Southend BC, 1977-86. B Oct 19 1952; ed Westcliff-on-Sea GS.

Andrew Symonds, chartered surveyor. B Jan 6 1939. FRICS.

Helen Jones, youth and community work project manager; mbr, PC nat exec; pty speaker on health and social services; treas, women's section; former constituency chmn and sec. B Jun 29 1960; ed Colchester HS; Caerernion HS: UCW, Aberystwyth. Nalgo, equal opportunities rep.

JARROW				No change		
Electorate % Turnout	62,611	74.4%	1992	62,845	74.4%	1987
*Dixon, D (Lab)	28,956	62.1%	-1.3%	29,651	63.4%	Lab
Ward, T F (C)	11,049	23.7%	+0.5%	10,856	23.2%	C
Orrell, J K (LD)	6,608	14.2%	+0.8%	6,230	13.3%	L/All
Lab to C swing 0.9%	46,613		38.4%	46,737		40.2%
		Lab maj	17,907		Lab maj	18,795

Donald Dixon was elected Opposn dep chief whip in 1987; an Opposn whip from 1984; chmn, PLP shipbuilding sub-cmte, 1985-7 and 1989- ; sec, trade union gp of Lab MPs. Shipyard worker, 1947-74; branch sec, GMB, 1974-9. Mbr, Select Cmtes on broadcasting, 1988-91; employment, 1983-7; Commons Services, 1979-83 and 1987-91; Selection, 1991- ; Commons catering, 1991- . Elected in 1979. B Mar 6 1929; ed Ellison Street C of E Elementary sch, Jarrow. Mbr, Jarrow BC, 1962-74 ; South Tyneside MDC, 1974-9. Freeman of Jarrow, 1972. Vice-pres, Jarrow and Hebburn Trades Cl. Mbr of and sponsored by GMB.

Terry Ward, teacher of economics and business studies; mbr, Middlesbrough BC, 1987-91; chmn, Brookfield Cons, 1983-9; has served on exec, Stockton S Cons Assocn. B Apr 23 1952; ed Birmingham, Keele and Cardiff univs.

Keith Orrell, head of unit for autistic children; mbr, S Tyneside Cl, 1990- (Opposn ldr, 1991-). B May 22 1944; ed Sunderland coll of ed; Open and Newcastle univs.

KEIGHLEY				No change		
Electorate % Turnout	66,358	82.6%	1992	65,831	79.4%	1987
*Waller, G P A (C)	25,983	47.4%	+1.7%	23,903	45.8%	C
Flanagan, Dr T B (Lab)	22,387	40.8%	+5.8%	18,297	35.0%	Lab
Simpson, I (LD)	5,793	10.6%	-8.7%	10,041	19.2%	L/All
Crowson, K M (Grn)	642	1.2%				
C to Lab swing 2.1%	54,805		6.6%	52,241		10.7%
		C maj	3,596		C maj	5,606

Gary Waller became jt vice-chmn, parly information technology cmte, in 1987 (its treas, 1981-87); sec, parly and scientific cmte, 1988-90; mbr, Commons information cmte, 1991- . Won this seat 1983; MP for Brighouse and Spenborough, 1979-83; contested Rother Valley, Feb and Oct 1974. Journalist. B Jun 24 1945; ed Rugby; Lancaster univ. Sec, all-pty Friends of Cycling parly gp; sec, Cons back-bench transport cmte, 1988- and 1985-7; mbr, jt cmte on consolidation bills, 1982- ; vice-chmn, parly food and health forum, 1985- . Vice-pres, Inst of Trading Standards Administration, 1988- ; Friends of Settle-Carlisle Railway, 1987- .

Thomas Flanagan, chartered civil engineer working for Kirklees Met Cl in highways division. Lab pty agent in 1987 at Keighley. Mbr, Bradford cl, 1984- (cl ldr); West Yorkshire police authority, 1985-8. B Aug 2 1959; ed De la Salle GS, Liverpool; Bradford Univ. Apex/GMB

Ian Simpson, landowner. B Sep 23 1941; ed Skipton GS; Manchester and New South Wales univs.

Mike Crowson, writer and researcher and former teacher, contested Hornchurch for Ecol Pty 1983; Thurrock for Libs 1979; Edmonton W in Canadian Fed elections 1972; Stony Plain, Alberta provincial elections 1970. Sec, Nat Cl, Ecol Pty, 1983-4; mbr, nat cl, Grn Pty, 1989-90. B Oct 13 1940; ed Bridlington GS; Oastler Coll, Huddersfield; Alberta univ, Edmonton, Canada; Bradford Univ.

KENSINGTON						No change
Electorate % Turnout	42,129	73.3%	1992	48,212	64.7%	1987
*Fishburn, J D (C)	15,540	50.3%	+2.8%	14,818	47.5%	C
Holmes, Ms A (Lab)	11,992	38.8%	+5.6%	10,371	33.2%	Lab
Shirley, C (LD)	2,770	9.0%	-8.3%	5,379	17.2%	SDP/All
Burlingham-Johnson, Ms A (Grn)	415	1.3%	-0.3%	528	1.7%	Grn
Hardy, A (NLP)	90	0.3%		65	0.2%	Human
Bulloch, Ms A (Anti-Fed)	71	0.2%		30	0.1%	PIP
C to Lab swing 1.4%	30,878		11.5%	31,191		14.3%
		C maj	3,548		C maj	4,447

Dudley Fishburn became PPS to Timothy Sainsbury, minr for trade, in 1990. Elected at by-election in 1988. Jt sec, all-pty leasehold reform parly gp, 1989- . Freelance journalist; with *The Economist*, 1969-88, being executive editor, 1979-88. Director, English National Ballet, 1988- ; HFC bank, 1990- ; British-American Arts Assocn, 1982-88; Harvard univ bd of overseers, 1990- (A univ director, 1985-88); trustee, Open univ foundation, 1982- . Consultant to Pepper Hamilton and Scheetz, US law firm, 1989- ; consultant to JP Morgan, 1989- . Contested Isle of Wight in 1979 and Oct 1974. B Jun 8 1946; ed Eton; Harvard. Pres, Harvard Club of London, 1975.

Ann Holmes, housing and community consultant, contested the 1988 by-election, Calder Valley 1983, and this seat 1979. Mbr, Islington BC, 1974-8. B Jul 22 1946; ed Whitcliffe Mount Sch, Cleckheaton; Hull univ. ACTSS.
Chris Shirley, company director; chmn, Kensington LDs, 1990-91. B May 16 1951; ed Kings Coll, London; Wharton univ, US.
Ajay Burlingham-Johnson, freelance systems analyst and computer consultant; Grn Pty conference organiser; local pty treas. B May 9 1963; ed Wadhurst Coll, Sussex; the Royal Masonic; Kingsway, Princeton.
Details of 1988 by-election on page 286

KENT MID						No change
Electorate % Turnout	74,459	79.7%	1992	72,456	71.9%	1987
*Rowe, A J B (C)	33,633	56.7%	+1.6%	28,719	55.1%	C
Robson, T (Lab)	13,984	23.6%	+5.5%	13,951	26.8%	L/All
Colley, G D (LD)	11,476	19.3%	-7.4%	9,420	18.1%	Lab
Valente, G (NLP)	224	0.4%				
C to Lab swing 2.0%	59,317		33.1%	52,090		28.4%
		C maj	19,649		C maj	14,768

Andrew Rowe joined select cmte on health in 1991; mbr, select cmte on employment, 1983-89; chmn (1989-), jt vice-chmn (1987-9) and jt sec (1983-6), Cons back-bench employment cmte. Chmn, parly panel on personal social services; chmn, 1990- , and former sec, all-pty franchise development gp. Elected in 1983. B Sep 11 1935; ed Eton; Merton Coll, Oxford. Pres, North Downs Rail Concern. Director of community affairs at Cons central office, 1975-9. Founder and director of Cons Small Business Bureau; Editor, *Small Business*, 1979-90. Consultant to Legal Protection Gp; adviser to Chevron Petroleum (UK) Ltd. Mbr, Swann Cmte, 1979-84; trustee, Community Service

Volunteers. IoJ.
Tim Robson, area engineering manager; mbr, Rochester upon Medway Cl, 1987-. B Sep 21 1955; ed Walderslade Sec Sch; Mid Kent Coll; Open univ. Mbr, Medway HA; MSF.
Graham Colley, solicitor and partner with wife in practice, contested the seat for L/All 1987. Mbr for Medway South, Kent CC, 1989-. Former membership sec, Lib Lawyers; treas, Southwark and Bermondsey Lib assocn; Maidstone Lib fund raising officer. B Jun 19 1953; ed Nottingham HS; Univ Coll of Wales, Aberystwyth; Coll of Europe, Bruges; Coll of Law, Chester.

KETTERING						No change
Electorate % Turnout	67,853	82.6%	1992	65,965	78.8%	1987
*Freeman, R N (C)	29,115	52.0%	+0.9%	26,532	51.1%	C
Hope, P I (Lab)	17,961	32.1%	+12.4%	15,205	29.3%	SDP/All
Denton-White, R (LD)	8,962	16.0%	-13.3%	10,229	19.7%	Lab
C to Lab swing 5.7%	56,038		19.9%	51,966		21.8%
		C maj	11,154		C maj	11,327

Roger Freeman was appointed minr for public transport, with rank of minister of state for transport, in 1990; under secretary of state for health, 1988-90; under secretary of state for armed forces, 1986-8. Elected in 1983; fought Don Valley, 1979. Chartered accountant.
Philip Hope, community worker and management consultant. Chairman and sec, Kettering CLP; mbr,

Kettering BC, 1983-7. B Apr 19 1955; ed Wandsworth comprehensive sch; Exeter univ. MSF.
Richard Denton-White, teacher in West London secure unit; mbr, Wootton Basset TC, Wilts, 1979-83. B Apr 11 1946; ed Bethaney sch, Goudhurst, Kent; City of Bath boys' sch; Roll coll, Exmouth; Exeter univ.

KILMARNOCK AND LOUDOUN				No change		
Electorate % Turnout	62,002	80.0%	1992	62,648	78.0%	1987
*McKelvey, W (Lab)	22,210	44.8%	-3.7%	23,713	48.5%	Lab
Neil, A (SNP)	15,231	30.7%	+12.5%	9,586	19.6%	C
Wilkinson, R M (C)	9,438	19.0%	-0.6%	8,881	18.2%	SNP
Philbrick, Mrs K (LD)	2,722	5.5%	-8.2%	6,698	13.7%	SDP/All
Lab to SNP swing 8.1%	49,601		14.1%	48,878		28.9%
		Lab maj	6,979		Lab maj	14,127

William McKelvey, chmn, Scottish gp of Lab MPs, 1985-6; former executive mbr of gp. Served on select cmte on Scottish affairs until 1986. Elected for this seat 1983; MP for Kilmarnock, 1979-83. Jt vice-chmn all-pty Scotch whisky industry parly gp; treas Scottish penal affairs gp. Chmn all-pty British-Cuban parly gp. Former full-time Lab party and union official; chmn Labour action for peace. B Jul 1934; ed Morgan Acad; Dundee coll of technology.

Sponsored by AUEW.
Alex Neil, economic consultant, contested Glasgow Central 1989 by-election; Chmn Network Scotland Ltd. B Aug 22 1951; ed Ayr Acad; Dundee univ. TGWU/ACTSS.
Richard Wilkinson, business consultant, contested Ayrshire Central 1979. Supplies manager, Lothian health bd, 1987-9; B Sep 7 1947; ed Irvine royal acad; Glasgow coll of commerce.

KINCARDINE AND DEESIDE				No change from **1987**		
Electorate % Turnout	66,617	78.7%	1992	63,587	75.2%	1987
Kynoch, G (C)	22,924	43.7%	+3.1%	19,438	40.6%	C
Stephen, N R (LD)	18,429	35.1%	-1.2%	17,375	36.3%	L/All
Macartney, Dr W J A (SNP)	5,927	11.3%	+4.9%	7,624	15.9%	Lab
Savidge, M (Lab)	4,795	9.1%	-6.8%	3,082	6.4%	SNP
Campbell, S (Grn)	381	0.7%	+0.1%	299	0.6%	Grn
LD to C swing 2.1%	52,456		8.6%	47,818		4.3%
		C maj	4,495		C maj	2,063

George Kynoch regained this seat for Cons 1992. Gp director, restructured G and G Kynoch plc, 1990- ; with company from 1971; Previously with ICI, Ardeer, Scotland. Pres, Scottish woollen industry, 1990-1; chmn, American panel of nat wool textile export corporation of UK, 1987-91. B Oct 7 1946; ed Cargilfield Sch, Edinburgh; Trinity Coll, Glenalmond; Bristol univ; Paisley tech coll. Chmn, Moray and W Banff Cons Assocn, 1990- ; vice-chmn, Northern Area Cons, 1991- .
Nicol Stephen, solicitor, gained this seat for LDs in 1991 by-election, losing it in 1992; contested seat in 1987. Mbr Grampian reg cl, 1982-92 Bd mbr Grampian Enterprise Ltd. B Mar 23 1960; ed Robert Gordon's Coll, Aberdeen; Aberdeen and Edinburgh univs.

Dr Allan Macartney, vice-pres of SNP. Contested 1991 by-election. Political scientist. Contested Scotland NE in 1989 Euro elections; Clackmannan in 1987; Tweeddale, Ettrick and Lauderdale 1983; Berwick and East Lothian 1979; Renfrewshire W 1970. B Feb 1941 in Accra, Ghana; ed Elgin Acad, Moray; Tubingen, Marburg, Edinburgh and Glasgow univs. AUT.
Malcolm Savidge, teacher, contested 1991 by-election; mbr Aberdeen city cl, 1980- . B May 9 1946; ed Wallington cty GS; Aberdeen univ; Aberdeen coll of ed. EIS; TGWU.
Steve Campbell, guest house owner, contested 1991 by-election. Chmn constituency Grn pty. B Apl 27 1959; ed Nottingham univ.
Details of 1991 by-election on page 288

KINGSTON UPON THAMES				No change		
Electorate % Turnout	51,077	78.4%	1992	54,839	78.5%	1987
*Lamont, N S H (C)	20,675	51.6%	-4.6%	24,198	56.2%	C
Osbourne, D (LD)	10,522	26.3%	-3.9%	13,012	30.2%	L/All
Markless, R H (Lab)	7,748	19.3%	+6.2%	5,676	13.2%	Lab
Amer, A (Lib)	771	1.9%		175	0.4%	CPWSML
Beaupre, D (Loony)	212	0.5%				
Woollcoombe, G (NLP)	81	0.2%				
Scholefield, A (Anti-Fed)	42	0.1%				
C to LD swing 0.3%	40,051		25.4%	43,061		26.0%
		C maj	10,153		C maj	11,186

Norman Lamont was appointed Chancellor of the Exchequer in 1990; joined cabinet as Chief Sec to Treasury in 1989; Financial Sec to Treasury, 1986-9; Minr of State for Defence Procurement, 1985-6; Minr of State for Industry, 1981-5; Under Sec of State for Energy, 1979-81. PC 1986. Mbr PAC, 1986-9. Merchant banker, N M Rothschild and Sons, 1968-79. Elected at 1972 by-election; contested Hull E, 1970. B May 8 1942; ed Loretto

Sch; Fitzwilliam coll, Cambridge (Pres of Union, 1964.)
Derek Osbourne, personnel/training consultant; mbr Kingston upon Thames BC, 1986- . B Mar 29 1954; ed Harold Malley GS; Bradford univ.
Robert Markless, research administrator, contested this seat 1987. Chmn SERA SW London (Grn section) and Kingston racial equality cl. B Feb 21 1950; ed Christ's coll, Finchley; Leeds univ. GMB/Apex.

KINGSWOOD						Lab gain
Electorate % Turnout	71,727	83.9%	1992	73,089	80.2%	1987
Berry, R L (Lab)	26,774	44.5%	+7.1%	26,300	44.9%	C
*Hayward, R A (C)	24,404	40.6%	-4.3%	21,907	37.4%	Lab
Pinkerton, Ms J (LD)	8,967	14.9%	-2.8%	10,382	17.7%	SDP/All
C to Lab swing 5.7%	60,145		3.9%	58,589		7.5%
		Lab maj	2,370		C maj	4,393

Roger Berry, a univ lecturer in economics, won the seat in 1992; contested it 1987, Weston-super-Mare 1983 and Bristol in 1984 Euro election. Mbr Avon CC 1981- (ldr Lab gp 1986- ; dep ldr of cl 1985-6; finance cmte chmn 1983-6). Vice-pres Bristol anti-apartheid movement. B Jul 4 1948; ed Dalton Cty Primary Sch, Huddersfield; Huddersfield New Coll; Bristol and Sussex Univs. MSF/AUT.
Robert Hayward held the seat 1983-92. Contested Carmarthen, Oct 1974. Jt sec Cons backbench aviation cmte 1990-2. PPS to Paul Channon, transport sec, 1987-9,

to corporate and consumer affairs minr 1985-7, and to industry minr 1986-7. Mbr select cmte on Cardiff Bay barrage bill, 1991-2 and energy 1983-5. Personnel manager, Esso Petroleum, 1971-5; Coca Cola Bottlers, 1975-9; GEC Large Machines, 1979-82. B Mar 11 1949; ed Abingdon Sch; Maidenhead GS; Univ of Rhodesia. Mbr Coventry City Cl, 1976-8. Qualified rugby referee.
Jeanne Pinkerton, newsagent. Mbr Bristol City Cl 1986-8; chmn Kingswood LDs 1988-90. B Mar 19 1946; ed sec mod sch.

KIRKCALDY						No change
Electorate % Turnout	51,762	75.1%	1992	53,439	76.5%	1987
*Moonie, Dr L G (Lab)	17,887	46.0%	-3.5%	20,281	49.6%	Lab
Hosie, S (SNP)	8,761	22.5%	+10.8%	8,711	21.3%	C
Wosley, S P (C)	8,476	21.8%	+0.5%	7,118	17.4%	SDP/All
Leslie, Ms S (LD)	3,729	9.6%	-7.8%	4,794	11.7%	SNP
Lab to SNP swing 7.2%	38,853		23.5%	40,904		28.3%
		Lab maj	9,126		Lab maj	11,570

Dr Lewis Moonie joined the Opposn front bench trade and industry team in 1989 as spokesman on technology. Elected in 1987. Mbr select cmte on social services 1987-9; on Treasury and civil service 1989. Vice-chmn PLP Treasury and civil service cmte 1988-9. Community medicine specialist with Fife health bd; worked as psychiatrist in Switzerland and Holland. Mbr Fife Reg Cl 1982-6 (vice-chmn finance); bd mbr of local co-op society. B Feb 25 1947; ed Grove Acad, Dundee; St Andrews and Edinburgh univs. ASTMS and TGWU. Sponsored by Co-op pty.

Stewart Hosie, information systems manager. SNP vice-convenor for youth affairs. B Jan 3 1963; ed Carnoustie HS; Bell St Coll of Tech, Dundee.
Stephen Wolsey is a mechanical engineer in electricity supply industry. Mbr Dunfermline DC, 1988- . B Oct 29 1957; ed The High School, Dunfermline; Napier Coll, Edinburgh. Vice-chmn Scottish Tory green initiative. EPEA.
Sue Leslie, teacher. Mbr exec PAT. B Mar 8 1961; ed Edinburgh univ; Moray House Coll of Ed, Edinburgh.

KNOWSLEY NORTH						No change
Electorate % Turnout	48,761	72.8%	1992	52,960	74.2%	1987
*Howarth, G E (Lab)	27,517	77.5%	+7.6%	27,454	69.9%	Lab
Mabey, S (C)	5,114	14.4%	+1.9%	6,356	16.2%	L/All
Murray, J (LD)	1,515	4.3%	-11.9%	4,922	12.5%	C
Lappin, Mrs K (Lib)	1,180	3.3%		538	1.4%	RF
Ruben, V (NLP)	179	0.5%				
C to Lab swing 2.9%	35,505		63.1%	39,270		53.7%
		Lab maj	22,403		Lab maj	21,098

George Howarth retained the seat at 1986 by-election. Opposn spokesman on environment 1990- dealing mainly with housing and planning. Jt vice-chmn all-pty Mersey barrage parly gp, 1990- . Mbr select cmte on parliamentary commissioner for administration 1987-90; on Environment, 1989-90. Director Wales TUC co-op centre voluntary management cmte 1984-6. Former mbr Huyton UDC; Knowsley BC 1975-86 (dep ldr, 1982). B Jun 29 1949; ed in Huyton; Kirkby CFE; Liverpool poly.

Sponsored by AEU.
Simon Mabey, chartered accountant, was Lord Mayor of Westminster 1989-90; mbr Westminster City Cl, 1982-90 (chmn social services cmte 1985-9; Westminster drugs task force, 1985-7). Mbr Bow Gp, 1978- (research sec 1982-3); soc of Cons accountants; Carlton Club and its political cmte. B Sep 29 1952; ed City of London Sch; Clare Coll, Cambridge. Freeman, City of London; mbr, City Livery Co.

KNOWSLEY SOUTH						No change
Electorate % Turnout	62,260	74.8%	1992	65,643	74.1%	1987
*O'Hara, E (Lab)	31,933	68.6%	+4.1%	31,378	64.5%	Lab
Byrom, L T (C)	9,922	21.3%	-0.3%	10,532	21.6%	C
Smith, I (LD)	4,480	9.6%	-4.3%	6,760	13.9%	SDP/All
Raiano, M (NLP)	217	0.5%				
C to Lab swing 2.2%	46,552		47.3%	48,670		42.8%
		Lab maj	22,011		Lab maj	20,846

Eddie O'Hara, head of curriculum studies, sch of ed and community studies, Liverpool poly, 1983-90, was elected at 1990 by-election. Mbr select cmtes on ed, science and arts, 1991- ; on Severn bridges bill, 1991. Principal lecturer and snr tutor, Dean of postgraduate studies, city of Liverpool coll of HE, 1974-83. Mbr Knowsley MBC, 1975-91; Merseyside coordinating cmte; AMA ed cmte and AMA planning and economic development cmte; Merseyside rep on exec cmte, regions Europeennes de tradition industrielle and mbr permanent cmte, assembly of European regions Working knowledge of several languages; second language Greek. Vice-chmn, all-pty British-Greek parly gp. B Oct 1 1937; ed Liverpool collegiate sch; Magdalen coll, Oxford;

London univ. AMMA.
Leslie Byrom, self-employed chartered surveyor, contested Sep 1990 by-election. Mbr Southport MBC, 1985- (ldr, Cons gp, 1991-); AMA policy cmte. B Apr 12 1956; ed Crosby cty sch; Southport tech coll. Mbr management cmte, Southport Cons assocn.
Ian Smith, teacher, contested seat 1983 and Sep 1990 by-election; St Helens 1979; mbr Prescot TC, 1983- (LD ldr; Mayor of Prescot, 1985-6); Whiston TC, 1983-7. B Jul 15 1951; ed Huyton Hey cty sec sch; Liverpool reg coll of art. NAS. Merseybeat record collector.
For details of 1990 by-election see page 287.

LAGAN VALLEY						No change
Electorate % Turnout	72,645	67.4%	1992	64,873	64.1%	1987
*Molyneaux, J H (UU)	29,772	60.8%	-9.2%	29,101	70.0%	UU
Close, S (All)	6,207	12.7%	-1.1%	5,728	13.8%	All
Lewsley, H (SDLP)	4,626	9.4%	+2.5%	2,888	6.9%	SDLP
Coleridge, T (C)	4,423	9.0%	2,656		6.4%	SF
Rice, P (SF)	3,346	6.8%	+0.4%	1,215	2.9%	WP
Lowry, Ms A (WP)	582	1.2%	-1.7%			
UU to All swing 4.0%	48,956		48.1%	41,588		56.2%
		UU maj	23,565		UU maj	23,373

James Molyneaux became ldr of the Ulster Unionist parliamentary party in 1974 and ldr of the Ulster Unionist pty in 1979; leader UUUC, 1974-7. Elected for this seat 1983; resigned it in 1985 in protest at Anglo-Irish agreement and re-elected at 1986 by-election; MP for S Antrim, 1970-83. UU member for S Antrim, N Ireland Assembly, 1982-6. PC 1983. Former partner in family firm of letterpress printers. B Aug 27 1920; ed Aldergrove sch, co Antrim. Dep grand master, orange order and hon PGM of Canada. Sovereign grand master, Commonwealth royal black institution, 1971. Mbr Antrim CC, 1964-73. Vice-pres UU Cl, 1974.

Seamus Close, financial director, contested this seat 1987, 1983 and Fermanagh and S Tyrone by-election 1981. Dep ldr Alliance pty, and spokesman on local govt. Mbr Lisburn DC, 1973- . B Aug 17 1947; ed St Malachy's coll; Belfast coll of business studies. Alliance assembly mbr S Antrim, 1982-6.
Timothy Coleridge, Lloyds underwriting agent; mbr Kensington and Chelsea BC, 1986- ; Kensington Cons assocn management cmte. B 1959; ed Eton; East Anglia univ.
Pat Rice, teacher, contested seat 1987. Lisburn cllr; SF speaker on ed, Irish language and culture.

LANCASHIRE WEST						Lab gain
Electorate % Turnout	77,462	82.6%	1992	76,094	79.7%	1987
Pickthall, C (Lab)	30,128	47.1%	+5.6%	26,500	43.7%	C
*Hind, K H (C)	28,051	43.9%	+0.2%	25,147	41.5%	Lab
Reilly, P (LD)	4,884	7.6%	-7.2%	8,972	14.8%	SDP/All
Pawley, P (Grn)	546	0.9%				
Morris, B (NLP)	336	0.5%				
C to Lab swing 2.7%	63,945		3.2%	60,619		2.2%
		Lab maj	2,077		C maj	1,353

Colin Pickthall, higher ed lecturer in Euro studies, won this seat in 1992; contested it 1987. Mbr Lancashire CC, 1989- . B Sep 13 1944; ed univs of Wales and Lancaster. Former mbr NW regional advisory cmte and Lancashire consultative cmte on higher ed and former chmn governors, Skelmersdale CFE. Early career included working in shipyards. NATFHE.
Kenneth Hind, barrister; MP for seat, 1983-92. PPS to Peter Brooke, Sec of State for N Ireland, 1990-2; to John Cope, Minr of State for Employment and then for N Ireland, 1987-90; and to Lord Trefgarne, Minr of State for

Defence Procurement, 1986-7. Chmn British-Irish environment, ed and culture cmte, and mbr steering cmte, British Irish inter-parly body, 1990-2. Sec Cons backbench legal cmte, 1986-90. Non-exec chmn De Keyser Europe Ltd, 1989- ; non-exec director, Doctus plc, 1990- . B Sep 15 1949; ed Woodhouse Grove sch, Bradford; Leeds univ; Inns of Court Sch of Law.
Peter Reilly, sixth form head teacher. B Dec 12 1945; ed Lancaster univ.

LANCASTER						No change
Electorate % Turnout	58,714	78.8%	1992	57,229	79.2%	1987
*Kellett-Bowman, Dame						
Elaine (C)	21,084	45.6%	-1.1%	21,142	46.7%	C
Henig, Mrs R B (Lab)	18,131	39.2%	+6.8%	14,689	32.4%	Lab
Humberstone, J C (LD)	6,524	14.1%	-5.8%	9,003	19.9%	L/All
Dowding, Ms G (Grn)	433	0.9%	-0.1%	473	1.0%	Grn
Barcis, R (NLP)	83	0.2%				
C to Lab swing 3.9%	46,255		6.4%	45,307		14.2%
		C maj	2,953		C maj	6,453

Dame Elaine Kellett-Bowman, farmer, social worker and barrister, won this seat 1970; contested Buckingham, 1966 and 1964; Norfolk SW, 1959 and 1959 by-election; Nelson and Colne, 1955. Mbr Euro Parliament, 1975-84, being MEP for Cumbria from 1979. B Jul 8 1924; ed Queen Mary's sch, Lytham; The Mount, York; St Anne's coll, Oxford. Alderman, Borough of Camden, 1968-74. Mbr of Lloyd's; press council 1964-8. No 1 Country Housewife, 1960.
Ruth Henig, lecturer in history at Lancaster univ, contested this seat 1979. Mbr Lancashire CC, 1981- (chmn, library, museums and arts cmte, 1985-9); chmn, Lancashire police authority, 1987-; sec/vice-chmn, Lancaster CLP. Vice chmn, Lancashire contract bridge assocn. B Nov 10 1943; ed Wyggestion Girls' GS, Leicester; Bedford coll, London univ. AUT.
John Humberstone, teacher. Mbr NW region LD exec. B Dec 9 1943; ed Hertford GS; Goldsmiths' and Birkbeck coll, London univ. AMMA.

LANGBAURGH						No change from 1987
Electorate % Turnout	79,566	83.1%	1992	79,193	78.8%	1987
Bates, M (C)	30,018	45.4%	+3.7%	26,047	41.7%	C
*Kumar, Dr A (Lab)	28,454	43.1%	+4.7%	23,959	38.4%	Lab
Allen, P J (LD)	7,615	11.5%	-8.4%	12,405	19.9%	L/All
C to Lab swing 0.5%	66,087		2.4%	62,411		3.3%
		C maj	1,564		C maj	2,088

Michael Bates, investment adviser, elected in 1992; contested by-election in 1991 and Tyne Bridge 1987. Consultant to Hogg Insurance Brokers. Pres Gateshead Cons assocn; chmn, Northern area YCs, 1985-7. Mbr Gateshead cl of churches; Newcastle literary and philosophical society. B May 26 1961; ed Heathfield Snr HS, Gateshead; Gateshead tech coll.
Ashok Kumar, snr research scientist formerly employed by British Steel Corporation, gained seat for Lab at 1991 by-election. Vice-chmn Langbaurgh CLP; Middlesbrough District Lab pty; mbr, Middlesbrough BC, 1987- . B May 28 1956; ed Aston univ, Birmingham; Imperial Coll, London univ. Mbr, Steel and Industrial Managers Assocn; Inst of Chemnical Engineering; Inst of Energy. Vice-chmn, Teesside Fabian Society. Sponsored by EETPU.
Peter Allen, univ lecturer, contested 1991 by-election. Former dep chmn, Northern reg LDs. B Oct 14 1959; ed Henry Smith sch, Hartlepool; Brunel univ; Cranfield Sch of Management. AUT, 1991- ; previously NATFHE. Methodist lay preacher.
For details of 1991 by-election, see page 288

LEEDS CENTRAL						No change
Electorate % Turnout	62,058	61.3%	1992	59,019	64.8%	1987
*Fatchett, D J (Lab)	23,673	62.2%	+6.6%	21,270	55.6%	Lab
Holdroyd, Mrs T C (C)	8,653	22.7%	-2.8%	9,765	25.5%	C
Pratt, D (LD)	5,713	15.0%	-2.9%	6,853	17.9%	SDP/All
				355	0.9%	Comm
C to Lab swing 4.7%	38,039		39.5%	38,243		30.1%
		Lab maj	15,020		Lab maj	11,505

Derek Fatchett joined Opposn front bench education team in 1987 as spokesman on secondary and tertiary ed. Dealt with youth affairs from 1988 when he was also in employment team spokesman on training; jt vice-chmn, all-pty parly youth affairs lobby; Opposn whip 1986-7, being then appointed dep campaigns co-ordinator. Elected in 1983; contested Bosworth, 1979. Lecturer in industrial relations, Leeds univ, 1971-83; chmn, PLP ed, science and arts cmte, 1985-6. B Aug 22 1945; ed Lincoln sch; Birmingham univ; LSE. Mbr, Wakefield MDC, 1980-4. Sponsored by MSF.
Tessa Holdroyd, director of employment training scheme; sales director, radio and TV company; mbr nat bd, YMCAs; cmte mbr Y Care International. Contested Leeds South and Morley 1987. Mbr parly sub-cmte Cons women's nat cmte; Yorkshire area women's GP cmte; patron, Colne Valley Cons assocn. B Jan 10 1939; ed St Andrews, Bedford; Bradford univ.
David Pratt, alarm company central station operator; mbr, Otley TC, 1979-87. Treas Leeds NW Lib assocn, 1982-7; chmn Otley and district YLs, 1978-80. B Dec 25 1957; ed Prince Henry's GS, Otley, W Yorks.

LEEDS EAST				No change		
Electorate % Turnout	61,695	70.0%	1992	61,178	70.2%	1987
Mudie, G (Lab)	24,929	57.7%	+9.0%	20,932	48.7%	Lab
Carmichael, W N (C)	12,232	28.3%	+1.8%	11,406	26.5%	C
Wrigley, P (LD)	6,040	14.0%	-10.8%	10,630	24.7%	L/All
C to Lab swing 3.6%	43,201		29.4%	42,968		22.2%
		Lab maj	12,697		Lab maj	9,526

George Mudie, union official, joined Nupe in 1968; former mbr AEU; former ldr Leeds city cl. Elected in 1992. B Feb 6, 1945; ed local state schs.
Neil Carmichael, farmer; mbr Northumberland CC, 1989- . Chmn Hexham Europe cmte; sec Northern area CPC; mbr exec cmte, Cons gp for Europe. Governor Kirkley Hall coll for agriculture. B Apr 15 1961; ed St Peter's sch, York;

Nottingham univ.
Peter Wrigley, teacher, contested Leeds Central for L/All in 1983; Batley and Morley Feb 1974 and 1970; W Yorkshire in 1989 Euro elections. Teaching with voluntary service overseas in Malawi, 1990-2. B Sep 4 1937; ed Batley GS; London and Bradford univs.

LEEDS NORTH EAST				No change		
Electorate % Turnout	64,372	76.9%	1992	64,631	75.3%	1987
*Kirkhope, T J R (C)	22,462	45.4%	-0.2%	22,196	45.6%	C
Hamilton, F (Lab)	18,218	36.8%	+11.6%	13,777	28.3%	SDP/All
Walmsley, C R (LD)	8,274	16.7%		12,292	25.3%	Lab
Noble, J (Grn)	546	1.1%	+0.2%	416	0.9%	Grn
C to Lab swing 5.9%	49,500		8.6%	48,681		17.3%
		C maj	4,244		C maj	8,419

Timothy Kirkhope was appointed an asst govt whip in 1990; solicitor and former company director. Elected in 1987; contested Darlington 1979 and Durham, Feb 1974. PPS to David Trippier, Minr for Environment and Countryside, 1989-90. Mbr select cmte on statutory instruments, 1987-90; Northumberland CC, 1981-5; Newcastle airport bd, 1982-5; Northern RHA, 1982-6. Jt vice-chmn Cons back-bench legal cmte, 1988-9; jt sec Cons environment cmte, 1988-9; sec all-pty solicitors' parly gp, 1989-90 . B Apr 29 1945; ed Royal GS, Newcastle-upon-Tyne; coll of law, Guildford. Former director Neto Costa (UK) Ltd, McGregor Utilities Ltd and Contact Personnel Ltd. Holder of private pilot's licence.

Fabian Hamilton, graphic designer; managing director of graphic design company; director of wines and spirits firm. Chmn Leeds West CLP, 1987-8, and Wortley branch, 1984-7. Mbr Leeds city cl, 1987- (chmn race equality cmte, 1988-). B Apr 4 1955; ed Brentwood sch, Essex; York univ. Sponsored by GPMU.
Christopher Walmsley, radio producer, contested Derbyshire W 1987 and 1986 by-election; High Peak Oct 1974. Mbr LD fed exec and conference cmte. B Jun 1943; ed St Joseph's coll, Blackpool; Univ coll, London (Pres of Union, 1969-70).
John Noble, student. B Sep 30 1967; ed Sunderland poly; Leeds univ.

LEEDS NORTH WEST				No change		
Electorate % Turnout	69,406	72.8%	1992	68,227	75.7%	1987
*Hampson, Dr K (C)	21,750	43.0%	-0.5%	22,480	43.5%	C
Pearce, Mrs B (LD)	14,079	27.8%	-5.6%	17,279	33.5%	L/All
Egan, Ms S (Lab)	13,782	27.3%	+5.5%	11,210	21.7%	Lab
Webb, D (Grn)	519	1.0%	-0.3%	663	1.3%	Grn
Nowosielski, N (Lib)	427	0.8%				
LD to C swing 2.5%	50,557		15.2%	51,632		10.1%
		C maj	7,671		C maj	5,201

Dr Keith Hampson, mbr select cmte on trade and industry, 1987- . Vice-pres WEA, 1978- , and of assocn of business executives, 1979- . Jt vice-chmn, 1988-9 and jt sec, 1985-8, Cons backbench defence cmte. Consultant to AUT, G.J.W. Ltd and White Young Consulting Gp Ltd; ed adviser to Elydon Ltd, export projects consultants; adviser to United Artists International; Yorkshire and Humberside building employers confed. Elected for this seat 1983; MP for Ripon, 1974-83, and contested 1973 by-election. Mbr education advisory cmte for Unesco, 1980-4. B Aug 14 1943; ed King James I GS, Bishop Auckland; Bristol and

Harvard univs. Lecturer in American history, Edinburgh univ, 1968-74.
Barbara Pearce, director of univ training, research and consultancy unit, contested 1989 Richmond (Yorks) by-election; nat pres, Student LDs, 1989- . B Mar 8 1942; ed Northumberland Heath sec mod sch; Erith GS; Nottingham and Leeds univs. AUT.
Sue Egan, asst to MEP and part-time adult ed tutor; mbr Leeds West CHC. B Sep 22 1954; ed Leeds univ. TGWU.
Dr David Webb, lecturer in computer aided engineering. B Mar 31 1949; ed Portsmouth poly; York univ. NATFHE.

LEEDS SOUTH AND MORLEY						No change
Electorate % Turnout	63,107	72.6%	1992	60,726	71.6%	1987
Gunnell, J (Lab)	23,896	52.2%	+2.6%	21,551	49.6%	Lab
Booth, G R (C)	16,524	36.1%	+1.9%	14,840	34.1%	C
Walmsley, Ms J (LD)	5,062	11.1%	-5.3%	7,099	16.3%	SDP/All
Thurston, R (NLP)	327	0.7%				
C to Lab swing 0.3%	45,809		16.1%	43,490		15.4%
		Lab maj	7,372		Lab maj	6,711

John Gunnell, chmn, Yorkshire and Humberside development assocn since 1981 and North of England regional consortium since 1982. Elected in 1992; contested Leeds NE twice in 1974. Mbr for Hunslet on Leeds city cl, since 1986, chmn, social services since 1990; mbr, West Yorkshire Met CC 1976-86, cl ldr, 1981-86, and spoke for met cty cls in their campaign against abolition, 1983-5. Taught in Leeds univ and at UN International sch, New York. B Oct 1 1933; ed King Edward's Sch, Birmingham; Leeds univ. Mbr, Audit Commission, 1983-90; Leeds Development Corporation, since 1988; Leeds Healthcare, 1990. Vice-chmn, Yorkshire Enterprise Ltd, since 1990

(chmn, 1982-90). Chmn, W Yorkshire Met Lab Pty, 1986-90. Director, Opera North, since 1982; Leeds Theatre Trust, since 1986. GMB.

George Booth, in partnership with wife, manufacturing floral giftware. Electrical engineer. Mbr, Scarborough DC, 1987; vice-chmn, Scarborough and Whitby Cons Assocn and York Cons Euro constituency cl. B Oct 8 1947; ed Elland GS, W Yorkshire; Huddersfield tech coll. Chmn, steering cmte, Nat Assocn of Village Shopkeepers.

Joan Walmsley, public relations consultant. B Apr 12 1943; ed Notre Dame HS, Liverpool; Liverpool univ; Manchester Poly.

LEEDS WEST						No change
Electorate % Turnout	67,084	71.1%	1992	66,344	73.3%	1987
*Battle, J D (Lab)	26,310	55.1%	+11.9%	21,032	43.2%	Lab
Bartlett, P (C)	12,482	26.2%	+3.0%	16,340	33.6%	L/All
Howard, G (LD)	4,252	8.9%	-24.7%	11,276	23.2%	C
Meadowcroft, M (Lib)	3,980	8.3%				
Mander, Miss A M (Grn)	569	1.2%				
Tenny, R (NF)	132	0.3%				
C to Lab swing 4.5%	47,725		29.0%	48,648		9.6%
		Lab maj	13,828		Lab maj	4,692

John Battle, nat co-ordinator for Church Action on Poverty, 1983-87, won this seat 1987; contested Leeds NW 1983. Chmn, PLP Treasury and Civil Service cmte, since 1991; chmn 1989-91 and vice-chmn since 1991. Chmn, PLP social security cmte, since 1989; jt vice-chmn, PLP health and social security cmte, 1987-9; campaign officer, Yorkshire gp of Lab MPs, 1989-90. Mbr, select cmte on environment, since 1991; Lab whip, 1988-90. Jt vice-chmn, all-pty charity laws parly panel; human rights gp; treas, overseas development gp. B Apr 26 1951; ed St Michael's Coll, Kirkby Lonsdale; Leeds univ. MSF.

Paul Bartlett, administrator employed by British Stan-

dards Institution, Milton Keynes; Euro information officer, Cons offices, Leeds, 1983-84. Mbr, Milton Keynes BC. B Feb 17 1961; ed Cardinal Wiseman boys' sch, Coventry; Solihull coll of tech; Hull univ.

Michael Meadowcroft was L/All MP for this seat, 1983-87; contested it, Feb and Oct 1974. Spokesman on housing and local govt in 1987 Alliance election team. In 1988 refused to join LDs and remained L. Mbr, Select Cmte on MPs Interests, 1986-7. Writer and journalist. B Mar 6 1942; ed King George V Sch, Southport; Bradford Univ.

Alison Mander, training officer. B Oct 25 1964; ed Leeds univ.

LEICESTER EAST						No change
Electorate % Turnout	63,434	78.4%	1992	66,372	78.6%	1987
*Vaz, N K A S (Lab)	28,123	56.5%	+10.4%	24,074	46.2%	Lab
Stevens, J C (C)	16,807	33.8%	-8.7%	22,150	42.5%	C
Mitchell, Mrs S A (LD)	4,043	8.1%	-3.2%	5,935	11.4%	SDP/All
Frankland, M (Grn)	453	0.9%				
Taylor, D (Homeland)	308	0.6%				
C to Lab swing 9.5%	49,734		22.8%	52,159		3.7%
		Lab maj	11,316		Lab maj	1,924

Keith Vaz won this seat 1987. Mbr, home affairs select cmte; jt vice-chmn, PLP ed, science and arts cmte, 1990-91; sec, all-pty Indo-British parly gp, since 1987; chmn, since 1990 and sec, 1987-90, all-pty footwear and leather industries parly and PLP wool and textiles gps. Contested Richmond and Barnes 1983; Surrey W, 1984 Euro elections. Solicitor. B Nov 26 1956; ed St Joseph's Convent, Aden; Latymer HS, Hammersmith; Gonville and Caius Coll, Cambridge; Coll of Law, Lancaster Gate. Chmn, PLP legal services gp; mbr, nat advisory cmte, Crime Concern, since 1989. Patron, Gingerbread, 1990; Pres, overseas

cricket club, Leicestershire. Sponsored, Nupe.

Jeff Stevens, solicitor, snr partner of firm, has served on Cons nat local govt advisory cmte. Mbr, Uttlesford DC, 1983-90; cl ldr; housing chmn. Pty offices include eastern area exec cmte; cmte, Saffron Walden constituency assocn and Saffron Walden town branch. Chmn, Cons eastern area social affairs forum. B Aug 6 1947; ed Friends Sch, Saffron Walden; City of London Coll.

Sheila Mitchell, teacher; chmn, Leicestershire foster care assocn; mbr, Leicester city cl, 1987-91. B Jul 28 1942; ed Ashford GS; Bristol Baptist Coll, Bristol univ.

LEICESTER SOUTH						No change
Electorate % Turnout	71,120	75.1%	1992	73,236	77.0%	1987
*Marshall, J (Lab)	27,934	52.3%	+8.1%	24,901	44.2%	Lab
Dutt, Dr M (C)	18,494	34.6%	-6.2%	23,024	40.8%	C
Crumbie, Mrs A (LD)	6,271	11.7%	-2.0%	7,773	13.8%	L/All
John, M (Grn)	554	1.0%	+0.3%	390	0.7%	Grn
Saunders, Ms P (NLP)	154	0.3%		192	0.3%	Ind Lab
				96	0.2%	WRP
C to Lab swing 7.2%	53,407		17.7%	56,376		3.3%
		Lab maj	9,440		Lab maj	1,877

James Marshall was appointed an Opposn spokesman on N Ireland in 1987; an Opposn spokesman on home affairs, 1982-3; an assistant govt whip, 1977-9. Mbr British-Irish inter-parly body. MP for this seat, Oct 1974-83, regained it in 1987; contested seat Feb 1974; Harborough, 1970. Lecturer. B Mar 13 1941; ed Sheffield city GS; Leeds univ. Mbr Leeds city cl, 1965-8; Leicester city cl, 1971-6 (ldr, 1974). Sponsored by GPMU.
Dr Michael Dutt, consultant physician, contested Strath-

clyde E in 1989 Euro elections. Mbr Westminster city cl, 1986-90 (housing cmte chmn, 1988-90). Pty ward chmn. B Apr 11 1951; ed John Lyon Sch, Harrow; King's Coll and St George's hosp medical sch, London. Mbr royal coll of physicians, since 1976. BMA.
Anne Crumbie, retired medical aid director, British Red Cross; former Samaritans director. Mbr Leics CC, 1985- ; Leics BC, 1987-91. B Jul 12 1927; ed Sowerby Bridge sec sch; Manchester univ.

LEICESTER WEST						No change
Electorate % Turnout	65,510	73.7%	1992	67,829	73.4%	1987
*Janner, G E (Lab)	22,574	46.8%	+2.3%	22,156	44.5%	Lab
Guthrie, J A (C)	18,596	38.5%	-3.5%	20,955	42.1%	C
Walker, G F (LD)	6,402	13.3%	-0.2%	6,708	13.5%	SDP/All
Wintram, Ms C (Grn)	517	1.1%				
Rosta, Ms J (NLP)	171	0.4%				
C to Lab swing 2.9%	48,260		8.2%	49,819		2.4%
		Lab maj	3,978		Lab maj	1,201

Greville Janner, QC, writer, journalist and company director. Mbr select cmte on employment, 1983- . Non-exec director, Ladbroke plc, 1986- ; director, JSB Gp, 1989- . Elected for this seat 1974; MP for Leicester NW, 1970-4; contested Wimbledon, 1955. B Jul 11 1928; ed Bishop's coll sch, Quebec; St Paul's sch, London; Trinity Hall, Cambridge; Harvard law sch. Pres bd of deputies of British Jews, 1979-85; Commonwealth Jewish cl, 1983- ; Jewish museum, 1985- ; hon vice-pres and mbr world exec, World Jewish congress, 1986- . Chmn all-pty parly industrial safety gp, 1975- ; jt sec interparly cl against anti-Semitism; war crimes gp, 1987- ; race and community parly panel; jt vice-chmn parly cmte for release of Soviet Jewry, 1971- ;

British-Israel gp, 1983- . Chmn holocaust ed trust, 1987- . Mbr magic circle. NUJ; NUM (Leics).
John Guthrie worked for Cadbury Schweppes and then Grand Metropolitan in personnel management. Chmn Tory reform gp, 1988-91; vice-chmn Bedfordshire SW Cons assocn, 1989; mbr exec Harrow West Cons assocn, 1985-7; nat union exec and general purposes cmtes, 1982-5; nat chmn YCs, 1984-5. B Oct 21 1957; ed Denbigh HS, Luton; Luton sixth form coll; Leicester univ (chmn univ Cons assocn, 1977).
Geoff Walker, teacher, is chmn, Leicester LDs; mbr Leicester city cl, 1987- . B May 14 1950; ed Shenfield tech HS; Northern counties coll, Newcastle univ. NAS/UWT.

LEICESTERSHIRE NORTH WEST						No change
Electorate % Turnout	72,414	86.1%	1992	70,633	82.9%	1987
*Ashby, D G (C)	28,379	45.5%	-2.1%	27,872	47.6%	C
Taylor, D L (Lab)	27,400	43.9%	+9.7%	20,044	34.3%	Lab
Beckett, J W R (LD)	6,353	10.2%	-7.0%	10,034	17.1%	L/All
Fawcett, J (NLP)	229	0.4%		570	1.0%	Grn
C to Lab swing 5.9%	62,361		1.6%	58,520		13.4%
		C maj	979		C maj	7,828

David Ashby, barrister, mbr of Lloyd's and company chmn, was elected in 1983. Mbr select cmte on home affairs, 1987- ; select cmte on parly commissioner for administration, 1983-90; jt select cmte on consolidation bills, 1983- . Vice-chmn, 1989-91 and 1987-8, Cons backbench legal cmte; vice-chmn 1989- , and sec 1987-9, Cons food and drinks sub-cmte. Mbr cl justice; chmn cmte of refugee cl. Chmn Drimont Ltd and subsidiaries. B May 14 1940; ed Royal GS, High Wycombe; Bristol univ. Sec all-pty civil liberties gp. Mbr Hammersmith BC, 1968-71; GLC,

1977-81; ILEA, 1977-81.
David Taylor, freelance accountant and computer manager; chmn CLP; mbr Leicestershire DC, 1981-7; Heather PC, 1987- . B Aug 22 1946; ed Ashby-de-la-Zouch GS; Coventry poly; Open univ. Nalgo, 1963- .
Jeremy Beckett, guest house/restaurant proprietor; freelance photographer; former teacher (nat chmn, PAT, 1979-82). Mbr Cromford PC; press officer, E Midlands LD region. B Apr 14 1952; ed King Edward VI GS, Bury St Edmunds; Dudley GS; St Paul's coll of ed, Cheltenham.

LEIGH						No change
Electorate % Turnout	70,064	75.0%	1992	69,155	74.1%	1987
*Cunliffe, L F (Lab)	32,225	61.3%	+2.7%	30,064	58.6%	Lab
Egerton, J R S (C)	13,398	25.5%	-0.8%	13,458	26.3%	C
Bleakley, R (LD)	6,621	12.6%	-2.5%	7,745	15.1%	SDP/All
Tayler, A (NLP)	320	0.6%				
C to Lab swing 1.7%	52,564		35.8%	51,267		32.4%
		Lab maj	18,827		Lab maj	16,606

Lawrence Cunliffe, an Opposn whip and mbr of nat exec NUM, was elected in 1979; contested Rochdale, Oct 1972 and Feb 1974. Mbr, exec cmte, UK branch, CPA, 1989- . Adviser, Club Institute Union. Jt chmn, all-pty parly minerals parly gp; non-profit making clubs gp; treas, Rugby League parly gp. B Mar 25 1929; ed St Edmund's RC school, Worsley, Manchester. Engineer with NCB, 1949-79. Mbr, Farnworth BC, 1960-74; Bolton MDC, 1974-9. Sponsored by NUM; chmn, miners' parly panel.
Joe Egerton runs corporate strategy consulting service;

former head of strategy services, Spicer and Oppenheim consulting gp. Research director, Hughended Foundation, 1985-7; Nato Research Fellow, 1984-5. B Apr 22 1952; ed Stonyhurst Coll; Merton Coll, Oxford. Economics director, Assocn of British Chambers of Commerce, 1977-82.
Robert Bleakley, administration asst, UCD, Ocean Estate, Trafford Park, Manchester. Vice-chmn, Leigh LDs; sec, Wigan area LDs; mbr, LD arts working gp. B Sep 20 1970; ed Fred Longworth HS, Tyldesley; St Johns Coll, Manchester.

LEOMINSTER						No change
Electorate % Turnout	70,873	81.7%	1992	69,977	77.5%	1987
*Temple-Morris, P (C)	32,783	56.6%	-1.2%	31,396	57.9%	C
Short, D (LD)	16,103	27.8%	-4.1%	17,321	31.9%	L/All
Chappell, C (Lab)	6,874	11.9%	+3.7%	4,444	8.2%	Lab
Norman, Ms F M (Grn)	1,503	2.6%	+0.6%	1,102	2.0%	Grn
Carlise, Capt E (Anti-Fed)	640	1.1%				
LD to C swing 1.4%	57,903		28.8%	54,263		25.9%
		C maj	16,680		C maj	14,075

Peter Temple-Morris, barrister, solicitor (admitted 1989), was elected jt vice-chmn, Cons back-bench Euro affairs cmte, in 1991. Mbr, select cmtes on Consolidation Bills, 1991- ; Foreign Affairs, 1987-90; Agriculture, 1982-3. UK chmn, British-Irish inter-parly body, 1988- ; jt chmn, all-pty release of hostages parly gp; jt vice-chmn (1982-90) and jt sec (1979-82), Cons back-bench foreign affairs cmte; jt vice-chmn, Cons N Ireland cmte, 1989- . Mbr, exec cmte, Society of Cons Lawyers, 1968-71, 1990- . Nat treas, UN Assocn (UK), 1987- . Mbr, exec, British Gp, IPU, 1977- (chmn, 1982-5). Elected in Feb 1974; contested Lambeth, Norwood, 1970; Newport, 1964 and 1966. B Feb 12 1938; ed Malvern Coll (governor, 1975- , and cl mbr,

1978-); St Catherine's Coll, Cambridge. Freeman, City of London; Liveryman, Basketmakers' Co.
Chris Chappell, a coordinator for Dial-a-Ride, contested seat 1987; mbr, Hereford employment creation project; Hereford and Dist Trades Cl. B Sep 19 1948; ed local schs; Hampshire Coll of Ag, Winchester. TGWU.
Felicity Norman, teacher, contested Hereford and Worcester in 1989 and 1984 Euro elections, and this seat in 1987 and 1983 gen elections. Mbr, Leominster DC. Convenor, Grn Pty elections cmte; W Midlands rep on pty cl. B July 27 1946; ed St Margaret's and St Helen's, Hastings; Univ Coll, London. NUT.

LEWES						No change
Electorate % Turnout	73,918	81.8%	1992	73,181	77.0%	1987
*Rathbone, J R (C)	33,042	54.6%	-2.2%	32,016	56.8%	C
Baker, N J (LD)	20,867	34.5%	+1.9%	18,396	32.6%	L/All
Chapman, Ms A (Lab)	5,758	9.5%	+0.7%	4,973	8.8%	Lab
Beaumont, A (Grn)	719	1.2%	-0.5%	970	1.7%	Grn
Clinch, N (NLP)	87	0.1%				
C to LD swing 2.0%	60,473		20.1%	56,355		24.2%
		C maj	12,175		C maj	13,620

John R (Tim) Rathbone was elected in Feb 1974. Mbr, Select Cmte on Sound Broadcasting, 1983-7. Chmn (1987-) and founding mbr (1984), all-pty cmte on drug misuse; consultant to Seeboard. B Mar 17 1933; ed Eton; Christ Church, Oxford; Harvard Business Sch. Chmn, advisory cmte, Inst of Management Resources, 1987- . Director, Charles Barker Gp Ltd, 1968-87; cl mbr, Nat Cmte for Electoral Reform. Mbr, delegation to Cl of Europe and WEU, 1987- . PPS to Minr for Health, 1979-82; to Minr of

Consumer Affairs, 1982-3; and to Minr for the Arts and Civil Service, 1985. FRSA.
Norman Baker is LD environment campaigner based in Commons and MP's researcher. Mbr, Lewes DC, 1987- (LD gp ldr); East Sussex CC, 1989- ; Beddingham PC, 1987- . B Jul 26 1957; ed Royal Liberty Sch, Gidea Park; Royal Holloway Coll, London univ.
Alison Chapman, research Fellow. B Jan 17 1943; ed Queen's Sch, Chester; London univ.

LEWISHAM EAST							Lab gain
Electorate % Turnout	57,674	74.8%		1992	59,627	73.9%	1987
Prentice, Mrs B T (Lab)	19,576	45.4%	+11.2%		19,873	45.1%	C
*Moynihan, C B (C)	18,481	42.8%	-2.3%		15,059	34.2%	Lab
Hawkins, J (LD)	4,877	11.3%	-9.4%		9,118	20.7%	SDP/All
Mansour, Ms G (NLP)	196	0.5%					
C to Lab swing 6.7%	43,130			2.5%	44,050		10.9%
		Lab maj	1,095			C maj	4,814

Bridget Prentice, teacher, won this seat in 1992; mbr Hammersmith and Fulham BC, 1986-; contested Croydon Central 1987. Chmn Fulham LP, 1982-5. B Dec 28 1952; ed Our Lady and St Francis sch, Glasgow; Glasgow and London univs; Sth Bank poly. Mbr of and sponsored by GMB; NUT. Mbr Lab women's network; women's legal defence fund; Lab campaign for criminal justice.
Colin Moynihan was Under Sec of State for Energy 1990-2; Minr for Sport with rank of Under Sec of State for Environment, 1987-90. MP for this seat 1983-92. PPS to Kenneth Clarke as Minr for Health and then for Employment, 1985-7. Mbr sports cl 1982-5. Vice-chmn

Ridgways tea and coffee merchants, 1983-6, and its chief exec, 1982-3; director of other companies until 1987; external consultant, Tate and Lyle plc, 1983-7. B Sep 13 1955; ed Monmouth sch; Univ coll, Oxford. Sec friends of the British cl, 1985-. Oxford double blue, rowing and boxing, 1976 and 1977. Won world gold medal for lightweight rowing, 1978; Olympic silver medal for rowing, 1980; world silver medal for rowing, 1981. Steward, British boxing bd of control, 1979-87. Freeman, City of London; Liveryman, Worshipful Co of Haberdashers.
Julian Hawkins, computer consultant; mbr Lewisham BC, 1990-. B Jan 21 1958; ed Cambridge.

LEWISHAM WEST							Lab gain
Electorate % Turnout	59,317	73.1%		1992	62,923	72.3%	1987
Dowd, J P (Lab)	20,378	47.0%	+9.1%		20,995	46.2%	C
*Maples, J C (C)	18,569	42.8%	-3.4%		17,223	37.9%	Lab
Neale, Ms E (LD)	4,295	9.9%	-6.0%		7,247	15.9%	L/All
Coulam, P (Anti-Fed)	125	0.3%					
C to Lab swing 6.2%	43,367			4.2%	45,465		8.3%
		Lab maj	1,809			C maj	3,772

Jim Dowd, telecommunications systems engineer, won this seat in 1992; contested it 1987 and Beckenham 1983. Mbr Lewisham BC, 1974-; dep mayor, 1987-; chmn finance cmte. B Mar 5 1951; ed Sedgehill comprehensive sch, London; London nautical sch. MSF; Co-op pty.
John Maples, lawyer and businessman, was Economic Sec to the Treasury, 1990-92. MP for this seat, 1983-92. PPS to Norman Lamont, Financial Sec and then Chief Sec to

the Treasury, 1987-90. B Apr 22 1943; ed Marlborough coll, Wiltshire; Downing coll, Cambridge univ; Harvard business sch. Director, SEP Industrial Holdings plc, 1989-90; former consultant to Alexander Stenhouse Gp.
Eileen Neale, lecturer in business ed; chmn campaigns cmte, Women LDs; fed rep, Dulwich branch. Ed Birmingham coll of commerce; Wolverhampton poly. NATFHE.

LEWISHAM, DEPTFORD							No change
Electorate % Turnout	57,014	65.1%		1992	58,151	64.9%	1987
*Ruddock, Mrs J M (Lab)	22,574	60.9%	+11.3%		18,724	49.6%	Lab
O'Neill, Miss T A J (C)	10,336	27.9%	-3.8%		11,953	31.7%	C
Brightwell, Ms J C (LD)	4,181	11.3%	-6.0%		6,513	17.2%	SDP/All
					568	1.5%	Grn
C to Lab swing 7.5%	37,091			33.0%	37,758		17.9%
		Lab maj	12,238			Lab maj	6,771

Joan Ruddock became an Opposn front bench transport spokesman in 1989. Elected 1987; contested Newbury 1979. Vice-chmn PLP defence cmte, 1987-9; jt vice-chmn, London gp of Lab MPs, 1987-. Mbr select cmte on televising Commons, 1988-91. Chmn, CND, 1981-85; a vice-chmn, 1985-86. Organiser, Reading Citizens Advice Bureau, 1979-86; Manpower Services Commission special programmes officer dealing with unemployed young people, 1977-79; director, Oxford Housing Aid Centre, 1973-77; with Shelter, 1968-73. B Dec 28 1943; ed

Pontypool GS for Girls; Imperial Coll, London univ. Sponsored by TGWU.
Teresa O'Neill, stockbroker clerk, was an officer and ward chmn in Lewisham East constituency; active within tenants movement; borough cl election candidate 1986 and 1990. B Jul 18 1961; ed St Theresa's RC Girls' Sch, Lewisham.
Johanna Brightwell, mother; pty press officer for Lewisham borough. B May 20 1964; ed Bristol and Leeds univs. C of E PCC and diocesan synod mbr.

LEYTON						No change
Electorate % Turnout	57,271	67.4%	1992	57,662	69.6%	1987
*Cohen, H M (Lab)	20,334	52.7%	+11.5%	16,536	41.2%	Lab
Smith, Miss C (C)	8,850	22.9%	-6.2%	11,895	29.6%	L/All
Fryer, J H (LD)	8,180	21.2%	-8.5%	11,692	29.1%	C
de Pinna, L (Lib)	561	1.5%				
Pervez, K (Grn)	412	1.1%				
Archer, R (NLP)	256	0.7%				
C to Lab swing 8.8%	38,593		29.8%	40,123		11.6%
		Lab maj	11,484		Lab maj	4,641

Harry Cohen was elected in 1983. Chmn PLP defence cmte in 1987- (jt vice-chmn, 1986-7); vice-chmn PLP Treasury and civil service cmte 1987-8; chmn Lab Friends of Palestine 1987-90. Accountant and local govt employee. B Dec 10 1949; ed secondary mod sch; part-time further ed. Mbr Waltham Forest BC 1972-84. Nalgo.
Christine Smith, company sec and administrator of car dealers; previously PA to director of sales of fashion menswear manufacturers. Press officer Leyton Cons Assocn 1986- , and dep chmn. Mbr Waltham Forest BC. B Jan 6 1952; ed Leyton Manor Sec Mod Sch.
Jonathan Fryer, writer and broadcaster, contested Orpington 1987; Chelsea 1983, and London SE in 1984 and 1979 Euro elections. Chmn Lib International (British gp) 1989- ; LD working pty on sustainable development; mbr Fed policy cmte 1989- . B Jun 5 1950; ed Manchester GS; St Edmund Hall, Oxford. Mbr Bromley BC 1986-90.
Khalid Pervez, management consultant. B Aug 20 1950; ed Panjab Univ, Lahore; London Sch of Accountancy; Financial Training Centre, Jersey.

LINCOLN						No change
Electorate % Turnout	78,905	79.2%	1992	77,049	75.6%	1987
*Carlisle, K M (C)	28,792	46.1%	-0.4%	27,097	46.5%	C
Butler, N J (Lab)	26,743	42.8%	+9.2%	19,614	33.7%	Lab
Harding-Price, D (LD)	6,316	10.1%	-9.3%	11,319	19.4%	SDP/All
Wiggin, Ms S (Lib)	603	1.0%		232	0.4%	RRPRC
C to Lab swing 4.8%	62,454		3.3%	58,262		12.8%
		C maj	2,049		C maj	7,483

Kenneth Carlisle was appointed under sec for transport 1992; under sec for defence 1990-2; a Lord Commissioner of the Treasury (govt whip), 1988-90; an asst govt whip 1987-8. Barrister, mbr of Lloyd's and farmer. PPS to Douglas Hurd 1983-7. Elected in 1979. Mbr select cmte Euro legislation 1981-2; on trade and industry 1980-2. B Mar 25 1941; ed Harrow; Magdalen Coll, Oxford. NFU.
Nick Butler, economist, contested this seat 1987. Chmn Fabian Society 1987-8. Chmn Streatham CLP 1981-2; ASTMS Westminster branch 1984-5 and 1987-9. B Nov 22 1954; ed Blackpool GS; Trinity Coll, Cambridge.
David Harding-Price, clinical nurse specialising in drug misuse; chmn under-16s working pty of northern drug services childcare gp. B Sep 7 1956; ed Lincoln GS; Cambridge Sch of Nursing; Manchester Poly. Chmn Grimsby branch and Yorkshire co-ordinating cmte RCN.

LINDSEY EAST						No change
Electorate % Turnout	80,026	78.1%	1992	74,027	75.2%	1987
*Tapsell, Sir Peter (C)	31,916	51.1%	-1.1%	29,048	52.2%	C
Dodsworth, J (LD)	20,070	32.1%	-4.6%	20,432	36.7%	L/All
Shepherd, D G (Lab)	9,477	15.2%	+4.0%	6,206	11.1%	Lab
Robinson, Ms R (Grn)	1,018	1.6%				
LD to C swing 1.7%	62,481		19.0%	55,686		15.5%
		C maj	11,846		C maj	8,616

Sir Peter Tapsell, mbr of London Stock Exchange, 1957- ; cl mbr, Inst of Fiscal Studies. Long-time adviser to Third World central banks; international adviser to Mitsubishi Trust Bank and to Nissho Iwai Trading Co; consultant to Nikko Securities Co. Hon vice-chmn Mitsubishi Trust Oxford Foundation, 1988- . Elected for this seat 1983; MP for Horncastle, 1966-83; for Nottingham W, 1959-64; contested Wednesbury, 1957. A Cons spokesman on Treasury and economic affairs, 1977-8 and on foreign and Commonwealth affairs, 1976-7. B Feb 1 1930; ed Tonbridge Sch; Merton Coll, Oxford (Hon Fellow, 1989). Librarian, Oxford Union, 1953; trustee, 1985- .
Jim Dodsworth, director of farming company. Mbr Lincolnshire CC 1981- (gp spokesman on planning); Burgh le Marsh PC 1979- . Chmn local NFU; local Methodist preacher; district vice-pres and local pres of the Scouts. B Nov 21 1932.
Dave Shepherd, factory shopfloor worker and GMB shop steward; branch sec and mbr regional cl; constituency trade union officer. Mbr Louth TC 1985- . B Oct 5 1956; ed Monks Dyke HS, Louth.
Rosemary Robinson, co-ordinator for community opportunities. Chmn Louth and District Grn pty. Mbr Donington-on-Bain PC 1982- . B Jun 11 1954; ed Coventry Poly.

LINLITHGOW						No change
Electorate % Turnout	61,082	78.7%	1992	59,542	77.6%	1987
*Dalyell, T (Lab)	21,603	45.0%	-2.4%	21,869	47.3%	Lab
MacAskill, K W (SNP)	14,577	30.3%	+5.4%	11,496	24.9%	SNP
Forbes, Miss E (C)	8,424	17.5%	+2.7%	6,828	14.8%	C
Falchikov, M G (LD)	3,446	7.2%	-5.5%	5,840	12.6%	SDP/All
				154	0.3%	Comm
Lab to SNP swing 3.9%	48,050		14.6%	46,187		22.5%
		Lab maj	7,026		Lab maj	10,373

Tam Dalyell was mbr Lab Pty NEC 1986-7. Jt vice-pres parly and scientific cmte; Opposn spokesman on science 1980-2. Elected for this seat 1983; MP for W Lothian 1962-83; contested Roxburgh, Selkirk and Peebles, 1959. Teacher and author; political columnist *New Scientist*, 1967- . B Aug 9 1932; ed Edinburgh Acad; Eton; King's coll, Cambridge; Moray House teachers' training coll, Edinburgh. MEP 1975-9. PPS to late Richard Crossman, 1964-70. Mbr cl Nat Trust for Scotland. Sponsored by RMT.
Kenneth MacAskill, lawyer, contested Livingston in 1987 and 1983 and Scotland Mid and Fife in 1989 Euro

elections. Mbr SNP nat exec since 1984, being SNP vice-convenor for policy. B Apr 28 1958; ed Linlithgow acad; Edinburgh univ.
Elizabeth Forbes, director of Northern Corporate Communications Ltd, Edinburgh, 1987- . Former foreign office employee, 1968-82. Vice-chmn Tory reform gp. B Aug 24 1946; ed Rosemead sch, Littlehampton; Edinburgh univ.
Mike Falchikov, snr lecturer in Russian, Edinburgh univ. Held office in Edinburgh S Libs and LDs; former election agent and on pty policy panels. B May 26 1937; ed Welwyn Garden City GS; Oriel coll, Oxford. AUT; Scottish civil liberties, Charter '88.

LITTLEBOROUGH AND SADDLEWORTH						No change
Electorate % Turnout	65,576	81.6%	1992	66,074	77.4%	1987
*Dickens, G K (C)	23,682	44.2%	+1.2%	22,027	43.1%	C
Davies, C (LD)	19,188	35.9%	+4.9%	15,825	30.9%	L/All
Brett, A J (Lab)	10,649	19.9%	-6.1%	13,299	26.0%	Lab
C to LD swing 1.9%	53,519		8.4%	51,151		12.1%
		C maj	4,494		C maj	6,202

Geoffrey Dickens was elected for this seat in 1983; MP for Huddersfield W, 1979-83; contested Ealing N, Oct 1974, and Teesside, Middlesbrough, Feb 1974. Mbr select cmte on energy 1985- . Non-exec director, Cunnington and Cooper Ltd; Nuclear and General Engineering Ltd, 1990- ; FEL Ltd. Parly consultant, Newhall Publications Ltd, Childwatch (Child Protection). B Aug 26 1931; ed Harrow; Acton Tech Coll. Treas all-pty pre-1973 war widows gp; mbr all-pty pensioners parly gp; all-pty childrens parly gp; campaigner for child protection. Holder of royal humane soc testimonial on vellum for having saved the lives of

children at sea.
Chris Davies, marketing consultant, contested this seat 1987. Mbr Liverpool city cl 1980-4 (chmn housing cmte 1981-3). B Jul 7 1954; ed Cheadle Hulme sch, Stockport; Cambridge univ.
Allen Brett, planning and leisure consultant; director, Gtr Manchester buses; part-time lecturer. Manchester area organiser, Co-op Pty. Mbr Gtr Manchester CC 1981-6; Rochdale MBC 1986-90. Euro agent in Lancs E 1984 and 1989. B Apl 29 1946; ed St Mary's coll; De la Salle coll of ed; Manchester univ. GMB; NAS/UWT.

LIVERPOOL, BROADGREEN						No change
Electorate % Turnout	60,080	69.6%	1992	63,091	75.9%	1987
Kennedy, Ms J (Lab)	18,062	43.2%	-5.4%	23,262	48.6%	Lab
Cooper, Ms R (LD)	11,035	26.4%	-9.6%	17,215	35.9%	L/All
*Fields, T (Soc Lab)	5,952	14.2%		7,413	15.5%	C
Roche, Mrs H L (C)	5,405	12.9%	-2.6%			
Radford, S (Lib)	1,211	2.9%				
Brennan, Mrs A (NLP)	149	0.4%				
LD to Lab swing 2.1%	41,814		16.8%	47,890		12.6%
		Lab maj	7,027		Lab maj	6,047

Jane Kennedy was elected for this seat in 1992. Nupe area organiser. Chmn, Oldham district Lab pty. B May 4 1958; ed Haughton comprehensive sch; Queen Elizabeth sixth form coll; Liverpool univ. Mbr Nupe; Ramblers assocn; Youth Hostel Assocn; Belgian shepherd dog assocn.
Rosie Cooper, buyer for Littlewoods chain stores; mbr Liverpool city cl 1973- (pty speaker on housing). Contested

Knowsley North 1987 and 1986 by-election; Liverpool Garston 1983. B Sep 5 1950; ed St Oswald's Jnr Sch; Bellerive convent GS.
Helen Roche, company secretary. Dep chmn Hornsey and Woodgreen Cons assocn 1988-90; chmn nat assocn of Cons graduates 1988-9. B Jun 15 1962; ed Felstead sch; Essex; Exeter Univ (chmn univ Cons assocn 1982-3).

LIVERPOOL, GARSTON						No change
Electorate % Turnout	57,538	70.6%	1992	61,280	75.7%	1987
*Loyden, E (Lab)	23,212	57.1%	+3.6%	24,848	53.6%	Lab
Backhouse, J E (C)	10,933	26.9%	+3.0%	11,071	23.9%	C
Roberts, W (LD)	5,398	13.3%	-9.1%	10,370	22.4%	SDP/All
Conrad, A (Lib)	894	2.2%		98	0.2%	WRP
Chandler, P (NLP)	187	0.5%				
C to Lab swing 0.3%	40,624		30.2%	46,387		29.7%
		Lab maj	12,279		Lab maj	13,777

Edward Loyden, re-elected in 1983; MP for the constituency, Feb 1974-9. Port worker, Mersey Docks and Harbour Co, 1946-74; Merchant Navy 1938-46. B May 3 1923; ed Friary RC elementary sch, Liverpool. Mbr Liverpool city cl 1960-74 and 1980- , dep leader 1983- ; Liverpool DC 1973; Merseyside Met CC 1973; Liverpool MDC 1980-3. Mbr nat exec TGWU 1968- and sponsored by union. Former mbr NUS.
John Backhouse, director of property and financial services company, contested Liverpool, W Derby 1987. Mbr Liverpool city cl 1988- . B Apr 28 1955; ed Merchant Taylor's sch; Kirkby CFE; Liverpool poly. Former treas Liverpool, Mossley Hill Cons assocn; finance officer, Merseyside W Euro constituency.
Bill Roberts, snr asst registrar and personnel officer; mbr Liverpool city cl 1987- ; nat public services standing cmte, inst of personnel management, 1985-91. B Jul 4 1943; ed St David's Coll, Lampeter.

LIVERPOOL, MOSSLEY HILL						No change
Electorate % Turnout	60,409	68.5%	1992	60,954	75.1%	1987
*Alton, D P P (LD)	19,809	47.9%	+4.2%	20,012	43.7%	L/All
Bann, N S (Lab)	17,203	41.6%	+2.7%	17,786	38.8%	Lab
Syder, S A (C)	4,269	10.3%	-7.2%	8,005	17.5%	C
Rigby, B (NLP)	114	0.3%				
Lab to LD swing 0.7%	41,395		6.3%	45,803		4.9%
		LD maj	2,606		L/All maj	2,226

David Alton was Lib and then LD spokesman on N Ireland, 1987-8; Alliance spokesman on N Ireland in 1987 election. Lib chief whip 1985-7. Vice-pres Life; co-founder movement for Christian democracy 1990; chmn all-pty Mersey barrage parly gp 1990- ; friends of Croatia gp 1991- ; treas HoC reform gp. Columnist *Catholic Pictorial*, 1982- ; *The Universe*, 1989- . Teacher of handicapped children, 1972-9; author. Elected for this seat 1983 and became LD MP in 1988; won Liverpool, Edge Hill, at Mar 1979 by-election; served for six days and was re-elected in gen election; contested that seat, Feb and Oct 1974. Patron, Jubilee campaign for release of prisoners of conscience, 1986- . B Mar 15 1951; ed Edmund Campion sch,
Hornchurch; Christ's coll of ed, Liverpool. Mbr Liverpool city cl 1972-80; Merseyside CC 1973-7. IoJ.
Neville Bann, lecturer; sec of CLP. Mbr and former full-time official of NATFHE. B Nov 24 1950; ed Lancaster sec mod and Gateway GS, Leicester; Liverpool univ; Edge Hill coll of ed.
Stephen Syder, computer analyst/programmer with business interests in information technology and insurance industry. Former hairdresser, selling business to attend univ. B Jan 30 1956; ed Prescot Boys' GS; Open univ; Liverpool univ (chmn univ Cons assocn 1987). Chmn NW Cons collegiate forum 1987-8; founder and organiser annual Cons conference for Liverpool.

LIVERPOOL, RIVERSIDE						No change
Electorate % Turnout	49,595	54.6%	1992	53,328	65.3%	1987
*Parry, R (Lab)	20,550	75.9%	+2.7%	25,505	73.2%	Lab
Zsigmond, A (C)	3,113	11.5%	-2.3%	4,816	13.8%	C
Akbar Ali, M (LD)	2,498	9.2%	-2.0%	3,912	11.2%	SDP/All
Brown, L (Grn)	738	2.7%		601	1.7%	Comm
Collins, J (NLP)	169	0.6%				
C to Lab swing 2.5%	27,068		64.4%	34,834		59.4%
		Lab maj	17,437		Lab maj	20,689

Robert Parry, former building trade worker and full-time organiser for Nupe, 1960-7, was elected for this seat 1983; MP for Liverpool, Scotland Exchange, Feb 1974-83; Liverpool Exchange, 1970-4. B Jan 8 1933; ed Bishop Goss RC School, Liverpool. Delegate to cl of Europe, 1984- and WEU, 1983- . Mbr standing orders cmte. Chmn Merseyside gp of Lab MPs 1976-87. Mbr Liverpool city cl 1963-74. Pres assocn for democracy in Hong Kong 1980- ; kids in need and distress (KIND) 1981- ; Liverpool and dist Sunday football league 1973- . Patron UNA Hong Kong 1977- . Vice-chmn Liberation 1981- ; Lab action for peace 1983- . Mbr of and sponsored by TGWU.
Dr Andrew Zsigmond, occupational health physician to
General Motors and private medical practitioner. Hon treas Liverpool medical institution; assocn of aviation medical examiners. Commander Merseyside order of St Lazarus of Jerusalem; sec world fed of Hungarian freedom fighters. Ward chmn Mossley Hill constituency. B Nov 17 1935; ed Liverpool univ; royal coll of physicians and surgeons.
Akbar Ali, retired chartered engineer, contested Blackburn for SDP/All 1987. Chmn Mossley Hill LDs 1989- ; Mossley Hill SDP 1987-8. Trustee, past pres Liverpool Muslim society; mbr Liverpool family health service authority. B Sep 15 1925; ed Osmania Univ, Hyderabad; Indian Inst of Science, Bangalore; Manchester univ.

LIVERPOOL, WALTON						No change
Electorate % Turnout	70,102	67.4%	1992	73,118	73.6%	1987
*Kilfoyle, P (Lab)	34,214	72.4%	+8.0%	34,661	64.4%	Lab
Greenwood, B J R (C)	5,915	12.5%	-1.9%	11,408	21.2%	L/All
Lang, J (LD)	5,672	12.0%	-9.2%	7,738	14.4%	C
Newall, T (Lib)	963	2.0%				
Carson, D J E (Prot Ref)	393	0.8%				
Raiano, Ms D (NLP)	98	0.2%				
C to Lab swing 4.9%	47,255		59.9%	53,807		43.2%
		Lab maj	28,299		Lab maj	23,253

Peter Kilfoyle, former Lab pty regional organiser in the North West of England, won the 1991 by-election. Joined staff of Lab pty in 1985; previously building labourer, teacher. Has held many posts within Lab pty and trade union movement. B Jun 9 1946; ed St Edwards Coll, Liverpool; Durham univ; Christ's Coll, Liverpool. MSFU, TGWU and Co-op pty.
Berkeley Greenwood contested the 1991 by-election. Management consultant and political analyst specialising in aviation, the economy and oil, since 1988; in Cons

research dept, 1987-8; series editor and reporter for programme on BBC Radio Merseyside, 1985-7. B Mar 20 1965; ed Shrubbery Sch, Cambridge; Hills Road Sixth Form Coll, Cambridge; Liverpool Univ (chmn univ Cons, 1986-7).
Joe Lang, pensioner; mbr, Liverpool City Cl, 1975-9 and since 1986 (LD gp whip). B Feb 28 1924; ed St Wilfreds RC Sch, Manchester.
Details of 1991 by-election on page 288

LIVERPOOL, WEST DERBY						No change
Electorate % Turnout	56,718	69.8%	1992	60,522	73.4%	1987
*Wareing, R N (Lab)	27,014	68.2%	+2.9%	29,021	65.3%	Lab
Fitzsimmons, S (C)	6,589	16.6%	-2.5%	8,525	19.2%	C
Bundred, Ms G (LD)	4,838	12.2%	-3.3%	6,897	15.5%	SDP/All
Curtis, D (Lib)	1,021	2.6%				
Higgins, C (NLP)	154	0.4%				
C to Lab swing 2.7%	39,616		51.6%	44,443		46.1%
		Lab maj	20,425		Lab maj	20,496

Robert Wareing became an Opposn whip in 1987. Lecturer at various colleges, 1957-83, including Central Liverpool Coll of FE, 1972-83. Elected for this seat 1983; contested Berwick-upon-Tweed, 1970; Liverpool, Edge Hill, 1979 by-election and gen election. Vice-chmn, British/Yugoslav parly gp since 1985; mbr all-pty disablement gp. B Aug 20 1930; ed Ranworth Square Sch, Liverpool; Alsop HS, Liverpool; Bolton Coll of Ed; London univ (external student). Mbr Merseyside CC 1981-6. Vice-pres AMA 1984-. Chmn Merseyside Economic Develop-

ment Co Ltd, 1981-6.
Stephen Fitzsimmons, computer manager, Elmgate Hotels Ltd; former security officer. Contested Liverpool, Riverside 1987. Mbr, Liverpool City Cl since 1988. B Aug 20 1956; ed Hillfoot Hey HS; Millbank Coll of Commerce. Chmn, Merseyside YCs, 1983-85. Chmn Merseyside YCs 1983-5; dep chmn, Riverside Cons Assocn since 1985.
Gillian Bundred, barrister; mbr Liverpool City Cl 1986. B Mar 14 1960; ed Univ Coll, London.

LIVINGSTON						No change
Electorate % Turnout	61,092	74.6%	1992	56,583	74.1%	1987
*Cook, R F (Lab)	20,245	44.4%	-1.2%	19,110	45.6%	Lab
Johnston, P J B (SNP)	12,140	26.6%	+10.0%	8,005	19.1%	L/All
Gordon, H (C)	8,824	19.4%	+0.6%	7,860	18.7%	C
Mackintosh, H F D (LD)	3,911	8.6%	-10.5%	6,969	16.6%	SNP
Ross-Smith, A (Grn)	469	1.0%				
Lab to SNP swing 5.6%	45,589		17.8%	41,944		26.5%
		Lab maj	8,105		Lab maj	11,105

Robin Cook became chief Opposn spokesman on health in 1989; chief spokesman on health and social security from 1987 to 1989. Member of shadow cabinet 1983-6, and since 1987. Spokesman on European and Community affairs, 1983-5; campaigns coordinator, 1985-6. A trade and industry spokesman, 1986-7; a Treasury and economic affairs spokesman, 1980-3. MP for Edinburgh Central, Feb 1974-83; contested Edinburgh North, 1970. Elected to Lab pty NEC in 1988 the year he was successful organizer of Neil Kinnock's leadership campaign against challenge of Tony Benn. B Feb 28 1946; ed Aberdeen GS; Royal HS, Edinburgh;

Edinburgh univ. Sponsored by RMT.
Peter Johnston, teacher; mbr W Lothian DC since 1985; former convenor Livington SNP. B Mar 10 1952; ed Callendar Park Coll of Ed, Falkirk. EIS.
Hugh Gordon runs own business development and strategic marketing consultancy; director, Cairngorm Chairlift Co; formerly with Ferranti in Edinburgh. B 1942; ed Cargilfield D.Sch, Edinburgh; Eton; St Andrews univ.
Fred Mackintosh, student, Edinburgh univ. Vice-chmn (policy), Scottish YLDs since 1990; mbr Scottish policy cmte since1991. B Feb 21 1970; ed Dulwich Coll, London; Edinburgh univ.

LLANELLI						No change
Electorate % Turnout	65,058	77.8%	1992	63,845	78.1%	1987
*Davies, D J D (Lab)	27,802	54.9%	-4.2%	29,506	59.2%	Lab
Down, G L (C)	8,532	16.9%	-0.3%	8,571	17.2%	C
Phillips, M (PC)	7,878	15.6%	+5.4%	6,714	13.5%	L/All
Evans, K (LD)	6,404	12.7%	-0.8%	5,088	10.2%	PC
Lab to C swing 2.0%	50,616		38.1%	49,879		42.0%
		Lab maj	19,270		Lab maj	20,935

Denzil Davies joined the public accounts cmte in 1991. Mbr shadow cabinet, 1985-8; chief Opposn spokesman on defence and disarmament and arms control, 1983-8, when he resigned; chief spokesman on Wales, 1983; a spokesman on defence 1982-3, on FCO affairs 1981-2, and on Treasury and economic affairs, 1979-81. Minr of State, Treasury, 1975-9. PC 1978. Barrister. Elected in 1970. B Oct 9 1938; ed Carmarthen GS; Pembroke coll, Oxford. Lectured at Chicago and Leeds univs.
Graham Down, accountant, held office in Bridgend Cons assocn; mbr Mid-Glamorgan HA 1986-90. B 1956; ed Bridgend Boys' GS; Brynteg comprehensive sch; Swansea coll of tech; Poly of Wales.
Marc Phillips, director, Dyfed Assocn of voluntary services; PC policy director on health; previously pty speaker on language and culture. B Dec 8 1953; ed Cyfarthfa HS, Merthyr Tydfil.
Keith Evans, economist and freelance writer, contested Bury S 1983. Dep chmn Llanelli constituency LDs; mbr Llanelli BC 1991- (sec, LD gp); Gtr Manchester CC 1981-86. B Apr 1 1956; ed Coleshill sch, Warwickshire; Wolverhampton poly; Univ coll, Swansea.

LONDONDERRY EAST						No change
Electorate % Turnout	75,559	69.8%	1992	71,031	68.7%	1987
*Ross, W (UU)	30,370	57.6%	-2.9%	29,532	60.5%	UU
Doherty, A (SDLP)	11,843	22.5%	+3.3%	9,375	19.2%	SDLP
Davey-Kennedy, Ms P (SF)	5,320	10.1%	-1.1%	5,464	11.2%	SF
McGowan, P (All)	3,613	6.9%	+0.2%	3,237	6.6%	All
Elder, A (C)	1,589	3.0%		935	1.9%	WP
				281	0.6%	Grn
UU to SDLP swing 3.1%	52,735		35.1%	48,824		41.3%
		UU maj	18,527		UU maj	20,157

William Ross, a farmer, was elected for this seat in 1983; MP for Londonderry, Feb 1974-83. Resigned seat in 1985 in protest at Anglo-Irish Agreement and was re-elected in 1986 by-election. UU whip and pty spokesman on Treasury matters; mbr jt cmte and select cmte on statutory instruments, 1991- ; Commons administration cmte, 1991-. Mbr apprentice boys of Derry, the orange and black institutions. B Feb 4 1936; ed Dungiven primary sch. Former mbr Limavady DC.
Arthur Doherty, former teacher, contested this seat 1987 and 1983. Mbr SDLP exec cmte 1974-80, and policy cmte; former chmn assocn of SDLP cllrs. Mbr Limacady BC, 1977- (dep mayor). B Jan 19 1932; ed St Columb's coll, Derry; St Mary's coll of ed, Belfast; Ulster univ.
Pauline Davey-Kennedy, mbr Magherafelt DC, SF speaker on women's issues.
Paddy McGowan, school principal, contested seat 1987. B Nov 2 1941; ed Belfast coll of art; Hornsey coll of art, London. Mbr Coleraine BC, 1981-.

LOUGHBOROUGH						No change
Electorate % Turnout	75,450	78.5%	1992	73,660	79.2%	1987
*Dorrell, S J (C)	30,064	50.7%	-4.0%	31,931	54.7%	C
Reed, A (Lab)	19,181	32.4%	+7.9%	14,283	24.5%	Lab
Stott, A (LD)	8,953	15.1%	-4.6%	11,499	19.7%	SDP/All
Sinclair, I (Grn)	817	1.4%	+0.3%	656	1.1%	Grn
Reynolds, P (NLP)	233	0.4%				
C to Lab swing 5.9%	59,248		18.4%	58,369		30.2%
		C maj	10,883		C maj	17,648

Stephen Dorrell was appointed Financial Secretary, Treasury in 1992. Under Sec of State for Health 1990-2; a Lord Commissioner of the Treasury (govt whip) 1988-90; an asst govt whip 1987-8. Former company director. PPS to Peter Walker, Sec of State for Energy, 1983-7 and personal asst in Feb 1974 election. Won this seat 1979; contested Hull E, Oct 1974. B Mar 25 1952; ed Uppingham; Brasenose coll, Oxford. Mbr select cmte on transport, 1979-83. Mbr bd Christian Aid 1985-7.
Andrew Reed, employment initiatives officer with Leics CC. B Sep 17 1964; ed Longsade community coll; Leicester poly. Nalgo; convenor, planning and transport dept, Leics cty branch, 1990-.
Tony Stott, lecturer at Leicester poly since 1979, is senior lecturer in public administration. Mbr Charnwood BC, 1986- ; Birstall PC, 1987- . B Oct 1930; ed Manchester and McGill univs.
Ian Sinclair, employed at Loughborough Univ, has been a Lab Pty cty treas and Grn Pty agent. District cllr, NW Leics, 1970-74. B Apr 27 1933; ed Kingston upon Thames Tech Coll; Regent St Poly; Loughborough Tech.

LUDLOW							No change
Electorate % Turnout	68,935	80.9%	1992	66,187	77.1%	1987	
*Gill, C J F (C)	28,719	51.5%	-2.4%	27,499	53.9%	C	
Phillips, I D (LD)	14,567	26.1%	-4.8%	15,800	31.0%	L/All	
Mason, Mrs B (Lab)	11,709	21.0%	+5.9%	7,724	15.1%	Lab	
Appleton-Fox, N (Grn)	758	1.4%					
LD to C swing 1.2%	55,753		25.4%	51,023		22.9%	
		C maj	14,152		C maj	11,699	

Christopher Gill, elected in 1987, joined select cmte on agriculture in 1989. Jt vice-chmn Cons backbench Euro affairs cmte 1989-91 (sec, 1988-9); jt vice-chmn 1991- , and sec 1990-1 Cons ag, fish and food backbench cmte; Cons food and drinks sub-cmte, 1989-90. Chmn of family meat processing business, F A Gill Ltd; mbr Wolverhampton BC, 1965-72; cl Wolverhampton chamber of commerce, 1984-7. B Oct 28 1936; ed Shrewsbury sch.

David Phillips, director of Sales Management Ltd, contested this seat for L/All 1987; Worcestershire S, 1983 and 1979, and Hereford and Worcester in 1984 Euro election. Chmn West Midlands LD reg exec. Mbr of and lecturer for electoral reform soc. B Feb 17 1933; ed Waverley GS, Birmingham.

Beryl Mason, administrator; former chmn Wrekin CLP, 1982-4 (vice-chmn 1985-); cty pty sec 1977-86; cty gp sec 1981-9. Mbr Shropshire CC 1973-7 and 1983- ; Lab gp ldr Wellington UDC 1971-4. B Oct 16 1938; ed Tom Hood comprehensive sch, Leytonstone. MSF.

Nic Appleton-Fox, archaeologist. B 1953; ed in Colchester.

LUTON NORTH							No change
Electorate % Turnout	76,857	81.9%	1992	74,235	77.6%	1987	
*Carlisle, J R (C)	33,777	53.7%	-0.2%	30,997	53.8%	C	
McWalter, A (Lab)	20,682	32.9%	+6.1%	15,424	26.8%	Lab	
Jackson, Dr J (LD)	7,569	12.0%	-7.4%	11,166	19.4%	SDP/All	
Jones, R (Grn)	623	1.0%					
Buscombe, K (NLP)	282	0.4%					
C to Lab swing 3.1%	62,933		20.8%	57,587		27.0%	
		C maj	13,095		C maj	15,573	

John Carlisle was elected for this seat in 1983; MP for Luton W 1979-83. Mbr select cmte on agriculture 1985-8. Consultant to Barry Simmons PR Ltd, 1987- ; non-exec director Bletchley Motors Gp plc, 1988- ; mbr all-pty motor industry gp. Mbr London corn exchange 1970-9 and 1987- . B Aug 28 1942; ed Bedford sch; St Lawrence coll, Ramsgate; London univ. Chmn Cons backbench sport cmte 1981-2, 1983-4, 1985- ; vice-chmn all-pty football gp 1987-9; mbr international exec cmte freedom in sport; governor, Sports Aid Foundation (Eastern), 1985- . Chmn 1987- and sec 1983-7, British-S Africa parly gp.

Tony McWalter, lecturer in philosophy and computing, contested St Albans in 1987; Bedfordshire S in 1989 Euro elections and Hertfordshire in 1984 Euro elections. Dist cllr 1979-83; sch governor 1983- . B Mar 20 1945; ed univ coll of Wales, Aberystwyth; McMaster univ, Canada; univ coll, Oxon. NATFHE (branch chmn 1981-90).

Dr Jane Jackson, public health physician, is vice-chmn, LD health assocn; mbr LD health panel. Hon sec medical art society, 1990- . B Feb 15 1933; ed Presbyterian Ladies coll, Perth, W Australia; Wroxall Abbey, Warwickshire; Trinity coll, Dublin; Linacre coll, Oxford; London sch of hygiene and tropical medicine.

LUTON SOUTH							No change
Electorate % Turnout	73,016	79.1%	1992	71,231	75.2%	1987	
*Bright, G F J (C)	25,900	44.8%	-1.4%	24,762	46.2%	C	
McKenzie, W D (Lab)	25,101	43.5%	+6.8%	19,647	36.7%	Lab	
Rogers, D W (LD)	6,020	10.4%	-6.7%	9,146	17.1%	L/All	
Bliss, Ms L (Grn)	550	1.0%					
Cooke, D (NLP)	191	0.3%					
C to Lab swing 4.1%	57,762		1.4%	53,555		9.6%	
		C maj	799		C maj	5,115	

Graham Bright was appointed PPS to John Major, prime minister, in 1990; PPS to Earl of Caithness, Paymaster Gen, 1989-90. Mbr Commons services cmte, 1990 and 1982-4. Chmn and managing director, Dietary Foods Ltd, 1970- . Elected in 1983; MP for Luton E, 1979-83; contested Dartford, Oct 1974; Thurrock, 1970 and Feb 1974. Chmn Cumberland Packing Corp Ltd, Cumberland Foods Ltd and Mother Nature Ltd. B Apr 2 1942; ed Hassenbrook cty sch; Thurrock tech coll. Mbr Thurrock BC 1966-79; Essex CC 1967-70. Chmn Eastern area CPC 1977-80; mbr Nat CPC 1980- ; pres Eastern area YCs, 1981- . PPS to home office minrs 1984-7. Mbr select cmte on broadcasting 1988-90. Jt sec 1984-5, and vice-chmn, 1987-8, Cons backbench aviation cmte; jt sec parly aviation gp 1984-90; chmn Cons cmte on smaller businesses, 1983-4 and 1987-8.

Bill McKenzie, chartered accountant, contested this seat 1987. Consultant to Price Waterhouse., Mbr Luton BC 1976- . B Jul 24 1946; ed Reading sch; Bristol univ. GMB.

David Rogers, company accountant; treas Chilterns region LDs. Mbr Aylesbury Vale DC, 1987-91. B Jul 8 1948; ed William Penn sch, Rickmansworth.

Lyn Bliss, analyst/programmer; local membership sec and pty contact. B May 15 1951; ed Luton Girls HS.

MACCLESFIELD						No change
Electorate % Turnout	76,548	82.3%	1992	76,093	77.4%	1987
*Winterton, N R (C)	36,447	57.9%	+1.5%	33,208	56.4%	C
Longworth, Ms M C (Lab)	13,680	21.7%	+2.1%	14,116	24.0%	L/All
Beatty, Dr P C W (LD)	12,600	20.0%	-4.0%	11,563	19.6%	Lab
Penn, Mrs C (NLP)	268	0.4%				
C to Lab swing 0.3%	62,995		36.1%	58,887		32.4%
		C maj	22,767		C maj	19,092

Nicholas Winterton was elected chmn, Select Cmte on Health, in 1991; on Select Cmte on Social Services, 1979-90; Select Cmte on Standing Orders, since 1981; and Chairmen's Panel. Non-exec director, Bridgwater Paper Co, since 1990; parly adviser to Construction Plant-hire Assocn, Baird Textile Holdings, British Paper Machinery Makers Assocn, Paper and Board Industry Fed, Emerson International; Scorpio Aviation and Marine Ltd. Elected in 1971 by-election; contested Newcastle-under-Lyme, 1969 by-election and 1970. B Mar 31 1938; ed Bilton Grange Prep Sch; Rugby. Chmn, all-pty gp for paper and board industry, since 1983; cotton and allied textiles gp; gp for pre-1973 war widows, and British Namibian gp. His wife Ann is Cons MP for Congleton.

Martina Longworth, part-time lecturer in business law. B Jan 30 1956; ed Notre Dame HS, Wigan; St John Rigby VI Form Coll, Orrell; Keele univ; Manchester Poly. Mbr, Christian Socialist Movement.

Dr Paul Beatty, medical physicist, contested Eccles 1987. Mbr, LD federal conference cmte. B Jan 25 1952; ed Handsworth GS, B'ham; Univ Coll, London. MSF. Methodist local preacher.

MAIDSTONE						No change
Electorate % Turnout	72,834	80.1%	1992	72,987	76.0%	1987
*Widdecombe, Miss A N (C)	31,611	54.2%	+1.7%	29,100	52.4%	C
Yates, Mrs P G (LD)	15,325	26.3%	-7.5%	18,736	33.8%	L/All
Logan, Mrs A F H (Lab)	10,517	18.0%	+5.5%	6,935	12.5%	Lab
Kemp, Ms P A (Grn)	707	1.2%	-0.1%	717	1.3%	Grn
Ingram, F (NLP)	172	0.3%				
LD to C swing 4.6%	58,332		27.9%	55,488		18.7%
		C maj	16,286		C maj	10,364

Ann Widdecombe was appointed an Under Sec of State for Social Security in 1990; mbr, Select Cmte on Social Services, 1988-90. Elected in 1987; contested Plymouth, Devonport, 1983 and Burnley, 1979. Snr administrator at London univ, 1975-87. Sec, Cons back-bench horticulture and markets sub-cmte, 1987-90. Was jt sec/research asst to Cons parly study gp on disablement benefits. B Oct 4 1947; ed La Sainte Union Convent, Bath; Birmingham univ; Lady Margaret Hall, Oxford. A founding mbr and vice-chmn, Women for Families and Defence. Mbr, Runny-mede DC, 1976-78.

Paula Yates, housewife; mbr, Maidstone BC, 1984- (cl ldr, 1987-92; chmn, policy and finance cmte, 1987-92). B Dec 27 1947; ed N London Collegiate Sch; Hull univ.

Anne Logan, CFE lecturer; vice-chmn Maidstone CLP and former branch sec. B May 16 1957; ed Tonbridge Girls' GS; Univ Coll of Wales, Aberystwyth; Birmingham univ; Kingston upon Thames Poly. NATFHE.

Penny Kemp, freelance writer and former teacher, contested this seat 1987 and Kent East in 1989 Euro elections. Co-chmn, UK Grn Pty Cl, 1988-89; mbr, pty Euro election cmte; convenor, media cmte, Grn Pty Cl, 1987-88. Headcorn parish cllr. B May 10 1949; ed privately.

MAKERFIELD						No change
Electorate % Turnout	71,425	76.1%	1992	70,819	75.8%	1987
*McCartney, I (Lab)	32,832	60.4%	+4.1%	30,190	56.3%	Lab
Dickson, Mrs D M (C)	14,714	27.1%	-0.2%	14,632	27.3%	C
Jeffers, S T (LD)	5,097	9.4%	-7.1%	8,838	16.5%	L/All
Cairns, Ms S (Lib)	1,309	2.4%				
Davies, C (NLP)	397	0.7%				
C to Lab swing 2.2%	54,349		33.3%	53,660		29.0%
		Lab maj	18,118		Lab maj	15,558

Ian McCartney joined Select Cmte on Social Security in 1991; mbr, Select Cmte on Social Services, 1989-91; chmn (1990-) and jt vice-chmn (1989-90), PLP employment cmte; chmn, all-pty home safety parly gp, 1988- ; child abduction gp, 1990- ; jt sec, leasehold reform gp, 1989- ; sec, prevention of solvent abuse gp and Tribune gp. "Head Waiter", Lab MPs Supper Club. Hon parly adviser to Greater Manchester Fire and Civil Defence Authority, 1986- ; unpaid adviser to Nat Assocn for Safety in the Home, 1989- ; cl mbr, Child Accident Prevention Trust. Elected in 1987 and became chmn, all-pty Rugby League parly gp. Hon pres, Childrens Wheelchair Fund. Spon-sored by TGWU; chmn, TGWU parly gp, 1989- .

Davina Dickson, solicitor, was voluntary Cons agent in Preston, 1987-90; NW environmental task force officer; campaign coordinator for Mr Michael Welsh MEP in 1989 Euro elections. Mbr, Cons NW women's cmte, 1989- ; Lancashire ed authority; Lancashire environmental forum. B Apr 19 1956; ed Brentwood Girls' Sch, Southport; Moreton Hall, Shropshire; Coll of Law, Chester.

Stephen Jeffers, pharmacist; mbr, Wigan MBC, 1987- (LD gp ldr, 1991-): W Lancs DC, 1979-81; chmn, Wigan and Leigh LDs. B Jul 2 1956; ed Upholland GS; Bath univ. Was in ASTMS.

MANCHESTER CENTRAL					No change	
Electorate % Turnout	56,446	56.9%	1992	62,928	63.9%	1987
*Litherland, R K (Lab)	23,336	72.7%	+4.5%	27,428	68.2%	Lab
Davies, P (C)	5,299	16.5%	-2.3%	7,561	18.8%	C
Clayton, M (LD)	3,151	9.8%	-3.2%	5,250	13.0%	SDP/All
Mitchell, Ms V (NLP)	167	0.5%				
Buchanan, A (CL)	167	0.5%				
C to Lab swing 3.4%	32,120		56.2%	40,239		49.4%
		Lab maj	18,037		Lab maj	19,867

Robert Litherland, former sales representative for a printing firm, has represented the seat since Sep 1979. Mbr, Unopposed Bills Panel. B Jun 23 1930; ed North Manchester HS for Boys. Mbr, Manchester City Cl since 1971; chmn, Manchester Direct Works Cmte, 1974-78. Dep chmn, Public Works Cmte, AMA, 1977-78. Sponsored by Sogat '82.
Peter Davies, managing director of The Vehicle Directory,

a specialist car company. Contested Farnham for Lab 1979 when he was research officer for Apex. B May 1 1951; ed RGS Newcastle; Oxford and Manchester univs.
Mark Clayton, data communications consultant and company director. Mbr, nat exec, NCCL, 1980-85; chmn and vice-chmn, Manchester gp, NCCL, 1979-85 and 1986-89. Contested Merseyside East in 1989 Euro elections. B Dec 7 1955.

MANCHESTER, BLACKLEY					No change	
Electorate % Turnout	55,234	69.3%	1992	58,814	72.9%	1987
*Eastham, K (Lab)	23,031	60.2%	+7.7%	22,476	52.4%	Lab
Hobhouse, W S (C)	10,642	27.8%	-1.0%	12,354	28.8%	C
Wheale, S (LD)	4,324	11.3%	-7.5%	8,041	18.8%	SDP/All
Kennedy, M (NLP)	288	0.8%				
C to Lab swing 4.4%	38,285		32.4%	42,871		23.6%
		Lab maj	12,389		Lab maj	10,122

Kenneth Eastham, former planning engineer with GEC, Trafford Park, has served on select cmte on employment since 1983; jt vice-chmn, PLP trade and industry cmte, 1987- , and of PLP employment cmte, 1985-87. An Opposn whip. Elected in 1979. B Aug 11 1927; ed Openshaw tech coll. Mbr, Manchester city cl, 1962-80; dep ldr, 1975-79, and chmn, ed cmte, 1978-79, and planning

cmte, 1971-74. Mbr, NW economic planning cl, 1975-79. Sponsored by AUEW.
William Hobhouse, manager in textile industry. Sec, Liverpool, Mossley Hill Cons Assocn, 1990- . B Jan 17 1963; ed Eton; Gonville and Caius Coll, Cambridge. Active in Prince's Youth Business Trust.

MANCHESTER, GORTON					No change	
Electorate % Turnout	62,410	60.8%	1992	64,243	70.4%	1987
*Kaufman, G B (Lab)	23,671	62.3%	+7.9%	24,615	54.4%	Lab
Bullock, J D (C)	7,392	19.5%	-3.8%	10,550	23.3%	C
Harris, C P (LD)	5,327	14.0%	-7.7%	9,830	21.7%	L/All
Henderson, T (Lib)	767	2.0%		253	0.6%	RF
Daw, M J (Grn)	595	1.6%				
Lawrence, Ms P (Rev Comm)	108	0.3%				
Mitchell, P (NLP)	84	0.2%				
Smith, Ms C (Int Comm)	30	0.1%				
C to Lab swing 5.9%	37,974		42.9%	45,248		31.1%
		Lab maj	16,279		Lab maj	14,065

Gerald Kaufman became chief Opposn spokesman on foreign and Commonwealth affairs in 1987; chief spokesman on home affairs, 1983-87. Elected to shadow Cabinet, 1980, being chief spokesman on environment, 1980-83; previously spokesman on housing, 1979-80. Mbr, Lab Pty NEC, 1991- . Minr of State, Dept of Industry, 1975-79; Under-Sec of State for Industry, 1975; and for Environment, 1974-75. PC 1978. Parly press liaison officer for Lab Pty, 1965-70. Elected for this seat 1983; MP for Manchester, Ardwick, 1970-83; contested Gillingham, 1959, and Bromley, 1955. B Jun 21 1930; ed Leeds GS; Queen's Coll, Oxford. Asst sec, Fabian Society, 1954-55. Political correspondent, New Statesman, 1964-65; political staff, Daily Mirror, 1955-64. Sponsored by GMB.

Jonathan Bullock, advertising director; account manager, Advanti Ltd, Nottingham, 1988- ; account exec, Jon Gordon advertising and Marketing Ltd based in Sheffield, 1986-88. Pres (1989-91) and chmn (1987-89), E Midlands YCs. B Mar 3 1963; ed Nottingham HS; Portsmouth Poly.
Phil Harris, snr lecturer and management consultant; chmn, Manchester Withington LDs, 1989- ; vice-chmn, Lib Pty, 1983-86. Trustee, Manchester Research Exchange, 1991- . B Mar 2 1952; ed Birkenhead Tech Coll; York univ (pres of union, 1977-78); Manchester Poly.
Mike Daw, trainee maths teacher; treas, Manchester Grn Pty. B Oct 23 1966; ed Boundstone Comprehensive, Lancing, Sussex; Manchester Poly. NAS/UWT.

163

MANCHESTER, WITHINGTON						No change
Electorate % Turnout	63,838	71.3%	1992	65,343	77.1%	1987
*Bradley, K J C (Lab)	23,962	52.7%	+9.7%	21,650	42.9%	Lab
Farthing, E (C)	14,227	31.3%	-5.0%	18,259	36.2%	C
Hennell, P G (LD)	6,457	14.2%	-5.6%	9,978	19.8%	L/All
Candeland, B A (Grn)	725	1.6%	+0.6%	524	1.0%	Grn
Menhinick, C (NLP)	128	0.3%				
C to Lab swing 7.3%	45,499		21.4%	50,411		6.7%
		Lab maj	9,735		Lab maj	3,391

Keith Bradley was elected in 1987 and appointed to Opposn front bench team on social security in 1991. Mbr Select Cmte on Agriculture 1989-91; sec and campaign officer NW gp of Lab MPs 1989- . Former health service administrator. Mbr Manchester City Cl, 1983-8. Former city cl director of Manchester Ship Canal and Manchester Airport plc. B May 17 1950; ed Manchester Poly; York Univ. MSF/Cohse.

Eric Farthing, local govt research officer, contested Merseyside E in 1989 Euro elections. Former police officer and coal miner. B Dec 24 1945; ed sec mod sch; Open Univ; Warwick Univ. Chmn Yorkshire area CPC 1988-91. Gordon Hennell, barrister and charity organiser. B Apr 12 1959; ed Burnage HS, Manchester; Trinity Coll, Cambridge; Inns of Court Sch of Law.

Brian Candeland, systems analyst, contested Greater Manchester Central in 1989 Euro elections. B Jan 20 1952; ed Loughborough Univ.

MANCHESTER, WYTHENSHAWE						No change
Electorate % Turnout	53,548	69.7%	1992	58,287	72.1%	1987
*Morris, A (Lab)	22,591	60.5%	+3.7%	23,881	56.8%	Lab
McKenna, K (C)	10,595	28.4%	-0.2%	12,026	28.6%	C
Fenn, S J (LD)	3,633	9.7%	-4.3%	5,921	14.1%	SDP/All
Otten, G N (Grn)	362	1.0%		216	0.5%	RF
Martin, Ms E (NLP)	133	0.4%				
C to Lab swing 2.0%	37,314		32.1%	42,044		28.2%
		Lab maj	11,996		Lab maj	11,855

Alfred Morris was elected in 1964; contested seat, 1959; Liverpool, Garston, 1951. Opposn spokesman on the disabled, 1970-4 and 1979- ; Minr for the Disabled, 1974-9, with rank of under sec. PC 1979. Chmn world planning gp that drafted charter for the 1980s for disabled people world wide, presented to all heads of govt in International Year of Disabled People 1981. Jt vice-pres 1991- and chmn 1988-91 Parly and Scientific Cmte; all-pty Anzac parly gp, 1982- (Awarded Queen's Service Order by New Zealand in 1990 and made officer of Order of Australia 1991); jt vice-chmn all-pty pre-1973 war widows gp; jt treas British-American gp 1983- . B Mar 23 1928; ed Manchester elementary schs; Ruskin and St Catherine's Colls, Oxford; post-graduate studies at Manchester Univ. Sponsored by Co-op pty.

Kevin McKenna, stockbroker. Former nat vice-chmn of Tory Reform Gp and former sec Manchester jnr chamber of commerce. Life mbr society for unborn child; mbr Tory green initiative. B Jun 19 1949; ed Marist Coll, Hull; Manchester Poly; Manchester Univ.

Steve Fenn, mature student. Mbr S Ribble BC 1983-5; Poynton PC 1987- . B Dec 23 1954; ed Northgate Sch, Ipswich; Bath Univ.

Guy Otten, solicitor. Former sec Manchester Grn pty; mbr Wythenshawe law centre management cmte. B Jul 7 1947; ed Downside RC public sch; Clare Coll, Cambridge; Manchester Univ and Poly.

MANSFIELD						No change
Electorate % Turnout	66,964	82.2%	1992	66,764	78.4%	1987
*Meale, J A (Lab)	29,932	54.4%	+16.9%	19,610	37.5%	Lab
Mond, G S (C)	18,208	33.1%	-4.3%	19,554	37.4%	C
Thompstone, Dr S R (LD)	6,925	12.6%	-9.6%	11,604	22.2%	SDP/All
				1,580	3.0%	ML
C to Lab swing 10.6%	55,065		21.3%	52,348		0.1%
		Lab maj	11,724		Lab maj	56

Alan Meale, elected in 1987, appointed to select cmte on home affairs 1990; mbr select cmte on European legislation 1988-90. Jt vice-chmn PLP employment cmte 1987- and PLP energy cmte 1989-90. Treas all-pty football gp 1989- ; jt sec all-pty cults gp 1989- . Parly and political adviser to Michael Meacher MP, 1983-7; former sec Campaign Gp of Labour MPs. Author. Personal asst gen sec Aslef 1980-3; nat employment development officer, Nat Assocn for Care and Resettlement of Offenders, 1977-80; engineering worker 1968-75; seaman, Merchant Navy, 1964-8. B July 31 1949; ed St Joseph's RC Sch; Ruskin Coll, Oxford. Sponsored by MSF.

Gary Mond, chartered accountant, contested Hamilton 1987. Chmn small leisure company; corporate finance relations and marketing gp. Chmn Greater London YCs 1985-6; cl mbr Bow Gp, 1987-9; asst treas, Chelsea Cons assocn, 1986-8. B May 11 1959; ed Univ Coll Sch, Hampstead; Trinity Coll, Cambridge. Former UK international butterfly swimmer (Olympic triallist 1976).

Dr Stuart Thompstone, univ lecturer, contested Sherwood 1987; Newark 1983. Jt owner of complex of holiday apartments in Italy. Mbr Newark and Sherwood DC 1991- ; Southwell PC 1987- . Former chmn Notts assocn of LDs; former sec Notts SDP. B Oct 18 1964; ed Forfar Acad; RAF Coll, Cranwell; Sch of Slavonic and E Euro Studies, London Univ; LSE. AUT.

MEDWAY						No change
Electorate % Turnout	61,736	80.2%	1992	64,103	73.0%	1987
*Fenner, Dame Peggy (C)	25,924	52.3%	+1.3%	23,889	51.0%	C
Marshall-Andrews, R G (Lab)	17,138	34.6%	+4.8%	13,960	29.8%	Lab
Trice, C L (LD)	4,751	9.6%	-8.5%	8,450	18.1%	SDP/All
Austin, M (Lib)	1,480	3.0%		504	1.1%	Grn
Kember, P (NLP)	234	0.5%				
C to Lab swing 1.7%	49,527		17.7%	46,803		21.2%
		C maj	8,786		C maj	9,929

Dame Peggy Fenner was elected for this seat in 1983; MP for Rochester and Chatham, 1979-83 and 1970-Oct 1974; contested Newcastle-under-Lyme, 1966. Parly Sec, Min of Ag, Fish and Food, 1981-6 and 1972-3. Mbr select cmte on members' interests, 1987- ; UK delegation Cl of Europe and WEU 1987- . Parly and legislative consultant to British Frozen Foods Fed. Chmn all-pty retail industry parly gp. B Nov 12 1922; ed LCC elementary sch, Brockley; Ide Hill Sch, Kent. Co-chmn women's national commission 1983-6. Mbr Sevenoaks UDC 1957-71; Euro Parliament, 1974-5.

Robert Marshall-Andrews, QC and writer, contested Richmond upon Thames Oct 1974; former chmn Richmond pty. Trustee Adamson Wildlife Trust and Geffrye Museum. B Apr 10 1944; ed Mill Hill Sch; Bristol Univ. Mbr Society of Lab Lawyers.
Cyril Trice, retired engineer. Mbr Rochester-upon-Medway City Cl, 1983-91; parish cllr, 1976-87. Former owner local mini-market food shop. B Jul 16 1931; ed at army sch, Chepstow. EPEA.

MEIRIONNYDD NANT CONWY						No change
Electorate % Turnout	32,413	81.5%	1992	31,632	82.1%	1987
Llwyd, E (PC)	11,608	44.0%	+3.9%	10,392	40.0%	PC
Lewis, G S (C)	6,995	26.5%	-1.9%	7,366	28.4%	C
Williams, D R (Lab)	4,978	18.8%	+1.9%	4,397	16.9%	Lab
Parry, Mrs R (LD)	2,358	8.9%	-5.8%	3,814	14.7%	SDP/All
Pritchard, W (Grn)	471	1.8%				
C to PC swing 2.9%	26,410		17.5%	25,969		11.7%
		PC maj	4,613		PC maj	3,026

Elfyn Llwyd retained this seat for Plaid Cymru in 1992. Solicitor with offices at Dolgellau, Barmouth and Bala. B Sep 26 1951; ed Ysgol Duffryn Conwy, Llanrwst; UCW, Aberystwyth; Christleton Coll of Law, Chester. Pigeon breeder.
Gwyn Lewis, agricultural merchant; catering manager, Nat Eisteddfod of Wales. Community cllr. Former mbr domestic animal medicines cl; cl animal health distributors assocn; chmn Llanrwst Nat Eisteddfod finance cmte 1989.

B Jun 10 1946; ed Llanrwst GS.
Rhys Williams, regional officer (Wales) of NUT, contested Caernarfon 1987. Former chmn Ceredigion and Pembrokeshire N CLP; mbr Tregaron community cl. B Jan 21 1948; ed Pontypridd Boys' GS; Exeter Univ; Coll of William and Mary, Virginia, US; Nottingham Univ. MSF.
Ruth Parry, owner/director of children's nursery. Mbr Welsh consumers cl, 1987-90. B Apr 7 1945; ed Cardiff Coll of Ed.

MERIDEN						No change
Electorate % Turnout	76,994	78.9%	1992	78,444	73.9%	1987
*Mills, I C (C)	33,462	55.1%	+0.0%	31,935	55.1%	C
Stephens, N J (Lab)	18,763	30.9%	+4.8%	15,115	26.1%	Lab
Morris, Mrs J A (LD)	8,489	14.0%	-4.8%	10,896	18.8%	SDP/All
C to Lab swing 2.4%	60,714		24.2%	57,946		29.0%
		C maj	14,699		C maj	16,820

Iain Mills, elected in 1979. Marketing planning manager with Dunlop responsible for marketing new tyre projects 1964-79; responsible for racing tyre development, 1966-70; now adviser to Nat Tyre Distributors Assocn and to Industrial Anti-Counterfeiting Gp, and Small Independent Brewers Assocn. Non-exec director, Interbrand Gp Ltd. Mbr select cmte on employment 1987- . Sec Cons transport cmte 1979-86; treas (1987-89) and vice-chmn (1984-87) all-pty transport safety gp; jt vice-chmn all-pty motor industry gp. B Apr 21 1940; ed Prince Edward Sch,

Bulawayo, Rhodesia; Cape Town Univ.
Nick Stephens, bank officer. Chmn Solihull CLP 1988-91 and treas 1982-8 and 1991- . Mbr Solihull MBC 1983- (sec of Lab gp 1986- ; vice-chmn ed cmte 1991-). Pres Central Midlands Co-op Society pty 1988-9 and vice-pres 1989- . B Apr 19 1958; ed Tudor Grange Sch, Solihull; Solihull Coll of Tech. BIFU. Sponsored by Co-op pty.
Judy Morris, housewife. Mbr Solihull MBC 1989-90 and 1991- . B Jun 25 1944; ed Riland Bedford HS, Sutton Coldfield; Warwick Univ.

MERTHYR TYDFIL AND RHYMNEY						No change
Electorate % Turnout	58,430	75.8%	1992	58,285	76.2%	1987
*Rowlands, E (Lab)	31,710	71.6%	-3.8%	33,477	75.4%	Lab
Rowland, R (LD)	4,997	11.3%	+3.2%	5,270	11.9%	C
Hughes, M (C)	4,904	11.1%	-0.8%	3,573	8.0%	L/All
Cox, A (PC)	2,704	6.1%	+1.4%	2,085	4.7%	PC
Lab to LD swing 3.5%	44,315		60.3%	44,405		63.5%
		Lab maj	26,713		Lab maj	28,207

Edward Rowlands was elected for this seat 1983; MP for Merthyr Tydfil 1972-83, and for Cardiff N 1966-70. Mbr select cmte on foreign affairs 1987- . An Opposn spokesman on energy 1980-8 and on foreign affairs 1979-80. Minr of state FCO 1976-9; under sec 1975-6; under sec for Wales 1974-5 and 1969-70. Vice-chmn all-pty book publishing gp 1987- (chmn 1983-84). Lecturer in modern history and govt, Welsh Coll of Advanced Tech. B Jan 23 1940; ed Rhondda GS; Wirral GS; King's Coll, London. Mbr governing body and exec Commonwealth Inst 1980- ; academic cl Wilton Park 1983- . Booker prize judge 1984.

Sponsored by Usdaw.

Mark Hughes, area development manager in computer industry; director, Lightning Skills Ltd; former communications manager with GKN. Mbr North Herts DC 1988- ; Royston TC 1987- (mayor 1990-1). B Sep 23 1961; ed Sheredes Sch, Herts; Kingsway Princeton Coll, London. Qualified football referee.

Alun Cox, unemployed. pty speaker on education; chmn conference steering cmte. B May 22 1964; ed Ysgol Gyfun Rhydfelen; UCW, Aberystwyth. Pres Welsh NUS 1989-91.

MIDDLESBROUGH						No change
Electorate % Turnout	58,844	69.9%	1992	60,789	71.0%	1987
*Bell, S (Lab)	26,343	64.1%	+4.4%	25,747	59.7%	Lab
Rayner, P R (C)	10,559	25.7%	+0.7%	10,789	25.0%	C
Jordan, Mrs R (LD)	4,201	10.2%	-5.1%	6,594	15.3%	L/All
C to Lab swing 1.9%	41,103		38.4%	43,130		34.7%
		Lab maj	15,784		Lab maj	14,958

Stuart Bell, barrister and writer, was an Opposn spokesman on N Ireland, 1984-7; founder mbr British-Irish inter-parly body 1990 and jt vice-chmn of its steering cmte 1990- ; vice-chmn Northern gp of Lab MPs, 1991- . Jt vice-chmn 1991- and exec cmte mbr 1990-1 British gp on IPU. Jt vice-chmn PLP Treasury and civil service cmte 1990- . Jt sec all-pty British-Israeli gp 1990- . Parly adviser to Merck, Sharp and Dohme. Mbr conciliation bd European Space Agency. Mbr Select Cmte on Cardiff Bay Barrage Bill, 1991- . Elected in 1983; contested Hexham, 1979. B May 16 1938; ed Hookergate GS, Durham.

Paul Rayner, quality assurance consultant and adviser to several information technology companies. Contested Rother Valley 1987. Variously chmn, vice-chmn, treas and cmte mbr Yorkshire Area CPC. B Oct 25 1946; ed Leeds GS; Bristol Univ; Bradford Univ Sch of Management. Chmn Computer Retailers' Assocn 1981.

Rosamund Jordan, teacher and fine art dealer, contested Scarborough in 1983. Ind mbr Stockton RDC 1970-4. B Apr 25 1943; ed Grangefield GS for Girls, Stockton-on-Tees; Darlington Coll of Ed; Open Univ. NAS/UWT.

MIDLOTHIAN						No change
Electorate % Turnout	60,255	77.9%	1992	60,549	77.2%	1987
Clarke, E L (Lab)	20,588	43.9%	-4.4%	22,553	48.3%	Lab
Lumsden, A (SNP)	10,254	21.9%	+11.3%	10,300	22.0%	SDP/All
Stoddart, W J (C)	9,443	20.1%	+1.9%	8,527	18.2%	C
Sewell, P L (LD)	6,164	13.1%		4,947	10.6%	SNP
Morrice, I D (Grn)	476	1.0%	+0.1%	412	0.9%	Grn
Lab to SNP swing 7.8%	46,925		22.0%	46,739		26.2%
		Lab maj	10,334		Lab maj	12,253

Eric Clarke was elected for this seat in 1992. Miner and former gen sec Scottish NUM. Former trustee Mineworkers Pension Fund; mbr of NUM, 1949- ; former mbr nat exec cmte Lab Pty. Mbr Midlothian CC 1962-75; Lothian reg cl 1974-8. JP for Midlothian, 1963-78. Former mbr Scottish cl for development and industry; South and West of Scotland Forestry Advisory Cmte. B Apr 9 1933; ed state schs; W M Ramsay Coll, Edinburgh; Esk Valley Tech Coll, Dalkeith, Midlothian. Hon Pres Mayfield Lab club.

Andrew Lumsden, lecturer in economics at Scottish Coll of Textiles, contested Tweeddale, Ettrick and Lauderdale 1987. Mbr SNP nat cl and mbr anti-poll tax cmte 1990-1; pty director of internal training and political education.

Mbr Borders reg cl 1986-8. Chmn Galawater SNP branch 1989-90. B May 11 1959; ed Galashiels Acad; Herriot-Watt Univ.

Jeff Stoddart, farmer. Independent mbr Loanhead BC for nine years (provost 1972-5); independent reg cllr, 1974-86. Trustee Edinburgh green belt trust. B Mar 2 1935; ed George Heriots Sch; Edinburgh Univ. Chmn Lothians area NFU; mbr of cl and past chmn Dalkeith agricultural society. Chmn Midlothian scout cl.

Paul Sewell, self-employed fleet consultant. B Feb 23 1964; ed Cuiken Primary Sch; Penicuik HS. Local pty vice-chmn.

Iain Morrice, computer programmer. Treas Scottish Grn pty. B Feb 10 1960; ed Aberdeen GS; Aberdeen Univ.

MILTON KEYNES NORTH EAST				New Seat
Electorate % Turnout	62,748	81.0%	1992	
Butler, P (C)	26,212	51.6%		
Cosin, Mrs M I (Lab)	12,036	23.7%		
Gaskell, P K (LD)	11,693	23.0%		
Francis, A H (Grn)	529	1.0%		
Kavanagh-Dowsett, Mrs M (Ind C)	249	0.5%		
Simson, M (NLP)	79	0.2%		
No swing calculation.	50,798	27.9%		
		C maj	14,176	

Peter Butler, solicitor; partner in a school for emotionally and behaviourally disturbed children. A vice-pres, local law society; cty cllr, 1975-79; constituency chmn. National chairman trainee solicitors of England and Wales, 1976-77. B Jun 10 1951; ed Adams GS, Newport, Shropshire; St Edmund Hall, Oxford.
Maggie Cosin contested Chingford in 1987. Mbr, Camden BC, since 1986; Waltham Forest Cl, 1971-74. Nat officer for Equity; mbr of and sponsored by GMB. B Jan 17 1941; ed St Gerald's Sch, Glasgow; LSE.

Peter Gaskell, editor of several publications about worldwide corporate investment. Agent for Milton Keynes in 1987; local pty exec mbr. B Jul 4 1965; ed John Rigby Coll, Orrell; Warwick univ.
Alan Francis, proprietor of consultancy in computer graphics and electronic publishing, contested Milton Keynes 1987 and 1983. B Jun 3 1948; ed Hitchin Boys' GS; Sussex univ. Held many Grn pty offices including convenor, 1988, and mbr, conferences cmte, 1991.

MILTON KEYNES SOUTH WEST				New Seat
Electorate % Turnout	66,422	77.0%	1992	
Legg, B (C)	23,840	46.6%		
Wilson, K J (Lab)	19,153	37.4%		
Pym, C (LD)	7,429	14.5%		
Field, Dr C (Grn)	525	1.0%		
Kelly, H (NLP)	202	0.4%		
No swing calculation.	51,149	9.2%		
		C maj	4,687	

Barry Legg is a main board executive director of Hillsdown Holdings plc, food manufacturers; accountant and associate, Inst of Taxation. Contested Bishop Auckland 1983. Treas, St Marylebone Cons Assocn. Co-founder and treas, Cons Way Forward. Former mbr, Westminster City Cl. B May 30 1949; ed Sir Thomas Rich's GS, Gloucester; Manchester univ. Mbr, Bow Gp and its industry standing cmte. Governor, Archbishop Tenison's GS. Mbr, Gloucestershire CCC.
Kevin Wilson, elected to Milton Keynes BC in 1978 (ldr of

cl, since 1990); mbr, Woughton PC, 1983- ; part-time teacher. Held all major branch and CLP posts, 1975-91. B Jun 4 1953; ed Ashton Sec Sch, Preston; Preston Sixth Form Coll; Madelly Coll of Ed. NUT.
Chris Pym, course manager, Open university; mbr, Milton Keynes BC, since 1983; Milton Keynes CHC. B Jan 13 1929; ed Marlborough Coll; Triunity Coll, Cambridge. AUT.
Caroline Field, social worker. B Apr 21 1963; ed Cambridge and Oxford univs.

MITCHAM AND MORDEN						No change
Electorate % Turnout	63,723	80.3%	1992	63,089	75.7%	1987
*Rumbold, Mrs A C R (C)	23,789	46.5%	-1.7%	23,002	48.2%	C
McDonagh, Ms S (Lab)	22,055	43.1%	+7.9%	16,819	35.2%	Lab
Field, J C (LD)	4,687	9.2%	-7.5%	7,930	16.6%	SDP/All
Walsh, T J (Grn)	655	1.3%				
C to Lab swing 4.8%	51,186	3.4%		47,751	12.9%	
		C maj	1,734		C maj	6,183

Angela Rumbold became Minr of State, Home Office, in 1990; Minr of State for Ed and Science, 1986-90; Under Sec of State for Environment, 1985-6; vice-chmn, Ministerial gp on women's issues. PC 1991. Elected at 1982 by-election. PPS to Nicholas Ridley, 1983-5. B Aug 11 1932; ed Notting Hill and Ealing HS; Perse School for Girls, Cambridge; Kings Coll, London. Former company director and adviser. Co-chmn, Women's Nat Commission, 1986-90. Mbr, select cmte, social services, 1982-3; Doctors and Dentists Review Body, 1979-82; Kingston upon Thames BC, 1974-83 Freeman, City of London, 1988.
Siobhain McDonagh, short-term housing consultant, contested this seat 1987. Mbr, Merton BC, 1982- . Voluntary adviser, Catholic Housing Advice Service,

Wandsworth; mbr, Merton Voluntary Service Cl. Chmn, Phipps Bridge youth centre and Merton bike scheme. B Feb 20 1960; ed Essex univ.
John Field, transportation planning consultant, fought London SW in 1989 Euro elections. Mbr, Wimbledon LD exec; LD transport policy working pty. Treas, Parly Advisory cl for Transport Safety; trustee, Christian trusts; elder, Wimbledon church. B Mar 14 1944; ed Sir Joseph Williamson's Maths sch, Rochester; Sheffield and Essex univs.
Tom Walsh, London taxi driver; dep rep to Grn Pty Cl for London. B Jan 24 1956; ed St Edward's Sch, Richmond; NE Surrey Coll of Tech.

MOLE VALLEY				No change		
Electorate % Turnout	66,949	82.0%	1992	67,715	77.0%	1987
*Baker, K W (C)	32,549	59.3%	-1.5%	31,689	60.8%	C
Watson, M D (LD)	16,599	30.2%	+0.3%	15,613	29.9%	L/All
Walsh, Dr T J (Lab)	5,291	9.6%	+0.3%	4,846	9.3%	Lab
Thomas, Ms J (NLP)	442	0.8%				
C to LD swing 0.9%	54,881		29.1%	52,148		30.8%
		C maj	15,950		C maj	16,076

Kenneth Baker resigned from the government immediately after the 1992 election. He had been home secretary 1990-2; Chancellor of the Duchy of Lancaster and chmn Cons pty 1989-90; education sec 1986-9; environment sec 1985-6; local govt minr 1984-5; minr for industry and for information technology 1981-4; parly sec civil service dept 1972-4. PC 1984. Elected for this seat 1983; MP for St Marylebone 1970-83; and for Acton 1968-70; contested that seat, 1966 and Poplar 1964. B Nov 3 1934; ed St Paul's Sch; Magdalen Coll, Oxford.

Michael Watson, chartered accountant. Mbr Mole Valley DC 1989- . B Dec 1 1952; ed Bristol GS; Exeter Univ.

Dr Tim Walsh, economist with the Post Office; previously with NEDO and Euro commission in Brussels. B Dec 1 1960; ed St Joseph's Primary Sch, Highgate Hill; St Aloysius' Coll, Highgate; Exeter and Bath Univs. Chmn Young Fabians 1989-90; exec mbr Fabian Society 1989- . MSF.

MONKLANDS EAST				No change		
Electorate % Turnout	48,391	75.1%	1992	49,644	74.8%	1987
*Smith, J (Lab)	22,266	61.3%	+0.3%	22,649	61.0%	Lab
Wright, J (SNP)	6,554	18.0%	+5.1%	6,260	16.9%	C
Walters, S (C)	5,830	16.0%	-0.8%	4,790	12.9%	SNP
Ross, P (LD)	1,679	4.6%	-4.6%	3,442	9.3%	L/All
Lab to SNP swing 2.4%	36,329		43.2%	37,141		44.1%
		Lab maj	15,712		Lab maj	16,389

John Smith, QC, was nominated as a contender for the leadership of the Labour pty after Neil Kinnock had announced that he was standing down. Mbr of shadow cabinet since 1979. Shadow chancellor 1987- ; shadow trade and industry sec 1985-7; shadow employment sec 1983-5; shadow energy sec 1982-3; shadow trade sec 1979-82. Trade sec 1978-9; minr Privy Cl Office 1976-8; minr for energy 1975-6; under sec for energy 1974-5. PC 1978. Elected for this seat 1983; MP for N Lanarkshire, 1970-83; contested E Fife, 1961 and 1964. Advocate. B Sep 13 1938; ed Dunoon GS; Glasgow Univ. Nat pres

industrial common ownership movement, 1988- . Sponsored by GMB.

Jim Wright, freelance management consultant, contested Motherwell S 1987 and 1983. B Dec 24 1942; ed Airdrie Acad; Glasgow Coll of Tech.

Stewart Walters, business consultant; managing director of marketing company; with Ferranti 1980-9. B Dec 10 1957; ed Liberton HS; Napier Poly.

Dr Philip Ross, hospital consultant and Edinburgh Univ reader. B Jun 6 1936; ed Robert Gordon's Coll; Aberdeen Univ.

MONKLANDS WEST				No change		
Electorate % Turnout	49,269	77.5%	1992	50,874	77.3%	1987
*Clarke, T (Lab)	23,384	61.3%	-1.0%	24,499	62.3%	Lab
Bovey, K (SNP)	6,319	16.6%	+5.7%	6,166	15.7%	C
Lownie, A J H (C)	6,074	15.9%	+0.2%	4,408	11.2%	SDP/All
Hamilton, Ms S (LD)	2,382	6.2%		4,260	10.8%	SNP
Lab to SNP swing 3.4%	38,159		44.7%	39,333		46.6%
		Lab maj	17,065		Lab maj	18,333

Tom Clarke was elected for this seat in 1983; MP for Coatbridge and Airdrie 1982-3. Appointed to health select cmte 1991. Mbr Opposn front bench health team 1987-90 as spokesman on personal social services; a spokesman on Scottish affairs, 1987. Sponsored Disabled Persons Act 1986. Mbr Scottish select cmte 1983-7. Chmn PLP foreign affairs cmte 1983-6; jt vice-chmn all-pty British-Netherlands gp; personal social services parly panel; sec all-pty UN gp. Governor British Film Inst. B Jan 10 1941; ed Columba HS, Coatbridge; Scottish Coll of Commerce.

Keith Bovey, solicitor, contested this seat 1987; Glasgow, Garscadden, 1978 by-election and Oct 1974; Glasgow,

Hillhead, Feb 1974. B Jul 31 1927; ed Paisley GS; Sch of Oriental and African Studies, London; Glasgow Univ. Been chmn, Scottish CND.

Andrew Lownie, literary agent and freelance journalist. Treas Cons gp for Europe 1990- ; former vice-chmn Holborn and St Pancras Cons assocn; treas NE London Euro constituency cl; cmte mbr Cons foreign affairs forum. B Nov 11 1961; ed Fettes Coll, Edinburgh; Westminster Sch; Magdalene Coll, Cambridge (pres of union 1984); Edinburgh Univ.

Shiona Hamilton is a housewife. Sec E Kilbride LDs. B Dec 30 1966; ed Uddingston GS.

MONMOUTH			No change from 1987			
Electorate % Turnout	59,147	86.1%	1992	58,468	80.6%	1987
Evans, R (C)	24,059	47.3%	-0.3%	22,387	47.5%	C
*Edwards, H (Lab)	20,855	41.0%	+13.3%	13,037	27.7%	Lab
David, Mrs F A (LD)	5,562	10.9%	-13.1%	11,313	24.0%	SDP/All
Witherden, M (Green/PC)	431	0.8%		363	0.8%	PC
C to Lab swing 6.8%	50,907		6.3%	47,100		19.9%
		C maj	3,204		C maj	9,350

Roger Evans, barrister, who contested 1991 by-election, regained seat for Cons in 1992; contested Ynys Mon 1987, Warley W 1979 and Oct 1974. Mbr exec cmte friends of friendless churches. Mbr Gwent CLA; assoc mbr Monmouthshire NFU. B Mar 1947; ed Clytha Park Sch, Newport; City of Norwich Sch; Bristol GS; Trinity Hall, Cambridge (pres of union 1970); chmn univ Cons assocn 1969.

Huw Edwards, lecturer and research consultant, gained the seat for Lab at the 1991 by-election. Mbr select cmte on Welsh affairs 1991-2; mbr Commons information cmte 1991-2. Research associate Low Pay Unit 1985- ; mbr exec

Shelter Cymru. Snr lecturer in social policy, Brighton Poly, 1988-91; lecturer in social policy, Manchester Poly, 1985-88; South Bank Poly, 1984-85; Sheffield Univ, 1983-84; Coventry (Lanchester) Poly, 1980-81. Open Univ tutor, 1987. B Apr 12 1953; ed Eastfields HS, Mitcham, Surrey; Manchester Poly; York Univ. Mbr Gwalia male voice choir. NATFHE.

Frances David, dep head teacher at comprehensive sch, became vice-pres of Welsh LDs in 1990. Contested 1991 Monmouth by-election; Newport E in 1987 and 1983. B Feb 4 1933; ed Sherborn Sch for Girls; St Hugh's Coll, Oxford.

MONTGOMERY			No change			
Electorate % Turnout	41,386	79.9%	1992	39,808	79.4%	1987
*Carlile, A C (LD)	16,031	48.5%	+1.9%	14,729	46.6%	L/All
France-Hayhurst, Mrs J (C)	10,822	32.7%	-5.8%	12,171	38.5%	C
Wood, S (Lab)	4,115	12.4%	+2.0%	3,304	10.5%	Lab
Parsons, H (PC)	1,581	4.8%	+0.3%	1,412	4.5%	PC
Adams, P (Grn)	508	1.5%				
C to LD swing 3.8%	33,057		15.8%	31,616		8.1%
		LD maj	5,209		L/All maj	2,558

Alex Carlile, QC, won the seat in 1983; contested Flint E, Feb 1974 and 1979. Appointed LD spokesman on trade and industry in 1990 and on legal affairs in 1989; spokesman on foreign and Euro affairs 1988-9; Lib and then LD spokesman on home and legal affairs 1984-8; Alliance spokesman on legal affairs in 1987 election. Jt sec all-pty barristers gp; treas all-pty UN gp; jt vice-chmn all-pty war crimes gp; charity laws parly panel; civil liberties gp. Lay mbr Gen Medical Cl 1989- . Mbr advisory cl on public records 1989- ; cl Howard League 1989- . Recorder since 1986. B Feb 12 1948; ed Epsom Coll, Surrey; King's Coll, London; Inns of Court Sch of Law. Adviser (unpaid) Overseas Doctors' Assocn.

Jeannie France-Hayhurst, barrister and businesswoman

running PR consultancy. Founder mbr women in enterprise; mbr Mensa; exec cmte 300 gp. B Jan 20 1950; ed Towyn GS; Univ of Wales; Inns of Court Sch of Law. Read law at Aberystwyth Univ.

Steve Wood, social worker and team ldr. B Feb 29 1952; ed state schs; Open Univ. Nupe.

Hugh Parsons, solicitor; mbr PC nat cl; exec cmte PC cllrs assocn. Mbr Llandrindod TC 1986- (mayor 1990-1). B Jan 16 1964; ed York Univ; Chester Coll of Law.

Patrick Adams, biologist and smallholder, contested N Wales for Grn pty in 1989 Euro elections. Lab mbr Oxford City Cl 1979-84. B Apr 1 1949; ed Oxford Sch; Wolverhampton Poly.

MORAY			No change			
Electorate % Turnout	63,255	72.5%	1992	62,201	72.6%	1987
*Ewing, Mrs W M (SNP)	20,299	44.3%	+1.1%	19,510	43.2%	SNP
Hossack, Mrs R L (C)	17,455	38.1%	+3.1%	15,825	35.0%	C
Smith, C (Lab)	5,448	11.9%	+0.6%	5,118	11.3%	Lab
Sheridan, J B (LD)	2,634	5.7%	-4.7%	4,724	10.5%	L/All
SNP to C swing 1.0%	45,836		6.2%	45,177		8.2%
		SNP maj	2,844		SNP maj	3,685

Margaret Ewing gained this seat in 1987 becoming leader of SNP parly gp and spokesman on defence (until 1990), health, social security, environment and Highlands and Islands; SNP MP for Dunbartonshire East (then Margaret Bain) Oct 1974-9, contesting that seat, Feb 1974, and Strathkelvin and Bearsden 1983. Mbr select cmte on Euro legislation 1990- . Jt vice-chmn all-pty Scottish sports gp 1987- ; low flying gp. Snr vice-chmn SNP 1984-7; vice-pres SNP 1987-90; mbr nat exec 1990- . B Sep 1 1945; ed Biggar HS; Glasgow and Strathclyde Univs. NUJ.

Roma Hossack, former BBC secretary. Mbr Moray DC

1974-91; Grampian regional cl 1977-90; Elgin TC 1972-4. B Sep 25 1937; ed Convent of Sacred Heart, Aberdeen; secretarial sch, Elgin.

Conal Smith, principal teacher of modern studies, contested seat 1987; mbr Moray DC 1988- ; Moray trades cl. B Aug 31 1947; ed Elgin Acad; Edinburgh Univ; Moray House, Edinburgh. EIS.

Brinsley Sheridan, quality and safety manager at offshore survival centre, Aberdeen. B Oct 31 1938; ed Hardyes Sch, Dorchester; Sch of Navigation, Southampton Univ.

MORECAMBE AND LUNESDALE				No change		
Electorate % Turnout	56,426	78.4%	1992	55,718	76.1%	1987
*Lennox-Boyd, M A (C)	22,507	50.9%	-1.7%	22,327	52.7%	C
Yates, Ms J (Lab)	10,998	24.9%	+2.4%	10,542	24.9%	SDP/All
Saville, A J (LD)	9,584	21.7%		9,535	22.5%	Lab
Turner, M (MBI)	916	2.1%				
Marriott, R (NLP)	205	0.5%				
C to Lab swing 2.1%	44,210		26.0%	42,404		27.8%
		C maj	11,509		C maj	11,785

Mark Lennox-Boyd was appointed Under Sec of State for Foreign and Commonwealth Affairs in 1990; PPS to Margaret Thatcher, 1988-90; a Ld Commissioner of Treasury (govt whip), 1986-8; an asst govt whip, 1984-86. PPS to Nigel Lawson, as Financial Sec to Treasury, Sec of State for Energy and Chancellor of Exchequer, 1980-4. Barrister and former company director. Elected for this seat 1983; MP for Morecambe and Lonsdale, 1979-83; contested Brent South, Oct 1974. B May 4 1943; ed Eton;

Christ Church, Oxford.
Jean Yates, night club owner; chmn, Heysham LP; sec Lancashire cty LP. Mbr Lancaster DC, 1974- . B Mar 14 1953; ed primary and sec schs. MSF.
Tony Saville, management consultant, was agent for this seat in 1987; mbr Lancaster city cl, 1987-91; chmn Morecambe alliance, 1986-8; sec Morecambe SDP, 1987-8. B Jul 8 1946; ed Hansom Boys' GS, Bradford; Panal Ash police coll, Harrogate. Director, Dukes Theatre, 1987- .

MOTHERWELL NORTH				No change		
Electorate % Turnout	57,290	76.7%	1992	57,632	77.3%	1987
*Reid, Dr J (Lab)	27,852	63.4%	-3.6%	29,825	66.9%	Lab
Clark, D A (SNP)	8,942	20.3%	+6.4%	6,230	14.0%	SNP
Hargrave, R (C)	5,011	11.4%	+0.3%	4,939	11.1%	C
Smith, Ms H (LD)	2,145	4.9%	-3.1%	3,558	8.0%	L/All
Lab to SNP swing 5.0%	43,950		43.0%	44,552		53.0%
		Lab maj	18,910		Lab maj	23,595

John Reid became an Opposn spokesman on defence, disarmament and arms control in 1990; mbr armed forces parliamentary scheme; a spokesman on children, 1989-90. Elected in 1987. Mbr PAC, 1988-90; jt vice-chmn PLP transport cmte, 1987-9. Scottish organiser, trade unionists for Lab, 1986-7; adviser to Neil Kinnock, 1983-5. B May 8 1947; ed St Patrick's senr sec sch, Coatbridge; Stirling univ. Sponsored by TGWU.
David Clark, section engineer (electrical), Clydebridge Steelworks, Glasgow; mbr Dalzell action cmte in campaign for investment. B Nov 1 1965; ed Hamilton GS; Strathclyde univ. Mbr steel and industrial managers'

assocn, former chmn, Dalzell centre; vice-chmn Scotland area branch; negotiating team mbr - British Steel General Steels.
Robert Hargrave, director of small structural company, contested this seat 1987 and 1983. Template maker, 1954-65; works manager, 1965-76. Former mbr exec cmte, Airdrie and Coatbridge Cons assocn. B Apr 27 1939; ed Dalziel HS, Motherwell.
Harriet Smith, policy development officer, prison reform Trust; parly press officer for LD MPs, 1988-9. B Oct 16 1954; ed St Denis sch, Edinburgh; Telford CHE; Edin univ.

MOTHERWELL SOUTH				No change		
Electorate % Turnout	50,042	76.2%	1992	52,127	75.5%	1987
*Bray, Dr J W (Lab)	21,771	57.1%	-1.2%	22,957	58.3%	Lab
Ullrich, Mrs K M (SNP)	7,758	20.4%	+5.0%	6,027	15.3%	SNP
McIntosh, W G (C)	6,097	16.0%	+1.5%	5,704	14.5%	C
Mackie, A G (LD)	2,349	6.2%	-5.2%	4,463	11.3%	SDP/All
Lettice, D (YSOR)	146	0.4%		223	0.6%	Comm
Lab to SNP swing 3.1%	38,121		36.8%	39,374		43.0%
		Lab maj	14,013		Lab maj	16,930

Jeremy Bray has been Opposn spokesman on science and technology since 1983; mbr select cmte on Treasury and civil service, 1979-83. Consultant to BIFU and to society of telecom executives. Visiting research fellow, Imperial coll, 1989- . Elected in 1983; MP for Motherwell and Wishaw, Oct 1974-83; and for Middlesbrough W, 1962-70; contested Thirsk and Malton, 1959. Jt vice-chmn all-pty engineering development parly gp; British-Chinese gp. Parly sec, Ministry of Technology, 1967-9, and to Ministry of Power, 1966-7. B Jun 29 1930; ed Aberystwyth GS; Kingswood sch, Bath; Jesus coll, Cambridge. TGWU.
Kay Ullrich, social worker employed by Strathclyde region,

contested Cunninghame S 1987 and 1983. Mbr nat cl; steel action cmte; nat sec, SNP/CND, 1984-6; Cunninghame S SNP press officer, 1978-87; chmn Ayr W branch, 1968-74. B May 5 1943; ed Ayr acad; Queen's coll, Glasgow. Qualified swimming coach. Nalgo.
Gordon McIntosh, instrument engineer. Vice-chmn Motherwell N Cons assocn, 1990- . B May 1 1954; ed Ardrossan academy. Worked in Saudi Arabia for seven years. EEPTU.
Alex Mackie, insolvency manager with international firm of accountants; past chmn Eastwood LDs. B Jun 11 1937; ed Eastwood sec sch, Clarkston, Glasgow.

NEATH						No change
Electorate % Turnout	56,392	80.6%	1992	55,261	78.8%	1987
*Hain, P G (Lab)	30,903	68.0%	+4.6%	27,612	63.4%	Lab
Adams, D R (C)	6,928	15.2%	-0.9%	7,034	16.1%	C
Evans, Dr D (PC)	5,145	11.3%	+4.9%	6,132	14.1%	SDP/All
Phillips, M (LD)	2,467	5.4%	-8.6%	2,792	6.4%	PC
C to Lab swing 2.8%	45,443		52.8%	43,570		47.2%
		Lab maj	23,975		Lab maj	20,578

Peter Hain, civil rights and anti-apartheid campaigner, author and unpaid director *Tribune* Newspaper, was elected at 1991 by-election; contested Putney 1987 and 1983. Head of research Union of Communication Workers 1976- . B Feb 16 1950; ed Pretoria Boys HS; Emanuel Sch, Wandsworth; Queen Mary's Coll, London Univ; Sussex Univ. Mbr anti-apartheid movement; nat chmn Young Libs 1971-3. Joined Lab pty in 1977. Press officer for anti-nazi league 1977-80; chmn Stop the '70 (South African) Tour campaign. GMB.
Rowland Adams, computer projects manager with GEC subsidiary EASAMS, Camberley. Mbr Surrey Heath BC

1987- (chmn leisure services and info tech cmtes). B Mar 21 1963; ed Mynachlog Nedd Primary Sch, Neath; France Hill Comprehensive, Camberley; NE London Poly, Barking.
Dr Dewi Evans, consultant paediatrician, contested 1991 by-election; PC spokesman on local govt; mbr W Glamorgan CC 1989- . B Jul 29 1949; ed Carmarthen GS; Univ of Wales Coll of Medicine. BMA.
The Rev Michael Phillips is pres Port Talbot Free Church Federal Cl; co-ordinator, Glamnorgan Christian ecology gp; exec mbr W Glamorgan community volunteer service. B Jul 15 1958.

NEW FOREST						No change
Electorate % Turnout	75,413	80.8%	1992	75,083	76.6%	1987
*McNair-Wilson, Sir P (C)	37,986	62.4%	-2.3%	37,188	64.7%	C
Vernon-Jackson, Mrs J K (LD)	17,581	28.9%	+2.0%	15,456	26.9%	L/All
Shutler, M J (Lab)	4,989	8.2%	-0.3%	4,856	8.4%	Lab
Carter, Ms F (NLP)	350	0.6%				
C to LD swing 2.1%	60,906		33.5%	57,500		37.8%
		C maj	20,405		C maj	21,732

Sir Patrick McNair-Wilson was elected for this seat in 1968; MP for Lewisham W, 1964-6. Chmn Jt Lords and Commons select cmte on private bill procedure 1987- ; mbr, select cmte on members' interests, 1985-6. Chmn Voucher Vault plc 1989-90; consultant to Union Carbide UK Ltd, Fawley Plant of Re-Chem International Ltd, and Rhone Poulenc plc. B May 28 1929; ed Hall Sch, Hampstead; Eton. Opposn spokesman on energy, 1974-6.
Jean Vernon-Jackson, retired nursing sister, was mayor of Lymington, 1987-9; mbr Lymington TC 1983-90. Mbr

Hampshire CC 1985- , and New Forest DC 1987- . Vice-chmn Lymington LD branch. B Apr 12 1930; ed Cranborne Chase Sch; Univ Coll Hospital.
Mike Shutler, local govt manual worker, contested Poole 1987; Bournemouth E 1983. Mbr Ringwood TC 1973- (cl chmn 1991); chmn Wessex reg bd CRS Ltd; vice-chmn Wessex Co-op pty cl; mbr southern sector bd Co-op Union Ltd. Former sec New Forest trade union cl; treas Hampshire Cty LP and Bournemouth/Poole Co-op pty. B Aug 27 1937; ed Harbridge C of C Sch. TGWU.

NEWARK						No change
Electorate % Turnout	68,801	82.2%	1992	67,555	77.6%	1987
*Alexander, R T (C)	28,494	50.4%	-3.1%	28,070	53.5%	C
Barton, D H (Lab)	20,265	35.8%	+8.1%	14,527	27.7%	Lab
Harris, P R B (LD)	7,342	13.0%	-5.8%	9,833	18.8%	SDP/All
Wood, Ms P (Grn)	435	0.8%				
C to Lab swing 5.6%	56,536		14.6%	52,430		25.8%
		C maj	8,229		C maj	13,543

Richard Alexander, solicitor, gained this seat for Cons in 1979; contested Lincoln 1966 and 1970. Mbr select cmte on agriculture 1988- ; select cmte on statutory instruments 1979- , and on environment 1983-7. Chmn E Midlands Cons MPs 1985- ; jt vice-chmn Cons backbench urban and inner cities cmte 1987-9; Cons home affairs cmte 1988- ; all-pty arts and heritage parly gp; non-profit making clubs gp. Parly adviser to Ancient Order of Foresters Friendly Society. Mbr exec cmte British gp IPU; chmn all-pty British-Romanian parly gp; jt vice-chmn Zambian gp; sec Bahrain and Kuwait gps; treas South Pacific gp. B Jun 29 1934; ed Eastbourne GS; Dewsbury GS; Univ Coll, London; Inst of Advanced Legal Studies, London Univ. Snr

partner Jones, Alexander and Co 1964-85. Mbr Bassetlaw DC 1975-9; Retford BC 1965-74; Notts CC 1967-74.
Dave Barton, college lecturer, contested this seat 1987. B Nov 15 1946; ed Guildford GS; Kingston Poly. Mbr Newark TC 1987- (gp ldr); Sherwood DC 1983- . Former chmn Newark CLP. NATFHE.
Peter Harris, educastion adviser; former head teacher; director of computer software and publishing houses. Speaker on economy for E Midlands LDs. Mbr Newark and Sherwood DC 1990- ; W Wiltshire DC 1986-8. B Apl 6 1955; ed Trinity Whitgift; Exeter and London Univs. NAHT.

NEWBURY						No change
Electorate % Turnout	80,252	82.8%	1992	75,187	78.0%	1987
Chaplin, Mrs J (C)	37,135	55.9%	-4.2%	35,266	60.1%	C
Rendel, D D (LD)	24,778	37.3%	+5.6%	18,608	31.7%	L/All
Hall, R J E (Lab)	3,962	6.0%	-2.2%	4,765	8.1%	Lab
Wallis, J (Grn)	539	0.8%				
C to LD swing 4.9%	66,414		18.6%	58,639		28.4%
		C maj	12,357		C maj	16,658

Judith Chaplin, political secretary since 1990 to John Major, prime minister, was his special adviser when he was Chancellor of the Exchequer, 1989-90, and to Nigel Lawson, Chancellor, 1988-9. Head of policy unit of inst of directors, 1986-8; in Cons research dept, 1983-6. Govt appointments have included interim advisory cl on teachers' pay, 1987-8, a review of the youth service, and the secondary exam cl responsible for GCSE, 1983-6. B Aug 19 1939; ed Wycombe Abbey; Girton coll, Cambridge. First worked in advertising; founded and ran independent sch for young children in Norfolk, 1967-74. Mbr Norfolk CC, 1974-85 (chmn ed cmte). Represented Norfolk on ACC, 1977-84, and was vice-chmn ACC ed cmte and on Burnham cmte.

David Rendel, management consultant; financial analyst with Esso Petroleum, contested this seat in 1987, Fulham 1983 and 1979. Mbr Newbury DC, 1987- . B Apr 15 1949; ed Eton and Oxford univ.

Richard Hall, researcher. B Aug 19 1964; ed Kennet comprehensive, Thatcham, Berks; Keele univ. MSF; former Apex branch chmn.

NEWCASTLE UPON TYNE CENTRAL						No change
Electorate % Turnout	59,973	71.3%	1992	63,682	72.5%	1987
*Cousins, J M (Lab)	21,123	49.4%	+5.2%	20,416	44.2%	Lab
Summersby, M A (C)	15,835	37.0%	-1.8%	17,933	38.8%	C
Opik, L (LD)	5,816	13.6%	-2.2%	7,304	15.8%	SDP/All
				418	0.9%	Grn
				111	0.2%	RF
C to Lab swing 3.5%	42,774		12.4%	46,182		5.4%
		Lab maj	5,288		Lab maj	2,483

Jim Cousins gained this seat in 1987. Joined select cmte on trade and industry in 1989; vice-chmn PLP Treasury and civil service cmte, 1989-90; chmn science sub-cmte of PLP ed, science and arts cmte. Researcher and lecturer. Mbr Tyne and Wear CC, 1973-86; Wallsend BC, 1969-73. Founder North low pay unit. B Feb 21 1944; ed Oxford univ; LSE. Sponsored by MSF.

Mike Summersby, company director; self-employed graph-ic designer. Mbr Newcastle city cl, 1983- (Cons gp dep ldr). Former reprographics services manager and print manager. B Sep 3 1937; ed Heaton tech sch, Newcastle; Newcastle coll of art and industrial design. Army service for 17 years included being lecturer in military accounting.

Lembit Opik is dep chmn northern region Lib Dems and vice-chmn Newcastle area Lib Dems. Ed Bristol Univ (Pres student union, 1985).

NEWCASTLE UPON TYNE EAST						No change
Electorate % Turnout	57,165	70.7%	1992	59,369	70.6%	1987
*Brown, N H (Lab)	24,342	60.2%	+3.8%	23,677	56.4%	Lab
Lucas, J R (C)	10,465	25.9%	-0.8%	11,177	26.6%	C
Thompson, A (LD)	4,883	12.1%	-4.0%	6,728	16.0%	L/All
Edwards, G L N (Grn)	744	1.8%		362	0.9%	Comm
C to Lab swing 2.3%	40,434		34.3%	41,944		29.8%
		Lab maj	13,877		Lab maj	12,500

Nicholas Brown became an Opposn spokesman on Treasury and economic affairs in 1987; a spokesman on legal affairs, 1985-7. Mbr jt select cmte on consolidation bills; treas parly and scientific cmte, 1991- . Elected in 1983. Legal adviser northern region of GMB, 1978-83. Mbr Newcastle upon Tyne city cl, 1980-4. B Jun 13 1950; ed Swattenden sec mod sch; Tunbridge Wells tech HS; Manchester univ. Sponsored by GMB.

Jeremy Lucas, educational consultant and theatrical publisher; former head of boarding and day prep sch. Mbr Essex CC, 1989- ; cl rep on Eastern region sports cl and eastern arts. Chmn trustees Mercury theatre, Colchester; pavilion and ground cmte, Essex cty cricket club (on gen cmte since 1974). B Aug 18 1944; ed Holmwood House prep sch, Colchester; Eton; Trinity coll, Dublin.

Alan Thompson, businessman with Thompson Business Equip Ltd, Thompson Coast Construction Ltd and Tolent Sea Defences Ltd. Chartered engineer. Contested Wansbeck 1983; Morpeth 1979 and E Dunbartonshire Oct 1974. B May 8 1936; ed Dicksons coll. Mbr Wansbeck DC, 1979-81; cty cl, 1981-9; Northumbria police authority, 1981-5.

Gareth Edwards, charity fundraiser; co-chmn Newcastle Grn pty; press officer NE area pty. B Aug 19 1966; ed Newcastle univ.

NEWCASTLE UPON TYNE NORTH				No change		
Electorate % Turnout	66,187	76.8%	1992	69,178	75.9%	1987
*Henderson, D J (Lab)	25,121	49.4%	+6.7%	22,424	42.7%	Lab
Gordon, I (C)	16,175	31.8%	+7.2%	17,181	32.7%	L/All
Maughan, P J (LD)	9,542	18.8%	-13.9%	12,915	24.6%	C
Lab to C swing 0.3%	50,838		17.6%	52,520		10.0%
		Lab maj	8,946		Lab maj	5,243

Douglas Henderson was elected in 1987. Appointed an Opposn spokesman on trade and industry in 1988. Chmn PLP Treasury and civil service cmte 1987-8; sec GMB parly gp 1987- . Regional organiser GMWU and GMB 1975-87; research officer GMWU 1973-5; clerk British Rail 1969; apprentice, Rolls-Royce 1966-8. Mbr exec Scottish cl of Lab pty 1979-87 (chmn 1984-5). B Jun 9 1949; ed Waid Acad, Anstruther, Fife; Central Coll, Glasgow; Strathclyde Univ. Sponsored by GMB.
Ian Gordon, chartered accountant; snr partner in BDO Binder Hamlyn; director, Northern Development Co; Tyne and Wear Development Corpn. Mbr North Tyneside MBC 1976- (Cons gp ldr 1982-). Leads Cons opposn gp on Northern region cls assocn. B Mar 21 1939; ed Carlisle GS. Mbr Northern Area local govt cmte; N Tyneside political cmte.
Peter Maughan, solicitor. Northern region LD spokesman on legal affairs. B May 16 1954; ed Dame Allan's Boys' Sch, Newcastle; Newcastle Poly.

NEWCASTLE-UNDER-LYME				No change		
Electorate % Turnout	66,595	80.3%	1992	66,053	80.8%	1987
*Golding, Mrs L (Lab)	25,652	47.9%	+7.4%	21,618	40.5%	Lab
Brierley, A D (C)	15,813	29.6%	+1.7%	16,486	30.9%	L/All
Thomas, A L (LD)	11,727	21.9%	-9.0%	14,863	27.9%	C
Lines, R (NLP)	314	0.6%		397	0.7%	ex Lab
C to Lab swing 2.9%	53,506		18.4%	53,364		9.6%
		Lab maj	9,839		Lab maj	5,132

Llin Golding, who won the 1986 by-election, became an Opposn whip in 1987. Mbr select cmte on broadcasting, 1990-1. Jt vice-chmn PLP home affairs cmte 1987- ; vice-chmn PLP parliamentary affairs cmte 1987- . Jt chmn all-pty homelessness parly gp; jt vice-chmn prevention of solvent abuse gp; children gp; war crimes gp; child abduction gp; sec industrial safety gp. Match sec Lords and Commons fly fishing club. Parly adviser to Nat Market Traders Assocn. B Mar 21 1933; ed Caerphilly Girls' GS; Cardiff Royal Infirmary Sch of Radiography. Mbr, Society of Radiographers; Nupe. Sponsored by Cermaic and Allied Trades Union.
Andrew Brierley, barrister. Director London Diocesan Fund Ltd. Mbr Cons Pty nat union exec cmte 1984-8; dep chmn Fulham Cons Assocn 1988-90; nat vice-chmn FCS 1984-5. B Sep 30 1961; ed King Edward VI Sch, Macclesfield; Torquay Boys' GS; Kingston Poly.
Alan Thomas, lecturer, contested this seat 1987, 1986 by-election and 1983; Stoke-on-Trent Central 1979 and Oct 1974. Mbr, Newcastle-under-Lyme DC 1980- ; Stafford-shire CC, 1981- . B Dec 1 1939; ed Wallasey GS; Hull and Keele Univs. NATFHE.

NEWHAM NORTH EAST				No change		
Electorate % Turnout	59,555	60.3%	1992	60,787	64.1%	1987
*Leighton, R (Lab)	20,952	58.3%	+6.4%	20,220	51.9%	Lab
Galbraith, J H (C)	10,966	30.5%	-0.2%	11,984	30.7%	C
Aves, Dr J J (LD)	4,020	11.2%	-6.2%	6,772	17.4%	L/All
C to Lab swing 3.3%	35,938		27.8%	38,976		21.1%
		Lab maj	9,986		Lab maj	8,236

Ronald Leighton has been chmn of the employment select cmte since 1984; chmn PLP employment cmte 1983-7; an Opposn whip 1981-4. Printer. Regained seat for Lab in 1979; contested Horsham and Crawley, Feb 1974, and Middleton and Prestwich, 1964. ChmnLabour's common market safeguards cmte 1975- ; sec Labour cmte for safeguards on common market 1967-70; director all-pty common market safeguards campaign 1970-3; national organizer of referendum campaign for No vote 1975. B Jan 24 1930; ed Monteagle and Bifrons Sch, Barking; Ruskin Coll, Oxford. Sponsored by GPMU.
Jeremy Galbraith, parliamentary consultant; personal asst to Cons MPs 1987-9. Chmn Cons friends of Israel. Vice-chmn Newham NE Cons assocn; former pty officer in Vauxhall, Leeds E and Leeds NW. B Aug 14 1966; ed Kings Sch, Worcester; Faculty of Law, Leeds Univ.
Dr Jonathan Aves, univ lecturer; vice-chmn constituency LDs; sch governor. B Sep 11 1959; ed City of London Sch; New Coll, Oxford; Sch of Slavonic and East European Studies, London Univ. Sec LD Eastern Europe gp. RIIA; AUT.

NEWHAM NORTH WEST						No change
Electorate % Turnout	46,471	56.0%	1992	47,568	59.4%	1987
*Banks, T L (Lab)	15,911	61.1%	+5.7%	15,677	55.4%	Lab
Prisk, M M (C)	6,740	25.9%	+0.5%	7,181	25.4%	C
Sawdon, A (LD)	2,445	9.4%	-8.0%	4,920	17.4%	SDP/All
Standford, Ms A J (Grn)	587	2.3%	+0.5%	497	1.8%	Grn
Jug, T (Loony G)	252	1.0%				
O'Sullivan, D (Int Comm)	100	0.4%				
C to Lab swing 2.6%	26,035	35.2%		28,275	30.0%	
		Lab maj	9,171		Lab maj	8,496

Tony Banks was an Opposn spokesman on social security with special responsibility for the European social charter, 1990-1. Mbr select cmte on Treasury and civil service, 1986-7; select cmte on standing orders, 1987- ; select cmte on procedure, 1987- ; cl of Europe and WEU, 1989- . Chmn London gp of Lab MPs, 1987- . Former asst gen sec assocn of broadcasting and allied staffs. Elected in 1983; contested E Grinstead, 1970; Newcastle N, Oct 1974; Watford, 1979. Chmn GLC, 1985-6; GLC mbr for Hammersmith, 1970-7, and Tooting, 1981-6. Former mbr Nat Theatre bd, English Nat Opera bd, London Festival Ballet bd. B Apr 8 1945; ed Archbishop Tenisons, Kennington; York univ; LSE. Mbr of, and sponsored by TGWU.

Mark Prisk, chartered surveyor and company director; vice-chmn Westminster N Cons assocn, 1989- ; mbr nat cmte, peace through Nato, 1983-7. B Jun 12 1962; ed Truro sch; Reading univ. Founder mbr Devon and Cornwall development co;

Amanda Sandford, information officer; coordinator, London region Grn pty. B Feb 16 1958; ed Congleton GS; Trent poly.

NEWHAM SOUTH						No change
Electorate % Turnout	51,143	60.2%	1992	50,244	59.1%	1987
*Spearing, N J (Lab)	14,358	46.6%	+3.1%	12,935	43.5%	Lab
Foster, Ms J R (C)	11,856	38.5%	+4.3%	10,169	34.2%	C
Kellaway, A J (LD)	4,572	14.9%	-7.4%	6,607	22.2%	SDP/All
Lab to C swing 0.6%	30,786	8.1%		29,711	9.3%	
		Lab maj	2,502		Lab maj	2,766

Nigel Spearing became chairman, select cmte on Euro legislation in 1983; mbr 1979- . Mbr select cmte on foreign affairs, 1979-87; bd Christian aid, 1987-91. Chmn PLP parly affairs cmte, 1989- ; jt vice-chmn, all-pty friends of cycling parly gp. Elected for this seat 1974 by-election; MP for Acton, 1970-Feb 1974; contested Warwick and Leamington, 1964. Teacher. B Oct 8 1930; ed Latymer upper sch, Hammersmith; St Catharine's coll, Cambridge. Chmn British anti-common market campaign, 1977-83; Pres socialist environment and resources assocn, 1977-86; Vice-pres, River Thames society. NUT.

Jacqueline Foster is vice-chmn, Greater London area Cons trade unionists and representative on nat cmte; vice-chmn Twickenham Cons assocn. Chmn British Airways "short haul" crew in Cabin Crew '89, a union for airline crews; mbr nat exec cl. Mbr BA cabin crew 1969- . B Dec 30 1947; ed Prescot Girls' GS. Mbr European Atlantic gp; Euro union of women; Bruges gp.

Alec Kellaway, economist and market researcher, contested this seat 1987 and Newham NW 1983. Mbr Newham cl, 1987- (Ldr of opposn, 1987-90; LD gp ldr, 1991-). B May 31 1953; ed East Ham GS for Boys; Christ Church, Oxford. Lay reader, C of E, 1985- . EETPU.

NEWPORT EAST						No change
Electorate % Turnout	51,603	81.2%	1992	52,199	80.1%	1987
*Hughes, R J (Lab)	23,050	55.0%	+5.9%	20,518	49.1%	Lab
Emmett, Mrs A (C)	13,151	31.4%	-0.8%	13,454	32.2%	C
Oliver, W A (LD)	4,991	11.9%	-5.7%	7,383	17.7%	SDP/All
Ainley, S (Green/PC)	716	1.7%		458	1.1%	PC
C to Lab swing 3.4%	41,908	23.6%		41,813	16.9%	
		Lab maj	9,899		Lab maj	7,064

Roy Hughes became mbr chairmen's panel and chmn of Welsh grand cmte in 1990, as in 1982-84. Mbr UK delegation, cl of Europe and WEU, 1991- ; British-Irish inter-parly body. An Opposn spokesman on Wales, 1984-8; jt vice-chmn PLP transport cmte, 1990- ; jt chmn all-pty motor industry parly gp; all-pty roads study gp; jt vice-chmn Commons motor club. Treas, 1990-1, and mbr, 1987-90, exec cmte, British gp, IPU. Elected for this seat 1983; MP for Newport, 1966-83. Former adminstrative officer in Coventry car firm, and officer in TGWU, 1959-66. B Jun 9 1925; ed Pontllanfraith sec sch; Ruskin coll, Oxford. Mbr Coventry city cl, 1962-6. Sponsored by TGWU.

Angela Emmett, employment specialist, chaired London west European union of women and Ealing Acton CPC; vice-chmn Gtr London area CPC. Former executive with BAT Industries plc, BOC ltd and Beecham Pharmaceuticals. B Aug 24 1952; ed Gumley House convent GS; Thames Valley management centre.

Will Oliver, former Euro official; software consultant. Membership sec Monmouth; branch chmn, Chepstow; community cllr, Mathern. B Oct 21 1935; ed Sir Joseph Williamson's mathematical sch, Rochester; RN Dockyard tech coll, Chatham. Former cl mbr union syndicale, Luxembourg, and of inst of professional civil servants.

NEWPORT WEST						No change
Electorate % Turnout	54,871	82.8%	1992	55,455	81.8%	1987
*Flynn, P P (Lab)	24,139	53.1%	+7.1%	20,887	46.1%	Lab
Taylor, A R (C)	16,360	36.0%	-4.1%	18,179	40.1%	C
Toye, A (LD)	4,296	9.5%	-3.6%	5,903	13.0%	L/All
Keelan, P (PC)	653	1.4%	+0.6%	377	0.8%	PC
C to Lab swing 5.6%	45,448		17.1%	45,346		6.0%
		Lab maj	7,779		Lab maj	2,708

Paul Flynn was an Opposn spokesman on social security, 1988-90. Gained this seat 1987; contested Denbigh, Oct 1974. Sec, all-pty dolphins parly gp, 1989- . Was research officer, 1984-7, for Llewellyn Smith, Labour MEP for SE Wales; steelworker, 1955-84. Has chaired broadcasting cl for Wales, and served on S Wales Docks Bd and cl, Univ Coll, Cardiff. Mbr, Lab Pty of Wales exec cmte; mbr, Gwent CC, 1974-82; former mbr, Newport BC. B Feb 9 1935; ed St Illtyd's; Univ Coll, Cardiff. Nupe.

Andrew Taylor, barrister, contested Wales S in 1989 Euro elections and Blaenau Gwent 1987. Been sec, Welsh Cons policy gp; mbr, Blaenau Gwent Cons Assocn; patron, Monmouth Cons Assocn. B Feb 14 1961; ed Tredegar comprehensive sch; Univ Coll, Cardiff. Cl for Legal Ed, London. Chmn, Abergavenny Lawn Tennis Club and playing mbr, Monmouthshire LT and Croquet Club (Penpergwm), 1986-9; now playing mbr, Stow Park LTC, Newport; sec, Tredegar RFC, 1987-88;

Peter Keelan, librarian, contested Cardiff West 1987 and S Wales in 1989 Euro elections. On PlC nat exec, 1987-91, and nat coordinator pty anti-poll tax campaign, 1988-91. B Dec 26 1953; ed in Newport; City Univ, London; UCW, Aberystwyth. AUT.

NEWRY AND ARMAGH						No change
Electorate % Turnout	67,508	77.9%	1992	66,027	79.2%	1987
*Mallon, S (SDLP)	26,073	49.6%	+1.5%	25,137	48.1%	SDLP
Speers, J (UU)	18,982	36.1%	-1.8%	19,812	37.9%	UU
Curran, B (SF)	6,547	12.5%	+0.6%	6,173	11.8%	SF
Bell, Mrs E (All)	972	1.8%	+0.6%	664	1.3%	All
				482	0.9%	WP
UU to SDLP swing 1.6%	52,574		13.5%	52,268		10.2%
		SDLP maj	7,091		SDLP maj	5,325

Seamus Mallon became a mbr of the Select Cmte on Agriculture in 1987. Dep Ldr, Social Democratic and Labour Party, 1978- . Won this seat at by-election in 1986, retaining it in 1987; contested it 1983. Teacher. B Aug 17 1936; ed St Mary's Coll of Ed, Belfast. Mbr, Anglo-Irish Inter-Parly Body, 1990- ; NI Assembly, 1973-4 and 1982; NI Convention, 1975-6; Irish Senate, 1981-2; Armagh DC, 1973- ; Irish Nat Teachers' Organisation.

Jim Speers, insurance broker, company director and farmer. chmn, Newry and Armagh UUs; mbr, Armagh DC, 1977- (ldr, UU gp). Contested NI Assembly 1982 and 1983 by-election. B May 20 1946; ed Armagh Sec Sch.

Brendan Curran, electrician, contested Upper Bann in 1987. Mbr, Newry and Mourne Cl; SF speaker on health and social services. SF mbr, Craigavon BC, 1985- . Ex-Maze prisoner.

Eileen Bell, administrator, Peace Train organisation; former general sec, Alliance Pty; mbr, central exec cmte; speaker on women's issues. B Aug 15 1943; ed St Kevin's, Falls Rd, Belfast; Dominican Coll, Belfast; Ulster Univ, Jordanstown.

NORFOLK MID						No change
Electorate % Turnout	80,336	81.6%	1992	73,893	78.2%	1987
*Ryder, R (C)	35,620	54.3%	-2.4%	32,758	56.7%	C
Castle, M V (Lab)	16,672	25.4%	+7.6%	14,750	25.5%	SDP/All
Gleed, M J (LD)	13,072	19.9%	-5.6%	10,272	17.8%	Lab
Waite, Mrs C (NLP)	226	0.3%				
C to Lab swing 5.0%	65,590		28.9%	57,780		31.2%
		C maj	18,948		C maj	18,008

Richard Ryder was appointed Parly Sec to the Treasury and govt Chief Whip in 1990; Paymaster General, 1990; Economic Sec to Treasury, 1989-90; Parly Secy, Ministry of Ag, Fish and Food, 1988-9; an asst Govt whip, 1986-8. PC 1990. PPS to Foreign Sec, 1984-6, and to Financial Sec to the Treasury, 1984. Chmn, Cons Foreign and Commonwealth Cl, 1984-9. Journalist; was also partner of family farming business. Political sec to Mrs Thatcher, 1975-81. B Feb 4 1949; ed Radley; Magdalene Coll, Cambridge. Elected in 1983; contested Gateshead E in both 1974 elections.

Mike Castle, financial consultant, former teacher, contested Poole 1983 and Hampshire Central 1984 Euro elections. Mbr, Norfolk CC, 1988- (chmn, Lab gp, 1989-91); Rushmoor BC, 1980-86. Director, Norwich Co-op Soc. B Dec 20 1949; ed Feklixstowe Cty GS; Southend HS for Boys; teacher training coll; Open univ. MSF, previously NUT.

Michael Gleed, farmer, is chmn, South Suffolk LDs; mbr, Babergh DC. B Oct 5 1930; ed Sherborne; Cambridge.

NORFOLK NORTH						No change
Electorate % Turnout	73,780	80.8%	1992	69,790	77.5%	1987
*Howell, R F (C)	28,810	48.3%	-5.0%	28,822	53.3%	C
Lamb, N P (LD)	16,265	27.3%	+2.3%	13,512	25.0%	SDP/All
Cullingham, M (Lab)	13,850	23.2%	+3.3%	10,765	19.9%	Lab
Zelter, A C (Grn)	559	0.9%	-0.8%	960	1.8%	Grn
Jackson, S (NLP)	167	0.3%				
C to LD swing 3.6%	59,651		21.0%	54,059		28.3%
		C maj	12,545		C maj	15,310

Ralph Howell won the seat in 1970; contested it in 1966. Appointed to environment select cmte in 1991; mbr Treasury and civil service select cmte 1982-7. Nominated mbr Euro Parlt 1974-9. Farmer and underwriting mbr of Lloyd's. Mbr exec 1922 Cmte 1984-90. Vice-chmn Cons backbench social security cmte 1991- ; chmn (1987-8) and jt sec (1985-7) Cons ag, fish and food cmte; jt sec (1987-90) and vice-chmn (1979-84) Cons finance cmte; chmn Cons backbench employment cmte 1984-7. B May 25 1923; ed Diss GS, Norfolk. Mbr Cl of Europe and WEU 1987-

Norman Lamb is a solicitor. Mbr Norwich City Cl 1987-91. Former chmn and sec Norwich S Lib Pty. B Sep 16 1957; ed Wymondham Coll, Norfolk; Leicester Univ.
Michael Cullingham is a teacher. Mbr N Norfolk DC 1990- ; Norfolk Natural Trust. B Jan 26 1946; ed Wymondham Coll, Norfolk; Sittingbourne Coll of Ed, Kent. NAS/UWT.
Angie Zelter, potter. B Jun 5 1951; ed St Albans Girls GS; Reading Univ.

NORFOLK NORTH WEST						No change
Electorate % Turnout	77,438	80.7%	1992	73,739	78.9%	1987
*Bellingham, H C (C)	32,554	52.1%	+1.6%	29,393	50.6%	C
Turner, Dr G (Lab)	20,990	33.6%	+16.1%	18,568	31.9%	SDP/All
Waterman, A M (LD)	8,599	13.8%	-18.2%	10,184	17.5%	Lab
Pink, S (NLP)	330	0.5%				
C to Lab swing 7.3%	62,473		18.5%	58,145		18.6%
		C maj	11,564		C maj	10,825

Henry Bellingham, a barrister, was elected in 1983. PPS to Malcolm Rifkind when transport sec 1990. Mbr enviroment select cmte 1987-91. Mbr British-Irish inter-parly body. B Mar 29 1955; ed Eton; Magdalene Coll, Cambridge; Inns of Court School of Law. Chmn Cons cl on E Europe 1989- . Parly adviser to Nat Assocn of Waste Disposal Contractors. Jt sec Cons backbench N Ireland cmte 1983-90; jt vice-chmn (1987-90) and jt sec (1983-7) Cons smaller businesses cmte. Founder mbr and sponsor W

Norfolk local enterprise agency, 1986- . Mbr of Lloyd's; partner in family farming and property business.
George Turner is a univ lecturer in electronic engineering. mbr Norfolk CC, 1977- (gp ldr 1985-90). B Aug 9 1940; ed Laxton GS, Oundle; Imperial Coll, London; Caius Coll, Cambridge. AUT.
Alan Waterman is a field centre proprietor. Regional rep British Trust for Ornithology. B Jun 28 1949; ed London and Exeter Univ.

NORFOLK SOUTH						No change
Electorate % Turnout	81,647	84.0%	1992	78,372	81.0%	1987
*MacGregor, J R R (C)	36,081	52.6%	-0.8%	33,912	53.4%	C
Brocklebank-Fowler, C (LD)	18,516	27.0%	-6.9%	21,494	33.9%	L/All
Needle, C J (Lab)	12,422	18.1%	+5.4%	8,047	12.7%	Lab
Ross-Wagenknecht, Mrs S (Grn)	702	1.0%				
Clark, N (NLP)	320	0.5%				
Peacock, R (Ind)	304	0.4%				
Watkins, R (Ind C)	232	0.3%				
LD to C swing 3.0%	68,577		25.6%	63,453		19.6%
		C maj	17,565		C maj	12,418

John MacGregor was appointed transport secretary in April 1992. Lord President of Council and Ldr of Commons 1990-2. Education sec 1989-90; agricultre minister 1987-9; Chief Sec to Treasury 1985; minr of state for ag, fish and food, 1983-5; under sec for industry 1981-3; PC 1985. Former director, Hill Samuel and Co Ltd, and Hill Samuel Registrars Ltd. Elected in Feb 1974. B Feb 14 1937; ed Merchiston Castle Sch, Edinburgh; St Andrews Univ; King's Coll, London.
Christopher Brocklebank-Fowler, management consultant; managing director, Cambridge Corporate Consultants 1985-7. Cons MP for King's Lynn 1970-4 and for Norfolk NW, 1974-81. Joined SDP and remained MP

1981-3. Defeated at Norfolk NW 1983 and contested seat 1987; also contested W Ham N 1964. Chmn overseas trade and development agency 1979-83; vice-chmn centre for world development of ed, 1980-3. B Jan 13 1934; ed Perse Sch.
Clive Needle, full-time organiser, sec/agent, Norfolk S CLP, since 1987; sec Norfolk Cty LP; mbr Port Glasgow community cl, 1984-6. B Sep 22 1956; ed Southend HS; Aston Univ, Birmingham. Mbr Labour organisers branch GMB/Apex.
Stephanie Ross-Wagenknecht, student; jt cty co-ordinator, Norfolk Grn pty; co-ordinator Chet Valley pty. B Jan 23 1955; ed Thorpe GS, Norwich. NUS.

NORFOLK SOUTH WEST				No change		
Electorate % Turnout	77,652	79.3%	1992	74,240	76.0%	1987
*Shephard, Mrs G P (C)	33,637	54.6%	-3.0%	32,519	57.6%	C
Page, Ms M E (Lab)	16,706	27.1%	+6.1%	12,083	21.4%	L/All
Marsh, J (LD)	11,237	18.2%	-3.2%	11,844	21.0%	Lab
C to Lab swing 4.6%	61,580		27.5%	56,446		36.2%
		C maj	16,931		C maj	20,436

Gillian Shephard was appointed Secretary of State for Employment in 1992. Minr of State, Treasury, 1990-2, and a dep chmn Cons Pty, 1991; Under Sec of State for Social Security, 1989-90; co-chmn women's nat Commission, 1990-1. Elected in 1987. PPS to Peter Lilley, Economic Sec to Treasury, 1988-9; mbr select cmte on social services, 1987-8; jt sec Cons backbench health and social services cmte, 1987-8. Chmn Norwich HA, 1985-7; W Norfolk and Wisbech HA, 1981-5. Mbr Norfolk CC, 1977-89. B Jan 22 1940; ed N Walsham Girls' HS, Norfolk; St Hilda's coll, Oxford. Former schools inspector and mental health act commissioner. Cambridge univ extra mural bd lecturer in European subjects, 1973- . Fluent in French.

Mary Page, teacher/translater, contested Norfolk in 1989 Euro elections and this seat in 1987. Director, Eurotranslate. Mbr Breckland DC, 1974-81; Thetford DC, 1974-81 and 1985-7; Mayor of Thetford, 1980-1. B May 15 1944; ed Bournemouth sch for girls; Southampton and London univs. NAS/UWT.

John Marsh runs his own food package engineering business. Mbr King's Lynn and W Norfolk DC, 1983-5. B May 25 1944; ed sec mod sch; Beeston Tech Coll; RAF tech courses.

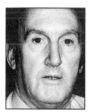

NORMANTON				No change		
Electorate % Turnout	65,562	76.4%	1992	62,899	74.8%	1987
*O'Brien, W (Lab)	25,936	51.8%	+2.3%	23,303	49.5%	Lab
Sturdy, R W (C)	16,986	33.9%	-0.1%	16,016	34.1%	C
Galdas, M (LD)	7,137	14.3%	-2.1%	7,717	16.4%	SDP/All
C to Lab swing 1.2%	50,059		17.9%	47,036		15.5%
		Lab maj	8,950		Lab maj	7,287

William O'Brien became an Opposn spokesman on environment in 1988 covering local government; former mbr public accounts cmte, 1983-8, and select cmte on energy, 1986-8. Sec all-pty inland waterways parly gp. Coalminer, 1945-83; NUM local branch official, 1956-83. Elected in 1983. Urban, county and metropolitan district councillor, 1951-83, B Jan 25 1929; ed St Joseph's sch, Castleford; Leeds univ (day release). Mbr NUM, 1945- .

Robert Sturdy, farmer, contested Lancashire East in 1989 Euro elections. B Jun 22 1944; ed Ashville coll, Harrogate. Chmn Yorks Cons Euro cl and of 1992 club; mbr Harrogate Cons exec and finance and gen purposes cmtes.

Mitchell Galdas, sales partner, Taurus Leather, Leeds. B Apr 30 1940; ed Pitmans Coll, Leeds.

NORTHAMPTON NORTH				No change		
Electorate % Turnout	69,139	78.5%	1992	69,294	74.6%	1987
*Marlow, A R (C)	24,865	45.8%	-2.2%	24,816	48.0%	C
Thomas, Mrs J M (Lab)	20,957	38.6%	+8.5%	15,560	30.1%	Lab
Church, R W (LD)	8,236	15.2%	-5.5%	10,690	20.7%	L/All
Spivack, B (NLP)	232	0.4%		471	0.9%	Grn
				156	0.3%	WRP
C to Lab swing 5.4%	54,290		7.2%	51,693		17.9%
		C maj	3,908		C maj	9,256

Anthony Marlow has been mbr select cmte on Euro legislation since 1983. Former development manager with grain shippers company. Gained seat for Cons in 1979; contested Normanton, Feb 1974, and Rugby, Oct 1974. B Jun 17 1940; ed Wellington coll; RMA Sandhurst; St Catharine's Coll, Cambridge. Jt vice-chmn, 1989-90 and jt sec, 1985-8, Cons backbench defence cmte. Vice-chmn allpty British-Palestine parly gp; sec British-Czechoslovak gp. Mbr steering cmte Cons European reform gp.

Janet Thomas, former social worker; Mbr Northampton CC, 1981- (dep gp ldr); Northampton BC, 1973-9; Anglian water authority, 1976-83; Oxford RHA, and gen Whitley cl, 1978-90. B Oct 16 1936; ed local state sch; Gosford HS. Post card collector.

Richard Church, shopkeeper, director, Church's China Stores. Mbr Northampton BC, 1983- (ldr, L and LD gp, 1983-); former chmn Northampton LD. B Apr 11 1958; ed Oakham sch, Rutland; Reading univ.

177

NORTHAMPTON SOUTH						No change
Electorate % Turnout	83,477	79.9%	1992	76,071	75.2%	1987
*Morris, M W L (C)	36,882	55.3%	-0.4%	31,864	55.7%	C
Dickie, J (Lab)	19,909	29.8%	+5.3%	14,061	24.6%	Lab
Mabbutt, G A G (LD)	9,912	14.9%	-3.7%	10,639	18.6%	SDP/All
				647	1.1%	Grn
C to Lab swing 2.8%	66,703		25.4%	57,211		31.1%
		C maj	16,973		C maj	17,803

Michael Morris was elected in Feb 1974; contested Islington N, 1966. Mbr public accounts cmte 1979- ; Commons chairmen's panel 1983- ; select cmte on energy 1982-5. Vice-chmn Cons backbench energy cmte 1981- . Director of Modern Personnel Ltd; consultant with AM International. B Nov 25 1936; ed Bedford sch (governor 1982- ; chmn of governors 1989-); St Catharine's coll, Cambridge. Mbr cl of Europe and WEU 1983-91. Chmn all-pty construction parly gp; treas all-pty parly food and health forum. Capt parly golf society 1988-91.

John Dickie, a teacher, contested this seat in 1987 and Northants in 1984 Euro election. Mbr Northampton BC 1973- (cl ldr; Lab gp ldr 1989-). Exec mbr Northampton community relations cl; bd mbr central festival opera. B Nov 28 1946; ed Wm Ellis sch, London; Brighton coll of ed; Sussex univ. NAS/UWT.

Graham Mabbutt, production controller in recording industry. Chmn/organiser/agent Milton Keynes SDP 1982-7; branch chmn Newport Pagnell LD, 1988-90. Mbr Lavenden PC 1982- (chmn 1987-). B Dec 20 1941; ed Moulton sec mod sch; Ousedale Adult ed centre; Ruskin coll, Oxford (postal course).

NORTHAVON						No change
Electorate % Turnout	83,496	84.2%	1992	78,483	80.2%	1987
*Cope, Sir John (C)	35,338	50.3%	-4.1%	34,224	54.4%	C
Larkins, Mrs H (LD)	23,477	33.4%	+1.7%	19,954	31.7%	L/All
Norris, Mrs J (Lab)	10,290	14.6%	+0.7%	8,762	13.9%	Lab
Greene, J (Grn)	789	1.1%				
Marx, P (Lib)	380	0.5%				
C to LD swing 2.9%	70,274		16.9%	62,940		22.7%
		C maj	11,861		C maj	14,270

Sir John Cope was appointed Paymaster General in the Treasury in April 1992. A dep chmn of Cons Pty 1990-2. Minr of state for N Ireland 1989-90; for employment and small firms 1987-9; Treasurer of HM Household and govt dep chief whip 1983-7; Ld Commissioner of Treasury (govt whip) 1981-3; asst govt whip 1979-81. PC 1988. Chartered accountant; former company director; adviser to Tacchi Investment Management Services. Hon vice-pres nat chamber of trade. Elected for this seat 1983; MP for S Gloucestershire, Feb 1974-83; contested Woolwich E, 1970. B May 13 1937; ed Oakham sch, Rutland.

Heather Larkin, teacher, was Avon cty cllr 1986-9; mbr Northavon DC 1991- . B Mar 13 1935; ed Colston Girls' sch, Bristol; Bristol univ. Branch rep AMMA.

June Norris, administrator, contested Northavon 1983. Mbr Avon CC 1988- . B Jun 13 1937; ed The Mount sch, York. Mbr of and sponsored by Nupe.

Jay Greene, mbr of Northavon DC's environment team; self-employed contractor since 1984; former social worker. Sec Northavon Grn pty. B Feb 2 1953; ed at convent, Bury St Edmunds; Warwick and York univs.

NORWICH NORTH						No change
Electorate % Turnout	63,308	81.8%	1992	62,725	79.2%	1987
*Thompson, H P (C)	22,419	43.3%	-2.6%	22,772	45.8%	C
Gibson, I (Lab)	22,153	42.8%	+12.6%	14,996	30.2%	Lab
Harrison, D (LD)	6,706	12.9%	-11.0%	11,922	24.0%	L/All
Betts, L (Grn)	433	0.8%				
Arnold, R (NLP)	93	0.2%				
C to Lab swing 7.6%	51,804		0.5%	49,690		15.6%
		C maj	266		C maj	7,776

Patrick Thompson was elected in 1983; contested Bradford N twice in 1974 and Barrow-in-Furness, 1979. PPS to minr for social security and minr for disabled, 1988-9; to minr of state for transport, and to under sec for transport, 1987-8. Mbr select cmte on statutory instruments 1990- ; ed, science and arts select cmte 1991- . Sec Cons backbench European affairs cmte 1991- . Jt sec Cons backbench arts and heritage cmte 1990- . Mbr Parly and Scientific Cmte 1983- ; founder mbr (now sec/treas) all-pty gp for engineering development. B Oct 21 1935; ed Felsted Sch,

Essex; Emmanuel Coll, Cambridge. Teacher and former engineer. AMMA.

Ian Gibson, Dean of Biological Sciences, Univ of East Anglia. B Sep 26, 1938; ed Dumfries local state schs; Edinburgh Univ. Exec cmte mbr ASTMS/MSF.

David Harrison, teacher and scientist. Mbr N Norfolk DC 1987- ; vice-chmn CHC 1987-9. B Nov 30 1937.

Lou Betts, press officer, Norfolk and Anglia Grn pty. B Nov 23 1952; ed City of Norwich Sch.

NORWICH SOUTH						No change
Electorate % Turnout	63,603	80.6%	1992	64,421	80.6%	1987
*Garrett, J L (Lab)	24,965	48.7%	+10.8%	19,666	37.9%	Lab
Baxter, D S (C)	18,784	36.6%	-0.6%	19,330	37.3%	C
Thomas, C (LD)	6,609	12.9%	-12.0%	12,896	24.9%	SDP/All
Holmes, A S (Grn)	803	1.6%				
Parsons, B (NLP)	104	0.2%				
C to Lab swing 5.7%	51,265	12.1%		51,892		0.6%
		Lab maj	6,181		Lab maj	336

John Garrett became Lab campaigns co-ordinator for Southern and Eastern England in 1989; an Opposn spokesman on trade and industry, 1988-9; a spokesman on energy 1987-8. Mbr select cmte on Treasury and Civil Service, 1989- . Regained seat for Lab in 1987; MP for the seat Feb 1974-83. Associate director, Inbucon Ltd, management consultants, 1983-7; manager, director of public services, Inbucon Ltd, 1963-74; now freelance associate to company. Director, Statesman and Nation Publishing Co 1986-7; W Midlands enterprise bd, 1986-7. Mbr Greenwich BC 1970-4. B Sep 8 1931; ed Sir George Monoux Sch, London; Oxford and California (Los Angeles) Univs.
David Baxter, deputy chmn Ipswich Cons assocn, 1987-9,

is a snr manager for British Telecom. Former marketing director, Miracom Ltd (info tech); Euro marketing director, UI Gp (US food corporation), and sales and marketing manager Mobil Plastics Europe, the industrial packaging division of Mobil Oil Corporation. Former officer of Esher, West Molesey and Surbiton Cons Assocns. B Feb 7 1955; ed Hinchley Wood Sch, Esher; Univ Coll, Cardiff. Mbr exec cl Cons family campaign; foreign affairs forum and environmental task force.
Christopher Thomas, teacher. Mbr Friends of the Earth and local environmental forum. B Apr 20 1948; ed Wolverhampton Poly; E Anglia Univ.
Adrian Holmes, computer programmer and consultant. B Aug 1 1956; ed Paston Sch, N Walsham; Leeds Univ.

NORWOOD						No change
Electorate % Turnout	52,496	65.9%	1992	56,602	67.0%	1987
*Fraser, J D (Lab)	18,391	53.2%	+4.7%	18,359	48.4%	Lab
Samways, J P E (C)	11,175	32.3%	-3.7%	13,636	36.0%	C
Lawman, Ms S J (LD)	4,087	11.8%	-2.9%	5,579	14.7%	SDP/All
Collins, W S B (Grn)	790	2.3%		171	0.5%	Rabies
Leighton, M (NLP)	138	0.4%		151	0.4%	CD
C to Lab swing 4.2%	34,581	20.9%		37,896		12.5%
		Lab maj	7,216		Lab maj	4,723

John Fraser became an Opposn spokesman on legal affairs in 1987; a spokesman on housing and construction, 1983-7; on trade, prices and consumer protection, 1979-83. Minr of state for prices and consumer protection 1976-9; under sec for employment 1974-6. Won the seat in 1966; contested it in 1964. Solicitor. B Jun 30 1934; ed Sloane GS, Chelsea; Co-operative Coll, Loughborough; Law Soc Sch of Law. Treas London gp of Lab MPs 1987- . Mbr Lambeth BC 1962-68. GMB.
Julian Samways, institutional fund manager, became

editor of *Crossbow* in 1990. Mbr gtr London area Cons cl 1989- ; Wimbledon Cons finance and gen purposes cmte 1989- . B Dec 29 1961; ed Wilmslow GS; Queen Mary Coll, London Univ. Nat vice-chmn FCS 1983-4.
Sandra Lawman, accounts supervisor. Mbr Lambeth BC 1990- . Former chmn nat schizophrenia fellowship Voices organization. B Sep 22 1958; ed Manchester HS for Girls; St Mary's Coll, Durham Univ.
Shane Collins, student. Co-sec Lambeth Grn pty. B Aug 16 1961; ed Allhallows Sch, Rousden.

NOTTINGHAM EAST						Lab gain
Electorate % Turnout	67,939	70.1%	1992	68,266	68.8%	1987
Heppell, J (Lab)	25,026	52.6%	+10.6%	20,162	42.9%	C
*Knowles, M (C)	17,346	36.4%	-6.5%	19,706	42.0%	Lab
Ball, T S (LD)	3,695	7.8%	-6.9%	6,883	14.7%	L/All
Jones, A (Grn)	667	1.4%		212	0.5%	RF
Roylance, C (Lib)	598	1.3%				
Ashforth, J (NLP)	283	0.6%				
C to Lab swing 8.6%	47,615	16.1%		46,963		1.0%
		Lab maj	7,680		C maj	456

John Heppell, a full-time cllr regained this seat for Lab in 1992. Mbr Nottinghamshire CC 1981- (dep Lab gp ldr; chmn equal opportunities cmte). B Nov 3 1948; ed Rutherford GS; Ashington Tech Coll. Mbr Co-op pty; Nottingham anti-apartheid; Edwards Lane community assocn; Longdale tenants and residents association. RMT (sponsored by union).
Michael Knowles was MP for this seat 1983-92; contested Merthyr Tydfil Feb 1974 and Brent E, Oct 1974. PPS to William Waldegrave 1987-8 and to Lord Elton 1985-6.

Mbr select cmte on Euro legislation 1988-92; on defence, 1991-2; on Severn Bridges Bill 1991-2. Jt sec Cons backbench home affairs cmte 1988-9; sec all-pty friends of Northern Cyprus gp. Mbr Kingston upon Thames BC 1971-83. Consultant to PPA International. Former export and home sales manager. B May 21 1942; ed Clapham Coll RC GS.
Tim Ball, computer analyst. B Sep 16 1959; ed Ilkeston GS, Derbyshire; Birmingham Univ.

NOTTINGHAM NORTH				No change	
Electorate % Turnout	69,494	75.0%	1992	69,620	72.6%	1987
*Allen, G W (Lab)	29,052	55.7%	+10.8%	22,713	44.9%	Lab
Bridge, I G (C)	18,309	35.1%	-6.5%	21,048	41.6%	C
Skelton, A (LD)	4,477	8.6%	-3.1%	5,912	11.7%SDP/All
Cadman, A (NLP)	274	0.5%		879	1.7%	Comm
C to Lab swing 8.7%	52,112		20.6%	50,552		3.3%
		Lab maj	10,743		Lab maj	1,665

Graham Allen won this seat in 1987. Appointed to Opposn social security team in 1991. Mbr select cmte on procedure 1990-1; on members' interests 1987-90; jt select cmte on consolidation bills 1987-91; public accounts cmte 1988-91. Chmn PLP Treasury and civil service cmte 1990-1. GMB official 1986-7; nat co-ordinator political funds campaign for trades union coordinating cmte 1984-6. GLC local govt officer 1983-4; Lab pty research officer 1978-83. B Jan 11 1953; ed Robert Shaw primary sch; Forest Fields GS; City of London Poly; Leeds Univ. Sponsored by TGWU.

Ian Bridge, proprietor of wine bar and restaurant. Contested Derbyshire NE 1983. Former production manager and planning and supplies manager with United Biscuits Ltd; former police officer and detective in Bedfordshire. B Jul 3 1952; ed Bushmead Sec Mod Sch, St Neots, Hunts; Mander Coll, Bedford; Durham Univ. Cons pty officer in Ashby area; former chmn Loughborough YCs. Former chmn Ashby-de-la-Zouch chamber of trade.
Tony Skelton, bus driver. Chmn assocn of LD trade unionists. Mbr TGWU. B Sep 6 1959; ed Top Valley Sch, Nottingham.

NOTTINGHAM SOUTH				Lab gain	
Electorate % Turnout	72,796	74.2%	1992	72,807	73.5%	1987
Simpson, A (Lab)	25,771	47.7%	+7.2%	23,921	44.7%	C
*Brandon-Bravo, N M (C)	22,590	41.8%	-2.9%	21,687	40.5%	Lab
David Long, G D (LD)	5,408	10.0%	-4.8%	7,917	14.8%SDP/All
Christou, Ms J (NLP)	263	0.5%			
C to Lab swing 5.0%	54,032		5.9%	53,525		4.2%
		Lab maj	3,181		C maj	2,234

Alan Simpson won this seat in 1992 having contested it in 1987. Information officer with Nottingham racial equality cl. Author of books and articles on racism and on housing policies. Mbr Notts CC 1985- . B Sep 20 1948; ed Bootle GS; Nottingham Poly. Nupe.
Martin Brandon-Bravo had been MP for this seat 1983-92; contested Nottingham E, 1979. Former PPS to Lord Waddington, to John Patten and to Earl Ferrers. Jt sec

Interparly cl against anti-semitism 1991-2. Mbr Nottingham City Cl, 1968-70 and 1976-87; bd of management nat water sports centre, Nottingham, of which he is a founding mbr 1972-83. B Mar 25 1932; ed Latymer Sch. Non-exec director Richard Stump Ltd 1983-89; parly adviser to ASL/Alliance (London).
Gary Long, public sector accountant,has held various party offices. B May 7 1957; ed Nottingham Univ.

NUNEATON				Lab gain	
Electorate % Turnout	70,906	83.7%	1992	68,287	80.4%	1987
Olner, W J (Lab)	27,157	45.8%	+11.2%	24,630	44.9%	C
*Stevens, L D (C)	25,526	43.0%	-1.9%	18,975	34.6%	Lab
Merritt, Ms R (LD)	6,671	11.2%	-8.0%	10,550	19.2%SDP/All
				719	1.3%	Grn
C to Lab swing 6.5%	59,354		2.7%	54,874		10.3%
		Lab maj	1,631		C maj	5,655

William Olner, an engineer, gained this seat for Labour in 1992. Mbr Nuneaton and Bedworth BC 1972- ; mayor of Nuneaton and Bedford 1986-7; chmn, environmental health cmte; former cl ldr and former chmn planning. AEU branch sec for many years and previously shop steward at Rolls-Royce, Coventry. Mbr Nuneaton and Bedworth trades cl. Co-founder Mary Ann Evans Hospice, Nuneaton, and chmn hospice trustees. B May 9 1942; ed Atherstone Sec Mod Sch; N Warwickshire Tech Coll.
Lewis Stevens, self-employed management and industrial engineering consultant, was MP for this seat 1983-92; fought it 1979. PPS to Colin Moyniham 1989-92 and to

David Heathcoat-Amory 1990-2. Mbr select cmte on employment 1987-9; on Channel tunnel bill 1986-7. Jt sec Cons backbench health and social services cmte 1986-8. B Apr 13 1936; ed Oldbury GS, Worcestershire; Liverpool Univ; Lanchester Coll, Coventry. Mbr Nuneaton BC 1966-72. Chmn of trustees Albert Herbert Pension Fund.
Ruth Merritt was elected to Warwickshire CC in 1989; mbr Stroud DC, 1990; Oakham Rutland TC 1974-81; dist cllr 1979-81. Mbr rivers advisory cmte NRA Severn Trent region. B Nov 17 1929; ed London and Open Univs. Avon AMMA recruiting officer, 1983-89.

OGMORE						No change
Electorate % Turnout	52,195	80.6%	1992	51,255	80.0%	1987
*Powell, R (Lab)	30,186	71.7%	+2.4%	28,462	69.4%	Lab
Edwards, D G (C)	6,359	15.1%	+0.1%	6,170	15.0%	C
Warman, J (LD)	2,868	6.8%	-2.8%	3,954	9.6%	SDP/All
McAllister, Ms L (PC)	2,667	6.3%	+2.0%	1,791	4.4%	PC
				652	1.6%	Ind Lab
C to Lab swing 1.1%	42,080		56.6%	41,029		54.3%
		Lab maj	23,827		Lab maj	22,292

Raymond Powell, an Opposn whip, was vice-chmn of PLP agriculture cmte, 1986-87; sec, Welsh gp of Lab MPs, 1984- . Chmn, Commons accommodation and works cmte, 1991- ; mbr, Commons Services Cmte, 1987-91 (chmn of new parly building sub-cmte, 1987-91); Select Cmtes on Employment, 1979-82; on Welsh Affairs, 1982-85. Chmn, S Wales Euro constituency, 1980- ; sec, all-pty fairs and showgrounds parly gp, 1989- . Elected in 1979. B Jun 19 1928; ed Pentre GS; Nat Cl of Labour Colls; LSE. With British Rail, 1945-50; shop manager, 1950-66; sec and agent to Walter Padley MP, 1967-69 (voluntary, 1969-79). Sponsored by Usdaw.
David Edwards runs own public relations and marketing business near Newtown, Md Wales. Represents Montgom-ery on N Wales Euro Cons Cl and on Wales Area Cl. Mbr, Newtown TC; Montgomeryshire DC, 1990- . B Nov 12 1965; ed Newtown HS; Harper Adams Agricultural Coll, Newport.
John Warman, boilermaker with British Steel. Mbr, Neath BC, 1972- (Mayor of Neath, 1988-9); Press Cl, 1983-89; Water Services Cmte for Wales. B Jun 20 1944; ed Cadoxton Sec Mod Sch. GMB shop steward.
Laura McAllister, postgraduate researcher and tutor in politics, Cardiff Univ, contested Bridgend 1987. Vice-chair, PlC political ed, 1989- ; nat chair, PlC youth movement, 1987-89; mbr, nat exec cmte. B Dec 10 1964; ed Bryntirion Comprehensive Sch, Bridgend; LSE; Univ Coll of Wales, Cardiff. Playing mbr, Cardiff Ladies FC.

OLD BEXLEY AND SIDCUP						No change
Electorate % Turnout	49,449	81.9%	1992	50,831	77.1%	1987
*Heath, Sir Edward (C)	24,450	60.3%	-1.8%	24,350	62.1%	C
Brierly, Ms D (Lab)	8,751	21.6%	+4.3%	8,076	20.6%	L/All
Nicolle, D J (LD)	6,438	15.9%	-4.7%	6,762	17.3%	Lab
Rose, B (Alt C)	733	1.8%				
Stephens, R (NLP)	148	0.4%				
C to Lab swing 3.1%	40,520		38.7%	39,188		41.5%
		C maj	15,699		C maj	16,274

Sir Edward Heath, father of the House of Commons, Leader of Cons Pty, 1965-75; Prime Minister, 1970-74, and Ldr of Opposition, 1965-70, and from Feb 1974-75. Chief Opposn spokesman on Treasury and economic affairs, 1964-65, and chmn, party's policy cmte and research dept. Sec of State for Industry, Trade and Regional Development, and President of Bd of Trade, 1963-64; Ld Privy Seal, 1960-63, being chief FCO spokesman in Commons and leading negotiations to join EC; Minr of Labour, 1959-60; Parly Sec to Treasury and Govt Chief Whip, 1955-59; Dep Govt Chief Whip, 1952-55; Govt whip, 1951-52. PC 1955. Elected for this seat 1983; MP for Bexley Sidcup, 1974-83, and for Bexley, 1950-74. Mbr of Lloyd's. B Jul 9 1916; ed Chatham House Sch, Ramsgate; Balliol Coll, Oxford (pres of Union, 1939). Musician, international yachtsman and author.
Donna Brierly, in public relations, was elected to Bexley BC in 1986. B Jan 12 1964; ed Bexley GS; Blackfern Sch for Girls; Bexley and Erith Tech HS. GMPU; Co-op Pty.
David Nicolle, retired adult ed principal. B Aug 28 1932; ed Elizabeth Coll, Guernsey; King Alfreds Coll, Winchester; St Lukes Coll, Exeter; London Univ. NAS/UWT.

OLDHAM CENTRAL AND ROYTON						No change
Electorate % Turnout	61,333	74.2%	1992	65,277	69.2%	1987
Davies, B (Lab)	23,246	51.1%	+2.9%	21,759	48.1%	Lab
Morris, Mrs P (C)	14,640	32.2%	-2.1%	15,480	34.3%	C
Dunn, Mrs A (LD)	7,224	15.9%	-1.7%	7,956	17.6%	SDP/All
Dalling, I (NLP)	403	0.9%				
C to Lab swing 2.5%	45,513		18.9%	45,195		13.9%
		Lab maj	8,606		Lab maj	6,279

Bryan Davies, secretary to the PLP since 1979, was MP for Enfield N, Feb 1974-1979; contested Newport W 1983; Norfolk Central, 1966. Asst Govt whip, 1979; mbr, Select Cmte on Overseas Development and Public Expenditure Cmte, 1975-79; Medical Research Cl, 1977-79. B Nov 1939; ed Redditch HS; Univ Coll, London; Inst of Ed, London; LSE. Lecturer, Middlesex Poly, Enfield, 1965-74; sec, E Herts CLP, 1970-74; teacher, Latymer Sch, 1962-65. NATFHE, 1962-79; TGWU, 1979 - .
Patricia Morris, cmte mbr of patrons and associates of Manchester City Art Galleries, 1982- ; mbr, Manchester N valuation and community charge tribunal. Technical analyst with Manchester stockbrokers, 1979-83. Mbr, Cons women's nat cmte, 1989- ; vice-chmn, NW area women's cmte; vice-chmn, Bolton W Cons Assocn, 1987-89. B 1953; ed Bolton Sch; Clifton and Didsbury Colls of Ed.
Ann Dunn, teacher, contested seat 1987. Parent governor and chair of sub-cmte for Oldham Comprehensive Sch. Elected rep to CSD, 1983-87. B May 6 1949; ed Hulme GS, Oldham; Keele Univ. AMMA.

OLDHAM WEST						No change
Electorate % Turnout	54,063	75.7%	1992	57,178	71.9%	1987
*Meacher, M H (Lab)	21,580	52.8%	+3.4%	20,291	49.4%	Lab
Gillen, J (C)	13,247	32.4%	-2.5%	14,324	34.9%	C
Smith, J D (LD)	5,525	13.5%	-2.3%	6,478	15.8%	L/All
Dalling, Ms S (NLP)	551	1.3%				
C to Lab swing 2.9%	40,903		20.4%	41,093		14.5%
		Lab maj	8,333		Lab maj	5,967

Michael Meacher, mbr of shadow cabinet since 1983, became chief Opposn spokesman on social security in 1989; chief spokesman on employment, 1987-9; on health and social security, 1983-7. Contested dep ldrship of Lab pty after 1983 election. Under Sec of State for Trade, 1976-9; for Health and Social Security, 1975-6, and for Industry, 1974-5. Regained seat for Lab 1970; contested Colchester 1966. B Nov 4 1939; ed Berkhamsted sch; New coll, Oxford; LSE. Mbr Labour NEC, 1983-8; chmn Labour coordinating cmte, 1978-83. Sponsored by Cohse.

Jonathan Gillen, director of investor relations and corporate public relations company. B Aug 2 1957; ed Kent univ. Former mbr nat cmte, fed of Cons students and chmn regional FCS.

John Smith, computer analyst/programmer. Mbr Oldham MBC, 1988- . B Apl 12 1948; ed The Hulme GS, Oldham.

ORKNEY AND SHETLAND						No change
Electorate % Turnout	31,472	65.5%	1992	31,047	68.7%	1987
*Wallace, J R (LD)	9,575	46.4%	+4.8%	8,881	41.7%	L/All
McCormick, Dr P (C)	4,542	22.0%	-1.2%	4,959	23.3%	C
Aberdein, J H (Lab)	4,093	19.8%	+1.1%	3,995	18.7%	Lab
McKie, Mrs F C (SNP)	2,301	11.2%		3,095	14.5%	OSM
Wharton, Ms C (NLP)	115	0.6%		389	1.8%	Grn
C to LD swing 3.0%	20,626		24.4%	21,319		18.4%
		LD maj	5,033		L/All maj	3,922

James Wallace became LD spokesman on employment and training and LD chief whip in 1988, and spokesman on fishing, 1989- . Lib chief whip, 1987-8; dep chief whip, 1985-7. Lib and then LD spokesman on defence, 1985-8; Alliance 1987 election team spokesman on transport. Non-practising advocate; parly adviser to inst of chartered accountants of Scotland; unpaid parly adviser to procurators fiscal society in Scotland. Elected in 1983; contested Dumfries, 1979; Euro candidate for South Scotland, 1979. Mbr Commons services cmte, 1985-7; liaison cmte, 1985- ; select cmte on procedure, 1988- . B Aug 25 1954; ed Annan acad, Dumfriesshire; Downing coll, Cambridge; Edinburgh univ.

Dr Paul McCormick, barrister. Mbr Havant BC, 1988- ; chmn Havant CPC, 1986-9. B Mar 17 1951; ed Chichester HS for Boys; Balliol and Nuffield colls, Oxford; City univ. Specialist adviser, Commons select cmte on employment, 1981.

John Aberdein, sec sch teacher of English, former herring fisherman and diver, contested this seat 1987. Supervised sea-canoeing centre at Calshot, Hampshire, 1980-2. Former sec Orkney trades cl; founder chmn Orkney's first tenants assocn. B Mar 23 1946; ed Robert Gordon's coll, Aberdeen; Aberdeen univ. EIS.

Frances McKie, teacher; SNP speaker on nuclear dumping. B Nov 14 1951; ed Edinburgh univ. EIS.

ORPINGTON						No change
Electorate % Turnout	57,318	83.7%	1992	59,608	78.5%	1987
Horam, J R (C)	27,421	57.2%	-1.1%	27,261	58.2%	C
Maines, C (LD)	14,486	30.2%	-0.8%	14,529	31.0%	L/All
Cowan, S J (Lab)	5,512	11.5%	+0.8%	5,020	10.7%	Lab
Almond, R (Lib)	539	1.1%				
C to LD swing 0.1%	47,958		27.0%	46,810		27.2%
		C maj	12,935		C maj	12,732

John Horam, economist; managing director, CRU Holdings Ltd, 1988- . Mbr Cons pty economic policy cmte. Labour MP for Gateshead West, 1970-81 and SDP MP for that seat, 1981-3; contested Newcastle Central 1983. Joined Conservative pty Feb 1987. Labour Under Secretary of State for Transport, 1976-9 and Lab spokesman on economic affairs, 1979-81. Managing director, Commodities Research Unit Ltd, 1968-70 and 1983-7. B Mar 7 1939; ed Silcoates sch, Wakefield; St Catharine's corr. AL coll, Cambridge. Former leader and feature writer, The Economist, 1965-8, and Financial Times, 1962-5.

Christopher Maines, credit controller, has been mbr Bromley BC since 1986; LD gp ldr on cl. B Jan 11 1958.

Steven Cowan, teacher, contested this seat 1987, Hampshire E 1983 and London SE in 1984 Euro elections. Mbr ILEA, 1983-90; sec Southall/Ealing CLP, 1990- ; B Sep 6 1951; ed Bristol and London univs. NUT and TGWU.

OXFORD EAST						No change
Electorate % Turnout	63,075	74.6%	1992	62,145	79.0%	1987
*Smith, A D (Lab)	23,702	50.4%	+7.4%	21,103	43.0%	Lab
Mayall, Dr M N A (C)	16,164	34.4%	-6.0%	19,815	40.4%	C
Horwood, M C (LD)	6,105	13.0%	-2.6%	7,648	15.6%	L/All
Lucas, Mrs C (Grn)	933	2.0%	+1.1%	441	0.9%	Grn
Wilson, Miss A (NLP)	101	0.2%		60	0.1%	CC
Thompson, K (Rev Comm)	48	0.1%				
C to Lab swing 6.7%	47,053		16.0%	49,067		2.6%
		Lab maj	7,538		Lab maj	1,288

Andrew Smith, elected in 1987, joined Opposn front bench ed team in 1988 as speaker on higher and continuing ed. Mbr Oxford city cl 1976-87 (chmn planning cmte 1984-87) Contested this seat 1983. Chmn bd of governors, Oxford poly. B Feb 1 1951; ed Reading sch; Oxford univ. Mbr of and sponsored by Usdaw.

Dr Mark Mayall, doctor at Guy's Hospital, London; mbr royal coll of psychiatrists, 1987-9, contested Livingstone 1987. B Dec 15 1958; ed St George's coll, Weybridge;

King's Coll London; Westminster Hosp.

Martin Horwood, fundraiser at Oxfam. Co-editor, *New Democrat International*, 1990-1; nat chmn, ULS, 1984-85. B Oct 12 1962; ed Cheltenham coll; Queen's coll, Oxford. ACTSS.

Caroline Lucas is an overseas development agency researcher. Co-chmn, Grn pty nat cl 1989-90; nat spokesman 1991- . B Dec 9 1960; ed Malvern Girls' coll; Exeter univ. NUJ.

OXFORD WEST AND ABINGDON						No change
Electorate % Turnout	72,328	76.7%	1992	69,193	78.4%	1987
*Patten, J H C (C)	25,163	45.4%	-1.0%	25,171	46.4%	C
Goodhart, Sir William (LD)	21,624	39.0%		20,293	37.4%	SDP/All
Kent, B (Lab)	7,652	13.8%	-1.1%	8,108	14.9%	Lab
Woodin, Dr M E (Grn)	660	1.2%	-0.1%	695	1.3%	Grn
Jenking, R (Lib)	194	0.3%				
Nelson, Miss S (Anti-Fed)	98	0.2%				
Wells, G (NLP)	75	0.1%				
C to LD swing 1.3%	55,466		6.4%	54,267		9.0%
		C maj	3,539		C maj	4,878

John Patten was appointed Secretary of State for Education in 1992. Minr of State, Home Office 1987-92; Minr for Housing, Urban Affairs and Construction, with rank of Minr of State, DOE 1985-7; Under Sec of State for Health and Social Security 1983-5; Under Sec of State for N Ireland 1981-3. PC 1990. PPS to Minrs of State, Home Office 1980-1. Elected for this seat 1983; MP for Oxford, 1979-83. B Jul 17 1945; ed Wimbledon coll; Sidney Sussex coll, Cambridge. Lecturer, Oxford univ 1969-79; Fellow and tutor 1972-81, and Fellow 1981- , Hertford coll, Oxford. Mbr Cl, Reading univ; Oxford city cl 1973-6. Editor, *Journal of Historical Geography* 1975-80.

Sir William Goodhart, barrister, contested Kensington in 1988 by-election 1987 and 1983. Chmn LD fed conference cmte 1988-91. B Jan 18 1933; ed Eton; Trinity coll, Cambridge; Harvard law sch.

Bruce Kent was chmn, campaign for nuclear disarmament 1987-90; vice-chmn 1985-7; gen sec 1980-5. Pres international peace bureau 1985- . B Jun 22 1929; ed Lower Canada coll, Montreal; Stonyhurst coll; Brasenose coll, Oxford. Resigned priesthood 1987. MSF.

Dr Mike Woodin, academic; psychologist, Oxford univ. Ed officer, Oxford Grn pty 1989-90. B Nov 6 1965; ed Gravesend GS; Manchester univ; Wolfson coll, Oxford..

PAISLEY NORTH						No change
Electorate % Turnout	46,403	73.4%	1992	49,487	73.5%	1987
*Adams, Mrs I (Lab)	17,269	50.7%	-4.8%	20,193	55.5%	Lab
Mullin, W A R (SNP)	7,940	23.3%	+10.4%	5,751	15.8%	C
Sharpe, D (C)	5,576	16.4%	+0.6%	5,741	15.8%	SDP/All
McCartin, Miss E (LD)	2,779	8.2%	-7.6%	4,696	12.9%	SNP
Mellor, G (Grn)	412	1.2%				
Brennan, N (NLP)	81	0.2%				
Lab to SNP swing 7.6%	34,057		27.4%	36,381		39.7%
		Lab maj	9,329		Lab maj	14,442

Irene Adams won this seat in a by-election in 1990, following the death of her husband, the former MP for the seat. Mbr Commons catering cmte, 1991- . Mbr Paisley TC 1970-4; Renfrew DC 1974-8; Strathclyde reg cl 1979-84. B Dec 27 1947; ed Stanley Green HS, Paisley. Widow of Allen Adams, MP for seat 1983-90, and for Paisley 1979-83.

Roger Mullin, partner in management consultancy, contested 1990 by-election; Kirkcaldy 1987; Ayrshire S twice in 1974. SNP spokesperson on environment; vice-

convenor, organisation. B Mar 12 1948; ed Edinburgh univ; Carrick acad.

David Sharpe, civil engineer, employed by Strathclyde reg cl roads dept. B Mar 26 1956; ed Jordanhill coll of ed; Glasgow coll. Mbr and former steward, Nalgo.

Eileen McCartin, a home economist employed by Strathclyde Reg Cl 1975- , contested seat 1987 and 1983. B May 6 1952; ed Notre Dame HS, Queens coll, Jordanhill coll and Glasgow tech coll. EIS 1974-5; Nalgo 1975- .

Details of 1990 by-election on page 288

PAISLEY SOUTH						No change
Electorate % Turnout	47,889	75.0%	1992	51,127	75.3%	1987
*McMaster, G (Lab)	18,202	50.7%	-5.5%	21,611	56.2%	Lab
Lawson, I M (SNP)	8,653	24.1%	+10.1%	5,826	15.1%	L/All
Laidlaw, Ms S (C)	5,703	15.9%	+1.2%	5,644	14.7%	C
Reid, A (LD)	3,271	9.1%	-6.0%	5,398	14.0%	SNP
Porter, S (NLP)	93	0.3%				
Lab to SNP swing 7.8%	35,922		26.6%	38,479		41.0%
		Lab maj	9,549		Lab maj	15,785

Gordon McMaster, snr lecturer in horticulture, retained the seat for Labour in the 1990 by-election. Former organiser of employment training project for mentally handicapped. Mbr Select cmte on procedure 1991- . Mbr euro standing cmte; Renfrew DC 1984-91 (cl ldr 1988-90; dep ldr 1987-8). Co-ordinator growing concern initiative, Strathclyde 1988-90. B Feb 13 1960; ed Cochrane Castle Primary Sch, Johnstone; Johnstone HS; Woodburn House FE Centre; W of Scotland Agricultural Coll; Jordanhill Coll of Ed. EIS; TGWU. Mbr Johnstone community cl, 1980-4 (chmn 1982-84). Sponsored by Co-op pty.
Iain Lawson, proprietor of pest control company in Paisley,
contested the 1990 by-election and Stirling for SNP 1987; Dumbarton for Cons in 1983, Glasgow Garscadden in 1979 and 1978 by-election. Joined SNP on day Gartcosh steel mill closed in 1986. Elected mbr SNP nat cl. B Oct 8 1952; ed Clydebank HS.
Sheila Laidlaw, professional florist. Pres Paisley Chamber of Commerce and Industry; director, Renfrew Development co. Mbr exec Paisley N Cons assocn; exec E Renfrewshire Cons assocn, 1970- . B Sep 15 1939.
Alan Reid, computer technician, contested 1990 by-election. Mbr Renfrew DC; Scottish LD exec. B 1954.

PECKHAM						No change
Electorate % Turnout	58,269	53.9%	1992	59,261	55.6%	1987
*Harman, Ms H (Lab)	19,391	61.8%	+7.2%	17,965	54.5%	Lab
Frazer, C M (C)	7,386	23.5%	-2.2%	8,476	25.7%	C
Colley, Mrs R E (LD)	4,331	13.8%	-4.0%	5,878	17.8%	L/All
Dacres, G (WRP)	146	0.5%	628	1.9%	Grn	
Emmanuel, V (Whiplash)	140	0.4%				
C to Lab swing 4.7%	31,394		38.2%	32,947		28.8%
		Lab maj	12,005		Lab maj	9,489

Harriet Harman appointed to Opposn front bench DHSS team in 1985 being responsible for health issues from 1987. Elected for Peckham in 1982 by-election. Solicitor and civil rights campaigner. Mbr PLP civil liberties group. B Jul 30 1950; ed St Paul's Girls Sch; York Univ. Legal officer, Nat Cl for Civil Liberties 1975-8. Sponsored by TGWU.
Christopher Frazer, barrister. Mbr City of London Corporation 1986- ; City of London police cmte. Chmn
Young Barristers of England and Wales 1991; trustee Lawaid '91. B Jun 17 1960; ed King's Coll Sch, Wimbledon; St John's Coll, Cambridge. Sec Society of Cons Lawyers 1988-9.
Rose Colley, solicitor. Mbr Southwark BC 1984- (dep gp ldr 1987-); LD Lawyers ed policy panel; ILEA mbr for Southwark and Bermondsey 1988-90. B Mar 4 1954; ed Ellington Sec Mod and Clarendon Hse GS, Ramsgate; UCW, Aberystwyth; Coll of Law; Garnett Coll.

PEMBROKE						Lab gain
Electorate % Turnout	73,187	82.9%	1992	70,360	80.8%	1987
Ainger, N R (Lab)	26,253	43.3%	+12.3%	23,314	41.0%	C
*Bennett, N J (C)	25,498	42.0%	+1.1%	17,614	31.0%	Lab
Berry, P G (LD)	6,625	10.9%	-15.2%	14,832	26.1%	L/All
Bryant, C L (PC)	1,627	2.7%	+0.7%	1,119	2.0%	PC
Coghill, R W (Grn)	484	0.8%				
Stoddart, M (Anti-Fed)	158	0.3%				
C to Lab swing 5.6%	60,645		1.2%	56,879		10.0%
		Lab maj	755		C maj	5,700

Nick Ainger, a rigger, won this seat in 1992. Mbr Dyfed CC 1981- . Former chmn and sec of CLP. B Oct 24 1949; ed Netherthorpe GS, Staveley. Snr TGWU stewart and branch sec 1978- .
Nicholas Bennett was Welsh under sec 1990-92. PPS to transport minr of state for 1990. Mbr Wesl select cmte 1987-90; procedure cmte 1988-90. Jt vice-chmn Cons backbench party organisation cmte 1989-90; jt sec Cons transport cmte 1987-8. MP for this seat 1987-92; contested Hackney Central 1979. . B May 7 1949; ed Sedgehill Sch, London; Southwark and Walbrook CFEs; N London Poly; London and Sussex Univs.
Peter Sain-Ley-Berry, business consultant, contested Pon-
typridd 1987 and Swansea W 1983. Sec Lloyd George society; mbr economic policy working gp and Welsh policy cmte. B May 9 1946; ed Magdalen Coll Sch, Oxford; Peterhouse, Cambridge; Birkbeck Coll, London. Former principal in Welsh Office.
Conrad Bryant, chief accountant of port authority and director of several subsidiary companies. Mbr, PC NEC and nat cl; former chmn Pembroke constituency pty. B Mar 11 1939; ed Tonyrefail GS.
Roger Coghill, director of research. Treas Torfaen Grn pty. B Jul 3 1940; ed City of London Sch; Emmanuel Coll, Cambridge.

PENDLE						Lab gain
Electorate % Turnout	64,063	82.9%	1992	63,588	81.8%	1987
Prentice, G (Lab)	23,497	44.2%	+8.9%	21,009	40.4%	C
*Lee, J R L (C)	21,384	40.3%	-0.1%	18,370	35.3%	Lab
Davies, A (LD)	7,976	15.0%	-9.3%	12,662	24.3%	L/All
Thome, Mrs V (Anti-Fed)	263	0.5%				
C to Lab swing 4.5%	53,120		4.0%	52,041		5.1%
		Lab maj	2,113		C maj	2,639

Gordon Prentice gained this seat for Labour in 1992. Worked as the Lab pty's local govt officer in policy directorate, Walworth Rd, London; mbr, Hammersmith and Fulham BC, 1982-90 (cl ldr 1986-88). Held CLP and branch offices; mbr Co-op pty. B Jan 28 1951; ed Glasgow univ (pres Univ union, 1972-3). TGWU.
John Lee was MP for this seat 1983-93; MP for Nelson and Colne 1979-83; contested Manchester, Moss Side, Oct 1974. Mbr select cmte on defence, 1990-2. Under Sec of State for Employment 1986-9, being Minr for Tourism 1987-9; Under Sec of State for Defence Procurement 1983-6. Former chmn all-pty tourism parly gp. Chartered accountant. Non-exec chmn Country Holidays Ltd, 1989-; non-exec director, Paterson Zochonis plc 1990-; PS Turner (Holdings) Ltd 1990-; MS International plc 1990-. Chmn assocn of leading visitor attractions 1990-. Consultant to Refuge Gp plc. B Jun 21 1942; ed William Hulme's GS, Manchester.

PENRITH AND THE BORDER						No change
Electorate % Turnout	73,769	79.7%	1992	70,994	77.5%	1987
*Maclean, D J (C)	33,808	57.5%	-2.7%	33,148	60.3%	C
Walker, K G (LD)	15,359	26.1%	-2.6%	15,782	28.7%	L/All
Metcalfe, J (Lab)	8,871	15.1%	+4.0%	6,075	11.0%	Lab
Gibson, R (Grn)	610	1.0%				
Docker, I (NLP)	129	0.2%				
C to LD swing 0.1%	58,777		31.4%	55,005		31.6%
		C maj	18,449		C maj	17,366

David Maclean was appointed Minister of State, Environment in 1992. Parly Sec Ministry of Agriculture, Fisheries and Food 1989-92; a Ld Commissioner of Treasury (govt whip) 1988-9; an asst govt whip 1987-8. Won the seat in 1983 by-election caused by elevation to House of Lords of William Whitelaw; contested Inverness, Nairn and Lochaber, 1983. PPS to Michael Jopling, Minr of Ag, Fish and Food 1986-7; mbr select cmte on agriculture 1983-6. B May 16 1953; ed Fortrose acad; Aberdeen univ.
Geyve Walker, solicitor in private practice; wine merchant. Nominated mbr Cumbria CC ed cmte 1990-; former chmn Penrith branch LDs. B Oct 15 1948; ed Arnold sch Blackpool; St Peter's coll Oxford.
John Metcalfe, trainman driver with BR, chmn Carlisle CLP 1988-90; sec CLP 1987-8. Mbr Carlisle city cl 1986-. B Oct 28 1963; ed Trinity sch, Carlisle. CPSA 1982-9; RMT 1989-.

PERTH AND KINROSS						No change
Electorate % Turnout	65,410	76.9%	1992	63,443	74.4%	1987
*Fairbairn, Sir Nicholas (C)	20,195	40.2%	+0.5%	18,716	39.6%	C
Cunningham, Ms R (SNP)	18,101	36.0%	+8.4%	13,040	27.6%	SNP
Rolfe, M J (Lab)	6,267	12.5%	-3.4%	7,969	16.9%	L/All
Black, M (LD)	5,714	11.4%	-5.5%	7,490	15.9%	Lab
C to SNP swing 3.9%	50,277		4.2%	47,215		12.0%
		C maj	2,094		C maj	5,676

Sir Nicholas Fairbairn, QC, was appointed chmn historic buildings cl for Scotland in 1988; trustee Scottish museums 1987-. Solicitor General for Scotland 1979-82. Mbr select cmte on Scottish affairs 1983-7. Elected for this seat 1983; MP for Kinross and West Perthshire, Oct 1974-83; contested Edinburgh, Central, 1964 and 1966. Vice-chmn Scottish Cons MPs 1983-. Journalist, painter, writer, broadcaster and director of three companies. Mbr Edinburgh Festival cl, 1971-. B Dec 24 1933; ed Loretto and Edinburgh univ. Vice-pres Scottish women's society of artists 1988-; chmn Scottish soc for defence of literature and the arts. Hon fellow, international academy of trial lawyers 1984.
Roseanna Cunningham, self-employed advocate and former local authority solicitor; on SNP nat exec; spokeswoman on non-nuclear environmental issues. B Jul 27 1951; ed state schs and univs in Scotland and Australia. Former Nalgo shop steward and branch chmn.
Mervyn Rolfe was elected to Tayside reg cl in 1986 (chmn of ed cmte 1986-; dep ldr 1990-). Chmn Angus East CLP 1980-5; treas Dundee E 1986-7. B Jul 31 1947; ed Buckhaven HS, Fife. TGWU.
Malcolm Black, former snr lecturer in public sector ed, contested Scotland Mid and Fife in 1989 Euro election; Kirkcaldy in 1983. Former independent town cllr; SDP/All regional cllr; held various SDP offices. B Feb 26 1936; ed Tobermory JS; Oban HS; Glasgow and London univs; Moray Hse and Jordan Hill colls. EIS (area chmn and treas); on nat exec assocn of lecturers in cols of ed in Scotland.

PETERBOROUGH						No change
Electorate % Turnout	87,638	75.1%	1992	84,284	73.5%	1987
*Mawhinney, Dr B S (C)	31,827	48.3%	-1.1%	30,624	49.4%	C
Owens, Ms J (Lab)	26,451	40.2%	+6.5%	20,840	33.6%	Lab
Taylor, Ms A (LD)	5,208	7.9%	-8.2%	9,984	16.1%	L/All
Murat, E (Lib)	1,557	2.4%		506	0.8%	Grn
Heaton, R (BNP)	311	0.5%				
Beasley, Mrs P I (PP)	271	0.4%				
Brettell, C (NLP)	215	0.3%				
C to Lab swing 3.8%	65,840		8.2%	61,954		15.8%
		C maj	5,376		C maj	9,784

Dr Brian Mawhinney was appointed health minr in 1992. N Ireland minr 1990-2; under sec 1986-90. Radiation biologist; snr lecturer, Royal Free Hospital Sch of Medicine, London, 1970-84. Gained seat in 1979; contested Stockton, Oct 1974. B Jul 26 1940; ed Royal Belfast Academical Inst; Queens Univ, Belfast; Univ of Michigan, US; Univ of London. Mbr Medical Research Cl, 1980-3; nat cl, Nat Soc for Cancer Relief, 1981-5; and exec of Cons medical soc. Pres Cons trade unionists, 1987-90;

mbr General Synod of Church of England, 1985-90. AUT.
Julie Owens, political researcher and administrator in European Parliament and former full-time official of Ucatt. B Feb 3 1955; ed Queen Elizabeth's Girls' GS, Mansfield; Aston and Sussex Univs.
Amanda Taylor, equipment consultant. Sec Peterborough LDs. B Jul 3 1962; ed Leeds Girls HS; St Aidan's and St John Fisher Sch, Harrogate; Leeds Univ.

PLYMOUTH, DEVONPORT						Lab gain
Electorate % Turnout	65,799	77.8%	1992	64,741	76.9%	1987
Jamieson, D C (Lab)	24,953	48.7%	+20.3%	21,039	42.3%	SDP/All
Simpson, K (C)	17,541	34.2%	+5.0%	14,569	29.3%	C
Mactaggart, M (LD)	6,315	12.3%		14,166	28.5%	Lab
Luscombe, H (Soc Dem)	2,152	4.2%	-38.1%			
Lyons, F (NLP)	255	0.5%				
C to Lab swing 7.6%	51,216		14.5%	49,774		13.0%
		Lab maj	7,412		SDP/All maj	6,470

David Jamieson, snr vice-principal of school, won this seat in 1992; contested Plymouth Drake 1987; Birmingham Hall Green, Feb 1974. Mbr Solihull CBC 1970-4. B May 18 1947; ed Tudor Grange GS, Solihull; St Peter's Coll, Saltley, Birmingham; Open Univ. NUT.
Keith Simpson was special adviser to defence sec 1988-90. Director Cranfield Security Studies Inst, Royal Military Coll of Science, Shrivenham, Wiltshire. Head of overseas and defence section Cons research dept 1986-8; snr lecturer in war studies and international affairs, RMA

Sandhurst, 1973-86. B March 29 1949; ed Thorpe GS, Norfolk; Hull Univ; King's Coll, London Univ; postgraduate research in war studies. Mbr Highlands and Islands malt whiskey club.
Murdoch Mactaggart, computer consultant, writer and software author, contested Somerset and Dorset W in 1989 Euro elections. Chmn and fund raiser Somerset and Dorset Theatre Co 1990- . Mbr Brympton PC 1985- . B Sep 15 1939; ed Edinburgh and Liverpool Univs.

PLYMOUTH, DRAKE						No change
Electorate % Turnout	51,667	75.6%	1992	51,186	76.6%	1987
*Fookes, Dame Janet (C)	17,075	43.7%	+2.4%	16,195	41.3%	C
Telford, P (Lab)	15,062	38.6%	+14.5%	13,070	33.3%	SDP/All
Cox, Mrs V A (LD)	5,893	15.1%	-18.2%	9,451	24.1%	Lab
Stanbury, D (Soc Dem)	476	1.2%		493	1.3%	Grn
Harrison, Ms A (Grn)	441	1.1%	-0.1%			
Pringle, T (NLP)	95	0.2%				
C to Lab swing 6.0%	39,042		5.2%	39,209		8.0%
		C maj	2,013		C maj	3,125

Dame Janet Fookes was elected for this seat 1974; MP for Merton and Morden, 1970-4. Mbr Speaker's panel of chairmen 1976- ; mbr, home affiars select cmte 1984- ; select cmte on broadcasting 1988-91. Chmn RSPCA 1979-81; vice-chmn 1981-3; mbr of cl since 1975; chmn all-pty gp for animal welfare 1985- (sec 1974-82); jt vice-chmn mental health gp. Teacher 1958-70. B Feb 21 1936; ed Hastings and St Leonards Ladies' Coll; Hastings HS; Royal Holloway Coll; Univ of London. Mbr cls SSAFA 1980- ; Commonwealth War Graves Commission, 1987- . Mbr Hastings CBC 1960-1 and 1963-70.
Peter Telford, barrister. Former branch and CLP sec and

chmn and youth organiser. B Mar 16 1959; ed Whitehaven GS; Keele Univ.
Val Cox, self-employed training consultant; radiotherapist andradiographer. Chmn N Cornwall LDs 1989-91; mbr Cornwall CC 1988- (chmn environmental gp 1990- ; vice-chmn personnel cmte 1989- ; LD gp press officer 1989-). Manager N Cornwall CAB 1979-88; vice-chmn Nat Assocn of CABs, Devon and Cornwall, 1988- ; mbr NACAB cl, 1982-8. B Mar 20 1942; ed Bournemouth Sch for Girls; Guy's Hosp Sch of Radiography; Poly of SW.
Anne Harrison, teacher/trainer. B Sep 25 1938; ed St Mary's Abbey, Mill Hill.

PLYMOUTH, SUTTON				No change		
Electorate % Turnout	67,430	81.2%	1992	64,120	79.0%	1987
Streeter, G (C)	27,070	49.5%	+3.7%	23,187	45.8%	C
Pawley, A (Lab)	15,120	27.6%	+11.2%	19,174	37.8%	L/All
Brett-Freeman, J P (LD)	12,291	22.5%	-15.4%	8,310	16.4%	Lab
Bowler, J (NLP)	256	0.5%				
C to Lab swing 3.8%	54,737		21.8%	50,671		7.9%
		C maj	11,950		C maj	4,013

Gary Streeter retained this seat for the Cons in 1992. Partner in Plymouth firm of solicitors. Mbr Plymouth City Cl, 1986- (chmn, housing cmte, 1989-91). B Oct 2 1955; ed Tiverton GS; Kings Coll, London Univ. Former chmn Mount Gould Cons assocn and mbr exec cl Sutton Cons assocn.

Andrew Pawley, insolvency examiner, was mbr Plymouth City Cl 1987-91. When elected at 23 became the youngest person to be elected to Plymouth cl. B Nov 3 1963; ed Plymouth GS: Coll of St Mark and St John; Bristol Poly. GMB; Co-op Pty.

Julian Brett-Freeman, housing management officer. Mbr Lib Pty Cl 1985-6; campaign officer, Gt Yarmouth, 1987-8; sec Battersea LDs 1987-8. B Nov 12 1960; ed Springfield Comprehensive, Portsmouth; S Downs Coll, Havant; Inst of Housing, final year.

PONTEFRACT AND CASTLEFORD				No change		
Electorate % Turnout	64,648	74.3%	1992	64,414	73.5%	1987
*Lofthouse, G (Lab)	33,546	69.9%	+3.0%	31,656	66.9%	Lab
Rockall, A G M (C)	10,051	20.9%	-0.3%	10,030	21.2%	C
Ryan, D L (LD)	4,410	9.2%	-2.1%	5,334	11.3%	L/All
				295	0.6%	RF
C to Lab swing 1.6%	48,007		48.9%	47,315		45.7%
		Lab maj	23,495		Lab maj	21,626

Geoffrey Lofthouse, was elected at 1978 by-election. MbrCommons Chairmen's Panel, 1987- ; select cmte on energy, 1983- ; Commons accommodation and works cmte, 1991- ; select cmte on broadcasting, 1990-1; Court of Referees; jt vice-chmn PLP energy cmte, 1985- . Sec, Yorkshire Labour MPs, 1985- . Personnel manager with the NCB at Fryston, 1970-8, having started in mining industry as haulage hand. B Dec 18 1925; ed Featherstone Sec Mod Sch; Leeds Univ. Mbr Pontefract BC 1962-74 (mayor, 1967-8); Wakefield MDC, 1974-9; NUM, 1939-64; Apex, 1970- ; BACM.

Anthony Rockall, managing director of Teloman Products Ltd, St Ives, Cambridgeshire. Mbr Cambridgeshire CC 1989- ; Huntingdon TC 1987- ; Huntingdonshire DC, 1987- . B Jul 8 1963; ed Oundle; Edinburgh Univ. Mbr Huntingdon Cons assocn.

David Ryan, teacher and teaching union official, being mbr nat exec county sec (1982-8) and field officer of AMMA. Sec Brigg and Cleethorpes LDs, 1990-1. B May 2 1937; ed Coatham Sch, Redcar; Leeds Univ.

PONTYPRIDD				No change		
Electorate % Turnout	61,685	79.3%	1992	61,255	76.6%	1987
*Howells, Dr K S (Lab)	29,722	60.8%	+4.5%	26,422	56.3%	Lab
Donnelly, Dr P D (C)	9,925	20.3%	+0.8%	9,135	19.5%	C
Bowen, Dr I D (PC)	4,448	9.1%	+3.8%	8,865	18.9%	SDP/All
Belzak, S (LD)	4,180	8.5%	-10.3%	2,498	5.3%	PC
Jackson, Ms E (Grn)	615	1.3%				
C to Lab swing 1.8%	48,890		40.5%	46,920		36.8%
		Lab maj	19,797		Lab maj	17,287

Kim Howells, a full-time official of S Wales Area NUM, 1982-9, was elected at 1989 by-election. Mbr PAC 1991- ; select cmtes on sittings of Commons, 1991-2; on environment, 1990-1; on Welsh affairs, 1989-90. Research officer, Swansea Univ, 1979-82; lecturer, 1975-9; coalminer, 1970-1; steel worker, 1969-70. B Nov 27 1946; ed Mountain Ash GS; Hornsey Coll of Art, Cambridge Coll of Advanced Tech; Warwick Univ.

Dr Peter Donnelly, medical practitioner, specialises in public health medicine. Mbr Cardiff City Cl, 1991- ; sch governor. B Jan 27 1963; ed Perth Acad; Edinburgh Univ.

Prof Delme Bowen, professor of cell biology, Univ of Wales Coll of Cardiff, contested seat 1987. Mbr, Mid-Glamorgan CC, 1989- ; Taff Ely BC, 1987; Llantrisant/Pontyclun Community Cl, 1978- (chmn 1991-2). B Mar 20 1944; ed Aman Valley GS; Univ Coll, Cardiff. AUT.

Steve Belzak, legal executive; mbr Taff-Ely BC 1983- . B May 15 1958; ed Pontypridd Boys GS.

POOLE				**No change**		
Electorate % Turnout	79,221	79.4%	1992	76,673	77.5%	1987
*Ward, J D (C)	33,445	53.2%	-4.3%	34,159	57.5%	C
Clements, B R (LD)	20,614	32.8%	+0.2%	19,351	32.6%	SDP/All
White, H R (Lab)	6,912	11.0%	+1.1%	5,901	9.9%	Lab
Steen, M (Ind C)	1,620	2.6%				
Bailey, A (NLP)	303	0.5%				
C to LD swing 2.3%	62,894		20.4%	59,411		24.9%
		C maj	12,831		C maj	14,808

John Ward, a chartered civil engineer and former director of building companies Taylor Woodrow (Arcon) Ltd and Arcon Building Exports Ltd, was elected in 1979; contested Portsmouth N, Oct 1974. Consultant to Taylor Woodrow Gp; with Taylor Woodrow Ltd, 1958-79. B Mar 8 1925; ed Romford County Tech Sch; St Andrew's Univ. PPS to John Moore when Sec of State for Social Services and for Social Security, 1987-9, and Financial Sec to the Treasury, 1984-6. Mbr exec cmte British gp IPU. UK delegate Cl of Europe and WEU 1983-7 and 1989- . Vice-chmn Cons backbench trade and industry cmte 1983-4; jt sec industry cmte, 1982-3.

Brian Clements, lecturer in computer engineering, contested seat for L/All 1983. Mbr Poole BC 1985- (cl ldr, 1991-); Western region LD exec; cl for regions of England; former chmn Wessex Euro Lib gp. B Jun 21 1938; ed Ilford Cty HS; Bournemouth Tech Coll; Portsmouth Poly; Garnett Coll, London. Former branch chmn, NATFHE.
Haydn White, head teacher, contested Dorset E and Hampshire W in 1989 Euro elections; Somerset N twice in 1974 gen election; Dorset N 1970. mayor of Blandford Forum, 1988-9. Chmn Dorset Cty and SW of England Lab pty. B Jun 27 1940; ed Maes-y-Dderwen Comprehensive Sch, Swansea Valley; UCW, Aberystwyth. NUT.

PORTSMOUTH NORTH				**No change**		
Electorate % Turnout	79,592	77.1%	1992	80,501	74.8%	1987
*Griffiths, P H S (C)	32,240	52.6%	-2.7%	33,297	55.3%	C
Burnett, Dr A D (Lab)	18,359	29.9%	+10.0%	14,896	24.7%	SDP/All
Bentley, A (LD)	10,101	16.5%	-8.3%	12,016	20.0%	Lab
Palmer, Mrs H (Grn)	628	1.0%				
C to Lab swing 6.4%	61,328		22.6%	60,209		30.6%
		C maj	13,881		C maj	18,401

Peter Griffiths was elected for this seat 1979; MP for Smethwick, 1964-6; fought Portsmouth N, Feb 1974, and Smethwick, 1959. Mbr Select Committee on MPs Interests 1983- . Former headmaster and snr lecturer in economic history. B May 24 1928; ed West Bromwich GS; City of Leeds Training Coll; London and Birmingham Univs. Mbr Smethwick BC 1955-64 (ldr, Cons gp, 1960-4) and alderman, 1964-6. Former pres YCs. Fullbright exchange professor of economics, Pierce Coll, Los Angeles, 1968-9.
Alan Burnett is a lecturer at Portsmouth Poly. Contested

Wight and Hampshire East in 1989 Euro elections. Elected to Portsmouth City Cl, 1986 (Lab gp ldr, 1990-); treas, Portsmouth Lab pty, 1969-70. JP. B Sep 30 1940; ed Durham, Indiana and Southampton Univs. NATFHE.
Alex Bentley, self-employed bespoke tailor; mbr, Portsmouth City Cl, 1989- (chmn environmental health). Chmn 1986-90, and vice-chmn 1990- , Portsmouth Arts Centre; chmn Portsmouth Aids link line 1991- . B Apr 18 1952; ed sec sch.

PORTSMOUTH SOUTH				**No change**		
Electorate % Turnout	77,645	69.1%	1992	76,292	71.3%	1987
*Martin, D J P (C)	22,798	42.5%	-0.8%	23,534	43.3%	C
Hancock, M T (LD)	22,556	42.0%	-0.9%	23,329	42.9%	SDP/All
Rapson, S (Lab)	7,857	14.6%	+1.7%	7,047	13.0%	Lab
Zivkovic, A (Grn)	349	0.7%		455	0.8%	657 Party
Trend, W (NLP)	91	0.2%				
LD to C swing 0.0%	53,651		0.5%	54,365		0.4%
		C maj	242		C maj	205

David Martin regained this seat for Cons in 1987; contested Yeovil 1983. Appointed PPS to Douglas Hurd, Foreign Secretary, in 1990; former PPS to Alan Clark, Minr of State for Defence Procurement. Mbr select cmte on statutory instruments, 1987-91. Director, Caravanes Martin SARL; director of family leisure/tourism business, Martins Caravan Co Ltd, and associated companies until 1989; partner in ADP & E Farmers. Barrister; called to Bar (Inner Temple) 1969, and practised, 1969-76. Mbr Teignbridge DC 1979-83. B Feb 5 1945; ed Norwood Sch, Exeter; Kelly Coll, Tavistock; Fitzwilliam Coll, Cambridge.
Michael Hancock won the seat for SDP/All in 1984 by-

election but was defeated in 1987. Director, Daytime Club, BBC, since 1987. Alliance spokesman on planning in 1987 election. Engineer. B Apr 9 1946; ed Hampshire, Oxford and London. Mbr Portsmouth City Cl, 1971- ; Hampshire CC, 1973- (LD gp ldr); leader Labour cllrs, 1977-81, joining SDP in 1981 and then LD. District officer for Mencap; chmn Southern branch NSPCC 1989- . Former mbr SDP nat exec.
Sydney Rapson, an aircraft fitter, was lord mayor of Portsmouth, 1990-1; mbr Portsmouth City Cl, 1971-8 and since 1979 (Lab gp ldr). B Apr 17 1942; ed Southsea Modern; Paulsgrove Modern.

PRESTON				**No change**		
Electorate % Turnout	64,158	71.7%	1992	64,459	69.0%	1987
*Wise, Mrs A (Lab)	24,983	54.3%	+1.8%	23,341	52.5%	Lab
O'Toole, S G (C)	12,808	27.8%	-0.7%	12,696	28.5%	C
Chadwick, W D (LD)	7,897	17.2%	-1.8%	8,452	19.0%	L/All
Ayliffe, Ms J (NLP)	341	0.7%				
C to Lab swing 1.3%	46,029		26.5%	44,489		23.9%
		Lab maj	12,175		Lab maj	10,645

Audrey Wise was elected for this seat 1987; MP for Coventry SW, Feb 1974-9; contested Woolwich 1983. Mbr, Lab Pty NEC, 1982-87. Appointed president of Usdaw in 1991 (sponsored by union). Mbr select cmte on health, 1991- ; mbr select cmte on social services, 1987-90. ChmnPLP health and personal social services cmte 1989- , and PLP health and social security cmte 1987-9; vice-chmn PLP social security cmte 1989-90. Former shorthand typist. Mbr select cmte on violence in the family 1976-8. B Jan 1935; ed Rutherford HS.

Simon O'Toole is a barrister. Warden (1988-91) Birmingham Univ Guild of Students and president 1981-2. Business interests in Lloyd's, insurance, shipping. Former pty officer in Vauxhall and Westminster S; sec Bow Gp home affairs cmte. B Sep 2 1957; ed St Thomas More, Eltham; Birmingham Univ; City Univ, London.
Bill Chadwick, personnel and training manager. Mbr Preston BC, 1990- ; Lancs CC 1985-9. B Jul 1 1954; ed St Cuthbert Mayne HS; Newcastle Univ; Manchester Poly.

PUDSEY				**No change**		
Electorate % Turnout	70,847	80.1%	1992	71,681	78.0%	1987
*Shaw, Sir Giles (C)	25,067	44.1%	-1.4%	25,457	45.5%	C
Giles, A (Lab)	16,095	28.3%	+7.9%	19,021	34.0%	L/All
Shutt, D T (LD)	15,153	26.7%	-7.3%	11,461	20.5%	Lab
Wynne, Ms J (Grn)	466	0.8%				
C to Lab swing 4.6%	56,781		15.8%	55,939		11.5%
		C maj	8,972		C maj	6,436

Sir Giles Shaw was elected in 1974; contested Hull W, 1966. Minr of state for industry at the DTI, 1986-7; minr of state, Home Office, 1984-6; under sec of state for energy, 1983-4, for environment, 1981-3, and for N Ireland, 1979-81. Mbr Commons chairmen's panel, 1988- ; Commons selection cmte, 1987- ; treas 1922 Cmte, 1988- . Director British Steel plc, 1990- ; Yorkshire Water plc 1990- ; Broadcasters Audience Research Bd 1989- ; consultant to Philip Harris Gp plc. B Nov 16 1931; ed Sedbergh Sch; St John's Coll, Cambridge (pres of union, 1954). Formerly with Rowntree Mackintosh (marketing director, confectionery division, 1970-4) and former director, North Riding Motors.
Arthur Giles, principal ed welfare officer, Leeds lea. Former chmn Pudsey CLP. B Dec 30 1940; ed Fircroft Coll; Manchester Poly. Nalgo.
David Shutt, chartered accountant, contested Calder Valley 1987 and 1983, Sowerby 1979, twice in 1974 and 1970. Mbr Calderdale MBC, 1973-90; mayor of Calderdale, 1982-83. B Mar 16 1942; ed Pudsey GS. Former chmn, Yorkshire Lib Fed; former mbr Lib pty cl exec and assembly cmtes. Trustee Joseph Rowntree Reform Trust Ltd and Joseph Rowntree Charitable Trust.

PUTNEY				**No change**		
Electorate % Turnout	61,914	77.9%	1992	63,108	75.9%	1987
*Mellor, D J (C)	25,188	52.2%	+1.7%	24,197	50.5%	C
Chegwidden, Ms J M (Lab)	17,662	36.6%	+0.5%	17,290	36.1%	Lab
Martyn, Dr J D F (LD)	4,636	9.6%	-2.8%	5,934	12.4%	L/All
Hagenbach, K M (Grn)	618	1.3%	+0.2%	508	1.1%	Grn
Levy, P (NLP)	139	0.3%				
Lab to C swing 0.6%	48,243		15.6%	47,929		14.4%
		C maj	7,526		C maj	6,907

David Mellor, QC, was appointed Secretary of State for national Heritage in 1992. Chief Sec to the Treasury in 1990-2; Minr of state, Privy Cl Office, and minr for the arts and for the civil service, 1990; minr of state, home office, 1989-90; for health, 1988-9; foreign and Commonwealth office, 1987-8; and home office 1986-7; Under Sec home office, 1983-6; energy 1981-3. PC 1990. Won seat in 1979; contested West Bromwich East, Oct 1974. B Mar 12 1949; ed Swanage GS; Christ's Coll, Cambridge. Special trustee Westminster Hosp 1980-7. Vice-chmn trustees London Philharmonic Orchestra, 1989- ; mbr cl Nat Youth Orchestra, 1981-6. Hon associate, British Veterinary Assocn, 1986; Fellow, Zoological Soc, 1981.

Judith Chegwidden, publisher of reports on metals and minerals economics; director Roskill Information Services Ltd; Exhibition Audience Audits Ltd; partner O W Roskill, industrial consultants. Former chmn Putney CLP. Mbr Wandsworth Cl, 1974-86. B July 22 1946; ed Truro HS; London Univ. MSF.
John Martyn, research consultant (energy marketing and market research). Chmn Putney SDP 1986-8; press officer Putney LDs, 1990- ; mbr Fulham BC 1961-4. B Apr 21 1927; ed Wallasey GS; LSE. Mbr Statistics Users Cl; EPEA.
Keith Hagenbach, author and dramatist. B Oct 24 1944; ed Rugby; Trinity Coll, Dublin.

RAVENSBOURNE						No change
Electorate % Turnout	57,259	81.2%	1992	59,365	75.7%	1987
*Hunt, Sir John (C)	29,506	63.4%	+0.5%	28,295	63.0%	C
Booth, P (LD)	9,792	21.0%		11,376	25.3%	SDP/All
Dyer, E W (Lab)	6,182	13.3%	+2.0%	5,087	11.3%	Lab
Mouland, I (Grn)	617	1.3%		184	0.4%	BN
White, P (Lib)	318	0.7%				
Shepheard, J (NLP)	105	0.2%				
LD to C swing 2.4%	46,520		42.4%	44,942		37.6%
		C maj	19,714		C maj	16,919

Sir John Hunt, a former stockbroker, was elected for Ravensbourne in Feb 1974; MP for Bromley, 1964-74; contested Lewisham S, 1959. Mbr chairmen's panel, 1980- ; select cmte on home affairs, 1980-7 and its sub-cmte on race relations and immigration. Parly adviser to Nat Hairdressers' Fed. B Oct 27 1929; ed Dulwich Coll. Mbr Bromley BC 1953-65; mayor 1963-4. Pres Inst of Administrative Accountants, later Financial Accountants, 1970-88. Former mbr exec cmte British gp IPU; chmn, Indo-British parly gp, 1979-91 (now jt pres); British-Caribbean Assocn, 1968-77 and 1984- . Freeman,

Haberdashers' Co and City of London. Mbr BBC general advisory cl, 1975-87; Cl of Europe and WEU, 1973-7 and 1988- .
Paul Booth, charity administrator. Mbr Bromley BC 1988- . B Oct 7 1951; ed Univ Coll, Cardiff. Mbr cl of management Keston Coll.
Erny Dyer, lithographic systems operator. Mbr Bromley Cl; Ravensbourne LP political ed officer. B Aug 26 1949; ed Horn Park Primary Sch and Northbrook Sec, Lewisham. GPMU.

READING EAST						No change
Electorate % Turnout	72,151	75.0%	1992	72,311	73.3%	1987
*Vaughan, Sir Gerard (C)	29,148	53.8%	+0.0%	28,515	53.8%	C
Parker, Ms G (Lab)	14,593	27.0%	+5.5%	12,298	23.2%	SDP/All
Thair, D A (LD)	9,528	17.6%	-5.6%	11,371	21.5%	Lab
McCubbin, Ms A (Grn)	861	1.6%	+0.3%	667	1.3%	Grn
C to Lab swing 2.7%	54,130		26.9%	52,976		30.6%
		C maj	14,555		C maj	16,217

Sir Gerard Vaughan was Minr of State for Trade (Minr for Consumer Affairs), 1982-3; Minr for Health, with rank of Minr of State, DHSS, 1979-82. Mbr select cmte on ed, science and the arts, 1983- ; chmn parly and scientific cmte and of parly office of science and tech (Post). Consultant, lecturer, author, mbr of Lloyd's. Elected for this seat in 1983; MP for Reading S, Feb 1974-83, and for Reading, 1970-4; contested Poplar, 1955. Consultant emeritus, Guy's Hosp, being on staff, 1958-79. Chmn Chingbury Ltd, a private family company; director, Spahealth Ltd, a medical film company. B Jun 11 1923; ed London Univ;

Guy's Hosp. Alderman GLC 1966-72, and LCC 1955-64. Pres Cons Medical Soc. Liveryman, Worshipful Co of Barbers (Upper Warden, 1991-92).
Gillian Parker, sub-editor with BBC monitoring unit. Mbr Reading BC 1986- . B Dec 8 1954; ed Essex and Birmingham Univs. BECTU and NUJ.
Denis Thair, local govt consumer protection officer. Chmn Wokingham constituency LDs, 1991-2; Wokingham Lib Assocn 1986-7. Mbr Wokingham DC 1986-91 (chmn, LD gp, 1989-91); Newbury DC 1979-85. B Mar 31 1931; ed Beckenham Cty Tech Sch; Crawley CFE. Nalgo.

READING WEST						No change
Electorate % Turnout	67,937	78.0%	1992	70,391	72.2%	1987
*Durant, Sir Tony (C)	28,048	52.9%	-2.4%	28,122	55.3%	C
Ruhemann, P M (Lab)	14,750	27.8%	+6.6%	11,369	22.4%	L/All
Lock, K H (LD)	9,572	18.1%	-4.3%	10,819	21.3%	Lab
Unsworth, P J (Grn)	613	1.2%	+0.1%	542	1.1%	Grn
C to Lab swing 4.5%	52,983		25.1%	50,852		32.9%
		C maj	13,298		C maj	16,753

Sir Anthony Durant was a government whip 1984-90, holding posts of Vice Chamberlain of Royal Household a Ld Commissioner of Treasury. Mbr exec 1922 Cmte; select cmte on parliamentary commissioner for administration 1974-83 and 1990- ; select cmte on health, 1991- . Director (unpaid) Kennington Palace Court. Political adviser, Nat Fed of Demolition Contractors. Chmn, Cons backbench environment cmte, 1991- and 1982-4. Elected for this seat in 1983; MP for Reading N, Feb 1974-83; contested Rother Valley, 1970. B Jan 9 1928; ed Dane Court Prep Sch; Bryanston Sch, Dorset. Mbr exec cmte, CPA UK branch (chmn 1988-90); all-pty gp on film industry; all-pty

gp on widows and single-parent families, 1977-85.
Peter Ruhemann, agent, Basingstoke CLP; chmn Reading Lab pty, 1985-90. Mbr Berkshire CC 1985- ; W Berks HA 1983-90. B Jun 8 1947; ed Altrincham GS, Cheshire; Imperial Coll, London Univ. TGWU and GMB/Apex.
Keith Lock, sales manager, Europe, for Reading based food gp, contested this seat 1987. Mbr Newbury DC 1973- ; Berkshire CC 1985-9. B Jun 29 1931; ed Colfe's GS, London; Woolwich Poly.
Philip Unsworth, occupational psychologist, contested this seat 1987. Has served on Grn pty cl. B Jan 1 1946; ed Blackpool GS; Leeds Univ.

REDCAR						No change
Electorate % Turnout	62,494	77.7%	1992	63,393	76.1%	1987
*Mowlam, Dr M (Lab)	27,184	56.0%	+8.6%	22,824	47.3%	Lab
Goodwill, R (C)	15,607	32.1%	+0.8%	15,089	31.3%	C
Abbott, C M (LD)	5,789	11.9%	-9.4%	10,298	21.4%	SDP/All
C to Lab swing 3.9%	48,580		23.8%	48,211		16.0%
		Lab maj	11,577		Lab maj	7,735

Marjorie Mowlam was appointed spokesman on City affairs in Opposition's DTI team in 1989; mbr team on N Ireland, 1988-9. Elected in 1987; asst co-ordinator, Lab Euro election campaign, 1989. Mbr, PAC, 1987-8. Administrative officer at Northern College, Barnsley, 1984-7. Chmn, Tyne Bridge CLP, 1982-3. B Sep 18 1949; ed Coundon Court Comprehensive Sch, Coventry; Durham Univ; Iowa Univ, US. Lecturer, Florida State Univ, 1977-8; Newcastle Univ, 1979-83. TGWU; sponsored by Cohse.

Robert Goodwill, farmer, has held branch, area and CPC offices; parish cllr, 1983- . Mbr Yorkshire water consumer consultative cmte, 1986-9. B Dec 31 1956; ed Bootham Sch, York; Newcastle Univ. Chmn NFU branch 1987-9, and NFU county cereals and livestock cmte 1986-8.
Chris Abbott, self-employed electrical contractor, contested Hartlepool 1979. Mbr Cleveland CC 1985- ; Langbaurgh-on-Tees BC 1987- ; Whitby TC 1978-84; Lib pty cl, 1986-8. B Jul 10 1950; ed Starbeck Sch, Harrogate.

REIGATE						No change
Electorate % Turnout	71,853	78.5%	1992	71,940	72.5%	1987
*Gardiner, Sir George (C)	32,220	57.1%	-2.2%	30,925	59.3%	C
Newsome, B (LD)	14,556	25.8%	+1.3%	12,752	24.4%	SDP/All
Young, Ms H (Lab)	9,150	16.2%	+1.9%	7,460	14.3%	Lab
Dilcliff, M (SD)	513	0.9%		1,026	2.0%	Grn
C to LD swing 1.8%	56,439		31.3%	52,163		34.8%
		C maj	17,664		C maj	18,173

Sir George Gardiner has been MP for this seat since 1974; contested Coventry S, 1970. Chmn 92 group of Cons backbenchers; chmn Cons backbench cmte on Euro affairs, 1980-7 (sec, 1976-9 and vice-chmn 1979-80); mbr exec 1922 Cmte, 1987- ; jt vice-chmn Cons backbench foreign and Commonwealth affairs cmte 1988-91. Journalist and public affairs consultant. Editor, Conservative News 1972-9; chief political correspondent Thomson Regional Newspapers 1964-74; author of biography on Margaret

Thatcher. B Mar 3 1935; ed Harvey GS, Folkestone; Balliol Coll, Oxford. Sec British-South African parly gp.
Barry Newsome, Nat West bank manager; mbr Reigate and Banstead BC 1986- (LD gp ldr). B May 12 1947; ed Bromley GS; Bromley Tech Coll.
Helen Young, computer sales account manager; mbr Reigate and Banstead DC, 1984- . B July 18 1948; ed local state schs. GMB.

RENFREW WEST AND INVERCLYDE						No change
Electorate % Turnout	58,122	80.3%	1992	56,189	80.5%	1987
*Graham, T (Lab)	17,085	36.6%	-2.1%	17,525	38.7%	Lab
Goldie, Miss A M (C)	15,341	32.9%	+3.1%	13,462	29.8%	C
Campbell, C M (SNP)	9,444	20.2%	+10.1%	9,669	21.4%	SDP/All
Nimmo, S (LD)	4,668	10.0%	-11.4%	4,578	10.1%	SNP
Maltman, D (NLP)	149	0.3%				
Lab to C swing 2.6%	46,687		3.7%	45,234		9.0%
		Lab maj	1,744		Lab maj	4,063

Thomas Graham gained this seat in 1987. Former office manager of firm of solicitors; former engineer with Rolls-Royce. Mbr Strathclyde Reg Cl, 1978-7. B Dec 5 1943; ed Fairfields Primary Sch, Govan; Crookston Castle Sch, Pollok; Stow Coll of Engineering. Mbr of and sponsored by Usdaw.
Annabel Goldie, solicitor, notary public and mbr cl of Royal Faculty of Procurators in Glasgow; partner in Glasgow firm since 1978. Chmn constituency assocn, 1989-90; vice-chmn, 1985-9. B Feb 27 1950; ed Kilmacolm Primary Sch; Greenock Acad; Strathclyde Univ. Elder, Church of

Scotland; Bishopton community cllr; mbr local crime prevention panel.
Colin Campbell, retired sec sch head, contested this seat 1987; Strathclyde W in 1989 Euro elections. Chmn Renfrew W and Inverclyde SNP and of Kilbarchan branch. B Aug 31 1938; ed Paisley GS; Glasgow Univ; Jordanhill Coll of Ed.
Alexander Nimmo, retired police officer; vice-chmn Renfrew West and Inverclyde LDs. Promotion co-ordinator child and family trust charity. Former exec mbr Scottish Police Fed. B Dec 9 1934; ed Dunbar Snr Sec Sch.

RHONDDA						No change
Electorate % Turnout	59,955	76.6%	1992	60,931	78.0%	1987
*Rogers, A R (Lab)	34,243	74.5%	+1.2%	34,847	73.3%	Lab
Davies, G (PC)	5,427	11.8%	+2.8%	4,261	9.0%	PC
Richards, J W (C)	3,588	7.8%	+0.2%	3,935	8.3%	SDP/All
Nicholls-Jones, P (LD)	2,431	5.3%	-3.0%	3,612	7.6%	C
Fisher, M (Comm GB)	245	0.5%		869	1.8%	Comm
Lab to PC swing 0.8%	45,934		62.7%	47,524		64.4%
		Lab maj	28,816		Lab maj	30,586

Allan Rogers became an Opposn spokesman on defence and disarmament and arms control in 1987; mbr select cmte on Euro legislation 1983-7; Channel tunnel bill select cmte 1986; PAC 1983-8; select cmte on Welsh affairs, 1983-7. Chmn (1987-8) vice-chmn (1986-7) and campaign officer (1989-) Welsh gp of Lab MPs. Elected for this seat 1983. Geologist; Fellow of Geological Soc. MEP for SE Wales, 1979-84; a vice-pres EP, 1979-82. B Oct 24 1932; ed Gelligaer Orimary Sch; Bargoed Sec Sch; Univ Coll, S Wales. Sponsored by Cohse.
Geraint Davies, pharmacist, contested the seat 1987 and

1983. Mbr Rhondda BC 1983- ; PC nat cl; chmn, constituency pty. B Dec 1 1948; ed Ysgol Gymraeg Ynyswen; Pentre GS; London Univ.
John Richards, managing director of management consultancy; director of Cardiff Marketing; Cardiff City Transport Services (Cardiff Bus). Mbr Cardiff City Cl, 1986- ; cl, Inst of Welsh Affairs. B Jun 14 1964; ed Llanishen HS; Bristol Univ; Univ of Wales Inst of Science and Tech. Trustee Cardiff charity for special relief.
Paul Nicholls-Jones, businessman. B Apr 8 1958; ed sec mod sch; Open Univ.

RIBBLE VALLEY					No change from	**1987**
Electorate % Turnout	64,996	85.7%	1992	62,644	79.1%	1987
Evans, N M (C)	29,178	52.4%	-8.5%	30,136	60.9%	C
*Carr, M (LD)	22,636	40.6%	+19.2%	10,608	21.4%	SDP/All
Pickup, R (Lab)	3,649	6.5%	-11.2%	8,781	17.7%	Lab
Beesley, D (Loony G)	152	0.3%				
Holmes, Ms N (NLP)	112	0.2%				
C to LD swing 13.8%	55,727		11.7%	49,525		39.4%
		C maj	6,542		C maj	19,528

Nigel Evans, newsagent and grocer, regained this seat for Cons pty in 1992 after unsuccessfuly contesting it in the 1991 by-election; contested the Pontypridd by-election in 1989 and Swansea West in 1987. Mbr West Glamorgan CC 1985-91. B Nov 10 1957; ed Dynevor Sch; Univ Coll, Swansea. Pres Swansea West Cons assocn; chmn, Welsh parly candidates policy gp, 1990.
Michael Carr, teacher, captured this seat for LD in 1991 by-election, contested it 1987 and 1983. Mbr Ribble Valley BC 1979-83. B Jan 31 1946; ed Catholic Coll, Preston;

Margaret McMillan Memorial Coll of Ed, Bradford. Mbr NAS/UWT 1975- ; mbr Lancs Fed NAS/UWT (press sec, 1984-7 and 1988-90); Rossendale NAS/UWT district sec, 1984-7; mbr, Lancs Fed exec cmte, 1990- .
Ronald Pickup, retired commercial accountant; mbr, Clitheroe TC and Ribble Valley BC 1988-91; Lancs CC 1989- . Exec trustee, Lancs Community Cl; director, Blackburn Groundwork Trust, B Feb 20 1931; ed Radcliffe Sec Mod Sch; Radcliffe Tech Coll. Nalgo.

RICHMOND (YORKS)						No change
Electorate % Turnout	82,879	78.4%	1992	79,277	72.1%	1987
*Hague, W (C)	40,202	61.9%	+0.6%	34,995	61.2%	C
Irwin, G (LD)	16,698	25.7%	-1.3%	15,419	27.0%	L/All
Cranston, R (Lab)	7,523	11.6%	-0.2%	6,737	11.8%	Lab
Barr, M (Ind)	570	0.9%				
LD to C swing 1.0%	64,993		36.2%	57,151		34.3%
		C maj	23,504		C maj	19,576

William Hague elected at 1989 by-election; contested Wentworth 1987. Appointed PPS to Norman Lamont, Chancellor of the Exchequer, in 1990. Management consultant with McKinsey and Co Ltd. Sec, Cons backbench ag, fish and food cmte, 1989-90; Yorkshire gp of Cons MPs, 1989- ; all-pty footwear and leather industries parly gp. Former director, Beale International Technology Ltd. B Mar 26 1961; ed Wath-upon-Dearne Comprehensive Sch, near Rotherham; Magdalen Coll, Oxford (Pres of Union and of Univ Cons Assocn, 1981); Institut Europeen

d'Administration des Affaires. Political adviser, Treasury, 1983. Former speech writer for Sir Geoffrey Howe, when Chancellor.
George Irwin, self-employed management consultant and chartered accountant, contested Bishop Auckland 1987. Mbr Richmondshire DC, 1984- . B Aug 17 1938; ed St Cuthberts GS, Newcastle upon Tyne.
Ross Cranston, barrister. B Jul 23 1948. Mbr AUT, Society of Lab Lawyers; Lab finance and industry gp.
Details of 1989 by-election on page 287

RICHMOND AND BARNES				**No change**		
Electorate % Turnout	53,081	85.0%	1992	54,700	83.2%	1987
*Hanley, J J (C)	22,894	50.7%	+3.0%	21,729	47.7%	C
Tonge, Dr J (LD)	19,025	42.2%	-1.7%	19,963	43.8%	L/All
Touhig, J D (Lab)	2,632	5.8%	-1.3%	3,227	7.1%	Lab
Maciejowska, Mrs J S M (Grn)	376	0.8%	-0.5%	610	1.3%	Grn
Cunningham, C (NLP)	89	0.2%				
Meacock, R (QFL)	62	0.1%				
Ellis-Jones, Ms A (Anti-Fed)	47	0.1%				
LD to C swing 2.3%	45,125		8.6%	45,529		3.9%
		C maj	3,869		C maj	1,766

Jeremy Hanley was appointed an Under Sec of State for N Ireland in 1990. Mbr select cmte on home affairs and sub-cmte on race relations and immigration, 1983-7; sec all-pty Europe parly gp, 1988-90; mbr exec cmte, UK branch, CPA, 1989-90. PPS to Richard Luce, Minr for the Arts, 1987-90, and briefly to Chris Patten when Sec of State for Environment. Chartered accountant; lecturer and broadcaster. Chmn Fraser Green Ltd, 1986-90; director of Financial Training Co Ltd, 1973-90 (being dep chmn). Elected in 1983; contested Lambeth Central, 1978 by-election and 1979. B Nov 17 1945; ed Rugby. Freeman, City of London. Mbr soc of Cons lawyers company law reform cmte, 1976-87.

Dr Jenny Tonge, medical practitioner, chmn constituency LDs; mbr for Kew, Richmond BC, 1980-90 (chmn social services, 1983-7, and personnel, 1987-9). B Feb 19 1941; ed Dudley Girls' HS, W Midlands; Univ Coll, London; Univ Coll Hosp. Chmn governors, Waldegrave sch. Friend of Kew Gardens and of Richmond Park. BMA.

Don Touhig, newspaper general manager and journalist; mbr Gwent CC, 1973- (chmn estates cmte, 1985-9, and finance cmte, 1991-). CLP pres and branch sec. B Dec 5 1947; ed St Francis Sch; East Mon Coll. TGWU; Guild of Newspaper Editors. TGWU.

ROCHDALE				**No change**		
Electorate % Turnout	69,522	76.5%	1992	68,703	74.6%	1987
Lynne, Miss E (LD)	22,776	42.8%	-0.6%	22,245	43.4%	L/All
Williams, A D (Lab)	20,937	39.4%	+1.4%	19,466	38.0%	Lab
Goldie-Scott, D J (C)	8,626	16.2%	-2.4%	9,561	18.6%	C
Henderson, K (BNP)	620	1.2%				
Lucker, V (NLP)	211	0.4%				
LD to Lab swing 1.0%	53,170		3.5%	51,272		5.4%
		LD maj	1,839		L/All maj	2,779

Elizabeth Lynne, speech consultant, contested Harwich for L/All in 1987. Nat junior LD social services speaker; NW speaker on housing, homelessness and community care. B Jan 22 1948; ed Dorking County GS. Chmn, Rochdale alliance for community care; on management cmtes, victim support, Rochdale CAB and voluntary action.

David Williams, lecturer/researcher, contested this seat 1987 and Colne Valley 1983. Lectures on trade union law and public administration; former scrapyard labourer and British Rail waiter. Mbr Rochdale MBC, 1979- . B May 1 1949; ed Cromwell Sec Sch; Salford GS; Newcastle and Manchester Univs. Sponsored by GMB.

Duncan Goldie-Scott, publisher; worked for Pearson plc. Direct marketing manager at Cons Central Office, 1986-8, and private sec to Norman Tebbit, then pty chmn. Mbr Westminster City Cl, 1990- (financial management and personnel cmte). B Mar 18 1956; ed Fettes coll, Edinburgh; Durham Univ; London Business Sch.

ROCHFORD				**No change**		
Electorate % Turnout	76,869	83.0%	1992	76,048	78.1%	1987
*Clark, Dr M (C)	38,967	61.1%	+0.6%	35,872	60.4%	C
Harris, N (LD)	12,931	20.3%	-7.0%	16,178	27.3%	L/All
Quinn, D (Lab)	10,537	16.5%	+4.2%	7,308	12.3%	Lab
Farmer, Ms L (Lib)	1,362	2.1%				
LD to C swing 3.8%	63,797		40.8%	59,358		33.2%
		C maj	26,036		C maj	19,694

Michael Clark, management consultant with PA Management Consultants Ltd, 1981-7, became chmn, select cmte on energy, 1989, mbr since 1983; vice-chmn, 1987-9 and jt sec, 1986-7, Cons backbench energy cmte. Parly consultant to PA Consulting Gp Ltd; parly adviser to royal soc of chemistry (fellow, 1987); British chemical engineering contractors assocn; MAT Gp Ltd. Chmn, 1990- and exec cmte mbr, 1987-90, British gp, IPU; mbr, cl, parly information technology cmte, 1984-90; vice-chmn, all-pty gp for chemical industry, 1990- (sec, 1985-90); sec, parly space cmte, 1989-91. Elected in 1983; contested Ilkeston, 1979. B Aug 1935; ed King Edward VI GS, Retford; King's Coll, London; Univ of Minnesota; St John's Coll, Cambridge.

Nicholas Harris, teacher. Mbr Rochford DC, 1988-92; vice-chmn, local pty, 1986-7. B Dec 12 1942; ed Bed Coll of HE. NAS/UWT.

Donald Quinn, unit manager for nat assocn for care and resettlement of offenders; chmn, Colchester clarion socialist cycle club, 1988- . B May 14 1949; ed Bedford and Essex Univs. MSF; TGWU.

193

ROMFORD						No change
Electorate % Turnout	54,001	78.0%	1992	55,668	72.9%	1987
*Neubert, Sir Michael (C)	23,834	56.6%	+0.6%	22,745	56.0%	C
Gordon, Ms E (Lab)	12,414	29.5%	+6.6%	9,274	22.8%	Lab
Atherton, Ms P (LD)	5,329	12.7%	-7.5%	8,195	20.2%	L/All
Gibson, F (Grn)	546	1.3%	+0.3%	385	0.9%	Grn
C to Lab swing 3.0%	42,123		27.1%	40,599		33.2%
		C maj	11,420		C maj	13,471

Sir Michael Neubert was Under Sec of State for Defence Procurement at the MoD, 1989-90; Under Sec of State for Armed Forces, 1988-9; Vice Chamberlain of Royal Household (Govt whip), 1988; a Lord Commissioner of Treasury (govt whip), 1986-8; asst govt whip, 1983-6. Parly adviser to Fed of Master Builders. Elected in Feb 1974; contested Romford 1970, Hammersmith N 1966. Former travel and industrial consultant. B Sep 3 1933; ed Queen Elizabeth's Sch, Barnet; Bromley GS; Downing Coll, Cambridge. Mbr Bromley BC 1960-3; London borough of Bromley Cl, 1964-8; alderman 1968-74; leader 1967-70; mayor 1972-3.

Eileen Gordon, constituency caseworker for Tony Banks MP. B Oct 22 1946; ed Harold Hill GS; Shoreditch Comprehensive; Westminster Coll of Ed. TGWU; Co-op pty.

Pat Atherton, retired head teacher, is mbr of LD ed policy gp and disability gp. Chmn Waltham Forest branch of 300 Gp. Mbr Waltham Forest BC, 1982-6. B Oct 18 1932; ed Birmingham Univ; Dudley Training Coll.

ROMSEY AND WATERSIDE						No change
Electorate % Turnout	82,628	83.2%	1992	79,136	79.0%	1987
*Colvin, M K B (C)	37,375	54.4%	-2.0%	35,303	56.4%	C
Dawson, G (LD)	22,071	32.1%		20,031	32.0%	SDP/All
Mawle, Ms A (Lab)	8,688	12.6%	+1.1%	7,213	11.5%	Lab
Spottiswood, J (Grn)	577	0.8%				
C to LD swing 1.1%	68,711		22.3%	62,547		24.4%
		C maj	15,304		C maj	15,272

Michael Colvin won this seat in 1983; MP for Bristol NW, 1979-83. Appointed select cmte on energy in 1990. PPS to minrs of state, FCO, 1983-5, and to Richard Luce, Minr for the Arts and Civil Service 1985-7. Farmer, landowner, mbr of Lloyd's, public house licensee. Chmn, cl for country sports, 1988- ; vice-chmn, British Field Sports Soc, 1987- ; sec, all-pty licensed trade parly gp. Parly adviser to Fed of Retail Licensed Trade (N Ireland). Qualified pilot and parachutist. B Sep 27 1932; ed Eton; RMA Sandhurst; Royal Ag Coll, Cirencester. Governor Enham Village Centre. Chmn Cons backbench aviation cmte 1987- and 1982-3; vice-chmn, 1990-. Jt sec 1987-90, Cons foreign and Commonwealth affairs cmte Mbr, Andover Cl, 1965-73; Test Valley Cl, 1973-5.

George Dawson, chemical engineer employed by Exxon Chemical, is vice-chmn Hants and Wight region of LDs and chmn Romsey and Waterside LD. Mbr New Forest DC 1987- ; Hythe Dibben PC 1987- . B Jun 11 1951; ed Castleford GS; Teesside Poly.

Angela Mawle, environmental scientist, contested Hampshire Central in 1989 Euro elections. Elected to Southampton City Cl in 1984 and chmn environment sub-cmte. B Aug 18 1945; ed Southampton Univ; Imperial Coll. Former health visitor and mbr Health Visitors Assocn.

ROSS, CROMARTY AND SKYE						No change
Electorate % Turnout	55,524	73.9%	1992	52,369	72.7%	1987
*Kennedy, C P (LD)	17,066	41.6%	-7.8%	18,809	49.4%	SDP/All
Gray, J (C)	9,436	23.0%	+3.3%	7,490	19.7%	C
Gibson, R M (SNP)	7,618	18.6%	+6.8%	7,287	19.1%	Lab
MacDonald, J T (Lab)	6,275	15.3%	-3.8%	4,492	11.8%	SNP
Jardine, D (Grn)	642	1.6%				
LD to C swing 5.6%	41,037		18.6%	38,078		29.7%
		LD maj	7,630		SDP/All maj	11,319

Charles Kennedy was elected party president in 1990. Became LD spokesman on health in 1989; spokesman on trade and industry, 1988-9; on social security, 1988; Alliance spokesman on health and social security in 1987 election team; SDP spokesman on health and social security and on Scotland, 1983-7; mbr select cmte on broadcasting, 1988- ; select cmte on social services, 1986-7. Won seat in 1983 and became LD MP in 1988. Chmn, SDP cl for Scotland, 1986-8. B Nov 25 1959; ed Lochaber HS, Fort William; Glasgow Univ (pres of union, 1980-81). Jt vice-chmn British Atlantic gp of Young Politicians. Formerly worked as radio news reporter and broadcaster in Inverness.

James Gray, writer; consultant to GNI Ltd and various City companies; visiting lecturer at several univs and polys. During 1985-1 was managing director, GNI Freight Futures Ltd; snr manager, GNI commodities and shipping division and director, Baltic Futures Exchange. Associate, Centre for Policy Studies. B Nov 7 1954; ed Glasgow HS; Glasgow Univ; Christ Church, Oxford. Freeman, City of London.

Rob Gibson, principal teacher of guidance, contested this seat 1987 and Inverness Feb 1974. Mbr Ross and Cromarty DC. SNP executive vice-convenor on policy. B Oct 16 1945; ed Dundee Univ. EIS.

Jimmy MacDonald, clinical services manager; Highland regional cllr since 1986. B Jan 22 1949; ed N Uist and Inverness. Cohse.

ROSSENDALE AND DARWEN — Lab gain

Electorate % Turnout	76,909	83.1%	1992	75,038	80.3%	1987
Anderson, Mrs J (Lab)	28,028	43.9%	+5.6%	28,056	46.6%	C
*Trippier, D A (C)	27,908	43.7%	-2.9%	23,074	38.3%	Lab
Connor, K (LD)	7,226	11.3%	-3.8%	9,097	15.1%	L/All
Gaffney, J E (Grn)	596	0.9%				
Gorrod, P (NLP)	125	0.2%				
C to Lab swing 4.2%	63,883		0.2%	60,227		8.3%
		Lab maj	120		C maj	4,982

Janet Anderson, housewife, part-time campaign organiser for Lab Pty, contested this seat 1987. Former personal asst to Barbara Castle, when MEP, and two MPs. B Dec 6 1949; ed Kingsfield comp, Bristol; Central London poly; Nantes Univ. TGWU; Natsopa/Sogat, 1971-74.

David Trippier was appointed Minr for the Environment and Countryside, with rank of Minister of State, DoE, in 1989; an Under Sec of State for Environment, 1987-9; and for Trade and Industry, 1983-5, moving to Dept of Employment as Under Sec of State in 1985 but remaining as Minr for Small Businesses. Dep chmn Cons pty, 1990. Former stockbroker and mbr of Stock Exchange from 1968. Elected for this seat 1983; MP for Rossendale, 1979-83; fought Rochdale in 1972 by-election and Oldham West, Feb and Oct 1974. B May 15 1945; ed Bury GS. Mbr, Rochdale Cl, 1969-78. Jt sec Cons back-bench defence cmte, 1980-2; sec all-pty footwear cmte, 1979-83.

Kevin Connor, quality laboratory technician, chmn constituency pty. B Jan 21 1946; ed Darwen Tech Coll. GMB

Jim Gaffney, self-employed market trader; E Lancs Grn Pty speaker and newsletter editor. B Oct 29 1955; ed St Michael's Coll, Leeds; Oxford Univ.

ROTHER VALLEY — No change

Electorate % Turnout	68,303	75.0%	1992	66,416	75.6%	1987
*Barron, K J (Lab)	30,977	60.5%	+4.1%	28,292	56.4%	Lab
Horton, T A W (C)	13,755	26.9%	+1.9%	12,502	24.9%	C
Smith, K (LD)	6,483	12.7%	-5.8%	9,240	18.4%	SDP/All
				145	0.3%	WRP
C to Lab swing 1.1%	51,215		33.6%	50,179		31.5%
		Lab maj	17,222		Lab maj	15,790

Kevin Barron became an Opposn spokesman on energy and particularly on the coal industry in 1988. PPS to Neil Kinnock, Ldr of the Opposition, 1985-8; chmn Yorkshire gp of Lab MPs, 1987- . Coal miner, 1962-83. Elected in 1983. Mbr select cmte on energy, 1983-6. B Oct 26 1946; ed Maltby Hall sec mod sch; Ruskin Coll, Oxford. Pres Rotherham and District TUC. Former NUM delegate for Maltby colliery. Sponsored by NUM.

Toby Horton is director, Allied Partnership Gp plc, York, and other companies; managing director, Radio Tees, 1979-83; corporate finance executive with Kleinwort, Benson Ltd and predecessor company, 1970-79. Contested Yorkshire SW in 1989 Euro elections; Sedgefield 1983; election agent, Bethnal Green and Stepney, 1987. Treas Stockton YMCA, 1979-83. B Feb 18 1947; ed Westminster; Christ Church, Oxford.

ROTHERHAM — No change

Electorate % Turnout	60,937	71.7%	1992	61,521	69.2%	1987
Boyce, J (Lab)	27,933	63.9%	+4.3%	25,422	59.7%	Lab
Yorke, S J D (C)	10,372	23.7%	+1.7%	9,410	22.1%	C
Wildgoose, D B (LD)	5,375	12.3%	-5.9%	7,766	18.2%	L/All
C to Lab swing 1.3%	43,680		40.2%	42,598		37.6%
		Lab maj	17,561		Lab maj	16,012

James Boyce, part-time travel asst; mbr Sheffield city cl, 1984- . Dep branch chmn of, and sponsored by AEU. Sheffield foundry section. Mbr War on Want. B Sep 6 1947; ed St Mirrens acad; Northern coll; Sheffield univ.

Stephen Yorke, political adviser in political office, 10 Downing St, and Cons research dept; barrister specialising in commercial, company and libel law. Legal adviser to *Sun, Today* and Sky TV during 1989. B Nov 14 1963; ed Eastbourne Coll; Magdalene Coll, Cambridge.

David Wildgoose, analyst/programmer, self-employed with own small computer software company. Mbrship sec Rotherham LDs. B Mar 13 1965; ed Oakwood comprehensive and Thomas Rotherham coll, Rotherham; Hull univ.

ROXBURGH AND BERWICKSHIRE				No change	
Electorate % Turnout	43,485	77.7%	1992	43,140	77.2%	1987
*Kirkwood, A J (LD)	15,852	46.9%	-2.3%	16,388	49.2%	L/All
Finlay-Maxwell, Mrs S (C)	11,595	34.3%	-2.9%	12,380	37.2%	C
Douglas, M (SNP)	3,437	10.2%	+5.4%	2,944	8.8%	Lab
Lambert, S (Lab)	2,909	8.6%	-0.2%	1,586	4.8%	SNP
C to LD swing 0.3%	33,793		12.6%	33,298		12.0%
		LD maj	4,257		L/All maj	4,008

Archy Kirkwood became convenor of the LD health, education and welfare team and social security and welfare spokesman in 1988; also appointed party's campaigns organiser; dep whip, 1989- ; Lib spokesman on Scotland and on fishing, 1987-8 Alliance spokesman on overseas development in 1987 election; Lib spokesman on health and social security, 1985-7. Elected in 1983 becoming LD MP in 1988. Sec/treas, all-pty pensioners parly gp; treas, gp on AIDS; European information marketplace gp; jt vice-chmn low flying gp. Mbr Court of Referees, 1987- . Notary Public; solicitor. B Apr 22 1946; ed Cranhill sec sch, Glasgow; Heriot-Watt Univ, Edinburgh. Trustee Joseph Rowntree Reform Trust, 1985- .

Shirley Finlay-Maxwell contested Tweeddale, Ettrick and Lauderdale in 1987. Worked as a bereavement counsellor

in hospice movement; snr exec with textile finishing co until 1984. Mbr Kirklees MDC, 1978-82 and 1983-6; vice-chmn Huddersfield E Cons assocn, 1980-2. B Feb 27 1935; ed St Leonard's Sch, St Andrews, Fife.

Marshall Douglas, accountant and audit manager, contested this seat 1987. Mbr Borders reg Cl, 1988-90. Treas Tweeddale, Ettrick and Lauderdale SNP; sec Tweeddale East branch. B 1957; ed Scottish Coll of Textiles.

Stephen Lambert, coll lecturer, contested Berwick-upon-Tweed 1987. CLP youth officer, membership sec, cl candidate, delegate to Newcastle Central CLP, 1984-92. B Dec 15 1958; ed Gosforth East sec mod sch; Warwick Univ; Bolton Coll of HE; Newcastle Poly. NATFHE.

RUGBY AND KENILWORTH				No change	
Electorate % Turnout	77,766	83.7%	1992	76,654	79.6%	1987
*Pawsey, J F (C)	34,110	52.4%	+0.8%	31,485	51.6%	C
Airey, J (Lab)	20,863	32.0%	+7.1%	15,221	24.9%	Lab
Roodhouse, J M (LD)	9,934	15.3%	-8.2%	14,343	23.5%	L/All
Withers, S (NLP)	202	0.3%				
C to Lab swing 3.1%	65,109		20.3%	61,049		26.6%
		C maj	13,247		C maj	16,264

James Pawsey was elected to exec of 1922 Cmte of Cons backbenchers in 1989. Director, Autobar Ltd (food services); St Martin's Hospitals, 1989- . Elected for this seat 1983; MP for Rugby, 1979-83. Chmn Cons back-bench ed cmte, 1985- ; mbr select cmtes on parly commissioner for administration, 1983- ; on standing orders, 1987- ; parly scientific cmte, 1982- . Jt vice-chmn, 1990- , and mbr 1984-90, exec cmte, British gp, IPU. Sec British Solidarity with Poland Campaign, 1982- . B Aug 21 1933; ed Coventry tech sch; Coventry Tech Coll. Mbr of Lloyd's.

John Airey, head of TU ed sch, Sandwell CFE, contested this seat 1987; chmn CLP, 1988- ; mbr Warwickshire CC, 1989- . B Jun 29 1949; ed Walton-le-Dale cty sec schl; Ruskin Coll; Pembroke coll, Oxford univ; Colton Coll of Ed. NATFHE; TGWU; Common Market Safeguards Cmte.

Jerry Roodhouse, sales engineer, contested Birmingham East in 1989 Euro elections. On exec of Euro region cmte; vice-chmn constituency LD. B Jun 26 1953; ed Harris Sch, Rugby; Rycotewood Coll, Thame. On nat exec, campaign for work and action trust.

RUISLIP, NORTHWOOD				No change	
Electorate % Turnout	54,151	81.9%	1992	56,365	77.7%	1987
*Wilkinson, J A D (C)	28,097	63.3%	+0.7%	27,418	62.6%	C
Brooks, Ms R (Lab)	8,306	18.7%	+5.2%	10,447	23.9%	L/All
Davies, H (LD)	7,739	17.4%	-6.4%	5,913	13.5%	Lab
Sheehan, M (NLP)	214	0.5%				
C to Lab swing 2.3%	44,356		44.6%	43,778		38.8%
		C maj	19,791		C maj	16,971

John Wilkinson was mbr select cmte on defence, 1987-90; chmn Cons back-bench aviation cmte, 1983-5; vice-chmn Cons defence cmte, 1990-91 and 1983-5; chmn Cons space sub-cmte, 1986-90 (vice-chmn, 1983-5). Business consultant, being chmn, EMC (Communications) Ltd, European marketing consultants, since 1984; director, International Partnerships Gp Inc, 1990- lecturer and author. Treas all-pty maritime parly gp. Elected for Ruislip-Northwood 1979; MP for Bradford W, 1970-Feb 1974; contested that seat, Oct 1974. B Sep 23 1940; ed Eton; RAF Coll, Cranwell; Churchill Coll, Cambridge. Chmn

Euro Freedom Cl, 1982-90; Horn of Africa Cl, 1984-8. Delegate to Cl of Europe (chmn space sub-cmte, 1984-8) and WEU (chmn cmte on scientific, tech and aerospace, 1986-9), 1979-90.

Rachel Brooks, trade union researcher; London rep on Lab Pty nat exec women's cmte; vice-chmn, Haringey local govt cmte, 1990- . B Mar 7 1962; ed Ranelagh sch, Bracknell; Oxford Univ. GMB; Co-op Pty.

Harry Davies, owner of local business and UK director of fine art company. Founder pres Northwood Lions club. B Apr 19 1939. Mbr Chartered Inst of Marketing.

RUSHCLIFFE					No change		
Electorate % Turnout	76,253	83.0%	1992	72,797	80.0%	1987	
*Clarke, K H (C)	34,448	54.4%	-4.4%	34,214	58.8%		C
Chewings, A (Lab)	14,682	23.2%	+6.6%	13,375	23.0%	SDP/All	
Wood, Dr A M (LD)	12,660	20.0%	-3.0%	9,631	16.5%		Lab
Anthony, S (Grn)	775	1.2%	-0.5%	991	1.7%		Grn
Maelor-Jones, M (Ind C)	611	1.0%					
Richards, D (NLP)	150	0.2%					
C to Lab swing 5.5%	63,326		31.2%	58,211		35.8%	
		C maj	19,766		C maj	20,839	

Kenneth Clarke, QC, was appointed Home Secretary in 1992. Sec of State for Education and Science in 1990; Sec of State for Health, 1988-90; Chancellor of the Duchy of Lancaster and chief spokesman in Commons for DTI as Minr for Trade and Industry, 1987-8; joined cabinet 1985 as Paymaster Gen and Minr for Employment, becoming dept's chief Commons spokesman, 1985-7; Minr for Health, with rank of Minr of State, DHSS, 1982-5; Parly Sec (1979-81) and Under Sec of State (1981-2) for Transport. PC 1984. Elected in 1970; contested Mansfield, 1966 and 1964. Ld Commissioner of Treasury (Govt whip) 1974; asst Govt whip, 1972-4. Barrister; Hon Bencher,

Gray's Inn, 1989. B Jul 2 1940; ed Nottingham HS; Gonville and Caius Coll, Cambridge (Pres of Union, 1963).
Alan Chewings, BIFU official; chmn, BIFU organisers (Apex) bargaining unit, 1987-9; mbr Rushcliffe BC, 1979-83; Cotgrave PC, 1976-86. B Feb 19 1955; ed W Bridgford CFE. GMB/Apex.
Dr Andrew Wood, family doctor. E Midland LD spokesman on constitutional reform; sec Nottingham cty gp. B Jun 11 1955; ed Eastwood HS, Glasgow; Glasgow Univ. BMA.
Simon Anthony, further ed computer lecturer; freelance video tape engineer. B Oct 30 1957.

RUTLAND AND MELTON					No change	
Electorate % Turnout	80,976	80.8%	1992	77,846	76.8%	1987
Duncan, A J C (C)	38,603	59.0%	-3.0%	37,073	62.0%	C
Taylor, Ms J (Lab)	13,068	20.0%	+5.5%	14,051	23.5%	L/All
Lustig, R E (LD)	12,682	19.4%	-4.1%	8,680	14.5%	Lab
Berreen, J (Grn)	861	1.3%				
Grey, R (NLP)	237	0.4%				
C to Lab swing 4.2%	65,451		39.0%	59,804		38.5%
		C maj	25,535		C maj	23,022

Alan Duncan, oil trader and adviser to govts and companies on oil supply, shipping and refining, contested Barnsley West and Penistone in 1987. Chmn and part-owner of Innovisions Ltd, a Yorkshire based video production company. With Shell International Petroleum, 1979-81. Lived in Singapore, 1984-6. B Mar 31 1957; ed Beechwood Park sch, St Albans; Merchant Taylors' Sch, Northwood; St John's Coll, Oxford (Pres of Union, 1979); Kennedy Scholar at Harvard Univ. Freeman, City of London; liveryman, Merchant Taylors' Co. Coxed coll first eight at Oxford and heavyweight crew at Harvard.

Joan Taylor, trade union mbr Lab pty reg exec. Mbr Nottinghamshire CC, 1973-7 and 1985- (chmn social services cmte, 1985-). B Apr 11 1944; ed Warren Farm sec sch, Birmingham; WEA; Open Univ. Mbr regional Apex cmte; branch sec nearly 25 years. Sponsored by GMB .
Richard Lustig is principal, Richard Lustig associates, management consultants. Contested Blaby 1987 and 1983; Derbyshire SE 1979. E Midlands reg LD spokesman on trade and industry; mbr cl of regions of England. Exec mbr, Nat Pure Water assocn. B Dec 17 1931; ed Salford GS; LSE.

RYEDALE					No change	
Electorate % Turnout	87,048	81.7%	1992	83,205	79.2%	1987
*Greenway, J R (C)	39,888	56.1%	+2.7%	35,149	53.3%	C
Shields, Mrs E L (LD)	21,449	30.1%	-8.4%	25,409	38.6%	L/All
Healey, J (Lab)	9,812	13.8%	+5.7%	5,340	8.1%	Lab
LD to C swing 5.6%	71,149		25.9%	65,898		14.8%
		C maj	18,439		C maj	9,740

John Greenway became PPS to Lady Trumpington, Minr of State for Agriculture, in 1991. Regained seat for Cons in 1987; mbr select cmte on home affairs, 1987-91. Jt vice-chmn, Cons back-bench ag, fish and food cmte, 1989-91; jt sec, Cons health cmte, 1988-91; jt vice-chmn, Cons home affairs cmte, 1990-1;; all-pty association football parly gp, 1990- . Sec all-pty financial services gp, 1991- . Director, Greenway Middleton and Co Ltd, registered insurance brokers; Pocknell and Co, graphic design consultants. Parly adviser to Inst of Insurance Brokers; Yorkshire Television plc, and British health care assocn. Consultant to Practice Financial Management, independent financial advisers. Mbr N Yorkshire CC, 1985-7. B Feb 15 1946; ed Sir John

Deane's GS, Northwich, Cheshire.
Elizabeth Shields was MP for this seat 1986-7 after winning by-election; contested seat 1983, and Howden, 1979. Chmn, Yorks and Humberside LD candidates cmte, 1988- . Lecturer/archivist; teacher, 1954-86; hd of dept at Malton Sch, N Yorkshire, 1976-86. B Feb 27 1928; ed Whyteleafe Girls' GS; Avery Hill Coll of Ed; Univ Coll, London; York Univ. Mbr, Ryedale DC, since 1980; chmn cl, 1989-90.
John Healey, campaigns manager in public/voluntary sector consultancy. B Feb 13 1960; ed St Peter's sch, York; Christ's Coll, Cambridge. NUJ; treas, Parly branch, 1983-86. Mbr campaigns cmte, NCCL.

SAFFRON WALDEN						No change
Electorate % Turnout	74,878	83.2%	1992	73,185	79.0%	1987
*Haselhurst, A G B (C)	35,272	56.6%	-1.1%	33,354	57.7%	C
Hayes, M P (LD)	17,848	28.6%	-0.3%	16,752	29.0%	L/All
Kotz, J (Lab)	8,933	14.3%	+2.8%	6,674	11.5%	Lab
Miller, M (NLP)	260	0.4%		816	1.4%	Grn
C to LD swing 0.4%	62,313		28.0%	57,813		28.7%
		C maj	17,424		C maj	16,602

Alan Haselhurst, mbr select cmte on Euro legislation; vice-chmn Cons backbench aviation cmte 1983-86 and 1988-,chmn, 1986-7; jt vice-chmn Cons ed cmte 1983- . Chmn trustees, community development foundation 1986- (trustee 1982-); chmn rights of way review cmte 1983- . Mbr Commons catering cmte 1991- . Elected at 1977 by-election; MP for Middleton and Prestwich 1970-Feb 74. Consultant to electronic engineering assocn, Albright & Wilson Ltd, Barrington Jay and Co, and Johnson Matthey plc. B Jun 23 1937; ed King Edward VI sch, Birmingham; Cheltenham coll; Oriel coll, Oxford (pres, univ Cons assocn 1958 and sec, treas and librarian of Union, 1959-60).

Mark Hayes, architect and regional manager national housing assoc, contested this seat 1987. Chmn LD English housing policy gp; former chmn Lib housing panel; LD coordinating cmte for England. Former mbr Lib pty cl; Cambridge city cl 1982-6. B 1956; ed Watford GS; Jesus coll, Cambridge. Lay preacher, United Reform Church. Regional officer salvation army housing assoc.

Jon Kotz, local govt officer; pty offices held include chmn Saffron Walden CLP and Hackney Central; Mbr Gtr London regional cl standing orders cmte. Mbr Hackney cl 1953-86 (mayor, ldr and dep ldr). Former chmn public works cmte, AMA. B Mar 21 1930; ed central sch of arts and crafts, Southampton Row, London. Nalgo.

SALFORD EAST						No change
Electorate % Turnout	52,616	64.4%	1992	58,087	66.0%	1987
*Orme, S (Lab)	20,327	60.0%	+1.2%	22,555	58.8%	Lab
Berens, D A (C)	9,092	26.8%	-0.5%	10,499	27.4%	C
Owen, N (LD)	3,836	11.3%	-2.0%	5,105	13.3%	SDP/All
Stanley, M (Grn)	463	1.4%		201	0.5%	WRP
Craig, C (NLP)	150	0.4%				
C to Lab swing 0.9%	33,868		33.2%	38,360		31.4%
		Lab maj	11,235		Lab maj	12,056

Stanley Orme was elected PLP chmn 1987. Mbr shadow cabinet 1979- ; chief Opposn spokesman on energy 1983-7; industry 1980-3 and on health and social security 1979-80. Mbr cmte on privileges 1989- ; Commons services cmte 1987-91; select cmte on sittings of Commons 1991- ; British-Irish inter-parly body. Chmn Commons administration cmte 1991- ; vice-pres parly and scientific cmte. Elected for this seat 1983; MP for Salford W 1964-83; contested Stockport S 1959. Minr for social security, with cabinet seat 1976-9; Minr of State, DHSS 1976; Minr of State for N Ireland 1974-6. PC 1974. Engineer. B Apr 5 1923; ed elementary and tech schs, nat cl of Lab colls and WEA classes. Sponsored by AEU; chmn AEU parly gp of MPs.

David Berens, solicitor, elected to Westminster city cl 1990 (mbr ed and social services cmtes). Vice-chmn Salford E Cons assocn 1981-3 and 1986-8. B Mar 16 1962; ed Durham univ.

SALISBURY						No change
Electorate % Turnout	75,916	79.9%	1992	76,221	75.6%	1987
*Key, S R (C)	31,546	52.0%	-2.9%	31,612	54.9%	C
Sample, P (LD)	22,573	37.2%	+2.2%	20,169	35.0%	SDP/All
Fear, S R (Lab)	5,483	9.0%	-0.4%	5,455	9.5%	Lab
Elcock, Dr S (Grn)	609	1.0%		372	0.6%	Ind
Fletcher, S (Ind)	233	0.4%	-0.3%			
Abbott, T (Wessex)	117	0.2%				
Martell, Ms A (NLP)	93	0.2%				
C to LD swing 2.5%	60,654		14.8%	57,608		19.9%
		C maj	8,973		C maj	11,443

Robert Key was appointed Under Sec of the newly-created National Heritage dept in 1992. Under Sec for Environment 1990-92; chmn inner cities religious cl 1991- ; PPS to Chris Patten, Minr for Overseas Development, and then Sec of State for Environment 1987-90; and to Minr of State for Energy, 1985-7. An asst master at Harrow 1969-83; political sec to Edward Heath, former Prime Minr 1984-5. Non-exec director Wessex Cable Ltd 1989-90. Mbr medical research cl 1989-90, and of its AIDS cmte 1988-90; jt vice-chmn all-pty parly gp on AIDS 1988-90. Mbr select cmte on ed, science and arts 1983-6. Jt parly chmn cl for ed in Commonwealth 1985-7. Elected in 1983; contested Camden, Holborn and St Pancras S, 1979. B Apr 22 1945; ed Sherborne sch; Clare coll, Cambridge. Mbr chorus of acad of St Martin-in-the-Fields 1975-89.

Paul Sample became head of public relations at Crime Concern in 1991; senior press officer of Help the Aged 1990-1; editor of Liberal News 1985-8 and founding editor of *Liberal Democrats News* 1988-9. Mbr Salisbury DC 1990- . B Mar 22 1961; ed City univ.

Steve Fear, lecturer; mbr Salisbury DC; chmn SW regional Lab pty. B Aug 1 1955; ed Ladysmith SM sch; Exeter coll; Reading univ; Wolverhampton poly. NATFHE.

SCARBOROUGH						No change
Electorate % Turnout	76,364	77.2%	1992	74,612	73.2%	1987
Sykes, J D (C)	29,334	49.8%	-0.9%	27,672	50.7%	C
Billing, D L (Lab)	17,600	29.9%	+6.2%	14,046	25.7%	SDP/All
Davenport, B (LD)	11,133	18.9%	-6.8%	12,913	23.6%	Lab
Richardson, Dr R (Grn)	876	1.5%				
C to Lab swing 3.6%	58,943		19.9%	54,631		24.9%
		C maj	11,734		C maj	13,626

John Sykes, company director with interests in property, agriculture, plastics manufacturing and petrol retailing, was elected in 1992. Former director, Leeds/Bradford airport. Contested Sheffield, Hillsborough 1987. Mbr, Kirklees MBC, 1987-91. Mbr, Yorkshire area Cons finance and gen purposes cmte; former vice-chmn, Yorkshire CPC; former chmn, Dewsbury Cons assocn. B Aug 24 1956; ed St David's sch, Huddersfield; Giggleswick sch, N Yorkshire. Was on Yorks and Humberside Tourist Bd.

David Billing, health service administrator; mbr, N Yorkshire CC, 1981- . B May 10 1950; ed London and Hull Univs. Nupe.

Bromley Davenport, social worker, contested Howden (E Yorks) in 1979 for Lab leaving pty in 1981 being an LD via SDP. Mbr, Skipton UDC, 1970-3. B Apr 18 1933; ed Radcliffe Tech Coll, Lancs); Queen's Univ, Belfast.

SEDGEFIELD						No change
Electorate % Turnout	61,024	77.1%	1992	60,866	76.1%	1987
*Blair, A C L (Lab)	28,453	60.5%	+4.5%	25,965	56.0%	Lab
Jopling, N M F (C)	13,594	28.9%	+1.1%	12,907	27.8%	C
Huntington, J G (LD)	4,982	10.6%	-5.5%	7,477	16.1%	SDP/All
C to Lab swing 1.7%	47,029		31.6%	46,349		28.2%
		Lab maj	14,859		Lab maj	13,058

Tony Blair, elected to shadow Cabinet in 1988, became chief Opposn spokesman on employment in 1989; chief spokesman on energy, 1988-9; a spokesman on trade and industry, 1987-8; on Treasury and economic affairs, 1984-7. Barrister (non-practising). Won seat in 1983; contested Beaconsfield by-election, 1982. B May 6 1953; ed Durham Choristers Sch; Fettes Coll, Edinburgh; St John's Coll, Oxford. Sponsored by TGWU.

Nicholas Jopling, farmer; mbr, Thirsk NFU cmte, 1986- ; branch delegate to NE region NFU, 1987- . Mbr, Hambleton DC, 1987- (finance chmn, 1991-). Son of former agriculture minister, Mr Michael Jopling, MP for Westmorland and Lonsdale. B Oct 4 1961; ed Bramcote sch, Scarborough; Eton; Newcastle univ. Been chmn, Pickhill and Sinderby district Cons assocn., and mbr, finance and gen purposes cmte, Richmond (Yorks) Cons assocn.

Garry Huntington, sales manager; has part share in hotel; mbr, Sedgefield DC, 1987- (LD ldr); Shildon TC, 1963-73; treas, Bishop Auckland LDs. B Dec 29 1940; ed Shildon All Saints sch; Bishop Auckland tech coll. Ex-mbr, GMWU.

SELBY						No change
Electorate % Turnout	77,178	80.2%	1992	71,378	77.7%	1987
*Alison, M J H (C)	31,067	50.2%	-1.4%	28,611	51.6%	C
Grogan, J T (Lab)	21,559	34.8%	+8.1%	14,832	26.7%	Lab
Batty, E (LD)	9,244	14.9%	-6.7%	12,010	21.7%	L/All
C to Lab swing 4.7%	61,870		15.4%	55,453		24.8%
		C maj	9,508		C maj	13,779

Michael Alison was appointed Second Church Estates Commissioner in 1987; PPS to Prime Minister, 1983-7; Minr of State for Employment, 1981-3; Minr of State for N Ireland, 1979-81. PC 1981. Sec, all-pty Christian Fellowship parly gp. An Opposn spokesman on environment, 1978-9, and on home affairs, 1975-8. Elected for this seat 1983; MP for Barkston Ash, 1964-83. Under Sec of State for Health and Social Security, 1970-4. B Jun 27 1926; ed Eton; Wadham Coll, Oxford; Ridley Hall, Cambridge.

John Grogan, personal asst to ldr of Leeds City Cl, contested this seat in 1987 and York in Euro elections 1989. Was asst to Dr Barry Seal, MEP for Yorkshire West and former ldr of Lab gp in European Parliament, and to ldr of Wolverhampton Cl. B Feb 24 1961; ed St Michael's Coll, Leeds; St John's Coll, Oxford. First Lab president of Oxford Univ students' union, 1982-3. Nupe.

Ted Batty, chartered arbitrator, chartered surveyor and specialist construction industry consultant in UK and abroad on resolving of disputes. Mbr, Selby DC, 1970-6 and 1987-92 (gp ldr, 1987-92). B Feb 5 1936; ed Cockburn GS, Leeds; London univ. Elder, Selby United Reformed Church.

SEVENOAKS					No change	
Electorate % Turnout	71,050	81.4%	1992	73,179	76.4%	1987
*Wolfson, G M (C)	33,245	57.5%	-1.4%	32,945	58.9%	C
Walshe, R F C (LD)	14,091	24.4%	-3.5%	15,600	27.9%	L/All
Evans, Ms J S (Lab)	9,470	16.4%	+3.2%	7,379	13.2%	Lab
Lawrence, Ms M E (Grn)	786	1.4%				
Wakeling, P (NLP)	210	0.4%				
LD to C swing 1.1%	57,802		33.1%	55,924		31.0%
		C maj	19,154		C maj	17,345

Mark Wolfson, a director of Hambros Bank Ltd, 1973-88, and its head of personnel, 1970-85, was elected in 1979; contested Islington N, Feb 1974; City of Westminster, Paddington, Oct 1974. PPS to Ian Stewart, Minr of State for the Armed Forces, 1987-8; to Minr of State for defence procurement, 1984-5; and to Minr of State for N Ireland, 1983-4. Partner, John Adair and Associates, managements consultants, 1988- . B Apr 7 1934; ed Eton; Pembroke Coll, Cambridge. Formerly with Canadian Pacific Railway and a teacher in an Indian reservation in British Columbia. Head of Brathay Hall centre, Lake District, 1962-6; head of youth services, Industrial soc, 1966-9. FRSA.

Roger Walshe, managing director of import/export agency; mbr Sevenoaks DC, 1987- ; Kent trust for nature conservation. B Apr 5 1935; ed Whitgift sch; London Univ.
Jeannie Evans, teacher; qualified assertiveness trainer; mbr Lab pty southern region exec, 1990- ; Kent Lab Pty women's officer; chmn Sevenoaks CLP. B Aug 17 1943; ed St Catherine's sch, Twickenham. Pres Kent division, NUT 1990-1; vice-chmn, nat advisory cmte on equal opportunities.
Margot Lawrence, Grn pty electoral returning officer, SE area; organiser, Sevenoaks pty. B Dec 11 1961; ed Walthamstow Hall, Sevenoaks.

SHEFFIELD CENTRAL					No change	
Electorate % Turnout	59,059	56.1%	1992	61,156	62.5%	1987
*Caborn, R G (Lab)	22,764	68.7%	+0.9%	25,872	67.7%	Lab
Davies, V (C)	5,470	16.5%	-0.6%	6,530	17.1%	C
Sangar, A (LD)	3,856	11.6%	-2.3%	5,314	13.9%	SDP/All
Wroe, G S (Grn)	750	2.3%		278	0.7%	RF
Clarke, M (EUVJJ)	212	0.6%		203	0.5%	Comm
O'Brien, Ms J (CL)	92	0.3%				
C to Lab swing 0.8%	33,144		52.2%	38,197		50.6%
		Lab maj	17,294		Lab maj	19,342

Richard Caborn, Lab campaigner on regional policy, was an Opposn spokesman on trade and industry, 1987-90. Elected in 1983; MEP for Sheffield, 1979-84. Mbr select cmte on Euro legislation, 1983-8. Unpaid director, Freedom Productions Ltd, 1988- ; Sheffield city trust, 1990- ; Sheffield festival, 1991- . B Oct 6 1943; ed Hurlfield comprehensive sch, Sheffield; Granville CFE; Sheffield poly. Chmn PLP anti-apartheid gp, 1987- ; sec all-pty southern Africa parly gp; vice-chmn, Tribune Gp, 1986-7. Convenor of shop stewards, Firth Brown Ltd, 1967-79. Sponsored by AEU. Chmn, Sheffield District Lab Pty.

Vernon Davies founded his own company in 1976 with interests in computers, finance, leisure and agriculture. Chmn, Essex SW Euro constituency, 1990- ; Epping Forest Cons Assocn, 1989- . B Feb 16 1944; ed Chigwell sch; Bristol Univ. Redbridge magistrate 1980- .
Andrew Sangar was elected to Sheffield city MBC in 1991; chmn, Yorks and Humberside YLDs, 1990-1. B Feb 18 1967; ed Sheffield Univ.
Graham Wroe, sec sch teacher; former Sheffield Grn press officer; now open meeting organiser. Recently spent year working in Uganda. B Apl 23 1959; ed Sheffield City Poly. NUT.

SHEFFIELD, ATTERCLIFFE					No change	
Electorate % Turnout	69,177	71.8%	1992	67,051	72.9%	1987
Betts, C J C (Lab)	28,563	57.5%	-0.3%	28,266	57.8%	Lab
Millward, G R (C)	13,083	26.3%	+3.7%	11,075	22.7%	C
Woolley, Mrs H E (LD)	7,283	14.7%	-4.9%	9,549	19.5%	SDP/All
Ferguson, G (Grn)	751	1.5%				
Lab to C swing 2.0%	49,680		31.2%	48,890		35.2%
		Lab maj	15,480		Lab maj	17,191

Clive Betts, economist and former local govt officer, was elected to Sheffield city cl in 1976 (ldr of cl, 1987- ; dep ldr, 1986-7; chmn of finance, 1986-8, and chmn of housing 1980-6). Former dep chmn, AMA and chmn of housing cmte, 1984-9. Mbr Lab housing gp. Contested Louth 1979; Sheffield, Hallam, Oct 1974. Was principal economist with S Yorkshire cty cl; previously an economist with TUC and Derbyshire CC. B Jan 13 1950; ed King Edward VII Sch, Sheffield; Pembroke Coll, Cambridge. Mbr of, and sponsored by TGWU. Been CLP chmn and

sec; mbr DLP exec.
Gordon Millward, managing director of two companies, contested this seat 1983. Mbr South Yorkshire CC, 1977-86; Sheffield chamber of commerce. Chmn, Sheffield industrial estate business assocn. B Set 14 1946; ed Birley sec sch. Vice-chmn, Attercliffe Cons assocn, 1989- .
Helen Woolley, landscape architect, contested this seat 1987. B Nov 15 1956; ed King Edward VI Camphill GS for Girls, Birmingham; Newcastle Univ. Associate of landscape inst.

SHEFFIELD, BRIGHTSIDE						No change
Electorate % Turnout	63,810	66.3%	1992	64,982	68.7%	1987
*Blunkett, D (Lab)	29,771	70.4%	+0.5%	31,208	69.9%	Lab
Loughton, T P (C)	7,090	16.8%	+1.1%	7,017	15.7%	C
Franklin, R (LD)	5,273	12.5%	-1.9%	6,434	14.4%	L/All
Hyland, D (Int Comm)	150	0.4%				
Lab to C swing 0.3%	42,284		53.6%	44,659		54.2%
		Lab maj	22,681		Lab maj	24,191

David Blunkett joined the Opposn front bench environment team in 1988 as a spokesman on housing and local govt; subsequently promoted to shadow minr of state for local govt. Elected in 1987; contested Sheffield Hallam Feb 1974. Jt vice-chmn, PLP environment cmte, 1987-8. Became Labour ldr of Sheffield City Cl in 1980, serving on cl, 1970-88; also on S Yorkshire CC, 1973-7. Mbr, Labour Pty NEC, 1983- , chairing its local govt cmte. Dep chmn, AMA, 1984-7. Parly adviser to Chartered Society of Physiotherapists. B Jun 6 1947; ed Royal Nat Coll for the Blind, Shrewsbury; Richmond CFE, Sheffield; Sheffield univ; Huddersfield Coll of Ed (Tech). Sponsored by Nupe,

mbr since 1974.
Tim Loughton, investment manager; vice-chmn, Battersea Cons Assocn, 1990- ; mbr, Gtr London area exec cmte. Was Lewes YC chmn and sec, Warwick and Cambridge univ Cons assocns. B May 30 1962; ed The Priory sch, Lewes; Warwick univ; Clare Coll, Cambridge. BIFU.
Richard Franklin, theatre director, actor, writer; contested 1991 Ribble by-election as Ind C against poll tax, and Twickenham in 1973 for Union of Ind People's Reps. B Jan 15 1936; ed Westminster sch; Christ Church, Oxford; Royal Acad of Dramatic Art. Equity.

SHEFFIELD, HALLAM						No change
Electorate % Turnout	76,584	70.8%	1992	74,158	74.7%	1987
*Patnick, C I (C)	24,693	45.5%	-0.8%	25,649	46.3%	C
Gold, Dr P J (LD)	17,952	33.1%	+0.6%	18,012	32.5%	L/All
Hardstaff, Ms V M (Lab)	10,930	20.1%	-0.2%	11,290	20.4%	Lab
Baker, M (Grn)	473	0.9%	+0.0%	459	0.8%	Grn
Hurford, R (NLP)	101	0.2%				
Clifford, Ms T (Rev Comm)	99	0.2%				
C to LD swing 0.7%	54,248		12.4%	55,410		13.8%
		C maj	6,741		C maj	7,637

Irvine Patnick was appointed a Lord Commissioner of the Treasury (Govt whip) in 1990; an asst Govt whip, 1989-90; jt vice-chmn, Cons back-bench environment cmte, 1988-9 being jt sec, 1987-8. Elected in 1987; contested Sheffield Hillsborough, 1979 and 1970. Chmn, Cons nat local govt advisory cmte, 1989-90; nat exec, Cons party, 1982-9; Sheffield City Cl, 1967-70; Sheffield MDC, 1971-88; S Yorkshire CC, being ldr of opposition, 1973-86, when it was abolished. B Oct 1929; ed Central tech sch; Sheffield poly. Governor, Sports Aid Foundation, Yorkshire and Humberside, 1980- .
Peter Gold, poly lecturer, contested this seat for L/All 1987. Chair, LD working gp on higher ed policy; vice-chair, LD

parly candidates assocn, 1990- . Treas, Nat Cl for Modern Languages. B Jun 20 1944; ed Harrow County Boys' GS; Christ Church, Oxford. APCT.
Veronica Hardstaff, modern languages teacher; mbr, Sheffield City Cl, 1971-8; coopted mbr, Sheffield ed cmte, 1981-3. Chmn, Sheffield Euro CLP; vice-chair, Sheffield District LP; sec, Hillsborough CLP, 1980-2. B Oct 23 1941; ed Bilston Girls' HS, S Staffs; Manchester and Cologne Univs. NUT (Sheffield assocn exec mbr, 1986, 1990).
Mallen Baker, freelance writer; Grn Pty speaker, 1990- ; co-chair, Grn Pty Cl, 1990-1. B May 23 1963.

SHEFFIELD, HEELEY						No change
Electorate % Turnout	70,953	70.9%	1992	73,931	72.0%	1987
*Michie, W (Lab)	28,005	55.7%	+2.3%	28,425	53.4%	Lab
Beck, D R (C)	13,051	25.9%	-0.3%	13,985	26.3%	C
Moore, P (LD)	9,247	18.4%	-1.9%	10,811	20.3%	SDP/All
C to Lab swing 1.3%	50,303		29.7%	53,221		27.1%
		Lab maj	14,954		Lab maj	14,440

William Michie, former maintenance electrician and laboratory technician, became redundant in 1981; was unemployed, 1981-3, and was elected for this seat in 1983. Treas, Campaign Gp of Lab MPs, 1987- ; vice-chmn, Yorkshire gp of Lab MPs, 1985-7. B Nov 24 1935; ed Abbeydale Secondary Sch, Sheffield. Mbr, Sheffield City Cl, 1970-84 (chmn, planning, 1974-81; employment, 1981-3, group sec and chief whip, 1974-83); South Yorkshire CC, 1974-1986 (chmn, area planning, 1974-

81). Sponsored by AEU.
David Beck, freelance journalist and public relations consultant. Mbr, N Yorkshire CC, 1989- ; Scarborough BC, 1976-9. Treas, Scarborough Cons assocn, 1987- ; chmn, Yorkshire YCs, 1979-81. B Sep 4 1950; ed Scarborough Boys HS.
Peter Moore, self-employed electrical engineer. Mbr, Rotherham BC, 1985-7; Sheffield MBC, 1990- . B Apr 5 1947; ed Ulverton GS.

SHEFFIELD, HILLSBOROUGH — No change

Electorate % Turnout	77,343	77.2%	1992	76,312	78.0%	1987
Jackson, Mrs H (Lab)	27,568	46.2%	+2.1%	26,208	44.0%	Lab
Chadwick, D (LD)	20,500	34.3%	-4.2%	22,922	38.5%	L/All
Cordle, S C (C)	11,640	19.5%	+2.0%	10,396	17.5%	C
LD to Lab swing 3.2%	59,708		11.8%	59,526		5.5%
		Lab maj	7,068		Lab maj	3,286

Helen Jackson, special education teacher, served on Sheffield city cl, 1980-91, chairing economic development cmte, 1983-91, and public works cmte, 1981-3; mbr Huyton UDC, 1972-4. Founder mbr and chmn, centre for local economic strategies; mbr Lab cmte on Ireland. B May 19 1939; ed Berkhamsted girls' sch; St Hilda's coll, Oxford. TGWU.

David Chadwick, further ed coll lecturer, fought this seat for L/All in 1987 and 1983; Penistone, 1979, 1978 by-election, and twice in 1974; Blackpool South, 1970; Nelson and Colne by-election, 1968. Mbr Sheffield city cl, 1975-

(gp ldr); S Yorkshire CC, 1980-5 (Lib gp ldr); Blackpool CBC, 1968-72. B Sep 2 1939; ed Blackpool CFE; Bolton coll of ed. NATFHE, being sec NATFHE liaison cmte, Rotherham. Mbr Peace through Nato.

Sid Cordle, customer service rep with Prudential, contested Sheffield Heeley 1983. Chmn, Yorkshire CTUs, 1989- ; mbr nat union exec cmte, 1989- ; Sheffield city cl, 1982-8 (shadow chmn, planning cmte, 1983-8); nat exec, nat union of insurance workers, 1986-90 (on section exec, Prudential, 1990-); TUC delegate, 1987 and 1989. B Jan 2 1956; ed Theale GS, Berks; Sheffield Univ.

SHERWOOD — Lab gain

Electorate % Turnout	73,354	85.5%	1992	71,378	81.9%	1987
Tipping, S P (Lab)	29,788	47.5%	+9.3%	26,816	45.9%	C
*Stewart, A S (C)	26,878	42.9%	-3.0%	22,321	38.2%	Lab
Howard, J (LD)	6,039	9.6%	-6.3%	9,343	16.0%	SDP/All
C to Lab swing 6.2%	62,705		4.6%	58,480		7.7%
		Lab maj	2,910		C maj	4,495

Simon (Paddy) Tipping, cllr; former community social worker, contested Rushcliffe 1987. Mbr Notts CC, 1981- (chmn, finance cmte). Director, Notts cooperative development agency; Nottingham development enterprise. B Oct 24 1949; ed Hipperholme GS; Nottingham Univ. Nupe.

Andrew (Andy) Stewart, a farmer, was elected in 1983. PPS to John MacGregor, as Minr of Ag, Fish and Food, Sec of State for Ed and Science and Ld Privy Seal and Ldr of

Commons, 1987- ; mbr select cmte on agriculture, 1983-7. B May 27 1937; ed Strathaven Acad, Lanark; W of Scotland agricultural coll. Mbr Nottinghamshire CC, 1974-83; Caunton PC, 1973-83. Mbr Newark branch, NFU, since 1961, and of county exec cmte, since 1966; Newark and Notts Agricultural Soc.

John Howard, self-employed consultant electrical and mechanical engineer. B Feb 5 1934; ed Trent Poly.

SHIPLEY — No change

Electorate % Turnout	68,816	82.1%	1992	68,705	79.2%	1987
*Fox, Sir Marcus (C)	28,463	50.4%	+0.9%	26,941	49.5%	C
Lockwood, Ms A (Lab)	16,081	28.5%	+5.2%	14,311	26.3%	L/All
Cole, J M C (LD)	11,288	20.0%	-6.3%	12,669	23.3%	Lab
Harris, C M (Grn)	680	1.2%	+0.3%	507	0.9%	Grn
C to Lab swing 2.2%	56,512		21.9%	54,428		23.2%
		C maj	12,382		C maj	12,630

Sir Marcus Fox, company director and consultant; elected chmn 1922 cmte of Cons backbenchers in 1992 (jt vice-chmn 1983-92); chmn, Commons cmte of selection, 1984- . Under Sec of State for Environment, 1979-81; Ld Commissioner of Treasury (Govt whip), 1973-4; asst Govt whip, 1972-3. Chmn, nat assocn of Cons clubs, 1988- ; United and Cecil Club. Elected in 1970; contested Dewsbury, 1959; Huddersfield W, 1966. B Jun 11 1927; ed Eastborough Cl sch, Dewsbury; Wheelwright GS, Dewsbury. Director, Westminster (Communications) Ltd, Care Services Gp, Hartley Investment Trust and other companies; consultant to 3M (UK) Ltd, Shepherd (Construction) Ltd, Onward Gp and Bristol Port Co. Jt vice-

chmn, Yorkshire Cons MPs, 1990- . Mbr Chorus of Acad of St Martin-in-the-Fields, 1975-89.

Annie Lockwood, citizens' advice bureau worker. Mbr N Tyneside cl, 1988- ; Northumbria police authority; Tyne and Wear fire authority. Wallsend CLP women's officer. B Jul 29 1949; ed Kent univ; Newcastle Poly. Nupe.

John Cole, teacher; head of economics, Salt GS, Shipley. Sec, Shipley LDs, 1988- ; sec (1985-8) and chmn (1980-5), Shipley Libs. B Jul 6 1944; ed Hampton sch, Middlesex; St Andrews univ. AMMA

Colin Harris, insurance and investment broker, contested this seat 1987. W Yorkshire Euro election treas, 1989. B Mar 19 1946; ed Salt GS.

SHOREHAM				No change		
Electorate % Turnout	71,252	81.2%	1992	71,318	77.5%	1987
Stephen, B M L (C)	32,670	56.5%	-4.4%	33,660	60.9%	C
King, M (LD)	18,384	31.8%	+1.8%	16,590	30.0%	L/All
Godwin, P (Lab)	6,123	10.6%	+1.4%	5,053	9.1%	Lab
Weights, W (Lib)	459	0.8%				
Dreben, J (NLP)	200	0.3%				
C to LD swing 3.1%	57,836		24.7%	55,303		30.9%
		C maj	14,286		C maj	17,070

Michael Stephen reatined this seat for Cons in 1992; contested Doncaster North 1983. Barrister. Former mbr Essex CC and former mbr ACC exec. Former vice-chmn Chelsea Cons Assocn. B Sep 25 1942; ed King Henry VIII Sch, Coventry; Stanford and Harvard Univs.
Martin King, head of travellers cheque operations, American Express; mbr Adur DC 1980- (cl ldr 1986-); ldr LD gp Assocn of DCs 1989- ; mbr management cmte cllrs assocn 1987- . B May 29 1951; ed Devizes Sch, Wilts; Harrow.
Paul Godwin, Nalgo trade union officer, contested this seat 1987. Mbr Hove BC 1979-91. Chmn Hove CLP. B May 2 1952; ed Brighton, Hove and Sussex GS; Brighton Poly. TGWU/ACTSS.

SHREWSBURY AND ATCHAM				No change		
Electorate % Turnout	70,620	82.5%	1992	70,689	77.0%	1987
*Conway, D L (C)	26,681	45.8%	-2.0%	26,027	47.8%	C
Hemsley, K A (LD)	15,716	27.0%	-4.2%	16,963	31.2%	L/All
Owen, Mrs E (Lab)	15,157	26.0%	+6.2%	10,797	19.8%	Lab
Hardy, G (Grn)	677	1.2%	-0.0%	660	1.2%	Grn
LD to C swing 1.1%	58,231		18.8%	54,447		16.6%
		C maj	10,965		C maj	9,064

Derek Conway was elected in 1983; contested Newcastle upon Tyne E, 1979; Durham, Oct 1974. PPS to Sir Wyn Roberts, minr of state for Wales, 1988-91. Mbr select cmte on transport 1987-8; select cmte on agriculture, 1986-7. Jt vice-chmn Cons backbench defence cmte, 1991- . Mbr exec cmte British gp, IPU. Major in 5th Bn (TA) Light Infantry. Parly adviser to British Shops and Stores Assocn and Nat Assocn of Bookmakers. Principal organiser of nat fund for research into crippling diseases 1974-83. B Feb 15 1953; ed Beacon Hill Boys' Sch; Gateshead Tech Coll; Newcastle Poly. Mbr Tyne and Wear Met CC1977-83 (ldr 1979-82); Gateshead BC 1974-8.
Kenneth Kemsley, retired senior lecturer in higher education, contested Burton 1987 for L/All and Eccles in 1983. Mbr Cheshire CC 1986- ; Congleton BC 1983- (mayor 1990-1); Congleton TC 1980-8. Chmn Congleton constituency pty 1984-6. B Feb 24 1926; ed Bridgnorth GS; Kirkby Coll of Ed; Manchester Univ. NUT/NATFHE.
Liz Owen, Mental Health Act commissioner, contested this seat in 1987. Mbr Shropshire CC 1981- . B Jan 13 1948; ed Central Newcastle HS; Seale Hayne Agricultural Coll; Trent Poly.

SHROPSHIRE NORTH				No change		
Electorate % Turnout	82,675	77.7%	1992	77,122	75.5%	1987
*Biffen, W J (C)	32,443	50.5%	-1.7%	30,385	52.2%	C
Stevens, H J (LD)	16,232	25.3%	-2.2%	15,970	27.4%	L/All
Hawkins, R J (Lab)	15,550	24.2%	+3.8%	11,866	20.4%	Lab
LD to C swing 0.2%	64,225		25.2%	58,221		24.8%
		C maj	16,211		C maj	14,415

John Biffen was Lord Privy Seal and Ldr of Commons, 1983-7; Lord President of Cl and Ldr of Commons 1982-3; Sec of State for Trade 1981-2; Chief Sec to Treasury 1979-81. PC 1979. Mbr Select Cmte on Privileges 1989- , and chmn 1982-7. Elected for this seat 1983; MP for Oswestry, 1961-83; contested Coventry E, 1959. Economist. B Nov 3 1930; ed Dr Morgan's GS, Bridgwater; Jesus Coll, Cambridge. Non-exec director, Glynwed International plc 1987- ; J Bibby & Sons plc 1988- . Mbr (unpaid), international advisory bd, International Assocn for Co-operation and Development in Southern Africa; unpaid adviser Euro-Turkish Corporation.
John Stevens, computer service manager, contested South Fylde for Libs in 1979, Bristol S Feb 1974 and Bristol NW 1970. B May 17 1943; ed Trowbridge HS.
Rob Hawkins, teacher, contested this seat 1987. B Mar 25 1949; ed in Worthing; Kesteven Coll of Ed. NAS/UWT.

SKIPTON AND RIPON						No change
Electorate % Turnout	75,628	81.3%	1992	72,199	77.8%	1987
*Curry, D M (C)	35,937	58.4%	-0.6%	33,128	59.0%	C
Hall, R (LD)	16,607	27.0%	-1.4%	15,954	28.4%	L/All
Allott, Ms K R (Lab)	8,978	14.6%	+3.4%	6,264	11.2%	Lab
				825	1.5%	Grn
LD to C swing 0.4%	61,522		31.4%	56,171		30.6%
		C maj	19,330		C maj	17,174

David Curry was appointed Minister of State for Agriculture, Fisheries and Food, in 1992. Parl Sec in dept 1989-92. Mbr select cmte on agriculture, 1987-9. Freelance journalist. Elected in 1987; contested Morpeth in Feb and Oct, 1974. Jt sec Cons backbench ag, fish and food cmte, 1987-9. MEP for Essex NE, 1979-89; Euro democratic gp and Cons spokesman, EP budgets cmte, 1985-9, and vice-chmn of cmte, 1984-5; rapporteur-general on 1987 EC budget. Chmn, EP agriculture cmte, 1982-4. B Jun 13 1944; ed Ripon GS; Corpus Christi Coll, Oxford; Kennedy inst of govt, Harvard. Former foreign correspondent and foreign news editor, *Financial Times*.

Richard Hall, lecturer in photography at York coll of arts and tech, contested Barnsley W and Penistone 1987. Mbr Harrogate BC, 1986- . B Mar 4 1942; ed Wennington Sch, Wetherby; Kitson Coll, Leeds; York univ. NATFHE.

Kate Allott, unemployed teacher; mbr N Yorks CC. 1989- . B Jul 3 1954; ed Queen Anne GS, York; Utd World Coll of the Atlantic; Bretton Hall Coll. Quaker. NUT.

SLOUGH						No change
Electorate % Turnout	73,889	78.2%	1992	73,424	75.9%	1987
*Watts, J A (C)	25,793	44.6%	-2.3%	26,166	46.9%	C
Lopez, E (Lab)	25,279	43.7%	+4.1%	22,076	39.6%	Lab
Mapp, P (LD)	4,041	7.0%	-6.4%	7,490	13.4%	SDP/All
Clark, J (Lib)	1,426	2.5%				
Alford, D (Ind Lab)	699	1.2%				
Carmichael, A (NF)	290	0.5%				
Creese, M (NLP)	153	0.3%				
Smith, Ms E (ERIP)	134	0.2%				
C to Lab swing 3.2%	57,815		0.9%	55,732		7.3%
		C maj	514		C maj	4,090

John Watts, chartered accountant, joined select cmte on Treasury and civil service in 1986. Jt vice-chmn, Cons backbench environment cmte, 1987-8; jt-chmn, all-pty non-profit making clubs parly gp. Mbr Hillingdon BC, 1973-86. Won this seat 1983. Director, Kenton & Middlesex building society, 1988- ; Global Satellite Communications plc, and Global Satellite Communications (Scotland) plc, 1991- ; parly adviser to Inst of Actuaries; Inst of chartered accountants in England and Wales; consultant to Rank Hovis McDougall plc and Wisdom Securities Ltd; adviser to Working Men's Club and Institute Union. B Apr 19 1947; ed Bishopshalt Sch, Hillingdon; Gonville and Caius Coll, Cambridge (chmn univ Cons Assocn, 1968).

Edward (Eddie) Lopez, full-time political organiser with Lab pty, contested this seat 1987. Trained as chartered accountant before being full-time organiser in Norwood. B Feb 7 1942; ed Affra Primary Sch, Brixton; Alleyns Sch, Dulwich. NULO/GMB.

Peter Mapp, management consultant with human resource management, IPM. Commissioned officer and instructor, RASFVR; officer, society of American military engineers. Exec cmte officer, Beaconsfield LDs. B Jan 27 1941.

SOLIHULL						No change
Electorate % Turnout	77,303	81.6%	1992	78,123	75.1%	1987
*Taylor, J M (C)	38,385	60.8%	-0.2%	35,844	61.1%	C
Southcombe, M J (LD)	13,239	21.0%	-3.0%	14,058	24.0%	L/All
Kutapan, Ms N (Lab)	10,544	16.7%	+1.7%	8,791	15.0%	Lab
Hards, C (Grn)	925	1.5%				
LD to C swing 1.4%	63,093		39.9%	58,693		37.1%
		C maj	25,146		C maj	21,786

John Mark Taylor was appointed Parliamentary secretary in Lord Chancellor's dept in 1992. Vice Chamberlain of HM Household 1990-92; a Lord Commissioner of the Treasury (govt whip), 1989-90; asst govt whip, 1988-9. PPS to Kenneth Clarke, Chancellor of the Duchy of Lancaster and Minr for Trade and Industry, 1987-8; jt vice-chmn, Cons back-bench Euro affairs cmte, 1986-7 (jt sec, 1983-6); mbr select cmte on environment, 1983-7; vice-chmn Cons back-bench sports cmte, 1985-7. Elected for this seat 1983; contested Dudley East, Feb and Oct 1974; MEP for Midlands East, 1979-84. Solicitor; former company director. B Aug 19 1941; ed Bromsgrove Sch. Mbr, Solihull CBC, 1971-74, and W Midlands CC, 1973-86. Vice-pres, AMA, 1979- .

Mike Southcombe, environmental analytical chemist, was mbr Chard TC, 1985-90; chmn LDs against apartheid; ex-chmn, Chard Libs and LDs. B Mar 9 1962; ed Holyrood sch, Chard; Royal Holloway coll, London univ. Nalgo.

Nicola Kutapan, training coordinator; mbr Camden BC, 1986-90; management bd, 300 Gp. Director, Seven Dials Monument Co; Fitzrovia Trust. B Apr 21 1958; ed state schs. TGWU.

SOMERTON AND FROME						No change
Electorate % Turnout	71,354	82.8%	1992	68,773	79.4%	1987
Robinson, M N F (C)	28,052	47.5%	-6.2%	29,351	53.7%	C
Heath, D W S (LD)	23,711	40.2%	+3.9%	19,813	36.3%	L/All
Ashford, R (Lab)	6,154	10.4%	+0.4%	5,461	10.0%	Lab
Graham, Ms L (Grn)	742	1.3%				
Pollock, Ms J (Lib)	388	0.7%				
C to LD swing 5.1%	59,047		7.4%	54,625		17.5%
		C maj	4,341		C maj	9,538

Mark Robinson was Under Sec of State for Wales 1985-7; PPS to Sec of State for Wales 1984-5; Mbr select cmte on foreign affairs 1983-4; hon sec UN parly gp 1983-5. MP for Newport W 1983-7; contested S Yorkshire in Euro elections 1979. Director, Leopold Joseph and Sons Ltd 1988- . Mbr Commonwealth development corpn 1988-92. Asst director, Commonwealth secretariat 1977-83; second officer, exec office, UN Secretary-General 1974-7; special asst to chief of UN emergency operation in Bangladesh 1972-3. Non-practising barrister. B Dec 26 1946; ed Harrow; Christ Church, Oxford; Middle Temple. Fellow, Industry and Parliament Trust.

David Heath, optician; parly consultant to World Wide Fund for Nature 1991, and to Age Concern 1991; company director. Mbr LD Fed exec 1989- ; Lib nat exec 1986-9; Somerset CC 1985- . B Mar 16 1954; ed Millfield sch; St John's Coll, Oxford; City Univ, London.
Bob Ashford, social work manager; mbr Frome TC and Mendip DC 1991- . B Jul 13 1953; ed Henbury comprehensive; Filton tech coll, Bristol; New univ of Ulster; Bristol univ. Nalgo.
Leona Graham, teacher and management consultant. B Aug 18 1942; ed univs in Ontario and British Columbia.

SOUTH HAMS						No change
Electorate % Turnout	83,061	81.1%	1992	78,583	78.6%	1987
*Steen, A D (C)	35,951	53.4%	-2.0%	34,218	55.4%	C
Evans, R V (LD)	22,240	33.0%	-1.1%	21,072	34.1%	L/All
Cohen, Ms E (Lab)	8,091	12.0%	+3.8%	5,060	8.2%	Lab
Titmuss, C (Grn)	846	1.3%	-0.6%	1,178	1.9%	Grn
Summerville, Mrs L (NLP)	227	0.3%		277	0.4%	Loony
C to LD swing 0.5%	67,355		20.4%	61,805		21.3%
		C maj	13,711		C maj	13,146

Anthony Steen, community worker and youth leader, non-practising barrister, Lloyd's underwriter. Coordinator Cons unit for marginal and critical seats 1982- . Won seat 1983; MP for Liverpool, Wavertree 1974-83. Adviser, Waggett and Co, management consultants; Airlines of Gt Britain; the English Vineyards Assocn; consultant Communication Gp. Mbr select cmte on environment 1991- . B Jul 22 1940; ed Westminster sch. Chmn Cons backbench inner cities and urban cmte 1979-80 and 1987- . Jt nat chmn Impact 80s Campaign; vice-pres (1988-) all-pty friends of cycling parly gp; chmn Commons and Lords cycle club. Mbr exec cl Nat Playing Fields Assocn.

Vaughan Evans, economist; independent consultant. B Sep 21 1951; ed Shrewsbury sch; Downing coll, Cambridge; London business sch.
Eleanor Cohen, art director and designer. Mbr Devon CC, 1989- ; chmn Lab pty, Plymouth St Peter ward. B Oct 10 1952; ed St Christopher sch Letchworth; Luton coll of art; Birmingham poly sch of theatre design. Equity 1978-82; BECTU (formerly ACTT) and on gen cl 1981-6, 1987-8 and 1990- .
Christopher Titmuss, teacher; S Hams pty press officer 1986-92. Co-founder, Gaia House trust, Denbury. B Apr 22 1944; ed John Fisher sch Purley.

SOUTH RIBBLE						No change
Electorate % Turnout	78,173	83.0%	1992	72,177	82.5%	1987
*Atkins, R J (C)	30,828	47.5%	+0.3%	28,133	47.2%	C
Smith, Dr G W T (Lab)	24,855	38.3%	+5.2%	19,703	33.1%	Lab
Jones, S N (LD)	8,928	13.8%	-6.0%	11,746	19.7%	L/All
Decter, Dr R (NLP)	269	0.4%				
C to Lab swing 2.5%	64,880		9.2%	59,582		14.1%
		C maj	5,973		C maj	8,430

Robert Atkins was appointed Minr of State for Northern Ireland in 1992. Minr for Sport with rank of Under Sec of State for Environment 1990 moving in Nov 1990 to Dept of Ed and Science until 1992; Minr for Roads and Traffic with rank of Under Sec of State for Transport, 1989-90; Under Sec of State for Trade and Industry, 1987-89. Former sales exec with Rank Xerox. Won this seat 1983; MP for Preston N, 1979-83; contested Luton W, Feb and Oct 1974. PPS to Lord Young of Graffham as minr without portfolio and Sec of State for Employment, 1984-87. B Feb 5 1946; ed Highgate Sch. Mbr, MCC; Middlesex and

Lancashire CCs; Lords and Commons Cricket. Mbr, Haringey BC, 1968-76. Mbr, Sherlock Holmes Society. Freeman, City of London.
Geoffrey Smith, retired consultant surgeon and retired Wing Cmdr RAF, contested Fylde 1987 and Lancs Central 1989 Euro elections. B Mar 18 1927; ed Downing Coll, Cambridge; St Bartholomew's Hosp, London. TGWU.
Simon Jones, coll lecturer; mbr, Chorley BC, 1990- ; Clayton-le-Woods PC, 1986- . Chmn, Save the Heart of Lancashire, 1989-91. B Feb 21 1955; ed Beechew Cliff Sch, Bath; Univ Coll, Cardiff; Worcester CHE. NATFHE.

SOUTH SHIELDS						No change
Electorate % Turnout	59,392	70.1%	1992	60,754	70.7%	1987
*Clark, Dr D G (Lab)	24,876	59.8%	+1.9%	24,882	57.9%	Lab
Howard, J L (C)	11,399	27.4%	+1.7%	11,031	25.7%	C
Preece, A (LD)	5,344	12.8%	-2.6%	6,654	15.5%	SDP/All
				408	0.9%	Dem
C to Lab swing 0.1%	41,619		32.4%	42,975		32.2%
		Lab maj	13,477		Lab maj	13,851

David Clark became chief Opposn spokesman on food, agriculture and rural affairs in 1987; elected to shadow cabinet 1986. Until 1987 held new and separate portfolio of Opposn spokesman on environmental protection and development. Director (1989-) and former adviser to Homeowners Friendly Soc. Elected for this seat 1979; MP for Colne Valley, 1970-Feb, 1974; contested Manchester, Withington 1966 and Colne Valley, Feb and Oct 1974. B Oct 19 1939; ed Windermere GS; Manchester and Sheffield Univs. Forester and univ lecturer. Pres Northern Ramblers; Northern region of YHA. Exec mbr Nat Trust; cl mbr Friends of Lake District and World Wildlife Fund UK. Sponsored by Nupe.

Jon Howard, company director and solicitor; co-founder and director of Cambridge Diet gp of companies, in assocn with Dr Alan Howard, father and inventor of Cambridge Diet. Chmn Leeds NW Cons assocn. B May 20 1956; ed Perse Sch, Cambridge; Downing Coll, Cambridge.

Arthur Preece, retired health service administrator; mbr, Hartlepool BC 1988- (gp ldr 1988-); Cleveland CC 1989- (gp chmn 1990-). B Feb 21 1928. Chmn LD advisory gp on health policy 1988- . B Feb 21 1928.

SOUTHAMPTON, ITCHEN						Lab gain
Electorate % Turnout	72,104	76.9%	1992	72,687	75.8%	1987
Denham, J V (Lab)	24,402	44.0%	+11.9%	24,419	44.3%	C
*Chope, C R (C)	23,851	43.0%	-1.3%	17,703	32.1%	Lab
Hodgson, J R T (LD)	7,221	13.0%	-10.6%	13,006	23.6%	SDP/All
C to Lab swing 6.6%	55,474		1.0%	55,128		12.2%
		Lab maj	551		C maj	6,716

John Denham, consultant to voluntary organisations on lobbying; was nat campaign officer for War on Want. Contested this seat in 1987 and 1983. Mbr Hampshire CC 1981-9; Southampton City Cl, 1989- . Former head of youth affairs, British Youth Cl. Formerly worked for Friends of the Earth. B Jul 15 1953; ed comprehensive sch; Southampton Univ. Mbr management cmte One World; chmn Eastpoint Centre Ltd, a community charity. MSF.

Christopher Chope was roads and traffic minister 1990-2; environment under sec 1986-90. Elected in 1983. PPS to Peter Brooke when minr of state, Treasury, 1985-6. Ldr Wandsworth BC 1979-83; mbr 1974-83. Barrister. B May 19 1947; ed St Andrew's Sch, Eastbourne; Marlborough Coll; St Andrew's Univs. Jt sec Cons environment cmte 1983-6; mbr select cmte on procedure 1984-6; mbr exec cmte Soc of Cons Lawyers 1983-6.

James Hodgson, mechanical engineer employed as project manager. Mbr Eastleigh BC 1988- . B Apr 2 1957; ed Stowe Sch; Brunel Univ; Cranfield Inst of Technology. Active in restoration of steam traction engines.

SOUTHAMPTON, TEST						No change
Electorate % Turnout	72,932	77.4%	1992	73,918	76.4%	1987
*Hill, S J A (C)	24,504	43.4%	-2.2%	25,722	45.6%	C
Whitehead, A P V (Lab)	23,919	42.4%	+9.1%	18,768	33.3%	Lab
Maddock, Ms D (LD)	7,391	13.1%	-8.1%	11,950	21.2%	L/All
Michaelis, J (Grn)	535	0.9%				
Plummer, D (NLP)	101	0.2%				
C to Lab swing 5.6%	56,450		1.0%	56,440		12.3%
		C maj	585		C maj	6,954

James Hill, director of two family private companies, regained the seat for Cons in 1979; mbr for the constituency 1970-Oct 1974; contested it 1968. Mbr Chairmen's Panel 1990- . Mbr select cmtes on procedure 1991- ; Euro legislation 1979-83; trade and industry 1979-83. Delegate and govt whip to cl of europe and WEU 1980-90. Pres Motor Schools Assocn 1980-5; mbr cl Inst of Advanced Motorists 1982-9. Chmn HoC Flying Club. B Dec 21 1926; ed Regents Park Sch, Southampton; N Wales Naval Training Coll; Southampton Univ. Chmn Cons backbench housing improvement sub-cmte, 1985- ; jt vice-chmn Cons constitutional affairs cmte 1990- . MEP 1973-5. Mbr Southampton City Cl 1966-70 and 1976-9.

Alan Whitehead, director of British Inst of Industrial Therapy, contested this seat 1987. Mbr Southampton City C 1980- (cl ldr since 1984). B Sep 15 1950; ed Isleworth GS; Southampton Univ. Mbr Labour Co-ordinating Cmte. Nupe.

Diana Maddock, teacher of English as a foreign language. Mbr Southampton City Cl 1984- (gp ldr). Mbr LD co-ordinating cmte for England 1991-2. B May 19 1945; ed Shenstone Training Coll; Portsmouth Poly.

Jonathan Michaelis, self-employed professional engineer, designer and manufacturer of aids for disabled people. Co-ordinator, Southampton Grn pty. B Mar 30 1964; ed Haberdashers' Aske's Sch, Elstree; Imperial Coll, London.

SOUTHEND EAST						No change
Electorate % Turnout	56,708	73.8%	1992	59,073	69.3%	1987
*Taylor, Sir Teddy (C)	24,591	58.8%	+0.8%	23,753	58.0%	C
Bramley, G J (Lab)	11,480	27.4%	+9.6%	9,906	24.2%	SDP/All
Horne, Mrs J (LD)	5,107	12.2%	+7,296		17.8%	Lab
Lynch, B (Lib)	673	1.6%				
C to Lab swing 4.4%	41,851		31.3%	40,955		33.8%
		C maj	13,111		C maj	13,847

Sir Edward (Teddy) Taylor has been jt sec, Cons back-bench home affairs cmte, since 1983. Elected at 1980 by-election; MP for Glasgow, Cathcart, 1964-79; contested Glasgow, Springburn, 1959. Journalist, adviser and company director. Chief Opposn spokesman on Scotland, 1977-9; Under Sec of State for Scotland, 1974, and in 1970-71 when he resigned in disagreement with govt policy on EC. Sec Cons Euro reform gp, 1980- . B Apr 18 1937; ed Glasgow HS; Glasgow univ. Adviser to Port of London Police Fed, 1972- ; Lawrence Building Co; Globtik Shipping; parly adviser to assocn for denture prosthesis; director, Shepherd Foods Ltd, and Ansvar (Temperance)

Insurance Co. NUJ.
Graham Bramley, teacher; mbr Barking and Dagenham BC, 1982- (chmn finance cmte, 1989-). Chmn governors, Barking coll of tech, 1987- ; governor, E London poly. SEA exec mbr, 1980-3. B Jun 3 1953; ed St Christopher's sec mod, Accrington; Accrington CFE; St Martin's coll of ed, Lancaster. NUT.
Jackie Horne, management training consultant particularly on Euro community studies, contested Dagenham 1983. Mbr Chelmsford BC, 1983-7 (Vice-chmn arts; ldr, SDP gp). Chaired central Essex SDP. B Nov 2 1935; ed Queen Mary coll, London univ.

SOUTHEND WEST						No change
Electorate % Turnout	64,198	77.8%	1992	68,415	75.3%	1987
*Channon, H P G (C)	27,319	54.7%	+0.3%	28,003	54.4%	C
Stimson, Mrs N J (LD)	15,417	30.9%	-7.2%	19,603	38.1%	L/All
Viney, G P (Lab)	6,139	12.3%	+4.7%	3,899	7.6%	Lab
Farmer, A (Lib)	495	1.0%				
Keene, C R (Grn)	451	0.9%				
Warburton, P (NLP)	127	0.3%				
LD to C swing 3.8%	49,948		23.8%	51,505		16.3%
		C maj	11,902		C maj	8,400

Paul Channon joined select cmte on procedure in 1990; jt vice-chmn Cons back-bench environment cmte, 1991- . Sec of State for Transport, 1987-9; Sec of State for Trade and Industry, 1986-7; Minr for Trade, with rank of Minr of State at DTI, 1983-6; Minr for the Arts, 1981-3; Minr of State, civil service dept, 1979-81. PC 1980. Minr for Housing and Construction, 1972-4; Minr of State for N Ireland, Mar-Nov 1972; Under Sec of State for Environment, 1970-2; Parly Sec, Ministry of Housing and Local Govt, Jun-Oct 1970. Elected at 1959 by-election, succeeding his father. B Oct 9 1935; ed Lockers Park, Hemel

Hempstead; Eton; Christ Church, Oxford.
Nina Stimson, editor of In Focus political magazine; L /All agent at Southend W, 1984-7; mbr LD campaigns and communications cmte; freelance consultant on fundraising for charities. B Jun 21 1947; ed Herts and Essex HS, Bishops Stortford.
Geoffrey Viney, teacher. Lab branch sec and constituency vice-chmn. B Aug 19 1956; ed Romford Tech HS; Birmingham Poly.
Chris Keene, lecturer; mbr UK Grn Pty campaigns cmte. B Oct 31 1951; ed Durham and London Univs.

SOUTHPORT						C gain
Electorate % Turnout	71,443	77.6%	1992	71,443	76.3%	1987
Banks, M R W (C)	26,081	47.0%	+2.5%	26,110	47.9%	L/All
*Fearn, R C (LD)	23,018	41.5%	-6.4%	24,261	44.5%	C
King, J (Lab)	5,637	10.2%	+3.8%	3,483	6.4%	Lab
Walker, J (Grn)	545	1.0%	-0.2%	653	1.2%	Grn
Clements, G (NLP)	159	0.3%				
LD to C swing 4.5%	55,440		5.5%	54,507		3.4%
		C maj	3,063		L/All maj	1,849

Matthew Banks, director of LBJ Ltd, won this seat in 1992; contested Manchester Central 1987. Mbr Wirral BC, 1984-8. Former Barclays bank employee and held commission in 1st Bn, Gordon Highlanders. B Jun 21 1961; ed Calday Grange GS, Sheffield; Sheffield city polytechnic; RMA Sandhurst.
Ronnie Fearn became LD spokesman on England, transport, housing and tourism, in 1991; also had local govt, 1989-1991; spokesman on health and tourism, 1988-9; Lib spokesman on health and social services, 1987-8; mbr select cmte on parly commissioner for administration, 1987- . Won this seat in 1987 becoming LD MP in 1988;

contested it in 1979, twice in 1974, and 1970. Pres YL Democrats, 1989- . Jt vice-chmn, all-pty parly gp for children, 1987- ; action on smoking and health (ASH) gp; alternative and complementary medicine gp; trans-Pennine gp; personal social services parly panel; treas Mersey barrage gp, 1990- ; UK-Manx gp, 1987- ; sec tourism gp. B Feb 6 1931; ed Norwood Rd cty sch; King George V GS, Southport. BIFU.
Jim King, administrator with Royal Mail. Vice-chmn, Salford E CLP; treas Gtr Manchester west Euro constituency. Mbr Salford city cl, 1984- . B Aug 11 1950; ed Clifden, Galway; Open Univ. UCW.

SOUTHWARK AND BERMONDSEY						No change
Electorate % Turnout	60,251	62.6%	1992	55,438	64.9%	1987
*Hughes, S H W (LD)	21,459	56.9%	+9.4%	17,072	47.4%	L/All
Balfe, R (Lab)	11,614	30.8%	-8.9%	14,293	39.7%	Lab
Raca, A J (C)	3,794	10.1%	-2.5%	4,522	12.6%	C
Tyler, S (BNP)	530	1.4%		108	0.3%	Comm
Blackham, T (NF)	168	0.4%				
Barnett, Dr G (NLP)	113	0.3%				
Grogan, J (CL)	56	0.1%				
Lab to LD swing 9.2%	37,734		26.1%	35,995		7.7%
		LD maj	9,845		L/All maj	2,779

Simon Hughes won this seat for the L/All at 1983 by-election and became LD MP in 1988. LD spokesman on environment 1990- ; spokesman on education 1988-90; on science, training and youth, 1989-90; LD dep whip, 1989- ; Lib and then LD spokesman on environment, 1983-8; Alliance spokesman on health and Church of England affairs in 1987 election. Vice-chmn parly youth affairs lobby 1984- ; all-pty Christian Fellowship gp. Director (unpaid) Rose Theatre Trust Co 1990- . Consultant to AMMA. Barrister. B May 17 1951; ed Llandaff Cathedral Sch, Cardiff; Christ Coll, Brecon; Selwyn Coll, Cambridge; Inns of Court Sch of Law; Coll of Europe, Bruges.
Richard Balfe has been MEP for London South Inner since 1979. Mbr EP cmtes on foreign affairs and security 1992- ; political affairs and institutional affairs cmte 1989-92; development and co-operation 1984-9; Lab spokesman on human rights and the Third World. Contested Paddington S in 1970. Chmn SE branch CWS 1987- . B May 14 1944; ed Brook Sec Modern Sch, Sheffield; LSE. Mbr exec London Lab Pty 1973- (chmn policy cmte 1983-5). MSF.
Andy Raca, export manager in family firm promoting business in Eastern Europe. Cons assocn chmn 1988-90; treas London S Inner Euro constituency 1988-90. B Apr 20 1964; ed Gateway Grammar Sixth Form Coll, Leicester; Bristol Univ.

SPELTHORNE						No change
Electorate % Turnout	69,343	80.4%	1992	72,967	74.1%	1987
*Wilshire, D (C)	32,627	58.5%	-1.5%	32,440	60.0%	C
Leedham, Ms A E (Lab)	12,784	22.9%	+5.9%	12,390	22.9%	SDP/All
Roberts, R (LD)	9,202	16.5%	-6.4%	9,227	17.1%	Lab
Wassell, Ms J (Grn)	580	1.0%				
Rea, D (Loony)	338	0.6%				
Ellis, D (NLP)	195	0.3%				
C to Lab swing 3.7%	55,726		35.6%	54,057		37.1%
		C maj	19,843		C maj	20,050

David Wilshire was returned fpr this seat in 1987. PPS to Alan Clark. defence procurement minr 1991-2. Jt vice-chmn Cons backbench environment cmte 1990-1; jt sec Cons N Ireland cmte 1990-1; sec Cons food and drinks industries sub-cmte 1990-1; jt vice-chmn all-pty Methodist gp 1990- ; chmn all-pty cults gp 1989- . Partner, Western Political Research Services 1979- ; visiting lecturer Inst of Local Govt Studies, Birmingham Univ; co-director, political management programme, Brunel Univ, 1986-90.
B Sep 16 1943; ed Kingswood Sch, Bath; Fitzwilliam Coll, Cambridge. Mbr Wansdyke DC Avon 1976-87; Avon CC 1977-81.
Ann Leedham, officer of Royal Coll of Nursing. B Jun 21 1952; ed Notting Hill and Ealing HS. Mbr of and sponsored by GMB.
Roger Roberts, training manager with BT; mbr Sutton BC 1986- . B Sep 12 1939; ed Open Univ.

ST ALBANS						No change
Electorate % Turnout	74,188	83.5%	1992	75,281	80.2%	1987
*Lilley, P B (C)	32,709	52.8%	+0.3%	31,726	52.5%	C
Howes, Mrs M (LD)	16,305	26.3%	-8.2%	20,845	34.5%	L/All
Pollard, K (Lab)	12,016	19.4%	+7.9%	6,922	11.5%	Lab
Simmons, C (Grn)	734	1.2%	-0.1%	788	1.3%	Grn
Lucas, D (NLP)	161	0.3%		110	0.2%	CPRP
LD to C swing 4.2%	61,925		26.5%	60,391		18.0%
		C maj	16,404		C maj	10,881

Peter Lilley was appointed social security sec in April 1992. Trade and industry sec 1990-2; financial sec, Treasury 1989-90; economic sec 1987-9. PC 1990. PPS to Nigel Lawson, Chancellor of the Exchequer, 1984-7; to Lord Bellwin and William Waldegrave, local govt minrs Jan-Oct 1984. Mbr PAC 1989-90. Chmn London Oil Analysts Co 1979-80. Elected in 1983; contested Tottenham Oct 1974. Consultant director Cons research dept 1979-83. B Aug 23 1943; ed Dulwich Coll; Clare Coll, Cambridge. Fellow Inst of Petroleum since 1978.
Monica Howes contested Ealing, Southall in 1987 and Mid-Bedfordshire 1983. Open Univ administrator. Former mbr nat exec and cl of Lib pty. Founder mbr 300 gp 1989- . B Sep 12 1938; ed Haberdashers' Aske's Sch; Johannesburg HS for Girls; Central London Poly. AUT.
Kerry Pollard, engineer. Mbr St Albans DC, 1982- ; Herts CC, 1989- . B Apr 27 1944; ed Thornleigh Coll, Bolton. Nalgo; MSF.
Craig Simmons, company director. B Oct 5 1959; ed Hatfield Poly, Herts.

ST HELENS NORTH				No change		
Electorate % Turnout	71,261	77.4%	1992	70,836	76.3%	1987
*Evans, J (Lab)	31,930	57.9%	+4.3%	28,989	53.7%	Lab
Anderson, B J (C)	15,686	28.5%	+1.2%	14,729	27.3%	C
Beirne, J (LD)	7,224	13.1%	-6.0%	10,300	19.1%	L/All
Lynch, Ms A (NLP)	287	0.5%				
C to Lab swing 1.5%	55,127		29.5%	54,018		26.4%
		Lab maj	16,244		Lab maj	14,260

John Evans was on Select Cmte on Defence, 1987-8; an Opposn spokesman on employment, 1983-7. Chmn, Lab Pty, 1991- (vice-chmn, 1990-1); mbr, Lab Pty NEC, since 1982; mbr, Lab working pty on electoral systems, 1990- . Political sec, Nat Union of Labour and Socialist Clubs. PPS to Mr Michael Foot, then Ldr of the Opposn, 1980-3; an Opposn whip, 1979-80; asst Govt whip, 1978-9. Elected for this seat 1983; MP for Newton, Feb 1974-83. MEP, 1975-9; chmn, Euro parliament regional policy and transport cmte, 1976-8. B Oct 19 1930; ed Jarrow Central Sch. Mbr, Hebburn UDC, 1962-74; South Tyneside MDC, 1973-4. Sponsored by AEU.

Brendan Anderson, barrister, was founding chmn, Cheshire Drugwatch. Former TA officer, 3rd (V) Battalion, Welsh Fusiliers. Sch governor in Chester, 1986-90. B Aug 2 1962. On Chester political cmte, 1986-8.

John Beirne, hairdresser; mbr, St Helens BC, 1990- . B May 2 1961; ed Parr HS.

ST HELENS SOUTH				No change		
Electorate % Turnout	67,507	73.8%	1992	69,449	71.3%	1987
*Bermingham, G E (Lab)	30,391	61.0%	+6.4%	27,027	54.6%	Lab
Buzzard, Mrs P M (C)	12,182	24.5%	-2.3%	13,226	26.7%	C
Spencer, B (LD)	6,933	13.9%	-4.8%	9,252	18.7%	SDP/All
Jump, Dr H (NLP)	295	0.6%				
C to Lab swing 4.3%	49,801		36.6%	49,505		27.9%
		Lab maj	18,209		Lab maj	13,801

Gerald Bermingham, a barrister, was elected in 1983; contested SE Derbyshire, 1979. Mbr, Select Cmte on Home Affairs, 1983- ; chmn (1987-) and jt vice-chmn (1985-87), PLP home affairs cmte; treas, all-pty space parly cmte. B Aug 20 1940; ed Cotton Coll, N Staffs; Wellingborough GS; Sheffield Univ. Mbr, Sheffield City Cl, 1975-79; 1980-82. Vice-pres, League Against Cruel Sports. Sponsored by Apex/GMB; mbr, TGWU.

Trisha Buzzard, legal executive; vice-chmn, Wallasey Cons assocn, 1989- ; chaired assocn's political cmte, 1986-9. Mbr, Wirral BC, 1987-8. Director of design and marketing services company, 1987-9; managed family hotel in Lake District, 1975-9, and worked in Canada. B Aug 4 1945; ed Maris Stella convent, New Brighton; Huyton Coll, Liverpool; Queens secretarial coll, London; Inst of Legal Executive, Liverpool Poly.

Brian Spencer, electrician; mbr, St Helens BC, 1980- (dep gp ldr, 1990-). B Jun 25 1947; ed St Helens Coll of Tech.

ST IVES				No change		
Electorate % Turnout	71,152	80.3%	1992	67,448	77.2%	1987
*Harris, D A (C)	24,528	42.9%	-5.4%	25,174	48.3%	C
George, A H (LD)	22,883	40.1%	+6.2%	17,619	33.8%	SDP/All
Warran, S (Lab)	9,144	16.0%	-1.8%	9,275	17.8%	Lab
Stephens, Dr G (Lib)	577	1.0%				
C to LD swing 5.8%	57,132		2.9%	52,068		14.5%
		C maj	1,645		C maj	7,555

David Harris was PPS to Sir Geoffrey Howe, Foreign Sec and then Ld President and Ldr of Commons, 1988-90; PPS to Lynda Chalker, Minr of State, FCO, and Tim Eggar, Under Sec of State, FCO, 1987-8. Mbr, Select Cmtes on Foreign Affairs, 1991- ; Broadcasting, 1988- ; Social Security, 1991- ; Sittings of Commons, 1991- ; Agriculture, 1983-7. Chmn (1987-) and sec (1985-7), Cons back-bench fisheries sub-cmte. Journalist. Elected in 1983; contested Mitcham and Morden, Feb 1974. MEP for Cornwall and Plymouth, 1979-84 B Nov 1 1937; ed Mount Radford Sch, Exeter. Mbr, GLC, 1968-77 Worked for *The Daily Telegraph* at Westminster, 1961-79, being chief political correspondent, 1976-9; chmn, lobby journalists, 1977-8; previously on *Western Morning News* and *Express and Echo*, Exeter.

Andrew George, voluntary sector field worker. Vice-chmn, Celtic League. B Dec 2 1958; ed Helston Sch; Oxford and Sussex univs.

Stephen Warran, electrican at local tin mine; mbr, Penwith DC, 1986- ; Penzance TC, 1987-91. Chmn, Penzance branch, Penwith dist Lab pty; vice-chair, St Ives CLP. B Aug 2 1963; ed Heamoor sec sch; Cornwall tech coll. GMB.

STAFFORD						No change
Electorate % Turnout	74,663	82.9%	1992	72,431	79.5%	1987
*Cash, W N P (C)	30,876	49.9%	-1.5%	29,541	51.3%	C
Kidney, D (Lab)	19,976	32.3%	+11.1%	15,834	27.5%	SDP/All
Calder, J (LD)	10,702	17.3%	-10.2%	12,177	21.2%	Lab
Peat, C (Hardcore)	178	0.3%				
Lines, P (NLP)	176	0.3%				
C to Lab swing 6.3%	61,908		17.6%	57,552		23.8%
		C maj	10,900		C maj	13,707

William Cash, a solicitor, was elected at 1984 by-election. Mbr employmenr select cmte 1989-90; Euro legislation 1985- ; statutory instruments 1986-90; consolidation bills 1987-90. Chmn Cons backbench Euro affairs cmte 1989-91; vice-chmn Cons small business bureau 1984- . B May 10 1940; ed Stonyhurst Coll; Lincoln Coll, Oxford. Adviser to Inst of Legal Executives, Inst of Company Accountants, Cl for Complementary and Alternative Medicine; Nat Market Traders' Fed; consultant to Radcliffe's and Co. Jt chmn all-pty complementary and alternative medicine gp 1989- ; all-pty jazz gp 1991- ; chmn gp on widows and one parent families 1984-9; general purposes cmte Primrose League 1985- . Mbr exec cl Royal Commonwealth Soc 1984- ; director Ironbridge Gorge Museum Trust 1980- .

David Kidney, solicitor. Mbr Stafford BC 1987- ; former mbr Stafford Moorlands PC. B Mar 21 1955; ed Stoke-on-Trent schs; Bristol Univ. MSF.

Jamie Calder, chartered accountant and managing director, Flairmet Ltd. Mbr Stafford BC 1987- (gp ldr 1991-); Staffs enterprise bd, 1991- ; district racial equality cl 1990- . B Apr 6 1954.

STAFFORDSHIRE MID					No change from	1987
Electorate % Turnout	73,414	85.7%	1992	71,252	79.4%	1987
Fabricant, M L D (C)	31,227	49.7%	-1.0%	28,644	50.6%	C
*Heal, Mrs S (Lab)	24,991	39.7%	+15.0%	13,990	24.7%	Lab
Stamp, B (LD)	6,432	10.2%	-12.9%	13,114	23.2%	L/All
Grice, Ms D (NLP)	239	0.4%		836	1.5%	Ind C
C to Lab swing 8.0%	62,889		9.9%	56,584		25.9%
		C maj	6,236		C maj	14,654

Michael Fabricant regained this seat, lost by Cons in 1990 by-election, in 1992. Until 1992 was a snr director and co-founder of an international broadcast and manufacturing gp with clients ranging from BBC to Radio Moscow. Economist and adviser to home office on broadcasting matters. Contested South Shields in 1987. Former BBC current affairs broadcaster; chartered engineer. Chmn Brighton Pavilion Cons Assocn for three years and form dep chmn. Mbr area CPC cmte. B Jun 12 1950; ed state schs; Loughborough, Sussex and London Univs and postgraduate research economics at Univ of Southern California, Los Angeles.

Sylvia Heal won the seat for Labour in 1990 by-elevtion. An Opposn spokesman on health 1991-2 and a spokesman on women's issues. Mbr select cmte on education, science and arts 1990-1. Mbr exec cl SSAFA. B Jul 20, 1942; ed Elfred Sec Modern Sch, Buckley, N Wales; Coleg Harlech; Univ Coll Swansea. Social worker, health service and dept of employment 1968-70 and 1980-90; medical records clerk, Chester Royal Infirmary, 1957-63. GMB/Apex.

Barry Stamp, advisory teacher with Staffs CC. Mbr Haughton PC 1987-91. Mbr LD ed policy gp. B Mar 22 1952; ed W Midlands CFE; Open Univ.

Details of 1990 by-election on page 287

STAFFORDSHIRE MOORLANDS						No change
Electorate % Turnout	75,036	83.7%	1992	74,302	80.4%	1987
*Knox, D L (C)	29,240	46.6%	-6.3%	31,613	52.9%	C
Siddelley, J E (Lab)	21,830	34.8%	+6.0%	17,186	28.8%	Lab
Jebb, Mrs C R (LD)	9,326	14.9%	-3.5%	10,950	18.3%	SDP/All
Howson, M (Anti-Fed)	2,121	3.4%				
Davies, P (NLP)	261	0.4%				
C to Lab swing 6.2%	62,778		11.8%	59,749		24.1%
		C maj	7,410		C maj	14,427

David Knox was returned for this seat in 1983; MP for Leek, 1970-83; contested Birmingham, Stechford, 1964 and 1966, and Nuneaton by-election, 1967. Mbr Commons chairmen's panel 1983- ; mbr select cmte on Euro legislation 1976- . Economist and management consultant. B May 30 1933; ed Lockerbie Acad; Dumfries Acad; London Univ. Jt vice-chmn all-pty home safety gp; world govt gp. Vice-chmn Cons Pty 1974-5. Vice-chmn Cons employment cmte 1979-80 (sec 1976-9); Cons Gp for Europe 1984-7.

James Siddelley, teacher. Sec Gtr Manchester Lab pty 1986- ; mbr NW reg exec Lab pty, 1988- (chmn environment policy gp); chmn Stockport Dist pty 1985-6 and 1987-90. B Apr 18 1944; ed Cty GS, Hyde; Wigan Mining Coll; London Univ; Manchester Poly; Salford Univ. Fellow, Royal Geographical Society. NAS/UWT and GMB.

Christina Jebb, former teacher. Mbr Staffordshire CC 1989- ; Staffs Moorlands DC 1991- ; Endon with Stanley PC 1991- . Chmn LD health assocn. B Jun 27 1949; ed St Agnes Convent HS and Holte GS, Birmingham; Doncaster Coll of Ed; Open Univ.

STAFFORDSHIRE SOUTH				No change		
Electorate % Turnout	82,758	81.5%	1992	79,261	78.2%	1987
*Cormack, P T (C)	40,266	59.7%	-1.2%	37,708	60.9%	C
Wylie, B A (Lab)	17,633	26.1%	+7.1%	12,440	20.1%	L/All
Sadler, I L (LD)	9,584	14.2%	-5.9%	11,805	19.1%	Lab
C to Lab swing 4.1%	67,483		33.5%	61,953		40.8%
		C maj	22,633		C maj	25,268

Patrick Cormack was appointed to Commons chairmen's panel in 1983; chmn, advisory cmte on Commons works of art, 1988- . Journalist, company director, consultant (Patrick Cormack & Partners). Elected for this seat Feb 1974; MP for Cannock, 1970-4; contested Grimsby, 1966; Bolsover, 1964. B May 18 1939; ed St James's Choir and Havelock schs, Grimsby; Hull univ. Jt chmn, all-pty arts and heritage gp, 1979- ; jt vice-chmn, release of hostages gp. Chmn, Cons pty advisory cmte on arts and heritage, 1988- ; Cl for Independent Ed, 1979- ; editorial bd, Parly Publications, 1983- . Mbr, cl, Georgian gp, 1985- ; cl, Winston Churchill Memorial Trust, 1983- . Vice-chmn, Heritage in Danger, 1974- . Mbr, Royal Commission on Historical Manuscripts, 1981- . Fellow, Soc of Antiquaries, 1978- . Rector's Warden, 1978-90, and Parly Warden, 1990- , St Margaret's Church, Westminster. Freeman, City of London; Hon. Citizen of Texas. IOJ.

Bruce Wylie, Oxfam campaign organiser. Programmer for Gtr Manchester CC, 1979-86. TGWU/ACTSS steward, exec mbr, 1986- ; Nalgo steward, 1979-86. B Apr 6 1950; ed Harrogate and Rickmansworth GSs; St Edmund Hall, Oxford; Birmingham Univ.

Ian Sadler, student services manager; LD press officer, South Staffs. Semi-finalist, Mastermind, 1991. Mbr, S Staffordshire DC, 1991- ; Wombourne PC, 1987- . B Apl 17 1949; ed Adams GS, Newport, Salop.

STAFFORDSHIRE SOUTH EAST				No change		
Electorate % Turnout	70,199	82.1%	1992	66,176	80.4%	1987
*Lightbown, D L (C)	29,180	50.7%	+3.5%	25,115	47.2%	C
Jenkins, B (Lab)	21,988	38.2%	+12.1%	14,230	26.7%	SDP/All
Penlington, Dr N (LD)	5,540	9.6%	-17.1%	13,874	26.1%	Lab
Taylor, Miss J (SD)	895	1.6%				
C to Lab swing 4.3%	57,603		12.5%	53,219		20.5%
		C maj	7,192		C maj	10,885

David Lightbown was appointed Comptroller of HM Household 9govt whip) in Dec 1990; Vice-Chamberlain of HM Household, 1990; a Lord Commissioner of the Treasury (Govt whip), 1987-90; an asst Govt whip, 1986-7; mbr, Commons accommodation and works cmte, 1991- ; Commons Services Cmte, 1989-91. Former chief engineer and director of Hampson Industries plc. Elected in 1983. B Nov 30 1932; ed Derby Sch of Art; Derby Tech Coll. Mbr, Lichfield DC, 1975-87; Staffordshire CC, 1977-85. Manager of his village football team until he became an MP.

Brian Jenkins, coll lecturer; mbr, Tamworth BC. B Sep 19 1942; ed Aston and Coventry Tech Colls; Coleg Harlech; LSE; Wolverhampton Poly. NATFHE.

Dr Napier Penlington, consultant anaesthetist, regional cardiothoracic unit. B Dec 22 1928; ed St John's, Cambridge. Pres, Coventry LDs, 1991- ; chmn, 1990-1; treas from merger to 1990. BMA.

STALYBRIDGE AND HYDE				No change		
Electorate % Turnout	68,189	73.5%	1992	67,983	74.2%	1987
*Pendry, T (Lab)	26,207	52.3%	+3.9%	24,401	48.4%	Lab
Mort, T S R (C)	17,376	34.7%	-2.5%	18,738	37.1%	C
Kirk, I M (LD)	4,740	9.5%	-5.0%	7,311	14.5%	SDP/All
Powell, R (Lib)	1,199	2.4%				
Poyzer, D (Loony)	337	0.7%				
Blomfield, E (NLP)	238	0.5%				
C to Lab swing 3.2%	50,097		17.6%	50,450		11.2%
		Lab maj	8,831		Lab maj	5,663

Tom Pendry has chaired the all-pty association football cmte since 1980 and PLP sports sub-cmte since 1984; jt vice-chmn, PLP environment cmte, 1988- ; co-chmn, all-pty jazz parly gp, 1991- . Mbr, Select Cmte on Environment, 1987- ; Select Cmte on MPs' Interests, 1983- . Steward, British Boxing Bd of Control, 1987- . Trustee, Tameside Community Care Trust. Under Sec of State for N Ireland, 1978-9; Lord Commissioner of the Treasury (govt whip), 1974-7. Mbr, nat advisory cmte, Duke of Edinburgh's Award Scheme. Full-time official, Nupe, 1960-70. Elected in 1970. B Jun 10 1934; ed St Augustine's Ramsgate; Oxford Univ. Mbr, Paddington BC, 1962-5. Sponsored by Nupe.

Simon Mort, management tutor and director of Simon Mort Reports Ltd, contested Sheffield in 1989 Euro elections. Mbr, Oxford City Cl, 1991- . Holds or recently held Cons Pty appointments as vice-chmn, Oxford W and Abingdon Cons Assocn; chmn, South Oxford branch and Oxford CPC; mbr, Cotswold Euro Cl and Oxford and Bucks Euro Cl; Oxford Exec Cl; Oxford W and Abingdon Constituency Cl; Wessex area cl; Wessex area CPC Advisory Cl; Oxford educational advisory cl. Mbr, Royal Utd Services Inst for Defence Studies; Assocn of Masters of Harriers and Beagles. B May 14 1941; ed Abberley Hall, Worcestershire; Malvern Coll; RMA Sandhurst; Gray's Inn (part-time); Staff Coll (including RMCS Shrivenham).

Ian Kirk, company director and software consultant. Former chmn, Cheadle Lib Pty. B Feb 25 1946; ed King Edward VII GS, Sheffield; Trinity Coll, Oxford.

STAMFORD AND SPALDING						No change
Electorate % Turnout	75,153	81.2%	1992	70,560	77.8%	1987
*Davies, J Q (C)	35,965	59.0%	+2.5%	31,016	56.5%	C
Burke, L C (Lab)	13,096	21.5%	+8.9%	17,009	31.0%	L/All
Lee, B D (LD)	11,939	19.6%	-11.4%	6,882	12.5%	Lab
C to Lab swing 3.2%	61,000		37.5%	54,907		25.5%
		C maj	22,869		C maj	14,007

Quentin Davies was elected for this seat 1987; contested B'ham, Ladywood by-election, 1977. PPS to Mrs Angela Rumbold, minr of state for Ed and Science and then at Home Office, 1989-92. Director, Dewe Rogerson Consultants Ltd, 1987- ; mbr, Market Access Panel; consultant to Morgan Grenfell and Co Ltd, merchant bankers, 1987- , having been a director, 1981-7; manager, then asst director, Morgan Grenfell, 1974-8; representative in France becoming Director-General and Pres, Morgan Grenfell France SA, 1978-81. Jt sec, Cons back-bench finance cmte, 1991- ; Cons trade and industry cmte, 1991- . B May 29 1944; ed Dragon ch, Oxford; Leighton Park;

Gonville and Caius Coll, Cambridge; Harvard univ, US. Liveryman, Goldsmiths' Co; Freeman, City of London.

Chris Burke, laboratory worker, contested Rutland and Melton 1987. Mbr, Stamford TC, 1988- . B Sep 9 1952; ed Garston, Liverpool. Gen elec agent, 1983. Chmn, Stamford CLP, 1990- , former constituency sec. RAF, 1970-82. MSF.

Bryan Lee, financial consultant; formerly chartered engineer in industrial consultancy. Mbr, LD regional exec and spokesman on housing, 1989- ; former chair, Stamford branch. B May 7 1932; ed Portsmouth Tech Coll; Cardiff Coll of Advanced Tech.

STEVENAGE						No change
Electorate % Turnout	70,233	83.0%	1992	69,525	80.5%	1987
*Wood, T J R (C)	26,652	45.7%	+3.6%	23,541	42.1%	C
Church, Ms J (Lab)	21,764	37.3%	+11.9%	18,201	32.5%	SDP/All
Reilly, A A (LD)	9,668	16.6%	-15.9%	14,229	25.4%	Lab
Calcraft, A (NLP)	233	0.4%				
C to Lab swing 4.1%	58,317		8.4%	55,971		9.5%
		C maj	4,888		C maj	5,340

Timothy Wood became a Ld Commissioner of Treasury (Govt whip) in 1992; asst Govt whip, 1990-92; PPS to Sec of State for N Ireland, 1989-90. Resigned as a senior project manager with international computer firm ICL, whom he joined in 1963, when he won this seat in 1983. PPS to Sir Ian Stewart, Minr of State for N Ireland, 1988-89 and to Sir John Stanley, when Minr of State for Armed Forces and then for N Ireland, 1986-88; jt sec, Cons back-bench environment cmte, 1985-6. B Aug 13 1940; ed King James's GS, Knaresborough; Manchester univ. Mbr,

Bracknell DC, 1975-83.

Judith Church, MSF union health and safety officer since 1986; former factory inspector. Chair, Hornsey and Wood Green CLP, 1989-90. B Sep 19 1953; ed St Bernard's GS, Slough; Leeds Univ; Huddersfield Poly; Aston Univ; Thames Valley Coll.

Andrew Reilly, publisher's editor, contested Newham S 1983; sec of charitable trust concerned with welfare of elderly. B Oct 18 1955; ed St Bonaventure's Sch, E7; Worthing Sixth Form Coll; Open Univ. AUT.

STIRLING						No change
Electorate % Turnout	58,266	82.3%	1992	57,836	78.7%	1987
*Forsyth, M B (C)	19,174	40.0%	+2.2%	17,191	37.8%	C
Phillips, Mrs K W (Lab)	18,471	38.5%	+2.0%	16,643	36.5%	Lab
Fisher, G (SNP)	6,558	13.7%	+2.9%	6,804	14.9%	L/All
Robertson, W B (LD)	3,337	7.0%	-8.0%	4,897	10.8%	SNP
Thomson, W R (Grn)	342	0.7%				
Sharp, R (Loony)	68	0.1%				
Lab to C swing 0.1%	47,950		1.5%	45,535		1.2%
		C maj	703		C maj	548

Michael Forsyth was appointed Minr of State for Employment in 1992; Minr of State, Scottish Office, 1990-92, following his resignation as chmn, 1989-90, of Scottish Cons Pty; an Under Sec of State for Scotland, 1987-90. Former company director. Won this seat 1983. Mbr, Select Cmte on Scottish Affairs, 1983-7; PPS to Sir Geoffrey Howe, Foreign Secretary, 1986-7; vice-chmn, Cons back-bench environment cmte, 1983-6. Mbr, Westminster City Cl, 1978-83. B Oct 16 1954; ed Arbroath HS; St Andrews univ. Chmn, FCS, 1976-7.

Kate Phillips, self-employed international education consultant specialising in education of adults; previously WEA tutor/organizer and Commonwealth TUC ed officer.

Contested Dumfries 1987. B Sep 4 1946; ed Glasgow Univ (adult student). MSF.

Gerry Fisher, computer manager, contested Bothwell, Feb 1974. Cl mbr and Fellow, past Pres, British Computer Society. Chmn, London branch, SNP, 1968-82; elected mbr, SNP nat cl. B Feb 8 1930; ed Whitehill Sch, Glasgow; Glasgow Univ.

Willie Robertson, owner of agricultural supply company; vice-chmn, Perth and Kinross LDs. B Sep 4 1949; ed Kinross HS; Perth HS; Edinburgh Coll of Commerce.

Bill Thomson, estate agent; Scottish Grn Pty economics speaker. B Jun 5 1954; ed Allan Glen's, Glasgow; Glasgow Univ.

STOCKPORT						Lab gain
Electorate % Turnout	58,095	82.3%	1992	60,059	78.1%	1987
Coffey, Ms M A (Lab)	21,096	44.1%	+8.8%	19,410	41.4%	C
*Favell, A R (C)	19,674	41.2%	-0.2%	16,557	35.3%	Lab
Corris, Mrs A C (LD)	6,539	13.7%	-8.4%	10,365	22.1%	SDP/All
Filmore, Ms J (Grn)	436	0.9%	-0.3%	573	1.2%	Grn
Saunders, D (NLP)	50	0.1%				
C to Lab swing 4.5%	47,795		3.0%	46,905		6.1%
		Lab maj	1,422		C maj	2,853

Anne Coffey, a local govt employee, won this seat for Labour in 1992. Mbr Stockport DC 1984- (Lab gp ldr 1988- ; former Lab spokesman on health, social services and education); local HA 1986-90. Contested Cheadle 1987. B Aug 31 1946; ed South Bank poly; Manchester univ. Nalgo.

Tony Favell, solicitor, company director and Halifax building society agent, was jt vice-chmn Cons back-bench Euro affairs cmte 1990-1. Elected in 1983; contested Bolsover 1979. PPS to John Major, when Minr for Social Security and Disabled, Chief Sec to Treasury, Foreign Sec and Chancellor of the Exchequer 1986-90. Director Broom Chemists Ltd, Sheffield Amusements Co Ltd; adviser to nat assocn of plumbing, heating and mechanical services contractors; consultant to solicitors, Favell & Smith, and Favell, Smith & Henson, B May 29 1939; ed St Bees, Cumbria; Sheffield univ. Treas 1985- and vice-chmn 1984-5, assocn of Cons clubs.

Anne Corris, housewife and former science teacher; mbr Stockport MBC 1987- (chmn leisure services cmte 1990-). B Aug 8 1954; ed Altrincham GS for girls; Umist.

Judith Filmore, social worker; NW pty organiser. B Apr 21 1958; ed Urmston GS, Manchester.

STOCKTON NORTH						No change
Electorate % Turnout	69,451	76.8%	1992	70,329	75.4%	1987
*Cook, F (Lab)	27,918	52.3%	+3.2%	26,043	49.1%	Lab
Brocklebank-Fowler, S E (C)	17,444	32.7%	+0.2%	17,242	32.5%	C
Fletcher, Mrs S (LD)	7,454	14.0%	-4.4%	9,712	18.3%	SDP/All
McGarvey, K (Ind Lab)	550	1.0%				
C to Lab swing 1.5%	53,366		19.6%	52,997		16.6%
		Lab maj	10,474		Lab maj	8,801

Frank Cook was a construction project manager with Capper-Neill International; former teacher, transport manager, gravedigger and Butlins redcoat. Elected in 1983. An Opposn whip; mbr select cmte on consolidation bills 1987-91; select cmte on procedure 1988- ; select cmte on employment 1983-7; advisory cmte on Commons works of art 1988- . Chmn 1989-90 and vice-chmn 1988-9 Northern gp of Lab MPs; jt vice-chmn all-pty parly gp for alternative energy strategies. B Nov 3 1935; ed Corby sch, Sunderland; De La Salle coll, Manchester; inst of ed, Leeds. Sponsored by MSF.

Simon Brocklebank-Fowler, merchant banker since 1986. Second Sec, Chancery, British Embassy, Madrid, 1984-6; in Western Euro dept FCO 1982-4. Mbr Westminster cl 1990- ; governor, Westminster city sch 1990- ; mbr exec cmte Cities of London and Westminster Cons assocn 1989-90. B Sep 26 1961; ed Westminster sch; Jesus coll, Cambridge.

Suzanne Fletcher, voluntary advice worker; mbr Stockton on Tees BC 1981- (LD gp ldr 1987-92). Rep to northern region LDs. B Feb 22 1945; ed Mexborough GS; Skipton HS; London univ (external).

STOCKTON SOUTH						No change
Electorate % Turnout	75,959	82.8%	1992	75,279	79.0%	1987
*Devlin, T R (C)	28,418	45.2%	+10.2%	20,833	35.0%	C
Scott, J M (Lab)	25,049	39.8%	+8.6%	20,059	33.7%	SDP/All
Kirkham, Mrs K R (LD)	9,410	15.0%	-18.8%	18,600	31.3%	Lab
Lab to C swing 0.8%	62,877		5.4%	59,492		1.3%
		C maj	3,369		C maj	774

Timothy Devlin, barrister and company director, gained the seat in 1987. Chmn all-pty panel on charity law; dep chmn Cons foreign affairs forum; jt vice-chmn all-pty release of hostages parly gp; chmn Northern gp of Cons MPs 1990-1; jt sec Cons backbench smaller businesses cmte 1990- ; Cons arts and heritage cmte 1988-90. Director, Fanedge Ltd, 1991- . B Jun 13 1959; ed Dulwich coll; LSE; City univ, London; Inns of Court sch of law, and Financial Training Ltd. Also educated in France. Hardwicke and Thomas More scholar at Lincoln's Inn.

John Scott, lecturer, contested this seat 1987. Mbr Thornaby-on-Tees, BC 1960-8 (mayor 1966-7); Stockton-on-Tees BC 1974- (mayor 1981-2); North region Lab exec cmte 1989- . B Oct 18 1925; ed Blackpool GS; Lincoln coll, Oxford. Chmn northern region cls assocn; bd mbr northern development co. TGWU.

Kay Kirkham, music teacher; sec to ASLDC; political sec in Stockton Sth. Mbr Cleveland CC 1985- (gp sec 1985-91, and gp dep ldr 1991-); Stockton BC 1987- . B Feb 11 1950; ed Watford GS for Girls; Sussex univ. Former mbr NUT.

STOKE-ON-TRENT CENTRAL						No change
Electorate % Turnout	65,527	68.1%	1992	65,987	68.8%	1987
*Fisher, M (Lab)	25,897	58.0%	+5.5%	23,842	52.5%	Lab
Gibb, N J (C)	12,477	27.9%	-3.1%	14,072	31.0%	C
Dent, M (LD)	6,073	13.6%	-2.8%	7,462	16.4%	SDP/All
Pullen, N (NLP)	196	0.4%				
C to Lab swing 4.3%	44,643		30.1%	45,376		21.5%
		Lab maj	13,420		Lab maj	9,770

Mark Fisher became Opposn spokesman on the arts in 1987; chmn PLP ed, science and arts beckbench cmte, 1984-6, and of PLP arts sub-cmte, 1984-6; vice-chmn PLP Treasury cmte, 1983-4. An Opposn whip, 1985-7. Elected for this seat 1983; contested Leek, 1979. Mbr select cmte on Treasury and civil service, 1983-6. Mbr cl policy studies inst, 1989- . Documentary film producer and script writer, 1966-75; principal, Tattenhall centre of ed, 1975-83. B Oct 29 1944; ed Eton; Trinity coll, Cambridge. Dep Pro-Chancellor, Keele univ, 1989- . Mbr Staffordshire CC, 1981-5; NUT (parly consultant to union).

Nicolas Gibb, tax consultant, chartered accountant; chmn Bethnal Green and Stepney Cons assocn, 1989, and treas 1988-9. B Sep 3 1960; ed Maidstone GS; Roundhay Sch, Leeds; Thornes House sch, Wakefield; Durham univ.

Martin Dent, retired Fellow, Keele univ; snr univ lecturer, 1963-90. B Jul 11 1925; ed Eton; Trinity coll, Cambridge; Worcester coll, Oxford. AUT.

STOKE-ON-TRENT NORTH						No change
Electorate % Turnout	73,141	73.4%	1992	74,184	72.9%	1987
*Walley, Ms J L (Lab)	30,464	56.7%	+9.6%	25,459	47.1%	Lab
Harris, L M (C)	15,687	29.2%	-2.1%	16,946	31.3%	C
Redfern, J (LD)	7,167	13.3%	-8.2%	11,665	21.6%	SDP/All
Morrison, A (NLP)	387	0.7%				
C to Lab swing 5.9%	53,705		27.5%	54,070		15.7%
		Lab maj	14,777		Lab maj	8,513

Joan Walley became an Opposn front bencher on transport in 1991; in Opposn front bench environment team, 1988-91, with responsibilities for environmental protection and conservation. Elected in 1987; jt vice-chmn PLP environment cmte, 1987-8; mbr Commons services cmte, 1987-91. jt sec, all-pty lighting parly gp, 1991- . Hon vice-pres inst of environmental health officers. Mbr Lambeth cl, 1982-6. B Jan 23 1949; ed Biddulph GS; Hull univ; Univ coll, Swansea. With alcoholics recovery project, 1970-3; Swansea city cl, 1974-8; Wandsworth BC, 1978-9. Sponsored by Cohse.

Laurence Harris, solicitor, has served on Cons nat union exec and general purposes cmtes; former YCs nat vice-chmn. Former research asst to Patrick McLoughlin MP. B Sep 6 1965; ed Solihull sch; Downing coll, Cambridge; Coll of law, Chancery Lane, London.

John Redfern, chef; mbr Staffs Moorlands cl, 1991- ; mbr Biddulph TC, 1991- (gp ldr). Capt Kidsgrove Chess Club, 1987- ; mbr Biddulph Sports Cl, 1990- . B Oct 10 1959; ed Univ of Wales; Warwick univ.

STOKE-ON-TRENT SOUTH						No change
Electorate % Turnout	71,316	74.3%	1992	70,806	73.7%	1987
Stevenson, G W (Lab)	26,380	49.8%	+2.3%	24,794	47.5%	Lab
Ibbs, R M (C)	19,471	36.7%	-1.1%	19,741	37.8%	C
Jones, F (LD)	6,870	13.0%	-1.7%	7,669	14.7%	L/All
Lines, Mrs E (NLP)	291	0.5%				
C to Lab swing 1.7%	53,012		13.0%	52,204		9.7%
		Lab maj	6,909		Lab maj	5,053

George Stevenson, bus driver, 1966-84, was first elected MEP for Staffordshire East in 1984 serving on the Euro parliament's cmte on transport until 1987; mbr cmte on budgets, 1987-9; cmte on agriculture, fisheries and rural development, 1989- . Chmn Lab gp of MEPs, 1987-8; South Asia EP delegation, 1989- (former vice-chmn). Mbr Stoke-on-Trent city cl, 1972-86; Staffs CC, 1981-5. Mbr TGWU, 1964- , branch shop steward, 1968-84, chmn, 1975-81; sponsored by TCWU. Transport driver, 1964-6; miner, 1957-64; pottery caster, 1953-7. B Aug 30 1938; ed Uttoxeter Rd primary sch; Queensberry Rd sec sch, Stoke-on-Trent. Mbr RIIA, assocn of western European parliamentarians against apartheid, Latin American solidarity campaign.

Roger Ibbs, chiropodist, contested Stoke-on-Trent North in 1983 and 1979. Mbr Staffordshire CC, 1985- (Cons highways spokesman); Stoke DC 1976-9. B Jan 19 1948; ed Christchurch jnr sch, Fenton; Alleyne's GS, Stone; northern coll of chiropody, Salford. Former chmn, Stoke South and Stoke North constituency parties.

Fred Jones, fork lift truck driver; former branch sec, area exec and nat cl mbr, union of democratic mineworkers. B Mar 20 1949; ed sec modern sch; adult ed coll.

STRANGFORD						No change
Electorate % Turnout	68,870	65.0%	1992	64,429	57.6%	1987
*Taylor, J D (UU)	19,517	43.6%	-32.4%	28,199	75.9%	UU
Wilson, S (DUP)	10,606	23.7%		7,553	20.3%	All
McCarthy, K (All)	7,585	16.9%	-3.4%	1,385	3.7%	WP
Eyre, S (C)	6,782	15.1%				
Shaw, D (NLP)	295	0.7%				
No swing calculation.	44,785		19.9%	37,137		55.6%
		UU maj	8,911		UU maj	20,646

John David Taylor, a civil engineer, was elected in 1983; resigned seat in 1985 in protest at Anglo-Irish Agreement and retained it at 1986 by-election. PC (NI)1970. Elected MEP, 1979-89. UU EC spokesman in Hse of Commons; jt sec Franco-British parly cmte. Unpaid chmn West Ulster Estates Ltd, 1968- ; Bramley Apple Restaurant Ltd, 1974- ; chmn Tontine Rooms Holding Co Ltd, 1978- . Publisher of *Tyrone Courier* and *Ulster Gazette*. Mbr Castlereagh BC, 1989- . B Dec 24 1937; ed Royal Sch Armagh; Queen's Univ, Belfast. MP, Stormont, 1965-72; NI Assembly, 1973-5; NI constitutional convention, 1975-6; NI Assembly, 1982-6; mbr select cmte on Euro legislation, 1983-6. Minr for home affairs in NI govt, 1970-2.

Sammy Wilson, DUP press officer; mbr Belfast city cl.

Kieran McCarthy, drapery and footwear retailer; mbr Ards BC, 1985- . B Sep 9 1942; ed St Josephs, Ballycran; Newtownards Tech Sch.

Stephen Eyre, barrister, contested Birmingham Hodge Hill 1987; mbr Solihull MBC, 1983- . B Oct 17 1957; ed Solihull sch; New coll, Oxford.

STRATFORD-ON-AVON						No change
Electorate % Turnout	82,824	82.1%	1992	81,263	76.5%	1987
*Howarth, A T (C)	40,251	59.2%	-2.7%	38,483	61.9%	C
Fogg, J N (LD)	17,359	25.5%	-2.3%	17,318	27.9%	L/All
Brookes, Ms S (Lab)	8,932	13.1%	+2.9%	6,335	10.2%	Lab
Roughan, R (Grn)	729	1.1%				
Saunders, A (Ind C)	573	0.8%				
Twite, M (NLP)	130	0.2%				
C to LD swing 0.2%	67,974		33.7%	62,136		34.1%
		C maj	22,892		C maj	21,165

Alan Howarth was appointed an Under Sec of State for Education and Science in 1989; Ld Commissioner of Treasury (govt whip), 1988-9; asst Govt whip, 1987-8. Elected for this seat 1983. PPS to Sir Rhodes Boyson, Minr of State for N Ireland and then Minr for Local Govt, 1985-7; sec Cons back-bench arts and heritage cmte, 1984-5. Public affairs adviser to Baring Brothers and Co Ltd, 1982-7. Governor, Royal Shakespeare Theatre, since 1984. B Jun 11 1944; ed Rugby; King's Coll, Cambridge. Mbr of Lloyd's. Vice-chmn Cons pty, 1980-1; director, Cons research dept, 1979-81. Senior research asst to Field Marshal Montgomery on A History of Warfare, 1965-67. Asst master, Westminster sch, 1968-74.

Nicholas Fogg, teacher; consultant to international affairs project based on Harvard Univ. Mbr Marlborough TC, 1981-91; Mayor of Marlborough, 1985-6; mbr Warwickshire CC, 1970-3; Founder-chmn St George community trust for homeless, 1977- ; Marlborough festival society, 1986- . B May 3 1941; ed Warwick sch; Nottingham univ; St John's coll, Oxford; King's Coll, London.

Sheila Brookes, quantity surveyor; mbr Solihull MBC, 1990- . Women's officer, 1984-6, and youth officer, 1987-8, Meriden CLP; women's officer Solihull CLP, 1988-90. B Oct 31 1949; ed Alcester GS. TGWU 1987- .

STRATHKELVIN AND BEARSDEN						No change
Electorate % Turnout	61,116	82.3%	1992	62,676	82.2%	1987
*Galbraith, S (Lab)	21,267	42.3%	+4.1%	19,639	38.1%	Lab
Hirst, M W (C)	18,105	36.0%	+2.6%	17,187	33.4%	C
Chalmers, T (SNP)	6,275	12.5%	+5.4%	11,034	21.4%	L/All
Waterfield, Mrs B (LD)	4,585	9.1%	-12.3%	3,654	7.1%	SNP
Whitley, D (NLP)	90	0.2%				
C to Lab swing 0.8%	50,322		6.3%	51,514		4.8%
		Lab maj	3,162		Lab maj	2,452

Samuel Galbraith became an Opposn spokesman on health in 1988; also joined front bench Scottish Office team in 1988. Won this seat in 1987. Neurosurgeon; was consultant neurosurgeon, institute of neurological sciences, Southern general hospital, Glasgow; consultant in neurosurgery, Gtr Glasgow health bd, 1978-87. Mbr medical campaign against nuclear weapons; Scottish medical campaign for Nicaragua. Pres. medical practitioners union and of NEC of ASTMS (now merged MSFU); health centre appeal fund. B Oct 18 1945; ed Greenock HS; Glasgow Univ. MSF.

Michael Hirst, chartered accountant, was MP for this seat, 1983-7; contested Dunbartonshire E, 1979; Dunbartonshire Central, Feb and Oct 1974. Mbr select cmte on Scottish affairs, 1983-7. Pres Scottish Cons assocn, 1990- ; vice-chmn, Scottish Cons pty, 1987-9. B Jan 2 1946; ed Glasgow Acad; Glasgow Univ.

Tom Chalmers, solicitor; nat treas SNP. B Apr 13 1964; ed Forrester HS, Edinburgh; Edinburgh univ.

Barbara Waterfield, teacher; mbr Bearsden and Milngavie DC, 1984-8. B Sep 18 1937; ed Sherborne; Glasgow Univ. EIS.

STREATHAM						Lab gain
Electorate % Turnout	56,825	70.8%	1992	60,519	69.5%	1987
Hill, T K (Lab)	18,925	47.0%	+7.8%	18,916	44.9%	C
*Shelton, Sir William (C)	16,608	41.3%	-3.7%	16,509	39.2%	Lab
Pindar, M J (LD)	3,858	9.6%	-6.2%	6,663	15.8%	L/All
Baker, R (Grn)	443	1.1%				
Hankin, A (Islamic)	154	0.4%				
Payne, Mrs C (ADS)	145	0.4%				
Parsons, J (NLP)	97	0.2%				
C to Lab swing 5.7%	40,230		5.8%	42,088		5.7%
		Lab maj	2,317		C maj	2,407

Keith Hill won this seat in 1992; contested Blaby 1979. Political officer, Rail, Maritime and Transport Workers (formerly NUR) 1976- ; research officer, Lab Pty international dept 1974-6. B Jul 28 1943; ed City of Leicester Boys' GS; Corpus Christi Coll, Oxford. RMT.
Sir William Shelton was MP for this sear Feb 1974-92; MP for Clapham 1970-4. PPS to Margaret Thatcher when Opposition ldr 1975-9. Ed and science under sec 1981-3. Mbr select cmte on MPs' interests; UK delegation, Cl of Europe and WEU, 1987- . Mbr of Lloyd's; director, Saracen Consultants Ltd; non-exec director, Mallerman-Summerfield Gp Ltd, 1989-90; consultant to McCann-Erickson Advertising Ltd. B Oct 30 1929; ed Radley Coll; Worcester Coll, Oxford; Tabor Univ, Mass; Texas Univ.
John Pindar, lecturer and international political consultant, contested London South Inner LD in 1989 Euro elections; and Southampton Itchen 1979. Mbr, exec, Streatham LD; exec, LD parly candidates' assocn. Apl 1 1955; ed Forest GS; Manchester and Newcastle Univs; Kings Coll, London; Temple Univ, Philadelphia.
Roger Baker interior decorator. Contested Dulwich 1983. Ed St Pauls. Vice-pres, Brixton West Indians cricket XI and captain Grn pty team.

STRETFORD						No change
Electorate % Turnout	54,467	68.8%	1992	57,568	71.9%	1987
*Lloyd, A J (Lab)	22,300	59.5%	+4.4%	22,831	55.2%	Lab
Rae, J C B (C)	11,163	29.8%	-2.6%	13,429	32.4%	C
Beswick, F C (LD)	3,722	9.9%	-2.4%	5,125	12.4% SDP/All
Boyton, A (NLP)	268	0.7%				
C to Lab swing 3.5%	37,453		29.7%	41,385		22.7%
		Lab maj	11,137		Lab maj	9,402

Tony Lloyd became an Opposn spokesman on employment in 1988; a spokesman on transport, 1987-88; previously an Opposn whip. Sec all-pty British-Japanese parly gp. Chmn PLP foreign affairs cmte 1986-7; mbr select cmte on home affairs and its sub-cmte on race relations and immigration, 1985-7; social services select cmte, 1983-5; jt vice-chmn PLP home affairs cmte 1985-7; sec, NW Gp of Lab MPs. Lecturer, Dept of Business and Admin, Salford Univ, 1979-83. B Feb 25 1950; ed Stretford GS; Nottingham Univ; Manchester Business Sch. Mbr, Trafford DC, 1979-84. Sponsored by GPMU.
Charles Rae, composer, author and broadcaster; lecturer in composition and analysis, Leeds Coll of Music, 1979- (a governor, 1986-90; mbr, academic bd, 1986- ; chmn, course development cmte, 1989-). Previously worked in family insurance broking firm. B Aug 10 1955; ed Moorfield Sch; Ghyll Royd prep sch, Ilkley; Ilkley GS; Sidney Sussex Coll, Cambridge; Chopin Acad of Music, Warsaw, 1981-83.
Francis Beswick is a writer of learning tapes and manuscript adviser. Chmn Stretford LDs, 1988- ; vice-chmn Trafford LD organisation, 1989- . B Jun 16 1950; ed Manchester Univ; Christ Coll, Liverpool; Open Univ. NAS/UWT.

STROUD						No change
Electorate % Turnout	82,553	84.5%	1992	81,275	80.6%	1987
*Knapman, R (C)	32,201	46.2%	-4.0%	32,883	50.2%	C
Drew, D E (Lab)	18,796	26.9%	+8.4%	20,508	31.3%	L/All
Robinson, M P (LD)	16,751	24.0%	-7.3%	12,145	18.5%	Lab
Atkinson, Ms S M (Grn)	2,005	2.9%				
C to Lab swing 6.2%	69,753		19.2%	65,536		18.9%
		C maj	13,405		C maj	12,375

Roger Knapman, chartered surveyor and farmer, was elected in 1987. PPS to Archie Hamilton, Minr of State for Armed Forces, 1991- . Jt vice-chmn, Cons backbench Euro affairs cmte, 1989-90; vice-chmn, 1990-91; and sec, 1988-90, Cons forestry sub-cmte. Jt sec, all-pty conservation parly gp; jt vice-chmn, all-pty East African parly gp. Partner, R J & R M Knapman, builders; associate partner, Carters, chartered surveyors; mbr, Lloyd's underwriting syndicates. B Feb 20 1944; ed Allhallows Sch, Lyme Regis; Royal Agricultural Coll, Cirencester.
David Drew, snr lecturer, Bristol Poly. Treas, Gloucs Lab Pty; mbr, exec, Stroud CLP; Stroud DC, 1987- ; Stevenage cllr, 1981-82. B Apr 13 1952; ed Kingsfield Sch, Kingswood, Bristol; Nottingham and B'ham Univs; Bristol Poly. NATFHE, Nupe.
Myles Robinson, chartered surveyor; director, industrial development company; mbr Gloucs CC, 1979- . Former chmn, Stroud LDs. B Mar 16 1950; ed Malvern Coll.
Sue Atkinson, teacher of special needs; Grn pty coordinator, local pty, area and cty. Town cllr. B Nov 10 1954; ed W Somerset Sch; Birmingham Poly.

SUFFOLK CENTRAL						No change
Electorate % Turnout	82,735	80.3%	1992	79,199	76.2%	1987
*Lord, M N (C)	32,917	49.6%	-4.1%	32,422	53.7%	C
Henniker-Major, Ms L (LD)	16,886	25.4%	-1.3%	16,132	26.7%	L/All
Harris, J W (Lab)	15,615	23.5%	+3.9%	11,817	19.6%	Lab
Matthissen, J E (Grn)	800	1.2%				
Wilmot, Ms J (NLP)	190	0.3%				
C to LD swing 1.4%	66,408		24.1%	60,371		27.0%
		C maj	16,031		C maj	16,290

Michael Lord joined select cmte on parliamentary commissioner for administration in 1990. PPS to John MacGregor, Minr of State for Agriculture and then Chief Sec to Treasury, 1984-7. Director, Palmer family trust, 1988- . Arboricultural consultant, Pres. arboricultural assocn; parly consultant to British printing industries fed and Country Houses Assocn Ltd. Sec all-pty forestry parly gp; mbr cl of Europe and WEU, 1987-91. Elected in 1983; contested Manchester, Gorton, 1979. B Oct 17 1938; ed William Hulme's GS, Manchester; Christ's coll, Cambridge. Mbr Beds CC, 1981-3; N Beds BC, 1974-7. BIM.
Lesley Henniker-Major, mbr Mid Suffolk DC, 1987- (gp

ldr); Suffolk CC, 1989- (dep gp ldr, 1989-91). B Sep 9 1948; ed Elizabeth HS, S Australia (last sch of 13); Australian nat univ.
John Harris, teacher; mbr Ipswich BC, 1989- ; pres Suffolk NUT, 1991-2. Mbr exec cmte and gmc, Ipswich Lab pty; Eastern cl sport and recreation; Ipswich sports cl. B Jun 18 1958; ed Harrow cty GS for boys, Middlesex; Lewes Priory comprehensive sch, Sussex; LSE; London inst of ed.
John Matthissen, accountant and computer consultant; director of software company. E Anglian mbr Grn pty cl; mbr Beyton PC. B Jul 5 1947; ed Ilford Cty HS; NE London Poly; Open univ.

SUFFOLK COASTAL						No change
Electorate % Turnout	79,333	81.6%	1992	75,684	77.9%	1987
*Gummer, J S (C)	34,680	53.6%	-2.1%	32,834	55.7%	C
Monk, P (LD)	15,395	23.8%	-6.0%	17,554	29.8%	SDP/All
Hodgson, T E (Lab)	13,508	20.9%	+8.1%	7,534	12.8%	Lab
Slade, A (Grn)	943	1.5%	-0.3%	1,049	1.8%	Grn
Kaplan, Ms F (NLP)	232	0.4%				
LD to C swing 1.9%	64,758		29.8%	58,971		25.9%
		C maj	19,285		C maj	15,280

John Gummer joined cabinet in 1989 when appointed Minr of Agriculture, Fisheries and Food; Minr for Local Govt, with rank of Minr of State, Dept of Environment, 1988-9; Minr of State for Ag, Fish and Food, 1985-8; Paymaster Gen, 1984-5; Minr of State for Employment, 1983-4; chmn of Cons pty, 1983-5; Under Sec of State for Employment, Jan-Oct 1983. PC 1985. Elected for this seat 1983; MP for Eye, 1979-83, and for Lewisham W, 1970-Feb 1974; contested Greenwich, 1964 and 1966. A Ld Commissioner of the Treasury (govt whip), 1981-3; asst govt whip, 1981. Mbr General Synod, C of E, 1979- . B

Nov 26 1939; ed King's sch, Rochester; Selwyn coll, Cambridge, pres of Union, 1962.
Peter Monk, fire technician with Essex CC. Nupe sec; B May 8 1945.
Terry Hodgson in electrical generation plant operation. Mbr Suffolk CC, 1990- ; Suffolk Coastal DC, 1983- ; Leiston TC, 1974-6 and 1979- ; Leiston UDC, 1972-4. Chmn, Suffolk Coastal CLP, 1984-6, and vice-chmn, 1981-4 and 1986-91. B Oct 11 1946; ed Saxmundham sec mod; Ipswich Civic Coll. AEU.

SUFFOLK SOUTH						No change
Electorate % Turnout	84,833	81.7%	1992	81,954	77.6%	1987
*Yeo, T S K (C)	34,793	50.2%	-3.3%	33,972	53.4%	C
Pollard, Mrs A K (LD)	17,504	25.2%	-2.6%	17,729	27.9%	L/All
Hesford, S (Lab)	16,623	24.0%	+5.3%	11,876	18.7%	Lab
Aisbitt, T (NLP)	420	0.6%				
C to LD swing 0.3%	69,340		24.9%	63,577		25.5%
		C maj	17,289		C maj	16,243

Timothy Yeo was appointed an Under Sec of State for Environment in 1990; PPS to Douglas Hurd, Home Secretary, and then Foreign Secretary, 1988-90. Director, Spastics Society, 1980-3, and on its exec cl, 1984-6; director, Worcester Engineering Co Ltd, 1975-86. Elected in 1983; fought Bedwellty, Feb 1974. Mbr select cmte on social services, 1985-8. B Mar 20 1945; ed Charterhouse; Emmanuel coll, Cambridge. Treas, international voluntary service, 1975-8, now a vice-pres; trustee, Tanzania development trust, 1980- . Led campaign to save Tadworth

Court children's hospital, Surrey; chmn Tadworth Court trust, 1984-90. Mbr independent development cl on mental handicap. Chmn charities VAT reform gp, 1982- .
Kathy Pollard, Babergh district cllr since 1987, works for British Telecom laboratories as a human factors consultant. B Dec 15 1951; ed Llwyn-y-Bryn HS, Swansea; Univ of Wales; Birmingham univ. Society of telecom executives.
Stephen Hesford, barrister; Altrincham branch LP chmn. B May 27 1957; ed Bradford univ; Central London poly. GMB/Apex.

SUNDERLAND NORTH						No change
Electorate % Turnout	72,874	68.9%	1992	75,674	70.5%	1987
Etherington, W (Lab)	30,481	60.7%	+5.0%	29,767	55.8%	Lab
Barnes, Miss J V (C)	13,477	26.9%	-1.4%	15,095	28.3%	C
Halom, V (LD)	5,389	10.7%	-5.2%	8,518	16.0%	L/All
Lundgren, Ms W (Lib)	841	1.7%				
C to Lab swing 3.2%	50,188		33.9%	53,380		27.5%
		Lab maj	17,004		Lab maj	14,672

William Etherington, vice-president, NE area of NUM, has been a full-time NUM official since Dec 1983. Fitter at Dawdon Colliery for 21 years; branch delegate of Durham mechanics branch, 1973-83, and also served as chmn and later sec of branch. B 1941; ed Redby Infants and Jnr schs; Monkwearmouth GS. Served apprenticeship at then Austin Pickersgill shipyard, Southwick, beginning in 1957. Mbr, Kelloe branch, Durham City CLP, from 1981; a ward treas, 1983-88; also served as CLP delegate and later elected to CLP exec cmte.

Judith Barnes, solicitor, was elected to Camden Cl 1986 (Cons gp ldr, 1990-). B Jan 17 1950; ed Oxford univ; coll of law. Former office holder in Holborn and St Pancras Cons Assocn.
Vic Halom, general manager of North Shields football club, played for Charlton, Leyton Orient, Fulham, Luton, Sunderland and Oldham, and managed Rochdale, Barrow and Burton Albion. B Oct 3 1948; ed Castle Gresley Sec Sch, Derbyshire.

SUNDERLAND SOUTH						No change
Electorate % Turnout	72,607	69.9%	1992	74,947	71.1%	1987
*Mullin, C J (Lab)	29,399	57.9%	+3.9%	28,823	54.1%	Lab
Howe, G E (C)	14,898	29.4%	-1.0%	16,210	30.4%	C
Lennox, J (LD)	5,844	11.5%	-3.1%	7,768	14.6%	SDP/All
Scouler, T (Grn)	596	1.2%	+0.2%	516	1.0%	Grn
C to Lab swing 2.5%	50,737		28.6%	53,317		23.7%
		Lab maj	14,501		Lab maj	12,613

Christopher Mullin, journalist and political novelist, was editor of Tribune, 1982-4. Elected for this seat in 1987; contested Kingston upon Thames, Feb 1974; Devon North 1970. Chmn, Britain-Vietnam Assocn; sec, all-pty British-Vietnam parly group; jt sec, Tibet group, since 1989. B Dec 12 1947; ed St Joseph's Coll, Birkfield, Ipswich; Hull univ. Sub-editor, BBC World Service, 1974-8. Exec mbr, Campaign for Lab Party Democracy, 1975-83. MSF and

NUJ.
George Howe, lecturer in adult ed; previously quality control engineer on N Sea and Middle East oil projects. Contested this seat 1987. Chmn, Sunderland Cons assocn, 1989- . B Jul 1 1936; ed Toronto univ; Sunderland Poly.
John Lennox, lecturer, Sunderland Poly; mbr Sunderland MBC, 1988- (gp ldr). B Jun 17 1947; ed Durham and Cambridge univs.

SURBITON						No change
Electorate % Turnout	42,421	82.4%	1992	45,428	78.3%	1987
*Tracey, R P (C)	19,033	54.4%	-1.4%	19,861	55.9%	C
Janke, Ms B (LD)	9,394	26.9%	-1.6%	10,120	28.5%	SDP/All
Hutchinson, R (Lab)	6,384	18.3%	+3.9%	5,111	14.4%	Lab
Parker, W (NLP)	161	0.5%		465	1.3%	Grn
LD to C swing 0.1%	34,972		27.6%	35,557		27.4%
		C maj	9,639		C maj	9,741

Richard Tracey was minr for sport, 1985-7. Director, Golf Design and Construction Co and Golflines International since 1989. Vice-pres, Special Olympics UK since 1989; public affairs adviser, 1978-83; BBC radio and television news and current affairs presenter and reporter, 1966-78. Chmn, Cons gp of London MPs, since 1990 (secretary, 1983-84); mbr, Select cmte on broadcasting, 1988-91. Won the seat 1983; contested Northampton N, Oct 1974. B Feb 8 1943; ed King Edward VI Sch, Stratford-upon-

Avon; Birmingham univ. Mbr, Economic Research Council, since 1981. Freeman, City of London.
Barbara Janke, teacher of modern languages; mbr, Kingston BC, since 1986 (chmn, finance and gen purposes cmte, 1986-7; speaker on ed, 1987-90; dep LD gp ldr, since 1990). B Jun 5 1947.
Robin Hutchinson, builder; mbr, Kingston BC, (Lab gp ldr, since 1988). B Oct 31 1958; ed Tiffin Boys, Kingston; Chelsea Sch of Art; Kingston poly. NUJ.

SURREY EAST				No change		
Electorate % Turnout	57,878	82.5%	1992	59,528	77.2%	1987
Ainsworth, P M (C)	29,767	62.3%	-1.1%	29,126	63.4%	C
Tomlin, R L (LD)	12,111	25.4%	+1.4%	11,000	23.9%	L/All
Roles, Mrs G (Lab)	5,075	10.6%	+0.2%	4,779	10.4%	Lab
Kilpatrick, I (Grn)	819	1.7%	-0.6%	1,044	2.3%	Grn
C to LD swing 1.2%	47,772		37.0%	45,949		39.4%
		C maj	17,656		C maj	18,126

Peter Ainsworth, director, Warburg Securities, investment banking, 1989- ; investment analyst, Laing and Cruickshank, stockbrokers, and Warburg Securities, 1981-9. Mbr, Wandsworth BC, 1986- (chmn, Cons gp and dep chmn, policy and finance cmte); Battersea Cons Assocn, 1985- ; cl of Bow Gp, 1984-86. B Nov 16 1956; ed Ludgrove Sch and Bradfield Coll, Berkshire; Lincoln Coll, Oxford. Research asst to Sir John Stewart-Clark, MEP, 1979-81.
Robert Tomlin, solicitor; mbr, Tandridge DC, 1986- ; vice-

chmn, Wireless for the Bedridden Society. B Mar 18 1948; ed St Ignatius Coll, London; UCW, Aberystwyth. Mbr, LD Christian Forum.
Gill Roles, biology teacher, contested Sussex E in 1989 Euro elections. Chmn, Wealden CLP, 1987- ; East Sussex Cty Lab Pty, 1988- . Governor, Oak Hall Special Sch, 1986- . B Nov 1950; ed Lady Margaret Sch, Fulham; Westfield Coll, London univ. NUT.
Ian Kilpatrick, computer systems programmer. B Mar 24 1964; ed Whitgift sch, Croydon.

SURREY NORTH WEST				No change		
Electorate % Turnout	83,648	78.3%	1992	83,083	72.5%	1987
*Grylls, Sir Michael (C)	41,772	63.8%	-0.2%	38,535	64.0%	C
Clark, Mrs C M (LD)	13,378	20.4%	-4.4%	14,960	24.8%	L/All
Hayhurst, R M (Lab)	8,886	13.6%	+2.4%	6,751	11.2%	Lab
Hockey, Mrs Y (Grn)	1,441	2.2%				
LD to C swing 2.1%	65,477		43.4%	60,246		39.1%
		C maj	28,394		C maj	23,575

Sir Michael Grylls, chmn, Small Business Bureau, 1979- , and director (unpaid), Small Business Bureau Ltd, 1990- ; chmn, Cons back-bench trade and industry cmte 1981- (vice-chmn, 1975-81); all-pty pharmaceutical industry parly gp. Elected Feb 1974; MP for Chertsey, 1970-4; contested Fulham, 1964 and 1966. Director, Le Carbone Lorraine (GB) Ltd, Sterling Winthrop Gp Ltd; Cape Ltd; consultant to Assocn of Authorised Public Accountants, Biwater Gp Ltd, Digital Equipment Co Ltd, Freight Complex Development and Management Ltd and other companies; adviser to Unitary Tax Campaign; parly spokesman, Inst of Directors, 1979- . B Feb 21 1934; ed RNC Dartmouth; univs in Paris and Madrid.

Mrs Chris Clark, teacher; mbr, constituency exec; sec, local UN, 1988- ; prison visitor, HMP Coldingley. B Aug 28 1948; ed Charles Edward Brooke Sch for Girls; Hockerill Coll of Ed.
Mark Hayhurst, teacher; mbr, Spelthorne BC, 1991- ; treas, Spelthorne CLP, 1990- ; Staines and Laleham branch chmn, 1989-91. B Sep 3 1964; ed Matthew Arnold sec sch, Staines; Strode's VIth Form Coll, Egham; Middlesex poly; Leeds univ. NUT.
Yvonne Hockey, technical consultant; local coordinator, Hart Grn Pty. Director, The Product Works Ltd. B Aug 8 1956; ed Aldershot Cty HS; Kingston Poly.

SURREY SOUTH WEST				No change		
Electorate % Turnout	72,288	82.8%	1992	73,018	78.4%	1987
*Bottomley, Mrs V H B M (C)	35,008	58.5%	-0.9%	34,024	59.5%	C
Sherlock, N R (LD)	20,033	33.5%	-0.9%	19,681	34.4%	L/All
Kelly, P J (Lab)	3,840	6.4%	+0.8%	3,224	5.6%	Lab
Bedrock, N (Grn)	710	1.2%		299	0.5%	Ind C
Campbell, K (NLP)	147	0.2%				
Newman, D (Anglo Sax)	98	0.2%				
C to LD swing 0.0%	59,836		25.0%	57,228		25.1%
		C maj	14,975		C maj	14,343

Virginia Bottomley became health secretary, 1992. Minister for health, 1989-92, and in 1991 appointed govt co-chmn, Women's National Commission; a junior environment minister, 1988-9. Elected at 1984 by-election; contested Isle of Wight, 1983. PPS to Sir Geoffrey Howe, foreign secretary, 1987-8; and to Christopher Patten 1985-7. Mbr, Medical Research Cl, 1987-8; vice-chmn, Nat Cl of Carers and their Elderly Dependants, 1982-8. Magistrate in inner London juvenile courts since 1975. Psychiatric social worker, Brixton and Camberwell child guidance units, 1973-84. B Mar 12 1948; ed Putney HS; Essex Univ; LSE. Mbr, ct of governors, LSE, 1985- . Wife of Peter

Bottomley, MP for Eltham.
Neil Sherlock, economist and management consultant; vice-chmn, Enterprise Europe. Adviser to Save the Children, 1990- . B Aug 13 1963; ed Esher Cty GS; Esher Coll; Christ Church, Oxford.
Phil Kelly, journalist; press officer for Mr Michael Meacher MP; former editor of *Tribune*. Mbr, Islington BC, 1984-86, 1990- . B Sep 18 1946; ed St Mary's Coll, Crosby; Leeds univ. NUJ.
Nigel Bedrock, well log analyst for oil company. B Oct 4 1959; ed Wirral GS for Boys; London univ.

SUSSEX MID				No change		
Electorate % Turnout	80,827	82.9%	1992	80,147	77.2%	1987
*Renton, R T (C)	39,524	59.0%	-2.1%	37,781	61.1%	C
Collins, Mrs M E (LD)	18,996	28.4%	-3.1%	19,489	31.5%	L/All
Gregory, Ms L (Lab)	6,951	10.4%	+3.0%	4,573	7.4%	Lab
Stevens, H G (Grn)	772	1.2%				
Berry, P (Loony)	392	0.6%				
Hodkin, P (PR)	246	0.4%				
Hankey, Dr A (NLP)	89	0.1%				
LD to C swing 0.5%	66,970		30.7%	61,843		29.6%
		C maj	20,528		C maj	18,292

Timothy Renton was appointed Minr for the Arts and Minr for the Civil Service in 1990 with rank of Minr of State, Privy Cl Office; Parly Sec to Treasury and Govt Chief Whip, 1989-90; Minr of State, Home Office, 1987-89; Minr of State, FCO, 1985-87; Under Sec of State, FCO, 1984-85. PC 1989. PPS to Sir Geoffrey Howe, Chancellor of Exchequer and then Foreign Sec, 1983-84; to Mr John Biffen, Chief Sec to Treasury and Secretary of State for Trade, 1979-81. Mbr of Lloyd's. Elected in Feb 1974; contested Sheffield Park, 1970. B May 28 1932; ed Eton; Magdalen Coll, Oxford. Nat Pres, Cons Trade Unionists, 1980-84. Chmn, Cons Foreign and Commonwealth Cl, 1982-84; mbr, Cl, Roedean Sch, 1982- . Trustee, Mental Health Foundation, 1985- . With wife, has tree nursery in Sussex. Apex.

Margaret Collins, teacher, contested Hove 1987. Mbr, W Sussex CC, 1985- . Founder chmn, SDP N Sussex area pty. B Nov 10 1940; ed Brondesbury and Kilburn HS for Girls; Trent Park Training Coll; Sussex Univ; Goldsmiths' Coll, London Univ. NUT (Pres, E Grinstead NUT, 1979-80).

Linda Gregory, union official since 1983, now with BIFU. B Dec 26 1959; ed Haywards Heath Sixth Form Coll; New Hall, Cambridge. MATSA (GMB).

Hugh Stevens, school bursar; partner in St Peter's Sch, Burgess Hill; sole director, Cambrian Tuition, Burgess Hill. B Sep 23 1961; ed Cranleigh Sch, Surrey; York Univ.

SUTTON COLDFIELD				No change		
Electorate % Turnout	71,410	79.5%	1992	72,329	74.5%	1987
*Fowler, Sir Norman (C)	37,001	65.2%	+1.2%	34,475	64.0%	C
Whorwood, J E (LD)	10,965	19.3%	-5.4%	13,292	24.7%	L/All
Bott-Obi, Ms J (Lab)	8,490	15.0%	+3.6%	6,104	11.3%	Lab
Meads, H (NLP)	324	0.6%				
LD to C swing 3.3%	56,780		45.9%	53,871		39.3%
		C maj	26,036		C maj	21,183

Sir Norman Fowler, appointed chmn, Conservative Party, 1992. Elected chmn, Cons back-bench European affairs cmte, 1991; employment secretary, 1987-90. Non-exec chmn, Midland Newspapers, 1991- ; non-exec director, Evered Bardon plc, quarrying and building materials gp, 1990- ; Group 4 Securitas, 1990- ; NFC plc, 1990- . Sec of State for Social Services, 1981-87; Sec of State (1981) and Minr (1979-81) of Transport. PC 1979. Journalist on The Times, 1961-70, being its Home Affairs Correspondent, 1966-70. On editorial board of Crossbow, 1962-70. Elected for this seat, Feb 1974; MP for Nottingham South, 1970-74. Mbr, Lloyd's. B Feb 2 1938; ed King Edward VI Sch, Chelmsford; Trinity Hall, Cambridge. NUJ.

Jim Whorwood, poly snr lecturer in manufacturing at Coventry Poly; chartered engineer; former managing director of manufacturing company. Mbr, Sutton Coldfield BC 1965-74; W Midlands CC, 1973-77. Pres, W Midlands Lib Pty, 1980-81; former sec and chmn, Sutton Coldfield Libs. B Oct 17 1934; ed Aston Univ; Bolton Coll of Ed; Aston Tech Coll.

Janet Bott-Obi, personal secretary; constuency women's officer since 1989. Mbr of and sponsored by GMB/Apex; financial sec, B'ham General Branch Apex, 1983- . B Sep 13 1944; ed John Willmott Mixwed GS; B'ham Univ.

SUTTON AND CHEAM				No change		
Electorate % Turnout	60,949	82.4%	1992	63,850	76.6%	1987
Maitland, Lady Olga (C)	27,710	55.2%	-5.6%	29,710	60.8%	C
Burstow, P (LD)	16,954	33.8%	+5.1%	13,992	28.6%	L/All
Martin, G C (Lab)	4,980	9.9%	-0.7%	5,202	10.6%	Lab
Duffy, J (Grn)	444	0.9%				
Hatchard, Ms A (NLP)	133	0.3%				
C to LD swing 5.4%	50,221		21.4%	48,904		32.1%
		C maj	10,756		C maj	15,718

Lady Olga Maitland, journalist with Sunday Express, contested Bethnal Green and Stepney 1987. Founder and chmn, Families for Defence, 1983- ; chmn, Conserve, 1991- ; vice-chmn, Why Campaign, 1987- ; vice-pres, Cons disability campaign, 1990- . B May 23 1944: ed St Mary and St Anne, Abbots Bromley; Lycee Francais de Londres. NUJ.

Paul Burstow, councillors officer, Assocn of LD Cllrs. Mbr, London reg LD exec; Fed policy cmte, 1988-90; Sutton BC, 1986- (chair, environment cmte, 1988-). B May 13 1962.

Geoff Martin, campaigns director; mbr, Merton BC, 1986- . Constituency vice-chair and various ward offices. B Sep 17 1962; ed Glyn GS, Ewell, Surrey. Nupe, 1981-87; NUJ, 1987- .

SWANSEA EAST — No change

Electorate % Turnout	59,196	75.6%	1992	57,200	75.4%	1987
*Anderson, D (Lab)	31,179	69.7%	+6.0%	27,478	63.7%	Lab
Davies, H L (C)	7,697	17.2%	-1.7%	8,140	18.9%	C
Barton, R (LD)	4,248	9.5%	-5.3%	6,380	14.8%	L/All
Bonner-Evans, Ms E (PC)	1,607	3.6%	+0.9%	1,145	2.7%	PC
C to Lab swing 3.8%	44,731		52.5%	43,143		44.8%
		Lab maj	23,482		Lab maj	19,338

Donald Anderson, barrister and former diplomat, Opposn spokesman on foreign affairs, 1983- . Treas (1988-90), vice-chmn (1985-8) and mbr, exec cmte, British gp, IPU; jt hon treas (1990-), mbr (1987-90) and vice-chmn (1986-7), exec cmte, CPA; snr vice-pres, Assocn of W European Parliamentarians for Action against Apartheid, 1984- . Chmn, all-pty Christian Fellowship parly gp. treas, Order of St John gp. Adviser, Directory Publishers' Assocn, and consultant, Royal Soc of Chemistry (both no personal financial benefit). Elected for this seat, Oct 1974; MP for Monmouth, 1966-70. B Jun 17 1939; ed Swansea GS; Univ Coll, Swansea (Hon Fellow; lecturer, 1964-66).

Sponsored by RMT.
Henri Lloyd Davies, managing director of estates company. Chmn, Wales Area CPC; mbr, Wales Area exec; Mid and West Wales Euro Cl. Vice-pres, Royal Welsh Agricultural Society and Utd Counties Agricultural Society; mbr, Royal Yachting Assocn; Aberaeron Yacht Club. B Dec 12 1946; ed Rugby; Bath Univ.
Robert Barton, principal lecturer in marketing. Former mbr, Woking BC. Ed London Business Sch.
Elenor Bonner-Evans, full-time student union officer. Pres, Powys, Dyfed and W Glamorgan area, Welsh NUS; mbr, cl, Univ of Wales. B Jul 10 1970.

SWANSEA WEST — No change

Electorate % Turnout	59,785	73.3%	1992	59,836	76.1%	1987
*Williams, A J (Lab)	23,238	53.0%	+4.5%	22,089	48.5%	Lab
Perry, R (C)	13,760	31.4%	-1.6%	15,027	33.0%	C
Shrewsbury, M J (LD)	4,620	10.5%	-4.9%	7,019	15.4%	L/All
Lloyd, Dr D (PC)	1,668	3.8%	+1.8%	902	2.0%	PC
Oubridge, B (Grn)	564	1.3%	+0.3%	469	1.0%	Grn
C to Lab swing 3.0%	43,850		21.6%	45,506		15.5%
		Lab maj	9,478		Lab maj	7,062

Alan Williams joined Public Accounts Cmte in 1990; an Opposn spokesman on Commons affairs and a deputy campaigns co-ordinator, 1988-9; spokesman on Wales, 1987-8; spokesman on Commons affairs, 1984-7; trade and industry, 1983-4; civil service, 1980-3; Wales, 1979-80. Industry minr 1976-9; prices and consumer protection minr 1974-6. PC 1977. Parly sec, MinTech 1969-70; under sec economic affairs dept 1967-9. Elected in 1964; contested Poole, 1959. B Oct 14 1930; ed Cardiff HS; Cardiff Coll of Tech; London and Oxford Univs. Adviser to Institution of Plant Engineers; adviser to Assocn of First Division Civil Servants, 1982- , and to TSSA.

Roy Perry, senior lecturer in politics. Mbr Cons nat local govt advisory cmte, 1991- . Mbr, Test Valley BC, 1979- (cl ldr 1985-); Eastleigh BC, 1970-74. B Feb 12 1943; ed Tottenham Cty GS; Exeter Univ. **Martyn Shrewsbury**, educational consultant and psycho therapist, contested Llanelli in 1987 and Swansea East 1983. B Apr 7 1938; ed Burton GS; Dynevor Comprehensive; Manchester and Swansea Univs. Fellow, Royal Anthropolotical Inst.
Dr David Lloyd, general practitioner; mbr, Welsh Cl, Royal Coll of GPs; BMA. B Dec 2 1956; ed Lampeter Comprehensive Sch, Dyfed; Welsh Nat Sch of Medicine, Cardiff.

SWINDON — No change

Electorate % Turnout	90,067	81.5%	1992	86,150	77.8%	1987
*Coombs, S C (C)	31,749	43.3%	-0.6%	29,385	43.8%	C
D'Avila, J P (Lab)	28,923	39.4%	+2.8%	24,528	36.6%	Lab
Cordon, S R (LD)	11,737	16.0%	-3.6%	13,114	19.6%	SDP/All
Hughes, W (Grn)	647	0.9%				
Gillard, R (Loony G)	236	0.3%				
Farrar, V (Ind)	78	0.1%				
C to Lab swing 1.7%	73,370		3.9%	67,027		7.2%
		C maj	2,826		C maj	4,857

Simon Coombs, a former marketing executive with BT, won this seat 1983. Mbr select cmtes on employment, 1987- ; on Cardiff Bay Barrage Bill, 1991- . Chmn, all-pty cable and satellite TV parly gp, 1987- (sec 1986-7); jt vice-chmn, Cons backbench tourism cmte, 1988- ; sec, Cons backbench employment cmte, 1991- ; treas , parly Info Tech Cmte, 1987- . Parly consultant to Blick Intl and British Telecom. Chmn (1989-) and sec (1985-89), parly Food and Health Forum. B Feb 21 1947; ed Wycliffe Coll;

Reading Univ.
Jim D'Avila, toolmaker at Rover car factory in Swindon; exec cmte mbr, Swindon CLP. Mbr, Thamesdown BC, 1976- . B Oct 18 1950; ed Moredon Primary and St Joseph's RC schs, Swindon. AEU mbr since 1969; convenor since 1977.
Simon Cordon, production planner. Mbr, Wilts CC, 1985-; Thamesdown BC, 1986- . B Aug 14 1963; ed London Univ; Goldsmiths' Coll.

TATTON						No change
Electorate % Turnout	71,085	80.8%	1992	71,904	76.7%	1987
*Hamilton, M N (C)	31,658	55.1%	+0.5%	30,128	54.6%	C
Kelly, J M (Lab)	15,798	27.5%	+6.2%	13,034	23.6%	SDP/All
Hancox, Mrs C (LD)	9,597	16.7%	-6.9%	11,760	21.3%	Lab
Gibson, M (FP)	410	0.7%	+0.2%	263	0.5%	FP
C to Lab swing 2.8%	57,463		27.6%	55,185		31.0%
		C maj	15,860		C maj	17,094

Neil Hamilton was appointed an Under Secretary at Department of Trade and Industry in 1992. Asst govt whip 1990-92; barrister (non-practising); mbr select cmte on Treasury and civil service, 1987-90. Elected in 1983; contested Abertillery, Feb 1974; Bradford N, 1979. PPS to David Mitchell, Minr of State for Transport, 1986-7. Former Euro and parly affairs director, inst of directors. Director, Plateau Mining plc, 1990. Vice-pres league for introduction of canine controls, 1984- ; small farmers' assocn, 1985- ; Cheshire agricultural soc, 1986- . Spectator 'parliamentary wit of the year', 1990. B Mar 9 1949; ed

Amman Valley GS; Univ Coll of Wales, Aberystwyth; Corpus Christi, Cambridge. Jt sec Cons backbench finance cmte, 1987-90; vice-chmn, small business bureau, 1985-90; jt vice-chmn, 1987-90 and 1984-6, and sec, 1983-4, Cons trade and industry cmte.
Jon Kelly, British Rail worker; chmn, Tatton CLP; sec Macclesfield district LP. Mbr Macclesfield BC, 1986-90. B Apr 13 1958; ed Wilmslow GS. RMT and TSSA.
Cathy Hancox contested Knowsley S by-election, Sep 1990. Mbr Liverpool city cl, 1980- ; chmn, Liverpool, Mossley Hill LDs. Ed St Augustins sch, Liverpool.

TAUNTON						No change
Electorate % Turnout	78,036	82.3%	1992	74,145	79.4%	1987
*Nicholson, D J (C)	29,576	46.0%	-5.3%	30,248	51.4%	C
Ballard, Mrs J (LD)	26,240	40.8%	+7.1%	19,868	33.7%	SDP/All
Hole, Mrs L J (Lab)	8,151	12.7%	-2.2%	8,754	14.9%	Lab
Leavey, P (NLP)	279	0.4%				
C to LD swing 6.2%	64,246		5.2%	58,870		17.6%
		C maj	3,336		C maj	10,380

David Nicholson became PPS to Mrs Lynda Chalker, Minr for Overseas Development, in 1990; jt vice-chmn, Cons back-bench social security cmte, 1989-90, jt sec, 1988-9); jt vice-chmn, 1990- , and sec, 1988-90, West Country Cons MPs. Jt sec all-pty population and development parly gp. Elected in 1987; contested Walsall S, 1983. Parly consultant to assocn of British chambers of commerce; on staff of assocn from 1982-7, as deputy director-general, 1986-7; parly adviser to Burson-Marsteller Ltd and to building employers confed. B Aug 17 1944; ed Queen

Elizabeth's GS, Blackburn; Christ Church, Oxford.
Jackie Ballard, adult basic ed organiser and psychology lecturer. Mbr LD fed policy cmte; S Somerset DC, 1987-91, cl ldr, 1990-1; dep ldr, 1988-90. B Jan 4 1953; ed Monmouth Sch for Girls: LSE.
Jean Hole, retired BT employee; mbr Taunton Deane DC, 1979- ; parish cllr, 1976-9. Hon pres Taunton assocn for homeless, 1986- . Ex-chmn and sec, Taunton CLP. B Oct 22 1930; ed St Andrews primary and Bishop Fox Girls' GS, Taunton; Open univ. NCU(C), 1979- .

TAYSIDE NORTH						No change
Electorate % Turnout	55,969	77.6%	1992	53,985	74.7%	1987
*Walker, W C (C)	20,283	46.7%	+1.3%	18,307	45.4%	C
Swinney, J R (SNP)	16,288	37.5%	+4.5%	13,291	32.9%	SNP
Horner, S A (LD)	3,791	8.7%	-4.2%	5,201	12.9%	L/All
Maclennan, T A S (Lab)	3,094	7.1%	-1.7%	3,550	8.8%	Lab
C to SNP swing 1.6%	43,456		9.2%	40,349		12.4%
		C maj	3,995		C maj	5,016

William Walker, mbr select cmtes on Scottish affairs and on parly commissioner for administration, 1979-87. Vice-chmn, Scottish Cons pty; jt vice-chmn, Cons backbench party organisation cmte, 1991- ; sec Scottish Cons backbench cmte, 1990- . Vice-chmn, world scout parly union. Chmn all-pty scout assocn parly gp; treas, Scotch whisky industry gp. Chmn Walker Associates, manage-ment, marketing and design consultancy company, 1975- ; director, Stagecoach Malawi Ltd ; Stagecoach Internation-al Services. Elected for this seat 1983; MP for Perth and E Perthshire, 1979-83; contested Dundee E, Oct 1974. B Feb 20 1929; ed Logie and Blackness schs, Dundee; Trades coll, Dundee; coll of arts, Dundee; coll for distributive trades, London. Parly adviser (unpaid), British gliding assocn and soc of procurator fiscals; also to British holiday

and home parks assocn ltd.
John Swinney, managing consultant, became nat sec of SNP in 1986; asst nat sec, 1984-6; sec, Young Scottish Nats, 1982-4; director, SNP Euro election unit, 1988-9. B Apr 13 1964; ed Forrester HS, Edinburgh; Edinburgh univ.
Simon Horner, EC commission official/journalist in development directorate, contested Scotland NE in 1989 Euro elections. B Mar 13 1959; ed Webster's HS, Kirriemuir; Edinburgh univ; Vrije Univ, Brussels; Euro univ inst, Florence.
Stewart Maclennan, parly researcher and political agent; mbr nec and Scottish reg chmn, CPSA; exec cmte Glasgow dist Lab pty, 1987- ; mbr Glasgow district trades cl, 1976- . B Aug 18 1950; ed Bell Baxter HS, Cupar. TGWU/ACTS.

TEIGNBRIDGE				No change		
Electorate % Turnout	74,892	83.4%	1992	71,872	80.3%	1987
*Nicholls, P C M (C)	31,272	50.0%	-3.2%	30,693	53.2%	C
Younger-Ross, R A (LD)	22,416	35.9%	+0.7%	20,268	35.1%	L/All
Kennedy, R (Lab)	8,128	13.0%	+1.9%	6,413	11.1%	Lab
Hope, A (Loony)	437	0.7%	+0.2%	312	0.5%	Loony
Hayes, N (NLP)	234	0.4%				
C to LD swing 1.9%	62,487		14.2%	57,686		18.1%
		C maj	8,856		C maj	10,425

Patrick Nicholls was under sec for environment, Jul-Oct 1990; under sec for employment, 1987-90. PPS to Mr John Gummer 1986-7; to home office ministers 1984-6. Appointed to Select Cmte on Social Security and Select Cmte on Procedure in 1991. Sec Cons backbench legal cmte, 1991- and 1983-4. Solicitor. Parly consultant to Hill and Smith Holdings plc; consultant to Port Enterprises Ltd, 1991- ; parly adviser to Fed of Assocns of Specialists and Sub-contractors. Elected in 1983. B Nov 14 1948; ed Redrice Coll, Andover; Coll of Law, Guildford. Mbr, East Devon DC, 1980-84. Sec West Country Cons MPs, 1984-5; vice-chmn Soc of Cons Lawyers, 1986-87.

Richard Younger-Ross, public relations consultant, contested Chislehurst 1987. Organising vice-chmn (1979-80) NLYL; mbr, Lib Pty Cl, 1979-84. Exec mbr, British Kurdish Friendship Society. B Jan 29 1953; ed Walton Sec Mod Sch, Walton-on-Thames; Ewell Tech Coll.

Robert Kennedy, retired schoolmaster; chmn, Teignbridge CLP, 1988-90. B Dec 29 1933; ed Bristol GS; Exeter Coll, Oxford; Leeds Univ Dept of Ed. NAS/UWT and then NUT.

THANET NORTH				No change		
Electorate % Turnout	70,978	76.0%	1992	69,723	72.2%	1987
*Gale, R J (C)	30,867	57.2%	-0.8%	29,225	58.0%	C
Bretman, A M (Lab)	12,657	23.5%	+6.8%	11,745	23.3%	SDP/All
Phillips, Ms J L (LD)	9,563	17.7%	-5.6%	8,395	16.7%	Lab
Dawe, Mrs H F (Grn)	873	1.6%	-0.4%	996	2.0%	Grn
C to Lab swing 3.8%	53,960		33.7%	50,361		34.7%
		C maj	18,210		C maj	17,480

Roger Gale became mbr, Select Cmte on Home Affairs, in 1987; mbr Select Cmte on Broadcasting, 1988-91. Jt sec, Cons backbench home affairs cmte, 1987-88; back-bench tourism cmte, 1985-88; all-pty cults gp, 1989- . Chmn (1990-), vice-chmn (1987-90) and sec (1985-7), Cons backbench media cmte; treas, all-pty licensed trade parly gp; jt vice-chmn, animal welfare gp. Parly consultant for Scottish and Newcastle Breweries plc; consultant to Rhone Poulenc Rorer Ltd and Organon UK Ltd. Elected in 1983; fought Birmingham, Northfield, in 1982 by-election. Founder mbr, E Kent Development Assocn, 1984- . B Aug 20 1943; ed Southbourne Prep Sch; Hardye's Sch, Dorchester; Guildhall Sch of Music and Drama. Producer with Thames TV, 1979-83. Mbr, nat cmte, Cons trade unionists, 1979- . Equity, NUJ, ACTT.

Alan Bretman, teacher, contested this seat 1987. Chmn, Faversham CLP, 1986-87; mbr, Queenborough TC, 1983-87 (chmn, 1984-87). B Sep 13 1949; ed Sir Geo Monoux GS, London; Fitzwilliam Coll, Cambridge; Nottingham Univ. TGWU; NUT.

Jo Phillips, radio journalist, is chmn Herne Bay and Whitstable crime prevention panel. B Aug 4 1956; ed Ashford Girls GS; Canterbury Coll. NUJ.

Hazel Dawe, job club administrator; Grn Pty monitor on Yugoslavia; union mbr in Austria for eight years. B Jul 12 1953; ed Cheshunt GS, Herts.

THANET SOUTH				No change		
Electorate % Turnout	62,441	78.2%	1992	62,761	73.7%	1987
*Aitken, J W P (C)	25,253	51.7%	-2.6%	25,135	54.3%	C
James, M S (Lab)	13,740	28.1%	+7.2%	11,452	24.8%	L/All
Pitt, W H (LD)	8,948	18.3%	-6.4%	9,673	20.9%	Lab
Peckham, Ms S (Grn)	871	1.8%				
C to Lab swing 4.9%	48,812		23.6%	46,260		29.6%
		C maj	11,513		C maj	13,683

Jonathan Aitken was appointed defence minr in APril 1992. Elected for this seat 1983; MP for Thanet E, Feb 1974-83; contested Meriden, 1966. Dep chmn, 1990- , and co-founder, Aitken Hume International plc, and a director of group's principal subsidiary and associate companies; director, TV-am plc, 1981-88; Al Bilad (UK) Ltd. Chmn, British Horn of Africa Cl. B Aug 30 1942; ed Eton; Christ Church, Oxford. Mbr, Select Cmte on Employment, 1979-82. Pres, London Road Runners Club, 1984- . Foreign correspondent, Evening Standard, 1966-71.

Mark James, corporate planning manager; mbr (Graves-end North Division), Kent CC, 1989- ; Bearsted PC, 1987-91; sec, Mid-Kent CLP, 1984-86. B Jul 10 1963; ed Bexleyheath Sch; Univ coll, London. MSF.

Bill Pitt contested this seat 1987; MP for Croydon NW, 1982-83; contested that seat 1979 and twice in 1974. Lib spokesman on home affairs, 1982-83. B Jul 1937; ed London Nautical Sch; S Bank Poly. Snr training adviser, Construction Industry Training Bd.

Sue Peckham, primary sch teacher; local Grn pty press officer. B Sep 1 1945; ed Barton Court, Canterbury; UCW Aberystwyth.

THURROCK						Lab gain
Electorate % Turnout	69,171	78.2%	1992	67,594	71.5%	1987
MacKinlay, A S (Lab)	24,791	45.9%	+4.8%	20,527	42.5%	C
*Janman, T S (C)	23,619	43.7%	+1.2%	19,837	41.0%	Lab
Banton, A J (LD)	5,145	9.5%	-7.0%	7,970	16.5%	SDP/All
Rogers, C (Pensioners)	391	0.7%				
Compobassi, P (Anti-Fed)	117	0.2%				
C to Lab swing 1.8%	54,063		2.2%	48,334		1.4%
		Lab maj	1,172		C maj	690

Andrew MacKinlay, trade union official, regained this seat for Lab in 1992; contested Peterborough 1987, Croydon Central 1983, Surbiton twice in 1974, and London S and Surrey E in 1984 Euro election. B Apr 24 1949; ed Salesian Coll, Chertsey. Mbr, Kingston upon Thames Cl, 1971-78; Chartered Inst of Secretaries and Administrators. TGWU. Collector of trade union and labour badges.
Tim Janman was MP for this seat 1987-92; mbr, Select Cmte on Employment, 1989-92; jt vice-chmn (1988-92) and jt sec (1987-88), Cons back-bench employment cmte; jt

sec, Cons home affairs cmte, 1989-92. Consultant (unpaid) to RFM Rock Radio. Salesman with IBM (UK) Ltd, 1983-87; formerly industrial relations officer with Ford Motor Co, 1979-83. B Sep 9 1956; ed Sir William Borlase GS, Nottingham Univ. Mbr, Southampton City Cl, 1987. Chmn, Selsdon Gp, 1983-87; nat senr vice-chmn, Fed of Cons Students, 1980-81.
Alan Banton, blood transfusion driver/clerk; mbr, Basildon DC, 1987- . B Oct 13 1948; ed sec sch. TGWU.

TIVERTON						No change
Electorate % Turnout	71,024	83.0%	1992	68,210	79.7%	1987
Browning, Mrs A F (C)	30,376	51.5%	-3.4%	29,875	54.9%	C
Cox, D N (LD)	19,287	32.7%	-5.3%	20,663	38.0%	L/All
Gibb, Ms S (Lab)	5,950	10.1%	+3.8%	3,400	6.3%	Lab
Morrish, D (Lib)	2,225	3.8%		434	0.8%	LO
Foggitt, P J (Grn)	1,007	1.7%				
Rhodes, B (NLP)	96	0.2%				
LD to C swing 0.9%	58,941		18.8%	54,372		16.9%
		C maj	11,089		C maj	9,212

Angela Browning retained the seat for the Cons in 1992; contested Crewe and Nantwich 1987. Management consultant specialising in training, communications and finance and a director of the Small Business Bureau. Mbr employment dept advisory cmte on women's employment, 1989-92. Nat chmn Women into Business. Former chmn Western Area CPC and former mbr Nat Advisory Cmte of CPC. Mbr, Nat Autistic Society; Thomas Hardy Society. B Dec 4 1946; ed Reading and Bournemouth Colls of Technology. Speaker for Peace through Nato. Fellow, Inst of Sales and Marketing Management.

David Cox, Post Office manager; mbr, Teignmouth TC, 1985-91. B May 21 1963; ed St Cutbert Mayne RC Sch; S Devon Coll of Advanced Tech. Sec, Teignmouth (Amalgamated) branch, UCW.
Susan Gibb, library asst at Exeter Univ; mbr, Tiverton TC, 1979-83. B Mar 4 1938; ed Manchester Univ. Nalgo: branch steward, 1985-89; delegate, Tiverton Trades Cl, 1985- . Mbr, Campaign for Advancement of State Ed.
Philip Foggitt, wholefood shop proprietor; mbr, East Devon DC, 1991- . B Aug 18 1952; ed London Univ; Oxford Poly.

TONBRIDGE AND MALLING						No change
Electorate % Turnout	77,292	82.7%	1992	76,797	77.8%	1987
*Stanley, Sir John (C)	36,542	57.2%	+0.3%	33,990	56.9%	C
Roberts, P D (LD)	14,984	23.5%	-6.0%	17,561	29.4%	SDP/All
O'Neill, Mrs M A (Lab)	11,533	18.1%	+5.0%	7,803	13.1%	Lab
Tidy, J (Grn)	612	1.0%		369	0.6%	BN
Hovarth, Mrs J (NLP)	221	0.3%				
LD to C swing 3.1%	63,892		33.7%	59,723		27.5%
		C maj	21,558		C maj	16,429

Sir John Stanley was Minr of State for N Ireland, 1987-88; and for Armed Forces, MoD, 1983-87; Minr for Housing and Construction, with rank of Minr of State at the DoE, 1979-83; PPS to Mrs Thatcher, 1976-79. PC 1984. Director, Conder Gp plc, 1989- ; Henderson Highland Trust plc, 1990- ; the Latin American Capital Fund Ltd; consultant to Metrolands Investments Ltd; Fidelity Investment Management Ltd; former financial executive with RTZ plc. Elected in Feb 1974; contested Newton, 1970. B Jan 19 1942; ed Repton; Lincoln Coll, Oxford. Trustee, Action Aid, 1989- .

Paul Roberts, sales and marketing manager with Kimberley-Clark Ltd; qualified accountant. Contested Bedfordshire in 1979 Euro elections. Mbr, Tonbridge and Malling BC, 1982- ; Wateringbury PC, 1982-91. B Jul 28 1947; ed Sevenoaks Sch; Aston Univ. Life master at bridge.
Margaret O'Neill, journalist; held various local pty offices and on cmtes. Sch governor. B Jun 21 1948; ed Howbury Grange Sch, Erith; Erith Coll of Tech. GMB.
Jim Tidy, who describes himself as a self-educated peasant, contested Kent West in 1989 Euro elections. B Dec 3 1922. Parish cllr. Usdaw.

TOOTING				No change		
Electorate % Turnout	68,306	74.8%	1992	68,116	71.2%	1987
*Cox, T M (Lab)	24,601	48.2%	+3.9%	21,457	44.2%	Lab
Winters, M A S (C)	20,494	40.1%	-1.1%	20,016	41.3%	C
Bunce, R J (LD)	3,776	7.4%	-5.8%	6,423	13.2%	SDP/All
Martin, Ms C (Lib)	1,340	2.6%		621	1.3%	Grn
Owens, P J (Grn)	694	1.4%	+0.1%			
Anklesalria, F (NLP)	119	0.2%				
Whitelaw, M (CD)	64	0.1%				
C to Lab swing 2.5%	51,088		8.0%	48,517		3.0%
		Lab maj	4,107		Lab maj	1,441

Thomas Cox was elected for this seat in 1983; MP for Wandsworth, Tooting Feb 1974-83 and for Wandsworth Central 1970-4; contested Stroud, 1966. Asst govt whip 1974-7; Lord Commissioner of the Treasury (whip) 1977-9. Delegate to Cl of Europe and WEU, 1985- . Jt vice-chmn 1987-91, and treas, 1991- , British gp IPU; chmn British Sengalese gp; vice-chmn Cameroon and Cyprus gps; jt vice-chmn, Kashmir, Nepalese, Pakistan and Togo gps. Jt vice-chmn, all-pty Order of St John gp; sec Limbless British Ex-Servicemen's Assocn gp. B 1930; ed state schools and LSE. Electrician. Former alderman, Fulham BC. Sponsored by EETPU.

Martin Winter, snr venture capital partner in London firm of solicitors, contested this seat 1987. Former chmn Tooting Cons assocn. Mbr, Wandsworth CHC, 1985-90; bd of management, Tooting youth project, 1986-88. Formerly with Waterloo legal advice service and Asian centre legal surgery, Wandsworth. B Apr 13 1954; ed Charterhouse; St Edmund Hall, Oxford.

Bob Bunce is a proof reader. Chmn Battersea and Tooting local pty. B Dec 19 1958; ed Sir Walter St John's Sch, Battersea; Queen Mary Coll, London; Central London Poly. Orthodox Christian.

Paul Owens, economic development officer. B Nov 9 1963; ed Sir Walter St Johns Sch, Battersea; South Bank and Middlesex Polys.

TORBAY				No change		
Electorate % Turnout	71,171	80.6%	1992	70,435	76.3%	1987
*Allason, R W S (C)	28,624	49.9%	-4.1%	29,029	54.0%	C
Sanders, A M (LD)	22,837	39.8%	+2.2%	20,209	37.6%	L/All
Truscott, P (Lab)	5,503	9.6%	+1.2%	4,538	8.4%	Lab
Jones, R (NF)	268	0.5%				
Thomas, Ms A (NLP)	157	0.3%				
C to LD swing 3.2%	57,389		10.1%	53,776		16.4%
		C maj	5,787		C maj	8,820

Mr Rupert Allason, as author writing as Nigel West principally about espionage, was elected in 1987; contested Battersea, 1983, and Kettering, 1979. Underwriting mbr of Lloyd's. European Editor of *Intelligence Quarterly* since 1985; and director of Westintel (Research) Ltd. Chmn all-pty British-Bermuda gp, 1989- . B Nov 8 1951; ed Downside Sch, Bath; Grenoble and London Univs. Mbr advisory bd, US National Intelligence Study Centre. Special constable, 1975-82. Worked for BBC television, 1978-82. NUJ.

Adrian Sanders, local govt researcher; political sec, Devon and Cornwall Reg Lib Pty, 1983-84; NLYL vice-pres, 1987; mbr, Torbay BC, 1984-86. B Apr 25 1959; ed Torquay Boys' GS.

Paul Truscott, team ldr, single homeless accommodation project in Essex; mbr, Colchester BC, 1988- . B Mar 20 1959; ed Newton Abbot GS; Exeter Coll; Oxford Univ. TGWU.

TORFAEN				No change		
Electorate % Turnout	61,104	77.5%	1992	59,896	75.6%	1987
*Murphy, P P (Lab)	30,352	64.1%	+5.4%	26,577	58.7%	Lab
Watkins, M C (C)	9,598	20.3%	+1.2%	9,027	19.9%	L/All
Hewson, M G (LD)	6,178	13.1%	-6.9%	8,632	19.1%	C
Cox, Dr J (Green/PC)	1,210	2.6%		577	1.3%	PC
				450	1.0%	Grn
C to Lab swing 2.1%	47,338		43.8%	45,263		38.8%
		Lab maj	20,754		Lab maj	17,550

Paul Murphy was elected in 1987; contested Wells, 1979. An Opposn spokesman on Wales 1988- . Mbr select cmte on Welsh affairs, 1987-9. Parly consultant to NATFHE. Jt sec, all-pty Franco-British Parly Relations Cmte. B Nov 25 1948; ed St Francis RC Primary Sch, Abersychan; West Monmouth Sch, Pontypool; Oriel Coll, Oxford. Lecturer in history and government at Ebbw Vale CFE, 1971-87; mbr, Torfaen BC, 1973-87 (chmn finance cmte, 1976-86).

Torfaen CLP sec, 1972-87. Sponsored by TGWU.

Mark Watkins, management consultant. Chmn, Torfaen YCs, 1979-82. B Jul 27 1961; ed West Monmouth Boys' GS; Univ Coll, Cardiff.

Malcolm Hewson, snr computing systems analyst; L/All agent for this seat 1987; Welsh LD spokesman. B Dec 31 1958; ed Leeds Univ. Society of Telecom Executives.

TOTTENHAM						No change
Electorate % Turnout	68,319	65.6%	1992	76,092	66.1%	1987
*Grant, B (Lab)	25,309	56.5%	+12.9%	21,921	43.6%	Lab
Charalambous, A L (C)	13,341	29.8%	-5.6%	17,780	35.4%	C
L'Estrange, A (LD)	5,120	11.4%	-6.4%	8,983	17.9%	L/All
Budge, P (Grn)	903	2.0%	+0.5%	744	1.5%	Grn
Obomanu, Ms M (NLP)	150	0.3%		638	1.3%	Ind Lab
				205	0.4%	WRP
C to Lab swing 9.2%	44,823	26.7%		50,271		8.2%
		Lab maj	11,968		Lab maj	4,141

Bernie Grant was elected in 1987 and in 1988 became jt vice-chmn, PLP home affairs cmte; chmn, Campaign Gp of Lab MPs, 1991- ; Standing Conference on Racial Equality in Europe, 1990- ; jt vice-pres, all-pty race and community parly gp; jt vice-chmn, all-pty British-Caribbean parly gp, 1989- . Chmn and founder mbr, parly Black Caucus, 1988- ; launched 'Black Parliamentarian' magazine, 1990, and is editor. Ldr of Haringey Cl, 1985-87; dep ldr, 1982-83; elected to cl, 1978. Strong supporter of black sections in Labour Party; development worker, Black Trade Unionists Solidarity Movement, 1983-4; mbr, nat exec cmte, Anti-Apartheid Movement, 1987- . B Feb 17 1944 in Georgetown, Guyana; emigrated to UK 1963; ed St Stanislaus Coll, Georgetown; Tottenham Tech Coll; Heriot Watt univ, Edinburgh. Former analyst, British Rail clerk,

telephonist and Nupe area officer. Newham senior district housing officer (community relations), 1985-7. Nupe.
Andrew Charalambous, barrister; partner, London and Metropolitan Finance, business consultants and corporate finance firm. B Mar 12 1967; ed Wm Forster Sch, Tottenham; Southgate Tech Coll; Queen Mary Coll, London univ; Inns of Court Sch of Law. Treas, Green Lanes ward, Haringey Cons Assocn.
Alex L'Estrange, retired; mature student on computer studies. Contested this seat for L/All 1983 when clerical officer with London shipbrokers. Chmn, Tottenham LDs. Mbr, Haringey BC, 1986-90. B Oct 21 1929; ed Collyer sch, Horsham; Sir John Cass coll, Whitechapel.
Peter Budge, accountant. B Jun 8 1942; ed Reed's Sch. Mbr, Musicians' Union.

TRURO						No change
Electorate % Turnout	75,101	82.4%	1992	72,432	79.9%	1987
*Taylor, M O J (LD)	31,230	50.5%	+1.5%	28,368	49.0%	L/All
St Aubyn, N F (C)	23,660	38.3%	-2.6%	23,615	40.8%	C
Geach, J (Lab)	6,078	9.8%	-0.3%	5,882	10.2%	Lab
Keating, L M (Grn)	569	0.9%				
Tankard, C (Lib)	208	0.3%				
Hartley, Ms M (NLP)	108	0.2%				
C to LD swing 2.0%	61,853	12.2%		57,865		8.2%
		LD maj	7,570		L/All maj	4,753

Matthew Taylor, who won this seat at the 1987 by-election, became LD spokesman on ed in 1990; spokesman on trade and industry, 1989-90; spokesman on England, covering local govt, housing and transport, 1988-9; Lib then LD spokesman on energy, 1987-8. Chmn, LD communications cmte, 1989- ; jt vice-chmn, all-pty parly youth affairs lobby. From 1986-7 was economic policy researcher for the Parly Lib pty and research assistant to the late David Penhaligan, MP for the seat 1974-86. B Jan 3 1963; ed St Paul's sch, Truro; Treliske sch, Truro; Univ Coll Sch,

London; Lady Margaret Hall, Oxford.
Nicholas St Aubyn contested this seat 1987 and by-election earlierin 1987. Mbr, Westminster City Cl, 1982-86. Chmn of small Cornish manufacturing company. B 1955; ed Eton and Trinity Coll, Oxford.
Jim Geach works in spray dept of Compair Maxam; mbr, Cornwall CC. B Feb 20 1951; ed Penwethers Truro SM Sch. AEU.
Liam Keating, horticulturist; sec, Truro Grn Pty. B Dec 15 1953; ed St Francis Xaviers GS, Liverpool.

TUNBRIDGE WELLS						No change
Electorate % Turnout	76,808	78.1%	1992	76,291	74.3%	1987
*Mayhew, Sir Patrick (C)	34,162	56.9%	-1.5%	33,111	58.4%	C
Clayton, A (LD)	17,030	28.4%	-1.6%	16,989	30.0%	L/All
Goodman, E (Lab)	8,300	13.8%	+2.3%	6,555	11.6%	Lab
Fenna, E (NLP)	267	0.4%				
Edey, R (ISS)	236	0.4%				
LD to C swing 0.0%	59,995	28.6%		56,655		28.5%
		C maj	17,132		C maj	16,122

Sir Patrick Mayhew, QC, was appointed Northern Ireland secretary, 1992; Attorney General 1987-92; Solicitor General, 1983-87; Minister of State, Home Office, 1981-83; junior employment minister, 1979-81. PC 1986. Mbr, privileges cmte since 1989. Elected in Feb 1974; fought Dulwich, Camberwell, 1970. Commissioner of Church of England. B Sep 11 1929; ed Tonbridge sch; Balliol coll, Oxford (Pres of Union, 1952). Mbr, exec, 1922 Cmte, 1976-9, and jt vice-chmn, Cons back-bench home affairs

cmte, 1976-9.
Tony Clayton, management consultant and industrial economist; mbr, Sevenoaks DC, 1987- ; Sevenoaks TC, 1987-; LD science policy gp. B Feb 4 1949; ed Sussex univ.
Ted Goodman, solicitor with business interests in forestry and company secretarial work. Mbr, Reigate and Banstead BC, 1990- . B Oct 26 1945; ed Kingston GS; N London Poly. Apex/GMB.

TWEEDDALE, ETTRICK AND LAUDERDALE						No change
Electorate % Turnout	39,493	78.0%	1992	37,875	77.2%	1987
*Steel, Sir David (LD)	12,296	39.9%	-10.0%	14,599	49.9%	L/All
Beat, L A (C)	9,776	31.7%	+2.1%	8,657	29.6%	C
Creech, Mrs C (SNP)	5,244	17.0%	+7.9%	3,320	11.4%	Lab
Dunton, E A (Lab)	3,328	10.8%	-0.6%	2,660	9.1%	SNP
Hein, J (Lib)	177	0.6%				
LD to C swing 6.1%	30,821		8.2%	29,236		20.3%
		LD maj	2,520		L/All maj	5,942

Sir David Steel was Ldr of Lib Party, 1976-88, when party merged with majority of SDP members to form Social and Liberal Democratic Pty - the Liberal Democrats; interim jt ldr, LDs, 1988. PC 1977. Convenor of LD foreign affairs team, 1988- ; spokesman on foreign affairs and overseas development, 1989- ; Lib chief whip, 1970-4. Director, Border Television, 1991- ; Lamancha Productions Ltd, 1991- ; journalist and broadcaster. Jt chmn, all-pty release of hostages parly gp. Elected for this seat 1983, being LD MP from 1988; MP for Roxburgh, Selkirk and Peebles, 1965-83; contested that seat, 1964. Sponsored Abortion Act, 1967. B Mar 31 1938 in Scotland; ed Prince of Wales Sch, Nairobi; George Watson's Coll, Edinburgh; Edinburgh univ. Vice-pres, Liberal International, 1978- .

Lloyd Beat, investment manager, UK equities, Edinburgh Fund Managers plc; mbr, exec cmte, Edinburgh S Cons Assocn, 1987- . Investment analyst, British Investment Trust plc, 1987-9 (merged with EFM 1988); with Standard Chartered Bank plc, 1986-87. Chmn, Scottish FCS, 1984-5; mbr, nat union exec cmte, 1985-6. B Mar 11 1964; ed Dundee univ.
Christine Creech, solicitor and former teacher. B Sep 9 1944; ed Edinburgh univ; Moray House.
Alan Dunton, teacher, social worker, criminologist and youth worker. Mbr, cl, Rotary International. Former branch chmn, CLP sec, agent; on Euro constituency exec. B Sep 23 1941; ed Hemel Hemstead GS; Hull Inst of Ed; London univ. GMB.

TWICKENHAM						No change
Electorate % Turnout	63,072	84.3%	1992	64,661	81.5%	1987
*Jessel, T F H (C)	26,804	50.4%	-1.4%	27,331	51.9%	C
Cable, Dr J V (LD)	21,093	39.7%	+1.3%	20,204	38.3%	L/All
Gold, Dr M D (Lab)	4,919	9.3%	+0.9%	4,415	8.4%	Lab
Gill, G (NLP)	152	0.3%		746	1.4%	Grn
Griffith, D (DLC)	103	0.2%				
Miners, A (Lib)	85	0.2%				
C to LD swing 1.4%	53,156		10.7%	52,696		13.5%
		C maj	5,711		C maj	7,127

Toby Jessel was elected in 1970; contested Hull N at by-election and general election, 1966, and Peckham, 1964. Mbr, Cl of Europe and WEU, since 1976; exec and organizing cmtes, European Music Year, 1985; Liveryman, Worshipful Company of Musicians. Chmn (1983- and jt vice-chmn (1979-82), Cons back-bench arts and heritage cmte; mbr, advisory cmte on Commons works of art, 1988- ; chmn, all-pty Anglo-Belgian parly gp; chmn (1991-) and jt vice-chmn (1987-91), Indo-British gp; jt sec, defence heritage gp; treas, Chilean gp, 1991- . B Jul 11 1934; ed RNC Dartmouth; Balliol Coll, Oxford.
Vincent Cable, snr economist, Shell International Oil Co, contested York 1987 and 1983; Glasgow, Hillhead for

Lab, 1970. Mbr, LD economics and environment policy panel. Previously adviser to Commonwealth Sec-General; dep director, Overseas Development Inst; special adviser to John Smith, when Sec of State for Trade. B May 9 1943; ed Nunthorpe GS, York; Trinity Coll, Cambridge (Pres of Union). Mbr, Glasgow City Cl, 1971-74. Former qualified pilot.
Michael Gold, snr lecturer at Central London Poly, contested Richmond and Barnes 1987. Chmn, London W Euro CLP; on regional exec, Gtr London Lab Pty, 1988-91; former chmn and sec, Richmond and Barnes CLP. B Mar 23 1953; ed state schs in St Albans and Reading; St Peter's Coll, Oxford; Edinburgh univ. NUJ/NATFHE.

TYNE BRIDGE						No change
Electorate % Turnout	53,079	62.6%	1992	58,152	63.1%	1987
*Clelland, D G (Lab)	22,328	67.2%	+4.1%	23,131	63.0%	Lab
Liddell-Grainger, C (C)	7,118	21.4%	+0.8%	7,558	20.6%	C
Burt, J (LD)	3,804	11.4%	-4.9%	6,005	16.4%	SDP/All
C to Lab swing 1.7%	33,250		45.7%	36,694		42.4%
		Lab maj	15,210		Lab maj	15,573

David Clelland was elected at 1985 by-election. Mbr, Select Cmte on Energy, 1989; Select Cmte on Home Affairs, 1985-9; Select Cmte on Parliamentary Commissioner for Administration, 1985-7. Chmn (1990-) and jt vice-chmn (1988-90), PLP environment cmte; hon sec and hon treas (1990-) and campaign officer (1989-), Northern gp of Lab MPs. Jt vice-chmn, tertiary colleges association parly gp; jt sec, British-Pakistan parly gp; exec mbr, all-pty clubs gp. B Jun 27 1943; ed Kelvin Grove Boys' sch, Gateshead;

Gateshead and Hebburn Tech colls. Electrical tester, 1964-81. Mbr, Gateshead BC, 1972-86. Mbr since 1963 of and sponsored by AEU.
Charles Liddell-Grainger, self-employed accountant, business consultant, and company director. Has served on Norwood Cons cmtes. B 1960; ed Millfield, Somerset; Central London poly.
John Burt, tree surgeon; Newcastle LD campaigns officer. B Jan 1 1962; ed Chesterfield Sch; Newcastle univ.

TYNEMOUTH						No change
Electorate % Turnout	74,955	80.4%	1992	74,407	78.1%	1987
*Trotter, N G (C)	27,731	46.0%	+2.8%	25,113	43.2%	C
Cosgrove, P (Lab)	27,134	45.0%	+6.2%	22,530	38.8%	Lab
Selby, P J S (LD)	4,855	8.1%	-9.9%	10,446	18.0%	L/All
Buchanan-Smith, A (Grn)	543	0.9%				
C to Lab swing 1.7%	60,263		1.0%	58,089		4.4%
			C maj 597			C maj 2,583

Neville Trotter, chartered accountant, has been mbr select cmte on transport since 1983. Director William Baird plc and subsidiary, Darchem Ltd; Romag Holdings plc; consultant with Grant Thornton; Bowring Gp and Go Ahead Northern; parly adviser to British marine equipment cl and British transport police fed. Chmn all-pty prevention of solvent abuse parly gp. Sponsored private bills on consumer safety, licensing amendment, and intoxicating substances supply (glue sniffing). Elected in Feb 1974; contested Consett 1970. B Jan 27 1932; Mbr Newcastle city cl 1963-74; Tyne and Wear MBC 1973-4. Mbr cl British maritime league; US naval inst. Freeman City of London; mbr worshipful co of chartered accountants. Ed Shrewsbury sch; King's coll, Durham.

Patrick Cosgrove, barrister and former teacher, contested this seat 1987, 1983 and 1979. Cllr Whitley Bay, then mbr North Tyneside cl, 1970- . B Apr 29 1947; ed St Cuthbert's GS, Newcastle; Leeds univ. TGWU.

Philip Selby, teacher, is former chmn Tynemouth LDs and northern counties YLs. B Jul 21 1947; ed Audenshaw GS; London and Newcastle upon Tyne univs. NUT.

Andrew Buchanan-Smith, solicitor. B Feb 10 1964; ed Forest sch, east London; Durham univ (pres univ SDP); Newcastle poly. MSF.

ULSTER MID						No change
Electorate % Turnout	69,071	79.3%	1992	67,256	77.4%	1987
*McCrea, Rev R T W (DUP)	23,181	42.3%	-1.8%	23,004	44.2%	DUP
Haughey, P D (SDLP)	16,994	31.0%	+4.8%	13,644	26.2%	SDLP
McElduff, B (SF)	10,248	18.7%	-5.2%	12,449	23.9%	SF
McLoughlin, J (Ind)	1,996	3.6%		1,846	3.5%	All
Gormley, Ms A (All)	1,506	2.8%	-0.8%	1,133	2.2%	WP
Hutchinson, H (LTU)	389	0.7%				
Owens, T (WP)	285	0.5%	-1.7%			
Anderson, J (NLP)	164	0.3%				
DUP to SDLP swing 3.3%	54,763		11.3%	52,076		18.0%
			DUP maj 6,187			DUP maj 9,360

Rev William McCrea, a minister of the Free Presbyterian Church of Ulster since 1967, was elected in 1983; resigned seat in 1985 in protest at Anglo-Irish agreement and retained it at 1986 by-election. Mbr Mid Ulster, N Ireland assembly 1982-6. Gospel recording artist; director Daybreak Recording Co. Received hon doctorate of divinity degree. B Aug 6 1948; ed Cookstown GS; theological coll, Free Presbyterian Church of Ulster. Mbr Magherafelt DC 1973- (chmn 1977-81).

Denis Haughey, former teacher now agent for pty ldr, John Hume, contested this seat 1987. B Oct 3 1944. Chmn SDLP 1973-8; exec mbr SDLP when formed in 1970 and international sec in 1978. Contested Fermanagh and South Tyrone Feb 1974 and Mid Ulster 1983. Ed St Patrick's coll, Omagh; Queen's univ, Belfast.

Barry McElduff, SF speaker on rural development and agriculture.

Ann Gormley, dental therapist; sec Alliance pty 1984 and 1989; sec women's issues gp. B Jul 1 1954; ed Convent GS, Omagh; New Cross hospital, London. MSF.

UPMINSTER						No change
Electorate % Turnout	64,138	80.5%	1992	66,613	75.2%	1987
*Bonsor, Sir Nicholas (C)	28,791	55.8%	+0.0%	27,946	55.8%	C
Ward, T (Lab)	14,970	29.0%	+6.9%	11,089	22.1%	SDP/All
Hurlstone, T (LD)	7,848	15.2%	-6.9%	11,069	22.1%	Lab
C to Lab swing 3.5%	51,609		26.8%	50,104		33.6%
			C maj 13,821			C maj 16,857

Sir Nicholas Bonsor, barrister, farmer, mbr of Lloyd's, and external mbr cl of Lloyd's of London, since 1987. Won this seat in 1983; MP for Nantwich 1979-83; fought Newcastle-under-Lyme Feb and Oct 1974. Chmn 1990- and vice-chmn 1987-90, standing cl of the baronetage. Chmn cyclotron trust for cancer treatment 1984- ; British field sports society 1988- ; Food Hygiene Bureau Ltd 1987- ; Cellar Solutions Ltd. B Dec 9 1942; ed Eton; Keble coll, Oxford. Mbr jt select cmte on consolidation bills; select cmte on Cardiff Bay barrage bill 1991- ; unopposed bills panel. Jt vice-chmn Cons backbench defence cmte 1987-90; trustee Baronets' trust 1986- ; Verdin trust for mentally handicapped, 1983- . Mbr royal yacht squadron. FRSA.

Terry Ward, teacher, chaired Brentwood and Ongar CLP, 1987-9. Pres Essex division NUT 1986-7; Brentwood NUT 1983 and 1990. B Mar 23 1947; ed Chase Cross sec sch; Co-op coll, Loughborough; York univ; inst of ed, London univ.

Terry Hurlstone, teacher; chmn Havering LDs. Contested Romford twice 1974. Chmn international autistic research organisation; director autism research. B Sep 20 1939; ed Hendon GS; Brentwood coll of ed.

UPPER BANN						No change
Electorate % Turnout	67,446	67.4%	1992	64,540	65.6%	1987
*Trimble, D (UU)	26,824	59.0%	-2.5%	26,037	61.5%	UU
Rodgers, Mrs B (SDLP)	10,661	23.4%	+2.9%	8,676	20.5%	SDLP
Curran, B P (SF)	2,777	6.1%	-1.3%	3,126	7.4%	SF
Ramsey, Dr W (All)	2,541	5.6%	-0.3%	2,487	5.9%	All
Jones, Mrs C (C)	1,556	3.4%	2,004	4.7%	WP	
French, T (WP)	1,120	2.5%	-2.3%			
UU to SDLP swing 2.7%	45,479		35.5%	42,330		41.0%
		UU maj	16,163		UU maj	17,361

David Trimble, non-practising mbr of the Bar of Northern Ireland, was elected at the by-election in 1990. Mbr N Ireland constitutional convention 1975-6. Senior lecturer faculty of law, Queen's univ, Belfast. B Oct 15 1944; ed Bangor GS; Queen's univ, Belfast.
Brid Rodgers contested this seat in 1990 by-election and 1987. Chmn SDLP 1978; pty gen sec 1981-3. Mbr Irish Republic senate 1983-6; Craigavon BC, 1985- .

Brendan Curran, mbr Craigavon cl.
William Ramsey, retired general practitioner, contested 1990 by-election; Armagh 1979. Mbr Craigavon cl 1973-85 and 1989- . Chmn Craigavon All assocn. B Sep 4 1930; ed Colerain acad inst; Queen's univ, Belfast.
Colette Jones, founder mbr Upper Bann Cons assocn, contested 1990 by-election. B 1946; ed Lisburn GS.
Details of 1990 by-election on page 287.

UXBRIDGE						No change
Electorate % Turnout	61,744	78.9%	1992	63,157	76.5%	1987
*Shersby, J M (C)	27,487	56.4%	-0.0%	27,292	56.5%	C
Evans, R J E (Lab)	14,308	29.4%	+5.9%	11,323	23.4%	Lab
Carey, S J (LD)	5,900	12.1%	-6.8%	9,164	19.0%	SDP/All
Flindall, I E (Grn)	538	1.1%	-0.0%	549	1.1%	Grn
O'Rourke, M (BNP)	350	0.7%				
Deans, A (NLP)	120	0.2%				
C to Lab swing 3.0%	48,703		27.1%	48,328		33.0%
		C maj	13,179		C maj	15,969

Michael Shersby became parly adviser to police fed of England and Wales in 1989. Mbr PAC and chairmen's panel 1983- ; chmn Cons backbench food and drinks sub-cmte 1979-89. Elected as MP for Hillingdon, Uxbridge, in 1972 by-election. Mbr exec cmte UK branch, CPA 1988- ; chmn all-pty British-Falkland Islands parly gp. Parly adviser to the sugar bureau 1988- (director general 1977-88 and a director 1966-72); vice-pres Corporation of Finance Brokers Ltd. B Feb 17 1933; ed John Lyon sch, Harrow-on-the-Hill. Pres London Green Belt cl 1989- . Trustee Harefield heart transplant trust 1989- . Director (unpaid) world sugar research organization; director Cadogan Management Ltd 1988- . Mbr Court, Brunel univ 1975- ; Paddington BC 1959-64; Westminster city cl 1964-71; dep Lord Mayor 1967-8.

Robert Evans, primary sch head teacher, contested Berkshire E 1987; London S and Surrey E in 1989 Euro elections. Former chmn Chertsey and Walton CLP (vice-chmn 1986-9); sec Hounslow SEA; mbr Croydon Co-op pty. B Oct 23 1956; ed cty sch, Ashford, Middlesex; London univ inst of ed; Shoreditch coll of ed. NUT (pres Leatherhead NUT 1983-5); GMB.
Steve Carey, govt relations consultant, chmn City LDs. Mbr Hillingdon BC 1986-90. B Mar 3 1955; ed Uxbridge coll; Salvatorian coll, Harrow.
Ian Flindall, energy conservation technician and partner in Chalkline Energy, contested this seat 1987 and Slough 1983. Mbr Hillingdon ecology forum 1989-90. B Oct 19 1952; ed Vyners GS; London univ.

VALE OF GLAMORGAN						No change from 1987
Electorate % Turnout	66,672	81.9%	1992	65,310	79.3%	1987
Sweeney, W E (C)	24,220	44.3%	-2.4%	24,229	46.8%	C
*Smith, J W P (Lab)	24,201	44.3%	+9.6%	17,978	34.7%	Lab
Davies, K (LD)	5,045	9.2%	-7.4%	8,633	16.7%	SDP/All
Haswell, D (PC)	1,160	2.1%	+0.3%	946	1.8%	PC
C to Lab swing 6.0%	54,626		0.0%	51,786		12.1%
		C maj	19		C maj	6,251

Walter Sweeney, solicitor and former law lecturer, regained this seat, lost by Cons at 1989 by-election. Contested Stretford 1983. Consultant with firm of solicitors. Mbr Rugby BC 1976-9; Vale of Glamorgan CHC; former mbr Bedfordshire CC. B Apr 23 1949; ed Lawrence Sheriff sch, Rugby; Darwin coll, Cambridge; Hull univ. Life mbr Cambridge univ Cons assocn. Former divisional chmn Rugby YCs and vice-chmn Rugby Cons assocn. Former chmn Rugby CPC, Hull univ FCS. Mbr law society.
John P Smith, senior lecturer in business studies, gained this seat for Labour at 1989 by-election; contested seat

1987. Mbr select cmte on broadcasting 1991-2; select cmte on Welsh affairs 1990-2; vice-chmn Welsh gp of Lab MPs 1991-2. Mbr Vale of Glamorgan BC (ldr Lab gp). B Mar 17 1951; ed Penarth cty sch; Gwent coll of higher ed; UCW Cardiff. Former mbr RAF, joiner, mature student, , univ tutor. Mbr WEA, anti-apartheid, AUT. Sponsored by MSF.
Keith Davies, fitter; mbr Neath BC 1985- . B Jul 24 1946.
David Haswell, teacher; constuency chmn. B Jan 6 1962; ed univ coll Cardiff; univ coll Swansea. NUT.
Details of 1989 by-election on page 287

VAUXHALL				**No change**		
Electorate % Turnout	62,473	62.4%	1992	66,538	64.0%	1987
*Hoey, Ms K (Lab)	21,328	54.7%	+4.6%	21,364	50.2%	Lab
Gentry, B A R (C)	10,840	27.8%	-1.2%	12,345	29.0%	C
Tuffrey, M W (LD)	5,678	14.6%	-3.7%	7,764	18.2%	SDP/All
Shepherd, Ms P A (Grn)	803	2.1%	+0.3%	770	1.8%	Grn
Khan, A (DOS)	156	0.4%		223	0.5%	Comm
Hill, Ms S (Rev Comm)	152	0.4%		117	0.3%	RF
C to Lab swing 2.9%	38,957		26.9%	42,583		21.2%
		Lab maj	10,488		Lab maj	9,019

Kate Hoey won the by-election in 1989 following the resignation of Stuart Holland; contested Dulwich in 1987. Joined select cmte on broadcasting in 1991; sec all-pty child abduction parly gp 1991- . Mbr advisory bd London Weekend Television. Former N Ireland athlete; educational adviser to London First Division football clubs 1985-9. Lecturer Southwark coll 1972-6; snr lecturer Kingsway Coll 1976-85. B Jun 21 1948; ed Lylehill primary sch; Belfast royal acad; Ulster coll of physical ed; City of London coll.
Bernard Gentry, London Underground booking clerk, was agent for this seat 1987; chmn Vauxhall Cons assocn 1988- ; vice-chmn Gtr London area CTU; London South Inner Euro constituency. B Dec 6 1959; ed Clapham coll. TSSA.
Michael Tuffrey, chartered accountant, contested 1989 by-election and Streatham 1987. Mbr Lambeth BC, 1990- . Chmn LD inner cities policy working gp. Freelance community affairs and charity consultant. B Sep 30 1959; ed Douai sch, nr Reading; Durham univ.
Penny Shepherd, computer consultant, contested London South Inner in 1989 Euro elections. Co-convenor Grn pty migration policy working gp 1989- . Mbr 300 Gp. B Jan 25 1954; ed St Anne's Convent sch, Southampton; Liverpool univ.
Details of 1989 by-election on page 287

WAKEFIELD				**No change**		
Electorate % Turnout	69,794	76.3%	1992	69,580	75.6%	1987
*Hinchliffe, D M (Lab)	26,964	50.6%	+4.0%	24,509	46.6%	Lab
Fanthorpe, D (C)	20,374	38.3%	-3.0%	21,720	41.3%	C
Wright, T J (LD)	5,900	11.1%	-1.0%	6,350	12.1%	SDP/All
C to Lab swing 3.5%	53,238		12.4%	52,579		5.3%
		Lab maj	6,590		Lab maj	2,789

David Hinchliffe joined Select Cmte on Health in 1991; jt vice-chmn PLP social security cmte 1990-1; all-pty personal social services parly panel; vice-chmn PLP health and personal social services cmte 1990- . Social work tutor Kirklees MBC 1980-7. Sec all-pty rugby league parly gp 1987- . Mbr Wakefield Met DC 1979- (Chmn employment and economic development cmtes); Wakefield health authority. B Oct 14 1948; ed Lawefield Lane primary sch, Wakefield; Cathedral sec mod sch, Wakefield; Leeds poly; Bradford univ. Social worker, Leeds 1968-79. Nupe.
David Fanthorpe, public affairs consultant; former dpty director Cons research dept; former mbr Wandsworth BC 1987-90. Vice-chmn Putney Cons assocn 1990- ; dpty chmn leisure and amenities cmte 1988-90. B Jul 23 1957; ed Nottingham HS; New coll Oxford.
Tim Wright, voluntary sector manager, contested Hull East 1987; mbr Humberside CC, 1985- (LD gp ldr 1989-); Beverley BC 1987-91. B Mar 22 1952; ed Hessle HS.

WALLASEY				**Lab gain**		
Electorate % Turnout	65,676	82.5%	1992	67,216	79.8%	1987
Eagle, Ms A (Lab)	26,531	49.0%	+7.0%	22,791	42.5%	C
*Chalker, Mrs L (C)	22,722	41.9%	-0.5%	22,512	41.9%	Lab
Thomas, N R L (LD)	4,177	7.7%	-7.9%	8,363	15.6%	SDP/All
Davis, Ms S (Grn)	650	1.2%				
Gay, G (NLP)	105	0.2%				
C to Lab swing 3.8%	54,185		7.0%	53,666		0.5%
		Lab maj	3,809		C maj	279

Angela Eagle, parliamentary liaison officer to the confederation of health service employees, won this seat for Labour in 1992. Employed by union since 1984, first as researcher and then as national press officer. Sponsored by union; mbr NUJ. Mbr trade union section Lab pty NEC women's cmte 1989- ; chmn nat conference of Lab women 1991. Mbr Labour's health forum; exec cmte socialist health association and Co-op pty. Sec Peckham CLP, 1989-91; mbr general cmte and chmn women's section. B Feb 17 1961; ed Formby HS; St John's coll, Oxford.
Lynda Chalker was Minr of overseas development, with rank of Minr of State for Foreign and Commonwealth Affairs 1989-92; in Dec 1990 given responsibilities covering Commonwealth and sub-Saharan Africa; Minr of State for Foreign and Commonwealth Affairs 1986-9; Minr of State for Transport 1983-6. PC 1987. Elected Feb 1974. B Apr 29 1942; ed Roedean; Heidelberg univ; Westfield coll, London univ.
Neil Thomas, sec and chief exec, charitable company providing vocational training. Contested Wallasey for L 1979 and Bebington and Ellesmere Port Oct 1974. Mbr Wallasey BC 1971-4; Wirral MBC 1973-9. B Jan 31 1934; ed Wallasey GS; Jesus coll, Cambridge.
Sally Davis, snr community occupational therapist in mental health; mbr British assocn of therapists; Oxfam 2000. B Jun 11 1963; ed St John's, York.

WALLSEND						No change
Electorate % Turnout	77,941	74.1%	1992	76,688	75.0%	1987
Byers, S J (Lab)	33,439	57.9%	+1.0%	32,709	56.8%	Lab
Gibbon, Miss M (C)	13,969	24.2%	+1.0%	13,325	23.2%	C
Huscroft, M J (LD)	10,369	17.9%	-2.1%	11,508	20.0%	SDP/All
C to Lab swing 0.0%	57,777		33.7%	57,542		33.7%
		Lab maj	19,470		Lab maj	19,384

Stephen Byers, senior lecturer in law, Newcastle Poly, contested Hexham in 1983. Elected to North Tyneside MBC in 1980; dep ldr of Cl, 1986- ; chmn, strategic planning and public services cmtes. Also chairs ed cmte of AMA and Cl of Local Ed Authorities. Leader, management panel of negotiating body for teachers and lecturers, the Nat Jt Cl for Further Ed. B Apr 13 1953; ed Chester CFE; Liverpool Poly. Nupe, 1984- ; NATFHE, 1975-84.
Mary Gibbon, teacher - head of business and information studies dept. Chmn, NE Area Cons ed advisory cmte, 1989-92. Chaired City of Durham Cons Assocn, 1986-90; branch chmn, City of Durham, 1982-86; CPC chmn, 1984-86. Parish cllr. B 1949; ed in Durham and Newcastle.
Mike Huscroft, insurance agent; mbr, Wallsend BC, 1969-74; North Tyneside MBC, 1973- (gp ldr, 1982-). B Jul 24 1943; ed St Columba's Tech Coll, Wallsend. Usdaw.

WALSALL NORTH						No change
Electorate % Turnout	69,604	75.0%	1992	68,331	73.8%	1987
*Winnick, D J (Lab)	24,387	46.7%	+4.2%	21,458	42.6%	Lab
Syms, R A R (C)	20,563	39.4%	+0.4%	19,668	39.0%	C
Powis, A (LD)	6,629	12.7%	-5.7%	9,285	18.4%	L/All
Reynolds, K (NF)	614	1.2%				
C to Lab swing 1.9%	52,193		7.3%	50,411		3.6%
		Lab maj	3,824		Lab maj	1,790

David Winnick,mbr, Select Cmte on Procedure, 1989- ; Treasury and Civil Service, 1987-89; Home Affairs, 1983-87; Environment, 1980-83. Jt vice-chmn, PLP foreign affairs cmte, 1985-87 and 1991- ; vice-chmn, W Midlands gp of Lab MPs, 1985- . Regained seat for Lab 1979; MP for Croydon S, 1966-70; contested Harwich 1964; Croydon Central, Oct 1974; Walsall, Nov 1976. B Jun 26 1933; ed sec schs; LSE. Chmn, Tribune Gp, 1984-85; chmn (unpaid), UK Immigrants Advisory Service, 1984-90. Mbr, Willesden Cl, 1959-64; Brent Cl, 1964-66. Vice-pres, Apex, 1983-88, and mbr, exec cl, 1978-88. GMB.
Robert Syms, director of family-owned building and plant hire gp; mbr, Wiltshire CC, 1985- ; Wessex RHA, 1988-90; N Wiltshire DC, 1983-87 (vice-chmn, 1984-87). Founder dir, N Wiltshire enterprise agency, 1986-89. Former chmn, N Wiltshire Cons Assocn. B Aug 15 1956; ed Colston's Sch, Bristol. Mbr, Bow Gp, British Atlantic Cmte, Peace through Nato.
Alan Powis, shop manager. LD spokesperson environmental health; secretary, Walsall LD. B Feb 26 1955; ed Darlaston Comp Sch; Sheffield Poly; Salford Univ.

WALSALL SOUTH						No change
Electorate % Turnout	65,642	76.3%	1992	66,746	75.5%	1987
*George, B T (Lab)	24,133	48.2%	+3.3%	22,629	44.9%	Lab
Jones, L (C)	20,955	41.9%	-0.8%	21,513	42.7%	C
Williams, G E (LD)	4,132	8.3%	-4.1%	6,241	12.4%	L/All
Clarke, R (Grn)	673	1.3%				
Oldbury, J (NLP)	167	0.3%				
C to Lab swing 2.1%	50,060		6.3%	50,383		2.2%
		Lab maj	3,178		Lab maj	1,116

Bruce George, mbr of Select Cmte on Defence since 1979, was elected in Feb 1974; contested Southport, 1970. Mbr, N Atlantic Assembly, 1982- , being rapporteur general of Political Cmte. Jt vice-chmn, defence heritage parly gp. Author and lecturer on defence and foreign policy subjects; editor, Jane's Nato Handbook. B Jun 1 1942; ed Mountain Ash GS; Univ Coll of Wales, Swansea; Warwick Univ. Visiting lecturer, Essex Univ, 1985-86; snr lecturer in politics, Birmingham Poly, 1970-74. Jt sec, all-pty social science and policy parly gp; British-Taiwan gp; treas, British-Nigerian gp; served on former Select Cmte on Violence in the Family; patron, Nat Assocn of Widows; vice-pres, Psoriasis Assocn; hon consultant, Confed of Long Distance Pigeon Racing Assocns; co-founder, sec and captain, House of Commons Football Club; pres, Walsall and District Gilbert and Sullivan Soc. Apex and NATFHE.
Laurence Jones, self-employed businessman, contested Warrington North 1987. Mbr, exec cl, Wirral S Cons Assocn. B 1948; ed Bebington Sec Sch; Wirral GS; Liverpool Poly.
Grant Williams, administrator; mbr, W Midlands LD regional exec; Walsall MBC, 1991- . Coordinator, Walsall NHS defence campaign, 1980- . B Apr 15 1965; ed Walton HS, Stafford; Wolverhampton Poly.

WALTHAMSTOW						Lab gain
Electorate % Turnout	49,140	72.3%	1992	48,691	72.4%	1987
Gerrard, N F (Lab)	16,251	45.7%	+11.0%	13,748	39.0%	C
*Summerson, H H F (C)	13,229	37.2%	-1.8%	12,236	34.7%	Lab
Leighton, P L (LD)	5,142	14.5%	-10.7%	8,852	25.1%	SDP/All
Lambert, J D (Grn)	594	1.7%		396	1.1%	DC
Wilkinson, V (Lib)	241	0.7%				
Planton, A (NLP)	94	0.3%				
C to Lab swing 6.4%	35,551		8.5%	35,232		4.3%
		Lab maj	3,022		C maj	1,512

Neil Gerrard, lecturer, won this seat in 1992; contested Chingford 1979. Mbr Waltham Forest BC 1973-90 (ldr Lab gp 1983-90; ldr of cl, 1986-90). Pty offices include CLP chmn, asst sec, and election agent. B Jul 3 1942; ed Manchester GS; Wadham Coll, Oxford. NATFHE (past branch membership sec and chmn).

Hugo Summerson was MP for this seat 1987-92; contested Barking 1983. Mbr select cmte on environment 1991-2. Mbr child abduction gp, 1991-2; sec Cons backbench agriculture, fisheries and food cmte, 1991-92; jt sec Cons back-ench urban and inner cities cmte 1989-91; treas, all-pty British-Latin-American gp, 1990-92. Chartered survey-or. Director, Palatine Properties, 1983- . B Jul 21 1950; ed Harrow; Royal Agricultural Coll.

Peter Leighton, barrister, contested this seat 1987 and 1983. Vice-chmn, LD Parly Candidates Assocn, 1990- ; London region LDs, 1988-90; mbr, coordinating cmte, England, 1989- . B Oct 16 1943; ed Leyton Cty HS; Univ Coll, London.

Jean Lambert is a teacher and leading Green pty speaker. Contested London NE in 1984 and 1989 Euro elections. Mbr Grn pty international cmte and Euro election cmte. B Jun 1 1950; ed Palmer's Girls GS, Grays, Essex; Univ Coll, Cardiff; St Paul's Coll, Cheltenham.

WANSBECK						No change
Electorate % Turnout	63,457	79.3%	1992	62,639	78.0%	1987
*Thompson, J (Lab)	30,046	59.7%	+2.2%	28,080	57.5%	Lab
Sanderson, H G H (C)	11,872	23.6%	+4.2%	11,291	23.1%	L/All
Priestley, B C (LD)	7,691	15.3%	-7.8%	9,490	19.4%	C
Best, N F (Grn)	710	1.4%				
Lab to C swing 1.0%	50,319		36.1%	48,861		34.4%
		Lab maj	18,174		Lab maj	16,789

Jack Thompson became an Opposn whip in 1990; mbr, Select Committee on Ed, Science and Arts, 1985-88; vice-chmn, PLP ed, science and arts cmte, 1985-86; chmn, 1991- , vice-chmn, 1990-91, and sec and treas, 1985-90, Northern gp of Lab MPs. Alternate mbr, UK delegation to Cl of Europe and WEU, 1987-91, and full mbr, 1991- , being chmn, WEU rules and privileges cmte, 1991- . Jt vice-chmn, all-pty Anglo-Belgian parly gp; treas, chemical industry gp, 1991- . Elected in 1983. B Aug 27 1928; ed Bothal Sch; Ashington Mining Coll. Mbr, Northumberland CC, 1974-83; Wansbeck DC, 1974-79; Newbiggin by the Seas UDC, 1970-74. Sponsored by NUM.

Glen Sanderson, farmer; mbr, Northumberland CC, 1989- . Dep vice-chmn, Northumberland NFU branch, 1990- . B Nov 24 1951; ed Ascham Hse, Gosforth; Trinity Coll, Glenalmond, Perthshire; Royal Agricultural Coll, Cirencester; Minnesota Univ, US.

Brian Priestley, schoolmaster; mbr, Castle Morpeth BC, 1983-91. Chmn, Wansbeck LDs, 1990-91; treas, Morpeth Libs, 1978-86. B Apr 6 1937; ed Bedlington GS; City of Leeds Training Coll. AMMA, 1966-91.

Nic Best, postal games designer. Chmn, Mid-Northumberland Grn pty. B Nov 19 1952; ed Dulwich Coll; St Catherine's Coll, Oxford; Edinburgh Univ.

WANSDYKE						No change
Electorate % Turnout	77,156	84.3%	1992	75,239	81.3%	1987
*Aspinwall, J H (C)	31,389	48.2%	-3.3%	31,537	51.6%	C
Norris, D (Lab)	18,048	27.7%	+4.5%	15,393	25.2%	L/All
Darby, Mrs D (LD)	14,834	22.8%	-2.4%	14,231	23.3%	Lab
Hayden, F E (Grn)	800	1.2%				
C to Lab swing 3.9%	65,071		20.5%	61,161		26.4%
		C maj	13,341		C maj	16,144

Jack Aspinwall joined the Select Cmte on Transport in 1988; mbr, Select Cmte on Parliamentary Commissioner for Administration, 1983-90; jt sec, Cons back-bench aviation cmte, 1985- . Director of investment company; and consultant to Rentokil plc, British Shoe Repairers Cl, BAA plc and GCI GP; director of family business of retail shops, 1956-66. Won this seat 1983; MP for Kingswood, 1979-83; contested it Feb and Oct 1974 as a Liberal. B Feb 1933; ed Prescot GS, Bootle; Marconi Coll, Chelmsford. Mbr, Avon CC; has also served on Kingswood DC. Owner of The Red Lion, Lambridge Buildings, Bath.

Dan Norris, child protection social worker and lecturer, contested Northavon 1987. Mbr, Bristol City Cl, 1989- . Fellow, Sussex Univ. B Jan 28 1960; ed Avon Comprehensive; Sussex Univ. Nupe.

Doreen Darby, partner in antiques business, contested Ruislip, Northwood 1987. Exec mbr, LD women's organisation. Mbr, Chiltern DC, 1979-83; Chalfont St Peter PC, 1979-90. B Nov 6 1926; ed Queen Elizabeth's Girls' GS, Barnet; Trafalgar Sch for Girls, Montreal.

Francis Hayden, engineer; in commercial aircraft design, British Aerospace; former teacher. B Oct 16 1952; ed Sevenoaks Sch; Bristol Univ (was on NUS exec and YL exec). MSF. Sec, local CND gp.

WANSTEAD AND WOODFORD				No change		
Electorate % Turnout	55,821	78.3%	1992	57,921	72.4%	1987
*Arbuthnot, J N (C)	26,204	60.0%	-1.3%	25,701	61.3%	C
Brown, Ms L (Lab)	9,319	21.3%	+4.7%	9,289	22.1%	L/All
Staight, G P (LD)	7,362	16.8%	-5.3%	6,958	16.6%	Lab
Roads, F (Grn)	637	1.5%				
Brickell, A (NLP)	178	0.4%				
C to Lab swing 3.0%	43,700		38.6%	41,948		39.1%
		C maj	16,885		C maj	16,412

James Arbuthnot was elected in 1987; contested Cynon Valley in 1983 and 1984 by-election. PPS to Peter Lilley in 1990; PPS to Archie Hamilton 1989-90. Mbr, Royal Borough of Kensington and Chelsea Cl 1978-87. Mbr of Lloyd's. Chancery barrister specialising in tax, company law, landlord and tenant law, probate and trust law. B Aug 4 1952; ed Wellesley House, Broadstairs; Eton; Trinity Coll, Cambridge. Pres, Cynon Valley Cons Assocn, 1983- .
Lyn Brown, local govt officer working in race relations unit. Mbr, Newham BC, 1988- (chmn direct services organisation cmte, 1989-90). B Apr 13 1960; ed local state sch,

Newham; Whitelands Coll, Putney. Nalgo.
Gary Staight, accountant; political organiser, Ilford N LDs; former press sec and ward organiser. Mbr, Redbridge BC, 1984-86 (gp ldr). B Nov 8 1952; ed King Coll, London Univ; Liverpool Univ. Qualified swimming coach, Chingford Swimming Club, 1984-7 and Romford SC, 1987-90.
Francis Roads, advisory music teacher; membership sec, Redbridge pty. B May 31 1943; ed Brentwood Sch; Permbroke Coll, Oxford.

WANTAGE				No change		
Electorate % Turnout	68,328	82.7%	1992	66,499	77.9%	1987
*Jackson, R V (C)	30,575	54.1%	+0.2%	27,951	54.0%	C
Morgan, R M C (LD)	14,102	25.0%	-5.5%	15,795	30.5%	SDP/All
Woodell, V S (Lab)	10,955	19.4%	+3.8%	8,055	15.5%	Lab
Ely, R J (Grn)	867	1.5%				
LD to C swing 2.8%	56,499		29.2%	51,801		23.5%
		C maj	16,473		C maj	12,156

Robert Jackson was appointed civil service minister in April 1992. Employment under sec 1990-2; under sec for ed and science 1987-90. Mbr select cmte on energy, 1987. Jt sec, Cons backbench ag, fish and food cmte, 1985-7; and to foreign affairs cmte, 1985-7. Political adviser to late Lord Soames when Governor of Rhodesia in 1980. Elected in 1983; contested Manchester Central, Oct 1974. MEP for Upper Thames, 1979-84. B Sep 24 1946; ed Falcon Coll, near Bulawayo; St Edmund Hall and All Souls, Oxford (Pres of Union, 1967; Fellow, 1968-86). Former consultant to Merck, Sharp and Dohme (Pharmaceuticals), Brewers' Society and Samuel Montagu plc. Mbr, Oxford City Cl, 1969-71.
Robert Morgan, retired managing director; mbr, Oxford-

shire CC, 1981- (cl chmn, 1991-); S Oxfordshire DC, 1979-83; vice-chmn Chiltern reg LDs. Director of Hebdon Royd Publications; partner in boarding kennels business; shop owned in partnership with wife. B Jan 3 1930; ed Wycliff Coll, Stonehouse; Bishop Gore GS, Swansea.
Vivian Woodell, social economy consultant, contested Hereford 1987. Director, Oxford and Swindon Co-op Society Ltd; three Industrial Common Ownership companies; Social Economy Consortium Ltd and three Co-op development companies. B May 8 1962; ed Dragon Sch, Oxford; Westminster Sch; Bristol Univ. MSF. Sponsored by Co-op Pty.
Robert Ely, electronics design engineer. B May 11 1952; ed E Barnet GS; Leeds and London Univs.

WARLEY EAST				No change		
Electorate % Turnout	51,717	71.7%	1992	55,706	69.4%	1987
*Faulds, A M W (Lab)	19,891	53.6%	+3.4%	19,428	50.2%	Lab
Marshall, G (C)	12,097	32.6%	-3.2%	13,843	35.8%	C
Harrod, A (LD)	4,547	12.3%	-1.7%	5,396	14.0%	SDP/All
Groucott, A (NLP)	561	1.5%				
C to Lab swing 3.3%	37,096		21.0%	38,667		14.4%
		Lab maj	7,794		Lab maj	5,585

Andrew Faulds, actor who, in the Register of MPs' Interests, says he has a 'valuable voice', was Opposn spokesman on the arts, 1970-3, and 1979-82. Sec and chmn (1974-87), Parly Assocn for Euro-Arab Co-operation, 1974- . Exec cmte mbr, GB-China Centre, 1976- ; IPU, British section, 1983- . Elected for this seat, Feb 1974; MP for Smethwick, 1966-74; contested Stratford upon Avon, 1963 and 1964. B Mar 1 1923; ed George Watson's, Louth GS, Daniel Stewart's, Edinburgh, Stirling HS and Glasgow Univ. Mbr, Commons Services Cmte, 1983-91. Delegate to Cl of Europe and WEU, 1975-80 and 1987- .

Mbr, Equity (cl mbr, 1966-69). Jt chmn, all-pty arts and heritage parly gp; jt dep chmn, complementary and alternative medicine gp; mbr, advisory cmte on Commons works of art, 1988- .
Giles Marshall, teacher; mbr, Camden BC, 1990- ; area chmn, West Midlands YCs, 1988-90; vice-chmn, Cons nat advisory cmte on ed, 1992- . B Sep 8 1965; ed Solihull Sch; Bristol Univ.
Alan Harrod, placement and development officer; mbr, Sandwell MBC, 1991- cllr. B Nov 30 1935; ed sec modern sch. Chmn TGWU, W Bromwich, 1972-87.

WARLEY WEST						No change
Electorate % Turnout	57,164	73.9%	1992	57,526	70.0%	1987
Spellar, J F (Lab)	21,386	50.6%	+1.4%	19,825	49.2%	Lab
Whitehouse, Mrs S A (C)	15,914	37.7%	+1.8%	14,432	35.8%	C
Todd, Miss E (LD)	4,945	11.7%	-3.3%	6,027	15.0%	L/All
Lab to C swing 0.2%	42,245	13.0%		40,284		13.4%
		Lab maj	5,472		Lab maj	5,393

John Spellar, EETPU nat official and union mbr since 1969, was MP for Birmingham Northfield 1982-3; contested Birmingham Northfield 1987 and Bromley 1970. Former mbr select cmte on energy. B Aug 5 1947; ed Bromley parish primary sch; Dulwich coll; St Edmund Hall, Oxford. Mbr Bromley BC 1970-4.
Sarah Whitehouse, investment banker; with Nat Westminster Bank 1983-5. Chmn Tooting Cons assocn; B Jan 13 1961; ed York coll for girls; Edgbaston C of E coll,

Birmingham; Felixstowe coll, Suffolk; St Andrews univ; Scotland (chmn univ Cons assocn 1981). Former vice-chmn Scottish FCS.
Elaine Todd, teacher, contested seat for L/All 1987. NAS/UWT, sec Dudley assocn 1989- . Former chmn Birmingham Northfield Lib Pty. B Aug 9 1950; ed Bolling sch, Bradford; N Counties coll of ed, Newcastle. Mbr Dudley racial equality cl.

WARRINGTON NORTH						No change
Electorate % Turnout	78,548	77.4%	1992	75,627	75.2%	1987
*Hoyle, E D H (Lab)	33,019	54.3%	+6.1%	27,422	48.2%	Lab
Daniels, C (C)	20,397	33.6%	-0.6%	19,409	34.1%	C
Greenhalgh, I (LD)	6,965	11.5%	-6.2%	10,046	17.7%	SDP/All
Davies, B (NLP)	400	0.7%				
C to Lab swing 3.3%	60,781	20.8%		56,877		14.1%
		Lab maj	12,622		Lab maj	8,013

Douglas Hoyle, mbr of select cmte on trade and industry since 1984, became chmn PLP trade and industry cmte in 1987; jt vice-chmn all-pty leasehold reform parly gp 1989- . Elected for this seat 1983; MP for Warrington 1981-3; and for Nelson and Colne, Oct 1974 to 1979; contested it in Feb 1974, and 1970; Clitheroe, 1964. Mbr Lab Party NEC 1978-82 and 1983-5. B Feb 17 1930; ed Adlington sch; Horwich tech coll; Bolton tech coll. Former sales engineer, Charles Weston Ltd, Salford. Jt pres MSFU 1988-91; Pres of ASTMS 1977-81 and 1985-8; vice-pres 1981-5; mbr nat exec 1968- , and union 1958- . Sponsored by MSFU.
Colin Daniels, marketing manager with national construction co; director and trustee of pension fund. Mbr Warrington BC 1979-87 (ldr Cons gp 1985-7); Thelwall

parish cl 1977- (chmn 1983-4); NW advisory cmte on local govt; exec Cheshire East Euro constuency. Chmn Warrington South Cons assocn 1983-8; Cheshire Cons coordinating cmte 1984- . Ed Boteler GS. Senior officer of Warrington and dist building employers' confed; mbr NW reg cl BEC, and its nat public sector monitoring gp.
Ian Greenhalgh, Cheshire and Wirral area organiser, Save the Children Fund; master butcher, former pres Bolton butchers' assocn. Contested Heywood and Middleton for SDP/All 1987. Founder mbr of SDP, former chmnconstituency and area SDP chmn, former area treas. Elected mbr Bolton chamber of trade. B Jul 9 1946; ed St Paul's primary sch; Smithills sec mod sch. Usdaw regional and nat delegate; MSF, Fund rep.

WARRINGTON SOUTH						Lab gain
Electorate % Turnout	77,694	82.0%	1992	76,219	77.6%	1987
Hall, M T (Lab)	27,819	43.6%	+7.8%	24,809	42.0%	C
*Butler, C J (C)	27,628	43.3%	+1.4%	21,200	35.9%	Lab
Walker, P (LD)	7,978	12.5%	-9.7%	13,112	22.2%	L/All
Benson, S (NLP)	321	0.5%				
C to Lab swing 3.2%	63,746	0.3%		59,121		6.1%
		Lab maj	191		C maj	3,609

Mike Hall, a teacher, gained this seat for Labour. Mbr Warrington BC, 1979- (cl ldr, 1985- ; chmn policy and resources cmte 1985-); unpaid director Warrington Borough Transport Ltd and Warrington Coachlines Ltd; chmn Warrington N CLP 1983-5. B Sep 20 1952; ed St Damian's sec mod sch Ashton-under-Lyne; Ashton-under-Lyne CFE; Stretford tech coll; Padgate coll of HE; N Cheshire coll; Bangor univ. NUT.
Christopher Butler joined select cmte on employment in 1990. Political adviser, market researcher and freelance journalist; parly consultant to Charities Trust plc as part of Littlewoods organisation. Mbr exec cmte UK branch, CPA 1991- . Elected in 1987; contested Brecon and Radnor

1985 by-election. Jt sec Cons backbench trade and industry cmte 1990- ; Cons tourism cmte 1991- ; sec Cons energy cmte 1988-90; Cons arts and heritage cmte 1987-8; jt vice-chmn all-pty leasehold reform parly gp 1989- ; jt sec parly cmte on drug misuse 1989- ; sec British-Bahamian gp; penal affairs gp 1990- ; treas Cuban gp 1991- . Mbr Cons research dept 1977-80; prime minister's political office 1980-3. B Aug 12 1950; ed Cardiff HS for boys; Emmanuel coll, Cambridge.
Peter Walker, marketing operations manager; mbr Cheshire CC 1989- (LD spokesman); Stockton Heath PC 1991- . Mbr cl Salford Univ. B Oct 7 1936.

WARWICK AND LEAMINGTON						No change
Electorate % Turnout	71,259	81.5%	1992	72,763	76.0%	1987
*Smith, Sir Dudley (C)	28,093	48.3%	-1.4%	27,530	49.8%	C
Taylor, M (Lab)	19,158	33.0%	+9.4%	13,548	24.5%	SDP/All
Boad, Mrs S E (LD)	9,645	16.6%		13,019	23.5%	Lab
Alty, Ms J A (Grn)	803	1.4%	-0.8%	1,214	2.2%	Grn
Newby, R (Ind)	251	0.4%				
Brewster, J (NLP)	156	0.3%				
C to Lab swing 5.4%	58,106		15.4%	55,311		25.3%
		C maj	8,935		C maj	13,982

Sir Dudley Smith was Under Sec of Defence for Army 1974; Under Sec of State for Employment 1970-4; an Opposn spokesman on employment and productivity, 1969-70; an Opposn whip 1964-6. Mbr cl of Europe and WEU 1979- (sec-general of European democratic gp 1983- ; chmn WEU defence cmte 1989- , and WEU budget cmte 1984-7). Management consultant. Elected at 1968 by-election; MP for Brentford and Chiswick 1959-66; contested Peckham, 1955. B Nov 14 1926; ed Chichester HS. Freeman City of London; liveryman horners' co; dep lieut of Warwickshire.
Matthew Taylor, research fellow; mbr Warwickshire CC

1985-9. B Dec 5 1960; ed Emanuel sch; Westminster coll; Southampton and Warwick univs. Nupe; AUT.
Sarah Boad, metallurgist; mbr Warwick DC, 1987- (gp ldr 1988-); Lliw Valley BC 1986-7. Former chmn and treas constituency pty. B Feb 22 1958; ed Monmouth sch for girls; univ coll of Swansea. MSF.
Janet Alty, lecturer, contested this seat 1987 and Midlands Central in 1989 Euro elections. Co-chmn Grn pty cl and convenor policy cmte 1987-9; pty speaker 1989-91. B Feb 20 1937; ed Manchester HS for girls; Bryn Mawr coll, Penn, US.

WARWICKSHIRE NORTH						Lab gain
Electorate % Turnout	71,473	83.8%	1992	70,687	79.9%	1987
O'Brien, M (Lab)	27,599	46.1%	+6.0%	25,453	45.1%	C
*Maude, F A A (C)	26,145	43.6%	-1.4%	22,624	40.1%	Lab
Mitchell, N (LD)	6,167	10.3%	-4.6%	8,382	14.8%	SDP/All
C to Lab swing 3.7%	59,911		2.4%	56,459		5.0%
		Lab maj	1,454		C maj	2,829

Michael O'Brien, solicitor, who gained the seast for Labour in 1992, contested the seat in 1987 and Ruislip Northwood 1983. Former chmn Worcester CLP; treas Colchester CLP. B Jun 19 1954; ed Worcester tech coll; North Staffs poly. GMB/Apex.
Francis Maude became Financial Sec to the Treasury in 1990; Minr of State for Foreign and Commonwealth Affairs with responsibility for European matters 1989-90; Minr for Corporate Affairs with rank of Under Sec of State

for Trade and Industry 1987-9; an asst govt whip 1985-7. Mbr PAC 1990- . Elected for this seat 1983. Barrister (not practising). B Jul 4 1953; ed Abingdon sch; Corpus Christi coll, Cambridge. Mbr Westminster city cl 1978-84. PPS to Peter Morrison, Minr of State for Employment 1984-5. Son of Lord Maude of Stratford-upon-Avon.
Noel Mitchell, PT teacher; retired sec head teacher. B Nov 14 1938; ed Leicester univ.

WATFORD						No change
Electorate % Turnout	72,291	82.3%	1992	73,540	77.9%	1987
*Garel-Jones, W A T T (C)	29,072	48.8%	+0.1%	27,912	48.7%	C
Jackson, M J (Lab)	19,482	32.7%	+4.5%	16,176	28.2%	Lab
Oaten, M (LD)	10,231	17.2%	-5.9%	13,202	23.0%	SDP/All
Hywel-Davies, J (Grn)	566	1.0%				
Davis, L (NLP)	176	0.3%				
C to Lab swing 2.2%	59,527		16.1%	57,290		20.5%
		C maj	9,590		C maj	11,736

Tristan Garel-Jones was appointed Minr of State for Foreign and Commonwealth Affairs in 1990; Treas of HM household and govt deputy chief whip 1989-90; comptroller of royal household (govt whip) 1988-9; Vice-Chamberlain of royal household (govt whip) 1986-8; a ld commissioner of the Treasury (ovt whip) 1983-6; an asst govt whip 1982-3. PC 1992. Mbr select cmte on broadcasting 1988-90. Former mbr of Lloyd's. Owner of language sch in Madrid, 1960-70. Gained seat for Cons in 1979; contested Caernarvon Feb 1974 and Watford Oct 1974. B Feb 28 1941; ed Llangennech primary sch; King's

sch, Canterbury.
Mike Jackson, Nupe official, contested this seat 1987. Mbr Watford BC, 1980- (cl ldr); SW Herts HA. Sec Watford anti-racist cmte. Chmn Watford CLP 1981-6; nat organisation of lab students 1977-8. B May 6 1948; ed Verulam sch, St Albans; Warwick univ. MSF; Nupe.
Mark Oaten, public affairs consultant; elected first SDP cllr in Watford 1986 and became LD cllr when pty formed; now gp ldr. B Mar 8 1964; ed Queens comprehensive; Hatfield poly; Watford coll.

WAVENEY					No change	
Electorate % Turnout	84,181	81.8%	1992	81,889	78.4%	1987
*Porter, D J (C)	33,174	48.2%	-0.2%	31,067	48.4%	C
Leverett, E C (Lab)	26,472	38.4%	+8.4%	19,284	30.0%	Lab
Rogers, A (LD)	8,925	13.0%	-8.6%	13,845	21.6%	SDP/All
Hook, D (NLP)	302	0.4%				
C to Lab swing 4.3%	68,873		9.7%	64,196		18.4%
		C maj	6,702		C maj	11,783

David Porter, former teacher and Cons party agent, was elected in 1987. Mbr select cmte on social security 1991- ; British-Irish inter-parly body. Director Etage Management Ltd 1988- . Sec Cons backbench fisheries sub-cmte 1987- . Mbr Waveney DC 1974-84 and 1985-7. B Apr 16 1948; ed Lowestoft GS; New college of speech and drama, London. Taught in East End of London 1970-2; director and co-founder vivid children's theatre 1972-8; head of drama Benjamin Britten HS, Lowestoft 1978-81. Became Cons Pty agent 1982 holding posts in Eltham 1982-3; Norwich N, 1983-4; Waveney, 1985-7.

Ezra Leverett, printer; mbr, vice-chmn, dep ldr and former ldr, Waveney DC; former mbr Halesworth UDC. Office holder Halesworth branch and Waveney CLP. B Jun 22 1946; ed Yoxford CP, Suffolk; Saxmundham sec mod sch; Chelmsford coll. Sogat (GPMU).

Adrian Rogers, bank auditor; mbr Forest Heath DC; chmn Newmarket branch Bury St Edmunds LDs. B Aug 5 1963; ed Newmarket upper sch; W Suffolk CFE. BIFU.

WEALDEN					No change	
Electorate % Turnout	74,665	80.8%	1992	73,057	75.0%	1987
*Johnson Smith, Sir G (C)	37,263	61.7%	-2.5%	35,154	64.2%	C
Skinner, M D (LD)	16,332	27.1%	-0.4%	15,044	27.5%	SDP/All
Billcliffe, S (Lab)	5,579	9.2%	+0.9%	4,563	8.3%	Lab
Guy-Moore, I (Grn)	1,002	1.7%				
Graham, Dr R (NLP)	182	0.3%				
C to LD swing 1.0%	60,358		34.7%	54,761		36.7%
		C maj	20,931		C maj	20,110

Sir Geoffrey Johnson Smith became chmn select cmte on members' interests in 1980; jt vice-chmn 1922 cmte, 1988- , and mbr of exec, 1979- ; chmn 1988- and jt vice-chmn 1980-8, Cons backbench defence cmte; jt treas all-pty British-American parly gp; jt pres race and community parly gp; jt vice-chmn defence heritage gp. Won this seat 1983; MP for E Grinstead 1965-83 and for Holborn and St Pancras S 1959-64. Non-exec director Brands Hatch Leisure plc; Taylor Alden Ltd; Glengate Holdings Ltd and MDA (Benelux) SA. Consultant to Eagle Star gp. B Apr 16 1924; ed Charterhouse; Lincoln coll, Oxford. Mbr N Atlantic assembly 1980- (chmn military cmte 1985-9; ldr of UK delegation 1987-).

Michael Skinner, banking systems officer; mbr Wealden DC 1987- ; Uckfield TC 1985- ; former vice-chmn Wealden. B Apr 19 1954; ed Battersea GS.

Steve Billcliffe, marketing manager for Unity Trust Bank; marketing manager for Lab pty 1984-8; contested Suffolk S 1983. B Oct 23 1950; ed Giggleswick sch, N Yorkshire; Salford coll of tech. TGWU; BIFU.

Ian Guy-Moore, part-time teacher and woodland manager; mbr Wealden Grn pty cmte 1989- ; Mayfield and Five Ashes PC 1991- . B Sep 16 1943; ed Tonbridge sch; St Paul's coll, Cheltenham; Bristol univ. NUT 1980-90.

WELLINGBOROUGH					No change	
Electorate % Turnout	73,875	81.9%	1992	70,450	78.1%	1987
*Fry, P D (C)	32,302	53.4%	+0.6%	29,038	52.7%	C
Sawford, P A (Lab)	20,486	33.9%	+6.7%	14,968	27.2%	Lab
Trevor, Ms J (LD)	7,714	12.7%	-7.3%	11,047	20.1%	L/All
C to Lab swing 3.0%	60,502		19.5%	55,053		25.6%
		C maj	11,816		C maj	14,070

Peter Fry, a former Cons spokesman on transport, joined the select cmte on transport in 1979. Chmn all-pty footwear and leather industries parly gp 1979-87; jt chmn roads study gp; Midland main line gp; sec road passenger transport gp. Consultant to Countrywide Political Communication, public affairs consultants; Whitworth Motor Holdings Ltd; adviser to PMS Ltd. Won seat at 1969 by-election; conested Nottingham N 1964; Willesden E 1966. Insurance broker. B May 26 1931; ed Royal GS, High Wycombe; Worcester coll, Oxford.

Philip Sawford, manager of training organisation; mbr Desborough TC 1977-91; Kettering BC 1979-83 and 1986-91. Held various district and CLP offices. B Jun 26 1950; ed Kettering GS; Ruskin coll; Leicester univ. NATFHE.

Julie Trevor, teacher; mbr Corby DC, Northants, 1991- . B Jan 18 1952; ed Maria Grey coll; Leicester univ.

WELLS						No change
Electorate % Turnout	69,833	82.7%	1992	67,195	79.6%	1987
*Heathcoat-Amory, D P (C)	28,620	49.6%	-4.0%	28,624	53.5%	C
Temperley, H (LD)	21,971	38.0%	+0.5%	20,083	37.6%	L/All
Pilgrim, J W (Lab)	6,126	10.6%	+1.9%	4,637	8.7%	Lab
Fenner, M (Grn)	1,042	1.8%		134	0.3%	Falk
C to LD swing 2.2%	57,759		11.5%	53,478		16.0%
		C maj	6,649		C maj	8,541

David Heathcoat-Amory was appointed Treasurer HM Household and deputy chief whip in April 1992; energy under sec 1990-2; environment under sec 1989-90; Ld Commissioner of Treasury (govt whip) 1989; asst govt whip, 1988-9. Chartered accountant, former underwriting mbr of Lloyd's and former company director. Elected in 1983; contested Brent S, 1979. PPS to Douglas Hurd, home sec, 1987-8, and to financial sec, Treasury, 1985-7. B Mar 21, 1949; ed Eton; Oxford Univ. Asst finance director, British Technology Gp, 1980-3. Director, Lowman Manufacturing Co Ltd, 1979-88.

Humphrey Temperley, sheep farmer; mbr, Somerset CC, 1985- (Opposn environment spokesman 1989-); S Somerset DC 1983- (chmn planning 1987-). Mbr Exmoor Nat Park bd, 1987- . B Dec 24 1948; ed Eton; Cambridge Univ.
John Pilgrim, agricultural development planner and social scientist. B Dec 3 1929; ed Sidcup and Chsilehurst GS; Birkbeck Coll, London; King's Coll, Cambridge.
Michael Fenner, actor; press officer, local pty. B Jun 21 1953; ed Reading GS; Central Sch of Speech and Drama. Equity since 1975.

WELWYN HATFIELD						No change
Electorate % Turnout	72,146	84.4%	1992	73,607	80.9%	1987
*Evans, D J (C)	29,447	48.4%	+2.7%	27,164	45.6%	C
Little, R A (Lab)	20,982	34.5%	+8.1%	16,261	27.3%	SDP/All
Parker, R G (LD)	10,196	16.7%	-10.6%	15,699	26.4%	Lab
Lucas, Ms E (NLP)	264	0.4%		401	0.7%	Ind C
C to Lab swing 2.7%	60,889		13.9%	59,525		18.3%
		C maj	8,465		C maj	10,903

David Evans, elected in 1987, was sec Cons backbench sports cmte, 1987-90. PPS to John Redwood 1991- ; to Lord Hesketh, Minr for Industry at DTI, 1990-1. Mbr Select Cmte on Members' Interests, 1990. Chmn Luton Town Football & Athletic Co Ltd, 1984-9, a director, 1976-90. Captained Club Cricket Conference, 1968-74, and tour to Australia, 1971; manager of 1975 tour. Chmn, Broadreach Services Ltd, 1990- ; Bradnam Enterprises Ltd, 1990- ; director, Leapsquare Ltd. Former director Initial plc; Trimoco plc (now consultant to Trimoco); founder, chmn and managing director (1960-86), Brengreen (Holdings) plc. Freeman, City of London; mbr,

Worshipful Co of Horners. B Apr 23 1935; ed Raglan Rd Sch; Tottenham Tech Coll.
Raymond Little, self-employed, runs small family decorating supplies shop; former production estimator for Hawker Siddeley Aviation. Contested Beds S Oct 1974; Sutton Coldfield Feb 1974. Mbr, Hatfield RDC, 1970-74; Welwyn Hatfield DC, 1973- (dep ldr of cl). B Jan 6 1949; ed Burleigh Sec Sch; St Albans CFE. MSF.
Robin Parker, teacher; mbr, Stevenage BC, 1982-90 and 1991- ; exec mbr, Stevenage SDP and then LDs. B Aug 8 1952; ed The Nobel GS, Stevenage; B'ham and Cambridge Univs. NUT, 1973- .

WENTWORTH						No change
Electorate % Turnout	64,914	74.0%	1992	63,886	72.5%	1987
*Hardy, P (Lab)	32,939	68.5%	+3.4%	30,205	65.2%	Lab
Brennan, M (C)	10,490	21.8%	+0.0%	10,113	21.8%	C
Roderick, Ms C (LD)	4,629	9.6%	-3.4%	6,031	13.0%	SDP/All
C to Lab swing 1.7%	48,058		46.7%	46,349		43.3%
		Lab maj	22,449		Lab maj	20,092

Peter Hardy was elected for this seat 1983; MP for Rother Valley, 1970-83; contested Scarborough and Whitby, 1964; Sheffield, Hallam, 1966. Teacher, 1953-70. Chmn, PLP energy cmte, 1974- . Delegate to Cl of Europe and WEU, 1976- (ldr, Lab delegation, 1983- ; chmn, cmte on environment, Cl of Europe, 1986-90; chmn, sub-cmte on natural environment, 1990- , and sub-cmte on terrorism, 1990- ; vice-chmn, Socialist gp, 1983-). B Jul 17 1931; ed Wath-upon-Dearne GS; Westminster Coll, London; Sheffield Univ. Vice-chmn, all-pty conservation parly gp; mbr, exec cmte, NSPCC, 1985- ; cl, Worldwide Fund for Nature (UK) Patron, Yorkshire Wildlife Trust. Mbr, Wath-upon-

Dearne UDC, 1960-70 (chmn, 1968-69). Sponsored by Nacods.
Michael Brennan, director of executive search company. B Nov 22 1965; ed Wath-upon-Deare Comprehensive Sch; Liverpool Univ (vice-chmn, univ Cons assocn and univ guild of undergraduates, 1984-87). Chmn, Wentworth YCs, 1983-85; and sec, NW Cons students. Ex-miner and mbr, NUM.
Chris Roderick, trainee solicitor; chair, local pty; mbr, Ravenfield PC. B Feb 1 1943; ed Sheffield Univ; Coll of Law, York. Has seven children.

WEST BROMWICH EAST						No change
Electorate % Turnout	56,940	75.3%	1992	58,239	73.2%	1987
*Snape, P C (Lab)	19,913	46.5%	+3.8%	18,162	42.6%	Lab
Blunt, C J R (C)	17,100	39.9%	-0.4%	17,179	40.3%	C
Smith, M (LD)	5,360	12.5%	-4.5%	7,268	17.1%	L/All
Lord, J (NF)	477	1.1%				
C to Lab swing 2.1%	42,850		6.6%	42,609		2.3%
		Lab maj	2,813		Lab maj	983

Peter Snape became an Opposn spokesman on transport in 1983; a spokesman on home affairs, 1982-3; and defence and disarmament, 1979-82. Lord Commissioner of Treasury (govt whip), 1977-9; asst Govt whip, 1975-7. Contested election of Opposn chief whip, 1990. Jt chmn, all-pty railways gp; all-pty Channel tunnel gp; chmn, Anglo-Iraqi gp; sec, Hungarian and Thai gps. Mbr of Select Cmte on Channel Tunnel Bill, 1986-7. Elected in Feb 1974. Clerical officer, British Rail, 1970-4; goods guard, 1967-70; regular soldier, 1961-67; railway signalman, 1957-61. B Feb 12 1942; ed St Joseph's sch, Stockport. Mbr, Bredbury and Romily UDC, 1971-4. Sponsored by NUR. Chmn, W Midlands Lab MPs, 1985- .

Crispin Blunt ended military career in 1990 to contest seat; was captain in Armoured Reconnaissance Regt, 13th/18th Royal Hussars and then studied at Cranfield. B Jul 15 1960; ed Wellington Coll; RMA Sandhurst; Durham Univ; Cranfield Sch of Management. Was hon sec, Royal Armoured Corps CC and captained regimental team.
Martyn Smith, CHC chief officer, contested this seat 1987, 1983 and 1979; Stoke-on-Trent N Oct 1974, Stoke-on-Trent S Feb 1974. B Feb 16 1946; ed Wyggeston Boys' Sch, Leicester; Jesus Coll, Cambridge. Mbr, Sandwell MBC, 1980- (Gp ldr); Newcastle-under-Lyme BC, 1972-74.

WEST BROMWICH WEST						No change
Electorate % Turnout	57,655	70.4%	1992	58,944	67.0%	1987
*Boothroyd, Miss B (Lab)	22,251	54.8%	+4.3%	19,925	50.5%	Lab
Swayne, D A (C)	14,421	35.5%	-1.6%	14,672	37.2%	C
Broadbent, Miss S (LD)	3,925	9.7%	-2.7%	4,877	12.4%	SDP/All
C to Lab swing 3.0%	40,597		19.3%	39,474		13.3%
		Lab maj	7,830		Lab maj	5,253

Betty Boothroyd was elected Speaker on April 27 1992, the first woman to hold the post. In July 1987 she had become the first woman Labour MP to be a Deputy Speaker, being appointed Second Deputy Chairman of Ways and Means. Mbr Commons Chairmen's Panel, 1979-87 and House of Commons Commission, 1983-7. Asst govt whip, 1974-6. Elected for this seat, Feb 1974; MP for West Bromwich, May 1973 to Feb 1974; contested Rossendale, 1970; Nelson and Colne by-election, 1968; Peterborough, 1959; Leicester SE by-election, 1957. Mbr BBC Gen Advisory Cl, 1987- . Euro MP1975-7. B Oct 8

1929; ed Dewsbury Coll of Commerce and Art. Mbr, exec cmte, UK branch, CPA, 1986- ; court, Birmingham Univ, 1982- .
Desmond Swayne, computer systems development manager at Royal Bank of Scotland, contested Pontypridd in 1987. B Aug 20 1956; ed Bedford Sch; St Andrews Univ. Mbr, Prayer Book Society. Serving TA officer. Prison visitor.
Sarah Broadbent, pension fund manager; worked in City for 10 years. B 1956; ed Appleton GS, Warrington; Bristol Univ; Insead, Fountainbleu.

WESTBURY						No change
Electorate % Turnout	87,356	83.0%	1992	84,860	78.2%	1987
Faber, D J C (C)	36,568	50.4%	-1.2%	34,256	51.6%	C
Rayner, Ms V A (LD)	23,962	33.1%	-3.3%	24,159	36.4%	L/All
Stallard, W (Lab)	9,642	13.3%	+1.3%	7,982	12.0%	Lab
Macdonald, P (Lib)	1,440	2.0%				
French, P R (Grn)	888	1.2%				
LD to C swing 1.1%	72,500		17.4%	66,397		15.2%
		C maj	12,606		C maj	10,097

David Faber was elected in 1992; contested contested Stockton N 1987. Co-founder and director of Sterling Marketing Ltd, a marketing consultancy Personal asst to Jeffrey Archer, then Cons deputy chmn, during 1987 election campaign; Cons research asst, Hse of Commons, 1984-5. Mbr of Lloyd's. B Jul 7 1961; ed Summer Fields, Oxford; Eton; Balliol Coll, Oxford. Former ward chmn, Cities of London and Westminster Cons Assocn; mbr, Foreign Affairs Forum. Grandson of the Earl of Stockton (Harold Macmillan).

Viv Rayner, business woman; employment agency proprietor; small business adviser. Contested Southampton Test for L/All 1987 and Wight and E Hants for LD in 1989 Euro elections. Mbr Isle of Wight CC, 1985-9 (gp sec). B Feb 17 1950; ed Godolphin and Latymer, Hammersmith.
William Stallard, lecturer in business studies. B Jan 28 1935; ed Strathclyde and Keele Univs. NATFHE.
Patrick French, writer; press officer for local pty. B May 28 1966; ed Ampleforth Coll; Edinburgh Univ.

WESTERN ISLES						No change
Electorate % Turnout	22,784	70.4%	1992	23,507	70.2%	1987
*MacDonald, C A (Lab)	7,664	47.8%	+5.1%	7,041	42.7%	Lab
MacFarlane, Ms F M (SNP)	5,961	37.2%	+8.7%	4,701	28.5%	SNP
Heany, R J (C)	1,362	8.5%	+0.4%	3,419	20.7%	SDP/All
Mitchison, N (LD)	552	3.4%	-17.3%	1,336	8.1%	C
Price, A (Ind)	491	3.1%				
Lab to SNP swing 1.8%	16,030		10.6%	16,497		14.2%
		Lab maj	1,703		Lab maj	2,340

Calum Macdonald won this seat in 1987 and joined select cmte on agriculture; jt vice-chmn PLP agriculture cmte 1987-9; chmn PLP Treasury and civil service cmte 1988-90; jt chmn and treas future of Europe trust parly gp; jt vice-chmn British-Atlantic gp of young politicians; all-pty British-Nicaraguan parly gp; sec world govt gp. Jt founder and jt chmn future of Europe trust. Former teaching fellow in political philosophy, univ of California. B May 7 1956; ed Bayble sch; Nicolson inst; Edinburgh univ. TGWU and Crofters union.

Frances MacFarlane, English teacher. . B Mar 28 1963; ed Nicolson inst, Stornaway; Glasgow univ; Jordanhill coll of ed, Glasgow.
Robert Heaney, chartered surveyor; mbr Edinburgh DC, 1988- . Chmn Stockbridge Cons branch, Edinburgh;. B Apr 5 1949; ed Holycross sch, Hamilton.
Neil Mitchison, journalist, broadcaster, computer consultant, EC official. Contested Highlands and Islands in 1989 Euro elections. B May 2 1951; ed Edinburgh acad; Trinity coll, Cambridge; Edinburgh univ.

WESTMINSTER NORTH						No change
Electorate % Turnout	58,847	75.8%	1992	59,263	71.1%	1987
*Wheeler, Sir John (C)	21,828	49.0%	+1.6%	19,941	47.3%	C
Edwards, Ms J F (Lab)	18,095	40.6%	+1.1%	16,631	39.5%	Lab
Wigoder, L J (LD)	3,341	7.5%	-4.6%	5,116	12.1%	SDP/All
Burke, Ms A (Grn)	1,017	2.3%	+1.2%	450	1.1%	Grn
Hinde, J (NLP)	159	0.4%				
Kelly, M (Anti-Fed)	137	0.3%				
Lab to C swing 0.3%	44,577		8.4%	42,138		7.9%
		C maj	3,733		C maj	3,310

Sir John Wheeler, director-general 1976-88 British security industry assocn ltd, and trustee of benevolent fund. Chmn home affairs select cmte 1987- (mbr 1979-). Elected for this seat 1983; MP for City of Westminster, Paddington 1979-83. Asst governor Wandsworth prison 1968-72 and Brixton 1972-3. Director Hunterprint plc 1990- , and other companies. Mbr of Lloyd's. B May 1 1940; ed cty sch Suffolk; Staff coll, Wakefield. Director nat supervisory cl for intruder alarms 1977-88. Ind chmn bd, nat inspectorate of security guard, patrol and transport services 1982- ; security systems inspectorate 1987-90. Mbr Home Office steering cmte on crime prevention 1986- . Chmn 1986- , vice-chmn 1979-86 all-pty penal affairs gp; jt vice-chmn 1987-90 and 1991- and jt sec 1980-7, Cons backbench home affairs cmte; chmn Cons Greater London MPs 1983-90; jt treas all-pty war crimes parly gp; chmn British-Pakistan gp; jt vice-chmn Nepalese gp; interparly cl against anti-Semitism 1991- . Mbr cl order of St John for London 1990- ;
Jenny Edwards, policy researcher for Jo Richardson, shadow Minr for women, contested this seat 1987. Mbr Westminster city cl 1990- . B Dec 26 1954; ed Torquay Girls' GS; Girton coll, Cambridge. TGWU.
Justin Wigoder, barrister. Mbr LD working gp on sport. B May 11 1951; ed Bryanston sch, Dorset; Oriel coll and Wolfson coll, Oxford.

WESTMORLAND AND LONSDALE						No change
Electorate % Turnout	71,865	77.8%	1992	70,237	74.8%	1987
*Jopling, T M (C)	31,798	56.9%	-0.7%	30,259	57.6%	C
Collins, S (LD)	15,362	27.5%	-1.7%	15,339	29.2%	L/All
Abbott, D J (Lab)	8,436	15.1%	+1.8%	6,968	13.3%	Lab
Johnstone, R (NLP)	287	0.5%				
LD to C swing 0.5%	55,883		29.4%	52,566		28.4%
		C maj	16,436		C maj	14,920

Michael Jopling joined select cmte on foreign affairs 1987 and cmte on privileges 1989; chmn select cmte on sittings of Commons 1991- ; sec all-pty British-American parly gp 1987- ; (vice-chmn 1983-86); jt vice-chmn Europe gp 1988- ; mbr exec cmte UK branch CPA 1974-9 (vice-chmn 1977-9) and 1987- . Minr of Agriculture, Fisheries and Food 1979-83. Parly Sec to Treasury and govt chief whip 1979-83; Won this seat 1983; MP for Westmorland 1964-83: contested Wakefield 1959. Director, Blagden Industries plc 1989- ; consultant to Hill and Knowlton (UK) Ltd. Farmer; mbr of Lloyd's. B Dec 10 1930; ed Cheltenham coll; King's coll, Durham univ. Pres auto cycle union 1990- . An Opposition spokesman on agriculture, 1974-9. Ld Commissioner of Treasury (govt whip) 1973-4; asst govt whip 1971-3. Former mbr select cmtes on science and tech and on ag. Mbr NFU nat cl 1962-4; Thirsk RDC, 1958-64.Jt sec Cons backbench ag cmte 1966-70. PPS Minr of Ag 1970-1.
Stanley Collins, business systems analyst; mbr South Lakeland DC 1979- . B Aug 10 1948; ed Umist.
Dickon Abbott, day centre officer; sec Windermere Lab pty. B Jan 9 1962; ed Kingdown, Warminster; Lincoln coll, Oxford. GMB.

WESTON-SUPER-MARE						No change
Electorate % Turnout	78,839	79.8%	1992	76,341	75.6%	1987
*Wiggin, A W (C)	30,022	47.7%	-1.7%	28,547	49.4%	C
Cotter, B (LD)	24,680	39.3%	+3.7%	20,549	35.6%	SDP/All
Murray, D (Lab)	6,913	11.0%	-0.4%	6,584	11.4%	Lab
Lawson, Dr R H (Grn)	1,262	2.0%	-1.6%	2,067	3.6%	Grn
C to LD swing 2.7%	62,877		8.5%	57,747		13.9%
		C maj	5,342		C maj	7,998

Jerry Wiggin joined Select Cmte on Agriculture and became chmn in 1987. Under Sec of State for Armed Forces, 1981-83; Parly Sec, Min of Ag, Fish and Food, 1979-81. Returned at 1969 by-election; contested Montgomeryshire, 1964 and 1966. Chmn, 1990- , and vice-chmn, 1989-90, economic cmte, N Atlantic Assembly (general rapporteur of cmte, 1976-79). B Feb 24 1937; ed Eton; Trinity Coll, Cambridge. Consultant to British Sugar and to Sears plc; adviser to British Marine Industries Fed; Nat Fed of Scale and Weighing Machine Manufacturers; mbr of Lloyd's (ceased underwriting 1992); former tenant farmer. Chmn, all-pty British-Swedish parly gp; jt vice-chmn, Chinese gp; retail trade gp; vice-chmn, photographic gp; jt sec, Turkish gp. PPS to Ld Balniel, Minr of State for Defence, 1970-74, and to Sir Ian Gilmour, Minr of State for Defence Procurement, 1971-73. Jt sec, Cons defence cmte, 1974-75; vice-chmn, Cons ag cmte, 1975-79; chmn, Cons Westcountry MPs, 1978-79.

Brian Cotter, managing director of plastics company; mbr, Woking BC, 1986-90. B Aug 24 1936; ed St Benedicts, Ealing; Downside Sch, Somerset.

David Murray, mental handicapped practitioner; mbr, Newport BC, 1986- . B Mar 8 1944; ed St Julian's HS, Newport; Open univ. Mbr, Mencap; TGWU.

Dr Richard Lawson, medical practitioner, contested Somerset and Dorset W in 1989 Euro elections, being runner-up, and Weston-super-Mare in 1987, obtaining record poll for Grn Pty. Speaker for Grn Pty, 1988; local govt speaker, 1989- . Mbr, Woodspring DC, 1987-91. B Jul 20 1946; ed Churchers Coll, Petersfield; King's Coll, London; Westminster Hosp. MSF.

WIGAN						No change
Electorate % Turnout	72,739	76.2%	1992	72,064	76.6%	1987
*Stott, R (Lab)	34,910	63.0%	+1.5%	33,955	61.5%	Lab
Hess, E J W (C)	13,068	23.6%	-0.9%	13,493	24.5%	C
Davies, G (LD)	6,111	11.0%	-3.0%	7,732	14.0%	L/All
White, K (Lib)	1,116	2.0%				
Taylor, Ms A (NLP)	197	0.4%				
C to Lab swing 1.2%	55,402		39.4%	55,180		37.1%
		Lab maj	21,842		Lab maj	20,462

Roger Stott, an Opposn spokesman on N Ireland, 1989- ; trade and industry, 1987-89; transport, 1980-83, and 1985-87; trade and industry with responsibilities for info tech, 1983-85. Vice-chmn and treas, N-West Lab MPs. Elected for this seat 1983; MP for Westhoughton, 1973-83; contested Cheadle, 1970. Telephone engineer, 1964-73. B Aug 7 1943; ed Rochdale Tech Coll; Ruskin Coll. Jt chmn, Settle-Carlisle parly gp; vice-chmn, all-pty British-Egyptian parly gp; jt sec, Mauritius and Turkish gps. Mbr, Rochdale Cl, 1970-74. Pres, Bass Wingates Band, since 1980. Sponsored by NCU.

Edward Hess, barrister, was sec, Society of Cons Lawyers, 1989-90; mbr, Kensington and Chelsea BC, 1988- . B Oct 29 1962; ed Rugby; Peterhouse, Cambridge (chmn, univ Cons assocn, 1984).

George Davies, hospital porter; mbr, Wigan MBC, 1987- (Dep ldr, LD gp). B May 31 1948; ed Cansfield HS; Wigan Tech Coll. Nupe shop steward.

WILTSHIRE NORTH						No change
Electorate % Turnout	85,851	81.7%	1992	80,712	79.3%	1987
*Needham, R F (C)	39,028	55.6%	+0.5%	35,309	55.2%	C
Napier, Mrs C (LD)	22,640	32.3%	-5.8%	24,370	38.1%	L/All
Reid, Mrs C (Lab)	6,945	9.9%	+3.1%	4,343	6.8%	Lab
Howitt, Ms L (Grn)	850	1.2%				
Hawkins, G (Lib)	622	0.9%				
Martienssen, S (Bastion)	66	0.1%				
LD to C swing 3.1%	70,151		23.4%	64,022		17.1%
		C maj	16,388		C maj	10,939

Richard Needham was appointed trade and industry min in April 1992. N Ireland under sec 1985-92. Elected for this seat 1983; MP for Chippenham, 1979-83; contested Pontefract and Castleford, Feb 1974; Gravesend, Oct 1974. Chmn, RGM Print Holdings Ltd, 1967-85; mbr of Lloyd's. Personal and political asst and later PPS to James Prior; PPS to environment sec 1984-5. Mbr, PAC, 1982-3; jt vice-chmn, Cons backbench employment cmte, 1981-3. B Jan 29 1942; ed Eton. Founder mbr, Anglo-Japanese 2000 Gp, 1984- . Mbr Somerset CC 1967-74. Governor, British Inst of Florence, 1983-85.

Christine Napier, management development consultant; mbr, N Wilts DC, 1982- . B Apr 19 1940; ed Montrose Acad; St Andrews and Lancaster Univs.

Christine Reid, a former teacher, runs a bed and breakfast establishment. Contested this seat 1987. Chmn CLP 1984- ; sec 1980-4. Mbr N Wilts DC and Corsham PC. B Aug 2 1943; ed Canonslade C of E GS, Bolton; Nottingham Univ. NUT.

WIMBLEDON						No change
Electorate % Turnout	61,917	80.2%	1992	63,353	76.1%	1987
*Goodson-Wickes, Dr C (C)	26,331	53.0%	+2.1%	24,538	50.9%	C
Abrams, K (Lab)	11,570	23.3%	+1.7%	13,237	27.5%	L/All
Willott, Mrs A L (LD)	10,569	21.3%	-6.2%	10,428	21.6%	Lab
Flood, V H (Grn)	860	1.7%				
Godfrey, H (NLP)	181	0.4%				
Hadley, G (Ind)	170	0.3%				
Lab to C swing 0.2%	49,681		29.7%	48,203		23.4%
		C maj	14,761		C maj	11,301

Dr Charles Goodson-Wickes, self-employed occupational physician and non-practising barrister, was elected in 1987; contested Islington Central 1979. PPS to Sir George Young, minister for housing and planning, 1992- . Unpaid director Merton Enterprise Agency 1987- . Chmn appeal bd asbestos licensing regulations 1982- . Mbr select cmte on consolidation bills 1987- . Jt vice-chmn 1991- , and jt sec 1990-1 Cons defence cmte; jt sec Cons arts and heritage cmte 1989- . Surgeon Captain, The Life Guards, 1973-7; on active service as Lt Col with HQ 7th Armoured Brigade in Saudi Arabia, Iraq and Kuwait during Gulf war, 1991. B Nov 7 1945; ed Charterhouse; St Bartholomew's Hosp;

Inner Temple. UK adviser, Norwegian Directorate of Health, 1983- . Mbr public affairs cmte, British Field Sports Soc 1980- .
Kingsley Abrams, policy and information officer for standing conf on Racial Equality in Europe. Mbr Merton BC. B Jan 31 1962; ed S Bank Poly, London. GMB.
Alison Willott, professional concert singer; teacher. B Feb 21 1946; ed Cheltenham Ladies Coll; Durham Univ; King's Coll, London Univ. AMMA.
Vaughan Flood, communications consultant. B Feb 5 1955; ed Dover GS for Boys; St Edmund Hall, Oxford.

WINCHESTER						No change
Electorate % Turnout	79,218	83.5%	1992	76,507	80.4%	1987
Malone, G P (C)	33,113	50.1%	-2.3%	32,195	52.3%	C
Barron, A D (LD)	24,992	37.8%	-2.4%	24,716	40.2%	SDP/All
Jenks, P J (Lab)	4,917	7.4%	+0.9%	4,028	6.5%	Lab
*Browne, J E D (Ind C)	3,095	4.7%		565	0.9%	Grn
LD to C swing 0.1%	66,117		12.3%	61,504		12.2%
		C maj	8,121		C maj	7,479

Gerald Malone was returned for this seat in 1992. MP for Aberdeen South, 1983-7; contested Glasgow, Provan, Feb 1974; Glasgow, Pollok, Oct 1974; Roxburgh, Selkirk and Peebles, 1979; Glasgow, Hillhead, 1982 by-election. Asst govt whip 1986-7; PPS to Sir Leon Brittan and other minrs 1985-6. Editor of *The Sunday Times Scotland*, 1989-90 and editorial consultant since 1990. Presenter, *Talk in Sunday*, Radio Clyde, 1988-90. Director of European affairs, energy and environmental center, Harvard Univ, 1987-90. Solicitor. B Jul 21 1950; ed St Aloysius' Coll, Glasgow; Glasgow Univ. Former mbr select cmtes on energy and European legislation.

Tony Barron, quantity surveyor. Mbr Hampshire CC 1985- ; regional pty cmte mbr 1990- . B Dec 27 1941; ed Crewe GS.
Peter Jenks, paramedic. Mbr Southampton City cl 1990- . Pres Southampton Lab pty 1989-91; Southampton TUC 1988-90. B Jun 2 1959; ed Bitterne Park Sec Mod Sch; Nothern Coll, Barnsley. Nupe.
John Browne was Cons MP for this seat, 1979-92. Deselected after being suspended from Commons. Mbr Treasury and civil service select cmte 1982-7 and on social security 1991-2. B Oct 17 1938; ed Malvern Coll; RMA Sandhurst; Cranfield Inst of Tech; Harvard Business Sch.

WINDSOR AND MAIDENHEAD						No change
Electorate % Turnout	77,327	81.7%	1992	79,319	75.4%	1987
Trend, M (C)	35,075	55.5%	-1.3%	33,980	56.8%	C
Hyde, J (LD)	22,147	35.1%	+8.1%	16,144	27.0%	L/All
Attlee, Ms C A M (Lab)	4,975	7.9%	-3.3%	6,678	11.2%	Lab
Williams, R (Grn)	510	0.8%	-0.4%	1,938	3.2%	Ind C
Askwith, D (Loony)	236	0.4%		711	1.2%	Grn
Bigg, Miss E (Ind)	110	0.2%		328	0.5%	BT
Grenville, M (NLP)	108	0.2%				
C to LD swing 4.7%	63,161		20.5%	59,779		29.8%
		C maj	12,928		C maj	17,836

Michael Trend, journalist, editor and broadcaster, retained the seat for the Conservatives., Contested London NE in 1989 Euro elections. Former chief leader writer, *The Daily Telegraph*; home editor of *The Spectator* from 1986; editor, House of Commons Magazine 1984-6, and of *History Today* 1981-4. In 1975 joined *The Times Literary Supplement* Chmn London NE Euro Cl 1985-8 and former finance officer; former sec Cons foreign affairs forum. Political aide to Norman Tebbit in Chingford in

1987 gen election. B Apr 19 1952; ed Westminster Sch; Oriel Coll, Oxford; Athens.
Jeremy Hyde, pharmacist, is managing director of pharmaceutical services company. Constituency chmn. B Nov 24 1952; ed St Pauls Sch, London; London Univ.
Cath Attlee, great neice of Clement Attlee, is a NHS manager. B Sep 9 1956; ed Farnborough Hill, Hants; Truro HS; City of London Poly; Manchester Univ. Nalgo.

WIRRAL SOUTH						No change
Electorate % Turnout	61,116	82.4%	1992	62,251	79.4%	1987
*Porter, G B (C)	25,590	50.8%	+0.6%	24,821	50.2%	C
Southworth, Ms H (Lab)	17,407	34.6%	+6.6%	13,858	28.0%	Lab
Cunniffe, E T (LD)	6,581	13.1%	-8.7%	10,779	21.8%	L/All
Birchenough, N (Grn)	584	1.2%				
Griffiths, G (NLP)	182	0.4%				
C to Lab swing 3.0%	50,344		16.3%	49,458		22.2%
		C maj	8,183		C maj	10,963

Barry Porter was elected in 1983; MP for Bebington and Ellesmere Port, 1978-83; contested Chorley Oct 1974; Newton Feb 1974; Liverpool, Scotland Exchange, Apr 1971. Appointed to select cmte on trade and industry in 1985; mbr Commons services cmte 1987-9; former mbr jt select cmte on consolidation bills. Solicitor. Director, County Seeds Ltd; Decision Makers Ltd. Sec, all-pty Mersey barrage parly gp, 1990- ; leisure and recreation gp; British-Gibraltar gp. B Jun 11 1939; ed Birkenhead Sch; Univ Coll, Oxford. Parly adviser to Hearing Aid Assocn, Wang (UK) Ltd and Impac plc; consultant to Air Boss Ltd; Groen Ltd. Mbr, Birkenhead CBC, 1967-74; Wirral BC, 1975-79.

Helen Southworth, director of Age Concern in St Helens; mbr, St Helems and Knowsley CHC. B Nov 13 1956; ed Larkhill Convent, Preston; Lancaster Univ. MSF.

Edward Cunniffe, company director and independent financial adviser. Chmn, Wirral Lib Club, 1989- . B Nov 3 1952; ed West Park GS, St Helens; St Helens Coll of Tech.

Nigel Birchenough, systems analyst; policy coordinator and speaker on energy, Wirral Grn Pty. B Mar 21 1951; ed Rydal, Colwyn Bay; Keele and Open Univs; Univ Coll of N Wales.

WIRRAL WEST						No change
Electorate % Turnout	62,453	81.6%	1992	63,597	77.9%	1987
*Hunt, D J F (C)	26,852	52.7%	+0.8%	25,736	51.9%	C
Stephenson, Ms H (Lab)	15,788	31.0%	+4.7%	13,013	26.3%	Lab
Thornton, J L (LD)	7,420	14.6%	-5.6%	10,015	20.2%	L/All
Bowler, Mrs G M (Grn)	700	1.4%	-0.3%	806	1.6%	Grn
Broome, N (NLP)	188	0.4%				
C to Lab swing 2.0%	50,948		21.7%	49,570		25.7%
		C maj	11,064		C maj	12,723

David Hunt was appointed to the cabinet as Welsh sec in 1990. PC 1990. Local govt minr 1989-90; Treas of HM Household and govt dep chief whip 1987-9; energy under sec 1984-7; lord commissioner of Treasury (govt whip) 1983-4; asst govt whip 1981-3. Mbr Commons services cmte 1987-9; select cmte on televising Commons, 1988-9. Vice-chmn, Cons pty 1983-5. Solicitor. Elected for this seat 1983; MP for Wirral, 1976-83; contested Bristol S 1970; Kingswood 1974. B May 21 1942; ed Liverpool Coll; Montpellier and Bristol Univs; Guildford Coll of Law.

Underwriting mbr of Lloyd's (external). Vice-pres, Cons Gp for Europe, 1984- (chmn 1981-2; vice-chmn, 1978-81).

Kath Stephenson, social worker employed as training officer. B Mar 13 1935; ed Whitley Bay GS; Manchester Univ; LSE. GMB/Apex.

John Thornton is retired. Mbr Wirral BC 1986-91 . B Jul 13 1930; ed Sherborne Sch, Dorset. Mbr, Inst of Personnel Management.

Garnette Bowler, part-time practice nurse; retired health visitor. B May 9 1926; ed state schs and tech coll.

WITNEY						No change
Electorate % Turnout	78,521	81.9%	1992	75,284	77.3%	1987
*Hurd, D R (C)	36,256	56.4%	-1.1%	33,458	57.5%	C
Plaskitt, J A (Lab)	13,688	21.3%	+4.6%	14,994	25.8%	L/All
Blair, I (LD)	13,393	20.8%	-4.9%	9,733	16.7%	Lab
Beckford, Ms C (Grn)	716	1.1%				
Catling, Ms S (NLP)	134	0.2%				
Brown, Miss M (FTA)	119	0.2%				
C to Lab swing 2.8%	64,306		35.1%	58,185		31.7%
		C maj	22,568		C maj	18,464

Douglas Hurd was appointed foreign sec in 1989. home secretary 1985-9; N Ireland sec 1984-5; minr of state, home office, 1983-4; minr of state, FCO, 1979-83. PC 1982. Contested party leadership in Nov 1990. Opposn spokesman on Europe, 1976-9; head of Sir Edward Heath's political office, 1968-74; Cons Research Dept, 1966-8 and head of foreign affairs section. Elected for this seat 1983; MP for Mid-Oxon, Feb 1974-83. B Mar 8 1930; ed Eton; Trinity Coll, Cambridge (Pres of Union, 1952). Trustee, Prayer Book Society. In Foreign Service, 1952-66. Author of political thrillers.

James Plaskitt, business consultant; mbr, Oxon CC, 1985- (ldr, Lab gp, 1990-). Chmn Oxford E CLP, 1988-90. B Jun 23 1954; ed Pilgrim Sch, Bedford; Univ Coll, Oxford. MSF.

Dr Ian Blair, physicist, contested Herts SW 1987 and 1983; Abingdon 1979. Mbr, Oxon CC, 1981- . B May 9 1936; ed King George V Sch, Southport; Oriel Coll, Oxford; Liverpool Univ.

Charlotte Beckford, anthropologist, company director, teacher. Sec, W Oxon Grn Pty. B Feb 4 1951; ed Godolphin and Latymer Sch, London; St Hilda's and St Anthony's Colls, Oxford.

WOKING						No change
Electorate % Turnout	80,842	79.2%	1992	82,476	75.1%	1987
*Onslow, C G D (C)	37,744	58.9%	+0.9%	35,990	58.1%	C
Buckrell, Mrs D A (LD)	17,902	28.0%	-3.4%	19,446	31.4%	L/All
Dalgleish, J M (Lab)	8,080	12.6%	+2.1%	6,537	10.5%	Lab
Macintyre, Mrs T (NLP)	302	0.5%				
LD to C swing 2.1%	64,028		31.0%	61,973		26.7%
		C maj	19,842		C maj	16,544

Cranley Onslow chmn of 1922 Cmte of Cons backbenchers 1984-92; mbr, its exec, 1968-72 and 1981-82 and 1983-4. PC 1988. Mbr, Cmte on Privileges, 1989- ; Select Cmtes on Procedure, 1988- ; on sittings of Commons, 1991-2. Elected in 1964. Director, Argyll Group plc, 1983- ; Redifon Ltd (formerly Rediffusion), 1985- (chmn, 1988-), Redifon Holdings Ltd and BET Security Services Ltd, 1988- ; Elmdale Investments Ltd and Scatsouth EO1-36, 1989- ; consultant to Bristow Helicopters, Generics Holdings Corporation; associate, LEK Partnership, management consultants. Chmn, Nautical Museums Trust, 1983- . Minr of State, FCO, 1982-83; Under Sec of State for Trade and Industry (Aerospace and Shipping), 1972-74. Cl mbr, British Field Sports Soc; Anglers' Co-op Assocn, Salmon and Trout Assocn, and Nat Rifle Assocn. Liveryman, Fishmongers' Company, 1991- . B Jun 8 1926; ed Harrow; Oriel Coll, Oxford; Geneva Univ.

Dorothy Buckrell contested Tunbridge Wells 1987. Employed in local govt. Mbr (Woking E), Surrey CC, 1981- (LD gp ldr). Was pres, Woking Lib Pty. B 1941; ed Willows City Sch, Morden; Exeter Univ. Nalgo.

James Dalgleish, nat organiser with EETPU. Former holder of various pty offices. B Dec 3 1953; ed Tonbridge Sch; Warwick Univ; City Univ Business Sch.

WOKINGHAM						No change
Electorate % Turnout	85,914	82.4%	1992	85,474	75.9%	1987
*Redwood, J A (C)	43,497	61.4%	+0.0%	39,808	61.4%	C
Simon, P G T (LD)	17,788	25.1%	-4.8%	19,421	29.9%	L/All
Bland, N T G (Lab)	8,846	12.5%	+3.8%	5,622	8.7%	Lab
Owen, P (Loony)	531	0.7%				
Harriss, P (WUWC)	148	0.2%				
LD to C swing 2.4%	70,810		36.3%	64,851		31.4%
		C maj	25,709		C maj	20,387

John Redwood was appointed minr of stae for environment in April 1992; trade and industry minr 1990-2; corporate affairs minr 1989-90. Industrialist and banker. Elected in 1987; contested Southwark, Peckham, 1982 by-election. Head of prime minister's policy unit, 1984-5. Non-exec chmn (1987-9), deputy chmn (1986-7) and director (1985), Norcros plc; investment manager and director, N M Rothschild and Sons, 1977-87, and non-exec director, 1987-9; investment adviser, Robert Fleming and Co, 1973-7. B Jun 15 1951; ed Kent Coll, Canterbury; Magdalen and St Antony's Colls, Oxford. Fellow, All Souls, 1972. Mbr Oxfordshire CC 1973-7.

Paul Simon, advertising manager for national computer journal. Treas LD parly candidates assocn, 1990- . B May 14 1965; St Birinus Sch, Didcot; Jesus Coll, Oxford.

Nelson Bland, multi-skilling training co-ordinator; mbr, Wokingham DC (Lab gp ldr); CLP chmn. B Dec 21 1953; ed St Richards RC Comprehensive Sch, Bexhill-on-Sea. TGWU.

WOLVERHAMPTON NORTH EAST						Lab gain
Electorate % Turnout	62,695	78.0%	1992	63,464	74.3%	1987
Purchase, K (Lab)	24,106	49.3%	+7.6%	19,857	42.1%	C
*Hicks, Mrs M P (C)	20,167	41.2%	-0.9%	19,653	41.7%	Lab
Gwinnett, M J (LD)	3,546	7.3%	-8.9%	7,623	16.2%	L/All
Bullman, K (Lib)	1,087	2.2%				
C to Lab swing 4.2%	48,906		8.1%	47,133		0.4%
		Lab maj	3,939		C maj	204

Kenneth Purchase, business development adviser, regained this seat for Lab in 1992; contested it 1987. Has worked for Aerospace, British Leyland and as a housing manager. Mbr, Wolverhampton Cl 1970-90; former mbr Wolverhampton DHA; Wolverhampton and Dist Manpower Bd; DHSS Benefits Tribunal. B Jan 8 1939; ed Wolverhampton Poly. TGWU(ACTS), 1955- .

Maureen Hicks was MP for this seat 1987-92; PPS to Earl of Caithness, Minr of State, FCO, and Mark Lennox-Boyd, Under Sec of State, FCO, 1990-2. Mbr, Select Cmte on Ed, Science and Arts, 1987-8; jt sec, Cons back-bench tourism cmte, 1987-90. Lecturer; tourism consultant; director, Stratford-upon-Avon Motor Museum, 1976-82. Mbr, Stratford on Avon DC, 1979-84; former mbr, Heart of England Tourist Bd executive. Asst area ed officer, 1974-6; asst staff manager, Marks and Spencer, 1970-4; secondary teacher of drama and English, 1969-70. B Feb 23 1948; ed Ashley Sec Sch; Brockenhurst GS; Furzedown Coll of Ed.

Malcolm Gwinnett, baker; mbr, Wolverhampton MBC, 1990- ; LD press officer for Wolverhampton and a ward chmn. Chmn, Wolverhampton Small Business Club, 1988-90. B Jan 10 1953.

WOLVERHAMPTON SOUTH EAST						No change
Electorate % Turnout	56,158	72.9%	1992	55,710	72.5%	1987
*Turner, D (Lab)	23,215	56.7%	+7.8%	19,760	48.9%	Lab
Bradbourn, P C (C)	12,975	31.7%	-1.4%	13,362	33.1%	C
Whitehouse, R F (LD)	3,881	9.5%	-8.5%	7,258	18.0%	L/All
Twelvetrees, Ms C (Lib)	850	2.1%				
C to Lab swing 4.6%	40,921		25.0%	40,380		15.8%
		Lab maj	10,240		Lab maj	6,398

Dennis Turner joined Select Cmte on Ed, Science and Arts in 1989; jt vice-chmn, PLP ed, science and arts back-bench cmte, 1991- . Director of Springvale sports, social and leisure cooperative; Springvale Training Ltd; unpaid director, W Midlands Co-op Finance Ltd; former unpaid director, W Midlands Enterprise Bd. Elected in 1987; contested Halesowen and Stourbridge, Feb and Oct 1974. Chmn, all-pty housing cooperatives parly gp; tertiary colleges assocn gp, 1990- . Mbr, West Midlands CC, 1974-86; Wolverhampton BC, 1966- . B Aug 26 1942; ed Stonefield Sec Mod Sch, Bilston; Bilston CFE. Sponsored by Co-op Pty.

Philip Bradbourn, local govt officer, being adviser to Cons gp ldr, Wolverhampton MBC; nat chmn, CPC; mbr, nat union exec and gen purposes cmtes; Cons local govt nat advisory cmte; W Midlands area exec cmte. B Aug 9 1951; ed Tipton GS; Wulfrun Coll; Worcester Coll.
Richard Whitehouse, teacher, contested this seat 1987 and Derby N 1979. Mbr, Wolverhampton MBC, 1984- (gp ldr, 1990-). Local govt officer, W Midlands LDs; former chmn and treas, Wolverhampton SE pty; chmn, Hull ULS, 1971-73; chmn, Hull Central, 1973. B Nov 27 1951; ed Hull Univ. NUT.

WOLVERHAMPTON SOUTH WEST						No change
Electorate % Turnout	67,288	78.3%	1992	68,586	75.5%	1987
*Budgen, N W (C)	25,969	49.3%	-1.4%	26,235	50.7%	C
Murphy, Dr S F (Lab)	21,003	39.9%	+9.1%	15,917	30.7%	Lab
Wiggin, M (LD)	4,470	8.5%	-10.1%	9,616	18.6%	SDP/All
Hallmark, C (Lib)	1,237	2.3%				
C to Lab swing 5.3%	52,679		9.4%	51,768		19.9%
		C maj	4,966		C maj	10,318

Nicholas Budgen, barrister and farmer, has been mbr of Select Cmte on Treasury and Civil Service, since 1983; Public Accounts Cmte, 1980-1. Consultant to Barnett International. Elected in Feb 1974; contested Birmingham, Small Heath, 1970. Asst govt whip, 1981-2. Sec, Cons backbench finance cmte, 1979. B Nov 3 1937; ed St Edward's Sch, Oxford; Corpus Christi Coll,

Cambridge. Chmn, Birmingham Bow Gp, 1967-68.
Simon Murphy, research/press officer to MEP. B Feb 24 1962; ed Sacred Heart Coll, Droitwich; N Worcs CFHE, Bromsgrove; UCW, Aberystwyth. Nupe, GMB.
Mark Wiggin, mature student. Editor, LD Focus. Mbr, Newport TC; NFU (ex-farmer). B Dec 4 1955; ed Adams GS, Newport, Shrops; Keele Univ.

WOODSPRING						No change
Electorate % Turnout	77,534	83.2%	1992	76,289	79.1%	1987
Fox, Dr L (C)	35,175	54.5%	-2.1%	34,134	56.6%	C
Kirsen, Mrs N E (LD)	17,666	27.4%	+0.4%	16,282	27.0%	L/All
Stone, R E (Lab)	9,942	15.4%	+1.0%	8,717	14.4%	Lab
Brown, N (Lib)	836	1.3%		1,208	2.0%	Grn
Knifton, Mrs R J (Grn)	801	1.2%	-0.8%			
Lee, B (NLP)	100	0.2%				
C to LD swing 1.2%	64,520		27.1%	60,341		29.6%
		C maj	17,509		C maj	17,852

Dr Liam Fox, a general practitioner, retained this seat for the Cons in 1992; contested Roxburgh and Berwickshire 1987. Mbr Royal Coll of General Practitioners, 1989. Former army medical officer; divisional surgeon, St John Ambulance. Former registrar, Hairmyres Hospital, East Kilbride; nat vice-chmn, Scottish YCs, 1983-4; mbr, central cmte, Families for Defence, 1987-9; Beaconsfield CPC. B Sep 22 1961; ed St Bride's HS, East Kilbride; Glasgow Univ (Pres, univ Cons club, 1982-83).
Nan Kirsen, former NHS medical sec/nursing and administration. Mbr, Woodspring DC, 1986- (gp ldr,

1987-); Easton-in-Gardano PC, 1981- . Part owner of graphics design studio run by husband. B Aug 23 1944; ed Abbotsleigh Primary Sch; Gordano Sec Mod Sch; took O-levels at night sch.
Ronald Stone, science technician; mbr, Avon CC, 1985- . B Dec 21 1942; ed Bristol Tech Sch; Brunel Tech Coll. ASTMS/MSF, being shop steward at Bristol Univ; former mbr, nat negotiating cmte, univ technicians.
Rosey Knifton, small holder and child minder; local Grn Pty treas. Mbr, Woodspring DC. B Jun 7 1947; ed St Brandons, Clevedon; Open Univ.

WOOLWICH						Lab gain
Electorate % Turnout	55,977	70.9%	1992	58,071	70.7%	1987
Austin-Walker, J (Lab)	17,551	44.2%	+7.2%	17,137	41.7%	SDP/All
*Cartwright, J C (SD)	15,326	38.6%	-3.1%	15,200	37.0%	Lab
Walmsley, K J T (C)	6,598	16.6%	-4.6%	8,723	21.2%	C
Hayward, Ms S (NLP)	220	0.6%				
Soc Dem to Lab swing 5.2%	39,695		5.6%	41,060		4.7%
		Lab maj	2,225		SDP/All maj	1,937

John Austin-Walker, popularly known as 'Jaws', won this seat for Lab 1992; contested it 1987. Race equality officer; nat chmn, Assocn of Community Health Cls, England and Wales, 1981-83. Chmn London Ecology Unit and of Emergency Planning Information Centre. Former sec/agent, Greenwich Lab Pty; former agent at Swindon. Mbr, Greenwich BC, 1970- (mayor 1987-9; ldr of cl, 1982-7). Vice-chmn, ALA, 1983-7; London Strategic Policy Unit, 1986-88. B Aug 21 1944; ed Glyn GS, Epsom; Goldsmiths Coll, New Cross. Past chmn, Greenwich MIND and British Youth Cl. MSF.
John Cartwright was SDP president 1988-90; Vice-Pres, 1987-8. Alliance spokesman on defence in 1987 election;

SDP spokesman on defence and foreign affairs, 1983-90, and environment, 1981-3. Non-exec director, SE London Cable Co, 1989-90. Mbr, Select Cmte on Defence, 1979-82 and 1986-92. SDP whip 1983-90. Sec all-pty retail trade gp, 1991-2; construction gp. Elected Lab MP for Woolwich E Oct 1974; resigned pty and joined SDP, 1981. SDP MP for this seat, 1983-90; Ind SD MP since pty dissolved in 1990. As Lab fought Bexleyheath Feb 1974 and Bexley 1970. B Nov 29 1933; ed Woking CGS.
Kevin Walmsley, snr tax manager with chartered accountancy practice. Mbr, Dartford BC, 1983- . Chmn, Dartford Cons Assocn, 1989-91. B Aug 20 1959; ed Southlands HS, Chorley; Runshaw Coll, Leyland; Liverpool Univ.

WORCESTER						No change
Electorate % Turnout	74,211	81.0%	1992	68,980	76.7%	1987
Luff, P J (C)	27,883	46.4%	-1.8%	25,504	48.2%	C
Berry, R E (Lab)	21,731	36.2%	+7.7%	15,051	28.4%	Lab
Caiger, J J (LD)	9,561	15.9%	-7.5%	12,386	23.4%	SDP/All
Foster, M J (Grn)	592	1.0%				
Soden, M (Brewer)	343	0.6%				
C to Lab swing 4.8%	60,110		10.2%	52,941		19.7%
		C maj	6,152		C maj	10,453

Peter Luff, public affairs consultant, contested Holborn and St Pancras in 1987. Head of Sir Edward Heath's private office, 1980-82; from 1977-79 research asst to Peter Walker, MP for Worcester from 1961 until this election. Asst managing director, Good Relations Ltd, 1990- ; former company sec of family stationery firm, Luff and Sons Ltd. B Feb 18 1955; ed Windsor GS; Corpus Christi Coll, Cambridge.
Roger Berry, social worker now employed as principal planning and development officer for social services dept. Worcester regional cmte mbr, Co-op Retail Services; pres, Worcester CLP, 1990- ; mbr, Worcester City Cl, 1974-76

and 1981- . Chair, Worcester branch, Co-op Pty and Co-op Society. B Aug 3 1945; ed The GS, Hanley Castle; Lanchester Coll of Tech, Coventry; Liverpool Univ; B'ham Poly. Nalgo.
John Caiger, professional charity fund raiser, contested the seat 1987. Director, Hambros Bank, 1984-90; Lt Colonel, Army (1955-84). B Jul 11 1936; ed Dover Coll; RMA Sandhurst.
Mike Foster, marketing manager; press officer, Worcester Grn Pty. B Sep 26 1948; ed Sir Wm Borlase GS, Marlow; Umist.

WORCESTERSHIRE MID						No change
Electorate % Turnout	84,269	81.1%	1992	80,591	76.6%	1987
*Forth, M E (C)	33,964	49.7%	-1.9%	31,854	51.6%	C
Smith, Ms J J (Lab)	24,094	35.3%	+7.8%	16,943	27.4%	Lab
Barwick, D (LD)	9,745	14.3%	-6.7%	12,954	21.0%	SDP/All
Davis, P (NLP)	520	0.8%				
C to Lab swing 4.9%	68,323		14.4%	61,751		24.1%
		C maj	9,870		C maj	14,911

Eric Forth was appointed under sec for education in April 1992; under sec for employment 1990-2; consumer affairs minr 1988-90. Elected in 1983; contested Barking, Feb and Oct 1974. MEP for North Birmingham, 1979-84. PPS to Minr of State for Ed and Science 1986-7. Chmn (1987-8) and vice-chmn (1983-6), Cons backbench European Affairs cmte. Mbr, Select Cmte on Employment, 1983-7; sec Cons backbench sports cmte, 1985-6. B Sep 9 1944; ed Jordanhill Coll Sch, Glasgow; Glasgow Univ. Mbr, Brentwood UDC, 1968-72.

Jacqui Smith, teacher. Mbr, Redditch BC. Constituency women's officer; previously Nat Organisation of Lab Students. B Nov 3 1962; ed Dyson Perrins CE HS, Malvern; Hertford Coll, Oxford.
David Barwick, adult ed coordinator; mbr, Redditch BC, 1986-90; LD reg exec. Has chaired constituency Libs and LDs. B Apr 23 1947; ed Caludon Castle Sch, Coventry; St Peter's Coll, B'ham; Open Univ.

WORCESTERSHIRE SOUTH						No change
Electorate % Turnout	80,423	80.0%	1992	77,237	75.6%	1987
*Spicer, W M H (C)	34,792	54.1%	-1.2%	32,277	55.3%	C
Chandler, P J (LD)	18,641	29.0%	-2.9%	18,632	31.9%	L/All
Knowles, N (Lab)	9,727	15.1%	+4.2%	6,374	10.9%	Lab
Woodford, G M H (Grn)	1,178	1.8%	-0.0%	1,089	1.9%	Grn
LD to C swing 0.9%	64,338		25.1%	58,372		23.4%
		C maj	16,151		C maj	13,645

Michael Spicer was Minr for Housing and Planning with rank of Minr of State for Environment in 1990; Under Sec of State for Energy, 1987-90; Under Sec of State for Transport, 1984-87, being Minr for Aviation, 1985-87. Pres, Assocn of Independent Electricity Producers, 1991- . Elected in Feb 1974; contested Easington, 1966 and 1970. Vice-chmn, Cons Party, 1981-83; dep chmn, 1983-85. PPS to Minrs of State for Trade, 1979-81. Mbr, Cons Research Dept, 1966-68; director, Cons Systems Research Centre, 1968-70. B Jan 22 1943; ed Wellington Coll; Emmanuel Coll, Cambridge.

Paul Chandler, tour operator, contested this seat 1987. Mbr, Malvern Hill DC, 1982-87; Hereford and Worcester CC, 1985- . B Nov 9 1949; ed Felsted Sch, Essex; Essex and Birmingham Univs.

Nigel Knowles, writer, contested Wyre Forest 1987, Hastings 1983, Bodmin 1979. Mbr, Wyre Forest DC, 1990- ; Hereford and Worcester CC, 1989- ; Haringey BC, 1982-87. B Dec 5 1946; ed King Charles I GS, Kidderminster; Bham Poly; Worcester CFE. MSF.

WORKINGTON						No change
Electorate % Turnout	57,597	81.5%	1992	56,911	80.6%	1987
*Campbell-Savours, D N (Lab)	26,719	56.9%	+4.5%	24,019	52.4%	Lab
Sexton, S E (C)	16,270	34.7%	-2.4%	17,000	37.1%	C
Neale, Ms C (LD)	3,028	6.4%	-4.1%	4,853	10.6%	L/All
Langstaff, D (Loony)	755	1.6%				
Escott, N (NLP)	183	0.4%				
C to Lab swing 3.5%	46,955		22.3%	45,872		15.3%
		Lab maj	10,449		Lab maj	7,019

Dale Campbell-Savours became Opposn deputy front bench spokesman on overseas development and cooperation and overseas aid in 1991. Served on Public Accounts Cmte, 1982-91; Select Cmte on MPs Interests, 1982- , and on Procedure, 1982-91. Former mbr, exec cmte, UK branch, CPA. Regained Workington for Lab 1979; contested seat 1976 by-election; Darwen, Feb and Oct, 1974. Director, clock manufacturing company, 1971-76. B Aug 23 1943; ed Keswick Sch; Sorbonne. Mbr, Ramsbottom UDC, 1972-74. TGWU. Sponsored by Cohse.

Stuart Sexton is director, education unit, Inst of Economic Affairs; was special adviser to then Sir Keith Joseph and Mark Carlisle as Sec of State for Ed and Science. Chmn, Ind Primary and Sec Ed Trust. Contested Warrington N 1983. Was executive with Shell International chemical company and Shell Italiana. Held RAF commission being head of chemistry dept, RAF Tech Coll. B Sep 14 1934; ed St Joseph's Coll, London; Imperial Coll of Science.

Christine Neale, housewife, part-time teacher; has arts and crafts business; formerly worked in City business administration. Aged 39; ed in London. Voluntary worker for environmental country gps.

WORSLEY						No change
Electorate % Turnout	72,244	77.7%	1992	73,208	77.2%	1987
*Lewis, T (Lab)	29,418	52.4%	+4.3%	27,157	48.1%	Lab
Cameron, N (C)	19,406	34.6%	-0.5%	19,820	35.1%	C
Boyd, R D (LD)	6,490	11.6%	-5.3%	9,507	16.8%	L/All
Connolly, P J (Grn)	677	1.2%				
Phillips, G (NLP)	176	0.3%				
C to Lab swing 2.4%	56,167		17.8%	56,484		13.0%
		Lab maj	10,012		Lab maj	7,337

Terry Lewis, a personnel officer, was elected in 1983. Mbr, Select Cmte on Environment, 1991- . Chmn, all-pty leasehold reform parly gp, 1989- ; jt sec, parly cmte for animal welfare, 1990- . B Dec 29 1935; ed Mount Carmel Sch, Salford. Mbr, Bolton BC, 1975- (education cmte chmn, 1982-83); Kearsley UDC, 1971-74. Sponsored by TGWU.

Neil Cameron, barrister; mbr, Lambeth BC, 1986-90. Underwriting mbr of Lloyd's. B 1959; ed Durham Univ (Pres, union society). Mbr, Bow Gp; Society of Cons Lawyers; Foreign Affairs Forum; British Atlantic Gp of Young Politicians.

Robert Boyd, retired tech coll chemistry teacher; hon life mbr, NATFHE; sec, Worsley LDs; mbr, LD NW region exec cmte. B Jan 10 1933; ed Hymers Coll, Hull; Hull Municipal Tech Coll — London External. Former vice-chmn, Salford SDP.

Philip Connolly, lecturer on building studies. Treas, Salford Grn Pty. B Apl 20 1960; ed Greenhilld, Rochdale; Exhall Grange, Coventry. Quaker.

WORTHING						No change
Electorate % Turnout	77,540	77.4%	1992	77,000	72.8%	1987
*Higgins, T L (C)	34,198	57.0%	-4.7%	34,573	61.7%	C
Bucknall, Ms S (LD)	17,665	29.4%	+0.7%	16,072	28.7%	L/All
Deen, J (Lab)	6,679	11.1%	+1.5%	5,387	9.6%	Lab
Beever, Mrs P (Grn)	806	1.3%				
Goble, N (Lib)	679	1.1%				
C to LD swing 2.7%	60,027		27.5%	56,032		33.0%
		C maj	16,533		C maj	18,501

Terence Higgins, economist, became chmn, Select Cmte on Treasury and Civil Service, in 1983; mbr since 1980. PC 1979. Chmn, HoC Liaison Cmte, 1984- . Governor, Nat Inst of Economic and Social Research, 1989- . Mbr, Cmte on Privileges, 1989- ; Public Accounts Commission, 1984- . Chmn, Cons back-bench transport cmte, 1979-82 and 1985-90. Financial Sec to the Treasury, 1972-4; Minr of State, Treasury, 1970-2. Elected 1964. B Jan 18 1928; ed Alleyn's Sch, Dulwich; Gonville and Caius Coll, Cambridge; Yale. Chmn, Langley Sports Ltd; director, Lex Service Group, 1980- ; Lex Employee Share Scheme Trustees Ltd and Owners Abroad Gp plc. Mbr exec 1922 Cmte 1980- . Former Olympic and Commonwealth Games

athlete. Cl mbr Inst of Advanced Motorists, 1980- . Governor, Dulwich Coll, 1980- .
Sue Bucknall, barrister; mbr, Adur Cl, 1987- (dep gp ldr; ch, community services and environment cmte, 1989-). B Dec 12 1947.
Jim Deen, group editor, contested this seat 1987. B Mar 6 1946; ed Queen Elizabeth GS, Wakefield; Manchester Univ. Mbr, Periodicals Training Cl; cl, Gardeners Royal Benevolent Society. NUJ.
Pauline Beever, snr environmental health officer with Arun DC; occupational safety and health specialist. B Jul 1 1954; ed Queen Anne GS, York; Ricards Lodge, Wimbledon; Bristol Poly; Kings Coll, London. Nalgo.

WREKIN, THE						No change
Electorate % Turnout	90,892	77.1%	1992	82,520	78.3%	1987
*Grocott, B (Lab)	33,865	48.3%	+5.5%	27,681	42.8%	Lab
Holt, Mrs E (C)	27,217	38.8%	-1.8%	26,225	40.6%	C
West, A C (LD)	8,032	11.5%	-5.2%	10,737	16.6%	SDP/All
Saunders, R (Grn)	1,008	1.4%				
C to Lab swing 3.6%	70,122		9.5%	64,643		2.3%
		Lab maj	6,648		Lab maj	1,456

Bruce Grocott became dep shadow Ldr of the House and dep Lab campaigns coordinator in 1987. Won this seat 1987; contested it 1983; MP for Lichfield and Tamworth, Oct 1974-9; contested it Feb 1974; SW Hertfordshire 1970. Television presenter and producer, 1979-87. Mbr, Select Cmte on Broadcasting, 1988- . Chmn, all-pty penal reform gp, 1976-79. Mbr, Select Cmte on Overseas Development, 1978-79; Bromsgrove DC, 1971-4 (chmn finance cmte). B Nov 1 1940; ed Hemel Hempstead GS; Leicester and Manchester Univs. Lecturer in politics, Manchester Univ, Birmingham Poly and N Staffordshire

Poly, 1964-74. NUJ.
Elizabeth Holt, communications company director, was a board mbr, Telford Development Corporation, 1975-91 (dpty chmn 1986-91). Contested Wolverhampton SE, Oct 1974. Mbr, Shropshire CC, 1973-81 and 1989- ; Wrekin DC, 1973-79; Petersfield RDC, 1961-66. Chmn Wrekin Cons; West Midlands Cons Social Affairs. B 1928; ed St Helen's Sch, Northwood.
Tony West, nurse tutor/lecturer; mbr, Newport West TC, 1991- ; vice-chmn, Newport (Shropshire) LDs. B Nov 10 1945; ed in Birmingham. RCN.

WREXHAM						No change
Electorate % Turnout	63,720	80.7%	1992	62,401	80.9%	1987
*Marek, Dr J (Lab)	24,830	48.3%	+4.4%	22,144	43.9%	Lab
Paterson, O W (C)	18,114	35.2%	-0.4%	17,992	35.6%	C
Thomas, A (LD)	7,074	13.8%	-5.7%	9,808	19.4%	L/All
Wheatley, G (PC)	1,415	2.8%	+1.7%	539	1.1%	PC
C to Lab swing 2.4%	51,433		13.1%	50,483		8.2%
		Lab maj	6,716		Lab maj	4,152

John Marek became an Opposn spokesman on Treasury and economic affairs and on Civil Service in 1987; in Opposn DHSS front bench team, 1985-87, as a health spokesman. Jt chmn, all-pty aviation parly gp; chmn, 1989-90, and vice-chmn, 1988-89, Welsh Lab MPs; mbr, Select Cmte on Welsh Affairs, 1983-86; PAC, 1985; all-pty road study gp. Jt vice-chmn, 1991- , and previously mbr, exec cmte, UK branch, CPA. Elected in 1983; contested Ludlow, Oct 1974. B Dec 24 1940; ed London Univ. Lecturer in applied maths, UCW, Aberystwyth, 1966-83. Mbr, Ceredigion DC, 1979-83; International Astronomical Union. Fellow, Industry and Parliament Trust. Sponsored by RMT.

Owen Paterson, tanner, has been director, British Leather Co, Birkenhead, since 1985; UK rep to Euro Tanning Fed. Mbr, Ellesmere Cottage Hospital action gp, 1988-89. B 24 1956; ed Radley; Corpus Christi Coll, Cambridge. Assisted John Biffen in North Shropshire in 1987 election.
Andrew Thomas, barrister. Mbr, Welsh LDs consumer affairs panel. B Oct 18 1965; ed Darland Comprehensive and Yale Sixth Form Coll, Wrexham; Cambridge Univ; Inns of Court Sch of Law. Son of Martin Thomas, QC, who contested this seat for L/All in 1987.
Gareth Wheatley, snr lecturer in NE Wales Inst. Ed Bishop Gore Sch; UCW, Aberystwyth.

WYCOMBE					No change	
Electorate % Turnout	72,564	78.0%	1992	71,918	72.8%	1987
*Whitney, R W (C)	30,081	53.1%	-0.7%	28,209	53.9%	C
Andrews, T W (LD)	13,005	23.0%		14,390	27.5%	SDP/All
Huddart, J R W (Lab)	12,222	21.6%	+2.9%	9,773	18.7%	Lab
Laker, J S (Grn)	686	1.2%				
Page, A (Soc Dem)	449	0.8%	-26.7%			
Anton, T (NLP)	168	0.3%				
LD to C swing 1.9%	56,611		30.2%	52,372		26.4%
		C maj	17,076		C maj	13,819

Raymond Whitney was Under Sec of State for Social Security, DHSS, 1984-85, and Under Sec of State for Health, DHSS, 1885-86; Under Sec of State for Foreign and Commonwealth Affairs, 1983-84. Chmn, Windsor Cable Television, 1989- ; Cable Corporation, 1989- . Elected at by-election in 1978. Chmn, all-pty British-Latin American parly gp, 1987- ; Cl for Defence Information, 1987- ; Mountbatten Community Trust; treas, all-pty cable and satellite TV parly gp. B Nov 28 1930; ed Wellingborough Sch; RMA Sandhurst; London Univ; Australian Nat Univ, Canberra; BIM. . In diplomatic service: First Sec, Peking, 1966-68; Hd of Chancery, British Embassy, Buenos Aires, 1969-72; Asst Hd, E African Dept, FCO, 1972-73; Dep High Commissioner and Economic Counsellor, Dacca, 1973-76; Hd of Information Research Dept and Overseas Information Dept, FCO, 1976-78.

Tim Andrews, management accountant; mbr, Wycombe DC, 1991- ; Marlow TC, 1987-91. Vice-chmn, Wycombe LDs; mbr, LD Christian Forum; Amnesty International, Greenpeace. B Jul 4 1965; ed John Hampden GS, High Wycombe.

John Huddart, retired business exec, contested this seat 1987. Mbr, Bucks CC, 1989- (Lab gp ldr); Newcastle City Cl, 1954-57. Chair, Wycombe Shelter gp, 1987- ; vice-chair, Wycombe Ed Concern. B May 25 1926; ed Rutherford Coll, Newcastle upon Tyne; Durham Univ; LSE. TGWU, MSF.

John Laker, managing director of ltd co. Co-chair, Grn Pty. B Aug 5 1946; ed state and private schs; college.

WYRE					No change	
Electorate % Turnout	67,778	79.5%	1992	67,066	75.4%	1987
*Mans, K D R (C)	29,449	54.6%	+1.6%	26,800	53.0%	C
Borrow, D (Lab)	17,785	33.0%	+11.8%	12,139	24.0%	SDP/All
Ault, J (LD)	6,420	11.9%	-12.1%	10,725	21.2%	Lab
Perry, R (NLP)	260	0.5%		874	1.7%	Grn
C to Lab swing 5.1%	53,914		21.6%	50,538		29.0%
		C maj	11,664		C maj	14,661

Keith Mans became PPS to Virginia Bottomley in 1990. Asst general inspector, 1987-9, and from 1978-87 retail manager with John Lewis Partnership. Elected in 1987; contested Stoke-on-Trent Central, 1983. Mbr, Select Cmtes on Cardiff Bay Barrage Bill, 1991- ; Environment, 1987-91. Vice-chmn, Cons backbench fisheries sub-cmte, 1987-90 ; jt sec, Cons backbench aviation cmte, 1987-90; Cons environment cmte, 1989-90. Sec, all-pty aviation parly gp; Cons NW mbrs gp. RAF pilot (Flight Lt), 1964-77; pilot in RAF Reserve, 1977- . B Feb 10 1946; ed Berkhamsted Sch; RAF Coll, Cranwell; Open Univ.

David Borrow, clerk to Merseyside valuation and community charge panel; mbr, Preston BC, 1987- . B Aug 2 1952; ed Mirfield GS; Manchester Poly.

John Ault is in hotel and catering trade; chmn Warrington YLDs 1991- ; mbr, nat exec, YLDs, 1989-91; Appleton PC, 1991- . B Aug 5 1970; ed Grange Sch, Hartford; Edge Hill Coll of HE.

WYRE FOREST					No change	
Electorate % Turnout	73,550	82.4%	1992	70,784	77.6%	1987
*Coombs, A M V (C)	28,983	47.8%	+0.7%	25,877	47.1%	C
Maden, R (Lab)	18,642	30.8%	+11.9%	18,653	34.0%	L/All
Jones, M (LD)	12,958	21.4%	-12.6%	10,365	18.9%	Lab
C to Lab swing 5.6%	60,583		17.1%	54,895		13.2%
		C maj	10,341		C maj	7,224

Anthony Coombs was elected in 1987; contested Coventry NW in 1983. PPS to David Mellor 1989- . Jt sec Cons backbench ed cmte 1987-9; sec, all-pty human rights gp. Managing director, Grevayne Properties Ltd, 1972- , and former director of several Midlands based companies including S & U Stores plc. Mbr Birmingham City Cl, since 1978. B Nov 18 1952; ed Bilton Grange Sch; Charterhouse Sch, Surrey; Worcester Coll, Oxford. Chmn of governors, Perry Common Sch, Birmingham, 1978- ; governor, King Edward Foundation, 1982-88; Birmingham Coll of Tourism, 1982-88. Pres, Wyre Forest 'Solidarity' campaign, 1987- .

Ross Maden, education adviser; mbr, Hereford and Worcs CC, 1985-91; chaired W Midlands regional Lab Pty, 1989-91; sec, CLP. B Mar 9 1947; ed Wolverhampton GS; Worcester Coll of Ed; Open Univ. NUT.

Mark Jones, volunteer bureau development officer. B Jun 12 1964. Vice-chmn, mobile ed project.

YEOVIL						No change
Electorate % Turnout	73,057	82.0%	1992	70,390	79.7%	1987
*Ashdown, J J D (LD)	30,958	51.7%	+0.3%	28,841	51.4%	L/All
Davidson, J (C)	22,125	36.9%	-4.3%	23,141	41.3%	C
Nelson, Ms V (Lab)	5,765	9.6%	+2.3%	4,099	7.3%	Lab
Risbridger, J (Grn)	639	1.1%				
Sutch, D (Loony)	338	0.6%				
Simmerson, R (APAKBI)	70	0.1%				
C to LD swing 2.3%	59,895		14.7%	56,081		10.2%
		LD maj	8,833		L/All maj	5,700

Paddy Ashdown was elected first Leader of the Liberal Democrats in 1988, defeating Mr Alan Beith by 41,401 votes (71.9%) to 16,202 (28.1%). PC 1989. LD spokesman on N Ireland, 1988-90; Lib and then LD spokesman on ed and science, 1987-8; spokesman on trade and industry, 1983-7. Alliance spokesman on education in 1987 election. Won this seat in 1983; contested it, 1979. B Feb 24 1941; ed Bedford Sch. Capt Royal Marines 1959-71; served with Commando units and Special Boat Service in Far East. Qualified Chinese (Mandarin) interpreter at MoD Chinese Language School, Hong Kong. First Secretary to UK mission to UN in Geneva 1971-6; employed at Westland Helicopters, Yeovil, 1976-8; senior manager, Morlands, Yeovil, 1978-81; local govt officer, Dorset CC 1981-3.

Julian Davidson, director, Davidson Gp, a family firm. Mbr Somerset CC (chmn performance review and special purposes cmte; vice-chmn resources cmte). Chmn Wyvern Waste Services Ltd. Mbr management cmte Taunton constituency Cons Assocn; chmn Taunton CPC, 1987-9. B Mar 21 1963; ed Gravesend GS; Hatfield Coll, Durham Univ.
Viv Nelson, snr lecturer in management and director of Pentlever Consultants Ltd. Former pty chmn and sec. B May 19 1954; ed Bootle GS; Univ Coll, Cardiff; Warwick Univ. NATFHE.
Jay Risbridger, company director, recycled paper industry. Mbr Grn pty cl. B Jun 21 1957; ed Lancing Coll, Sussex; Bradford Univ.

YNYS MON						No change
Electorate % Turnout	53,412	80.6%	1992	52,633	81.7%	1987
*Wyn Jones, I (PC)	15,984	37.1%	-6.1%	18,580	43.2%	PC
Price Rowlands, G (C)	14,878	34.6%	+1.3%	14,282	33.2%	C
Jones, Dr R O (Lab)	10,126	23.5%	+6.6%	7,255	16.9%	Lab
Badger, Mrs P E (LD)	1,891	4.4%	-2.3%	2,863	6.7%	SDP/All
Parry, Mrs S (NLP)	182	0.4%				
PC to C swing 3.7%	43,061		2.6%	42,980		10.0%
		PC maj	1,106		PC maj	4,298

Ieuan Wyn Jones, solicitor and partner in practice, 1974-87, won this seat in 1987; contested it 1983, West Denbigh in 1979 and Oct 1974, and North Wales in Euro elections, 1979. Mbr select cmte on Wesh affairs, 1989- ; jt vice-chmn all-pty Friends of Croatia gp 1991- . Nat chmn PC 1990- and 1980-2; nat vice-chmn 1975-9. B May 22 1949; ed Pontardawe GS; Ysgol-y-Berwyn, Y Bala, Gwynedd; Liverpool Poly.

Gwyn Price Rowlands, barrister. B 1951; ed Friars and Brynhyfryd Schs; Liverpool and London Univs. Former North Wales youth public speaking champion.
Robin Jones, univ lecturer. B Jan 10 1936; UCNW, Bangor; Edinburgh Univ.
Pauline Badger, occupational therapist. B Jun 12 1947; ed Wallasey HS; Liverpool Coll of Occupational Therapy.

YORK						Lab gain
Electorate % Turnout	79,242	81.0%	1992	79,297	78.4%	1987
Bayley, H (Lab)	31,525	49.1%	+7.7%	25,880	41.6%	C
*Gregory, C R (C)	25,183	39.2%	-2.4%	25,733	41.4%	Lab
Anderson, Mrs K J (LD)	6,811	10.6%	-5.3%	9,898	15.9%	SDP/All
Kenwright, S (Grn)	594	0.9%	-0.1%	637	1.0%	Grn
Orr, Ms P (NLP)	54	0.1%				
C to Lab swing 5.1%	64,167		9.9%	62,148		0.2%
		Lab maj	6,342		C maj	147

Hugh Bayley, health economist, univ lecturer, and freelance TV producer, won the seat for Labour in 1992 having contested it in 1987. Director (unpaid) York cl for voluntary service. Mbr and former sec, exec cmte Lab co-ordinating-cmte; chmn Yorkshire region Fabian Society. Nat officer Nalgo 1977-82. Mbr York HA 1988-90; Camden cl 1980-6 (chmn employment cmte 1981-2 and Lab gp 1982-5). B Jan 9 1952; ed Haileybury Sch; Bristol and York Univs. Founder and sec International Broadcasting Trust 1982-6. AUT.
Conal Gregory, Master of Wine and company director, won

the seat 1983. Jt vice-chmn (1990-2 and 1987-9) and jt sec (1983-7), Cons backbench transport cmte; chmn (1989-92) and vice-chmn (1985-9), Cons food and drinks industries sub-cmte; jt vice-chmn Cons tourism cmte 1985- ; all-pty hospice gp 1990- ; jt vice-chmn 1991- , and sec 1983-91, tourism cmte.. B Mar 11 1947; ed King's Coll Sch, Wimbledon; Sheffield Univ; Worshipful Co of Vintners.
Karen Anderson, teacher; social care development officer for Diocese of York. B Nov 23 1960; ed Queen Elizabeth Sch, Wimborne; St John's Coll, Oxford. AMMA.

Abbreviations

The following abbreviations have been used in the biographies of MPs and candidates:

ABA	Amateur Boxing Association
Acad	Academy
ACC	Association of County Councils
ACTT	Association of Cinematograph, Television and Allied Technicians
AHA	Area Health Authority
ALC	Association of Liberal Councillors
AMA	Association of Metropolitan Authorities
AMP	Advance management programme
Apex	Association of Professional Executive clerical and Computer Staff
APCT	Association of Polytechnic and College Teachers
APT	Association of Polytechnic Teachers
ASLDC	Association of Social and Liberal Democratic Councillors
Aslef	Associated Society of Locomotive Engineers and Firemen
Assocn	Association
Asst	Assistant
AUEW/TASS	Amalgamated Union of Engineering Workers (Technical Administrative and Supervisory Section)
AUT	Association of University Teachers
B	Born
BC	Borough Council
Bd	Board
BEC	Building Employers' Confederation
BIFU	Banking Insurance and Finance Union
BMA	British Medical Association
BR	British Rail
CAB	Citizens Advice Bureau
CBC	County Borough Council
CBI	Confederation of British Industries
CC	County Council
CFE	College of Further Education
CHC	Community Health Council
CHE	College of Higher Education
Chmn	Chairman
Cl	Council
CLA	Country Landowners' Association
Cllr	Councillor
CLP	Constituency Labour Party
Cmte	Committee
CND	Campaign for Nuclear Disarmament
Cohse	Confederation of Health Service Employees
Coll	College
Confed	Confederation
Cons	Conservative
Co-op	Co-operative Party
Corp	Corporation
Cosla	Convention of Scottish Local Authorities
CPA	Commonwealth Parliamentary Association
CPSA	Civil and Public Service Association
CPC	Conservative Political Centre
CSD	Council for Social Democracy
Cty	County
DC	District Council
Dept	Department
DHA	District health authority
DHSS	Department of Health and Social Security
Dist	District
Div	Division
DLP	Divisional Labour Party
DSS	Department of Social Security
DTI	Department of Trade and Industry
EC	European Community
Ed	Education
EEC	European Economic Community
EETPU	Electrical, Electronic, Telecommunications, and Plumbing Union
EIS	Educational Institute of Scotland
EPEA	Electrical Power Engineers Association
Euro	European
Exec	Executive
FBU	Fire Brigades Union
FCO	Foreign and Commonwealth Office
FCS	Federation of Conservative Students
Fed	Federation
FIMechE	Fellow, Institute of Mechanical Engineers
FOC	Father (chairman) of Chapel (branch), NUJ
FRS	Fellow of Royal Society
GLC	Greater London Council
GMB	General, Municipal, Boilermakers and Allied Trades Union
GMC	General management committee
Govt	Government
Gp	Group
GPMU	Graphical, Paper and Media Union
GS	Grammar School
HS	High School
ICE	Institution of Civil Engineers
ILEA	Inner London Education Authority
Info	Information
Inst	Institute
IOJ	Institute of Journalists
IPCS	Institution of Professional Civil Servants
IPU	Interparliamentary Union
IRSF	Inland Revenue Staff Federation
ISTC	Iron and Steel Trades Confederation
Jt	Joint
L and Lib	Liberal
Lab	Labour
Lancs	Lancashire
Ld	Lord
LD	Liberal Democrat
Ldr	Leader
LSE	London School of Economics
Mass	Massachusetts
MATSA	Managerial Administrative Technical Staff Association
MBC	Metropolitan Borough Council
Mbr	Member
MDC	Metropolitan District Council
MEP	Member of European Parliament
Minr	Minister
MSFU	Manufacturing, Science and Finance Union
Nacods	National Association of Collierymen etc
NAHT	National Association of Head Teachers
Nalgo	National Association of Local Government Officers
NAS	National Association of Schoolmasters
Nat	National
NATFHE	National Association of Teachers in Further and Higher Education
NCB	National Coal Board
NCER	National Council for Electoral Reform
NCU	National Communications Union
NEC	National executive committee
NFBTE	National Federation of Building Trades Employers
NFU	National Farmers' Union
NI	Northern Ireland
NLVA	National Licensed Victuallers' Association
NLYL	National League of Young Liberals
NUJ	National Union of Journalists
NUM	National Union of Mineworkers
Numast	National Union of Marine and Shipping Transport Officers
Nupe	National Union of Public Employees
NUR	National Union of Railwaymen (now RMT)
NUS	National Union of Seamen (now RMT)
NUS	National Union of Students
PAC	Public Accounts Committee
Parly	Parliamentary
PAT	Professional Association of Teachers
PC	Privy Councillor/Parish Council
PLP	Parliamentary Labour Party
Poly	Polytechnic
PPS	Parliamentary Private Secretary
Pres	President
Pty	Party
RCN	Royal College of Nursing
RCVS	Royal College of Veterinary Surgeons
RDC	Rural District Council
Reg	Regional
Rep	Representative
RHA	Regional Health Authority
RMA	Royal Military Academy
RMT	National Union of Rail, Maritime and Transport Workers
RNC	Royal Naval College
Sch	School
SD	Social Democrat
SDP	Social Democratic Party
SEA	Socialist Educational Association
Sec	Secretary
Sec Mod Sch	Secondary Modern School
SFHEA	Scottish Further and Higher Education Assocn
SLD	Social and Liberal Democratic Party
SLP	Scottish Liberal Party
Snr	Senior
Soc	Society
SSAFA	Soldiers', Sailors', and Airmen's Families Association
SSTA	Scottish Secondary Teachers Association
TA	Territorial Army
TC	Town Council
Tech	Technical or Technology
TGWU	Transport and General Workers' Union
Treas	Treasurer
TSSA	Transport Salaried Staffs Association
TV	Television
Ucatt	Union of Construction, Allied Trades and Technicians
UCW	University College of Wales
UDC	Urban District Council/Urban Development Corporation
ULS	Union of Liberal Students
UMIST	Univ of Manchester Inst of Science and Tech
UNA	United Nations Association
Univ	University
USDAW	Union of Shop, Distributive and Allied Workers
WEA	Workers Educational Association
WEU	Western European Union
YHA	Youth Hostels Association
YCs	Young Conservatives
YLs	Young Liberals

How the Nation Voted — April 1992

	C	Lab	LD	Nat	Other	Total
England						
Electorate						36,041,516
Votes	12,796,652	9,551,236	5,398,071	0	401,290	28,147,249
% of vote/turnout	45.5	33.9	19.2	0.0	1.4	78.1
MPs	319	195	10	0	0	524
Candidates	524	524	522	0	757	2,327
						Swing -2.6%
Scotland						
Electorate						3,888,033
Votes	751,954	1,142,866	383,856	629,552	23,327	2,931,555
% of vote/turnout	25.7	39.0	13.1	21.5	0.8	75.4
MPs	11	49	9	3	0	72
Candidates	72	72	72	72	53	341
						Swing +2.5%
Wales						
Electorate						2,195,029
Votes	499,677	865,633	217,457	154,439	11,590	1,748,796
% of vote/turnout	28.6	49.5	12.4	8.8	0.7	79.7
MPs	6	27	1	4	0	38
Candidates	38	38	38	35	31	180
						Swing -2.7%
Northern Ireland						
Electorate						1,125,143
Votes	44,608	0	0	0	740,485	785,093
% of vote/turnout	5.7	0.0	0.0	0.0	94.3	69.8
MPs	0	0	0	0	17	17
Candidates	11	0	0	0	89	100
United Kingdom						
Electorate						43,249,721
Votes	14,092,891	11,559,735	5,999,384	783,991	1,176,692	33,612,693
% of vote/turnout	41.9	34.4	17.8	2.3	3.5	77.7
MPs	336	271	20	7	17	651
Candidates	645	634	632	107	930	2,948
						Swing -1.9%

How the Nation Voted — June 1987

	C	Lab	ALL	Nat	Other	Total
England						
Electorate						35,988,364
Votes	12,521,998	8,006,466	6,467,350	0	137,708	27,133,522
% of vote/turnout	46.1	29.5	23.8	0.0	0.5	75.4
MPs	357	155	10	0	1*	523
Candidates	522	523	523	0	214	1,782
						Swing -1.2%
Scotland						
Electorate						3,952,465
Votes	713,091	1,258,132	570,043	416,473	10,069	2,967,808
% of vote/turnout	24.0	42.4	19.2	14.0	0.3	75.1
MPs	10	50	9	3	0	72
Candidates	72	72	72	71	21	308
						Swing -5.8%
Wales						
Electorate						2,151,332
Votes	501,316	765,199	304,230	123,599	3,742	1,698,086
% of vote/turnout	29.5	45.1	17.9	7.3	0.2	78.9
MPs	8	24	3	3	0	38
Candidates	38	38	38	38	6	158
						Swing -4.5%
Northern Ireland						
Electorate						1,089,159
Votes	0	0	0	0	730,152	730,152
% of vote/turnout	0.0	0.0	0.0	0.0	100	67.0
MPs	0	0	0	0	17	17
Candidates	0	0	0	0	77	77
United Kingdom						
Electorate						43,181,320
Votes	13,736,405	10,029,797	7,341,623	540,072	881,671	32,529,568
% of vote/turnout	42.2	30.8	22.6	1.7	2.7	75.3
MPs	375	229	22	6	18*	650
Candidates	632	633	633	109	318	2,325
						Swing -1.7%

* Including the Speaker

Swing from C to Lab in both tables

Doubts cast on two-party system

by Ivor Crewe

The 1992 election returned a Conservative government with a majority of 64 over Labour and of 21 over all parties, enough to sustain it against by-election losses and backbench defectors for a full parliament.

The Conservatives won 336 seats, compared with 375 in 1987, arising from a net loss of 39 to Labour and 2 to the Liberal Democrats. (They also won the extra seat carved out of the over-sized Milton Keynes constituency by the Boundary Commissioners.) To its 39 net gains from the Conservatives, Labour added the three seats held by the rump of the former SDP — Greenwich, Woolwich and Plymouth Devonport — to increase its parliamentary strength from 229 to 271. The Liberal Democrats lost two seats to the Conservatives (Southport and Brecon and Radnor) and one to Plaid Cymru (Ceredigion and Pembroke North), but gained four West Country seats from the Conservatives (Bath, Cheltenham, Cornwall North and Devon North) to end with a total of 20. This is one more than the 19 defended by Liberal Democrats but two down on the 22 won by the Liberal/SDP Alliance in 1987. Plaid Cymru increased its parliamentary representation from three to four, while the number of Scottish Nationalist MPs stayed at three, despite a substantially increased vote. In Northern Ireland the SDLP ousted Sinn Fein from Belfast West, winning four seats altogether; the remaining 13 seats were divided between the Protestant parties in the same proportion as before: nine Official Unionists, three Democratic Unionists, and one independent Unionist.

The election set two records. It was the first occasion since the arrival of the mass franchise that a party had won four elections in a row. By the next election the Conservatives will have held office for 17 or 18 years, the longest spell of continuous government by the same party since the 1820s. The 14.1 million votes obtained by the Conservatives were the largest number ever cast for one party at a British general election.

Despite the record Conservative vote, the result was a less than full-hearted endorsement of the outgoing Conservative government. Its 1987 overall majority of 101 was slashed. The Conservative share of the UK vote slipped from 42.2 to 41.9 per cent, its fourth lowest level since the war, and the smallest vote share on which it has won an election since 1922. In the 1950s it won elections with 48 to 49 per cent of the vote and in 1970, under Edward Heath, it won a similar majority (30) with 46 per cent of the vote.

In one sense the 1992 election was a considerable stride forward for the Labour party. For the second consecutive election it advanced in votes and its gain in seats was its largest since 1966. It finally quashed the challenge from the centre parties. In 1983 Labour's vote share was only 2 points ahead of the Alliance's; in 1987 the gap opened to 8 points; in 1992 it widened further to 17 points.

But the interpretation of election results depends on one's choice of starting point and of performance indicators. Labour's vote share of 34.4 per cent represents only a fairly modest rise from its 30.8 per cent in 1987 and its low point of 27.6 per cent in 1983, and remains well below the 36.9 per cent it obtained in 1979 when Mrs Thatcher first came to power. Since then Labour has failed to make inroads into the Conservative vote, which has remained remarkably steady at 42-44 per cent. Its advance since 1983 has consisted of retrieving most (but not all) of the ground it ceded to the Alliance in 1983. Adjusting for the number of seats it contested, 1992 marks Labour's third worst performance since 1918, the two worse results being 1983 and 1987.

The modest swing to Labour varied across regions and constituencies (see table):

The Conservative vote fell furthest in the South West (-3.0%) and East Midlands (-2.0%) but rose fractionally in Yorkshire and Humberside (+0.5%), the North East (+1.1%) and Scotland (+1.7%) — the first electoral fruits, perhaps, of industrial regeneration after the 1980-2 recession. The Labour vote rose most in the East Midlands (+7.4%), where the miners' strike had damaged it in 1987, in East Anglia (+6.3%), where it regained the considerable

Regional changes (%) 1987-1992

	Cons	Lab	Lib/ Dem	Con-to Lab
South	-1.4	+4.5	-4.4	3.0
Midlands	-1.3	+6.3	-5.8	3.8
Wales	-0.9	+4.4	-5.5	2.7
North	+0.4	+4.1	-4.0	1.9
Scotland	+1.7	-3.4	-6.1	-2.5

ground it had lost to the Alliance in the 1980s, and in London (+5.6%) where it appears to have benefited from the decline of "loony Left" councils.

The result was a setback for the Liberal Democrats who, on the basis of the campaign polls, hoped to win a fifth of the vote and up to 30 seats. In the event their 17.8 per cent of the vote fell 4.5

points below the Alliance's 1987 level and was less than that obtained by the Liberals under Jeremy Thorpe in February 1974 (19.3 per cent) and October 1974.

The departure of the SDP hurt the Liberal Democrats, whose vote collapsed in constituencies where there had been no Liberal tradition but where the SDP had performed well in the 1980s, such as Norfolk North West (-18.1%), Stevenage (-15.9%) Plymouth Drake (-18.2%) and Plymouth Sutton (-15.4%)

Their one compensation was to concentrate their vote somewhat more effectively than before, winning 20 seats compared with 13 to 14 in 1974. Their vote generally fell furthest where it mattered least (where the 1987 election had put them in a distant third place), and held up best where they were the clear challenger or (outside Scotland) already held the seat. They lost only two of the seven seats that would have fallen on a uniform swing.

The Liberal Democrats' hopes of benefiting from tactical voting were generally not realised. Their inability to squeeze the Labour vote any further in Portsmouth South, Hazel Grove, Hereford and, most notably, Falmouth and Camborne, allowed the Conservatives to cling on.

The election put paid to the Liberal Democrats' claim to have replaced Labour as the main challenger in Conservative seats. In 1987 Labour was runner-up in 142 Conservative seats, the Alliance in 230; this time Labour came second in 188 and the Liberal Democrats in only 145.

The result was an even more bitter disappointment for the Scottish Nationalists, who entered the campaign buoyed up by the endorsement of *The Sun* and by 27-28 per cent levels of support in the opinion polls. Their actual vote share was 21.5 per cent, half as much again as in 1987 (14.0 per cent) but well below their peak in October 1974 (30.4 per cent) and no better than February 1974 (21.9 per cent). They held the 3 seats they won in 1987 but gained no extra; Jim Sillars, their by-election victor at Govan, and Dick Douglas, the Labour MP for Dunfermline West who defected to the Nationalists, both failed to be re-elected. The electoral system treated the SNP harshly; in February 1974 with the same share of the vote they won seven seats.

Nor did the SNP's advance in votes provide a strong potential for breakthrough next time. They took second place in 37 of the 72 Scottish seats but came within 10 per cent of the winner in only four.

Plaid Cymru also increased their vote, but very slightly, from 7.3 to 8.8 per cent, their highest share since October 1974. They held their three existing seats in north west Wales and, in perhaps the biggest surprise of the election, jumped from fourth place in 1987 to gain Ceredigion and Pembroke from the Liberal Democrats' Welsh-speaking sheep farmer, Geraint Howells. In the rest of Wales, Plaid's vote share reached double figures in only five seats and was over 25 per cent behind the winner in all but one, its former seat of Carmarthen, where it reduced Labour's lead to five per cent. Carmarthen apart, Plaid appears to have maximised its potential parliamentary strength.

In Northern Ireland it was a good election for the SDLP. It ousted Gerry Adams, the leader of Sinn Fein, from the increasingly Catholic enclave of Belfast West, leaving Sinn Fein with no Westminster MPs. The SDLP probably owed its narrow majority to tactical voting by the constituency's diminishing Protestant minority — a rare example of cross-over voting in the divided province. In the twelve constituencies contested by both parties there was a 1.9 per cent swing from Sinn Fein to the SDLP who always came out ahead.

The total Loyalist vote rose slightly, from 54.8 to 56.1 per cent, while the non-sectarian Alliance party saw its vote drop from 11.4 to 10.0 per cent. With little encouragement from London, local Conservatives contested the Northern Ireland election for the first time, obtaining 10.1 per cent of the vote in the 11 seats they contested, more at the expense of the official Unionists than of the DUP. The Conservative leader won 32 per cent in Down North, coming a strong second to the independent Unionist, James Kilfedder. As in 1987, a stand-down pact between the official Unionists and Democratic Unionists enabled the two parties to hold Fermanagh and South Tyrone and Mid Ulster, where Catholics and Protestants are evenly balanced, against a divided Catholic opposition.

The official turnout, 77.7 per cent, was higher than in 1987 (75.3 per cent), and fractionally above average for elections since February 1974 (when the Liberals and Nationalists first contested most seats). The increase since 1987 was largely the product of a younger and more efficiently compiled electoral register, and the non-registration of approximately 250,000 poll-tax evaders who probably contained a disproportionate number of people who, if registered, would not have voted.

Turnout rose throughout the country, but unevenly. It increased by most in the South, excluding London (+ 3.6 per cent), the Midlands (+3.2 per cent) and London (+ 3.0 per cent) and least in the North (+ 0.9 per cent) and Scotland (+ 0.3 per cent). It also varied markedly across constituencies, being higher in marginal than safe seats, in rural than urban areas, in Wales, the East Midlands and the South West than elsewhere, and in seats with a recent history of a by-election. The highest turnouts were in constituencies which combined two or three of these features: Leicestershire North West (86.1 per cent), Monmouth (86.1 per cent), Brecon and Radnor (85.9 per cent). The lowest turnouts were in inner-city seats: Peckham (53.9 per cent), Liverpool Riverside (54.6 per cent) and Newham North West (56.0%).

Neither the level nor change in turnout appears to have affected the election result. There is no evidence to support the speculation by some commentators that superior organisation on the ground enabled the Conservatives to mobilise a higher proportion than Labour could of their respective supporters, and thus save vital marginal seats. Turnout was indeed higher in Conservative than Labour seats, but this pattern is usual and was no more pronounced in 1992 than in the past. At the constituency level, increases in turnout correlated with above-average, not below-average, swings to Labour, although the association was weak.

Britain's simple-plurality (first-past-the-post) electoral system once again produced a distribution of seats that was markedly unrepresentative of the distribution of votes. The Conservatives won 52 per cent of the seats on 42 per cent of the vote, Labour won 42 per cent of the seats on 34 per cent of the vote, but the Liberal Democrats 3 per cent of the seats on 18 per cent of the vote. Under proportional representation (assuming a 2 per cent threshold of representation) the result would have been Conservative 274, Labour 225, Liberal Democrat 117, SNP 15, Plaid Cymru 3, others 17, leading to either a Conservative-Liberal Democrat or a Labour-Liberal Democrat coalition government.

Not all the minor parties were penalised by the electoral system. Plaid Cymru's tally of four seats was one more than its 8.8 per cent of the vote in Wales "deserved" and the SDLP's total of four seats was exactly proportional to its 23.5 per cent of the vote in Northern Ireland — the end of Protestant gerrymandering in Ulster. Both parties benefited from the fact that their vote is geographically concentrated. But the SNP won only three of the 15 seats its 21 per cent of the Scottish vote "entitled" it to and the Liberal Democrats won only 20 of the 117 seats that 18 per cent of the vote would have earned under a system of proportional representation. They suffered because their vote was distributed too evenly.

One of the electoral system's usual distortions did not materialise. In past elections it has over-represented both major parties, but always rewarded the winner much more handsomely than the runner-up. This distortion followed the so-called "cube law" up to 1970: the ratio of Conservative to Labour seats was the cube of the ratio of Conservative to Labour votes. In 1992 the electoral system over-rewarded the Conservative and Labour parties, but equally. The Conservative:Labour ratio of the vote was 55:45 and the Conservative:Labour ratio of seats was also 55:45.

As a result, the Conservative-Labour gap in the popular vote produced a much smaller Conservative-Labour gap in seats than in the past. In 1959, the Conservatives were 5.6 per cent ahead of Labour in the vote, but won 107 seats more; in 1979, they were 7.0 per cent ahead and won 71 seats more; in 1992, they were 7.7 per cent ahead, but won only 65 seats more.

Labour benefited more from the electoral system than at previous elections it has lost, for three reasons. Firstly, the swing to Labour was higher in Conservative-Labour marginals (3.5 per cent) than in the country as a whole (1.9 per cent). Had the national swing applied uniformly across all constituencies Labour would have taken 19, not 39, Conservative seats, leaving the Conservatives with an overall majority of 61.

Secondly, the over-representation of Scottish and Welsh constituencies, and population movement since 1976, the base year on which the current boundaries were drawn, means that Labour seats have a smaller electorate than Conservative seats. In addition, turnout was, as usual, lower in Labour seats than Conservative seats. As a result, Labour distributed its national vote more efficiently than the Conservatives. In the past, it has wasted its vote with superfluously large majorities in its own safe seats, while the majority of seats with small majorities have been won by the Conservatives. This time, the pattern was reversed. Of seats with majorities over 20,000 C won 41, Lab 25; of seats with majorities under 3,000 C won 42, Lab 46.

However, more seats than usual were won with tiny majorities, to the benefit of the Conservatives. They won 21 of the 39 seats won with majorities of under 1,000, and all four seats won by under 100 votes. Their overall majority of 21 rests on their 11 most marginal seats, all won with majorities of under 600 votes. The government may have been saved by the local MP's personal vote. The Conservative vote share fell by 1.6 per cent where the incumbent retired, but by 1.1 per cent where the incumbent stood again, a small difference, but one equal to about 300 votes.

There were some notable personal performances by sitting MPs. The Labour left-winger, Alan Meale, raised his majority in Mansfield from 56 to 11,724. Malcolm Moss, who gained Cambridgeshire North East from the Liberals in 1987, increased his majority from 1,428 to 15,093. Simon Hughes, the Liberal Democrat MP for Southwark and Bermondsey, defied the national trend and widened his majority from 2,779 (7.7 per cent) to 9,845 (26.1 per cent). The prime minister increased his majority in his fast-growing Huntingdon constituency from 27,044 to 36,230, easily the biggest margin of votes in the country.

The 1992 election cast doubt on the traditional picture of Britain as a balanced two-party system, in which regular swings of the electoral pendulum enable the Conservative and Labour parties to alternate in office. By the next election, the Conservatives will have been in office for 59 of the 79 years since modern party system emerged in 1918. The Labour party, by contrast, has failed to reach 40 per cent of the vote in the last six elections and the Liberal Democrats have, once again, been unable to achieve a breakthrough for the centre. Britain's two-party system appears to consist of a natural party of government and a natural party of opposition.

Ivor Crewe is professor of government at the University of Essex.

Regional, metropolitan, city and county voting

The Times has calculated the following analyses of voting in the general election on April 9 1992 in which 651 seats were contested compared with 650 in 1987. The constituency of Milton Keynes was split into two along with a major change to the Buckingham seat. There are 524 parliamentary seats in England, 72 in Scotland, 38 in Wales and 17 in Northern Ireland. The separate analysis of voting in Ulster is on Page 292.

The election statistics for England have been divided into the official standard nine regions of the country: East Anglia (20 seats); East Midlands (42 seats); Greater London (84 seats); North-West (73 seats); Northern (36 seats); South-East (109 seats - 108 in 1987); South-West (48 seats); West Midlands (58 seats) and Yorks and Humberside (54 seats);

Statistics are also set out for the metropolitan areas; non-metropolitan counties; and UK cities and boroughs with three or more seats. Scotland has been analysed on a regional basis and Wales by county.

The regional analysis for England is as follows:

EAST ANGLIA			C	Lab	LD	Other	Total
1992	Electorate	1,556,863	Votes	635,774	348,353	242,886	18,388	1,245,401
	Turnout %	80.0	Votes %	51.0	28.0	19.5	1.5	100.0
	Swing %	-3.7	Seats	17	3	0	0	20
	C to Lab		Candidates	20	20	20	42	102
1987	Electorate	1,495,371	Votes	601,421	249,894	297,041	5,217	1,153,573
	Turnout %	77.1	Votes %	52.1	21.7	25.7	0.5	100.0
			Seats	19	1	0	0	20
			Candidates	20	20	20	7	67
			Change 87-92	-1.1	6.3	-6.2	1.0	

Bury St Edmunds, Cambridge, Cambridgeshire North East, Cambridgeshire South East, Cambridgeshire South West, Great Yarmouth,Huntingdon, Ipswich, Norfolk Mid, Norfolk North, Norfolk North West, Norfolk South, Norfolk South West, Norwich North,Norwich South, Peterborough, Suffolk Central, Suffolk Coastal, Suffolk South, Waveney.

EAST MIDLANDS			C	Lab	LD	Other	Total
1992	Electorate	3,060,360	Votes	1,149,504	922,392	376,603	17,851	2,466,350
	Turnout %	80.6	Votes %	46.6	37.4	15.3	0.7	100.0
	Swing %	-4.7	Seats	28	14	0	0	42
	C to Lab		Candidates	42	42	42	38	164
1987	Electorate	2,992,872	Votes	1,127,208	696,780	487,164	9,128	2,320,280
	Turnout %	77.5	Votes %	48.6	30.0	21.0	0.4	100.0
			Seats	31	11	0	0	42
			Candidates	42	42	42	17	143
			Change 87-92	-2.0	7.4	-5.7	0.3	

Amber Valley, Ashfield, Bassetlaw, Blaby, Bolsover, Bosworth, Broxtowe, Chesterfield, Corby, Daventry, Derby North, Derby South,Derbyshire North East, Derbyshire South, Derbyshire West, Erewash, Gainsborough and Horncastle, Gedling, Grantham, Harborough,High Peak, Holland with Boston, Kettering, Leicester East, Leicester South, Leicester West, Leicestershire North West, Lincoln,Lindsey East, Loughborough, Mansfield, Newark, Northampton North, Northampton South, Nottingham East, Nottingham North,Nottingham South, Rushcliffe, Rutland and Melton, Sherwood, Stamford and Spalding, Wellingborough.

GREATER LONDON			C	Lab	LD	Other	Total
1992	Electorate	4,876,604	Votes	1,630,320	1,332,421	542,733	89,364	3,594,838
	Turnout %	73.7	Votes %	45.4	37.1	15.1	2.5	100.0
	Swing %	-3.0	Seats	48	35	1	0	84
	C to Lab		Candidates	84	84	82	160	410
1987	Electorate	5,111,379	Votes	1,655,952	1,136,903	770,117	50,869	3,613,841
	Turnout %	70.7	Votes %	45.8	31.5	21.3	1.4	100.0
			Seats	57	23	3	1	84
			Candidates	83	84	84	63	314
			Change 87-92	-0.5	5.6	-6.2	1.1	

Barking, Battersea, Beckenham, Bethnal Green and Stepney, Bexleyheath, Bow and Poplar, Brent East, Brent North, Brent South, Brentford and Isleworth, Carshalton and Wallington, Chelsea, Chingford, Chipping Barnet, Chislehurst, City of London and Westminster South, Croydon Central, Croydon North East, Croydon North West, Croydon South, Dagenham, Dulwich,Ealing North, Ealing Acton, Ealing Southall, Edmonton, Eltham, Enfield North, Enfield Southgate, Erith and Crayford,Feltham and Heston, Finchley, Fulham, Greenwich, Hackney North and Stoke

Newington, Hackney South and Shoreditch, Hammersmith, Hampstead and Highgate, Harrow East, Harrow West, Hayes and Harlington, Hendon North, Hendon South, Holborn and St Pancras,Hornchurch, Hornsey and Wood Green, Ilford North, Ilford South, Islington North, Islington South and Finsbury, Kensington, Kingston upon Thames, Lewisham East, Lewisham West, Lewisham Deptford, Leyton, Mitcham and Morden, Newham North East, Newham North West, Newham South, Norwood, Old Bexley and Sidcup, Orpington, Peckham, Putney, Ravensbourne, Richmond and Barnes, Romford, Ruislip Northwood, Southwark and Bermondsey, Streatham, Surbiton, Sutton and Cheam, Tooting, Tottenham, Twickenham, Upminster, Uxbridge, Vauxhall, Walthamstow, Wanstead and Woodford, Westminster North, Wimbledon, Woolwich.

NORTH-WEST			C	Lab	LD	Other	Total
1992	Electorate	4,780,134	Votes	1,395,718	1,660,051	582,177	56,319	3,694,265
	Turnout %	77.3	Votes %	37.8	44.9	15.8	1.5	100.0
	Swing %	-2.0	Seats	27	44	2	0	73
	C to Lab		Candidates	73	73	73	119	338
1987	Electorate	4,842,068	Votes	1,401,459	1,518,680	758,143	8,996	3,687,278
	Turnout %	76.2	Votes %	38.0	41.2	20.6	0.2	100.0
			Seats	34	36	3	0	73
			Candidates	73	73	73	19	238
			Change 87-92	-0.2	3.7	-4.8	1.3	

Altrincham and Sale, Ashton-under-Lyne, Birkenhead, Blackburn, Blackpool North, Blackpool South, Bolton North East, Bolton South East, Bolton West, Bootle, Burnley, Bury North, Bury South, Cheadle, Chester City of, Chorley, Congleton, Crewe and Nantwich, Crosby, Davyhulme, Denton and Reddish, Eccles, Eddisbury, Ellesmere Port and Neston, Fylde, Halton, Hazel Grove, Heywood and Middleton, Hyndburn, Knowsley North, Knowsley South, Lancashire West, Lancaster, Leigh, Littleborough and Saddleworth, Liverpool Broadgreen, Liverpool Garston, Liverpool Mossley Hill, Liverpool Riverside, Liverpool Walton, Liverpool West Derby, Macclesfield, Makerfield, Manchester Central, Manchester Blackley, Manchester Gorton, Manchester Withington, Manchester Wythenshawe, Morecambe and Lunesdale, Oldham Central and Royton, Oldham West, Pendle, Preston, Ribble Valley, Rochdale, Rossendale and Darwen, Salford East, South Ribble, Southport, St Helens North, St Helens South, Stalybridge and Hyde, Stockport, Stretford, Tatton, Wallasey, Warrington North, Warrington South, Wigan, Wirral South, Wirral West, Worsley, Wyre.

NORTHERN			C	Lab	LD	Other	Total
1992	Electorate	2,366,686	Votes	603,893	914,712	281,236	8,704	1,808,545
	Turnout %	76.4	Votes %	33.4	50.6	15.6	0.5	100.0
	Swing %	-1.6	Seats	6	29	1	0	36
	C to Lab		Candidates	36	36	36	17	125
1987	Electorate	2,378,984	Votes	578,996	830,785	376,675	4,635	1,791,091
	Turnout %	75.3	Votes %	32.3	46.4	21.0	0.3	100.0
			Seats	8	27	1	0	36
			Candidates	36	36	36	9	117
			Change 87-92	1.1	4.2	-5.5	0.2	

Barrow and Furness, Berwick-upon-Tweed, Bishop Auckland, Blaydon, Blyth Valley, Carlisle, Copeland, Darlington, Durham North, Durham North West, Durham City of, Easington, Gateshead East, Hartlepool, Hexham, Houghton and Washington, Jarrow, Langbaurgh, Middlesbrough, Newcastle upon Tyne Central, Newcastle upon Tyne East, Newcastle upon Tyne North, Penrith and the Border, Redcar, Sedgefield, South Shields, Stockton North, Stockton South, Sunderland North, Sunderland South, Tyne Bridge, Tynemouth, Wallsend, Wansbeck, Westmorland and Lonsdale, Workington.

SOUTH-EAST			C	Lab	LD	Other	Total
1992	Electorate	8,041,908	Votes	3,519,049	1,341,298	1,507,298	88,124	6,455,769
	Turnout %	80.3	Votes %	54.5	20.8	23.3	1.4	100.0
	Swing %	-2.5	Seats	106	3	0	0	109
	C to Lab		Candidates	109	109	109	178	505
1987	Electorate	7,988,668	Votes	3,382,849	1,023,521	1,653,514	27,603	6,087,487
	Turnout %	76.2	Votes %	55.6	16.8	27.2	0.5	100.0
			Seats	107	1	0	0	108
			Candidates	108	108	108	44	368
			Change 87-92	-1.1	4.0	-3.8	0.9	

Aldershot, Arundel, Ashford, Aylesbury, Banbury, Basildon, Basingstoke, Beaconsfield, Bedfordshire Mid, Bedfordshire North, Bedfordshire South West, Berkshire East, Bexhill and Battle, Billericay, Braintree, Brentwood and Ongar, Brighton Kemptown, Brighton Pavilion, Broxbourne, Buckingham, Canterbury, Castle Point, Chelmsford, Chertsey and Walton, Chesham and Amersham, Chichester, Colchester North, Colchester South and Maldon, Crawley, Dartford, Dover, Eastbourne, Eastleigh, Epping Forest, Epsom and Ewell, Esher, Fareham, Faversham, Folkestone and Hythe, Gillingham, Gosport, Gravesham, Guildford, Hampshire East, Hampshire North West, Harlow, Harwich, Hastings and Rye, Havant, Henley, Hertford and Stortford, Hertfordshire North, Hertfordshire South West, Hertfordshire West, Hertsmere, Horsham, Hove, Isle of Wight, Kent Mid, Lewes, Luton North, Luton South, Maidstone, Medway, Milton Keynes North East, Milton Keynes South West, Mole Valley, New Forest, Newbury, Oxford East, Oxford West and Abingdon, Portsmouth North, Portsmouth South, Reading East, Reading West, Reigate, Rochford, Romsey and Waterside, Saffron Walden, Sevenoaks, Shoreham, Slough, Southampton Itchen, Southampton Test, Southend East, Southend West, Spelthorne, St Albans, Stevenage, Surrey East, Surrey North West, Surrey South West, Sussex Mid, Thanet North, Thanet South, Thurrock, Tonbridge and Malling, Tunbridge Wells, Wantage, Watford, Wealden, Welwyn Hatfield, Winchester, Windsor and Maidenhead, Witney, Woking, Wokingham, Worthing, Wycombe.

SOUTH-WEST			C	Lab	LD	Other	Total
1992	Electorate	3,600,654	Votes	1,387,921	561,847	916,844	52,191	2,918,803
	Turnout %	81.1	Votes %	47.6	19.2	31.4	1.8	100.0
	Swing %	-3.2	Seats	38	4	6	0	48
	C to Lab		Candidates	48	48	48	100	244
1987	Electorate	3,506,075	Votes	1,386,857	436,358	906,288	13,048	2,742,551
	Turnout %	78.2	Votes %	50.6	15.9	33.0	0.5	100.0
			Seats	44	1	3	0	48
			Candidates	48	48	48	22	166
			Change 87-92	-3.0	3.3	-1.6	1.3	

Bath, Bournemouth East, Bournemouth West, Bridgwater, Bristol East, Bristol North West, Bristol South, Bristol West, Cheltenham, Christchurch, Cirencester and Tewkesbury, Cornwall North, Cornwall South East, Devizes, Devon North, Devon West and Torridge, Dorset North, Dorset South, Dorset West, Exeter, Falmouth and Camborne, Gloucester, Gloucestershire West, Honiton, Kingswood, Northavon, Plymouth Devonport, Plymouth Drake, Plymouth Sutton, Poole, Salisbury, Somerton and Frome, South Hams, St Ives, Stroud, Swindon, Taunton, Teignbridge, Tiverton, Torbay, Truro, Wansdyke, Wells, Westbury, Weston-super-Mare, Wiltshire North, Woodspring, Yeovil.

WEST MIDLANDS			C	Lab	LD	Other	Total
1992	Electorate	3,969,970	Votes	1,390,246	1,203,352	466,048	45,124	3,104,770
	Turnout %	78.2	Votes %	44.8	38.8	15.0	1.5	100.0
	Swing %	-3.1	Seats	29	29	0	0	58
	C to Lab		Candidates	58	58	58	54	228
1987	Electorate	3,943,327	Votes	1,346,505	984,667	615,699	10,401	2,957,272
	Turnout %	75.0	Votes %	45.5	33.3	20.8	0.4	100.0
			Seats	36	22	0	0	58
			Candidates	58	58	58	17	191
			Change 87-92	-0.8	5.5	-5.8	1.1	

Aldridge-Brownhills, Birmingham Edgbaston, Birmingham Erdington, Birmingham Hall Green, Birmingham Hodge Hill, Birmingham Ladywood, Birmingham Northfield, Birmingham Perry Barr, Birmingham Selly Oak, Birmingham Small Heath, Birmingham Sparkbrook, Birmingham Yardley, Bromsgrove, Burton, Cannock and Burntwood, Coventry North East, Coventry North West, Coventry South East, Coventry South West, Dudley East, Dudley West, Halesowen and Stourbridge, Hereford, Leominster, Ludlow, Meriden, Newcastle-under-Lyme, Nuneaton, Rugby and Kenilworth, Shrewsbury and Atcham, Shropshire North, Solihull, Stafford, Staffordshire Mid, Staffordshire Moorlands, Staffordshire South, Staffordshire South East, Stoke-on-Trent Central, Stoke-on-Trent North, Stoke-on-Trent South, Stratford-on-Avon, Sutton Coldfield, Walsall North, Walsall South, Warley East, Warley West, Warwick and Leamington, Warwickshire North, West Bromwich East, West Bromwich West, Wolverhampton North East, Wolverhampton South East, Wolverhampton South West, Worcester, Worcestershire Mid, Worcestershire South, Wrekin The, Wyre Forest.

YORKS AND HUMBERSIDE			C	Lab	LD	Other	Total
1992	Electorate	3,788,337	Votes	1,084,227	1,266,810	481,246	25,225	2,857,508
	Turnout %	75.4	Votes %	37.9	44.3	16.8	0.9	100.0
	Swing %	-1.6	Seats	20	34	0	0	54
	C to Lab		Candidates	54	54	54	49	211
1987	Electorate	3,729,620	Votes	1,040,751	1,128,878	602,709	7,811	2,780,149
	Turnout %	74.5	Votes %	37.4	40.6	21.7	0.3	100.0
			Seats	21	33	0	0	54
			Candidates	54	54	54	16	178
			Change 87-92	0.5	3.7	-4.8	0.6	

Barnsley Central, Barnsley East, Barnsley West and Penistone, Batley and Spen, Beverley, Boothferry, Bradford North, Bradford South, Bradford West, Bridlington, Brigg and Cleethorpes, Calder Valley, Colne Valley, Dewsbury, Don Valley, Doncaster Central, Doncaster North, Elmet, Glanford and Scunthorpe, Great Grimsby, Halifax, Harrogate, Hemsworth, Huddersfield, Hull East, Hull North, Hull West, Keighley, Leeds Central, Leeds East, Leeds North East, Leeds North West, Leeds South and Morley, Leeds West, Normanton, Pontefract and Castleford, Pudsey, Richmond (Yorks), Rother Valley, Rotherham, Ryedale, Scarborough, Selby, Sheffield Central, Sheffield Attercliffe, Sheffield Brightside, Sheffield Hallam, Sheffield Heeley, Sheffield Hillsborough, Shipley, Skipton and Ripon, Wakefield, Wentworth, York.

TOTALS			C	Lab	LD	Other	Total
1992	Electorate	36,041,516	Votes	12,796,652	9,551,236	5,398,071	401,290	28,147,249
	Turnout %	78.1	Votes %	45.5	33.9	19.2	1.4	100.0
	Swing %	-2.6	Seats	319	195	10	0	524
	C to Lab		Candidates	524	524	522	757	2327
1987	Electorate	35,988,364	Votes	12,521,998	8,006,466	6,467,350	137,708	27,133,522
	Turnout %	75.4	Votes %	46.1	29.5	23.8	0.5	100.0
			Seats	357	155	10	1	523
			Candidates	522	523	523	214	1782
			Change 87-92	-0.7	4.4	-4.7	0.9	

METROPOLITAN ANALYSIS

Although the G L C and the six Metropolitan County Councils have been abolished, the metropolitan county boundaries are still in place and thus these areas continue to provide a good basis for comparison of voting between 1987 and 1992 in the areas of heaviest population in England.

The Metropolis has been divided into two areas - Outer London and Inner London and the two have also been combined to give a Great London area table among the regional tables. Outside London there are 36 metropolitan city and borough authorities in the six metropolitan county areas. None of the parliamentary constituencies crosses a metropolitan county boundary but six city/borough area constituencies cross city/borough boundaries.

Seats making up Metropolitan counties and the voting in them was as follows:

GREATER MANCHESTER			C	Lab	LD	Other	Total
1992	Electorate	1,899,993	Votes	511,945	682,848	226,075	22,445	1,443,313
	Turnout %	76.0	Votes %	35.5	47.3	15.7	1.6	100.0
	Swing %	-1.9	Seats	9	20	1	0	30
	C to Lab		Candidates	30	30	30	49	139
1987	Electorate	1,945,586	Votes	526,361	644,948	290,883	2,113	1,464,305
	Turnout %	75.3	Votes %	35.9	44.0	19.9	0.1	100.0
			Seats	10	19	1	0	30
			Candidates	30	30	30	6	96
			Change 87-92	-0.5	3.3	-4.2	1.4	

Altrincham and Sale, Ashton-under-Lyne, Bolton North East, Bolton South East, Bolton West, Bury North, Bury South, Cheadle, Davyhulme, Denton and Reddish, Eccles, Hazel Grove, Heywood and Middleton, Leigh, Littleborough and Saddleworth, Makerfield, Manchester Central, Manchester Blackley, Manchester Gorton, Manchester Withington, Manchester Wythenshawe, Oldham Central and Royton, Oldham West, Rochdale, Salford East, Stalybridge and Hyde, Stockport, Stretford, Wigan, Worsley.

INNER LONDON			C	Lab	LD	Other	Total
1992	Electorate	1,631,434	Votes	408,597	519,972	148,134	51,984	1,128,687
	Turnout %	69.2	Votes %	36.2	46.0	13.2	4.6	100.0
	Swing %	-2.9	Seats	8	20	1	0	29
	C to Lab		Candidates	29	29	27	72	157
1987	Electorate	1,717,109	Votes	424,538	470,700	241,424	12,593	1,149,255
	Turnout %	66.9	Votes %	36.9	41.0	21.0	1.1	100.0
			Seats	13	13	3	0	29
			Candidates	29	29	29	37	124
			Change 87-92	-0.8	5.1	-7.8	3.5	

Battersea, Bethnal Green and Stepney, Bow and Poplar, Chelsea, City of London and Westminster South, Dulwich, Eltham, Fulham, Greenwich, Hackney North and Stoke Newington, Hackney South and Shoreditch, Hammersmith, Hampstead and Highgate, Holborn and St Pancras, Islington North, Islington South and Finsbury, Kensington, Lewisham East, Lewisham West, Lewisham Deptford, Norwood, Peckham, Putney, Southwark and Bermondsey, Streatham, Tooting, Vauxhall, Westminster North, Woolwich.

MERSEYSIDE			C	Lab	LD	Other	Total
1992	Electorate	1,079,446	Votes	232,147	411,412	134,878	21,248	799,685
	Turnout %	74.1	Votes %	29.0	51.4	16.9	2.7	100.0
	Swing %	-2.0	Seats	4	12	1	0	17
	C to Lab		Candidates	17	17	17	33	84
1987	Electorate	1,117,029	Votes	242,437	397,647	195,653	2,696	838,433
	Turnout %	75.1	Votes %	28.9	47.4	23.3	0.3	100.0
			Seats	4	11	2	0	17
			Candidates	17	17	17	5	56
			Change 87-92	0.1	4.0	-6.5	2.3	

Birkenhead, Bootle, Crosby, Knowsley North, Knowsley South, Liverpool Broadgreen, Liverpool Garston, Liverpool Mossley Hill, Liverpool Riverside, Liverpool Walton, Liverpool West Derby, Southport, St Helens North, St Helens South, Wallasey, Wirral South, Wirral West.

OUTER LONDON

			C	Lab	LD	Other	Total
1992	Electorate	3,245,170	Votes	1,221,723	812,449	394,599	37,380	2,466,151
	Turnout %	76.0	Votes %	49.5	32.9	16.0	1.5	100.0
	Swing %	-3.2	Seats	40	15	0	0	55
	C to Lab		Candidates	55	55	55	88	253
1987	Electorate	3,394,270	Votes	1,231,414	666,203	528,693	38,276	2,464,586
	Turnout %	72.6	Votes %	50.0	27.0	21.5	1.6	100.0
			Seats	44	10	0	1	55
			Candidates	54	55	55	26	190
			Change 87-92	-0.4	5.9	-5.5	-0.0	

Barking, Beckenham, Bexleyheath, Brent East, Brent North, Brent South, Brentford and Isleworth, Carshalton and Wallington, Chingford, Chipping Barnet, Chislehurst, Croydon Central, Croydon North East, Croydon North West, Croydon South, Dagenham, Ealing North, Ealing Acton, Ealing Southall, Edmonton, Enfield North, Enfield Southgate, Erith and Crayford, Feltham and Heston, Finchley, Harrow East, Harrow West, Hayes and Harlington, Hendon North, Hendon South, Hornchurch, Hornsey and Wood Green, Ilford North, Ilford South, Kingston upon Thames, Leyton, Mitcham and Morden, Newham North East, Newham North West, Newham South, Old Bexley and Sidcup, Orpington, Ravensbourne, Richmond and Barnes, Romford, Ruislip Northwood, Surbiton, Sutton and Cheam, Tottenham, Twickenham, Upminster, Uxbridge, Walthamstow, Wanstead and Woodford, Wimbledon.

SOUTH YORKSHIRE

			C	Lab	LD	Other	Total
1992	Electorate	1,003,827	Votes	186,270	418,747	113,692	4,585	723,294
	Turnout %	72.1	Votes %	25.8	57.9	15.7	0.6	100.0
	Swing %	-0.5	Seats	1	14	0	0	15
	C to Lab		Candidates	15	15	15	11	56
1987	Electorate	997,096	Votes	180,327	405,192	136,323	1,085	722,927
	Turnout %	72.5	Votes %	24.9	56.0	18.9	0.2	100.0
			Seats	1	14	0	0	15
			Candidates	15	15	15	4	49
			Change 87-92	0.8	1.8	-3.1	0.5	

Barnsley Central, Barnsley East, Barnsley West and Penistone, Don Valley, Doncaster Central, Doncaster North, Rother Valley, Rotherham, Sheffield Central, Sheffield Attercliffe, Sheffield Brightside, Sheffield Hallam, Sheffield Heeley, Sheffield Hillsborough, Wentworth.

TYNE AND WEAR

			C	Lab	LD	Other	Total
1992	Electorate	866,508	Votes	181,296	359,060	86,122	2,724	629,202
	Turnout %	72.6	Votes %	28.8	57.1	13.7	0.4	100.0
	Swing %	-1.1	Seats	1	12	0	0	13
	C to Lab		Candidates	13	13	13	4	43
1987	Electorate	887,856	Votes	177,639	344,987	119,452	1,815	643,893
	Turnout %	72.5	Votes %	27.6	53.6	18.6	0.3	100.0
			Seats	1	12	0	0	13
			Candidates	13	13	13	5	44
			Change 87-92	1.2	3.5	-4.9	0.2	

Blaydon, Gateshead East, Houghton and Washington, Jarrow, Newcastle upon Tyne Central, Newcastle upon Tyne East, Newcastle upon Tyne North, South Shields, Sunderland North, Sunderland South, Tyne Bridge, Tynemouth, Wallsend.

WEST MIDLANDS

			C	Lab	LD	Other	Total
1992	Electorate	1,957,966	Votes	622,505	650,483	177,618	28,082	1,478,688
	Turnout %	75.5	Votes %	42.1	44.0	12.0	1.9	100.0
	Swing %	-2.4	Seats	10	21	0	0	31
	C to Lab		Candidates	31	31	31	25	118
1987	Electorate	1,991,176	Votes	616,375	575,279	249,433	4,384	1,445,471
	Turnout %	72.6	Votes %	42.6	39.8	17.3	0.3	100.0
			Seats	14	17	0	0	31
			Candidates	31	31	31	10	103
			Change 87-92	-0.5	4.2	-5.2	1.6	

Aldridge-Brownhills, Birmingham Edgbaston, Birmingham Erdington, Birmingham Hall Green, Birmingham Hodge Hill, Birmingham Ladywood, Birmingham Northfield, Birmingham Perry Barr, Birmingham Selly Oak, Birmingham Small Heath, Birmingham Sparkbrook, Birmingham Yardley, Coventry North East, Coventry North West, Coventry South East, Coventry South West, Dudley East, Dudley West, Halesowen and Stourbridge, Meriden, Solihull, Sutton Coldfield, Walsall North, Walsall South, Warley East, Warley West, West Bromwich East, West Bromwich West, Wolverhampton North East, Wolverhampton South East, Wolverhampton South West.

WEST YORKSHIRE			C	Lab	LD	Other	Total
1992	Electorate	1,563,354	Votes	455,513	542,044	179,116	14,911	1,191,584
	Turnout %	76.2	Votes %	38.2	45.5	15.0	1.3	100.0
	Swing %	-2.1	Seats	9	14	0	0	23
	C to Lab		Candidates	23	23	23	27	96
1987	Electorate	1,543,576	Votes	441,722	478,135	242,848	4,177	1,166,882
	Turnout %	75.6	Votes %	37.9	41.0	20.8	0.4	100.0
			Seats	9	14	0	0	23
			Candidates	23	23	23	8	77
			Change 87-92	0.4	4.5	-5.8	0.9	

Batley and Spen, Bradford North, Bradford South, Bradford West, Calder Valley, Colne Valley, Dewsbury, Elmet, Halifax, Hemsworth, Huddersfield, Keighley, Leeds Central, Leeds East, Leeds North East, Leeds North West, Leeds South and Morley, Leeds West, Normanton, Pontefract and Castleford, Pudsey, Shipley, Wakefield.

TOTALS			C	Lab	LD	Other	Total
1992	Electorate	13,247,698	Votes	3,819,996	4,397,015	1,461,234	183,359	9,861,604
	Turnout %	74.4	Votes %	38.7	44.6	14.8	1.9	100.0
	Swing %	-2.2	Seats	82	128	3	0	213
	C to Lab		Candidates	213	213	211	309	946
1987	Electorate	13,593,698	Votes	3,840,813	3,983,091	2,004,709	67,139	9,895,752
	Turnout %	72.8	Votes %	38.8	40.3	20.3	0.7	100.0
			Seats	96	110	6	1	213
			Candidates	212	213	213	101	739
			Change 87-92	-0.1	4.3	-5.4	1.2	

NON-METROPOLITAN COUNTIES

There are 39 non-Metropolitan counties containing 311 parliamentary constituencies, none of which cross county boundaries. The Isle of Wight has just one seat (its detailed analysis is in the election results).
The analysis in these counties in comparison with 1987 is as follows:

AVON			C	Lab	LD	Other	Total
1992	Electorate	722,632	Votes	261,772	161,952	155,733	8,891	588,348
	Turnout %	81.4	Votes %	44.5	27.5	26.5	1.5	100.0
	Swing %	-3.5	Seats	6	3	1	0	10
	C to Lab		Candidates	10	10	10	20	50
1987	Electorate	722,493	Votes	271,205	135,627	152,739	6,227	565,798
	Turnout %	78.3	Votes %	47.9	24.0	27.0	1.1	100.0
			Seats	9	1	0	0	10
			Candidates	10	10	10	8	38
			Change 87-92	-3.4	3.6	-0.5	0.4	

Bath, Bristol East, Bristol North West, Bristol South, Bristol West, Kingswood, Northavon, Wansdyke, Weston-super-Mare, Woodspring.

BEDFORDSHIRE			C	Lab	LD	Other	Total
1992	Electorate	385,188	Votes	167,325	95,402	46,548	5,256	314,531
	Turnout %	81.7	Votes %	53.2	30.3	14.8	1.7	100.0
	Swing %	-3.6	Seats	5	0	0	0	5
	C to Lab		Candidates	5	5	5	10	25
1987	Electorate	378,631	Votes	159,155	71,026	62,047	1,257	293,485
	Turnout %	77.5	Votes %	54.2	24.2	21.1	0.4	100.0
			Seats	5	0	0	0	5
			Candidates	5	5	5	2	17
			Change 87-92	-1.0	6.1	-6.3	1.2	

Bedfordshire Mid, Bedfordshire North, Bedfordshire South West, Luton North, Luton South.

BERKSHIRE			C	Lab	LD	Other	Total
1992	Electorate	547,835	Votes	242,594	86,863	103,072	6,358	438,887
	Turnout %	80.1	Votes %	55.3	19.8	23.5	1.4	100.0
	Swing %	-1.9	Seats	7	0	0	0	7
	C to Lab		Candidates	7	7	7	14	35
1987	Electorate	543,926	Votes	230,951	70,618	101,798	4,311	407,678
	Turnout %	75.0	Votes %	56.7	17.3	25.0	1.1	100.0
			Seats	7	0	0	0	7
			Candidates	7	7	7	6	27
			Change 87-92	-1.4	2.5	-1.5	0.4	

Berkshire East, Newbury, Reading East, Reading West, Slough, Windsor and Maidenhead, Wokingham.

BUCKINGHAMSHIRE			C	Lab	LD	Other	Total
1992	Electorate	471,168	Votes	216,219	72,684	83,745	6,868	379,516
	Turnout %	80.5	Votes %	57.0	19.2	22.1	1.8	100.0
	Swing %	-1.9	Seats	7	0	0	0	7
	C to Lab		Candidates	7	7	7	16	37
1987	Electorate	455,378	Votes	196,565	53,246	93,182	1,570	344,563
	Turnout %	75.7	Votes %	57.0	15.5	27.0	0.5	100.0
			Seats	6	0	0	0	6
			Candidates	6	6	6	2	20
			Change 87-92	-0.1	3.7	-5.0	1.4	

Aylesbury, Beaconsfield, Buckingham, Chesham and Amersham, Milton Keynes North East, Milton Keynes South West, Wycombe.

CAMBRIDGESHIRE			C	Lab	LD	Other	Total
1992	Electorate	492,526	Votes	209,831	89,734	75,974	9,622	385,161
	Turnout %	78.2	Votes %	54.5	23.3	19.7	2.5	100.0
	Swing %	-1.7	Seats	5	1	0	0	6
	C to Lab		Candidates	6	6	6	20	38
1987	Electorate	468,911	Votes	189,284	66,061	99,359	1,977	356,681
	Turnout %	76.1	Votes %	53.1	18.5	27.9	0.6	100.0
			Seats	6	0	0	0	6
			Candidates	6	6	6	3	21
			Change 87-92	1.4	4.8	-8.1	1.9	

Cambridge, Cambridgeshire North East, Cambridgeshire South East, Cambridgeshire South West, Huntingdon, Peterborough.

CHESHIRE			C	Lab	LD	Other	Total
1992	Electorate	734,282	Votes	268,313	234,353	91,956	5,315	599,937
	Turnout %	81.7	Votes %	44.7	39.1	15.3	0.9	100.0
	Swing %	-2.4	Seats	5	5	0	0	10
	C to Lab		Candidates	10	10	10	14	44
1987	Electorate	725,907	Votes	254,639	195,389	117,190	1,424	568,642
	Turnout %	78.3	Votes %	44.8	34.4	20.6	0.3	100.0
			Seats	7	3	0	0	10
			Candidates	10	10	10	3	33
			Change 87-92	-0.1	4.7	-5.3	0.6	

Chester City of, Congleton, Crewe and Nantwich, Eddisbury, Ellesmere Port and Neston, Halton, Macclesfield, Tatton, Warrington North, Warrington South.

CLEVELAND			C	Lab	LD	Other	Total
1992	Electorate	414,282	Votes	120,080	161,764	41,329	550	323,723
	Turnout %	78.1	Votes %	37.1	50.0	12.8	0.2	100.0
	Swing %	-1.0	Seats	2	4	0	0	6
	C to Lab		Candidates	6	6	6	1	19
1987	Electorate	417,669	Votes	107,007	141,469	66,115	1,786	316,377
	Turnout %	75.7	Votes %	33.8	44.7	20.9	0.6	100.0
			Seats	2	4	0	0	6
			Candidates	6	6	6	1	19
			Change 87-92	3.3	5.3	-8.1	-0.4	

Hartlepool, Langbaurgh, Middlesbrough, Redcar, Stockton North, Stockton South.

CORNWALL

			C	Lab	LD	Other	Total
1992	Electorate	366,826	Votes	127,678	41,593	124,553	5,133	298,957
	Turnout %	81.5	Votes %	42.7	13.9	41.7	1.7	100.0
	Swing %	-2.9	Seats	3	0	2	0	5
	C to Lab		Candidates	5	5	5	14	29
1987	Electorate	351,115	Votes	131,194	34,994	111,064	373	277,625
	Turnout %	79.1	Votes %	47.3	12.6	40.0	0.1	100.0
			Seats	4	0	1	0	5
			Candidates	5	5	5	1	16
			Change 87-92	-4.5	1.3	1.7	1.6	

Cornwall North, Cornwall South East, Falmouth and Camborne, St Ives, Truro.

CUMBRIA

			C	Lab	LD	Other	Total
1992	Electorate	381,046	Votes	142,126	113,401	49,086	2,302	306,915
	Turnout %	80.5	Votes %	46.3	36.9	16.0	0.8	100.0
	Swing %	-2.8	Seats	2	4	0	0	6
	C to Lab		Candidates	6	6	6	7	25
1987	Electorate	377,178	Votes	142,339	97,876	55,480	319	296,014
	Turnout %	78.5	Votes %	48.1	33.1	18.7	0.1	100.0
			Seats	3	3	0	0	6
			Candidates	6	6	6	1	19
			Change 87-92	-1.8	3.9	-2.7	0.6	

Barrow and Furness, Carlisle, Copeland, Penrith and the Border, Westmorland and Lonsdale, Workington.

DERBYSHIRE

			C	Lab	LD	Other	Total
1992	Electorate	718,805	Votes	244,939	256,097	87,028	2,416	590,480
	Turnout %	82.1	Votes %	41.5	43.4	14.7	0.4	100.0
	Swing %	-4.5	Seats	6	4	0	0	10
	C to Lab		Candidates	10	10	10	6	36
1987	Electorate	712,462	Votes	241,079	201,785	114,593	291	557,748
	Turnout %	78.3	Votes %	43.2	36.2	20.5	0.1	100.0
			Seats	6	4	0	0	10
			Candidates	10	10	10	1	31
			Change 87-92	-1.7	7.2	-5.8	0.4	

Amber Valley, Bolsover, Chesterfield, Derby North, Derby South, Derbyshire North East, Derbyshire South, Derbyshire West, Erewash, High Peak.

DEVON

			C	Lab	LD	Other	Total
1992	Electorate	786,921	Votes	303,232	122,854	193,787	18,229	638,102
	Turnout %	81.1	Votes %	47.5	19.3	30.4	2.9	100.0
	Swing %	-4.1	Seats	9	1	1	0	11
	C to Lab		Candidates	11	11	11	26	59
1987	Electorate	763,638	Votes	297,174	78,426	219,748	5,415	600,763
	Turnout %	78.7	Votes %	49.5	13.1	36.6	0.9	100.0
			Seats	10	0	1	0	11
			Candidates	11	11	11	9	42
			Change 87-92	-1.9	6.2	-6.2	2.0	

Devon North, Devon West and Torridge, Exeter, Honiton, Plymouth Devonport, Plymouth Drake, Plymouth Sutton, South Hams, Teignbridge, Tiverton, Torbay.

DORSET

			C	Lab	LD	Other	Total
1992	Electorate	520,248	Votes	222,031	54,613	127,061	3,766	407,471
	Turnout %	78.3	Votes %	54.5	13.4	31.2	0.9	100.0
	Swing %	-2.7	Seats	7	0	0	0	7
	C to Lab		Candidates	7	7	7	8	29
1987	Electorate	507,372	Votes	222,200	43,414	118,346	244	384,204
	Turnout %	75.7	Votes %	57.8	11.3	30.8	0.1	100.0
			Seats	7	0	0	0	7
			Candidates	7	7	7	1	22
			Change 87-92	-3.3	2.1	0.4	0.9	

Bournemouth East, Bournemouth West, Christchurch, Dorset North, Dorset South, Dorset West, Poole.

DURHAM			C	Lab	LD	Other	Total
1992	Electorate	467,749	Votes	101,621	204,437	50,883	1,167	358,108
	Turnout %	76.6	Votes %	28.4	57.1	14.2	0.3	100.0
	Swing %	-2.5	Seats	0	7	0	0	7
	C to Lab		Candidates	7	7	7	2	23
1987	Electorate	463,800	Votes	99,928	183,306	69,379	0	352,613
	Turnout %	76.0	Votes %	28.3	52.0	19.7	0.0	100.0
			Seats	1	6	0	0	7
			Candidates	7	7	7	0	21
			Change 87-92	0.0	5.1	-5.5	0.3	

Bishop Auckland, Darlington, Durham North, Durham North West, Durham City of, Easington, Sedgefield.

ESSEX			C	Lab	LD	Other	Total
1992	Electorate	1,173,526	Votes	510,710	222,675	205,219	9,187	947,791
	Turnout %	80.8	Votes %	53.9	23.5	21.7	1.0	100.0
	Swing %	-2.4	Seats	15	1	0	0	16
	C to Lab		Candidates	16	16	16	17	65
1987	Electorate	1,167,472	Votes	481,794	168,591	237,369	3,061	890,815
	Turnout %	76.3	Votes %	54.1	18.9	26.6	0.3	100.0
			Seats	16	0	0	0	16
			Candidates	16	16	16	6	54
			Change 87-92	-0.2	4.6	-5.0	0.6	

Basildon, Billericay, Braintree, Brentwood and Ongar, Castle Point, Chelmsford, Colchester North, Colchester South and Maldon, Epping Forest, Harlow, Harwich, Rochford, Saffron Walden, Southend East, Southend West, Thurrock.

GLOUCESTERSHIRE			C	Lab	LD	Other	Total
1992	Electorate	411,245	Votes	160,244	78,221	95,646	3,984	338,095
	Turnout %	82.2	Votes %	47.4	23.1	28.3	1.2	100.0
	Swing %	-4.0	Seats	4	0	1	0	5
	C to Lab		Candidates	5	5	5	8	23
1987	Electorate	399,484	Votes	159,609	57,557	99,450	283	316,899
	Turnout %	79.3	Votes %	50.4	18.2	31.4	0.1	100.0
			Seats	5	0	0	0	5
			Candidates	5	5	5	1	16
			Change 87-92	-3.0	5.0	-3.1	1.1	

Cheltenham, Cirencester and Tewkesbury, Gloucester, Gloucestershire West, Stroud.

HAMPSHIRE			C	Lab	LD	Other	Total
1992	Electorate	1,286,031	Votes	549,183	179,840	282,054	11,874	1,022,951
	Turnout %	79.5	Votes %	53.7	17.6	27.6	1.2	100.0
	Swing %	-2.5	Seats	15	1	0	0	16
	C to Lab		Candidates	16	16	16	17	65
1987	Electorate	1,256,929	Votes	530,021	133,506	300,022	1,393	964,942
	Turnout %	76.8	Votes %	54.9	13.8	31.1	0.1	100.0
			Seats	16	0	0	0	16
			Candidates	16	16	16	3	51
			Change 87-92	-1.2	3.7	-3.5	1.0	

Aldershot, Basingstoke, Eastleigh, Fareham, Gosport, Hampshire East, Hampshire North West, Havant, Isle of Wight, New Forest, Portsmouth North, Portsmouth South, Romsey and Waterside, Southampton Itchen, Southampton Test, Winchester.

HEREFORD AND WORCESTER			C	Lab	LD	Other	Total
1992	Electorate	524,113	Votes	216,841	105,080	98,412	6,228	426,561
	Turnout %	81.4	Votes %	50.8	24.6	23.1	1.5	100.0
	Swing %	-3.8	Seats	7	0	0	0	7
	C to Lab		Candidates	7	7	7	8	29
1987	Electorate	504,138	Votes	200,824	69,574	115,061	2,191	387,650
	Turnout %	76.9	Votes %	51.8	17.9	29.7	0.6	100.0
			Seats	7	0	0	0	7
			Candidates	7	7	7	2	23
			Change 87-92	-1.0	6.7	-6.6	0.9	

Bromsgrove, Hereford, Leominster, Worcester, Worcestershire Mid, Worcestershire South, Wyre Forest.

HERTFORDSHIRE			C	Lab	LD	Other	Total
1992	Electorate	737,054	Votes	322,667	157,252	123,161	5,619	608,699
	Turnout %	82.6	Votes %	53.0	25.8	20.2	0.9	100.0
	Swing %	-2.5	Seats	10	0	0	0	10
	C to Lab		Candidates	10	10	10	14	44
1987	Electorate	744,762	Votes	305,252	116,404	163,027	2,113	586,796
	Turnout %	78.8	Votes %	52.0	19.8	27.8	0.4	100.0
			Seats	10	0	0	0	10
			Candidates	10	10	10	4	34
			Change 87-92	1.0	6.0	-7.5	0.6	

Broxbourne, Hertford and Stortford, Hertfordshire North, Hertfordshire South West, Hertfordshire West, Hertsmere, St Albans, Stevenage, Watford, Welwyn Hatfield.

HUMBERSIDE			C	Lab	LD	Other	Total
1992	Electorate	666,567	Votes	208,810	201,792	87,062	2,855	500,519
	Turnout %	75.1	Votes %	41.7	40.3	17.4	0.6	100.0
	Swing %	-2.8	Seats	4	5	0	0	9
	C to Lab		Candidates	9	9	9	6	33
1987	Electorate	653,219	Votes	202,100	168,061	111,537	1,087	482,785
	Turnout %	73.9	Votes %	41.9	34.8	23.1	0.2	100.0
			Seats	4	5	0	0	9
			Candidates	9	9	9	2	29
			Change 87-92	-0.1	5.5	-5.7	0.3	

Beverley, Boothferry, Bridlington, Brigg and Cleethorpes, Glanford and Scunthorpe, Great Grimsby, Hull East, Hull North, Hull West.

KENT			C	Lab	LD	Other	Total
1992	Electorate	1,146,298	Votes	488,399	223,225	195,859	12,035	919,518
	Turnout %	80.2	Votes %	53.1	24.3	21.3	1.3	100.0
	Swing %	-2.9	Seats	16	0	0	0	16
	C to Lab		Candidates	16	16	16	29	77
1987	Electorate	1,144,091	Votes	468,984	167,612	226,508	4,959	868,063
	Turnout %	75.9	Votes %	54.0	19.3	26.1	0.6	100.0
			Seats	16	0	0	0	16
			Candidates	16	16	16	8	56
			Change 87-92	-0.9	5.0	-4.8	0.7	

Ashford, Canterbury, Dartford, Dover, Faversham, Folkestone and Hythe, Gillingham, Gravesham, Kent Mid, Maidstone, Medway, Sevenoaks, Thanet North, Thanet South, Tonbridge and Malling, Tunbridge Wells.

LANCASHIRE			C	Lab	LD	Other	Total
1992	Electorate	1,066,413	Votes	383,313	331,438	129,268	7,311	851,330
	Turnout %	79.8	Votes %	45.0	38.9	15.2	0.9	100.0
	Swing %	-2.9	Seats	9	7	0	0	16
	C to Lab		Candidates	16	16	16	23	71
1987	Electorate	1,053,546	Votes	378,022	280,696	154,417	2,763	815,898
	Turnout %	77.4	Votes %	46.3	34.4	18.9	0.3	100.0
			Seats	13	3	0	0	16
			Candidates	16	16	16	5	53
			Change 87-92	-1.3	4.5	-3.7	0.5	

Blackburn, Blackpool North, Blackpool South, Burnley, Chorley, Fylde, Hyndburn, Lancashire West, Lancaster, Morecambe and Lunesdale, Pendle, Preston, Ribble Valley, Rossendale and Darwen, South Ribble, Wyre.

LEICESTERSHIRE			C	Lab	LD	Other	Total
1992	Electorate	667,442	Votes	261,339	177,438	91,864	6,359	537,000
	Turnout %	80.5	Votes %	48.7	33.0	17.1	1.2	100.0
	Swing %	-4.6	Seats	6	3	0	0	9
	C to Lab		Candidates	9	9	9	15	42
1987	Electorate	658,556	Votes	270,098	141,617	105,091	2,564	519,370
	Turnout %	78.9	Votes %	52.0	27.3	20.2	0.5	100.0
			Seats	6	3	0	0	9
			Candidates	9	9	9	6	33
			Change 87-92	-3.3	5.8	-3.1	0.7	

Blaby, Bosworth, Harborough, Leicester East, Leicester South, Leicester West, Leicestershire North West, Loughborough, Rutland and Melton.

LINCOLNSHIRE			C	Lab	LD	Other	Total
1992	Electorate	457,485	Votes	194,470	93,869	71,840	3,121	363,300
	Turnout %	79.4	Votes %	53.5	25.8	19.8	0.9	100.0
	Swing %	-3.8	Seats	6	0	0	0	6
	C to Lab		Candidates	6	6	6	3	21
1987	Electorate	436,369	Votes	177,182	60,789	90,160	1,337	329,468
	Turnout %	75.5	Votes %	53.8	18.5	27.4	0.4	100.0
			Seats	6	0	0	0	6
			Candidates	6	6	6	3	21
			Change 87-92	-0.2	7.4	-7.6	0.5	

Gainsborough and Horncastle, Grantham, Holland with Boston, Lincoln, Lindsey East, Stamford and Spalding.

NORFOLK			C	Lab	LD	Other	Total
1992	Electorate	586,027	Votes	233,410	147,954	88,229	4,557	474,150
	Turnout %	80.9	Votes %	49.2	31.2	18.6	1.0	100.0
	Swing %	-5.0	Seats	7	1	0	0	8
	C to Lab		Candidates	8	8	8	13	37
1987	Electorate	562,950	Votes	224,842	101,027	113,612	960	440,441
	Turnout %	78.2	Votes %	51.0	22.9	25.8	0.2	100.0
			Seats	7	1	0	0	8
			Candidates	8	8	8	1	25
			Change 87-92	-1.8	8.3	-7.2	0.7	

Great Yarmouth, Norfolk Mid, Norfolk North, Norfolk North West, Norfolk South, Norfolk South West, Norwich North, Norwich South.

NORTHAMPTONSHIRE			C	Lab	LD	Other	Total
1992	Electorate	434,501	Votes	183,101	118,634	50,436	1,438	353,609
	Turnout %	81.4	Votes %	51.8	33.5	14.3	0.4	100.0
	Swing %	-3.2	Seats	6	0	0	0	6
	C to Lab		Candidates	6	6	6	3	21
1987	Electorate	417,140	Votes	166,926	87,433	67,049	1,274	322,682
	Turnout %	77.4	Votes %	51.7	27.1	20.8	0.4	100.0
			Seats	6	0	0	0	6
			Candidates	6	6	6	3	21
			Change 87-92	0.0	6.5	-6.5	0.0	

Corby, Daventry, Kettering, Northampton North, Northampton South, Wellingborough.

NORTHUMBERLAND			C	Lab	LD	Other	Total
1992	Electorate	237,101	Votes	58,770	76,050	53,816	1,961	190,597
	Turnout %	80.4	Votes %	30.8	39.9	28.2	1.0	100.0
	Swing %	-1.5	Seats	1	2	1	0	4
	C to Lab		Candidates	4	4	4	3	15
1987	Electorate	232,481	Votes	52,083	63,147	66,249	715	182,194
	Turnout %	78.4	Votes %	28.6	34.7	36.4	0.4	100.0
			Seats	1	2	1	0	4
			Candidates	4	4	4	2	14
			Change 87-92	2.2	5.2	-8.1	0.6	

Berwick-upon-Tweed, Blyth Valley, Hexham, Wansbeck.

NOTTINGHAMSHIRE			C	Lab	LD	Other	Total
1992	Electorate	782,127	Votes	265,655	276,354	75,435	4,517	621,961
	Turnout %	79.5	Votes %	42.7	44.4	12.1	0.7	100.0
	Swing %	-6.5	Seats	4	7	0	0	11
	C to Lab		Candidates	11	11	11	11	44
1987	Electorate	768,345	Votes	271,923	205,156	110,271	3,662	591,012
	Turnout %	76.9	Votes %	46.0	34.7	18.7	0.6	100.0
			Seats	7	4	0	0	11
			Candidates	11	11	11	4	37
			Change 87-92	-3.3	9.7	-6.5	0.1	

Ashfield, Bassetlaw, Broxtowe, Gedling, Mansfield, Newark, Nottingham East, Nottingham North, Nottingham South, Rushcliffe, Sherwood.

COUNTY ANALYSIS

OXFORDSHIRE			C	Lab	LD	Other	Total
1992	Electorate	418,794	Votes	171,208	79,168	78,269	4,900	333,545
	Turnout %	79.6	Votes %	51.3	23.7	23.5	1.5	100.0
	Swing %	-2.4	Seats	5	1	0	0	6
	C to Lab		Candidates	6	6	6	14	32
1987	Electorate	408,019	Votes	166,089	63,961	84,012	1,196	315,258
	Turnout %	77.3	Votes %	52.7	20.3	26.6	0.4	100.0
			Seats	5	1	0	0	6
			Candidates	6	6	6	3	21
			Change 87-92	-1.4	3.4	-3.2	1.1	

Banbury, Henley, Oxford East, Oxford West and Abingdon, Wantage, Witney.

SHROPSHIRE			C	Lab	LD	Other	Total
1992	Electorate	313,122	Votes	115,060	76,281	54,547	2,443	248,331
	Turnout %	79.3	Votes %	46.3	30.7	22.0	1.0	100.0
	Swing %	-3.6	Seats	3	1	0	0	4
	C to Lab		Candidates	4	4	4	3	15
1987	Electorate	296,518	Votes	110,136	58,068	59,470	660	228,334
	Turnout %	77.0	Votes %	48.2	25.4	26.0	0.3	100.0
			Seats	3	1	0	0	4
			Candidates	4	4	4	1	13
			Change 87-92	-1.9	5.3	-4.1	0.7	

Ludlow, Shrewsbury and Atcham, Shropshire North, Wrekin The.

SOMERSET			C	Lab	LD	Other	Total
1992	Electorate	363,847	Votes	134,983	38,561	119,774	4,539	297,857
	Turnout %	81.9	Votes %	45.3	12.9	40.2	1.5	100.0
	Swing %	-3.0	Seats	4	0	1	0	5
	C to Lab		Candidates	5	5	5	10	25
1987	Electorate	347,983	Votes	138,541	32,545	104,587	134	275,807
	Turnout %	79.3	Votes %	50.2	11.8	37.9	0.0	100.0
			Seats	4	0	1	0	5
			Candidates	5	5	5	1	16
			Change 87-92	-4.9	1.1	2.3	1.5	

Bridgwater, Somerton and Frome, Taunton, Wells, Yeovil.

STAFFORDSHIRE			C	Lab	LD	Other	Total
1992	Electorate	800,541	Votes	281,715	267,799	85,695	5,527	640,736
	Turnout %	80.0	Votes %	44.0	41.8	13.4	0.9	100.0
	Swing %	-4.4	Seats	6	5	0	0	11
	C to Lab		Candidates	11	11	11	11	44
1987	Electorate	781,841	Votes	271,589	205,572	127,594	1,233	605,988
	Turnout %	77.5	Votes %	44.8	33.9	21.1	0.2	100.0
			Seats	7	4	0	0	11
			Candidates	11	11	11	2	35
			Change 87-92	-0.9	7.9	-7.7	0.7	

Burton, Cannock and Burntwood, Newcastle-under-Lyme, Stafford, Staffordshire Mid, Staffordshire Moorlands, Staffordshire South, Staffordshire South East, Stoke-on-Trent Central, Stoke-on-Trent North, Stoke-on-Trent South.

SUFFOLK			C	Lab	LD	Other	Total
1992	Electorate	478,310	Votes	192,533	110,665	78,683	4,209	386,090
	Turnout %	80.7	Votes %	49.9	28.7	20.4	1.1	100.0
	Swing %	-4.1	Seats	5	1	0	0	6
	C to Lab		Candidates	6	6	6	9	27
1987	Electorate	463,510	Votes	187,295	82,806	84,070	2,280	356,451
	Turnout %	76.9	Votes %	52.5	23.2	23.6	0.6	100.0
			Seats	6	0	0	0	6
			Candidates	6	6	6	3	21
			Change 87-92	-2.7	5.4	-3.2	0.5	

Bury St Edmunds, Ipswich, Suffolk Central, Suffolk Coastal, Suffolk South, Waveney.

SURREY			C	Lab	LD	Other	Total
1992	Electorate	777,509	Votes	373,343	84,942	158,821	6,597	623,703
	Turnout %	80.2	Votes %	59.9	13.6	25.5	1.1	100.0
	Swing %	-1.5	Seats	11	0	0	0	11
	C to Lab		Candidates	11	11	11	14	47
1987	Electorate	792,847	Votes	361,831	68,173	165,039	2,369	597,412
	Turnout %	75.4	Votes %	60.6	11.4	27.6	0.4	100.0
			Seats	11	0	0	0	11
			Candidates	11	11	11	3	36
			Change 87-92	-0.7	2.2	-2.2	0.7	

Chertsey and Walton, Epsom and Ewell, Esher, Guildford, Mole Valley, Reigate, Spelthorne, Surrey East, Surrey North West, Surrey South West, Woking.

SUSSEX EAST			C	Lab	LD	Other	Total
1992	Electorate	545,086	Votes	225,284	74,797	117,248	9,163	426,492
	Turnout %	78.2	Votes %	52.8	17.5	27.5	2.1	100.0
	Swing %	-3.7	Seats	8	0	0	0	8
	C to Lab		Candidates	8	8	8	16	40
1987	Electorate	550,235	Votes	235,529	61,887	107,244	2,795	407,455
	Turnout %	74.1	Votes %	57.8	15.2	26.3	0.7	100.0
			Seats	8	0	0	0	8
			Candidates	8	8	8	5	29
			Change 87-92	-5.0	2.3	1.2	1.5	

Bexhill and Battle, Brighton Kemptown, Brighton Pavilion, Eastbourne, Hastings and Rye, Hove, Lewes, Wealden.

SUSSEX WEST			C	Lab	LD	Other	Total
1992	Electorate	553,419	Votes	252,117	64,450	113,302	10,267	440,136
	Turnout %	79.5	Votes %	57.3	14.6	25.7	2.3	100.0
	Swing %	-2.8	Seats	7	0	0	0	7
	C to Lab		Candidates	7	7	7	17	38
1987	Electorate	546,378	Votes	246,678	48,497	113,266	2,579	411,020
	Turnout %	75.2	Votes %	60.0	11.8	27.6	0.6	100.0
			Seats	7	0	0	0	7
			Candidates	7	7	7	2	23
			Change 87-92	-2.7	2.8	-1.8	1.7	

Arundel, Chichester, Crawley, Horsham, Shoreham, Sussex Mid, Worthing.

WARWICKSHIRE			C	Lab	LD	Other	Total
1992	Electorate	374,228	Votes	154,125	103,709	49,776	2,844	310,454
	Turnout %	83.0	Votes %	49.6	33.4	16.0	0.9	100.0
	Swing %	-4.2	Seats	3	2	0	0	5
	C to Lab		Candidates	5	5	5	7	22
1987	Electorate	369,654	Votes	147,581	76,174	64,141	1,933	289,829
	Turnout %	78.4	Votes %	50.9	26.3	22.1	0.7	100.0
			Seats	5	0	0	0	5
			Candidates	5	5	5	2	17
			Change 87-92	-1.3	7.1	-6.1	0.2	

Nuneaton, Rugby and Kenilworth, Stratford-on-Avon, Warwick and Leamington, Warwickshire North.

WILTSHIRE			C	Lab	LD	Other	Total
1992	Electorate	428,935	Votes	177,981	64,053	100,290	7,649	349,973
	Turnout %	81.6	Votes %	50.9	18.3	28.7	2.2	100.0
	Swing %	-1.3	Seats	5	0	0	0	5
	C to Lab		Candidates	5	5	5	14	29
1987	Electorate	413,990	Votes	166,934	53,795	100,354	372	321,455
	Turnout %	77.6	Votes %	51.9	16.7	31.2	0.1	100.0
			Seats	5	0	0	0	5
			Candidates	5	5	5	1	16
			Change 87-92	-1.1	1.6	-2.6	2.1	

Devizes, Salisbury, Swindon, Westbury, Wiltshire North.

YORKSHIRE NORTH				C	Lab	LD	Other	Total
1992	Electorate	554,589	Votes	233,634	104,227	101,376	2,874	442,111
	Turnout %	79.7	Votes %	52.8	23.6	22.9	0.7	100.0
	Swing %	-2.4	Seats	6	1	0	0	7
	C to Lab		Candidates	7	7	7	5	26
1987	Electorate	535,729	Votes	216,602	77,490	112,001	1,462	407,555
	Turnout %	76.1	Votes %	53.1	19.0	27.5	0.4	100.0
			Seats	7	0	0	0	7
			Candidates	7	7	7	2	23
			Change 87-92	-0.3	4.6	-4.6	0.3	

Harrogate, Richmond (Yorks), Ryedale, Scarborough, Selby, Skipton and Ripon, York.

TOTALS				C	Lab	LD	Other	Total
1992	Electorate	22,793,818	Votes	8,976,656	5,154,221	3,936,837	217,931	18,285,645
	Turnout %	80.2	Votes %	49.1	28.2	21.5	1.2	100.0
	Swing %	-3.1	Seats	237	67	7	0	311
	C to Lab		Candidates	311	311	311	448	1381
1987	Electorate	22,394,666	Votes	8,681,185	4,023,375	4,462,641	70,569	17,237,770
	Turnout %	77.0	Votes %	50.4	23.3	25.9	0.4	100.0
			Seats	261	45	4	0	310
			Candidates	310	310	310	113	1043
			Change 87-92	-1.3	4.8	-4.4	0.8	

UNITED KINGDOM CITIES AND BOROUGHS

Voting in principal cities and boroughs in England, Scotland, Wales and Northern Ireland, together with comparison with polling in 1987, was as follows:

BARNSLEY				C	Lab	LD	Other	Total
1992	Electorate	172,798	Votes	26,717	85,359	13,330	970	126,376
	Turnout %	73.1	Votes %	21.1	67.5	10.5	0.8	100.0
	Swing %	-0.4	Seats	0	3	0	0	3
	C to Lab		Candidates	3	3	3	1	10
1987	Electorate	170,498	Votes	24,832	81,585	17,819	0	124,236
	Turnout %	72.9	Votes %	20.0	65.7	14.3	0.0	100.0
			Seats	0	3	0	0	3
			Candidates	3	3	3	0	9
			Change 87-92	1.2	1.9	-3.8	0.8	

Barnsley Central, Barnsley East, Barnsley West and Penistone.

BELFAST				UU	DUP	All	SF	SDLP	Other	Total
1992	Electorate	214,536	Votes	38,342	18,437	17,950	23,321	31,296	15,913	145,259
	Turnout %	67.7	Votes %	26.4	12.7	12.4	16.1	21.5	11.0	100.0
	Swing %	-0.3	Seats	2	1	0	0	1	0	4
	UU to DUP		Candidates	3	1	3	4	3	14	28
1987	Electorate	227,283	Votes	40,918	20,372	20,408	23,603	24,704	13,394	143,399
	Turnout %	63.1	Votes %	28.5	14.2	14.2	16.5	17.2	9.3	100.0
			Seats	2	1	0	1	0	0	4
			Candidates	3	1	3	4	3	5	19
			Change 87-92	-2.1	-1.5	-1.9	-0.4	4.3	1.6	

Belfast East, Belfast North, Belfast South, Belfast West.

BIRMINGHAM				C	Lab	LD	Other	Total
1992	Electorate	728,044	Votes	213,466	243,072	68,805	3,983	529,326
	Turnout %	72.7	Votes %	40.3	45.9	13.0	0.8	100.0
	Swing %	-2.9	Seats	3	9	0	0	12
	C to Lab		Candidates	12	12	12	9	45
1987	Electorate	746,200	Votes	215,285	214,068	87,486	3,595	520,434
	Turnout %	69.7	Votes %	41.4	41.1	16.8	0.7	100.0
			Seats	6	6	0	0	12
			Candidates	12	12	12	8	44
			Change 87-92	-1.0	4.8	-3.8	0.1	

Birmingham Edgbaston, Erdington, Hall Green, Hodge Hill, Ladywood, Northfield, Perry Barr, Selly Oak, Small Heath, Sparkbrook and Yardley, Sutton Coldfield.

BOLTON

			C	Lab	LD	Other	Total
1992	Electorate	195,603	Votes	62,311	73,738	17,743	3,605	157,397
	Turnout %	80.5	Votes %	39.6	46.8	11.3	2.3	100.0
	Swing %	-1.7	Seats	2	1	0	0	3
	C to Lab		Candidates	3	3	3	4	13
1987	Electorate	195,157	Votes	60,931	66,906	24,157	0	151,994
	Turnout %	77.9	Votes %	40.1	44.0	15.9	0.0	100.0
			Seats	2	1	0	0	3
			Candidates	3	3	3	0	9
			Change 87-92	-0.5	2.8	-4.6	2.3	

Bolton North East, Bolton South East, Bolton West.

BRADFORD

			C	Lab	LD	Other	Total
1992	Electorate	341,823	Votes	107,029	113,119	38,607	3,338	262,093
	Turnout %	76.7	Votes %	40.8	43.2	14.7	1.3	100.0
	Swing %	-3.2	Seats	2	3	0	0	5
	C to Lab		Candidates	5	5	5	7	22
1987	Electorate	342,317	Votes	109,365	98,980	47,774	507	256,626
	Turnout %	75.0	Votes %	42.6	38.6	18.6	0.2	100.0
			Seats	2	3	0	0	5
			Candidates	5	5	5	1	16
			Change 87-92	-1.8	4.6	-3.9	1.1	

Bradford North, Bradford South, Bradford West, Keighley, Shipley.

BRISTOL

			C	Lab	LD	Other	Total
1992	Electorate	270,191	Votes	83,494	85,883	40,391	3,122	212,890
	Turnout %	78.8	Votes %	39.2	40.3	19.0	1.5	100.0
	Swing %	-6.0	Seats	2	2	0	0	4
	C to Lab		Candidates	4	4	4	9	21
1987	Electorate	277,806	Votes	92,948	69,919	48,076	2,265	213,208
	Turnout %	76.7	Votes %	43.6	32.8	22.5	1.1	100.0
			Seats	3	1	0	0	4
			Candidates	4	4	4	5	17
			Change 87-92	-4.4	7.5	-3.6	0.4	

Bristol East, Bristol North West, Bristol South, Bristol West.

CARDIFF

			C	Lab	LD	Nat	Other	Total
1992	Electorate	234,819	Votes	67,069	87,281	24,366	3,617	1,502	183,835
	Turnout %	78.3	Votes %	36.5	47.5	13.3	2.0	0.8	100.0
	Swing %	-6.0	Seats	1	3	0	0	0	4
	C to Lab		Candidates	4	4	4	4	6	22
1987	Electorate	223,761	Votes	67,968	66,367	37,987	2,562	0	174,884
	Turnout %	78.2	Votes %	38.9	37.9	21.7	1.5	0.0	100.0
			Seats	2	2	0	0	0	4
			Candidates	4	4	4	4	0	16
			Change 87-92	-2.4	9.5	-8.5	0.5	0.8	

Cardiff Central, Cardiff North, Cardiff South and Penarth, Cardiff West.

COVENTRY

			C	Lab	LD	Other	Total
1992	Electorate	227,727	Votes	60,953	78,936	18,360	15,925	174,174
	Turnout %	76.5	Votes %	35.0	45.3	10.5	9.1	100.0
	Swing %	0.8	Seats	1	3	0	0	4
	Lab to C		Candidates	4	4	4	5	17
1987	Electorate	238,016	Votes	61,386	82,359	32,218	789	176,752
	Turnout %	74.3	Votes %	34.7	46.6	18.2	0.4	100.0
			Seats	1	3	0	0	4
			Candidates	4	4	4	2	14
			Change 87-92	0.3	-1.3	-7.7	8.7	

Coventry North East, Coventry North West, Coventry South East, Coventry South West.

DONCASTER

			C	Lab	LD	Other	Total
1992	Electorate	219,949	Votes	49,909	93,938	19,764	987	164,598
	Turnout %	74.8	Votes %	30.3	57.1	12.0	0.6	100.0
	Swing %	-1.0	Seats	0	3	0	0	3
	C to Lab		Candidates	3	3	3	2	11
1987	Electorate	217,185	Votes	48,818	88,419	22,425	0	159,662
	Turnout %	73.5	Votes %	30.6	55.4	14.0	0.0	100.0
			Seats	0	3	0	0	3
			Candidates	3	3	3	0	9
			Change 87-92	-0.3	1.7	-2.0	0.6	

Don Valley, Doncaster Central, Doncaster North.

DUDLEY

			C	Lab	LD	Other	Total
1992	Electorate	239,631	Votes	87,647	81,476	20,787	1,583	191,493
	Turnout %	79.9	Votes %	45.8	42.5	10.9	0.8	100.0
	Swing %	-4.1	Seats	2	1	0	0	3
	C to Lab		Candidates	3	3	3	2	11
1987	Electorate	235,012	Votes	84,730	64,151	32,100	0	180,981
	Turnout %	77.0	Votes %	46.8	35.4	17.7	0.0	100.0
			Seats	2	1	0	0	3
			Candidates	3	3	3	0	9
			Change 87-92	-1.0	7.1	-6.9	0.8	

Dudley East, Dudley West, Halesowen and Stourbridge.

EDINBURGH

			C	Lab	LD	Nat	Other	Total
1992	Electorate	334,654	Votes	80,302	85,507	41,657	37,295	6,385	251,146
	Turnout %	75.0	Votes %	32.0	34.0	16.6	14.8	2.5	100.0
	Swing %	1.5	Seats	2	4	0	0	0	6
	Lab to C		Candidates	6	6	6	6	10	34
1987	Electorate	352,964	Votes	85,059	98,564	59,956	18,531	878	262,988
	Turnout %	74.5	Votes %	32.3	37.5	22.8	7.0	0.3	100.0
			Seats	2	4	0	0	0	6
			Candidates	6	6	6	6	2	26
			Change 87-92	-0.4	-3.4	-6.2	7.8	2.2	

Edinburgh Central, Edinburgh East, Edinburgh South, Edinburgh West, Edinburgh Leith, Edinburgh Pentlands.

GATESHEAD AND NEWCASTLE-UPON-TYNE CITY

			C	Lab	LD	Other	Total
1992	Electorate	366,803	Votes	74,848	150,042	40,367	744	266,001
	Turnout %	72.5	Votes %	28.1	56.4	15.2	0.3	100.0
	Swing %	-1.4	Seats	0	6	0	0	6
	C to Lab		Candidates	6	6	6	1	19
1987	Electorate	384,635	Votes	73,397	143,820	58,238	891	276,346
	Turnout %	71.8	Votes %	26.6	52.0	21.1	0.3	100.0
			Seats	0	6	0	0	6
			Candidates	6	6	6	3	21
			Change 87-92	1.6	4.4	-5.9	-0.0	

Blaydon, Gateshead East, Newcastle upon Tyne Central, Newcastle upon Tyne East, Newcastle upon Tyne North, Tyne Bridge.

GLASGOW

			C	Lab	LD	Nat	Other	Total
1992	Electorate	518,716	Votes	51,016	198,228	30,197	72,905	8,872	361,218
	Turnout %	69.6	Votes %	14.1	54.9	8.4	20.2	2.5	100.0
	Swing %	4.3	Seats	0	11	0	0	0	11
	Lab to C		Candidates	11	11	11	11	12	56
1987	Electorate	566,845	Votes	50,772	249,600	59,965	41,015	2,262	403,614
	Turnout %	71.2	Votes %	12.6	61.8	14.9	10.2	0.6	100.0
			Seats	0	11	0	0	0	11
			Candidates	11	11	11	11	7	51
			Change 87-92	1.5	-7.0	-6.5	10.0	1.9	

Glasgow Central, Glasgow Cathcart, Glasgow Garscadden, Glasgow Govan, Glasgow Hillhead, Glasgow Maryhill, Glasgow Pollok, Glasgow Provan, Glasgow Rutherglen, Glasgow Shettleston, Glasgow Springburn.

HULL

			C	Lab	LD	Other	Total
1992	Electorate	196,510	Votes	33,162	77,850	20,421	884	132,317
	Turnout %	67.3	Votes %	25.1	58.8	15.4	0.7	100.0
	Swing %	-4.1	Seats	0	3	0	0	3
	C to Lab		Candidates	3	3	3	3	12
1987	Electorate	197,581	Votes	37,949	72,937	26,203	0	137,089
	Turnout %	69.4	Votes %	27.7	53.2	19.1	0.0	100.0
			Seats	0	3	0	0	3
			Candidates	3	3	3	0	9
			Change 87-92	-2.6	5.6	-3.7	0.7	

Hull East, Hull North, Hull West.

KIRKLEES

			C	Lab	LD	Other	Total
1992	Electorate	288,903	Votes	93,969	93,228	36,680	3,336	227,213
	Turnout %	78.6	Votes %	41.4	41.0	16.1	1.5	100.0
	Swing %	0.7	Seats	2	2	0	0	4
	Lab to C		Candidates	4	4	4	10	22
1987	Electorate	281,795	Votes	84,933	87,190	46,832	1,941	220,896
	Turnout %	78.4	Votes %	38.4	39.5	21.2	0.9	100.0
			Seats	2	2	0	0	4
			Candidates	4	4	4	3	15
			Change 87-92	2.9	1.6	-5.1	0.6	

Batley and Spen, Colne Valley, Dewsbury, Huddersfield.

LEEDS

			C	Lab	LD	Other	Total
1992	Electorate	529,127	Votes	146,847	171,319	64,717	6,966	389,849
	Turnout %	73.7	Votes %	37.7	43.9	16.6	1.8	100.0
	Swing %	-3.5	Seats	4	4	0	0	8
	C to Lab		Candidates	8	8	8	8	32
1987	Electorate	520,830	Votes	143,078	140,050	99,754	1,434	384,316
	Turnout %	73.8	Votes %	37.2	36.4	26.0	0.4	100.0
			Seats	4	4	0	0	8
			Candidates	8	8	8	3	27
			Change 87-92	0.4	7.5	-9.4	1.4	

Elmet, Leeds Central, Leeds East, Leeds North East, Leeds North West, Leeds South and Morley, Leeds West, Pudsey.

LEICESTER

			C	Lab	LD	Other	Total
1992	Electorate	200,064	Votes	53,897	78,631	16,716	2,157	151,401
	Turnout %	75.7	Votes %	35.6	51.9	11.0	1.4	100.0
	Swing %	-6.6	Seats	0	3	0	0	3
	C to Lab		Candidates	3	3	3	6	15
1987	Electorate	207,437	Votes	66,129	71,131	20,416	678	158,354
	Turnout %	76.3	Votes %	41.8	44.9	12.9	0.4	100.0
			Seats	0	3	0	0	3
			Candidates	3	3	3	3	12
			Change 87-92	-6.2	7.0	-1.9	1.0	

Leicester East, Leicester South, Leicester West.

LIVERPOOL

			C	Lab	LD	Other	Total
1992	Electorate	354,442	Votes	36,224	140,255	49,250	12,043	237,772
	Turnout %	67.1	Votes %	15.2	59.0	20.7	5.1	100.0
	Swing %	-2.2	Seats	0	5	1	0	6
	C to Lab		Candidates	6	6	6	13	31
1987	Electorate	372,293	Votes	47,568	155,083	69,814	699	273,164
	Turnout %	73.4	Votes %	17.4	56.8	25.6	0.3	100.0
			Seats	0	5	1	0	6
			Candidates	6	6	6	2	20
			Change 87-92	-2.2	2.2	-4.8	4.8	

Liverpool Broadgreen, Garston, Mossley Hill, Riverside, Walton, West Derby.

MANCHESTER AND TRAFFORD			C	Lab	LD	Other	Total
1992	Electorate	473,519	Votes	112,600	170,956	44,012	4,699	332,267
	Turnout %	70.2	Votes %	33.9	51.5	13.2	1.4	100.0
	Swing %	-2.8	Seats	2	6	0	0	8
	C to Lab		Candidates	8	8	8	15	39
1987	Electorate	500,352	Votes	125,558	168,932	69,300	993	364,783
	Turnout %	72.9	Votes %	34.4	46.3	19.0	0.3	100.0
			Seats	2	6	0	0	8
			Candidates	8	8	8	3	27
			Change 87-92	-0.5	5.1	-5.8	1.1	

Altrincham and Sale, Davyhulme, Manchester Central, Manchester Blackley, Manchester Gorton, Manchester Withington, Manchester Wythenshawe, Stretford.

NOTTINGHAM			C	Lab	LD	Other	Total
1992	Electorate	210,229	Votes	58,245	79,849	13,580	2,085	153,759
	Turnout %	73.1	Votes %	37.9	51.9	8.8	1.4	100.0
	Swing %	-7.4	Seats	0	3	0	0	3
	C to Lab		Candidates	3	3	3	5	14
1987	Electorate	210,693	Votes	65,131	64,106	20,712	1,091	151,040
	Turnout %	71.7	Votes %	43.1	42.4	13.7	0.7	100.0
			Seats	2	1	0	0	3
			Candidates	3	3	3	2	11
			Change 87-92	-5.2	9.5	-4.9	0.6	

Nottingham East, Nottingham North, Nottingham South.

OLDHAM AND ROCHDALE			C	Lab	LD	Other	Total
1992	Electorate	307,670	Votes	74,501	98,792	59,975	2,676	235,944
	Turnout %	76.7	Votes %	31.6	41.9	25.4	1.1	100.0
	Swing %	-0.8	Seats	1	3	1	0	5
	C to Lab		Candidates	5	5	5	6	21
1987	Electorate	316,719	Votes	76,444	96,715	59,457	0	232,616
	Turnout %	73.4	Votes %	32.9	41.6	25.6	0.0	100.0
			Seats	1	3	1	0	5
			Candidates	5	5	5	0	15
			Change 87-92	-1.3	0.3	-0000023		

Heywood and Middleton, Littleborough and Saddleworth, Oldham Central and Royton, Oldham West, Rochdale.

PLYMOUTH			C	Lab	LD	Other	Total
1992	Electorate	184,896	Votes	61,686	55,135	24,499	3,675	144,995
	Turnout %	78.4	Votes %	42.5	38.0	16.9	2.5	100.0
	Swing %	-5.6	Seats	2	1	0	0	3
	C to Lab		Candidates	3	3	3	6	15
1987	Electorate	180,047	Votes	53,951	31,927	53,283	493	139,654
	Turnout %	77.6	Votes %	38.6	22.9	38.2	0.4	100.0
			Seats	2	0	1	0	3
			Candidates	3	3	3	1	10
			Change 87-92	3.9	15.2	-21.3	2.2	

Plymouth Devonport, Plymouth Drake, Plymouth Sutton.

ROTHERHAM			C	Lab	LD	Other	Total
1992	Electorate	194,154	Votes	34,617	91,849	16,487	0	142,953
	Turnout %	73.6	Votes %	24.2	64.3	11.5	0.0	100.0
	Swing %	-1.4	Seats	0	3	0	0	3
	C to Lab		Candidates	3	3	3	0	9
1987	Electorate	191,823	Votes	32,025	83,919	23,037	145	139,126
	Turnout %	72.5	Votes %	23.0	60.3	16.6	0.1	100.0
			Seats	0	3	0	0	3
			Candidates	3	3	3	1	10
			Change 87-92	1.2	3.9	-5.0	-0.1	

Rother Valley, Rotherham, Wentworth.

SALFORD CITY AND WIGAN

				C	Lab	LD	Other	Total
1992	Electorate	403,998	Votes	83,809	177,069	33,990	5,596	300,464
	Turnout %	74.4	Votes %	27.9	58.9	11.3	1.9	100.0
	Swing %	-2.1	Seats	0	6	0	0	6
	C to Lab		Candidates	6	6	6	11	29
1987	Electorate	410,294	Votes	87,549	169,267	47,851	201	304,868
	Turnout %	74.3	Votes %	28.7	55.5	15.7	0.1	100.0
			Seats	0	6	0	0	6
			Candidates	6	6	6	1	19
			Change 87-92	-0.8	3.4	-4.4	1.8	

Eccles, Leigh, Makerfield, Salford East, Wigan, Worsley.

SANDWELL

				C	Lab	LD	Other	Total
1992	Electorate	223,476	Votes	59,532	83,441	18,777	1,038	162,788
	Turnout %	72.8	Votes %	36.6	51.3	11.5	0.6	100.0
	Swing %	-2.0	Seats	0	4	0	0	4
	C to Lab		Candidates	4	4	4	2	14
1987	Electorate	230,415	Votes	60,126	77,340	23,568	0	161,034
	Turnout %	69.9	Votes %	37.3	48.0	14.6	0.0	100.0
			Seats	0	4	0	0	4
			Candidates	4	4	4	0	12
			Change 87-92	-0.8	3.2	-3.1	0.6	

Warley East, Warley West, West Bromwich East, West Bromwich West.

SEFTON

				C	Lab	LD	Other	Total
1992	Electorate	223,288	Votes	66,370	60,562	42,881	3,905	173,718
	Turnout %	77.8	Votes %	38.2	34.9	24.7	2.2	100.0
	Swing %	-2.7	Seats	2	1	0	0	3
	C to Lab		Candidates	3	3	3	7	16
1987	Electorate	227,122	Votes	65,601	50,450	56,919	653	173,623
	Turnout %	76.4	Votes %	37.8	29.1	32.8	0.4	100.0
			Seats	1	1	1	0	3
			Candidates	3	3	3	1	10
			Change 87-92	0.4	5.8	-8.1	1.9	

Bootle, Crosby, Southport.

SHEFFIELD

				C	Lab	LD	Other	Total
1992	Electorate	416,926	Votes	75,027	147,601	64,111	2,628	289,367
	Turnout %	69.4	Votes %	25.9	51.0	22.2	0.9	100.0
	Swing %	0.2	Seats	1	5	0	0	6
	Lab to C		Candidates	6	6	6	8	26
1987	Electorate	417,590	Votes	74,652	151,269	73,042	940	299,903
	Turnout %	71.8	Votes %	24.9	50.4	24.4	0.3	100.0
			Seats	1	5	0	0	6
			Candidates	6	6	6	3	21
			Change 87-92	1.0	0.6	-2.2	0.6	

Sheffield Central, Sheffield Attercliffe, Sheffield Brightside, Sheffield Hallam, Sheffield Heeley, Sheffield Hillsborough.

STOCKPORT AND TAMESIDE

				C	Lab	LD	Other	Total
1992	Electorate	383,881	Votes	124,585	113,706	60,513	5,478	304,282
	Turnout %	79.3	Votes %	40.9	37.4	19.9	1.8	100.0
	Swing %	-2.0	Seats	2	4	0	0	6
	C to Lab		Candidates	6	6	6	11	29
1987	Electorate	390,064	Votes	123,904	100,761	76,542	919	302,126
	Turnout %	77.5	Votes %	41.0	33.4	25.3	0.3	100.0
			Seats	3	3	0	0	6
			Candidates	6	6	6	2	20
			Change 87-92	-0.1	4.0	-5.4	1.5	

Ashton-under-Lyne, Cheadle, Denton and Reddish, Hazel Grove, Stalybridge and Hyde, Stockport.

STOKE-ON-TRENT

STOKE-ON-TRENT				C	Lab	LD	Other	Total
1992	Electorate	209,984	Votes	47,635	82,741	20,110	874	151,360
	Turnout %	72.1	Votes %	31.5	54.7	13.3	0.6	100.0
	Swing %	-3.9	Seats	0	3	0	0	3
	C to Lab		Candidates	3	3	3	3	12
1987	Electorate	210,977	Votes	50,759	74,095	26,796	0	151,650
	Turnout %	71.9	Votes %	33.5	48.9	17.7	0.0	100.0
			Seats	0	3	0	0	3
			Candidates	3	3	3	0	9
			Change 87-92	-2.0	5.8	-4.4	0.6	

Stoke-on-Trent Central, Stoke-on-Trent North, Stoke-on-Trent South.

SUNDERLAND

SUNDERLAND				C	Lab	LD	Other	Total
1992	Electorate	224,806	Votes	42,300	94,613	18,579	1,437	156,929
	Turnout %	69.8	Votes %	27.0	60.3	11.8	0.9	100.0
	Swing %	-2.0	Seats	0	3	0	0	3
	C to Lab		Candidates	3	3	3	2	11
1987	Electorate	228,527	Votes	43,917	91,395	26,376	516	162,204
	Turnout %	71.0	Votes %	27.1	56.3	16.3	0.3	100.0
			Seats	0	3	0	0	3
			Candidates	3	3	3	1	10
			Change 87-92	-0.1	3.9	-4.4	0.6	

Houghton and Washington, Sunderland North, Sunderland South.

WAKEFIELD

WAKEFIELD				C	Lab	LD	Other	Total
1992	Electorate	255,683	Votes	55,278	116,388	21,906	0	193,572
	Turnout %	75.7	Votes %	28.6	60.1	11.3	0.0	100.0
	Swing %	-1.9	Seats	0	4	0	0	4
	C to Lab		Candidates	4	4	4	0	12
1987	Electorate	251,844	Votes	54,925	107,327	25,969	295	188,516
	Turnout %	74.9	Votes %	29.1	56.9	13.8	0.2	100.0
			Seats	0	4	0	0	4
			Candidates	4	4	4	1	13
			Change 87-92	-0.6	3.2	-2.5	-0.2	

Hemsworth, Normanton, Pontefract and Castleford, Wakefield.

WALSALL

WALSALL				C	Lab	LD	Other	Total
1992	Electorate	198,650	Votes	69,949	65,927	17,264	1,454	154,594
	Turnout %	77.8	Votes %	45.2	42.6	11.2	0.9	100.0
	Swing %	-1.9	Seats	1	2	0	0	3
	C to Lab		Candidates	3	3	3	3	12
1987	Electorate	197,206	Votes	67,615	58,125	24,610	0	150,350
	Turnout %	76.2	Votes %	45.0	38.7	16.4	0.0	100.0
			Seats	1	2	0	0	3
			Candidates	3	3	3	0	9
			Change 87-92	0.3	4.0	-5.2	0.9	

Aldridge-Brownhills, Walsall North, Walsall South.

WIRRAL

WIRRAL				C	Lab	LD	Other	Total
1992	Electorate	251,927	Votes	86,649	88,824	22,595	3,142	201,210
	Turnout %	79.9	Votes %	43.1	44.1	11.2	1.6	100.0
	Swing %	-2.7	Seats	2	2	0	0	4
	C to Lab		Candidates	4	4	4	8	20
1987	Electorate	258,726	Votes	85,859	77,266	36,252	806	200,183
	Turnout %	77.4	Votes %	42.9	38.6	18.1	0.4	100.0
			Seats	3	1	0	0	4
			Candidates	4	4	4	1	13
			Change 87-92	0.2	5.5	-6.9	1.2	

Birkenhead, Wallasey, Wirral South, West.

WOLVERHAMPTON			C	Lab	LD	Other	Total
1992	Electorate	186,141	Votes	59,111	68,324	11,897	3,174	142,506
	Turnout %	76.6	Votes %	41.5	47.9	8.3	2.2	100.0
	Swing %	-4.7	Seats	1	2	0	0	3
	C to Lab		Candidates	3	3	3	3	12
1987	Electorate	187,760	Votes	59,454	55,330	24,497	0	139,281
	Turnout %	74.2	Votes %	42.7	39.7	17.6	0.0	100.0
			Seats	2	1	0	0	3
			Candidates	3	3	3	0	9
			Change 87-92	-1.2	8.2	-9.2	2.2	

Wolverhampton North East, Wolverhampton South East, Wolverhampton South West.

TOTALS			C	Lab	LD	Nat	Other	Total
1992	Electorate	9,983,568	Votes	2,449,531	3,533,639	1,053,334	113,817	254,745	7,405,066
	Turnout %	74.2	Votes %	33.1	47.7	14.2	1.5	3.4	100.0
	Swing %	-1.8	Seats	35	118	2	0	4	159
	C to Lab		Candidates	158	155	155	21	223	712
1987	Electorate	10,167,774	Votes	2,482,618	3,309,353	1,459,431	62,108	166,390	7,479,900
	Turnout %	73.6	Votes %	33.2	44.2	19.5	0.8	2.2	100.0
			Seats	44	107	4	0	4	159
			Candidates	155	155	155	21	75	561
			Change 87-92	-0.1	3.5	-5.3	0.7	1.2	

SCOTLAND

There are 72 parliamentary constituencies in Scotland. The analysis of the voting in the nine regions of Scotland is as follows:

BORDERS			C	Lab	LD	Nat	Other	Total
1992	Electorate	82,978	Votes	21,371	6,237	28,148	8,681	177	64,614
	Turnout %	77.9	Votes %	33.1	9.7	43.6	13.4	0.3	100.0
	Swing %	-0.1	Seats	0	0	2	0	0	2
	C to Lab		Candidates	2	2	2	2	1	9
1987	Electorate	81,015	Votes	21,037	6,264	30,987	4,246	0	62,534
	Turnout %	77.2	Votes %	33.6	10.0	49.6	6.8	0.0	100.0
			Seats	0	0	2	0	0	2
			Candidates	2	2	2	2	0	8
			Change 87-92	-0.6	-0.4	-6.0	6.6	0.3	

Roxburgh and Berwickshire, Tweeddale Ettrick and Lauderdale.

CENTRAL			C	Lab	LD	Nat	Other	Total
1992	Electorate	209,273	Votes	41,649	74,885	11,093	36,688	410	164,725
	Turnout %	78.7	Votes %	25.3	45.5	6.7	22.3	0.2	100.0
	Swing %	2.9	Seats	1	3	0	0	0	4
	Lab to C		Candidates	4	4	4	4	2	18
1987	Electorate	209,705	Votes	36,871	78,595	20,230	25,165	0	160,861
	Turnout %	76.7	Votes %	22.9	48.9	12.6	15.6	0.0	100.0
			Seats	1	3	0	0	0	4
			Candidates	4	4	4	4	0	16
			Change 87-92	2.4	-3.4	-5.8	6.6	0.2	

Clackmannan, Falkirk East, West, Stirling.

DUMFRIES AND GALLOWAY			C	Lab	LD	Nat	Other	Total
1992	Electorate	115,619	Votes	39,770	20,440	9,575	23,184	419	93,388
	Turnout %	80.8	Votes %	42.6	21.9	10.3	24.8	0.4	100.0
	Swing %	-0.6	Seats	2	0	0	0	0	2
	C to Lab		Candidates	2	2	2	2	2	10
1987	Electorate	112,776	Votes	35,377	16,590	14,065	19,310	579	85,921
	Turnout %	76.2	Votes %	41.2	19.3	16.4	22.5	0.7	100.0
			Seats	2	0	0	0	0	2
			Candidates	2	2	2	2	2	10
			Change 87-92	1.4	2.6	-6.1	2.4	-0.2	

Dumfries, Galloway and Upper Nithsdale.

FIFE			C	Lab	LD	Nat	Other	Total
1992	Electorate	262,788	Votes	47,089	81,308	34,435	36,117	379	199,328
	Turnout %	75.9	Votes %	23.6	40.8	17.3	18.1	0.2	100.0
	Swing %	2.0	Seats	0	4	1	0	0	5
	Lab to C		Candidates	5	5	5	5	2	22
1987	Electorate	264,033	Votes	47,133	89,929	43,883	21,042	0	201,987
	Turnout %	76.5	Votes %	23.3	44.5	21.7	10.4	0.0	100.0
			Seats	0	4	1	0	0	5
			Candidates	5	5	5	5	0	20
			Change 87-92	0.3	-3.7	-4.5	7.7	0.2	

Dunfermline East, West, Fife Central, North East, Kirkcaldy.

GRAMPIAN			C	Lab	LD	Nat	Other	Total
1992	Electorate	393,946	Votes	102,753	53,864	55,348	72,456	381	284,802
	Turnout %	72.3	Votes %	36.1	18.9	19.4	25.4	0.1	100.0
	Swing %	3.5	Seats	2	1	1	2	0	6
	Lab to C		Candidates	6	6	6	6	1	25
1987	Electorate	387,573	Votes	90,584	62,313	69,791	54,533	299	277,520
	Turnout %	71.6	Votes %	32.6	22.5	25.1	19.7	0.1	100.0
			Seats	1	2	1	2	0	6
			Candidates	6	6	6	6	1	25
			Change 87-92	3.4	-3.5	-5.7	5.8	0.0	

Aberdeen North, South, Banff and Buchan, Gordon, Kincardine and Deeside, Moray.

HIGHLAND			C	Lab	LD	Nat	Other	Total
1992	Electorate	210,153	Votes	31,524	34,315	50,483	32,491	2,014	150,827
	Turnout %	71.8	Votes %	20.9	22.8	33.5	21.5	1.3	100.0
	Swing %	0.9	Seats	0	1	4	0	0	5
	Lab to C		Candidates	5	5	5	5	4	24
1987	Electorate	204,945	Votes	28,530	33,751	60,869	18,565	4,503	146,218
	Turnout %	71.3	Votes %	19.5	23.1	41.6	12.7	3.1	100.0
			Seats	0	1	4	0	0	5
			Candidates	5	5	5	4	4	23
			Change 87-92	1.4	-0.3	-8.2	8.8	-1.7	

Caithness and Sutherland, Inverness Nairn and Lochaber, Orkney and Shetland, Ross Cromarty and Skye, Western Isles.

LOTHIAN			C	Lab	LD	Nat	Other	Total
1992	Electorate	583,782	Votes	122,494	173,480	61,304	82,042	7,330	446,650
	Turnout %	76.5	Votes %	27.4	38.8	13.7	18.4	1.6	100.0
	Swing %	1.4	Seats	2	8	0	0	0	10
	Lab to C		Candidates	10	10	10	10	12	52
1987	Electorate	594,684	Votes	122,752	186,679	92,030	45,670	1,895	449,026
	Turnout %	75.5	Votes %	27.3	41.6	20.5	10.2	0.4	100.0
			Seats	2	8	0	0	0	10
			Candidates	10	10	10	10	5	45
			Change 87-92	0.1	-2.7	-6.8	8.2	1.2	

East Lothian, the Edinburgh seats of Central, East, South, West, Leith and Pentlands, Linlithgow, Livingston, Midlothian.

STRATHCLYDE			C	Lab	LD	Nat	Other	Total
1992	Electorate	1,726,033	Votes	271,479	643,723	115,211	260,407	10,895	1,301,715
	Turnout %	75.4	Votes %	20.9	49.5	8.9	20.0	0.8	100.0
	Swing %	2.7	Seats	2	30	1	0	0	33
	Lab to C		Candidates	33	33	33	33	24	156
1987	Electorate	1,796,515	Votes	261,464	723,545	213,361	156,387	2,485	1,357,242
	Turnout %	75.5	Votes %	19.3	53.3	15.7	11.5	0.2	100.0
			Seats	2	30	1	0	0	33
			Candidates	33	33	33	33	8	140
			Change 87-92	1.6	-3.9	-6.9	8.5	0.7	

Argyll and Bute, Ayr, Carrick Cumnock and Doon Valley, Clydebank and Milngavie, Clydesdale, Cumbernauld and Kilsyth, Cunninghame N and S, Dumbarton, Eastwood, E Kilbride, the Glasgow seats of Central, Cathcart, Garscadden, Govan, Hillhead, Maryhill, Pollok, Provan, Rutherglen, Shettleston and Springburn, Greenock and Port Glasgow, Hamilton, Kilmarnock and Loudoun, Monklands E and W, Motherwell N and S, Paisley N and S, Renfrew W and Inverclyde, Strathkelvin and Bearsden.

TAYSIDE				C	Lab	LD	Nat	Other	Total
1992	Electorate	303,461	Votes	73,825	54,614	18,259	77,486	1,322	225,506
	Turnout %	74.3	Votes %	32.7	24.2	8.1	34.4	0.6	100.0
	Swing %	2.3	Seats	2	2	0	1	0	5
	Lab to C		Candidates	5	5	5	5	5	25
1987	Electorate	301,219	Votes	69,343	60,466	24,827	71,555	308	226,499
	Turnout %	75.2	Votes %	30.6	26.7	11.0	31.6	0.1	100.0
			Seats	2	2	0	1	0	5
			Candidates	5	5	5	5	1	21
			Change 87-92	2.1	-2.5	-2.9	2.8	0.5	

Angus East, Dundee East, West, Perth and Kinross, Tayside North.

TOTALS				C	Lab	LD	Nat	Other	Total
1992	Electorate	3,888,033	Votes	751,954	1,142,866	383,856	629,552	23,327	2,931,555
	Turnout %	75.4	Votes %	25.7	39.0	13.1	21.5	0.8	100.0
	Swing %	2.5	Seats	11	49	9	3	0	72
	Lab to C		Candidates	72	72	72	72	53	341
1987	Electorate	3,952,465	Votes	713,091	1,258,132	570,043	416,473	10,069	2,967,808
	Turnout %	75.1	Votes %	24.0	42.4	19.2	14.0	0.3	100.0
			Seats	10	50	9	3	0	72
			Candidates	72	72	72	71	21	308
			Change 87-92	1.6	-3.4	-6.1	7.4	0.5	

WALES

Wales has 38 parliamentary seats in its eight counties and the analysis of voting in the Principality is as follows:

CLWYD				C	Lab	LD	Nat	Other	Total
1992	Electorate	318,746	Votes	99,446	114,943	31,995	10,103	1,297	257,784
	Turnout %	80.9	Votes %	38.6	44.6	12.4	3.9	0.5	100.0
	Swing %	-3.3	Seats	1	4	0	0	0	5
	C to Lab		Candidates	5	5	5	5	5	25
1987	Electorate	308,892	Votes	96,042	94,600	48,051	8,309	0	247,002
	Turnout %	80.0	Votes %	38.9	38.3	19.5	3.4	0.0	100.0
			Seats	2	3	0	0	0	5
			Candidates	5	5	5	5	0	20
			Change 87-92	-0.3	6.3	-7.0	0.6	0.5	

Alyn and Deeside, Clwyd North West, Clwyd South West, Delyn, Wrexham.

DYFED				C	Lab	LD	Nat	Other	Total
1992	Electorate	273,312	Votes	59,530	84,571	31,209	43,482	642	219,434
	Turnout %	80.3	Votes %	27.1	38.5	14.2	19.8	0.3	100.0
	Swing %	-2.0	Seats	0	3	0	1	0	4
	C to Lab		Candidates	4	4	4	4	2	18
1987	Electorate	262,598	Votes	59,679	75,213	46,432	26,512	1,302	209,138
	Turnout %	79.6	Votes %	28.5	36.0	22.2	12.7	0.6	100.0
			Seats	1	2	1	0	0	4
			Candidates	4	4	4	4	2	18
			Change 87-92	-1.4	2.6	-8.0	7.1	-0.3	

Carmarthen, Ceredigion and Pembroke North, Llanelli, Pembroke.

GLAMORGAN MID				C	Lab	LD	Nat	Other	Total
1992	Electorate	405,020	Votes	55,524	207,971	26,217	25,554	860	316,126
	Turnout %	78.1	Votes %	17.6	65.8	8.3	8.1	0.3	100.0
	Swing %	-1.1	Seats	0	7	0	0	0	7
	C to Lab		Candidates	7	7	7	7	2	30
1987	Electorate	402,890	Votes	55,869	200,021	37,491	18,204	1,521	313,106
	Turnout %	77.7	Votes %	17.8	63.9	12.0	5.8	0.5	100.0
			Seats	0	7	0	0	0	7
			Candidates	7	7	7	7	2	30
			Change 87-92	-0.3	1.9	-3.7	2.3	-0.2	

Bridgend, Caerphilly, Cynon Valley, Merthyr Tydfil and Rhymney, Ogmore, Pontypridd, Rhondda.

GLAMORGAN SOUTH

			C	Lab	LD	Nat	Other	Total
1992	Electorate	301,491	Votes	91,289	111,482	29,411	4,777	1,502	238,461
	Turnout %	79.1	Votes %	38.3	46.8	12.3	2.0	0.6	100.0
	Swing %	-6.0	Seats	2	3	0	0	0	5
	C to Lab		Candidates	5	5	5	5	6	26
1987	Electorate	289,071	Votes	92,197	84,345	46,620	3,508	0	226,670
	Turnout %	78.4	Votes %	40.7	37.2	20.6	1.5	0.0	100.0
			Seats	3	2	0	0	0	5
			Candidates	5	5	5	5	0	20
			Change 87-92	-2.4	9.5	-8.2	0.5	0.6	

Cardiff Central, Cardiff North, Cardiff South and Penarth, Cardiff West, Vale of Glamorgan.

GLAMORGAN WEST

			C	Lab	LD	Nat	Other	Total
1992	Electorate	284,254	Votes	50,389	135,652	20,989	11,997	1,907	220,934
	Turnout %	77.7	Votes %	22.8	61.4	9.5	5.4	0.9	100.0
	Swing %	-2.5	Seats	0	5	0	0	0	5
	C to Lab		Candidates	5	5	5	5	5	25
1987	Electorate	283,448	Votes	52,436	126,443	33,693	7,304	469	220,345
	Turnout %	77.7	Votes %	23.8	57.4	15.3	3.3	0.2	100.0
			Seats	0	5	0	0	0	5
			Candidates	5	5	5	5	1	21
			Change 87-92	-1.0	4.0	-5.8	2.1	0.7	

Aberavon, Gower, Neath, Swansea East, Swansea West.

GWENT

			C	Lab	LD	Nat	Other	Total
1992	Electorate	333,442	Votes	73,614	163,637	26,153	4,388	2,904	270,696
	Turnout %	81.2	Votes %	27.2	60.5	9.7	1.6	1.1	100.0
	Swing %	-3.5	Seats	1	5	0	0	0	6
	C to Lab		Candidates	6	6	6	3	4	25
1987	Electorate	332,443	Votes	73,565	142,740	41,219	5,328	450	263,302
	Turnout %	79.2	Votes %	27.9	54.2	15.7	2.0	0.2	100.0
			Seats	1	5	0	0	0	6
			Candidates	6	6	6	6	1	25
			Change 87-92	-0.7	6.2	-6.0	-0.4	0.9	

Blaenau Gwent, Islwyn, Monmouth, Newport East, Newport West, Torfaen.

GWYNEDD

			C	Lab	LD	Nat	Other	Total
1992	Electorate	185,869	Votes	43,086	31,628	19,605	52,139	1,577	148,035
	Turnout %	79.6	Votes %	29.1	21.4	13.2	35.2	1.1	100.0
	Swing %	-2.5	Seats	1	0	0	3	0	4
	C to Lab		Candidates	4	4	4	4	5	21
1987	Electorate	182,788	Votes	44,904	26,353	21,486	52,487	0	145,230
	Turnout %	79.5	Votes %	30.9	18.1	14.8	36.1	0.0	100.0
			Seats	1	0	0	3	0	4
			Candidates	4	4	4	4	0	16
			Change 87-92	-1.8	3.2	-1.6	-0.9	1.1	

Caernarfon, Conwy, Meirionnydd Nant Conwy, Ynys Mon.

POWYS

			C	Lab	All	Nat	Other	Total
1992	Electorate	92,895	Votes	26,799	15,749	31,878	1,999	901	77,326
	Turnout %	83.2	Votes %	34.7	20.4	41.2	2.6	1.2	100.0
	Swing %	-0.5	Seats	1	0	1	0	0	2
	C to Lab		Candidates	2	2	2	2	2	10
1987	Electorate	89,202	Votes	26,624	15,484	29,238	1,947	0	73,293
	Turnout %	82.2	Votes %	36.3	21.1	39.9	2.7	0.0	100.0
			Seats	0	0	2	0	0	2
			Candidates	2	2	2	2	0	8
			Change 87-92	-1.7	-0.8	1.3	-0.1	1.2	

Brecon and Radnor, Montgomery.

TOTALS

			C	Lab	All	Nat	Other	Total
1992	Electorate	2,195,029	Votes	499,677	865,633	217,457	154,439	11,590	1,748,796
	Turnout %	79.7	Votes %	28.6	49.5	12.4	8.8	0.7	100.0
	Swing %	-2.7	Seats	6	27	1	4	0	38
	C to Lab		Candidates	38	38	38	35	31	180
1987	Electorate	2,151,332	Votes	501,316	765,199	304,230	123,599	3,742	1,698,086
	Turnout %	78.9	Votes %	29.5	45.1	17.9	7.3	0.2	100.0
			Seats	8	24	3	3	0	38
			Candidates	38	38	38	38	6	158
			Change 87-92	-0.9	4.4	-5.5	1.6	0.4	

Marginal seats

The Conservatives regained the Vale of Glamorgan seat, which they had lost in a by-election, by the narrowest of margins — a mere 19 votes. Three other Tory seats were won by fewer than a hundred votes and at the next election the Conservatives will be defending 92 seats which would be lost on a swing of no more than 5 per cent.

Of the 651 MPs, 170 have majorities of 10 per cent or less, compared with 151 in 1987. Labour have 62, the Liberal Democrats 11, SNP three, Plaid Cymru and SDLP (N Ireland) one each. The most marginal Labour seat is at Rossendale and Darwen. Janet Anderson beat David Trippier, the former minister, by 120 votes.

The table shows the majority both as a percentage and number of votes over the runner-up.

Conservative marginals

Seat	%	Votes
Vale of Glamorgan	0.03	19 Lab
Hayes and Harlington	0.03	53 Lab
Bristol North West	0.08	45 Lab
Ayr	0.16	85 Lab
Brecon and Radnor	0.29	130 LD
Bolton North East	0.38	185 Lab
Portsmouth South	0.45	242 LD
Norwich North	0.51	266 Lab
Corby	0.60	342 Lab
Slough	0.89	514 Lab
Tynemouth	0.99	597 Lab
Southampton, Test	1.04	585 Lab
Amber Valley	1.20	712 Lab
Edmonton	1.24	593 Lab
Luton South	1.38	799 Lab
Dover	1.45	833 Lab
Bury South	1.46	788 Lab
Stirling	1.47	703 Lab
Leicestershire NW	1.57	979 Lab
Hazel Grove	1.70	929 LD
Edinburgh West	1.80	879 LD
Bolton West	1.81	1,079 Lab
Chester, City of	2.07	1,101 Lab
Isle of Wight	2.29	1,827 LD
Batley and Spen	2.31	1,408 Lab
Conwy	2.36	995 LD
Langbaurgh	2.37	1,564 Lab
Basildon	2.75	1,480 Lab
Coventry South West	2.82	1,436 Lab
St Ives	2.88	1,645 LD
Lincoln	3.28	2,049 Lab
Mitcham and Morden	3.39	1,734 Lab
Aberdeen South	3.69	1,517 Lab
Swindon	3.85	2,826 Lab
Blackpool South	3.79	1,667 Lab
Brentford & Isleworth	3.86	2,086 Lab
Eltham	4.09	1,666 Lab
Perth and Kinross	4.16	2,094 SNP
Erith and Crayford	4.96	2,339 Lab
Plymouth, Drake	5.16	2,013 Lab
Harlow	5.19	2,940 Lab
Taunton	5.19	3,336 LD
Stockton South	5.36	3,369 Lab
Southport	5.52	3,063 LD
Galloway and Upper Nithsdale	5.55	2,468 SNP
Elmet	5.60	3,261 Lab
Falmouth and Camborne	5.70	3,267 LD
Devon West and Torridge	5.77	3,614 LD
Hereford	6.03	3,413 LD
Cardiff North	6.22	2,969 Lab
Monmouth	6.29	3,204 Lab
Lancaster	6.38	2,953 Lab
Oxfrd West and Abingdon	6.38	3,539 LD
Exeter	6.41	4,045 Lab
Chorley	6.53	4,246 Lab
Keighley	6.56	3,596 Lab
Derbyshire South	6.62	4,658 Lab
Blackpool North	6.75	3,040 Lab
Brighton, Kemptown	6.96	3,056 Lab
Northampton North	7.20	3,908 Lab
Somerton and Frome	7.35	4,341 LD
Gloucestershire West	7.39	4,958 Lab
Derby North	7.55	4,453 Lab
Birmingham, Hall Green	7.80	3,665 Lab
Calder Valley	7.98	4,878 Lab
High Peak	8.04	4,819 Lab
Bury North	8.08	4,764 Lab
Dudley West	8.14	5,789 Lab
Peterborough	8.17	5,376 Lab
Brighton, Pavilion	8.30	3,675 Lab
Westminster North	8.37	3,733 Lab
Stevenage	8.38	4,888 Lab
Littleborough and Saddleworth	8.40	4,494 LD
Weston-super-Mare	8.50	5,342 LD
Richmond and Barnes	8.57	3,869 LD
Leeds North East	8.57	4,244 Lab
Kincardine and Deeside	8.57	4,495 LD
Davyhulme	8.77	4,426 Lab
Eastbourne	8.89	5,481 LD
Erewash	9.00	5,703 Lab
Milton Keynes S W	9.16	4,687 Lab
Tayside North	9.19	3,995 SNP
South Ribble	9.21	5,973 Lab
Battersea	9.26	4,840 Lab
Gravesham	9.30	5,493 Lab
Gloucester	9.37	6,058 Lab
Wolverhampton S W	9.43	4,966 Lab
Edinburgh, Pentlands	9.63	4,290 Lab
Burton	9.66	5,996 Lab
Waveney	9.73	6,702 Lab
Staffordshire Mid	9.92	6,236 Lab
Great Yarmouth	9.98	5,309 Lab

Labour marginals

Seat	%	Votes
Rossendale and Darwen	0.19	120 C
Warrington South	0.30	191 C
Birmingham, Yardley	0.38	162 C
Ipswich	0.49	265 C
Halifax	0.83	478 C
Ilford South	0.94	402 C
Southampton, Itchen	0.99	551 C
Dewsbury	1.09	634 C
Cambridge	1.15	580 C
Birmingham, Northfield	1.17	630 C
Pembroke	1.24	755 C
Thurrock	2.17	1,172 C
Warwickshire North	2.43	1,454 C
Cannock and Burntwood	2.46	1,506 C
Lewisham East	2.54	1,095 C
Nuneaton	2.75	1,631 C
Stockport	2.98	1,422 C
Lancashire West	3.25	2,077 C
Ellesmere Port and Neston	3.30	1,989 C
Feltham and Heston	3.32	1,995 C
Hampstead and Highgate	3.39	1,440 C
Coventry South East	3.59	1,311 C
Delyn	3.67	2,039 C
Birmingham, Selly Oak	3.73	2,060 C
Renfrew W and Inverclyde	3.74	1,744 C
Croydon North West	3.77	1,526 C
Greenwich	3.80	1,357 SD
Kingswood	3.94	2,370 C
Pendle	3.98	2,113 C
Hyndburn	3.99	1,960 C
Lewisham West	4.17	1,809 C
Crewe and Nantwich	4.39	2,695 C
Sherwood	4.64	2,910 C
Darlington	5.06	2,798 C
Carmarthen	5.13	2,922 PC
Copeland	5.32	2,439 C
Bristol East	5.35	2,692 C
Edinburgh Central	5.43	2,126 C
Dulwich	5.49	2,056 C
Woolwich	5.61	2,225 SD
Nottingham South	5.89	3,181 C
Streatham	5.91	2,317 C
Strathkelvin and Bearsden	6.28	3,162 C
Walsall South	6.35	3,178 C
Barrow and Furness	6.43	3,578 C
West Bromwich East	6.56	2,813 C
Cunninghame North	6.86	2,939 C
Wallasey	7.03	3,809 C
Carlisle	7.10	3,108 C
Walsall North	7.33	3,824 C
Walthamstow	7.82	2,796 C
Tooting	8.04	4,107 C
Wolverhampton N E	8.05	3,939 C
Cardiff Central	8.07	3,465 C
Newham South	8.13	2,502 C
Leicester West	8.24	3,978 C
Bradford South	9.27	4,902 C
Hornsey and Wood Green	9.29	5,177 C
Edinburgh South	9.37	4,176 C
Wrekin, The	9.48	6,648 C
York	9.88	6,342 C
Clwyd South West	10.00	4,941 C

Liberal Democrat marginals

Seat	%	Votes
Gordon	0.46	274 C
Inverness, Nairn & Lochaber	0.90	458 Lab
Devon North	1.36	794 C
Cheltenham	2.60	1,668 C
Cornwall North	3.07	1,921 C
Rochdale	3.46	1,839 Lab
Liverpool, Mossley Hill	6.30	2,606 Lab
Bath	7.17	3,768 C
Argyll and Bute	7.19	2,622 C
Fife North East	7.91	3,308 C
Tweeddle, Ettrick & Lauderdale	8.18	2,520 C

SNP marginals

Seat	%	Votes
Angus East	2.01	954 C
Moray	6.20	2,844 C
Banff and Buchan	8.89	4,108 C

Plaid Cymru marginals

Seat	%	Votes
Ynys Mon	2.57	1,106 C
Ceredigion and Pembroke North	6.24	3,193 LD

SDLP marginal

Seat	%	Votes
Belfast West	1.47	589 SF

Ministers in House of Lords

Lord Mackay of Clashfern became Lord Chancellor in 1988; a Lord of Appeal in Ordinary from 1985; Lord Advocate of Scotland, 1979-84; PC 1979; Life peer, created 1979; QC (Scot) 1965; former Standing Junior Counsel to Queen's and Lord Treasurer's Remembrancer, Scottish Home and Health Dept, Commissioners of Inland Revenue in Scotland; Sheriff Principal, Renfrew and Argyll, 1972-4; Vice-Dean Faculty of Advocates, 1973-6; Dean, 1976-9; a Senator of College of Justice in Scotland, 1984-5. Parttime mbr, Scottish Law Commission, 1976-9. Hon Master of the Bench, Inner Temple, 1979. Fellow, International Academy of Trial Lawyers and of Royal Society of Edinburgh; Hon Fellow, Inst of Taxation and of Society of Public Teachers of Law. Director, Stenhouse Holdings Ltd, 1976-7. Mbr, Insurance Brokers Registration Cl, 1977-9. A Commissioner of Northern Lighthouses, 1975-84. B Jul 2 1927; ed George Heriot's Sch, Edinburgh; Edinburgh Univ. Mathematics lecturer, St Andrews Univ, 1948-50; Major then Senior Scholar in mathematics, Trinity Coll, Cambridge.

John Wakeham, Lord Privy Seal and Leader of the House of Lords, was appointed following the 1992 election when he retired from the Commons. He had been given responsibility for co-ordinating government policies in June 1990. Secretary of State for Energy 1989-1992; Lord Privy Seal and Leader of the Commons 1987-8; Parliamentary Secretary, Treasury and Government Chief Whip, 1983-7; Minister of State, Treasury, 1982-3; Under Secretary of State, Industry, 1981-2; Assistant Government Whip, 1979-81. B June 22, 1932, ed Charterhouse. Chartered accountant and former company director.

The Earl of Caithness was appointed Minister of State for Transport, April 1992. Minister of State for Foreign and Commonwealth Affairs 1990-2; Paymaster General, 1989-90; Minister of State for Environment, 1988-9; Minister of State, Home Office, 1986-8; Under Secretary of State for Transport, 1985-6; a Lord-in-Waiting (Govt whip), 1984-5. PC 1990. B Nov 3 1948; ed Marlborough; Royal Ag Coll, Cirencester.

Lynda Chalker was made a life peer after losing seat as Conservative MP for Wallasey at the 1992 general election. She retained the post of Minister for Overseas Development which she had held in the Commons since 1989. Deputy Foreign Secretary, 1987-9, as Minister of State, to which post she was appointed in 1986 with special responsibility for sub-Saharan Africa, the Commonwealth, Europe, international trade and economic relations and personnel. Minister of State, Transport, 1983-6; Under Secretary, Transport, 1982-3. B April 29, 1942. Ed, Roedean and Heidelberg and London Univs and Central Poly. Former executive director, International Market Research Co. Vice-chairman, National Young Conservatives, 1970-1; Former governor, Roedean Sch. Former mbr, BBC advisory cttee and of BPA advisory panel.

Baroness Blatch was appointed Minister of State for Education in 1992. She was a Minister of State, Environment, 1991-2; an Under Secretary of State for Environment, 1990-1; formerly a whip. Mbr, Cambridgeshire CC, 1977-89 (ldr, 1981-5); bd, Peterborough Development Corporation, 1984-8; Euro Economic and Social Cmte, 1986-7; Cons nat local govt advisory cmte, 1988- . Pres, Nat Benevolent Inst, 1989- ; chmn, Anglo-American Community Relations Cmte, RAF Alconbury, 1985- . B Jul 24 1937; ed state sec sch for girls, Prenton, Birkenhead; Huntingdonshire Coll. Air traffic control asst, WRAF, 1955-9, and Aircraft and Armament Experimental Establishment, Boscombe Down, 1959-63.

Earl Ferrers was appointed Minr of State, Home Office, and Dep Ldr of House of Lords, in 1988. High Steward of Norwich Cathedral, 1979- ; chmn, Royal Commission on Historical Monuments (England), 1984-8. Minr of State for Agriculture, Fisheries and Food and Dep Ldr of Hse of Lords, 1979-83; Parly Sec, Min of Agriculture, Fisheries and Food, 1974; Lord-in-Waiting (Govt whip), 1971-4 and 1962-4. PC 1982. Chmn, British Agricultural Export Cl, 1984-8; mbr, Armitage Cmte on political activities of civil servants, 1976- ; cl, Food from Britain, 1984-8; cl, Hurstpierpoint Coll, 1959-68; director, Economic Forestry Gp, 1985-8; Chatham Historic Dockyard Trust, 1984-8. B Jun 8 1929; ed Winchester Coll; Magdalene Coll, Cambridge. Director, Norwich Union Insurance Gp, 1983-8 and 1975-9. Chmn, Trustee Savings Bank of Eastern England, 1977-9; mbr, TSB Central Bd, 1977-9; director, Central TSB, 1978-9; TSB Trustcard Ltd, 1978-9.

Lord Fraser of Carmyllie was appointed Minister of State, Scottish Office in 1992; Lord Advocate, 1989-92; Solicitor General for Scotland, 1982-9. PC 1989. Cons MP for Angus East, 1983-7, and for Angus South, 1979-83; contested Aberdeen North, Oct 1974. PPS to Sec of State for Scotland, 1981-2. QC (Scot), 1982. B May 29, 1945; ed St Andrews Prep Sch, Grahamstown, S Africa; Loretto Sch, Musselburgh; Gonville and Caius Coll, Cambridge; Edinburgh Univ. Standing Junior Counsel in Scotland to Foreign and Commonwealth Office, 1979; lecturer in constitutional law, Heriot-Watt Univ, 1971-75; chmn, Scottish Cons Lawyers Reform Gp, 1976.

Alan Rodger was made a life peer on being appointed Lord Advocate in April 1992. Solicitor General for Scotland 1989-92. B September 1944; ed Kelvinside Acad, Glasgow; Glasgow Univ; New College, Oxford. Fellow, Balliol, 1969-70; New College, Oxford, 1970-2. Member, Faculty of Advocates 1974; Clerk of the faculty, 1976-9; Advocate Depute, 1985-8; Home Advocate Depute, 1986-8; Mbr, Mental Welfare Commission, Scotland, 1981-4.

Earl Howe was appointed Parliamentary Secretary for Agriculture in April 1992; Lord-in-waiting (Govt whip) 1991-2. B Jan 1951, ed Rugby and Christ Church, Oxford. Arable and dairy farmer; dir, Adam & Co, 1987-90; dir, Provident Life Assocn, 1988-91; Barclays Bank, 1983-7 (senior man, 1984-7); associate, Inst of Bankers, 1976-; govr, William IV Naval Foundation, 1984-; vice-presdt, National Socty for Epilepsy 1984-6, presdt, 1986-.

Viscount Ullswater was appointed an Under Secretary of State for Employment in 1990; a Lord-in-Waiting (Govt whip), 1989-90. B Jan 9 1942; ed Eton and Trinity Coll, Cambridge. Capt, Royal Wessex Yeomanry, TAVR, 1973-8.

Lord Strathclyde was appointed an Under Secretary of State for Scotland in 1990; Under Secretary of State for Environment, 1990; Under Secretary of State for Employment, 1989-90; a Lord-in-Waiting (Govt whip) 1988-9. B Feb 22 1960; ed Wellington Coll; East Anglia Univ; Universite d'Aix-en-Provence. Insurance broker, Bain Dawes, subsequently Bain Clarkson Ltd, 1982. Contested Merseyside East for Conservatives in 1984 Euro elections.

Baroness Cumberlege was appointed Under Secretary for Health in Apr 1992. B Jan, 1943; ed Convent of Sacred Heart, Tunbridge Wells; mbr East Sussex AHA, 1977-81; chmn, Brighton HA, 1981-8; mbr, Cl, National Assocn of Hlth Authorities, 1982-8. Chmn, Review of Community Nursing for England, 1985; Mbr UK Cen Cl Nursing, Midwifery and Health Visiting, 1989 and of NHS policy brd, 1989.

Lord Henley was appointed Under Secretary of State for Social Security in 1989; a Lord-in-Waiting (Govt whip), 1989. Barrister. Mbr, Cumbria CC, 1986-9. Chmn, Penrith and the Border Cons Assocn, 1987-9; pres, Cumbria Assocn of Local Cls, 1981-9. B Nov 22 1953; ed Dragon Sch, Oxford; Clifton Coll; Durham Univ.

Baroness Denton of Wakefield was appointed Under Secretary for Trade and Industry in Apr 1992; Baroness-in-Waiting (Govt whip) 1992. B Dec 1935. Ed Rothwell GS and LSE. Dep chmn, Black Country Development Corporation, 1987-91; racing and rally driver, 1969-72; external affairs director, Austin Rover, 1985-6; marketing director, Heron Motor Gp, 1978-80; Huxford gp, 1972-8. Director, British Nuclear Fuels, 1987-91; Burson-Marsteller, 1987-91; London and Edinburgh

Insurance Gp, 1989-91; Triplex Lloyd, 1990-91; Think Green, 1989-91; Ordnance Survey, 1985-8. Chmn, Women on Move agst Cancer, 1979-91. Governor, LSE, 1982-91; Mbr, NHS Policy Brd, 1991; Mbr, Teachers Review Body, 1991.

Lord Hesketh was appointed Government Chief Whip and Captain, Gentleman at Arms, in 1991; Minister for Industry, 1990-1; Under Secretary of State for Environment, 1989-90; a Lord-in-Waiting (Govt whip), 1986-9. B Oct 28 1950; ed Ampleforth. Ran his own Formula One motor racing team.

The Earl of Strathmore and Kinghorne was appointed Captain, Yeoman of the Guard and Govt dep chief whip in 1991; a Lord-in-Waiting (Govt whip), 1989-91. Capt, Scots Guards, in which he was commissioned in 1980. Page of Honour to HM Queen Elizabeth, the Queen Mother, 1971-3. B Jun 7 1957; ed Aberdeen Univ.

Baroness Trumpington moved to the Whips' Office in Apr 1992 and appointed to the Privy Council. Minister of State for Agriculture, Fisheries and Food, 1989-92; Parliamentary Secretary, 1987-9. Baroness-in-Waiting (Govt whip), 1983-5; Under Secretary of State for Health and Social Security, 1985-7. B Oct 1922; ed privately in England and France. Mbr, Cambridge City Cl, 1963-73; Mayor of Cambridge, 1971-2; Cambridgeshire CC, 1973-5. Pres, Assocn of Heads of Independent Schs, 1980-90; Steward, Folkestone Racecourse, 1980-.

The Earl of Arran was appointed Under Secretary of State, Northern Ireland Office in Apr 1992; Under Secretary of State for the Armed Forces in 1989-92; a Lord-in-Waiting (Govt whip), 1987-9. Co-founder, Gore Publishing Ltd, 1980; co-chmn, Children's Country Holidays Fund. B Jul 14 1938; ed Eton and Balliol Coll, Oxford.

Viscount Long, a Lord-in-Waiting (Government whip), 1979- ; Opposition whip, 1974-9. B Jan 30 1929; ed Harrow.

Lord Cavendish of Furness was appointed a Lord-in-Waiting (Govt whip) in 1990. Chmn, Holker Estate gp of companies, 1971-90. Mbr, Cumbria CC, 1985-90. B Nov 2 1941; ed Eton. In international banking, 1961-71. Chmn, Morecambe and Lonsdale Cons Assocn, 1975-8; governors, St Anne's Sch, Windemere, 1983-9.

Viscount Astor was appointed a Lord-in-Waiting (Govt whip) in 1990. B Dec 27 1951; ed Eton.

Viscount St Davids was appointed Lord-in-Waiting (whip), 1992. Investment analyst, member of Stock Exchange, 1965. Director of Citicorp Scrimgeour Vickers (Securities) 1985-88, responsible for European equity sales department. B Jan 30, 1939. Ed Haverford West GS, Sevenoaks Sch and King's College, London. Held various offices in Scout movement.

Record year for women

by Roger Wood, Parliamentary Editor of *The Times*

Equal representation in the House of Commons still looks a long way off, but women contested the 1992 election in record numbers and there are signs that some real progress is being made. There are now 60 women MPs, a record number and three times more than there were 20 years ago.

A total of 568 women stood for election, compared with 327 in 1987. Among the main parties the Liberal Democrats led the way with 143, followed by Labour with 137. The Conservatives fielded 63 candidates. Labour now has 37 women in the Commons, the Conservatives have 20, Liberal Democrats 2 and Scottish Nationalists 1.

At the 1987 general election 41 women were successful and they were joined by the winners of three subsequent by-elections. With the exception of Margaret Thatcher all the women MPs stood for re-election in 1992 and 39 retained their seats. The most notable defeat was that of Lynda Chalker, the overseas development minister, who was defending a majority of just 279 at Wallasey. She lost to another woman, Angela Eagle, a trade union official. It was announced after the election that Mrs Chalker would go to the House of Lords and retain her ministerial post.

The other defeated MPs were Sylvia Heal, who won Mid-Staffordshire for Labour in a 1990 by-election, Maureen Hicks, Tory MP for Wolverhampton North East since 1987, and Rosie Barnes, whose defeat at Greenwich (coupled with that of John Cartwright at Woolwich) marked the end of Social Democrat representation in the Commons.

Among the 21 new women MPs was Oscar-winning actress Glenda Jackson who overturned a Conservative majority to win Hampstead and Highgate for Labour. The safe Conservative seat at Newbury was won by Judith Chaplin, former political secretary and special adviser to John Major.

Immediately after the election the prime minister appointed his first cabinet and included Virginia Bottomley as health secretary and Gillian Shephard as employment secretary. This move countered widespread criticism of John Major when he failed to appoint any women in his first cabinet 16 months earlier.

Some campaigners for equal representation now feel that a realistic target would be 100 women MPs by the end of the decade. Failure to achieve this will not be due to any lack of enthusiasm. The 1992 election set new records for women, both in terms of candidates standing and members elected. The 1987 election was hailed as a breakthrough for exactly the same reasons despite the often-repeated complaints by women's groups that the long hours and male club atmosphere of the Commons put up barriers to women.The women MPs in this Parliament are:

Conservative

Virginia Bottomley (Surrey SW); Angela Browning (Tiverton); Judith Chaplin (Newbury); Edwina Currie (Derbyshire S); Dame Peggy Fenner (Medway); Dame Janet Fookes (Plymouth, Drake); Cheryl Gillan (Chesham and Amersham); Teresa Gorman (Billericay); Dame Elaine Kellett-Bowman (Lancaster); Angela Knight (Erewash); Dame Jill Knight (Birmingham, Edgbaston); Jacqui Lait (Hastings and Rye); Lady Olga Maitland (Sutton and Cheam); Emma Nicholson (Devon West and Torridge); Elizabeth Peacock (Batley and Spen); Marion Roe (Broxbourne); Angela Rumbold (Mitcham and Morden); Gillian Shephard (Norfolk SW); Ann Widdecombe (Maidstone); Ann Winterton (Congleton)

Labour

Diane Abbott (Hackney N and Stoke Newington); Irene Adams (Paisley N); Janet Anderson (Rossendale and Darwen); Hilary Armstrong (Durham NW); Margaret Beckett (Derby S); Betty Boothroyd (West Bromwich W); Anne Campbell (Cambridge); Ann Clwyd (Cynon Valley); Anne Coffey (Stockport); Jean Corston (Bristol E); Gwyneth Dunwoody (Crewe and Nantwich); Angela Eagle (Wallasey); Maria Fyfe (Glasgow, Maryhill); Llin Golding (Newcastle-under-Lyme); Mildred Gordon (Bow and Poplar); Harriet Harman (Peckham); Kate Hoey (Vauxhall); Glenda Jackson (Hampstead and Highgate); Helen Jackson (Sheffield, Hillsborough); Lynne Jones (Birmingham, Selly Oak); Tessa Jowell (Dulwich); Jane Kennedy (Liverpool, Broadgreen); Joan Lestor (Eccles); Alice Mahon (Halifax); Estelle Morris (Birmingham, Yardley); Marjorie Mowlam (Redcar); Bridget Prentice (Lewisham East); Dawn Primarolo (Bristol S); Joyce Quin (Gateshead E); Jo Richardson (Barking); Barbara Roche (Hornsey and Wood Green); Joan Ruddock (Lewisham, Deptford); Clare Short (Birmingham, Ladywood); Rachel Squire (Dunfermline W); Ann Taylor (Dewsbury); Joan Walley (Stoke-on-Trent N); Audrey Wise (Preston)

Liberal Democrat

Elizabeth Lynne (Rochdale); Ray Michie (Argyll and Bute)

Scottish National Party

Margaret Ewing (Moray)

Year	No of women candidates	C	Number of women members of Parliament				Total elected
			Lab	Lib and L/SDP All	Others		
1945	87	1	21	1	1		24
1950	126	6	14	1	-		21
1951	74	6	11	-	-		17
1955	87	9	14	-	1		24
1959	75	12	13	-	-		25
1964	89	11	17	-	-		28
1966	80	7	19	-	-		26
1970	97	15	10	-	1		26
1974 (Feb)	143	9	13	-	1		23
1974 (Oct)	150	7	18	-	2		27
1979	206	8	11	-	-		19
1983	276	13	10	-	-		23
1987	327	17	21	2	1		41
1992	568	20	37	2	1		60

Nine ministers defeated

Despite winning the election, the Conservatives suffered a severe blow when Christopher Patten, the party chairman, lost his seat at Bath to the Liberal Democrats. Mr Patten had faced the daunting task of running the national campaign from Conservative Central Office in London and flying to Bath daily to defend his majority of 1,412.

Lynda Chalker, the overseas aid minister, was beaten at Wallasey, but was elevated to the House of Lords and retained her post. The Conservatives lost a further seven ministers: Francis Maude (financial secretary) at North Warwickshire; John Maples (economic secretary) at Lewisham West; Christopher Chope (transport) at Southampton, Itchen; Colin Moynihan (energy) at Lewisham East; Nicholas Bennett (Welsh office) at Pembroke; Michael Fallon (education) at Darlington; and David Trippier (environment) at Rossendale and Darwen.

Both independent Social Democrat members, Rosie Barnes and John Cartwright, lost their south-east London seats. Dave Nellist and Terry Fields, who had been expelled from the Labour party, and Ron Brown, John Hughes, and Sydney Bidwell, who had been deselected all lost to official Labour candidates..

Liberal Democrat victors at by-elections, David Bellotti (Eastbourne), Mike Carr (Ribble Valley) and Nicol Stephen (Kincardine and Deeside) saw their seats revert to the Conservatives. Labour, too, lost their four by-election gains to the Conservatives. John Smith lost the Vale of Glamorgan, Huw Edwards was beaten at Monmouth, Sylvia Heal was beaten at Mid Staffordshire, and Ashok Kumar lost at Langbaurgh.

The Scottish Nationalists lost their deputy leader, Jim Sillars, whose Glasgow Govan seat returned to Labour, and Dick Douglas, who had defected from Labour to the SNP, was also beaten. Richard Livesey, leader of the Welsh Liberal Democrats, saw his 1987 majority of 56 at Brecon and Radnor turned into a Conservative majority of 130.

John Browne, who stood as an unofficial Conservative in Winchester after he had been deselected, was defeated.

Sixty MPs lost their seats: 38 Conservative; six Liberal Democrats; five Labour; and eleven others.

The full list of defeated MPs is:

Conservative
Anthony Beaumont-Dark *Birmingham, Selly Oak*
Nicholas Bennett *Pembroke*
Gerald Bowden *Dulwich*
Martin Brandon-Bravo *Nottingham South*
Christopher Butler *Warrington South*
Lynda Chalker *Wallasey*
Christopher Chope *Southampton, Itchen*
Tony Favell *Stockport*
Michael Fallon *Darlington*
Cecil Franks *Barrow and Furness*
David Gilroy Bevan *Birmingham, Yardley*
Conal Gregory *York*
Ian Grist *Cardiff Central*
Patrick Ground *Feltham and Heston*
Kenneth Hargreaves *Hyndburn*
Robert Hayward *Kingswood*
Maureen Hicks *Wolverhampton N E*
Kenneth Hind *Lancashire West*
Gerald Howarth *Cannock and Burntwood*
Michael Irvine *Ipswich*
Tim Janman *Thurrock*
Roger King *Birmingham, Northfield*
Michael Knowles *Nottingham East*
John Lee *Pendle*
Humfrey Malins *Croydon North West*
John Maples *Lewisham West*
Francis Maude *Warwickshire North*
Colin Moynihan *Lewisham East*
Sir Gerrard Neale *Cornwall North*
Christopher Patten *Bath*
Jonathan Sayeed *Bristol East*
Sir William Shelton *Streatham*
Tony Speller *Devon North*
Lewis Stevens *Nuneaton*
Andrew Stewart *Sherwood*
Hugo Summerson *Walthamstow*
Neil Thorne *Ilford South*
David Trippier *Rossendale and Darwen*

Labour
Frank Doran *Aberdeen South*
Huw Edwards *Monmouth*
Sylvia Heal *Mid Staffordshire*
Ashok Kumar *Langbaurgh*
John Smith *Vale of Glamorgan*

Liberal Democrat
David Bellotti *Eastbourne*
Mike Carr *Ribble Valley*
Ronnie Fearn *Southport*
Geraint Howells *Ceredigion & Pembroke N*
David Livsey *Brecon and Radnor*
Nicol Stephen *Kincardine and Deeside*

Scottish National
Jim Sillars *Glasgow, Govan*
Dick Douglas *Glasgow, Garscadden*

Ind SD
Rosie Barnes *Greenwich*
John Cartwright *Woolwich*

Sinn Fein
Gerry Adams *Belfast West*

Others
Sydney Bidwell *Ealing, Southall*
John Browne *Winchester*
Terry Fields *Liverpool, Broadgreen*
John Hughes *Coventry North East*
Dave Nellist *Coventry South East*
Ron Brown *Edinburgh, Leith*

Mrs Thatcher leaves the Commons

The new House of Commons is without many prominent political figures who had been on its green benches for several decades, notably Margaret Thatcher, prime minister from 1979 to 1990, and Michael Foot, leader of the Labour party from 1980 to 1983. Mrs Thatcher was accompanied by ten former members of her cabinet, among them Sir Geoffrey Howe, her foreign secretary from 1983 to 1990, and Nigel Lawson, Chancellor of the Exchequer, from 1983 to 1990.

Besides Mr Foot, the Labour benches have lost the formidable political figure of Denis Healey, former Chancellor and defence secretary and shadow foreign secretary. He had spent 28 years on the front benches. He was joined by Merlyn Rees, former home secretary and Northern Ireland secretary. The SDP leader and Labour foreign secretary, Dr David Owen, went with them.

Among the other eight Tory former cabinet ministers to leave the Commons were four who had been Secretary of State for Trade and Industry: Norman Tebbitt, who was also party chairman, Cecil Parkinson, another former party chairman, Nicholas Ridley and Peter Walker, who had been a Tory front bencher for 22 years, from 1968 until 1990. To these can be added Sir Ian Gilmour (Lord Privy Seal), John Moore (Secretary of State for Social Services), John Wakeham (Secretary of State for Energy). He was the only member of Mr Major's cabinet not to seek re-election but continued in the government as Leader of the Lords. George Younger, who had been Secretary of State for Scotland and for Defence, also retired from the Commons.

Sir Bernard Braine, Father of the House, who entered the Commons in 1950, called it a day. His successor as Father is Sir Edward Heath, the former prime minister. At the end of the last Parliament, MPs paid warm tributes to the retiring Speaker, Bernard Weatherill, who had been in the chair since 1983 and whose face became familiar through the televising of Commons proceedings. Sir Paul Dean, a deputy Speaker, and five members of the Chairmen's Panel who preside over standing committees, retired with him.

A number of other former Conservative ministers also stood down, including Sir Richard Luce (arts), Sir Timothy Raison (overseas development) and Alan Clark (defence). Three select committee chairmen went: Sir Hugh Rossi (environment), Sir Anthony Buck (Ombudsman) and Kenneth Warren (trade and Industry). Ivor Stanbrook, chair

man of the Conservative back bench committee on Northern Ireland, has also gone. Among the Tory backbenchers leaving was Sir Anthony Meyer (Clwyd North West) who challenged Mrs Thatcher for the leadership in 1989.

From the Labour benches the party's solitary knight, Sir Patrick Duffy, a former Royal Navy minister, gave up his Sheffield seat. Other former ministers to leave were Denis Howell, sports minister and spokesman for many years; Peter Archer QC, solicitor-general, 1974-9; Alex Eadie and Harry Ewing. Jack Ashley, the deaf campaigner for the disabled, decided to take a well-earned rest along with the popular Liberal Democrat from Rochdale, Sir Cyril Smith. Three deselected Labour MPs, two expelled Labour MPs and a deselected Tory MP decided to fight on, but all were defeated. The following MPs did not seek re-election at the 1992 general election:

Conservative (56):

Julian Amery: *Brighton, Pavilion*
Alan Amos: *Hexham*
William Benyon: *Milton Keynes*
Sir Peter Blaker: *Blackpool South*
Robert Boscawen: *Somerton and Frome*
Sir Bernard Braine: *Castle Point*
Sir Antony Buck: *Colchester North*
Alan Clark: *Plymouth Sutton*
Sir William Clark: *Croydon South*
Sir Paul Dean: *Woodspring*
Sir John Farr: *Harborough*
Sir Geoffrey Finsberg: *Hampstead and Highgate*
Sir Ian Gilmour: *Chesham and Amersham*
Sir Alan Glyn: *Windsor and Maidenhead*
Sir Philip Goodhart: *Beckenham*
Sir Eldon Griffiths: *Bury St Edmunds*
Christopher Hawkins: *High Peak*
Sir Barney Hayhoe: *Brentford and Isleworth*
Sir Geoffrey Howe: *Surrey East*
Sir Charles Irving: *Cheltenham*
Michael Latham: *Rutland and Melton*
Nigel Lawson: *Blaby*
Sir Ian Lloyd: *Havant*
Sir Richard Luce: *Shoreham*
Sir Neil Macfarlane: *Sutton and Cheam*
Sir Robert McCrindle: *Brentwood and Ongar*
Sir Michael McNair-Wilson: *Newbury*
Sir Robin Maxwell-Hyslop: *Tiverton*
Sir Anthony Meyer: *Clwyd North West*
Sir Hal Miller: *Bromsgrove*
Norman Miscampbell: *Blackpool North*
John Moore: *Croydon Central*
Sir Charles Morrison: *Devizes*
Sir Peter Morrison: *City of Chester*
David Mudd: *Falmouth and Camborne*

Cecil Parkinson: *Hertsmere*
Sir David Price: *Eastleigh*
Keith Raffan: *Delyn*
Sir Timothy Raison: *Aylesbury*
Robert Rhodes James: *Cambridge*
Nicholas Ridley: *Cirencester and Tewkesbury*
Sir Julian Ridsdale: *Harwich*
Sir Hugh Rossi: *Hornsey and Wood Green*
Peter Rost: *Erewash*
Sir Michael Shaw: *Scarborough*
Ivor Stanbrook: *Orpington*
Ian Stewart: *Hertfordshire North*
Sir John Stokes: *Halesowen and Stourbridge*
Norman Tebbit: *Chingford*
Mrs Margaret Thatcher: *Finchley*
John Wakeham: *Colchester South and Maldon*
Peter Walker: *Worcester*
Sir Dennis Walters: *Westbury*
Kenneth Warren: *Hastings and Rye*
Michael Woodcock: *Ellesmere Port and Neston*
George Younger: *Ayr*

Labour (19):
Peter Archer: *Warley West*
Jack Ashley: *Stoke-on-Trent South*

Robert Clay: *Sunderland North*
Stanley Crowther: *Rotherham*
Sir Patrick Duffy: *Sheffield, Attercliffe*
Alex Eadie: *Midlothian*
Harry Ewing: *Falkirk East*
Martin Flannery: *Sheffield, Hillsborough*
Michael Foot: *Blaenau Gwent*
Ted Garrett: *Wallsend*
Frank Haynes: *Ashfield*
Denis Healey: *Leeds, East*
Denis Howell: *Birmingham, Small Heath*
David Lambie: *Cunninghame South*
James Lamond: *Oldham Central and Royton*
Ted Leadbitter: *Hartlepool*
Allen McKay: *Barnsley West and Penistone*
Merlyn Rees: *Leeds South and Morley*
Michael Welsh: *Doncaster North*

Liberal Democrats:
Sir Cyril Smith: *Rochdale*

Ind Social Democrat:
Dr David Owen: *Plymouth, Devonport*

Pl Cymru:
Mr Dafydd Thomas: *Meirionnydd Nant Conwy*

Speaker:
Mr Bernard Weatherill: *Croydon North East*

Conservatives hit in by-election upsets

The Conservatives suffered seven defeats in by-elections between 1987 and 1992, but regained all the seats in the general election. The most surprising were at Mid-Staffordshire and Ribble Valley, both regarded as safe Tory seats.

The first severe jolt to the government came in March 1990 when the Labour candidate, Sylvia Heal, riding along on the crest of Thatcher Government unpopularity over the poll tax and high interest rates, overturned a 14,654 Conservative majority to win by 9,449 votes. It prompted Mrs Heal to declare that the "dark age of Thatcherism is drawing to a close".

The by-election swing to Labour was 21.33 per cent. But that victory was put in the shade by Liberal Democrat victories at Ribble Valley in 1991 when Mike Carr swept home on a swing of 24.7 per cent and at Eastbourne in 1990 when David Bellotti won with a 20 per cent swing against the Tories in a by-election caused by the IRA murder of Ian Gow. Ribble Valley, on the basis of 1987 voting, was the fourteenth safest Tory seat.

With the general election getting closer, the Tories found no comfort when in November 1991 they lost Langbaurgh to Labour. Ashok Kumar overturned a Tory 1987 majority of 2,088 to win the seat by 1,975. But the 3.5 per cent swing fell short of that needed to put Neil Kinnock and Labour in power with a clear Commons majority.

The 1991 Liberal Democrat triumph in Kincardine and Deeside was much more ominous. It reduced the Tories to nine seats in Scotland compared with Labour's 48, the Liberal Democrats' 10 and the SNPs' five. It was a result that brought campaigns for devolution and then independence for Scotland to the fore.

The Conservatives could only take comfort that all three of Labour's previous by-election gains from them since 1970 had been reversed at the subsequent general election. Mid-Staffordshire, in 1990, was the fifth seat Labour gained in by-elections from the Tories since the early 1960s and this was followed by successes in 1991 at Monmouth and Langbaurgh. Others were the Vale of Glamorgan (1989), Fulham (1986), Birmingham Northfield (1982) and Bromsgrove (1971).

In stark contrast, the first major political upset in the by-elections of the 1987-92 Parliament embarrassed the Labour Party much more than the Tories. Neil Kinnock conceded it was a bad result. In Glasgow, Govan, in November 1988, Jim Sillars, a former Labour MP, swept the SNP to victory by turning a 1987 Labour majority of 19,509 into a 3,554 nationalist majority.

Labour had cause for rejoicing when they captured Vale of Glamorgan, John Smith turning the 6,521 Tory 1987 majority into a 6,028 Labour majority. The swing was 12.4 per cent, at that time the best for Labour since Mrs Thatcher came to power in 1979. In 1991, the Labour majority at Neath fell heavily but even so, the seat remained a party stronghold.

The Conservatives retained Epping Forest in December 1988 although their majority fell markedly and in February 1989 at Richmond, Yorks, their support collapsed even more. They held both seats only because the SDP and Liberal Democrats each fielded candidates. At Richmond the Tories had a majority of only 2,634 compared with 19,576 in 1987. The SDP came second and they and LD combined polled 28,498 votes while the winner, William Hague, polled 19,543. There were calls for pacts, but they came to nothing.

On Euro election voting day, June 15 1989, Labour safely retained their Westminster seats at Vauxhall and Glasgow Central, the latter with a satisfying margin over the SNP. The gloomy future of the SDP came starkly to the fore in the Bootle by-election in May 1990 when the party's candidate polled fewer votes than Lord David Sutch's Monster Raving Loony Party.

On May 24 1990, Mike Carr held the safe Labour seat of Bootle but on July 20 Mr Carr died having been an MP for only 57 days. Labour MPs in three other safe seats died leading to by-elections in Knowsley South, Paisley North and Paisley South and the death of Pat Wall led to a contest in Bradford North, a marginal. Labour safely held them all along with Neath, Liverpool Walton (easily shrugging off a Militant intervention) and Hemsworth where the Labour Party executive imposed Derek Enright, a former Member of the European Parliament, as official candidate.

The following by-elections took place in the 1987-92 Parliament:

1988
July 14: **Kensington** (caused by the death on May 18 1988 of Sir Brandon Rhys Williams): Total vote 23,693 (51.04%). D Fishburn (C) 9,829 (41.4%); Mrs A Holmes (Lab) 9,014 (38.0%); W Goodhart (LD) 2,546 (10.7%); J Martin (SDP) 1,190 (5.0%); P Hobson (Grn) 572; Ms Cynthia Payne (Payne & Pleasure) 193; Lord David Sutch (Loony) 61; J Duignan (London Class War) 60; B Goodier (Anti-Left) 31; B McDermott (Free Trade Lib) 31; W Scola (Leveller) 27; J Crowley (Anti-Yuppie) 24; J Connell (Stop ITN) 20; Dr Kailish Trivedi (Ind

Janata) 5 (Others 4.3%). C maj 815 (3.4%). Swing C to Lab 10.1%.

November 10: **Glasgow, Govan** (caused by the appointment of Bruce Millan as European Commissioner):
Total vote 30,104. J Sillars (SNP) 14,677; B Gillespie (Lab) 11,123; G Hamilton (C) 2,207; B Ponsonby (LD) 1,246; G Campbell (Grn) 345; D Chalmers (Comm) 281; Lord David Sutch (Loony) 174; F. Clark (Rainbow) 51. SNP maj 3,554. Swing from Lab to SNP 28.1%. SNP gain from Lab.

December 15: **Epping Forest** (caused by the death on Sep 17 1988 of Sir John Biggs-Davison):
Total vote: 33,415 (49,0%). S J Norris (C) 13,183; A J Thompson (LD) 8,679; S W Murray (Lab) 6,261; M G Pettman (SDP) 4,077; A M Simms (Grn) 672; Ms Tina Wingfield (INF) 286; Lord David Sutch (Loony) 208; Ms Jakki Moore (Rainbow All) 33; B G Goodier (Ind) 16. C maj 4,504. Swing C to LD/SDP 17.9%. Swing figure assumes LD/SDP combined by-election votes compared with Alliance vote in 1987.

1989

February 23: **Richmond, Yorks** (caused by the appointment of Sir Leon Brittan as European Commissioner):
Total vote: 52,561 (63.0%). W Hague (C) 19,543 (37.1%); M Potter (SDP) 16,909 (32.1%); Mrs B Pearce (LD) 11,589 (22.0%); F Robson (Lab) 2,591 (4.9%); Dr R Upshall (Grn) 1,473; Lord David Sutch (Loony) 167; A Mills (University) 113; Lindi St Claire (Corrective) 106; N Watkins (Off Lib) 70. C maj 2,634 (5.0%). Swing C to LD/SDP 25.6%. Swing figure assumes LD/SDP combined by-election vote compared with Alliance vote in 1987.

February 23: **Pontypridd** (caused by the death on Dec 13 1988 of Brynmor John):
Total vote: 38,551 (62%). K Howells (Lab) 20,549 (53.4%); S Morgan (PlC) 9,755 (25.3%); N Evans (C) 5,212 (13.5%); T Ellis (LD) 1,500 (3.9%); T Thomas (SDP) 1,199 (3.1%); D Richards (Comm) 239; D Black (Ind) 57. Lab maj 10,794 (28.1%). Swing Lab to PlC 13.0%.

May 4: **Vale of Glamorgan** (caused by the death on Feb 22 1989 of Sir Raymond Gower):
Total vote: 47,746. J W P Smith (Lab) 23,342 (48.9%); R Richards (C) 17,314 (36.3%); F Leavers (LD) 2,017 (4.2%); J Dixon (PlC) 1,672 (3.5%); K Davies (SDP) 1,098 (2.3%); Ms M Wakefield (Grn) 971 (2.0%); C Tiarks (Ind) 847 '/(1.8%); Lord David Sutch (Loony) 266 (0.5%); E Roberts (Welsh Ind) 148 (0.3%); Ms Lindi St Claire (Ind) 39 (0.08%); D Black (Ind) 32 (0.07%). Lab maj 6,028 (12.6%). Lab gain from C. C to Lab swing 12.35%.

June 15: **Glasgow Central** (caused by the death on Mar 23 1989 of Robert McTaggart):
Total vote: 26,535 (53.3%). M Watson (Lab) 14,480 (54.5%); A Neil (SNP) 8,018 (30.2%); A Hogarth (C) 2,028 (7.6%); Ms I Brandt (Grn) 1,019 (3.8%); R McCreadie (LD) 411 (1.5%); P Kerr (SDP) 253 (0.9%); Ms L Murdoch (Rev

Comm) 141; W Kidd (Scot Soc) 137; D. Lettice (Workers Rev) 48 (last three candidates totalled 1.2%). Lab maj 6,462 (24.3%). Lab to SNP swing 15.0%.

June 15: **Vauxhall** (caused by the resignation in May 1989 of Stuart Holland): Total vote 28,795 (45.1%). Ms K Hoey (Lab) 15,191 (51.9%); M Keegan (C) 5,425 (18.5%); M Tuffrey (LD) 5,043 (17.2%); H Bewley (Grn) 1,767 (6.0%); H Andrew (People's) 302; D Allen (Greens) 264; R Narayan (Ind) 179; D Milligan (Rev Comm) 177; P Harrington (Off NF) 127; Lord David Sutch (Loony) 106; D Black (Christ All) 86; T Budden (NF) 83; G Rolth (Fellowship) 24; W Scola (Leveller) 21 (last 10 candidates totalled 6.2%). Lab maj 9,766 (13.4%). C to Lab swing 6.1%.

1990

March 22: **Staffordshire Mid** (caused by the death on Dec 19 1989 of John Heddle): Total vote 57,359 (77.5%). Mrs S L Heal (Lab) 27,649 (49.1%); C C L Prior (C) 18,200 (32.3%); T A Jones (LD) 6,315 (11.2%); I W Wood (SDP) 1,422 (2.5%); R Saunders (Grn) 1,215 (2.2%); J G Bazeley (Anti-PM C) 547; Lord David Sutch (Loony) 336; C J G Hill (NF) 311; C A Abel (NHS Supporters) 102; N Parker-Jarvis (Anti-Immigration) 71; S B F Hughes (Raving Loony) 59; L St C Love (Nat Ind Correct) 51; B R A Mildwater (Save the 2CV) 42; D M Black (Christian All) 39. Lab maj 9,449 (16.8%). Lab gain from C. C to Lab swing 21.3%.

May 17: **Upper Bann** (caused by death on Feb 11 1990 of Harold McCusker): Total vote 35,364 (54.76%). D Trimble (UU) 20,547 (58.1%); Mrs B Rodgers (SDLP) 6,698 (18.9%); Ms S Campbell (Sinn Fein) 2,033 (5.8%); Rev H Ross (Ulster Independence) 1,534 (4.3%); T French (Workers) 1,083 (3.1%); Mrs C Jones (C) 1,038 (2.9%); W Ramsey (All) 948; G McMichael (UDP) 600; P Doran (Gr) 576; E Holmes (Right to vote Lab) 235; A Dunn (SDP) 154 (Others, 7.1%). UU maj 13,849 (39.2%).

May 24: **Bootle** (caused by death on Mar 21 1990 of Allan Roberts): Total vote 35,477 (50.2%). M Carr (Lab) 26,737 (75.4%); W J Clappison (C) 3,220 (9.1%); J Cunningham (LD) 3,179 (9.0%); S Brady (Grn) 1,267; K White (L) 474; Lord David Sutch (Loony) 418; J Holmes (SDP) 155; T Schofield (Ind) 27 (Others 6.6%). Lab maj 23,517 (66.3%). C to Lab swing 9.7%.

Sep 27: **Knowsley South** (caused by death on Jun 25 1990 of Sean Hughes): Total vote 21,207 (33.6%). E O'Hara (Lab) 14,581 (68.8%); L Byrom (C) 3,214 (15.1%); Ms C Hancox (LD) 1,809 (8.5%); R Georgeson (Grn) 656; I Smith (L) 628; Lord David Sutch (Loony) 197; Lady Cash Whiplash (Corrective) 99 (Others 7.5%). Lab maj 11,367 (53.7%). C to Lab swing 9.7%.

Oct 18: **Eastbourne** (caused by killing by IRA car bomb on Jul 30 1990 of Ian Gow): Total vote 46,072 (61.0%), D Bellotti (LD) 23,415 (50.8%); R S Hickmet (C) 18,865 (40.9%); Ms

C Atkins (Lab) 2,308 (5.0%); D Aherne (Grn) 553; Ms T Williamson (L) 526; Ms L St Claire Miss Whiplash (Corrective) 216; J McAuley (NF) 154; E Page (Ironside) 35 (Others 3.2%). LD maj 4,550 (9.9%). LD gain from C. C to LD swing 20.0%.

Nov 8: **Bootle** (caused by death on Jul 20 1990 of Michael Carr who won May by-election): Total vote 28,145 (39.8%). J Benton (Lab) 22,052 (78.2%); W J Clappison (C) 2,587 (9.1%); J Cunningham (LD) 2,216 (7.8%); S Brady (Grn) 557 (2.0%); Lord David Sutch (Loony) 310 (1.1%); K White (L) 291 (1.0%); D Black (Christian All) 132 (0.5%). Lab maj 19,465 (69.1%). Swing from C to Lab since previous by-election 1.5%.

Nov 8: **Bradford North** (caused by death on Aug 6 1990 of Patrick Wall): Total vote 36,029 (53.4%). T Rooney (Lab) 18,619 (51.6%); D Ward (LD) 9,105 (25.2%); Mrs J Atkin (C) 6,048 (16.7%); D M Pidcock (Islamic GB) 800 (2.2%); M Knott (Grn) 447 (1.2%); R Tenney (NF) 305 (0.8%); J Floyd (Christian All) 219 (0.6%); W Beckett (Loony) 210 (0.6%); N Nowosielski (L) 187 (0.5%); M Wrigglesworth (Ind C Anti-Poll Tax) 89 (0.2%). Lab maj 9,514 (26.4%). Swing from C to Lab 15.8%.

Nov 29: **Paisley North** (caused by death on Sep 5 1990 of Allen Adams): Total vote 25,828 (53.7%). Mrs I Adams (Lab) 11,353 (43.9%); R Mullin (SNP) 7,583 (29.4%); E Marwick (C) 3,835 (14.8%); J Bannerman (LD) 2,139 (8.3%); D Mellor (Grn) 918 (3.6%). Lab maj 3,770 (14.5%). Lab to SNP swing 14.05%.

Nov 29: **Paisley South** (caused by death on Oct 23 1990 of Mr Norman Buchan): Total vote 27,062 (55.O%). G McMaster (Lab) 12,485 (46.1%); I Lawson (SNP) 7,455 (27.5%); J Workman (C) 3,627 (13.4%); A Reid (LD) 2,660 (9.8%); Ms E Collie (Grn) 835 (3.1%). Lab maj 5,030 (18.6%). Lab to SNP swing 11.8%.

1991

March 7: **Ribble Valley** (following appointment in Nov 1990 of David Waddington as Lord Privy Seal and Leader of the House of Lords): M Carr (LD) 22,377 (48.5%); N Evans (C) 17,776 (38.5%); Ms J Farrington (Lab) 4,356 (9.4%); D Brass (Ind C) 611 (1.3%); H Ingham (Grn) 466 (1.0%); Lord David Sutch (Loony) 278; S Taylor (L) 133; Ms L St Clair (Corrective) 72; S B F Hughes (Rav L) 60 (last

four 1.2% of vote). LD maj 4,601 (10.0%). LD gain from C. Swing from C to LD 24.7%.

April 4: **Neath** (caused by the death on Jan 14 1991 of Donald Coleman): Total vote 34,753 (64.0%). P Hain (Lab) 17,962 (51.7%); D Evans (PlC) 8,132 (23.3%); R Evans (C) 2,995 (8.6%); D Lloyd (LD) 2,000 (5.8%); J Warman (SDP) 1,826; R Jeffreys (Ind Lab) 1,253; Lord David Sutch (Loony) 263; B Kirk (Bean Pty) 262 (Others, 10.4%). Lab maj 9,830 (28.7%). Lab to PlC swing 14.0%.

May 16: **Monmouth** (caused by death on Mar 29 1991 of Sir John Stradling Thomas): Total vote 45,100 (76.0%). H Edwards (Lab) 17,733 (39.3%); R Evans (C) 15,327 (34.0%); Mrs F David (LD) 11,164 (24.8%); Lord David Sutch (Loony) 314; M Witherden (PlC/Grn) 277; P Carpenter (Unitax) 164; Ms L St Clair (Corrective) 121 (Others 1.9%). Lab maj 2,406 (5.3%). Lab gain from C. Swing C to Lab 12.6%.

July 4: **Liverpool Walton** (caused by death on May 27 1991 of Eric Heffer): Total vote 40,183 (56.5%). P Kilfoyle (Lab) 21,317 (53.0%); P Clark (LD) 14,457 (36.0%); Ms L Mahmood (Walton Real Lab) 2,613 (6.5%); B Greenwood (C) 1,155 (2.8%); Lord David Sutch (Loony) 546 (1.3%); E G Lee-Deslisle (Ind) 63 (0.1%). Lab maj 6,860 (17.0%). Lab to LD swing 13.1%.

November 7: **Kincardine and Deeside** (caused by death on Aug 29 1991 of Alick Buchanan-Smith): Total vote 42,393 (65.7%). N Stephen (LD) 20,779 (49.0%); M Humphrey (C) 12,955 (30.6%); A Macartney (SNP) 4,705 (11.1%); M Savidger (Lab) 3,271 (7.7%(); S Campbell (Grn) 683 (1.6%). LD maj 7,824 (18.4%). LD gain from C. C to LD swing 11.4%.

November 7: **Hemsworth** (caused by death on Sep 14 1991 of George Buckley): Total vote 23,971 (42.8%). D Enright (Lab) 15,895 (66.3%); Ms V Megson (LD) 4,808 (20.1%); G Harrison (C) 2,512 (10.5%); P Ablett (Ind Lab) 648 (2.7%); T Smith (Corrective) 108 (0.4%). Lab maj 11,087 (46.2%). No change. Lab to LD swing 2.5%.

November 7: **Langbaurgh** (caused by death on Sep 20 1991 of Richard Holt): Total vote 52,363 (65.4%). A Kumar (Lab) 22,442 (42.9%); M Bates (C) 20,467 (39.1%); P Allen (LD) 8,421 (16.1%); G Parr (Grn) 456 (0.9%). Lab maj 1,975 (3.8%). Lab gain from C. C to Lab swing 3.6%.

So near . . . so far

By Robert Worcester

Reasonably enough, most people believe that the polls got it wrong in 1992, more wrong than in any election since the war. In a way, they are right, as never before have the opinion polls been so wrong in their prediction of the outcome. Over the 14 elections since 1945, the average error per share of the parties of the final polls published on the eve of the election has been 1.4 per cent. In 1992 it was 2.8 per cent. Worse, while the five major polling organisations, Gallup, Harris, ICM, Mori and NOP, averaged a 1.3 per cent Labour lead, the final result was a 7.6 per cent lead for the Conservatives. The polls backed the wrong winner, by a wider margin, than ever before, and by more than can be accounted for by sampling error.

In another way, the polls were nearly right in indicating a hung parliament as the most likely result. How can this be? The Conservative margin of victory was a 21-seat majority. If just 11 seats had not been held by the Conservatives and instead had gone to their opponents, a hung parliament would have been the result. In fact, in the 11 most marginal seats held by the Tories, from the 19 vote majority in the Vale of Glamorgan to the 585 in Southampton Test, if just 1,241 voters out of the 32,825,306 who voted in Great Britain had voted for the opposition, the hung parliament expected from the final polls would have been the election's result.

Some 104 national voting intention measures had been taken during the year between the Monmouth by-election and March 11 when the prime minister announced the election date. Of these, no fewer than 75 would have delivered a hung parliament if the election had been held when the polling was taken.

So it was no surprise when the first poll of the election was published in *The Times* indicating a 3 per cent Labour lead, enough to make Labour the largest party, but insufficient for a working majority. In fact, research showed that in four of the past ten elections there had been no net change between the last poll taken before the election call and the outcome, in eight out of the ten there had been less than a 2 per cent swing and in only one, 1970, had there been a shift of the magnitude of this election.

Much has been made of Labour's "mountain to climb", with psephologists pointing out that no party had recovered from an 11.8 per cent defeat to win the following election; less was made of the fact that no party had ever recovered from a 23 per cent trough in their rating in the poll, to win a subsequent election, and Labour had led the Conservatives by 54 per cent to 31 per cent two years before the election was called. Either way, psephological history was going to be made.

There were 50 mainstream polls published during the 1992 election, compared with 54 in 1987. There were 74,490 interviews taken in these national polls, slightly fewer than the 83,083 interviewed in 1987. In addition, there were another 30 or so national, regional and local constituency polls which interviewed another 30,000 electors, making a total of approximately 100,000 interviews. With an electorate of 42.58 million it is no wonder that many people believe that "I've never been polled and I don't know anybody who has been either."

The fact that the final polls of the campaign, all taken one or two days before polling day, were so consistent — all five had the Tories at 38 per cent +/- 1 per cent, Labour at 40 per cent +/- 2 per cent, and the Liberal Democrats at 18 per cent +/- 2 per cent — suggests that neither sample size nor sampling "error" were responsible for the magnitude of the difference between the final polls and the actual result. Many other hypotheses have been put forward including mass economy with the truth, late swing, and media effect. All probably played their part.

Polls are snapshots at a point in time, and that point is when the fieldwork was done, not when the results were published. One indicator was that Mori's final poll for *The Times* was in three independent matched samples, and the Tuesday night sample was considerably more Labour inclined than the interviews done on the Wednesday. Another was that the Harris exit poll for ITN found a steadily declining level of support for Labour through polling day — the 3pm cut-off figures had Labour at 39 per cent, the 5pm figures were 38 per cent; the 8pm results, the ones that were broadcast, reported Labour at 37 per cent, and the 10pm "finals" showed Labour at the 36 per cent they finally got. Another was that the recall interviews done on the day following the election with two independent samples of electors interviewed the week before to see *if* they had switched, *how* they had switched, and *why* those who had switched were consistent and accounted for some 3 of the 4 per cent error. Perhaps the other 1 per cent were lying. I doubt it.

The Conservatives spent nearly all of their advertising money in the final three days, the Tory tabloids bashed away, the Tories themselves levelled all of their guns at the threat that Liberal Democrat voters were "letting Labour in". Labour's peak came on "Red Wednesday", eight days before polling day, with a lead sufficient for an overall majority. The Sheffield rally proved the beginning of the end for Labour and the dawning of a fourth term for the Conservatives.

Robert M Worcester is Chairman of Mori and visiting professor of government at the London School of Economics

The Poll of Polls

Budget - March 10   Election called - March 11

Fieldwork date		Sample	Sampling points	Con	Lab	LDem	Other	Con lead over Lab	C/Lab swing	Publication
11.3	NOP	1,050	(54)	41	40	15	4	+1	6	Mail o Sun
11-12.3	Mori	1,054	(53)	38	41	16	5	-3	7	The Times
11-12.3	Harris	1,054	(100)	40	43	12	5	-3	7	Observer
11-13.3	Harris	1,086	(98)	39	40	16	5	-1	6	D Express
11-13.3	Harris	2,186	(100)	37	41	17	5	-4	7.5	LWT
12-13.3	Mori*	1,544	(65)	40	39	16	5	+1	5	S Times
12-13.3	NOP*	2,155	(133)	40	41	14	5	-1	6	Ind on S
13.3	ICM	1,059	(54)	39	40	16	5	-1	6	S Express
15-16.3	Harris	1,081	(98)	41	38	17	4	3	4	D Express
16.3	Mori	1,099	(54)	38	43	16	3	-5	8	Times
17.3	ICM	1,100	(54)	38	43	16	3	-5	8	Guardian
17-18.3	Gallup	984	(100)	40.5	38.5	18	3	2	4.5	D Tel
17-18.3	NOP	1,262	(82)	38	42	17	3	-4	7.5	Ind
18-20.3	Mori*	1,257	(63)	38	41	19	2	-3	7	S.Times
19-20.3	Harris	1,096	(100)	40	39	17	4	1	5	Observer
20.3	ICM	1,115	(54)	37	42	16	5	-5	8	S. Express
19-21.3	NOP*T	1,004	(133)	39	41	15	5	-2	6.5	Ind on Sun
20-21.3	NOP	1,085	(54)	38	40	16	6	-2	6.5	Mail o Sun
21-23.3	Harris	1,000	(99)	43	38	15	4	+5	3	D Express
22-23.3	Harris	2,158	(100)	38	42	16	4	-4	7.5	ITN
23.3	Mori	1,109	(55)	38	41	17	4	-3	7	Times
23-24.3	Gallup	1,092	(100)	40	40.5	16.5	3	-0.5	5.7	D Tel
24.3	ICM	1,096	(54)	39	40	17	4	-1	6	Guardian
24.3	NMR	1,105	(55)	38	39	19	4	-1	6	Europn
24-25.3	NOP	1,326	(84)	39	42	14	5	-3	7	Ind/BBC
25-27.3	Mori*	1,292	(65)	38	40	20	2	-2	6.5	S Times
26-27.3	Harris	1,057	(99)	40	38	17	5	2	4.5	Observer
27.3	ICM	1,136	(54)	36	38	20	6	-2	6.5	S Express
27-28.3	NOP	1,099	(54)	37	41	18	4	-4	7.5	Mail o S
26-29.3	NOP*T	1,000	(133)	39	40	16	5	-1	6	Ind on S
28-30.3	Harris	1,108	(100)	40	39	17	4	+1	5	D Express
29-30.3	Harris	2,152	(100)	35	41	19	5	-6	8.5	ITN
30.3	Mori	1,080	(54)	35	42	19	4	-7	9	Times
31.3	ICM	1,126	(54)	37	41	18	4	-4	7.5	Guardn
31.3-1.4	Gallup	1,095	(100)	38	37.5	20.5	4	+0.5	5.2	D Tel
31.3-1.4	NOP	1,302	(83)	37	39	19	5	-2	6.5	BBC/Ind
31.3-3.4	ICM	10,460	(330)	36	39	20	5	-3	7	PA
1-3.4	Mori*	1,265	(65)	37	39	21	3	-2	6.5	S Times
2-3.4	Gallup	1,043	(95)	37.5	37.5	22	3	0	5.5	S Tel
2-3.4	NOP*T	1,006	(133)	38	41	17	4	-3	7	Ind on S
3.4	ICM	1,139	(54)	37	39	18	6	-2	6.5	S Express
3-4.4	NOP	1,104	(54)	35	41	20	4	-6	8.5	Mail o Sun
3-4.4	Harris	1,090	(100)	38	40	17	5	-2	6.5	Observer
4-6.4	Harris	1,093	(100)	37	38	21	4	-1	6	D Express
4-7.4	Harris	2,210	(100)	38	40	18	4	-2	6.5	ITN
6-7.4	Mori	1,065	(53)	37	40	20	3	-3	7	YTV
7-8.4	Mori	1,731	(164)	38	39	20	3	-1	6	Times
7-8.4	NOP	1,746	(85)	39	42	17	2	-3	7	Ind/BBC
7-8.4	Gallup	2,748	(198)	38.5	38	20	3.5	+0.5	5.25	D Tel
8.4	ICM	2,186	(103)	38	38	20	4	0	5.5	Guardn
9.4	RESULT	(GB)		42.8	35.2	18.3	3.7	7.6	2.0	

ABBREVIATIONS: Mail o Sun-*Mail on Sunday*; D Express-*Daily Express*; LWT-London Weekend Television; S Times-*Sunday Times*; Ind on S-*The Independent on Sunday*; S Express- *Sunday Express*; D Tel-*The Daily Telegraph*; Ind-*The Independent*; ITN-Independent Television News; Europn-*The European*; Newsnt-Newsnight; PA-Press Association newsagency; YTV-Yorkshire Television. *=Panel T=Telephone poll

Minor changes mask upheaval in Scotland

by Peter Riddell

The election result in Scotland showed the smallest change in seats of any region, and was the most surprising for that reason. Compared with the 1987 election, the Tories gained one seat, Aberdeen South (for a total of 11); Labour lost one (down to 49); while the Liberal Democrats and Scottish Nationalists were unchanged at nine and three MPs respectively. The Tories and Labour each regained their by-election losses since 1987 — the Tories from the Liberal Democrats, who had won at Kincardine and Deeside in November 1991, and Labour from the SNP, who had won Glasgow, Govan, in November 1988.

But these minor changes masked upheavals in Scottish politics dating back to the 1987 general election when Tory representation was cut in half and several ministers lost their seats. Labour and the other opposition parties claimed that the Tories therefore had no mandate to govern Scotland. Successive Scottish secretaries, first Malcolm Rifkind and, from November 1990, Ian Lang were forced on the defensive. The Scottish select committee was not set up because the Tories could not find sufficient MPs from north of the border to serve, while intense arguments broke out within the Scottish Conservative party, notably surrounding the appointment in 1989 and removal in 1990 of Michael Forsyth as party chairman. He was seen as a strong Thatcherite.

The opposition side also experienced tensions. Labour leaders under the cautious Donald Dewar sought to maintain unity by promising an elected Scottish parliament with limited tax-raising powers. But they faced both the continued scepticism about devolution of a minority such as Tam Dalyell and demands for direct action from the hard left. There were calls for civil disobedience over the introduction of the poll tax.

Demands for devolution grew within the Scottish church, media, educational, legal and artistic communities, leading to the formation of a Scottish Constitutional Convention including leading members of both the Labour and Liberal Democrat parties, though not the SNP, as well as prominent churchmen, local government leaders and others. That was reflected in a flowering of debate and writing about the Scottish national identity.

After a number of internal ructions, the Scottish Nationalists repositioned themselves as a left-of-centre party seeking independence for Scotland within Europe. The fortunes of the SNP, which had fallen for much of the 1980s after their losses in 1979, revived, especially following the victory of Jim Sillars at the Govan by-election.

Opinion polls showed both that the Tories had fallen below their 1987 level of support and that there was a sharp rise in backing both for the SNP and for the principle of independence. These surveys, particularly one or two showing very high figures for separation, attracted national notice to the Scottish question. John Major promised to take stock of the situation after the election, though he strongly defended the benefits of the union and gave a warning that a devolved assembly would represent a slippery slope towards separation and a loss of influence for Scotland.

The constitutional issue dominated most reporting about the election, even though polls showed that, as in the rest of Britain, the public was more worried about education, health and unemployment. For most of the campaign, the Tories looked like losers, with widespread predictions that they would be down to only four or five MPs and a poll showing that Mr Lang would lose his seat.

In the event, the Tories increased their share of the vote by nearly 1.7 points to 25.7 per cent, while Labour slipped by 3.4 points to 39 per cent. The SNP jumped 7.4 points to 21.5 per cent, while the Liberal Democrats dropped by 6.1 points to 13.1 per cent. There was a much smaller change in the balance of seats, partly because of the impact of four-party competition under a first past the post system. Electoral history was, for example, made in Inverness, Nairn and Lochaber where Sir Russell Johnston of the Liberal Democrats held his seat with just 26.05 per cent of the vote. His three main rivals were behind in a range of 22.6 per cent to 25.15 per cent.

The apparent swing back to the Tories in the last few days probably reflected a combination of the general recoil against the prospect of a Labour government and the rallying to the Tories after the strong last minute warnings by Mr Major and Mr Lang over the threats to the union.

Because the result was unexpected it strengthened Mr Lang's position even though nearly three-quarters of Scottish voters had supported parties seeking a change in the constitutional status quo. Opposition leaders continued to argue that the Tories still had no authority to govern Scotland. Labour leaders, eager to avoid losing the initiative to some of their own MPs who demanded direct action and to the SNP, backed a call for a referendum to sound out opinion on Scotland's future. The election had left Scotland's political future more unstable than the bald result implied.

Support grows for SDLP

by Edward Gorman, Ireland Correspondent of *The Times*

The General Election in Northern Ireland produced significant gains for the Social Democratic and Labour Party at the expense of Sinn Fein, the political wing of the IRA.

The SDLP increased its share of the vote in 13 of the province's 17 constituencies and inflicted an historic reversal on Sinn Fein in West Belfast where it took the seat held by Gerry Adams, the party president, since 1983.

Overall the election demonstrated that moderate parties in both communities continue to hold their ground, giving further encouragement to the British and Irish governments that a new agreement in Belfast on devolved government may be attainable in the lifetime of this Parliament.

The campaign was marked by the first appearance of Northern Ireland Conservatives in a Westminster election since organising in the province in 1989. The party did not return an MP and polled 5.7 per cent of the vote, a performance which does not guarantee it a permanent foothold in Ulster politics.

The gains made by the SDLP — it was up 2.4 per cent on 1987 — indicate growing support in the Nationalist and Republican minority community for that party's rejection of violence and strategy of achieving a united Ireland by peaceful, democratic means.

They were seen in Dublin as bolstering the already thriving Anglo-Irish process and the Anglo-Irish agreement which now looks like a permanent feature of the political landscape.

At the same time, the election underlined the gradual decline of Sinn Fein. Its vote share was cut from 11.4 per cent to 10 per cent, a loss of around 5,000 on its performance in 1987. Since 1983 when the party secured 13.4 per cent of the vote across the province amounting to 102,000 votes, its share has fallen by a quarter to just 78,000 in 1992.

Sinn Fein lost most heavily to the SDLP in the rural west of the province. In Fermanagh and South Tyrone it was once well ahead of its moderate rival, but the SDLP has now drawn level. In Mid-Ulster, again a constituency where Sinn Fein was once well ahead, the SDLP has established a convincing lead, suggesting to some observers that it might take this seat from the sitting Unionist MP at the next election.

In Belfast the defeat for Mr Adams was offset by the fact that the Sinn Fein vote remained solid. Mr Adams polled only 36 votes less than in 1987 but lost the seat to Joe Hendron of the SDLP largely as a result of unexpected tactical voting by around 3,000 Protestants on the Shankhill Road.

In the Unionist community the election provided no evidence of dissatisfaction with the way its political leaders had handled the inter-party talks process in the month leading up to the poll. The Ulster Unionist Party's vote held up well at 34.5 per cent, down just 3.3 per cent while Ian Paisley's Democratic Unionist Party polled 13.1 per cent of the vote, up 1.4 per cent on 1987. Mr Paisley's party fielded candidates against the UUP in only three constituencies and clearly hoped to wrest East Antrim from Roy Beggs, the sitting UU MP, but failed.

The DUP's electoral fortunes continue to indicate a slow decline, suggesting that when Mr Paisley finally leaves the political scene his party may well split at least two ways leaving the field clear for the larger and more moderate UUP.

Much of the interest in the run-up to polling day had been in the role the Unionist parties might have played had there been a hung parliament. The Conservative party made clear that it would not discount a deal with Unionists, though in the end this proved unncessary.

Jim Molyneaux, the UU leader, ruled out any formal deals with a minority government but said his support would be available on an issue-by-issue basis. His party's election manifesto began with what amounted to a long shopping list of requirements. The main elements were measures to improve the way Northern Ireland is governed at Westminster with the abolition of Orders in Council and the establishment of a select committee.

Mr Paisley who more openly enthused at the prospect of a post-election deal, laid greater emphasis on the security aspect and would have been looking for a more interventionist and draconian approach designed to stifle the IRA.

It would undoubtedly have been to the detriment of healthy Anglo-Irish relations and to the prospects for establishing a new agreement of devolution in Belfast had the Conservatives been forced into a deal with Unionists. The decisive election result was welcomed for this reason in nationalist quarters and especially in Dublin.

The non-sectarian Alliance party had an unremarkable election, polling 8.7 per cent of the vote, a fall of 1.2 per cent on 1987, and again failed to return its first MP.

Part of its vote share was lost to the Conservative party, fighting a general election in Northern Ireland for the first time sinceits decision to organise in the province in 1989. The party ran candidates in 11 constituencies but had a realistic chance only in North Down, where Jim Kilfedder the sitting Ulster Popular Unionist Party MP, held on to the seat.

The Best Future for Britain

FOREWORD

Mr John Major, prime minister and leader of the Conservative Party, said in his foreword that at the end of this Parliament a new millennium would be in view. "We must raise our sights high. This manifesto is about making our country respected and secure, and helping you achieve a better, safer and more prosperous future. For I believe — strongly — that you, and not the government, should be in charge of your life. That's what Conservatism stands for. That principle underlies all the policies in this Manifesto."

He declared: "Only Conservatives can truly claim to be the party of opportunity; choice; ownership and responsibility. Socialists like to keep people under the government's thumb. Conservatives want to give them independence. But we also want to put government at your service, giving you what you've paid for — good public services, responsible to you. You know I believe in choice and in this election, as always, there is another choice. You can vote for our opponents, and watch them take Britain back to the 1970s. Back to socialism. Back to strikes. Back to strife. Back to the world's pity, or worse still, contempt. I don't believe Britain wants that. I know the world doesn't want that for Britain. I hope you will choose a different path — to go forward, not back; to go for the best, knowing that Britain can be the best and do it best. My belief is clear. Only the best is good enough for Britain."

TAKING RESPONSIBILITY FOR BRITAIN

The world has been transformed in recent years. Communism has collapsed in Eastern Europe, and the Soviet Union has fallen apart. Everywhere socialism is in retreat and democracy, human rights and market economics are advancing. The authority of the UN has been bolstered and Iraqi aggression seen off. Talks are under way in the Middle East and South Africa. It is a time of great opportunity, but also of new dangers. Britain needs firm leadership at this time. We must be represented by a team of quality and experience. A team which can help shape the world for the next century. A Conservative team.

Under the Conservatives, Britain has regained her rightful influence in the world. We have stood up for the values our country has always represented. We have defended Britain's interests with vigour and with success. The respect with which Britain is regarded in the world has rarely been higher. We play a central part in world affairs as a member of the European Community, Nato, the Commonwealth and the Group of 7 leading industrial countries, and as a permanent member of the UN Security Council. No other country holds all these positions.

We are taking a leading role in recasting all the main international institutions to which we belong: the United Nations, the European Community, Nato, and the Commonwealth. The prime minister convened the first ever meeting of the UN Security Council at heads of government level. Between now and the end of 1992 there will be seven summits where issues of critical importance to our future will be determined: two EC councils, at Lisbon and Edinburgh, the G7 summit, the CSCE summit, EC summits with the US and Japan, and the Earth Summit at Rio de Janeiro. Britain will be at the centre of these negotiations.

The Need for Leadership

The end of the cold war has enabled the UN to act with new unity and authority. Under the authority of the UN, British forces played a leading and courageous part in the Gulf War and the liberation of Kuwait. At the prime minister's instigation, the UN also backed the operation to protect the Kurds. Britain has led the world in helping the reforms in the former Soviet Union. The prime minister gave full and immediate support to President Yeltsin in the August coup attempt, and was the first Western leader to visit Moscow after the coup failed. Britain has led the way in building up relations with the republics of the new Commonwealth of Independent States. We have provided valuable economic and humanitarian aid to ease the transition to a market economy.

● We will support an enhanced role for the UN in peace-keeping and combating state-sponsored terrorism.

● We are determined that Iraq should comply with the terms of the Gulf War cease-fire agreement, and in particular that it should co-operate with the UN in dismantling its weapons of mass destruction.

● We support early Russian membership of the IMF and World Bank, as well as a stabilisation fund for the rouble.

● We are co-operating with our partners to provide urgent help to the former Soviet Union and Eastern Europe to upgrade the safety of their nuclear power stations.

● We strongly support the peace process in the Middle East. The outcome of the talks must safeguard the security of Israel and achieve self-determination for the people of the occupied territories.

● We will safeguard the prosperity of Hong Kong, nuture democratic institutions and work with the Chinese government within the terms of the joint declaration.

● We seek a solution to the dispute which has divided Cyprus since 1974. A settlement must recognise that Cyprus is indivisible and that the rights of both communities must be assured. We will support the UN's efforts to secure a fair and lasting solution.

● The problems of Kashmir cannot be resolved by violence. We urge both India and Pakistan to address and resolve the issue, and we stand ready to help.

Our Influence for Good

All over the world countries are turning to democracy and free markets. Last October in Harare, the Commonwealth took on a new role as a promoter of democracy, the rule of law, and respect for individual freedoms. Already the Commonwealth is monitoring elections to ensure that they are free and fair. Britain is taking the lead in encouraging these trends.

We give substantial aid to the relief of poverty and to help the struggling economies of the developing world. Our aid programme next year (excluding aid to Eastern Europe and the CIS) will reach £1,800 million. Britain also makes more direct private investment in the developing world than any other EC country — some £2,400 million in 1989. We are urging the international community to take decisive action on debt relief, the liberalisation of world trade and support for good government.

We continue to accept the long-term UN target for aid of 0.7 per cent of GNP, although we cannot set a timetable for its achievement. The quality of Britain's overseas aid programme is second to none. It is well targeted and highly effective. Eighty per cent of our bilateral aid goes to the poorest countries. New aid to the poorest is given as grants, not loans.

We are supporting projects designed to build efficient institutions and accountable government. We are helping to improve public administration and the legal system in a number of countries. The English language is one of our nation's greatest assets — culturally, politically and commercially. The BBC World Service has unrivalled standing around the globe. The British Council acts as a cultural ambassador for Britain and for the English language.

● We will use overseas aid to promote good government, sensible economic policies, the rooting out of corruption, and — crucially — respect for human rights and the rule of law.

● We will press creditor countries to accept the prime minister's proposal — the "Trinidad Terms" — for a two-thirds reduction in the official debt of the poorest countries.

● We will promote the development of multi-party systems through the new Westminster Foundation for Democracy.

● We will promote the English language by strengthening both the British Council and the BBC World Service. We will encourage both to become more entrepreneurial in order to finance their activities in developing markets.

The Risks We Face Now

The collapse of the old Soviet Union has dramatically vindicated Conservative defence policy. We have always put the security of our country first. We have kept the peace by staying strong. Today the threat of a massive surprise attack from Eastern Europe has gone. But we still face grave risks to our security. We cannot drop our guard. Under the Conservatives, Britain will never do so.

Within the former Soviet Union there remains a huge military force. Democracy and the rule of law are yet to be firmly established. Control over these armed forces and the massive nuclear capability is uncertain. The events in Yugoslavia show what can happen when communism collapses in disorder.

Increasingly, threats come from outside Europe — as we saw so clearly in the Gulf. Many more countries are acquiring large stocks of modern arms. Some are trying to obtain nuclear, biological and chemical weapons. Britain must be able to respond to any unexpected danger.

The Conservatives are the only party who recognise both the opportunities and the threats of the new world. For over forty years, our security has been based firmly on Nato, the most successful defensive alliance ever. We will work with our allies to ensure that Nato remains the cornerstone of our defence. Britain will command a new Nato Rapid Reaction Corps ready to deploy quickly to counter any sudden threat. As Europeans we must accept a greater role in safeguarding the peace in our continent.

We will promote arms control and reduction initiatives. On Britain's initiative, the UN is establishing a register of arms transfers in order to monitor any dangerous arsenals of weapons.

Britain has always been strongly opposed to nuclear proliferation. We will back an enhanced role for the International Atomic Energy Agency in inspecting nuclear sites and for the UN Security Council in acting against those nations which break their non-proliferation obligations.

● We will work to strengthen the Western European Union as the European pillar of Nato. We will press for a European reaction force.

● We will intensify the co-ordination of security policies within the Twelve.
● We will work through the CSCE to safeguard the security of Europe.
● We will support a comprehensive and verifiable ban on chemical weapons, and further controls on the export of items which could be used in making biological weapons.
● We will help Russia in her efforts to dismantle nuclear weapons.

Our Armed Forces

Only the Conservatives can be trusted to maintain the quality and capability of our armed forces. We are proud of the skill, courage and professionalism which they displayed in the Gulf and which they show daily in Northern Ireland. We are the only party unambiguously committed to the preservation and modernisation of our independent nuclear deterrent.

Our defence would be unsafe in the hands of the opposition parties. Labour have opposed our defence policies at every turn. They have twisted and turned in their attitude to our nuclear deterrent. They would devastate our conventional forces by cuts of at least 27 per cent, which would lead to huge job losses in the defence industries.

The Liberal Democrats would cause even more damage to Britain's defences. Their aim is to cut our defence spending by half by the end of the decade.

We insist that our forces have the modern, effective equipment that they need. The Gulf War showed that the services must have the latest technology to give them maximum flexibility and mobility. That is why we have ordered the new Challenger II tank for the Army, the Merlin helicopter for the Navy, the Asraam air defence missile for the RAF and a wide range of other new equipment for our forces.

Our reappraisal of Britain's defence needs will result in a major restructuring of our armed forces to take account of the changing world situation. In future our forces will be smaller, but better equipped. Our services deserve the excellent pay and conditions which we have secured for them and will maintain.

● We will complete the deployment of the next generation of Britain's minimum nuclear deterrent. We will order and complete the fourth Trident submarine.
● We will ensure the forces have the best and most modern equipment.
● We will improve the quality and management of service housing and help those in the forces save towards buying a home of their own.
● The reserves will play an even more important role and we will introduce legislation to allow their more flexible use.

The European Community

The Conservatives have been the party of Britain in Europe for 30 years. We have argued when argument was necessary; but we have not wavered nor changed our views. We have ensured that Britain is at the heart of Europe; a strong and respected partner.

We have played a decisive part in the development of the community over the past decade. It was a British initiative which launched the single market programme and our insistence which reformed the community's finances. Britain has promoted co-operation on foreign policy and in combating terrorism. Britain has also persuaded our partners to welcome new countries who apply for community membership.

The Maastricht Treaty was a success both for Britain and for the rest of Europe. British proposals helped to shape the key provisions of the treaty, including those strengthening the enforcement of community law, defence, subsidiarity and law and order. But Britain refused to accept the damaging social chapter proposed by other Europeans, and it was excluded from the Maastricht Treaty.

All member states must live up to their obligations under community law. At Maastricht, we secured agreement that the European Court will be able to fine any member state which fails to do so.

● We will work closely with our partners in foreign policy and in the war on international crime.
● We will continue to resist changes to the Treaty of Rome that would damage British business.
● We will resist commission initiatives which run counter to the principle that issues should be dealt with on a national basis wherever possible.
● Britain is a great trading nation. We prosper through the maintenance of an open trading system. We will work for a successful outcome to the Gatt negotiations.
● We will redouble our efforts to reform the common agricultural policy and will stoutly defend the interests of British farmers and consumers.
● We will insist on more effective control over community spending and will resist pressure to extend community competence to new areas.
● We will work to strengthen the external frontiers of the community whilst maintaining the checks needed at our own borders against illegal immigration, drugs, terrorism and disease.

The British Presidency

In the second half of 1992 Britain will take the chair of the council of ministers. The British presidency comes at a turning point in the community's history. It gives us the opportunity to shape the direction of the community and to establish its priorities. We shall use it to promote our vision of an outward looking community based on free enterprise.

Our presidency will reach its climax at the Edinburgh meeting of the European council, which we will hold in the historic palace of Holyrood House. While the attention of Europe is focused on Edinburgh, the strength of our union will be visible to all.

Our priorities will be:

● To start negotiations with those Efta countries who want to join the Community so that they can join by 1995.

● To build on the EC's association agreements with Czechoslovakia, Hungary and Poland so that we can welcome them to full membership by the year 2000.

● To conclude EC trade and co-operation agreements with the main republics of the former Soviet Union.

● To complete the single market and extend it to the seven countries of Efta. Over half our trade is with the rest of the community. The single market will create an open market of 350 million customers for British goods and services. To complete the single market we shall aim to:

— open up the market for life insurance to free competition;

— liberalise air travel to bring down air fares in Europe closer to those in America;

— free up the shipping and road transport markets so that British operators can carry freely within the EC;

— increase competition in the European energy sector.

● We will provide guidance and help to any British company encountering a trade barrier illegal under European law.

● We will press for progress on the environment, including the fifth environment action programme.

● We will chair the negotiations on the future spending priorities of the community to ensure value for money. We will safeguard the abatement negotiated by Mrs Thatcher which has so far brought some £12,000 million in budget rebates to Britain.

WEALTH AND OWNERSHIP

The 1990s present a great economic opportunity for Britain. We have got the scourge of inflation under control. We have cut direct tax rates. And a stable currency gives industry a chance to realise the potential released by the reforms of the 1980s.

We have extended ownership more widely — of homes, savings and shares — with millions more sharing directly in Britain's success. We will promote enterprise through low taxes, sound money and a stable currency.

When the exchange-rate mechanism was being created, during the final days of the last Labour government, the then prime minister decided Britain could not take part. It was easy to see why. The economy was too weak. Inflation was too high. In 1974-9, the inflation rate averaged over 15 per cent. It peaked at 27 per cent. Public borrowing rose to nearly 10 per cent of national income — equivalent to £55,000 million today. Penal taxes blunted enterprise. Britain was a byword for strikes.

The Conservatives have changed all that. Since 1979, our inflation rate has averaged 7.5 per cent. Now it is only just over 4 per cent — below the average for the European community. In the 1960s and 1970s, Britain had the slowest growth rate in the European community. But in the 1980s, we grew faster than either France or Germany. Industrial disputes became rare events. And in 1990 a Conservative government joined the ERM.

Penal taxes have been abolished. A man on average earnings, with a wife and two children, has an income today which after tax and inflation is 39 per cent higher than it was in Labour's last year. That great advance in the standard of living is at risk in this election.

Since the war, living standards have always risen faster under Conservative governments than under Labour. Now we are pledged to cut tax rates again — and have made a start on the road to 20p income tax.

Corporate tax rates have been cut, too. Our business investment has increased more rapidly than in any other major economy except Japan. Britain attracts by far the biggest share of Japanese and American investment in Europe. That, too, is at risk in this election.

Britain's Opportunity

We are now members of:

— The biggest free market in the world. British industry is again respected in Europe.

— A zone of low inflation, in which we can compete with the best.

Britain must not throw this opportunity away by electing a Labour government. The world recession has been tough for all of us, at home and abroad. Unemployment has risen. But in Britain we have laid the foundations for recovery. What is needed to trigger confidence and growth is a Conservative victory with a decisive majority. What would postpone recovery, and turn this promise of growth into the certainty of hard times, is the election of our opponents whose policies would mean higher taxes, higher inflation, higher interest rates, more bureaucratic regulation and more strikes.

In the 1990s, the Government's task will be to provide an economic environment which encourages enterprise — the mainspring of prosperity. Our aims must be:

● To achieve price stability.
● To keep firm control over public spending.
● To continue to reduce taxes as fast as we prudently can.
● To make sure that market mechanisms and incentives are allowed to do their job.

Price stability does not mean a frozen economy in which no price ever moves. But we must drive inflation down so low that it no longer affects the decisions made by ordinary people, businesses and government. When inflation rises, so do bankruptcies. When inflation falls, industry can plan again for a profitable future. Inflation creates strife, as different groups in society struggle to restore their living standards. It destroys jobs. It erodes savings and social benefits and threatens our currency.

Inflation and Europe

Membership of the ERM is now central to our counter-inflation discipline. But the ERM is not a magic wand. It would not protect Labour, it would merely expose the folly of Labour policies. Some Labour politicians know that all too well — others simply don't. They — and some of the unions — would put irresistible spending pressure on a Labour government.

Some members of the European community are anxious to hurry on from the ERM to economic and monetary union. Others have doubts. Quite apart from the constitutional issues, they do not want to take risks with what is being achieved in the ERM.

The treaty negotiated at Maastricht laid down the process under which the Community can, if its members meet certain economic conditions, create a monetary union with a single currency for some or all of them. Together with Germany, we fought for tough criteria. We believe a monetary union would collapse, with damaging consequences, if it were imposed on economies that were too diverse.

A union will only come about by 1997 if a substantial majority of community members agree it should. It would only include those members who were judged to have met specified conditions. And it would only come about if a majority of members were judged to have done so.

But the treaty goes on to say that monetary union will come about automatically in 1999, for all who meet the conditions. We did not want to exclude ourselves from membership; but we could not accept such an automatic commitment. By the end of this decade the EC's membership will have changed; the economic performance of many of its members may have changed. We cannot tell who the members of such a union might be.

We therefore secured the freedom to make a proper judgment on events. We are as free to join if we wish as any other member. We would have to meet the same conditions — no more, no less. We will play our full part in the discussions of the monetary institutions Europe may create in the 1990s. But we are not obliged to join in a single currency if we do not want to.

● In due course, we will move to the narrow bands of the ERM.
● We will play our full part in the design and discussion of monetary institutions for Europe.
● When or if other members of the EC move to a monetary union with a single currency, we will take our own unfettered decision on whether to join. That decision will be taken by the United Kingdom parliament.

The Route to Lower Taxes

Economic growth is created by people's hard work, ingenuity, thrift and willingness to take risks. An enterprise economy rewards the industrious and thrifty. We believe that government should not gobble up all the proceeds of growth, and that those who create prosperity should enjoy it, through lower taxes and more opportunity to build up personal wealth.

Our policy is therefore to reduce the share of national income taken by the public sector. In the mid-1970s, public spending peaked at over 49 per cent of our gross national product. In the early 1980s, it peaked at over 47 per cent. In this recession, it is peaking at only 43 per cent. We aim to reduce this steadily as the recovery gets under way.

Keeping control of public spending will enable us to cut taxes while bringing the Government's budget back towards balance in the years ahead. Excessive government borrowing can lead to inflation. Government should always he on guard against that danger. However, when demand in the economy is weak, public borrowing will tend to rise.

Because companies pay taxes according to how well they did the previous year, the deficit tends to be deepest just as we come out of recession. We must make sure that as the economy grows, borrowing slows.

By bringing tax and spending decisions together in a unified Budget from next year, we will make the choices clearer. But lower taxes and a prudent approach to borrowing do not mean public spending must fall; quite the reverse. A lightly taxed economy generates more economic growth, and more revenue. High taxes kill the goose that lays the golden eggs. In the course of its last five years in office, Labour was forced to cut public spending, in real terms. By contrast, the Conservatives have been able to raise public spending by nearly a quarter in real terms.

Higher tax rates do not always bring in more money. In practice, they can bring in less. The Conservative government has more than halved the top rate of tax. Yet top rate taxpayers today provide a bigger share of our tax revenues than they did before. Lower taxes have encouraged more people to work harder — not to spend their time working out how to avoid penal taxes.

During the past 13 years we have cut, simplified or abolished a whole range of direct taxes.

— We have cut the basic rate of income tax from 33p to 25p, and the top rate from 83p to 40p

— We have now announced a new starting income tax rate of 20p.

— We have raised the basic single person's tax allowance by 27 per cent more than would be needed to keep pace with inflation.

— We have simplified and reduced the burden of taxation on capital.

— We have cut corporation tax from 52 per cent to 33 per cent (and from 42 per cent to 25 per cent for small companies).

— We have reduced the burden of national insurance on low earners.

— We have introduced independent taxation of husbands and wives, giving married women full eligibility for tax allowances.

— We have introduced new tax incentives for savings.

— We have abolished several taxes completely, including the surcharge on income from savings, the national insurance surcharge, development land tax, and capital transfer tax.

We are the only party that understands the need for low taxation. Labour and the Liberals openly advocate increased taxation. Yet lower taxes clearly create a more productive economy. They also achieve another prime objective of Conservative governments, which is to transfer power from the state to the people. Labour would:

— Reverse our cut in the starting rate of income tax to 20p.

— Raise the top rate.

— Abolish the national insurance ceiling.

— Introduce a new savings surcharge.

● We announced in the Budget an important first step towards a basic income tax rate of 20p. By applying a 20p rate to the first £2,000 of taxable income, we have cut taxes for all 25 million taxpayers, and taken the four million on lowest incomes out of 25p tax altogether.

● We will make further progress towards a basic income tax rate of 20p.

● We will reduce the share of national income taken by the public sector.

● We will see the budget return towards balance as the economy recovers.

The Right to Own

Since 1979, wealth has been spread more widely through the community. Home ownership, share ownership and the build-up of personal pensions have all contributed. Over two-thirds of people live in homes that they own, 10 million people own shares, six million of them in newly privatised industries. About 2.5 million have benefited from tax incentives to encourage employee share schemes. And over 4.5 million people are now building up their own personal pensions. But these freedoms are at risk. Labour would:

— Halt the privatisation programme and threaten the value of shares in privatised industries with renationalisation and new government controls.

— Bring back credit rationing, leading to mortgage queues.

— Turn the pensions market on its head, making pension provision costly and difficult.

These changes would drive savings overseas and make wealth again the prerogative of the few.

By contrast, we want to do more to encourage the wider distribution of wealth throughout society. Sustaining not just a home-owning but a capital-owning democracy is crucial to our vision for the 1990s. We intend to spread the ownership of shares, homes, pensions and savings. We will do so through future privatisations, help for would-be home owners in council tenancies and further encouragement for the spread of personal pensions. We intend to lighten the burden of capital taxes and reform the taxation of savings.

We believe inheritance tax is particularly inequitable. It falls only on those who do not dispose of their assets seven years or more before their death. It is inevitably the case that these tend to be people who are not rich enough to engage in high-powered tax planning, or who, for lack of knowledge or advice, fail to take the necessary precautionary action.

In the Budget, we announced that we would take most family businesses out of inheritance tax altogether. During the new parliament, we will aim to lessen the burden on families to whom home ownership has brought the threat of this erratic tax.

● We will aim to bring home ownership, share ownership and personal pensions within the reach of more families.

● We will continue to reform the taxation of savings, building on the success of Peps and Tessas.

● We will raise the tax threshold for inheritance tax so that the homes and savings of an increasing number of our citizens can pass unencumbered from one generation to another.

● Whenever possible, we will ensure that future privatisations offer opportunities to employees to secure a stake in the ownership of their business.
● We will encourage companies to make dealing in their own shares easier, especially for small shareholders, and encourage wider share ownership, through, for example, the establishment of share shops.
● We will abolish stamp duty on share transactions.

Setting the Economy Free

Starting with the abolition of exchange controls in 1979, the government has created new incentives for every part of our economy. Manufacturing industry suffered particularly badly from the harm inflicted on the British economy by Labour governments in the 1960s and 1970s. To a far greater extent than service industries, it was the victim of militant trades unionism, restrictive practices, nationalisation, state intervention, tax distortion, planning controls and over-regulation. We believe strongly that a vigorous manufacturing sector is essential to a healthy British economy. Over the past 13 years, we have steadily dismantled barriers to its growth.

The competitiveness and performance of British manufacturing have been transformed. Its impressive recovery was recognised by the Confederation of British Industry, in its report aptly titled *Competing with the World's Best*. Manufacturing productivity has risen by more than half since 1979 — faster than in any other major industrial country. Over the past 10 years, British manufactured exports have grown faster than those of France, Germany, the United States or even Japan. The British motor industry has achieved an astonishing revival. By 1996, Britain should again be exporting more cars than we import — for the first time since 1974. We have given the industry yet more encouragement in the Budget, by halving the special tax paid on new cars.

The British standard for quality management has effectively become the international standard. But that is only the beginning. We have set up a team of senior business people to pursue the idea of a new British quality award.

The City is Europe's greatest financial centre. It contributes £11,000 million net to our balance of payments. Financial services employ 12 per cent of our workforce. London's capital markets and financial services have grown vigorously because they are innovative and highly competitive. We will continue our efforts to break down the barriers that prevent them from competing freely throughout Europe and in the wider world. The European Bank for Reconstruction and Development is now based in London. It puts us in the forefront of encouraging investment in the developing markets of central and Eastern Europe.

Service industries make a vital contribution to our economy and to our balance of payments. Tourism, for example, today employs 1.5 million people, 20 per cent more than in 1980. It is an industry which boasts many famous companies — but it is also driven by the dynamism of many small firms. We will continue to help them by simplifying rules and regulations on business and through the DTI enterprise initiative and a range of other schemes.
● We will continue to reduce tax burdens on business, as we have done this year for the motor industry, whenever it is possible to do so.
● We will abolish unnecessary licences and reduce the need for specific approvals for product design.
● We will back British companies encountering any discrimination, trade barriers or state subsidies that should no longer exist within the single market.
● We will back the regulators of the financial services industry in their efforts to achieve high standards while keeping the rule books down to manageable size.

Privatisation

Competition and private ownership are the most powerful engines of economic efficiency, innovation and choice. They lead to the creation of world-class companies. We have returned to private enterprise two-thirds of the companies once owned by the state: 46 businesses employing about 900,000 people. This programme has been the model for governments across the whole world. The work of liberalising markets which were once monopolised goes on. In 1984 we privatised British Telecom but only Mercury was given a licence to carry services over fixed links. In 1991 we decided to end this duopoly. The UK now has one of the most open and dynamic telecommunications markets in the world.

But much greater economic efficiency is not the only gain. Employees have been able to take a direct stake in the newly privatised companies. Millions of people have been given the same chance to own a real share in the nation's assets. Companies which looked inwards to Whitehall are now listening to their customers and shareholders.

Some activities of government must always be provided in the public sector. But in central government, Next Steps agencies and local government, management is increasingly buying in services from the private sector. Our proposals for developing this policy have been set out in the white papers on *Competing for Quality* in central and local government.
● We will continue our privatisation programme. British Coal will be returned to the private sector. So will local authority bus companies. We will encourage local authorities to sell their airports. We will end British Rail's monopoly. We will sell certain rail services and franchise others.

● The Ports Act 1991 has paved the way for the privatisation of the Trust Ports by competitive tender. Tees and Hartlepool, Tilbury, Medway, Forth and Clyde have already been privatised.
● We are privatising Northern Ireland Electricity and will privatise the Northern Ireland water and sewage services. We will look for ways of bringing private sector skills into the management of Northern Ireland railways.
● We will bring private sector enterprise into the public services by encouraging contracting out and competitive tendering throughout government.
● We will require all government departments to report annually on their plans for market-testing, and progress in achieving it, in their own services and in those of their associated agencies.
● We will maintain our programme of compulsory competitive tendering of local authority services. We will ensure that unfair terms are excluded and will discourage investment to protect in-house services when better, more cost effective services are available through the private sector.
● We will ensure that competitive tendering is extended to white collar local authority services such as those offered by lawyers, accountants, architects and surveyors.
● We will tackle all anti-competitive and restrictive practices with vigour. We will introduce new legislation giving stronger powers to deal with cartels.

Deregulation

We are concerned that at every level of government — in Europe, in Whitehall and in local authorities — some regulations may have been adopted in answer to legitimate concerns, but without proper regard to their overall impact on businesses and individuals. A proper balance needs to be struck between essential protection for the public, and over-zealous and intrusive controls aimed at the elimination of all conceivable risk. It is wrong that new regulations, designed to deal with isolated problems, should interfere with the private arrangements of citizens or with reasonable commercial practices that have earned broad public acceptance.
● The compliance costs of new UK and EC regulations must be assessed properly. Existing regulations which are outmoded and burdensome must be simplified or removed. We will give priority to the work of the DTI deregulation unit in these areas.
● We will examine ways in which the uniform scope of regulation could be eased to safeguard traditional local products or practices.
● We will examine whether certain regulations affecting individual citizens within their own homes could be made advisory, rather than mandatory.

Energy

Our energy policies have brought the consumer both lower prices and better service. We have privatised British Gas and the electricity industry in a way that has opened these markets to competition. These policies are now being seized upon in Europe as essential extensions of the single market. Domestic customers are now protected by a price formula, and high standards of service are enforced by the independent regulators. For instance, electricity disconnections for debt have fallen by 43 per cent since the launch of privatisation.

We have ensured that the safety of employees comes first, and have given thousands the opportunity of acquiring a stake in their industry.

The future of the coal industry depends crucially on the competitiveness of coal as a fuel for electricity generation. British Coal has made enormous progress in increasing productivity since the end of the 1985 strike — but there is still further to go. We will support the efforts of British Coal and its workforce to improve the industry's performance. The long-term future of the industry lies in the private sector. We have invested in clean coal technology to safeguard the environment. Renewable energy projects have received unprecedented support. North Sea oil and gas are enjoying a record expansion thanks to our policies of deregulation and low taxation.
● Safety will remain our highest priority throughout the energy sector.
● We will continue to encourage competition in energy markets. We will progressively reduce the British Gas monopoly of the retail gas market, to give small users the same rights as big firms.
● We will privatise British Coal in a way that enables employees to enjoy a stake in the industry.
● We will increase our support for British Coal Enterprise which promotes economic regeneration in areas affected by the closure of mines, and has successfully assisted 76,000 people in finding new jobs.
● We will review the future of the nuclear industry in 1994. We are committed to safe and economical nuclear power. The existing strict arrangements for nuclear waste will be maintained.
● We will maintain a guaranteed market for renewable energy projects and fund research in this area.
● We will consult on new building regulations to improve energy use. Together with British Gas and some of the regional electricity companies, we will establish an independent energy savings trust to promote energy efficiency. Our grants scheme for low income households will receive record funding next year.

Science and Innovation

British science has an unrivalled reputation for ground-breaking research. We believe in investing in scientific research because it enriches the quality of our lives and provides the feedstock of industrial innovation. The science budget has grown by 24 per cent in real terms since 1978-9. Increasingly, funding will reflect the quality of the research output so that the best centres can truly be world leaders. The Government spends nearly £3,000 million a year on civil research and development — at least as high a proportion of national income as the Japanese or Americans. And since 1978, British industry's spending on R&D has increased by 37 per cent in real terms.

● We will continue to support our science base to maintain the excellence of our science and to ensure that we produce the skilled technical people we need.

● We will encourage the transfer of people and technology from universities to businesses and upgrade the Link scheme, which funds joint research.

● We will encourage the establishment of centres of technological excellence linking industrial research organisations with universities and polytechnics.

● We will continue to develop new innovation schemes for small and medium-sized businesses, including the highly regarded Spur programme to provide help with the development of new products and processes.

Regional Policies

In recent years, the United Kingdom has attracted five times as much Japanese investment as Germany or France, which powerfully demonstrates that we have created the most attractive environment in Europe for investors. Our positive policy towards inward investment will be maintained, in contrast to that of the TUC and the Labour party. The government will continue to invest in a strong infrastructure and boost technology expertise in the regions.

● We will ensure that regional policy is well targeted.

● We will continue to support all parts of the United Kingdom in their campaigns to attract inward investment.

● We will give additional emphasis to upgrading skills and technology when allocating funds.

Small Businesses

Small businesses are the seedcorn of the economy. Their numbers have grown by more than a third since 1979, while the number of self-employed people has grown to over 12 per cent of the workforce. We will continue to recognise the special needs of small and medium-sized companies, and to ensure that government delivers useful services to them. Our tax regime for small businesses is one of the most favourable in Europe. We have raised the VAT threshold every year since 1979 and reduced the small companies rate of corporation tax from 42 per cent to 25 per cent.

Training and enterprise councils (and local enterprise companies in Scotland) have developed a wide range of services for business and enterprise which assist over 150,000 small companies each year. We have developed the popular enterprise initiative, under which 40,000 companies have been helped to buy in outside expertise offering key management skills. We now propose to develop this initiative further.

We also propose to help businesses by easing the transfer of commercial tenancies.

● We announced in the Budget new measures to help small businesses, including full relief against inheritance tax on most business assets, reductions in business rates and proposals to speed up the payment of outstanding bills.

● During the new parliament, we will develop a new enterprise service to give small and medium-sized companies help in diagnosing their most important strategic needs. A new consultancy brokerage service will supply information to small companies. We will also develop a technology audit which will provide small firms with a plan for change. And we will continue to support total quality management consultancies.

● TECs and LECs will be closely involved in developing and implementing this new initiative.

● The independent Law Commission has recommended that a commercial tenant should in general be freed from any future liability under a lease when he assigns away his interest under it. We will consider how this principle could be put into effect for new commercial leases.

Consumer Affairs

Consumers want choice, quality and value for money. Competition only works effectively if consumers have the information they need to make sensible decisions. Our food safety policy promotes consumer choice and consumer safety. We introduced the 1990 Food Safety Act to ensure the highest standards of food hygiene.

● We will introduce legislation designed to give consumers confidence that what they purchase is properly described — and that adequate compensation is offered where these requirements are not met.

● We will enable the courts to override unfair terms in contracts and improve our powers to deal with rogue traders.

● We will ensure that guarantees mean what they say, and that manufacturers or importers share responsibility with the people who sell their goods.

CONSERVATIVE MANIFESTO

● We will tighten up the rules on holiday brochures and contracts, and introduce a cooling-off period into timeshare contracts.
● We will introduce legislation to simplify trade mark registration and extend the rights they confer.
● We will enforce science-based controls on the use of chemicals in food production and will maintain our policy of open access to information on pesticide safety.
● We will improve standards of food labelling in close consultation with consumer representatives.

CHOICE AND THE CHARTER

The Citizen's Charter is the most far-reaching programme ever devised to improve quality in public services. It addresses the needs of those who use public services, extends people's rights, requires services to set clear standards — and to tell the public how far those standards are met.

The Citizen's Charter:
— widens popular choice;
— helps people to exercise that choice in a properly informed way;
— expects all public services to put the customer first;
— promotes the challenge of competition within the public sector;
— requires clear performance standards to be set and for services to be measured against them;
— insists on a proper response to complaints and on action to set right the problems behind them.

The charter will be at the centre of government's decision-making throughout the 1990s. No one doubts the professionalism of the vast majority of public servants. But too often the system's outdated working methods and attitudes prevent them from giving their best. The charter's commitment to modern, open services will help them to win the respect that good service deserves.

In less than a year since the white paper, 18 detailed charters have been published. Each sets out tough new standards and gives new information and rights to the public. Each will be revised regularly to check on progress, and raise standards higher. But, already, results are clear.
— In hospitals, from April, every out-patient will have a fixed appointment time and our guarantee of maximum waiting times for operations will be steadily improved.
— On council estates every tenant will have the right to call in a private contractor if the council fails to do a minor repair.
— In schools, all parents will have the right to a report on their child's performance and details on that of the school.

Rights such as these should not have been denied to the public. The Citizen's Charter, steadily but surely, is changing all that.

Knowledge, Standards, Choice

The next Conservative government will carry the charter still further. There will be more information about standards and performance; clear standards set within public services which are still shrouded in mystery; more choice built into public services and proper complaints procedures introduced. Many of these are outlined later in the manifesto under Education, Health, Local Government and Transport. Here are a few examples from the programme for the next two years:
● The Audit Commission will be able to publish league tables of performance including each local council and health authority so that people can compare the quality of service.
● We will ensure that inspection reports are published and widely available. All councils will have to respond in public to criticism from auditors.
● We will introduce a new 'Charterline' that people with questions or problems with a public service will be able to ring.
● We will require British Rail to tighten its targets for reliability and punctuality on all lines, and report monthly to passengers on how it is doing. London Underground will publish its own charter.
● We will expect Post Offices and Job Centres to set out standards of service and levels of achievement.
● A new Charter Mark award will give recognition to those parts of the public service that best meet charter standards.
● British Rail and London Underground are introducing compensation systems for travellers.
● We will review the powers of the local government ombudsman to ensure that findings of maladministration are properly dealt with by all local authorities.
● We will consult on a new Lay Adjudicators scheme to help the public resolve difficulties and disputes.

We will extend competition and accountability in public services. Those who provide public services will have to prove they can give the right quality at the right cost.
● We will extend compulsory competitive tendering to local authority housing management, and examine how to apply it to white-collar services.
● We will act to ensure that private firms bidding to improve local authority public services are not obstructed by unscrupulous practices in councils or by unfair contracts.

● We will pursue more competitive tendering for central government services.

● We will encourage the wider use of performance pay inside the civil service and in other parts of the public service. A link between a person's effort and his or her pay is a powerful means of improving performance.

● Civil servants dealing with the public will normally identify themselves by name.

● We will toughen inspection of key public services where choice and competition must inevitably be limited. We will introduce, for the first time, regular independent inspection of all schools.

● We will act to ensure that the inspectorates of police, fire, probation, and social services, together with any new inspectorates that are established, will be truly independent of the service which they inspect.

● We will ensure that the reports from these systematic regular inspections are published. More lay inspectors, drawn from other professions and from the general public, will bring fresh insights into service improvement.

● We will publish later this year new proposals for the inspection of social work in England, setting up arrangements for systematic independent inspection of all care services and every local authority social services department.

● Inspections of local authority homes will be carried out by teams that contain lay inspectors and are independent of the influence of the management of the homes.

All of the privatised utilities have a specialist regulator who is responsible for promoting competition, reviewing prices and protecting the public interest. We have introduced legislation to increase the powers of these regulators to the level of the strongest.

● We are ensuring that the regulators have the powers they need to promote competition and safeguard the interests of the customer by controlling price increases. We will increase competition in the gas and water markets.

● We are giving the regulators powers to set standards of service, covering such matters as fixed appointment times for service calls.

The Post Office

The Post Office is among the best in Europe for speed and reliability of its letter services. Traffic has grown by 50 per cent in a decade in which it has operated without a subsidy. Last year the first-class letter service achieved record improvements in reliability. The local post office is a vital and valued feature of the rural community. In 1981 we introduced private competition for deliveries costing over £1. This led to the rapid growth of the private courier industry, with substantial benefits to business users. We believe that further benefits to consumers would flow from additional competition.

● We are committed to maintaining a nation-wide letter service with delivery to every address in the United Kingdom, within a uniform structure of prices, and with a nation-wide network of post offices.

● We will legislate to set up a new independent regulator to advise on issues affecting Post Office customers, and on the progressive introduction of competition.

● We will set performance targets for the Post Office and ensure they are published in all offices, together with results achieved.

● We will ensure there is effective redress for customers where services fail.

● We will lower the limit on the Post Office monopoly much closer to the level of the first class stamp.

● We will provide improved scope for contractors to carry mail to final delivery offices.

● We will consider requests to license limited specialist services to compete within the Post Office monopoly.

Whitehall & Westminster

Whitehall must move with the times. It is over a decade since the last major restructuring of the departments of government. Since then:

— Two-thirds of the state industrial sector has been privatised, transferring about 900,000 jobs to the private sector.

— Government has reduced the burden of regulation and the need for central bureaucracy.

— Civil service manpower has been reduced by almost a quarter.

— Many of the functions of government have been devolved from Whitehall

— The Citizen's Charter programme is bringing new quality to public services.

We will continue to reorganise central government in tune with its modern role, while devolving and contracting-out executive functions. We want to ensure that the drive to save money, to reduce bureaucracy and raise quality is powerfully led from the centre of government.

● We will give a Cabinet minister responsibility for the Citizen's Charter programme and reforming the civil service, taking charge of the Citizen's Charter unit, efficiency unit, the programme for creating agencies and the public competition and purchasing unit. This will make it easier to raise quality and efficiency in government and see that contracting-out and market-testing are energetically pursued.

● We intend to create a new department, under a Cabinet minister, with responsibility for broadcasting, arts, sport, tourism, the national heritage and the film industry. This department will aim to encourage private sector enterprise in all these fields. The national lottery and the millennium fund will also bring new responsibilities to government in these areas.

● We will transfer the core responsibilities of the Department of Energy to the Department of Trade and Industry and responsibilities for energy efficiency to the Department of the Environment, ending the need for a separate department.

● Small businesses are the seedcorn of our future prosperity. We believe the Department of Trade and Industry should take over responsibility for them. We also want to strengthen the links between the DTI and the highly successful training and enterprise councils.

● Responsibility for overseeing all financial services will be brought together in the Treasury, in line with the practice adopted in most other advanced countries.

● New programmes for regenerating our inner cities are outlined in this manifesto. Responsibilities will be brought together in the Department of the Environment.

● We are determined to ensure that women in the work-force realise their full potential. We will transfer from the Home Office to the Department of Employment the lead responsibility for co-ordinating government policy on issues of particular concern to women.

Open Government

Government has traditionally been far too reluctant to provide information. This secrecy extends from the processes of Cabinet government to schools which refuse to release exam results. Under the Citizen's Charter, a great deal more information is now being made available on the services provided by government.

We have also:

— replaced the catch-all provisions of the 1911 Official Secrets Act with narrower offences depending on specific tests of the harm likely to be caused by disclosure, while giving special protection to vital information relating to our national security;

— introduced rights to check certain personal records held on computer, and supported new rights of access to a range of government records;

— committed ourselves to a public right of access to information about the environment, including water supply, air quality, dumping at sea and radioactive substances;

— made available more reports on matters of public concern such as food safety and industrial risks.

We intend to carry forward this move towards greater openness.

● We will review the 80 or so statutory restrictions which exist on the disclosure of information — retaining only those needed to protect privacy and essential confidentiality.

● We will seek to provide greater access to personal records held by government.

● We will be less secretive about the workings of government. For example, when the committees of the Cabinet are reconstituted after the election we will, for the first time, set out their names and membership. We will update and — for the first time — publish the guidance for ministers on procedure.

The Workings of Parliament

It is not just Whitehall that must change. Parliament, too, has to keep its working methods under review to make sure it attracts the best people to the service of their country and uses their talents to best effect.

● We will propose appropriate parliamentary reforms to ensure that the House of Commons conducts its business more efficiently and effectively, taking into account the benefit of modern technology, the increasing constituency demands upon Members of Parliament and the need to attract more women to stand for election.

OPPORTUNITY FOR ALL

Conservatives believe that high standards in education and training are the key to personal opportunity and national success. We believe in partnership with parents, choice in schools and a good grounding in the basic skills all children need to make a success of their lives. We are committed to widening opportunities without compromising academic standards. We will continue to expand higher education and training. We will reinforce the rights of the individual in the world of work, and break down artificial barriers to advancement. By extending opportunity and arming people with the power to choose, we will give valuable freedoms and a powerful spur to achievement.

Schools, Pupils & Parents

We are now seeing real improvements in our education system. One in four young people goes on to higher education; at the beginning of the 1980s, it was only one in eight. Sixty per cent of 16-year-olds stay on in full-time education, up from only 40 per cent in 1979. And we have embarked on the most important and wide-ranging reforms since the 1940s. For the first time in our history, we will soon have a national curriculum which will require all the main school subjects to be covered thoroughly. The testing of seven-year-olds is well under way and tests for older children are now being developed. Starting this September, GCSE courses will be steadily integrated with the national curriculum.

Under the parent's charter, all schools will have to provide at least one written report on the progress of each child each year. Information on the performance of all local schools will be given to parents, enabling them to exercise choice more effectively. We believe all parents have the right to choice in education — not only those who can afford school fees. Young people differ in their interests and aptitudes, and we need a range of schools to offer them the best opportunities. We have always fought to maintain diversity in education, protecting the right of local people to preserve their grammar schools, and defending independent schools against mindless Labour attacks. And we have always valued the important contribution made by the churches to our children's education.

We have further increased diversity by:
— Giving schools control over their own budgets and encouraging new types of school.
— Allowing schools to become independent of local councils, by applying for grant-maintained status if the parents involved so wish. By mid-1992, over 200 GM schools will be up and running.
— Creating a number of highly popular city technology colleges.
— Launching the highly successful initiative under which schools are able to bid directly for the resources to become technology schools.

We intend to take all these initiatives farther and offer parents more choice in the new parliament. Popular schools will be allowed to expand, and more schools will be able to apply for technology funding. We will make it easier for small schools to enjoy the benefits of GM status by grouping together.
● We will complete the introduction of the national curriculum offering 10 subjects at a nationally-defined standard — English, mathematics, science, history, geography, technology, art, music, PE and, in secondary schools, a foreign language.
● Regular and straightforward tests will be in place for all seven, 11 and 14-year-olds by 1994.
● GCSE at age 16 will be integrated into the national curriculum, with a new A+ grade to test the most able. The majority of marks will come from a written exam.
● We will continue to encourage the creation of nursery places. For the first time, over 50 per cent of three and four-year-olds have places either in nursery or primary schools.
● Full information will be published annually about the performance of all local schools in each area.
● Independent inspection of schools will provide parents with straightforward reports on their child's school, together with an action plan from governors to remedy any weaknesses.
● Popular schools which are oversubscribed will be given the resources to expand.
● GM schools will be able to change their charter if that is what parents clearly want and the change fits in with the wider needs of the local area.
● The technology schools initiative will be expanded across the country.
● Existing schools which opt for GM status will be able to emulate city technology colleges and attract private technology sponsorship.
● We will maintain the assisted places scheme, which gives access to independent education to many families who could not otherwise afford it.
● We will ensure that the partnership between the state and the churches in education is maintained and strengthened.
● We will enable small schools to apply for GM status in groups.
● We will pay particular attention to raising educational standards in areas of deprivation in our cities.

Teaching

We are determined to reinforce the professionalism of teachers and the esteem in which they are held. We have created an independent teachers' pay review body. We accepted in full its first recommendations; nearly half of all teachers are now earning over £20,000 a year. We will press ahead with regular appraisal of teachers to encourage high standards and develop professional skills.

As a first step in the reform of teacher training, postgraduate students will spend much more time in school classrooms, learning their skills under the practised eye of senior teachers. It is vital that the education system should attract back women who have taken a career break to raise a family. Through grants to local authorities, we are financing schemes to introduce more flexible working practices — such as job-sharing.
● We will undertake reform of the teacher training system to make it more effective in developing classroom skills.
● We will develop measures to encourage women with family responsibilities to enter or return to teaching.

After 16

We believe that young people should be free to choose between college, work-based training and sixth form studies. We are giving further education colleges and sixth form colleges in England and Wales autonomy, free from council control. We also value our school sixth forms, and will ensure they retain their place in the new system. And we will allow them to attract older students as well. FE colleges will continue to receive support for adult education, while local authorities will retain the resources to respond to local demand for leisure courses.

We will defend the well-respected A-level examinations, which Labour would destroy. We will continue to encourage participation in AS examinations. We will also continue to develop new high-quality national vocational qualifications, and introduce a new post-16 diploma which recognises achievement in both vocational and academic courses.

● We will develop an advanced diploma which can be earned by students pursuing either academic or vocational courses, and a new general national vocational qualification.

● We intend to allow school sixth forms to open their doors if they wish to older students, and to accept training credits or fees from them.

● From April next year, further education and sixth form colleges will be independent of local government control.

● Mature students will enjoy a wider choice of courses.

Higher Education

Britain maintains the best university system in Europe. We have also developed a thriving network of polytechnics, whose student numbers have increased nearly sixfold since the end of the 1960s. By the year 2000, one in three young people will follow full-time higher education courses. Meanwhile, the number of mature entrants to higher education has risen by 65 per cent since 1979. And our universities are attracting increasing numbers of foreign students. Despite this huge expansion, our students enjoy one of the most generous support systems in the world. The introduction of student loans has given students 30 per cent more money for their living costs than the former system of grants alone. The new system will steadily reduce the proportion of students' living costs that their parents are expected to meet.

● We will continue to expand the number of students in higher education. We are abolishing the artificial "binary line" between universities and polytechnics.

● We are putting in place new mechanisms to ensure that academic standards are maintained in higher education.

● We will continue to provide generous support for students and to expand our student loans commitment.

The Training Revolution

A training revolution is under way in Britain. The government's job is to create a framework within which men and women of all ages can develop skills, gain qualifications and shape their own futures.

We have already brought the world of work and the world of school into closer harmony. Government and industry are working together. Employers already spend over £20,000 million a year on training. Government spending on training has increased 2.5 times in real terms since 1979, to £2,800 million. The government's effort is being channelled through the 82 new training and enterprise councils (and the local enterprise companies in Scotland) — the most significant peacetime partnership between government and industry this century.

— 'Compacts' have resulted in many young people working to goals for attainment and attendance in school. In return, they are guaranteed a job with training — or training leading to a job.

— This year, two million students will participate in the technical and vocational education initiative.

— Investors in People is the new national standard for companies making a commitment to training. TECs play an important role in helping companies attain it.

— Employer-led TECs and LECs are delivering Government-funded training programmes which reflect industry's understanding of local needs.

— Industry is working closely with the national council for vocational qualifications.

— The CBI's training targets for Britain's workforce demonstrate a new partnership between business and education.

Seventy-five per cent of 16-year-olds stay on in full-time education or youth training schemes, up from 46 per cent in 1979. Since 1983, over three million young people have taken up youth training places. And 82 per cent go into jobs or further education when they complete YT. Now we are offering young people aged 16 and 17 vouchers they can use to buy approved courses of education or training, and which will put the power of choice in their hands.

In 1988, we launched employment training, the largest programme of its kind in Europe, which has since helped 1.2 million people. While local programmes are the responsibility of the TECs, the government guarantees the offer of help to particular groups of unemployed. Last year, we launched the new employment action programme, which will help more than 61,000 people in a full year. This is a new addition to a range of measures which include Jobclubs, the job interview guarantee scheme and other tested methods of helping unemployed people back to work.

We are also supporting individual training effort. Since 1988, when we launched career development loans (interest-free for up to 15 months), over 25,000 people have benefited. Last year's Budget gave tax relief on training fees — a boost to the 250,000 people a year who finance their own training. Now, with the TECs, we intend to introduce new financial help for career and training guidance.

● By the end of the new Parliament, the new system of national vocational qualifications should cover virtually every occupation in the economy. The CBI's training targets envisage 80 per cent of young people reaching NVQ level 2 by the end of the Parliament.

● We intend to make training credits available to all 16-year-olds and 17-year-olds within the lifetime of the new Parliament. The TECs will continue to be responsible for the YT programme for this age group.

● We will continue to finance training programmes for the long-term unemployed and those who face particular difficulties.

● We will launch with the TECs a new initiative, giving people a voucher with which they can buy a 'skill check', providing assessment and guidance on how to make the most of their working lives.

Workers and Unions

Over the past 13 years, we have legislated to lift regulatory burdens from the shoulders of those who create jobs in Britain. To industry's relief, we shunned the job-destroying European social charter. And we reject Labour's job-destroying notion of a national minimum wage. We have also legislated five times to transform industrial relations, returning power from militants to ordinary union members. As a result, the number of days lost each year through strikes has fallen from an average 12.9 million in the 1970s to less than a million last year — the lowest figure since records began a century ago.

Labour would disrupt industrial peace by weakening the power of management and the courts. They propose to take away the courts' most important sanction — the power to take over a union's assets. Sympathy strikes would be legalised by Labour, and employers would be prevented from dismissing strikers who broke their contracts.

The workers' rights we believe in are those which enhance an individual's status and opportunities. We believe people should be informed and consulted by employers about issues which affect their work. No one should be allowed to deduct trade union fees automatically from an employee's pay without written authorisation. Individuals must be given greater rights to belong to the union of their choice. We also believe strongly that employers, employees and customers should not have their lives and businesses disrupted by wildcat strikes. In the new Parliament, we will legislate to enforce and enhance these rights.

● We will require employers to give everyone who works for them for more than eight hours a week a clear written statement of their terms and conditions of employment.

● We will make automatic deduction of union membership dues without written authorisation unlawful.

● We will take measures to give individual greater freedom in choosing a union.

● We will legislate to require that all pre-strike ballots are postal and subject to independent scrutiny, and that at least seven days' notice of a strike is given after a ballot.

● People who use public services will have the right to restrain the disruption of those services by unlawful industrial action.

A Share in the Future

We also believe that people at work should be helped to build security for themselves and their families. Employees should be given every opportunity to acquire a stake in the business for which they work. We have ruled that executive share option schemes may grant options at a discount only if the employer also runs an all-employee scheme.

Saving for a pension reduces reliance on the state. We welcome the provision of occupational schemes covering over 11 million workers. There are already important safeguards, which we have improved, for the rights of members in such schemes. But we believe that a full review of the arrangements is now needed. We also believe the new freedoms for scheme members will strengthen accountability and benefit investors.

● We will establish a review of the framework of law and regulation within which occupational schemes operate.

● We will give every member of an occupational scheme the right to an annual statement of the value of their savings.

● In addition we will examine ways of giving those who retire with lump sum payments more choice as to how their savings are invested.

Women and Opportunity

A higher proportion of women go out to work in Britain than in any other EC country except Denmark. Many women choose to work part-time, and our policies have encouraged the development of part-time work within a framework which safeguards employees from exploitation.

CONSERVATIVE MANIFESTO

Throughout Europe, the UK is recognised to have the most comprehensive legislation to combat sex discrimination. We are also committed to breaking down artificial barriers to women's advancement based on prejudice or lack of imagination. As an employer, government must continue to set an example.

The tax relief we have introduced on training fees is constructed to ensure that non-tax payers — who include many married women — will be able to benefit, too. Many training and enterprise councils already have specific plans to help women trainees. We will involve them further in helping employers to help with childcare.

We believe mothers should be treated equally by government, whether they work outside the home or not. We are fully committed to maintaining the real value of child benefit. And we will act where a push by government is needed to stimulate the provision of childcare.

All employers who meet childcare costs can set these off against their liability for corporation tax. In addition, we have relieved employees from paying income tax on the benefit of workplace nurseries.

After-school childcare is an area of particular importance to many working mothers. We will introduce a new initiative to encourage the provision of after-school facilities by schools, employers and voluntary groups across the country.

● The government will amend the law relating to the employment rights of pregnant women to give effect to the EC directive on pregnant workers. This addition to our already extensive legal provision will give a right to at least 14 weeks' maternity leave and protection against dismissal on grounds of pregnancy.

● We will take forward our public appointments initiative. Departments will publish plans for between a quarter and a half of public appointments to be held by women by 1996.

● We will ensure that all parts of government adopt a strategic approach to the employment and development of women staff. We will encourage them to participate in the Opportunity 2000 initiative.

● We will continue to oppose EC measures which would discourage part-time employment, valued by so many women.

● We will encourage all TECs to adopt plans to help women trainees have equal access to training opportunities.

● We will introduce a new grant, paid through TECs, to help employers, voluntary groups or schools to set up after-school care and holiday arrangements. We will ensure that schools are free to participate.

FREEDOM UNDER THE LAW

The Conservative party has always stood for the protection of the citizen and the defence of the rule of law. Society is entitled to a sense of security; individuals to peace of mind; the guardians of that peace to our whole-hearted support. Our policies on law and order, and the rights of individuals, are designed to protect the people of this country and their way of life.

Britain experiences less violent crime than many comparable countries. But crime has continued to rise in Britain. And the challenge for the 1990s is to step up the fight against lawlessness and violence, so that our citizens can live free from fear.

We must continue to ensure that the sentence fits the crime — with long sentences for dangerous criminals, and fines and a tougher regime for punishment outside prison available as an alternative for less serious crime. And we must maintain confidence in our legal system.

We must tackle crime at its roots. Two-thirds of the offences dealt with by our courts are committed by only 7 per cent of those convicted. Most of these constant offenders started down the path of crime while still of school age.

We have launched a reform of our prisons, improving the prospect that those who serve custodial sentences will not return to crime.

But above all, we must remember that it is our policemen and women who are in the front line of the battle. To combat crime effectively, the police need the full support of the government and the public.

Police and the Community

We Conservatives can be proud of our record in supporting the police. Since 1979 we have increased spending on the police by 74 per cent in real terms. Uniformed manpower has increased by 16,000 and civilian manpower by 12,000. We have launched a campaign to recruit 10,000 special constables.

Over the next few years we want to see a major reform which will help provide what the public wants and needs: a visible, local police presence.

We will be encouraging police forces to develop local community policing, to link the force more closely with the communities they protect. The Metropolitan Police will be reorganised on this basis by the spring of 1993. Two-thirds of English and Welsh forces are already preparing similar plans. Pilot schemes suggest they can add greatly to the citizen's sense of security and build support for the police.

Community policing will involve local residents, listen to their views and engage their help in the fight against crime. It will mean:

— smaller police units with officers serving the same area for longer. That way, people can really get to know their local police officers;

— each police force devolving its management and operational control to local units, and streamlining its chain of command;

— getting police back on the beat, and in close contact with the neighbourhoods under their care.

It will be supported by an extension of neighbourhood watch schemes, which are vital in deterring theft and burglaries.

Public confidence in the police is enhanced when people know what they can expect from their local police force, and when outsiders are let into the process of inspecting how they work. At least five police forces are already leading the way with charters setting out their targets.

● We are continuing to increase police numbers. There will be 1,000 extra police officers this year.

● We will continue to give the police the support and resources they need to carry out their duties effectively and efficiently.

● We will be seeking the nation-wide introduction of community policing.

● We will encourage civilianisation as a means of freeing police officers for operational duties.

● We will encourage the extension of neighbourhood watch to more residential areas.

● We will continue to increase the special constabulary, which has seen a rise in recruitment this year of ten per cent.

● We want each police force to produce a charter telling local people, for example, how quickly the police will aim to respond to emergency calls.

● We will introduce lay inspectors with management experience into the police inspectorate.

Protectors and Victims

We look to the police to protect us. They risk their lives to do so. Police officers are entitled to the protection of the community they serve. Those who indulge in the shameful practice of 'ambushing', or seeking to frustrate the work of the emergency services, deserve to face severe penalties. We welcome the findings of a study by the Home Office and Crown Prosecution Service which shows that assaults on policemen attract consistently heavier penalties. But we will examine ways of introducing further protection for the police.

We must also pay special attention to the needs of the victims of crime, in the courts and in rebuilding their lives. We have increased funding for victim support. The number of people directly affected by violent and sexual crime remains relatively small. But fear of crime can have a devastating effect on people's lives, and particularly on women's lives. We are determined to reduce this fear.

● We will set up a working party to examine what more can be done to protect the police and members of other emergency services from assault.

● We will encourage victims to report sexual offences by giving them statutory anonymity.

● Under our safer cities programme, there are 124 schemes to improve street lighting, which has been shown to reduce the fear of crime significantly.

● Women-only taxi services are being encouraged under the same safer cities programme.

Penalties and Prevention

Our armoury of criminal law and penalties requires constant review. We have just introduced a new law specifically aimed at the so-called joy-rider. This places the responsibility for dangerous driving, damage, injury or death following from the taking of a vehicle squarely on the shoulders of those in it. Even where joy-riding is not involved, causing death through dangerous or drink driving is a very serious offence. We believe that the maximum sentence for such a crime should reflect its gravity.

Squatting is nothing less than the seizure of another's property without consent. Having consulted widely on the subject, we have decided to extend the criminal law dealing with squatting. Illegal camping by gypsies or other travellers can affect the lives of whole communities. We believe that this problem must be tackled.

We are concerned about the small but persistent minority, particularly of young people, who re-offend while already on bail. We have announced new measures to deter them from repeated crime. Young people who find themselves on probation for shop-lifting, vandalism or petty thuggery should be shown where the path of crime may lead. They should be given a brief personal experience of the nature of prison life.

● Joy-riders will now face prison sentences of up to five years, unlimited fines and unlimited driving bans.

● We will extend the maximum sentence for causing death through dangerous or drink driving.

● We will create a new criminal offence of squatting, to give greater protection to the owners and occupants of shops, commercial premises, houses and flats.

● The 1968 Caravan Sites Act will be reviewed with the aim of reducing the nuisance of illegal encampments.

● As part of a community sentence, young offenders will be taken to see what life is really like inside one of our prisons — a sobering experience for them.
● We will introduce a new police power to make an arrest for breach of police bail.
● We will give the courts the statutory power to increase sentences for those who offend while on bail.
● We will increase the number of bail hostel places, to enable closer supervision of those on bail.
● We will mount a drive against school truancy, and set up a task force to find the best ways of co-ordinating the work of local agencies helping young people at risk of becoming offenders.

Reforming our Prisons

Prisons should be places which are austere but decent, providing a busy and positive regime which prepares prisoners for their ultimate release. We have been reversing the Labour party's neglect of the prison service in the 1970s. Since 1985, 14 new prisons have been opened. Seven more will open over the next two years. The end of overcrowding is now in sight.

We have already taken steps to implement the key recommendations of the Woolf report on the future of our prisons. We will bring private sector skills in to enhance efficiency and increase value for money. We have put out to tender the contract for prison escort services, an approach which has worked well in other countries. The first contract for a privately managed remand centre has been awarded.

● We will sustain our massive prison reform and building programme.
● A reconstruction programme will end the degrading need for "slopping out" by the end of 1994.
● We will reorganise prisoners' education, training and work opportunities.
● We will establish the prison service as a separate agency, whose director will have the clear responsibility for day-to-day operations. The home secretary will remain ministerially accountable to Parliament for prison policy.
● We will increase the use of private sector management skills.

Our Legal System

As a free society we must have a justice system that is fair, accessible and responsive to the citizen. We have introduced new powers for the Court of Appeal to increase sentences for crime. And in response to public concern about a small but significant number of miscarriages of justice, we have appointed a royal commission to review aspects of the criminal justice system, including the conduct of investigations, the handling of forensic evidence, and the powers of the Court of Appeal.

We have already reduced the opportunity for abuse by our introduction of tape-recorded interviews of suspects by the police. At the same time, we are concerned that police investigations should not be made more difficult by the misuse of certain rights. We have already introduced a wide range of reforms following our civil justice review. Extending the jurisdiction of the county courts has helped speed up justice. The success of the small claims system in these courts has shown that simplified procedures can enable people to conduct their own cases or rely on a lay adviser. We have also introduced a reform which will give people more choice as to who represents them legally in court.

We are committed to enabling people with limited means to have access to legal services. We are determined to ensure that these services are delivered efficiently, in a way which provides the best value for money. The principles of the Citizen's Charter are being applied to our legal system. We will shortly be publishing a courts charter. We are overhauling the way in which family matters are handled in our courts. The new family code will be applied by magistrates and judges especially trained in family law.

Our Sunday trading laws have come into question as a result of a possible conflict with Article 30 of the Treaty of Rome. This matter is now before the European Court of Justice, and we are awaiting a judgment. The government brought forward proposals in 1986 to reform the shopping laws, but Parliament was not able to agree a conclusion. Parliament will be given the opportunity to consider this issue again.

● We will introduce a major criminal justice bill in the lifetime of the new parliament.
● We will extend the types of cases which can be handled by the county courts in a simplified way.
● We will consult on a lay adjudicators scheme to make it easier for citizens to settle disputes with service providers.
● We will provide a code of family law that will continue to underpin the institution of marriage, give priority to the welfare of the child, and emphasise the primary responsibility of parents for the welfare of children and the family.
● We will bring forward proposals for reform of the Sunday trading laws once the legal position has been made clear by the European Court of Justice.

Pornography, Privacy, Libel

We have the toughest anti-pornography laws in Western Europe, and we will keep them that way. Every year, about 300,000 people — mostly women — request advice and assistance in dealing with obscene or malicious phone calls. We intend to do more to deter this harassment, in conjunction with the telecommunications industry.

The Press Complaints Commission is now in operation, and we will monitor its work carefully to see if self-regulation succeeds. The public's dislike of unprincipled press behaviour has sometimes been expressed in the award of erratically large libel damages. While this is understandable, it has led to an inordinate number of successful appeals. We therefore propose to simplify the law relating to libel in the light of the recommendations of the Neill Committee.

● British domestic controls on pornography will remain in place even after the completion of the single European market.

● We will increase the maximum penalties for making obscene or malicious phone calls.

● We propose to allow judges to settle the level of damages in libel cases where the defendant offers to pay to make amends.

Community Relations

Racial harmony demands restraint on all sides, and a tolerant understanding of the legitimate views of others. Everybody, regardless of ethnic background, religious or personal belief, has the right to go about his or her life free from the threat of intimidation and assault. We are determined that everyone lawfully settled in this country should enjoy the full range of opportunities in our society. That requires openness on the part of the majority, and, on the part of the ethnic minorities themselves, a determination to participate fully in the life of the wider community.

The Home Office invests £129 million in grants designed to encourage those running public services to ensure that people from ethnic minorities can enjoy the full range of public services — such as health, housing and social services. We believe that these grants would be more effective if responsibility was transferred to those departments which can make best use of the money.

● Racial and sexual discrimination have no place in our society. We have given the police stronger powers to deal with racial hatred. We will continue to ensure that the full force of the law is used to deal with racial attacks.

● We will transfer the education share of the Home Office's 'Section 11' money to the Department of Education, to focus help on those from ethnic minority backgrounds who need additional English language teaching.

Immigration and Refugees

Good community relations in this country depend upon a clear structure of immigration controls which are fair, understandable and properly enforced. We are determined to maintain our present system of immigration controls unless we have evidence that other arrangements would be equally satisfactory and cost-effective. But an increasing number of would-be immigrants from Eastern Europe and other parts of the world seek to abuse our openness to genuine refugees. The number of people seeking refugee status has risen from 5,000 a year to 45,000 over the past four years. We will continue to honour our commitent to the 1951 UN Convention, and give refuge to those who reach our shores with a well-founded fear of persecution.

● In the new parliament we must therefore reintroduce the Asylum Bill, opposed by Labour and the Liberal Democrats, to create a faster and more effective system of determining who are genuine political refugees and who are not.

● We will provide a fair and expeditious system for examining claims for refugee status. This will include a workable appeal system for applicants under which those with manifestly unfounded claims will be returned quickly to their own country or to the country they came from.

● Finger-printing will be introduced for asylum applicants, to prevent multiple applications and fraudulent benefit claims.

The Danger of Drugs

Illegal drug abuse poses a major threat to the fabric of our society. It can destroy the health and lives of young people in particular. We will tackle this problem with vigour. We have already taken action on a wide front:

— we have set up co-ordinators in every local education authority to train teachers about the harm drugs can do, and to bring the fight against drug abuse into the classroom;

— we have set up 16 local drug prevention teams in inner cities to tackle particular problem areas;

— we have created the national drugs intelligence unit at New Scotland Yard;

— we have taken the lead in Europe in pressing for the establishment of a Europe-wide drugs unit, as a first step towards a creation of a 'Europol';

— we have set up a network of 31 drug liaison officers in 19 different countries, tracking the international drugs traffickers who threaten Britain with their trade.

We now have the toughest sanctions in Western Europe against drug traffickers. A number of public services and voluntary bodies are engaged in fighting drug misuse at local level. Such efforts need co-ordination to ensure that local effort and dedication is directed to best effect.

● We will not legalise any banned drugs.

● We will bring forward proposals to ensure that the control of drug misuse is co-ordinated effectively.

● We intend to strengthen our confiscatory powers still further. And we will ensure that our

controls against drug-trafficking are not weakened by any changes in Europe.
● We will make it an offence to supply anabolic steroids to minors.

The Threat of Terrorism

Tragic and dangerous events remind us only too frequently of the need for the special measures provided by the Prevention of Terrorism Act. While Labour proposes to weaken or dismantle them, we know that for the safety of our citizens they must be continued, and the police effort against terrorism must be reinforced. We have set up in New Scotland Yard arrangements to co-ordinate the activities of all our police forces in the fight against terrorism.

We will provide the necessary measures and resources to combat terrorism, whether it comes from the IRA or other evil groups who seek to undermine our democracy.

RESPONSIBILITY FOR OTHERS

Conservatives believe we have responsibility one for another. We will continue to care for those in need and work to establish a society that is generous, as well as prosperous. Our health, care and social security systems are fundamental to government responsibilities; and we believe strongly in fostering voluntary services too.

The NHS Present and Future

The Conservative party is totally committed to the National Health Service. The government has set out in the patient's charter the principles on which the NHS is based. The most fundamental of these is that need, and not ability to pay, is and will remain the basis on which care is offered to all by the NHS. Since 1979, there have been great improvements in the health of the nation.
— Life expectancy has increased by two years.
— Deaths among babies and very young children have gone down by 40 per cent.
— Hospitals are treating well over a million more people a year as in-patients.
— Hospitals are treating over two million more people a year as out-patients.
— Kidney transplants have more than doubled.
— Hip replacements have increased by over 50 per cent.
— Coronary artery by-passes have nearly tripled.
Since 1979 the government has vastly increased the resources available to the NHS.
— We have increased overall funding for the NHS by 55 per cent after allowing for inflation. The cash increases in each of the three years up to 1992-3 have been the biggest ever.
— The number of doctors and dentists has been increased by 17,000, and the real resources committed to GP services have doubled since 1979.
— The number of nurses and midwives has gone up by 69,000.
— We have established the independent pay review body which nurses had sought for so long and increased their pay by 43 per cent. It is hard now to remember that Labour actually cut nurses' pay.
— We have restored the hospital building programme so savagely cut by Labour at the end of their last term of office.
But the Conservative Government has not simply spent more money on the NHS.
— We have reformed the organisation of the NHS to encourage those working in the service to respond to what patients want and need, and to get the most out of the increased money which the taxpayer provides.
At local level, health authorities now have the task of buying health care with their local share of the National Health budget. Hospitals can now be run by their own local team of doctors, nurses and managers. By April there will be 156 NHS Trusts, whose local boards will have extra freedoms to develop local NHS services. Another 156 hospitals have applied to become trusts from April 1993.
We have acted to reduce the long hours worked by junior doctors in hospitals. For the first time limits are being set on the number of hours which may be worked continuously. Good nursing is the essential complement to good medicine. We have introduced Project 2000 - a new approach to the professional training of nurses.
The GP has a crucial role to play in the development of health services. Under the Government's fund-holding initiative, doctors have control over their own spending on behalf of patients for the first time. Over 3,000 GPs will be fundholders by April, caring for 14 per cent of NHS patients. A further 2,500 are preparing to become fundholders in April 1993. As a result, new services are being offered at local surgeries and health centres. Many general practitioners have said that they would like to become involved in fund-holding. We have already extended the scope of the fund-holding scheme to allow general practitioners to provide services such as community nursing.
● We will, year by year, increase the level of real resources committed to the NHS. Savings made through greater efficiency will be ploughed back into the service.
● We will develop a comprehensive research and development strategy for the NHS.
● We will continue to develop the NHS Trust movement which places responsibility for managing hospitals and other services with local teams who are closest to patients.

● We will continue to encourage the involvement of doctors and other medical staff in the management of services.

● We will introduce powers for nurses to prescribe where appropriate.

● We will complete the implementation of Project 2000 training for nurses.

● We will set goals for the employment of women in professional and managerial posts in the NHS.

● We will ensure that, following maternity leave or a career break, all women working in the NHS, including those returning to nursing on a part-time or job-sharing basis, are able to return to work of a similar status or level to that which they left.

● We will ensure that the benefits of fund-holding arrangements are available to any GP who wishes to apply, and we will be ready to extend the scope of the scheme further as it develops.

The Patient's Charter

No one questions the dedication of those who work in the NHS. But before the government's reforms, the system did not always allow that dedication to produce the service which people should be able to expect. The patient's charter sets out clearly what is now expected from the NHS. We have already pledged that in future no one will wait more than two years for treatment on the NHS. In many parts of the country, for most treatments, the waiting time is much shorter than this; and we will seek further progress in reducing waiting times.

● Binding guarantees will be set locally for in-patient waiting times, starting with the operations where waiting causes most distress. To ensure that progress on waiting times continues, we intend that from March 31 1993, no one should have to wait more than 18 months for a hip or knee replacement, or a cataract operation. We are sure that, as now, many hospitals will be able to do better than this.

● We will move to a system under which a named nurse or midwife will be responsible for your care while you are in hospital.

● We will set specific targets for out-patient waiting times.

● We will make it easier for patients to find out what services are available from the NHS via a new national NHS information service.

● We will ensure that comparative information about the health standards achieved by health authorities is available to the public.

● Simple systems will be set up to allow complaints to be registered and responses given if things go wrong.

Strategy for Health

This government has embarked on the first ever strategy for health. Good health requires more than good NHS care when people are sick. A variety of factors — including preventive medicine, diet, exercise, sensible drinking and not smoking — can contribute substantially to improving health across the whole population.

● We will set health objectives to be achieved by the end of the century, including reductions in illness and death from heart disease and cancers.

● We will add new health objectives as the strategy develops.

Care Services

Care services for children, the elderly and the handicapped are provided by local government, health authorities, the private sector and voluntary groups, not directly by central government. But government is indirectly involved as the provider of taxpayers' money, and through its duty to set standards for publicly and privately provided care.

As the number of elderly people in the population grows, there will be more frail and vulnerable citizens who need support. Many of them will want to be cared for at home. Others will need residential or nursing home care. It is vital that people should have choice in the type of care available. In all cases people must be able to rely on the quality of care. As we move towards implementation of *Caring for People* in April 1993:

● We will take steps to ensure that individuals who need residential or nursing care continue to have a choice of homes, including independent homes. Money transferred from the social security budget to local social services departments will be used for this purpose.

● We will ensure that all local authorities publish information about the social services that are available, including information on standards and complaints procedures.

● We will provide choice in domiciliary and day care.

● We will provide further funding for voluntary organisations to play their vital part in the development of community care services.

● We will support the organisations which help those who care for friends and relatives at home.

Children

This government introduced the Children Act, a landmark in legislation to protect children. The Act requires childcare facilities to be registered to ensure that standards are maintained throughout the country. We believe that the diversity of childcare provision in the UK is one of its strengths. It offers parents real choice. Over 90 per cent of three to four-year-olds are engaged in some form of group activity. We shall continue to encourage the development of childcare arrangements in the voluntary and independent sectors.

● Each local authority will be asked to produce a local childcare plan setting out the provision available in their area.

● We will ensure that the standards implemented through the Children Act are applied sensibly, and do not discourage private or voluntary arrangements which are often best suited to the needs of children and parents.

● We will carry forward a family support initiative, encouraging the voluntary sector to work in partnership with families and local authorities.

Social Security

Our aim is to improve further and modernise Britain's social security system. We are providing more support than ever before — £14 for every £10 spent in 1979, after allowing for inflation. More importantly, this extra help is more clearly focused on those groups with the greatest needs — less well-off pensioners, disabled people and low income families. We have also sought to provide those on social security with better incentives to earn, and gain independence. All too often the old system created barriers to work and penalised the thrifty.

The benefit structure is now more flexible and easier to understand. The new benefits agency is simplifying forms and widening choice in methods of payment. We will complete the massive investment in new technology — Europe's biggest computerisation project — that has made it possible to raise the quality of service to the public. And we will extend 'Helplines' and other means of assistance with individual difficulties.

● We will continue to simplify social security forms wherever possible.

● We will set up a new family credit telephone advice service to support working families.

● We will establish a new agency to carry out all social security war pensions work with the aim of providing a better, more efficient service to war pensioners and war widows.

Security in Retirement

Britain's pensioners recognise the security that Conservative government brings — low inflation, savings that grow, firmness in the face of crime, public services that put the customer first. Those who have dedicated their lives to the service of the community deserve that stability. We will continue to give the fight against inflation our first priority. The basic state retirement pension will remain the foundation for retirement. We will continue to protect its value against price rises, as we have for the last 13 years.

We also recognise that some pensioners who have no savings or pensions from their jobs need extra help. So we will increase the additional support, already up by over £300 million a year since 1989, available to less well-off pensioners. The number of those over pensionable age will be far higher in the next century than it is today. If we do not make provision now, the burden we will place on our children will be too great. That is why we must encourage people to build up savings, investments, and occupational and personal pensions.

But Labour policy is hostile to such personal effort; Labour wants pensioners to depend on the state. Failure to control inflation meant that pensioners' incomes from savings were cut under the last Labour government.

About eight in 10 pensioners have some sort of second income to top up their state pension. By abolishing the hated earnings rule we have enabled pensioners to keep their retirement pension, even if they take a job in retirement. And we have increased the level of savings that is disregarded in working out entitlement to benefits for pensioners. Personal pensions have brought real choice into retirement provision. Over 4.5 million people have set up their own pensions since 1988. We want to see both occupational and personal provision expand much further in the course of the 1990s.

● As evidence of our continuing commitment to poorer pensioners, we have announced in the Budget an increase of £2 a week for single people, £3 a week for couples, in income support for pensioners. Combined with the increases this April, this measure will provide less well-off pensioners with between £5.75 and £10.70 a week extra.

● We will continue to pay, from April 1993, a rebate at the level recommended by the Government Actuary for all those who contract out of the State Earnings Related Pension Scheme.

● We will legislate to provide a new one per cent incentive for holders of personal pensions aged 30 and over from April 1993, when the existing incentive ends.

● We will consider proposals for a new system of rebates to come into effect from April 1996 with the aim of ensuring that personal pensions remain attractive across the age range.

● We are firmly committed to equal treatment for men and women in pensions. Following assessment of the responses to our discussion paper, we will bring forward legislation to achieve this.

Supporting Families

Our reforms have cut away the barriers that meant many breadwinners lost money if they went to work. Family credit has transformed the prospects of 350,000 low-income families. As a result of improvements since 1988, we have made available an extra £600 million a year in real terms to low-income families with children. But we also recognise that all families face extra costs in bringing up children. So we have raised child benefit. For a two-child family the increases we are making will, by April 1992, have raised the total value of child benefit by almost £3 in a single year, to £17.45 a week.

Our new child support agency will make sure that absent parents make a proper contribution — and that far more lone parents and their children get the maintenance that is theirs by right. And benefit changes make it easier for more families — including single parents — to combine work and family responsibilities.

● Child benefit will remain the cornerstone of our policy for all families with children. Its value will increase each year in line with prices.

● Child benefit will continue to be paid to all families, normally to the mother, and in respect of all children.

Help for Disabled People

Under the Conservatives, more disabled people than ever before are getting the help they need and deserve. Since 1979, the number receiving attendance allowance has more than trebled; the number receiving mobility allowance has risen six-fold; the number receiving invalid care allowance has risen 25-fold. Today we spend some £12,000 million a year on benefits for long-term sick and disabled people. Even after allowing for inflation, that is two-and-a-half times as much as Labour spent in the 1970s.

— Disability living allowance will bring together the existing attendance and mobility allowance, providing new help to many disabled people who at present get no such help. Disability working allowance will make it easier for disabled people to take up a job.

● We are introducing new disability benefits which will, in the next parliament, bring extra help to at least 300,000 people. By 1993-4 these and other improvements will mean that we will be directing an extra £300 million a year to long-term sick and disabled people.

● The independent living fund has proved a great success in giving severely disabled people an opportunity to live in the community. We are committed to maintaining a fund which supports the most severely disabled people.

The Voluntary Sector

Charities and voluntary groups play a vital role in our national life. Britain is rich in its citizens' willingness to give time, effort and money to helping others. We have a great tradition of voluntary work at home and overseas. There are now about 350,000 voluntary groups in Britain — and personal donations to charities now amount to some £5,000 million a year. We have done much to boost charitable giving.

— Under the payroll giving scheme, employees can now contribute up to £50 a month tax-free.

— Gifts and bequests have been exempted from inheritance tax.

— The gift aid scheme allows charities to claim tax relief on one-off gifts of more than £400 — a change just announced in the Budget.

— The maximum limit on single charitable gifts qualifying for income and corporation tax relief has been abolished.

The new charities legislation will ensure that charities are better managed and properly regulated. We believe this will enhance public confidence in charities and further boost charitable giving.

The government gives some £2,500 million a year to support the activities of the voluntary sector (including housing associations). Industry has been generous with its sponsorship and with technical support. But money is not the only contribution that government and business can make. Businesses have become much more practically involved in work in the community. And government could do more to encourage new forms of volunteering, to encourage the most effective use of the money it gives, and to bring together voluntary effort at the local and national level.

● We will continue to support the work of the voluntary sector and promote volunteering.

● We will work with voluntary agencies to develop, over the life of the next parliament, a national bank of information on opportunities for volunteering.

● We will encourage efforts to improve the co-ordination and promote the growth of local volunteer support, building on the success of neighbourhood watch to develop a network of voluntary help in local communities.

Animal Welfare

We are leading the European community in our achievements in improving animal welfare. We have also taken action at home and abroad to improve conservation, and will continue to do so. English Nature, which advises the government on wildlife issues, has embarked on an ambitious programme to restore endangered species. The Wildlife and Countryside Act 1981 provides special protection for 304 species of birds and animals, as well as protecting our heritage of wild plants.

We are firmly opposed to international trade in rare and protected species such as rhinoceroses, cheetahs, leopards, and bears. We have pushed successfully for an EC ban on large-scale drift nets that threatened dolphins, and we support the UN resolution calling for a moratorium on their use. We support the extension of the moratorium on commercial whaling and have co-sponsored resolutions against 'scientific' hunting of whales. We have successfully pressed for an EC ban on the import of baby seal products and of furs from those countries which permit leghold traps.

We have set up the farm animal welfare council and have brought in welfare codes covering livestock on farms and in transit. We are establishing an ethical committee to look at the effects of advanced techniques in animal breeding. We have banned the use of veal crates, and taken action to ensure humane slaughter. We insisted that we should retain our power to stop the export of live horses. At Maastricht we secured a landmark in animal welfare: our partners' agreement to a declaration that the welfare of animals should be taken into account in the framing of EC legislation.

We now have the toughest set of controls on animal experimentation in Europe, and the number of animals used in experiments has fallen steadily. We have supported stronger laws to protect badgers and stop cruel tethering, and have increased the penalties for organising animal fights and for cruelty.

● We will introduce a wildlife enhancement scheme and expand the species recovery scheme, both to be run by English Nature.

● We have tightened controls on the import of wild birds and will press the EC to do the same.

● We oppose resumption of the trade in ivory or elephant products, and will provide additional support for elephant conservation projects in Africa.

● We will urge our EC partners to bring animal welfare standards up to UK levels, for example by banning veal crates and stalls and tethers for pigs. We will press them to put into practice the principles of the Maastricht declaration.

● We will use our EC presidency to toughen up EC regulations and improve EC compliance with rules governing animal experiments.

● We will press for higher EC standards for the keeping of battery hens and for the care of animals in transit.

● We will not accept any weakening of our rabies prevention safeguards.

A BRIGHTER BRITAIN

Making Britain a brighter and better place in which to live requires a high quality physical environment — including housing, transport and reinvigorated urban areas. The Conservative commitment is both to the re-creation of our civic pride and also to the preservation and integrity of our rural heritage, founded on the core industry of agriculture. Our aim is to enhance life for the British people.

Home Ownership

The opportunity to own a home and pass it on is one of the most important rights an individual has in a free society. Conservatives have extended that right. It lies at the heart of our philosophy. We want to see wealth and security being passed down from generation to generation. Some four million more householders own their own homes compared with 1979. The number of former council tenants who have bought their homes has risen to 1.4 million.

We now need to make it easier for those council tenants living in high-cost areas or on low incomes to move gradually into home ownership, without taking on too heavy a financial burden at any one time. This will bring the benefits of home ownership within the reach of more people and introduce more diversity in local authority estates. We also want to help more leaseholders to own and control the management of their property.

But we recognise that not everyone can, or will want to, buy his or her home. So we are determined to encourage a strong private rented sector while continuing to safeguard the rights of existing regulated tenants. Bringing empty private sector dwellings back into use will extend choice, make it easier for people to move jobs, and help tackle homelessness.

● We will maintain mortgage tax relief.

● We will continue 'right to buy' discounts and ensure that local authorities respond reasonably and rapidly to applications.

● We will introduce a new nation-wide 'rents to mortgages' scheme, enabling council tenants to take a part-share in their home, gradually stepping up to full ownership.

● We will put more of the Housing Corporation's £2,000 million budget into do-it-yourself shared ownership. This will enable first time buyers to choose a home and buy a share of it — usually 50 per cent — with a housing association paying rent on the rest until they wish to increase their stake in the property.

● We will introduce commonhold legislation, giving residential leaseholders living in blocks of flats the right to acquire the freehold of their block at the market rate. Leaseholders of higher rated houses will also be given the right to buy the freehold of their property. Leaseholders who live in a block which does not qualify will have a new right to buy an extended lease.

● We will introduce statutory time limits for answers by local authorities to standard enquiries by house-buyers, and explore the idea of a new computerised property data bank bringing together information held by the Land Registry and other public bodies.

● We will extend nation-wide the scheme we have piloted to increase private renting, whereby housing associations manage properties, building trust between tenant and private sector landlord.

● As soon as possible in the new parliament, we will introduce a new 'rent a room' scheme under which home-owners will be able to let rooms to lodgers without having to pay tax on the rent they receive.

Meeting Housing Need

We are also committed to securing a better deal for council tenants and increasing the supply of affordable housing for those in housing need. We will introduce more choice, improve management of estates and create new rights as part of the tenant's charter. Our aim will be to give tenants a choice of landlord wherever possible, and make management of both council and housing association stock more responsive to the needs of tenants.

We will improve the way in which council housing is managed by bringing in new private sector providers operating on contract to the local authority. We will introduce more competition and choice, thereby improving services to the tenant and increasing accountability. And we intend to give council tenants new opportunities themselves to improve the flat or house in which they live.

We have already begun a process of large-scale voluntary transfer which allows local authority tenants to opt to transfer to a housing association. We wish to see this result in diversity, not local monopoly, and will therefore act to limit the size of blocks that can be transferred.

Nearly all new social housing is now being built by housing associations. Over the next three years, we are committed to spend nearly £6,000 million through the Housing Corporation to provide 153,000 homes. We will do more to bring into use properties owned by central and local government which are standing empty for no good reason. This will enable us to house more people on the waiting list and, in some cases, to provide more opportunities for homesteading.

Through estate action and housing action trusts we have invested £1,000 million in recent years in a concentrated attack on the country's worst housing estates. Some 360,000 dwellings have been improved as a result. As part of those programmes, on which we are committed to spend a further £1,400 million over the next three years, we are demolishing or redesigning tower blocks and deck access estates, rebuilding on a more human scale. Wherever we can, whenever tenants want it, and where resources allow, we will pull down the eyesores which have blotted our cityscapes and too often provided breeding grounds for crime and delinquency.

The government is spending about £100 million tackling the problem of rough sleeping in our cities. As a result we have seen a sharp fall in the numbers who sleep rough on our streets. Working closely with the voluntary sector we will continue to provide help for those sleeping rough, particularly in the capital.

● We will revolutionise the management of council houses and flats. Compulsory competitive tendering will oblige local authorities to bring in managers who demonstrate their ability to deliver the best services to tenants.

● We will continue our programme of large-scale voluntary transfer of council properties to housing associations. But in order to bring management closer to tenants, we intend to reduce the limit on the number of properties transferred in a single batch.

● We will give tenants a new 'right to improve', so they can receive compensation for certain home improvements which they undertake. And we will improve the existing 'right to repair'.

● We will continue our estate action and housing action trust programmes which concentrate resources on the worst council estates.

● We will enable tenants to apply for housing action trusts to take over and improve the worst estates.

● We will work with the Housing Corporation to establish a new ombudsman for housing association tenants. We will also encourage the corporation to extend opportunities for tenant involvement in the management of housing association properties.

● We will set up a task force — headed by an independent chairman — to help bring empty government residential properties back into use. These will either be sold or let on short term leases to those in housing need.

● As part of estate action we will introduce a new pilot scheme to promote homesteading. Local authorities will be encouraged to offer those in housing need the opportunity to restore and improve council properties. In exchange, homesteaders will pay a lower rent or be able to buy at a reduced price.

Transport

Under the Conservatives, transport in Britain is being transformed. More competition on the roads and in the air has led to better services and more choice. Our successful policies of deregulation and privatisation have gone hand-in-hand with a sustained and growing programme of investment. Over 1,000 miles of new trunk roads and motorway have been built, more than 100 bypasses constructed, and some 750 miles of railway electrified. Airlines now operate 50 per cent more flights. More people travel farther and more easily than ever before.

Over the next three years we are committed to the biggest investment in Britain's transport infrastructure in our history. We will also seek further opportunities for the private sector to contribute, as it has for example with the Channel tunnel, the Queen Elizabeth II bridge at Dartford, the second Severn bridge and the Birmingham northern ring road. We intend the proposed new rail link from the Channel tunnel to King's Cross to be taken forward by the private sector.

The Railways

We believe that the railways can play a bigger part in responding to Britain's growing transport needs, and are investing accordingly. Next year alone, British Rail's external finance will top £2,000 million. The new passenger's charter will help to raise the quality of service. For the first time ever performance targets will be set, widely published and rigorously monitored; fare levels will reflect the standards set; and discounts will be paid to regular travellers where performance targets are not met.

We believe that the best way to produce profound and lasting improvements on the railways is to end BR's state monopoly. We want to restore the pride and local commitment that died with nationalisation. We want to give the private sector the opportunity to operate existing rail services and introduce new ones, for both passengers and freight. A significant number of companies have already said that they want to introduce new railway services as soon as the monopoly is ended. We will give them that chance.

Our plans for the railways are designed to bring better services for all passengers as rapidly as possible. We believe that franchising provides the best way of achieving that. Long term, as performance improves and services become more commercially attractive as a result of bringing in private sector disciplines, it will make sense to consider whether some services can be sold outright. In the next parliament:

● By franchising, we will give the private sector the fullest opportunity to operate existing passenger railway services.

● Required standards of punctuality, reliability and quality of service will be specified by franchises; subsidy will continue to be provided where necessary; arrangements to sustain the current national network of services will be maintained; and through-ticketing will be required.

● A new rail regulator — who will ensure that all companies have fair access to the track — will award the franchises and make sure that the franchisees honour the terms of the contract.

● BR's accounting systems and internal structures will be reorganised. One part of BR will continue to be responsible for all track and infrastructure. The operating side of BR will continue to provide passenger services until they are franchised out to the private sector.

● The franchise areas will be decided only after technical discussions with BR. But our aim will be to franchise out services in such a way as to reflect regional and local identity and make operating sense. We want to recover a sense of pride in our railways and to recapture the spirit of the old regional companies.

● We will sell BR's freight operations outright. We will also sell its parcels business.

● We will be prepared to sell stations which we want to be centres of activity — either to franchisees or independent companies.

● The railway inspectorate will be given full powers to ensure the highest standards of safety.

Roads

Nine out of every ten journeys, whether passenger or freight, are made by road. We must therefore continue to provide an efficient road network. In the years ahead we will concentrate particularly on the bypass programme. As part of the Citizen's Charter, we will bring forward reforms which will enable the private sector to start filling the gaps in the motorway service area network and to introduce more variety. Rather than large, intrusive stations at long intervals we should see smaller, more frequent service areas providing a much wider range of facilities.

We will investigate ways of speeding up, within the Department of Transport, the procedures for building new roads. We will continue our campaign to keep 'coning off' on motorways to a minimum by extending lane rental schemes, under which contractors who fall behind schedule incur financial penalties. Next year two-thirds of all motorway maintenance work will be carried out in this way. Britain has the best road safety record in the EC. In spite of the vastly increased volume of traffic, fewer people are now killed on our roads than at any time since 1948. Our aim is to improve on that record still further.

In spite of the benefits they bring, cars carry an environmental cost. In Britain catalytic converters will be compulsory on all new cars from the end of 1992. This will eliminate virtually all harmful exhaust gases, except for the emission of CO^2. The only certain way of cutting CO^2 emissions is to encourage fuel efficiency. Action is needed at international level and we will play our full part. Buses have an increasingly important part to play. The deregulation of long-distance coach services has led to a major expansion in reliable and cheap services. Bus deregulation outside London has increased milage by 16 per cent. We now propose to take deregulation and privatisation further.

We will improve road transport by:
● Investing £6,300 million in our trunk road and motorway network over the next three years, concentrating particularly on bypasses. Some 40 new ones will be opened by 1995 on trunk roads alone.
● Increasing penalties for those convicted of drink driving.
● Installing cameras at dangerous road junctions to film those who drive through red traffic lights.
● Encouraging local councils, assisted by a special budget we have set aside, to introduce pedestrian priority areas and cycle lanes.
● Privatising the remaining 39 local authority bus companies.
● Deregulating buses in London and privatising the London Buses subsidiaries. A new London Bus Executive will be responsible for bus-stops, stands and stations and for contracting out socially necessary services. The concessionary fares scheme in London will continue.
● Changing the system under which motorway service areas are provided.
● Encouraging action internationally, and within our own motor industry, to promote more fuel efficient vehicles.

Aviation and Shipping

More competition in aviation means more choice, better services and lower fares. That is why we have been pressing within the EC for full liberalisation of services. We also want to see more transatlantic flights, particularly to regional airports. People in the regions should not have to travel to London in order to fly to the United States. Direct flights would boost local economies and apply downward pressure on fares. The key regional airports are still in local authority ownership. They should be well placed to benefit from an increase in the number of direct point-to-point flights. But if they are really to grow and prosper, they need access to private capital, freed from the constraints of public ownership.

Air safety cannot be compromised. Over the next five years the Civil Aviation Authority will invest £750 million in modernising its systems.

More can be done to cut some of the regulatory burdens our shipping industry faces. We will ensure that the recommendations of the government-industry joint working party are put into effect as rapidly as possible.
● We will further liberalise transatlantic air services and encourage more international flights to and from regional airports.
● We will encourage local authorities to sell their airports.
● We will reduce airport congestion by increasing the capacity of our air traffic control.
● We will continue to campaign within the EC for further liberalisation, particularly of cabotage, so that there are more commercial opportunities for British companies.

London's Transport

A major programme of renewal and modernisation is transforming public transport in London — including the biggest expansion of London's rail network since the 1930s. The £750 million upgrading of the Central Line is already under way, to be followed by a similar programme on the Northern Line; the Jubilee Line extension and Crossrail will follow. London Underground is planning to invest £3,500 million over the next three years. It has introduced an ambitious company plan which will lead to better service, cleaner trains and more staff at stations and on platforms. Their new charter will be published shortly.

Responsibility for the Docklands Light Railway has been transferred to the London Docklands Development Corporation. As its performance continues to improve, we expect to see growing private sector interest in purchasing it outright.
● We will seek to privatise the Docklands Light Railway during the lifetime of the next Parliament.
● The new Jubilee Line is being extended to Docklands and South East London and will be followed by the East-West Crossrail, linking Paddington to Liverpool Street. The Docklands Light Railway is being extended at an eventual cost of £800 million.
● London Underground's charter will set out tougher new standards and what it will do to compensate passengers should it fail to meet those standards.

Local Government

Local councillors — some 25,000 men and women throughout Britain — are responsible for some of our most important public services. Since 1979 we have sought to create an accountable local government system capable of delivering high quality local services at a price that local people are prepared to pay. Conservatives councils in shires, districts and cities have been at the forefront of

these reforms. In a responsive and efficient manner, they have demonstrated how to deliver good services at an affordable price. Over the past 13 years, we have:
— held down unjustified rises in the cost of local government;
— abolished the power of local councils to shift the burden of taxation on to local business, for the first time limiting the overall rise in business rates to no more than the rate of inflation;
— abolished an expensive and bureaucratic layer of government in London and other big cities;
— developed the local authority role from direct provider to effective enabler, encouraging many tenants to buy their own homes, allowing schools the freedom to manage their own affairs and improving the quality of local services by allowing private business to compete for contracts.

Labour threaten all these reforms. They would uncap local spending, leading to higher local and national taxes. They would uncap business rates, threatening a return to the 1980s when the English rate poundage rose 37 per cent more than inflation. They would abolish the requirement on local authorities to seek value for money through competitive tendering. They would remove the freedom of local communities to preserve their grammar schools. They would introduce a new, expensive layer of government bureaucracy at regional level. They would return local government finance to the bad old days of domestic rates, with unrestrained power for local councils to charge householders as much as they like. And they would abolish the Audit Commission, which not only maintains the probity of local government accounting, but also pioneered the drive for better quality of service and value for money in local government.

We now propose further reforms in the structure, finance and accountability of local government. In the meantime, we have transferred a further share of the burden of financing local services to central government. Today, local community chargepayers bear only a small proportion of the cost of local councils.

● We will set up a commission to examine, area by area, the appropriate local government arrangements in England. Local communities will be fully consulted and their loyalties and interests will be central to the commission's task in deciding whether in any area a single tier of local government could provide better accountability and greater efficiency.

● We are looking at ways in which the internal management of local authorities might become more effective.

● We are applying the principles of the Citizen's Charter to local government, requiring the publication of more information which will enable local people to judge the efficiency of their councils in providing services.

● We will continue to cap local spending where necessary.

● As we announced in the Budget, no one's uniform business rate will go up this year by more than the rate of inflation — 4.1 per cent. And we have speeded up the benefits of revaluation for those businesses who gain from it.

● In future years, we will maintain our pledge to prevent UBR poundage rising by more than inflation.

● We will replace the community charge with a new council tax in April 1993. The council tax will be simple and straightforward to administer. It will be fair and will rightly reflect both the value of the property and the number of adults who live in it.

● Single householders, who suffered under the rates, will receive a 25 per cent discount. By grouping properties into a limited number of bands, the council tax also avoids the punitive bills which would be imposed by an unfettered rating system of the kind proposed by Labour. Students and people on low incomes will not have to pay.

Cities

We take pride in our cities. Right across Britain they have been given a new lease of life. From London to Glasgow, from Cardiff to Newcastle, historic buildings have been restored and areas which had been run down have been transformed. The £4,000 million 'action for cities' programme underlines the Conservative commitment to our inner cities and the people who live there. It highlights our determination to spread opportunity as widely as possible. We want all our people to share in growing prosperity and to have a stake in the country's future. Much has been achieved in recent years. The urban development corporations and the wide range of central government grants have helped to regenerate many of our inner city areas. But more remains to be done.

The best way to restore the spirit of enterprise which first made our cities great is for local people, the private sector, the voluntary sector and local and central government, to work together in partnership. That is the principle which lies behind City Challenge. Its new approach of competitive bidding has already galvanized towns and cities into bringing forward imaginative proposals for regeneration. It has improved co-ordination, secured better value for money and encouraged programmes which tackle problems on a number of fronts.

● We will continue to extend City Challenge and allocate a greater proportion of resources by competitive bidding.

● We will support urban development corporations in their critical task of urban regeneration.

● We will bring together resources for targeted inner city programmes into a single budget. This will mean that funding will go where it is most needed locally rather than according to a set of priorities determined in Whitehall.

● We will strengthen the machinery for co-ordination in the regions. New, integrated regional offices of the appropriate Whitehall departments will be established so that business and local government will have only one port of call.

● We will establish a new urban regeneration agency to pull together our efforts to clear up and develop derelict land, helping to bring it back into commercial use and provide new opportunities for local people.

Working in the urban areas, the URA will administer much of the urban programme of the Department of the Environment. It will have a dual function. First, outside the existing UDC areas, it will reclaim derelict land, assembling suitable sites for redevelopment using vesting or compulsory purchase powers where necessary. Second, it will itself be able to develop land in partnership with the private sector. This represents a major step forward in unlocking the commercial potential of our inner cities and of breathing new life into areas which may have been derelict for many years.

But our focus is not just on physical regeneration. We want to see more opportunities for training, more encouragement to enterprise, better education and more measures to tackle drugs and crime. Encouraging enterprise, improving the environment and providing new opportunities for the unemployed are central to our inner city policies. Remotivating individuals and providing the right conditions for business are the only ways to make lasting change.

● We will offer the loan guarantee scheme for small firms on more generous terms in inner city areas. The scheme will be extended from task force areas to include successful City Challenge bidders.

● We will make more people eligible for our successful job interview guarantee scheme, which links unemployed people with local jobs.

● We will carry out pilot projects for the 'foyer' concept, whereby young people are given a place in a hotel if in exchange they give a commitment to train and look for work.

● We will pilot a number of 'back to work' bonus schemes in inner city areas for the long-term unemployed.

● We will extend customised training under the job link programme to include City Challenge areas.

● We will make inner city task force and City Challenge areas eligible for regional innovation grants.

We are also determined to raise standards in our inner city schools, to crack down on truancy, and to help prepare young people for the world of work. The city technology colleges show what can be done. They are overwhelmingly popular with parents and pupils and are doing much to raise standards for children of all abilities in the inner cities. Under the Citizen's Charter, we shall soon be able to identify much more precisely than ever before those schools which are delivering unacceptably low standards. So will parents. We will publish test results, exam results and truancy rates and ensure that there is regular independent inspection. This will enable us to put the spotlight on those inner city local education authorities and schools which are failing their pupils.

● We will continue to seek opportunities to open new CTCs in deprived inner city areas.

● We will ensure that more schools, especially in the inner cities, have the opportunity to develop their technological expertise.

Tackling crime and the fear of crime forms a vital part of the strategy to make our inner cities better places to live and work. The safer cities initiative, launched in 1988, has successfully brought together local groups and agencies to tackle crime in some of our worst affected urban areas. Twenty schemes are already in operation.

● We will double the number of safer cities schemes to cover 40 urban areas.

London

London is a magnet to visitors and business from across the world. Since 1979 we have invested heavily to secure that status. Billions of pounds have gone into improving air, rail and underground links. We will continue that programme of modernisation. We are determined to sustain into the next century London's special position as one of the world's leading capital cities. We reject Labour's plan to recreate a bureaucratic and wasteful GLC. Instead, as part of our millennium programme, we will launch a London 2000 initiative. The Secretary of State for the Environment will convene a new private sector forum to promote London internationally as a business, tourist and cultural centre.

The secretary of state will also chair a new Cabinet sub-committee to bring together ministers from all key departments and co-ordinate policy for the further improvement of London. A single minister will be given responsibility for co-ordinating London's transport services. London's place as a world centre for financial and insurance services is pre-eminent; we intend to keep it that way. And we will support the vigorous cultural life of the capital, which has seen new galleries, theatres and museums opening over the last decade.

● We will launch a London 2000 initiative.

● We will convene a new private sector forum to promote London's position internationally.
● We will establish a new cabinet subcommittee to coordinate policy on London.
● We will give a single transport minister responsibility for services in London. He will chair a new transport working group which will bring together public transport operators — from both public and private sectors — to discuss transport issues in London.

The Countryside

We have always cared for the countryside. We support its major industries and way of life, while recognising the place it holds in the hearts of those who live in towns. We want to protect our most beautiful landscapes, conserve the abundance and variety of our wildlife and habitats, promote access and public enjoyment of the countryside, and encourage public participation in caring for the countryside.

But the countryside is more than just a pretty picture. It is a place where people live and work, as they have done in the past and will do in the future. In providing our public services, we will continue to recognise the particular needs of people who live in the countryside. We will continue to promote a diverse rural economy, balancing the need for jobs, housing and services in rural areas with protection of the rural environment.

Agriculture

Centuries of farming have shaped our countryside. Now farming is at a crossroads, both here and in the rest of the European community. World-wide pressure to reduce protectionist measures, and the need to contain the cost of the common agricultural policy, mean that farmers will face reduced support and increased competition. We believe that farming in the UK can meet these challenges. But many farmers will need help to adapt to the new conditions, and we will continue to provide assistance. It will become increasingly important for farmers to obtain a greater proportion of their income from the market. We will encourage farmers, retailers and manufacturers to work together to increase our share of the European food market.

We are committed to reducing the burden of regulation on business in general, and farming in particular. We will not accept UK farmers being put at a disadvantage by EC laws being applied differently in other countries. Responsible farmers have always combined efficient farming with care for the countryside. We will continue to encourage this approach through schemes to protect landscape and habitats of special importance. We will also maintain direct support for farming in the less favoured areas in ways which encourage good environmental practice.

● We will seek a reform of the CAP which brings agriculture closer to the market; reduces the costs to taxpayers and consumers; is implemented at a pace which the industry can bear; affects all community farmers equitably, regardless of size or location; and recognises the importance of environmental protection.
● We will build on the producer marketing initiatives which we have already launched, including the group marketing grant.
● We will assist the Milk Marketing Board's move to a new structure which will be better able to protect the interest of producers and consumers in the single market.
● We will publish target response times for grant and licence applications made to the Ministry of Agriculture.
● We will take forward proposals for radical liberalisation of the agricultural tenancy laws in order to make more land available for rent, especially for new entrants.
● We will enforce effective pollution control regulations while helping farmers to meet the high standards required.
● We will press for an agreement in the EC's agricultural council which will allow us to provide financial encouragement for organic agriculture.

Forestry

Forestry is a traditional rural industry, which also affects the landscape, and gives pleasure to millions of people. The needs of a successful industry, landscape conservation, and public access must all be accommodated; and we will reorganise the Forestry Commission to reflect these objectives more effectively.
● We will plant a new national forest in the Midlands and community forests elsewhere.
● We will review the effectiveness of the current incentives for forestry investment.
● We will produce guidance on the preparation of local indicative forestry strategies designed to encourage new woodlands, while steering planting away from sensitive areas.

Fishing

Fishing is a vital industry in many parts of our islands. Many fishermen have done well in recent years but they now face great pressure on the fish stocks. This means that fishing quotas are likely to fall in coming years in order to preserve the long-term future of the fisheries. We will continue to work for the profitable and sustainable future of our fishing fleet.
● We are determined to see that the renegotiation of the Common Fisheries Policy protects the interests of UK fisherman and retains our share of the Community's fishing opportunities.

● We will introduce a balanced package of measures, including decommissioning and controls on fishing activity, to conserve fish and safeguard the future of the industry.

Rural Jobs and Services

Changes in agriculture and other traditional industries will affect employment opportunities in the countryside. We will continue to target help through the rural development commission, and ask the RDC to review the rural development areas to ensure that its efforts are targeted on the areas of most need. We are committed to developing tourism in ways which provide all-year-round jobs and bring benefit to less well-known parts of our countryside, without damaging the environment. We have recently published new planning policy guidance which makes it clear how the countryside can benefit from new businesses and jobs, if the location and design of development are handled with sensitivity.

In local government, many of our shire counties and districts have led the way in raising the quality of public service. Local post offices, local transport and local schools all have an important role to play in sustaining rural life.

● We will consult on our recently published draft planning policy guidance designed to provide a clear framework for decisions on developments to aid tourism.

● We will widen the availability of the rural development commission's successful redundant buildings grant scheme, and strengthen other RDC programmes.

● We will maintain our special programmes to promote affordable homes in rural areas.

● We are fully committed to maintaining a national network of post offices.

● We will continue to assist local authorities who want to subsidise rural transport.

● We will enable village schools that wish to apply for grant maintained status to do so in small groups, thus enabling them to share management tasks while still enjoying the benefits of independence.

● The expansion of GP fund-holding will bring particular benefits to rural areas because of the convenience of different services — such as physiotherapy and consultant appointments — being offered in the GP's surgery.

Caring for the Countryside

Some of our finest landscapes are designated as national parks. All national park authorities will become independent boards, which will make it easier for them to carry out their tasks effectively. The New Forest will be given a statutory status which will give it as great a level of protection as any national park. Last summer the government launched an experiment in 'countryside stewardship'. This aims to conserve, enhance and re-create fine landscapes so that they may be enjoyed and appreciated by the public. The response from farmers, landowners and environmental bodies has been very positive. We therefore propose to expand the scheme and to introduce a new scheme to preserve hedgerows — a much valued feature of the English landscape, and a haven for wildlife.

The government endorsed and supported the Countryside Commission's target designed to bring 120,000 miles of rights of way into good order by the end of the century. At parish level, individuals can work together either to safeguard the character of their local village, or to improve its appearance. Local action can also preserve local wildlife and habitats. Under the rural environmental action scheme, grants of up to £2,000 per project will be available to support local environmental action.

The government is keen to promote the fullest possible use of inland waterways for leisure, recreation and amenity, in the regeneration of inner cities and for freight transport where appropriate. But we recognise that the various uses of canals and rivers must be properly managed to protect the character and environment of the waterways.

● We will expand the countryside stewardship scheme to cover the conservation of historic landscapes, meadows, pasture and hedgerows. Public access to qualifying schemes will be encouraged.

● We will introduce a hedgerow incentive scheme to help preserve hedgerows of particular historic, landscape or wildlife importance.

● We will contribute to the Countryside Commission's 'new parish path partnership' designed to stimulate local maintenance and improvement schemes.

● We will continue to support the development and redevelopment of our canals, as well as enhancing the environmental standards of our waterways.

The Environment

The Conservative party's commitment to the environment is beyond doubt. Other parties promise the earth. We have taken action — both nationally and internationally — to preserve it. Environmental protection can impose financial costs on producers, consumers and taxpayers, so we must make sure the threat of damage is a real one. But we also accept the precautionary principle — the need to act, where there is significant risk of damage, before the scientific evidence is conclusive. And we recognise that higher environmental standards can offer new opportunities for business. We published the first comprehensive white paper on the environment in 1990. It covered everything from the stratosphere to the street corner. We will continue to publish annual progress reports.

This Conservative government has taken a lead in working to protect the ozone layer. We will strive to accelerate the eradication of ozone depleting substances. One of the most important issues facing all countries is the threat of global warming. Effective action to combat global warming must be international action. Again we have taken a lead. The prime minister was the first world leader to announce his intention to attend the Earth Summit in Rio de Janeiro this June. We have said that we will consider stabilising our CO_2 emissions earlier than our existing conditional target of 2005. We have promised to provide new and additional resources to help the developing countries to tackle their environmental problems.

Within Britain, and ahead of other European countries, we have introduced the concept of integrated pollution control. We have set up, for the first time, powerful coordinating machinery within Whitehall to ensure that environmental considerations are given due weight in all decision-making. We are committed to openness on environmental matters. We support the establishment of a European environment agency to provide a Europe-wide environmental database. We believe that the public should have access to information held by the pollution control authorities. Public registers are now provided by bodies such as the National Rivers Authority and Her Majesty's Inspectorate of Pollution.

● We will establish a new environment agency which will bring together the functions of the National Rivers Authority, Her Majesty's Inspectorate of Pollution and the waste regulation functions of local authorities.

● The new EA will have a statutory duty to publish an annual state of the environment report.

● Within the European community we will press for the introduction of integrated pollution control on the UK model.

TOWARDS THE MILLENNIUM

A more prosperous Britain can afford to be ambitious. We can aspire to excellence in the arts, broadcasting and sport. We can use our increased leisure time, energy and money, to improve life for ourselves and our families. The national lottery we propose to introduce can be used to restore our heritage and promote projects which will become a source of national pride. National lotteries have been found useful at several times in our history. The British Museum was founded out of the proceeds of such a lottery. Fourteen years ago, a royal commission recommended the creation of a national lottery in Britain to provide extra money for deserving causes. The case has become even stronger as British people gain more opportunities to participate in foreign lotteries — thus increasing the risk that funds which we could put to good use in Britain will be diverted abroad.

We believe a well-run, carefully controlled form of national lottery would be popular, while raising money for many good causes. We will canvass views on how such a lottery should be run and controlled, and how it would fit within the pattern of charitable fund-raising in Britain. We believe that the funds generated by a national lottery should be used to enhance the life of our nation. People who enjoy the arts, sport, Britain's heritage and fine countryside could all benefit from the proceeds from a national lottery. Charities, right across the country and covering such areas as medical research, will also be potential beneficiaries.

The Millennium Fund

We will be consulting widely on the best way to distribute the proceeds of a lottery. But we have decided that part of the proceeds should be put aside, year by year, into a millennium fund specifically dedicated to projects which will commemorate the start of the twenty-first century and will be enjoyed by future generations.

● We therefore propose to introduce a national lottery from 1994, which would help provide funds for a number of good causes in the artistic, sporting, heritage and charitable fields — and from which some funds would be put aside for a millennium fund.

The millennium fund could be used, for example:

● To restore the fabric of our nation: our great inheritance of buildings which symbolise and enrich our national life.

● To help endow our cities and regions with facilities to enhance the celebration of United Kingdom 2000, such as the sporting facilities Manchester would need to host the 2000 Olympics.

● To help another major city — chosen by competition — to hold an international trade fair designed to be a showcase of British innovation for the twenty-first century.

● To enable voluntary groups and local communities to bid for funding for their own millennium projects for local restoration schemes, or for improving the amenities of canals and rivers, as a source of enjoyment for local people and a habitat for wildlife.

● To provide millennium bursaries for young people (and newly retired people) offering their time, energy and commitment to schemes designed to change the face of the United Kingdom by the year 2000.

The Arts

Britain has a great artistic heritage and a lively contemporary arts scene. The arts have flourished in recent years, with growing attendance at theatre, opera, dance and arts festivals. We have supported this by increasing the public funding of the arts, by 60 per cent in real terms since 1979, and introducing new incentives to personal giving. The arts have also forged new partnerships with local authorities, businesses and private patrons. Business sponsorship in particular has expanded hugely.

We have set up new regional arts boards and supported the Scottish and Welsh Arts Councils in order to diversify and enrich cultural life throughout the country. We have financed the European arts festival to be held throughout Britain during our presidency of the community in the second half of this year, as well as the first national music day in June. In this year's Budget, we announced further tax relief on film-making in this country. Our aim is to make the performing arts, museums and our heritage accessible to all. We will encourage the young to become involved and will facilitate access for the disabled.

● The national lottery will provide a new source of finance for the arts.

● We will maintain support for the arts and continue to develop schemes for greater sponsorship in co-operation with business and private individuals.

● We will re-examine the role of the Arts Council, as many of its functions are now carried out regionally.

● We will continue our support of libraries as educational, cultural and community centres, and urge local authorities to keep up standards. We will complete the new British Library building for which we have provided £450 million.

Sport

Success in sport is a source of national pride. Enjoyment of sport can enrich every life. We have given strong support to the Sports Council and its efforts to raise participation in sport. We actively support Manchester's bid to bring the Olympic Games to Britain. We want to restore the good image of football. Tough action has cut down football hooliganism. We have helped to establish the Football Trust, which now devotes £20 million a year to improving the safety of grounds.

Under the national curriculum all primary and secondary age pupils will follow a course of PE. All pupils will be taught to swim by the age of 11.

We will continue to encourage private sector sponsorship of sport. We will encourage more effective use of local sport and leisure facilities through compulsory competitive tendering. We want to see more dual use of school playing fields and halls and will give schools more freedom in their management. We are asking local education authorities not to make sales of school playing fields in future unless there is no evidence of long-term need.

● Sport, too, will benefit from the resources generated by the national lottery.

● We will actively support Britain's bid to host the 2000 Olympic Games in Manchester. We will provide £55 million towards the preparation of the site and key facilities in the first stage of the bid, and we will ensure that the project, whether successful or not, contributes to the effective regeneration of east Manchester.

● We will set up a new business sponsorship for sport scheme. This is expected to raise £6 million in its first year to support local and youth sport.

Our Heritage

Public interest and involvement in Britain's heritage has never been greater. We have created in the past decade English Heritage and the National Heritage Memorial Fund to give greater focus and drive to the government's policies. The National Trust and private owners take a leading part in preserving our almost unrivalled heritage. Government will work in partnership to secure our heritage for the benefit of future generations.

Our cathedrals are among our national glories. We therefore launched the cathedral repair grant scheme in April 1991, providing £11.5 million over three years.

We have increased, to £12 million, the grant to the NHMF for the purchase of historic properties, objects and collections. The government also provides help to private owners through English Heritage repair grants, and tax relief in return for commitments on upkeep and public access. We want to preserve the special character of our old town and city centres. We will encourage councils to ensure that new developments are in character with the past; to maintain buildings of importance to the character of towns and cities; to limit unnecessary street furniture and signs; and to plant trees and preserve historic patterns and open spaces.

● The national lottery will also provide funds for the preservation of our heritage.

● We will continue to provide substantial financial assistance for the protection and preservation of the heritage.

● Together with the heritage agencies, we will work to make heritage sites accessible to the public.

Broadcasting

We are proud of our record of extending choice, encouraging new producers and maintaining high standards in broadcasting. We opened the way to the setting-up of Channel 4, independent radio, satellite television and multi-channel cable TV networks. The 1990 Broadcasting Act means

Broadcasting

that three new independent radio services and a fifth television channel will be set up during the next Parliament. Over two million homes already receive satellite TV. We have now licensed well over 100 cable TV networks and this new industry expects to invest £3,000 million over the next five years. In coming years, British viewers will have an increasing choice of channels and programmes. The new and sophisticated cable networks will open the way not only to new telecommunication services, but also to the spread of emerging technologies such as high definition television.

We attach great importance to the work of the Broadcasting Standards Council, which we set up under the 1990 Act. All television and radio companies accept the need to maintain standards of taste and decency in their treatment of sex and violence and their use of bad language.

The European community regulates standards in satellite broadcasts originating from each member state. We were one of the first countries to ratify a new Council of Europe convention applying similar rules to all its member states. We also, in the Broadcasting Act, brought in sanctions against the transmission of offensive satellite broadcasts from abroad, and made it an offence for advertisers and equipment suppliers to support such programmes.

Independent television producers are benefiting from the requirement put on the BBC and ITV to commission a quarter of all their programmes, excluding the news, from outsiders. There are now great opportunities for independent producers to sell their programmes to new television channels and international markets, and there is much greater choice for viewers as a result.

In 1996, the BBC's Charter comes up for renewal. This will be considered against the background of the much more varied and competitive broadcasting environment which our policies have created. It is important that there should be a wide public debate about the future direction the BBC should take.

● We will back the work of the Broadcasting Standards Council and remain vigilant about ensuring high standards in satellite broadcast from abroad.

● We will publish a discussion paper on the future of the BBC recognising its special responsibilities for providing public service broadcasting.

A UNITED KINGDOM

The United Kingdom is far greater than the sum of its parts. Over many centuries its nations have worked, and frequently fought, side by side. Together, we have made a unique mark on history. Together, we hold a special place in international affairs. To break up the union now would diminish our influence for good in the world, just at the time when it is most needed.

Nationalist plans for independence are a recipe for weakness and isolation. Higher taxes and political uncertainty would deter investment and destroy jobs. The costly Labour and Liberal devolution proposals for Scotland and Wales have the same drawbacks. They do not intend to bring about separation, but run that risk. They could feed, but not resolve, grievances that arise in different parts of Britain. They would deprive Scotland and Wales of their rightful seats in the United Kingdom cabinet, seats the Conservatives are determined to preserve. We believe strongly that we should go on working together in full partnership in a Union that has served every part of the United Kingdom well.

The plans for devolution put forward by the other parties would have a grave impact not just on Wales, but also on England. They propose new and costly regional assemblies for which there is no demand. We will oppose all such unnecessary layers of government. The Union has brought us strength both economically and politically. Yet it has preserved the historic and cultural diversity of our islands. Our constitution is flexible, fair and tolerant. It has made this country one of the best places in which to live, work and bring up our children. These benefits cannot be tossed away lightly. We will fight to preserve the union, a promise which only the Conservatives can give at this election.

Scotland

Scotland has achieved an economic and cultural regeneration over the past 13 years. The Scottish economy has responded vigorously to the policies we have introduced to liberate enterprise, and many more people are now saving, investing and owning their homes. The public services are better funded and more efficient. There has been a flowering of Scottish culture.

Scotland enjoys a rich and distinct tradition and her own institutions, which we have preserved and strengthened. Scotland has its own framework for the encouragement of enterprise, investment and training; its own education system which continues to excel, with more pupils leaving school better qualified and more going on to further and higher education; its own health budgets which deliver high standards of care; and its own glorious inheritance of buildings and countryside.

A separate manifesto for Scotland sets out our record in detail and our proposals for building on these achievements. In this document, therefore, we list only a selection.

● Business in Scotland has received a boost from our creation of Scottish Enterprise and the local enterprise companies. We have formed Scottish Trade International to help our exporters, as

Locate in Scotland does for inward investors. To assist business further, we will complete the harmonisation of business rates in Scotland with those in the rest of the country.

● The massive bureaucracies and layers of local government have few supporters in Scotland. We will continue to press local authorities to provide the value for money and the quality of services that people expect. We will press ahead with the reform of the current burdensome system of local government by introducing single tier councils throughout Scotland.

● We will continue to strengthen Scotland's education system for the benefit of parents, pupils and teachers. We will respond to the proposals of the Howie committee to ensure that upper secondary education matches the best in Europe. We will continue to increase the number of places in higher and further education and will complete our reforms of the system.

● We will extend our reforms to improve NHS patient care in Scotland. Scotland has led the way in setting limits to waiting-times for operations and will now be reducing these further.

● We are creating a new body, Scottish Natural Heritage, with overall responsibility for conserving the natural environment. We will go further, and will create a Scottish environmental protection agency to bring together powers to ensure the quality of our air, rivers and bathing waters.

Wales

Since 1979, the economy of Wales has changed spectacularly. With only five per cent of the United Kingdom's population, Wales has consistently enjoyed 20 per cent of its inward investment. New industries have sprung up. Self-employment has risen by two-thirds. Welsh manufacturing now has the highest productivity of any part in the United Kingdom.

Land made derelict by old industries has been reclaimed on a massive scale. The Cardiff Bay development and the Ebbw Vale garden festival are outstanding examples, together with the programme for the Valleys. Since 1979, we have spent more than £3,000 million on roads in Wales. Spending on health has increased by 60 per cent in real terms since 1979. We have spent more than £5 million on our radical 'waiting times initiative', leading to the treatment of 35,000 extra patients. In school we are spending nearly half as much again, in real terms per pupil, as in 1979. And there has been an enormous expansion in the training budget.

More Welsh homes — 72 per cent — are owned by those who live in them than in the United Kingdom as a whole. Since the right to buy was introduced in 1980, we have enabled almost 90,000 council and housing association tenants to buy their own homes.

A separate manifesto, in both English and Welsh, sets out our full programme for building on these achievements for Wales.

● We will set up a Welsh economic council to bring together the various bodies with interests in inward investment, tourism and small business to advise the secretary of state.

● We aim to remove all significant dereliction from Wales by the end of the new Parliament.

● We will promote the work of the Countryside Council for Wales, in order to protect the countryside and those who earn their livelihood there.

● We will give further resources to our rural initiative. And we will continue to support hill farmers through the hill livestock compensatory allowances.

● We will continue to invest heavily in road improvements, including the second Severn bridge, completing the M4 in South Wales and the A55 in North Wales.

● We will continue with our record hospital building programme.

● We will continue to offer generous funding for housing for Wales and concentrate our efforts on the special needs of rural Wales. All major publicly funded housing developments will make adequate provision for the less well off.

● We will introduce a new Welsh Language Act.

● We will publish a white paper on local government reform this autumn with a view to establishing unitary authorities, based on the historic counties and county boroughs. We will ensure a full role for community councils under these arrangements.

Northern Ireland

We have upheld our pledge that Northern Ireland will remain an integral part of the United Kingdom in accordance with the democratically expressed wishes of the majority of the people who live there. It is a pledge that only the Conservative and Unionist Party can give. Conservative candidates are standing in our name and in that cause.

Our overriding objective in Northern Ireland is to eliminate the evil of terrorism. This requires progress in four areas: security, economic, social and political. The security forces in Northern Ireland perform their duties with courage and professionalism. They are entitled to expect all the necessary encouragement, and legal and material support from the government. Under the Conservatives, the strength of the RUC has been increased, while the Emergency Provisions Act 1991 contains new powers to combat terrorist funding.

Northern Ireland is sharing in the economic transformation of the United Kingdom as a result of Conservative policies. Belfast is attracting significant new private investment. Harland and Wolff and Shorts have been successfully privatised. Major work is also under way to regenerate

Londonderry and many of Ulster's smaller towns. We will continue to pursue policies to encourage enterprise and bring new jobs — by contrast with Labour, whose plan for a national minimum wage would hit the province particularly hard.

In the new parliament we will continue to seek to re-establish stable institutions of government in Northern Ireland, so that powers currently exercised by ministers in the Northern Ireland Office can be returned to locally elected politicians.

● We will always give the security forces our full backing within the rule of law, and — against Labour opposition — ensure that they have the special powers they need to protect the whole community from violence.

● We will complete the privatisation of Northern Ireland Electricity, transfer the water and sewage services to the private sector, and examine ways of bringing private sector skills into the management of Northern Ireland Railways.

● We will continue to pursue policies designed to alleviate social needs, to promote equity of treatment and to widen the sense of common purpose which is growing in the province.

● We will build on the close security cooperation that has been established with the Republic of Ireland under the Anglo-Irish agreement.

● We will continue to work strenuously for a political agreement which is acceptable to all the parties involved in the talks which the secretary of state has had during the past year with the main constitutional parties in Northern Ireland and the government of the Republic of Ireland. They have provided a firm basis for political progress in Ulster, and for building new relationships both between Northern Ireland and the Republic, and in these islands as a whole.

YOUR CHOICE AT THIS ELECTION

This election is about the future. Your future. Britain's future. Our future role in the world. This is a time to go forward with conviction and confidence, not to go back to the failure and bitter controversies of the past. It is difficult to remember the Britain we were elected to transform in 1979. The country we did transform. It was a depressed and divided country, accustomed to failure and suspicious of change.

During the succeeding parliaments, we have curbed inflation, reformed trade union law, encouraged enterprise, cut taxes, modernised our education and training, improved the management of our health service, given more help to the needy, extended ownership, helped through our vigilance to end the Cold War, widened our influence in Europe, and earned the respect of the world.

A decade of success ended with the problems of recession — a world recession. We know how tough it has been for many but we are poised to move forward again, lacking only the spark of confidence with which a Conservative victory would ignite recovery.

The Challenge Ahead

The challenges of the 1990s demand a responsible and sure-footed government which understands the nature of the achievements of the 1980s and is ready to build successfully on them. A government committed to the principles of choice, ownership, responsibility and opportunity; committed to low inflation and low taxes; committed to better quality and value in our public services; committed to strong defences. Labour cannot provide that leadership. They lack experience, principle and vision.

With socialism everywhere in rout or retreat, it is unclear what the Labour party stands for. For public consumption, Labour leaders purport to have jettisoned the principles of a life-time. But how much can they be trusted? How genuine is the conversion and what do they actually believe?

It is clear only that Labour would threaten our achievements, undo our reforms and hamstring Britain. They would turn the clock back to policies that impoverished and divided our country. Socialism here and abroad is the regret of yesterday not the hope of tomorrow.

Only the Best for Britain

We believe that only the best is good enough for Britain, and that the best will only be accomplished if we give the British people the freedom and the opportunity they need to succeed.

We have a new leader, proven in office, and a new agenda — yet a tried set of principles. Those principles reflect our conviction that Britain has done best when the people of Britain have been given the personal incentive to succeed. National success has not been primarily the result of accidents of geography, landscape and natural resources. Nor has it been the result of government action and state control. Success has been won when we have given our people their head: when their natural skills, talents, energy, thrift and inventiveness have been released, not suppressed. That was true when this century began; it is still true as this century draws to its close.

Britain should approach the millennium with head and spirits high, with a strong economy, with a high standard of living, with generously endowed and well managed public services, and with secure defences. We want Britain to be an example to the world of how a free people can make the very best of their destiny. That prospect is within the grasp of us all. We must now make it happen.

The prize is great, the hope invigorating, the dream attainable. We want, with you, to make the dream a reality. A Conservative government will help you to achieve the very best. The very best future for Britain.

Time to get Britain working again

In his foreword to the Labour Party manifesto, Mr Neil Kinnock, party leader and leader of the Opposition, said that the general election was a choice between a Conservative government paralysed by recession, and a Labour government determined to get on with building recovery.

He declared: "Gripped by the longest recession since the war, Britain needs a government with a clear sense of direction and purpose. A government with the people and the policies to get Britain working again and to achieve sustained recovery - strength with staying power. Labour will be such a government."

The country faced clear alternatives, he added. "A Conservative government would mean a repeat of the same stale policies which brought economic insecurity, privatised and underfunded public services and increased social division. The Conservatives have no policies which would mean sustained recovery, higher health care or improved educational standards. The arrogance remains which brought us the poll tax, centralisation in Britain and isolation in Europe. If they can't get it right in 13 years, they never will.

"The Labour government will mean a fresh start for Britain. It will mean strong and continued emphasis on investment for economic strength. It will mean action to help families, fair taxation, incentives for enterprise and support for essential community services. It will mean greater freedom, security and opportunity. It will mean change for the better.

"It's time to make that change. It's time for Labour."

IMMEDIATE ACTION FOR NATIONAL RECOVERY

Britain faces a huge task of national reconstruction. From day one, the new government must start to get Britain working again. It must get the economy out of recession, it must lay foundations for the future. Recovery must be based on investment, for only investment will create lasting prosperity.

Today, millions of people fear losing their job, their home or their business. The new Labour government's national recovery programme will start to remove that fear, with immediate action on investment, jobs and training. It will combat recession now and build sustained and sustainable recovery for the future.

Britain's economic problems are deep-seated. We will not be able to do at once everything that we would like to do. But we will get down to business right away. And as with any properly run business, our immediate programme will be part of a strategy for long-term success.

Action for industry

1. We will provide enhanced capital allowances to encourage companies immediately to bring forward manufacturing investment in new machinery and plant, innovation and design. This will last for a limited period.
2. We will introduce an investment tax incentive tailored to the special needs of small businesses.
3. We will immediately begin the phased release of receipts from the sale of council houses, land and property receipts to allow local authorities to build new homes and improve old ones. More building workers in the recession-savaged construction and building supply industries will be employed and more families rehoused. Equivalent arrangements will be made in Scotland.
4. We will allow British Rail to proceed with a leasing scheme of 188 new Networker trains on the North Kent line — the first step in securing private investment to help modernise Britain's railways and protect our environment.

Action for jobs

5. Housing investment will generate jobs. We will also establish a work programme, combining three days a week work for the unemployed — paid at the proper rate — with two days' training and job seeking. This will benefit the community and ensure that unemployed people are offered a range of employment and training opportunities. The programme, which can be quickly and easily established, will allow us to start bringing down unemployment immediately. Our aim is to prevent long-term unemployment, rather than just trying to cope with it after it has occurred.

Action for skills and schools

6. We will restore last year's training cuts which caused so much damage to training for young people and the unemployed. We will establish a new cash-limited *Skills for the 90s* fund, with an initial budget of £300 million, to upgrade the training of those in work. Investment will be targeted

particularly at areas of skill shortages and will give people who are now unskilled the chance to acquire basic skills.

7. Over the next 22 months, additional resources of at least £600 million will be available for investment in education. Amongst other projects, this will help to tackle equipment shortages and the backlog of school repairs.

Action for the NHS

8. Over the next 22 months, additional resources of at least £1 billion will be available for investment in the National Health Service. This will help the NHS to make real advances in care and treatment.

Action for children

9. We will start to increase nursery education places for three and four year olds by making sure that local councils actually use the money they receive for nursery education to create new places and by switching capital funds earmarked for the city technology college programmes. This will lead to the rapid creation of 25,000 new places.

10. We will extend the exemption from tax which applies to workplace nurseries to all forms of employer assistance with childcare.

Getting Results

Every action we propose makes sense by itself. Together, our proposals add up to a co-ordinated programme for recovery.

By investing in house-building and repairs, we start to rehouse homeless people.

By investing in public transport, we start to transform commuters' lives and create a cleaner environment.

By investing in the NHS, we offer new security to the patients and the public.

By investing in education, we nourish the talents of children and lay the basis for future success.

With each step, we employ more workers in industries from construction and computer software, to high-tech engineering, printing and publishing. We enable businesses to thrive. We save taxpayers' money on benefits. We transform unemployment claimants into employed contributors.

Labour's programme for national recovery will this year help bring Britain out of recession. Public investment will modernise services, help business and industry and stimulate private investment. It will make you and your family better off.

BUILDING A STRONG ECONOMY

Labour's economic policy rests on one simple, commonsense fact. The only way for Britain to build a strong economy is to make the goods and services which people at home and abroad want to buy.

Britain is in a race for economic survival and success. Faced with intense competition, companies and countries can succeed only by constantly improving their performance. Every employee in every enterprise must be involved in a new partnership so that trained and talented people can use the most modern technologies to create top-quality products.

But none of this will happen with a government that believes that the best thing is to do nothing. Three-thousand men and women have lost their jobs every working day since John Major became Prime Minister. Every week, 900 businesses go bankrupt. Every day, 200 families lose their homes.

The Conservatives have created the longest recession for 60 years. They have no idea how to get us out of it and even less idea how to stay out of it. Britain needs a Labour government which will back British industry in the way our competitors back theirs.

A Government which Business can do Business with

Modern government has a strategic role, not to replace the market but to ensure that the market works properly. Other competitors in Europe and elsewhere recognise that industrial policy must be at the heart of economic policy. It is the government's responsibility to create the conditions for enterprise to thrive.

Business needs sustained and balanced growth, stable exchange rates, steady and competitive interest rates and low inflation. We will deliver them.

Business must have a high level of education, science and skills. Incentives for high-tech investment. Modern transport. Strong regional economies for new developments. We will deliver them.

We will Keep Prices Down

Inflation has been suppressed by recession. But it has not been cured.

To curb inflation, Labour will maintain the value of the pound within the European Exchange Rate Mechanism. We will manage credit sensibly. We will stop excessive price rises in water, electricity, telephones, transport and NHS prescriptions.

The only way to defeat inflation in the medium term is to raise productivity substantially. By promoting investment and improving skills, we will tackle the underlying causes of inflation.

We will Introduce Fair Taxes

Attacking poverty is an essential component of Labour's programme for national recovery and prosperity. The most effective way to reduce poverty quickly is to increase child benefit and pensions and take low-paid people out of taxation. To achieve these goals, we will reform the national insurance and income tax system.

We will increase child benefit to £9.95 a week for all children, with the full value going to every family. This measure will benefit seven million families and is worth £127.40 a year to a family with two children.

We will increase the basic retirement pension by an extra £5 a week for a single person and £8 for a married couple. All pensioners will receive the full increase, which will also go to widows and others on benefits linked by statute to the basic pension level. Twelve million people will benefit.

We will abolish the two per cent national insurance contribution on earnings under £54 a week — effectively a £56 annual entry fee into the national insurance system.

At present, employees earning less than £405 a week pay contributions on all their earnings, while above that level no contributions are paid at all. This is an unfair anomaly in our tax structure. The ceiling on contributions will therefore be abolished.

We will take 740,000 taxpayers out of taxation altogether by increasing the personal allowance and wife's earned income allowance by more than inflation. Married couples will have the option of splitting the married couple's allowance between them as they choose.

The basic rate of tax will remain unchanged at 25 per cent, as will the 40 per cent rate. A new top rate income tax of 50 per cent will apply to individuals with an income of at least £40,000 this year.

Labour's tax and benefit changes are self-financing. They are fair. And they will make every individual employee on earnings up to at least £22,000 a year better off.

We will Reform Decision Making

Britain urgently needs a better way of making economic decisions. Government must decide at the same time how much to spend and how to pay for spending. The Budget should decide both.

Every autumn, we will make a *State of the Nation* report on the British economy. Our national economic assessment will then allow employers, trade unions and other social partners to consider Britain's competitiveness and the competing claims on national output. These considerations will be an important influence on collective bargaining.

In order to provide honest information about the state of the British economy, we will make the Central Statistical Office independent and free from political interference.

We will halt the deterioration which has taken place in the pay and conditions of many public service workers — often through pay settlements which have been arbitrarily imposed upon them. We will seek fairer and more rational ways of determining public sector pay within clearly defined budget limits.

We will Cut Unemployment

We are determined to make a swift reduction in unemployment and have explained in our national recovery programme just how this will be done. It includes immediate action for unemployed people, as well as direct investment — for instance, in construction — to create thousands of new jobs.

Steady and sustained economic growth will generate jobs that last. Better training will help people get back to work.

Unemployment must be tackled by the European Community as a whole. We will use our influence in Europe to secure the necessary policies for co-ordinated growth.

We will Modernise Britain's Industries

It is time to rebuild Britain's industrial strength. For lasting recovery, Britain needs a modern industrial policy designed to build skills, upgrade technology, encourage industry in every region and expand exports.

An investment decade for Britain will start with the immediate introduction of enhanced investment allowances. We will help Britain's high-technology industries with a 25 per cent tax credit for additional investment in research and development. Small firms will be assisted with a new investment scheme, combining a cash-limited fund for new investments with tax incentives tailored to their special needs.

Britain's industrial future depends on transforming our inventive genius into manufacturing strength. Labour will work with industry to establish British Technology Enterprise and create technology trusts throughout Britain, building bridges between industries and universities and helping firms turn good ideas into commercial products. We will encourage the development of the most modern telecommunications networks.

Labour's Minister for Science will develop a national strategy to promote high-quality science and technology, so that Britain can better anticipate and respond to the challenges of the future.

All over the world, industries face unprecedented environmental challenges. We will support new research into environmentally friendly technologies and launch a great environment exhibition to publicise and to promote sales of the cleanest British technologies.

We will Strengthen our Regional Economies

We will establish new regional development agencies in England, strengthen Scottish Enterprise and the Welsh Development Agency and modernise regional incentives. Regional agencies will become powerhouses for industrial development, encouraging investment, technology and skills. The Scottish parliament will have a vital role in building the competitive strength of the Scottish economy. Our new Welsh assembly will also have important economic responsibilities .

Labour's national investment bank, operating on strictly commercial lines, will bring public and private sector together to invest in long-term regional and national infrastructure projects.

Small and growing businesses will have a new deal. As well as the lowest possible interest rates, they need the backing on which their competitors can rely in France and Germany. Labour will establish a network of one-stop advice centres providing them with access to high-quality specialist assistance.

We will give special attention to the establishment of small businesses by women, and members of the ethnic minority communities, who often face difficulties raising venture capital.

Under the Conservatives, Britain has moved from manufacturing trade surplus to manufacturing trade deficit. The recent privatisation of the Export Credit Guarantee Department can only do further damage. Labour will create modern export services for the nation and the regions.

We will Invest in Modern Transport

Commuters and companies need fast, safe transport. Labour will act to make sure they get it.

It is absurd that French Railways can raise funds for new investment in the City of London, when British Rail is not allowed to do so. We will remove these restrictions. Leasing schemes will allow large-scale investments to be financed at relatively little cost to the public sector borrowing requirement.

Private finance will also be mobilised for a high-speed rail network which will eventually link every region to the Channel Tunnel, with proper environmental safeguards.

We will Improve Energy Supplies

Families, commerce and industry need heat, light and power at prices they can afford. Britain is well placed with reserves of coal, oil and gas which must be husbanded in a national energy policy to balance the needs of the present with those of the future. We will encourage enhanced recovery of oil from the North Sea and avoid becoming too dependent on imported fuel. We will meet our international obligations to reduce harmful chimney emissions.

We will restore public control of the National Grid and give it new duties and powers to ensure the long-term security of electricity supplies. We will secure the long-term future of the coal industry by reducing imports, stopping the 'dash for gas' and reining back on open-casting. We will retain the Department of Energy and move its petroleum engineering directorate to Aberdeen. We will require the energy companies to invest in R&D, and encourage the development of clean-burn coal technology.

We will Invest in People at Work

The key to a successful modern economy is a well-educated and motivated workforce. We cannot compete on the basis of low educational standards or poor working conditions. Britain's future must be high skill, high wage and high tech.

Two things are needed: a training revolution to modernise people's skills, and rights for employees to fair treatment at work.

We will offer unemployed people a range of employment and training opportunities. Our aim is to ensure that anyone who is unemployed for more than six months has a choice of job experience or training. We will also help the people often left out of good training opportunities, including the disabled, women returning after caring for children, and those with special educational needs.

Expanded childcare will help women return to work and undertake training. A critical task is to upgrade the skills of people in work. Training and enterprise councils will be retained, reformed and made more broadly representative of their local communities and given stable budgets.

Instead of the present series of piecemeal initiatives we will establish a coherent national training policy to meet the needs of industry and provide people with real equal opportunities at work. All employers, except for very small businesses, will be obliged to invest a minimum amount on training their workforce or make a contribution to the local or national training effort. Training will be a real partnership between government and industry, not an excuse to shift all the burden on to employers.

We will transform the Careers Service to make careers advice available to everyone, young or old, employed or unemployed.

Britain cannot get the best performance from our employees by giving them the worst treatment. There will be a fair framework of law for both employers and unions. There will be no return to the trade union legislation of the 1970s. Ballots before strikes and for union elections will stay. There will be no mass or flying pickets. But our individual employees are entitled to be treated at least as fairly as their colleagues in Europe.

We will opt in to the Social Chapter of the new European Treaty and introduce employment standards common in successful economies, including the best health and safety legislation. The existing protection provided for people engaged in especially hazardous work will be retained.

Women and men must be able to care for their family as well as earn a living. We will give all employees equal rights and status under the law, whether they are full-time or part-time, permanent or temporary. We aim to guarantee every woman in employment the right to 14 weeks' maternity leave on full pay, and to give fathers paternity leave, bringing Britain into line with the better provision elsewhere in the European Community.

Employees will have new rights to be consulted and informed about decisions which affect them, as well as the right to union membership and representation. We will restore union rights at GCHQ. Anti-discrimination law will be strengthened and we will consider as part of that law outlawing discrimination in employment on the grounds of age.

Britain's Wages Councils set minimum wages for about 2.5 million people. But there is no minimum wage for all employees. We will end the scandal of poverty pay and bring Britain into line with the rest of Europe by introducing a statutory minimum wage of £3.40 an hour. This is a major but long overdue reform which will benefit around four million low-paid people, 80 per cent of whom are women. We will consult widely to ensure smooth implementation.

We will Promote a Stake for Employees

Employees should have the opportunity to own collectively a significant stake in the company for which they work, through a democratic employee share ownership plan (ESOP) or a co-operative. We will strengthen support for such schemes and consult about the possibility of creating a new tax incentive to encourage companies to establish or extend an ESOP or set up a co-operative.

Recent pension fund scandals have shown how right Labour has been to call for stronger legal protection. We will reform the law so that pension funds belong to their members, not to employers. Half of the pension trustees will be employees, with an independent chairman, and pensioners will be represented.

MODERNISING THE NATIONAL HEALTH SERVICE

This election will decide the future of the NHS. Indeed, it will decide whether or not we continue to have a NHS of the kind that the British people want.

The Conservatives would continue to commercialise and privatise the NHS until it is run as just another business. With Labour, it will be modernised and restored as a high-quality public service, accountable to the community.

Labour will stop the privatisation of the NHS and return opted-out hospitals and other services to the local NHS. We will halt the commercial market which is creating a two-tier health service.

Our Commitment to the NHS

For a decade, the Conservatives have persistently underfunded the health service. It may well take at least the lifetime of a parliament to put things right, but Labour will start immediately. Instead of cutting income tax, we will make additional resources of at least £1 billion available for investment in the NHS over the next 22 months. Each year thereafter, we will continue to tackle underfunding. Unlike the Conservatives, we will not impose any new health charges.

Labour will recognise the additional claims on the NHS from the growing number of very elderly people and the development of medical technology and knowledge. We will retain the pay review bodies. We will not cheat health authorities by agreeing pay awards which are not fully funded and leaving managers to bridge the gap by cutting patient care. We will invest in the modernisation of our hospitals and tackle the backlog of repairs and maintenance.

We will also launch a new programme to invest £60 million in the modernisation of Britain's cancer services, using the resources we will save by scrapping the Conservatives' tax handout on private medical insurance. Within our overall budget, we will tackle the shortage of intensive care beds with a special programme providing an additional £25 million to expand this life-saving service.

A Healthy Britain

Labour will launch a national health initiative to promote physical and mental health from birth to old age. This initiative will be led by the Department of Health and Community Care and by a new Cabinet committee that will cut through departmental boundaries.

We will set new targets to cut the inequalities in health between social classes and ethnic groups. Our health initiative will set targets for better health, backed by effective action. We will, for instance:

● strengthen screening by restoring the free eye test;

- cut cancer by banning tobacco advertising;
- encourage healthy diets by introducing clearer food labelling;
- promote health at work by creating a modern occupational health service within the NHS.

GPs have a vital role to play in health promotion. We will increase the time they have for each patient by reversing the financial pressures to take on too many patients. We will make sure every community has access to dentists, with the resources to provide full NHS cover, and we will restore the free dental check.

By improving family planning services, we will reduce unwanted pregnancies and help achieve our target of cutting the number of abortions by at least a quarter. We will ensure that access to abortion is equally available in every region.

A Modern NHS

We will create a modern, efficient NHS with incentives to improve performance — but without the queue-jumping and waste created by a market in health care.

We will provide more services through local health centres and other community settings. We will give GPs the power to insist on improvements in service to all the patients in a neighbourhood.

We will give the outcome of treatment the same importance as the throughput of treatment. Our new health quality commission will monitor the quality of care and raise standards.

The continuing care of very elderly and chronically sick patients will be a higher priority. We will halt the reduction in NHS services for long-term care and community health services which support elderly and disabled patients at home.

To achieve this change of direction, we will negotiate performance agreements with each health authority and back them with an incentive fund to reward authorities which perform well. These agreements will set local targets which reflect local priorities, for instance, to cut waiting lists or switch mental health services into the community. Hospital managers, who will be accountable for meeting their targets, will otherwise be given maximum freedom of decision making.

We will create new community health authorities, representative of local people, which bring together both GP services and hospital care.

A First-Class Service to Patients

In Labour's health service, power will belong to patients, not accountants. We will restore the right of patients to be treated in the hospital of their choice. Women will have the right to be seen by a woman GP and we will encourage the development of well women clinics. Ethnic minorities will have the right to obtain the diet required by their religious beliefs.

We will set four new standards for a better service to:

- cut cancelled operations;
- improve cleanliness in hospitals;
- make it easier to phone for an ambulance;
- increase early admissions from waiting lists.

As part of our commitment to a quality service to patients, we will end compulsory competitive tendering for hospital support services, which has driven down standards of cleanliness and catering.

We will invest £25 million from within our overall budget to purchase several hundred more new, fully equipped ambulances.

A Community Service

Labour will expand the services which elderly people and their carers need for long-term support in the community, such as home helps, care assistants and community services. Our Department of Health and Community Care, with a new minister of state for community care, will develop a high-quality programme of community care which responds to what users want.

We will introduce a new earmarked grant for community care which will support the work of Labour councils in providing care for people at home, and oblige Conservative councils to use the grant to improve those services. We will end the pressure on councils to privatise their residential homes by providing funding for local authorities equivalent to the benefits paid to private homes.

We will insist that the first call on income from the sale of mental health hospitals is the provision of better accommodation and services in the community for mental health users and people with learning disabilities. We will end the neglect that has allowed some former patients to end up sleeping rough and led to others being placed on remand. Labour will ensure that these services are in place before patients who will benefit from life in the community are transferred out of long-term hospital care.

RAISING STANDARDS IN OUR SCHOOLS

Good education is the best investment in Britain's future. All girls and boys, from every background, must be able to discover their talents and fulfil their potential.

We want every child to get qualifications that count. We need safe, disciplined schools, where professional teachers work closely with parents. Learning must become a lifetime opportunity, with new chances to update skills at work.

That is our vision of a well-educated Britain.

But, under the Conservatives, Britain today invests a smaller share of our national wealth in education than in 1979. More and more parents are now being forced to pay for essentials in a system which should be free.

Labour will modernise Britain's schools. Over the next 22 months, additional resources of at least £600 million will be made available for investment in education. We will then continue steadily to increase the share of Britain's national wealth invested in education.

We will Offer Nursery Education to Three and Four Year Olds

By the end of the decade, all three and four year olds will have the opportunity of nursery education if their parents so wish.

Within six months, every local education authority will have to set targets for steadily increasing nursery and childcare services. Childhood partnerships between councils, parents, schools, local businesses and community groups will help extend a wide range of childcare and nursery education services.

The immediate investment in childcare described earlier is only the beginning. Our ministry for women will have a central role in helping to develop a nationwide childcare strategy, including out-of-school and holiday provision as well as care for younger children.

We will Raise Standards in our Schools

By investing in better teaching, smaller classes and modern books and equipment, we will raise education standards.

Teachers will be guaranteed a proper salary and career structure. A general teaching council for England and Wales will help them achieve the highest professional standards. Higher quality training will be followed by proper support for newly qualified teachers. A national in-service training programme will ensure that all teachers are fully qualified in the subject they are teaching.

Within 12 months, we will end the scandal of primary school classes of over 40 children. We will then establish and steadily reduce maximum limits on class sizes, until no primary school child is taught in a class of more than 30.

To make sure that children are reading by the age of seven, we will create a national reading standards programme, with a national reading recovery programme to help those in difficulty. £20 million will be invested in reading recovery in the first year. National tests must provide the information needed to help pupils, and to judge schools' effectiveness, without wasting good teaching time. Children with special needs or special abilities will receive the extra attention they deserve.

Nine out of 10 secondary school children are in comprehensive schools. We will end selection at 11 where it still exists. We will introduce a fairer system for all school reorganisations, with independent public enquiries. We will phase out the assisted places scheme (without affecting pupils currently on a place, or offered one from September 1992) and redirect the savings to meet wider educational needs.

Because the national curriculum cannot be properly taught without new textbooks, we will earmark funds for class and library books. Every child needs a good grounding in science and technology. We will introduce a programme to improve equipment and laboratories. We will start to tackle the backlog of school repairs. For instance, we will invest £30 million to ensure that within 12 months, no child has to use an outside lavatory.

Guaranteed Standards

Conservative plans to privatise the schools' inspectorate will be scrapped. Our education standards commission, together with Her Majesty's Inspectors, will monitor the performance of every school. If a school is under-performing, the commission, which will be answerable to Parliament, will have the powers to ensure that it is brought up to standard.

National awards, similar to the Queen's Award for Industry, will encourage excellence in schools.

We will reform the Conservatives' scheme for the local management of schools. All schools will be free to manage their day-to-day budgets, with local education authorities given a new strategic role. Opted-out schools will be freed from central government control and brought together with city technology colleges into the mainstream of the local school system.

New Rights for Parents

We will reform the Conservatives' scheme for the local management of schools. All schools will be free to manage their day-to-day budgets, with local education authorities given a new strategic role. Opted-out schools will be freed from central government control and brought together with city technology colleges into the mainstream of the local school system.

Home-school contracts will tell parents exactly what the school undertakes to deliver and what their responsibilities are. If they are dissatisfied with the school or education authority, they will be able to call in the education standards commission and get action taken.

We wish to see the key role of church and other voluntary-aided schools secured and available equally and on the same criteria to all religions.

We will Modernise the Curriculum

Labour will modernise the national curriculum and apply it in all schools. From the age of 14, pupils will study five essential subjects: English, mathematics, science, a modern language and technology. In schools teaching in Welsh, the study of Welsh will be included. Every pupil will also be offered a wide range of academic, technical and other options.

Taking account of the views of parents, employers, teachers, pupils and the recommendations of the Higginson report, we will establish a five-subject A level and bring it together with technical qualifications into our new advanced certificate. Open to part-time and full-time students of any age, it will include 'credits' which can be transferred between different institutions. We will consult widely about the detailed structure of this new qualification, and finalise proposals quickly.

Young people must have real opportunities to widen their experience and skills. Sixteen year olds not in full-time education will be entitled to a new traineeship lasting for up to two years, with an option of a further two years. Every young person in employment will be guaranteed the right to 'Learn while you earn'.

Labour's Education Targets

We have set ourselves four education targets. They are the basis for our strategy and the benchmark against which progress will be judged.

First, a nursery education for all three and four year olds whose parents wish, by the year 2000.

Second, within five years, we want four out of five 16 to 18 year olds to be able to achieve at least five GCSEs at grades A, B or C, or their equivalent.

Third, by the end of the decade, we want half of Britain's 16 to 19 year olds to be able to qualify at the new advanced certificate level A levels or the equivalent in BTEC and other post-16 opportunities for study.

Fourth, within 20 years, we will double the number of students in higher education, with at least one in three young adults participating by the year 2000.

The student loan scheme deters many bright youngsters from poor families. We will replace it with a fairer system of student grants and targeted help for housing and vacation hardship. We will take effective steps to safeguard standards throughout higher education.

We will stop the Conservatives' adult education cuts and encourage local authorities to develop adult and community education and access courses, particularly for mature students. People over 50 who missed earlier opportunities will be able to apply for a 'return to learn' grant towards further or higher education.

THE BEST FUTURE FOR FAMILIES AND COMMUNITIES

Britain's families deserve the support which families receive in other European countries. We will create a new sense of community and social cohesion.

We will make families better off

As we explained earlier, we will increase child benefit for seven million families. Higher pensions and related benefits will benefit another 12 million people. We will reform the tax and national insurance system, and take 740,000 low-paid people out of tax. After the first year's extra increases we will restore the link between increases in the basic pension and prices or earnings, whichever is higher.

Britain's national insurance system is far more efficient than private insurance. We will open it up to new groups such as low-paid and part-time workers.

Labour will end the Conservatives' freeze on benefits for widowed mothers and other lone parents. We will encourage parents on income support to claim maintenance by allowing them to keep part of it before benefit is cut.

We will restore nutritional guidelines for school meals and reverse the cuts in free school meals as soon as possible.

We will reform benefits for people with disabilities and make it easier for those available for work to take employment. As resources allow, we will improve and extend invalid care allowance.

Labour will develop a flexible decade of retirement between the ages of 60 and 70, so that men and women can choose to retire on a full pension or continue in work without discrimination .

Our new national pensions plan, building on the state earnings related pension scheme, will offer people now in work a pension based on their 20 best years' earnings. Those who are self-employed will also be able to join. Occupational and personal pension schemes will have to guarantee a minimum pension before they can contract out, and guarantee equal treatment for men and women.

We will reform means-tested benefits, replace the social fund, and restore benefit rights to 16 and 17 year olds as soon as possible. To relieve anxiety about funeral costs, we will introduce a funeral payment of £600, available on request. The costs will in most cases be recovered from the deceased's estate, although small estates will be disregarded.

We will Abolish the Poll Tax

Labour will abolish the poll tax immediately. We will replace it with our fair rates system, related to people's ability to pay. We reject the Conservatives' unfair banding and discount system, which would create a property poll tax. We will modernise the valuation system to ensure that properties are fairly assessed.

Abolition of the minimum 20 per cent contribution — which will be of particular help to young people — will be followed by an improved rebate system, with special help to retired people on low incomes living alone. Business rates will become a local tax again, with rate rebates for small firms.

People Need Decent Homes

Labour will establish mortgage rescue schemes throughout the country, enabling home buyers to remain as tenants or part-owners. Mortgage interest tax relief will continue at the present rate. We will seek new arrangements to enable first-time buyers to concentrate relief in the early years. Housing log books and an end to gazumping will also help home buyers. We will also ensure that home-buyers receive proper advice about the potential cost of their mortgages in future years.

Councils and housing associations will be allowed to lease or buy empty homes in order to provide accommodation for homeless people. Homes left empty without good reason by any public authority will be transferred to a better social landlord.

We will restore housing benefit to people under 18 and provide more refuges for women escaping domestic violence.

Labour will keep the right to buy. We will increase the number of homes for rent by establishing a housing bank to facilitate the balanced use of councils' capital receipts and offer investment capital at attractive rates of interest. Tenants will be offered the option to 'part rent, part buy'. Steps will be taken to improve sub-standard housing.

Council tenants will be guaranteed real rights over their homes. Councils will set rents at a reasonable level, reflecting income levels in the different regions and localities. We will eliminate racial discrimination in housing allocation and improve safety on estates.

In the private sector there is a need both for homes at market rents and those where rents are regulated and housing benefit payable. We will consult fully before introducing reforms and will not legislate retrospectively.

All tenants must be protected against noise, nuisance, harassment and shoddy service.

Leaseholders will have new rights, either to extend their lease, or collectively buy the freehold of their property from non-resident freeholders.

We will Protect People Against Crime

Crime in Britain has more than doubled since 1979. Over five million crimes were recorded last year, but the real total is certainly higher.

Labour will insist that local councils work with the police to improve crime prevention by:
● modernising vulnerable estates;
● improving street lighting;
● demolishing derelict buildings;
● fencing off waste land.

Planning applications will be examined against crime prevention criteria. The sale of replica guns will be banned.

Elected police authorities will use the extra resources available for the war against crime to ensure that more police officers are visible on the beat, backed up by the modern technology which is essential to crime prevention and detection.

We will implement the recommendations of the Woolf report to improve prison conditions. Prison must offer training for employment, not for crime. We will promote non-custodial sentences for non-violent crimes and take steps to eradicate the discrimination in sentencing policy which particularly affects women and ethnic minority offenders.

People Have a Right to First-Class Services

We will develop customer contracts for local services, along the lines pioneered by Labour authorities. Local communities will help design services to meet their needs, with voluntary groups playing a key role in delivering services.

Our new quality commission, incorporating the work of the audit commission, will ensure councils provide high-quality, value-for-money services, with clear avenues for complaint and redress. We will not tolerate shoddy service, inefficiency or waste. Councils will have to carry out an annual survey of customer satisfaction, published just before local elections.

The contracts of chief officers will be linked to quality targets, with senior managers required to sample the service they provide. Compulsory competitive tendering will be abolished, but the quality commission will have the power, where services have broken down, to insist that they are put out to tender, with contractors required to meet conditions such as quality thresholds and fair employment.

Local planning must reflect what people, not developers, want. The Conservatives' bonfire of planning controls has led to ill-thought out development, often against the wishes of local people. Labour will give people more say in drawing up plans for their area and create a new right of appeal for residents against developments which fly in the face of their local plan. Beneficial development will be speeded up, damaging development checked and the green belt safeguarded. We will reverse the present planning presumption in favour of opencast coal mining and give top priority to local people and their environment.

Councils Must be Accountable to Local People

We shall introduce annual elections in England and Wales, with one third of councillors elected each year. Councillors must get proper support, to ensure that they are drawn from all parts of the community and are not financially disadvantaged.

Labour will sign the European charter of local self government and give local councils a general power of competence, in line with other European countries, so that councils can develop new and imaginative services.

We will reform the system for allocating grants to local councils and introduce less centralised rules on capital spending, enabling councils to make prudent long-term investment.

We will Support Arts and Leisure

Building on the example of many Labour councils which have developed imaginative arts initiatives, we will make the arts a statutory responsibility for local authorities. Labour's ministry for the arts and media will encourage Britain's arts and their associated industries, including broadcasting and the press, to develop new ideas and attract more people. Government will commission the best designers, artists and architects, for instance, to help communities transform run-down city centres.

We will renew the BBC's Charter in a way which guarantees continuation of high-quality public service broadcasting — available in all parts of the country and covering a wide spectrum of programmes. The licence fee remains the best way of financing the BBC and preserving its independence. A concessionary fee will be introduced for all pensioners.

As people have more leisure, they also need better facilities for sport. We will encourage councils to invest in modern, well-staffed sports centres for the enjoyment of people of all ages and abilities, and give mandatory rate relief to voluntary sports clubs.

New facilities and better backing for people with outstanding talent will help put Britain back on the international sporting map. We will review sports taxation, reform the sports councils and make football grounds safe for spectators. We will stop the wanton sale of school playing fields and ensure that sport takes its proper place within the curriculum.

We will Protect Consumers

Our consumers' charter will cover all goods and services. It will include:
● tougher health and safety standards;
● compensation for injury from dangerous products;
● comprehensive guarantees;
● a fast, simple remedy if things go wrong.

We will press for similar standards throughout the European Community and strengthen the work of consumer groups and advice centres so that aspirations and standards are met.

Every utility will be required to provide a customer contract, with compensation if standards are not met. Gas and electricity disconnections will be banned completely where young children or elderly people are concerned. We will regulate telephone services which demean women and corrupt children.

We will strengthen the regulation of the utilities, enforce standards through our consumer protection commission, and ensure prices are cut or other action taken where profits are excessive so that the customer gets a fair deal. We will establish a petroleum products regulator. Government and parliament will have a stronger role to work on the consumer's behalf. We will help consumers have a voice locally and nationally.

We will Create a Cleaner, Safer Environment

The greatest challenge we face is the responsibility to ensure the survival of the planet.

Economic progress goes hand in hand with environmental responsibility. Labour will embrace the goal of sustainable development, with environmental modernisation an integral part of our industrial strategy.

Labour's prime minister will go to the earth summit in June, with a commitment to stabilising emissions of CO_2 (the main source of global warming) at their 1990 levels by the end of the decade and a recognition that significant cuts will be needed in the early years of the new century. We will adopt the tightest possible timetable for eliminating CFCs and other chemicals which deplete the ozone layer.

Our tough pollution standards, based on the health and safety of children, will be enforced by an independent environmental protection executive. We will develop a national waste strategy promoting waste minimisation, re-use and recycling. Business will be encouraged to have environmental audits. The trade in toxic waste will be banned.

We will establish a new legal right to a clean environment, ensure environmental freedom of information, implement European environmental standards such as environmental impact assessment and promote a European environmental charter. Every government policy will be subjected to environmental appraisal, co-ordinated by a cabinet minister for environmental protection. An annual green book assessing the environmental impact of government economic policy will accompany the traditional financial red book.

Improving Inner Cities

We will reverse the unfair treatment which has meant that the inner cities have lost out in terms of local government finance, housing investment and support for employment. Labour will pull together the present unco-ordinated initiatives into a coherent urban programme which will strengthen local economies, generate jobs and improve the quality of people's lives.

We will encourage local councils to create enterprise partnerships with employers, trade unions and the community, which will mobilise the commitment and the enthusiasm of local people. The composition and terms of reference of urban development corporations will be changed immediately and they will in due course be wound up in an orderly way.

At the local level, we will tackle litter and graffiti and start to transform inner city environments by establishing neighbourhood action areas where local communities can develop their own plans for regenerating the area.

Clean Water, Healthy Food

We will ensure that our drinking water, beaches and rivers meet the highest European standards and end the dumping of industrial waste at sea. The provision of water is so fundamental that it is a priority for return to public control. In the meantime, we will protect consumers against high prices and poor service and give greater priority to environmental problems.

Labour's independent food standards agency will ensure high food quality standards. Our department of food and farming will offer British farmers and consumers a better deal. Subsidies for production will gradually be replaced with green premium payments to promote environmentally sound management of the countryside.

We will Invest in Decent Public Transport

We will transform transport policy by ensuring, for the first time, that all road, railway, aviation, shipping and inland waterways projects are judged on the basis of their environmental, social and economic impact. Within six months we will review the roads programme and mobilise private capital for large-scale public transport investment. All major transport projects will be subject to environment impact assessment and we will fully observe the requirements of the European directive on EIAs. Road building proposals for sensitive areas such as Oxleas Wood and Twyford Down must be subject to full environmental assessment.

We reject Conservative plans to privatise British Rail. Instead, we will modernise, setting clear performance targets to improve the quality of service and shift more freight from road to rail.

We will tackle the problem of congestion and environmental damage by enabling local authorities to provide better quality transport. We will end the deregulation of buses, introduce bus priority measures integrated with new rapid transit systems within a 'green light' programme designed to encourage people to transfer to public transport. Proper concessionary fare schemes will be developed in every area. Traffic management schemes to cut unnecessary car use and better facilities for cyclists and pedestrians will make town centres safer and more attractive.

We will reform transport taxation in order to encourage smaller, cleaner cars and the use of catalytic converters. The subsidy to company cars will be phased out.

In London and the south east, congestion costs the economy over £10 billion a year. We will stop bus deregulation and privatisation of London Transport and promote efficient public transport.

We will seek to reverse the unacceptable decline in Britain's merchant navy and encourage the greater use of British-owned and crewed vessels, adding to Britain's security and reducing the cost to our balance or payments.

All transport services will be required to meet high standards of service and safety, with effective avenues for complaint and compensation where appropriate. We will establish a new independent transport safety inspectorate within the health and safety legislation to improve the safety environment which has led to the terrible tragedies of recent years. Increased security measures and better staffing will be particularly welcome to women, elderly and disabled people.

Saving Energy

Labour will give top priority to energy saving rather than energy sales. We will set up an energy efficiency agency and a renewable energy agency. We will require the gas and electricity companies to invest in insulation and other energy-saving measures.

We will not invest in new nuclear power stations, continue with those in the planning process or extend the lives of existing nuclear stations beyond their safe life span. Britain's dependence on nuclear power will therefore steadily diminish. We will use the most modern technology to deal with the problems of decommissioning and nuclear waste.

A Better Life in the Country

We will expand affordable housing in rural areas, develop countryside colleges to meet wider training needs and invest in workshops and small business units. We will support rural schools and improve public transport. The work of the Rural Development Commission and the Development Board for Rural Wales will be boosted.

The ecological richness of our countryside must be protected. We will give people a new right of access to open country, create new national parks and step up protection for special sites. We will consult widely on the best way forward for nature conservation and countryside bodies, including independent boards for all national parks. We will safeguard Britain's rivers and canals and improve leisure facilities. Anglers will benefit from and contribute to our plans for improved river quality.

We will Protect Animals

We will reduce cruelty to animals within Britain and Europe. We will ban the testing of beauty aids on animals, outlaw fur farming and ensure better treatment of farm animals and animals in transit. Our national dog registration scheme will provide the money for a warden service.

As part of our programme to outlaw cruelty to wild mammals, we will allow a free vote in the House of Commons on a proposal to ban the hunting of live quarry with hounds and, if that is passed, provide parliamentary time for the necessary legislation. There will be no new limitations on the country sports of angling or shooting.

A MODERN DEMOCRACY

It is time to modernise Britain's democracy. Central to Labour's purpose in government is our commitment to radical constitutional reform.

Our charter of rights, backed up by a complementary and democratically enforced bill of rights, will establish in law the specific rights of every citizen.

We will start in our first parliamentary session with a freedom of information act which will open up government to the people. Exceptions will be tightly drawn.

We will Give Power to the Nations and Regions

We will move immediately to establish an elected Scottish parliament. It will have powers to legislate for and administer Scotland's domestic affairs and modernise Scotland's economy and the ability to represent Scotland within the United Kingdom and Europe.

Labour's legislation will be firmly based on the proposals agreed in the Scottish constitutional convention. The Parliament will be elected on an additional member system. It will be responsible for local government, health, housing, education, transport, environmental and other policies within Scotland.

In our first year, we will introduce a new Welsh language act. We will establish, in the lifetime of a full parliament, an elected Welsh assembly in Cardiff with powers and functions which reflect the existing administrative structure. Local government in Wales will be reformed to create between 25 and 30 'most purpose' authorities.

A regional tier of government in the English regions will take over many powers now exercised nationally, such as regional economic planning and transport. These new administrations will later form the basis for elected regional governments. To simplify local government in England, we will establish 'most purpose' authorities generally based on district councils. In some areas, a county-wide authority or the amalgamation of districts may be more appropriate. We will consult widely before finalising proposals.

London is now the only European capital without the advantage of its own elected authority. Labour will give Londoners the right to elect a new greater London authority, responsible for making London a better place to live and work.

We will Safeguard Press Freedom

We will remove unjustified restrictions on broadcasting and establish an urgent enquiry by the Monopolies and Mergers Commission into the concentration of media ownership. If the press fail to deal with abuses of individual privacy, we will implement the Calcutt report's recommendations for statutory protection.

Individuals must be able to control personal information about themselves. We will strengthen Britain's Data Protection Act in line with European practice. The security services will be brought under the scrutiny of a Parliamentary select committee.

We will See That Justice is Done

There is widespread concern about the miscarriages of justice which have imprisoned innocent people. As part of our sweeping programme of law reform, we will establish an additional appeals tribunal, including lay members as well as lawyers, to examine the most contentious convictions.

The Police and Criminal Evidence Act will be reformed. Convictions will no longer be possible on uncorroborated confession evidence.

We will improve access to legal aid and, when resources allow, extend it to tribunal hearings. We will encourage the expansion of voluntary advice centres and invest in better support for victims. We will appoint from the House of Commons a minister for legal administration, who will initially be part of the Lord Chancellor's department. We will go on to create a department of legal administration headed by a minister in the Commons who will be responsible for all courts and tribunals in England and Wales. Future reform of the distinctive Scottish legal system will be the responsibility of the Scottish parliament.

We will work with the legal profession to open up new opportunities to women and to black and ethnic minority groups, and create an independent judicial appointments commission. A sentencing council will bring some consistency into what is now often a haphazard process. A court inspectorate will improve the efficiency of our often outdated judicial system.

We will Offer Everyone a Fair Chance

Stronger sex and race discrimination laws will ensure that organisations awarded government contracts take positive steps to promote equal treatment. We will introduce a new law dealing with discrimination on grounds of sexuality, repeal the unjust Clause 28 and allow a free vote in the House of Commons on the age of consent.

In order to safeguard the rights of people with disabilities, we will appoint a minister for the disabled and extend anti-discrimination laws to cover this group.

We will establish a children's minister within the Home Office to co-ordinate policies for children across departments. One independent children's commissioner will promote the interests of all children. Protecting children will be high on the agenda, as will the full implementation of the children act and the UN Convention to promote childrens rights.

Labour's Ministry for Women

Following the successful example of France, Germany and many other countries, Labour will appoint a cabinet minister for women. She will ensure that women's voices are heard at the highest level. She will monitor the work of all other departments and co-ordinate action for equal opportunities across government.

The ministry will also initiate legislation for women. In particular, we will introduce a new sex equality act which will combine and strengthen the current equal pay and sex discrimination laws.

The ministry for women will have special responsibility for co-ordinating childcare policy, improving women's safety and encouraging more women to participate in public life.

The Black and Ethnic Minority Communities

We are determined to ensure that women and men from ethnic minority groups are full and equal members of the community.

As well as strengthening the race discrimination laws and extending the powers of the Commission for Racial Equality, we will press for similar laws throughout the European Community. We will not tolerate the present level of racial harassment and attacks, and will ensure that more effective protection is given to vulnerable groups. Contract compliance laws will be the first step towards guaranteeing the black and Asian British their fair share of jobs.

A Fair Citizenship Law

We will introduce fair immigration and citizenship laws which restore the right to British citizenship for every child born in Britain. Our laws, which will not discriminate on grounds of sex or race, will respect the right to family life. A new act will guarantee sanctuary to genuine refugees but prevent bogus applications for asylum.

We are determined to see that equally fair laws apply throughout the European Community and will oppose any attempt to remove voting rights from Commonwealth citizens in European elections.

Northern Ireland

Labour will continue the present talks on Northern Ireland. In the long term, we want to see a united Ireland achieved by consensus and without violence. We support the commitment in the Anglo-Irish Agreement that 'any change in the status of Northern Ireland would only come about with the consent of a majority in Northern Ireland'. We will work within the agreement to achieve our policy of unity by consent, and strengthen measures against injustice, discrimination and deprivation.

We will fight terrorism by every lawful means, repealing the counter-productive Prevention of Terrorism Act and replacing it with a measure which is more effective and genuinely acceptable in a democratic society.

A Modern Parliament

Westminster must become more effective in protecting citizens and holding government to account. We will therefore improve the procedures and facilities of the House of Commons, strengthen scrutiny of EC legislation, and end ministerial misuse of the Royal Prerogative.

We will give shareholders the right to vote upon all political donations made by public companies, require donations to political parties to be declared in a public register, require the accounts of political parties to be published and, as recommended by the Houghton Report, introduce state aid for political parties.

Further constitutional reforms will include those leading to the replacement of the House of Lords with a new elected second chamber which will have the power to delay, for the lifetime of a Parliament, change to designated legislation reducing individual or constitutional rights.

We will continue to encourage a wide and well-informed public debate on the electoral system. The working party on electoral systems which we established in opposition under the distinguished chairmanship of Professor Raymond Plant will continue its work with an extended membership and enhanced authority and report to the next Labour government.

This general election was called only after months of on-again, off-again dithering which damaged our economy and weakened our democracy. No government with a majority should be allowed to put the interests of party above country as the Conservatives have done. Although an early election will sometimes be necessary, we will introduce as a general rule a fixed parliamentary term.

BRITAIN IN A NEW WORLD

We need a new government to grasp new opportunities. A Labour government ready to exploit Britain's unique, interlinking membership of the United Nations Security Council, NATO, the Commonwealth, the European Community and the G7.

It's a New Chance to Enhance Peace in the World

Labour, which in opposition joined our Nato allies in rejecting the Conservative government's cold war nostalgia, will in government partner the United States in negotiating to reduce the world's stocks of nuclear weapons. We shall seek to involve the four former Soviet nuclear republics, together with France and China. Until elimination of those stocks is achieved, Labour will retain Britain's nuclear capability, with the number of warheads no greater than the present total .

With the increase in major nuclear powers from five to eight, proliferation is a dangerous reality and may become an even greater threat to peace and stability. The Tory government contributed to proliferation when it permitted the supply of nuclear weapons material to Saddam Hussein. The Labour government will work in the United Nations for a strengthened nuclear non-proliferation treaty, backed by meaningful sanctions and by a comprehensive nuclear test ban treaty. We will in addition work for a global ban on chemical and biological weapons and stronger controls to prevent proliferation of ballistic missiles. Meanwhile, we will join Russia in ending nuclear tests.

We will actively support the peace-making role of the UN — for example, in Cambodia and Somalia — and work for a permanent United Nations peace-keeping force.

It's a New Chance to Solve Long Running Disputes

The Labour government will work in the United Nations and the European Community to enhance peace prospects in the Middle East. Our aims are security for Israel and self-determination for the Palestinians. There must be strict control on arms sales to the region.

Labour will work in the United Nations, the Commonwealth, the European Community and Nato to help bring about the peaceful reunification of Cyprus, on the federal basis advocated by the sovereign government of Cyprus. The Labour government will make itself available to our friends in India and Pakistan to assist in achieving a negotiated solution to the problem of Kashmir that is acceptable to all the people of Kashmir — Moslems, Hindus and Buddhists.

We will, as a matter of urgency, discuss with Hong Kong's representatives what measures may best enhance democracy and confidence during Britain's five remaining years of responsibility for the colony.

It's a New Chance to Provide Genuine Security for Britain

As the party which took Britain into Nato, Labour will base its defence policies on UK membership of the alliance. We will provide whatever resources are needed for effective defence for our country, providing the necessary level of forces with the appropriate equipment and weapons.

Unlike the Tories, we recognise that disarmament negotiations and technological change can bring about problems for our defence industries. Nearly 100,000 jobs have already been lost during the past two years and 123,000 more are in danger.

Selling more arms to poor countries is not an acceptable or effective way of maintaining Britain's defence industries. We will stop sales to countries which might use them for internal repression or international aggression.

The Labour government will set up a defence diversification agency to assist workers, communities and companies affected by change. The agency will ensure that resources made available by reductions in defence spending — reductions already planned by the Conservative government - are used in the first instance for rebuilding and investing in our manufacturing base. From the fruits of this investment can stem finance for health and the social services.

It's a New Chance for a New Europe

The Labour government will promote Britain out of the European second division into which our country has been relegated by the Tories. Our first chance will be the United Kingdom's six-months' presidency of the Community, starting on 1 July. We shall use that presidency to end the Tories' opt-out from the social chapter, so that the British people can benefit from European safeguards. We will also use our presidency to help ensure that poorer countries are not disadvantaged as a result of the single market.

We shall play an active part in negotiations on economic and monetary union. We shall fight for Britain's interests, working for Europe-wide policies to fight unemployment and to enhance regional and structural industrial policy. The elected finance ministers of the different countries must become the effective political counterpart to the central bank whose headquarters should be in Britain.

As part of the evolving role of the regions of Europe, we will establish a Scottish representative office in Brussels and seek appropriate representation for the Scottish parliament in European institutions. We shall seek fundamental changes in the wasteful common agricultural policy. Savings can help finance other Community projects.

We shall make the widening of the Community a priority, and shall advocate speedy admission for Austria, Sweden, Finland and Cyprus, whose membership applications have been or are about to be lodged. We shall seek to create conditions in which, at the appropriate time, the new democracies of Central and Eastern Europe can join the Community.

It's a New Chance for Human Rights

Labour will set up a human rights division in the Foreign and Commonwealth Office and require all Britain's diplomatic posts abroad to appoint an officer to monitor human rights. There will be an annual report to Parliament. Decisions on economic aid and arms sales will be linked to human rights records.

It's a New Chance to Win Friends Abroad

Labour will end Tory government meddling in the valuable work of the British Council. Within carefully controlled costings, Labour will consider new scope for the BBC World Service, praised by listeners such as Terry Waite and Mikhail Gorbachev, and for the BBC's World Service Television Service.

It's a New Chance to Fight World Hunger and Poverty

Under the Tories, Britain's aid budget has been cut to its lowest ever. The Labour government will aim to meet the United Nations aid target of 0.7 per cent of GNP within five years — the lifetime of a full parliament. Labour will establish a separate department of state for international development, whose minister will be in the cabinet.

Tackling poverty will be the top priority of our aid programme. We will make aid more effective, work more closely with non-governmental agencies, put women at the heart of our programme and, in co-ordination with other donors, reduce the share of tied aid. Labour will promote environmentally sustainable development and encourage new approaches to reduce Third World debt. We will restore funding for development education in the UK.

We will promote greater and fairer trade for poor countries, to enable their economies to grow and diversify. UN and European Community action to help the world's poor must become more effective. Labour will take Britain back into Unesco.

The Labour government will work within the G7 and the European Community to win support for a new Marshall plan to assist the former communist countries of central and Eastern Europe and of the ex-Soviet Union. Instability in those countries, caused by shortages and discontent, could be as great a threat to world peace as the armed communism that has now disappeared.

It's a New Chance for Britain in the Commonwealth

The Tories have regarded the Commonwealth as a wearisome obligation. Labour believes that this unique inter-racial and inter-hemispheric organisation can play a central role in righting racism, hunger and human rights violations. We shall play an active part in the Commonwealth and join the South Africa committee of foreign ministers which the Tories have boycotted.

It's a New Chance to Safeguard the Environment

The Tories have been laggardly and reluctant in international moves to protect our planet's environment. Labour will set the pace in pressing for international action to safeguard the ozone layer, to combat acid rain, to tackle the problem of global warming, to face up to the environmental needs of the poorest people of the world. We will scrap the Tory government's opt-out on European Community environmental protection measures and deadlines. Labour will adamantly oppose any attempts to permit commercial exploitation of the virgin continent of Antarctica.

Changing Britain for good

After the headline "Be warned: this manifesto may not be what you expect", the introduction of the Liberal Democratic Manifesto declared:

This manifesto does not promise good times just around the corner. It does not avoid difficult questions out of fear of unpopularity. It simply tells the truth; the truth about what Liberal Democrats believe has to be done in order for Britain to succeed.

If you want Britain to stay the same then you probably won't like this manifesto. But if you want real change, if you long for a better future for yourself, your family, your community and your country, then read on.

But Britain will only succeed when its political leaders start treating voters as informed citizens with shared concerns, not as ignorant consumers to be manipulated. Now is the time for change. So this manifesto is different from others you may read.

We do not shrink from the real choices for our country. We are not afraid to say what needs to be said. We are not afraid to do what needs to be done. And we are clear that if we want to make a modern Britain, we must first *change* Britain.

WHAT LIBERAL DEMOCRATS STAND FOR

The Manifesto began: Liberal Democrats put people first. We aim to create a society in which all men and women can realise their full potential and shape their own successes. We believe that if we could liberate this wealth of talent we would transform our economy and create a shared society of which we should all be proud.

Liberal Democrats know that this cannot be achieved without fundamental reform.

We must change our political system to give the citizen more power and the government less; our economic system to confer power on consumers and to provide employees with a share in the wealth they create; our public services to guarantee choice and dignity to each of us; and our education system to equip us better for the modern world.

Liberal Democrats recognise the importance of the things we own in private but we also know the value of what we hold in common. We believe that people are at their best as members of communities, where they care about each other and for those less fortunate than themselves. So our policies are designed to strengthen communities, tackle crime and poverty, build up the common wealth and improve the shared quality of life.

In the economic sphere we know that the free market is the best guarantee of responsiveness to choice and change. But we believe the market should be our servant not our master. So we see the role of government as crucial in making the market work properly, by creating the conditions for success, promoting competition, breaking up monopolies and spreading information. And government has to be ready to make the investments which private enterprise will not, whether in transport, education or public works.

Liberal Democrats know that we have a duty, not only to each other but to the generations which follow us, to protect the environment. We believe that this is best achieved not by making people poorer or less free but by building true environmental costs into the market so as to reward those who conserve and penalise those who pollute.

Liberal Democrats are uncompromisingly internationalist. We know that there is a limit to what Britain can achieve alone and we are committed to building in the wider world the sort of society we strive for at home, founded on mutual cooperation, political liberty and shared prosperity.We have long been committed Europeans, believing that Britain can only be secure, successful and environmentally safe if we play our full part in building a more united and democratic Europe.

Globally, Liberal Democrats will work to strengthen international cooperation. We reject outdated notions of national sovereignty, believing that they now stand in the way of common action to deal with the scourges of disease and hunger, the deterioration of the Earth's environment and the continuing angers of the post-cold war world.

We believe that all government, whether local, national, or increasingly European, should be bound by the rights of the individual and should be fully accountable.

Because Liberal Democrats alone understand that we shall not change Britain's future unless and until we change Britain's electoral system, we are committed to electoral and constitutional reform. We shall not rest until the government of Britain fully belongs to the citizens it is there to serve.

BRITAIN'S BALANCE SHEET

In drawing up this manifesto, we have begun from where Britain is today. Like any good auditor, we have been realistic about national achievements and failures, about opportunities and problems. The result is a balance sheet which shows our country's strengths and weaknesses.

Despite some points of promise and potential, Britain's balance sheet shows how much still needs to be done. The following pages reveal the extent to which, in the economy, in the environment, in education, and in local services, successive British governments have failed to realise the opportunities of the past decades. Although there are bright spots, the general picture is one of relative decline in relation to other advanced democracies. Forty years of failure are the result not only of misjudged policies from both Conservative and Labour governments. Even more crucially, they are the product of an outdated political system which has consistently sacrificed the long term to the short term and abandoned principles for expediency.

The economic balance sheet

UK exports in 1991: £103,804m. But imports have grown even more, to £113,770m. The balance of trade has been negative since 1982, and in 1989 hit a record £24 billion.

Industrial relations: Although industrial relations, as measured by strikes, have improved, there has still been relatively little progress towards involving employees in the success of their enterprises — through profit-sharing, share ownership and structures of participation.

Positives: 1 In some ways British industry is thriving. In 1991 exports climbed to a record level of £103,804 million.

2 Industrial relations have improved markedly since the 1970s. Trade unions have become more responsible and democratic. Days lost through strikes fell from more than 29 million in 1979 to under a million in the year to October 1991.

3 The excessively high income-tax rates inherited from the last Labour Government have been brought down — from a top rate of 83 per cent in 1979 to 40 per cent in 1992.

Negatives: 1 Unemployment has been the most obvious cost of the current recession. The latest figures show 2,604,100 out of work. The number unemployed for more than six months has doubled in the past year.

2 The recession is biting deeply into industry. Business bankruptcies have jumped from 28,935 to 47,777 in 1991.

3 High interest rates are throttling the chances of economic recovery. British three-month rates stood at 10.7 per cent in February, compared to 9.5 per cent in Germany, 5.3 per cent in Japan and 4.3 per cent in the US. Short-term management of the economy has meant that governments manipulate interest rates to ensure re-election, rather than with the long term interests of the economy in mind. Interest rates fell before each of the last two general elections, only to rise again afterwards.

4 Britain is failing to invest for the long term. Investment in manufacturing industry fell from £3.1 billion in the first quarter of 1990 to £2.5 billion in the last quarter of 1991. This decline is not just a feature of the current recession. From 1979 to 1983 the annual level of manufacturing investment fell by 33 per cent. It recovered to its 1979 level only in 1988.

5 This failure to invest for the long term can be seen also in innovation, the development of new ideas and products. In 1984-8 only 3.4 per cent of patents granted in the US to other nationals went to Britons (3.7 per cent in 1979-83). By comparison, France had grown from 3.3 per cent to 3.4 per cent and Japan managed 18.8 per cent (against 12.9 per cent in the earlier period).

6 Britain's record of economic growth is very poor. The UK economy contracted by 2.2 per cent in 1991 — the biggest annual fall since the 1930s — while Italy's grew by 1.3 per cent and Germany's by 1.9 per cent.

7 Conservative management of the economy has stoked the biggest credit boom in Britain's history. Average personal debt as a proportion of disposable household income mushroomed from 57 per cent in 1980 to 114 per cent in 1990.

8 Conservative taxation policies may have reduced high marginal income-tax rates, but it was the rich who benefited, not the country as a whole. From the beginning to the end of the 1980s, take-home pay rose by 41.4 per cent for those on 1½ times the national average, by 37 per cent for those on the national average and by only 32 per cent for those on half the average.

The environmental balance sheet

Renewable energy generation: 45 per cent of electricity demand could be met from wind power. In fact the amount of electricity produced by renewable sources in the UK has steadily declined over the past five years. While France produces almost 20 per cent of its energy from renewable sources the UK manages only 1.3 per cent.

Unleaded petrol: As in so many environmental matters, Britain was late in introducing tax differentials for unleaded fuel. In 1989, sales of unleaded fuel in Germany were more than double those in the UK.

Positives: 1 Britain has a massive advantage in natural resources that give it the potential to be at the forefront of renewable energy generation. Government estimates show that up to 45 per cent of electricity demand could be met from wind power.

2 Government action can significantly affects standards of environmental protection. The market share of unleaded petrol rose from 1.1 per cent to 43.0 per cent between August 1988 and November 1991, due to widening tax differentials.

3 Britain has a positive record on protecting its countryside. More of our land is protected in national parks than any other EC member, and one more has recently been announced, in the New Forest.

Negatives: 1 In too many ways Britain unfortunately deserves its nickname of The Dirty Man of Europe. Carbon dioxide emissions — the main source of global warming — increased in the UK from 525 million tonnes in 1986 to 530 million in 1989. The UN estimates that a reduction in carbon dioxide emission of 20 per cent by 2005 will be necessary to avoid potentially disastrous effects of global warming. Yet the Government has committed Britain merely to *stabilise* emission by 2005 — well behind the majority of EC countries.

2 The UK produces more sulphur dioxide, the main cause of acid rain, than any other EC member, but is only now beginning to install pollution-control devices to power stations. Germany started in 1984.

3 Prosecutions for water pollution more than doubled between 1981 and 1988, while an additional 40 beaches were found not be complying with EC standards in 1990 — making a total of 20 per cent of all British beaches.

4 The Government has failed to invest in the development of renewable energy sources — despite the fact that they avoid the pollution problems associated with coal, oil and gas. Currently, just over £20 million is spent annually on renewable energy research and development, compared to more than £200 million a year on nuclear power.

5 Even worse, the Government has cut the budget of the energy efficiency office, while investment in energy conservation would save money and reduce pollution. The 1990-1 level of funding, a meagre £23 million, is lower than it was four years before.

6 Pollution from road transport has risen from 884 million tonnes of nitrogen oxides in 1980 to 1,298 million tonnes in 1989. Congestion on the roads costs an estimated £15 billion a year, yet the Government continues to do nothing to curb the rate of growth of car use — estimated at 142 per cent between 1990 and 2005.

7 At the same time, the proportion of freight carried on the railways between 1989 and 1990 dropped from 9 per cent to 7 per cent, while the proportion using road transport rose to 83 per cent.

8 Rail transport is placed at a disadvantage in Britain. Levels of government support for the railways fell throughout the 1980s, from £1,262 million in 1980-1 to £462 million in 1990-1.

The educational balance sheet

Number of teachers: The retention rate of teachers is very bad. More than half of the country's qualified teachers have left the profession.

Pupil-teacher ratios: In recent years, the pupil-teacher ratio has turned up once again — from 16.9 in 1990 to 17.2 in 1991.

Positives: 1 In some ways educational standards are improving. The number of teachers in nursery and primary education grew from 176,228 in 1986 to 193,516 in 1991.

2 Similarly, pupil-teacher ratios fell from 18.2 in 1980-1 to 16.9 in 1990-1.

3 Some of the Government's changes have been for the better. The idea of local management of schools has, in some places, produced school management of imagination and quality.

Negatives: 1 Overall, government funding of education is inadequate. The proportion of Britain's gross domestic product devoted to education fell from 5.6 per cent in 1981-2 to 5 per cent in 1990-1. In the same year France invested 5.7 per cent of GDP, the US 6.7 per cent and Ireland 7.1 per cent. The government has been quite happy to invest when it suits its own ideological ends. Pupils in opted-out schools are funded at an average of four times the level of LEA pupils.

2 The number of secondary school teachers fell from 224,618 in 1986 to 198,030 in 1991.

3 There has been a serious decline in the number of people qualifying as teachers, down from 25,000 in 1980 to 18,500 in 1988. The government is planning further cuts in teacher-training facilities.

4 British children lose out in critical areas of education. The proportion of children in pre-compulsory education in 1987-8 was a mere 3.6 per cent, compared to 13.5 per cent in Germany, 17 per cent in Belgium and 18.4 per cent in France.

5 Compared to our competitors, not enough of our young people stay on to post-compulsory education. The proportion of 16-18 year olds in full-time education or training was 35 per cent in Britain in 1988, compared to 47 per cent in Germany, 66 per cent in France and 79 per cent in the US.

6 Investment in scientific research and development has fallen from 0.35 per cent to 0.28% of GDP (while in Germany it stands at 0.40%), not only affecting our higher education system but creating a knock-on effect throughout the British economy.

The social balance sheet

Home ownership: Government help has been directed to home owners at the expense of others. Investment in local authority housing has collapsed and no help is available to the private rented sector.

Police: Insufficient effort has been devoted to making sure policemen are on the beat. A more visible police presence in communities is essential to combat both crime and the fear of crime.

Positives: 1 Overall, British standards of health are improving. Life expectancy for men rose from 70.8 years in 1981 to 73.2 years in 1991, and for women from 76.8 to 78.8 years.

2 Home ownership in Britain rose from 55.8 per cent of households in 1981 to 67.3% in 1991.

3 The size of the police establishment has increased by 15 per cent since 1978-9. Expenditure on the police rose by 55 per cent in real terms over the same period, and police pay showed a 29 per cent real rise.

Negatives: 1 While the NHS hospital sector's real purchasing power grew by 15.6 per cent between 1980-1 and 1990-1, expenditure requirements (due to demographic change and the rising costs of medical technology) in fact increased by 21.3 per cent. The cumulative shortfall in the hospital and community health services sector in England alone now stands at £4.44 billion.

2 The total number of people waiting for NHS treatment in the UK rose to more than one million in March 1990. Twenty-five per cent of inpatients wait for longer than a year for treatment.

3 The number of sight tests has fallen by 21 per cent since the introduction of charges in 1988.

4 The Government has withdrawn funding for new house building, and refused to allow councils to spend the receipts they have gained from new home owners. As a result, the amount of local authority housing built has fallen from more than 65,300 homes in 1979 to a mere 8,600 in 1990.

5 The number of people accepted by local authorities as homeless rose from 70,000 in 1979 to almost 170,000 in 1990 — and this does not include the single homeless.

6 With the massive expansion of mortgage lending and the subsequent use of interest rates to bring down inflation, the number of mortgages over 12 months in arrears rose from 59,690 in June 1991 to 91,740 by the end of the year. The number of properties repossessed rose by 74 per cent over the 1990 figure to 75,540 in 1991.

7 Outcomes have failed disastrously to match the input of additional resources to law and order. Recorded rates of notified crime have increased year on year by 5.5 per cent on average, and by a massive 16 per cent in 1990-91.

8 At the same time, crime clear-up rates have declined to 32 per cent.

9 Britain has proportionately the largest prison population of any EC country — and we also have more prisoners serving life sentences than the rest of the EC combined. Not only is imprisonment of doubtful value for many offenders, it is also extremely expensive. Better value for money would result from less use of custody for many classes of offender.

Policies for the new century

It is clear from our analysis of Britain's balance sheet that Britain needs change. Here are our first steps, the key measures which we believe must be taken straight away if we are to break the cycle of Britain's decline, unlock the full scope of Britain's potential and pave the way to future success.

● Britain's political institutions need thorough-going reform: stable and representative government, elected parliaments in Scotland and Wales, decentralisation of power to the English regions and to local government, freedom of information and a bill of rights. As the essential measure to secure and entrench lasting reform we will introduce fair votes by proportional representation for parliamentary elections.

● In the middle of the recession, the economy needs new impetus not a tax cut. We will immediately introduce an emergency programme of investment in the infrastructure and in public works in order to get companies and people back to work, thus reducing unemployment by 600,000 over the next two years.

● Lower inflation and a stable climate for industry to plan and prosper will lead to long-term prosperity. We will give the Bank of England independent responsibility for monetary policy, with a requirement to promote price stability. We will put the pound into the narrow band of the exchange rate mechanism.

● Environmental priorities must be built into all economic decision-making, ensuring that economic success goes hand in hand with environmental responsibility. We will introduce new environmental incentives.

● The skills and capabilities of the British people must be adequate to meet the challenges of the new century. We will increase investment in education by £2 billion, funding this by an increase of 1p on income tax.

● Older people deserve greater security. We will protect private pensions, and increase the basic state pension, making it payable as of right without means testing.

● Britain's future must be safeguarded by active membership of a European Community which is united and democratic and in which decisions are taken as close to the people as possible. We will take decisive steps towards the economic, monetary and political union of a democratic Europe.

Only when these key steps have been taken will government and individuals alike be able to plan for the long term, instead of focusing on the short term and the next election. The balance of this manifesto sets out the Liberal Democrat vision of the future: our long-term programme for government. The detailed costing and revenue-raising effects of our proposals are contained in a separate supplement.

1. BRITAIN'S PROSPERITY: PUBLIC INVESTMENT; PRIVATE ENTERPRISE

Liberal Democrats aim to encourage a competitive and enterprising economy which is environmentally sustainable, founded on partnership and advanced skills and closely integrated with Europe.

What the economy needs is a new impetus. The Government's proposed tax cut will not achieve this. Only new investment will provide the kick-start needed to escape from recession and reduce the waste of talent and energy which results from unemployment.

But Liberal Democrats also recognise Britain's long-term needs. We are committed to the free market, to free trade and to the creation of a competitive and enterprising economy. We do not believe it is government's job to run business — people do that much better. We see government's role as enabling firms and entrepreneurs to have the best possible chance. That means encouraging competition, investing in skills, involving employees in the success of their companies, nurturing small businesses, playing a positive part in the construction of the new European economy and, above all, bringing greater stability to national economic management.

Our long-term aim is to shift the burden of taxation away from the things the country needs more of — income, savings and value added — and on to the things we want less of, such as pollution and resource depletion.

Turning Britain round

The current recession is undermining Britain's competitiveness and future success. Unemployment and business closures lead to a wastage of talent and a loss of resources. At the same time, essential investment in our country's future, in infrastructure, in education and training and in innovation, is being neglected.

Liberal Democrats will introduce an emergency programme of investment to end the slump. We will immediately put in hand a major programme of public capital investment, funded by reversing the Tory tax cut together with a prudent increase in borrowing.

This, combined with a freeze in business rates and new investment in education to increase the nation's skills, will kick-start recovery and create jobs. We will:

● Attack unemployment by creating new employment opportunities. Our emergency programme should reduce unemployment by at least 600,000 over two years. We will increase spending on public transport, housing, hospitals and schools, on energy efficiency and conservation projects and on education and training - all sensible investments for the country's future.We will aim to guarantee everyone out of work for six months or more a place on either a high quality training programme or on a work programme with a strong element of training.

● Invest in infrastructure. We will provide support for transport infrastructure, including a dedicated high-speed rail link from the Channel Tunnel to connect with the major routes to the north and west of Britain, and the extension of electrification throughout the country. We will encourage the expansion of airports outside the south east.

● Freeze business rates this year, thus effectively reducing them in real terms, a larger reduction than that promised by the Government.

● Create a training incentive for firms through the introduction of a levy equal to 2 per cent of payroll, from which they would deduct their expenditure on training. We will require employers to release their employees aged under 19 for a minimum of two days a week further education and/or training for nationally recognised qualifications.We will establish a fully integrated system of skills training, leading to recognised qualifications for a broad range of skills. We will increase access courses for mature students and retraining for women returners and those in mid-career. We will fund crash courses in the main areas of skill shortage, aimed in particular at the long-term unemployed.

● Invest in local economies. We will set up and fund new regional development and local enterprise agencies. We will encourage TECs to become strong, locally based, employer-led organisations providing business services, acting as an effective voice for business at local level, and overseeing training of those in employment.We will encourage decentralisation of banks and other financial institutions. We will end the present government's policy of clawing back from local authorities amounts equivalent to those they receive from the European Community's regional development fund.

● Invest in research, innovation and design. We will increase immediately the government science budget to 0.35 per cent of GDP and raise it steadily thereafter. We will establish regional technology transfer centres to bring together the resources of industry, colleges, and government labs. We will encourage industry to invest in innovation and to improve the provision of seedcorn capital. We will reverse cuts in design consultancy schemes and provide additional funding for the Design Council.

Making Britain competitive

A climate of enterprise and competition is vital if British industry and products are to compete effectively in overseas markets. Yet the current government has concentrated instead on converting public into private monopolies. We will:

● Stimulate competition. We will take tough action against monopolies, mergers and financial raids. The Monopolies and Mergers Commission will be combined with the Office of Fair Trading and made independent of government, increasing its effectiveness. We will introduce a Restrictive Practices Act to penalise anti-competitive behaviour and end price-fixing by cartels. We will encourage greater competition in the banking sector.

● Break up monopolies. We will break up the monopoly providers of services such as British Telecom and British Gas. We will permit access by private operators to the British Rail track network. We will liberalise the coal industry by transferring ownership of coal reserves to the Crown (in line with other minerals), and issuing licences to operate pits to other groups, as well as British Coal.

● Promote consumer rights. We will take the lead within the EC to ensure that all products come with accurate, full and simple product and service information. We will give consumer watchdogs, including the regulators and the standards departments, greater powers, and improve redress for inadequate goods and services.

● Encourage decentralised wage bargaining. Our plans to spread employee ownership and participation will encourage wages to be set according to the profitability of individual firms rather than to some national "going rate". In addition, we will encourage moves towards greater decentralisation of wage bargaining at company level and, in the longer term as national and regional government develops, in the public sector.

Serving customers

Many financial institutions, and particularly some of the high-street banks, have a poor record of customer service, for individuals and businesses. It is still far too common to see charges applied to accounts, or interest rates changed, without customers being fully informed, and to see new types of accounts opened without existing customers being told that they could benefit from them.

Banks which are responsive to their customers will be good for the economy. We will ensure that commercial borrowers are entitled to a full contract specifying the terms, conditions and duration of the services provided. We will introduce rights for customers of all financial institutions, ensuring they are fully informed when changes are made which do or might affect them.

Promoting enterprise

Government needs to provide an immediate impetus to get the economy moving. But long-term private investment in the production of high-quality tradable goods and services is essential for long-term success. This will only be possible if we encourage a climate of investment, enterprise and partnership. We will:

● Reform taxation to increase investment. We will increase investment substantially in schemes such as SMART to encourage innovation in industry, particularly small and medium-sized enterprises, especially those involved in manufacturing. We will reform corporation tax and the taxation of savings to achieve even treatment of different forms of savings. This will reduce the current tax penalties on investment in industry.

● Encourage a long-term approach to private investment. We will reverse the burden of proof for acquisitions away from the target company towards the predator, and require companies to ballot their shareholders on bid plans.We will reform company law to require greater disclosure of information such as expenditure on research and development. We will define the responsibilities of non-executive directors and insist that all publicly quoted companies have them on their boards.

● Encourage small businesses and the self-employed, and ensure a "level playing field" for them in competing with their larger counterparts. This will include relieving the administrative burden on small businesses, legislating to make interest payable on overdue debt, and encouraging TECs, chambers of commerce and local enterprise agencies to reorganise to form a network of business-led "one-stop shops".We will encourage, and if necessary legislate for, banks to treat small businesses fairly by agreeing contracts for services.

● Encourage flexibility in working patterns, including part-time and flexi-time work, job-sharing and homeworking, adequate backup for carers of the young or old, and access to appropriate training. We will encourage a new system of tax-free child-care vouchers for parents of children under five, given by employers and usable in workplace, local authority and private nurseries and for individual qualified carers.

● Share success in industry. We will legislate to establish the right of every private sector employee in a substantial company to have access to a share in ownership and/or in the profits they help to create. We will encourage profit-related pay, employee share-ownership schemes and employee buy-outs. We will relaunch the cooperative development agency.

● Build partnership in industry. We will ensure that every employee has a right to participate in decision-making in their enterprise. We will set up a new industrial partnership agency to help companies and their employees find the precise forms of partnership which best suit them.

Creating long-term prosperity

We will change the ways in which economic policy is made and implemented, to bring greater stability and a sensible framework to economic management — ending the present "boom, bust"approach. This requires fuller integration with the European Community. Our key changes are:

● Establishing an operationally independent Bank of England to become the central bank of the UK, to ensure disciplined economic management, to end political manipulation of the economy and to form the rock upon which a long-term anti-inflationary strategy can be built. This will also help progress towards an independent European central bank.

● Moving sterling to the narrow band of the European exchange rate mechanism as soon as possible, helping stable progress towards lower interest rates.

● Taxes and public spending to be set to reach a "savings target" for the nation over a period of years. We will set a target as a total of private and public-sector savings, and adjust fiscal policy to achieve the target over the medium term. If the country does not save enough to achieve the target, we will alter taxes and public spending accordingly, to ensure adequate long-term investment and keep the economy developing in a non-inflationary way. We will encourage individual savings by giving tax relief on all income paid into new registered savings accounts.

● Reform of the annual Budget. We will publish a draft Budget four months before the final version, to promote open discussion of economic and taxation policy.This will facilitate the integration of spending and revenue-raising, a measure we have long advocated. This will also make it easier to measure the impact of economic policy on the environment. We will establish an independent national statistical commission to collect and publish statistics and improve their quality.

● Working towards European economic and monetary union, including the establishment of an independent European central bank and a single European currency. We will renounce the Conservatives' Maastricht "opt-out" clause, accept the timetabled approach to EMU, and renegotiate the social chapter with a positive British input.

Changing the economy for good

Liberal Democrats recognise that if we are to improve Britain's disappointing economic performance we have to change the governmental system which produces it. Our proposals for electoral and constitutional reform are a prerequisite for better economic performance. Proportional representation will produce greater stability in government, ending the economic disruption caused by sudden sharp swings in government policies before and after elections. Home rule and decentralisation will ensure that economic power and prosperity is spread throughout Britain. Integration within Europe will create the framework for long-term economic strength. Freedom of information legislation and open government will improve competition and encourage informed debate. A written constitution will ensure that politicians can no longer ignore long-term priorities for short-term expediency and political advantage.

Childcare vouchers

Britain seriously lags behind its Continental neighbours in provision for child care for working parents. This not only unfairly impedes opportunity for the people concerned. It holds back the contribution to the economy of many highly skilled workers.

We will encourage the introduction of a system of child care vouchers, provided by employers to parents with children under school age. They will be usable to pay for child care in a range of places — workplace, local authority or private nurseries, play groups or by individual qualified carers. The parent will choose, topping up the value if they wish. Child care vouchers will be deductible expenses for the employers and tax free for the parents. Self-employed people will be able to purchase vouchers and receive similar tax advantages. In due course the principle could be extended to cover child care for older children.

2. BRITAIN'S ENVIRONMENT: ENVIRONMENTAL PROTECTION AND CONSERVATION

Liberal Democrats are determined to ensure that Britain changes its ways so that it becomes a leader, not a laggard, in facing the environmental challenge. Polluters will pay and conservers will be rewarded. Taxation will be gradually shifted from the things we want more of — income, savings and value added — to the things we want less of: pollution and resource depletion.

The accelerating destruction of the environment is one of the most serious challenges we face today. Its symptoms are becoming clearer with every year, from global warming and holes in the ozone layer to poisoned rivers and polluted air at home. They threaten not just our ability to enjoy our towns and countryside but our health and our children's future. Liberal Democrats aim to cut pollution and clean up the local environment.

We aim to build a society that does not create wealth at the expense of the environment. Our economy currently functions unsustainably, producing unacceptable levels of pollution and rates of resource depletion. We will create new incentives to follow environmentally sensitive strategies and behaviour.

Protecting our heritage

Conserving and enhancing the physical environment, countryside and townscape alike, is of crucial importance to everyone's quality of life. Liberal Democrats will:

● Improve countryside, protection policies for national parks, heritage coasts, areas of outstanding natural beauty, and sites of special scientific interest. We will tighten controls against exploitation, we will create more national parks and we will improve access to the countryside.

● Introduce countryside management agreements for farmers and landowners who wish to take them up. These will be drawn up in conjunction with local planning authorities with the aim of managing the countryside to develop sustainable agriculture, safeguard plant and animal wildlife, and preserve traditional landscape features, such as woods, hedgerows and dry-stone walls.

● Reform land use planning so that the protection of the natural environment becomes a major feature of the planning system. We will decentralise planning decisions as much as possible, giving a key role to the local plan drawn up by the local authority.

● Clean up the cities. We will improve public transport, reduce traffic congestion, and encourage pedestrianisation and cycling schemes. We will encourage more parks, gardens and green spaces. We will provide more resources for councils to deal with noise complaints and make compensation for excessive commercial noise more widely available.

● Promote better waste management. We will provide grants for recycling schemes, introduce regulations on the use of packaging materials, and encourage local authorities to clean up litter. We will clean up beaches and coastlines by ensuring full treatment of sewage.

● Improve standards of animal protection. We will set up an animal protection commission to enforce and recommend changes to legislation. We will phase out battery cages and unacceptable systems of factory farming, tighten controls on the export of live animals for slaughter, and establish a dog registration scheme.We will prohibit experiments involving pain or distress for non-medical and non-veterinary purposes, promote alternatives to the use of animals in research and education, and ensure that laws against badger-baiting and dog-fighting are enforced.On hunting with hounds, Liberal Democrats as a party have declared their opposition, but recognise, like the Conservative and Labour parties, that legislation is a matter of conscience for each individual MP.

Controlling pollution

We will use market mechanisms, where feasible, to reduce pollution by ensuring that environmental costs and benefits are fed into the economy. Direct controls will still be needed in some cases. We will:

● Set targets for cutting pollution. These include a 30 per cent reduction in carbon dioxide emissions from the UK by the year 2005; our energy policy is geared to this target. We will ban the use of CFCs and halons by 1994.

● Introduce a system of tradable emission licences. We will issue factories and power stations with licences setting a ceiling on permitted emissions of pollutants such as sulphur dioxide. These will be tradable: those who are most efficient at reducing pollution would have surplus licences which they could then sell either to those less efficient, or back to government. The targets for emissions — and therefore number of licences available — will be reduced year by year, leading to a steady fall in pollution.

● Create a new department of natural resources with sole responsibility for environmental protection, leaving the Department of the Environment to cover local government and housing. We will set up an independent and powerful environmental protection agency to work with the new European environment agency.

● Put forward plans for a powerful United Nations environment programme to lead global efforts to protect the environment, operating within the framework of an "Earth charter".We wish to see a world market in tradable emission licences for carbon dioxide and other pollutants. This would not only provide incentives to cut pollution but also act as a channel for transferring resources to developing countries.

Conserving energy

Without an effective energy policy, government cannot have an effective environment policy. Britain's national energy strategy must be set within an overall European framework, with the aim of reducing pollution, improving energy efficiency and boosting the use of renewables. We will:

● Support a Community-wide energy tax on all energy sources. This will be related to levels of carbon dioxide emitted and will provide a strong incentive for saving energy and investing in cleaner sources. Extra revenue raised through the tax will be fed back into the economy reducing other taxes such as Vat and by protecting those least able to adapt to the higher price of energy.

● Invest in energy conservation and efficiency. We will set new energy efficiency standards for homes, offices and factories, and for products such as light bulbs, fridges and cookers.We will give grants for home insulation and the installation of solar panels, and introduce energy audits of buildings. We will encourage combined heat and power and district heating schemes.

● Double government spending on renewable energy research. We will establish a renewable energy office to promote research, development and application, in particular of wave power, hot rocks geothermal energy, passive solar design of buildings, small-scale hydropower schemes and wind energy. We will complete the study on the construction of a Severn barrage.

● Start to phase out nuclear fission power stations, which are prohibitively expensive and potentially hazardous. We aim to complete the phase-out at the latest by the year 2020 (and earlier if feasible), and we will not proceed further with the construction of the Sizewell B PWR. We will continue nuclear research, but at a lower cost. Reprocessing spent nuclear fuel rods increases the volume of waste and should be undertaken only when necessary for safety reasons.

We aim to build a society that does not create wealth at the expense of the environment. We will create new incentives to follow environmentally sensitive strategies and behaviour.

Air pollution index

Air pollution threatens the health of millions of people — particularly children, elderly people and anyone with a respiratory problem such as asthma. Government monitoring stations measure levels of pollutants such as nitrogen oxides or low-level ozone but fail to publicise them widely. When levels exceed World Health Organisation guidelines, the result is described as "good" — in other countries it would be called "poor".

We will increase the number of monitoring stations, ensuring that all major urban areas are covered. We will publish a regular air pollution index and encourage newspapers and TV and radio weather forecasts to use it. This will increase public consciousness of the pollution issue and prove of real benefit to the health of vulnerable people.

Making transport clean and efficient

By expanding the provision and quality of public transport and reducing society's dependence on the private car, we will improve travel efficiency and protect the environment. We will achieve this by:

● Investment in public transport, increasing its frequency of service, speed and safety, and reducing its cost to the individual — especially in isolated rural areas where the need is greatest. We will encourage new schemes, using light railways and trams in cities. We will require local authorities to define minimum standards of accessibility in their areas and draw up transport plans which meet them.

● Immediate improvements in the rail network, allowing more movement of goods and passengers by rail and less environmental damage. We will construct a high-speed link from the Channel Tunnel to connect with the major rail routes to the north and west, and extend electrification throughout the country.We oppose the privatisation of British Rail, but will allow private operators access to the rail network, while giving BR the freedom to raise investment capital on the open market.

● A reduction in fuel consumption. All political parties accept that long-term increases in petrol prices are not only environmentally necessary but unavoidable. We will phase these in gradually by applying our Energy Tax to petrol, while at the same time graduating vehicle excise duty and car tax according to fuel efficiency — so that the most efficient vehicles pay least. These price increases will not be brought in unless and until compensation schemes for individuals and rural communities which have no alternative to the use of cars are ready to be introduced. We will scrap the remaining tax breaks for company cars and apply tougher limits to permitted emissions.

● Assisting people in rural areas by making concessionary fares on local public transport widely available. We will encourage the use of village minibuses, "post and passenger" buses and taxi services. People who have no alternatives to private cars will be helped by our plans to graduate vehicle excise duty and by specific target measures to help isolated communities.

● Action against traffic congestion in urban areas. We will encourage local authorities to introduce peak-hour bans on cars, traffic calming measures, car-sharing schemes and further pedestrianisation. We will introduce a variety of road-pricing schemes, in which motorists pay to use highly congested roads at busy times of the day.

● New priorities for road building. We will approve motorway or trunk road investments only where it can be demonstrated that alternative transport provision cannot meet the need at lower economic and environment cost. Essential new roads and improvements will still proceed but the creation of a "level playing field" in decision-making between rail and road will ensure some switch of passenger and freight transport to the railways.

● The expansion of airports outside the south east while at the same time freezing further development at Gatwick and Stansted.

● Reversing the decline in the merchant fleet. For economic and defence reasons, we will boost British shipping and promote recruitment and training for the merchant navy.

● Environmental planning policies. We will introduce planning policies which will encourage the building of homes near workplaces, leisure facilities, shops and other services. Where this is not possible, public transport must be easily accessible. We will encourage the use of information technology to decentralise work.

Water district discount

According to the government, water bills will rise by 50 per cent within the next few years. For many households (in Wales, for example), water bills are now higher than bills for all local government services put together. Since 1989 nearly a million summonses have been issued to people who could not pay their water bills.

At present water companies have a bulk supply discount for commercial customers — a "wholesale price" for their water. Liberal Democrats will alter the licensing conditions for water companies to extend this to groups of domestic consumers who live on large estates and in sheltered housing complexes. This district discount will keep down bills for elderly people and many low-income inner-city residents living on large estates.

Building a sustainable economy

Liberal Democrats aim to build an economy which is not only competitive and enterprising but also environmentally sustainable, leaving future generations a wealth inheritance — of knowledge, technology, capital and environment assets — at least as great as that inherited by the current generation. Our proposals are:

● A better method of measuring economic progress. The conventional target of growth in GDP is a poor indicator progress. We will modify GDP by incorporating measurements of pollution and resource depletion to create a figure for sustainable national income. We will also use indicators of social and personal quality of life such as changes in life expectancy, literacy rates and education attainments to give a better measure of progress. The prime minister will present an annual report on changes in these indicators to parliament.

● A system of environmental incentives and penalties. We will make available grants and subsidies for environmentally friendly activities, such as home insulation, and to help individuals and industry adjust to our new stricter standards for pollution control. We will penalise activities which harm the environment or deplete stocks of raw materials through taxation, so that prices reflect the damage they do. Our new energy tax is this manifesto's key proposal in this area. The revenue raised will be used to reduce other taxes such as Vat.

● Enable consumers to identify and choose sustainable products. We will introduce new product labels, showing information such as energy consumption during use and the environmental impact of the production process. We will introduce strict standards of life expectancy for consumer durables and encourage deposit-refund schemes. We will improve recycling and waste-disposal systems. We will encourage environmental audits for companies, showing the environmental impact of their activities.

Reviving rural communities

Our policy for the countryside aims both to protect Britain's natural environment and to recreate success in one of Britain's greatest industries, agriculture. The farming industry is passing through a period of profound change; most farmers recognise that the industry must achieve a better balance with the market and the environment. We will help this transition by:

● Working for fundamental reform of the common agricultural policy. We want to ease the adjustment from the present price support mechanism towards market prices and direct support aimed at assisting the farming industry in transition and at environmental and social goals. These will be funded by savings made out of the present intervention mechanisms of the CAP.

● New incentive payments for environmental objectives, in particular for extensifying food production (using land less intensively), and reduced-input and organic farming. Countryside management agreements, described above, will be a key feature in this shift of CAP resources from price support to environmental goals.

● Reformed systems of direct support, aimed in particular at helping family farms and crofts.

● Introducing renewable limited-term tenancies for agricultural land, encouraging new entrants to farming. We will encourage local councils to continue to provide smallholdings and to introduce part-time holdings for new entrants.

● Expanding forestry. We support the long-term aim of doubling the area of the UK under forestry, but this must include a higher proportion of broad-leafed hardwoods. We oppose the privatisation of the Forestry Commission. We will create more community forests near large towns.

● Encouraging fishing and fish farming. We will improve the government's decommissioning proposals and appraise, with the industry, effective technical conservation measures. We should move towards fisheries licensing and management on a more regional basis to help traditional fishing communities and protect those who fish sustainably, such as mackerel handliners. We will transfer full planning responsibility for fish farming to local authorities, and we will increase research into the environmental aspects of fish farming and diversification. We will work with the EC to counter the dumping of stocks into the Community.

● The extension of rural development agencies. These will be responsible for coordinating development and diversification, in partnership with local authorities, the private and voluntary sectors and local communities.

● Tougher action on food safety. We will transfer responsibility for food standards from the agriculture ministry to a new food and drugs commission. We will bring in much tighter labelling requirements for all foods, and make funding available for food research and scientific establishments. We will improve consumer representation on government advisory committees.

3. BRITAIN'S SKILLS: EXCELLENCE FOR ALL

Britain's citizens are our greatest asset. Liberal Democrats will invest in people to enable every individual to fulfil their potential, and, in so doing, build the nation's economic and social strength. We aim to create a first-class education system for all, not just by providing adequate public funding, but also through reforms which increase choice and opportunity for each citizen.

Liberal Democrats start from the belief that every individual, whatever their age, sex, background or ability, possesses a unique potential and a valuable contribution to offer society. Our target is excellence for all. This requires more relevant courses, higher standards and improved provision. Excellence also has a cost. We will guarantee that Liberal Democrats will increase investment in education by £2 billion in the first year, even though this will require an extra penny in the pound on income tax. Our priorities for investment are pre-school education, education and training for 16-19 year olds, and adult education.

Aiming high; raising standards

Our aim is simple — to give Britain a world-class education system, in which high quality is the key, by the year 2000. We will:
● Create the framework for high standards by establishing a single department of education and training with oversight of all education and training. We will set up a national qualifications council to coordinate a single system of academic and vocational courses for 14-19 year olds, and a new higher education standards council to monitor quality in higher education.
● Improve inspections. We will ensure that a fully independent HM Inspectorate of Education and Training, properly staffed and funded, reports on the entire range of public and private provision from pre-school education to universities. Local inspectors of schools will be answerable to the inspectorate, which will also have a new role as education ombudsman. We will carry out a school buildings audit alongside the regular four-yearly local school inspection, to assess the physical state of schools and equipment. We will reinstate the buildings standards suspended in 1989.
● Support teachers. We will set up a statutory general teaching council to improve professional qualifications and set standards for teacher training and retraining. We will improve provision for in-service training and career breaks for women teachers with children. We supported the introduction of the teachers' pay review body and believe it will ensure that teachers are properly rewarded.

Putting education at the heart of the community

Liberal Democrats pioneered local management of schools. Now we aim to increase further the day-to-day independence of schools and colleges within a democratically accountable framework of local education authorities. This includes:
● A new independence for schools and further education colleges. We will give schools increased administrative support in return for the wider opening of their facilities to the local community. We will fully fund individual teacher costs. We will encourage every school to enhance its character, ethos and areas of special interest within a more flexible national curriculum framework. Within this context of greater freedom for all schools, we will end the two-tier system created by grant maintained schools and city technology colleges by returning them to the strategic planning framework of the local elected education authority. Strategic responsibility for adult and further education will remain with the LEA. LEA representatives on school governing bodies will reflect fairly the political balance of the authority.
● A new role for local democracy. We will require LEAs to guarantee a suitable place, with proper support, for every child in education and training up to the age of 19. This will include responsibility for ensuring that schools and colleges meet the highest standards of academic performance, discipline and behaviour, and for providing special services for schools, such as peripatetic music, language development, or behaviour support. Published information about schools and colleges will recognise achievement on the basis of "education value added" — progress made by pupils — rather than crude "league tables" of results.
● Independent schools. We recognise the contribution to excellence which the best of these schools make, and the right of those who wish to pay for private education to do so, but this should not be subsidised from public resources. We will phase out the assisted places scheme without affecting those already in it, and restore the money saved to state schools. We will review the charitable status of independent schools with the intention of ensuring that the benefits of charitable status are only awarded to those institutions that make a genuine contribution to the wider community.

Opening schools to the community

Schools should be seen as a valuable resource, not just for their pupils but for the communities around them. Access to their libraries, computers, meetings rooms, sports halls, playing fields and swimming pools could make a big contribution to community life.

We will encourage all schools to open up these facilities to local people in the evenings, at weekends and in school holidays. Some of our proposed expansion of adult education will be organised in this way. Local authorities — particularly community councils where they exist — will help to provide the administrative support needed to manage such open access.

Educating the individual

Liberal Democrats will ensure that every individual can receive high-quality education and training throughout their life from before school to retirement. But the current system places too little emphasis on vocational achievements. We will:

● Guarantee pre-school education for every child. We will guarantee every child access to two years' pre-school education with a choice of pre-school provision.

● Introduce a national record of achievement. We will ensure that every pupil has a national record of achievement so that progress is properly documented and shared between parents and schools. Supplemented by individual diagnostic testing, this will replace the current standard assessment tasks in order to raise standards.

● Reduce class sizes. We aim to reduce maximum class sizes so that no registration class in the country need have more than 30 pupils.

● Reward academic and vocational achievements. Our new national qualifications council will develop a modular, credit-based course and examination structure for the 14-19 age group, covering both vocational and academic courses. This will build on a simpler, more flexible national curriculum and a revised and extended system of national curriculum levels. Pupils from the age of 14 will study a balanced curriculum around a core of maths, English, science and a foreign language, adding specialisms in academic, vocational or technical courses, some delivered by employers in the workplace. We will ensure that all 14-19 year olds have a personal tutor and careers advice, helping them build the foundations for personal fulfilment and success.

● Broaden post-16 education. We will give all 16-19 year olds in work the equivalent of at least two days a week education or training. Courses will be selected by both the employer and the individual and will be accredited as part of our new 14-19 system. Those studying full-time will study up to three major and two subsidiary subjects, adding work experience, parenting and citizenship to build a baccalaureate-style programme.

● Improve special educational needs provision. We will give every LEA a separate special educational Needs service with its own budget for which schools will bid for funding. We will require schools to prepare, for every child with special needs who is not currently covered, an indicative statement to identify needs, set targets and report progress. The service will be monitored by specialists in the local inspection team and in HMI.

● Enable education for life. We will give every citizen an entitlement to a period of retraining or education at a time of their choice during their adult lives, based on distance learning costs. We will start by giving this guarantee to those groups most in need, including the long-term unemployed and single parents.

Opening the doors to higher education

Britain's higher education system still provides excellent standards of education, but does so for too few people. Liberal Democrats aim to increase both participation and flexibility in studying for degrees, because not all students want to follow traditional three-year courses. We will:

● Increase the number of students in higher education to two million by the year 2000. As well as more young people, we will particularly encourage the participation of women, people from minority ethnic and poorer backgrounds, and people with disabilities.

● Increase flexibility in courses. We will introduce a credit-based system, enabling students to achieve a diploma after the equivalent of two years, with the option of a further one or two years' study leading to a degree. We will make financial assistance available for part-time study.

● Open up new opportunities for study. We will develop distance learning opportunities and extend the franchising of higher education courses so that courses can start at local colleges — helping people who wish or need to study from home.

● Fund students properly. We will abolish student loans and restore student entitlement to housing benefit and income support. As our plans for the reform of tax and benefits are implemented, we will establish a student income entitlement and a student allowance to which all students, both full and part-time will be eligible.

● Guarantee quality. Our new higher education standards council will ensure that, as numbers rise, quality does not suffer. We will establish a proper career structure for research fellows and set up a pay review body for academic and non-academic staff to halt the brain drain.

● Invest in research. We will immediately increase the science budget to 0.35% of GDP, and raise it steadily thereafter. We will establish a new humanities research council.

4. BRITAIN'S PEOPLE: HEALTHIER, SAFER AND BETTER HOUSED

Liberal Democrats will invest in local services to enable communities to thrive. Our aim is to ensure that individuals of all backgrounds and means can live free of the fear of sickness, poverty and crime.

The steps we outline in this paper are necessary to create a fair, democratic and prosperous society, in which individuals are able to make their voice heard and develop their talents and skills to the full. But we believe that people can realise their potential best not as isolated individuals, but as members of thriving and responsible communities. We will invest in the network of community services — health, housing, crime prevention, social security, arts and sport — to improve quality, choice and opportunity for everyone.

Guaranteeing high-quality health care

Liberal Democrats remain steadfastly committed to the original aims of the NHS: to enable everyone to live free of the fear of illness, injury and disability; to provide health care free at the point of delivery and regardless of ability to pay.

The government's "reforms" mean that patients are made to follow the money; under our proposals, money will follow the patients. We especially oppose the two-tier health service which the government is creating. Our priorities are:

● A decent level of health service funding, including an annual real increase to match the costs of new technology and the growing number of elderly people. We will start to replace the underfunding suffered by the health service under the Conservatives, invest more in renovating and constructing new health service buildings, and increase spending in the priority areas listed below. We will abolish tax relief for private health insurance, whilst protecting the rights of existing policy-holders.

● Health promotion — keeping people healthy, and treating the root causes of ill health. We will provide resources for preventive medicine, health education and occupational health, invest in screening programmes for the prevention of disease, tackle the problems of drug abuse, ban tobacco promotion, remove charges for eye tests and dental checkups, and both freeze and extend exemptions from prescription charges. We will increase resources for primary care. We will restore a comprehensive dental screening service in schools and improve the dentists' NHS contract. We will require all government departments to take account of the impact on health of their decisions — of crucial importance in areas such as industrial investment, housing, social security and environmental protection.

● Real choice in health care. We will introduce an effective Patient's Charter, including rights to hospital treatment within a specified time, a choice of GP, guaranteed access to health records, and a comprehensive no-fault compensation scheme. We will require health authorities to publish a charter of services, defining basic entitlements, and provide redress where these are not satisfied. We will establish a new national inspectorate for health to guarantee a quality service.

● Better health care for women. We will ensure access to clinics providing health promotion, counselling, family planning and screening services, particularly for cervical and breast cancer, and advice on maternity and child care. We will increase the availability both of treatment by women health professionals and of home birth.

● High-quality community care, available through voluntary, private and local authority services to people unable to care for themselves. We will give users control over the options for care and provide services in a way which guarantees individuals maximum independence while retaining existing community links. We will provide bridging finance for local authorities for the transition to the new legislative arrangements on community care.

● Investment in NHS staff, including in-service training, especially in areas of significant shortage and changing roles. We will reform medical staffing and training to replace the consultant-led hierarchy with teams of accredited specialists.

● A health service for all. We will ensure that the assessment of health-care needs and the strategic planning of all services are the responsibility of democratically accountable health authorities. We will replace the so-called "internal market" with service agreements between authorities and hospitals and other health units. We will replace GP fundholding with a system which guarantees GPs freedom to refer patients outside the service agreements negotiated by health authorities. We will create a common structure of local management of hospitals and community units, ending the ability of NHS trusts to dispose of their capital assets, to set their own terms and conditions of service for staff, and to withdraw from local planning of health services.

Providing good housing

Decent, affordable and safe housing is vital to personal happiness and family life. We will encourage home ownership, but we recognise that the housing market has been distorted by mortgage tax relief, and we believe that choice in housing means providing more rented accommodation in both public and private sectors. We will:

● Introduce housing cost relief weighted towards those most in need and available to house buyers and renters. This will replace mortgage tax relief for future home buyers, which often helps most those who need it least, and causes enormous distortions in the savings and housing markets. People holding mortgages will be protected: they will have the choice of moving to housing cost relief or continuing to receive mortgage interest tax relief.

● Boost house building and renovation. We will relax controls on local authority capital receipts, especially for new council building, for houses built in cooperation with housing associations, and for renovation and repair work. We recognise that the urgent need for homes can only be met by mobilising both private investment and public spending. We will therefore create a new partnership housing sector to ensure high-quality affordable rented housing.

● Improve tenants' rights to better standards of repair and maintenance in the public and private sectors. We will encourage councils to create more tenants' cooperatives. We will retain the right of council tenants to opt for a change of landlord, but only after a fair ballot.

● Take urgent action on homelessness. We will pay income support to claimants in advance and assist with initial deposits, extend the duty of local authorities to provide accommodation for 16-18 year olds, and encourage councils to assist each other with housing needs. We will fund the provision of short-term rented housing to reduce the use of bed and breakfast accommodation. We will legislate to bring into use dwellings left empty without reasonable cause for more than a year.

● Adopt new environmental standards for all buildings, commercial and domestic. We will introduce a requirement for energy audits on all new buildings as a precondition of grants for home insulation, solar heating and other energy-saving measures. Homes which meet the new standards will be exempt from stamp duty on house purchase. We will encourage shared combined heat and power schemes, and encourage those planning new houses to take into account the scope for passive solar heating.

Home energy efficiency discount

Saving energy in the home makes good environmental sense, and will save money on electricity and gas bills. We will make houses which meet high standards of energy efficiency exempt from the first £1,000 of stamp duty when they are sold. Their energy standard will be assessed by an energy audit carried out by the local authority's energy efficiency unit.

If a home does not meet the minimum standard, the owner will be able to claim back all money spent within the first year after purchase on raising it to that level, through, for example, home insulation, up to the amount of stamp duty they paid when they bought the property (up to the maximum of £1,000). This will help to cut pollution and save energy and give a valuable boost to the housing market.

Protecting the community

Over the past ten years recorded crime has risen faster than at any time in our history. Meanwhile, prison conditions have deteriorated and the public has lost confidence in the criminal justice system. Liberal Democrats will reverse this trend by:

● Creating safe and secure communities. We will give local authorities the powers to develop comprehensive community crime prevention programmes, improve services to victims and encourage neighbourhood watch and safer city programmes. We will pay special attention to the underlying social problems in high-crime areas, particularly to prevent young people drifting into crime.

● Putting more police officers on the beat. We will redeploy police resources in order to increase police presence in local communities and establish local neighbourhood offices. We will decentralise budgetary control to police subdivisions. We will encourage recruitment campaigns and training for promotion to increase the number of women and ethnic minority officers in the police force and especially in the higher ranks. Multicultural and anti-racism training will also increase confidence in the police among minority ethnic communities. We will support the creation by the police of new racial attacks squads to monitor and coordinate action against racially motivated attacks.

● Reforming the criminal justice system. We will establish a ministry for justice, merging the relevant functions of the Home Office and the Lord Chancellor's Department. We will create the post of public defender, equivalent in status to the DPP and responsible for investigating alleged miscarriages of justice. We will extend legal aid, ensuring that justice is more widely available. We will encourage "restorative justice", in which mediation between victims and offenders provides reparations for those who suffer from crime.

● Radically reforming conditions inside prisons, reducing overcrowding, improving prison officers' morale and punishing offenders where possible within the community. We will create women's units in prisons where feasible. We will extend the rights and responsibilities of prisoners along the lines recommended by the Woolf report, and create the post of prison ombudsman.

● Amend the provision of the asylum bill. We will introduce improved welfare and legal rights for genuine asylum seekers and establish substantive rights of appeal.

A citizen's pension

At present many people do not receive the full basic state pension. If they have not paid enough tax because they have not earned enough during their working lives, people have to rely on means-tested benefits when they retire. Women in particular are badly affected, because they tend to have the lowest paid jobs and to spend several years looking after children.

Liberal Democrats believe that a pension should be a right for everyone. We will ensure that the basic state pension is paid as of right and end means testing for our poorest senior citizens.

Ensuring a decent income for all

The tax and social security systems are long overdue for reform. Our objectives are to simplify and integrate the two systems, to mount a determined assault on poverty and dependence, and to protect our citizens from want. We will work towards the eventual creation of a new "citizen's income", payable to all irrespective of sex or status. For pensioners, the citizen's income will be well above the present pension, and for everyone else it will be about £12.80 a week (at present prices).

Unpaid work will at last be recognised as valuable. Women caring in the home, for example, will receive an independent income from the state for the first time. The citizen's income will be buttressed by a single benefit for those in need, unifying income support and family credit, with supplements for people with disabilities and for child-care support. These reforms will ensure that every citizen is guaranteed a decent minimum income, whether or not they are in employment. Our immediate priorities, which will act as steps towards the citizen's income, include:

● Immediate improvements in benefits. We will increase child benefit by £1 per week for each child. Income support for under-25s will be paid at the full rate, an increase of £8.50 per week. We will give back to 16 and 17 year olds the right to claim income support. We will end immediately the minimum poll tax level of 20 per cent, prior to the abolition of the tax itself. We will reform the social fund, removing its cash limit and converting most loans into grants.

● Increasing the basic state pension immediately by £5 a week for single pensioners, and by £8 a week for married couples. This higher basic pension will be paid to every pensioner, regardless of their contributory record, to end the indignity of means testing. After the initial increase, we will uprate the basic pension every year in line with average earnings. This will be paid for by abolishing Serps, which does not help the poorest pensioners. People who have already built up Serps entitlements will of course still receive their Serps pension.

● Protecting the rights of members of occupational pension schemes. We will provide a statutory framework protection, including employee representation on occupational pension trusts.

● Creating a comprehensive disability income scheme to give people with disabilities real financial freedom. We will increase invalidity benefit by 15 per cent, extend mobility allowance and base payments on medical records rather than national insurance contributions. In the longer term we aim to reimburse individuals in full for the additional costs of their disability.

● Creating a carer's benefit for the many individuals who forgo normal earnings to look after elderly or disabled relatives. We will convert invalid care allowance into a carer's benefit, increasing its value by an immediate 15 per cent, indexing its future level to earnings and altering the entitlement rules to enable carers to combine caring with part-time or even full-time jobs and to ensure that people will still be eligible even if the caring starts after the carer reaches pensionable age.

● Further improvements in benefits. We will, over the lifetime of a parliament, phase out the differential in child benefit between the first child and subsequent children; reintroduce death and maternity grants; increase the family premium for income support and family credit, and reform the system of cold-weather payments.

● Unifying income tax and employees' national insurance contributions so that the two taxes are collected and administered together and paid on the same income, whether from earnings, investments, capital gains or perks.

● Making the investment needed to end the recession, using the money borrowed by the Conservatives to pay for their pre-election tax cuts. We will also raise the basic rate of income tax by one penny in the pound to pay for the improvements essential to education. Our new tax rates will be as follows:

—About 80 per cent of tax payers will pay 26 per cent income tax plus the 9 per cent from national insurance (a combined rate of 35 per cent).
—On earnings above £33,000, a combined rate of 42 per cent will apply.
—On earnings above £50,000 a combined rate of 50 per cent will be paid.
—Pensioners and ordinary savers will not pay the 9 per cent national insurance element on their incomes. Special provisions will also ensure that those on modest incomes most of which comes from investments, such as people who have been made redundant, do not pay this 9 per cent on their savings.

Widening horizons: investing in the arts

The arts benefit society in two ways. First, access to the arts is intrinsic to a high quality of life. Second, the cultural sector — the arts, crafts, design, and audiovisual industries — makes as great a net contribution to the economy as does the oil industry. We will:

● Create a new Ministry of Arts and Communications headed by a minister in the cabinet. Liberal Democrats will raise investment in the arts to the EC average over five years.

● Reform and decentralise arts funding and organisation. We will decentralise many of the responsibilities of the Arts Council, increasing the roles of regional arts boards and local authorities.

● Strengthen links between the arts and education. We will enhance practical arts teaching and library provision in schools and extend the provision of adult education for the arts and crafts. We will restore funding for public libraries to 1980 levels. We will abolish museum charges for school parties.

● Transfer responsibility for broadcasting to the new ministry. The BBC is a major patron of the arts, and broadcasting itself combines a variety of arts and crafts. We will reform recent legislation affecting the independent channels to entrench the interests of quality broadcasting and to guarantee political independence. These interests will also be reflected in the impending review of the BBC's Charter, and our plans for cable television.

● Encourage participation within Europe — including in particular cooperation in the film industry, in protecting and enhancing our common heritage and in expanding opportunities for young artists of all kinds.

Encouraging a fit, active and healthy society

Sport is important for the economic, social and health benefits which it can bring and for its ability to enhance community identity. Liberal Democrats will:

● Create a UK sports commission to provide a voice for participants, spectators and administrators. State sports councils will continue to receive their core funds from government but the commission will raise and distribute additional resources for the promotion of participation and excellence.

● Encourage sport across the community. We will encourage schools to invest in sports facilities and open them up to the local community. We will establish community sports plans offering tax relief to sports clubs that share facilities and coaching resources with local schools. We will encourage local authorities to transform football grounds into multi-sport venues.

● Encourage individual and corporate sponsorship, review the role of the Foundation for Arts and Sport and reconsider the Conservatives' hasty proposal for a national lottery.

● Maintain Britain's leading role in the fight against drug abuse in sport, ensuring adequate funding for testing programmes and education campaigns directed at participants.

● Enhance safety in the provision of sports grounds. We will put the safety of spectators first in any legislation and make standards mandatory. We will take into account the size of grounds when setting safety standards. We will raise revenue for investment in safety by increasing levies on football pools and betting. We will require local authorities to include sports spectators on ground safety committees.

Guaranteeing equal opportunities

A forward-looking society places an equal value on the contribution of all its citizens — and benefits from the participation of all. Yet in today's Britain many groups of individuals are systematically discriminated against by a society which fails to recognise their right to equality of opportunity. Liberal Democrats will:

● Fight discrimination by incorporating the European convention on human rights into UK law and then extending it into a full UK bill of rights. This will reinforce existing protection in British courts against discrimination on the grounds of sex, race, age, disability, religion or sexual orientation. We will set up a commission of human rights to assist individuals to take legal action in cases of discrimination or other breaches of the rights guaranteed in the convention.

● Strengthen the rights of women. We will guarantee equal pay for work of equal value; require public authorities and private contractors holding public contracts to be equal-opportunity employers and improve child-care support and facilities. Proportional representation for elections and modernising parliamentary procedures will help to end the discrimination against women on elected bodies and in government at European, national and local levels.

● Extend the opportunities of young people. We will entrench young people's rights of representation on organisations which affect their lives and well-being such as college governing bodies. We will place a statutory obligation on local authorities to provide a comprehensive youth service in partnership with the voluntary sector, and we will invest in leisure and recreation facilities. Young people will have the right to confidential medical advice and treatment.

● Make old age a time of opportunity. We will introduce a flexible "decade of retirement" for men and women, in which people may choose to retire and take a state pension at any time between ages 60 and 70 (the value of the pension increasing with the age of retirement). We will increase choice for elderly and retired people by encouraging openings in voluntary and part-time work, and widening the availability of education, the arts and recreational facilities.

● Protect the rights of ethnic minorities. We will reinforce legislation to ensure equal opportunities for all, in housing, employment, education and training, especially in inner-city areas. PR will greatly increase the possibilities of participation in the political process. We will repeal the 1981 Nationality Act, reform immigration legislation to make it free from racial discrimination and restore the right of entry to British passport holders. We will push for the extension of EC race discrimination legislation and ensure that the rights of black and Asian British citizens are respected throughout the EC. We will encourage changes to the education system which place a positive value on a pluralist, diverse and multicultural society.

● Guarantee equal rights for gay men and lesbians through changes to criminal law, anti-discrimination legislation and police practices. We will repeal Section 28 of the 1988 Local

Government Act. We will create a common age of consent regardless of gender or sexual orientation.
● Work with people with disabilities and their organisations to draw up a charter of rights for people with disabilities. We will implement the 1986 Disabled Persons Act in full, giving priority to the development of advocacy schemes.

5. BRITAIN'S PARTNERS: EUROPEAN PARTNERSHIP FOR THE NEW CENTURY

Liberal Democrats will take decisive steps towards a fully integrated, federal and democratic European community. We believe that by sharing sovereignty and pooling power, Britain and its partners will be better able to achieve common goals for the economy, the environment, society and security than by acting alone. Our aim is to create a citizens' Europe in which power lies as close to the citizen as possible.

Making Britain's European presidency work

Very few of the proposals that we have set out in the preceding sections will be successful unless Britain is prepared to work in partnership within the community. Following Maastricht, yet again Britain risks being left behind while the rest of Europe moves on. Liberal Democrats want Britain to play a full role in creating a dynamic and democratic Europe. We will use Britain's six-month tenure of the presidency of the community's council of ministers to make a start on the real tasks that lie ahead: building a prosperous and integrated economy; correcting the democratic deficit, making Europe work for its citizens, not its institutions: widening the community's membership; and helping to create a peaceful and stable new world order.

We cannot expect Britain to influence the direction the community takes in the next decade unless it is a full and enthusiastic member.

Our vision of the new Europe is of a federal community, where power is exercised at the lowest level consistent with good government. For us, federalism means decentralisation: passing powers down more than passing them up. The creation of Scottish, Welsh and English regional parliaments therefore goes hand in hand with the promotion of more European cooperation and partnership, ensuring access to power for individuals and their communities right across Europe.

Building a citizens' Europe

January 1993 will bring the single market. Economic and monetary union will follow by the end of the decade. Yet the community is still too much an organisation for businessmen and bureaucrats instead of citizens and communities. We want to mould Europe's future in the interests of Europe's people. Our priorities are:
● Economic and monetary union including the establishment of an independent European central bank and a single European currency. We will renounce the Conservatives' "opt-out" clause and accept the timetable for EMU.
● Cooperation in research and innovation. We will encourage further collaboration within the EC on major scientific projects and the development of new technologies such as telecommunications, information technology and environmentally sustainable innovations.
● Action on the environment. Our environmental goals cannot be successfully achieved unless action is taken across the community. The proposed European environment agency must be established, a European energy policy drawn up and environmental subsidies and penalties applied community-wide.
● An active regional and social policy. The single market and economic and monetary union will expose regions and firms to greater competition. This will be beneficial in the long run, but the EC must assist in the transitional period. We will renounce Britain's social chapter "opt-out" and argue for a more flexible framework of social policy across the Community. The EC should set down minimum standards of health and safety and employee rights, leaving national governments and enterprises to decide how to meet them, subject ultimately to the judgement of the courts.
● Fundamental reform of the Common Agricultural Policy. We will ease the transition from the present wasteful and inefficient price support mechanism to market prices and direct support for farmers' incomes to achieve environmental and social goals, to be funded by savings made from the present intervention payment system.

Creating a new democracy in Europe

The community's structure gives far too much weight to the council of ministers at the expense of the European parliament, and, most importantly, of the individual citizen. Further moves to European union, and enlargement, must depend on the institutions of the EC becoming truly democratic. We will:
● Set out the rights of the European citizen. We will work for a clear definition of the rights of the European citizen, and insist that these are common to all community nationals. This must include common voting rights at local, national and European levels.
● Increase the democratic powers of the European parliament. We will ensure that the parliament becomes an effective partner with the council in law-making, exercising in full the power of "co-decision".

● Introduce fair votes for the 1994 British elections to the European parliament. The British citizen must no longer be denied the fair voting systems enjoyed by the citizens of every other European country.

● Make the commission more accountable. The parliament must have the power to confirm or deny the council's nominee as president of the commission, and then to approve or not the president's choice of commissioners — and subsequently to sack them if necessary. We welcome the provisions of the Maastricht treaty as a first step.

● Increase democracy and accountability in the council of ministers. We will argue to extend majority voting in the council to cover all areas of community policy other than constitutional and crucial security matters. When passing laws, the council should meet in public.

● Improve national scrutiny of ministers' actions in Europe. We will create a new Europe committee of the House of Commons, and give our reformed House of Lords a special role in scrutinising developments in the community.

● Prepare for community enlargement, welcoming EFTA members and, when they are ready, the new democracies of central and Eastern Europe. A community with more members requires reformed and dynamic institutions. Further moves to European union, and enlargement, must depend on the institutions of the European community becoming truly democratic.

Sharing security; working for peace

The Gulf War and its aftermath have shown the crucial need for stronger and more effective world institutions capable of upholding international law and enforcing respect for human rights. Britain must ensure that the community plays a pivotal role in the construction of a new security order in Europe, following the democratisation of Eastern and central Europe. New initiatives for disarmament and for sharing security burdens will enable further reductions in levels of armaments to be made without endangering security. On the global stage, a stronger United Nations will be needed to underpin cooperation in tackling the world's problems. We will:

● Develop common European community foreign and security policies. This will include a common approach to defence procurement and the gradual integration of community members' armed forces under a joint military command. The burden of collective security in Western Europe should be shared more equally; we will press for contributions from all nations to the costs of joint forces such as Nato's proposed rapid reaction force — of which Britain will provide almost half.

● Promote democracy and reform in Eastern and central Europe by coordinating generous economic assistance to countries introducing democracy, guaranteeing human rights and reforming their economies.

● Assist the peaceful evolution of the commonwealth of independent states, the former USSR. We will help not just with food and financial aid and technical assistance, but also with the provision of military resources to shift food and supplies, and with scientific assistance to dismantle nuclear weapons.

● Develop a pan-European security framework. We will encourage the conference on security and cooperation in Europe to develop monitoring, verification and mediation duties within the continent. We will press for Nato to guarantee the borders of Poland, Czechoslovakia and Hungary and to enter into talks with other governments in the region for similar guarantees.

● Instigate a comprehensive review of UK defence policy which will be dictated by a rigorous analysis of defence needs rather than by fixed monetary targets. The review will cover the continuing need for contributions to collective security, the value of Britain's remaining extra-European commitments, and the potential for increasing our contribution to UN peacekeeping missions. Given the present hopeful international situation, we believe that further reductions in levels of armaments will be able to be made without in any way endangering security. Since the review will set out the framework for defence policy for years to come, we will halt any defence cut, and any order for a new weapons system, which might prejudice its outcome.

● Establish an arms conversion agency to help arms manufacturers to diversify and convert out of the defence field, funded by savings made in the defence budget. Our proposed regional development agencies will also provide help to areas particularly affected. We will reduce spending on military research and development, and shift the resources saved into the civilian sector.

● Maintain a minimum nuclear deterrent. We believe that the UK needs to retain its independent nuclear deterrent, but that the escalation of firepower represented by the scale of the Trident replacement for Polaris is unnecessary and unhelpful. We will ensure that the total number of warheads on the four-boat Trident system is limited to no more than that currently deployed on the Polaris system, and our defence review will consider whether we can reduce this further without threatening security. Our review will also examine the possibilities of future European cooperation in the provision of a deterrent force. We reject the government's proposed replacement of British free-fall nuclear bombs with air-to-surface missiles.

● Propose new disarmament initiatives covering all categories of conventional and nuclear weapons. These will aim to eliminate non-strategic nuclear weapons from Europe, and to reduce the strategic weapons possessed by the US, the former Soviet Union, Britain, France and China —

a vital step towards the day when individual nations' possession of nuclear deterrents ceases to be necessary.

● Act against the arms trade. Together with our community partners, we will establish a register of all international arms sales, eventually to become a UN register. We will place a total embargo on arms sales to regimes which violate human rights, and work for further global agreements among suppliers to control arms sales and technology transfer. We will close the Defence Export Services Organisation and ensure that overseas aid is not linked in any way to arms purchases.

● Make the United Nations more effective. The UN security council should take a proactive role in peace-keeping before confrontation develops into conflict. We will work with our community partners to ensure that funds are available for maintaining peace and security. The UN military staff committee should be reinstated and a permanent peacekeeping force established, with member states contributing contingents on an annual basis. Because of the need to assign British forces to this and to European policing and disaster roles (on top of their present commitments), more general purpose infantry battalions will be required than the number currently planned by the Conservative government.

Developing global prosperity

A secure, democratic and peaceful world can never be created while so much of the globe remains so desperately poor. Britain must play its part in developing prosperity, protecting the world environment, eradicating poverty, famine and disease, and promoting human rights and international cooperation. This will include:

● Increasing overseas aid to reach the UN target of 0.7 per cent of GNP over five years. We will increase aid especially to democratic countries carrying out policies which benefit the poorest, are environmentally sustainable and respect human rights. We will raise the proportion of aid given as grants instead of loans and place greater emphasis on supporting small-scale, community-based, labour-intensive projects. We will promote closer European cooperation, to make the best use of national and community aid, and avoid wasteful duplication. We will rejoin UNESCO.

● Ending the commercialisation of aid which the current government has practised and which substantially reduces its value to the world's poorest. We will reduce the proportion of UK aid tied to the purchase of UK goods and services and ensure that help to British exports is solely a function of the Department of Trade and Industry, rather than the ODA.

● Encouraging environmentally sustainable development. This includes the transfer of appropriate technology, the development of sustainable agriculture and forestry, sustainable use policies for the tropical rain forests and projects to prevent desertification, and the promotion of energy conservation and renewable energy schemes. We will provide technical help to develop methods of resource accounting and environmental protection and ensure that measures of sustainability are incorporated in decisions on development projects and programmes.

● Urgent action to tackle the growth in the world's population. Having doubled in the past 50 years to five billion, the world's population is expected to increase by a further one billion in the 1990s alone. We will give priority to support for family-planning programmes, education and employment opportunities for women, and basic provision for old age.

● Reform of the world trading and financial systems. We see the successful conclusion of the Uruguay round of the Gatt world trade talks as an urgent priority. Global prosperity also requires the reversal of the net flow of resources from the global south. We will press the EC to coordinate international action to resolve the debt crisis, including reducing government-to-government debt, introducing regulatory and tax regimes to encourage commercial banks to reduce or write off debt, extending eligibility to IMF and World Bank loans, and encouraging, where appropriate, debt for development and debt for environment swaps. We will press for the progressive reduction of all tariff and non-tariff trade barriers, and in particular the removal of unfair trading barriers against developing countries.

6. BRITAIN'S DEMOCRACY: ELECTORAL AND CONSTITUTIONAL REFORM

Liberal Democrats, alone in British politics, recognise that unless we change Britain's system of government, we cannot change Britain's future. Without constitutional reform, we will not achieve our other objectives. We believe in citizenship, not subjecthood — in the ability of all individuals to exercise power over the institutions that govern their lives. The creation of a modernised democracy therefore lies at the heart of all our proposals. We recognise too that Britain's success in the next century will depend not just on changing what we do, but in changing the way in which we do it. However worthy its intentions, and however able its personnel, no government will be able to put Britain right unless and until it has modernised our constitution.

Fair voting for an effective parliament

Our current "winner takes all" system of voting has many faults. It is unfair, unstable and divisive. Government by minority is usually bad government: in no truly democratic country could a disaster like the poll tax have been pushed through in defiance of public opinion, wasting billions of pounds and causing misery to millions of people. Our top priority is therefore the introduction of fair votes for all elections at all levels of government.

Fair votes will make every elector's vote count. It will increase citizens' control over their elected representatives, by abolishing safe seats. It will eradicate the power of the extremist minority in political parties. It will lead to a better choice of candidates and ensure that more women and candidates from minority ethnic communities are elected. Above all, it will reduce tit-for-tat politics and introduce much greater stability into government, allowing individuals and businesses alike to plan for their future with confidence. We will:

● Bring in fair votes. We will introduce proportional representation for all elections at local, national and European levels. We propose the single transferable vote, by which electors cast their votes in multi-member constituencies based on natural communities.

● Introduce fixed-term parliaments of four years, with a known date for the next election, subject to an earlier election only if the government loses a special "explicit" vote of no confidence.

● Reform the House of Lords. We will maintain a second chamber as a senate, primarily elected by the citizens of the nations and regions of the United Kingdom. It will have power to delay all legislation other than money bills for up to two years.

● Improve the way parliament works. We will give MPs greater influence over the executive by boosting the powers of select committees, improving staff backup for backbenchers and increasing financial and civil service support for opposition parties. We will improve the quality of legislation by establishing pre-legislative committees and better scrutiny of delegated legislation. We will improve the quality of debates by allocating time for business more fairly, timetabling committee sessions of bills and ending parliament's late-night sittings.

Bringing power to the people

Our system of government is far too centralised, and fails to make effective use of the talents and skills available across the country. We believe that political power is best exercised at the most local level possible, consistent with good government. We will:

● Introduce home rule for Scotland, with the immediate creation of an elected Scottish parliament.

● Introduce home rule for Wales, with the immediate creation of an elected Welsh senedd.

● Reform and strengthen local government, removing unnecessary tiers, restoring councils' independence and ensuring they are accountable to the people through a fair voting system.

● Create the framework for regional government in England. We will enable the establishment of fully democratic regional governments throughout England. We will set up a strategic authority for London as a priority. Preceding the new regional governments, we will establish regional development agencies throughout England, helping to boost economic development and prosperity.

● Decentralise power to the new national and regional governments. Economic development, housing, health, social services, roads and public transport, education and planning are functions which should be devolved from Whitehall and brought nearer the people they most affect.

Consulting local citizens

Liberal Democrats want local councils to be as responsive and accountable to their local citizens as possible. We will introduce across the country an initiative pioneered by Liberal Democrat-run councils such as South Somerset and Richmond.

We will require every council to conduct an annual survey of all its residents to gauge their views on the quality of local services. A summary of the results of the survey, compared to the previous year's findings, will be published with the annual demand for the local income tax, so that every resident is able to tell what their council is achieving with the money they pay.

Strengthening local government

The current government's approach to local government finance — most notably through the poll tax fiasco — has been to destroy the independence of local authorities by reducing their powers to raise and spend revenue. The Liberal Democrat approach is exactly the opposite: we aim to take power away from Westminster and Whitehall, giving new powers to stronger, more independent and more democratic local councils — elected by fair votes. We will:

● Abolish the poll tax, cancel plans for the proposed council tax and introduce a local income tax, related to ability to pay and collected by the Inland Revenue. Local income tax is easy to understand, easy to administer, and fair. It works effectively in many other countries.

● Replace the uniform business rate with site value rating — locally administered and based on the taxation of land values (with exemption for agricultural land and domestic properties). This will create incentives to improve property, rather than leave it undeveloped. Administration will be easier and local accountability will be restored.

● Reform and strengthen local government. We will reform principal local councils into a unitary system based on natural communities and the wishes of local people. We will give the new authorities greater responsibilities — for example, over education, health, and planning — and freedom to ensure the delivery of services in ways they think best. Local authorities will be given a "general power of competence", which will allow them to carry out any beneficial local action which neither duplicates the work of other public bodies nor breaks the law.

● Bring local government nearer to the people, by enabling the formation of a full network of community, parish, town or neighbourhood councils. We will ensure that all tiers of regional and local government publish a charter of services, giving citizens clear rights to standards of service, and remedies if these are not met.

Ensuring citizens' rights and opportunities

No citizen is truly free unless all are. Individual citizens and minority communities themselves need protection against the power of the state and against discrimination and unfair treatment. Citizens must have rights of access to information about decisions taken by public authorities in their name. We will:

● Introduce a freedom of information act, placing responsibility on government and other authorities to justify secrecy. We will reverse the present government's encroachments on freedom of speech and association, such as the banning of trade unions at GCHQ. We will legislate to give individuals the right of access to their personal files, except in matters relating to national security, whether held by public or private bodies. Security services and intelligence agencies should be accountable to a committee of senior privy councillors.

● Enact a bill of rights by immediately incorporating the European convention on human rights and its protocols into UK law. We will create a commission of human rights to help people bring proceedings under the bill and to recommend changes in existing law and practice. In due course we will add rights and freedoms not currently included in the convention, extending into a full UK bill of rights.

● Take tougher action against discrimination. Our bill of rights will guarantee effective protection against discrimination on the grounds of sex, race, age, disability, religion or sexual orientation. Our commission of human rights will help individuals take legal action in cases of discrimination.

● End the bias against women's participation in the present political system. The introduction of fair votes and of sensible parliamentary conditions will increase both the number of women candidates and the number of women MPs. In addition, we will use government's powers of appointment to ensure fair representation of women on public bodies.

● Improve the administration of the legal system with the establishment of a ministry of justice, separating responsibility for civil liberties and justice from that for order and security. We will establish a judicial services commission to appoint judges.

● Adopt a written constitution, of which the bill of rights will form the centrepiece. We will create a supreme court to entrench and defend these fundamental reforms to the relationship between the citizen and the state.

Working for peace: Northern Ireland

Liberal Democrats reject simplistic solutions for Northern Ireland. We aim to confront the legitimate fears and aspirations of both communities. We accept that both the unionist and nationalist traditions are valid and legitimate; that Northern Ireland should remain a part of the UK until the free consent of the majority of its people is given to change; that the Republic of Ireland has a legitimate interest in the future of Northern Ireland; and that a partnership in government which allows both communities to participate is the only practical way in which to make progress.

Together with the Alliance party, our sister party and the only non-sectarian political party in Northern Ireland, we believe that mutual respect, shared responsibilities and decentralised government are the only basis for a lasting solution to the troubles of Northern Ireland. We will work together to:

● Maintain the Anglo-Irish agreement, unless and until an improved agreement emerges from cross-party talks to replace it.

● Strengthen the constitutional rights of individuals within Northern Ireland. The case for fair voting for all elections, to bring together communities and encourage cooperation, and for a bill of rights to protect individuals, is even more pressing in Northern Ireland than it is in the rest of the UK. We will reform the Diplock system, so that three judges preside over non-jury trials, and encourage the use of juries wherever possible. We will introduce a 110-day limit on the length of time for which a prisoner may be held before trial, repeal the broadcasting ban, and provide for the videotaping of police interviews with terrorist suspects.

● Support community-based organisations striving for peace and reconciliation and working to eliminate sectarianism and discrimination in religious life, education, housing and politics.

● Welcome the opportunities offered by the development of the European community, in terms of economic assistance to Northern Ireland and also because it creates a framework for progress in the relationship between the UK and the Republic of Ireland.

OUR PLEDGE

What has been set out in these pages is a programme which could change Britain for good. We could become a country of citizens, not subjects, striving for excellence rather than settling for second best. We could be economically prosperous, environmentally responsible and educated to our full potential. But the obstacle to national success is the British system of government itself. Until that outdated charade is swept away, Britain's decline will continue, whatever government may be in power. That is why Liberal Democrats are putting constitutional change at the heart of our election campaign. The reform of our outdated and undemocratic voting system in particular is the change which will make other reforms possible and is the key to a successful future.

Because we believe in stable democratic government supported by a majority of the British people, we shall not only campaign wholeheartedly for fair votes in the coming weeks, we also make a pledge for the period after the election. Our aim will be the creation of stable government for a whole parliament and a more democratic basis for future elections. Liberal Democrats will neither support nor participate in a government which turns its back on reform. Any minority government which tries to play games with the constitution in order to cling to power, promoting instability and dodging the moral challenge of democracy, will have to contend with us.

That is our pledge.

Liberal Democrat appointments

The Liberal Democrat leader, Paddy Ashdown, announced the party's reshuffled front bench team on May 5, 1992. This involved appointments for the new MPs elected on April 9.

Paul Tyler, who won Cornwall North, became the new Liberal Democrat spokesman on agriculture, succeeding Geraint Howells, who was defeated at Ceredigion and Pembroke North. Don Foster, a former teacher and university lecturer, who defeated Chris Patten, Tory party chairman, at Bath became education spokesman; Liz Lynne, who succeeded Sir Cyril Smith at Rochdale, was named as the new health spokesman.

Nick Harvey, who won Devon North, was appointed transport spokesman, and Nigel Jones, victor at Cheltenham, spokesman on England, local government and housing.

The other national spokesmen are: Jim Wallace and Ray Michie (Scotland); Lord Holme of Cheltenham (Northern Ireland, and Alex Carlile (Wales).

Mr Ashdown retained the front bench team system which he introduced after becoming party leader. The new teams, with their portfolios, are:

Economic and resources: Alan Beith (treasury and civil service); Malcolm Bruce (trade, industry, employment); Paul Tyler (agriculture, rural affairs); Simon Hughes (environment, natural resources); Nick Harvey (transport).

Home affairs: Robert Maclennan (home affairs and national heritage); Nigel Jones (England, local government, housing); Matthew Taylor (citizen's charter, youth issues); Ray Michie (women's issues); Menzies Campbell (sport).

Public services: Archy Kirkwood (social security, older people, disabled); Liz Lynne (health, community care); Don Foster (education, training).

Foreign affairs: Sir David Steel (foreign affairs); Menzies Campbell (defence, disarmament); Sir Russell Johnston and Charles Kennedy (Europe, East/West relations); Lord Bonham-Carter (overseas development).

Independence in Europe

The Scottish National Party manifesto said:

Independence in Europe is the only policy which will bring stability to Scotland. The status quo is thoroughly discredited. Devolution would result in endless feuds with Westminster. Independence is the immediate, logical and clear cut answer to the question of how Scotland should be governed. The path to independence has been well mapped out by other countries. In this century, nearly 50 Commonwealth nations have harmoniously untied the knot linking them to London.

An independent Scotland will have a written constitution, like most other modern democracies, which will include a bill of rights clearly setting out the rights and responsibilities of citizens and state alike. This will include guaranteed fundamental rights at least as extensive as the European Convention on Human Rights.

Only with independence in Europe can Scotland be put on the road to full employment. Scotland is an inherently rich country; our problem is that we lack control of our own assets and resources. Since 1979, £100 billion of our North Sea oil and gas revenues have been wasted by Westminster. An SNP government will use some of the vast resources which remain to help fund full employment.

Education is one of the cornerstones of a developed society. An SNP government will ensure it is freely available to all our people. All students will have the right to a free education. Repair and modernisation of buildings will be made a priority. Tory legislation, such as national testing and opting out, will be repealed.

The SNP regards the arts as a vital part of our national life. We will encourage the widest possible enjoyment of and participation in all forms of the arts. The SNP will create a Scottish ministry for the arts. A National Theatre in Scotland and a Scottish Academy of the Arts will be established, to provide leadership and stimulation in the arts.

The SNP will retain and develop the National Health Service. In an independent Scotland, comprehensive health care of the highest standard will be free to all at time of need and point of need. An SNP government will abolish charges for prescriptions, eye care and essential dental work.

The SNP is committed to a non-nuclear Scotland. An independent Scotland will immediately withdraw from the UK's Trident programme, and will order nuclear weapons and installations off our soil. The existing Polaris nuclear weapons fleet will be removed from Scotland as soon as is possible. An independent Scotland will have strong conventional defence forces. But there will be no place for scandalously expensive, impractical and ultimately useless nuclear weapons.

The SNP is also completely opposed to the dumping of imported nuclear waste in Scotland. We will not let Scotland become the world's nuclear dustbin. But other urgent measures are also required to safeguard our environment. An SNP government will establish an environmental protection agency responsible to Parliament and independent of the executive. Its job will be to control pollution and make certain that all new developments are environmentally sound.

Poor public housing is the scourge of Scotland. Dampness, long waiting lists, lack of funding and run-down properties have created a legacy of intolerable misery. Nearly two-thirds of council rent collected is paid straight back out in loan charges. This crippling capital debt must be written off to meet the immediate and crying need for decent homes. An SNP government will write off this burden over the four years of the first Scottish parliament. This move will help Scottish councils to provide a decent home for every family. In addition, new houses will be built and an effective modernisation and repair programme undertaken.

Scotland's rural economy has been under siege for generations. An SNP government will recognise the vital importance of our rural areas, and take positive steps to maintain the rural population and provide new opportunities for young people who would otherwise have to leave. For farming, which is the backbone of the rural economy, the SNP will act to reduce farmers' exposure to short term interest rates by establishing an agricultural finance bank. Fishing is ten times more important to the Scottish economy than to the UK. Thirty thousand jobs are dependent on the success of the industry. An SNP government will reject any scheme for transferable quotas.

An SNP government will undertake a comprehensive review of the social security system. Benefits will be raised in real terms by 10 per cent over four years, with child benefit increased to £10 a week for every child.

An SNP government will reinstate pensions in full in relation to earnings over a four-year period. The SNP will increase the basic state pension immediately by £6.35 — on top of the proposed rates — to £60.50 for a single person, and by £10.10 to £96.80 for a married couple.

Provision for the needs of disabled people will be an important part of the economic and social programme in an independent Scotland. There should be an element of positive discrimination in terms of employment.

To help the low paid, the SNP will introduce a 20 per cent low basic rate of income tax on the first £3,000 of taxable income.

DUP seeks 'ring of steel'

The Ulster Unionist Party election manifesto entitled *The People's Choice*, placed its main emphasis on the constitutional position of Northern Ireland and the party's aim of strengthening its place within the United Kingdom.

The UUP called for a return of democratic accountability in the Province but warned the government that any system of devolution prepared for Northern Ireland must be similar to mechanisms proposed for elsewhere in the UK.

It went on to call for a formal restatement of Northern Ireland's position. "It must be manifestly substantiated that the citizens of Northern Ireland are, like their colleagues in England, Scotland, and Wales, citizens of the United Kingdom with all the rights and obligations which go with that status." The government must campaign to persuade the Irish government to drop its territorial claim to Northern Ireland. This claim remained an encouragement to terrorists and a justification for their actions.

The manifesto includes a call for the scrapping of the Anglo-Irish Agreement and its replacement by a wider British-Irish agreement which would take the "totality of relationships in these islands" into account.

On economic matters the UUP called on the government to treat as a priority job creation in the Province.

The Democratic Unionist Party manifesto entitled *Raise The Standard* called for the "elimination" of the IRA. "The Provisional IRA will not be talked out of existence nor will any constitutional device cause them to go away," the document said. "They must be militarily defeated."

The document called for a more military-driven strategy, for tighter border security, for an increase in resources to the police and army, for the creation of a part-time civilian militia to back up the security forces and the creation of a "ring of steel" around Republican areas. Other recommendations included surprise search and seizure operations, the introduction of identity cards, the proscription of Sinn Fein and the imposition of selective curfews. The manifesto restated the DUP's hostility to the Anglo-Irish Agreement and to what it sees as interference in Northern Ireland's affairs by the Irish government.

In other areas the DUP stated its opposition to the introduction of a national lottery which it said was immoral and its determination to preserve Sunday as a day of rest. The Social Democrat and Labour Party manifesto entitled *A New North, A New Ireland, A New Europe*, emphasised the success the party believes it has enjoyed in defining the debate and the way to move forward on Northern Ireland over the last ten years.

The party recorded its concern about the behaviour of British soldiers on duty in Northern Ireland and what it claimed is the persistently high level of harassment by the police and army, particularly against young people in certain areas. The party said that the greatest contribution to civil and human rights would be for the paramilitary groups to call off their campaigns.

On the economy the SDLP described Northern Ireland as facing a "grave crisis" which amounted to a human tragedy for people living there. The party called for a more locally focused industrial investment strategy to generate jobs and for greater cross-border cooperation with industry in the Irish Republic.

On equality of opportunity the SDLP said equal representation at the work place had not yet been achieved and discrimination was still practised in many companies.

The Alliance manifesto entitled *The Vote of Peace* stressed the party's preparedness to make "fair, realistic and honest compromises" in the cause of peace.

The party said that political agreement was a prerequisite for peace because it would provide the opportunity for the community to unite against terrorism. A vote for the Alliance was a way out of the stalemate perpetuated by the main parties. The manifesto called for the creation of a regional government for Northern Ireland which would become a vehicle for a new common loyalty between Roman Catholics and Protestants. This would be an "administration open to all the major elected groupings opposed to violence, selected in proportion to their electoral strength, (which) would create a political structure which all reasonable sections of this community could support." The manifesto said Northern Ireland would remain within the United Kingdom but with "good neighbourly relations" with the Irish Republic. The Sinn Fein manifesto entitled *Towards a Lasting Peace in Ireland*, called for a new approach by the government to solving the Northern Ireland question based on "comprehensive negotiations between all the parties." The manifesto noted Sinn Fein's belief that every effort to rule Ireland by Britain had failed and that partition has been a recipe for what it called "permanent crisis".

Sinn Fein said the three key requirements for creating the conditions in which peace could flourish in Northern Ireland were a British government which made the ending of partition its political objective, a Dublin government with the same view, and cooperation between the two governments to bring about in the shortest possible time the reunification of Ireland.

Towards 2000

The Plaid Cymru manifesto, published in Welsh and English, declared that Plaid Cymru, approaching the year 2000, was in step with the progressive mainstream of European politics. Throughout Wales they had seen towns and villages changing. Discrepancies in employment levels and personal incomes had led to massive immigration of wealthy people who could outbid local people for businesses and homes. As part of the pattern, moral values rooted in Welsh history had been attacked by a philosophy of greed and selfishness. The values that identified Wales must be defended.

The manifesto sets out policies under various headings:

Environment: Fifty wind farms to be provided, 15 to 20 tidal generators; offshore wind or wave generators. Wide distribution of bottle and waste-paper banks, kerbside collection of recyclable waste; purchase of recycled material; recycling and repair industries to be established; energy and environment audits by local authorities. Extending planning authority jurisdiction beyond low-water mark; coastal regional plans; improving beaches and coastal water; forums for public participation.

Europe and the Economy: A central EC bank under controlled by European parliament; increased regional and social funds; regional budget under control of Welsh parliament; aims of the EC redefined towards continuing growth in use of non-renewable resources and a balanced, equitable and sustainable economy.

Economy of Wales: More investment in energy conservation and renewables; new sector of recycling schemes; development of high-technology industries.

Charter for small businesses: Financial help for start-up and expansion; local income tax; abolition of automatic inflation in water cost; support for businesses threatened by foreclosure; flexible planning policies to meet local needs; public sector-led investment to stimulate economy in areas of high unemployment; simplification of tax procedures.

Education and training: Training network with all organisations involved forming where employers, unions, Welsh Office, Action Wales, higher and local education and voluntary organisations form partnership; data bank to match career opportunities throughout Wales; support for locally initiated training and employment; entry for women to all training schemes.

Transport and communications: Reopening of stations in growing towns and of local services; reopening of lines matching heavy commuter traffic and other lines; a high-speed link with Channel tunnel.

Completion of heads-of-valleys road; upgrading of roads and building by-passes; three Irish ferries and regular sea limks to south of France and Iberia to be developed .

Financing: By present taxation in Wales; by increased central income tax, earmarked for investment; by redirection of arms spending and combined European and local regional funds.

Agriculture: Commitment to maintain the family farm; fair payment for maintaining environment; promotion of ecologically healthy farming and emphasis on agriculture within integrated rural policy. Ensuring reasonable farmers' incomes; stronger support for less-favoured areas; more emphasis on structural policy; financial support for changing to organic farming and development of processing food into value-added products in rural areas. Start-up grants and other measures for young farmers' initiative.

Local government: Urgent creation of elected body to speak for all Wales; enhanced planning role for local authorities. Local income tax.

Social justice: Comprehensive equality act and integrated national policy for equality in education and training.

Health: Single free service for all in Wales with free prescriptions, dental and eye tests.

Animals: All food animals to be slaughtered as near as possible to where they are raised; EC-wide improvement of welfare standards;.

Education: State responsibility for education at all levels. Promotion of Welsh language at nursery schools. Village schools to be preserved. Independent funding council for higher and further education.

Fair voting: Most members of elected bodies should represent a geographically defined constituency but overall result should reflect votes cast for each party as closely as possible.

Bill of rights: To secure freedom of expression; right to assemble; right to join political party, trade union or employers' organisation; freedom from discrimination; right to see and obtain copies of any document containing personal information; right to legal advice, to trial by jury and to reply to any broadcast or published report lowering standing of individual in public's eye.

The manifesto ends with the party's aim for a self-governing Wales in Europe. " In the 1990s, full self-government is no longer a distant aim but an urgent necessity. The tide of history is moving fast in our direction. By the end of the century Wales will have a government of its own. In this programme we present our vision of a self-governing Wales within a democratic European confederation; a vision that inspires us with hope and confidence".

Votes, but no MPs

Several parties fielded candidates nationally and attracted many votes, but not enough to win a seat at Westminster.

The Green party's manifesto was launched with a foreword by Jonathon Porritt, the environmental campaigner, saying that progress on environmental issues had been "bitterly disappointing" since the 1989 European elections when the party gained 15 per cent of the vote.

Voters and some businesses were realising that the critical state of the world was the bedrock of all politics, said the manifesto, *New Directions: The Path to a Green Britain Now.* Under the Green party, there would be a shift from income tax and VAT to taxes on energy, pollution and raw materials. A levy would be imposed on all packaging materials to cover the cost of local recycling schemes. Every person, whether employed or unemployed, would receive automatic payments, replacing existing benefits, tax allowances and tax relief, to ensure a minimum level of economic security for all.

Proceeds from shutting down nuclear power would be used for energy conservation and home insulation schemes and electricity companies would make profits through "increased efficiency" rather than building capacity to produce more electricity.

All but the most essential road-building schemes would be cancelled, with money channelled instead into public transport.

Rural communities would be revived and farmers paid for habitat protection schemes, reduced chemical use, renewal of hedgerows and lower stocking densities on sensitive uplands.

Firm commitments would be made to halting global warming, reducing carbon dioxide emissions by up to 80 per cent and banning ozone-depleting gases. The General Agreement on Tariffs and Trade, through its proposed multilateral trading organisation, planned to challenge national legislation aimed at improving the environment and therefore should be wound up as soon as possible.

Other parties called for economic recovery but the Green party wanted revival "for the victims of uncaring industrialism, for the soul of our communities, for the beauty and magnificence of Planet Earth."

● The Liberal party produced a simple one-sheet manifesto that pointed out the differences that keep it apart from the Liberal Democrats with whom its members refused to merge in 1988 and which they describe as illiberal.

The manifesto also showed how the party differs from other parties in British politics. " . . . by remaining true to its principles, the Liberal party has always been the conscience of British politics. The continuous existence of a Liberal party, even with reduced support, has ensured the presence on the political agenda of key issues that would otherwise have been conviently forgotten."

The manifesto outlined policy on national issues, including the rejection of national sovereignty and expressed the belief that federations of communities hold the key to peace and prosperity; supported the creation of a single European economy based on a unified market; in education opposed the national curriculum as a dangerous concentration of power in Whitehall; urged that environmental pollution must not be taxed, but stopped; and urged reform of voting systems.

The manifesto called for a body to police animal welfare protection; offered re-organisation of administration of arts and sport and rationing of energy to conserve finite resources; switching of subsidies in farming and fishing from quantity to quality; democratic election of health authorities; restoration to local authorities of decisions on whether to sell council houses and to spend the money on building new ones.

The rights of the individual were declared to be paramount. The manifesto sought a programme of investment in industry staffed by a well-educated and adaptable work force with a stake in their industries.

● The Natural Law party offered the first governent in the world based on sound scientific principles; administration based on natural law, capable of satisfying everyone; support of natural law for national life and creation of the supreme quality of life — heaven on earth — in the nation. Among its detailed aims were low taxes for all.

● The last of the Social Democrat MPs who declined to join the Liberal Democrats disappeared from the Commons. David Owen, former leader, did not stand and Rosie Barnes and John Cartwright lost their seats, fighting as independent Social Democrats without a national manifesto.

● The British National party campaigned for repatriation of black immigrants, the execution of drug smugglers, fewer black faces in sports teams and for a prime minister to be elected indefinitely.

● The Democratic Left, a party that survives from the end of British communism, 42 years after the last Communist MP served in the British parliament, fielded no candidates, but urged its supporters to vote Labour.

Index to Candidates

Those elected are named in bold type

371

N

Y

Z